The Palgrave Handbook of Global Social Work Education

"This book is an important contribution to the body of literature not only on social work education, but social work and social development praxis. It has been written at a critical juncture when the world seems to be inundated with new and old threats such as *inter alia*: racism, xenophobia, gender-based violence, climate change, a migrant crisis, and reactionary politicians ascending to power in the traditional liberal democracies and in other parts of the globe. More than ever, social work education needs to adequately equip students with relevant knowledge and skills to respond to the aforementioned challenges. This book will be useful to many educators, practitioners, policy-makers and students as it practically covers sixty chapters from forty-three countries located in different regions of the world. I strongly recommend this book to anyone who wants to have both a panoramic view and deeper understanding of social work education across the globe."

—Ndangwa Noyoo, *Head of the Department of Social Development,*
University of Cape Town, South Africa

"The editors and contributors to this handbook are to be commended for compiling such a helpful and accessible source of information about social work education around the world today. They also provide an insightful analysis of how social work education has evolved and how it seeks to prepare students to serve their communities in many different countries. It will be a vitally important resource for social work educators, students, and researchers everywhere."

—James Midgley, *Professor of the Graduate School and Dean Emeritus of the School of*
Social Welfare, University of California, Berkeley, USA

"While sharing many similarities and common characteristics, such as the global definition and standard with their counterparts in other countries, social work in each country has its own uniqueness due to local socio-politico-cultural factors. In this post-colonial era, we have tried to decentre the Eurocentric discourse of social work. Knowing how social work is practiced and institutionalized in different countries will be one of the decentring strategies. Throughout the years, several sets of edited volumes have been published to introduce the social work of various countries. This new handbook is an exciting and most updated reference that documents and introduces the social work practice of forty-three countries from around the world, many of which have rarely been introduced in the existing literature. I congratulate the editorial team on this meaningful and important contribution to the global social work community."

—Miu Chung Yan, *Professor of the School of Social Work,*
University of British Columbia, Canada

Sajid S. M. · Rajendra Baikady ·
Cheng Sheng-Li · Haruhiko Sakaguchi
Editors

The Palgrave Handbook of Global Social Work Education

palgrave
macmillan

Editors
Sajid S. M.
Jamia Millia Islamia
New Delhi, Delhi, India

Cheng Sheng-Li
Department of Social Work
Shandong University
Shandong, China

Rajendra Baikady
Paul Baerwald School of Social Work
and Social Welfare
Hebrew University of Jerusalem
Jerusalem, Israel

University of Johannesburg
Johannesburg, South Africa

Haruhiko Sakaguchi
Department of Social Welfare
Ryukoku University
Kyoto, Japan

ISBN 978-3-030-39965-8   ISBN 978-3-030-39966-5   (eBook)
https://doi.org/10.1007/978-3-030-39966-5

FOREWORD

The establishment of institutions that educate and train new social workers is, without doubt, a critical component of the social work professionalization project. Shortly after the notion of the "social worker" emerged in
the last two decades of the nineteenth century, schools intended to convey
the knowledge and skills required by budding social workers to address the
needs of individuals and families and to alleviate the social problems that led
to these, were established. Following the first schools of social work, which
opened during the initial decade of the twentieth century in Amsterdam,
London, New York, Chicago, and Berlin, additional schools were established
in Europe and other continents. During the subsequent two decades, a major
effort was undertaken by social work education entrepreneurs to further the
internationalization of the profession through conferences and professional
associations and networks, publications, and visits. At the same time, educators in schools of social work in different countries sought to move beyond
existing knowledge in their efforts to train social workers. Pioneering research
projects undertaken by the faculty and students at these institutions focused
on gathering data in order to shed light on the conditions of service users and
their communities, to highlight their living conditions, and to identify practices and policies required to improve these.

Alice Salomon, the key figure in the establishment of social work in
Germany and the President of the International Committee of Schools of
Social Work at the time, undertook the first effort to document the internationalization of social work education and to offer, what she described, as
"a sociological interpretation" of this process. In a book published in 1937,
Salomon offered details of 179 schools of social work in 32 countries. Not
surprisingly, the schools that existed at the time were predominantly in
Western countries. European schools of social work tended to be the model
for the handful of schools in Asia, Africa, or Latin America. The establishment

of these was often motivated by Christian religious beliefs, and they generally operated with the support of colonial administrations.

The Palgrave Handbook of Global Social Work Education, edited by Sajid S. M., Rajendra Baikady, Cheng Sheng-Li, and Haruhiko Sakaguchi, is clear evidence of how far social work and social work education has come since then. Eighty years after the publication of Salomon's study, the editors of this volume have brought together a superb collection of chapters that document the achievements and the challenges faced by social work education today in 42 countries. The most striking difference between the two volumes is, of course, the way the focus has moved from the original core nations, in which social work emerged, to the Global South. Thus, *The Palgrave Handbook of Global Social Work Education* enables the reader to appreciate not only the marked proliferation of social work and social work education across the globe but also the ways in which professional education has evolved and moved away from its strongly Eurocentric origins to reflect this process. The editors' conscious decision to include chapters that deal primarily, though not exclusively, with social work education in the Global South reflects the truly global nature of the social work profession. But it also speaks to the fact that, despite the tremendous growth of social work in the Global South, the focus of much of the academic literature is still upon social work and social work education in North America and Europe.

This volume seeks to address the numerous contemporary issues, concerns, dilemmas, and challenges faced by social work education. These reflect a period in which globalization has created, in its wake, possibilities and problems that were inconceivable in the past. Increased wealth in many countries offers a path to addressing poverty in a way not seen before. The growth in trade, the movement of people, and the accessibility of information technology as a means to facilitate the transnational movement of ideas, knowledge, and practice can be tools for improving peoples' lives across the globe. Yet growing inequality within nations and between them, negative reactions to intensive competition and migration, and the growing power of multinationals threaten lives and livelihoods across the world. Similarly, the threat of dramatic climate change and the devastating impact that can wreak is already being felt across the world.

The editors of *The Palgrave Handbook of Global Social Work Education* are to be lauded in their efforts to bring together in this volume chapters that explore the ways in which social workers and social work education in different countries, and in collaboration between countries and through the good offices of the profession's international organizations, seek to contribute to efforts to address these challenges. In doing so, the chapters in the book offer readers a better understanding of the ways in which social work educators prepare students to further social justice in a future that may differ much from what existed not only in the past but in the present, as well. They provide us within insights into the innovative ideas and practices that are emerging within the profession and its training efforts across the world.

Despite the tremendous growth in social work over the last eighty years, the growing internationalization of the profession, and the transfer of knowledge across boundaries, this book underscores that social work is both a global and, at the same time, a local profession. The challenges faced by social workers across the globe are clearly interconnected and often similar. But they are not the same and indeed they can be very different. While social work education in all countries is influenced by values, ideas, knowledge, and practices elsewhere, it also does, and should, reflect the specific needs and challenges and the indigenous culture of its immediate environment. As the chapters here show, more than even before this is the case for social work education in the Global South. In this sense, Alice Salomon's hopes, regarding the impact of her survey of social work education so many decades ago, remain as pertinent today as it was then: "[The survey] should help to bring about an understanding of the fact that the methods of education for social work do not differ on account of different opinions of the leaders of the movement, but because each nation seeks to express and satisfy the needs of civilization and culture which are characteristic for her" (Salomon, 1937, p. 8).

Jerusalem, Israel   John Gal
                                                        Idit Weiss-Gal

REFERENCE

Salomon, A. (1937). In ICSSW (Ed.), *Education for social work: A sociological interpretation based on an international survey*. Zurich: Verlag fur Recht und Gesellschaft.

ACKNOWLEDGMENTS

The idea of this book originated from a discussion between two of the editors (Sajid S. M. and Rajendra Baikady) in mid-2017 and later including Shengli and Sakaguchi as all of us share the same research and professional interest. After reasonable amount of discussion, we put together a proposal with the intention to gather a reasonable number of chapters on social work education at the international level. Interestingly for the first call to express an expression of interest, we received an overwhelming number of contributors, which finally resulted in 60 completed and submitted chapters spanning into 42 countries across the world. We are thankful to all our contributing authors for their enthusiasm, commitment, and support throughout this book project.

As the volume of submission was very high, finding reviewers to peer review the submitted manuscripts was a real challenge. We are grateful to our peer review team for supporting us to maintain the quality and helping the authors to strengthen their arguments and presentations. We have not mentioned any individuals here, for want of space, but we are thankful to all our colleagues, peers, and students who have from time to time contributed to our learning by either asking thought-provoking questions or answering them.

We are thankful to entire editorial team at Palgrave Macmillan and especially Milana Vernikova and Linda Braus for helping us at every step of completing this handbook.

Each one of us thanks our families and colleagues for emotional and intellectual support they provided us throughout the project.

We have greatly enjoyed interacting with the authors and benefiting from their thoughts on social work education and practice.

In essence, this book is a product of excellent teamwork. However, for any shortcomings and limitations in it, we are responsible.

Thank you,

November 2019

Sajid S. M.
Rajendra Baikady
Cheng Sheng-Li
Haruhiko Sakaguchi

Editor's Note

All chapters in *The Palgrave Handbook of Global Social Work Education* have undergone blind peer review. Chapters were given to the reviewers blindly so that none of the reviewers knew the authors. All reviewers had expertise in social work, and the reviews were returned to the authors only after removing the reviewer's identity. Further, when a review suggested major revision, such chapters were sent for another round of review for a third opinion. On account of high number of chapters submitted and difficulty in finding reviewers who can return the review on time, we followed the cross-referring method, i.e., referring the chapter of one author to another author without identifiable information. However, we chose to give chapters for review to only senior and experienced social work educators. In some cases, an outsider was also requested to read and provide review for the chapters. Nevertheless, all reviewers were from social work academia and were from different countries across the globe. Our intention was to provide constructive feedback to assist our authors and make their work stronger and more scholarly. So, we asked our reviewers five questions regarding: relevance of the chapter to the handbook, critique/argument or insight, international relevance, structure of the chapter, and readability. This process was applied to all authors, including the editors who were also chapter authors. Overall, the Introduction, Conclusion, and section introductions by editors were deliberately sent to senior social work educators for their comments and suggestions.

Contents

Editors and Contributors

About the Editors

Professor Sajid S. M. has been associated with the Department of Social Work, Jamia Millia Islamia since 1982, and is currently a professor since 2001. He obtained his master's and doctorate degrees in Social Work from Jamia Millia Islamia, New Delhi (India), and Bachelor's degree from the University of Delhi. He served as Pro-Vice-Chancellor of Jamia Millia Islamia w.e.f. June 01, 2013, to May 15, 2014, and officiated as the Vice-Chancellor of Jamia Millia Islamia, New Delhi, w.e.f. July 09, 2013, to May 15, 2014. He has also served as Registrar (administrative head) of Jamia Millia Islamia, from January 2010 to May 2013. In addition, he also held positions of Hony. Advisor, Centres of Higher Learning and Research, Jamia Millia Islamia, from 2008 to 2011 and as the Director, Academic Staff College, Jamia Millia Islamia, during 2007–2008, Founding Director of the Nelson Mandela Centre of Peace and Conflict Resolution, JMI and Officer on Special Duty (OSD), AJK Mass Communication Research Centre, JMI. He has carried out several research projects, which include Religion and Peace Building, Madrasah Education, Minorities Education, Social Work Education, Drug Abuse and Child Labour, etc. He was appointed as "True Visitor" by York University, Toronto, Canada during May–June 2015. He taught a summer course on "Critical International Social Work from a Global South Perspective" at York University, in this capacity. He recently organized "International Conference on Social Work Education and Practice" during February 20–22, 2017. A book titled "Reflections on Social Work Profession" comprising some of the papers presented at the conference has been edited by him and is under print.

Dr. Rajendra Baikady is a Social Work educator and researcher. He is the winner of Golda Meir Post-Doctoral Fellowship at Hebrew University of Jerusalem, Israel (2019–2020), and Confucius Studies Understanding China Fellowship (Post-Doctoral Research) at Shandong University Peoples Republic of China (2018–2019). He was one among the 20 selected candidates for the Short-Term Research Award (STRA) by the Ministry of Education, Government of Taiwan, and conducted research at National Chengchi University, Taiwan, during June–July 2018. He was awarded the prestigious INLAKS foundation Research Travel Grant 2015 and Indian Council of Social Science Research, Collect Data abroad Scholarship, 2015 for conducting his research at Shandong University, China. His most recent books (co-edited) are: Social Welfare Policies and Programmes in South Asia (Routledge) and Building Sustainable Communities-Civil Society Response in South Asia (Palgrave Macmillan). He is co-editing the Journal Special issue of *Social Work and Society* (to be published in 2020) and has ongoing international collaboration with researchers from China, Bangladesh, Israel, Japan, Slovenia, Switzerland, and South Africa. Presently, he is at the Hebrew University of Jerusalem Israel and conducting research under the supervision of Prof. John Gal. In addition to this Dr. Baikady is affiliated to the University of Johannesburg, South Africa as Senior Research Associate to the Department of Social Work.

Cheng Sheng-Li is Professor in the Department of Social Work, School of Philosophy and Social Development, Shandong University, People's Republic of China and has been in postgraduate teaching for more than 25 years. He has carried out research projects funded by international agencies such as UNESCO, Washington University in St. Louis in the USA, University of British Columbia in Canada, and Taiwan Dongwu University. He was a Visiting Professor for many international university departments. He has 6 books, 37 research articles (in both English and Chinese), and 5 international projects to his credit. His areas of work are urban poverty and social assistance, social policy and social welfare, social psychology, family, child, and youth.

Haruhiko Sakaguchi is Professor, Department of Social Welfare, Ryukoku University Junior College, Japan. Since 1997, he has been offering courses on different semesters in addition to conducting academic research and providing academic supervision and consultation of students and researchers. Both of his Bachelor of Arts (B.A.) and Master of Arts (M.A.) were in Social Welfare, Osaka Prefecture University. He gained his Ph.D. in Social Welfare from Osaka Prefecture University. He has published a number of journal articles and book chapters dealing in a range of debates in social work, social welfare, and social policy. He has participated in many seminars, workshops, and conferences and has been a member of several professional networks, journal editorial boards, research institutes, and civil society organizations. His research interests are macro social work, social work education, and international social work. He is the immediate past treasurer of Asian and Pacific Association for Social Work Education.

Contributors

Iftakhar Ahmad Department of Social Work, Shahjalal University of Science and Technology, Sylhet, Bangladesh

Isahaque Ali Social Work Section, School of Social Sciences, Universiti Sains Malaysia, Penang, Malaysia

José Luis Almeida Centre for Transdisciplinary Development Studies (CETRAD), University of Tras Os Montes E Alto Douro (UTAD), Vila Real, Portugal

K. Anuradha Department of Social Work, Sri Padmavati Mahila Visvavidyalayam (Women's University), Tirupati, India

Bini Araia Investing in People and Culture, London, UK

Maik Arnold University of Applied Science, Dresden, Germany

Seda Attepe Özden Department of Social Work, Faculty of Health Sciences, Baskent University, Ankara, Turkey

Azlinda Azman Social Work Section, School of Social Sciences, Universiti Sains Malaysia, Penang, Malaysia

Ismail Baba School of Social Sciences, Universiti Sains Malaysia (USM), George Town, Malaysia

Peter Beresford Brunel University London, London, UK; University of Essex, Essex, UK

Olga I. Borodkina Saint Petersburg University, Saint Petersburg, Russian Federation

Julie Byrne Trinity College Dublin, The University of Dublin, Dublin, Ireland

Annamaria Campanini International Association of Schools of Social Work (IASSW), Dipartimento di Sociologia e Ricerca Sociale, Università Milano Bicocca, Milan, Italy;
Senior Research Associate, University of Johannesburg, South Africa

Helen Casey Faculty of Wellbeing, Education and Language Studies, The Open University, Milton Keynes, UK

Cecilia Lai Wan Chan Department of Social Work and Social Administration, The University of Hong Kong, Pokfulam, Hong Kong

Jonas Christensen Department of Social Work, Malmö University, Malmö, Sweden

Oldřich Chytil Faculty of Social Studies, University of Ostrava, Ostrava, Czech Republic

Bishnu Mohan Dash Department of Social Work, Bhim Rao Ambedkar College, University of Delhi, Delhi, India

Gil "Jake" I. Espenido Department of Social Work, College of Social Work and Community Development, University of the Philippines, Quezon City, Philippines

Hans van Ewijk Emeritus Professor Social Work Theory, University of Humanistic Studies, Utrecht, The Netherlands;
Visiting Professor Social Work Policy, Tartu University, Tartu, Estonia

Adi Fahrudin Department of Social Welfare, University of Muhammadiyah Jakarta, South Tangerang, Indonesia

Ziad Faraj University of Birmingham, Birmingham, UK

Luca Fazzi Department of Sociology and Social Research, University of Trento, Trento, Italy

M. Gail Augustine Associate Faculty (IUPUI), Indiana University-Purdue University Indianapolis, Indianapolis, IN, USA

Carolyn Gentle-Genitty Indiana University School of Social Work, Indianapolis, IN, USA

Kateřina Glumbíková Faculty of Social Studies, University of Ostrava, Ostrava, Czechia

Alice Gojová Faculty of Social Studies, University of Ostrava, Ostrava, Czechia

Emilio José Gómez-Ciriano Universidad de Castilla-La Mancha, Ciudad Real, Spain

Sharif Haider The Open University, Milton Keynes, UK

Zulkarnain A. Hatta Faculty of Social Science, Arts and Humanities, Lincoln University College, Petaling Jaya, Malaysia

Stephanie Holt Trinity College Dublin, The University of Dublin, Dublin, Ireland

Md Ismail Hossain Department of Social Work, Shahjalal University of Science and Technology, Sylhet, Bangladesh

Teoh Ai Hua School of Applied Psychology, Social Work and Policy, College of Arts and Sciences, Universiti Utara Malaysia, Sintok, Malaysia

M. Rezaul Islam Institute of Social Welfare and Research, University of Dhaka, Dhaka, Bangladesh

Wassie Kebede School of Social Work, Addis Ababa University, Addis Ababa, Ethiopia

Gloria Kirwan National University of Ireland, Maynooth, Ireland

Mayio Konidaris Department of Social Work, Monash University, Melbourne, VIC, Australia

Ivana Kowaliková Faculty of Social Studies, University of Ostrava, Ostrava, Czech Republic

Jerzy Krzyszkowski Department of Social Policy, Social Work and Tourism, Jan Dlugosz University in Czestochowa, Czestochowa, Poland

Yazan Laham Al-Quds Open University, Jerusalem, Palestine

Janet T. Y. Leung Department of Applied Social Sciences, The Hong Kong Polytechnic University, Hong Kong, Hong Kong

Joe Cho Bun Leung Department of Social Work and Social Administration, The University of Hong Kong, Pokfulam, Hong Kong

Wan-I Lin Department of Social Work, National Taiwan University, Taipei, Taiwan

Kana Matsuo Asian Research Institute for International Social Work, Shukutoku University, Chiba, Japan

Kalyani K. Mehta S R Nathan School of Human Development, Singapore University of Social Sciences, Singapore, Singapore

Bojana Mesec University of Ljubljana, Ljubljana, Slovenia

Jing Min School of Social and Public Administration, East China University of Science and Technology, Shanghai, China

Mariola Mirowska Department of Social Policy, Social Work and Tourism, Jan Dlugosz University in Czestochowa, Czestochowa, Poland

Edmos Mtetwa Department of Social Work, University of Zimbabwe, Harare, Zimbabwe

Munyaradzi Muchacha Department of Social Work, University of Zimbabwe, Harare, Zimbabwe

Rodreck Mupedziswa Department of Social Work, University of Botswana, Gaborone, Botswana

Majdy Nabahin Al-Quds Open University, Jerusalem, Palestine

Ksenija Napan School of Social Work, College of Health, Massey University, Auckland, New Zealand

Karene-Anne Nathaniel Department of Behavioural Sciences, Faculty of Social Sciences, University of the West Indies, St Augustine, Republic of Trinidad and Tobago

Pavel Navrátil Department of Social Policy and Social Work, Masaryk University, Brno, Czech Republic

Jitka Navrátilová Department of Social Policy and Social Work, Masaryk University, Brno, Czech Republic

Carolyn Noble Australian College of Applied Psychology (ACAP), Sydney, Australia

Keitseope Nthomang Department of Social Work, University of Botswana, Gaborone, Botswana

Jonathan Parker Department of Social Sciences and Social Work, Bournemouth University, Bournemouth, UK

Stavros K. Parlalis Department of Psychology and Social Sciences, School of Education and Social Sciences, Frederick University, Nicosia, Cyprus

Sylvia Parusel Qualitative and Community Based Research Unit, British Columbia Centre on Substance Use, Vancouver, BC, Canada

Melissa Petrakis Senior Lecturer at the Department of Social Work, Monash University, Melbourne, VIC, Australia;
Senior Research Fellow at St Vincent's Hospital (Melbourne), Mental Health Service, Melbourne, VIC, Australia

Jarosław Przeperski Centre for Family Research, Nicolaus Copernicus University, Torun, Poland

Corinne Renguette Indianapolis School of Engineering and Technology, Indiana University-Purdue University, Indianapolis, IN, USA

Claudia Reyes-Quilodrán Escuela de Trabajo Social, Pontificia Universidad Católica de Chile, Santiago, Chile

Liljana Rihter Faculty of Social Work, University of Ljubljana, Ljubljana, Slovenia

Angela Rosignoli Department of Sociology and Social Research, University of Trento, Trento, Italy

Maria Roth Social Work Department, Babes-Bolyai University, Cluj-Napoca, Romania

Shorena Sadzaglishvili Ilia State University, Tbilisi, Georgia

H. Unnathi S. Samaraweera Department of Sociology, University of Colombo, Colombo, Sri Lanka

Tatiana Saruis University of Modena and Reggio Emilia, Reggio Emilia, Italy

Caroline Schmitt Institute of Education Working Group "Social Work", Johannes Gutenberg-University Mainz, Mainz, Germany

Fuziah Shaffie School of Applied Psychology, Social Work and Policy, College of Arts and Sciences, Universiti Utara Malaysia, Sintok, Malaysia

Nasreen Aslam Shah Department of Social Work, Centre of Excellence for Women's Studies, University of Karachi, Karachi, Pakistan

Mohd Shahid Department of Social Work, School of Arts and Social Sciences, Maulana Azad National Urdu University, Hyderabad, Telangana, India

S. Shamila School of Social Work, NISD, Colombo, Sri Lanka

Odireleng Shehu Department of Social Work, University of Botswana, Gaborone, Botswana

Anne-Margrethe Sønneland VID Specialized University, Oslo, Norway

Paula Sousa Centre for Transdisciplinary Development Studies (CETRAD), University of Tras Os Montes E Alto Douro (UTAD), Vila Real, Portugal

Helle Strauss Faculty of Social Science and Pedagogy, Institute of Social Work, University College Copenhagen, Copenhagen, Denmark

Béla Szabó Babeş-Bolyai University, Cluj-Napoca, Romania

Khalid Mohammad Tabish Jamia Millia Islamia, New Delhi, India

Melike Tekindal Department of Social Work, Faculty of Health Sciences, Izmir Katip Çelebi University, Izmir, Turkey

Ciwang Teyra Department of Social Work, National Taiwan University, Taipei, Taiwan

Soňa Vávrová Faculty of Social Studies, University of Ostrava, Ostrava, Czechia

Stella Volturo University of Bologna, Bologna, Italy

Matthias D. Witte Institute of Education Working Group "Social Work", Johannes Gutenberg-University Mainz, Mainz, Germany

Yong Xiang Xu School of Social and Public Administration, East China University of Science and Technology, Shanghai, China

Amit Kumar Yadav Nava Kshitiz College, Bardibas, Nepal

Raj Yadav University of the Sunshine Coast, Sunshine Coast, QLD, Australia

Buğra Yıldırım Department of Social Work, Faculty of Health Sciences, Manisa Celal Bayar University, Manisa, Turkey

Husmiati Yusuf Center for Social Welfare Research and Development, Jakarta, Indonesia

Oğuzhan Zengin Department of Social Work, Faculty of Economics and Administrative Sciences, Karabük University, Karabük, Turkey

List of Figures

List of Tables

Introduction: Social Work—A Profession Without Boundaries: Debates on Global and Contextual Social Work

Sajid S. M., Rajendra Baikady,
Cheng Sheng-Li and Haruhiko Sakaguchi

This is a book that sheds light on social work education and its development in 42 countries across the globe. The book documents the status of social work education and examines context-specific challenges faced by the profession in both developed and developing economies. This book, which targets social work educators in an international context, aims at developing a global perspective in social work education and collaboration in teaching and research. It is written at a time when social work education across the globe is in transition and facing several challenges such as professionalism,

S. S. M.
Jamia Millia Islamia, New Delhi, New Delhi, India
e-mail: ssajid@jmi.ac.in

R. Baikady (✉)
Paul Baerwald School of Social Work and Social Welfare,
Hebrew University of Jerusalem, Jerusalem, Israel
e-mail: rajendra.baikady@mail.huji.ac.il

University of Johannesburg, Johannesburg, South Africa

C. Sheng-Li
Department of Social Work, Shandong University, Shandong, China

H. Sakaguchi
Department of Social Welfare, Ryukoku University, Kyoto, Kyoto, Japan
e-mail: antonkun@human.ryukoku.ac.jp

© The Author(s) 2021
S. S. M. et al. (eds.), *The Palgrave Handbook of Global Social Work Education*, https://doi.org/10.1007/978-3-030-39966-5_1

1

accreditation, curriculum content, sharp focus, and field education. It provides cross-national perspectives on how the challenges faced by social work education are addressed in countries across the globe. In doing so, we intend to bring international social work educators together to learn from each other and to develop some standard ways in which to address specific social work education challenges.

Social work education is continuously evolving in terms of curriculum development, accreditation standards, and transferability across countries. The emphasis of social work education across the globe is to develop qualified social work professionals who will then address the contemporary social issues and problems in both local and global societies. Social work education aims at achieving integration of social work knowledge, attitude, and skills among the graduates that are relevant to contemporary social realities. However, at present, the social work education and practice across the world, especially in the developing countries, are facing many challenges, which pose hurdles in the process of modernisation, professionalisation, and standardisation of social work education and practice. Globalisation in the twenty-first century has triggered several changes in the world. Countries across the world are facing issues such as climate change, overpopulation in some countries, and negative growth of population in several others, rapid ageing, and issues related to immigration, migration, mental illness, and rising income inequality. In addition, established world order and global dominance of the West-centric development agenda and modernity and the unequal distribution of the world's resources have created tremendous problems for many people living in both global and local communities in the developed and developing countries.

Professionally trained social workers strive to achieve equality and social justice in the world's societies (International Federation of Social Workers [IFSW], International Association of Schools of Social Work [IASSW], and International Council on Social Welfare [ICSW], 2012b). Developing culturally competent social workers who have cross-national perspectives is the need of the hour. Among the human service professionals, social workers are most committed to achieving social justice, human dignity, and worth (Bonnycastle, 2011; Van Voorhis & Hostetter, 2006). Social workers across the globe fight against social economic and political injustice and assist the affected population with a variety of social issues (McBeath, 2016). Further, the core purpose of the social work profession is to meet the needs of the disadvantaged and populations that are at risk. Fundamentally, grounded in the principles of dignity and worth of all people, social workers practice micro- and macro-social work in pursuit of well-being of people at risk in all national contexts (Keenan, Limone, & Sandoval, 2017). Thus, both micro- and macro-social work practices are believed to help in alleviating individual suffering and bringing the essential changes in the systems that are responsible for human suffering (Austin, Anthony, Tolleson Knee, & Mathias, 2016). Training culturally competent social workers who will then respond to human suffering, irrespective of national boundaries, is a need that has been created by neoliberal economic and political development. Questioning and reimagining the social work educational programmes across the world societies is most required now, at a time when efficacy and effectiveness of social workers and social work methods are contested globally (Lorenz, 2014), in line with neoliberalism, austerity policies, and new public management (Houston, 2016; Virokannas, Rauhala, & Harrikari, 2014). The world is in chaos and peaceful human existence is in uncertain. Issues related to human suffering across national boundaries are on the rise, and the need for human service professionals to address these issues is higher now than ever. Hence, there is a need for social work to develop and deliver educational programmes that will have the most effect on social issues. *The Palgrave Handbook of Global Social Work Education* is about such efforts to educate social workers across different nation societies, who will respond to the world's needs, either directly or indirectly. The book casts light on social work education and its delivery in different countries and in different socio-economic and political contexts.

INTERNATIONAL SOCIAL WORK—THE DEBATES

The importance of this book in these times, when social work across the globe is in transition and status and the credibility and existence of the profession is challenged in many countries across the world, hardly needs to be emphasised. Further discussion on internationalisation of social work education and practice on the one hand, and indigenisation and culturally specific social work on the other, makes social work in the twenty-first century a closely contested profession. Since this book, *The Palgrave Handbook of Global Social Work Education,* deliberates the issues related to international and global social work, in this part we will discuss the origin, development, and the present status of internationalisation of social work in the globe. Internationalisation of social work programmes and curriculum across the world started in 1996 (Johnson, 1996), and the movement influenced the countries across the world. The early years of internationalisation of social work started with faculty and student exchanges on the topics related to global concerns and outreach programmes in and around the neighbouring countries (Johnson, 1996). The effort then started to reflect the dominant global models of social work education in the Asia and Pacific region (Healy, 2001; Midgley, 2000). The internationalisation of social work is increasingly an important aspect as the profession responds to issues related to marginalisation that have spread across borders (Dominelli, 2010; Healy, 2008; Hugman, Moosa-Mitha, & Moyo, 2010; Lyons, Hokenstad, Pawar, & Huegler, 2012).

In the present globalised world, with new emerging orders, social work programmes around the world are emerging at a faster rate. The current trends occurring across the world provide very compelling evidence of the demand for new approaches to social work education and practice internationally. Pressing current global trends include the dramatic rise in global poverty, disparity, and continued issues of extreme famine across the globe; the growth of political and economic refugees in the world; war, terrorism, and human rights violations such as the growing world problem of human enslavement; global warming; global pandemics; problems of homelessness, combined with increased unemployment and underemployment; child abuse; and human trafficking. Many of the most challenging domestic social problems confronting social workers in the world today are rooted in transnational forces that originated in other regions of the world. Social work today is a global profession, and the education of social workers takes place in countries throughout the world; the aim of social work is to find a solution to the social problems which are hindering the development of the country in general, and the individual in specific. Social work as a discipline developed to find innovative ways to achieve social justice and human right entitlement for the general public. Social work education developed as a response to the growing social problems all over the globe, and trained social workers are expected to deal with these social problems on the micro- and macro-levels.

A number of social work educators have argued that it is important to internationalise social work teaching and learning. Two decades ago, Asamoah, Healy, and Mayadas (1997) gave a call for the internationalisation of the social work curriculum for training social workers, enabling them to then practice in the global context. However, at the forefront of global transformation, it is also important to understand that in academia, the idea of internationalisation of social work is not very well conceived of, as it has not been achieved in the schools of social work, especially in the Global South. As a result, despite the growing importance and advancement of social work in academia and professional practice at the international level, no widely accepted definition of the term *international social work* exists (Healy, 2012; Nagy & Falk, 2000, p. 52). Social work scholars refer to international social work as comparative studies and research. However, Ife (2001) argued that international social work practice is something that goes beyond the comparative approach. Lyons' argument in 1999 was that 'international social work is not restricted by boundaries; it is about going beyond the boundaries and practicing social work'. Further, the aim of social work is social work practice across borders and efforts to influence policy and practice at a global level (Lyons, 1999). In 1943, George Warren used the term international social work to refer the practices undertaken by the agencies at the international level (Healy, 2008). In the absence of a well-articulated definition, the social work dictionary defines international social work as—a loosely used term applied to—international organisations using social work methods or personnel; social work cooperation between countries; and the transfer of methods or knowledge about social work between countries (Barker, 1991).

While there is no specific description about what international social work is all about, and scholars have given different explanations in different contexts, we are working with the concept that international social work is something that can be regarded as a specific sub-branch of social work that equips social work graduates with the set of skills and knowledge required for practice at the international context. While reading this book, you will get to know how social work approaches are different and varied across the world, even with the delivery of programmes at each level. In many countries, even the duration and the for-credit, practice hours required for trained social workers are different than that of rest of the world. While there are also concerns about what international social work does and where workers find their space for service and practice, the growing literature on globalisation and international social work explicitly links social work practice to (re)settlement, issues of citizenship, inclusion, and participation in civil society. At the macro-level, international social work practice involves human rights, social justice, and advocacy work; at the meso-level, it deals with community development; and at the micro-level, problem-solving with individuals and their families (Nash, 2005).

Interestingly, a few studies have looked at teaching programmes in social work with global issues and concerns (Bye, Prom, Tsybikdorzhieva, & Boldonova, 2006), course work and activities (Johnson, 2004), and international field placements (Baikady, Cheng, & Channaveer, 2016; Lager, Mathiesen, Rodgers, & Cox, 2010). Further establishment of international social work associations, and the preparation and implementation of the *Global Agenda for Social Work and Global Standards for Social Work Education*, are the milestones for bringing together local and global practitioners, researchers, and educators from different parts of the world (IFSW, IASSW, & ICSW, 2012a, b). In 2004, the International Association of Schools of Social Work (IASSW) and the IFSW adopted a set of Global Standards for Social Work Education and Training. The standards address the mission, programme objectives, outcomes, curriculum, and the structure of educational programmes. Standards for cultural and ethnic diversity and gender inclusiveness, as well as social work values and ethical codes of conduct, are also included in the document. The purpose of developing the standards was to assure high-quality education for social workers around the globe. They were established to provide a framework that can be adapted to local conditions and contexts in different parts of the world. Many of the institutions across the globe are incorporating these global standards in their teaching, learning, and practising of social work education.

While discussing the internationalisation of social work education, one must focus on resource mobilisation and resource flow from the Global North to the Global South. Problems faced by countries in the Global South, along with their social realities and coping abilities are largely different from that of the countries in the Global North. It is also important to make sure that while propagating the internationalisation of social work education and practice, the effort does not lead to a 'one size fits all' approach, which may then lead to 'colonialization' (Gray & Coates, 2010; Hugman, 2008). There is an emerging discussion about bringing balance between the universal and local principles, approaches, and ideas in social work practice (Gray & Coates, 2010; Hugman, 2008).

Further, the difficulties in developing international social work teaching programmes have been addressed by scholars in diverse contexts. The teaching of international social work needs more resources in terms of money, time, material, and trained personnel with skills and knowledge (Pawar, 2010, p. 904). Developing and promoting social work teaching programmes on international issues is quite difficult, as bringing international perspectives among learners and educators is a complex task and the contextual differences make it complicated to bring accuracy, complexity, and sensitivity among the stakeholders. However, the terms 'international', 'transnational', 'global', and 'cross-cultural', which are used in social work education and practice, have direct implications on the internationalisation of the social work curriculum and teaching programme (Rasell et al., 2019). Research has also showed that international social work has failed to understand the social realities at a local level (e.g. Koch, 2013; Seckinelgin, 2012). International social work in general lacks a Global South perspective, which may be better able to address the social issues that are hindering the growth and prosperity of countries in the Global South. This lack is also because 'by and large, the international social work agenda appears to have originated from the West' (Pawar, 2010, p. 905), and because the dominant voice of academics is from the Global North (Wehbi, Parada, George, & Lessa, 2016, p. 285). Further, conceptualising, developing, and teaching international social work programmes in any part of the world require a strong understanding of local realities that shape the social work practice and knowledge. More research on social work education in a north–south relationship is much needed, as still there is a strong dominance of Global North knowledge and priorities. Greater reciprocity, mutual influence, and collaborations in social work education can yield more for international social work education in the future (Zuchowski, Gopalkrishnan, King, & Francis, 2017).

THE CHANGING GLOBAL ORDER: EMERGING ISSUES AND NEED FOR A SOCIAL WORK RESPONSE

Global warming, climate change, and natural disasters are increasing at a very alarming rate. The social work profession in many countries has notably contributed to the resettlement of disaster victims and reconstruction of social order after major disasters. These initiatives have also helped the profession to gain notable recognitions in society and among the public. However, apart from five national contexts, professional recognition of social workers is very poor, and in many cases, legal or state recognition is still unavailable. Professionals are serving the people, but they are not able to make a big impact on society as a whole because of the lack of support by the state. Hence, social work education and professional training need to incorporate the issues pertaining to climate change, disaster, and natural calamities and need to equip professionally trained graduates to address these issues in diverse national and cross-national contexts. Further research studies have proven that in order to attain environmental sustainability, a more holistic curriculum need to be cultivated and future organisational leaders need to be trained for sustainability leadership (Lertpratchya et al., 2017; Schein, 2015).

The world leaders have formulated and adopted a set of sustainable development goals for the betterment of global society. The 2030 agenda was adopted by the United Nations on 25 September 2015. The principle aim of this agenda was centred on achieving sustainable development through several development goals collectively called the *Sustainable Development Goals* (SDGs). The agenda is applicable to all countries as endorsed by a group of 193 member nations of the General Assembly, including both developed and developing countries. Poverty and hunger reduction are one of the primary and foremost important goals. Unfortunately, many countries in the world are unable to reduce poverty, even after decades of efforts by both state and no-state actors. However, doing away with poverty is an essential need for the world, as research studies have shown living in poverty leads to complex mental health issues (Ackerman, Brown, & Izard, 2004; Blair, 2010), and well-being of the population is an important aspect of any developing or developed nation. Social work programmes across the globe have a greater responsibility to train social workers who have the required skills and knowledge to contribute to building sustainable societies across the globe.

Irrespective of economic development, societies across the globe are under threat and undergoing violence and transformation. Incidents of violence, terrorism, and attacks on human dignity and life have become a part of some societies in the Global South, as well as in the north. Countries in the Middle East, countries in the south Asian region, and some countries in the west continuously face attacks on human life and dignity. Social workers need to be trained in order to advocate for greater dignity and social justice, and to bring people together, out of religious, social, and economic affiliations, and build a just society. There is a greater need for social workers with the skills and knowledge to deal with extremist powers and socially deviant behaviour in both developed and developing countries.

Social media has developed very extensively in contemporary society. The influence and impact of social media platforms, such as Facebook, Twitter, and blogs, have been studied and documented for their contribution in bringing larger social and political change in societies across the world.

These media are not only useful for coordinating and organising people in large numbers, but they also help to bring people together from different parts of the world and create solidarity with marginalised groups in need of support. Many campaigns, including the recent #metoo, the earlier Occupy Movement, and the Arab Spring of 2011, were significantly influenced by social media advocacy. In a fast-changing world, the lack of social justice, equality, and dignity for human life poses many challenges for prosperity and peaceful existence in any society. Training programmes for social workers need to incorporate digital literacy skills development, along with the effective and ethical use of social media platforms in advocacy and social service initiatives. Earlier research studies have proven that social media, such as Facebook and Twitter, had the capacity to contribute towards the coordination of large events related to public debates and to mobilise people into action (boyd, 2011; Levine, 2000; Varnelis & Friedberg, 2008). Further studies have also proven social media's role in bringing about political and social change (Fuchs, 2014a, b; Valenzuela, 2012).

THE UNRESOLVED ISSUES—SOCIAL WORK IN TRANSITION

Social work in the contemporary world is facing numerous challenges, including the very fundamental question of professional existence in some countries, and a stronghold by the authoritative government in some other. Today societies across the globe are undergoing transformation. The gap between the Global South and Global North is larger than ever. Further discussion on the capability, credibility, and nature and role of social work in societal development, indigenisation, and development of contextual and culturally appropriate social work are in the forefront. On the other hand, scholars are also advocating for a single unified definition of practice (Association of Social Work Boards [ASWB], 2015; Holosko, Winkel, Crandall, & Briggs, 2015; Lightfoot, Nienow, Moua, Colburn, & Petri, 2016) where social work itself needs to be different, context-specific, and culturally relevant. In many countries, social work is still not recognised as a profession by the state, the general public, employers, or other professions. Low wages, lack of research, absence of professional associations and regulatory professional bodies to set and enforce minimum standards of social work education and practice, and a lack of distinct contribution of the profession, coupled with a blurred focus of the profession, and educational programmes characterised by a vague understanding of knowledge and skill requirements to be imparted to social work graduates are some of the major factors responsible for a lack of recognition of the profession. (e.g. Pawar, 2010 on Asia; Iarskaia-Smirnova & Rasell, 2014 on Russia). In addition to this, the social work profession in many countries has failed to gain the support and confidence of the state and state actors, and as a result, it is not yet a state-recognised profession, and hence, working with government programmes is more than impossible for social workers in these countries. According to the international definition of social work, social workers have a greater responsibility for promoting social change, achieving social justice, and ensuring social functioning (IFSW, 2014). However, without consensus between the professional associations at the regional, national, and international level, achieving these core aspirations of the profession is more than impossible in a constantly changing world society.

In sum, social work education and the profession both have a greater responsibility in the process of community development. Connected and reciprocal support between education and field practice can contribute to the welfare of the various sections of the society. Therefore, there is a need for well-qualified, practice-oriented, and committed social workers in countries across the world. Thus trained, skilled social workers can work towards improving the socio-economic status and quality of life for community members. In addition, social work education and practice needs cross-cultural collaboration and cooperation in training future social work graduates. The book *The Palgrave Handbook of Global Social Work Education* is targeted at social work educators involved in international and cross-country teaching, as well as scholars interested in debates about the balance of local–global dimensions in social work practice and education.

Organisation of the Book

The uniqueness of *The Palgrave Handbook of Global Social Work Education* is that it addresses the issues and challenges in the delivery of social work education across the world. As such, it tackles a very broad brief, switching the lens away from a West-centric focus to engage with a much broader audience in countries that are in the process of modernisation and professionalisation, alongside those where social work education is more developed. The book also offers several perspectives that are largely unrehearsed, or at least under-rehearsed, in the dominant literature. The book includes 60 specially commissioned chapters covering social work education from 42 countries, most of which are not documented in the dominant literature. Social work education aims at achieving the integration of social work knowledge, attitude, and skills among graduates, which are relevant to contemporary social realities. However, at present, the social work education and practice across the world, especially in developing countries, is facing many challenges, which are hurdles in the process of modernisation, professionalisation, and standardisation of social work education and practice.

The objectives of this book are, among others,

 i. to define social work education in contemporary society;
 ii. to gain an understanding of what the emerging areas are for social work education and training, in order to address the social realities in the contemporary world;

iii. to determine the major challenges that exist with respect to curriculum, teaching, practice, and training in the light of globalisation;

iv. to gain an understanding of the issues, challenges, and concerns of social work education in the context of globalisation;

v. to analyse the curriculum, pedagogy, and practice of social work in diverse contexts;

vi. to explore the ways in which the courses address the complex political and social problems in contemporary society; and

vii. to examine the extent to which the programme curriculum addresses local and diverse cultural issues relating to the poorest and most marginalised groups, such as Dalits and minorities in India.

The focuses of the chapters are theoretical, evidence-based, and empirical in nature, and all the authors of this handbook make an effort to discuss, deliberate, and document the happenings in social work academia in their respective country, while there are also efforts to compare social work beyond boundaries and cultural ethos. The book is divided into nine parts:

Part I: Defining and Redefining Social Work: Social Work Education in East Asia and South East Asia

Part II: Advancement of Social Work Education in the West—Lessons Learnt

Part III: Social Work Education in Developing Economies—Challenges and Opportunities

Part IV: Socio-Political and Economic Conflicts and Social Work in a Contemporary World

Part V: Researching Social Work in the Global South—Implications for Education

Part VI: Social Work Education for the Next Generation—Hope over Fear

Part VII: Marginalised Communities in Diverse Contexts and Social Work Education

Part VIII: Pedagogical Issues in Social Work—Rethinking Practice Teaching

Part IX: Social Work with People in Difficult Circumstances—A Step Towards Sustainability

Each of these segments will be introduced with an overview that sets forth the context. This book will serve as a reference to universities throughout the world that are offering academic programmes in social work at doctoral, post-graduate, and master's levels. This book will be equally useful for students, faculty, and researchers in these universities. Anyone interested in the study of social work education and development, and the challenges of social work and the contemporary issues faced by the social work profession across the globe will find this book immensely helpful. The book will also provide insightful resources and materials for other helping professions that rely on interdisciplinary perspectives and an integrated approach to human problem-solving. This book can help readers to gain comprehensive, comparative perspectives on social work education, the content, curriculum, course structure, course delivery, fieldwork practicum, internships, and professionalisation of the discipline in both developing and developed countries. We hope that the students, educators, and especially researchers doing comparative and cross-country studies and exchange programmes find this collection interesting and insightful.

References

Ackerman, B. P., Brown, E. D., & Izard, C. E. (2004). The relations between contextual risk, earned income and the school adjustment of children from economically disadvantaged families. *Developmental Psychology, 40*, 204–216. https://doi.org/10.1037/0012-1649.40.2.204.

Asamoah, Y., Healy, L. M., & Mayadas, N. (1997). Ending the international-domestic dichotomy: New approaches to a global curriculum for the millennium. *Journal of Social Work Education, 33*, 389–402. https://doi.org/10.1080/10437797.1997.10778879.

Association of Social Work Boards. (2015). *Model social work practice act.* Retrieved from https://www.aswb.org/wp-content/uploads/2013/10/Model_law.pdf.

Austin, J. A., Anthony, E. K., Tolleson Knee, R., & Mathias, J. (2016). Revisiting the relationship between macro and micro social work practice. *Families in Society, 97*, 270–277. https://doi.org/10.1606/1044-3894.2016.97.33.

Baikady, R., Cheng, S., & Channaveer, R. M. (2016). Social work students' field work experience in Bhutan: A qualitative study. *Asian Journal of Development and Governance, 2*(2), 65–82.

Barker, R. (1991). *The social work dictionary* (2nd ed.). Silver Spring, MD: NASW Press.

Blair, C. (2010). Stress and the development of self-regulation in context. *Child Development Perspectives, 4*(3), 181–188.

Bonnycastle, C. R. (2011). Social justice along a continuum: A relational illustrative model. *Social Service Review, 85*, 267–295. https://doi.org/10.1086/660703.

boyd, d. (2011). Social networking sites as networked publics: Affordances, dynamics, and implications. In Z. Papacharissi (Ed.), *A networked self: Identity, community, and culture on social network sites* (pp. 39–58). New York, NY: Routledge.

Bye, L., Prom, K. B., Tsybikdorzhieva, B., & Boldonova, I. (2006). Utilizing technology to infuse international content into social work curriculum: A Siberian correspondent model. *Journal of Teaching in Social Work, 26*(3/4), 41–55. https://doi.org/10.1300/J067v26n03_03.

Dominelli, L. (2010). Globalization, contemporary challenges and social work practice. *International Social Work, 53*(5), 599–612.

Fuchs, C. (2014a). Social media and the public sphere. *Triple C: Communication, Capitalism and Critique: Journal for a Global Sustainable Information Society, 12*(1), 57–101.

Fuchs, C. (2014b). *Social media: A critical introduction.* London, UK: Sage.

Gray, M., & Coates, J. (2010). Indigenization' and knowledge development: Extending the debate. *International Social Work, 53*(5), 613–627.

Healy, L. M. (2001). *International social work: Professional action in an interdependent world.* New York: Oxford University Press.

Healy, L. (2008). *International social work: Professional action in an interdependent world* (2nd ed.). New York: Oxford University Press.

Healy, L. M. (2012). Defining international social work. In L. Healy & R. Link (Eds.), *Handbook of international social work* (pp. 9–15). New York, NY: Oxford University Press.

Holosko, M., Winkel, M., Crandall, C., & Briggs, H. (2015). A content analysis of mission statements of our top 50 schools of social work. *Journal of Social Work Education, 51*, 222–236. https://doi.org/10.1080/10437797.2015.1012922.

Houston, S. (2016). Beyond individualism: Social work and social identity. *The British Journal of Social Work, 46*(2), 532–548.

Hugman, R. (2008). Ethics in a world of difference. *Ethics and Social Welfare, 2*(2), 118–132.

Hugman, R., Moosa-Mitha, M., & Moyo, O. (2010). Towards a borderless social work: Reconsidering notions of international social work. *International Social Work, 53*(5), 629–643.

Iarskaia-Smirnova, E., & Rasell, M. (2014). Integrating practice into Russian social work education: Institutional logics and curriculum regulation. *International Social Work, 57*(3), 222–234.

Ife, J. (2001). Local and global practice: Relocating social work as a human rights profession in the new global order. *European Journal of Social Work, 4*(1), 5–15.

International Federation of Social Workers (IFSW). (2014). *Global definition of social work*. Melbourne: International Federation of Social Workers.

International Federation of Social Workers (IFSW), International Association of Schools of Social Work (IASSW), & International Council on Social Welfare (ICSW). (2012a). *The global agenda for social work and social development*. Retrieved from http://cdn.ifsw.org/assets/globalagenda2012.pdf.

International Federation of Social Workers (IFSW), International Association of Schools of Social Work (IASSW), & International Council on Social Welfare (ICSW). (2012b). *Global standards for the education and training of the social work profession*. Retrieved from http://ifsw.org/policies/global-standards/.

Johnson, A. K. (2004). Increasing internationalization in social work programs: Healy's continuum as a strategic planning guide. *International Social Work, 47*, 7–23. https://doi.org/10.1177/0020872804036445.

Johnson, W. H. (1996). International activity in undergraduate social work education in the United States. *International Social Work, 39*, 189–199.

Keenan, E. K., Limone, C., & Sandoval, S. L. (2017). A "just sense of well-being": Social work's unifying purpose in action. *Social Work, 62*, 19–28. https://doi.org/10.1093/sw/sww066.

Koch, E. (2013). *Free market tuberculosis: Managing epidemics in post socialist Georgia*. Nashville, TN: Vanderbilt University Press.

Lager, P. B., Mathiesen, S. G., Rodgers, M. E., & Cox, S. E. (2010). *Guidebook for international field and student exchanges*. Alexandria, VA: Council on Social Work Education.

Levine, P. (2000). The Internet and civil society. *Report from the Institute for Philosophy and Public Policy, 20*, 1–9. Retrieved from http://www.puaf.umd.edu/ippp.

Lertpratchya, A. P., Besley, J. C., Takahashi, B., Zwickle, A., & Whitley, C. T. (2017). Assessing the role of college as a sustainability communication channel. *International Journal of Sustainability in Higher Education, 18*(7), 1060–1075.

Lightfoot, E., Nienow, M., Moua, K. N. L., Colburn, G., & Petri, A. (2016). Insights on professional identification and licensure from community social workers.

Journal of Community Practice, 24, 123–146. https://doi.org/10.1080/107054 22.2016.1165328.

Lorenz, W. (2014). Is history repeating itself? Reinventing social work's role in ensuring social solidarity under conditions of globalization. In E. Virokannas, P.-L. Rauhala, & T. Harrikari (Eds.), *Social change and social work: The changing societal conditions of social work in time and place*. Farnham, UK: Ashgate.

Lyons, K. (1999). *International social work: Themes and perspectives*. Aldershot: Ashgate.

Lyons, K., Hokenstad, T., Pawar, M., & Huegler, N. (Eds.). (2012). *SAGE Handbook of international social work*. London: Sage.

McBeath, B. (2016). Re-envisioning macro social work practice. *Families in Society, 97*, 5–14. https://doi.org/10.1606/1044-3894.2016.97.9.

Midgley, J. (2000). Globalisation, capitalism and social welfare [Special issue]. *Canadian Social Work Review, 2*, 13–28.

Nagy, G., & Falk, D. S. (2000). Dilemmas in international and cross-cultural social work education. *International Social Work, 43*, 49–60. https://doi.org/10.1177/ a010520.

Nash, M. (2005). Response to settlement needs: Migrants and refugees and community development. In M. Nash, R. Munford, & K. O'Donoghue (Eds.), *Social work theories in action* (pp. 140–154). London and Philadelphia, PA: Jessica Kingsley Publishers.

Pawar, M. (2010). Looking outwards: Teaching international social work in Asia. *Social Work Education, 29*(8), 896–909.

Rasell, M., Join-Lambert, H., Naumiuk, A., Pinto, C., Uggerhoj, L., & Walker, J. (2019). Diversity, dialogue, and identity in designing globally relevant social work education. *Social Work Education, 38*(6), 675–688. https://doi.org/10.1080/026 15479.2019.1570108.

Schein, S. (2015). *A new psychology for sustainability leadership*. Sheffield, UK: Greenleaf Publishing Ltd.

Seckinelgin, H. (2012). The global governance of success in HIV/AIDS policy: Emergency action, everyday lives and Sen's capabilities. *Health and Place, 18*(3), 453–460.

Valenzuela, S. (2012, July). *Protesting in the age of social media: Information, opinion expression and activism in online networks*. Paper presented to the 5th Latin American Public Opinion Congress, Bogota, Colombia.

Van Voorhis, R. M., & Hostetter, C. (2006). The impact of MSW education on social worker empowerment and commitment to client empowerment through social justice advocacy. *Journal of Social Work Education, 42*, 105–121. https://doi. org/10.5175/JSWE.2006.200303147.

Varnelis, K., & Friedberg, A. (2008). Place: The networking of public space. In K. Varnelis (Ed.), *Networked publics* (pp. 15–42). Cambridge: MIT Press.

Virokannas, E., Rauhala, P.-L., & Harrikari, T. (2014). *Social change and social work: The changing societal conditions of social work in time and place*. Farnham, Surrey: Ashgate.

Wehbi, S., Parada, H., George, P., & Lessa, I. (2016). Going home: Social work across and about borders. *International Social Work, 59*(2), 284–292.

Zuchowski, I. S., Gopalkrishnan, N., King, J., & Francis, A. (2017). Reciprocity in international student exchange: Challenges posed by neo-colonialism and the dominance of the Western voice. *Aotearoa New Zealand Social Work, 29*(1), 77–87.

PART I

Defining and Redefining Social Work: Social Work Education in East Asia and South East Asia

There are several challenges for social work education in East Asia and South East Asia today. Fundamentally, social work in the region is struggling to get its professional recognition. The professional status of social work is especially low in the countries where western democracy is not fully adopted, and social work has been seen as just an instrument to promote social stability and social control. Fundamentally, social work is regarded as an important tool to promote social development, social justice, equality human rights and human dignity (IFSW, 2014). This part of the book includes chapters from, Indonesia, China, Malaysia and Taiwan. Social work education in each of these countries has a varying history. Three countries in the region began social work education in the 1950s (Taiwan 1950, Thailand 1950 and Indonesia 1957), whereas Malaysia started its first social work education programme only in 1970s. Further, the development of social work in most of these countries is influenced by the West, mostly from the United States either directly or indirectly. For example, social work development in Indonesia and Taiwan had an indirect influence by the United States whereas social work development in Japan and China has direct influence. Among all these countries, social work education in China has an interesting history and had gone through interesting milestones in terms of its origin and development. Unlike any other country in the region, social work in China had seen an interruption of 40 years and was resumed only in the 1980s by the central government. Thereafter social work in socialist China is seen as a means of social control and as an instrument to achieve social stability and establish a harmonious society. At present, social work education programmes, community programmes, and social service agencies are controlled and monitored by the central government.

Looking at the experience of Chinese social work, one may wrongly argue that the development of social work as a profession needs states support. However, the growth and development of any profession does not happen in a vacuum. The development of social work needs interaction between economic, social, and political aspects of the country. The development and growth of social work is mostly influenced by the type of government that a country has, further the level of economic development and social life of the people that a country reflects, and influence the kind of social work programme it develops and supports. For example, the democracy across the world promotes social work with a distinct ideology of social justice and social equality, whereas countries with non-democratic government restrain themselves from promoting the principles of social justice and equality in their social work profession. However, it is also interesting that only the support by state cannot develop social work in the fullest. Evident to this despite overwarming state support social work in Mainland China is facing numerous challenges. As noted by existing literature, there are lack of acceptance by the public (Wang, 2000, 2013); lack of experienced social workers (Li, 2016; Shi, 2011); issues related to social work field education (Chiller & Crisp, 2012; Hung, Ng, & Fung, 2010; Mo & O'Donoghue, 2018; Ng, 2013; Tsui, O'Donoghue, Boddy, & Pak, 2017); low salary and unclear career prospects (Zeng, Cheung, Leung, & He, 2016). Scholars have also noted that still social work is not an attractive profession of choice for the university graduates (Bai & Daley, 2014).

Societies in the East Asia and South East Asia face similar social issues such as poverty, ageing, issues related to child and women welfare (apart from five localized problems such as one child issue, rural poverty, lonely elderly, human trafficking young progeny, early marriage, youth delinquency, discrimination against migrant, health issues, child labour, border issue and internal conflict, undocumented labourers, and huge number of non-formal labour force). However, social work in all of these countries is different in terms of both education and practice. Further cultural barriers are also obvious in the region for the effective practice of social work. Social work in most of the countries in East Asia and South East Asia is still confused with charity and volunteerism. The attitude of general public is causing more obstacles in the professional growth of the social work, whereas the state has no provisions for creating public awareness in many of these countries. Japan and China have a social work licensing system for practising social work; it did not really help the profession to gain the confidence of general public. As a result, even today social work in China is not a fascinating profession for the graduates (Bai & Daley, 2014).

The problems encountered by the social work programmes in the region are context specific and unique to each country; however, in general all social work programmes face some very fundamental developmental challenges in common. Lack of professional recognition is most common factor effecting the development of social work education in the region. Evidences from Indonesia (Fahrudin, 2009) and China (Wang, 2000, 2013) show that social work is still struggling to achieve the professional status despite its presence for many decades. In some countries, the lack of government support is affecting the professional growth of social work, whereas in China the profession fails to grow and develop because of the governmental control (Liu, 2003; Yip, 2007), at the level of both practice and education (Chiller & Crisp, 2012; Hung et al., 2010; Mo & O'Donoghue, 2018; Ng, 2013; Tsui et al., 2017).

One of the common problems faced by the social work profession is the lack of trained educators with social work qualifications. As reported in China, social work programmes taught by educators without social work background are suffering from poor quality of social work education (Chan et.al. Chapter 4 in this volume). Similarly, in Taiwan, Malaysia and Indonesia a large number of social work educators are from social sciences and not with social work or social welfare background. Further, there is a tension in some countries on, whether the social work should focus on developing context-specific practitioners or practitioners for cross-boarder practice. Nevertheless, Taiwan focuses mainly on developing social workers who can qualify the national social work practice examination and china prepares social workers to ensure social control and social stability in the country.

For the coming millennium, social work in China and Japan needs to focus more on rapid ageing population, whereas social work in Indonesia needs more focus on poverty and inequality. Nevertheless, entire social work fraternity in the region need a focused training and teaching on disaster, natural calamities, and other human sufferings. Incidents of disaster such as earthquakes, floods, and other natural calamities had a greater impact on the development of the region. Social work as a service profession needs to find supporting mechanisms to the victims of these calamities and needs to develop programmes in reintegrating affected population to the mainstream. Social work programmes in the region should learn from the experiences of Japan, Taiwan and China in disaster management and response to these. Further, social work in general in East Asia and South East Asia learns from Chinese social work development. In a short span of 30 years, social work education in China achieved 339 higher education institutions producing undergraduates (Zhang, 2017), and 148 masters programmes (China Philanthropy Times, 2018) producing post graduate social workers as of 2017. Keeping apart the drawbacks the rapid establishment of the programmes and introducing social work practice license and social work service purchase system in China has much to teach to rest of the world. Across the region, there are uniqueness and best practices that each country can learn from each other. Indonesia is the only country that offers social work in its secondary schools (Midgley, 1981). However, Japan has social work programmes in universities, colleges, junior colleges, vocational colleges, and other general training facilities for Certified Social Workers. Indonesia and Malaysia still don't have licensing system for the practitioners and Japan, China, and Taiwan still struggling to enhance the professional practice despite established certification mechanism.

This part of the book explores the development of social work education and its challenges in East Asia and the South East Asian countries. Chapters in this part are an interplay between the local challenges and its global relevance, whereas chapters in this volume further describe the realities of social work education from South Africa to Palestine, Japan to Germany, and Nepal to Trinidad and Tobago. Written by subject specialists, each chapter in this part provides an in-depth analysis of social work education, historical background, cultural and economic aspect that either supports or hinders the development of the social work alongside the national context of social work education. In addition, all these chapters discuss the contemporary challenges and struts of the social work education.

However, the development of indigenous knowledge in social work, the professionalization of social work education and practice, standardization of social work curriculum, collaboration and cooperation between the schools of social work needs further examination and enquiry. The chapters in this part as well as in this volume make an effort in filling the gap in available literature on context-specific challenges for social work education.

References

Bai, J. R., & Daley, J. (2014). A snapshot of the current status of social work education in Mainland China. *Journal of Social Work Education, 50*, 525–534, https://doi.org/10.1080/10437797.2014.916932.

Chiller, P., & Crisp, B. R. (2012). Professional supervision: A workforce retention strategy for social work? *Australian Social Work, 65*, 232–242, https://doi.org/10.1080/0312407X.2011.625036.

China Philanthropy Times. (2018, January 3). Social work: Year of balanced development. Retrieved from http://www.gongyishibao.com/html/yaowen/13161.html.

Fahrudin, A. (2009). Future challenges and direction of social work education and practice in Indonesia. *Proceeding of Seoul international conference on social work (deans conference) "social work education and practice development in the Asia and Pacific region". Seoul Korea, 15–18 April 2009.* Organized by Korean Association of Social Workers, Korean Council on Social Welfare Education, and APASWE.

Hung, S. L., Ng, S. L., & Fung, K. K. (2010). Functions of social work supervision in Shenzhen: Insights from the cross-border supervision model. *International Social Work, 53*, 366–378, https://doi.org/10.1177/0020872809359864.

International Federation of Social Workers (IFSW). (2014). *Global definition of social work.* Melbourne: International Federation of Social Workers.

Li, Y. S. (2016). *Social work development in the new era: Needs, challenges and countermeasures* (in Chinese, Xīn chángtài shíqí shèhuì gōngzuò fāzhǎn xūqiú tiǎozhàn yǔ yìngduì). Retrieved from http://big5.xinhuanet.com/gate/big5/news.xinhuanet.com/gongyi/201603/29/c_128830876.htm.

Liu, J. (2003). Literature review: Ten critical issues on the social work education development in China. *The Hong Kong Journal of Social Work, 37*, 41–59.

Midgley, J. (1981). *Professional imperialism: Social work in the third world.* London: Heinemann.

Mo, Y. H., & O'Donoghue, K. (2018). Nurturing a budding flower: External supervisors' support of the developmental needs of Chinese social workers in Shenzhen, China. *International Social Work*, 1–15.

Ng, K. F. (2013). *A comparison between the internal and external supervisory process conducted by supervisor of Hong Kong and Shenzhen: An example of Guangzhou and Shenzhen* (Unpublished Master thesis). Guangzhou: Polytechnic University.

Shi, X. H. (2011). Researching the social work brain drain. *Journal of Reform & Opening, 1,* 35–36.

Tsui, M. S., O'Donoghue, K., Boddy, J., & Pak, C. M. (2017). From supervision to organisational learning: A typology to integrate supervision, mentorship, consultation and coaching. *The British Journal of Social Work, 47,* 2406–2420, https://doi.org/10.1093/bjsw/bcx006.

Wang, S. B. (2000). A preliminary discussion on indigenization of social work in China. In K. L. Ho & S. B. Wang (Eds.), *An exploration of social work in Chinese societies* (pp. 173–190). River Edge, NJ: Global Publishing.

Wang, S. B. (2013). Social work experience and development in China. *Chinese Education and Society, 46*(6), 79–91, https://doi.org/10.2753/CED1061-1932460612.

Yip, K. S. (2007). Tensions and dilemmas of social work education in China. *International Social Work, 50,* 93–105. https://doi.org/10.1177/0020872807071485.

Zeng, S. C., Cheung, M., Leung, P., & He, X. (2016). Voices from social work graduates in China: Reasons for not choosing social work as a career. *Social Work, 61,* 69–78.

Zhang, Y. (2017, December 10). There are 339 universities and colleges in China that set up social work majors and 105 MSW colleges (In Chinese: Wǒguó gòngyǒu 339 suǒ gāoděng yuàn xiào shèzhì shèhuì gōngzuò zhuānyè,105 suǒ MSW bànxué yuàn xiào). Retrieved from https://www.060694.com/p/clrm20.html.

CHAPTER 2

Social Work Education in Contemporary Indonesia: Issues, Challenges, and Concerns

Adi Fahrudin and Husmiati Yusuf

INTRODUCTION

Indonesia is an archipelagic country of 17,508 islands that stretch along the equator in Southeast Asia. The five major islands are Sumatra, Kalimantan, Java, Sulawesi, and Papua. Based on the National Census in 2010 the population of Indonesia is 237.6 million and based on the World Bank the population estimate for 2018 was 268 million many of whom are descendants of people who migrated from various areas creating a diversity of cultures, religions, ethnicities, and languages. The official language of Indonesia is Indonesian (Bahasa Indonesia). It is the language that unifies Indonesia with its 350 ethnic groups and 750 native languages and dialects. The archipelago's landforms and climate have significantly influenced agriculture, trade, and the formation of the state. Indonesia is divided administratively into provinces and districts. Until 2001 the number of provinces was only 27, but expanded to 34 in 2013 (Ministry of Domestic Affairs, 2013). Indonesia proclaimed independence from Japanese colonial rule on August 17, 1945. Since then the country has experienced several profound political developments. Indonesia's founder President Sukarno was succeeded by President Suharto in 1966. A "new order" government was established in 1967 and was oriented toward direct overall development. In 1997 and 1998

A. Fahrudin (✉)
Department of Social Welfare, University of Muhammadiyah Jakarta,
South Tangerang, Indonesia

H. Yusuf
Center for Social Welfare Research and Development, Jakarta, Indonesia

S. S. M. et al. (eds.), *The Palgrave Handbook of Global Social Work Education*, https://doi.org/10.1007/978-3-030-39966-5_2

Indonesia went through its worst economic crisis since independence (CBS, 2010). After more than three decades in power President Suharto resigned in 1998. The political situation underwent a rapid transition. Suharto's last vice president B. J. Habibie succeeded him as president from 1998 to 1999. He was followed by Abdurrahman Wahid from 1999 to 2001 and Megawati Soekarnoputri, daughter of President Sukarno, from 2001 to 2004. A historic direct presidential election took place for the first time in October 2004 when President Susilo Bambang Yudoyono came into office. He was reelected for a second term (2009–2014). From 2014 the active Jakarta governor was elected as President of Indonesia (2014–2019). Indonesia is plagued by a number of fundamental social problems such as poverty and malnutrition, unemployment, children's issues, drug abuse, HIV/AIDS, natural and social disaster, disability, and an explosion in the number of older people. These problems need social work intervention by professional social workers. Although social work in Indonesia is not something new, it still struggles to get established.

To understand social work education in Indonesia we must fully understand the history and dynamics of the national education system. National education is divided into three levels: basic, secondary, and higher. Based on the National Education System Law No. 20 Year 2003 higher education institutions in Indonesia can take the form of academies, polytechnics, colleges, institutes, or universities. Higher education is provided by the Ministry of Research, Technology and Higher Education (MORTHE), other ministries or government institutions, and a community of private agencies. In the National Education System higher education is divided into two types known as academic education and professional education. Academic education is higher education based on innovative science and development with more emphasis on quality improvement and a broader science vision. Academic education is usually offered by a college, institute, or university, while professional education is higher education that exists to equip students with specific skills with emphasis on improving competency and work skills regarding applied science and technology. Professional education is offered by an academy, polytechnic, college, institute, or university. Academic education is mostly under the administration of MORTHE, while professional education is generally under the administration of other ministries. The main purpose of academic education is to produce graduates with academic degrees at the undergraduate (S1–Bachelor) and postgraduate (S2–Master and S3–PhD) levels, while the aim of professional education is to give graduates the label of professional (Diploma 1 to 4) up to the label of specialist (Specialist 1 to 2). The quality of social work and how it is practised is regulated by government. Quality assurance regarding social work education and how it should be practised is very important to maintaining standards in the future and to ensuring that graduates from social work programs become qualified and competent social workers.

HISTORY OF SOCIAL WORK EDUCATION

Social work education in most countries is offered at the college or university level. Indonesia is a major exception in offering social work courses not only in universities and colleges but also in secondary schools (Midgley, 1981). Formal social work education in Indonesia starts at the secondary level. Under Ministry of Education Decree No. 24/C (04-09-1946) the Sekolah Pembimbing Kemasyarakatan (SPK) were established in Solo (Central Java).[1] These were the first types of schools to offer 4-year courses in social work education at secondary school level. Such schools were the result of collaboration between the Ministry of Social Affairs and the Ministry of Education and were tasked with training Ministry of Social Affairs staff of both sexes. In 1950 these schools expanded their curriculum from basic social work education to include theory and practice. Most students were Ministry of Social Affairs staff. In 1952 some 25 graduates from these schools were sent by the Ministry of Social Affairs to study further at the School voor Maatschapelijk Werk in the Netherlands. One of these students was Mr D. Drajat who went on to teach a 1-year course in basic social vocational training called Kursus Dinas Sosial Menengah dan Atas (KDSMA) that was extended to become the Kursus Kejuruan Sosial Tingkat Menengah dan Tinggi (KKSTMT), a 2-year training programme.[2] This course was considered as early formal education and training necessary to improve the quality of human resources at the Ministry of Social Affairs (Fahrudin, 1997; Sulaiman, 1985). The first Director of the KDSMA was Mr H. A. Romlie (1957–1963). In 1964 these schools were upgraded to college university status under the Ministry of Social Affairs. One of them the Bandung School of Social Welfare now has college university status and students can gain a 3-year Bachelor's degree and a 2-year postgraduate *doctorandus.*

In 1955 an SPK was established in Jakarta. In 1959 these schools changed their names to Sekolah Pekerjaan Sosial Atas (SPSA, Social Work High Schools) and were established in other parts of Indonesia such as Medan, Palembang, Semarang, Malang, Banjarmasin, and Makasar. In 1976 these schools had another name change to Sekolah Menengah Pekerjaan Sosial (SMPS, Social Work Secondary Schools). These schools continued to offer 4-year courses. In 1994 the names of these types of schools were further changed to Sekolah Menengah Kejuruan (SMK) Kesejahteraan Masyarakat (Vocational Secondary Schools of Community Welfare). Under Ministry of Education and Culture Decree No. 036/O/1997 (07-03-1997) the social work programme in these schools was merged with other programmes under the Sekolah Menengah Kejuruan (Vocational Secondary Schools) with one of the majors being a 3-year course on social work/social care. The establishment of the Sekolah Pembimbing Kemasyarakatan (SPK) and the course Kursus Dinas Sosial Menengah dan Atas (KDSMA) was not only as a result of the need for skilled human resources to implement the work of the then relatively newly formed Ministry of Social Affairs but also to shape a response to the two previous UN International Surveys of Training for Social Work. The surveys were titled Documents of Training for Social Work: An International Survey (UN Publication Sales No. 1950.IV.11) and Training for Social Work: Second International Survey (UN Publication Sales No. 1955.IV.9) and were both very clear that the education and training of social workers in Indonesia still required much to be desired. This was a consequence, first, of Indonesia being a relatively new independent state and post-independence political turmoil meant there was no time to think about the need for experts skilled in the field of social work when leaders of the country needed to be put in place. The second reason is the countries that once colonized Indonesia such as the Netherlands and Japan did not prepare a system of social welfare services— let alone one preparing trained professionals in social work! Many policies were implemented by the United Nations to expand social work to developing countries especially in the Third World. Midgley (1981) noted that among the earliest activities of the United Nations in the field of social policy was an international survey of the need for social work training. This survey was designed to determine the extent of and need for social work education throughout the world. Although it dealt with industrial countries too, special attention was paid to the Third World (p. 57). Brigham (1982) noted that in 1981 only four universities and colleges had social work programmes at the Bachelor and Doctorate levels in Indonesia. These courses were offered by the University of Indonesia, Bandung School of Social Welfare, University of Muhammadiyah Jakarta, and Widuri School of Social Work. By the 1990s more public and private universities offered social work education programmes under the label social welfare. According to Sisworahardjo (1993) only 27 universities and colleges had social work/social welfare programmes registered with the Indonesian Association for Social Work Education. As of 2011 there were 33 universities/colleges offering social work/social welfare programmes (IASWE, 2012). However, according to Sulaiman (1985) the quantity of social work/social welfare programmes did not lessen the quality of social work education programmes.

Political, social, and economic changes in Indonesia influenced social work education. As a result of the New Order Regime of General Suharto more changes and reforms occurred in the education system and social service delivery models (Fahrudin, 1999). Earthquakes and the tsunami disaster in 2004 in Indonesia provided opportunities for higher education institutions to cooperate with national and international agencies. For example, the State Islamic University in Yogyakarta (which is under the control of the Ministry of Religious Affairs), the McGill University, and the Canadian International Development Agency (CIDA) jointly set up and offered postgraduate interdisciplinary Islamic studies focusing on social work without an undergraduate social work programme (Fatimah & Wildan, 2013).

DEVELOPMENT OF SOCIAL WORK EDUCATION

Social work education in Indonesia is varied in terms of programmed content, teaching methods, student admission qualifications, duration of study, career outcomes, and student intakes each year (Fahrudin, 1999). According to Brigham (1982) the number of social work schools correlates with a country's size, development level, socioeconomic status, cultural factor, colonial history, and poverty level. Therefore, Brigham's study has relevance to the Indonesian social work education system. Social work education in Indonesia is very varied, has been slow to develop, and is still struggling to achieve professional education status relevant to its national development. The major problem with social work education in Indonesia is the education system's struggle to attain a professional standard and curriculum that is relevant to the country's needs (Fahrudin, 2009). Moreover, it lacks the human resources necessary to teach social workers (especially, qualified lecturers and instructors for fieldwork). Colonization is also known to influence the development of social welfare systems and social work education (Fahrudin, 2013). For example, the Malaysian social welfare system and social work education were influenced by the British. However, in the case of Indonesia colonization by the Dutch and the Japanese had little impact on the country's social welfare system and social work education (Fahrudin, 1999, 2005, 2009). From the very start social work education in Indonesia was strongly influenced by the American model. Most of the social work curriculum is now based on the curriculum, approaches, and modified models of practice from the United States (Fahrudin & Yusuf, 2016). The curriculum content is more clinical in that it makes use of a problem-solving approach and model. The early years were marked by social work experts from the United States such as Professors Brigham, Irvin Tebor, T. Bisno, David Drucker, and Mildred Sikema mainly guiding and supervising the establishment of the social work education curriculum under the UN Development Programme (UNDP). Moreover, most pioneering social work educators in Indonesia (particularly, those from the Bandung School of Social Welfare) such as J. Marsaman, Holil Sulaiman, and Irawan Soehartono graduated from universities in the United States (Sulaiman, 1985). They incorporated knowledge and experiences gained from the United States into the Indonesian social work curriculum and training, adapting and modifying them to the local context.

SOCIAL WORK EDUCATION: ISSUES AND CHALLENGES

Despite the many imminent issues affecting social work education in Indonesia, this chapter will highlight only a few selected issues that are currently affecting and will continue to affect the development and direction of social work practice in Indonesia. If these issues and challenges are not addressed the status quo will clearly remain and will have adverse effects on young social worker practitioners specifically and other social workers generally. This will both directly and indirectly affect the welfare of the clients they serve.

Social Work Curriculum

Historically, social work education in Indonesia has accepted and adapted many models from Western social work education. This has relevance to Kendall's (1986) study where evidence shows that Asian schools are still struggling with the problems of indigenisation and the implementation of social development objectives in social work education. No serious effort is being made to search for a core or supplementary social work curriculum that is more relevant to national development. Efforts to change curriculum patterns to increase their relevance is occurring—though very slowly. Formulation of a social work education standard and core curriculum equivalent to the International Association of Schools of Social Work (IASSW) global standard for social work education and training still remains as a major issue. This has relevance to Coulshed's (1993) and Hammoud (1988) statement that the universal problem in social work curriculum design is how to include more variety in subject matter into courses and the issues involved in applying such subject matter to the teaching of social work students and how to integrate methods of teaching and learning that can be applied to social work. There is no difference in the social work/social welfare education programme in both public and private universities. For example, students at the Bachelor level at the University of Indonesia require 144 credit hours to complete the course—the same required for students at the Diploma IV level at the Bandung School of Social Welfare. Social work education in Indonesia is very varied. The structure of higher education is divided into academic and professional education and has implications for the social work education system since this is also divided into two main streams. A programme of academic education is carried out by public and private universities that have educational programmes such as a social welfare science programme, while a programme of professional social work education is carried out by schools such as the Bandung School of Social Welfare.

Standard and Accreditation

Social work/social welfare programmes are delivered through regular classes in both universities and colleges. There is no online education or distance education system. Even today the accreditation of social work education and the licensing for social work practice is not clear—let alone implemented. Indonesia has established the Badan Akreditasi Nasional-Perguruan Tinggi (BAN-PT, Higher Education Institution National Accreditation Board) administered by the Ministry of National Education for the accreditation of education programmes, in general, in both universities and colleges. Indonesia also has a semi-government institution under the administration of the Ministry of Manpower and Transmigration called the Badan Nasional Sertifikasi Profesi (BNSP, National Board for Profession Certification). The function of this board is not specific to social work but applies to all professions and occupations. Because there is no specific standard and accreditation of social work education it is difficult to ensure the quality of social work education or that of social work practice. This will pose problems for social work students who want to further their studies overseas and for social work graduates who wish to practise or work in other countries.

Multicultural Education

Indonesia is a multicultural country made up of people from different racial, ethnic, socioeconomic, religious, and cultural backgrounds. The programme for social work education faces challenges in teaching cultural sensitivity to social work students. Issues include how to design and implement a social work curriculum relevant to a multicultural society. The main responsibility of social work educators regarding this issue is to help in the transition from student to professional social worker and ensure the physical and academic environment for learning is favorable and provides them with relevant practice knowledge and skills. One of the most important issues facing social work education in Indonesia today relates to how students can be taught social work in a way that is personally meaningful to them and directly related to the developmental functions of the country and its own cultural context. If the answer could be given in one word, then it would be indigenisation. It is necessary to indigenise teaching methods and teaching materials. As a result of the Asian and Pacific Association for Social Work Education/International Federation of Social Workers (APASWE/IFSW) Asia Conference in Jakarta the Indonesian Association for Social Work Education (IASWE) organized in 1987 a national workshop on National Social Work Education Curriculum standard in Bandung (Sulaiman, 1987). The outcome was a document on setting up a core social work curriculum and the indigenisation of teaching material. The debate on Western social work education and indigenisation will continue for some time to come.

Indigenisation

An issue regarding indigenous social work in Indonesia is related to religion and local culture. In 2004 the State Islamic University in Yogyakarta jointly made available a new postgraduate programme with McGill University and CIDA. The programme was a Master of Arts in interdisciplinary Islamic studies with a major in social work. This programme is interesting in that it combines Islam as a religion with social work and views it from a secular perspective. However, the development of indigenous social work in Indonesia has not generally been very successful. The curriculum, teaching materials, reference books, and fieldwork model are still being adapted from those of the United States and other countries. Social work education and practice in Indonesia has largely been influenced by social workers, volunteers, and international humanitarian organisation workers who provided assistance after the tsunami disaster in Aceh. Change in and awareness of the global environment particularly in relation to the multicultural, globalisation, and sustainable development in the country have influenced social work education and practice. However, universities and colleges modify and adapt their programmes according to their own perceptions and interests without direction and guidance from the Indonesia Association for Social Work Education.

Fieldwork

The curriculum and fieldwork system in Indonesia differs between the academic (university) and professional (college) mainstream. The typical curriculum for social work education at the Bachelor level involves generic social work. The curriculum and fieldwork system of the academic and professional mainstream differs in terms of length of fieldwork, supervision, method of evaluation, etc. However, it contradicts generic social work education. For example, fieldwork placement of social work students is a compulsory subject for all students at university. However, there is a problem with the structure and content of this fieldwork placement when fieldwork is not systematically supervised by a social work educator from the university or by a trained social worker in the respective social welfare agency of placement. Universities providing a programme of academic education in social welfare are more flexible in that supervision from the university and the agency is not strict. Hence students often do fieldwork without completing the minimum hours required. Some other colleges offering professional education in social work treat fieldwork systematically. Students from such colleges only take the subject when they have experienced three fieldwork options and completed a minimum total of 600 hours. This subject consists of three types of fieldwork: Fieldwork I in the agency and community with concurrent placement, Fieldwork II in the community with block placement, and Fieldwork III in the agency with block placement. Such fieldwork placements give students the opportunity to apply their theoretical knowledge in practice. Such fieldwork involvement teaches students the basic skills necessary for working with an individual, group, or community. Generally, the major handicap in fieldwork education in Indonesia is the lack of professionally qualified social workers to take on the supervisory role for students on field placements. Unlike the case in developed countries Indonesia still lacks a cohort of trained personnel to supervise students in their fieldwork environment. The lack of such trained professionals invariably burdens the academic staff with the task of supervising students in their field placement as well (Fahrudin, 2004a, 2004b).

Social Work Distance Education

Distance education is important in social work education. Since Indonesia is an archipelago it needs to develop a distance social work education system. A programme of social work/social welfare is only delivered through regular classes at universities and colleges. Distance education in social work is not driven by technology but by the profession's obligation to educate social workers in a way that will ensure their ability to provide needed services to persons and communities effectively (Abels, 2005). Indonesia is the world's largest archipelago and is estimated to have about 18,000 islands. Therefore, distance education in social work would provide an ideal way of bringing improved educational opportunities to rural and island areas (especially, for individuals keen to become social workers who would otherwise be left out due to diverse economic and geographical constraints). There are 33 schools in Indonesia that provide courses on social work most of which are found on Java. Distance education in social work would promote social access, equality, and social justice for everyone. Distance education in social work in this context would not only provide a medium for the teaching of social work, it would also help in fulfilling the commitment of social work to equality and social justice.

Student Selection

Another issue in social work education worthy of mention is the mechanism used to select students. Currently there is no systematic mechanism to select students wanting to receive social work education in Indonesia. Having selection criteria in place for entry to any programme or profession is important in determining who are selected or rejected. This represents for those selected entry to the first stage of a professional career and preparation for this career. This will involve changes in the social status, income, lifestyle, and life chances of the candidate in addition to membership of the professional community (Fahrudin, 2004b).

SOCIAL WORK EDUCATION: QUO VADIS AND CONCERN

The development of social work education in Indonesia has witnessed a series of historical moments in which different ideas as to the purpose of social workers still continues to be debated. There is still no national standard for social work education such as a basic curriculum, accreditation, fieldwork system, and fieldwork supervision nor any national definition of what social work is to guide universities, colleges, and other stakeholders. The Ministry of Research, Technology and Higher Education (MORTHE) and the Ministry of Social Affairs have played very important roles in the development of social work education for the future. Although the historical and current situation of social work education in Indonesia have similarities with other countries such as Malaysia, Vietnam, Bangladesh, and China, there are still major differences. In Malaysia, for example, professional social work was introduced by the British as early as the 1930s, but it was mainly focussed on problems of migrant labourers from India and China (Yasas, 1974). It was only after World War II, when social problems of displacement, juvenile delinquency, and poverty became more prominent, that the Department of Social Welfare was formally established in 1946. Social work services were introduced to provide financial aid for the needy, probation programmes for juvenile delinquents, care homes for women and girls, and residential care for the disabled and the aged. However, social work education did not formally start at the University of Malaya in Singapore until 1952 (Yasas, 1974). According to Baba (1998) the development of programmes of social work education in the country also varied from programme to programme. It appears that the programme of social work education at the University of Science Malaysia was the only programme meeting the standards of the IASSW. In terms of academic staff trained in social work many universities still rely on non-trained social work academic staff from other disciplines (Baba, 1992). However, the situation changed as a result of socioeconomic progress between 1985 and 2000 with social work education in Malaysia developing very fast compared with most ASEAN countries except the Philippines. This was also the case in Vietnam when the importance of social work to national development gathered momentum in 1986 and the process of economic reform called *doi moi* began. However, social work education did not formally start in Vietnam until 1995 when the Ministry of Education and Training approved two higher education institutions to teach social work as part of a broader social science programme (Hugman, Lan, & Hong, 2007). Social work education in Vietnam today is available in other universities despite there being no national standard for social work education such as a curriculum, academic staff, and fieldwork. By comparison, social work education in Bangladesh originated in the days of the Pakistani regime (Moore, 1958). Such education had two key objectives: to build a professional leadership capable of solving acute and large-scale social problems and of criticising how the existing social welfare structure operated in response to various human needs and to guide the future development programme. A 3-month introductory course in social work was first started in Bangladesh (then known as East Pakistan) in 1953. This was followed between 1955 and 1956 by professional education in social work being introduced as a 9-month training course on community development and medical social work at Dhaka University. With the completion of the 9-month on-the-job training course under the country's first Urban

Community Development Project the establishment of a school of social work under Dhaka University was proposed. Samad and Faruque (2009) noted that all the above initiatives were undertaken under the auspices of the UN Technical Assistance Programme in the Social Service Sector and guided by UN experts (namely, Dr J. J. D. Moore, Mr Shawty, Ms Anana Tooll, Ms Lucky, and Mr Dumpson).

Although social work education used to be provided in a few universities in China such as Yanjin University of Nanjing, during the 1950s and 1960s communist ideologies conflicted with capitalist ideologies and social work was removed from the university curriculum. Nevertheless, social work education and training in China developed much faster than in other countries when the government adopted an open door policy in 1978, sociology teaching was resumed, and social work was reintroduced to higher education (Law & Gu, 2008). Social work education in China rapidly expanded in 1988 when the Ministry of Education formally allowed universities to establish a social work programme. The Ministry of Civil Affairs was instrumental in setting up the Civil Affairs Social Work Education Research Center in 1987, the China Social Worker Association in 1991, and the China Association of Social Work Education in 1994. The development of social work education took a unique path in China. In the absence of trained social work academics there was rapid growth of social work programmes at all levels of training institutions including universities under the ambit of the Ministry of Education, provincial and district level universities, and local vocational and technical training institutes. According to Law and Gu (2008) approximately 30 social work programmes had been established by 1999. Although they were mostly under the auspices of the sociology departments of respective universities, 9 of them formed an independent Social Work Department. However, as of 2006 there were more than 200 institutions across the country providing social work training at various levels. The number is expected to rise. In the absence of an explicit government policy acknowledging social work as an accredited vocation the rationale for universities to add social work to their teaching subjects is pragmatic (i.e., fulfilling the government's requirement to expand higher education by increasing the intake of undergraduate students despite the lack of relevant teaching staff and job opportunities for graduates). In Thailand the history and development of social work were also unique. According Mongkolnchaiarunya (2009), social work education has been taught in two universities in Thailand: Thammasat University, which is the second oldest public university, started this programme in 1954 and established the Faculty of Social Administration; and the Faculty of Social Work and Social Welfare, which belonged to a private university called Hua Chiew Chalermprakiat University, made available a social work programme in 1990. Both institutions are quality accredited by the Commission on Higher Education of the Ministry of Education. In actual fact, the first programme of social work training in Thailand was launched in 1942. It was a 1-year program administered by the Council of Women's Culture at the time of the Marshal Pibulsongkram government. The council offered a Diploma (Certificate) for those who completed the programme. Trainees were government servants who worked for the council. Lots of difficulties such as lack of appropriate teachers led to the programme being terminated after 3 years of operation. The development of social work education in Indonesia, Malaysia, Vietnam, Bangladesh, China, and Thailand is varied in system, curriculum, fieldwork, academic staff, and government support. Contributions from experts under the UN Development Programme in Early Social Work Education played an important role in the development of social work education. Economic progress has been found to correlate with the development of social work education in Malaysia and China. Vietnam social work education started at the same time as economic reform. In contrast with the situation in Malaysia, China, and Vietnam, social work education in Indonesia and Bangladesh was not accompanied by economic progress in the country. Although social work education in Malaysia and China developed very quickly, in Indonesia it was very slow. The major issues here for Indonesia are what direction should social work education in Indonesia take and how should the system, curriculum, staff development, fieldwork, etc. be reformed.

CONCLUSION

The history of social work education in Indonesia started with independence. Although the history, development, and current situation of social work education varies widely from country to country, colonisation did not significantly influence development of the social welfare system and social work education in Indonesia. Development of social work education and the social work profession is still struggling to attain maturity as a profession. Social work education needs a new direction for it to achieve the international standard in curriculum, fieldwork, student selection, indigenisation, multicultural perspective, and distance education. The future direction of social work education in Indonesia will not be successful without strategic alliance and cooperation from higher learning institutions that offer a programme of social work education, as well as support by government. Many stakeholders (especially, government institutions, the School of Social Association, and the National Association of Social Workers) need to play their respective roles and give their support to promote, improve, and enhance the quality of social work education and practice in Indonesia.

NOTES

1. Ministry of Education Decree No. 24/C (04-09-1946).
2. Generally, in BSSW history publicly only known as KKST, but in formal document as Kursus Kejuruan Sosial Tingkat Menengah dan Tinggi.

REFERENCES

Abels, P. (2005). The way to distance education. In Paul Abels (Ed.), *Distance education in social work: Planning, teaching and learning*. New York: Springer.

Baba, I. (1992). Social work—An effort towards building a caring society. In C. K. Sin & I. M. Salleh (Eds.), *Caring society: Emerging issues and future direction*. Kuala Lumpur: ISIS Malaysia.

Baba, I. (1998). *The need for professionalism in social work: In the case of Malaysia*. Paper presented at Advancing Social Work Education, Universiti Malaysia Sarawak, Kota Samarahan.

Brigham, T. M. (1982). Social work education pattern in five developing countries: Relevance of US Microsystems model. *Journal of Education for Social Work, 18*(12), 21–26.

Central Bureau of Statistics. (2010). *National population census report*. Jakarta: CBS.

Coulshed, V. (1993). Adult learning: Implications for teaching in social work education. *British Journal of Social Work, 23*, 1–13.

Fahrudin, A. (1997). *Pendidikan tinggi pekerjaan sosial: Sejarah, agenda masalah dan kegayutannya dengan pembangunan nasional* [*Social work higher education: A history, problems agenda and relevance with national development*]. Dalam Prosiding Seminar Ilmiah Perhimpunan Pelajar Indonesia (PPI) se—Malaysia. Perhimpunan Pelajar Indonesia, Universiti Sains Malaysia, Penang.

Fahrudin, A. (1999). *Komitmen profesional dikalangan pelajar kerja sosial di Indonesia* [*Professional commitment among social work students' in Indonesia*] (Unpublished PhD thesis, Social Work). Institute of Postgraduate Studies, Universiti Sains Malaysia, Penang.

Fahrudin, A. (2004a). *Global standard in social work education and critic to social work education curriculum in Indonesia*. Paper presented at International Seminar on Social Work Education Curriculum Development, Joint organized by Bandung School of Social Welfare and La Trobe University, Australia.

Fahrudin, A. (2004b). *Pendidikan dan latihan pekerjaan sosial berbasis kompetensi*. Makalah disajikan dalam Seminar Pendidikan dan Pelatihan Berbasis Komptensi.

Fahrudin, A. (2005). *Mainstreaming social development in national policy and program*. Paper presented at International Conference on Social Development, State Islamic University, Jakarta.

Fahrudin, A. (2009, April 15–18). Future challenges and direction of social work education and practice in Indonesia. *Proceeding of Seoul International Conference on Social Work (Deans Conference), Social work education and practice development in the Asia and Pacific region*. Seoul Korea. Organized by Korean Association of Social Workers, Korean Council on Social Welfare Education, and APASWE.

Fahrudin, A. (2013). Social work and social welfare in Indonesia. In E. Furuto (Ed.), *Social work and social welfare in Asia and Pacific*. Washington, DC: Columbia University Press.

Fahrudin, A., & Yusuf, H. (2016, March). Social work education in Indonesia: History and current situation. *International Journal of Social Work and Human Services Practice Horizon Research Publishing, 4*(1), 16–23.

Fatimah, H., & Wildan, M. (2013). *Personal interview regarding international collaboration in social work education between UIN Sunan Kalijaga and McGill University*. Yogyakarta.

Hammoud, H. R. (1988). Social work education in developing countries: Issues and problems in undergraduate curricula. *International Social Work, 31,* 195–210.

Hugman, R., Lan, N. T. T., & Hong, N. T. (2007). Developing social work in Vietnam. *International Social Work, 50*(2), 197–211.

Indonesian Association for Social Work Education (IASWE). (2012). *Profile social work and social welfare education program in Indonesia.* Bandung: Bandung College of Social Work.

Kendall, K. A. (1986). Social work education in the 1980s: Accent on change. *International Social Work, 29*(1), 15–28. https://doi.org/10.1177/00208728 8602900104.

Law, K. C. A., & Gu, J. X. (2008). Social work education in Mainland China: Development and Issues. *Asian Social Work and Policy Review, 2,* 1–12.

Midgley, J. (1981). *Professional imperialism: Social work in the third world.* London: Heineman.

Ministry of Domestic Affairs. (2013). *List of provinces, districts, cities, and subdistricts in Indonesia.* Retrieved June 10, 2013, from http://www.depdagri.go.id/media/filemanager/2013/01/29/0//0.indukkec.pdf.

Mongkolnchaiarunya, J. (2009, April 15–18). *Social work education and profession in Thailand: Sunrise or sunset.* Paper presented at the Seoul International Social Work Conference—Dean's Forum: *Social work education and practice development in Asia Pacific region* in Seoul, South Korea. The conference is jointly organized by the Asia Pacific Association for Social Work Education (APASWE), Korean Council on Social Welfare Education (KCSWE) and Korean Association of Social Workers (KASW).

Moore, J. J. O. (1958). *The report and the prospect from which it arose: A tentative and unpublished report.* Prepared for the Government of Pakistan, Dhaka.

Samad, M., & Faruque, C. J. (2009, April 15–18). Development of social work education in Bangladesh and need for international cooperation. *Proceeding of Seoul International Conference on Social Work (Deans Conference), Social work education and practice development in the Asia and Pacific region.* Seoul Korea. Organized by Korean Association of Social Workers, Korean Council on Social Welfare Education, and APASWE.

Sisworahardjo, S. (1993). School members of the Indonesian association for social work education. *Asian Pacific Journal of Social Work, 3*(1), 106–108. https://doi.org/10.1080/21650993.1993.9755631.

Sulaiman, H. (1985). *Pemikiran Ke Arah Peningkatan dan Pengembangan Pendidikan Pekerjaan Sosial di Indonesia.* Bandung: Sekolah Tinggi Kesejahteraan Sosial.

Sulaiman, H. (1987). *Pemikiran ke arah peningkatan dan pengembangan pendidikan pekerjaan sosial di Indonesia.* Bandung: Sekolah Tinggi Kesejahteraan Sosial.

Yasas, F. M. (1974). *Report to the government of Malaysia on the establishment of a professional course in social work and community development training at the bachelor's level at the Universiti Sains Malaysia.* Bangkok: ESCAP.

CHAPTER 3

Challenges in Social Work Education in the Context of Social Work in Japanese Society

Kana Matsuo

Introduction

Japanese social work education started before World War II. However, after the war it changed its shape and goals. American theories such as casework, community work, and group social work were established within the Japanese curriculum of social work schools. This chapter reviews the context of social work/welfare system and describes recent challenges in social work education in Japan.

Concept of Social Work in Japan

Although English literature distinguishes between the meanings of social work, social welfare, and social wellbeing, in Japanese all these terms are commonly described by one word *fukushi* "[福祉]."

Social welfare–related activities and facilities take many forms in Japan; however, not all such activities are equivalent to what is called social work in the United States. Nakamura (2007) defined social work as that carried out by social work professions that have workers trained in the skills and knowledge of social work. Moreover, social *fukushi* activities extensively embrace professional social work. Regrettably, workers in social work

K. Matsuo (✉)
Asian Research Institute for International Social Work,
Shukutoku University, Chiba, Japan
e-mail: kana.matsuo@soc.shukutoku.ac.jp

© The Author(s) 2021
S. S. M. et al. (eds.), *The Palgrave Handbook of Global Social Work Education*, https://doi.org/10.1007/978-3-030-39966-5_3

professions have been officially termed certified social workers, although they have not yet been recognised as belonging to the social work profession in governmental labour statistics in Japan. Statistics show that only guidance workers in facilities belong to the Japanese social work profession (Ministry of Internal Affairs and Communications, 2009).

Why is social work such a complex concept in Japan? Is it because of the lack of comprehensive legislation on social work? No it is not, although the language gap between Japanese and English is undoubtedly a major factor.

As mentioned above, the terms social work, social welfare, and social well-being are all described by one Japanese word *fukushi* "[福祉]" (Ichibangase, 1968).

Before World War II the concept of social work was evoked after the Rice Riot in 1918. It focussed on providing relief from poverty by undertaking charitable acts and was social reformistic in character. The Settlement House Movement and social work system were introduced from the United States and other Western countries. These activities translated as *shakai jigyou* "[社会事業]" in Japanese. The term described organizational activities carried out mostly to improve the lot of vulnerable people in society. *Shakai jigyou* has been operational in voluntary private and public facilities ever since. Social work and its translated term *shakai jigyou* have been explained in the narrow sense of *shakai fukushi* "[社会福祉]" in Japan (Ichibangase, 1964, 1971, 1994).

After World War II the Japanese social welfare system was amended to align with the new constitution adopted by the government. *Fukushi* was translated as "welfare" in the English version of the constitution. Therefore, in Japanese legislation *fukushi*, social work, and social welfare can all be used to mean "welfare" in English.

BACKGROUND TO SOCIAL WORK/WELFARE/FUKUSHI IN JAPAN AFTER WORLD WAR II

From 1945 to 1954 the General Headquarters (GHQ)[1] had an undeniable impact on policy making in Japan. The main issue they had to tackle was emergency relief and rebuilding in post-war confusion.

Social work in Japan was made up of two streams that began at that time. One stream was to build the social *fukushi* organisational system. It was well matched with the policy making and social needs of the post-war period. Discussions on social welfare states, social welfare policy, and social security were vigorous among social *fukushi* academic circles. They quoted articles and took onboard legislation from Sweden and the United Kingdom. They focussed on establishing a social security system that included health and nutrition control, medical delivery, and the social *fukushi* system.

The other stream focussed on providing social workers with the practical skills necessary to be engaged in the social workforce. Social casework, social group work, and community work theories from the United States were introduced to Japan.[2] Japanese social work textbooks are responsible for introducing the roots of social work theories from the United States (Kitajima, Soeda, Takahashi, & Watanabe, 2002; Editorial Committee on the Certified Social Workers' Training Courses, 2010; Okamura, 2011).

From 1955 to 1965 the Japanese economy grew rapidly and people's daily lives changed likewise. People from rural areas moved to cities in search of job opportunities. A comprehensive social security system was established and modified in this period. National Health Insurance covered the medical care requirements of all citizens. The National Pension Scheme likewise formed the core of the Japanese social *fukushi* policy discussion.

In the period of high economic growth (1965–1974) people's lives became largely stabilized with higher wages and higher standards of living. The population in cities increased rapidly and, conversely, the rural population decreased and the number of elderly got bigger. The number of women who worked after bearing children also increased and this highlighted the need for childcare facilities during the day. This led to the Children's Nursery Care and the Child Allowance System.

"The First Year of Welfare," as it was called, was 1973. Until 1973 medical services were free for the elderly and the national pension system had been revised. Social *fukushi* legislation had been enacted and divided into six types for the poverty stricken, children, physically and mentally disabled, the elderly, women, and single-parent families. However, somewhat ironically the same year marked a turning point in welfare policies due to sudden stagnation in the economy referred to as the Oil Shock in Japan. The resultant fiscal austerity meant that social *fukushi* policies that had been expanded were reexamined, transferred to become community-based policies, and moved from large public institutions to private social resources.

Care provided by large institutions shifted to in-home care in an effort to maintain and improve quality of life (QOL) (MHLW, 1996) in the mid-1980s. The official social welfare budget was cut off and led to new service delivery systems such as small non-profit organisations (NPOs).

With this background the Certified Social Worker (CSW) and Certified Care Worker Act was enacted in 1987, and in 1997 under Act 131 a certified examination system was established for psychiatric social workers as well.

The situation changed dramatically after the mid-1990s. The structural reform of social security in Japan started at that time. The aim was to prepare for an ageing society with fewer children. Social welfare services began to be delivered as user-oriented services that were available to all citizens. Citizens could basically choose the service they needed.

The Long-term Care Insurance Act (1997, enacted in 2000) and the amended Social Welfare Act (1951) strongly reflected the concept of user-oriented services and represented a milestone in the social *fukushi* system in Japan.

An ageing society with fewer children was the basis for Japanese social welfare and security policies. In addition, social welfare policies for disabled people were reexamined and several task force groups were established in 2003 so that the UN Convention on the Rights of Persons with Disabilities in 2014 could be ratified. The first act for developmental disabilities was enacted in 2004 (Act on Support for Persons with Developmental Disabilities, Act No. 167 of 2004). The Services and Support for Persons with Disabilities Act came into force in 2005 and represented new welfare legislation to provide comprehensive support for people with disabilities.

The once traditional extended family system in Japan shifted to that of a nuclear family. Younger generations in rural areas moved away from their parents. They had to bring up their children in cities without support from their parents. They were also isolated in their own living areas because most people lived far from their workplaces. The Child Welfare Act was amended in 2008 to take this into consideration; however, the shortage of childcare facilities continues to be a serious social problem in Japan.

Moreover, many people face various challenges in bringing up a family of their own and continuing with their career. The younger generation, in particular, find it difficult to maintain their working environment and support their family as well.

The elderly live without the support of their children and their children find it hard to bring up their own family. The family style has seen another shift from nuclear families to non-children families in recent times in Japan. This has led to programmes being set up to support families with children in an effort to avoid a society in which parents feel obliged not to have children.

On 11 March 2011 a massive earthquake and tsunami impacted the northeast area of Japan. The Great East Japan Earthquake killed 19,630 people (2569 were never found) and injured 6230 (as of March 2018).[3] This tragic disaster highlighted a lack of preparedness on the part of the state and the vulnerability of the community.

Social security and tax have been comprehensively reformed since 2011. The purpose of such reform is to ensure that all civilians live in harmony *kyo-sei* "共生" and receive the benefits of social security in this period of rapid social economic change in Japan.

In 2014 the Long-term Care Insurance Act was amended to include a new programme titled the Community-based Integrated Care System. This reform reflected the new system of social welfare and healthcare for the elderly.

As a result of these trends certified social workers (CSWs) are now reassuming their role in the community. CSWs are expected to be real social workers and not merely perform a consultation role.

SOCIAL WORKERS IN JAPAN

Although officers in municipal welfare offices and child guidance centers are not required to be CSWs or psychiatric social workers (PSWs), they are trained in higher education (to at least college/university Bachelor level) and then work professionally in their respective workplaces.

Since the 1990s CSWs and PSWs have been recognised as trained and professional social workers in Japan. As of March 2018 there were 221,251 CSWs, 80,891 PSWs, and 1,558,897 certified care workers registered in Japan.[4]

The main workplaces of social workers are social welfare corporations,[5] which are considered juridical by the Social Welfare Act. Such corporations deliver various services mainly through institutions and facilities such as homes for the elderly, mentally/physically disabled, and children. Many social workers also work in hospitals and municipal/governmental authorities and more than 50% of PSWs work in hospitals and clinics. The number of workplaces and job opportunities for social workers have rapidly spread in private enterprises and in educational and legal fields.

Certified workers are organised by professional groups. Such groups and medical social workers have reorganised themselves into a single professional social worker association.

Social Work Education in Japan

As mentioned earlier, social work education in Japan started in the nineteenth century and was overhauled to suit the certification exam in mid-1980. Japanese social work education is strictly regulated as per the Certified Social Workers Act. A fieldwork practicum currently requires 180 credit hours and coursework for instruction and supervision of fieldwork is 90 credit hours. Note that schools provide the coursework necessary to become eligible to take the national examination. However, not all students take the national examination; hence the pass rate is only 30% for CSWs. Social work education in Japan is provided at universities, colleges, junior colleges, vocational colleges, and other general training facilities for certified social workers. Three associations were formerly established to promote social work education, academic research, social work, and social welfare development. They were then integrated and reorganised as one organisation called the Japan Association for Social Work Education (JASWE) in 2016. As of May 2018 it has 283 member schools.[6]

JASWE research into the careers of students who graduate from social work schools found that 48.9% of students selected job opportunities in social welfare/medical fields and 26.8% selected general enterprise companies. It was found that choices made by students depended on their education levels. University students tended to choose general companies not related to their studies in the university, while junior college students and vocational college students tended to take up jobs in the social welfare/medical fields.

The term social work "ソーシャルワーク" has only really been seen in textbooks and papers in Japanese since 2000. However, the term has not fully replicated the original model and concepts as used in the United States. The main function of certified social workers is "to provide advice, guidance, or welfare services in consultations about the welfare" of needy people, as per the act.[7] Social work/welfare discussion in Japan continues to be split into two streams: social welfare and policy discussion and social work theory discussion (Ohashi, 2005). Discussion on social work theories continues to rely on concepts and theories borrowed from overseas (Nakamura, 2007), as original Japanese theory discussion hardly ever takes place (Iwasaki, 2011).

ISSUES AND CHALLENGES

Rapid economic growth in Japan saw the introduction of several new trends and changes affecting the people. These changes can be represented by keywords such as diversity of the social welfare service delivery system, ageing and shrinking population, and the reduced function of family. Therefore, the challenges facing Japanese social work lie in comprehensively supporting citizens in a society that is ageing and has a decreasing birthrate. Certified social workers as professional social workers in Japan have various *needs* that have been overlooked by respective bureaucratic legislation in communities.

Although Japanese households now have fewer members, households with elderly people are increasing rapidly. It is reported that households with elderly people represent 48.4% of total households as of 2016, while 58.2% of households have single occupants or couples without children (MHLW, 2017a, 2017b, 2017c, 2017d). There are reports of domestic violence on the elderly perpetrated by their unmarried children—their so-called carers. These numbers show that nuclear families are ageing, isolated, and lack support from their community (Kikuchi, 2018).

Social work services are currently provided by various organisations scattered across Japan. In addition to the traditional institutions for the elderly/people with disability/children and single mothers, there are also schools, hospitals, private/enterprises, local authorities, correction facilities, NPOs, and so on. The national government's system of care has been shifted to a community-based integrated care system (MHLW, 2017a, 2017b, 2017c, 2017d). By 2025 the elderly population is expected to be very high; hence the need to ensure a long-term care insurance (LTCI) system. Emphasis must be on the necessity to establish a comprehensive system of healthcare and nursing care and prevent rapid increase in the number of LTCI users. This reflects the need for the "socialization function of the family." Social welfare services for families are developing and spreading widely. A serious social challenge is how to protect children from domestic violence and abuse. The younger generation live in the city, are sometimes isolated, live far from their parents, and are forced to take care of their children by themselves with little help from the state. This implies that society/community is required to develop support systems for children and their families.

Moreover, Japan's national government needs to put in place the necessary qualified human resources.

A comprehensive social welfare/social security system has been established in Japan since 2017 based on something called a regional symbiosis society *Chiiki Kyo-sei Shakai* "地域共生社会." Such a system reflects a society where there are fewer children yet more elderly people. It has been specifically developed to meet the social function needs of children, the elderly, and the handicapped. However, such a society will inevitably lead to a reduction in the size of the workforce (especially, in the suburbs) and weaken community networks. The regional symbiosis society concept is expected to resolve the difficulties people face to balance their work–life experience. However, the new concept can only be brought about if social workers take on new perspectives as experts and establish respective networks of supporters and receivers of social welfare services. They would function not only in their consultation capacity, as mentioned in the Certified Social Worker Act, but also in their full capacity as professional social workers as per the global definition of the social work profession.

NOTES

1. Many social workers working in the GHQ were educated in the United States. Under the control of the GHQ Japanese social welfare services received a boost after World War II.
2. American theories were translated into Japanese by people with links to the United States. In this way American social work researchers such as M. Richmond, H. Perlman, J. Adams, and F. Biestek became part and parcel of Japanese social work history.
3. Retrieved from the Fire and Disaster Management Agency (2018).
4. http://www.sssc.or.jp/touroku/pdf/pdf_t04.pdf.
5. https://www.mhlw.go.jp/english/wp/wp-hw11/dl/08e.pdf.
6. http://www.jaswe.jp/jascsw_members_list.html.
7. Article 2(1) of Certified Social Worker and Certified Care Worker Act.

REFERENCES

Certified Social Worker and Certified Care Worker Act. (1987). Amendment of Act No. 83 of 2014.

MHLW. (1996). *The Japanese experience in social security*. Retrieved from http://www1.mhlw.go.jp/english/ssp_in_j/index.html.

MHLW. (2017a). *Comprehensive survey of living conditions*. Retrieved from http://www.mhlw.go.jp/toukei/saikin/hw/k-tyosa/k-tyosa16/dl/16.pdf.

MHLW. (2017b). *Establishing "the community-based integrated care system".*

MHLW. (2017c). *Outline of the revision of the long-term care insurance system, etc. to strengthen the community-based integrated care system in 2017–18*. Retrieved from http://www.mhlw.go.jp/english/policy/care-welfare/care-welfare-elderly/dl/ltcis_2017_e.pdf.

MHLW. (2017d). 「地域共生社会」の実現にむけて. Retrieved from https://www.mhlw.go.jp/stf/houdou/0000150538.html.

Services and Supports for Persons with Disabilities Act. (2005). Amendment of Act No. 94 of 2006.

Social Welfare Act. (1951). Amendment of Act No. 85 of 2008.

一番ヶ瀬康子 [Ichibangase, Y.]. (1964, 1994). 社会福祉事業概論 社会福祉とはなにか (Vol. 1, pp. 42–147): 労働旬報社.

一番ヶ瀬康子 [Ichibangase, Y.]. (1968). 社会福祉への視点 社会福祉論 (pp. 3–16): 有斐閣.

一番ヶ瀬康子 [Ichibangase, Y.]. (1971, 1994). 社会福祉学序説—社会福祉学の科学とは何か 社会福祉とはなにか (Vol. 1, pp. 175–256): 労働旬報社.

岡村重夫 [Okamura, S.]. (1955, 2011). ソーシャル・ワーカーの本質的機能. In 岩田正美監修, 白澤成和, & 岩間伸之 (Eds.), ソーシャルワークとはなにか (Vol. 4, pp. 21–29): 日本図書センター.

北島英治 [Kitajima, E.], 副田あけみ [Soeda, A.], 高橋重広 [Takahashi, S.], & 渡部律子 [Watanabe, R] (Eds.), (2002). ソーシャルワーク実践の基礎理論. 東京: 有斐閣.

岩崎晋也 [Iwasaki, S.]. (2011). 社会福祉原論研究の活性化にむけて. In 岩田正美監修 & 岩崎晋也 (Eds.), 社会福祉とは何か 理論と展開 (Vol. 1, pp. 3–40): 日本図書センター.

菊池信子 [Kikuchi, N.]. (2018). 要介護高齢者と家族支援 (特集 家族支援とソーシャルワーク) [Older adults with nursing care and the family support]. ソーシャルワーク研究: 社会福祉実践の総合研究誌, 43(4), 275–283.

総務省 [Ministry of Internal Affairs and Communications.]. (2009). Standard occupational classification for Japan. Retrieved from http://www.soumu.go.jp/toukei_toukatsu/index/seido/shokgyou/kou_h21.htm#grp16.

総務省消防庁 [Fire and Disaster Management Agency, Ministry of Internal Affairs and Communications.]. (2018). 平成 23 年 (2011 年) 東北地方太平洋沖地震(東日本大震災)について (第 157 報). Retrieved from http://www.fdma.go.jp/bn/higaihou/pdf/jishin/157.pdf.

大橋謙策 [Ohashi, K.]. (2005). わが国におけるソーシャルワークの理論化を求めて (特集: わが国におけるソーシャルワークの理論化を求めて). ソーシャルワーク研究, 31(1), 4–19.

社会福祉士養成講座編集委員会 [Editorial Committee on the Certified Social Workers' Training Courses.] (Ed.). (2010). 相談援助の理論と方法II (2 ed.): 中央法規出版.

仲村優一 [Nakamura, Y.]. (2007). 日本のソーシャルワークの課題 (ソーシャルケアサービス従事者研究協議会 Ed.): 相川書房.

CHAPTER 4

Social Work Education in Taiwan: Issues, Challenges, and Prospects

Wan-I Lin and Ciwang Teyra

INTRODUCTION

In, the mid-nineteenth century, capitalism brought about the impoverishment of the working class and the substantial growth of urban populations. The significant role played by the bourgeoisie in maintaining capitalism led to the development of Charity Organization Society, using moral education (especially teaching values of thriftiness and self-reliance) to discipline the poor. Control and management of public and private philanthropy served as a means of distinguishing between those deserved to be relieved and those who were not (Bailey & Brake, 1975). The development of capitalism quickly spread from England to the United States (USA), leading the USA to become the first country that established the professional social work. As the influence of colonisation and imperialism, social work theories and practices spread quickly from the West to different parts of the world. As Midgley (1981, pp. xi–xii) mentioned that "social work is established also in many developing countries; it has been exported to these countries over the last thirty years and while social workers in the Third World do not command the same salaries or enjoy the same degree of recognition, they share a common professional identity with their western counterparts. This has been fostered large through social work education, …. Here students are trained to apply the principles of social work in the same way as are students in western

W.-I. Lin · C. Teyra (✉)
Department of Social Work, National Taiwan University, Taipei, Taiwan
e-mail: linwani@ntu.edu.tw

C. Teyra
e-mail: ciwang@ntu.edu.tw

© The Author(s) 2021
S. S. M. et al. (eds.), *The Palgrave Handbook of Global Social Work Education*, https://doi.org/10.1007/978-3-030-39966-5_4

countries; they study the same textbooks, read the same journals and are taught the same theories and methods. They find employment subsequently in public and voluntary welfare organisations which attempt to deal with social problems in the same way as do social welfare agencies in the West". Therefore, the effectiveness of social work in the Third World is questionable due to different social and structural contexts.

Like many other colonised countries or least developed countries, social work in Taiwan was transplanted through a colonial mother country, Japan, which also originally adapted social work from the West. Social work in Taiwan was also highly influenced by social work practices in a capitalist core country, especially the USA. Since the 1960s, social work education in the USA has been introduced into Taiwan, and since became a professional pursuit. Social work education in Taiwan quickly expanded until the Social Worker Act (shehui gongzuo shi fa) was implemented in 1997, leading to an expansion in social work departments, and an increase in Master of Social Work (MSW) programmes. Wilensky (1964) asserts that in the process of professionalisation based on structural-functional and processual perspectives, there are typically several stages of development: (1) to have a demand for full-time positions, (2) to press for establishment of a training school, (3) to form a professional association, (4) to win the support of law for the protection of the job territory, and (5) to carry out a formal code of ethics. In examining the situation, by 1980, we can conclude that social work had entered a professional field in Taiwan and by 1997, Taiwan had already reached the fourth stage of this process, that of legislation being drawn up to defend against professions sharing similarities. However, as Midgley (1981, p. xi) argued, even with this process of professionalisation, this does not necessarily mean that social work in each country is accorded the same professional status and community sanction as US social work. The process of social work education development differs in every country, confronting social, political, economic, and educational differences, as well as different controversies and responses to such controversies. This paper will discuss the issues and challenges of social work education in the pursuit of the professionalisation of social work in Taiwan.

THE DEVELOPMENT OF SOCIAL WORK EDUCATION IN TAIWAN

The beginnings of social work education in Taiwan can be traced back in September 1950 with the establishment of the Department of Social Administration at the Taiwan Provincial College of Administration. This was a two-year diploma programme with 84 credits. However, most teachers/ faculty members were not social work professional background, and the students trained in the programme mainly provided to the government's needs in social administration. It is very different than today's social work education which underscores social work profession. In 1955, the Taiwan Provincial

College of Administration was merged into the Taiwan Provincial Law and Business College and the Department of Social Administration was changed into the Department of Sociology. This was split three years later between Sociology and Social Administration, the latter of which later became the Department of Social Work. Such was the beginnings of how social work education became a part of college. In 1956, Taiwan Provincial Normal University established a "social work unit" (shehui shiye zu) as part of the Department of Social Education, the term used for "social work" coming from the Japanese translation for social work (Lin, 2013).

Higher education in Taiwan gradually offered social work courses since the 1950s. For instance, Tunghai University, National Taiwan University, Fu Jen University, and Soochow University established department of sociology in 1955, 1960, 1969, and 1973, respectively. These universities also offered social administration and social work courses among their departments of sociology. There are three primary reasons that social work education began in Taiwan parasitically within departments of sociology (Lin, 1991, 1994, 2013). First, it is because of the influence of China's experience. In 1929, Yenching University in China expanded its sociology department to become the "Department of Sociology and Social Work". Later on, in China, Ginling College, Ginling Women's College, Fudan University, Qilu University, and Hujiang College came to have social work courses underneath their sociology departments. After Kuomintang government relocated from China and took over Taiwan in the 1940s, they also brought China's social work educational experiences to Taiwan. Second, at the time, there was a severe lack of qualified social work teachers/faculty members, and it was very hard to set up an independent department. Even then, social work courses were often taught by sociology faculties. Third and lastly, at the time, the government, universities, and society had difficulty distinguishing social work from sociology.

According to Wilensky (1964), only when there is a demand for a form of full-time position could there be the establishment of social work education. In 1967, the Taiwan Government set up a regulation that in residential institutions, for every 200 clients, there needed to be one social worker and that in county governments for every 500 poor households, there needed to be one social worker. These regulations began to be implemented in 1971. The Taiwan Government began to experiment with appointing social workers to support community development and poverty relief. For the sake of promoting community development and combating poverty, In July 1969, Taiwan's Ministry of the Interior invited United Nations advisor Porthy Moses and various Taiwanese social work teachers/faculty members to meet, discuss, research, and develop social work education in Taiwan. Subsequently, in February 1971, Taiwan's Ministry of the Labor and the United Nations Development Programme jointly held a "Conference on Social Work Teaching, Learning, and Practice" in Taipei. This conference was to provide a comprehensive review and plan for social work education (Ministry of the

Interior, 1971). This conference also led to US social work education entering Taiwan. Introduction to social work, social work with individuals, social work with groups, community organising and community development, social welfare administration, social welfare policy, social work research methods, human behaviour in social environment, and social work field practicum were made into nine required core classes—to be taken in the course of social work professionalisation. This laid the foundation for social work education in Taiwan.

In 1973, National Taiwan University's Department of Sociology started teaching Sociology and Social Work separately and other universities followed suit. In 1979, Tunghai University established a Department of Social Work and other colleges did the same. The National Association of Medical Social Workers began to be established in 1983 and in 1989, a nationwide social worker organisation was founded, the predecessor of today's Taiwan Association of Social Workers (TASW).

After the formation of a professional organisation, advocates began to push the government to form an independent social welfare department, rather than having a Social Affairs Division under the Ministry of Interior in charge of social welfare administration. At the same time, a team headed by Lin, one of the authors of this paper, began drafting a Social Worker Act to standardise the qualifications and core responsibilities of social workers, in order to distinguish them from professions sharing similarities. The Social Worker Act passed into law in March 1997 and the President announced its implementation on April 2. As a result, April 2 became celebrated as "Social Work Day" by social workers in Taiwan.

In anticipation of the Social Worker Act passing through legislature, starting in 1992, many schools that previously did not offer classes in social work began to establish departments of social work. Up until 1998, Taiwan already had 21 social work and social welfare-related departments. After passage of the Social Worker Act, more social work departments were established up until in 2017, and social work-related departments include 33 BSW programmes, 23 MSW programmes, and 6 Ph.D. programmes (these numbers do not include religious institutes). Every year, there are over 3300 BSW, 400 MSW, and 20 Ph.D. openings for students' recruitments. In fact, there are more students graduated than needed in the job market for social workers each year.

Apart from the TASW, which is similar to the US National Association of Social Workers, there is also the Taiwanese Social Work Education Association, which is similar to US Council of Social Work Education (CSWE). However, social work departments are not set up like in the USA, where accreditation from the CSWE is required. Instead, each university sets up a proposal for establishing a department, then seeks approval from the Taiwan's Ministry of Education. After receiving this application to set up a department, the Ministry of Education requests two experienced social work professors to inspect this proposal. If approved, the department can get ready for preparation and begin to enrol new students in the second year. If the basic conditions are met, the request of setting up a department can also take place after revision, or after additional materials are added. Schools that apply generally, to the extent of their ability, compile proposals in accordance with requirements; for example, they will assess the social work labour market, set aims, devise a curriculum, find teachers, arrange practicum sites, and arrange for library and teaching equipment. Although having qualified teachers/faculty members is the primary indicator of this, it is very easy for forgery to take place. In the proposal, a number of qualified teachers may be listed as faculty members, but in reality, this may only be for short-term employment instead of tenure track jobs. This is the reason as to why social work departments have greatly increased in number since 1990.

CHALLENGES OF PROFESSIONALISATION IN SOCIAL WORK

As such, which universities should be the type of university to teach social work? Should be general universities (academic discipline) and/or vocational colleges (applied practice)? Also, what should be included in social work education? A significant debate regarding this took place in the 1900s. In 1907, sociology and economics professor Samuel M. Lindsay became head of the New York School of Philanthropy. Lindsay strongly emphasised training in the social sciences and allowed social work students to enrol in as sociology and economics students in Columbia University. However, in 1912, the New York School of Philanthropy's board of directors did not agree with Lindsay's plan of incorporating Columbia University, as a result of which Lindsay resigned his position. However, he warned that without social sciences and university-based education, this type of schools has no way of becoming a national leader in social work (Shoemaker, 1998, p. 186).

WHAT KIND OF HELPING PROFESSION
SHOULD SOCIAL WORKERS BE TAUGHT?

In 1905, Harvard University integrated with Simmons Female College to form the Boston School for Social Workers. This school divided in 1916, because of dispute views on the academic apprenticeship of social work. A fundamental difference was divergences in view regarding the relation gender and social work. Simmons Female College saw social work as a natural extension of women's traditional roles and strongly argued that many women are motivated by a missionary spirit and in this way are willing to take on work in spite of low salaries (Shoemaker, 1998). It was something men were not seen as suited for. Harvard wanted no part of this and Simmons became a traditional casework school. This kind of gender stereotype affected the professionalisation of social work, causing social work to develop under conditions shaped by the gender inequality of the period, contributing to low wages for social workers and for social work to be seen as a low-end form of work. In particular, Simmons Female College wished for social work to move in the direction of technical and vocational training, with a specific focus on skill-based education, but this was something that Harvard University could not accept. Harvard University took the view that social work should reflect social theory and diverse points of view, and that the professionalisation of social work should not be thought of solely in gendered terms. This demonstrates the means by which the technicalisation and professionalisation of social work were intimately bound up with tension over gender roles.

Outside of this, in 1903, Graham Taylor, the head of the Chicago Commons Settlement House, established the Chicago School of Civics and Philanthropy In 1907, Sophonisba Breckinridge and Edith Abbott, who were both professors, were appointed to research positions. Abbot believed that social work should keep in mind reforms and state-building work of the Progressive Era. She disagreed with what she perceived as overemphasis on individual casework in social work training at the time, saying that social change as coming through research and knowing how to influence policy. Abbott and Breckenridge wanted social workers to be administrators and policy leaders, no matter male or female. Based on the idea of professionalism, even though they developed a casework curriculum their focus was still on the social structure and changing it as a way to ameliorate problems. For the sake of pursuing professionalisation, the New York School of Philanthropy was later merged into Columbia University and became a school of social work. But this further established the professionalisation of social work education, with an emphasis on basic training in the social sciences, while at the same time attending to casework and the formulation of social policy.

Unlike the American experience would be that of German social work education. Early on, like America, German social work education also did not first appear as a form of college-level education. By 1970 to 1971, some vocational-school level subjects, such as social work, commerce, machinery, management, were changed into higher education subjects and integrated into higher education (*Fachhochschulen*). For social workers, it was something hoped for that they would be upgraded to a high-level of training which includes social work practical skills and scientific and professional knowledge, although for employers, consideration of raising salaries, positions, and qualifications led them to strongly criticise raising social work to the college level. Before the unification of Germany, social work training took place in another form of professional school (*Berufsakademien*). However, this did not lead to the acknowledgement of social work as a professional field, primarily because social work was not allotted enough credits (Krammer, 1998).

In Taiwan, the higher education is divided between the two types: general universities and universities of science and technology, the former of which primarily recruits students who graduated from high school, and the recruitment from the later one are students who graduated from vocational schools. As the guidance of social work education established in around 1910 in the USA, social workers are required to obtain practice skills as well as a general university degree for general scientific knowledge sets. As a result, in Taiwan, Bachelor of Social Work (BSW) programmes in general universities emphasise on both basic scientific and professional knowledge and practice skills trainings, while programmes in universities of science and technology tend to focus exclusively towards practice skills.

In anticipation of the passage of the Social Worker Act, in 1996, the National Pingtung University of Science and Technology began to train social workers under the auspices of the department of life science and technology (in 2000, this formally became the department of social work). This began the first department of social work in Taiwan that was part of a university of science and technology. After Pingtung University of Technology began to train social workers, Chia Nan University of Pharmacy and Science in 1999, Chaoyang University of Technology in 2000, Toko University of Technology in 2003, Tajen University of Technology in 2007, Yu Da University of Technology in 2011, Taipei College of Maritime Technology in 2013, and Shu Te University of Technology in 2014 began to form departments of social work programmes, or establish or health care and social work departments. Outside of Pingtung University of Science and Technology, which is public, these universities of science and technology were all private schools. These social work departments in private universities of science and technology also enrolled two-year technical degree students, established evening programmes, and usually recruited 100–200 students each year, which is two to four times more than public schools' annual recruitments. As an increase number of social work programmes being offered across different types of universities, there are some debates regarding the differences of social work education between general universities and universities of science and technology.

Social work education should emphasise on the competencies cultivation of both practice skills and basic scientific knowledge and ability, and these two competencies should be acknowledged in both universities and universities of science and technology education systems. Although the BSW programmes established in two different education systems in Taiwan, the differences in curriculums are minor because of the passage of Social Worker Act. The structure for the curriculum design of BSW programmes primarily focuses on qualifying students for taking licensure exam by fulfilling the criteria for Social Worker Act. The curriculum design will also be based on faculty members' specialised areas. As a result, the biggest division between two social work education systems would be the qualities and quantities of social work faculty members.

Several studies examine the quality of social work faculty members in Taiwan from 1997 to 2010 to see if it is improved by implementation of the

Social Worker Act (Lin, 2010; Lin & Wang, 2010). The findings indicated no progress as evidence by the fact only 50% faculty members possess social work, social welfare, or social welfare policy backgrounds (Lin, 2010; Lin & Wang, 2010). The result is even worse by adding on departments established after 2011, which is included but not limited to: Toko University of Technology with only 28% faculty with social work background, Tatung University of Technology with 0%, Yu Da University of Technology with 37.5%, National Changhua University of Education with 4.5%, Nanhua University with 7.7%, National Quemoy University with 60%, Taipei University of Marine Technology with 33%, and Shu-Te University of Technology with 40%. Even though there had been a large growth in social work departments, the professional quality of social work faculties had not improved but regressed.

In comparison with international experiences, Barretta-Herman (2008) sent a questionnaire to International Association of Schools of Social Work (IASSW) members and received responses from 147 social work schools or departments in 28 countries, discovering that of teachers that had a degree of social work, America had 83%, Africa had 74%, Asia and Pacific countries had 54%, as well as 48% in Europe. The percentages of faculty who obtained a degree in social work in Asia and Pacific countries were on the lower end, and many faculties had backgrounds in sociology, social policy, and pedagogy. Currently, the percentage of social work faculty in Taiwan who obtained a degree in social work is relatively low comparing to other countries.

On note of this, with the expedite expansion of social work departments in Taiwan, many schools neglected to recognise the importance of the quality of faculty. While the quantity of faculties who obtained a social work degree remaining to be an issue, the primary gap of hiring qualified faculty in schools is the misinterpretation by the mainstream society about social work profession, which is perceived as a warm and loving charity work but professional career. Several universities in Taiwan, in order to establish a social work department, ended up shifting surplus teachers from other department to the social work department, or drawing teachers from sociology, pedagogy, counselling, or other related backgrounds to social work department to make it work. Many schools adopted the above approaches, as a result, some social work departments may only have one or two faculty that actually possess a background in social work, who then must take up core courses, and hire adjuncts from the fields to cover other classes. The phenomenon happens especially more frequently among universities of science and technology system. This compromised education system will result in many not fully trained students who will graduate without proper professional skill sets, knowledge, and ethics by the time they enter the job market. The harm will go towards not only students, but also agencies and clients who received services from these trained students.

Professionalism vs. Unionism

Taiwan's social work education does not demonstrate clear radicalism. The earliest individuals to introduce the notion of radical social work were Lin and Ku (1992), publishing the Chinese-language book Radical Social Work based on the concepts from Bailey and Brake (1975), Throssell (1975), Corrigan and Leonard (1978), Pritchard and Taylor (1978), Halmos (1978), Joyce, Corrigan, and Hayes (1988). Although there is no course titled Radical Social Work currently offered in Taiwanese social work departments, Taiwan has not allowed Radical Social Work to rot away. Like that in the experiences of American and English, some grass-roots social workers advocated to unionise and challenged the design of social work professionalisation. However, their statements lack criticisms towards the macro-context of capitalism and new public administration.

The rank-and-file movement in America in the 1930s took place under the Great Depression, initiated by grass-roots social welfare workers and left-wing labour organisers, aimed to (1) awakening the political consciousness of social workers, (2) pursuing an integrated national social security and social welfare system, and (3) promoting the legalisation of social worker unions (Selmi & Hunter, 2001).

Case Con founded by English social workers in the 1970s. The name itself was a provocation and criticism, it played on the term "case conference", the "con" of groups of concerned professional social workers sitting around a table and reducing structural problems to individual "cases", a form of victim blaming (Weinstein, 2011). The organisation believed that social workers and their "clients" should share in joint struggle. In the Case Con Manifesto that they released, first, they advocated that social workers do not have easy answers and should not simplify the issues and demands of "clients". Second, they agreed with left-wing criticisms of the welfare state, believing that the welfare state was only a means for the capitalist system to appease the working class and did not actually have any real interest in improving conditions for the working class. Third, professionalisation would hurt the ability of professional social workers and non-professional social workers to work together, as well as that professionalism would impede the relationship between social workers and their "clients". This would introduce a business model into life structure, with certain correct behaviour considered professional, including detachment and controlling one's feelings. Fourth, social work organisations had to be independent of the government and needed to stand on the side of their "clients", not hesitating to protest the capitalist nation and its administrative tools. Last, they supported social workers forming a rank-and-file trade union (Weinstein, 2011). Case Con ended its work in 1977. Case Con fundamentally advocated a form of deprofessionalisation, overthrowing the hegemony of the professional system, and returning social work to care work for the proletariat, as realising a form of social justice.

In England, Radical Social Workers became the Social Work Action Network (SWAN) in 2004, as frontline, grass-roots workers, scholars, and users of social work that aimed establish a platform that aimed to take action regarding the crisis of social work. What they protested was not a simplified notion of professionalism, but was now focused on new public managerialism and neoliberalism (Weinstein, 2011). They had the demand of reclaiming social policy (de Haan, 2007), a new framework for rights-based social policy, and also advocated reclaiming social work (Ferguson, 2008), using SWAN as a platform to push for this, calling for a return to the basic premise of social work, against what was distorted due to neoliberalism.

In Taiwan, a group of social workers, working on the recovery of a large earthquake took place on 21 September 1999, killing 2415 individuals, referred to themselves as "Drifting Social Workers" (Piaoliu social workers). They issued an online newsletter, organised workshops for social workers, and published Taiwan's first publication specifically discussing issues of rank-and-file in social work. Against how mainstream social workers discussed social work issues in terms of "professionalism", "philanthropy", "helping professionals", the "Drifting Social Workers" opposed the hegemony of the nation, and did not agree with the "public-private partnership" that mainstream social workers had with the nation. As a result, they took on a position of reflecting and criticising the hegemony of the nation (Fang, 2013). The "Drifting Social Workers" also criticised professionalisation as controlled by the nation and they believed that this was a form of establishment. Tao (1999) believed that this establishment of social work profession was a kind of submission or attachment to state governing authority, that professionalisation had raised professional self-autonomy, in spite of that these were two different directions. The Social Worker Act seems to have seen the social work profession as lacking in deal and aspiring towards social reform. Wang and Tao (2006), stating that "The Social Worker Act has considerably blocked the ability of grass-roots community-based social workers, especially those who have not trained in the academic discipline of social workers and obtained certification. However, several grass-roots community-based social workers are closer in relation to those that they serve, with less differences in language and culture, and are more successful in social work practice than those academically trained" (Wang & Tao, 2006).

The "Drifting Social Workers" not only challenged professionalisation from the nation state; but they also challenged the associations formed by certificated social workers. To support labour rights especially those who do not have social work certificates but practice in fields, they supported and encouraged social workers organising labour unions. Similar to the rank-and-file movement in the USA in the 1930s which was concerned with the rights of social workers, the "Drifting Social Workers" concerned themselves with labour rights and emphasised that social workers are also workers, have the right to form labour unions, and should work together with other labours, to fight for labour rights. Starting in 2007, a small group of grass-roots social workers in the Taipei, Taoyuan, Kaohsiung, Taichung, New Taipei, and Hualien gradually joined in labour unions which differentiated from certificated social worker associations. The growing of Drifting Social Workers and social work labour unions offered different perspectives of social work professionalisation and also drove public attention to the issues regarding legitimate of social work examination and certificate.

The purpose of social work education in Taiwan is primarily to train students to pass examinations to be admitted as social workers. This system is based on social worker qualifications in America and Japan, with the requirement of a paper and pencil test. Testing responsibilities are in the hands of the central government in Taiwan and not through professional organisations for social workers holding such tests, although professors of social work and experienced social workers are asked to form testing committees to come up with questions and topics for the test. The passing rate for social workers is less than 16%, around the same level for nutritionists, less than the 60% or so for clinical psychiatrist and counsellor. Why should the passing rate of social workers be so low? The primary reason is because the qualification for social worker is BSW. As mentioned above, a large number of social work schools have been set up, but some schools have a shortage of professional educators/faculty. This may impact students' growth of social work knowledge, which in turn may affect their performance of examination. Additionally, although examination system seems to offer equal opportunities for test takers, the system itself utilises dominant approach to evaluate who is qualified social worker that might not be applicable to certain populations in Taiwan, especially indigenous peoples who share different worldviews and ways of knowing.

What is more, before 2013, only college graduates who had taken more than 20 credits of courses in social work were allowed to take certification exams for social workers. Consequently, this led to the proliferation of short-term courses or continuing education that provided 7 classes and 20 credits. This allowed graduates who had not studied social work but wanted to become social workers to participate in exams especially for social workers. However, this kind of short-term social work education was difficult to provide adequate training which combines both scientific and professional knowledge and practice skills for nurturing qualified social workers due to limited courses. In response, the examination institutions and the social work community could only restrict the rate of those that passed to compensate. This low rate of passage has caused several social work departments in universities of science and technology to be dissatisfied, because the rate their students pass these examinations is very low. Some schools have only a very few students that pass the exam in a year and some have none at all.

In order to respond to this issue of complaints about the low rate of passage while maintaining the expertise of social workers, strengthening the content and profession of social work education would be the primary aim. Using 20 credits was as a means of setting a threshold to increase the strictness for qualifying for the national social worker examinations, and the amendment of "Rules for the Higher Professional Examinations for Technical and Professional Social Work Education" is also due to the efforts of the social work community. The examination qualifications have been changed to requisites for 5 fields, with each subject covering at least 3 credits and 15 subjects totalling 45 credits or more, which was effective from January 2013 onwards. We look forward to these rules raising the standards for professionality. Although this reform has lowered the incentives for providing short-term classes that offer credits, this is unable to address the issue of quality of social work students, and there will continue to lead to doubts about regarding raising the qualification for the exam and the rate of passage.

SPECIALIST APPROACH VS. GENERALIST APPROACH

Not long after the Social Worker Act passed in 1997, continual pressures came from adjacent professions. The Clinical Psychologist and Counsellor Act took effect in November of 2001; its eligibility requirements are much more stringent than those for social workers. First, the examination requirements of clinical psychologist and counsellor are a master's in clinical psychology or counselling. Second, the agencies in which clinical psychologist is practised are designated by the central authorities, and two years of clinical internship is required. Third, the clinical psychologist and counsellor require continuing education training, with a document proving continued education issued every six year for licence renewal. Fourth, the code of ethics for psychologists practice is rather strict and it contains 131 clauses. Lastly, the Social Worker Act's thirteenth clause's first paragraph states that, "A social worker shall engage in the following tasks: social and psychological assessment and treatment of the problems about behavior, social relationship, marriage, social adjustment and so on". This is an important aspect of the tasks of social workers. And this also means that social workers are directly in competition with clinical psychologists and counsellors, and it will depend on whose ability is better, and who is more competent for these responsibilities (Lin & Shen, 2008).

In reality, during the planning and investigation for the first version of the Social Worker Act, the social workers were divided into two levels: basic social workers and advanced social workers. Due to the lack of maturity in social work practice fields at the time, the social work community was worried that there were too many examinations. As a result, at the time, only a primary-level generalist approach or basic social worker was adopted. However, in the face of more competitive market, for social workers to pursue their survival in the professional market (quasi-market), they had to adjust their strategy. Nothing else could be done but raising their educational level, raising qualification standards for testing, instituting multiple levels of specialisation, reinforcing supervision, and improving working conditions to attract talent for the long term and so on. The field of social work practice in Taiwan has gradually matured, and consequently, the voice of specialised professionals has emerged. Japan developed social welfare specialisation ten years before Taiwan and has long distinguished between different fields and levels of expertise. Even South Korea, which passed legislation regarding social welfare workers later than Taiwan, has already implemented the development of specialisation (Lin & Shen, 2008). If social workers in Taiwan still cling to being afraid of examinations, divisions between basic and advanced levels, or division of labour, or in the name of proletarianisation push for deprofessionalisation, neglecting the facts of different divisions in social work, social workers in Taiwan can only continue to work under wretched conditions in which they are forced to work in other specialised fields. In such a case, citing professional autonomy or seeking justice for the disadvantaged is being unable to see the forest for the trees. At the same time, this does not mean that all fields need to take on a specialist approach, in reality, this could be more deliberate. Some fields are not suited for specialist approaches, such as community work, public welfare service, social care, and agency-based social work.

Even if this meets resistance from some groups, due to the amendment of the law pushed for TASW as well as advocated by hospital and mental health social workers, division between levels of social workers has taken effect after 2008. Specialised social workers are distinguished by five fields: medical, mental health, children and families, the elderly, and disabilities, from 2007 onwards. But the implementation of this has not been smooth. Outside of medical social work and mental health social work, social workers in other fields are not fully supportive of these divisions. One reason is because specialisation for field of medical treatment is very detailed, and divisions have existed for a long time.[1] However, other social work fields, for example, disability services, elderly care, child social work, school social work, family services, indigenous social work etc., are still adopted by a generalist approach, instead of dividing into fields of specialty. Indeed, not every social work field needs to have specialised social workers. A generalist approach might align with its necessity. However, there are also some fields requesting to be recognised its specialist. For instance, in recent years, indigenous and grass-roots community social workers have been arguing the neglect of considering indigenous social work as a specialisation. Given that indigenous peoples have their own unique histories, cultures, and experiences, social workers who work with indigenous individuals, families, and communities may require to have different knowledge, methods, and abilities. From this, it can be seen that the path to specialisation in Taiwanese social work has not been smooth and still has room for improvement.

Prospects of Social Work Education in Taiwan

Outside of Chia Nan University of Pharmacy and Science, Tajen University of Technology, Tatung University of Technology, Toko University of Technology, and Taipei University of Maritime Technology, and other universities of technology, and Quemoy University, which lacks a MSW programme, all other colleges have MSW programmes. This has visibly raised the levels for social work training in Taiwan to the master level. MSW students consist of a total of 11% of social work students; however, regarding the labour market demand for social workers, the supply amount of qualified social workers greatly surpasses demand. Consequently, whether social work students engage in social work after graduating is uncertain. As MSW students have a relatively greater interest in pursuing social work as a profession after graduation, this demonstrates that in Taiwan, the MSW will become the mainstream on the job market, much like the experience of the USA.

Despite every year there continue to be over 3700 students that graduate from BSW and MSW and one half of them would participate in the national social worker examination, a significantly high proportion of social work graduates is still unable to obtain social work certification and then apply for licensee given low passing rates of the examination. Currently, social work certification is not a necessary qualification for social welfare mechanisms in hiring social workers. Although the government aims to promoting hiring certified social workers, in short term, it is less likely to block social work/welfare agencies from hiring social workers without certificate of qualification in social work, it only needs to contract out as a means of gradually raising the hiring ratio of certified social workers in social welfare agencies. In the field of practice in Taiwan, there are more non-certified social workers in social welfare agencies or organisations, particularly in the civil sector. The relatively low passing rate towards the national social worker examination leads to disputes and controversies towards the exam.

In the process of promoting the professionalisation of social work, social work education is crucially important. It would be ideal if there is a criterion similar to the CSWE of the USA to check mechanism for the quality of social work education across different universities. Since Taiwan has not developed the criteria yet, it might still need to rely on today's national social worker examination to assess foundational social work knowledge prior to a better and more comprehensive system being established even though there are some arguments towards the examination. If it is only at the testing level that there are check mechanisms, although this may have its effectiveness, the process is admittedly painful, and this is controversial. For example, the test questions and grading of each exam which normally is conducted by different test committee members greatly influence the rate of passage. As we observe with that there was nearly a threefold difference rates of passage for the two tests held in 2017.[2] The protests of students taking these examinations are very worrisome for the testing committee. Other than the addressed disputes, current exam contents neglect to address cultural diversity perspective and its implications in social work fields, and it fails to reflect the diversity abilities. In Taiwan, it is very common that the education content is primarily influenced by exam content. If the mainstream education in schools lacks emphasising on diversity perspectives and related issues, it will hinder cultural competencies cultivation among students and eventually will produce social workers who lack diversity knowledge and harm the communities and individuals by projecting their own stereotypes. What's more, the current exam system is constituted by mainstream Han culture, which creates underlying social exclusion to diverse communities in Taiwan, specifically towards those practitioners with different language and cultural backgrounds. The society in Taiwan is constituted by diverse ethnic groups; sixteen indigenous tribes have been officially recognised by Taiwan Government and these tribes represent different traditions, languages, and cultures. Although over 90% of the population use Han Chinese language, approximately 2.3% of the entire population are indigenous peoples who possess their own languages, cultures, and worldviews.

The current licensure exam only designed in Chinese language version, and it also not designed as a standard exam; it's consisted of multiple choices and essay questions in every subject. Therefore, in order to pass the exam, individuals would require to conduct essay writing for long paragraphs in Chinese to answer the questions. The comprehension and the ability to write long statements in Chinese create social exclusion for indigenous people when taking the exam since this format doesn't fit in their culture contexts. Many indigenous practitioners, who speak fluent native language and have extensive working experiences in tribes, ended up failing this exam due to the unfamiliarity of expressing their perspectives in Chinese language and context. The overall exam design overlooks cultural sensitivity and deprives the opportunities for indigenous social worker to success. It will not only reduce the motivations for social workers who have diverse backgrounds to pursue social work profession, but also limit the opportunities for those making impact at work. Additionally, since current social work education is highly influenced by the content of national social worker examination, which is built based on dominant perspectives, it would provide students with compromised diversity perspectives resulting in confusion upon working in fields.

To foster social work education development and cultivate diversity perspectives, some social work advocacy groups starting advocating culture diversity as one of the domains to be included in the social work education and exam, and even promote the idea of developing the certification system to replace the current examination system to ensure cultural sensitivity and clients' best interests were validated and protected by services providers.

To sum up, social work education plays key role in social work professional development in Taiwan. Although there are challenges, disputes, and rooms to grow, those voices and different perspectives mature the social work profession in Taiwan to respond to diversity and tolerance.

NOTES

1. Social work entered into the hospital system in 1906. After becoming part of the medical care team, it became custom for medical social workers to divide labor.
2. In 2017, the national social worker examination passing rate was 7.77% in April and 21.24% in August.

REFERENCES

Bailey, R., & Brake, M. (1975). *Radical social work*. London: Edward Arnold.

Barretta-Herman, A. (2008). Meeting the expectations of the Global Standards: A status report on the IASSW membership. *International Social Work, 51*(6), 823–834.

Corrigan, P., & Leonard, P. (1978). *Social work practice under capitalism: A Marxist approach*. London: Macmillan.

De Haan, A. (2007). *Reclaiming social policy: Globalization, social exclusion and new poverty reduction strategies*. Hampshire: Palgrave.

Fang, Y. (2013). *Wo wang nali zou, yinwei nali kan bujian lu: Wo de shinian shegong xiao geming*. Taipei: China Times Publishing Co.

Ferguson, I. (2008). *Reclaiming social work: Challenging neo-liberalism and promoting social justice*. London: Sage.

Halmos, P. (1978). *The personal and the politics: Social work and the politics*. London: Hutchinson.

Joyce, P., Corrigan, P., & Hayes, M. (1988). *Striking out: Trade unionism in social work*. London: Macmillan.

Krammer, D. (1998). Social work in Germany. In S. Shardlow & M. Payne (Ed.), *Contemporary issues in social work: Western Europe*. Aldershot: Arena.

Lin, W. I., & Wang, Kate Y. T. (2010). What does professionalization mean? Tracing the trajectory of social work education in Taiwan. *Social Work Education, 29*(8), 869–881.

Lin, W. I. (1991). Woguo shehui fuli shiye yu yanjiu de fazhan. *Chinese Journal of Sociology, 15*, 74–119.

Lin, W. I., & Ku, Y. W. (Trans.). (1992). *Radical social work*. Taipei: Wu-Nan Book Inc.

Lin, W. I. (1994). *Fuli guojia-Lishi bijiao de fenxi*. Taipei: Chuliu.

Lin, W. Y., & Shen, S. H. (2008). Specialized approach: The next step of Taiwan's social work development. *Community Development Journal, 121*, 199–233.

Lin, W. Y. (2010). The development of social work education in Taiwan: Issues of the post-professionalism. *NTU Social Work Review, 12*, 153–196.

Lin, W. Y. (2013). *Dangdai shehui gongzuo: Lilun yu fangfa* (3rd ed.). Taipei: Wu-Nan Book Inc.

Ministry of the Interior, Taiwan ROC. (1971). Shehui gongzuo jiaoxue zuo yantao huiyi shilu.

Midgley, J. (1981). *Professional imperialism: Social work in the third world*. London: Heinemann.

Miller, S. E. (2010). A conceptual framework for the professional socialization of social workers. *Journal of Human Behavior in the Social Environment, 20*(7), 924–938.

Morales, A., & Sheafor, B. (1998). *Social work: A profession of many faces.* Boston: Allyn & Bacon.

Perlman, H. H. (1969). *Helping: Charlotte Towle on social work and social casework.* Chicago: University of Chicago.

Pritchard, C., & Taylor, R. (1978). *Social work: Reform or revolution?* London: RKP.

Selmi, P., & Hunter, R. (2001). Beyond the rank and file movement: Mary van Kleeck and social work radicalism in the Great Depression, 1931–1942. *Journal of Sociology & Social Welfare, 28*(2), 75–101.

Shoemaker, L. M. (1998). Early conflicts in social work education. *Social Service Review, 72*(2), 182–191.

Tao, F. Y. (1999). Shehui gongzuo zhuanye fazhan de fenxi yu zhanwang. *Community Development Journal, 88,* 190–196.

Tao, F. Y. (2012). Critiques upon ways of licensing to social workers in Taiwan. *Journal of Community Work and Community Studies, 2*(1), 65–78.

Throssell, H. (1975). *Social work: Radical essays.* St. Lucia, QLD: University of Queensland Press.

Valutis, S., Rubin, D., & Bell, M. (2012). Professional socialization and social work values: Who are we teaching? *Social Work Education, 31*(8), 1046–1057.

Wang, T. Y., & Tao, F. Y. (2006). Zhuanye hua = Zhengzhao = Zhuanye zizhu? *Research in Applied Psychology, 30,* 201–224.

Weinstein, J. (2011). Case con and radical social work in the 1970s: The impatient revolutionaries. In M. Lavalette (Ed.), *Radical social work today: Social work at the crossroads.* Bristol: The Policy Press.

Wilensky, H. (1964). The professionalization of everyone? *The American Journal of Sociology, LXX*(2), 137–158.

CHAPTER 5

China: From Ideological Focused Education to Professional Social Work Education

Cecilia Lai Wan Chan⦿, *Joe Cho Bun Leung,*
Jing Min and Yong Xiang Xu

INTRODUCTION

From the establishment of the Communist China, the limited professional social work services and social work education came to a total halt since the Cultural Revolution (1960s). Before the Open Door Policy in the 1980s, social work education was restricted to cadres training institutions for the Communist Youth League, Women's Federation, Labour Union, and Civil Affairs workers. This chapter describes how social work education in China evolved through several important historical periods since the early 1900s from a purely Western Christian-based social work education (before 1949) to an ideologically driven human service cadre training (before Open Door Policy) and then towards aligning more with professional social work education internationally (Gao & Yan, 2014; Li, Han, & Huang, 2013; Wang & Tsang, 2016; Xiong & Wang, 2007).

Yong Xiang Xu: Deceased–

C. L. W. Chan (✉) · J. C. B. Leung
Department of Social Work and Social Administration,
The University of Hong Kong, Pokfulam, Hong Kong
e-mail: cecichan@hku.hk

J. Min · Y. X. Xu
School of Social and Public Administration,
East China University of Science and Technology, Shanghai, China

© The Author(s) 2021
S. S. M. et al. (eds.), *The Palgrave Handbook of Global Social Work Education*, https://doi.org/10.1007/978-3-030-39966-5_5

Driven by high pressure of social problems arising from the rapid economic growth and urbanisation, the development of professional social work education in China in the past two decades was rapid. By the end of 2018, there were more than 348 undergraduate and 150 diploma social work programmes, and 147 Master of Social Work (MSW) programmes, as well as 17 PhD programmes graduating over 40,000 social work graduates each year. The China Association for Social Work Education (CASWE) has a current membership of over 380 institutions. The total social service workforce has reached 1.24 million. Since the establishment of public professional social work examination system, 439,266 had passed the examination and registered as social workers and senior social workers in China (*China Philanthropy News*, March 22, 2019). Concomitantly, this thriving social work workforce has been employed in a variety of emerging social welfare services, requiring social work professional input. Although there are issues on the lack of standardisation of curriculum design and fieldwork practice, ill-equipped social work teachers, and the weak career prospects for social work graduates, the development of professional social work education has been phenomenal. Being the second largest economy with the largest population in the world, there is ample room for the further growth and improvement of the quality of professional social work services and social work education in China.

This chapter will review the historical development of social work education during three period of time in China, 1910–1978, 1979–2005, and 2006–date. These landmark periods were closely linked to the sociopolitical context of China in the last century. The situation of Hong Kong, Macao, and Taiwan will not be included as the development of social work education was not affected by the political scene in mainland China. Standard and level of professionalisation in these three places were much higher. Professors from these Chinese communities were an important driving force after the Open Door Policy in fostering re-connection of the social service sector with professional social work organisations internationally.

Truncated Early Development of Professional Social Work Education (1910–1978)

Social work was non-existent in traditional China, Ching Dynasty, until the establishment of the Republic of China in 1910. Social work education was introduced into China by a group of American Missionary teachers through the sociology programme of St. John's University, Shanghai in 1908. Headed by an American missionary Daniel Kulp, the social work programme was established in the sociology department of the Shanghai Wujiang University in 1914, together with the establishment of a university-based community service centre. The Young Men's Christian Association (YMCA) (established in China in 1895), under its secretary, John Burgees set up a social service organisation (the Social Progress Club) for students in Beijing 1912.

Together with other missionary teachers from Princeton University, they later set up the sociology department at Peking University in 1922. Financed by the Rockefeller Foundation, a religious and social service department was established in the Xiehe Hospital, Beijing in 1918. The Department of Sociology of Peking University with a social work programme set up was renamed as Department of Sociology and Social Services in 1925. Xiehe Hospital offered fieldwork placements for social work students from Peking University. By the 1930s, there were 12 missionary-related universities in China offering social work education within the departments of sociology. These programmes were initially taught by missionaries from America, and later by local social work teachers educated in America (Gao & Yan, 2014; Leung & Nann, 1995). Professor Jieqiong Lei, widely known as the "mother of social work education in China", graduated from America and returned to China to help promoting social work services in the 1930s. The first independent department of social work (Department of Social Welfare) was established in Nanjing Jinling University in 1948.

As illustrated above, major features of the early stage of social work education were: subordinating under sociology (social work programmes were offered within the sociology departments), missionary-led (early programmes were set up and taught by American missionaries), limited in scale (there were only 12 universities with social work programmes in 1930), modelled after the West (American-based curriculum with social casework as the major social work method taught), with limited government recognition and support (there were basically no social work jobs available in the society at that time). The primary purpose of social work education was to provide trained workforce supporting university-based social service projects initiated by Christian missionaries from the West (Wang & Tsang, 2016).

After the establishment of the People's Republic of China (PRC) in 1949, Western-oriented social work practice under the previous capitalistic regime was regarded as an "iron fist behind a velvet glove" that oppressed the working-class people. Labelled as "bourgeois or pseudo-science", social work together with other social science disciplines, such as psychology and sociology were abolished in university education in 1953. Only Marxist economics were taught to university students as a required subject in political education for all.

At the same time, missionaries had to leave and most social welfare organisations were either closed down or taken over by the PRC government. Under the "iron-rice bowl" system of the centrally planned economy, work units were responsible for the provision of social, cultural, and educational services, including social welfare services ranging from child care to family support services. As life expectancy was short, there was little need for services for the elderly. New groups of government-employed and administration-oriented non-professional "social workers" were established. They were cadres in trade unions, women's federations, communist youth leagues and the neighbourhoods who employed administrative procedures and ideological education to resolve social contradictions/conflicts and personal problems. To resolve family and individual issues, people involved had to undergo people's mediation in which the "client" would face public and open criticisms, and directive instructions to learn from the role models of being a good citizen under the socialist system of New China. Administrative procedures would discipline (job demotion, salary deduction, and transfer to unfavourable positions) or reward (job promotion, selection as learning model, and housing or welfare benefits) the client to induce "desirable" individual behaviorial and ideological "changes" (Leung & Lam, 2000).

The American National Association of Social Workers made its first visit to China in 1977. According to its report, China was apparently seen as an utopia without Western types of social problems, such as poverty, juvenile delinquencies, abandon babies, mental illnesses, obesity, unwed marriages, and family breakdown. On the surface, there was no need of "professional social workers" (Chauncey & Sally, 1979). For three decades, the term "social work" was recognised as a type of non-paid volunteering work. Professional social work and social work education were absent from China's social welfare and educational system.

REINSTATING SOCIAL WELFARE AND SOCIAL WORK EDUCATION (1979–2005)

In adopting the Open Door Policy (1978) and market-oriented economic reform in the 1980s, the traditional welfare protection offered by the collectives, notably work units in the cities and communes in the rural areas, was eroding rapidly. Under a more pluralistic economy, people's livelihood became less secure due to rising unemployment, inadequate labour market protection, and income instability (Chan & Chow, 1992). Pension support and healthcare protection had become either inaccessible or less reliable. Even worse, the traditional family support had been broken down rapidly due to higher population mobility, increased family breakdown and divorces, draconian family planning policy and ageing population. Unprecedented social issues emerge. They include income inequalities, urban poverty, family violence, care of the elderly and the disabled persons, drug abuse, juvenile delinquency, abandoned babies, homeless vagabonds, left-behind children, and frail older persons in villages due to migration of young people to cities for jobs (Leung & Xu, 2015, Chapters 2 and 3).

Facing rapid escalating of social demands and the need for effective social control, the Ministry of Civil Affairs (MoCA) was then established in 1978 to take charge of formulating social policy for the welfare of the deprived and under-privileged populations. At the same time, sociology was restated in universities in 1979. Prominent sociology scholars, such as Professor Xiaotong Fei and Professor Jieqiong Lei, advocated for the establishment of social work education programmes. In the first textbook on sociology published in 1984 by Professor Fei, there was a chapter on "applied sociology", referring to social work as a professional discipline under sociology.

The Ministry of Civil Affairs (MoCA) was aware of the need to have better trained and equipped cadres to cope with the profound social challenges. It established the national Cadre Training College in 1983. Study tours were organised, especially to Hong Kong to learn about the design and operation of social welfare services outside China. After a national conference in 1987 on the need of social work education, the MoCA supported the setting of social work programmes in four universities in 1988. In the same year, the Asia–Pacific Association for Social Work Education (APASWE) collaborated with Peking University organised an international conference on social work education in Beijing. Participants were mainly professors from the four universities, cadres training colleges of Women's Federation, Communist Youth League, Labour Union, and others from sociology departments of various universities with interests in developing social work education. That conference was portrayed as an icebreaking contact for Chinese social work educators with their Western counterparts.

In 1986 to 1989, the University of Hong Kong (HKU) collaborated with Sun Yat-sen University to launch the first social work programme after 1949 in Guangzhou. Courses were taught by social work teachers from HKU. Meanwhile, HKU MSW students were arranged to have fieldwork placements, supervised by HKU supervisors at work units, such as the street offices and cadre colleges in Guangzhou. The evaluation report on the Project observed that sociology students and government cadres were suspicious of China's need of Western-based social work found in capitalistic societies. Yet they were fascinated by the variety of "soft" skills of social work in relating with people. They included skills in interviewing, counselling, running small groups and simulation games, as well as organising social activities. However, as the local teachers were not professional social workers, there were no practicum requirements in the programme. As there were no social work jobs, few of the students seemed interested in pursuing a social work career. Many of the graduates of Sun Yat-sen University took up civil service jobs that had a brighter and clearer career path. Without fieldwork placements, students treated social work teaching as an academic discipline rather than professional education (Leung, Nann, & He, 1990).

Following the beginning of the negotiation on the future of Hong Kong between China and the UK in the mid-1980s, Guangzhou, a major city close to Hong Kong, had shown more interests in learning more about social work operated welfare service model. Neighbourhood-based welfare services for children, the disabled, and the older people began to emerge particularly in those relatively wealthy communities, and some of the traditional NGOs, such as the YMCA and Young Women's Christian Association, under the sponsorship of the Communist Party, were re-invigorated to provide social services (Chan, 1993). In learning from Hong Kong, the MoCA promoted community services and implemented "welfare lotteries" to generate funds for social services in 1986. The general public could buy the lottery tickets and the winners would receive cash payments. After paying the prizes, the remaining sum would be allocated for funding social welfare and natural disaster relief projects. In 2017, welfare lotteries raised a total of 63 billion yuan (around US$9M) (MoCA, 2018).

Under the leadership of the MoCA, with support from social workers and social work teachers within and outside China, the China Association of Social Workers (CASW) was established in 1991. The CASW joined as a country member of the International Federation of Social Workers (IFSW) in 1992. With the support from the Ministry of Education, the professional organisation coordinating social work education institutions in the development of social work education, the China Association of Social Work Education (CASWE) was formed in the following year (1995) and participated as a member of the International Association of Schools of Social Work (IASSW). Funded by the Keswick Foundation, Hong Kong, CASWE was responsible for organising pilot social service networks to serve as practice base for students, social work conferences, overseas study tours, textbook publications, and training workshop for teachers.

Despite increased international contacts and support, initial responses in setting up new social work education programmes remained cautious. By 1997, there were only about 21 social work undergraduate programmes established, with about 1000 graduates a year. To tackle unemployment issues of high-school graduates, the government started policy to rapidly expand higher education and enrolment in 1999. Social work was re-classified as a "non-controlled development" subject, local governments and universities had the discretion to set up occupation-oriented programmes. Social work programmes soared immediately from only 36 in 2001, 90 in 2002, 172 in 2003, and further to 211 in 2007, producing over 10,000 graduates each year. The phenomenal growth of social work education programmes was not a response to the employment demands from the social welfare sector. Until then, there were still no formal social work positions for the employment of social work graduates. In fact, the government, specifically the MoCA, was still cautious about promoting social work as a profession. The situation was described as an "education-led" social work development. Most social work graduates, particularly those from prestigious universities, could not enter into employment as professional social workers. In other words, social work education was evolved independently by detaching itself from the social welfare field (Leung, 2013).

In general, the design of the social work curriculum was modelled after the Hong Kong or the international framework, including basic courses on social work practice, fieldwork placements, social policy, human behaviour and social environment, research and management. Despite the high growth in number, programme quality remained poor. Hindering factors included the lack of social work teachers with practice experiences and formal social work education; inadequate standardisation of curriculum (lacking accreditation mechanism); insufficient locally produced textbooks and teaching material, as well as qualified fieldwork supervisors and practice settings (Leung, 2007, 2013; Wang & Tsang, 2016). More importantly, the government had no formal social work positions, and the development of NGOs was very limited. The lack of career prospects had greatly discouraged high-school students from choosing social work programmes and entering social work jobs after graduation.

There were criticisms that the social work curriculum was directly and implanted into the Chinese society without going through the process "indigenization". Professor Shi, the former secretary of CASWE, was critical of the situation. He concisely pointed out that China's social work education development was "born late but grew fast; led by educational institutions; insufficient quality teachers; and conveniently swallowed the whole curriculum package without adequate digestion" (Shi, 2004, p. 31). The whole social work education was growing too fast. Yet it lacked the capacity and environment to build up a competent educational system supporting the development of the social welfare services and social work profession. Described as "Great Leap Introduction" of social work values and knowledge of social work from Hong Kong and the West, the former President of the CASWE, Professor Si Bin Wang showed concern over the lack of quality of social work education (Wang, 2012). Prominent Chinese social work educators, such as S. B. Wang, B. N. Shi, R. X. Xu, and Y. G. Xiong, have queried that social work education in China has been adopting international standards without going through a systematical process of indigenisation (Leung, 2007, 2013).

As most social work teachers in universities had backgrounds of sociology, political science or philosophy without any professional social work education, the need of improving the quality of social work teachers became paramount. In the beginning of the 1990s, a number of university teachers of social work programmes were sent to Hong Kong, mostly University of Hong Kong and Chinese University of Hong Kong, for their Doctoral or Master research degrees. The Hong Kong Polytechnic University, in collaboration with Peking University, set up the Master of Arts programme in social work (later retitled as MSW), produced more than 230 graduates since 2000. The University of Hong Kong, in collaborating with Fudan University, introduced two master programmes in social work and social service management in Shanghai 2001. Six teachers of Fudan University took the MSW programme and became the programme with the largest number of professionally trained social work institution in China during that time. This was the first social work programme operated by an outside Mainland China institution registered under the Ministry of Education. In short, Hong Kong played a key role in facilitating and empowering the early stage of social work education in Mainland China.

In 2001, social work was formally recognised as an "occupation" by the Ministry of Labour (2001). In 2003, MoCA encouraged local governments to set up pilot projects and employ social workers. In 1995, Shanghai Pudong district government contracted Shanghai YMCA to manage a community service centre. In 2003, the first independent welfare non-government organisation (NGO) in China was set up in Shanghai. Both of them employed social work graduates and received professional consultation and supervision from NGOs in Hong Kong. Shanghai, as a pioneer in the development of social work practice, set up an examination-based system for the accreditation of social workers in 2003. Three semi-governmental NGOs were set up, employing over 1300 social workers in 2006. Through government purchase of services, these social work-based "correctional services" for young people (drug users, discharged prisoners, juvenile delinquents) were formally introduced into Shanghai (Leung, 2013). Despite calling those social work jobs, the persons hired were not necessarily professionally trained. Many of the social work professors took on a CEO or Chairperson of newly established NGOs to establish new services and evaluate programme effectiveness. Social work teachers also took on as leaders in the NGOs, conduct research, and provide services to the population.

During this period of time, professional social work was only beginning to be recognised academically as a sub-discipline of sociology and occupationally under the Ministry of Civil Affairs (MoCA). Besides acting as a training base for social work teachers from China, Hong Kong performed the bridging role connecting China to the international social work community. More importantly, a group of Hong Kong scholars specialised on research studies on China's social welfare and social work practice has emerged (Chan, 1993; Chan & Chow, 1992; Chow and Xu, 2001; Leung, 1994; Leung & Nann, 1995). Emerging international publications on social issues, social policy, and social work facilitated more international interests on and collaboration with China.

SOCIAL GOVERNANCE REFORMS AND PHENOMENAL GROWTH IN SOCIAL WORK SERVICES, WORKFORCE AND SOCIAL WORK EDUCATION (2006–2018)

After a decade of phenomenal growth in social work education and limited development in the development of social work jobs, the year 2006 was a turning point. In that year, the Communist Party of China (CPC) Congress pledged to build up a harmonious society and there was a need to construct a large social work workforce. In the same year, the government published the occupational standards and methods for qualifying examinations for social workers. According to the *2012 Code of Social Work Practice* published by MoCA, social work was recognised as an occupation to implement social policy of the government and the CPC, mitigate social tension, resolve social

problems, maintain social stability, promote social justice, and construct harmonious society (MoCA, 2012). More importantly, social work seems to
promise the CPC the "soft power" to resolve social contradictions, ideological conflict, and maintain social stability after the rapid economic reform,
with reduction of the life-time employment (breaking of iron-rice-bowl) and
associated employment security due to the large-scale privatisation of state
enterprises.

Being officially recognised as an important agent in the building of social
cohesion and harmony, number of universities in China offering social work
programmes rapidly expand. The number of institutions offering BSW and
MSW programme increased rapidly from 227 in 2008 to 348 in 2018. More
social work programme teachers were professionally qualified from overseas
or locally. Fieldwork experiences were required as standards of practice in professional programmes, although the quality of the fieldwork supervision varied across institutions. Local professional organisations are being established
in the areas of medical social work, palliative care social work, community
social work, industrial social work, clinical social work, and family social work
were being established. In order to regulate professional standards, all social
workers, trained or non-trained, would take a national public examination to
get themselves registered.

There are two levels of expectation in the public examination for registered
social workers: assistant social worker level and social worker level. Assistant
social workers are required to sit examination on basic social work "integrated
abilities" and practice. Social workers are required to be examined on senior
levels of the above together with social work legislation and policy. In the
first national qualifying examination in 2008, 24,840 (18% of the 137,800
total number who took the examination) were qualified as registered social
workers. With the government recognising the need for good quality social
service due to rapid ageing of the population and growing income disparities, the *Framework on National Medium-and Long-Term Talent Development
Plan (2010–2020)* issued by the CPC and government ministries included
social work as one of the six key workforce to be promoted in the year 2010.
It also put forward the goal of having 1.5 million social workers by the year
2015 and three million social workers by the year 2020. Again, the *Opinions
on Strengthening the Construction of Social Work Professional* (2011) and the
*Medium- and Long-Term Plan for the Construction of Social Work Professional
Talents (2011–2020)* (2012) put forward specific requirements for the education, training, assessment, and employment of social workers. The targets
were revised to having 0.5 million social workers by the year 2015 and 1.45
million by the year 2020. Table 5.1 provides the figures on the phenomenal
growth of social workers and social work programmes from 2006 to 2018.

This is the stage of formal recognition of social work into the social
infrastructure of society. The development of social work services has been
acknowledged and promoted under the auspicious of the CPC and facilitated

Table 5.1 Development of social workers personnel, professional educational programs and schools in China (2008–2018)

	2008	2010	2012	2014	2015	2016	2017	2018
Participants in soical worker examinations	137,800	69,000	126,866	207,694	276,500	299,300	331,800	424,500
Social work workforce	–	0.2M	0.3M	0.4M	0.5M	0.76M	1.02M	1.24M
Registered social workers	–	45,000	72,086	113,907	184,865	200,000	312,089	439,000
Social work organizations	–	500	1247	3521	4686	6600	7511	–
Social work educational institutions	227	261	292	313	324	338	339	348
MSW programmes	–	58	61	104	104	105	105	147
No. of SW graduates	10,000	–	20,000	30,000	30,000	30,000	30,000	40,000
Investment (billion RMB)	–	0.7	1.25	2.22	2.67	4.268	5.11	–

Sources CASW (2009, 2010, 2013) and MoCA (various years)

by the MoCA through two major channels. First, local governments were encouraged to develop social work jobs. Second, regulations on social governance reforms included facilitating the formation and registration of social service and welfare organisations, notably social work organisations. The government deploy public funds to purchase social services from social work organisations to strengthen and standardise social service provision in the community.[1] To strengthen the social infrastructure, a series of programmes and policies were established. Regulations and guidelines published to promote social work practice include: social work ethics (2013), social work leadership (2015), children work guidelines (2014), elderly work (2015, 2016), development of social work positions (2016), and community work guidelines (2017), social casework and group work practice guidelines (2018), and standards for senior social workers (2018). The role of social work practice in specific fields includes remote marginal regions (2012), volunteering (2013), rehabilitation in natural disasters (2013), enterprises (2013), youth work (2014), correction services (2013), drug abuse (2014), social assistance (2014, 2017), mental health (2015, 2017), domestic violence (2015), and protection of left-behind children (2015). The strategy for effective social work intervention to tackle various social needs and problems in society was being clearly articulated and turned into policy standards.

According to the *China Social Work Development Report 2011–2012* edited by the China Social Work Research Center (CSWRC) of the MoCA, there are 11 recognised fields of social work practice (CSWRC, 2013). They are social assistance, post-natural disaster rehabilitation, work with the disabled persons, women, older persons, young people, medical social work, rural social work, correctional services, union social work, and drug abuse services. The 2008 Wenchuan earthquake has prominently publicised the contribution of social work in post-natural disaster rehabilitation. Nationally, community-based campaigns on linking up social organisations, social workers, and volunteers are thriving. Coastal provinces with ample resources have been more vigorous in promoting non-governmental social work organisations, developing a variety of community-based welfare services, encouraging innovations, implementing government purchase of services, and promoting social work jobs and careers (Leung & Xu, 2015, Chapter 7; CSWRC, 2013).

In the Greater Bay Area with major cities like Shenzhen, Dongguan, and Guangzhou, social service organisations employed experienced professional social work supervisors from Hong Kong to help them in developing a robust system of social welfare services (Law & Liu, 2018; Mo & Tsui, 2016, 2018; QCSWS, 2018). Urban management with private housing estates and owners' involvement also enhance quest for more market-oriented community service provisions. Private housing estates hired social workers and professionals in running club facilities to cater for needs of retired persons and families with young children (Xu & Hou, 2015; Xu & Xu, 2016). Based on standardisation of government purchase of services, more social work organisations emerged employing a large number of social workers. Now Guangdong tops the country in terms of the number of social workers and non-governmental social work organisations, as well as the amount of funds allocated by the local governments for the purchase of welfare services for their citizens (Gong, Jiang, & Leung, 2019; Law, 2019; Lei & Chan, 2018). In essence, more specialised social work services have been emerging particularly in coastal cities, demanding better-equipped social workers, and more specialised social work educational programmes.

Government purchase of service is regarded as a "double-edged sword". It has provided the necessary funding support to develop much needed welfare services and a greater role of non-governmental organisations in social welfare, leading to further social governance reforms. However, if the contribution of professional social work cannot be demonstrated and government funding support may facilitate corruption and collusion in the service delivery process, then, credibility of the government in social work can be eroded (Wang, 2018a). With limited fund-raising and revenue generation capacity, social work organisations are largely dependent on government funding for the delivery of social welfare services. By becoming the "servant" of the government and struggling to obtain funds through competitive bidding, they have limited ability for service innovation and respond to newly emerging needs, not to mention advocacy (Gong et al., 2019; Xiong & Wang, 2007).

Relationship of social workers with the government can be described as "embeddedness" in which social workers are grafted into the existing government-dominated social and governance system (Wang, 2011; Wang & Tsang, 2016). Social workers have to be dependent on government patronage, trust, and funding. Under the government administrative leadership and funding control, professional discretion is severely threatened (Wang, 2011). In practice, social work projects, particularly those based in the community, have to be supervised and monitored by local government officials. Community centres in some cities, such as Shenzhen, have been renamed as "Community Centers of the Party". A key requirement for social work organisations bidding for family services centres in Guangzhou is that the organisation has to set up a CCP party branch, i.e. the need to have party member social workers in charge. In a nutshell, social work currently is functioned as an integral part of the government and the Communist Party system. The issue of how to effectively collaborate with the Party becomes a key challenge for the further development of the social work profession (Wang, 2018b). As more political cadres are becoming social workers through qualifying examinations and more professionally trained social workers have to take up political duties of maintaining social stability, the dividing line between professional intervention and political education is becoming increasingly blurred.

Future Challenges (2019 and Beyond)

There is profound and remarkable development of social work professionalisation and social work education in the past decade. The growth of social work workforce, social work teachers, social welfare services, and social work programmes has been impressive and unprecedented; and yet they are not without challenges (Liu, Lam, & Yan, 2012). Instead of relying on textbooks and material imported from Hong Kong and Taiwan, as well as translated materials from the West, local teachers have contributed to building new knowledge, produced impressive locally relevant textbooks, published their research in newly established local social work journals, and oftentimes in international journals as well. Indisputably, more and more social work teachers are better equipped with formal social work education received in China, Hong Kong and overseas. China has become an active player in the international social work community, including the International Federation of Social Workers (IFSW) and International Association of School of Social Work (IASSW). Engagement includes the sponsoring and participation in international and regional conferences, making overseas study trips, sabbatical arrangements, and collaborative agreements in research and student/staff exchange.

The example of the Five-year China Collaborative (2012–2017) by American Council on Social Work Education, International Social Work Education, the International Association of Schools of Social Work, with consultation from the China Association of Social Work Education guided and monitored the development of seven regional partnerships between social work programmes in China and the United States, is a good illustration of the vibrant development of international collaboration. Established programmes in top universities in the United States, such as New York University and University of Southern California, are establishing their respective programme in China, online and off-line. Universities in China are resourced to hire international scholars as permanent and/or visiting faculty. Start up grants and large funding for social science impact studies are easily available as a result of rising expectations of the middle class and growing affluence of the society. The future development of social work education in China is going to be interesting, fluid, and dynamic. However, there are challenges confronting the development of social work education in China.

1. *Enhancing the academic status of social work education*: Currently, many social work programmes are still subordinated under the departments of sociology. Social work needs to be recognised as an independent academic and professional discipline with its own department or school. Academic status of social work can only be enhanced through active research and publications, admission of quality students, and improvement of employment prospects of social work graduates. Social work teachers now are often distracted by their active involvement in establishing and operating social work organisations, delivering government

financed welfare projects and working on large research grants on social problems. Although these projects can provide teachers with direct service experiences and offer social work students with better fieldwork opportunities, the incentives of receiving remunerations can divert teachers' motivations and efforts to improve teaching and research output. The termination of two BSW programmes in prestigious universities in Guangzhou in 2017 was a clear indication that the university administration was not satisfied with the academic performance of social work teachers as well as with the employment prospects of the social work graduates.

2. *Moving towards accreditation of social work programmes*. Currently, the establishment and monitoring of a social work programme are regulated and monitored only by the Ministry of Education, university administration, and facilitated by CASWE. There are still programmes with no professionally qualified social work teachers, and fieldwork placements requirements and supervision are not standardised. Following international good practice and to ensure quality professional education, there should be an independent professional mechanism, with explicit criteria established to accredit social work programmes.

3. *Improving employment prospects and career for social workers*. Based on a public examination system to qualify social workers, the value of social work education would be in doubt. It is estimated that the majority of the social work workforce, including those registered social workers, are not necessarily having formal social work education. A more differentiated job classification system should be formulated to provide favourable employment and career prospects for social workers with formal social work training. The current MSW programmes enrol students with both social work and non-social work undergraduate degrees. There should be clear distinctions between the MSW and BSW programmes in curriculum design and preferably in employment prospects. Different programme concentrations and advanced practice programmes can be provided to provide the required and specialised expertise in the field.

4. *Promoting international collaborations*. To widen exposures of social work teachers, more teachers can seek their attachments overseas, Hong Kong and Taiwan. These opportunities to travel overseas might be affected by the Sino-US tension started in 2019. Getting an international visiting scholar visa to the United States may be more difficult. Overseas fieldwork placements possibilities for students and especially for master and doctoral students should be explored in order to broaden perspective of locally trained social workers. There is new funding from the government for universities to hire renowned overseas social work scholars and experienced social work practitioners to share their experiences and good practice. However, the relevance of the research and practice of visitors who are willing to visit China may need a process of integration

into the Chinese context. In fact, more fee-charging courses on practice skills taught by overseas experienced social workers can be found in China now. International travel and international exchange will have to be rebuilt under the new normal post-covid-19 pandemic as well.

Finally, social work education has been caught in a vicious circle. Poorly developed social work jobs with low pay and limited job promotion prospects cannot attract highly motivated and quality students to enrol in social work programmes and enter social work jobs. Dropout rate in the social welfare field has been high. Oftentimes, receiving social work education from loosely structured social work curriculum and fieldwork arrangements taught by professionally incompetent teachers with limited direct social work practice experiences, social work graduates are ill-equipped for social welfare jobs. Evidence-based programme evaluation is rare. Without the evidence to demonstrate the value of social work, employers would find it difficult to raise salary and improve working conditions for social workers. Unless there is a breakthrough in this vicious circle, the maturity of social work profession and social work education may take a long and winding road.

NOTE

1. Examples of these Regulations are: *Circular on Promoting the Development of Non-governmental Social Work Organization*s (MoCA, 2009); *Opinion Concerning Strengthening and Innovating Social Management* (CPC, 2011); *Guiding Opinion Concerning Government Purchase of Social Work Services* (MoCA, 2012); *Guiding Opinion Concerning the Purchase of Services from the Society* (State Council, 2013); *Options on Reform and Transfer of Functions of the Organization of the State Council* (State Council, 2013); *Guiding Opinion on Government Purchase of Services from the Social Sector* (State Council, 2013); *Opinion on Speeding Up the Promotion of Community Social Work Services* (MoCA, 2014); *Opinion on Further Promoting the Development of Non-governmental Social Work Organizations* (MoCA, 2014); *Management Methods for Foreign NGO* (State Council, 2017); *Opinion Concerning the Strengthening and Perfecting Urban and Rural Community Governance* (CPC, 2017); *Opinion of the MoCA on Further Strengthening and Improving the Management of Social Service Organization* (MoCA, 2018); *Opinion on Reforming the Management System for Orderly and Healthy Development of Social Organizations* (State Council and CPC, 2018); and *Circular on Innovating Social Innovation and Services* (MoCA, 2018).

REFERENCES

CASW (China Association of Social Workers). (2009, 2010, 2013). *Annual Report on Development of Social Work in China*. Beijing: Social Sciences Publishers.

Chan, C. (1993). *The myth of neighbourhood mutual help: The contemporary Chinese community-based welfare system in Guangzhou*. Hong Kong: Hong Kong University Press.

Chan, C., & Chow, N. (1992). *More welfare after economic reform? Welfare development in the People's Republic of China.* Hong Kong: Centre of Urban Planning and Environmental Management, University of Hong Kong.

Chauncey, A., & Sally, A. (Eds.). (1979). *China view: First NASW study tour.* Washington, DC: National Association of Social Workers.

Chow, N., & Xu, Y. B. (2001). *Socialist welfare in a market economy: Social security reforms in Guangzhou, China.* London: Ashgate.

CSWDR. (2018). *China Social Work Development Report.* http://www.chinadevelopmentbrief.org.cn/news-22678.html.

CSWRC (China Social Work Research Center, MoCA). (2013). *China Social Work Development Report 2011–2012.* Beijing: China Social Sciences Publishers.

Gao, J. G., & Yan, M. C. (2014). Social work in making: The state and social work development in China. *International Journal of Social Welfare., 24*(1), 93–101. https://doi.org/10.1111/ijsw.12089.

Gong, H., Jiang, H., & Leung, J. (2019). The changing relationship between the Chinese Government and non-governmental organizations in social service delivery: Approaching partnership? *Asian Pacific Journal of Social Work and Development.* http://doi.org/10.1080/02185385.2018.1525762.

Law, A. (Ed.). (2019). *Guangdong social work.* Beijing: China Social Science Publishers.

Law, K. T., & Liu, X. L. (Eds.). (2018). *The Blue Book of Guangdong* (Annual Report on Social Work Development in Guangdong). Beijing: China Social Sciences Publisher.

Lei, J., & Chan, C. K. (Eds.). (2018). *Welfare reform revolution: Contracting out social services.* New York: Routledge.

Leung, J. (1994). Dismantling the iron rice bowl: Welfare reforms in the PRC. *Journal of Social Policy, 23*(3), 341–361.

Leung, J. (2007). An international definition on social work for China. *Journal of International Social Welfare, 16,* 391–397.

Leung, J. (2013). The development of social work and social work education in China: Issues and prospects. In C. Noble, M. Henrickson, & Y. Han (Eds.), *Social work education in the Asia Pacific region: Issues and debates* (pp. 175–206). Sydney: University of Sydney Press.

Leung, J., & Lam, D. (2000). Enforcing family care obligations for the elderly in China through mediation. *Asia Pacific Journal of Social Work, 10*(1), 77–89.

Leung, J., & Nann, R. (1995). *Authority and benevolence: Social welfare in China.* Hong Kong and New York: The Chinese University Press and St. Martin's Press.

Leung, J., Nann, R., & He, X. F. (1990, August). *Introducing social work and social work education in the PRC* (A Report on a Three-Year Cooperative Project in Social). Work Education and Research between the University of Hong Kong and Zhongshan University, Research Series of the Department of Social Work and Social Administration, The University of Hong Kong.

Leung, J., & Xu, Y. (2015). *China's social welfare—The third turning point.* Cambridge: Polity Press.

Li, Y., Han, W. J., & Huang, C. C. (2013). Development of social work education in China: Background, current status, and prospects. *Journal of Social Work Education, 48*(4), 635–653. https://doi.org/10.5175/JSWE.2012.201100049.

Liu, Y., Lam, C. M., & Yan, M. C. (2012). A challenged professional identity: The struggles of new social workers in China. *China Journal of Social Work, 5*(3), 189–200.

Mo, K., & Tsui, M. S. (2016). External supervision for social workers in another socio-political context: A qualitative study in Shenzhen. *China. China Journal of Social Work, 9*(1), 62–74.

Mo, K., & Tsui, M. S. (2018). Toward an indigenized external supervision approach in China. *International Social Work, 8,* 1–18.

MoCA (Ministry of Civil Affairs). (2012). *Social work code of practice.* http://xxgk.mca.gov.cn:8081/new_gips/contentSearch?id=46213.

MoCA (Ministry of Civil Affairs). (2018). *Annual Report on Social Services 2017.* http://www.mca.gov.cn/article/sj/tjgb/2017/201708021607.pdf.

MoCA (Ministry of Civil Affairs). (various years). *Annual Report on Social Service Statistics.* http://www.mca.gov.cn/article/sj/tjgb/.

QCSWS (Qi Chuang Social Work Service). (2018). *Annual Report 2018 and Qi Chuang Tenth Anniversary (2008–2018),* Special Issue (in Chinese).

Shi, B. N. (2004). A new century: Choices facing China's social work education. *Journal of University of Science and Technology, Beijing, 20,* 1. http://210.31.160.111:82/paper/2014/05/26/20140526143341203.pdf.

Wang, S. B. (2011, September 28). The embedded development of China's social work. *China Sociology Website.* http://sociology.cssn.cn/webpic/web/sociology/upload/2011/09/d20110928170036421.pdf.

Wang, S. B. (2012, July). Going though our meaningful history. *China Social Work.* http://blog.sina.com.cn/s/blog_4c670d3d0102e2kx.html.

Wang, S. B. (2018a, October 8). Government purchase of service is an innovation, but it can also be a trap. *China Society Press.* http://theory.swchina.org/research/2018/1008/32312.shtml.

Wang, S. B. (2018b, September 25). Facilitating the synergy of development between social work and party work. *China Social Work.* http://theory.swchina.org/research/2018/0925/32256.shtml.

Wang, S. B., & Tsang, A. (2016). Development of social work education in China in an era of rapid reform and transformation. In I. Taylor, M. Bogg, M. Lefevre, & B. Treater (Eds.), *Routledge international handbook of social work education* (pp. 73–83). London: Routledge.

Xiong, Y. G., & Wang, S. B. (2007). Development of social work education in China in the context of new policy initiatives: Issues and challenges. *Social Work Education, 26*(6), 560–572.

Xu, X., & Xu, Y. (2016). The connotation, mechanism and practical logic of "Three Society Linkage" in grassroots Governance: An empirical research of H Community in Shenzhen. *China Social Science Journal, 7,* 87–96.

Xu, Y. Q., & Hou, L. W. (2015). Analysis of paths in urban neighbourhood management. *Social Sciences Journal, 219,* 33–38.

CHAPTER 6

The Development of Social Work Education in Malaysia

Fuziah Shaffie, Teoh Ai Hua and Ismail Baba

Introduction

As part of Southeast Asian archipelago, Malaysia with the states of Sabah and Sarawak was established in 1963, combining Malaya, Singapore, Sabah, and Sarawak. The term 'Malaya' to the British colonial period, and the term 'Malaysia' to the period since 1963, are used accordingly in this chapter. Singapore joined Malaysia in 1963 and then separated from the latter in 1965 to form an independent state. Consisting of two regions separated by some 640 miles of the South China Sea, Malaysia is a federation of 13 states and three federal territories. The country is dominated by ethnic Malay, Chinese, with Indians forming a tinier section, with an estimated population of 32 million in 2019 (http://worldpopulationreview.com). In Sarawak, the predominant ethnic group is the Ibans, followed by the Chinese and Malays. Sabah is predominantly comprised of the ethnic group Kadazan-Dusun followed by Bajau and Malays.

Though Islam is the official religion enshrined in the Malaysian constitution, there are several other religions practised including Christianity and various tribal religions. Malay is the official language but English is widely spoken in most parts of the country. Malaysia is very much a multi-ethnic,

F. Shaffie (✉) · T. A. Hua
School of Applied Psychology, Social Work and Policy,
College of Arts and Sciences, Universiti Utara Malaysia, Sintok, Malaysia
e-mail: fuzi484@uum.edu.my

I. Baba
School of Social Sciences, Universiti Sains Malaysia (USM),
George Town, Malaysia

© The Author(s) 2021   79
S. S. M. et al. (eds.), *The Palgrave Handbook of Global Social Work Education*, https://doi.org/10.1007/978-3-030-39966-5_6

multicultural, and multiracial country whose social integration has become a model for the rest of the world. The different races have their own traditions and customs which give Malaysia a colourful heritage.

Most of the issues currently faced by social work professions today have references to the past, characterising much of the professions' development. Scholars in Malaysia do not devote much attention to this aspect. Social work as a profession does not appear to have developed as much as in other developed or developing countries. Thus, to better understand the current structure of social work education in Malaysia, it is helpful to consider the past. Historical study or viewing from the historical perspective would increase knowledge concerning social work professions, provide an understanding of the organisational, individual, social, political, and economic circumstances in which a particular phenomenon occurs and depict the emergence and development of social work education (Fuziah, 2006).

Social work education, looking from the historical perspective, is an under-researched area in Malaysia and thus, this writing will serve to provide a comprehensive understanding about social work during the colonial period until present day. At the moment, few studies suggest that social work and social welfare in Malaysia was originally moulded by the British colonial policy (DSW, n.d.; Davis, Doling, & Zainal, 2000; Fuziah, 2006; Lee, 2011). The studies have the intention of making an original and substantive contribution to the literature on the origin of social welfare services.

Social Welfare Work During the Colonial Period

The nation was juggled by a series of colonial hands, with the Portuguese, Dutch, British, and Japanese beginning in the middle of the sixteenth century. British ruled the country from 1786 until 1941, and then it was under the Japanese occupation that ended in 1945. In 1945, it was ruled once again by the British until its independence in 1957. Since 1946, the basic structure of the social welfare system in Malaya was laid down by the colonial administrators. More than 150 years of British colonisation in Malaya has had a tremendous impact on the country's administration, economic, and social system.

What constituted the most important outcome from colonisation was that Britain ultimately became the dominant power in Malaya, even though the country was colonised by other Imperial powers. The British incursions into the country brought far greater infiltration of Western institutions, culture, and values, which resulted in drastic changes of the existing traditional systems of administration, economy, and structure of the society.

Malaysia is a very complex social structure, because of the different cultural values and practices of three major communities. The presence of the three main ethnic groups was rather unique compared to other British colonies because no other colonies were comprised of such ethnic composition. Each ethnic group relied on its own ways in dealing with welfare issues. It may be argued that the existence of a multi-ethnic society had a significant effect on the establishment and execution of social welfare services in Malaysia since the government needs to consider the implications of the services for each ethnic group which perhaps may include the provision of social work education in the country.

British colonisation provided the country with various social services, such as education to support and uphold 'colonial duty'. Social welfare development was characterised by residual approach that is, which targeted the needy group in the society. The government also made attempts for a more comprehensive welfare provision to the Malayan population. The aftermath of the Second World War created a multitude of social problems. Thousands of families were left destitute and traditional welfare services were no longer capable of meeting the needs of the people. The authorized or obligatory organisation and resources to handle the aftermath of the war 'with any effect clearly lay in the hands of the government' (Sushama, 1992, p. 56). It was the responsibility of the colonial government to organise measures for the relief and recovery of the Malayan people. The government indicated a move to provide welfare services to the whole population of Malaya, irrespective of ethnic groups (Fuziah, 2006). Apart from marking the British re-occupation of Malaya, the Department of Social Welfare (DSW) was established in 1946 as a major government agency authorised to provide social welfare services.

The emergence of social work education in the country has been carried out through textbooks, curricula, and theories which were imported from Western countries by educators, who studied in Europe, the United States, and Australia. Though we have learned much from the West, the discussion so far has shown that the British colonial government was concerned about the importation of Western ideas and practices about welfare to suit the local circumstances. It has also revealed the underlying factors of resolving welfare provision such as religion, traditions, and values, indicating the need to modify Western welfare ideas and practices to the Malayan circumstances. Although their knowledge of local circumstances was insufficient, the colonial officers used their judgement as to what was right, trialling to see to what extent their ideas were workable and acceptable.

On training of social welfare workers, the existing literature revealed that no active steps were taken by the colonial government to examine and discuss the needs of the local people with representatives of the indigenous groups, even though the literature showed the colonial government had sent a Malay, a Chinese and an Indian for training in the UK (Fuziah, 2006). The colonial government had taken an initiative to train a representative of each major ethnic group. By doing so, the government had hoped these three candidates would be able to learn the UK welfare ideas and apply them to Malaya.

The content of training, both in the UK and in Malaya, consisted of theoretical and practical work. Voluntary bodies such as the British Red Cross workers contributed to the training programme by giving lectures and training facilities to course participants. One significant difference between the training in the UK and that in Malaya was regarding the places where the participants carried out the practical component of the course. In the case of the UK, the students were placed in different parts of the UK, and thus they would have been greatly exposed to the UK welfare ideas and experiences. They would then have to translate these ideas and adapted them to the local conditions when they came back to Malaya. On the other hand, participants who were trained in Malaya were placed at various parts of Malaya, in an 'unstructured as well as structured settings, where in addition to the traditional agencies, where there were supervisors, there was developed wider geographical and social settings in the community, the district, the aboriginal settlement and the housing estate' (Robertson, 1980, p. 75). Thus, these groups of students have had the opportunity to gain a variety of interests and experiences within the local context which would not be available otherwise.

As the first Chief Social Welfare Officer in the DSW (1946–1947), J. A. Harvey held the view that social welfare workers should be properly trained and knowledgeable about the East, in relation to its religion and outlook. He suggested that workers could only derive all this knowledge from years of experience in the field. A social worker new to the country should not only be very careful before implementing any new policy, but also needed to consult local opinion. Interestingly, Harvey exhibited an endeavour to understand the local cultures when he stressed that any attempt to apply Western experience without tempering it to local conditions and opinions would only lead to difficulties and resentment (Malaysia National Archives, MU 2247/46). Harvey pointed out the importance of local opinion in matters concerning their welfare, and he was cautious as evidenced by his remarks '...new facets of welfare work are a different matter but in each case we must bear in mind the fact that local opinion and modern thought are not necessarily at one on this matter' (Malaysia National Archives, MU 2247/46).

Harvey also revealed that the local Chinese in Malaya, at any rate, had never accepted work of this kind as an obligation to the country. In fact, it was questionable whether they wanted to accept the work because in doing so, it would mean that they would have to make a break with tradition (Malaysia National Archives, MU 2247/46). For instance, in order to maintain their own culture and tradition within Malaya, the Chinese built their own schools, erected their own maternity hospitals, and their own homes for orphans. In various ways, the Chinese, through their clans, exhibited strong independence of government aid in welfare matters. On the other hand, the Indians, according to Harvey, although generally accepted responsibility for the welfare and upbringing of the underprivileged and the neglected members of their community, indicated a willingness to accept the state's intervention in welfare services.

Harvey had spoken out about the importance of knowledge about local circumstances among the welfare officers. If his views were taken up by the government, on the one hand, it would have had funding implication because it would have needed research and repeated meetings to consider local needs within the welfare policy, which the government could not afford to do so. On the other hand, the colonial power would not have wanted to provide welfare to the people of Malaya at a similar, or almost similar, scale as what was being done in Britain that is by resorting to a universal approach. Moreover, it needs to be borne in mind that Britain, a colonial power, had always considered itself (and its people) as superior and Malaya was only one of its many colonies.

The colonial government's role in the provision of welfare also changed after the war. It began to take charge of the welfare work that had been, to a considerable extent, sustained and managed by voluntary bodies preceding the war. For instance, the government intervened by supporting the establishment and operation of some welfare homes and by encouraging voluntary and non-governmental bodies to aid in providing welfare services. Nevertheless, the colonial government's involvement in the provision of welfare services was minimal and welfare provision was provided to the needy group only such as orphans, destitute, and delinquent in the homes administered by the DSW, whereas the bulk of the welfare work (48 children homes, for example) was still undertaken by the voluntary bodies (Fuziah, 2006).

Non-governmental bodies significantly contributed to the development of early social welfare services in Malaya. Hardiman and Midgley (1982) and MacPherson and Midgley (1987) claimed that provision in the early welfare services was not provided by the colonial governments but by missionary organisations such as the London Missionary Society (LMS). An integrated relationship between the voluntary sectors and the government existed during the period of (1946–1957). The government had relied heavily on the cooperation and support of the voluntary bodies. Midgley's (1981, 1997) views on the importance of the non-governmental sector, whereby the colonial government was content to let voluntary organisations cater for welfare needs of the colonised people while its own interventions were kept to a minimum.

Fuziah's (2006) has illustrated the models in which welfare ideas and practices of the UK were diffused. The transfer of welfare knowledge, ideas, and practices was done by modifying and adapting them to fit the local circumstances, needs, and culture. For instance, when training the personnel to deal with social welfare matters in Malaya, there was the issue of local familiarisation that the locally employed social welfare personnel 'should have a thorough knowledge of the subjects they will have to deal with' in the country later on (Malaysia National Archives, FS 12857). In a sense, basic and compulsory knowledge of social welfare were imparted to the trainees with the expectations that they applied the learned knowledge to manage social welfare issues within their local social context. As highlighted by Robertson (1980), the course content involved 'an exposure to various tapestries of life, both urban and rural; to different ethnic groups; to different priorities in meeting social needs as between the then primarily rural and urban situations' in the country (1980). It was believed that the characteristics of the course could certainly fit the local context. This seemingly supports Midgley's (1984) conjecture that the diffusion of the colonial government's welfare ideas, practices, and experiences took place in either an 'uncritical replication of alien welfare policies', or through a mode of diffusion that would be described as a 'discerning adaptation of foreign experience'.

This is in line with the view that social policies and welfare services in the colonies were not only limited in scope but also were characterised by a residual nature (Hardiman & Midgley, 1982; Harper, 1991; Hodge, 1973; MacPherson, 1982; MacPherson & Midgley, 1987; Midgley, 1981, 1990; Rodney, 1972). Though they did not specifically refer to Malaya, nevertheless the literature had supported their assertion (Fuziah, 2006). On welfare matters, the measures undertaken by the government suggested the government did not have specific welfare guidelines for Malaya that could be relied on when resolving welfare matters that arose. Thus, the government resorted to adapt existing legislation and adapted British welfare ideas to suit the local circumstances. On training workers, the government showed a move to consider its welfare ideas and practices that were worthy of being translated and adapted to suit local context. Hence, Midgley's (1981) assertions that within colonialism, knowledge, and skills were identified, selected, and modified before resolving local issues is accurate.

It can be said that, generally, the post-independent government's approach towards welfare provision in Malaysia has not significantly changed from that during the British rule during the period of 1946–1957. In a sense, the post-independent social welfare policy is never fully elucidated by the pre-independent government. Nevertheless, Malaysia's post-independence policy is intent on enacting welfare policies according to the nation's multi-ethnic population because the tensions as well as the opportunities inherent in the ethnic mix have had a profound influence on the post-independence period shaping the Malaysian approach to welfare provision (Doling & Omar, 2000).

The Introduction of Social Work

Social work was introduced to Malaysia in the form of social welfare during the British colonial period. The British Colonial Office in Malaya established the Department of Social Services in 1937 where all the social workers were made up by expatriates from the UK who were professionally trained in social work from the London School of Economics (LSE) (Fuziah & Baba, 2013). After the end of the Second World War, the British returned to Malaya and established the Department of Social Welfare (DSW) in the Federation of Malaya in 1946.

Due to the lack of trained local social workers and no training facilities of such discipline at that time, four local officers were selected to do a two-year course in Social Welfare at LSE in the same year. Subsequently, small badges of officers were sent for their social work education and training in the UK annually until the 1950s. In 1952, a School of Applied Social Studies was established at the National University of Singapore (NUS) (formerly known as the University of Malaya (UM) to train local social workers through a diploma programme (Fuziah & Baba, 2013). At that time, the department only offered a diploma programme under the School of Applied Social Studies (*The Straits Times*, 22 September 2012; Yasas, 1974).

Nevertheless, the Diploma of Applied Social Studies stayed at the Singapore campus in a restructuring exercise where the campus in Singapore was renamed to University of Singapore (now known as the National University of Singapore [NUS]) while the Kuala Lumpur campus maintained the name of University of Malaya in 1962. Although the social work education was only offered in Singapore, it did not affect the training of social workers for Malaysia, even after Singapore and Malaysia separated in 1965. The discontinuation of NUS in providing Malaysians to study social work at NUS has facilitated Malaysia to set up its own first social work education at the Universiti Sains Malaysia (USM) in 1975 (Fuziah & Baba, 2013; Sinnasamy, 2006).

Social Work Education in Malaysia: 1975–1995

Establishment of social work education at the degree level at USM was a joint effort between the Ministry of Social Welfare and USM following an idea which was mooted from a United Nation Conference of Social Welfare Ministers in 1968 in Bangkok, Thailand (Baba, 2011). Some of the key people involved in the formation of the social work programme at USM were Mr. S. Sockanathan, Director of Social Welfare Department Malaysia; Miss Frances Maria Yasas, the Regional Advisor on Training in Social Work and Community Development of the United Nations Economic Commission for Asia and the Far East (UNECAFE); Dr. Blake, Dean of the Faculty of Social Science of USM; Miss P. C. Sushama, executive committee member of the Malaysian Association of Social Workers (MASW); and a group of deputy directors from the Ministry of Social Welfare (Fuziah & Baba, 2013).

Even though the initial name proposed for the programme was 'Social Work and Community Development', eventually the name 'Social Development and Administration' (SDA) was adopted as social development was the preferred term among developing countries at that time. However, SDA could not portray the clear identity of social work and has created confusion for many people and organisations who wanted to know about social work in Malaysia. It was finally changed to 'Social Work Programme' in 1995 (Baba, 2011; Fuziah & Baba, 2013).

As the sole social work programme in Malaysia for almost two decades, USM has played an active role not only in producing local professional social workers, but has also involved with various international social work activities by joining the membership of IASSW and the Asia and Pacific Association for Social Work Education (APASWE), and hosted two APASWE seminars over the years (Fuziah & Baba, 2013).

THE DEVELOPMENT OF SOCIAL WORK EDUCATION AFTER 1995

The development of social work education at the institutions of higher learning in Malaysia intensified in the 1990s following the pronouncement of Vision 2020 where it outlined establishing a fully caring society as one of the challenges, as well as the establishing of new public universities in the 1980s and 1990s. Social work was seen fit to produce the human resource that addresses social ills and lead to the creation of a caring society.

Social work education was established at Universiti Malaysia Sarawak (UNIMAS) in 1993 with a Bachelor of Social Science (Social Work) (Sinnasamy, 2006), followed by Universiti Utara Malaysia (UUM) in 1997 with a Bachelor of Social Work Management in 1997. It was then followed by Universiti Kebangsaan Malaysia (UKM) which offers Master in Medical Social Work in 2000, catering to the training needs of social workers working at the public hospitals. At the same time, two public universities also started to offer programmes related to human services and human development. University Malaya (UM) introduced a Department of Social Administration and Justice in 1993, which later introduced a Bachelor of Arts (Social Administration and Justice) in 1993 and Universiti Putra Malaysia (UPM) offer minor in social work for its Bachelor of Science (Human Development) in 2000 that provides some courses related to social work. All these five institutions are all public universities.

The increase of social work programmes in a short time has raised concerns over the differences in curriculum design and the lack of qualified and experienced social work educators. Hence, under the initiative of USM, these five (USM, UNIMAS, UUM, UKM, and UM) universities came together in 2000 and form the National Joint Consultative Council on Social Work Education (NJCCSWE) with the inclusion of the Malaysian Association of Social Workers. The objective of this grouping is to provide support to less experienced social work programmes to ensure quality and standardisation of social work education in the country (Fuziah & Baba, 2013).

The formation of NJCCSWE in 2002 has provided a platform for the social work educators to discuss issues pertaining to social work education and training in the country. However, as a non-registered network, it has not achieved the status nor influence like other formal institutions such as the Council on Social Work Education (CSWE) in the US. For example, the NJCCSWE has no capacity to run periodic training programs. Therefore, social work educators were engaged in their individual capacity, rather than through the NJCCSWE, by government agencies or non-government welfare organizations to conduct skill training for their social welfare workforce.

Social Work Curriculum

World Conference on Social Work and Social Development in Melbourne (2014) concluded that both IFSW and IASSW adopted a new global definition of social work in their respective General Meeting:

> Social work is a practice-based profession and an academic discipline that promotes social change and development, social cohesion, and the empowerment and liberation of people. Principles of social justice, human rights, collective responsibility and respect for diversities are central to social work. Underpinned by theories of social work, social sciences, humanities and indigenous knowledge, social work engages people and structures to address life challenges and enhance wellbeing. (www.iassw-aiets.org)

The lengthy global definition encapsulated the complexities that the social work profession has to deal with, and the wide-ranging knowledge that social workers must acquire. It reinforces that social work cannot simply be carried by anyone without proper training and education (Social work, 2010). The NJCCSWE has produced a guideline on the components of the social work curriculum which is in line with the standards set by IASSW. The guidelines also stipulate other requirements like qualifications of the faculty members and the procedure for field instruction and supervision. The summary is as shown in Table 6.1.

It is important for Malaysian social work curriculum not only to be on par with the international standards but also able to develop indigenous knowledge and practices (Ling, 2007). In order to standardise the social work curriculum of the five universities in Malaysia, it was suggested that these universities should use the curriculum that were stipulated in Table 6.1. There is also a growing trend of social workers movement between borders (Bodde & Duke, 2009), meaning social workers can be engaged or employed to practise in other countries. The liberalisation of the service sector in ASEAN also put a demand on social workers trained in Malaysia to be equipped and recognised in order to provide social work service in the ASEAN community later on. At present, ASEAN member states have been working since 2011 to improve the standard of social services in its member states (https://asean.org/asean-social-work-consortium-kicks-off/Jakarta, 4 March 2011).

Table 6.1 Four components of social work curriculum

Component	Focus area	Examples/names of subject
Foundational subjects	Social sciences and humanities: understanding of human behaviour and society, and contemporary social issues	• Psychology • Sociology • Human Development • Cultural diversity • Race relations • Policy and law
Social work core subjects	Theories and skills: knowledge, skills, and values in social work	• Ethics and values of social work • Social work intervention: individual casework, family work, group work, and community work. • Social welfare and policy • Communication and counselling skills • Working in organizations
Practice settings subjects	Area of services relevant to social workers	• Children and families • Health and mental health • Drugs and substance abuses • Disabilities • School • Elderly • Minority and marginalized community • Offending and criminal justice system
Practicum/Field instruction	Crucial and integral part of professional training in social work involving placement and supervision	• Minimum 2 placements with a total of 800–1000 hours on fieldwork practice • Minimum 1 hour per week of professional supervision

The Role of Social Work Educators in Advancing the Social Work Profession

As discussed earlier, the development of social work in Malaysia started with the establishment of the Department of Social Welfare in 1946, followed by the introduction of social work education in 1952 in Singapore. The Malaysian Association of Social Workers (MASW), the national social work professional body, was only formed in 1973 and registered in 1974, a year before the first social work education programme started at USM. P. C. Sushama, who retired as the Head of the Medical Social Work of the University Malaya Hospital, joined USM and became the first Malaysian social work educator at USM.

Over the years, MASW has been promoting and advocating for professional social work practice in the country despite its limited human and monetary resources. It is a member organisation of the International Federation of Social Workers (IFSW), Commonwealth Organisation for Social Work (COSW), Balai Ikhtisas Malaysia (BIM) (Malaysia Professional Centre), and the Malaysian Council of Social Welfare and Social Development (MAKPEM).

For almost 20 years after its inception, the MASW leadership has always been led by social workers from the DSWM until 1995 when Siti Hawa Ali from USM became the first social work educator being elected as the President for 1995–1997. It took another 12 years before another social work educator, Teoh Ai Hua, to be elected as President (2009–2017). Two other educators have since taken helm of the leadership of MASW, namely Ismail Baba (2017–2019) and Mohamad Suhaimi from UKM (2019–2021).

Social work educators from Malaysia are also active internationally. The social work educators of USM engaged with global social work through its association with IASSW and APASWE. Siti Hawa Ali was the first social work educator from Malaysia to serve as committee member of APASWE. This was followed by Zulkarnain Hatta, also from USM, who served as Honorary Secretary of APASWE, and eventually being the first Malaysian to be elected as President of APASWE in 2018. On the other hand, although UUM is member of APASWE, two of its social work educators are mainly active with the IFSW-Asia Pacific. Sharima Ruwaida Abbas serves in the Disaster Response Sub-Committee while Teoh Ai Hua serves as the Asia Pacific representative in the IFSW Ethics Commission and Nomination Committee. This networking enables social work community in Malaysia constantly keeping up to date with the latest social work education standards and development globally.

Despite the increase of tertiary social work education at the local universities, there was concern over the competency of social workers in the field due to the lack of qualified social work being employed in both the government and non-government sector (Baba, 1992, 2011; Lee, 2011). In responding to the need of competent workforce in social work, the DSWM has collaborated with USM in 1993 to initiate a diploma programme at its Training Institute of Welfare (ILK). The teaching staffs consisted of both social work lecturers like Angeline Cheah, Siti Hawa Ali, and Siti Norhayati from USM, and senior social welfare officers in the training division. Unfortunately, the diploma programme stopped a year after when the Public Service Department didn't agree to recognise it as qualification for promotion. Nevertheless, social work educators at USM were constantly engaged by the DSWM as to conduct social work training for social welfare officers at ILK in the 1990s until it ceased operation in early 2000 and replaced by the Institut Sosial Malaysia (ISM) in 2002.

Besides USM, UNIMAS has also taken the initiative to address the need of social work education for social workers by organising the 'Advancing Social Work Education Seminar' in 1998, followed by the 'Advancing Indigenous Social Work Seminar' in 2003. The 1998 Seminar raised the need for closer collaboration and coordination among social work educators from different universities and subsequently led to the idea of forming the NJCCSWE.

In 2004, MASW and the DSWM have embarked on a project to develop the national competency standards for social work practice with the assistance of an Australian social work consultant Dr. Pauline Meemeduma (Lee, 2011; Teoh, 2014). The draft national competency standards for social work practice were completed in 2005 and later included in the 9th Malaysia Plan in 2006. From 2006 to 2008, under the guidance of Pauline and the funding from DSWM, MASW conducted series of training on the Professional Accountable Practice (PAP) Model at ISM to social welfare officers, social welfare assistants as well as NGOs workers as an introductory practice framework of the competency standards. The late Angeline Cheah from USM was involved as one of the master trainers of the PAP Model.

In addition, Pauline also facilitated the NJCCSWE in 2006 in drafting the National Policy and Educational Standards for Social Work Education in Higher Learning Institutions of Malaysia. It was the first major project for the NJCCSWE since it was formed. Upon completion, the policy was presented to the Director General of Ministry of Higher Education in the same year and all social work programmes use it as the principle guide in planning their social work curriculum.

At the same time, after series of dialogue and discussion with various stakeholders, MASW realised that the key to advance the social work profession in the country is through a legislated regulatory system. Although social work has been recognised as a profession by being accepted as member of the Malaysia Professional Centre (BIM) since 1974, it is one of the few that yet to have its own legislation. In addition, as social work is a caring profession (Hugman, 1991) that operates in a non-profit setting, it is seen as philanthropic or charitable activities and does not have a strong market support. This can also be shown that all social work programmes are offered by the public universities but not by the private universities. As a result, social work is misperceived of low professional credential and image, and more critically, lacking control over education, employment, and professional development all these years.

Working closely with the DSWM, social work educators and other stakeholders including UNICEF Malaysia, a memorandum consisting six measures to enhance the social work profession which include establishing the National Social Work Competency Standards, enacting a Social Workers Bill, establishing a national social work regulatory body, recruitment of qualified social workers, standardisation of social work education and development of social work courses was submitted to the Cabinet through the Ministry of Women,

Family and Community Development. On 23 April 2010, the government approved the six measures (Proposed, 2010). Subsequently, a Technical Committee on Improving Social Work Professionalism in Malaysia chaired by the Director General of Social Welfare was set up to work on these measures. The social work educators were represented in the Technical Committee through Azlinda Azman (USM) and Ling How Kee (UNIMAS).

Social Work Education Challenges and Way Forward

The development of social work education in Malaysia as a whole appears to be slow, difficult, and complex as compare to the development of social work practice in Malaysia. Part of the problems stamped from the fact that the social work education was interrupted when the University of Malaya in Singapore had to discontinue taking Malaysians to study social work in 1975. The separation between Singapore and Malaysia had forced Malaysia to start its own professional training in social work and this has some impact on the development of social work in Malaysia.

Social work education in MalaysiaMalaysia, since its early development, was adapted from various international curricula. The theories, knowledge, and practices of the social work educators who had obtained their trainings— diplomas, degrees, Masters, and PhDs—from countries outside Malaysia (e.g. UK, United States, Australia) were brought back to Malaysia and had been adapted and modified to fit the local context. As pointed out by Midgley (1984), a 'discerning adaptation of foreign experience' had indeed happened within the social work education in Malaysia. In a sense, the knowledge gained from the West and United States was taken to 'meet the needs of this country [Malaya]' which indeed had supported what Robertson (1980) had voiced out. Thus, within the context of Malaysia, social work education was disseminated from the West and/or United States but with modification—to fit the local context of the country—a very much a multi-ethnic, multicultural, and multiracial country.

As a whole, social work as a profession is still having its own problems. As a profession, social work needs to build its own identity. The public still perceives social work as a voluntary work that does not require professional training. As a result, many claims that they are 'social workers' when the actual that fact they are merely volunteers.

Although social work education has managed to establish itself at the tertiary level, social work as a profession still faces a lot of challenges in the country (Baba, 2011). Accreditation of social work education is still an issue. For example, MASW and NJCCSWE have no jurisdiction to be an accrediting body on social work education. Fortunately, social work educators who are appointed by the Malaysia Qualifying Agency (MQA) to review new social work programmes can give their professional opinions on the proposed curriculum, thus there are still some measures to ensure standardisation and quality.

Moreover, MASW and NJCCSWE also have no control over the employment of qualified social workers in both the public and the non-government sector. Over the years, low numbers of qualified social workers being employed, and the recruitment of non-qualified social workers in the field has further weakened the image of the profession which already faces poor public understanding of its professional nature. The challenge for the profession is how to get social work graduates to be the first choice for employers when recruiting new staffs because many organisations do not use the term social worker in their organisational structure. For example, the term 'social development officer' is used by the Public Service Commission when advertising for the recruitment of social welfare officer. The medical social workers use 'medical social work officer' as their job title although their occupation in the public service refers as social development officer. Social work graduates who got recruited into the National Anti-Drug Agency (AADK) are called AADK Officers in both their occupation and job title. In the NGO sector, only a handful of organisations, like Women's Aids Organisation, Yayasan Chow Kit and OrphanCare use the term 'social worker' and specifically employ social work graduates for these positions.

In addition, due to the non-existence of legislation that regulates social work, many of these positions that fit and need the skills of social work are always opened to graduates from other disciplines. Consequently, many of the services provided by social welfare organisations only cater to the basic needs of the clients like monetary assistance and shelter, except for organisations and individuals who are willing to invest both money and time in training to equip their staffs with relevant skills to deal with complex issues like domestic violence, child abuses, mental illness, homelessness, learning disabilities, drug and substance abuses, and the combination of more than one problem.

With the employment of non-social work qualification workers, the social work programmes at the universities also faced problem when arranging social work students to do their practicum or field placement. As indicated in the guideline of NJCCSWE, the students are expected to be supervised by qualified social work supervisors at least 1 hour per week during placement. If the supervisors at the organisations themselves are not familiar with the theories, skills, and values of social work, they would not be able to provide adequate supervision and, as a result, the students would not be able to relate their academic learning with the actual practice on the ground effectively.

Thus far the standardisation of social work education at the bachelor level is more or less determined, with the exception of number of years of study and frequency of practicum. Some programmes are four years while the other are three years. Some programmes have up to three field placements or practicum while some only have one block placement. However, there are still much to be done to improve the quality and availability of social work education in Malaysia. First, the National Social Work Competency Standards must be understood by social work educators before they can be incorporated into the curriculum. The challenge for social work programmes is to produce social work graduates who not only excel academically but are also competent in practice when compare with non-social work graduates. This will eventually shift the benchmarking of social work education and training towards competency practice. In this regard, social work educators must take the leadership role in devising the evaluation mechanism of the competency standards that suits both the multicultural society of Malaysia as well as the universal values of social work. Full utilisation of the National Social Work Competency Standards by the profession is crucial as it demonstrates the value of professional education and training.

The second challenge is the availability and opportunity of social work education for existing workers without quitting their job. Thus far, all the social work degrees are offered on a full-time basis. Social work or social welfare equivalent education at non-graduate diploma level is non-existence. However, there are many experienced workers who may not have sufficient academic qualification or have no resources to do a full four-year time degree. Furthermore, there is also a large group of non-graduate social welfare assistants employed by DSWM that are looking for suitable social work education at diploma level. With regard to that, in 2013, DSWM and UUM started a cooperative programme named Executive Certificate in Social Work Practice (SPEC). The creation of SPEC was in line with the point memorandum of creating more social work training courses at the certificate and diploma level, as well as to cater for the shortage of social work training courses at ISM. Later in 2016, UKM and ISM came up with Postgraduate Diploma in Social Work where the courses are taught at ISM by social work educators from UKM. It was also during that period of time that the MASW and a few non-government welfare organisations started to work with one private college, Methodist College Kuala Lumpur (MCKL), in offering a Diploma in Social Work. This programme was designed for the workforce (working adults) in the NGO settings who may not be able to pursue a full-time social work degree at the public universities to gain recognition when the Social Work Profession Bill is implemented. The Diploma received its first batch of students in April 2017.

The third challenge will be Continuous Professional Education (CPE) for social workers. One of the requirements of social work regulatory system is that all registered social workers to attend recognised training courses or seminars annually to accumulate CPE points for renewal of practising certificate or licence. Although MASW conducts training workshops from time to time, it is unrealistic for it to run CPE courses all over the country. In this regard, all the social work programmes at the universities must be ready to offer CPE for working social workers. It will require close cooperation and coordination to ensure that all social workers can receive the calendar of training courses at the beginning of each year for their CPE purposes. It also requires a lot of resources to ensure all CPE courses will not pose heavy financial burden to all social workers.

CONCLUSION

Social work education in Malaysia has progressed slowly and steadily to established itself as a discipline at the universities. Nevertheless, it still has a long way to go as compared to other developed countries. Both generic and specialist programmes at the postgraduate level are still lacking. Employment of qualified social workers is still not definite in the social service, and social work has yet to establish itself as a career and fulfil its full potential as a profession. The professionalisation project currently in plan can provide the platform for social work educators to play a leading role in research, design and delivery of training courses, evaluation of competency standards, and strengthening the profession in years to come.

REFERENCES

ASEAN Social Work Consortium Kicks Off. (March 4, 2011). Retrieved from https://asean.org/asean-social-work-consortium-kicks-off/Jakarta.

Baba, I. (1992). An effort towards building a caring society. In K. S. Cho & M. S. Ismail (Eds.), *Caring society: Emerging issues and future directions*. ISIS: Kuala Lumpur.

Baba, I. (2011). Kerja sosial di Malaysia: perkembangan, halatuju dan cabaran [Social work in Malaysia: Development, and challenges]. In E. Suharto & A. Azman (Eds.), *Pendidikan dan praktik pekerjaan sosial di Indonesia dan Malaysia [Education and social work practice in Malaysia and Indonesia]* Yogyakarta: Samudra Biru.

Bodde, L., & Duke, J. (2009). Registration in New Zealand social work: The challenge of change. *International Social Work, 52*(6), 785–797.

Davis, A., Doling, J., & Zainal, K. (2000). Britain and Malaysia: The development of welfare policies. In J. Doling & R. Omar (Eds.), *Social welfare East and West: Britain and Malaysia*. Aldershot, UK: Ashgate.

Department of Social Welfare. (n.d.). *History of the department of social welfare Malaysia 50 Years 1946–1996*.

Doling, J., & Omar, R. (2000). *Social welfare east and west: Britain and Malaysia*. Aldershot, England: Ashgate.

Fuziah, S. (2006). *British colonial policy on social welfare in Malaya 1946–1957: Child welfare services* (PhD thesis). University of Warwick, Coventry, United Kingdom. Retrieved from http://go.warwick.ac.uk/wrap/4113.

Fuziah, S., & Baba, I. (2013). Internationalization of social work education in Malaysia. In *Internationalization of social work education in Asia*. Joint International Joint Research Project. Social Work Research Institute Asian Center for Welfare in Society (ACWeIS), Japan College of Social Work, and Asian and Pacific Association for Social Work Education (APASWE). Retrieved from http://id.nii.ac.jp/1137/00000206/.

Hardiman, M., & Midgley, J. (1982). *The social dimensions of development: Social policy and planning in the third world*. New York: Wiley.

Harper, T. N. (1991). *The colonial inheritance: State and society in Malaya, 1945–1957* (PhD thesis). University of Cambridge, UK.

Hodge, P. (1973). Social policy: An historical perspective as seen in colonial policy. *Journal of Oriental Studies, XI*(2), 207–219.

Hugman, R. (1991). *Power in caring profession*. London: Macmillan Education.

Lee, P. N. (2011). *Development of medical social work practice in Malaysia: A historical perspective* (Master thesis). Universiti Sains Malaysia, Pulau Pinang, Malaysia.

Ling, H. K. (2007). *Indigenising social work: Research and practice in Sarawak*. Petaling Jaya: Strategic Information and Research Development Centre.

MacPherson, S. (1982). *Social policy in the third world: The social dilemmas of underdevelopment*. Sussex: Wheatsheaf.

MacPherson, S., & Midgley, J. (1987). *Comparative social policy and the third world*. Sussex: Wheatsheaf.

Malaysia National Archives. (1946). Malayan Union Secretariat 2247/46 Labour and social policy.

Malaysia National Archives. (1950). Federal Secretariat 12857 Social welfare training school.

Malaysian Population. (2019). Retrieved from http://www.worldpopulationreview.com.

Midgley, J. (1981). *Professional imperialism: Social work in the third world*. London: Heinemann.

Midgley, J. (1984). Diffusion and the development of social policy: Evidence from the third world. *Journal of Social Policy, 13*(2), 167–184.

Midgley, J. (1990). International social work: Learning from the third world. *Social Work, 35*, 295–301.

Midgley, J. (1997). *Social welfare in global context*. Thousand Oaks: Sage.

Proposed social workers act gets the govt's nod. (2010, May 5). *The Star*, p. 6.

Robertson, J. M. (1980). Problems related to practical training in social work. In P. Hodge (Ed.), *Community problems and social work in South East Asia*. Hong Kong: Hong Kong University.

Rodney, W. (1972). *How Europe underdeveloped Africa*. Dar-es-Salaam: Tanzania.

Sinnasamy, M. (2006). *Human resource development on social work: A study of Malaysia* (Working paper series, WP-2006-01-E). Nihon Fukushi University. Retrieved from http://www.n-fukushi.ac.jp/gp/coe/report/pdf/wp-kuno.pdf.

Social work can't be for 'just anyone'. (2010, September 19). *New Straits Times*, pp. 32.

Sushama, P. C. (1992). The caring society: Institutional history and prospects. In K. S. Cho & M. S. Ismail (Eds.), *Caring society: Emerging issues and future directions*. ISIS: Kuala Lumpur.

Teoh, A. H. (2014). Social work education in Malaysia: The past, present and future. In L. Q. S. Hee, R. Balan, D. Edward Kissey, & J. S. E. Lee (Eds.), *A decade of achievement of voluntary welfare services in Sabah* (2005–2014) (pp. 3–11). Kota Kinabalu, Sabah: Sabah Council of Social Services.

The Straits Times, 22 September 2012, Singapore.

Yasas, F. M. (1974). A report to the government of Malaysia on the establishment of a professional course in social work and community development training at the bachelor's level at the Universiti Sains Malaysia, Pulau Pinang. In co-operation with United Nations Economic Commission for Asia and the Far East.

PART II

Advancement of Social Work Education in the West: Lessons Learnt

Introduction

This part of the book comprises eight chapters that describe, dissect, and critically examine the nature of social work education and its development in the West. The authors in this part provide thought-provoking analysis based on their empirical research and evidence-based understanding from various parts of the world. Since the introduction of social work education, it was believed to be the best, and rest of the world started following the curriculum, teaching-learning, pedagogy, research, and practice components used in the West. Thus, the social work across the world was largely influenced by the 'west', and soon, it became a 'western centric' profession. However, scholars from different countries started realizing the lack of efficacy of such borrowed models of social work education and practice in the wake of radically different local realities and social problems. Moving ahead many social work educators and international experts started creating the awareness regarding 'contextual social work' or 'indigenization' of social work at the local, national, and international levels.

Social work education in the twenty-first century had seen several path-breaking innovations in the West, whereas the East is still struggling to replace the Western models by locally developed knowledge base and practice wisdom. This part of the book tries to capture the debate on universal vs contextual social work. Evident to this, the chapters in this part highlight the challenges faced by social workers in the Western countries and thus help the readers to understand that the challenges are not new to the profession but the magnitude and the approach towards challenges are different given the different sociopolitical and economic conditions.

Despite its present status and advancement, social work across the globe had innumerable challenges in the initial development phase. Analysing the developmental path of social work education in any country helps us to understand the milestones achieved and difficulties faced during the development. *Luca Fazz* and Angela Rosignoli provide an in-depth analysis of such challenges faced by social work during its development in Italy. The advancement of social work education is also contributed by an interdisciplinary and interprofessional collaboration within the country, region, and beyond the borders. As argued by many researchers, the interdisciplinary collaboration across the globe resulted in the development of social work faculty and students learning opportunities. These collaborative initiatives have also resulted in the development of cross-cultural teaching, learning and research paradigms within international social work. Mike Arnold examines the relationship between management education and change management practice in social work institutions within the framework of three inseparably linked dimensions, namely: (1) change management as an object of social management research, (2) social management research as a resource for the justification of change strategies in social work organizations, and (3) professional competence as integral component of management education in social work degree programmes.

With the advancement of society, social problems effecting people also advanced. Social work as a human service profession then expected to equip its graduates with newly acquired skills in dealing with contently changing social order. As a result, institutions across the globe, especially in the West, developed innovative online teaching programmes in social work where learners engage in learning without attending regular lectures. Shareef Haider examined the challenges and possibilities of using practical tools and techniques in imparting social work skills to students through online teaching. Knowledge exchange and two-way learning in social work are possible through international collaborations and co-learning. This approach will allow the knowledge and resource flow from both West–East and facilitate the learning from each other's advancements, success, and failures. Despite advancement in international social work over last many decades, learning from East or developing economies has not been focused much by the practitioners, educators, and researchers in the West. More attention to the efforts made by the practitioners and researchers dealing with major challenges like poverty, discrimination, and inequalities will help in developing a more critical understanding of intervention strategies and their efficacy. This will also help in examining comparative advantages and strengths of different approaches followed in the West or east and learning from each other for better role performance. Social work programmes in many developing economies may have advanced thinking despite working with few resources, but working well with grass-roots communities, social development strategies, working more collectively with local communities than the social work programmes in many advanced countries. *Jonas Christensen* explores the internationalization of social work education in Sweden and documents the local and global challenges faced by the social work with special reference to Swedish context.

This chapter helps the reader to understand how the social work programmes in the West are internationalized and what challenges they face during the transition from local to the global and what the social work in the Global South can learn from this.

In spite of advanced welfare state, societies in the West continue to face innumerable social problems that hinder the human development. Social workers in many Western countries serve as welfare advocates and thus contribute to the transformation of people's lives. However, there are considerable differences in terms of social welfare and social policy, social work delivery, and the population that are served by the social workers in the West and in the East. Understanding these differences needs the comparative analysis, and *Hallen Ingrid Strauss* documents the differences between social work in a Danish context compared with social work in other parts of the world. This comparison helps in understanding the challenges for social work programme delivery and future opportunities for social work in Denmark. Further, globalization, liberalization, and privatization of means of production have led to a major shift in the welfare provisions in many developing countries. In many developed countries, the state is escaping from its welfare responsibilities, and as a result, many welfare provisions are outsourced to the private companies. Health, education, housing, and social security in many countries are not ensured by the state rather outsourced to the private agencies. This shift in welfare has resulted in changing social welfare and social work education in many countries in the world. *Anne Margrethe* explores how recent changes in the welfare state matter for social work in Norway and tries in understanding that how changes in ideology and values, apparent in the 'work line' in social policies, have led to a partial shift in responsibility for welfare from the state to the individual.

While most of the chapters in each part of this handbook examine the challenges faced by social work education at some point of discussion, the focus of this part is to examine the development of social work in Western countries with an intention to learn from both the advancement and challenges in delivering social work programmes. These learnings are intended to develop an understanding of the issues faced and interventions developed and to make a wise decision while replicating the West. The basic understanding is that both developing and developed countries can learn from each other as well as the learnings for developing and less developed countries include learning from the failures in the West and not replicating them in the conception, designing, and delivery of social work interventions.

CHAPTER 7

Change Management Education in Social Work Degree Programmes in Germany: Bridging the Gap Between Management Science and Professional Practice

Maik Arnold

Since the 1990s, change management has received considerable attention as the new paradigm for the management of organisational transformations as well as behavioural and motivational changes within both for-profit and non-profit organisations. As a result, change management has been included in most bachelor's and master's degree programmes in social work and pedagogics in Germany, either as additional courses or as an area of specialisation. However, its interdisciplinary and intersectional nature has, so far, not been thoroughly considered in the development of managerial and social competences. In particular, the relationship between management science and professional practice was not given much attention, even though the development of change strategies in Human Service Organisations (HSO) must be based on research findings from both social sciences and management studies. In addition, management research and education need to draw conclusions from experiences gained in professional practice (e.g. Raelin, 1997).

Research on the theory of transfer in the field of change management has not kept pace with the practice of leading change. So far, existing research has failed to develop a satisfactory concept of theory-practice transfer and ignored the relationship of the justification and development of change strategies as part of the management of social organisations. A number of important questions for researchers, educators, practitioners, consultants, etc. are

M. Arnold (✉)
University of Applied Science, Dresden, Germany

S. S. M. et al. (eds.), *The Palgrave Handbook of Global Social Work Education*, https://doi.org/10.1007/978-3-030-39966-5_7

left unanswered, such as: How do we theorise from practice and how can practitioner's experiences induce new fruitful theoretical insights into the change management of HSO? More generally, we could also ask: How can we best understand the theorising of the complex practice in leading change? What kind of framework do we need to understand theory, practice, and education that supports developing best practices? How do we best approach the theory-practice transfer that enables practitioners and researchers to see their tasks steadily from different perspectives? How can research findings have an impact on the practice and policy in the change environment?

The relationship between theory and practice in social management has, for a long time, been made the object of a vast and multifaceted reflection that has characterised social work from its initial steps as a professional practice (Schön, 2017). Functioning on the fundamentals of an independent, obscure, and theoretic corpus of knowledge has often been accepted as one of the initial important features of a practice to be defined as a profession. Getting guidance from theory has strongly been linked with the effectiveness of practice. Correctly or wrongly, the evaluation of the significant impact of the profession—on the problems dealt with—has been associated with the use of theory in practice (Vanderlinde & Braak, 2010). In social management, it is impossible to isolate hypothesis from research. Practice encompasses the course of utilising theory and understanding to impact precise forms of alteration. A practice not informed by hypothesis appears to be sterile and recurring, while theory not informed by both actualities of research and practice appears to be only exciting and often extraneous (Danielson, 2011).

A variety of models, theories, and perspectives influence social workers' practice in social management. The theories of social work evaluate the occupation and describe its objective, realm, and nature in the world (Moon, 2013). They give a description of what the profession entails, how it impacts, and why it operates like it does. In comparison, those theories meant for social changes concentrate on associates and assisting processes. They elucidate the behaviour of human beings, the social environment, the way transformation happens, and how social workers facilitate it, so it can be helpful to the clients (Manners, 2017).

In social management, practice frameworks and orienting theories are employed by the social workers. The orienting theories give a description and an explanation of the behaviour and the way and why given problems develop (Bolton, 2014). According to Pickering (2010), these frameworks and theories give significant background comprehension and are normally obtained from other fields, like sociology, psychology, biology, economics, and cultural anthropology, among others. Examples comprise of the different theories associated with human development, socialisation, personality, organisational functioning, family systems, and political power, as well as the theories linked to certain forms of plights, like shortage, crime, domestic violence, psychological issues, teenage pregnancy, and ethnic inequity (Deutsch, Coleman, &

Marcus, 2014). Orienting theories give minimal guidance on how to stimulate change. Guidance is obtained from research and practice perspectives.

The practice perspectives are explained as conceptual lens that are applied in social management to view behaviours of human beings and social structure and, concurrently, steer the assortment of intercession methods (Van Manen, 2016). A practice viewpoint acts to assess or amplify specific characteristics while putting other characteristics in the setting. Research is applied in social management to assist in evaluating the connections between people and their environment. They assist in the evaluation of values and the procedures to be adopted in the working towards change. Research frameworks provide descriptions of specific behaviours or environments and extensive instructions regarding how those circumstances or behaviours may be transformed (Dalkir, 2013). Theories of social management, formulated through research, serve as a guidance framework for an intercession that brings about a specific form of transformation. In social management, a majority of the practice theories are incorporated in one or several theories for orientation. Examples include the psychosocial technique that is founded majorly on psychodynamic presumption, personality psychology, and the behavioural psychotherapy that is founded on the learning theories (Danielson, 2011).

In filling the gap between management science and professional practice, research helps in the formulation of practice models applied by social workers as sets of concepts and domains helpful in guiding specific interventions (Smith, 2015). In comparison with practice theory, the models are not incorporated to a specific justification of behaviour. For instance, an approach that is task-centred is perceived as a practice concept instead of a practice presumption since the action phases of the intercession are not incorporated to any single description of predicament situations. Similarly, the intervention crisis is described to be a theory instead of a practice. Research in sociology argues that model develops from a real experience or experimentation instead of evolving from a given theory or behaviour (Babbie, 2016).

It is rare to apply a sole-orienting hypothesis or a sole practice structure in practice or isolate them from the research practices upon where they are founded. Instead, a majority of the practitioners use a broad diversity of orienting theory and a set of well-matched and corresponding viewpoints, presumptions, and research findings in an integrative manner (Gay, 2010). This implies that, as a way of boosting efficiency, social workers apply a blend of science and art. It is identified that a practitioner brings specific aspects to the practice field that influence the procedure and result. Simultaneously, the social workers are needed to combine their artistic capabilities with the knowledge and scientific base of the profession. With no art, the knowledge base is of minimal significance (Wenger, 2011). However, with no knowledge, the art is of limited efficiency. Thus, merging art and science into a practice framework is important.

Against the background of the literature review, this paper explores the relationship between management sciences and professional practice of managing change in HSO within the framework of the following three inseparably linked dimensions: (1) change management as an *object* of social management research (e.g. Schmid, 2004), (2) social management research as a *resource* for the justification of change strategies in social work organisations, and (3) *professional competence* as integral component of management education in social work degree programmes. These three dimensions help to adequately explicate the relationship between science and practice. Eventually, it is demonstrated that *reflective, translational competence* acquired in management education in social work degree programmes will be effective, if only the individuals' capacity to act is both scientifically sound and saturated in professional practice experiences. This conceptual paper is largely based on findings drawn from experiences in the development of degree programmes in social work, pedagogics, and management at undergraduate and postgraduate levels in different German universities.

SCIENCE AND PRACTICE OF CHANGE MANAGEMENT IN HUMAN SERVICE ORGANISATIONS

What Is an Organisation?

The term 'organisation' is linked to three related terms: organisation, organisations (both meaning: entities, states, and conditions), and organising (such as an activity situated in time and place). As Howard E. Aldrich (1979) described in his book, *Organisations and Environments*, '[o]rganisations are goal-directed, boundary-maintaining, activity systems' (Aldrich, 1979, p. 4). In the course of history in organisational studies, this term has been used regularly in combination with a wide range of metaphors: we can talk about organisations as machines, organisms or living systems, cultures, psychic prisons, brains, complex systems, and instruments of domination (Morgan, 1997). In this paper, we will refer to organisations as complex social entities that entitle individuals to work on and achieve commonly shared goals. Organisations, in this regard, are often more effective than individuals' own activities. They are vital means to accomplish routinised or planned tasks. As specialised entities, they aim for serving clients' demands, especially in the human service sector. They not only safeguard the survival of individuals working in organisations but also provide opportunities and places for innovation.

Furthermore, we deal with the so-called HSO, whose 'business is addressed to human condition' (Austin, 2002, p. 2). They are created to provide social services in order to address the needs of individuals, groups, and social problems that aim for the prevention, improvement, or resolution of health, social, and environmental problems. Their services focus, in general,

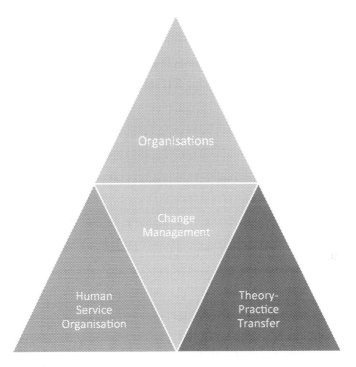

Fig. 7.1 Basis terminology (Author's own research)

on societal needs and concerns, defined either by law or the social welfare community at large, for example, mental health services, family services, psychosocial therapy, children with learning disabilities, homeless people, etc.

Since the 1990s, change management approaches received considerable attention as the new paradigm for the management of behavioural, motivational, and institutional changes in organisations. Human service organisations, as any other type of organisation, underlie permanent changes that need to be managed. In this context, 'Change Management' is regarded as a goal-oriented action that aims at the realisation of organisational changes, development, and transformation, for example, of strategies, processes, structures, organisational culture, and relations to externals. Its success will depend on behaviour and attitudes of personnel. In this view, change management is a way to target permanent changes; it is not temporary and not a single project. Figure 7.1 summarises the terminology used in this paper.

CHANGE MANAGEMENT IN HUMAN SERVICE ORGANISATIONS

Research has shown that organisational change has become a *normality* for all organisations in both for-profit and non-profit sectors (e.g. Mossholder, Settoon, Armenakis, & Harris, 2000). However, why do organisations need to change? Changes do happen because of several factors and causes (e.g. Beck & Schwarz, 2011), such as: (1) shifts in the external environment and of internal factors, for example, financial crisis, changes in social welfare laws, introduction of new members of board, merges, buy-outs, over-bureaucratisation, etc.; (2) the orientation of welfare service providers towards quality development, while the quality of services will depend on the needs of the clients, which are often hard to measure and difficult to standardise; (3) an introduction of strategic concepts, such as service-mindedness and customer relationship management; and (4) difficulties in the recruitment, motivation, and development of personnel.

With regard to the question of what aspects can be altered in the life of an organisation, we often observe changes in *work settings* (e.g. formal structures, procedures, communication rules, job descriptions, and office space) and *attitudes or behaviours of individuals* working in or for an organisation (e.g. improvement of required skills and competences, professionalisation, values, principles and vision of the organisation) (Porras & Silvers, 1991, p. 56).

Even if changes and transformations happen, however, there are limitations to the success and how organisations manage to deal with these changes: the average lifespan of an organisation has declined in the last two decades from 20 to 12.5 years (Have, Have, Huijsmans, & van der Eng, 2015). Organisations mainly disappear because of environmental changes to which they were not able to adapt. However, even if an organisation aims for an adaption, only about 30–50% of all changes will usually succeed (Have et al., 2015). The questions that can be raised are: Can a better scientific knowledge help to increase the percentage of successful organisational developments? Why do many organisations fail in the process of change and transformation? If we want to answer these questions, we need to investigate the relationship between science and professional practice.

Relationship Between Science and Practice: A Theory-Practice Transfer Model

As in other contexts, strategies for managing change in HSO have to be developed on the basis of research findings from both social sciences and management studies. Vice versa, research also needs to draw its conclusions from experiences gained in professional practice. In the following, we will focus primarily on this special relationship between science and professional practice and do not want to repeat social science and business studies literature on change management, often related to approaches, such as: lean management as a consequent value-chain orientation, business process re-engineering as optimisation of the four aspects cost quality service time, Kurt Lewin's three-phase model of organisational development (i.e. unfreezing, moving, and refreezing), or approaches that understand changes as organisational learning processes (Burnes, 2004).

From a theoretical perspective, science and practice can be understood as two domains that are linked to one another as partly related, permeable, mostly autonomous fields of actions that both strive for different logics of rationality (Bosch, Kraetsch, & Renn, 2001). *Science* is eased from the burden of an application of findings; it can be theoretical-oriented, conceptual, systematising, methodical-controlled, primarily descriptive of problems, driven by the fundamental decisions of 'true and false' (Bosch et al., 2001, p. 208) and connected to 'implicit knowledge and own implicit rules'; for example, in surveys we want to understand why and how organisations need to change (Bosch et al., 2001, p. 209). *Practice* is, per se, oriented towards efficiency and the fundamental differentiation of 'efficient and non-efficient'; it looks for practical applications, seeks for problem solutions, and is usually action-oriented. The two domains, science and practice, cannot be separated from each other, but they can be understood as 'moments of the action process' (Bosch et al., 2001, p. 206), while between both domains' various 'translations' (Bosch et al., 2001, p. 207) this process of translation requires a specific competence: actors from science and practice need to have knowledge, skills, and experiences to a greater extent not only of one's own but also of the other fields of action. Insights drawn within the different domains can be gained, for example, in higher education contexts, in internships during studies at university (i.e. students can gain work-related experiences in a protected setting and under practical guidance), work-life visits in HSO, and teaching research projects (i.e. students learn to use and apply research methodology to practical problems).

THREE DIMENSIONS OF THE RELATIONSHIP BETWEEN SCIENCE AND PROFESSIONAL PRACTICE[1]

It is assumed in this paper that strategies of change management in HSO cannot be justified and developed without back reference to research in social sciences and business studies; vice versa, research can also learn from experiences gained in professional practice. Therefore, the relationship between management research and professional change management will be explored within the framework of three inseparably linked dimensions: (1) change management, as an *object* of social management research; (2) management research, as a *resource* for the justification and development of change strategies and leading change in HSO; (3) professional competence, as a *component* for the development and implementation of change strategies in HSO. The next three subsections will focus on each one of these dimensions.

Change Management as an Object of Management Research

Research in organisational studies has shown that we can distinguish various *types of change processes* (Porras & Silvers, 1991). On the one hand, the term *organisational development* (OD) (synonymous to planned change of first order) can be characterised as follows: it aims for partially changing work conditions, often with references to scientific concepts, in order to provoke changes in behaviour and attitudes of the personnel. It can also be understood as a reaction to internal needs of developmental and environmental demands for adaptation due to changing market conditions. OD leads to a new developmental status quo of an organisation. On the other hand, *organisational transformation* (OT) (synonymous to change of second-order) is regarded as a paradigmatic change of the whole organisation, for example, its vision, structures, processes, and of work conditions with reference to scientific concepts. It aims at behavioural and attitudinal changes of the personnel in order to shape desired future relations to the organisational environment. As Porras and Silvers (1991) have pointed out, each type of change will depend on different variables on at least two levels that moderate the change process: the organisational level (e.g. corporate philosophy, work conditions, and leadership principles) or the individual level (e.g. personal development of required skills or the introduction of new quality standards).

According to Weick and Quinn (1999), we can also distinguish various *forms of intervention*. Firstly, episodic change is a punctual, less systematic change that happens if internal structures and demands from environment are disproportionate. Such organisational change can be characterised with, for example, Kurt Lewin's model of organisational development. Episodic changes address short-term adaptations. The change agent is responsible for the introduction of new issues, step by step. Critically speaking, episodic changes do not permit long-term developments because it assumes a stable environment and involves mostly normative approaches or assumes rational, linear, and not circular processes of change (Burnes, 2004). Secondly, 'continuous change' (Orlikowski, 1996) refers to permanent modifications on the level of organisational processes and structures (e.g. adjustments of the product line, according to the demand of market or welfare services). It is characterised by cyclical and long-term process orientation. The change agents need to be sense-makers and translators of change. Thirdly, planned change underlies the concept of 'think to act', and it assumes a stable context, while processes need to be clearly structured. Planned change is a popular concept in the field of change management. Fourthly, improvised change is closely related to the concept of 'act to think', where changes are anticipated: if a problem emerges, the change agent is responsible for the exploitation of opportunities for successful changes. Improvised changes happen in typical phases or sequences: anticipation of problems, emergence of problem, exploit opportunity, and so forth.

Change management is described by few authors as a 'generic task of controlling' (Schreyögg & Koch, 2014), which involves three types of change management concepts: (1) change through objectives, highlighting the formal level of an organisation; (2) behaviour-oriented changes in order to overcome resistance towards change, highlighting the informal level of an organisation; and (3) change through organisational learning, which highlights learning as attitude and perception.

Furthermore, research has shown that the success of organisational changes depends on various success factors that mediate the change process (Beck & Schwarz, 2011). First of all, the staff is the primary success factor and less often the factual level of new structures, processes, and strategies. If staff is in doubt, not convinced or if the expected changes and vision are not clearly communicated, it is very likely that organisational change activities are doomed to failure. Other factors identified as challenges in the process of leading change are insufficient monitoring and resistance of staff due to anxieties of losses. Hence, top management and change leaders should not only ensure the need of change, provide a plan, and organise internal support for change in order to overcome resistances, but they should also gain support from top management, build external support capacities (e.g. consultancy, political and financial stakeholder), provide resources, safeguard the implementation of changes, pursue comprehensive, and integrate change on all levels of the organisation (Fernandez & Rainey, 2006, pp. 169–173). Besides the various studies on the success factors of organisational change, experts in the field of OD often refer to transparency of objectives, participation of staff at all levels and stages of the process and the provision of spaces of innovation as success factors.

In HSO, the change management need to be equipped by different factors that support the initiation of a change process. Especially, Wilfried Krüger's (2009) '3W-Model' includes the following components: a demand for change ('Wandlungsbedarf', for example, in the form of an internal or external situational analysis), a willingness to change ('Wandlungsbereitschaft', based on values like participation and commitment), and the ability to change ('Wandlungsfähigkeit', based on values like flexibility and adaptation). These three intermediating factors of the change process are embedded in a process model consisting of five interrelated phases (Krüger, 2009): (1) initiation (i.e. a demand for change), (2) conceptualisation (i.e. setting objectives), (3) mobilisation (i.e. communication and a willingness to change), (4) realisation (e.g. project management, quality management, and personnel development), and (5) implementation (i.e. the safeguarding of institutionalising results and planned changes).

The organisational change activities are not only an object of management research, but also research can be regarded as a resource for the development of change strategies in HSO.

Management Research as a Resource for the Justification and Development of Change Management Strategies in HSO

In general, the management literature provides a large repertoire of models, concepts, and approaches to describe organisational change. If we make use of such research findings for the justification and development of change management strategies or for the optimisation of professional practice (social management) research can become a *resource*. Due to the limitation of this paper, we do not provide an overview on the different theories of organisational change and the various models developed in research and practice (see Hatch, 2011; Van de Ven & Poole, 2004), but we will focus hereafter only on the St. Gallen Management Model in its third edition (Rüegg-Stürm, 2003).[2] This model is somehow related to a systemic-constructivist perspective and is widely used as an orientation framework that enables change agents to reduce the complexity of an organisation and entangle its system environment. Additionally, the model also aids for the determination of specific challenges related to organisational change processes.

As all such models, also the St. Gallen Management Model, cannot be claimed as a true or false representation of reality, but it can be claimed—more or less—as an appropriate and inappropriate extract from the complex nature of change processes. We refer to this model, therefore, because it supports the structuration of different levels of an organisation and provides us a ground for dialogue on the involved elements, parts, and individuals in the organisational transition process. According to this model, the author assumes that an organisation is a supra-individual, multifunctional, and purpose-oriented entity as well as a complex socio-technical system, in which all elements interact with each other and are inseparably linked within a dynamic web of meanings.

As shown in Fig. 7.2, the St. Gallen Management Model consists of six system elements or perspectives of an organisation: the external environment, stakeholder, themes of interaction, internal structures, processes, and two possible modes of organisational development. According to Rüegg-Stürm (2003), these elements can be understood as follows: (1) The *External Environment* is the organisational context in which all entrepreneurial activities are embedded. Often it is the systemic environment that initiates a demand of change. (2) *Stakeholders* comprise of the individuals, organised groups, and institutions that are affected by the organisations' activities in positive or negative ways. In Fig. 7.2, we can see, on the left, the suppliers including service provider (taker) and, on the right, the people and groups affected (giver). (3) The *Themes of Interaction*, which are the objects and content of exchange between actors inside and outside of the organisation that constitute the relationship and communication between stakeholder and the organisation (e.g. issues, themes of cooperation, interests, goods, norms, and values). (4) *Internal structures*, in which the centre of the model is the organisation at hand, characterised by its everyday activities. In line with the internal structure, *strategies* safeguard the short- and long-term success of an enterprise, for example, by the areas of expertise, fields of cooperation, core competences, range of services, and demands of the stakeholder. *Structure* refers to the structural and process organisation, including the allocation of responsibilities and resources. An organisational *culture* is responsible for

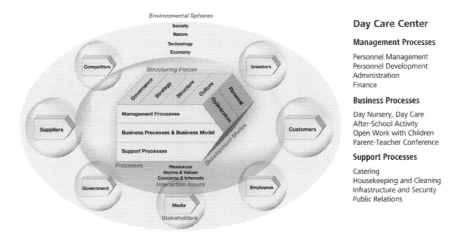

Day Care Center

Management Processes

Personnel Management
Personnel Development
Administration
Finance

Business Processes

Day Nursery, Day Care
After-School Activity
Open Work with Children
Parent-Teacher Conference

Support Processes

Catering
Housekeeping and Cleaning
Infrastructure and Security
Public Relations

Fig. 7.2 St. Gallen Management Model (Rüegg-Stürm, 2003) applied to Day Care Centre (Author's own research)

the creation of horizons of meaning (e.g. conjunctive experiences, implicit contacts of cooperation, values, attitudes, myths, rules of speech, and stories of success or failure). (5) *Processes*, which refers to the horizontal und customer-oriented processes of an organisation include: management processes, business operation processes (i.e. market-oriented core activities), and support processes.

(6) *Modes of development*, which distinguishes organisational changes into the alternating phases of *renewal* as meaning revolutionary, radical, and fundamental change in the patterns of thinking and action or guiding principles (transformations) and *optimisation* as meaning evolutionary and incremental changes of only parts and within an organisation in form of fine-tuning (development).

In Table 7.1, the St. Gallen Management Model (Rüegg-Stürm, 2003) has been applied to the situation and context of a specific HSO: a day care centre for children at preschool age. In order to successfully implement changes in HSO, a specific professional competence is required by not only the change agents but also by staff and all stakeholders involved in the process. Such a competence supports the development and implementation of change strategies.

Professional Competence as an Integral Component for the Development and Implementation of Social Work Degree Programmes in Germany

As the third dimension of the relationship between management sciences and professional practice, we investigate *professional competence* as an integral part of the education in social work degree programmes. Such a competence is

Table 7.1 St. Gallen Management Model (Rüegg-Stürm, 2003), as applied to Day Care Centre and After-School Activities

Element	Sub-criteria	Transfer to context of day care centre for children
External Environment	Society, politics, laws	Increasing need for day care, development of quality management, changes in social laws, and jurisdiction
Stakeholder	Supplier Affected people	Municipality or city, responsible body of child and youth care, youth welfare office, and child benefit agency Employees, management of day care institution, children, and parents council
Themes of Interaction	Resources Norms and values Concern and interests	Pedagogical material, education, and professional *self-perception* Child-oriented development and educational plan child care ratio and implementation of quality management system
Internal Structures	Strategies Structure Culture	Institutions' mission, e.g. fundamentals of cooperation with parents, welfare office, therapist, and municipal institutions Structural organisation, responsibilities, group size, and use of quality manuals Child-orientation, processes of organisational learning, social inclusion, individual development, satisfaction of parents and employees, and case conferences
Processes	Management process Business operation process Support processes	Personnel management, administration, controlling, and finances Care process such as nursery, child day care, open day care, and parents' evening Catering, equipment, cleaning, housekeeping, public relations, and security, infrastructure
Modes of Development	Renewal optimisation	New conception, change of responsible body, and generational change/recruitment Quality management circles, project days, international contacts, qualification and development of personnel, and team training to sensitise for changes

required because, frequently, scientific findings cannot simply be applied to concrete practical contexts. Moreover, a competence to translate from one domain of action to the other is needed in order to adjust, integrate, and transfer the scientific knowledge into practice and to provide a ground for decision-making processes. Research can only provide suggestions and models for orientation, such as the St. Gallen Management Model, but translations have to be made in order to apply such models in professional practice. Bosch et al. (2001, p. 209) made clear that professional competence is substantiated 'in the capacity of practically engaged people who speak two kinds of languages and "translate" explicitly prepared elements of knowledge *in actu*, meaning sensible to the situation'. As mentioned earlier, it is necessary to connect one domain of action to the other. Due to the limitations of this paper, we will refer hereafter to two exemplary relationships between professional practice and education as well as to the few principles for organisational change from a leadership perspective. In order to support the development and acquisition of professional competence in management sciences and practice, the following aspects need to be considered for the development and implementation of social work degree programmes: (1) integration of management education in study regulations of degree programmes for social workers, social pedagogics, and early childhood education; (2) incorporating experiential learning objectives into the curriculum; (3) promoting cooperation between universities, non-university research, and further training institutions; and (4) change management education in social work degree programmes should take seriously the principles of change leadership.

Firstly, in the field of HSO, the quality of change management will largely depend on the professional and managerial skills and qualifications of social workers, pedagogues, nurses, and managers, etc. In this regard, in many study regulations of bachelor's and master's degree programs in the field of social work, early childhood education, and nursing in Universities of Applied Sciences, 'professional competence' is often referred to as the core objective. Its curricula should also adopt topics, such as introduction to management in the social economy, stakeholder management, accounting, marketing, organisational management, personnel development, and personnel recruitment. Students need to be made familiar with methods like organisational analysis, appraisal interviews, survey techniques, and action research. The development of skills and competences should support the acquisition of analytical, empirical-methodical, reflective, and translational competencies.

Secondly, one effective way to acquire professional competences is to integrate experiential learning objectives into the curriculum, so that students are actively involved in processing and transferring knowledge and skills between theory and practice, while being intensely involved in the learning situation. Unlike lectures and traditional case studies, simulations and games are, for example, powerful teaching methods to help students to learn about managing organisations as well as to understand the complexity, ambiguity, and interpersonal relations in real-life contexts. In addition to instructive, situational, and constructivist perspectives, experiential learning promotes the acquisition of knowledge as a process of learning through experience and the reflexion on doing things. The experiential learning cycle is best described by David Kolb (1984): A learner acquires knowledge not by heart, lecture, or audition alone, but by experiencing a learning object. After (i) a concrete new experience is encountered (e.g. by doing or having experiences or by reinterpretation of existing experiences), a learner (ii) reflects on its observations of this new experience (e.g. by reviewing; of importance, here, are possible inconsistencies between experiences and its understanding, (iii) draws an abstract conceptualisation (e.g. concluding, its lessons learnt from experience; this may lead to new ideas or help to refine or modify existing abstract concepts), and (iv) will try later in active experimentation (e.g. planning or trying out what he has learnt in the real world and see what will be the result of it, in order to make new experiences, etc.). In higher education, experiential learning can be triggered by discussing case studies, reflecting on group work in the course, or by reflecting on professional experiences. The latter reflections on past professional experiences are possible, especially in courses of further education and professional degree programmes. If learning in such courses is guided by experiential learning, a knowledge transfer between theory and practice and back is possible. Beside others, management teaching should include blended learning concepts, such as flipped classrooms (Großkurth & Handke, 2014) that are often more effective than traditional classrooms (Bergfjord & Heggernes, 2016; Mason, Shuman, & Cook, 2013), simulations (Rollag & Parise, 2015), war games, case studies, learning labs, and excursions.

Thirdly, not only today but also in the future, cooperation between universities, applied research, and further training institutions is vital. Research and training projects should be oriented towards the demands of professional practitioners, such as the development of part-time, extra-occupational, and in-service study programmes, provision of continuing education, practice development within research projects. In all these kind of projects, components of practicable change models can be developed, tested, and revised. This can include different outreach activities, such as practitioner's lectures, cooperation with schools, projects of service learning, and certified further education. Additionally, practitioner research should be part of the management education, such as teaching or research projects, student research in practical-oriented theses, and projects with third-party funding.

Finally, change management education in social work, social pedagogics, and early childhood education degree programmes should seriously consider the principles of organisations' change leadership, highlighted in the works of John Kotter (1995). He described eight principles that also refer to the various competences that change agents must have to communicate and implement changes in organisations. According to Kotter (1995, p. 61), leaders need to: (1) *establish a sense of urgency* (i.e. a potential crisis caused by challenges for the organisations' environment, and the artificial preservation of the status quo is often dangerous); (2) *form powerful coalitions within and outside the organisation* (i.e. it is vital for the change process to have a heterogeneous group of people including staff as well as HRM and QM management); (3) *create a shared vision* that is powerful enough to survive a long period of time and helps to combine analytical thinking and dreaming; (4) *communicate the vision clearly and creditably*, using all communication channels, words, and deeds available; (5) *empower staff and stakeholder to act on the vision* (i.e. it needs to be acknowledged that we cannot be freed completely from all resistances; therefore, all people in the process need to be treated fairly, regardless of who resist changes); (6) *plan for and create short-term wins* (i.e. hoping for changes is not sufficient; instead, visions can be revised, adjusted, refined, and elaborated; (7) *consolidate improvements and produce more changes* (i.e. success can also be a danger to changes; therefore, a good plan for change includes small and large milestones); (8) *institutionalise new approaches* (i.e. leaders should show employees how change will happen and how the quality of organisations' results can be increased; therefore, leaders must have clear objectives). As can be seen, professional competence occupies a central role as a component for the development and implementation of change strategies in HSO.

CONCLUSION

The conditions and speed of change will depend on the time frame, budget, knowledge, qualifications, willingness to change, urgency of change, and translational competences. As has been shown, the justifications and implementation of change strategies in HSO are largely determined by the relationship between science and practice. In this paper, the hypothesis was developed that the science-practice relationship can be defined within three dimensions: (1) change management as an *object* of research, (2) research as a *resource* for the justification and development of change strategies, and (3) professional competence as an integral *component* of the development of leading change. This threefold relationship and its relevance for social management research seem to be the key to success, especially with regard to the development of science and practice. Such science-practice transfer can be promoted best by a research-oriented as well as practical-oriented training of students in the field of personnel and organisational development.

NOTES

1. This three-dimensional approach has been described earlier as 'purpose-guided research' (Kölbl, 2007).
2. Although a fourth edition of the St. Gallen Management Model has been published quite recently (see Rüegg-Stürm & Grand, 2015), we refer to the third edition of the model, because it can be better applied to change management.

References

Aldrich, H. E. (1979). *Organizations and environments*. Englewood Cliffs, NJ: Prentice Hall.

Austin, D. M. (2002). Getting to know the human service organization. In D. M. Austin (Ed.), *Human services management: Organizational leadership in social work practice* (pp. 1–21). New York, Chichester et al.: Columbia University Press.

Babbie, E. (2016). *The practice of social research*. Bosten, MA: Cengage Learning.

Beck, R., & Schwarz, G. (2011). *Organisationswandel und Change Management* (3rd ed.). Brandenburg: Service-Agentur des Hochschulverbundes Distance Learning.

Bergfjord, O. J., & Heggernes, T. (2016). Evaluation of a 'flipped classroom'. Approach in management education. *Journal of University Teaching & Learning Practice, 13*(5). http://ro.uow.edu.au/jutlp/vol13/iss5/17. February 6, 2020.

Bolton, G. (2014). *Reflective practice: Writing and professional development*. Thousand Oaks, CA: Sage.

Bosch, A., Kraetsch, C., & Renn, J. (2001). Paradoxien Des Wissenstransfers. Die 'Neue Liaison' Zwischen Sozialwissenschaftlichem Wissen und sozialer Praxis durch pragmatische Öffnung und Grenzerhaltung. *Soziale Welt 52*(2), 199–218.

Burnes, B. (2004). Kurt Lewin and the planned approach to change: A re-appraisal. *Journal of Management Studies, 41*(6), 977–1002. https://doi.org/10.1111/j.1467-6486.2004.00463.x.

Dalkir, K. (2013). *Knowledge management in theory and practice*. Amsterdam et al.: Elsevier.

Danielson, C. (2011). *Enhancing professional practice: A framework for teaching*. Alexandria, VA: ASCD.

Deutsch, M., Coleman, P. T., & Marcus, E. C. (Eds.). (2014). *The handbook of conflict resolution: Theory and practice* (3rd ed.). San Francisco, CA: Wiley.

Fernandez, S., & Rainey, H. G. (2006). Managing successful organizational change in the public sector. *Public Administration Review, 66*(2), 168–176. https://doi.org/10.1111/j.1540-6210.2006.00570.x.

Gay, G. (2010). *Culturally responsive teaching: Theory, research, and practice*. New York and London: Teachers College Press.

Großkurth, E., & Handke, J. (2014). *The inverted classroom model: The 3rd German ICM-conference—proceedings*. Berlin: Walter de Gruyter Verlag.

Hatch, M. J. (2011). *Organizations: A very short introduction*. Oxford and New York: Oxford University Press.

Have, S. T., Have, W. T., Huijsmans, A.-B., & van der Eng, N. (2015). *Change competency: Implementing effective change*. New York, NY and Abingdon, Oxon: Routledge.

Kolb, D. A. (1984). *Experiential learning: Experience as the source of learning and development* (Vol. 1). Englewood Cliffs, NJ: Prentice-Hall.

Kölbl, C. (2007). *Zur Professionalität Interkultureller Trainings*. Unpublished conference paper. Chemnitz: Chemnitz University of Technology.

Kotter, J. P. (1995). Leading change: Why transformation efforts fail. *Harvard Business Review, 73*(2), 59–67.

Krüger, W. (2009). *Excellence in change: Wege Zur Strategischen Erneuerung* (4th ed.). Wiesbaden: Gabler Verlag.

Manners, R. A. (2017). *Professional dominance: The social structure of medical care*. New York: Routledge.

Mason, G. S., Shuman, T. R., & Cook, K. E. (2013). Comparing the effectiveness of an inverted classroom to a traditional classroom in an upper-division engineering course. *IEEE Transactions on Education, 56,* 430–435.

Moon, J. A. (2013). *A handbook of reflective and experiential learning: Theory and practice.* London, New York: Routledge.

Morgan, G. (1997). *Images of organization.* Thousand Oaks, CA: Sage.

Mossholder, K. W., Settoon, R. P., Armenakis, A. A., & Harris, S. G. (2000). Emotion during organizational transformations: An interactive model of survivor reactions. *Group and Organization Management, 25*(3), 220–243. https://doi.org/10.1177/1059601100253002.

Orlikowski, W. J. (1996). Improvising organizational transformation over time: A situated change perspective. *Information Systems Research, 7*(1), 63–92. https://doi.org/10.1287/isre.7.1.63.

Pickering, A. (2010). *The mangle of practice: Time, agency, and science.* Chicago: University of Chicago Press.

Porras, J. I., & Silvers, R. C. (1991). Organization development and transformation. *Annual Review of Psychology, 42,* 51–78.

Raelin, J. A. (1997). A model of work-based learning. *Organization Science, 8,* 563–578.

Rollag, K., & Parise, S. (2005). The Bikestuff simulation: Experiencing the challenge of organizational change. *Journal of Management Education, 29*(5), 769–787.

Rüegg-Stürm, J. (2003). *Das Neue St. Galler management-modell* (2nd ed.). Bern: Haupt.

Rüegg-Stürm, J., & Grand, S. (2015). *Das St. Galler management-modell.* Berlin: Haupt.

Schmid, H. (2004). Organization-environment relationships: Theory for management practice in human service organizations. *Administration in Social Work, 28*(1), 97–113.

Schön, D. A. (2017). *The reflective practitioner: How professionals think in action.* London and New York: Routledge.

Schreyögg, G., & Koch, J. (2014). *Grundlagen Des Managements. Basiswissen Für Studium Und Beruf* (3rd ed.). Wiesbaden: Springer Fachmedien.

Smith, J. A. (Ed.). (2015). *Qualitative psychology: A practical guide to research methods.* Thousand Oaks, CA: Sage.

Van de Ven, A., & Poole, M. (2004). *Theories of organizational change and innovation processes. Handbook of organizational change and innovation.* Oxford and New York: Oxford University Press.

Vanderlinde, R., & Braak, J. (2010). The gap between educational research and practice: Views of teachers, school leaders, intermediaries, and researchers. *British Educational Research Journal, 36*(2), 299–316.

Van Manen, M. (2016). *Researching lived experience: Human science for an action sensitive pedagogy.* London and New York: Routledge.

Weick, K. E., & Quinn, R. E. (1999). Organizational change and development. *Annual Review of Psychology, 50,* 361–386. https://doi.org/10.1146/annurev.psych.50.1.361.

Wenger, E. (2011). *Communities of practice: A brief introduction.* STEP Leadership Workshop, University of Oregon. http://hdl.handle.net/1794/11736. February 6, 2020.

CHAPTER 8

Social Work Education in Italy: Problems and Perspectives

Luca Fazzi and Angela Rosignoli

INTRODUCTION

Social work education in Italy is strongly influenced by the history of the profession and by the characteristics and evolution of the national welfare system. Unlike other Western countries, until the 1990s the education of social workers in Italy took place within a system of institutions parallel with those of universities and the discipline was considered to be a practical rather than an academic subject. The process of academisation, which became necessary as a result of university reforms, has consequently been difficult and guided by interests largely unrelated to those of the profession.

Analysis of the Italian case highlights that without a solid welfare system and institutional legitimisation of the profession it is very difficult to make the educational system coherent with the needs and expectations that concern the professional development of social work. The first part of the chapter describes the history and characteristics of social work in Italy. The second part analyses the process of building the educational system for social workers from its birth to its integration within universities. Finally, the dynamics that have led to the current crisis of educational pathways and the main challenges to be faced in constructing a new model of social work education in Italy are described and discussed.

L. Fazzi (✉) · A. Rosignoli
Department of Sociology and Social Research,
University of Trento, Trento, Italy
e-mail: luca.fazzi@unitn.it

© The Author(s) 2021   119
S. S. M. et al. (eds.), *The Palgrave Handbook of Global Social Work Education*, https://doi.org/10.1007/978-3-030-39966-5_8

SOCIAL WORK IN ITALY:
EVOLUTION AND CHARACTERISTICS

Social work in Italy is performed by a specific professional known as a social worker (Campanini, 2007). The figure of the social worker was first created at the end of World War II. At that time the need to address the economic and social consequences of the war was strongly felt and social work was developed in the form of pioneering community work undertaken by a limited number of people. The policies of post-war reconstruction and international aid provided the funding to launch the first educational paths of social work, while awareness of the need to introduce social welfare programmes to help the weakest social groups slowly emerged. Until the beginning of the 1970s the Italian welfare model was characterised by a marked familism and low coverage of services (Naldini, 2003). The development of social work coincided largely with the spread of social services at the regional level that began with the launch of the administrative decentralisation process following the institution of regional authorities in Italy. In 1977 local administrations were granted direct authority in the area of welfare. Thus, staff dedicated to management of the new responsibilities had to be established quickly. The figure of the social worker was the only one that seemed sufficiently formalised to allow access to the role of public official and this created the conditions for the rapid rise of the profession.

The first generations of social workers who entered public administrations between the end of the 1970s and the 1980s were largely composed of figures driven by strong political and social motivations typical of the culture that existed at the time. That period is also remembered as a time when rights were reformed. Between 1975 and 1978 the Italian parliament approved fundamental laws that pursued for the first time a universal logic of the creation of a national system of social protection in such an explicit way. Therefore, employment in the public sector within this political and cultural framework was for many social workers the professional fulfilment of a project guided by values such as inclusion and social justice embodied symbolically in the rising social status. The public nature of social work helped to reinforce the conviction that the "natural" position of the profession was within the public sector and that the sense of professional identity was to be sought within the boundaries of the state. Employment in other areas such as the third sector (i.e., voluntary sector) were seen instead progressively as fallback positions chosen by a very small number of social workers.

The 1990s in Italy involved considerable reformism within the scope of social policies that culminated in 2000 with the approval of the first national framework legislation on welfare (L. 328/00). The role of social work was recognized as central to implementation of the new legislation and public administrations were driven to reinforce their staff bodies further by recruiting new personnel. Around the start of the new millennium investment in social services seemed to open up new perspectives for the profession. At the local level there was the development of social programmes, while national funding schemes in areas such as the protection of children and families allowed many social workers to experiment with planning at this level.

With the progressive development of social policies public professional social work became an increasingly broad employment opportunity and a professional profile of interest among many young people. In 2001 the *First Report on Social Services* recorded 27,174 professional social workers showing a growth rate of 600% compared with the 1970s (Sgroi, 2001).

Public social policies continued to develop, though at a progressively slower pace, up to the end of the first decade of the new millennium. A new national survey in 2009 revealed the existence of 35,000 social workers representing a further increase on the previous decade (Facchini, 2010).

Local authorities were still the main source of employment for the profession. Most social workers were employed in frontline positions with fewer than 10% in positions of service management or coordination. Unlike early stages in the development of the profession, the tasks of community building and advocacy are not very widespread, while social planning also involves a smaller number of professionals because of the first local authority expenditure cuts. Bureaucratisation has a widespread influence on professional practice. Responsibility for the assessment of social needs remains in the hands of social workers, but it is often undertaken within agencies that operate with targets, procedures, and resources that have a considerable effect on the discretionary powers of operators.

As a final point, social work is a profession with a pronounced gender connotation. Almost 90% of social workers are women.

SOCIAL WORK EDUCATION IN ITALY: ORIGINS AND EARLY DEVELOPMENTS

Unlike other Western countries, social work education is a relatively recent tradition in Italy (Campanini, 2015). The first schools of social work were founded in the post–World War II period on the initiative of secular and religious associations involved in post-war economic and social reconstruction. From the outset the schools sought, though not without difficulty, to build an extensive network of contacts to develop a common educational programme. While secular and religious schools maintained different cultural orientations, the cultural exchanges gave rise to the formation of a progressive shared awareness of the importance of vocational training for social work.

The teaching programmes of social work schools were originally markedly multidisciplinary. Alongside social work subjects students were taught statistics, demography, accident prevention, law, and economics. This approach was the result of the way in which the primary founders were trained. Unlike other countries, social work education in Italy was not launched by specialists on the subject, but mainly by figures involved in the democratic and civil reconstruction of the nation after the war. It took involvement in the international debate for new theories on social work to be introduced to the curriculum and classroom learning to be combined with work placements. In this way programmes progressively developed a clear professional profile.

The lack of tradition of social work studies and practices meant that the introduction of educational programmes was influenced above all by schools in English-speaking countries. The first students of social work were promoters of schools that were able to benefit from scholarships from international bodies committed to funding reconstruction of the country. Such students spent lengthy periods studying in the United States. These international experiences proved decisive in shaping the early stages of the development of social work education.

Despite intellectual fervour and the attempt to define educational paths the number of students enrolled at schools of social work remained relatively low until the mid-1970s. Since that time the management bodies of social work were transformed into *scuole dirette a fini speciali* (special purpose schools). This was the time when Italy witnessed the start of the process of decentralisation of welfare responsibilities to local authorities with an increase in demand for specialists in the public social sector. Social workers are the only figures who can boast a structured educational pathway and are thus identified as most capable of meeting requirements in the newly developing system of local public services.

Institutionalisation of the figure of social worker increased pressure for formal recognition of an academic qualification. Thus, at the beginning of the 1990s a university diploma of social work was established contributing significantly to the legitimacy and visibility of the educational pathway and becoming the prerequisite for taking part in public sector employment competitions. In 1993 social work acquired the official status of profession and a professional register was legally established where social workers had to register to practise the profession. In 1999 Decree No. 509 of the Ministry of Universities further consolidated recognition of academic qualifications by instituting a 3-year degree course in social work and a specialist degree course in planning and management of policies and social services.

The title "social worker" thus acquired full formal recognition and its value in the labour market increased considerably. In just a few years the number of 3-year and specialist degree courses increased massively and Italy experienced what Tynjälä, Välimaa, and Sarja (2003, p. 147) described as "massification" in higher education systems. Thousands of students enrolled on social work courses increasing the pressure to launch new programmes even in more peripheral universities.

The Path of Academisation

Academisation resulted in the structure of educational programmes undergoing profound changes. Study plans in special purpose schools required mandatory inclusion of specific professional disciplines of social work. This gave considerable weight to specialist subjects in the professional development of social workers in terms of the educational curriculum of students. The new academic rules gave broad discretionary powers to individual universities to define the curriculum and incorporate professional social work subjects within the field of sociological studies. Programmes that first focussed mainly on professional subjects were consequently often redesigned according to the expertise of the teaching body associated with the main disciplines of individual departments. The result was that of the 36 Bachelor degree courses and 35 Master's degree courses active in the academic year 2017 there were on average only four basic courses in social work (principles and foundations of social services, social service methods and techniques, organisation of social services, and social policy). Although a few universities offer five courses, only two universities offer multiple basic courses. When it comes to Master's degree courses professional courses in social work are even more fragmented.

As far as teachers are concerned, social worker course leaders from old special purpose schools have largely been excluded from university recruitment. They have been replaced by teachers qualified in other disciplines or continue to teach as lecturers alternating teaching with practising their profession within social services.

The result is establishment of a dual level of teaching. The first level (higher in number and permanently based in faculties and departments) is made up mainly of teachers of so-called social work–related subjects (sociology, psychology, management, law, etc.). The second level is made up of guest lecturers who teach social work. Working in social services means many guest lecturers are tasked with pursuing studies and research and developing curricula appropriate to the role of formally qualified teacher.

In Bachelor and Master's degree courses professional social work subjects are currently taught by around 120 teachers 75% of whom are teachers qualified in social work and 33% in other disciplines. However, permanent teachers qualified as social workers number just 16 including 1 full professor, 4 associate professors, and 11 associate researchers. All the others are professionals employed in social services who lecture on temporary contracts and who are paid little to lecture.

Teachers who undertake full-time studies and research in universities are consequently very few. The low number of social workers in permanent teaching positions in universities greatly reduces the academic power of the scientific community. The governing bodies of the departments of many universities include only teachers on annual contracts who have no decision-making power. This situation of disablement has contributed to creating a lack of trust between teachers qualified as social workers and teachers and researchers associated with other scientific disciplines and to undermining the foundations of mutual collaboration.

The small number of social workers who belong to the scientific community is also a primary cause of the difficulty in increasing the production of empirical research and expanding social work research in new areas. Although the number of articles in prestigious international journals has increased in the last 5 years, the total number of publications is still extremely low in relation to that of the scientific communities of other countries. This trend contrasts sharply with what is seen at the international level where over the past 20 years there has been a strong increase in scientific production in the field of social work (Howard & Garland, 2015). The weakness of the scientific community also slows the construction of a scientific discipline open to collaboration with other disciplines. In countries where the tradition of research on social work is better established there is an attempt to define the profession in a more open manner (Brekke, 2014), whereas in Italy the debate is still highly focussed on identifying specific features of research on social work.

The still fragile role of scientific research is clearly visible in the study plans of social work courses. Subjects that in other countries are widely taught as part of university social work curricula such as service user perspective, evidence-based social work, methodology of research in social work, and contemporary social work practice are either absent or are covered only superficially within 3-year and Master's degree courses.

One of the consequences of the increasing weakness of teaching programmes is the widespread accusation by the professional community of the inadequacy of theoretical education in providing new professionals with the skills needed to cope with changes in problems at work.

Practice Education

In addition to classroom education social work students must spend a minimum number of hours of work placement within the social services under the supervision of an experienced professional.

Work placement allows students to link theory to practice through the creation of what Bogo and Vayda (1998) defined a virtuous "loop" of thinking, feeling, and doing. For Wilson and Campbell (2013) the space between the classroom and practice education is the most challenging experience of the entire educational process of social work students. As a result of the reduced presence of social work subjects in the classroom work placement in Italy is particularly important in students' educational process.

Although the number of credit hours needed for Bachelor and Master's degree courses varies, the hours of training as a proportion of total hours of teaching is very limited when compared with that of many European countries. In Bachelor courses the number of hours dedicated to work placements is worth a maximum of 18 credits out of a total of 180 credits, while in a

Master's degree the hours of practical work drops to 10 credits out of a total of 120.

There is no uniform standard concerning the hours of direct supervision by placement supervisors.

For work placements to be undertaken universities are required to search for and identify social workers available to act as volunteer student supervisors within social services.

The organisation of work placements is also very varied across the country. Some universities use specialised staff on temporary contracts to manage work placements and supervisor relations. Although the number of staff can vary, in many cases it is too small to cope with the number of work placements to be managed. Instead of professionals on temporary contracts some universities use teaching staff who have to divide their workload between teaching and managing staff work. The result is the often tiring relationship between supervisors and staff. Supervisor training and updating is often occasional or completely absent. In addition, the relationship between university staff and supervisors is discontinuous and poorly structured (Fazzi & Rosignoli, 2012).

The few studies on the subject indicate that supervision is also seen by most social workers as an activity that above all requires work experience in the field to be managed effectively. Educational elements of the supervision process are vastly undervalued (Giarola & Neve, 2009). The dominant approach to supervision is characterised by attitudes replicating typical dynamics found in the relationship between operator and customer (Fazzi & Rosignoli, 2016). On the one hand, supervision thus assumes an "administrative and regulatory" character and the concept of learning is tied to the ability of the skilled professional to transmit to the student the technical knowledge needed to carry out the tasks assigned to the social worker by institutions. On the other hand, the prevailing attitude is that which Payne (2007) called "reflective therapeutic" focussing predominantly on the emotional and relational dimension of the learning process. The most effective supervision practices considered in the literature that emphasise the collaboration between experienced professional and student, mutual learning, and experimentation of reflective critical thinking (Kanno & Koeske, 2010) are instead scarcely adopted and interest in their dissemination appears limited.

Therefore, field education in Italy is a very fragile pillar of social work education unlike the case in other countries.

Effects of the Crisis

The economic crisis was an important watershed that resulted in an explosion of contradictions in the way social work education in Italy was changing and imposed the need for it to be profoundly rethought.

Between 2008 and 2016 the number of people in poverty doubled and there was a sharp increase in unemployment. Unemployment hit young people in particular. They became a veritable army of unemployed estimated on the order of 2 million people. Loss of employment and increase in poverty were accompanied by very significant social upheavals that weakened the familist structure of the Italian welfare system. The traditional family was in rapid decline. Increased separations, reduced birth rates, and increased numbers of the elderly multiplied the need for care and assistance and revealed a series of problems in interweaving complex healthcare, employment, and social needs. In the last 20 years there has also been a rapid increase in migratory flows most of which came from outside the European Union. In 2014 the landings began of hundreds of thousands of refugees from Africa and the Middle East, which have sorely tested hospitality and generated strong xenophobic sentiment.

The size and complexity of problems to be faced put social workers under great professional pressure at a time when they found themselves operating within bodies that were in turn subjected to in-depth reorganisation. Working conditions in welfare agencies generally deteriorated with the financial crisis. The system witnessed a widespread increase in workload, difficulty in replacing outgoing staff, and an increase in occupational stress (Bertotti, 2016).

The most recent research reveals that in the post–economic crisis period the vast majority of social workers expressed great concern about the reduction in resources, narrowing of services, and the reduction in personnel. These considerations created an emotional climate of widespread frustration and lack of confidence for the future.

At the same time the culture of social rights that characterised the rise of public welfare policies was subject to a frontal attack by new right-wing populist movements (Ruzza & Fella, 2009). The economic crisis and austerity policies in Italy encouraged the emergence of political parties whose programmes explicitly target erosion of the rights of marginal social groups, foreigners, and refugees. Consequently, social workers (especially, in northern regions of the country where the populist movements are stronger) often operate in institutional contexts that hinder hospitality, empowerment, and advocacy (Fazzi, 2015).

In this new scenario the need for social work to find new strategies and skills to tackle change is becoming a central theme for the future of the profession. Exposure to increasing work pressures implies the need to prepare professionals to be resilient in the face of adversity (Beddoe & Adamson, 2016). Educational programmes should therefore provide skills for coping, stress management, subjective wellbeing, and the ability to maintain work–life balance (Grant, Kinman, & Baker, 2014). Managerial pressure and reduced funds to play with in turn force professionals to build formal and informal partnerships with others to respond to their needs. Thus, community work regains significant importance in the organisation of effective interventions in a regime of scarce resources (Fazzi, 2018). Work with migrants and asylum seekers in turn involves thorough reorganisation of the skills of social workers. Not only does it involve interaction with cultures and complex needs it also involves encouraging participation in and access to welfare policies (Barberis & Boccagni, 2014). Moreover, the emergence of populism together with the drive toward rationalisation puts at risk the ethics and principles of social work (Gray & Webb, 2013). Consequently, it is increasingly important to base professional practice on human rights and anti-oppressive theory and to promote the acquisition of skills to facilitate professional activism (Noble, 2007).

This clearly shows how change is particularly relevant to the practice of social work in this current phase in history. Therefore, the development of congruent educational programmes is a priority for the academic system, the professional community, and the services sector.

Changes in the Labour Market

Transformations in the labour market must take centre stage on the agenda concerning the adequacy of knowledge and skills needed to cope with change. The economic crisis brought about progressive resizing of public policies. The number of officials recruited under a permanent contract in public administration have thus undergone rapid transformation.

When the economic crisis started 70% of social workers were still employed under permanent contracts in the public sector (Fiore & Puccio, 2010). National research on employment opportunities for graduates in social work in the period 2006–2012 revealed that of those employed in positions consistent with their academic qualifications 45% in the public sector were on fixed term contracts. Similar figures were found for those employed in the private sector and in the third sector (Tognetti, 2015). Moreover, the public sector is no longer the favoured employment opportunity of newly qualified social workers. In 2008 approximately 85% of social workers worked in public administration. For those who graduated after 2010 the rate of employment in the public sector dropped to about 30% of newly employed.

At the same time there has been an increase in the proportion of graduates who work in jobs where their academic qualification is of no use to them, who are unemployed, and who are increasingly employed in fields other than the public sector. The proportion of people employed in the third sector, in particular, has almost tripled.

The third sector is also under pressure from cuts to public spending and rationalisation policies. Public services are being outsourced because of the need for cost savings resulting in lower wages and poorer working conditions for operators. However, available research points to the requirement for greater flexibility and broadening of the tasks of social workers as characteristic features of the new employment sector (Fazzi, 2012). Third-sector professionals are more engaged in tasks that go beyond casework. Although it remains a fundamental part of their work, third-sector employees appear more engaged in other tasks such as promotional activities, community work, and project writing.

A further difference regarding traditional work in the public sector is that third-sector social workers are often also partners in the organisations in which they operate and therefore have greater power to influence organisational decisions. This influence is given in many cases by granting specific professional status to social workers. Unlike public bodies in which administrative and technical/management professions enjoy a status superior to that of social professions, social workers in third-sector organisations tend to be considered more as qualified professionals. As a result it is easier for them to occupy positions that have greater decision-making powers and this presupposes greater competence regarding matters such as organisation, staff management, or economic and financial planning.

A further change is growth in the number of social workers who practise as self-employed professionals. This is an emerging phenomenon linked mainly to liberalisation of the labour market that drives many young people to work as self-employed providers of services to organisations or directly to private customers. The independent management of work becomes the professional priority for this new category of social workers.

Stalling of the University System

Faced with the demand for new skills the university system has reached an impasse. The need to provide new social workers with skills that are more solid and articulated than those required in the past has become a subject of debate on the future of social work. As far back as 2012 the Italian National Association of Social Workers (Ordine nazionale degli assistenti sociali) proposed a draft law to deal with this situation (never discussed in parliament) aimed at strengthening university educational paths in social work. The objective was to reinforce social work skill areas of the curricula and promote plans to recruit teachers with social worker experience.

However, the post-crisis priorities of university policies in Italy were almost entirely focussed on rationalising the organisation of departments and cutting costs. Thus, degree courses in social work were reduced in number, while at the same time the teaching of professional social work, which had become weak, showed no improvement. Although the average age of social worker teachers on permanent contracts rose to 50, the need to establish PhD courses in social work to encourage qualification of a new teaching body has not yet been translated into launching specific initiatives.

Moreover, education is still strongly influenced by traditional teaching models. The frontal lectures that characterise university teaching in Italy are widespread, while innovative teaching practices such as lessons that involve the active involvement of users, the use of audiovisual aids, or case simulations are almost completely absent.

Recent research highlights how focus on the procedural and formal aspects of social work still tends to be central to teaching programmes. Creativity and orientation toward innovation are topics barely touched upon as is experimentation with new educational models such that transferable skills of value in learning how to deal with new tasks can be acquired (Fazzi, 2016). Reappropriation of the political view of social work is also found more in professional practice than in the curricula of university courses.

A further effect of cuts on university policies is a phenomenon already identified at the international level: marginalisation of the role of field education in social work education (Morley & O'Connor, 2016). As demonstrated by Globerman and Bogo (2003), changes to the culture and priorities of welfare agencies directly influence the inclination of professionals to perform the role of supervisors. In a climate where there is growing pressure toward productivity and cost savings many professionals have less time to devote to students. Furthermore, it often happens that supervision is viewed by management of the organisation as too expensive for the bodies in which social workers are employed. Therefore, such activity receives little support or is even discouraged. The increase in pressure means supervisors have more need for support from university tutoring staff. The staffing and coordination of work placements nevertheless continue to be performed mostly by temporary staff. Moreover, in many universities effective collaboration with supervisors is increasingly hampered by the lack of resources. Therefore, supervision tends to be carried out increasingly with what is essentially a "blank mandate" on the part of universities regarding supervisors with the consequent increase in responsibility borne by professionals already pressed by the policies of reorganisation and cuts to services. The task of the supervisor tends to become more difficult and many social workers put under pressure withdraw their offer of availability to universities for student supervision.

CHALLENGES AND PROSPECTS

As several authors have highlighted, in a fast-changing world social workers are required to have different and additional forms of knowledge and practices than those used in the welfare state era (Harms Smith & Ferguson, 2016). The lack of such knowledge prevents the seizing of opportunities for transformation and leads to the risk of favouring the status quo and the dissemination of attitudes of frustration and demotivation among professionals.

Social work education in Italy has been established over time through a non-linear and often contradictory process. Alongside significant progress there are also limitations that have prevented the building of a truly autonomous body of knowledge and a fully recognised education system. Before the economic crisis the expansion of public welfare was the driver for the growth of social work in Italy in various dimensions. Contradictions in the educational system thus remained latent. The idea that the growth of public policies alone would be enough to justify and promote the development of the profession was simultaneously instilled in the culture of the professional community.

With the economic crisis of 2008 the situation changed rapidly. The schism between the knowledge and skills of new social workers and the complexity of problems and challenges to be faced got dramatically larger.

Overcoming the current difficulties will involve addressing and resolving the numerous challenges. Absolutely necessary is acceptance of the importance of social work as indispensable to dealing with new social problems. The changes that characterise society such as the increase in migratory flows, ageing of the population, and the spread of poverty create new opportunities for action by social workers. It is important for social workers to be involved in the discussions. They should be protagonists of actions aimed at tackling these new phenomena. Social workers need to carry out their everyday practice in full view and not the offices where they are often confined. Giving the profession new political and social visibility is necessary to returning the problem of skills development and the solidity of the profession's educational pathways back to the centre of the debate.

A number of objectives should be pursued when configuring social work education. Teaching programmes should be profoundly renewed according to the social challenges then emerging. Subjects such as intercultural social work, budget management, and organisation of services, as well as practices based on empirical evidence, should be incorporated in graduate curricula to increase the effectiveness of work and open up new employment opportunities for the profession. As far as the relationship with universities is concerned it is essential to increase interdisciplinary training, collaboration, and research to foster the construction of alliances with other disciplines and to develop greater interest and skills within academe regarding the themes of social work. Finally, the issue of alliances is central to the relationship with agencies that provide social services. The purpose should be to design training courses that, on the one hand, promote practical learning by the students and, on the other, make the presence of the trainees and the commitment of their supervisors compatible with solution of the problems addressed by the institutions.

References

Barberis, E., & Boccagni, P. (2014). Blurred rights, local practices: Social work and immigration in Italy. *British Journal of Social Work, 44*(1), 70–87.

Beddoe, L., & Adamson, C. (2016). Educating resilient practitioners. In I. Taylor, M. Bogo, M. Lefevre, & B. Teater (Eds.), *Routledge international handbook of social work education* (pp. 343–355). London: Routledge.

Bertotti, T. (2016). Resources reduction and welfare changes: Tensions between social workers and organisations—The Italian case in child protection services. *European Journal of Social Work, 19*(6), 963–976.

Bogo, M., & Vayda, E. (1998). *The practice of field instruction in social work: Theory and process* (2nd ed.). Toronto: University of Toronto.

Brekke, J. S. (2014). A science of social work, and social work as an integrative scientific discipline: Have we gone too far, or not far enough? *Research on Social Work Practice, 24,* 517–523.

Campanini, A. (2007). Social work in Italy. *European Journal of Social Work, 76*(1), 107–116.

Campanini, M. (2015). Social work education in Italy: History and the present scenario. *The Indian Journal of Social Work, 76*(1), 57–74.

Fazzi, L. (2012). Social work in the public and non-profit sectors in Italy: What are differences? *European Journal of Social Work, 5,* 629–644.

Fazzi, L. (2015). Exclusionary populism, xenophobia and social work in Italy. *International Social Work, 4,* 595–605.

Fazzi, L. (2016). Are we educating creative professionals? The results of some experiments on the education of social work students in Italy. *Social Work Education, 1,* 89–99.

Fazzi, L. (2018). Social workers' views on community involvement in child protection work in Italy. *Child & Family Social Work, 24*(1), 1–9.

Fazzi, L., & Rosignoli, A. (2012). *Guida per i supervisori di tirocinio per il servizio sociale.* Milano: FrancoAngeli.

Fazzi, L., & Rosignoli, A. (2016). Reversing the perspective: When the supervisors learn from the students. *British Journal of Social Work, 1,* 204–221.

Fiore, B., & Puccio, R. (2010). Quanto vale una professione altruista? I mutamenti nella regolazione del mercato del lavoro. In C. Facchini (a cura di), *Tra impegno e professione* (pp. 143–158). Bologna: Il Mulino.

Giarola, A., & Neve, E. (2009). Una ricerca sulla supervisione agli assistenti sociali in servizio: i risultati. *Rassegna di servizio sociale, 2–3,* 24–43.

Globerman, J., & Bogo, M. (2003). Changing times: Understanding social workers' motivation to be field instructors. *Social Work, 48*(1), 65–73.

Grant, L., Kinman, G., & Baker, S. (2014). Put on our own oxygen mask before assisting others: Social work educators perspectives on an emotional curriculum. *British Journal of Social Work, 45*(8), 2351–2367.

Gray, M., & Webb, S. A. (2013). *The new politics of social work.* New York: Palgrave.

Harms Smith, L., & Ferguson, I. (2016). Practice Learning: Challenging neoliberalism in a turbolent world. In I. Taylor, M. Bogo, M. Lefevre, & B. Teater (Eds.), *Routledge international handbook of social work education* (pp. 209–291). London: Routledge.

Howard, M. O., & Garland, E. L. (2015). Social work research: 2044. *Journal of the Society for Social Work and Research, 6,* 173–200.

Kanno, H., & Koeske, G. F. (2010). MSW students' satisfaction with their field placements: The role of preparedness and supervision quality. *Journal of Social Work Education, 46*(1), 23–38.

Morley, C., & O'Connor, D. (2016). Contesting field education in social work: Using critical reflection to enhance student learning for critical practice. In I. Taylor, M. Bogo, M. Lefebre, & B. Teater (Eds.), *Routledge international handbook of social work education* (pp. 220–232). London: Routledge.

Naldini, M. (2003). *The family in the mediterranean welfare states.* London: Frank Cass.

Noble, C. (2007). Social work collective action and social movements. In L. Dominelli (Ed.), *Revitalising communities in a globalising world*. London, UK: Ashgate.

Payne, M. (2007). *What is professional social work*. Chicago, IL: Lyceum Books.

Ruzza, C., & Fella, S. (2009). *Re-inventing the Italian right: Territorial politics, populism and 'post-fascism'*. New York: Routledge.

Sgroi, E. (2001). Introduzione: Il servizio sociale come professione. Identità e percorsi nel contesto sociale del nostro Paese. In EISS (Ed.), *Primo rapporto sulla situazione del servizio sociale*. Roma: EISS.

Tognetti, M. (2015). *Voglio fare l'assistente sociale. Formazione e occupazione dei laureati in Servizio sociale in tempi di crisi e discontinuità*. Milano: FrancoAngeli.

Tynjälä, P., Välimaa, J., & Sarja, A. (2003). Pedagogical perspectives on the relationship between higher education and working life. *Higher Education, 46*, 147–166.

Wilson, G., & Campbell, A. (2013). Developing social work education: Academic perspectives. *British Journal of Social Work, 43*(5), 1005–1023.

CHAPTER 9

The Concept of Professional Identity in Selected Approaches to the Education of Social Workers

Jitka Navrátilová and Pavel Navrátil

INTRODUCTION

In the Czech Republic, the education of social workers as well as the practice of social work itself has undergone dramatic development in the last three decades. In the early 1990s, following the Velvet Revolution, which ended nearly 40 years of Communist ideology domination, there was a gradual renewal of the higher education of social workers, as well as a new demand for the development of social work as a specific profession (Brnula, Kodymová, & Michelová, 2014). However, this development was marked by the consequences of the previous period, which affected social work. In regard to the development of social work in the Czech Republic, Navrátil (2001) states that the socialist (i.e. communist) establishment not only caused a violent interruption of the natural development of social work, which took place in democratic societies, but if any awareness of social work or social workers persisted in society at all, it was gradually deformed and distorted ideologically. Hardly anything remained of its original professional mission or identity. This "ideologization" also meant that "institutions were not interested in professional social workers and gradually the public awareness of the

J. Navrátilová (✉) · P. Navrátil
Department of Social Policy and Social Work, Masaryk University,
Brno, Czech Republic
e-mail: jitkanav@fss.muni.cz

P. Navrátil
e-mail: 17824@mail.muni.cz

133
S. S. M. et al. (eds.), *The Palgrave Handbook of Global Social Work Education*, https://doi.org/10.1007/978-3-030-39966-5_9

professional profile of this vocation was fading (...)". As a result, the awareness of the characteristics of social work disappeared and its identity became totally unclear (Schimmerlingová, 1991, p. 10).

In addition to the communist ideological ballast describing social work as an unnecessary profession, the 40 years of the liquidation of practical social work also resulted in the interruption of the training of social workers. Social change in 1989 created space for the development of social work, and questions regarding the identity of the field and the appropriate education of social workers emerged with renewed urgency. These questions became important in connection with the establishment of the Association of Educators in Social Work in 1993.

Although it could have seemed that democratic processes enabled the new development of social work, there were some critical challenges that emerged. Due to the unsuccessful negotiation among social work practitioners, educators, and employers, there was no agreement in the sector on the identity of social work in the Czech Republic (Musil, 2013). The situation was complicated by the legislative definition of social work, which led rather to the fact that social work was perceived as a social service. The absence of agreement on the nature of social work among the most important actors in social work has had its serious consequences to this day. Nearly thirty years after social work began to be retaught in the Czech Republic, it is not entirely clear what social work is, or what its domain is (Chytil, 2007; Navrátil & Navrátilová, 2008; Punová, 2012; Matulayová & Musil, 2013; Musil, 2013).

Even though ambiguities surrounding the identity of social work persist to this day, it does not mean that social work has ceased to be taught or practised. This text is based on the assumption that the lack of agreement among stakeholders on their professional identity does not mean a loss of identity, but rather a space for the construction of a plurality of identities. From this perspective, we try to reflect on how the identity of social work is shaped and formed by education. We ask this basic question: "*What types of professional identities are developed by schools educating social workers in the Czech Republic?*"

RESEARCH METHODOLOGY

In this article, we rely on the data collected in 2010 for a study aimed primarily to find out what educational approaches were chosen by the educators of social work in the Czech Republic. In the framework of that research, a set of case studies was carried out to understand which educational models were favoured by schools educating social workers. We utilised a mixed research strategy and data were collected through questionnaires and interviews.

The selection set of the cases in the first phase involved schools training social workers and cooperating with the Association of Educators in Social Work. This association is the most important social player, which systematically affects on the long-term the level of education of social work in the Czech Republic. Each of the schools connected with this association was approached with the offer to participate in the study. The schools, in turn, approached their teachers. Those teachers who were willing to cooperate in this research and responded positively to the offer of participation were the ones to become the subjects of inquiry. Our research consisted of 18 case studies, consisting of qualitative and quantitative data. Each of the case studies represented one of the schools that prepares social workers for their future profession.

The role of our respondents was twofold. In the first place, they acted the role of "the expert" who, thanks to their familiarity, could provide insight information about rules, structure, or school practices, as they are part of their curriculum at school. In the second role, they acted as informants whereby through the set of research questions, they expressed their attitudes, opinions, and topics that were part of the survey.

The first stage of the research helped identify the three main educational approaches that are being applied in the Czech Republic (evidence-based, competency-based, and reflective approaches) in social work education.

Although this knowledge brought us a significantly better understanding on educational situation in social work, we started to recognise that identified educational models could rely on different assumptions and images of social work, so we decided to shed more light on it. We have decided to conduct the second part of the research. This follow-up study covers a secondary analysis collected data to answer the question, what discourses and professional identities are inherently present in the educational models we had identified in 2010. At this stage, we used all the data but chose a new interpretative framework for them to help distinguish the discourses and identity types. Also, we focused on identification of the preferred values that were explicitly or implicitly present in each approach. The new interpretative perspective helped us to look at the earlier findings from a new perspective and to recognise the discourses and identities that the schools created, both deliberately and unintentionally.

In the subsequent part of the text, we will briefly introduce the educational approaches we have discovered in the first part of the research.

Approaches to the Education of Social Workers in the Czech Republic (Summary of the First Stage of the Research)

The question of the identity of social work is becoming increasingly difficult to answer under postmodern conditions. The social construction of the identity of social work is affected by various influences, contexts, and discourses. It is precisely the postmodern *super-diversity* that allows the formulation of different concepts of social work identities (Navrátil, 1998, 2013). However, the plurality of identities makes it more difficult to define the aims of social work with definitive validity (at least to the extent of a particular group or territory); similarly, it does not allow for the definitive delimitation of the content of the activities of social workers (McDonald, 2006) and poses new challenges regarding the legitimacy of the field of social work (Musil 2013).

With regard to the fact that the area of university education is absolutely fundamental in forming and shaping the identity of social work (Etzkowitz & Dzisah, 2012), a particular method of education was at the centre of the empirical research, specifically "school-based approaches to the education of future social workers". We realise that the area of education is characterised by a diversity of views as to what are appropriate ways and content of education. Over the history of social work education, many different and often contradictory approaches on how to teach and train social workers (Lishman, 2011) have evolved. Although the education at its general level focuses on "helping clients to manage to interact with their social environment", schools begin from a variety of premises and emphasise different elements of education. Some of these approaches emphasise the importance of theoretical knowledge; others prefer the training of practical skills; while others focus on topics of self-development, critical thinking, or the ability to foster the active participation of clients in changing their difficult life situations (Navrátilová & Navrátil, 2016). The educational approach most preferred by schools shows what values are considered to be key in the preparation of social workers for their future profession.

Many authors involved in the training of social workers (Doel, Shawdon, & Morrison, 2002; Evans, 1999; Shardlow & Doel, 1996; Sheafor & Jenkins, 1982) point to the idea that the area which undergoes the most debate as to what the form of education should be is the field of professional practice. The value that individual schools attribute to practice is, in our work, also a starting point for distinguishing individual approaches to education and recognising the identities that are supported by the schools of social work. Based on the key dimensions, we differentiate individual learning approaches and consider their consequences for creating discourses and shaping the identity of social work for students.

With the array of approaches that have been created over the course of educating social workers, we have specifically focused on the three below, which concern the fundamental position in the education of social workers in the Czech Republic. In this section, we summarise the basic results of the empirical research from 2010.

Evidence-Based Approach to Education

This type of education emphasises a close *connection with scientific methods.* Although other approaches to social work education can also be seen to involve research, this approach is primarily based on the fact that the basis for the decision-making of social workers must be *scientifically verified evidence* (Griffiths, 1999; Sackett et al., 1996; Sheldon, 2001; Webb, 2001).

Evidence-based social work is presented by a number of authors as a process in which evidence is used as a tool for deciding on the choice of intervention in the assisting process. The burden of this decision is transferred to the best possible piece of evidence (Gambrill, 1999; Gibbs & Gambrill, 1999), which it is supposed is based primarily on quantitative research (Barber, 2008; McNeece & Thyer, 2004). The most important are those interventions that have the highest level of empirical support, in contrast to those that are based on the mutual consensus of experts with an interpretative understanding of the situation (Rosen & Proctor, 2003; Shaw, 1999; Smith, 2004). Social workers are expected to be able to provide procedures and instructions that are measurable and provide the certainty of objectivist knowledge. Although some of the writers grounded in the "evidence-based" approach consider it important when creating new knowledge also to include ideas based on practical experience and wisdom (Roberts & Yeager, 2004, 2006), it is not considered to be a very reliable resource that should serve as the basis for selecting interventions.

In practice, social work proceeds systematically and rationally from assessment to intervention, followed by evaluations based on the need to choose the most effective intervention (Gray, Plath, & Webb, 2009). The research that social workers rely on in making their decision must include dual information: on the one hand, information about the problem itself, which they are confronting, about its etiology and their knowledge of it; on the other hand, information about what kind of interventions within this problem area can be used by individual types of social services. These research aids eliminate the risks associated with the uncertainty that social workers face in decision-making, and at the same time, provide them with the confidence to find functional solutions when making decisions.

"Finding evidence" in a specific way has influenced how we think about the requirements for students' knowledge and skills. They are primarily cultivated through the students' cognitive abilities, which enable them to successfully pass through the process of finding the best evidence.

In terms of the goal, evidence-based education and practice in social work focus on acquiring skills for using scientific resources and evidence, which serve as support for decision-making on intervention. Over the course of study, during which students should be learning to find the best evidence, Jarolímková (2004) emphasises the information literacy of the users. Students are encouraged to systematically search for sources of information about the target population and their problems in order to be able to consider their credibility, reliability, and applicability in their work with the client.

Evidence-based education emphasises the ability to argue with regard to data and other credible sources. The position of the theoretical framework is more influential in this approach than the experience acquired in practice.

Competence-Oriented Approach to Education

The competence approach has been occupying a prime position for social workers in practice and in the education of social workers for several decades. This approach to competences is evident not only in the Czech Republic but in many other European countries as well (Chytil, 2007; Kearney, 2000; Lorenz, 2007; Shardlow & Doel, 1996; Webb, 2001). Competency models based on the behavioural movement began to appear in the 1920s, pervading the education system in the 1950s (Ainsworth, 1977; Kuhlmann, 2009; Parker, 2006; Pierson, 1996), and particularly massively influencing the education of social workers in the last four decades, when it became dominant in educational programs and accreditation standards in diverse areas of education (Kuhlmann, 2009).

The main popularity of the competency models is that it provides workers with clear and specific guidelines (Kanter, 1983). The education system, which was based on developing specific instructions on how to act in certain situations, was soon applied in most areas of social work. For this to take place, a broad system of competencies had to be created to cover the wide range of activities that occupy social workers (Reid, 1992). The sense of competence is to model the capabilities and practices of the idealised actors, who behave rationally and who perfectly handle the rules that underlie a particular kind of behaviour. This involves the formalisation of basic skills (Fay, 2002). Handling certain competences means that one has mastered certain rules or norms of rationality relating to a particular activity.

The use of competence models in practice means that it is preferable to apply pre-prepared solutions for the problems that clients bring. Competence-oriented social work is not primarily concerned with deeper connections affecting the problem that the client has come to a social worker with, but rather takes it like an isolated problem that can be solved using a solution that is known in advance. As a result, social workers do not rely on critical thinking as an inherent part of their intervention. This concept relies on the fact that certain solutions simply work for certain problems. Competency models simplify the various elements of complex and dynamic social interactions and reduce their social nature to individual components (Dominelli, 1997).

In the competency approach, the core of the education is in practical lessons and training. Students learn how to respond in certain situations, acquire skills and behavioural habits. They acquire a wide range of competences focused on specific goals, learn how to respond in certain situations, acquire pre-defined skills and habits that they then improve and refine in practice. Social work is understood as a "craft". Clark (1976, in Shardlow & Doel, 1996) points out that, although the competence approach in individual study programs is conceived in different ways, it is likely that these programs will include the following characteristics: *focus on outputs rather than the process of learning*. Students are supposed to demonstrate the proficiency of certain pre-defined competencies. Learning methods through which these competences are achieved do not play such a role. It is the achievement of results that is essential. *Teaching and learning are defined in terms of performance.* The student must demonstrate an ability to perform that is determined in advance. There are *clear performance measurement criteria* that indicate various levels of competence. Competence-based education does not primarily address the reflection of student experience (Bogo & Vayda, 1987). It is necessary only to reflect the accuracy or inaccuracy, suitability or inappropriateness of the use of a particular skill.

Reflective Approach to Education

Reflective approaches are inspiring greater interest and high expectations in numerous areas of professional activities involving work with people. Interest in reflective processes was sparked by authors who began to cast doubt on the usefulness of linear technical thinking in applied professions, but which, in addition to academic knowledge, need to take into account the experience of professionals and their clients (Schön, 1983). Reflective approaches quickly permeated scholarly and educational texts in social work. Since the idea that a social worker when making decisions should take into account not only their experience but also the stimuli on the part of clients, reflective approaches appeared very natural in the context of social work (Chow, Lam, Leung, Wong, & Chan, 2011; D'Cruz, Gillingham, & Melendez, 2007; Ferguson, 2003; Nixon & Murr, 2006).

Although the requirements for critical reflection appeared much earlier (Dewey, 1916, 1930, 1933), its growth and expansion occurred especially during the late modern times (D'Cruz et al., 2007; Ferguson, 2008; Fook, 2002; Howe, 1994; Navrátil & Navrátilová, 2008; Payne, 2008; Parton & O'Byrne, 2000; Thompson, 2002; Thompson & Thompson, 2008) and in conjunction with the need to focus attention on the structural contexts that affect the lives of individuals and the work of social workers with clients (Chytil, 2007; Ferguson, 2008; Fook, 2002; Freire 1996; Keller, 2007; Lorenz, 2007; Payne, 2008; van der Laan, 1998). The postmodern era, which offers the opportunity to choose a variety of perspectives from which to interpret one's own life, has brought social workers not only a variety of possible interpretations and choices, but also greater uncertainty as to which of the chosen perspectives is the right approach for their work with clients.

The work of Donald Schön (1983, 1990) was very important in the practice of social workers. He identified and described two basic approaches to creating new knowledge related to working with people. The first is based on reflection after acting, that is, reflection-on-action, and the second on reflection during acting, or reflection-in-action. Within these approaches, he emphasises the importance of the work experience and practical skills that are gained in practice. Schön emphasises the idea that the art of practice—mastery—is a better starting point for professional education than technical rationality based on systematic, theory-based knowledge acquired through academic education (Redmond, 2006).

Reflective approaches also implied a new perspective on the education of social workers, which began to focus mainly on the process of learning (Mezirow, 1985, 1991; Brookfield, 1987, 1995). As part of the learning process, students are led to reflectively assess their experiences and interpretations. This process focuses primarily on the transformation of knowledge and learning, in which there should be a critical confrontation of possible interpretations of the gained experience. Reflective education is therefore oriented to developing the abilities of future social workers to become aware of different aspects, levels and interpretations of their experience and that of their clients.

Within reflective education, there are a number of models applied to the training of social workers. In the preparation of students of social work, emphasis is placed on reflection in three main fields: (a) cognitive, (b) affective, and (c) value-based (Thompson & Thompson, 2008), although cultural reflection has also been of great consideration lately (Payne, 2008). Even though reflection plays a crucial role in the above-mentioned areas in the education of social workers, another key is the willingness to bring openness into the education process and the ability to integrate the diversity of human experience as a source of creativity and innovative practices.

In the next section, we will focus on elucidating the characteristics of discourses and identities that are part of the ideological background of individual approaches. This involves presenting the value aspects of discursive constructions as we could identify and differentiate them in the data.

DISCOURSES AND IDENTITIES OF SOCIAL WORK (SECONDARY ANALYSIS)

Based on the secondary analysis of the data, we identified four types of discourse and identity that are strengthened and created through the educational approaches described above, which are applied by schools to the education of social workers in the Czech Republic.

Discourse 1: Social Work as a (Natural) Science

As part of the secondary analysis, we identified a discourse that is anchored in scientific rhetoric. This means that the training of social workers emphasises the need to use scientific support in assessing the client's life situation and the choice of the most effective interventions. Although we have found only one piece of evidence showing social work to be anchored in scientific discourse, it is evident that there is also some permeation of such conceived social work in the education of social workers in the Czech Republic, as the following citations show.

In practical training, students are encouraged to find **research resources** about the target group they are working with. (Case study 18)

In social work, it is necessary to look at specific aspects of life situations with the **help of theory and research**. On this basis, we can indicate appropriate and objectively functioning interventions. (Case study 18)

The findings of **research and theoretical resources** should be (critically) reflected and confronted (by students) with their practical experience gained in practice and used to identify interventions. (Case study 18)

These quotations suggest that theories and research findings play an important role in determining the intervention. The value here is the objective systems of knowledge that are a frame of reference of each intervention. Knowledge in this mode tends more to being applied than that it would originate within the framework of practice. The power of the knowledge system is therefore crucial here. At the same time, some aspects of scientific discourse also appear to be part of a reflective discourse, in which, alongside theory and experience, research reflection is also of consideration.

Researcher Identity (Key Word: Proof)

In this identity model, the basic identifying feature is that social work is a science. Scientific social work is such that the social workers apply knowledge derived from basic research, as would be the case for a doctor who, on the basis of pharmaceutical research, knows that, for example, the administration of a certain substance (medicine) results in the relief of psychological stress in 90% of patients. After making the diagnosis (psychological stress), the physician would probably prescribe such a substance (medicine) to most of his patients with this diagnosis, as he would expect, based on the studies, that it would work with 90% of the patients. A part of the expert identity is a belief in empirical evidence that confirms the correctness of a process and determines the direction of intervention. The opinion of the patient is less relevant in this case because the patient does not know what substances could positively affect his illness. In such a model, there is a dominance of the positivist approach, which believes that reality can be well-described, explained, and expressed in a more or less accurate theory based on this explanation. According to this theory, trained professionals proceed and lead their intervention into the client's life situation.

Discourse 2: Social Work as a Craft

Providing unified instructions for solving client problems, specifying individual professional knowledge, and emphasising measurable behaviour, which are typical features of the competency models, have comprised the most widespread approach to social worker education in our research. This discourse is also confirmed in the language of the competency models, which schools often describe in their curricula. For this reason, we come across expressions such as adopting/acquiring and certifying/verifying competence, a set of practical competencies, creating tools for standardisation, and learning objectives.

Examples of such expressions are shown in the following quotations:

> Our school works with the concept of **practical competencies** used in the Czech Republic, which we want to develop for the needs of our school .... The practice, which is an integral part of social work study, requires the creation of **tools for standardization** and the improvement of quality and effectivity. (Case study 4)

> Our graduates must **master the practical skills and competences** of the profession of social worker. (Case study 13)

> As part of the practical training, **students acquire and demonstrate their competence** in the skills of a social worker. During their practice, these competences are reflected in actual practice ... Our ultimate goal is to **verify and evaluate the competences** acquired in the practice of social work, to verify the documents obtained during the practice, according to **predetermined criteria**. (Case study 13)

The discourse that lies behind these respondents' statements shows that social workers are expected to undergo some training that will teach them the craft of social work. There is a hidden assumption that the complex and dynamic social interactions of our clients' lives can be reduced to individual components that social workers can learn to work with by mastering certain skills or competences (see Dominelli, 1997). The value lies in the skill, in the craft-based ability to solve the problem.

Craftsman Identity (Motto: Competence and Skill)

The identity of a technical profession is related to the logic of the competence discourse. It implies that the social worker should be a skilled (social) craftsman who can employ the appropriate skills to solve the problem of his client. The social worker should be a master of empathy and communication and can apply technically correct procedures at the right time. It is not necessary to be intellectually pervasive, as it is the craftsmanship that makes the person a sought-after assistant. As a result of the brilliance of his competences, the social worker can effectively solve the client's difficulties and problems. Social work in this model of identity is similar to computer repair technicians. In the event of a problem, he is sought out to detect and correct the defective part. Similar to the scientific mode, a diagnostic routine is used to help the repairer to identify the location of the error. As a result, the social repairer can perform the expected action, providing in-depth information, training the client in better communication, and revealing alternatives in order to achieve the desired goal.

Discourse 3: Social Work as a Philosophy

Social work, in this sense, is understood as an activity in which a social worker considers each step, and its practical and symbolic consequences. The behaviour of the social worker should be subject to the critical verification of the assumptions and circumstances that are part of their work with the client. This concept is not about the discovery of the (only) objective truth but opens up the space to take into account the various (parallel) truths with which and in which all participants and, above all, the clients live. This type of discourse in social work aims not only to support the reflection in the work of social workers but also aims to help clients reflect on their diverse life situations and be familiar with the dynamically changing structures and networks that are part of their clients' lives. The social worker must be able to learn to respond to and handle the constantly new problems, risks, and challenges generated by the conditions of the postmodern world.

Below are the statements that represent this type of discourse:

> In practice, we support the professional growth of a student to become, on the basis of his efforts, a **reflective helping professional** who is able to assess a social situation and **react to the ever-changing human problems** at an individual and structural level. (Case study 18)

The emphasis on reflection is also evident from the statements of the following respondents:

> The ultimate goal of practical instruction is to **teach the student to critically reflect** on the profession of social worker, leading to self-reflection as well as personal and professional growth. (Case study 13)

> We strive to equip our students with theoretical tools for the **critical reflection of their own practice** and to create a context for the administrative and organizational aspects of practice. (Case study 4)

Reflective social work is the opposite of proceduralised work. This kind of discourse emphasises the assessing of the uniqueness of the client's situation and his life situation. Using reflective thinking, clients are perceived as equal partners of the social worker. Social workers are encouraged to share their insights into the life situation with their clients. The purpose of such social work is to empower people to take responsibility for their lives and learn to handle the confusing living conditions of late modernity. The value of this discourse is the ability to view diversity and practice perspectivism.

Thinker Identity (Motto: Reflection)

With this concept of identity, a social worker resembles a thinker who must explore numerous hypotheses and theories to choose the one that he can trust. The reflective way of working entails the ability to look at the client's situation as well as at possible ways of working with him from various angles and perspectives. However, the research work requires one to talk to the largest possible range of conversation partners (respondents), who could help the researcher gain completely unexpected perspectives on a situation. Likewise, the reflective social worker is not afraid to reveal entirely new ways of interpreting a situation and takes into consideration which one will provide the client with the most opportunities, possibilities, and benefit. The reflective social worker, however, does not shy away from theory or research. They are understood as other possible points of view that can explain the situation in a useful way. The reflective identity, however, values one voice in particular; that is, the voice of the client, who from the beginning, is invited to work together. The client can and should, from the beginning, take part in solving his own detective mystery. That is why the participatory principle is sometimes considered a key feature of this concept of social work.

Discourse 4: Social Work as Education

A specific discourse that does not directly relate to the initially identified approaches in education is the educational discourse. Certain schools that we have previously identified as schools promoting scientific, matrix, or craft discourse have placed into the forefront, among other principles, the value of personal maturing and student growth, and the willingness of the student to overcome the social exclusion of his clients. As such, we have labelled this set of considerations as a separate discourse.

Educational discourse aims to train experts to deepen their critical consciousness with their clients, to be sensitive to various forms of discrimination, and to conceive strategies to overcome them and develop the client's potential. In this discourse, the social worker is often defined as an agent of social change, who coordinates social groups using educational strategies to help citizens understand and participate in their social, political, economic, and cultural environment and fully integrate into society.

Educational discourse emphasises the readiness of adepts of the field to operate in a very wide variety of contexts: to have the ability to respond to the needs of all groups of people, to have access to culture and the material assets of society, and to promote their client's daily participation in society. Social work in this type of discourse has an educational character as well as an anti-discriminatory dimension. The two basic tasks of this type of social worker include education and social support in the environment. The following citations represent this discourse:

We teach students to learn to **perceive themselves as a tool of assistance** that needs to be developed. (Case study 13)

... Our **goal is the personal growth** of students. (Case study 13)

... Students must also be **able to educate** themselves outside the classroom and **provide care** for socially challenged individuals (children and youth, abandoned individuals, people in crisis situations). (Case study 13)

The goal is the personal growth of students so that they are **able to stimulate their clients**. (Case study 13)

Educator Identity (Motto: Knowledge and Growth)

The educator identity can be compared to an orchardist. The orchardist is characteristic by the ability to breed trees, to promote their growth, occasionally prune them, and provide water or other necessary external resources. The aim of the orchardist is, however, to ensure that the tree has healthy growth and makes use of its potential. Similarly, educative social workers attaching to this concept of social work, use their skills to stimulate the development of individuals, groups, and communities. They want to release the client's internal resources and possibly remove external limits in an environment that prevents them from realising this.

Discourses—Summary

Each of the discourses represents a different image of the profession. In the case of scientific discourse, social work is depicted as an expert profession. Competence (skills) discourse portrays social work as a profession of technically competent experts who solve life's problems. Reflective discourse represents the vision of social work as a thinker profession in which the best solution is achieved by proper thinking. Scientific discourse sets out the ideal of a social worker as an expert who "knows" and can obtain valid information. Skills discourse formulates the idea of the ideal worker as a technically competent craftsman who can solve problems. The ideal of the philosophical discourse is an expert striving to understand the multifaceted dimensions of the client's situation. Educational discourse creates a picture of social work as a profession whose aim is to empower individuals and communities, as well as their growth and development of potential.

Conclusion

Our study was to answer the question: *"What types of professional identities are developed by schools through the educational approaches applied to the training of social workers in the Czech Republic?"* Based on secondary analysis, we

Table 9.1 Overview of discourses and identities of social work

	Scientific discourse	Craftsman discourse	Philosophical discourse	Educational discourse
General points of view	Social work as science	Social work as craft	Social work as reflective thinking	Social work as education
Key values	Proof	Competence	Thinking	Power/grow
Approach to education	The goal is to educate an expert who knows what is best for the client	The goal is to educate an expert who can technically solve the problem	The aim is to educate an expert who seeks understanding in the context	The aim is to educate an expert who can educate others
Identity in short	Scientist	Craftsman	Thinkers	Educator

Source Own research

have newly interpreted the data of our own empirical survey, which originally dealt with the concept of social worker education. Based on the reanalysis of these data, we were able to identify four main images or identities of social work to which Czech educators are trying to orientate their education.

These are identity models that can be referred to in short as (1) scientist identity, (2) craftsman identity, (3) thinkers identity, and (4) educator identity. For each identity, we have tried to outline its general starting point, key value, approach to education and concept of professional identity. We briefly summarise the findings that are presented in Table 9.1.

A key aspect of scientific discourse is the ability of the social worker to find evidence that enables him to conceive the best possible intervention. Craftsman discourse then assumes that it is essential that the social worker master the skill as a craft that will provide the client with the best assistance. Philosophical discourse is based on the premise that the best service can only come from reflective thinking. The discursive starting points are also reflected in the image of appropriate social worker education. The educational approach in social work emphasises the aspect of knowledge transfer, which empowers clients and promotes their growth.

It is not possible to clearly identify which of the social worker identity types prevail in the Czech context. From the point of view of our research, however, this is not absolutely essential. We wanted to report on the spectrum of identities that have developed in our environment, as we believe it is very important to have an awareness of what type of social worker identity we are promoting in the educational process. This is not merely about having a technically adequate study structure, but rather of further identifying the values that are related to the preferred type of social work identity.

BIBLIOGRAPHY

Ainsworth, D. (1977). Examining the basis for competency-based education. *The Journal of Higher Education, 48*(3), 321–332.

Barber, J. (2008). What evidence-based practise is. In B. W. White (Ed.), *Comprehensive handbook of social work and social welfare: The profession of social work*. Hoboken, NJ: Wiley.

Bogo, M., & Vayda, E. (1987). *The practice of field instruction in social work*. Toronto: University of Toronto Press.

Brnula, P., Kodymová, P., & Michelová, R. (2014). *Marie Krakešová: Priekopníčka teórie sociálnej práce v Československu*. Bratislava: Iris.

Brookfield, S. D. (1987). *Developing critical thinkers: Challenging adults to explore ways to thinking and acting*. San Francisco: Jossey-Bass.

Brookfield, S. D. (1995). *Becoming a critically reflective teacher*. San Francisco: Jossey-Bass.

Chow, A. Y. M., Lam, D. O. B., Leung, G. S. M., Wong, D. F. K., & Chan, B. F. P. (2011). Promoting reflexivity among social work students: The development and evaluation of a programme. *Social Work Education, 30*(2), 141–156.

Chytil, O. (2007). Důsledky modernizace pro sociální práci. *Sociální práce/Sociálna práca, 8*(4), 64–71.

D'Cruz, H., Gillingham, P., & Melendez, S. (2007). Reflexivity, its meanings and relevance for social work: A critical review of the literature. *The British Journal of Social Work, 37*(1), 73–90.

Dewey, J. (1916). *Democracy and education.* New York: The Free Press.

Dewey, J. (1930). *Human nature and conduct.* New York: Modern Library.

Dewey, J. (1933). *How we think.* New York: Heath.

Doel, M., Sawdon, C., & Morrison, D. (2002). *Learning, practice and assessment: Signposting the portfolio.* London: Jessica Kingsley.

Dominelli, L. (1997). *Sociology for social work.* London: Macmillan Press.

Etzkowitz, H., & Dzisah, J. (2012). *The age of knowledge: The dynamics of universities, knowledge and society.* Leiden: Brill.

Evans, D. (1999). *Practice learning in the caring professions.* Brookfield: Ashgate Publishing.

Fay, B. (2002). *Současná filosofie sociálních věd: multikulturní přístup.* Praha: Slon.

Ferguson, H. (2003). Welfare, social exclusion and reflexivity: The case of child and women protection. *Journal of Social Policy, 32*(2), 199–216.

Ferguson, H. (2008). The theory and practice of critical best practice in social work. In K. Jones, B. Cooper, & H. Ferguson (Eds.), *Best practice in social work: Critical perspectives.* Houndmills, Basingstoke, Hampshire, New York: Palgrave Macmillan.

Fook, J. (2002). *Social work: Critical theory and practice.* London: Sage.

Ford, K., & Jones, A. (1987). *Student supervision.* London: Macmillan Education Ltd.

Freire, P. (1996). *Pedagogy of the oppressed.* London: Penguins Books.

Gambrill, E. (1999). Evidence-based practice: An alternative to authority based practice. *Families in Society, 80,* 341–350.

Gibbs, L., & Gambrill, E. (1999). *Critical thinking for social worker: Exercises for the helping professions.* Thousand Oaks, CA: Pine Forge Press.

Gray, M., Plath, D., & Webb, S. A. (2009). *Evidence-based social work: A critical stance.* London and New York: Routledge.

Griffiths, P. (1999). The challenge of implementing evidence-based health care. *British Journal of Community Nursing, 4*(3), 142–147.

Howe, D. (1994). Modernity, postmodernity and social work. *The British Journal of Social Work, 24*(5), 513–532.

Jarolímková, A. (2004). Evidence based medicine a její vliv na činnost lékařských knihoven a informačních středisek. *Knihovnická revue, 15*(2), 75–81.

Kanter, J. S. (1983). Reevaluation of task-centered social work practice. *Clinical Social Work Journal, 11*(3), 228–244.

Kearney, J. (2000). Social Work education in Britain: A history of the commodification of social work practice and education. In W. W. Kruszyńska & J. Krzyszkowski (Eds.), *Education of social workers on the eve of the European Union's enlargement.* Absolwent: Lodž.

Keller, J. (2007). *Teorie modernizace.* Praha: Slon.

Kuhlmann, E. G. (2009). Competency-based social work education: A thirty-year retrospective on the behavioral objectives movement. *Social Work a Christianity, 36*(1), 70–76.

Lishman, J. (2011). *Social work education and training.* London: Jessica Kingsley Publishers.

Lorenz, W. (2007). Teorie a metody sociální práce v Evropě – profesní profil sociálních pracovníků. *Sociální práce/Sociálna práca, 1,* 62–71.

Matulayová, T., & Musil, L. (Eds.). (2013). *Social work, education and postmodernity: Theory and studies in selected Czech, Slovak and Polish issues.* Liberec: Technical University of Liberec.

McDonald, C. (2006). *Challenging social work: The context of practice.* New York: Palgrave Macmillan.

McNeece, C. A., & Thyer, B. A. (2004). Evidence-based practice and social work. *Journal of Evidence-Based Social Work, 1*(1), 7–25.

Mezirow, J. (1985). A critical theory of self-directed learning. In S. Brookfield, *Self-directed learning: From theory to practice* (pp. 17–30). San Francisco: Jossey-Bass.

Mezirow, J. (1991). *Transformative dimensions of adult learning.* San Francisco: Jossey-Bass.

Musil, L. (2013). Challenges of postmodern institutionalisation for education in social work. In T. Matulayová & L. Musil (Eds.), *Social work, education and postmodernity: theory and studies in selected Czech, Slovak and Polish issues.* Liberec: Technical University of Liberec.

Navrátil, P. (1998). Sociální práce jako sociální konstrukce. *Sociologický časopis, XXXIV*(1), 37–50.

Navrátil, P. (2001). *Teorie a metody sociální práce.* Brno: Marek Zeman.

Navrátil, P. (2013). Sociální konstruktivismus. In O. Matoušek, et al. (Eds.), *Encyklopedie sociální práce* (pp. 26–31). Portál: Praha.

Navrátil, P., & Navrátilová, J. (2008). Postmodernita jako prostor pro existenciálně citlivou sociální práci. *Časopis sociální práce/Sociálna práca, 8*(4), 124–135.

Navrátilová, J. (2010). *Pojetí praktického vzdělávání sociálních pracovníků* (Doctoral theses, Dissertations). Brno: Masaryk University, Faculty of Social Studies.

Navrátilová, J., & Navrátil, P. (2016). Educational discourses in social work. *Sociální pedagogika/Social education, 4*(1), 38–56.

Nixon, S., & Murr, A. (2006). Practice learning and the development of professional practice. *Social Work Education, 25*(8), 798–811.

Parker, J. (2006) Developing perceptions of competence during practice learning. *British Journal of Social Work, 36,* 1017–1036.

Parton, N., & O'Byrne, P. (2000). *Constructive social work.* London: Macmillan Press.

Payne, M. (2008). *Social care practice in context.* New York: Palgrave Macmillan.

Pierson, J. (1996). The behavioural approach to social work. In Ch. Hanvey & T. Philpot (Eds.), *Practising social work.* London and New York: Routledge.

Punová, M. (2012). Standardy vzdělávání v sociální práci a jejich naplňování v praktickém vzdělávání studentů sociální práce na katedře sociální politiky a sociální práce FSS MU Brno. *Aula, revue pro vysokoškolskou a vědní politiku, 20*(2), 48–61.

Redmond, B. (2006). *Reflection in action: Developing reflective practice in health and social services.* Hampshire: Ashgate Publishing.

Reid, W. J. (1992). *Task strategies: An empirical approach to clinical social work.* New York: Columbia University Press.

Roberts, A. R., & Yeager, K. R. (Eds.). (2004). *Evidence-based practice manual: Research and outcome measures in health and human services.* New York: Oxford University Press.

Roberts, A. R., & Yeager, K. R. (Eds.). (2006). *Foundations of evidence-based social work practice*. New York: Oxford University Press.

Rosen, A., & Proctor, E. (2003). *Developing practice guidelines for social work intervention*. New York: Columbia University Press.

Sackett, D. L., Rosenberg, W. M. C., Gray, J. A. M., Haynes, R. B., & Richardson, W. S. (1996). Evidence based medicine: What it is and what it isn't. *BMJ, 312*(7023), 71–72.

Schimmerlingová, V. (1991). Nové pojetí práce sociálních pracovníků. *Sociální Politika, 17*(8), 10.

Schön, D. A. (1983). *The reflective practitioner: How professionals think in action*. London: Temple Smith.

Schön, D. A. (1990). *Educating the reflective practitioner: Toward a new design for teaching and learning in the professions*. San Francisco: Jossey-Bass.

Shardlow, S., & Doel, M. (1996). *Practice learning and teaching*. London: Macmillan Press LTD.

Shaw, I. (1999). *Qualitative evaluation*. London: Sage.

Sheafor, B. W., & Jenkins, L. E. (1982). An overview of social work field instruction. In B. W. Sheafor, Ch R Horejsi, & G. A. Horejsi (Eds.), *Social work practice: Techniques and guidelines for social work practice*. Needham Heights: A Pearson Education.

Sheldon, B. (2001). Validity of evidence based practice in social work: A reply to Stephen Webb. *British Journal of Social Work, 31*, 801–809.

Smith, D. (2004). *Social work and evidence based practice*. London: Jessica Kingsley.

Thompson, N. (2002). *People skills*. Basingstoke: Palgrave Macmillan.

Thompson, S., & Thompson, N. (2008). *The critically reflective practitioner*. New York: Palgrave Macmillan.

van der Laan, Gert. (1998). *Otázky legitimace sociální práce: Pomoc není zboží*. Boskovice: Albert.

Webb, S. A. (2001). Some consideration on the validity of evidence-based practice in social work. *British Journal of Social Work, 31*, 57–79.

CHAPTER 10

Danish Welfare State and Social Work Education and Practice: Development and Challenges

Helle Strauss

INTRODUCTION

Denmark is a small wealthy country of 5.8 million people who live in a temperate coastal climate. Democracy is well established and stable and the population is well educated. Undergraduate degrees in subjects such as social work, teaching, pedagogies, and nursing is undertaken by 20% of the population. Postgraduate education is undertaken by 12%. In 2017 some 8000 more women than men were enrolled in postgraduate education (Statistics Denmark: "Denmark in Figures 2018," www.dst.dk/pubomtale/28923).

Participation in the workforce is among the highest in Europe, especially due to the high representation of women. In 2017 the number of people participating in the workforce aged 15–64 years was for men 1,441,000 or 81.5% and for women 1,318,000 or 76.1%.

In addition to relative high salaries, well-regulated working conditions such as a 37-hour working week, 5 weeks of holidays yearly, and 52 weeks of maternity leave for parents the Danish workforce is highly competitive. Success seems to be linked to high efficiency, know-how, innovation, and a trusted public sector (Askeland & Strauss, 2014).

Although the Danish system is often called a social democratic model, the formation and development of the welfare state has been influenced by all

H. Strauss (✉)
Faculty of Social Science and Pedagogy, Institute of Social Work,
University College Copenhagen, Copenhagen, Denmark
e-mail: helle.strauss@webspeed.dk

© The Author(s) 2021
S. S. M. et al. (eds.), *The Palgrave Handbook of Global Social Work Education*, https://doi.org/10.1007/978-3-030-39966-5_10

major political parties in Denmark including the Liberal and Conservative parties on the right wing of the parliament. Currently (2018) 13 different political parties constitute the Danish parliament and the government is formed as a coalition between different parties. Currently (2020) the social democrats form the government, but without majority in the parliament. But it is a tradition that legislation is adapted by negotiation and consensus between most or all of the elected parties.

What characterises the Danish welfare state? In this chapter the Danish system is compared with other welfare systems and it will be addressed how solidarity, equality and universality traditionally are understood as welfare columns.

WELFARE MODELS

It seems to be generally agreed that welfare is about how a country creates, regulates, and finances social institutions. The responsibility for executing welfare lies in cooperation between the state, civil society, and the market. How responsibility is divided between those three areas defines which welfare model the state operates.

Three different models of welfare systems are employed in the West:

1. The Liberal/Anglo-Saxon model, which is exercised in the United States, the United Kingdom, Canada, Australia, and New Zealand. The model reserves social benefits for the neediest and the state is responsible only for core services that are delivered mostly in cooperation with non-governmental organisations. Self-responsibility and individual freedom are highly valued.
2. The corporatist/Conservative model, which is also called the continental model. According to this social security is mainly funded by mandatory insurances linked to work. Germany is an example of this model. Social problems in Mediterranean countries are more often expected to be taken care of by the family, the church, or voluntary organisations.
3. The Nordic welfare model, which is characterised by universality (i.e., everyone is entitled to rights). The state is responsible for most social welfare that is financed by a progressive tax system. Norway, Sweden, Finland, Iceland, and Denmark have developed similar welfare systems.

Although these three "classical" models have today changed into blended forms that are much more different, several characteristics linked to the Nordic model are still recognisable in the Danish model (Askeland & Strauss, 2014).

Social welfare especially relates to how people feel about living in their country. Their experience of wellbeing is the goal of the welfare regime. Welfare can be defined as:

... the highest possible access to economic resources, a high level of well-being, including the happiness of the citizens, a guaranteed minimum income to avoid living in poverty, and, finally, having the capabilities to ensure the individual a good life. (Greve, 2013, p. 3)

Wellbeing is also about trust and confidence in the future. The welfare state can be seen as an investment in the future through education and health-care to bring up a new generation of citizens capable of providing not only for themselves but also for the elderly and their own children. The *World Happiness Reports* measure people's experience of happiness regarding con-fidence, security, prosperity, freedom, community health, and work–life bal-ance. For several years Denmark has kept its ranking on the world's happiness index as among the top-three countries alongside other Nordic countries and Switzerland (Helliwell, Layard, & Sachs, 2018, Fig. 2.2, p. 20).

The Danish welfare system has been criticised for being expensive. However, when the state provides for the long-time care of an individual, it has been found to be cheaper than if individuals insure themselves for sit-uations such as unemployment, illness, disability, or sudden death (Greve, 2013). It is also not possible to predict how many years individuals will need long-time support, so it is less expensive for the people to share the risk either through taxation or mandatory social insurance.

Background and Development of the Danish Welfare System

Social Reforms

The first social reforms took place in Denmark in 1891 when the country moved from an agricultural economy to an industrialised society and the sov-ereign surrendered power to parliament. These reforms aimed to care for poor and sick people in need by providing them with support in the form of alms as a means of addressing poverty.

Free public education from primary school to further educational pro-grammes and universities was already a tradition.

In 1933 major social reforms were instigated by political settlements reached between elected parties with the goal of giving benefits from the *principles of rights perspective* rather than giving alms and offering more human support to those in need, although appropriate strictness was to be executed toward irresponsible or anti-social behaviour (Schiermarcher & Høgh, 2006). Over the next decades the public health system grew in scope and function supported by tax funding and individual insurance fees. Laws were passed about disability pensions and old age benefits for people above 65 years that would also be funded by taxes. Although the state would provide some help in case of unemployment, people could also be covered for their loss of income by subscribing to the unemployment system administered by the unions. As a result union membership increased. Strengthened in this way unions were able to secure better working conditions for their members. These developments were to influence future social reforms in the growth of social welfare reforms in Denmark.

The 1960s and 1970s have been called the "golden time" of the welfare state (Greve, 2013). Nordic welfare ideology about solidarity, prevention, rehabilitation, and social security underpinned new social reforms during this period. Public health insurances were abandoned and healthcare and welfare services were fully funded by tax. The size and scope of welfare and health benefits were more comprehensive than before. Social care, childcare, and family support were included in state-supported public institutions, although some private social institutions also existed with public financial support. The welfare and health system and its services and benefits were financed by a complicated progressive tax system letting higher income individuals pay a higher percentage of their income than low-income individuals such that "broader shoulders bear the heavier burdens." In this way some redistribution of wealth took place. The core characteristics of the traditional Nordic welfare policy are outlined below.

Equality

Denmark is one of the most equal countries in the world. On a list of the richest countries in the world by Global Finance 2016 Denmark's relative poverty is rated at 5.5, the lowest listed (Organisation for Economic Co-operation and Development or OECD, http://www.oecd.org/social/inequality.htm).

Despite inequality continuing to be low in Denmark it has been increasing since the mid-1990s from a level around 20 to 26 in 1993 (0 = complete equality in income). This is a rise of around 6–7 points or approximately 30% (Schytz Juul, 2015). The poor, defined by an income 50% below the median, has grown from 240,000 to 350,000 people or around 45% (Schytz Juul, 2015). If this development continues, then it will be a threat to coherence of the community in the long run.

Equality is a good indicator of how social problems present themselves in relation to crime, substance abuse, mental health, teenage motherhood, etc. The greater the inequality the greater the number of social problems that show up in society (Wilkinson & Pickett, 2010). At the same time greater equality contributes to the wellbeing of people. Equality of rights does not necessarily lead to equality of outcome (Holtung, 2009). Although more children from disadvantaged families in Denmark are entering higher education, this seems to be partly linked to expansion in higher education, in general. Inequality in higher education measured by parental income has been on the rise, although it is still fairly small. This change is the reason attention should be paid to the impact of a universalist welfare state without tuition fees and governmental grants for studies (Thomsen, 2015).

In the European Union greater understanding of the advantages of having an equal society seem to offer mobility across generations:

> We have reached a tipping point. Inequality can no longer be treated as an after-thought. We need to focus the debate on how the benefits of growth are dis-tributed. Our report 'In it Together' and our work on inclusive growth have clearly shown that there doesn't have to be a trade-off between growth and equality. On the contrary, the opening up of opportunity can spur stronger economic performance and improve living standards across the board! (OECD Secretary-General, http://www.oecd.org/social/inequality.htm)

Solidarity

The key and enduring concept of solidarity is a fundamental principle. Mutual trust is still relatively high between Danish people. The expectation is that nobody will exploit the system, that everybody will do their duty, and that everyone will receive rights. This allows the welfare state to provide every-one with the equal right to access social benefits (Askeland & Strauss, 2014). Everyone agrees that all citizens at different times in their lives will need support and care from the free welfare system by providing such services as childcare institutions, schools, education, hospitals, support with rent, and specialised residential care for the disabled and elderly. People believe the state will provide for their needs. Solidarity between the people and the state as provider of their long-term care is the result of such mutual trust. Indeed, the responsibility of the state to provide for all its citizens is enshrined in law. For example, the inclusion of service users' perspectives is enshrined in the Consolidation Act on Legal Protection and Administration in Social Matters of 2012. According to this act citizens have the right to be heard, have access to their own journal, and have the right to appeal (http://eng-lish.sm.dk/media/14899/consolidation-act-on-legal-protection-and-admin-istration-in-social-matters.pdf). Moreover, children have the right to be heard too. In 2012 a childcare office was established to protect the rights of chil-dren and young adults and facilitate their access to an ombudsman to make criticisms, recommendations, and process their perspectives (http://boerne-kontoret.ombudsmanden.dk/laesestof/).

Universality

The state provides universal benefits to families to help them bring up their children. Children and young people have universal rights to free education in schools and universities and are given economic support to cover living expenses while they study when they have reached 18 years of age.

The rights to welfare such as child benefit are independent of the income and wealth of parents. When it comes to special care of disabled children, the state will provide support by assessing the impairment—not the income of the family. Because of the high participation of women in the labour force there is public support of an institutional childcare system providing such services as nurseries, kindergartens, and after-school programmes taught by professional pedagogical staff. Social security provides for people unable to provide for themselves due to illness, accident, unemployment, or old age. Some ongoing benefits are subject to assessment such as free daycare institutions, leisure activities supporting children at risk, rent subsidies, and pension supplements.

Denmark has become a much wealthier country over the last 20 years, but the support and level of benefits from welfare policy have become less generous since the 1990s. This paradox is linked to the advent of New Public Management.

Those three hallmarks of the Danish welfare state correspond very well with the traditional social work principles of human rights, social justice, and combating poverty.

Impact of New Public Management

In 1998 new reforms were introduced that reflected a new era in welfare thinking. The neoliberalist movement that found inspiration in the United States and the United Kingdom emerged in Denmark as well and changed not only social work but also other systems such as the healthcare system and the education system in the way they were governed. The essence of the New Public Management approach was privatisation, contracting, outsourcing, standardisation, efficiency, control, and documentation. The approach gradually dominated the welfare sector and leadership in public administration changed from professional leadership to leadership by lawyers and economists. Responsibility was gradually moved from the state to service users who had to assume more responsibility for their situations. Self-support was to underpin service delivery. The change was criticised for making individuals responsible for their social problems despite the fact that conditions such as illness and unemployment could be linked to sociopolitical and economic structures rather than individual failings.

This legislative change was considered a reintroduction of old concepts such as self-inflicted need (Reintoft, 1998). A potent example of the 1998 reform was the requirement that people who lost their jobs would need to attend educational or work-related programmes as a condition for getting social benefits. Even if involved full time in programmes, people would not receive a regular salary nor gain rights to the higher unemployment benefit to which a person fully employed would be eligible. The transformation was called "from Well-fare to Work-fare."

Although benefits for people without work have generally been reduced, this is especially true of people who have not lived in Denmark for 7 of the last 8 years. This rule clearly targets migrant people as did the earlier introduced and abandoned "Start Help" (Ejrnæs & Strauss, 2014). The government believed reduced benefits would discourage potential migration into Denmark. As the cost of living in Denmark is high migrant families are at risk of becoming marginalised and unable to participate in normal activities in the community.

Professional individual assessment of people's problems and needs from a holistic perspective has been replaced in many instances by ticking of boxes in standard schemes. People working in social services and the health service are required to document their work tasks in detail. Such documentation is very time consuming and many working hours have been lost from direct contact with and support of service users.

The tradition of having the social welfare system provided by public institutions at the national or municipality level has gradually changed and some social care has been outsourced to private organisations though still funded by taxes. The education sector is still mainly public. Some private schools and gymnasiums (i.e., preparatory schools for university) exist but private universities do not.

The argument for privatising the social sector has been to provide better, more effective, and cheaper care under market conditions. Today some private enterprises provide good support, some have made a lot of money by providing care for children and adults in need of special support, while others have gone bankrupt leaving public authorities in the lurch. Documentation on how to improve the sector in light of the problems brought about by privatisation is still missing.

Education has experienced continuous cuts over the years. The significant decrease in preparation time needed by social work educators to keep abreast of advances has made it more difficult for them to find the time to update their knowledge base through literature, new research, and participation in relevant academic activities. As a consequence teachers will often need to reuse material that is no longer up to date. This may lead to more stressed or less engaged teachers, less engaged students, and a general decline in the quality of social work education.

Although resources for measuring quality such as accreditation, evaluations, and reviews of curricula are much more extensive than earlier, resources for quality production such as preparation time for teaching have been declining.

Despite the growing prosperity of the country over the last decades severe cuts have taken place in the public sector including daycare institutions, primary schools, and further education. A recent research study among 35,000 people employed in private and public workplaces found that the number of Danes showing symptoms of work-related stress has increased. This is especially true of public employees the proportion of whom with stress symptoms has increased by 20% compared with 2012, which means that almost one in four public employees working in public service suffers from symptoms of stress. This is a rise of 17% since 2012. The study found that employees directly working with people (such as teachers and pedagogues) are especially vulnerable as a result of not being allowed to perform well enough because of cuts (Lichtenberg, 2018).

History and Development of Social Work Education in Denmark

Since the administration of social legislation needed professional and skilled staff the need arose for a social work profession. The first qualified social helper in Denmark was Manon Lüttichau who was educated in the United States and took up employment in the Psychiatric Department of the Municipality Hospital in Copenhagen in 1934. The first course on social work education was established in 1937 and the following year the Danish Association for Social Workers was set up. The association today has 18,000 members. Since 1942 social work education has been called social advisor education. In this chapter the English terms social worker and social work education are used (Buss & Strauss, 2004).

In 1962 a 3-year course on social work education began and in 2001 it obtained the status of a Bachelor degree. The course was extended to 3.5 years by ministerial order in 2002. The degree is offered in six different schools: Aalborg, http://www.en.aau.dk/; Århus, https://en.via.dk/; Copenhagen, https://www.kp.dk/; Esbjerg, https://www.ucsyd.dk/international; Odense, https://international.ucl.dk/; and Roskilde, https://phabsalon.dk/english/.

Social work courses are usually taught in university colleges in Denmark the exception being Aalborg where they take place in a university.

The faculty in Danish social work education extends beyond the field of social work to such subjects as sociology, law, economy, psychology, and anthropology. The constitution of faculty in this way offers an opportunity for a more holistic understanding of social problems, people, and surrounding society.

In 1968 two social work schools established a full-time, 1-year postgraduate course (Buss & Strauss, 2004). These courses continued until a social work candidate degree became available at Aalborg University in 1992. Although social workers can get a Ph.D. degree in Denmark, only traditional universities are allowed to offer Master's degrees, candidate degrees, and Ph.D.s.

Different specialisations in diploma courses are awarded 20 ECTS (European Credit Transfer and Accumulation System) credits on transfer to university colleges. Moreover, social workers can study various Master's degrees in universities.

Some Danish social workers opt for a doctoral degree from Lund University in Sweden, which is located 65 km from Copenhagen.

Research

Increased academisation of the social work profession has led to research becoming an integral part of education and practice, as well as to increasing expectations of faculty members to include research in their teaching (Askeland & Strauss, 2014).

Research takes place in university colleges, universities, and institutions such as VIVE—the Danish Centre for Social Science Research, https://vive.dk/english/, which is an independent analysis and research centre working within the principal welfare fields.

The theoretical and scientific knowledge base for social work has grown considerably during the last 25 years. Social work students mainly study Danish or Nordic social work literature because it directly relates to the context of local welfare systems and structures. A number of books written in English are also used—mostly after having been translated though.

International Influence

Since 1965 social work education in Denmark has been closely connected with other Nordic social work education systems through the Nordic Association of Schools of Social Work, which is made up of member schools from Norway, Sweden, Finland, Iceland, and Greenland (International Association of Schools of Social Work or IASSW, www.iassw.socwork.org/en/). The European Association of Schools of Social Work has also been an important platform arranging biannual conferences and providing a professional network. *The Global Standards for Social Work Education and Training* were published by the IASSW and the International Federation of Schools of Social Work (ifsw.org) and the document has been used in curriculum development in Copenhagen. *Ethics in Social Work, Statement of Principles* (www.iassw-aiets.org/eng/) published by the same international association is also used in teaching and projects. These regional and global organisations have been important platforms for the exchange of knowledge and ideas to promote excellence in social work education as well as student and staff exchange. The Association for Research on Social Work (Forsa) was established as a special forum to facilitate social work research in Sweden in 1987 (Swedish Association for Social Work Research, http://www.forsa.nu/In-english.aspx) and in Denmark in 1999 (Forsa Denmark, https://forsa.dk/om-forsa).

The professional international organisations founded by social work schools, professionals, teachers, and researchers had to conform to the European Bologna Declaration for Further Education that was agreed by politicians in 1999. This regulation aimed at facilitating and encouraging student and staff mobility and through this develop a more skilled and flexible workforce. The European education system has been highly influenced by introducing a joint system for higher education that can be broken down into Bachelor degrees, Master's degrees, and Ph.D.s and a joint system (the European Credit Transfer and Accumulation System or ECTS) that facilitates the comparison of different modules and semesters across European borders. The mobility of students and staff is supported by Erasmus funding and has led to some mobility over recent decades. Such financial support has encouraged the development of more international modules (described in the following sections).

DANISH SOCIAL WORK EDUCATION TODAY

Local social problems in a globalised world need to be seen within a broad context. This may be even more evident from the perspective of a small country. Having an awareness of roots that are increasingly global necessitates change in social work curricula not only in Denmark but in other Nordic countries too. Reorganisation of the welfare state and neoliberal influences have created new conditions for the organisation, education, and practice of social work. Global awareness requires a curriculum for social work that includes knowledge of global structural transformations and their human consequences. Students need to embrace new perspectives on the global/local dialectic and knowledge on structural power imbalances—globally and locally—and to understand how these may construct stereotypes of otherness (Flem, Jönsson, Alseth, Strauss, & Antczak, 2017).

New topics such as climate, green social work, and sustainability are crucial to social work practice today and in the future.

The Institute of Social Work at University College Copenhagen has a tradition of including international perspectives in social work education courses. The makeup of some of these courses is explained in the following. First, social work education in general is briefly introduced.

In 2017 a total of 2237 social work students started their Bachelor degrees in different social work schools in Denmark. As in many other Western countries social work is a female-dominated profession—only around 7% are males (Als Research, 2013; http://www.alsresearch.dk/English; http://www.alsresearch.dk/uploads/Publikationer/Rapport%20-%20M%C3%A6nd%20p%C3%A5%20socialr%C3%A5dgiveruddannelsen.pdf).

Since students should reflect the community they are going to serve clearly there need to be more male students.

The Danish state influences all parts of the education system such as course duration, course content, and exams. Representatives from various stakeholders take part in committee work together with educational staff and students when a new ministerial order for education is developed. The ministerial order for social work education is changed on a regular basis. The last time was in June 2011, but the length of 3.5 years corresponding to 210 ECTS was maintained. The new ministerial order was:

> The aim of the Bachelor's Degree Programme in Social Work is to qualify graduates to carry out tasks in all aspects of social work. Graduates must be able, in an independent manner and in cooperation with other sectors and professions, to contribute to the prevention and resolution of social problems, as well as to plan, coordinate, carry out, evaluate and further develop measures within social work at the individual, group, organisational and societal levels in the context of public administration, including measures related to employment, actions to be taken, and the private sector. (Ministry of Education, Ministerial Order concerning Professional Bachelor Programmes in Social Work No. 766 of 24/06/2011, section 1 (1), https://www.phmetropol.dk/Uddannelser/Socialraadgiver/Uddannelsen/Studieordninger)

The ministerial order for social work education allows for slightly different interpretations of the order in the six different schools of social work in Denmark. Note that university colleges in Denmark are accredited by the Public National Accreditation Council.

Two Danish schools (Aarhus and Copenhagen) in 2000 established special lines for intercultural–international social work education that could be taught parallel with classical lines. Today only University College Copenhagen offers a fully international–intercultural Bachelor degree in social work.

Changes in society and new possibilities for social workers to gain employment in international social care organisations triggered development of these special lines. Confronting social problems of people with immigrant backgrounds and vulnerable groups in international contexts resulted in growing awareness of how social problems in local contexts are linked to the global structures and institutional arrangements of any society (Payne & Askeland, 2008). The need for more knowledge of international and intercultural perspectives on social work became increasingly more important.

Until the 1970s social work education served a monocultural community. However, in 2018 13.3% of the population were counted as migrants or descendants (descendants are defined as born in Denmark of parents who are neither Danish citizens nor born in Denmark). Society has been unable to support migrants sufficiently well when it comes to their inclusion and full participation in the community. As a consequence some migrant families have become marginalised and vulnerable.

The School of Social Work (Den Sociale Højskole) in Copenhagen was an independent school until 2008 when it merged to become Metropolitan University College (Metropol). After the merger it had almost 10,000 students. In 2018 Metropol merged with University College Copenhagen to become the Institute of Social Work. It now has 20,000 students, 2000 employees, and runs 21 different degree courses. Some 4500 students gain Bachelor degrees here every year. The Institute of Social Work has today around 1500 social work students. Despite changes in the organisational framework the Institute of Social Work has preserved a special focus on international perspectives in education.

Let us now consider the international parts of the social work programme undertaken at University College Copenhagen and explain them further (https://www.kp.dk/om+os/organisation/tal+og+fakta).

The Bachelor curriculum for both the classical and international lines was translated from English (https://www.phmetropol.dk/Uddannelser/Socialraadgiver/Uddannelsen/Studieordninger). Although the international–intercultural line has not been independently translated from English since 2012, special module descriptions of some parts will now be explained.

The social work programme is constructed around themes of more weeks, and different professions support with their special knowledge into a broad knowledge base of the theme. The approach to teaching is similar for both lines of the programme and constructed not only around lectures, but also places a lot of emphasis on students' responsibility for their own learning. They are expected to achieve the required competencies partly on their own through theoretical studies, group discussions, group exercises, written exercises, writing synopses, and writing Bachelor theses under supervision. Some written assignments can also take place in groups. The expectation is that students will learn from each other by engaging in discussions and reflections. Students are invited to present theory in class, to engage with other students, and to share their opinions. This has the added benefit of improving their competencies in expressing themselves and developing their personal and professional competencies to perform well in future positions. All students in internships are required to reflect upon their experiences by writing three reflective log assignments about (1) their personal experience from the social, political, cultural, organisational, and regulatory context; (2) alternative actions and decisions that could have been taken and underlying assumptions as to why they could have been taken; and (3) their personal emotions, dynamics between themselves and people they work with, and power to be had in relationships.

Attendance by students at such interstudent discussions is not mandatory and their participation is sometimes quite low. At the same time their reading of academic texts seems to be declining too. This can be attributed to students being accustomed to the Internet and virtual platforms that provide entertaining, illustrated, quick, and easily accessible information. The various pedagogical tools currently being used may not to be sufficient today. Teachers will need not only high academic skills and professional experience, but the competency to make teaching more entertaining to hold the interest of students. The lack of preparation time (as mentioned above) may also affect attendance and preparation among students.

International Exchange of Students

Danish social work students in University College Copenhagen are encouraged to go abroad to carry out some of their theoretical or practical studies as it is believed that they will benefit both professionally and personally through theoretical studies or internship in Europe or other regions of the world. Although the European Union gives some funding for studies in its member states, Danish state funding supports studies outside Europe. However, only around 4% or around 60 students per year take advantage of the opportunity.

International–Intercultural Bachelor Program in Copenhagen: Introduction

The introduction to this program is written in Danish. My translation of it in English is: "The international–intercultural Bachelor specialisation programme focusses on international– intercultural perspectives. Teaching addresses social problems and social work in a diverse globalised world. Although the legal framework and the modules are the same as those of the classical line, intercultural–international perspectives are more in the focus. Understanding of social problems and social work from an intercultural and international perspective within Denmark, outside Denmark, and in the European Union forms a significant part of the programme. Students become engaged with social work and social problems within a global perspective and they are challenged to bring global perspectives into local work. Although internship abroad is an opportunity, it is not mandatory" (the Danish original is available at https://www.phmetropol.dk/uddannelser/socialraadgiver/uddannelsen/uddannelsens_opbygning/den_interkulturelle_og_internationale_studieretning). The international Bachelor degree is taught in Danish. There has been growing interest in establishing such an international specialisation in Copenhagen and other places of study during the last couple of years.

Comparative Perspectives on Social Work with Young People (Elective Module)

For the last 15 years a course on social work with young people has been taught in English as part of the Copenhagen social work programme. It is taught as an elective module to around 20 students. The students comprise Danish students and students from other European social work schools. Over the last couple of years some American students have attended part of the module. Allowing students to mix in this way gives them the possibility to gain comparative perspectives on social work in different countries and to reflect on the impact different welfare systems have on people. In addition, they learn first-hand what differences in culture means from their international fellow students.

There are obstacles to including students from developing countries in social work courses other than migrant students now resident in Denmark. If students from developing countries could participate in such courses, then fellow students would not only get a more comprehensive worldview they would also learn much more about social work elsewhere.

The aim of the Social Work with Young People course is to explore and qualify such work. This topic is important to social work everywhere and of special interest to almost all young students. It is a field in which all students already have some knowledge from their home countries emboldening them not just to follow the course but to contribute to it. Danish and international comparative perspectives on policies, theories, methods, and social practices are applied throughout the course. The course focusses on three themes: (1) welfare policies and rights, (2) the constitution of identities, and (3) young people in vulnerable positions and at risk of marginalisation from mainstream society. The course includes lectures, workshops, field visits, written and digital assignments, and practice-related exercises. Students must submit an individually prepared synopsis for individual oral examination. The module lasts 10 weeks (or 15 ECTS) and is taught in English.

International Social Work (Elective Module)
The International Social Work elective module lasts 10 weeks (or 15 ECTS) and widens professional perspectives of social work by looking beyond the borders of Denmark and seeking to prepare the student for international social work and social work linked to war, conflict, emergency aid, support, and developmental work. The focus is on a collective approach to methods and the interplay between health, poverty, and social problems. The course is taught in Danish.

Social Work in Urban Areas (Semester)
Four different European schools of social work from four different countries developed the Social Work in Urban Areas international semester (30 ECTS) to be taught in English. The schools in the partnership were the Copenhagen School of Social Work (Denmark), Amsterdam School of Social Work (the Netherlands), Helsinki School of Social Work (Finland), and Artevelde School of Social Work (Belgium). Representatives from the faculty of each school participated in meetings about programme planning over a period of two preparatory years. It was hoped joining forces to develop a course lasting a semester where specialist knowledge acquired by the schools involved would offer a learning opportunity that was both high quality and full of expert

knowledge. The expectation was that this would be a learning process for all faculty members that would also impact other modules in the schools. The semester was taught for the first time during fall 2017 in Copenhagen.

The four partners presented cities as a new point of departure for contemporary social work. The programme puts forward the proposition that social workers are key to organising a world in which all voices are heard especially those of vulnerable and marginalised citizens and communities in any city. To this end social workers must be co-producers in creating what UN-Habitat calls "a new urban paradigm for the city we need" (UN-Habitat, 2014). Promoting everyone's right to the city is the idea underlying intervention at the city level. This programme offers perspectives and tools on how social work can link the global agenda (IASSW, 2010) to an urban context and thereby motivate future social workers to envision the type of city we need.

The introduction to the curriculum states:

> Globalisation and associated processes of urbanisation have far-reaching consequences for the majority of the population. More than 50% of the European population lives in urban areas, a number that will increase to 75% by 2050. Migration, economic recession and increasing inequalities among others, are factors that change our cities. The city is involved in global processes but at the same time local enough to have impact on the decision-making processes that influence the life of citizens. This context challenges social work practitioners who experience limits and constraints on influencing the situation.

The *UN-Habitat 2012 Manifesto for Cities* accordingly argues, "the battle for a more sustainable future will be won or lost in cities" (UN-Habitat, 2014).

The Social Work in Urban Areas course will rotate between the four different schools every fall semester. Although each school has expertise in specific themes, one or more faculty members from every school teaches a part of the course every semester as a guest teacher.

European funding supports the exchange of European students as well as staff. Having students from different countries in the same classroom for a longer course is one way of supporting these aspirations. Funding the participation of students from developing countries in the classroom would increase the potential.

Concluding Remarks

The development and creation of the Danish welfare system has taken around 100 years. The ethics of the profession adheres to human rights and fits well with the traditional principles of universality, equality, and solidarity of the Danish welfare system.

Although the Danish welfare system has been able to prevent and reduce social problems linked to children at risk, marginalised families, people without work, mental health patients, and other people exposed to risk for much longer, a holistic assessment of individual social problems was the starting point for professional support.

New public management and privatisation do not fit well with the classical ideas of solidarity, equality, and universality of the Danish welfare system. Neoliberalism made Denmark a more unequal nation. Severe cuts in welfare have taken place at the same time as Denmark became more prosperous. Cuts have affected the conditions of children in daycare institutions, primary schools, the educational system overall, and the health system.

Since welfare cuts affect people at risk and in need of support of the welfare system, their opportunities to be compensated by social support and thereby overcome their problems have diminished. Moreover, people's lives in general have been affected since a significant part of the working population today is suffering from stress-related symptoms, which can be linked to demands for high-level efficiency every day in workplaces despite fewer staff.

It should always be kept in mind that education is investment in the future and that maintaining Denmark as a dynamic, rich, and innovative country is highly dependent on education.

Global awareness requires a curriculum for social work that includes knowledge of global structural transformations and their human consequences. International social work organisations are important to continuous development of professional papers on ethical principles, definition of social work, and global standards for social work education and training. Social work education in Copenhagen has prioritised innovation and the development of international elements by bringing students of different nationalities together in the classroom in a process that underpins global awareness and understanding.

REFERENCES

(Danish titles translated into English)

Askeland, G. A., & Strauss, H. (2014) The Nordic Welfare model. In C. Noble, H. Strauss, & B. Littlechild (Eds.), *Global social work—Crossing borders, blurring boundaries.* Sydney, NSW: Sydney University Press.

Buss, L. G., & Strauss, H. (2004). Socialrådgiverprofessionen. In *Relationsprofessioner.* **Eng**: The social work profession. In L. Moos, J. Krejsler & P. F. Lauersen (Eds.), *Professions of relations.* Copenhagen, Denmark: Danish Pedagogical University.

Ejrnæs, M., & Strauss, H. (2014). Challenges to human rights and social justice in Denmark: An analysis of the "start help" program. In L. Dominelli & M. Moosa-Mitha (Eds.), *Reconfiguring citizenship.* Farnham, UK: Ashgate.

Flem, A. L., Jönsson, J. H., Alseth, A.-K., Strauss, H., & Antczak, H. (2017). Revitalising social work education through global and critical awareness—Examples from three Scandinavian schools of social work. *European Journal of Social Work, 20*(1), 76–87.

Greve, B. (2013): What is welfare and public welfare? In B. Greve (Eds.), *The Routledge handbook of the welfare state*. Abingdon: Routledge.

Helliwell, J., Layard, R., & Sachs, J. (2018). *World Happiness Report 2018*. New York: Sustainable Development Solutions Network.

Holtung, N. (2009). Lige muligheder som ideal i politisk filosofi. I *Lige muligheder for alle – social arv, kultur og retfærdighed*. In Holtung & Lippert-Rasmussen (Eds.), *Nyt fra Samfundsvidenskaberne*. Frederiksberg, DK. **Eng**: Holtung, N. (2009). Equal opportunities as an ideal in political philosophy. In Holtung & Lippert-Rasmussen(Eds.), *Equal opportunities for everyone: Social enheritage, culture and justice*. Frederiksberg, Denmark.

International Association of Schools of Social Work. (2010). www.iassw-aiets.org.

Lichtenberg, E. (2018). https://translate.google.com/translate?hl=en&sl=da&u= www.ae.dk/sites/www.ae.dk/files/dokumenter/analyse/ae_flere-oplever-stress-isaer-blandt-offentligt-ansatte_.pdf&prev=search.

Payne, M., & Askeland, G. A. (2008). *Globalization and international social work: Postmodern change and challenge*. London, UK: Ashgate.

Reintoft. (1998). *Træd Varsomt. Dansk socialpolitik ved en korsvej*. **Eng**: Take care: Danish social policy at a crossroad Hans Reitzel. Copenhagen, Denmark.

Schiermarcher, I., & Høgh, H. (2006). *Moralske begrundelser for forandringer af socialhjælp*. **Eng**: Moral reasons for changes of social help. Den Sociale Højskole. Copenhagen, Denmark.

Schytz Juul, J. (2015). Udvikling i økonomisk ulighed i Danmark. Samfundsøkonomen. **Eng:** Development of inequality in Denmark. *Journal of Economics of Society, 3,* 12–17.

Thomsen, J. P. (2015). Maintaining inequality effectively? Access to higher education programs in a universalist welfare state in periods of educational expansion 1984–2010. *European Sociological Review, 31*(6), 683–696.

UN-Habitat. (2014). unhabitat.org/urban-thinkers-the-city-we-need.

Wilkinson, R., & Pickett, K. (2010). *The spirit level: Why greater equality makes societies stronger*. New York, NY: Bloomsbury Press.

CHAPTER 11

Teaching Social Work Skills Online

Sharif Haider

Rapid advancement of ICTs is impacting on every walk of our life. Social work is not immune to it, but the adoption of ICTs in social work is slow (e.g. Baker, Warburton, Hodgkin, & Pascal, 2014). Resource deficiency, practitioners' attitudes and understanding, confidence in using ICTs, inadequate infrastructure, and lack of professional development are some of the few reasons why ICTs are not fully immersed with social work practice. However, research regarding adopting ICTs has suggested that potentially ICTs could improve the provision of social work and support practitioners to become efficient and productive. Not only social work practice but also education could gain much out of the advancement of ICTs to deliver social work education creatively and meaningfully. It is because ICTs opened up a new frontier whereby its flexibility diminished the idea of specific time and space to deliver social work education. Undoubtedly ICTs opened up a number of technological innovation to:

- support problem-centred learning and enable students to apply life experience and previous learning;
- offer flexibility in relation to time, space, mode, and pacing to accommodate students' needs;
- provide a platform to collaborate with and learn from peers;
- allow teachers to become creative in the way they deliver, transfer, and disseminate knowledge;
- provide the platform to feedback students regularly and constructively.

S. Haider (✉)
The Open University, Milton Keynes, UK
e-mail: s.m.haider@open.ac.uk

S. S. M. et al. (eds.), *The Palgrave Handbook of Global Social Work Education*, https://doi.org/10.1007/978-3-030-39966-5_11

169

For the above reasons and because of the increased expectations of students and pressure on savings money, a number of universities and colleges are now adopting ICTs fully or partially to deliver social work education. Some pedagogical debate has indicated that face-to-face contact is important to cognitive and meta-cognitive skills to teach social work students (Lyons, 1999); it is based on a belief that a vocational qualification such as social work focuses on relationship building and working jointly with individuals to make positive changes to their life. That means interpersonal skills development is vital as well as their communication, problem-solving, critical thinking, decision-making, teamwork, and critical reflection skills. Questions have been raised as to whether online technologies are adequate to teach students those skills. A number of research (e.g. Al-Mubaid, 2014; Oterholm, 2009) now indicate that this is not only possible technically but also it is preferred by some students and employers due to the flexibility it offers in relation to time and space to engage students who are not able to attend face-to-face sessions. Also, this mode of learning is cost effective in reaching out to hard-to-access student groups.

The aim of the chapter is to explore how core social work skills can be taught and facilitated via online media. In order to achieve this, the chapter discusses critical reflection which will be used as a framework to demonstrate how problem-solving, critical thinking, decision-making, communication, and team working could be taught to social work students. With this in mind, the chapter will initially discuss what is critical reflection and its significance in social work. This will lead to a discussion of an array of models of critical reflection. Discussion will then focus on how students can learn core social work skills online through the framework of critical reflection. A range of teaching strategies based on research evidence are incorporated to demonstrate how teachers play a pivotal role in developing an effective learning environment and supporting students in learning core social work skills. Challenges of teaching core social work skills online as well as a way forward are explored at the end of the chapter. Before understanding critical reflection it is vital to grasp the concept of reflection.

REFLECTION

An experienced driver changes gear and drives a car according to the road condition without thinking about the mechanism of changing gear—he or she will push the clutch all the way down and release it steadily so the car does not judder when turning right or left. Simultaneously he or she holds the steering wheel, looking at the mirror before signalling to turn right or left. An experienced driver performs these tasks unconsciously but learner drivers first need to learn, then try, and evaluate whether they are doing these procedures correctly and safely; they then amend their action if required.

Similarly, when we walk, we do not think about the mechanisms of walking. But when we stop and think how we walk—i.e. what the body goes through physiologically to permit us to walk; which law of motion explains walking; how we could walk better or differently on a different road and in different circumstance—we start to reflect. Reflection entails thinking about and analysing one's experience and action with an aim to improve understanding and practice. Active thinking about our experiences leads us to explore what worked and what did not. Then we are in a position to put an improved plan into action. An unconscious student social worker becomes a conscious student social worker and develops his or her practice through reflection. Autopilot mode of social work practice stops when students start to reflect and take the responsibility of changing their practice, i.e. start to develop themselves.

Reflective practice enables a student social worker to learn from his or her experience and continuously develop his or her practice. It is an ongoing mechanism to transform social work practice. It is like a confession and self-interrogation of one's own self.

Prerequisite to becoming a social work professional is to open to new challenges, explore different and alternatives avenues, and recognise how these interact with the existing, political, economic, social, and technological environment. As a result of this, social work will become an authoritative discipline.

Benefits of Reflection

Reflection (Kolb, 1984) could bring the following benefits to the practice of a student social worker:

- It enables students to become conscious about their own practice. This is important because it breaks the status quo of practice and changes their social work practice. Consequently, they become better practitioners.
- It involves the social work practice becoming person-centred.
- It clarifies what students are doing well and what knowledge and skills they need to develop further and the reason why.
- It allows students to become evidenced-based practitioners.
- It develops students' own repository of tips, techniques, and tools for best social work practice.
- Most of us read articles, research papers, and reports that are useful to put into practice, but some of us do not do this. Reflection creates that opportunity to absorb new ideas and concepts and to assess their effectiveness upon our own practice
- Reflection enables a student social worker to plan for a social work session way ahead; so that, the session can be managed effectively.
- It can deter students from repeating mistakes.
- It enables them to challenge their own beliefs and assumptions, which could prevent them from providing good quality services.

REFLECTIVE VS REFLEXIVE

Some writers have argued that the concepts 'reflective' and 'reflexive' are identical and can be applied interchangeably. However, there are fundamental differences between these two terms. Reflection is related to reflection, i.e. the process of thinking or reviewing actions, of analysing an incident. Thompson and Thompson (2008) perceive 'reflective' as being 'self-aware'. On the other hand, "reflexive" means the ability to reorganise one's own influence on practice. We all have certain values, beliefs, experience, and culture; they affect the way we practise social work. Recognising these underlying but fundamental factors enables a student of social work to explore the reason for his or her behaviours and actions. Unearthing this will involve a student social worker delving deeper into his or her social work practice. This is a deeper level of reflection. That means that reflexivity is part of reflection or a consequence of reflection (Ingram, Fenton, Hodson, & Juindal-Snape, 2014). For example, when a student social worker is asked to explain their values, they became reflective.

- How I influenced the outcome of my social work practice?
- Why I behaved in this way?
- Why I felt the way I felt during my practice and now?
- What beliefs and values I have that affected my action?
- What beliefs and values I need to challenge to see an alternative or different perspective other than mine?

Deeper level of reflection is what a student social worker should strive for. In order to achieve this, students need to aim to use reflexive practice in reflection.

CRITICAL REFLECTION

Critical reflection is 'a process which is partially based on, and integrates elements of deconstructive thinking. It can provide a means of reconstructing, and thus change the ways in which individuals perceive and relate to their social worlds' (Fook, 2004, p. 16). When students uncover power dynamics in relationships and challenge their implicit assumptions and values, they become critically reflective (Brookfield, 1995). The aim to reflect critically is to apply theories and research to practise. By doing so students challenge underlying assumptions of their social work practice.

The next section focuses on a range of frameworks to support reflection. These frameworks need to be taught to students to reflect critically; they act as a vehicle to learn core social work skills online.

The Gibbs Framework

Gibbs (1988) provided six stages of a reflection framework:

Description of the event: The first stage of Gibbs reflective cycle is to describe an event (Fig. 11.1). The following questions would enable a student social worker to focus on the reflective event:

- What role I played?
- What was the context of the event?
- Who were involved and what were their role and responsibilities?
- What exactly happened?
- What outcomes I planned to achieve?
- What were the outcomes?

Feelings and Thoughts: At this stage, a student social worker would think about his or her emotions, the feelings and thinking at the time of social work. Basically, this stage enables a social worker to become self-aware:

- How did you feel during the event?
- What were your thinking?

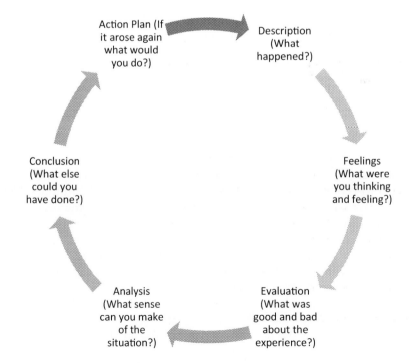

Fig. 11.1   Gibb's (1988) reflective cycle

- How did it make you feel or how did a team member make you feel?
- What did you think about the outcome you achieved?
- What are your thinking and feeling now?

Evaluate: Now a student social worker needs to evaluate the event or incident; i.e., they need to make a judgement regarding what has happened by exploring both positive and negative aspects of that incident.

Analysis: Information from the previous stage will support this stage because in this stage a student social worker will explore critically what worked, what did not work, and then why that worked or didn't work. Also, questions, such as what should have happened, need to be asked. Honesty and transparency are vital to obtain the best outcome from this stage.

Conclusion: As information and analysis are available now, this is the ultimate question, what a student social worker might have done differently.

Action Plan: In this stage, an action plan needs to be devised to learn from the experience. It could be that a learning gap will be identified from the reflection. An action plan will then enable the student social worker to move forward so that practice will improve in future.

This reflective cycle can be applied in reflection-on-action as well as reflection-for-action.

5 Whys

Using questions, to start with 'why' enables a student social worker to delve deeper into the underlying issues and problems. This is flexible and easy to remember. There is no set of prescribed questions but one needs to bear in mind that this is the main strength of this approach. It enables us to formulate questions depending on the circumstances.

These can be used in conjunction with other techniques. It does not need to be 5 whys; it can be less or more, until an answer cannot be found.

It is vital that a student social worker knows the reason why he or she is engaged in certain things. Sometimes these can be invisible until a student social worker constantly asks question 'why' to go right into the heart of the issue. The 5 whys framework would provide them with a rationale that is probably ingrained in a deeper level of their intentions. However, the 'why' question is not a nice one; it can feel threatening when it is repeated 5 times. An example of how this framework can be applied about a line manager's behaviour is shown below:

- Why am I feeling annoyed?
  – It is because he did not follow what he agreed last time.
- Why can't I allow …It is a voluntary agreement?
  – I know he won't do it; as his line manager, I know that he always says 'yes' to everything but does not deliver on time.

- Why do I think he would do the same thing, if I let him, again?
  - Because he did not follow all his action plan.
- Why I would not ask him to stop him doing all the unnecessary tasks on a regular basis?

Depending on the answer of the last question you can ask another question by using 'why'.

REHEARSING

This technique is good for reflect-for-action in planning stage of a session. Student social workers could rehearse what and how they are going to perform certain tasks. They may rehearse what they do if things do not go according to their plan as well rehearsing the plan. This technique gives confidence to the student social worker before an event, because they have prepared for the event.

5 Ws 1H

5 Ws 1H is a simple technique, easy to remember but effective for critical reflection. It can be adaptable to various circumstances in three reflective frameworks: 5 Ws 1H stands for,

What?
Why?
When?
Where?
Who?
How?

They are the prefixes for questions based on an incident or circumstance or practice. This technique can be used to gather information as well as to achieve a particular outcome.

What—a question starting with 'what' enables student social workers to focus their reflections and set the parameter for reflection as well as enabling them to gather available information. What needs to be reflected and why can be explored easily by using 'what' at the beginning of the questions:

- What am I trying to achieve for reflection on this incident?
- What am I trying to achieve from this session?
- What do I want to learn from this session or this practice?
- What outcome do I want from the practice?
- What do I want to reflect (a critical incident, an incident, a circumstance, a specific practice, a session, etc.)?

- What framework is appropriate for reflection?
- What are the consequences of using a particular framework?

Why—'why' question allows us to delve deeper into an incident or event. It goes right into the heart of reflection—why I am reflecting, i.e. significance of reflection. As stated earlier in this chapter, reflection should not be an onerous chore for student social workers as they have many things that they need to do to manage the team. Reflection should be part and parcel of their role. Hence, reflecting upon every little practice or an incident is not a good use of their valuable time. They need to pick and choose. This question would enable them to select the reason why they need to reflect on a specific practice and incident.

In social work, the 'why' question enables social workers to explore why they did or what they did or why they are doing or what they are doing or why they want to go this way. This will lead student social workers to unpack their theoretical and practical knowledge and enables each of them to establish his or her suitability in practice, i.e. effectiveness of their practice will be revealed by posing this question. It will also inform a student social worker about his or her cultural norms, values, assumptions, and understanding of certain matters that he or she practise.

When—In relation to reflection, the question starting with 'when' allows a student social worker to be specific regarding when to explore and reflect on a specific practice and incident, when to take action to improve practice. Specifically in reflect-in-action student social workers may want to take action straight away to change their practice. Questions starting with 'when' encourage them to prioritise their action with commitment. When we reflect while working, we are reflecting-in-action, i.e. we are reflecting in the midst of an event. However, we reflect-on-action when we reflect after the incident or event.

Where—this question permits a student social worker to identify a space for reflection. Also, this question is helpful to identify a space for group reflection. For group reflection space can be an important factor so that everyone can attend without disruption to their reflection. This is for fixed and formal reflection.

Who—questions that start with 'who' allow a student social worker to consider how his or her decision and action impact on whom. Also, this question enables a student social worker to decide with whom he or she wants to do the reflecting:

– Who is going to be affected by the outcome?

How—questions that start with 'how' lead us to understand the best way to reflect as well as the way student social workers can learn from their reflection:

– How can I reflect effectively?

BORTAN'S FRAMEWORK

Bortan's (1970) framework can be used in three aspects of reflection: reflect-for-action, reflect-in-action, and reflect-for-action. It is very simple and easy to remember, and it does not suggest particular types or questions; rather, it is open and flexible. Similar to the 5Ws 1H the prefixes of the question are:

- What
- So what
- Now what

What: Questions that start with 'what' enable student social workers to explore their practice or an incident. For example, they want to ask questions like:

- What is happening, what happened, and what is my plan.
- What am I doing, what did I do, what were my values, what were my assumptions, what was my feeling, what were the consequences of my actions, and what did other workers do.

This is descriptive phase of reflection but allows student social worker to focus on specific issues and incidents.

So What: So what influences a student social worker to ask challenging questions: it will also challenge the way student social workers carry out social work and how they do it.

- So what I did this
- So what my decision was this
- So what I do not achieve what I wanted to achieve
- So what I need to do differently
- So what were my alternative interventions
- So what knowledge, research, and values I applied.

Now What: The last question starts with 'now what'. This is to move student social workers to develop an action plan:

- Now what action do I need to take?
- Now what needs to change?
- Now what do I need to learn or develop further?

This framework can be applied in reflection-in-action but this section is suitable only for reflection-on-action.

OPERATIONAL MATTERS

Online Media

Generally online forums and live online tutorials are widely used to facilitate fundamental social work skills online. Mostly live online tutorials replicate the face-to-face classroom environment using a conferencing software programme (Fig. 11.2). On the other hand, communication in online forums are mostly text-based where students put their views, comments, answers, questions, and opinions and reply to other students/teachers posts.

Some distance learning institutes have different forums. For example, the Open University in the UK has tutor group forums, module wide forums, and welcome café or forum. They have different purposes. For example, welcome café or welcome forum or opening forum is time limited; it opens generally four weeks before students start their course and ends one or two weeks after the start date then the forums become 'read only'; it deals with initial queries and advice about the course before students officially start. A tutor group forum is specific to a tutor group. Only students from that group have access to the forum; mostly this for is used to facilitate and teach social work skills. Usually an allocated teacher of the group facilitates and supports students to carry out critical reflection and learn fundamental social work skills. Last but not least is the module wide forums where students' posts queries not related to their tutorial group, e.g. sharing ideas with other fellow students outside their own tutor group. It stays open across the whole presentation of a course or module and all students of the module or course have access to this forum (Fig. 11.3).

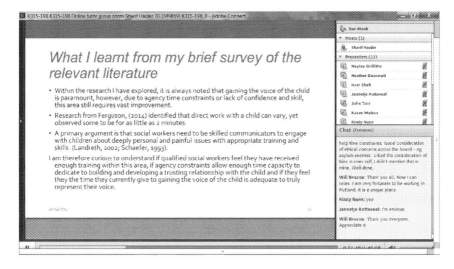

Fig. 11.2 A screenshot of the author's online tutorial

There are other types of forums, for example, study skills forums, guest forums, ICT support forums, etc. (Fig. 11.4).

Teachers need to focus on three areas to facilitate or teach social work skills online:

- Developing or creating the online environment;
- Use appropriate teaching strategies;
- Provide online support.

Netiquette: Both online forums and online live tutorials can be used, i.e. to facilitate social work skills sessions virtually. In order to create a conducive environment for students to interact, engage, and be involved in the forum it is vital for teachers to include welcome messages and ice breakers and set the ground rules. Research shows that engaging students from distance fully depends on creating a relaxed environment in which students feel a sense of belonging. In order to achieve this teachers need to develop a safe space in which students feel at ease and comfortable to discuss matters freely without anxiety and fear (Haider, 2015).

At the start of the course, teachers can co-develop ground rules with students. Ground rules set the tone for online interaction. These rules are a contract between teachers and students about online netiquette. They are vital

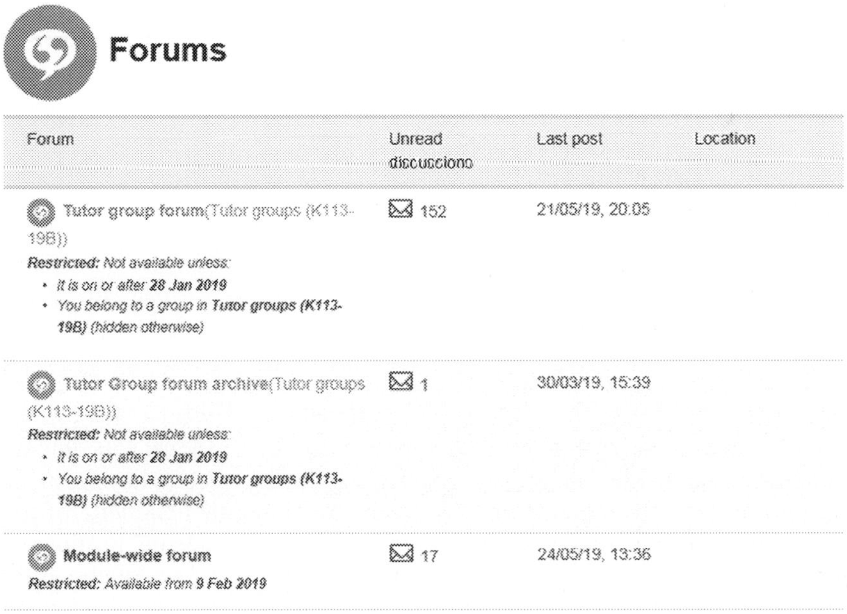

Fig. 11.3   An example of a screenshot of types of forums (OU, 2019)

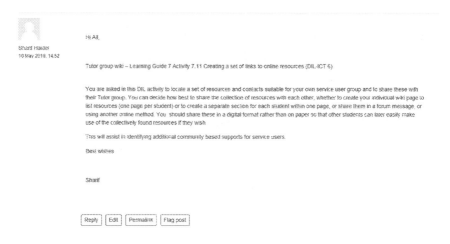

Fig. 11.4 An example of a tutor group forum

because students discuss and debate about service users, carers and family members' private and confidential matters. Some of the ground rules could be:

- Commitment to respecting and valuing others.
- Rights to keep confidentiality.
- Listen to each other.
- Appreciate different opinions.
- Be willing to share and accept.
- Get involved—workshops and forums.
- No such thing as a 'daft' question.
- Respect boundaries and confidentiality with sensitivity.
- Learning environment—challenge the ideas but not the people.
- Respect the group—turn up on time, mobiles off/silent.

Buelens, Totte, Deketelaere, and Dierickx (2009) found that establishing netiquette or ground rules did not make any difference to students' postings but it is vital to create a climate and environment required to learn fundamental social work skills. They suggested providing guidelines about how to make postings informative and academically acceptable alongside netiquette of students' postings; they observed that guidelines improve students' postings. It is highly recommended that teachers set the boundaries and netiquette at the initial stage of the course to minimise conflict and problems at a later stage. Furthermore, it is important to keep netiquette information simple and short;

as Haider (2015) showed, long posting could be off-putting for some students and reduce students' online level of engagement.

Clarifying the purposes, expectations and how students might use forums enable them to take control of their studies and not to feel lost. Students may not understand—especially those who are distance learning social work students—the pedagogical benefits of interaction freely available in online forums and subsequently their impact on their overall learning and development.

> **Tips**
>
> Research showed that regular virtual contact via online forums reduces students' isolation (Sainsbury & Barnes, 2014). Creating a thread in online forums allows teachers to disseminate vital information about the course, e.g. contents, assessments, and making criteria. This technique reduces students' anxiety and fear.

Case Study or Critical Incident analysis: In order to facilitate and teach social work skills online-critical thinking, critical reflection, problem-solving, non-verbal communication, and team working—teachers should use problem focused and relevant case studies or a critical incident analysis. Learning objectives and outcomes should be established before a case study or critical incident analysis is used. Before using a case study or a critical incident analysis teachers need to provide guidance and instructions on how to analyse the case or deconstruct a critical incident for students. Before analysing case studies students need to learn how they should reflect by using reflective frameworks.

> **Tips**
>
> Posting an example about how to reflect and then critically reflect on an incident enables students to engage in the online forums and they will start to learn the skills. It helps students to get started. Also, adding a start message that demonstrates to the students what the teacher is aiming to achieve helps to keep the discussion in the forum focused.

Guidance: With ground rules, it is important to inform students of the purpose of online forums or live online tutorials. Clarifying expectations helps teachers to manage the virtual learning environment. Thorpe (2012) prescribed to establish the purpose of forums or live sessions so that students understand their roles and responsibilities, and what to expect from the forums and sessions. Setting the goal will also enable tutors to manage the sessions or forums.

Effective management and participation of online forums can develop a learning 'community' in which even distance learning students will not become isolated from learning social work skills.

Online forums should be developed in such a way that students and teachers can construct knowledge by sharing their views, experiences, ideas, simultaneously challenging existing knowledge. By doing all these they become part of the learning community.

Ice breaking activities: An ice breaking activity makes students feel at ease and comfortable (Ter-Stepanian, 2012) and the learning environment becomes less threatening. Ice breaking and first online activities do not need to be based on deep cognitive questions and topics. They could be personal and social questions or/and reflection (Anderson, 2009). The aim should be to engage students in a friendly and supportive manner to interact freely with their teachers and fellow students early in the course. Anderson (2009) perceived that virtual interaction builds up the relationships between students, and between students and their teachers.

Research has suggested (e.g. Barnes & Sainsbury, 2015; Haider, 2015) that when teachers provide examples of what students need to do, and what and how to contribute, students find it easy to get started. For example, teachers could participate in the ice breaking activity then students would follow. Modelling like this not only encourages students to engage, interact, and create a conducive environment, but also provides a direction and reduces uncertainty, anxiety, and initial fear. As Dennen (2005) stated, 'discussion participation will not just happen on its own. Learners look to the instructor to shape their interactions'.

Teachers' initial messages and their subsequent response to their students also set the tone of the forum. The use of words, phrases, and contents of language should be supportive. Teachers need to be extra vigilant and careful specifically in the language they use in online forums. Absence of non-verbal cues makes it difficult for students to understand some of the words, phrases, concepts, and ideas in online forums. From research findings (Haider, 2015), we now know that simple, short, concise, and supportive words and phrases allow students to effortlessly understand messages from teachers. It does not need to be formal; it can be relaxed. Concise and succinct messages enable students to become engaged; lengthy or too wordy messages could disengage students. For this reason, effective distance learning teachers should create two to three threads in online forums to welcome students, disseminate essential course information, and break the ice.

Online environment can create an effective and productive environment for learning and practice social work skills as long as it designs and manages to empower and engage students.

Questioning and interrogating: In a face-to-face classroom environment, students ask question to clarify ideas and concepts but in online forum this is difficult to achieve. However, in live online tutorials via a conferencing software programme, students can use microphones and speakers to question, discuss and debate with their teachers or fellow students.

After analysing case studies students provide their views, opinions, and solutions about the problems in the case study. A teacher's role is to encourage students to discuss and debate in the online forums. If it is a live online tutorials students could discuss and debate virtually through their microphone and speaker. It is vital for teachers to provide guidelines to students about how to questions their peers regarding their comments, views, and solutions.

> **Tips**
>
> Ensure that students are clear about the purpose and expectations of the forums and online tutorials. A joint activity to develop the purpose and expectations of online forums and online tutorials sets the boundary and make students' responsible and accountable.

- What are the issues and concerns of the case?
- How are these issues and concerns constructed in your social work practice setting?
- What personal, social, historical, cultural, institutional, and political values support this construction?
- What knowledge, values, skills, and research evidence informed your practice?
- Why did you use specific knowledge, values, skills, and research evidence in your practice?
- How your intervention impact on service users, carers, and family members?
- Who benefits from your interventions?
- Who became disadvantaged because of your intervention?
- How has this practice impacted on service users, carers, public, and your organisation?
- What are the power relations between you and service users or cares or family members or all, you and your organisation?
- What are the alternatives to your intervention?
- What do you need to do to apply alternative?
- How will you change your practice?
- How will you maintain, monitor, and evaluate new changes?
- What are your justifications for alternative options?

Box 1 Examples of Critical Reflective questions

Research showed (e.g. Haider, 2015) that some teachers use Socratic style questions to support students:

1. Questions for clarification;
2. Questions that probe assumptions;
3. Questions that probe reasons and evidence;
4. Questions about viewpoints and perspectives;
5. Questions that probe implications and consequences;
6. Questions about the question.

These questions encourage students to challenge each other's positions. Asking appropriate questions is vital to develop critical and analytical thinking. It also supports deep learning because students are not only trying to solve the problems in the case study but also to explore alternatives solutions and justifications of their arguments.

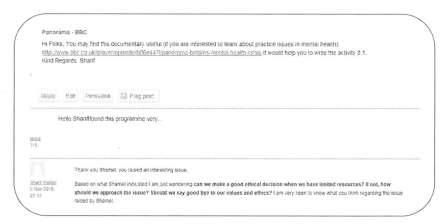

Box 2 An example of asking challenging questions.

Teachers need to carefully read students' posts and ask them questions to support them in their debate. Sometimes teachers use challenging questions to encourage students to think differently or explore alternative perspectives and solutions; sometimes they use testing question to assess students' understanding of issues and concepts (Haider, 2015).

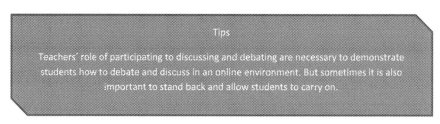

Haider (2015) also found that teachers need to proactively look at the messages and answer them with the three types of questions (illustrated in previous section) to improve students' engagement and interaction in online forums.

Social Presence: Social presence is about forum users' awareness and understanding of each other as 'real people' and as community members (Gunawardena, 1995). Social presence is critical for learning and teaching fundamental social work skills online. Such presence enables students to have dialogue, discussion, and debate with their fellow students and teachers. By doing so their ability to think analytically, critically, and reflectively improves. As a result students' performance improves. Research (e.g. Kear, 2010) indicated that delay in responses to messages and lack of visual cues does not provide students with a sense of social presence. In order to improve the sense of social presence, Kear (2010) suggested creating online profiles, with photos, and some personal information to make forums less threatening. However, sharing photos and personal information could be perceived as disclosing private information but as long as students and tutors agree to do so then it could positively impact a social presence.

Tips

Use supportive, encouraging and motivating language to engage and involve students in online forums.

After learning about how to create a conducive environment and ways to support students to learn core social work skills, the focus of the next section will be exploring a range of challenges that teachers will encounter and how they should overcome them.

CHALLENGES OF USING ONLINE FORUMS TO TEACH SOCIAL WORK SKILLS

Using forum to criticise teachers and managers: Artis (2014) and Barnes and Sainsbury (2015) in their research found that some students had a tendency to share their assignment results and in some instances, criticise teachers and workplace managers in online forums. Undoubtedly teachers should be vigilant and address these matters straight away because the forum should be focused on teaching social work skills. In order to prevent such circumstances, teachers should develop and clarify expectations, and the purpose of the forums as well as set the ground rules at the start of the course. When students start to discuss matters in the live online tutorials, teachers need to diplomatically ask students to stop and to request that they restrict such discussion to one-to-one sessions.

Personal disclosure: Research (Barnes & Sainsbury, 2015; Haider, 2015) suggested that initially disclosing personal information could break the ice and enable teachers to create a conducive environment. Some students feel that the online forums are right media to air their views and their experiences honestly; some feel uneasy about that; some reflect and share their own difficult personal experiences. So, online forums serve different purposes for different participants; it is unlikely that teacher will meet everyone's specific needs if it is a large-scale forum. The teachers' role here is to carefully and sensitively support students and reduce disruption. Barnes and Sainsbury (2015) suggested that probably teachers should first model how information can be shared without breaching confidentiality before they ask students to share their own experiences.

Challenging messages: Online forums could create an environment in which some students dominate the forum or wish to show themselves as perfect students; some act like a spokesperson for other students; some may act like a 'tutor' in the forum. Hodgson and Reynolds (2005) suggested that teachers should value differences and disagreement within forums since this can become a good and stimulating learning experience. Uniformity of opinion should not be praised to manage the online forums or discussion in the online tutorials; rather, differences of opinions and views should be celebrated to co-create social work knowledge. However, that does not mean that teachers should put up with the disruptive behaviours of a handful of students; rather, they can address these matters diplomatically, in some instances outside the forums and online tutorials.

The teachers' role is pivotal to facilitate social work skills sessions online. It is demanding but rewarding. Research by Haider (2015) suggested that teachers need to think spontaneously to answer students' questions posted in online forums. They may have to think on their feet and to find a creative way to answer some of the online messages because messages are not hidden and all students in the course can see them. They have to invest a great deal of time to train some students who have not fully grasped social work theories, methods, and models and bring those students to a standard where they can start to apply them in their practice, also, reflect on them to develop the social work skills.

Use of current information and communication technologies could enable teachers to support students to learn a range of social work skills online. One way of achieving this is using critical reflection frameworks to analyse contemporary social work case studies and critical incidents analysis. This chapter has focused on how teachers could use a range of reflections frameworks with a case study or critical incident analysis or both to initiate, engage, and involve students in learning social work skills, such as written communication, team working, problem-solving, decision-making, critical thinking, critical reflection, and analytical skills. Developing a supportive virtual environment is vital to encourage students to learn and master social work skills. This chapter has suggested an array of teaching strategies that could be utilised to support students. Also, discussion in this chapter has touched on the pivotal role teachers play in facilitating and teaching social work skills online. Teachers need to be spontaneous, agile, adaptable, proactive, and responsive to establish their presence in online learning; so that, students engage and involve with discussions and debates.

References

Anderson, T. (2009). The dance of technology and pedagogy in self-paced distance education. Paper presented at the 17th ICDE World Congress, Maastricht.

Al-Mubaid, H. (2014). A new method for promoting critical thinking in online education. *International Journal of Advancement Corporate Learning, 7*(4), 34–37.

Artis, J. (2014). *Issues in a module-wide student forum* (HSC Teaching Online Panel Investigation). Milton Keynes: The Open University.

Baker, S., Warburton, J., Hodgkin, S., & Pascal, J. (2014). Re-imagining the relationship between social work and information and communication technology in the network society. *Australian Social Work, 67*(4), 467–478.

Barnes, F., & Sainsbury, K. (2015). *A teaching online panel project exploring good practice in moderating large scale forums within the Faculty of Health and Social Care* (Teaching Online Panel (TOP) Project Report). Milton Keynes: The Open University.

Borton, T. (1970). *Reach, teach and touch.* London: McGraw-Hill.

Brookfield, S. (1995). *Becoming a critically reflective teacher.* San Francisco: Jossey-Bass.

Buelens, H., Totte, N., Deketelaere, A., & Dierickx, K. (2009). Electronic discussion forums in medical ethics education: the impact of didactic guidelines and netiquette. *Medical Education, 41*(7), 711–717.

Dennen, V. P. (2005). From message posting to learning dialogues: Factors affecting learner participation in asynchronous discussion. *Distance Education, 226*(1), 127–148.

Fook, J. (2004). Critical reflection and transformative possibilities. In L. Davies & P. Leonard (Eds.), *Social Work in a corporate era: Practice, power and resistance.* Aldershot: Ashgate.

Gibbs, G. (1988). *Learning by doing: A guide to teaching and learning methods.* Oxford: Oxford Further Education Unit.

Gunawardena, C. N. (1995). Social presence theory and implications for interaction and collaborative learning in computer conferences. *International Journal of Educational Telecommunications, 1*(2/3), 147–166.

Haider, S. (2015). *Critical reflection in online forums.* Milton Keynes: The Open University.

Hodgson, V., & Reynolds, M. (2005). Consensus, difference and multiple communities' in networked learning. *Studies in Higher Education, 30*(1), 11–24.

Ingram, R., Fenton, J., Hodson, A., & Juindal-Snape, D. (2014). *Reflective social work practice.* Basingstoke: Palgrave Macmillan.

Kear, K. (2010, May 3–4). Social presence in online learning communities. In *Proceedings of the 7th International Conference on Networked Learning 2010.* Aalborg, Denmark.

Kolb, D. A. (1984). *Experiential learning: Experience as a source of learning and development.* Upper Saddle River, NJ: Prentice Hall.

Lyons, K. (1999). *Social work in higher education: Demise or development? (Centre for Evaluative Development Research).* Aldershot: Ashgate.

Oterholm, I. (2009). Online critical reflection in social work education. *European Journal of Social Work, 12*(3), 363–375.

Ter-Stepanian, A. (2012). Online or face to face: Instructional strategies for improving learning outcomes in e-learning. *The International Journal of Technology, Knowledge, and Society, 8*, 2.

The Open University. (2019). *K113 19B list of forums.* https://learn2.open.ac.uk/course/view.php?id=207490&area=forums. Accessed 24 May 2019.

Thompson, S., & Thompson, N. (2008). *The critical reflective practitioner.* Basingstoke: Palgrave Macmillan.

Thorpe, M. (2012). Educational technology: Does pedagogy still matter? *Educational Technology Magazine: The Magazine for Managers of Change in Education, 52*(2), 10–14.

CHAPTER 12

Social Work Education in Portugal

Paula Sousa and José Luis Almeida

INTRODUCTION

The purpose of this chapter is to present the background of social work education in Portugal, highlighting the main milestones that influenced it and the constraints and challenges it faces today.

The chapter is organised as follows:

- Background of social work education in Portugal;
- Social work education after the advent of democracy in 1974;
- Higher education system and structure;
- The three study cycles: bachelor's, master's, and doctorate;
- Bologna Process impact on social work education;
- Impact of Agency for Assessment and Accreditation of Higher Education on social work education; and
- Critical points and challenges.

BACKGROUND OF SOCIAL WORK EDUCATION IN PORTUGAL

The origins of social work education in Portugal can be traced to the official creation of the first specific schools of social work in the 1930s, particularly with the founding of the Institute of Social Work in Lisbon (1935) and

P. Sousa (✉) · J. L. Almeida
Centre for Transdisciplinary Development Studies (CETRAD), University of Tras Os Montes E Alto Douro (UTAD), Vila Real, Portugal

S. S. M. et al. (eds.), *The Palgrave Handbook of Global Social Work Education*, https://doi.org/10.1007/978-3-030-39966-5_12

the Social Normal School in Coimbra (1937). Almost two decades later, the Social Service Institute of Porto was founded (1956).

The establishment of these schools, which were targeted specifically at social work education, took place at a time when Portugal was under a dictatorial political regime called the New State from 1933 until 1974—an authoritarian and oppressive regime. It should also be noted that this political regime had a strong connection with the Catholic Church.

The first social work schools were founded to some extent to serve the ideological purposes of the regime; that is, to specifically train women to work towards maintaining order and social harmony, in a context where the majority of the population faced difficult conditions with high socio-economic needs. Therefore, in order to control "social assistance" and make it essentially charitable and corporatist assistance, the political regime consented to the opening of the first schools of social work, under the seal of the Catholic Church. This would determine a programme of education administered in such a way that social assistance was provided in accordance with the ideological orientation of the regime, with a publicity campaign aimed at gaining public support and preventing social conflict. It should also be emphasised that education in social work was grounded in theological thinking and broadly based on the social doctrine of the Church.

With the purpose of regulating education for social services, in 1939 the State declared its intention to:

> [establish the] general principles of guidance and coordination to which education establishments for social services are to be subjected, and [approve] the general plan of studies and programs, all for the training of suitable and responsible leaders in the environment for which they are intended, at the same time conscious and active cooperators of the National Revolution [...] so that it can never deviate from the corporative and Christian human sense. (Martins, 2009, p. 27)

The courses were recognised; the schools were given official licenses and called the "Social Normal School" and the "Institute of Social Service of Lisbon".

According to Branco (2009), the official recognition of schools and social service courses led to:

> the orientation of the training according to a three-year study plan and the diploma and professional title of Social Worker, exclusive to graduates in Social Work. In this first phase, the training comprised the medical–sanitary, legal, philosophical and social service dimensions. (2009, p. 62)

Therefore, the orientation of the training and the mission that was intended for social workers assumed a strongly doctrinal, corporate, and conservative character. In 1956, a review was carried out of the public regulation of social work education and the courses began to have a duration of four years (Branco, 2009, p. 63).

Despite the country still being under a dictatorship, in 1961, the social work course was recognised as a higher education course and, in 1969, social work schools became higher institutes (Fernandes, 1985, p. 145).

In the 1960s, some attempts were made to renew education in social work, and the directors of the social service institutes presented "various proposals for changes to the study plan in Social Work, contemplating the international guidelines for this training, but can not that the Ministry of National Education meets its pretensions" (Martins, 2009, pp. 27–28). This rejection is related to the dictatorship's refusal to institutionalise the social sciences, which resulted in conditioning the "academic education of social work and its relationship with the public university" (Martins, 2009, p. 29).

In the same decade, a process began of untying social work institutes from the Catholic Church and its more conservative thinking, thus breaking with the subordination to the Catholic Church and reinforcing the institutes' progressive autonomy. At first it was deemed that, "the disciplines of religious orientation are no longer required in the course of Social Work" (Martins, 2009, p. 31), removing from progressive social work education guidelines of a moral–religious nature. However, there was still no autonomy from the political regime and the monitoring and control of social work education continued until the end of the dictatorial political regime in 1974.

Social Work Education After the Advent of Democracy in 1974

The revolution of 1974 put an end to the dictatorship and led to profound changes in Portuguese society. Freedom and democracy had a strong impact on all sectors, including the education system. With regard to social work education, according to Branco, "the influence of the currents of critical and radical social work, and more particularly of the so-called reconceptualization movement of social work of Latin American origin" (2009, p. 64) deepened in this new context.

It was at this time that the three private schools of social work education mobilised efforts for their integration into public universities; this also triggered a movement towards the recognition of an undergraduate degree.

In 1989, it became possible to obtain a university degree and education in social work was extended from four to five years of academic training. According to Carvalho (2010), this training

> included two years with a theoretical basis with subjects in the fields of social work, sociology, psychology of personal and organizational behavior, as well as law, methods, and techniques of scientific research. In the following two years, in addition to these disciplinary contents, the training integrated a practical dimension, internship with the development of specific social work methodologies in the context of sectoral policies with monitoring seminars. The last year was devoted exclusively to scientific research process which culminated with a research work. (Carvalho, 2010, p. 155)

It was precisely at this stage that postgraduate training in social work began, specifically with the establishment of master's degrees and doctorates in social work in 1986–1987, under protocols with the Pontifical Catholic University of São Paulo, Brazil (Fernandes, 1985; Negreiros, 1999).

In 1995, "the first master's degree course in Social Work in Portugal was recognized and in 2003 the first doctorate" (Santos & Martins, 2016, p. 327).

Since the 2000s, there has been a profound transformation of social work education, particularly with the proliferation of social work courses in other private higher educational institutions and with the opening of social work courses in higher public education, thus increasing from three to twenty-two social work courses (Santos & Martins, 2016).

A decisive milestone at the time for social work education was the Bologna Declaration (1999), which consisted of a political declaration signed by 29 countries which sought to establish a European Higher Education Area (EHEA) in which the governments of the signatory countries undertook to reorganise their countries' higher education systems in accordance with the established principles.

Among the Bologna Declaration's objectives are to:

- Establish a transferable and cumulative credit system (ECTS credits), common to European countries;
- Adopt a system based on two study cycles, but this structure has been extended to three cycles.[1] The Bologna three-cycle system is structured as follows:
  - First cycle, lasting six to eight semesters (180–240 ECTS credits)—assigning the degree of Bachelor;
  - Second cycle, lasting a year and a half to two years (90–120 ECTS credits)—assigning the degree of Master;
  - Third cycle, lasting two years (180 ECTS credits)—assigning the degree of Doctor (PhD).

According to the *Bologna Process Implementation Report*, "the majority of first-cycle programs have a workload corresponding to 180 ECTS credits. Another quite widespread model is the 240 credits model, which applies to most first-cycle programs in around one-third of all EHEA countries" (European Commission/EACEA/Eurydice, 2018, p. 125).

At the master's level (second cycle), there are significant differences between countries in terms of the participation in masters programmes; "the workload of these programs is most commonly set at 120 ECTS credits" (European Commission/EACEA/Eurydice, 2018, p. 125).

In almost all EHEA countries, a doctoral programme, "follows the commonly agreed principles (the so called 'Salzburg Principles'), i.e. doctoral studies are expected to last three to four years full-time" (European Commission/EACEA/Eurydice, 2018, pp. 125–126).

In Portugal, the Bologna degree structure maintained the designations (bachelor's, master's, and doctoral degree) that the universities used in the structure of degrees prior to Bologna. However, the duration of the first cycle according to Bologna (in Portugal designated as *licenciatura*) is, as a rule, shorter than the duration of existing degrees before Bologna. Masters' degrees in Bologna have a more flexible duration and are not supposed to have the same level of requirement compared to the structure prior to Bologna, because the master's degree prior to Bologna was intended for students who had completed a course lasting four or five years. In this way, it is not possible to compare formations that, although maintaining the same designations, have different assumptions and different durations.

HIGHER EDUCATION SYSTEM AND STRUCTURE

Portuguese higher education is organised in a binary system, which integrates university education and polytechnic education, and has a structure based on four cycles: a cycle of short studies, which does not confer an academic degree, and three cycles of studies leading to the academic degrees of Bachelor's (BA), Master's (MSW), and PhD (Fig. 12.1).

We will present a brief description of the Portuguese higher education system taken from the website of the *Direção Geral do Ensino Superior* (https://www.dges.gov.pt/) designed for the purpose of providing information about the Portuguese higher education system for international students. The system of higher education is described on the page entitled "Study & Research in Portugal" (DGES, 2016).

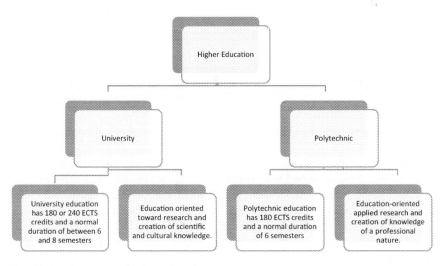

Fig. 12.1 Portuguese higher education system

The first steps towards the legal reform of the system of higher education were made in 2005, with the introduction of the new credit system (ECTS) for cycles of study, mobility mechanisms, and diploma supplement, among others. Changes were also made to the Basic Law for the Education System in order to implement the Bologna Process.

The new structure, which divided education into three cycles of study, was created in 2006 and it was completely implemented in Portugal in 2009/2010. Generic qualification descriptors were also defined for each of the cycles of study, based on acquired competences, as well as the structure for the first and second cycles of study in terms of typical ECTS intervals.

Portuguese higher education includes university and polytechnic education. University education is offered by public and private university institutions while polytechnic education is offered by public and private non-university institutions. Private higher education institutions must be subject to the previous recognition of the Ministry of Education and Science. The higher education system also includes a concordatory institution.

As a result of the Bologna Process, three cycles of study were established: the first cycle corresponds to the bachelor's degree; the second cycle corresponds to the master's degree; and the third cycle corresponds to the PhD.

The following is a brief description of the three study cycles: *Licenciado, Mestre, and Doutor.*[2]

Licenciado *Degree (Bachelor's)*

Both university and polytechnic institutions confer the degree of *licenciado* (bachelor's). In polytechnic education, the cycle of studies that leads to the degree of *licenciado* has 180 credits and a normal length of six curricular semesters. In certain cases, specifically those covered by internal legislation or by European legislation, the cycle of studies can have up to 240 credits with a normal length of up to seven or eight curricular semesters.

In university education, the cycle of studies that leads to the degree of *licenciado* has from 180 to 240 credits and a normal length of between six to eight curricular semesters.

In the first cycle of studies, the degree of *licenciado* is conferred by universities or polytechnics institutions to those who, after concluding all the curricular units that are integrated into the study programme of the *licenciatura* course, have obtained the established number of credits. In this cycle of studies, the degree of *licenciado* (bachelor) is conferred to those who have obtained 180 credits, corresponding to the first six semesters of work.

The combined workload of first- and second-cycle programmes does not imply that students necessarily study in a second-cycle programme once they complete a first-cycle degree.

Mestre *Degree (Master's)*

Both university and polytechnic institutions confer the degree of *mestre* (master's). The cycle of studies that leads to the degree of *mestre* has from 90 to 120 credits and a normal length of between three to four curricular semesters or, in exceptional circumstances, 60 credits and a duration of two semesters, resulting from a stable and consolidated practice in that specific field at an international level.

In polytechnic education, the cycle of studies that leads to the *mestre* degree must predominantly ensure that the student acquires a professional specialisation. In university education, the cycle of studies that leads to the *mestre* degree must ensure that the student acquires an academic specialisation involving research, innovation, or expansion of professional competences. In university education, the *mestre* degree may also be conferred after an integrated cycle of studies, with 300–360 credits and a normal length of 10–12 curricular semesters in cases for which the access to the practice of a certain professional activity depends on a length of time established by legal EU standards or resulting from a stable practice consolidated in the European Union.

The degree of *mestre* is conferred to those who, after concluding all the curricular units integrated into the study programme of the *mestrado* course, have obtained the established number of credits and successfully publicly defended their dissertation, their project work, or their traineeship report.

Doutor *Degree (PhD)*

The *doutor* (doctor) degree is conferred by universities and university institutes. The degree of *doutor* is conferred to those who have concluded all the curricular units integrated into the study programme of the *doutoramento* (doctoral) course, when applicable, and successfully defended their thesis in public.

Doctoral training differs from first- and second-cycle studies by its intensive research component. For this reason, the third cycle is covered by specific policy guidelines known as the Salzburg Principles (EUA, 2005).

In Portugal, according to the *Bologna Process Implementation Report,* "less than 5% of second-cycle graduates eventually enter a doctoral-degree program" (European Commission/EACEA/Eurydice, 2018, p. 105).

THE THREE STUDY CYCLES IN SOCIAL WORK EDUCATION

The current state of educational provision in social work is presented in the following tables, specifically of the three study cycles: bachelor's, master's, and doctorate.

Data collected from the institutional website of A3ES, regarding the Accreditation of Study Programs (A3ES, n.d.) of social work courses allows us to aggregate and synthesise relevant information about the social work courses.[3]

Bachelor's Degree in Social Work

According to data from the *Direção-Geral do Ensino Superior* (DGES, 2016), in the academic year 2017/2018 there were 15 higher education institutions offering social work courses, of which 10 were public and five private.

Table 12.1 presents a general characterisation of social work courses at the undergraduate level (first cycle).

In 2018, 17 degrees are available (first cycle). In public education there are 10 bachelors' degrees, of which five are in the university system and the other five in the polytechnic system. The remaining seven courses belong to the private education system.

The duration of the courses ranges from six to seven semesters, with a corresponding number of ECTS credits; that is, between 180 and 210. All degrees are accredited for a period of six years, although on different dates.

Table 12.1 Higher education institutions with bachelor's degree in social work (first cycle)

Higher education institutions (HEIs)	Public/ private	Semesters	ECTS credits	Date of accreditation
University of Trás-os-Montes and Alto Douro (UTAD)	Public	7	210	2014
University of Coimbra	Public	7	210	2014
University of Lisbon—ISCSP	Public	7	210	2015
University Institute of Lisbon—ISCTE	Public	6	180	2014
University of the Azores	Public	7	210	2015
Polytechnic Institute of Beja	Public	6	180	2014
Polytechnic Institute of Castelo Branco	Public	6	180	2015
Polytechnic Institute of Leiria	Public	6	180	2014
Polytechnic Institute of Portalegre	Public	6	180	2014
Polytechnic Institute of Viseu	Public	6	180	2012
Higher Institute Miguel Torga	Private	7	210	2014
Higher Institute of Social Service of Porto (ISSSP)	Private	7	210	2012
Catholic University of Portugal—Lisbon and Braga (*)	Private	7	210	2015
Lusíada University	Private	6	180	2015
Lusófona University—Lisbon and Oporto (*)	Private	6	180	2014
Total: 15 HEIs and 17 Courses				
(*) Institutions offering two courses in different cities				

Sources DGES (n.d.) and A3ES (n.d.)

It should be noted that these results from accreditation and audit procedures may change depending on whether or not the recommendations for improvement and changes made by the external assessment teams have been complied with.

In Portugal, the completion of a bachelor's degree (first cycle) enables graduates to exercise a professional practice and, as such, it is not required to do a master's degree (second cycle). Indeed, the Bologna Declaration emphasises that the degree awarded after the first cycle should be relevant not only to second-cycle studies, but also to the European labour market. In other words, first-cycle graduates should have a choice between pursuing their studies and starting out in employment.

Transition to the labour market. A bachelor's degree in social work (first cycle) allows graduates to enter the labour market in the public sector or the private non-profit sector. However, "until the end of the 1990s, unemployment of social workers in Portugal was residual. From the middle of the first decade of the twenty-first century it ceases to be" (Castro, Tomé, & Carrara, 2015, p. 110). The reduction of the public offer of jobs resulting from the reconfiguration of the welfare state and the deregulation of the profession are the predominant reasons for the increasing unemployment of social workers.

The *Direção-Geral de Estatísticas de Educação e Ciência* (DGEEC, 2017) provides statistical data on registered unemployed with higher qualifications by study area. However, the social work course does not appear separately, but is included in a broad study area called "Social Services", in which several different courses are included. In 2017, at the IEFP (Institute for Employment and Vocational Training), 11.8% recent graduates in this area registered as unemployed (InfoCursos, 2018).

Master's Degree in Social Work

The master's degree in social work has existed since 1995; it is authorised by the Ministry of Education and administered by the Higher Colleges of Social Work, Lisbon and Porto, with Ordinance n. 182/1995 (Fernandes, 1985; Negreiros, 1999, p. 36).

As with undergraduate courses (first cycle), with the emergence of A3ES in 2007, masters' degrees in social work have also been the subject of successive evaluations and reformulations in accordance with the recommendations of the external evaluation teams.

Table 12.2 presents a general characterisation of social work courses at the master's level (second cycle).

In 2018, eight social work master's degree courses (second cycle) are available. In public education, there are four masters' degrees and the other four are in private education.

Table 12.2 Higher education institutions with master's degree in social work (second cycle)

Higher education institutions (HEIs)	Category	Duration (semesters)	ECTS credits	Date of accreditation	Accredited years
University of Tras-os-Montes and Alto Douro	Public education	3	90	2017	2
University of Coimbra	Public education	3	90	2014	6
University of Lisbon—ISCSP	Public education	4	120	2014	6
University Institute of Lisbon—ISCTE	Public education	4	120	2012	6
Higher Institute Miguel Torga	Private education	3	90	2015	6
Catholic University of Portugal	Private education	3	90	2015	6
Lusíada University	Private education	4	120	2012	6
Lusófona University	Private education	4	120	2015	6
8 IES					

Source A3ES

The duration of the master's degree varies between three and four semesters, with a corresponding number of ECTS credits; that is, between 90 and 120.

It should be noted that these results from accreditation and audit processes may change depending on whether or not the recommendations for improvement and changes made by the external assessment teams have been complied with.

PhD in Social Work

In addition to the bachelor's and master's degrees (first and second cycles), it is also possible to complete a PhD in social work (third cycle).

The first doctoral courses in social work in Portugal were established in 1997, in the framework of an international interuniversity partnership between the Higher Institute of Social Service of Lisbon (ISSSL), Portugal, and the Pontifical Catholic University (PUC) of São Paulo, Brazil.

Since 2004, new doctoral programmes in social work have been established which are provided solely by Portuguese higher education institutions; these are the Higher Institute of Social Work of Lisbon (ISSSL), Higher Institute for Labour and Business Sciences (ISCTE), the Portuguese Catholic University (UCP), and the Higher Institute of Social Work of Porto (ISSSP).

Table 12.3   Higher education institutions with PhD/Doctorate degree in social work (third cycle)

Higher education institutions (HEIs)	Category	Duration (semesters)	ECTS credits	Date of accreditation	Accredited years
University Institute of Lisbon—ISCTE	Public education	6	180	2015	6
Catholic University of Portugal + University of Coimbra	Private education + public education (Interuniversity program)	6	180	2015	6
Lusíada University	Private education	6	180	2013	6

Source A3ES

In 2018, three PhD courses in social work are available to students. In public education, there are two PhD courses (although one of these is in partnership with a private educational institution) and in private education there is one PhD course.

These PhD courses last six semesters, with 180 ECTS credits. Again, it should be noted that these results from accreditation and audit processes may change depending on whether or not the recommendations for improvement and changes recommended by the external assessment teams are complied with.

In Portugal, PhD courses and doctorates in social work are rare. Table 12.3 provides a general characterisation of doctoral studies in social work (third cycle).

Bologna Process Impact on Social Work Education

Following the Bologna Declaration, higher education was organised into three training cycles (first cycle: undergraduate degree; second cycle: master's degree; third cycle: doctoral degree) which already existed. In the case of social work courses, these courses were already attributed a bachelor's degree (with a duration of five years); however, when the Bologna Process came into effect, the degree had a shorter duration (six to seven semesters). Thus, there was a shortening of the training level of the bachelor's degree, which in turn was reflected in the new study plans because all higher education institutions were obliged to present to the *Direção Geral de Ensino Superior*[4] (DGES) proposals for restructuring the courses—for registration of adequacy and operating authorisation, within the framework of Bologna—to start operating from 2006/2007 and 2007/2008.

The reduction from five to three years of the degree (*licenciatura*) in social work implied cuts to the programme content and the time for internship. This reduction in training was considered unfavourable with regard to the quality of teaching and courses, and, as such, in 2006 the Association of Social Work Professionals (APSS) expressed its concern regarding the adequacy of social work training after the Bologna Process, defending the need for the undergraduate degree (first cycle) to have "preferably eight semesters" (Carvalho & Pinto, 2015, p. 83); however, this aspiration did not materialise and the undergraduate courses in social work began to oscillate between six and seven semesters. As a general rule, in university higher education, the social work courses now have seven semesters (210 ECTS credits) and in polytechnic higher education these courses have six semesters (180 ECTS credits; see Table 12.1).

One of the major areas of higher education reform throughout the Bologna Process was the development of quality assurance and that "continues to be an area of dynamic evolution in the European Higher Education Area" (European Commission/EACEA/Eurydice, 2018, p. 151).

Following the developments of quality assurance systems, specifically those in the European area, the Portuguese state decided to create the Agency for Assessment and Accreditation of Higher Education (A3ES)[5] with the purpose of promoting and ensuring the quality of higher education.

Therefore, another important milestone for social work education in Portugal was the establishment of the A3ES in 2007.[6]

Thus, A3ES bridged the gap which existed in terms of evaluation and accreditation of existing social work courses, because there was no public or private entity which evaluated or accredited social work courses. Indeed, social work courses until then were freely created by private and public higher education institutions, which had full autonomy to define the study plans of the courses, which were approved by the ministry responsible for higher education. Such autonomy and lack of regulation led to a multiplicity of study plans and courses in social work education and, therefore, the creation of the A3ES agency was intended to bridge the gap that existed in terms of the regulation and quality of social work education.

IMPACT OF AGENCY FOR ASSESSMENT AND ACCREDITATION OF HIGHER EDUCATION IN SOCIAL WORK EDUCATION

The main objective of the Agency for Assessment and Accreditation of Higher Education (A3ES) is to promote the improvement of the performance of higher education institutions and their study programmes, and to guarantee the fulfilment of the basic requirements for their official recognition. Thus, the creation of the A3ES had a strong impact on social work education because it was through this agency that a rigorous evaluation of the programmes of study of social work courses and their accreditation was carried out.

Two of the specific objectives of the A3ES agency should be highlighted (A3ES, n.d.-b):

- To develop the quality assessment of the performance of higher education institutions and their study programmes;
- To determine the accreditation criteria in order to translate their results into qualitative appreciations as well as to define the consequences of assessment for the operation of study programmes and institutions.

The assessment and accreditation regime to be developed by the agency was defined in Law no. 38/2007 of the 16th of August, and the procedures for the assessment and accreditation of higher education institutions and their study programmes must comply with the normative framework.[7]

There are guidelines (A3ES, n.d.-c) for accreditation and certification processes carried out by A3ES, namely:

- Prior accreditation of new study programmes
- Assessment/accreditation of study programmes in operation
- Audit of internal quality assurance systems

These guidelines are supplemented by an assessment handbook (A3ES, n.d.-d) which provides explanations and the basic structure of the entire process of accreditation and quality assurance systems.

The functioning of A3ES had a major impact on social work education in Portugal because it addressed a gap in relation to the lack of regulation in this area, particularly at the level of the first cycle, which was "a domain crossed by weaknesses and risks regarding the quality of training provided, requiring attention and basic regulation" (Branco, 2009, p. 74).

In fact, before the existence of A3ES, accreditation of social work courses was made without any prior assessment by agencies or experts of the disciplinary field of social work attesting the reliability of the study plans. Therefore, there was only a mitigated state regulation of social work education by the Ministry of Higher Education, which was limited to single accreditations and not based on social work education standards.

The emergence of the A3ES in 2007 brought to an end this single mode of accreditation of courses, introduced requirements and standards regarding the accreditation of study programmes in social work, and—above all—established requirements regarding the quality of educational provision in social work.

In the evaluation process conducted by A3ES, it is worth highlighting the external evaluations, which are carried out by assessment panels—the external assessment teams, comprising independent experts who evaluate a set of study programmes in the field of social work and whose activities involve analysis of the self-assessment report, visits to the educational establishments, and collection and analysis of data and information needed for the assessment and accreditation of the course. It should be noted, however, that evaluation of study programmes is guided by the Global Standards for the Education and

Training of the Social Work Profession (IASSW & IFSW, 2004) because there are no national standards in Portugal.

These external evaluation teams constitute a strong input to the evaluation and accreditation system of social work courses in Portugal.

After the evaluation process is completed, there are consequences for the study programme. The external assessment team may draft conditional recommendations and establish a probationary accreditation period for a given number of years, thus allowing assessment of the degree of compliance with the recommendations in that period. A decade after the first assessments of social work courses by the A3ES, some courses were discontinued and others had significant improvements as a result of the recommendations made by the external evaluation teams.

CRITICAL POINTS AND CHALLENGES

In Portugal, social work education had a long period of time with no effective regulation; this made possible the existence of study programmes which did not respect the minimum legal requirements. Fortunately, this problem has been minimised with the emergence of the A3ES; however, there is still a problem regarding the lack of standards and guidelines for accreditation of social work education which makes possible the existence of a plurality of study programmes. Although the assessment panels, comprising social work experts, guide the evaluation according to the Global Standards for the Education and Training of the Social Work Profession (IASSW & IFSW, 2004), there remains a diversity of curricula. However, it should be noted that reports of the first evaluations made by the external evaluation teams made several recommendations for conditional accreditation of these study programmes, with the main recommendations related to the strengthening and curricular development of the predominant scientific area—that is, social work.

The multiplicity of study programmes has to do mainly with the fact that, in Portugal, there are no standards for social work education at the national level which define the guiding principles underpinning social work, the vision for social work, and the transferable skills which students should acquire—that is, an official document that sets out the learning requirements that each programme of social work education in Portugal must meet.

Standards in social work education should set out what students need to learn to do, what they need to be able to understand, and the competences they must have when they complete their training to be prepared for the labour market.

The lack of these national standards for accreditation can be considered the main critical factor of social work education in Portugal, because this lack of basic curricular guidelines specific to the Portuguese context allows each educational institution to design its study programmes for the social work course, without following a specific curricular guide related to a basic curricular matrix or the support of an educational policy on social work education.

Therefore, the challenge for the field of social work education in Portugal is to define national standards for social work education, like those that already exist in many other countries. Two brief examples are England and the USA. In England, there are the *Standards of Proficiency* of the HCPC (Health and Care Professions Council) and the *Professional Capabilities Framework* of the College of Social Work which outline the curriculum and professional standards. In the USA, the CSWE's Commission on Accreditation (COA) is responsible for developing accreditation standards that define competent preparation and ensuring that social work programmes meet these standards.[8] The Council on Social Work Education (CSWE, n.d.) uses the *Educational Policy and Accreditation Standards* (EPAS, 2015) to accredit baccalaureate and master's level social work programmes.

Creating standards and guidelines for accreditation is a challenge that should be transformed into a project and placed as a priority on the agenda of those involved in social work education in Portugal because quality assurance requires that effort.

FUNDING

This work is supported by the European Structural and Investment Funds in the FEDER component, through the Operational Competitiveness and Internationalisation Program (COMPETE 2020) [Project No. 006971 (UID/SOC/04011)]; and national funds, through the FCT—Portuguese Foundation for Science and Technology under the project UID/SOC/04011/2013.

NOTES

1. Commitment made in 2003 in Communiqué of the Conference of Ministers responsible for Higher Education, Berlin, 19 September 2003.
2. The words in italics are the terms used in the Portuguese language.
3. The information refers to the date of consultation and collection (10 May 2018) and therefore there may be a slight discrepancy regarding the data to be updated.
4. Decree-Law 74/2006 of 24 March is the basis of adequacy of higher education courses in Portugal.
5. For more information about A3ES, see http://www.a3es.pt/en/about-a3es.
6. The legislation put in place to establish this agency is Decree-Law no. 369/2007 of 5 November.
7. For more information on the normative framework, see http://www.a3es.pt/en/accreditation-and-audit/normative-framework.
8. See CSWE Accreditation https://www.cswe.org/Accreditation [Accessed 24 may 2018].

REFERENCES

A3ES. (n.d.-a). *Accreditation of study programs.* Retrieved from http://www.a3es.pt/en/accreditation-and-audit/accreditation-process-results/accreditation-study-programs.

A3ES. (n.d.-b). *Objectives.* Retrieved from http://www.a3es.pt/en/about-a3es/objectives.

A3ES. (n.d.-c). *Guidelines.* Retrieved from http://www.a3es.pt/en/accreditation-and-audit/guidelines.

A3ES. (n.d.-d). *Assessment handbook* [pdf]. Retrieved from http://www.a3es.pt/sites/default/files/Assessment%20Handbook_Final.pdf.

Bologna Declaration. (1999). Retrieved from http://www.magna-charta.org/resources/files/BOLOGNA_DECLARATION.pdf.

Branco, F. (2009). A profissão de Assistente Social em Portugal. *Revista Locus Soci@l, 3,* 61–89. Retrieved from http://cesss.fch.lisboa.ucp.pt/images/site/locus-social/locus-social-n3-2009.pdf#page=55&zoom=80.

Carvalho, M. I. (2010). Serviço Social em Portugal: Percurso Cruzado entre a Assistência e os Direitos. *Revista Serviço Social & Saúde, IX*(10), 147–164.

Carvalho, M. I., & Pinto, C. (2015). Desafios do Serviço Social na atualidade em Portugal. *Serviço Social & Sociedade, 121,* 66–94.

Castro, A. M. M., Tomé, R. M., & Carrara, V. A. (2015). A emigração dos assistentes sociais portugueses: Faces do trabalho e do desemprego em tempos de crise e austeridade. *Serviço Social & Sociedade, 121,* 95–124. https://doi.org/10.1590/0101-6628.015.

CSWE. (n.d.). *Accreditation.* Retrieved from https://www.cswe.org/Accreditation.

DGEEC (Direção-Geral de Estatísticas de Educação e Ciência). (2017). *Caracterização dos desempregados registados com habilitação superior – junho de 2017.* Retrieved from http://w3.dgeec.mec.pt/dsee/Desemprego/D201706/DGEEC_DSEE_DEES_2017_Desemprego_jun2017.htm.

DGES (Direção Geral do Ensino Superior). (2016). *Study & research in Portugal* [Online]. Retrieved from http://www.studyinportugal.edu.pt/index.php/study/portuguese-higher-education.

DGES (Direção Geral do Ensino Superior). (n.d.). Retrieved from https://www.dges.gov.pt/pt.

EUA (European University Association). (2005). *Salzburg 2005—Conclusions and recommendations* [pdf]. Retrieved from https://eua.eu/downloads/publications/salzburg%20recommendations%202005.pdf.

European Commission/EACEA/Eurydice. (2018). *The European higher education area in 2018: Bologna process implementation report.* Luxembourg: Publications Office of the European Union.

EPAS. (2015). *Educational policy and accreditation standards.* Retrieved from https://www.cswe.org/Accreditation/Standards-and-Policies/2015-EPAS.

Fernandes, E. (1985). Evolução da formação dos assistentes sociais. *Intervenção Social, 2*(3), 123–142.

InfoCursos. (2018). *Dados e Estatisticas de Cursos Superiores.* Retrieved from http://infocursos.mec.pt/.

Martins, A. (2009). 70 Anos de Formação em Serviço Social em Tempos de Ditadura e de Democracia: Da Escola Normal Social ao Instituto Superior Miguel Torga. *Interacções, 17,* 21–44.

Negreiros, M. A. (1999). Qualificação académica e profissionalização do Serviço Social: o caso português. In M. Negreiros, et al. (Eds.), *Serviço Social profissão e identidade, que trajetória* (pp. 13–44). Lisboa/S. Paulo: Veras.

Santos, C. M., & Martins, A. (2016). A formação do assistente social em Portugal: tendências críticas em questão. *Revista Katálysis, 19*(3), 324–332.

LEGISLATION

Lei n.º 46/86, de 14 de outubro - Lei de Bases do Sistema Educativo.

Lei n.º 62/2007, de 10 de setembro - Regime Jurídico das Instituições de Ensino Superior.

Decreto-Lei n.º 74/2006, de 24 de março - Graus e Diplomas do Ensino Superior.

ALTERADO POR:

Decreto-Lei, nº 107/2008, de 25 de junho.

Decreto-Lei, nº 230/2009, de 14 de setembro.

Decreto-Lei, nº 115/2013, de 7 de agosto.

Decreto-Lei, nº 63/2016, de 13 de setembro.

Decreto-Lei n.º 42/2005, de 22 de fevereiro - Princípios reguladores de instrumentos para a criação do espaço europeu de ensino superior (ECTS).

Decreto-Lei n.º 369/2007, de 5 de novembro - Agência de Avaliação e Acreditação do Ensino Superior.

IASSW, & IFSW. (2004). *Global standards for the education and training of the social work profession*. Available at http://www.iassw-aiets.org.

Lei n.º 38/2007, de 16 de agosto - Avaliação do Ensino Superior.

CHAPTER 13

Social Work in a Local and Global Context: A Swedish Approach

Jonas Christensen ⓘ

Background

The need for international education on the subject of social work is clear, although achieving it may be complex (Merrill & Frost, 2011). Although social workers are faced with new responsibilities, it is important for education to go beyond the national level (Healy, 2008). Nagy and Falk (2000) claim that the impact of ongoing global processes on the social work profession is dramatic and that reformulating education to include more international and cross-border cultural content is needed. While the internationalisation of social work is a contested idea, it is nonetheless seen as an evolving and indeterminate project (Harrison & Melville, 2010). The principal reason for the pressure on internationalisation in social work might be a very practical one: today social workers around the world have greater opportunities to bring about social action in a globalised world either individually or through agencies and organisations (Healy, 2008). With a view to putting concepts into practice Nilsson (2003) defines internationalisation as "the process of integrating an international dimension into the research, teaching and services function of higher education. Social work might be one of the most international field of all and International social work is a growing field of interest." Contemporary social work has not fully recognised the extent to which its practice and professional environment are shaped by interdependence. Neither has the profession seized available opportunities for increasing its impact internationally (Nilsson, 2003). It could be suggested that these

J. Christensen (✉)
Department of Social Work, Malmö University, Malmö, Sweden
e-mail: jonas.christensen@mau.se

S. S. M. et al. (eds.), *The Palgrave Handbook of Global Social Work Education*, https://doi.org/10.1007/978-3-030-39966-5_13

opportunities present practical opportunities to develop internationalisation of social work as a real opportunity for shared meaning and understanding. As pointed out by Cox and Pawar (2006), dimensions in international social work need to have a local as well as a global face (i.e., the reality of globalisation demands a dimension of localisation). Righard (2013) discusses how the various definitions of international social work have changed over time and she categorizes these changes into three groups: modernisation, radicalisation, and globalisation. In the last category (i.e., where we are now) a big challenge for the social worker is to find strategies to face the challenges that arise in a global society. Globalisation affects the social policy discussion in many ways (Cousins, 2005) and therefore also affects social work and social work education. The need for international education in social work is clear, although achieving it may be complex (Merrill & Frost, 2011). Nagy and Falk (2000) suggest that international issues be incorporated into mainstream social work education, that comparisons be made between the approaches, theories, and programmes of other countries, and that more specialised professional programmes be created. According to Faruque and Ahmmed (2013) the social work profession by its very nature stresses a mutual interaction among individuals, groups, and communities that has expanded to include exchanges, discussion, research, and understanding of the social work profession among countries and continents.

AIM AND RESEARCH QUESTION

The aim of this chapter is to consider internationalisation and social work education from a Swedish context. Malmo University (MaU) is used as the local example. The research question posed in this chapter is: How can social work knowledge be understood on the basis of the concepts of reflexivity and reflectivity in the local and global classroom?

SOCIAL WORK EDUCATION IN A SWEDISH AND LOCAL CONTEXT

Academic emphasis on social work education in Sweden is rather strong and tied closely to the university system. The Swedish National Agency for Higher Education gives universities and colleges the authority to issue degrees. Some professions stipulate requirements for accreditation (e.g., psychologists, doctors, and nurses). However, professional degrees without accreditation also have special requirements to fulfil. This is the case for the degree in social work called Socionom. The length of study programmes is related to the length of academic career programmes (at the Bachelor level this can be estimated at 3.5 years). Social work is an academic subject that has its own autonomous position and can be seen as being the "parent discipline"

(Juliusdottir & Petrsson, 2003) in which the core subjects are psychology, sociology, and pedagogy. Internships take a full semester (usually the fifth semester). Students in the last semester of the social work programme at the Bachelor level ought to deepen their graduation profile into eligible themes dependent on a single university.

The professional university degree awarded in the field of social work is formally named the Degree of Bachelor of Science in Social Work (i.e., Socionom). There are 20 universities and colleges approved to provide undergraduate social work study programmes in Sweden. Many deliver decentralised and distance education such that programmes are available more broadly. The programme takes 3.5 years to complete. There are on average more than eight applicants per social work place and just over three applicants per social care place. Approximately 1800 students are accepted each year of whom 90 to 95% complete their degree. The programmes include applied studies and provide both academic and professional training. Some universities and university colleges run courses in the field of social work without being accredited to provide professional degrees. Instead they provide general Bachelor and Master's degrees. Consequently, they attract approximately 2000 applicants wanting to do social work each year.

Since 2006 the concepts underlying social work and social care have been integrated into both the Socionom degree and its title. Previously they were separated in two different degrees (social work and social pedagogy). This is the reason the social work degree has not only been developed and understood somewhat differently in Sweden compared with several countries in Europe. The growth of higher education in Sweden is evident in the number of professional degrees within the field of social work burgeoning by approximately 40% over the past 15 years.

MAGISTER PROGRAMMES

Magister has had many different meanings in the Swedish educational system from a doctorate to a graduate degree. Since 2007 in Sweden the Magister examination (*magisterexamen*) is a 1-year graduate degree requiring at least 3 years of undergraduate studies. In Sweden a Magister (*filosofie magister*) was historically the highest degree at faculties of philosophy and was equivalent to a doctorate used in theology, law, and medicine. The Magister degree for those subjects was abolished in 1863 and replaced with the Doctor of Philosophy. Programmes for achieving a Magister degree in social work in Sweden differ in length and content from 1 year full time to 2 years part time. The Swedish funding system makes Magister programs financially risky for universities. A Magister is not recognized or needed for promotion to higher positions nor is it important in career planning for all employees.

Only around 10% of all social workers have a Master's degree showing that the added value in sense of salary and opportunities in career is relatively low (Höjer, 2007). However, although a Magister is not formally needed professionally, it is a prerequisite for applicants to apply and enter doctoral programmes in social work if they are offered at a university.

Research: PhD Education in Social Work

Social work research education leading to a Ph.D. in social work started in the late 1970s in Sweden. It is now offered in seven universities. The first full Professor of Social Work qualified in Sweden in 1977. Today some 40 years later Sweden has around 200 full Professors of Social Work. The ongoing process of professionalisation in social work is the consequence of robust links between research, education, and practice. Doctoral students are offered courses not only on scientific methods used in the study of social work, but also on research writing and presentation. The Ph.D. is a 4-year full-time programme. In practice all doctoral students in Sweden are employed during their doctoral studies. At the MaU around 25 Ph.D. students in social work are registered and as a part of the introduction course it could be mentioned that Ph.D. education in social work in comparison globally is a part.

Local Context of Internationalisation in Social Work Education

Eligible courses on social work studies using MaU as an example focus on social policy, children and family, drug addiction, migration, and care of the elderly. Around 100 social worker students enter MaU each semester and around 800 are in the study programme. The main idea behind the continuous development of internationalisation in social work education in the social work curriculum at MaU in general is that social workers need to be prepared to address social work in a local and global context by studying internationally related cases and community problems that arise in their domestic practice. Although social work is described contextually as bound to national traditions, laws, and local culture (Lorenz, 1994), the content of social work education in Sweden is to a large extent governed by national guidelines due to the professional title of Socionom. International perspectives on social work in the Bachelor-level social work curriculum at MaU have become integrated parts of single lectures during the first and second semesters. This is much the same at the Master's level with invited guest lecturers speaking about related themes and often on a comparative basis. Apart from the programmes two courses "Social Work: Social Policy and Welfare" and "Social Work in a Local and Global Context" are offered at the Bachelor level and integrate an intercultural perspective focussing on social science, the welfare state in comparison, and social work practice. Since social work needs to be understood in its local context by gaining a global understanding the term *glocal* (global and local) is used in this chapter. Parts of these individual courses are therefore also integrated as campus-based modules in ordinary full social work programmes. Such cases contribute to mutual exchange not only about solving global social problems but also gaining knowledge of other countries and their social systems. Although the term internationalisation in social work education is well established and the need for further international education in social work is viewed as essential, the way in which it can be brought about is complex.

Cross-national comparison of social work according to Meeuwisse and Swärd (2008) is a question of assumptions and levels. Although focus could be on the macro level where comparisons are based on social policy, it could also be on profession (micro–meso level) or on practice-oriented differences (micro–meso level). This makes sense because it may be more relevant and useful to use the term "cross-national and global social work" instead of internationalisation. Faruque and Ahmmed (2013) discussed whether internationalisation of social work should be seen as a method to address new and complex social problems that arise from the complexities of international contexts.

MaU is a young urban university (established in 1998) that reflects the local and regional community, embraces diversity as a quality, and educates and prepares students to become change agents ready to act on behalf of a sustainable global society. The university collaborates with other stakeholders in society to create, share, and make use of knowledge contributing to sustainable societal improvement both locally and globally. MaU considers the interplay between the individual, institutional, and societal level of understanding as important to research and challenge-based learning. It does so by integrating practice and theory through collaborative, interdisciplinary research methods and theories of learning into both digital and analogue learning environments and by creating sustainable platforms to enable learning to expand in partnership. Teachers, researchers, and students at MaU are engaged in putting in place processes that ensure lifelong learning and promote knowledge acquisition in which research is integrated, holistic, and sustainable coupled with educational and professional development. To bring this about social work students should be encouraged to develop their abilities to identify, initiate, and lead processes of change to address and handle complex societal issues. This is the reason the term "students as change agents" is used at MaU. Striving for a sustainable and more equitable world and contributing to make education and lifelong learning naturally integrated parts of society as a whole is related to this. In social work education there is a need to adjust to the needs of next-generation students by putting in place processes that ensure lifelong learning throughout a working life marked by constant change. Our approach to learning has to be scrutinized and critically reflected on regarding how it accords with both societal and citizens' needs. Social work education therefore needs to develop border-crossing meeting spaces and to concretise if the aim is to research social professional education and the development of professions within welfare sectors. Therefore, such a project is aimed at making sure these societal challenges focus on challenge-based learning and approaches and lead to growing demand for availability, flexibility, and funding. At the same time such fundamental societal changes should shine the light on how research, education, and continued professional development can and should be organised so as to secure more reflective, reflexive, holistic, and sustainable understanding (Tragardh, 2012). MaU social work education is a part of this.

Theoretical Frame

Defining our own values is often difficult as they dwell deep inside us. Our selective perception is an unaware consequence of the variety of information that characterises our surrounding environment. A frame of theories, methods, and empirical observations chosen when looking at specific objects is highly dependent on the result of the selective process that every human being undergoes in their upbringing, working life, education, etc. Dewey (1934) argued, "all direct experience is qualitative, and qualities are what make life-experience itself directly precious." Building on Knowles and Dewey, Schön's concept of reflective practice considered the pre-service process of learning and suggested that any reflective practicum requires that students plunge into the doing and try to educate themselves before they know what it is they're trying to learn (Schön, 1987). Knowledge creation through the development of mutually productive forms of collaboration has for a long time been an important issue for educators and practitioners in different sectors of working life (Inkpen, 1996). In the social sciences there is also a long tradition of criticism of traditional learning models and corresponding interest in different models of action-based, collaborative learning (Bruffee, 1993). Mainstream social science education is too frequently mired in the nineteenth century ideals of Wilhelm von Humboldt that include a linear relationship between theory and practice and a view of the educator as basically detached from the field of practice (Sörlin, 1996). Accordingly, traditional models of learning tend to objectify the participants and are too inflexible, closed, specialised, of insufficient practical relevance, etc. (Gibbons et al., 1994). In contrast, meaningful learning from the viewpoint of informal and formal processes directed at learning to understand is probable. This approach could enable strategies and tools to see new patterns. Reflection refers to an activity in which an experience is recalled. It is a response that involves the conscious recall and examination of experiences as a basis for evaluation and as a source for planning and action (Schön, 1983). The reflective approach nurtures the ability to (re)build and (re)elaborate creatively the pathways of new understanding. It implies paying attention to routine practices that through reflective analysis assume a different meaning or are perceived under a new light (Martins, Coimbra, Pinto, & Serradas, 2015). One way of expanding a reflective practice is to move toward a practice of reflexivity. Engaging in reflexivity requires critical thought and careful consideration followed by action rooted in understanding. Engaging in mindfulness and introspection with careful and open consideration to the complexity of situations and events that present themselves frequently generates reflexive practice. While reflection is often individual, reflexivity is decidedly relational. Being reflexive and discussing reflexivity in education increases the credibility of research and professional development, yet it is important to illuminate and describe the different kinds of reflexivity. Reflexivity has deep roots and breadth in most disciplines especially in the social sciences. We find out that "systematic reflexivity is the constant analysis of one's own theoretical and methodological presuppositions" (Coghlan & Brannick, 2005). Reflexivity is a movement from awareness to connectedness. It invites us not only to develop a stronger sense of attentiveness to who we are and who we are becoming, but it also provides an opportunity to explore other worldviews. Following these deeper questions reflexivity leads to the realisation that individual experiences are integral to perceiving the world and our connection to it. It is a process that includes attention to beliefs about ontology (the study of what it means to exist) and epistemology (the study of what it means to know). Reflexivity requires attention to an object while at the same time attending to our own role in how that object is being constructed or constituted (Davies, 2004). When people meet, many types of exchanges take place including social, academic, and cultural exchanges. Personal meetings on different levels are key factors. They make the assimilation of knowledge and resources possible (Christensen, 2016).

METHODOLOGY

Research data were collected from a group of 30 social work students from Sweden, Germany, England, Scotland, Austria, and the United States. This group of students participated in a 2-week short-term campus-based Bachelor course entitled "Social Work: Social Policies and Welfare." The course is an independent course offered by the MaU since 2010 and has an estimated value of 7.5 ECTS (European Credit Transfer and Accumulation System). The course is a full international course, which means it covers issues and phenomena that have arisen in an increasingly globalised world. Consequently, the course curriculum has as its aim to develop students' knowledge and understanding in relation to social policies within a global

context with particular focus on their relevance to social work and their implications for social work practice. For international students coming to Malmo
it is an elective course. The course takes place over 2 weeks (11 days: Monday
to Friday of the following week) each spring semester in January/February.
The course schedule starts each day at 9:30 a.m. and ends at 4:30 p.m.
Research data on students' experiences were collected by spontaneous classroom observations during the 2-week course together with written replies.
Written replies were made in the classroom (before a scheduled lecture took
place) as part of the course and at the end of the course. The replies were
collected anonymously. The written question was: What does the concept
of internationalisation in social work education mean to you? The students
were each given 40 minutes for the written reply. Thereafter, interpretation
and analysis were undertaken. Written replies were ethically conducted in an
established and commonly accepted educational setting and students were
informed in advance that the results were to be interpreted and analysed
anonymously for research purposes.

Findings

The reflective learning process enables participants to see and understand
themselves in many ways from a broader perspective. The research question
for this study was: How can knowledge in social work be understood on
the basis of the concepts of reflexivity and reflectivity in the local and global
classroom?

By reflective learning we mean the processes by which students engage
with one another to discuss, reflect, and learn from each other. In contrast,
reflexivity is the process by which they begin applying their emergent knowledge in a more spontaneous fashion. In this way the reflexive is almost contrary to the reflective. While the reflective tends to reinforce pre-existing
beliefs, the reflexive is a manifestation of evolving understanding and an
emergent professional identity. Participant feedback, views, and reflections
of those students who attended the module of the international course are
highlighted. The starting point in defining glocal knowledge is that it is theoretical, practical, and processual. It is shown that understanding the concepts
of reflexivity and reflectivity can be useful in understanding students' knowledge construction. The interplay between participating social work students
encourages them to develop their capacity for self-reflectivity as a part of their
professional understanding and development on different levels of knowledge
acquisition.

The following statement can be seen as macrosocial since it speaks of culture, nations, traditions, and language: "Internationalisation in social work
education for me is about gaining a deeper insight into different cultures, differences, and similarities to use in the field of practice and professional situations." At the microsocial level the individual and the focus on interaction

are central: "We try to understand each other, but we tend to create barriers instead." Statements from some of the students relate to social work occupations that relate to the individual and focus on interaction wherein the microsocial level can be seen: "Language exchange, cultural encounters between people, listen, be curious, raise questions, discuss and develop, learn from each other, reduce prejudice, overcome abandonment, come up with new ideas, confirm old ideas, learn about social work in different countries, and learn from each other." An exchange of knowledge characterised by mutual interest may also include a "resistor," as stated by some of the respondents: "We cannot understand that particular term in social work in that way" and "We are not doing social work in that way in our country." In the process of change (especially if handled correctly) this resistance can represent a significant driving force for the reflective student to develop a local understanding. Individuals and the way they interact in their environment are the starting point of learning. Such interaction occurs at different levels that in an academic session may be seen as individual, organisational or institutional, and societal. According to Meeuwisse and Swärd (2008) this shows that cross-national comparison of social work is a question of assumptions and levels. The focus could be on the macro level where comparisons are based and related to the profession (micro–meso level) or on practice-oriented differences (micro–meso level).

The capacity for resilience shown by students at the intrapersonal level can be seen in the following statement made by one of them: "There's a hill you have to overcome. It is a challenge and necessity for development and challenges." The exosocial level can be seen in the following statement: "So, I imagine a picture of a network that stretches across borders where it is more possible than ever to communicate and collaborate between different NGOs and authorities and this relates to society on the whole as well as institutions … No matter where we come from, we all want to feel good." Our students seem to like their role as social workers but view it in a critical way. They set up a connection between the local and the global. They ask each other how such-and-such is done in each other's countries and learn that they do not have to do this in a prescriptive and anticipated way. Since social work today is under financial pressure, borders are closed, and states are no longer prepared to help, social workers will have to push boundaries and try to extend discourse. They will have to mirror what they face on the doorstep and reflect at the same time on the "global sound" and on alternative approaches.

Since social work is an international profession and one that social workers are committed to, all the students felt it was very important for them to have a module on internationalisation embedded in their curriculum. The main conclusion is that "thinking globally, acting locally" should be key to developing social work education. Developing reflective and reflexive capacities when meeting others can be seen among students as adding momentum to this. This demands in-depth knowledge about individual driving forces and views on what is essential when it comes to international social work education. The importance of allowing students to meet on a transnational basis to social work education built upon internationalisation at home as a part of domestic local programmes that have global understanding—a glocalized view on social work—should not be underestimated when developing professional skills. Students are stimulated by being part of a community that reflects on the learning practices of other cultures. This may create a new framework for innovative learning through collaboration. It is through inclusive encounters where diverse backgrounds, cultures, and frameworks are represented that we are challenged in our notions—not least in learning environments and contexts. A challenge-based learning approach connecting local knowledge and understanding with global awareness is foreseen. By integrating reflection and reflexivity in social work education in a way where local knowledge and global awareness interact with challenge-based learning, we can identify how this can be achieved and at the same time enable sustainable lifelong learning by (a) taking a critical, creative, and holistic approach to learning and knowledge; (b) having a diversity of perspectives; (c) using collaborative methods of research and education; (d) identifying challenges, tasks, problems, and processes; and (e) keeping internationalisation firmly in mind.

Limitations of the Study

A qualitative weakness of the study was in assuming that a group of students would be likely to have a high degree of interest in internationalisation issues prior to participating despite the course being elective. Although this was an open issue, it did allow respondents to freely express themselves thus strengthening reliability. Although there were limitations to the study, the key thing is to be aware of them and try to deal with them in the best possible way in line with the purpose of the study. Limitations could be lack of time, the group selected was too small, and the environment created stress. However, students did not ask for more time, the materials and input transcribed reached a saturation point mainly due to analysis rather than the number of students, and participants did not show any signs of stress due to lack of time.

Conclusion

Universal challenges facing social work education call for a shift in focus to internationally shared knowledge. The purpose of the social worker profession is in many ways to assist, intervene, and strengthen people's capacity to understand diversity at the micro, macro, and meso level. In an increasingly global society the development of reflective learning processes and activities to support such an understanding locally will be increasingly crucial. A challenge-based learning approach where societal and social challenges are defined and integrated is essential. The reflective learning process in many ways enables participants to see and understand themselves from a broader perspective. Reflective learning relates to the processes by which students engage with one another to discuss, reflect, and learn from each other from a local and global context. In contrast, reflexive learning is the process by which they begin applying their emergent knowledge in a more spontaneous fashion. In this way the reflexive is almost contrary to the reflective. While the reflective tends to reinforce pre-existing beliefs, the reflexive is a manifestation of evolving understanding and an emergent profession identity. Although social work practice is very much about acting locally, an understanding of global awareness is more important than ever—glocal knowledge.

Acknowledgements We thank Dr Bret Weber of the University of North Dakota, Dr Joachim Thönnessen of the University of Applied Science in Osnabrück, Dr Eberhard Raithelhuber of the University of Salzburg, and Dr Lucy Grimshaw of the University of Dundee for their contributions to discussions.

References

Bruffee, K. A. (1993). *Collaborative learning: Higher education, interdependence, and the authority of knowledge.* Baltimore: Johns Hopkins University Press.

Christensen, J. (2016) *A critical reflection of bronfenbrenner's development ecology Model, problems of education in the 21st century*, Scientific Methodical Centre "Scientia Educologica", Lithuania; The Associated Member of Lithuanian Scientific Society, European Society for the History of Science (ESHS) and ICASE, vol. 69.

Coghlan, D., & Brannick, T. (2005). *Doing action research in your organization.* London: Sage.

Cousins, M. (2005). *European welfare states: Comparative perspectives.* London, UK: Sage.

Cox, D., & Pawar, M. (2006). *International social work: Issues, strategies and programs.* Thousand Oak: Sage.

Davies, M. G. (2004). *Multiple voices in the translation classroom: Activities, tasks, and projects.* Amsterdam: John Benjamin's Publishing Company.

Dewey, J. (1934). The need for a philosophy of education. In J. Dewey (Ed.), *Art as Experience* (35–57). New York: Capricorn Books.

Faruque, C., & Ahmmed, F. (2013). Development of social work education and practice in an era of international collaboration and cooperation. *Journal International Social Issues 2*(1), 61–70.

Gibbons, M., Limoges, C., Nowotny, H., Schwartzman, S., Scott, P., & Trow, M. (1994). *The New Production of Knowledge: The Dynamics of Science and Research in Contemporary Societies.* Thousand Oaks, CA: Sage.

Harrison, G., & Melville, R. (2010). *Rethinking social work in a global world.* Basingstoke: Palgrave Macmillan.

Healy, L. (2008). *International social work: Professional action in an interdependent world* (pp. 43–47). Oxford and New York: Oxford University Press.

Höjer, S. (2007) *Social work in Sweden.* EUSW Listening conference, Gothenburg.

Inkpen, A. C. (1996). Creating knowledge through collaboration. *California Management Review, 39*(1), 123–140.

Juliusdottir, S., & Petrsson, J. (2003). Common social work education standards in the Nordic countries—Opening an issue. *Social Work and Society, 1*(1), 6–10.

Lorenz, W. (1994). *Social work in a changing Europe.* London, UK: Routledge.

Martins, A. O., Coimbra, M. N., Pinto, I. P., & Serradas, R. (2015). How teachers experience practical reflectivity in schools: A case study. *American Journal of Educational Research, 3*(7), 918–922. http://pubs.sciepub.com/education/3/7/16.

Merril, M. C., & Frost, C. J. (2011). Internationalizing social work education: Models, methods and meanings. *Frontiers: The Interdisciplinary Journal of Study Abroad, 21,* 189–210.

Meeuwisse, A., & Swärd, H., (2008). *Cross-national comparisons of social work— A question of intial assumptions and levels of analysis.* London: European Journal of Social work.

Nagy, G., & Falk, D. S. (2000). Dilemmas in international and cross-cultural social work education. *International Social Work, 43*(1), 49–60.

Nilsson, B. (2003). Internationalization at home from a Swedish perspective: The Case of Malmö. *Journal of studies in International Education, 7*(1), 27–40.

Righard, E. (2013). Internationellt socialt arbete – *Definitioner och perspektivval i historisk belysning* [*International social work—Definitions and choice of perspectives in a historical context*]. Socialvetenskaplig tidskrift no 2.

Schön, D. (1983). *The reflective practitioner: How professionals think in action.* London: Temple Smith.

Schön, D. (1987). *Educating the reflective practitioner.* San Francisco: Jossey-Bass.

Sörlin, S. (1996). Universiteten som drivkrafter. Globalisering, kunskapspolitik och den nya intellektuella geografin [*Universities as driving forces. Globalization, policy in knowledge acquisition and the new intellectual geography*]. Stockholm: SNS Förlag.

Tragardh, L. (2012). "Framtidsutmaningar - Det nya Sverige", i Stromback, et al., *Framtidsutmaningar: det nya Sverige,* Volante publ.

CHAPTER 14

Social Work in a Changing Scandinavian Welfare State: Norway

Anne-Margrethe Sønneland

Norway is what Esping-Andersen (1990) called a social democratic or Scandinavian welfare state. It is characterised by an extensive welfare state, relatively egalitarian income distribution (Halvorsen & Stjernø, 2008), and a high level of services (Kjølsrød, 2005). Universal social rights to relatively generous benefits provide protection against social risks (Botten, Elvebakken, & Kildal, 2003). Norwegian welfare policies make up an extensive system of redistribution of resources based on arguments of social justice and equality (Sinding Aasen, 2018). The state plays an extensive role in welfare arrangements that clearly demonstrates itself in extensive public services, public employment, and taxation-based income–benefit schemes. Social services are mainly organised at the municipal level (Alestalo, Hort, & Kuhnle, 2009).

Since 1945 the welfare state has gradually defined more risks as responsibilities of the state and identified legitimate needs that warrant protection (Ervik & Kildal, 2016). The aim has been to create a security network that applies to everyone independent of their economic status and at the same time improve conditions for those who have less (Kjølsrød, 2010). Scandinavian welfare states are "work-friendly" in that their social security systems and labour market policies are designed to promote full employment (Alestalo et al., 2009). The focus on equality and universalism is a main feature of the Norwegian welfare state (Botten et al., 2003). Universalism is a system in which the principle of social rights is extended to cover the whole population (Alestalo et al., 2009). It ensures everyone a minimum living

A.-M. Sønneland (✉)
VID Specialized University, Oslo, Norway
e-mail: a.m.sonneland@vid.no

standard (Botten et al., 2003) and that public welfare applies to everyone (Briseid, 2019).

Despite the stability of European welfare states (Kuhnle, 2000) and huge support for tax-financed welfare policies (Hernes & Hippe, 2007), the sustainability of a universally oriented, egalitarian, and high-cost welfare state is increasingly questioned (Ellingsæter & Leira, 2006). Over recent decades, there have been changes in society as well as in ideas about social policies and some areas of the welfare state (Kildal, 2018). Individualisation and increased emphasis on personal responsibility and contractual thinking have entered the debate (Ervik & Kildal, 2016) and there is more emphasis on the duty of individuals to take care of themselves (Botten et al., 2003).

Since Norwegian social work is by and large a welfare state profession (Dahle, 2010) and the development of social work in Norway is closely linked to development of the welfare state (Misje, 2019), changes in the welfare state are important not only to social work but also to the education of social workers. This chapter explores how recent changes in the welfare state matter to social work in Norway. Central to the argument is that changes in ideology and values that are apparent in the work line of social policies have led to a partial shift in responsibility for welfare from the state to the individual. This chapter goes on to explore some ways in which such changes in social policy influence and change social work.

The Norwegian Welfare State: A Historical Introduction

The Norwegian welfare state developed and matured after the Second World War (Ervik & Kildal, 2016), its development in the post-war years constituted a visionary project for societal change and optimism about the future. There was a strong belief in the possibilities of politics to improve society (Christoffersen, 2017a). The aim was to develop economic and political arrangements that could ensure a decent standard of living for the whole population (Lysestøl, 2002). Central ideas were work and welfare for everyone through good and universal systems such as economic support for persons who were unable to work (Seip, 1981). An important aim was to replace stigmatising systems with broader systems of economic support (Hjelmtveit, 2005). There was a strong belief in education as a way of increasing productivity and stimulating economic growth. Moreover, equal access to education would also serve to counteract social differences and make it possible for the working class to gain influence and participation in society (Hagen & Skule, 2007). Health policies were aimed at ensuring the population had equal access to high-quality health services (Stamsø, 2005).

Economic equality was a goal (Seip, 1981, pp. 53–57). Inequality was understood as being structural—as a problem that had its roots mainly at the societal level. This understanding represented a shift from earlier ideas about inequality as the result of choices made by and low morale of the individual. This structural understanding of inequality was crucial to the development of the welfare state and to general acceptance that the state should take on larger responsibility for the welfare of citizens. An understanding of inequality as unfair together with a feeling of unity after World War II contributed to giving the welfare state legitimacy (Christoffersen, 2017a, 2019).

One of the main aspects of the emerging welfare state was an emphasis on good-quality universal systems. For a system to be universal Briseid (2019) argues that three factors have to be present: (1) all those in need of welfare services have the right to such services independent of age, economy, and family resources; (2) all those who need services have access to them; and (3) services are of good quality, are not too expensive, and the majority of the population find them to be more attractive than private services. A central feature of a universal welfare state is that all legal residents have an equal right to health services and that health services are publicly financed (Halvorsen & Stjernø, 2008). There are both idealistic and pragmatic reasons for the universality of the Norwegian welfare state, and particularly since World War II there has been a tendency to avoid excluding people with poor means in Scandinavia. There has also been a pragmatic tendency to favour universal schemes instead of extensive means-testing to minimise administrative costs (Alestalo et al., 2009). Several important systems of economic support have been introduced since 1946 such as universal child allowance in 1946, old age pension in 1957, and national insurance in 1967. National insurance was not a new system, but merged several systems and changed old age pensions to partly reflect earlier income (Ervik & Kildal, 2016; Hjelmtveit, 2005). Expansion of the welfare state represented a restructuring of the relationship between state and family since the welfare state took on a larger part of the responsibility (Leira, 2012).

Social work as an educational course was first taught in 1950 in answer to demands from the welfare state. The state needed competent workers and in 1947 a state committee was established to discuss the need for a school of social work that would teach municipal administration and direct work with clients (Dahle, 2010; Jóhannesdóttir & Aamodt, 2019). Optimal ways of administering public resources dominated in discussions of social work during the 1950s and 1960s. In the 1960s there was a shift toward developing systems directed at helping the needy (Dahle, 2010) and the main focus was on individual social treatment (Hanssen, 2005). Living standards became more equal throughout the 1950s and 1960s and it was generally felt the welfare state had overcome poverty (Christoffersen, 2017b). Since the 1960s municipalities have been required to establish a means of administering social services including coordination of services to the elderly, distribution of social benefits, and child protection. Since the 1970s social services took over responsibilities from elected representatives in municipalities. This laid the ground for professional social workers in municipalities since modern social treatment built on methods from psychotherapy required professional knowledge (Hanssen, 2005).

The expansion of the welfare state continued until the late 1970s. There were systems in place to compensate for loss of income in most risk situations including illness (Fløtten, Grønningssæter, Hippe, & Christensen, 2007). Employment for all was a central goal (Furre, 1991), most of the population—men and women—already participated in the labour market (Fløtten et al., 2007). Radical ideas were introduced in social work coupled with analysis of how existing structures and ideologies about health and welfare contributed to "clientification" and powerlessness among those who used social services (Finnseth, 2005).

THE 1980s: TOWARD "WELFARE CONSUMERISM" AND A NEW WELFARE CONTRACT?

Since the 1980s the market has occupied a more prominent place in the Norwegian welfare state (Ervik & Kildal, 2016). The OECD report "The Welfare State in Crisis" (published in 1981) analysed demographic and economic challenges. It argued that too generous welfare programmes and too strict regulations of markets had led to oversized, inefficient, bureaucratic, and costly welfare states. The report was influential and led to changes in the Norwegian welfare state (Botten et al., 2003). It suggested that the welfare state itself produced counterproductive effects such as dependency, passivity, and disincentives to work. Thus, the idea of a "new welfare contract" between citizens and the state grew in popularity: access to public benefits should be more closely linked to certain duties citizens were obliged to meet as a condition for eligibility (Ervik & Kildal, 2016).

Sejersted (2004) pointed out two important changes that took place during the 1980s. There was a shift toward what he called "welfare consumerism" where what had been considered a collective system of security was seen more as a system of individual rights. This shift implied that people related to services in a different manner. The other change was what Sejersted called a "freedom revolution" in which old ideas about equality and unity were replaced with ideas about freedom, individualism and pluralism. During the years of the social democratic welfare state (1945–1970) high-quality standard solutions had been the goal. Since the 1980s there have been increasing demands for liberty to choose between schools for the children, which doctor to see, and when to do the shopping.

In the 1980s and 1990s, the perspective of redistributive equality as a matter of justice was increasingly challenged by ideas of productive inequality, where inequality is seen as a productive force that can lead to economic growth. In such a perspective, a central idea is that the economic outcome should reflect the effort of the individual, and that economic differences can be just if they reflect the effort. Such ideological changes led to welfare increasingly becoming an individual project depending on individual responsibility. This shift is present in the work line of social policies (Christoffersen, 2017b), which will be discussed in the next section. Ideas about justice changed during the same period from policies of social rights to policies of right and duty. Policies of social rights expressed an egalitarian, resource-based notion of justice that included ideas about redistribution, equal respect, and equal opportunity. The shift was toward policies of right and duty that were more concerned with establishing the limits to granting such goods (Ervik & Kildal, 2016).

Municipalities carry out many of the welfare services granted to the population. Moreover, since the 1990s there has been increased attention to differences in services and subsidies between municipalities. Such differences contrast with the idea of universality and equality (Hanssen, 2005). Briseid (2017) found that communal care was not always universal and suggested a weakening of public services in fields with low status such as mental care for the elderly could be seen. Municipalities are required and expected to carry out services of a high standard within economic limits and have to prioritise (Kjølsrød, 2010). Briseid argued that there was a mismatch between the legal duties of municipalities and the economic resources they are given: they cannot uphold the services they are responsible for with the resources they have available. Thus, she held that the task of dismantling or downsizing universalism was left to municipalities since they are given responsibility for choosing what to prioritise. What she interpreted as a weakening of universalism was easier because of the trust that Norwegians have in the state as a protector of such universalism.

As shown by Ellingsæter & Pedersen (2013) in their article on how parenthood is organised. Hernes and Hippe (2007) held that the mentality in Norway is one of collectivistic individualism. Established collective arrangements and institutions promote individual liberty, social equality, and coherence in society. Social and political systems are not only practical solutions but inherent in norms and behaviour. Central to collectivistic individualism is an egalitarian view of others—the notion that all members of society depend on each other and that collective solutions might lead to more individual freedom.

Work Line in Norwegian Social Policy

Inclusion in the workforce and greater emphasis on the responsibility of individuals have been central to social policy reforms since the 1990s (Kjørstad, 2005). Moreover, the arguments used relate to strengthening work morale and to reducing public expenditure (Sinding Aasen, 2018). A renewed work approach was launched that placed emphasis on active measures rather than so-called passive benefits and on citizens' obligations rather than their rights (Ervik & Kildal, 2016). Such policies often refer to activation, participation, responsibility, rights and duties, and benefits and are more often seen as being traded for work (Kjørstad, 2005).

While some of the reforms implemented in the 1990s imply stricter criterias for welfare policies, others have led to more generous policies (Kildal

& Kuhnle, 2005). The state has withdrawn from its monopoly in running services and there is now more room for the market and for private solutions. Although there has been a general increase in prosperity, an increasing number of people face new risks and new uncertainties (Botten et al., 2003). Socioeconomic inequalities are increasing despite continuing to be small compared with other OECD countries (Trommald, 2017).

When claimants have to perform some prescribed activity to receive benefits the term active conditionality is used. It is increasingly often used when granting welfare benefits in Norway and in other European welfare states. Such activity can be to apply for jobs, to follow courses or study, or carry out work. Such policies come with sanctioning regimes directed at claimants who fail to maintain or fulfil the prescribed activity (Hagelund, Øverbye, Hatland, & Terum, 2016). When active conditionality requires that the claimant work in exchange for receiving benefits this is often referred to as workfare. Although workfare regimes differ, they are all rooted in what Peck and Theodore (2001, p. 429) called workfareism. Workfareism is based on an analysis of welfare dependency where "dysfunctional lifestyles and malformed work ethics of the poor are cited as the fundamental policy problem." Although the myth of welfare dependency has an Anglo-American origin, it has been suggested that Nordic welfare states are especially at risk of encouraging welfare dependency due to the relatively high level of benefits. Vogt (2018) argued that the myth was based on an individualistic and static understanding of people's lives and a narrow understanding of welfare. Workfareism entails the imposition of mandatory work requirements with a view to enforcing work while residualising welfare (Peck & Theodore, 2001). Activation requirements are often presented as being empowering and ways of enhancing the human capital of the claimant (Hagelund et al., 2016).

Workfare policies in Norway are not overtly controversial since they are linked to positive concepts that promote human development and concern for the wellbeing of clients (Kjørstad, 2005). Justifying the new focus on responsibilities of the unemployed is mainly linked to the idea that such responsibilities are beneficial for the claimants themselves (Ervik & Kildal, 2016). Report to the Parliament No. 30 (1994–1995) stated that "The balancing of rights and duties will also contribute to increased dignity and a greater degree of autonomy" (in Ervik & Kildal, 2016, p. 112). Thus, Ervik and Kildal (2016, p. 112) argued the main concern becomes how to change individuals' behaviour in a way that can make them help themselves. Changes in the Norwegian welfare state not only reflect political, economic, and social changes in society, but also changes in ideology, values, and ideas about welfare. What are considered to be social questions have changed as have ideas about equality and inequality (Christoffersen, 2017a).

Whether or not the Norwegian welfare state changed fundamentally as a result of the increasing marketization of the 1990s is a moot point. Some argue that the institutional characteristics of Scandinavian-type welfare states are likely to remain intact despite the changes and reforms that have taken place since the 1990s (Kuhnle, 2000 in Alestalo et al., 2009). Others hold that Nordic countries now have more in common with continental welfare states due to reforms such as shorter periods of eligibility for sickness and unemployment and the introduction of workfare systems (Kamali & Jönsson, 2018, p. 8). Despite the privatisation of some services, there are also popular claims for expansion of rights related to the welfare state such as health services, maternity and paternity leave, and studies at university level (Hernes & Hippe, 2007).

Norwegian Labour and Welfare Administration and New Individualism

Reform of the Norwegian Labour and Welfare Administration (NAV) was the most extensive reform carried out in the history of the Norwegian welfare state (Røysum, 2013). The new administration merged Public Employment Services, National Insurance Services, and Municipal Social Assistance Services into a one-stop service. The aim was to get more people into work or some other activity, achieve more coordinated services, and to make services more easily accessible. There were three general characteristics of the reform: employment orientation, user orientation, and efficiency. The administrative goal was to facilitate individual follow-up of users (Andreassen, 2005; Ervik & Kildal, 2016; Røysum, 2017).

NAV is in charge of one-third of the state budget state and responsible for more than 60 different economic support systems including old age pensions, child benefits, municipal financial social assistance programmes, and employment qualification programmes (Andreassen, 2005; Røysum, 2017). NAV is the main organiser of activation policies.

The qualification program is targeted at persons who are long-time unemployed and long-term recipients of social assistance. It is one of the main programmes in NAV. The programme aims at helping people with complex and substantial problems and helping them get work through a 2-year programme. During these 2 years participants receive a standardised qualification benefit and follow an individually designed programme that should equal full-time activity. Another important programme is Work Assessment Allowance that has the aim of helping people with medical problems enter the labour market. Both these programmes offer contract-based, conditional rights to economic benefits, as well as close individual follow-up and guidance. Thus, balancing rights and duties is central to both programmes. Violations of the duties of activity by the recipient may be financially sanctioned (Ervik & Kildal, 2016).

Social assistance constitutes the final safety net in Norway and provides economic assistance when other sources of aid fail to provide help or the help provided is not sufficient to meet human needs. Since 2017 there have been activation requirements for persons under the age of 30 who apply for social assistance. Moreover, municipalities can also require activation for persons who are 30 years or older. The aim is to help those who receive such support to find employment (Arbeids- og sosialdepartementet, 2017). Vogt (2018) held that the myth of welfare dependency seemed to have influenced the introduction of activation requirements for this group. Participants can be sanctioned if they do not follow up the prescribed activity in which case their economic benefits may be shortened but not withdrawn (Dahl & Lima, 2018).

SOCIAL WORK IN A CHANGING WELFARE STATE

Primary ethical principles in social work are related to social justice and respect (Røysum, 2017) and to the obligation to put the client's interests in the centre (Kjørstad, 2005, p. 383). Social work education is characterised by critical thinking. Students are trained to analyse complex challenges and problems they encounter in social work and to identify situations of injustice and misrecognition (Jensen & Føssestøl, 2005).

NAV has brought about a change in the way standardisation, counting, and reports are viewed. Such changes challenge the ideas social workers have about how they should do social work (Øvrelid, 2018; Terum, Tufte, & Jessen, 2012). The implementation of NAV reform has put the professional identity of social workers under pressure and highlighted a conflict between two views of social work: (1) a standardised way of working; and (2) social work based on relationships with individual clients and an ability to see and analyse the situation of individuals in their social and political context (Øvrelid, 2018, p. 105).

Several social work academics argue that social work has altered as a result of changes in social policies. Rugkåsa and Ylvisåker (2018) argued that social work has become individualised and depoliticised. Røysum (2017) held that social workers who are employed in the public sector increasingly have to adapt to an environment defined by market values and meet demands owing to economic principles and public service reforms. According to Alseth and Flem (2017) social workers are employed in a context where neoliberal policies have led to changes in the frameworks within which social work acts and such changes sometimes contradict values in social work.

Policies of activation are put into action by social workers on the frontline (Moen Gjersøe, 2019). Moreover, social workers have considerable discretion over when and how they implement sanctions (Kjørstad, 2005). In her study of how social workers implement activation policies related to the qualification program Brodtkorb (2017) found that social workers do not only focus on whether the participant has complied with the demands of activation when deciding whether or not to impose sanctions, they also take into consideration other factors such as the reasons the participant has not followed up.

Another element to be considered is an analysis of the consequences of such sanctions for the participant. When consequences could be severe for participants, social workers are known to be very restrictive with sanctions since internal rules and policies within municipalities are important to the practice of social workers (Kjørstad, 2005). Moen Gjersøe (2019) studied how social workers decide whether people are eligible for pension based on ill health and whether they are able to get paid work. This has traditionally been the responsibility of the medical profession. Social workers take such decisions based on information about the participant and knowledge about the labour market. The dilemma faced by social workers is when to decide that a participant does not have the capacity to work when the person does not fulfil the criteria for a pension based on the medical situation alone and when no jobs are available. Social workers follow up participants closely and might allow participants to continue in programmes where they do not quite fit. All these studies suggest that social workers attempt to balance their loyalty to ethical principles in social work such as their wish to place the clients' interest before loyalty to employers and political signals (see also Kjørstad, 2005; Terum et al., 2012).

How are social workers responding to such practices? In his study of social workers involved in NAV, Øvrelid (2018, p. 112) found there was little opposition to the NAV system. In contrast, he described how social workers stayed loyal and adapted to the system. Social workers tend to take on personal responsibility and believe that if they have problems managing the job, then it has to do with their lack of knowledge. Thus, although they might criticise a lack of training in NAV, they define the problems they encounter as their own individual, professional problems (Øvrelid, 2018, pp. 112, 113). Rugkåsa and Ylvisåker (2018) found that social workers often feel powerless when confronted with the conflicting pressures of remaining loyal to service users' needs and dealing with the demands of the welfare system at the same time. Lidén and Trætteberg (2019), on the other hand, found that most social workers in charge of implementing activation policies for young people who apply for social assistance hold a positive view of activation policies. They give two reasons for this: the tools provided by activation policies and increased resources that came with the law. Social workers describe the new law as ensuring NAV offices provide meaningful activities for participants (Lidén & Trætteberg, 2019). Brodtkorb (2017) described the mixed signals sent out by laws when it comes to who should be included and how sanctions should be carried out. Social workers have to find ways of dealing with this and do so, as found by Brodtkorb, by being more restrictive in implementing sanctions than the system would suggest.

Social workers are gatekeepers in charge of making decisions about who is included in different programmes and in charge of implementing sanctions if participants do not follow up on their duty to carry out activities. Kjørstad (2005) thus held that the ethical position of social workers is important to the quality of decisions taken and to the legitimacy of the system. Kroken (2006) claimed that social workers wield more influence over social work practice when they clearly demonstrate the consequences of contemporary policies. Rugkåsa and Ylvisåker (2018) argued that social workers need to be provided with knowledge about political and institutional circumstances. They also argued that critical reflection can serve as a tool to help social workers scrutinise the values and theories underpinning social work and thereby resist the mechanisms that lead to increasing inequalities and social problems.

Challenges Facing Social Work Education: Final Remarks

The Norwegian welfare state is changing and has implications for social work and social work education. The Norwegian welfare state is a Nordic or social democratic welfare state (Esping-Andersen, 1990) where emphasis has traditionally been on universal systems and services. Universality (i.e., access to good-quality services for the entire population) has been among the main features of the welfare state. The welfare state and rights to welfare have broad support in the population. Since the 1990s activation policies have been increasingly used. This together with increased standardisation in social work presents challenges both for social work and for social work education.

Bibliography

Alestalo, M., Hort, S. E. O., & Kuhnle, S. (2009). *The Nordic model: Conditions, origins, outcomes, lessons.* Berlin: Hertie School of Governance.

Alseth, A. K., & Flem, A. L. (2017). Sosialarbeiderutdanning i et mangfoldig studiefellesskap - en ressurs for barnevernet? *Tidsskriftet Norges Barnevern, 94*(3), 186–205.

Andreassen, T. A. (2005). NAV - Arbeids- og velferdsforvaltningen. In M. A. Stamsø (Ed.), *Velferdsstaten i endring.* Oslo: Gyldendal akademisk.

Arbeids- og sosialdepartementet. (2017). Aktivitetsplikt for mottakere av sosialhjelp. Retrieved October 18, 2019, from regjeringen.no website: https://www.regjeringen.no/no/tema/pensjon-trygd-og-sosiale-tjenester/innsikt/sosiale-tjenester/okonomisk-sosialhjelp/aktivitetsplikt-for-mottakere-av-sosialhjelp/id2009224/.

Botten, G., Elvebakken, K. T., & Kildal, N. (2003). The Norwegian welfare state on the threshold of a new century. *Scandinavian Journal of Public Health, 31,* 81–84.

Briseid, K. (2017). *On the old and the new: An ethnographic study of older people's mental health services in a changing welfare state.* (PhD thesis). University College of South East Norway. Doctoral dissertation no. 19, 2017.

Briseid, K. (2019). Personorientering i en norsk velferdsstatskontekst. *Tidsskrift for velferdsforskning, 5*(1), 1–17.

Brodtkorb, E. (2017). *Individualisering av tjenester i et aktiveringsprogram - en studie av veilederfellesskapet i kvalifiseringsprogrammet* (PhD thesis). Høgskolen i Oslo og Akershus, Oslo.

Christoffersen, H. (2017a). *Likhet i forandring: en begrepshistorisk analyse av Høyres og Arbeiderpartiets valg- og prinsipprogrammer for perioden 1933–2013* (HIoA avhandlinger). Høgskolen i Oslo og Akershus, Oslo.

Christoffersen, H. (2017b). *Likhet i forandring: Institutt for sosialfag* (PhD thesis). OsloMet Skriftserien, 2017: 9. Oslo, VID Specialized University.

Dahl, E. S., & Lima, I. (2018). *NAV-kontorenes erfaringer med aktivitetsplikt for unge sosialhjelpsmottakere* (No. 4). Retrieved from NAV website: https://www.nav.no/no/NAV+og+samfunn/Kunnskap/Analyser+fra+NAV/Arbeid+og+velferd/Arbeid+og+velferd/nav-kontorenes-erfaringer-med-aktivitetsplikt-for-unge-sosialhjelpsmottakere.

Dahle, R. (2010). Sosialt arbeid - en historie om kjønn, klasse og profesjon. *Tidsskrift for Kjønnsforskning, 34*(1), 41–56.

Ellingsæter, A. L., & Leira, A. (2006). Introduction: Politicising parenthood in Scandinavia. In A. L. Ellingsæter & A. Leira (Eds.), *Politicising parenthood in Scandinavia: Gender relations in welfare states.* Bristol: Policy Press.

Ellingsæter, A. L., & Pedersen, E. (2013). Fruktbarhetens fundament i den norske velferdsstaten. *Tidsskrift for Samfunnsforskning, 54*(1), 3–29.

Ervik, R., & Kildal, N. (2016). From collective to individual responsibility? Changing problem definitions of the welfare state. In R. Ervik & N. Kildal (Eds.), *New contractualism in European welfare State policies.* London: Taylor & Francis.

Esping-Andersen, G. (1990). *The three worlds of welfare capitalism.* Cambridge: Polity Press.

Finnseth, A. (2005). *Engasjert for mennesket. Innsteg i Diakonhjemmets historie 1890–2000.* Oslo: Forlaget Snorre.

Fløtten, T., Grønningsæter, A., Hippe, J. M., & Christensen, J. (2007). Den reformerte velferdsstaten - en ny samfunnskontrakt. In J. E. Dølvik, T. Fløtten, G. Hernes, & J. M. Hippe (Eds.), *Hamskifte. Den norske modellen i endring.* Oslo: Gyldendal akademisk.

Furre, B. (1991). *Vårt hundreår.* Oslo: Det Norske Samlaget.

Hagelund, A., Øverbye, E., Hatland, A., & Terum, L. I. (2016). Sanksjoner - arbeidslinjas nattside? *Tidsskrift for Velferdsforskning, 19*(1), 24–43.

Hagen, A., & Skule, S. (2007). Den norske modellen og utviklingen av kunnskapssamfunnet. In J. E. Dølvik, T. Fløtten, G. Hernes, & J. M. Hippe (Eds.), *Hamskifte. Den norske modellen i endring.* Oslo: Gyldendal akademisk.

Halvorsen, K., & Stjernø, S. (2008). *Work, oil and welfare.* Oslo: Universitetsforlaget.

Hanssen, J.-I. (2005). Kommunal sosialpolitikk. In M. A. Stamsø (Ed.), *Velferdsstaten i endring.* Oslo: Gyldendal akademisk.

Hernes, G., & Hippe, J. M. (2007). Kollektivists individualisme. In J. E. Dølvik, T. Fløtten, G. Hernes, & J. M. Hippe (Eds.), *Hamskifte. Den norske modellen i endring.* Oslo: Gyldendal akademisk.

Hjelmtveit, V. (2005). Sosialpolitikk i historisk perspektiv. In M. A. Stamsø (Ed.), *Velferdsstaten i endring.* Oslo: Gyldendal akademisk.

Jensen, K., & Føssestøl, B. (2005). Et språk for de gode gjerninger? Om sosialarbeiderstudenter og deres motivasjon. *Nordisk Sosialt Arbeid, 25*(1), 17–30.

Jóhannesdóttir, H., & Aamodt, L. G. (2019). *Pionerer i sosialt arbeid. Samtaler om profesjonalisering og yrkesidentitet.* Bergen: Fagbokforlaget.

Kamali, M., & Jönsson, J. H. (2018). Introduction: Neoliberalism and social work in the Nordic welfare states. In M. Kamali & J. H. Jönsson (Eds.), *Neoliberalism, Nordic welfare states, and social work.* London: Routledge.

Kildal, N. (2018). Hvor(for) forsvant velferdsstatens normative spørsmål? *Norsk Sosiologisk Tidsskrift, 2*(1), 5–7.

Kildal, N., & Kuhnle, S. (2005). Introduction. In N. Kildal & S. Kuhnle (Eds.), *Normative foundations of the welfare state: The Nordic experience*. Abingdon, Oxon: Routledge.

Kjølsrød, L. (2005). En tjenesteintensiv velferdsstat. In I. Frønes & L. Kjølsrød (Eds.), *Det norske samfunn*. Oslo: Gyldendal akademisk.

Kjølsrød, L. (2010). Velferdsstaten under press. In I. Frønes & L. Kjølsrød (Eds.), *Det norske samfunn. 6. utgave* (6th ed.). Oslo: Gyldendal akademisk.

Kjørstad, M. (2005). Between professional ethics and bureaucratic rationalilty: The challenging ethical position of social workers who are faced with implementing a workfare policy. *European Journal of Social Work, 8*(4), 381–398.

Kroken, R. (2006). Nye perspektiver på sosialarbeideres samfunnsoppdrag. *Nordisk Sosialt Arbeid, 26*(4), 306–316.

Kuhnle, S. (2000). European welfare lessons of the 1990s. In S. Kuhnle (Ed.), *Survival of the European welfare state*. London: Routledge/ECPR Studies in European Political Science.

Leira, A. (2012). Omsorgens institusjoner, omsorgens kjønn. In A. L. Ellingsæter & K. Widerberg (Eds.), *Velferdsstatens familier. Nye sosiologiske perspektiver*. Oslo: Gyldendal akademisk forlag.

Lidén, H., & Trætteberg, H. S. (2019). *Aktivitetsplikt for unge mottakere av sosialhjelp. Delrapport 1* (No. 12; p. Institutt for Samfunnsforskning). Retrieved from Rapport_12_19_Aktivitetsplikt_for_unge_mottakere_av_sosialhjelp.pdf (908.5Kb).

Lysestøl, P. M. (2002). Velferdsstatens framtid. *Nordisk Sosialt Arbeid, 22*(2), 102–107.

Misje, T. (2019). Migrantar med avgrensa rettar i den norske velferdsstaten: Ei utfordring for sosialt arbeid og for sosialarbeidarar. In A. M. Sønneland (Ed.), *Alle skal med? Om likhet, arbeidslinje og alles rett til velferd i et samfunn i endring*. Oslo: VID Specialized University.

Moen Gjersøe, H. (2019). Komplekse vurderinger i førstelinjen: Arbeidsevnevurdering som aktiveringspolitisk virkemiddel. In A. M. Sønneland (Ed.), *Alle skal med? Om likhet, arbeidslinje og alles rett til velferd i et samfunn i endring*. Oslo: VID Specialized University.

Øvrelid, B. (2018). Profesjonsidentitetens vilkår. Sosialt arbeid i NAV. *Tidsskrift for Velferdsforskning, 21*(2), 103–118.

Peck, J., & Theodore, N. (2001). Exporting workfare/importing welfare-to-work: exploring the politics of Third Way policy transfer. *Political Geography, 20*, 427–460.

Røysum, A. (2013). The reform of the welfare services in Norway: One office—One way of thinking? *European Journal of Social Work, 16*(5), 708–723.

Røysum, A. (2017). 'How' we do social work, not 'what' we do. *Nordic Social Work Research, 7*(2), 141–154.

Rugkåsa, M., & Ylvisåker, S. (2018). Resisting neoliberal changes in social work education. In M. Kamali & J. H. Jönsson (Eds.), *Neoliberalism, Nordic welfare states, and social work*. London: Routledge.

Seip, A. L. (1981). *Om velferdsstatens framvekst*. Oslo: Universitetsforlaget.

Sejersted, F. (2004). Sosialdemokratiets tidsalder. *Nytt Norsk Tidsskrift, 21*(3–4), 250–263.

Sinding Aasen, H. (2018). Fra rettsstat til velferdsstat - normative utviklingslinjer. *Norsk Sosiologisk Tidsskrift, 2*(1), 84–93.

Stamsø, M. A. (2005). Helsetjenester. In M. A. Stamsø (Ed.), *Velferdsstaten i endring*. Oslo: Gyldendal akademisk.

Terum, L. I., Tufte, P. A., & Jessen, J. T. (2012). Arbeidslinja og sosialarbeiderne. In S. Stjernø & E. Øverbye (Eds.), *Arbeidslinja. Arbeidsmotivasjonen og velferdsstaten*. Oslo: Universitetsforlaget.

Trommald, M. (2017). *Økte forskjeller - gjør det noe? In Oppvekstrapporten 2017*. Oslo: Barne- og familie.

Vogt, K. C. (2018). Myten om velferdsavhengighet. In K. Christensen & L. J. Syltevik (Eds.), *Myter om velferd og velferdsstaten*. Oslo: Cappelen Damm akademisk.

PART III

Social Work Education in Developing Economies: Challenges and Opportunities

This section of the book particularly focuses on the contemporary challenges faced by social work education in the developing countries. The problems faced by social work education and practice in the developing countries are different from the problems that are experienced by the social work profession in the developed countries. Thus, the issues within the developing countries need a more intensive intervention and state support in developing the profession and achieving the fullest professional identity. Professional recognition is one of the most important challenges that are discussed throughout this handbook. Social work in both the North and the South face issues related to professional recognition; however, the professional issues in the West are much related to advanced pay, advanced working condition, and advanced representative opportunities whereas professionalization issues in the developing countries are much related to minimum pay, basic trust among the service users, and identity as professional social workers.

Contributions in this part of the book discuss a wide variety of issues pertaining to the development of social work education in Zimbabwe, Ireland, Georgia, Poland, India, Nepal, Bangladesh, Pakistan, and Sri Lanka. Interestingly, five of these are South Asian countries where social work is still in a developing stage and searching for an identity. Many of the challenges faced by countries in South Asia are common; however, they also face some peculiar problems. Nepal being a landlocked country faces several internal conflicts and issues such as poverty, unemployment, and lack of basic social security that threatens almost all people in Nepal. Given these condition, social work education in Nepal is expected to prepare social work professionals equipped to effectively address these conflicts and other above-mentioned issues. The importance of decolonizing social work education in Nepal is well articulated by Rajkumar Yadav and Amit Kumar Yadav, who carried out a content analysis of social work curriculums taught across Nepal's social work educational institutions and conceptualized what decolonization of social work education in Nepal entails and what are its prospects and challenges. Further, *Bishnu Mohan Dash* examines the social work education and its development in India and questions the effectiveness and universality of the Western knowledge that is widely practised and incorporated into Indian social work curriculum since its inception in 1936. The chapter argues that there is an urgent need for 'bharatiyakaran' of social work education to make social work more responsible to changing social, economic, and political condition of the country.

Further, *Ishahaque Ali* and colleagues in Bangladesh, *Nasreen Aslam Shah* in Pakistan examine the challenges for social work development and growth in the respective countries and try to capture the debates in the light of social, economic, and religious background. Both authors discuss social work practice in the context of a dominant Islamic state. Ishahaque Ali and colleagues try to explore the influence of Islam on social work development in Bangladesh and examines the Islamic perspective on social work activities or programs that were operated by Muslim orphanages and mosques. Researchers have already noted the influence of Devolution (Mizrahi, 2001; Sanfort, 2000), changing demographics, growing disparities between rich and poor (Fisher & Karger, 1997), and reduced philanthropic funding for the economically disadvantaged (Foundation Center, 2003) on social work practice. Furthering this understanding, *Nasreen Aslam Shah* examines the social work educational achievements and challenges in Pakistan and provides a historical analysis of the social work in Pakistan.

Changes in the socio-economic contexts, the political conflict and uncertainty, privatization of means of production, and lack of resources within the nation had greater impact on social welfare delivery in many countries in recent decades. Shifting economic development, i.e. public sector undertaking to private sector undertaking in many countries, especially in the Global South, leads to disasters changes and challenges for the marginalized sections. Interestingly, social work as a service profession centred its curriculum and teaching towards social problems in many parts of the world and thus aimed for training the workforce to address these emerging social problems. This effort by social work academia is further explored by Edmos Mtetwa and Munyaradzi Muchacha in Zimbabwe. They analyse to what extent social work education in Zimbabwe responds to the political and economic imperatives obtaining in the African country. Further, *Sajid S. M. and Khalid Mohammad Tabish* critically examine the pedagogy and methodologies of social work interventions at various level and their relevance to changing sociopolitical and cultural condition in India. This further develops an understanding of how contextual realities of the Global South influence the social work education and practice. It is quite important that in this time of global transformation and varied political power shift, social work education across the globe needs to focus on training social workers with political sensitivity and training them to work with the governmental agencies and bureaucrats at different levels of policy formulation and welfare delivery.

Nevertheless, despite numerous challenges faced by social work in the developing countries, there are innovations and uniqueness *Julie Byrne, Stephanie Holt and Gloria Kirwan* highlights unique features of the system of social work education in Ireland. They explore a system which has been shaped by the wider social context, including key economic, political, and social developments at a time of rapid social change in Ireland. It also provides the evidence of social work education responding to the myriad of competing demands raised by rapid socio-economic and political changes. Different political regimes across the globe had both positive and negative impacts on the social work development. For example, the social work education in China had 40 years of absence because of the 'communist regime' which literally banned social work departments and teaching programmes; however, later in 1980s same communist party of China re-introduced social work education to China with an intention to develop harmonious society. *Jerzy Krzyszkowski* discusses the similar challenges faced by the social work education in post-communist Poland. The rapid social transformation that took place in Poland resulted in the establishment of social work teaching programmes as an autonomous field of study since 2006.

The group of chapters which follow takes us to the understanding of our differing and similar challenges in social work education across the borders. These understandings basically help the social work educators, students, and researchers to highlight commonality and co-learning from each other's experiences. Finally, there is a hope for the social work education in the Global South, as many countries in the Global South are experiencing a growing demand for professional social workers and social workers are getting involved in the policy influencing process and advocacy, though at a slower pace and in fewer numbers than what is desired. New educational programmes are being implemented at the masters and doctoral level in many parts of the developing world. Internationalization and collaborative teaching and research initiatives are opening for the developing world in the new millennium. These hopes are also reflected by Shorena Sadzaglishvili by gives us an account of social work development and the innovations that are taking place in Georgia within the modern international context and examines methods of increasing the visibility of doctoral education and translational research opportunities in Georgia to prepare qualified new generations of social workers and, consequently, promote a balanced social welfare system, broader social and economic equality, and the dignity and worth of all the Georgian people.

REFERENCES

Fisher, R. & Karger, H. J. (1997). *Social work and community in a private world: Getting out in public*. White Plains, NY: Addison Wesley Longman.

Foundation Center. (2003). *Foundation giving trends: Update on funding priorities*. New York, NY: Foundation Center.

Mizrahi, T. (2001). The status of community organizing in 2001: Community practice context, complexities, contradictions, and contributions. *Research on Social Work Practice, 11,* 176–189.

Sanfort, J. (2000). Developing new skills for community practice in an era of policy devolution. *Journal of Social Work Education, 36*(2), 183–186.

CHAPTER 15

Social Work Education for Social Justice and Poverty Reduction in Africa

Edmos Mtetwa and Munyaradzi Muchacha

INTRODUCTION

The social work profession was borne out of the need to protect the poor and most vulnerable groups in society. Since then, a plethora of developments have since occurred in the focus and orientation of the profession. Most importantly was the shift towards developmental social work. This brought forth the need to address human rights and social justice as critical indicators of social well-being. This paper critically assesses the extent to which social work as practised in Africa has been able to stand up to the task of the protection of human rights in its pursuit to achieving social justice. The paper begins by conceptualising social work. Thereafter, the paper moves to scrutinise the place of social work in championing the cause of social justice.

CONCEPTUALISING SOCIAL WORK

Over time, social work has evolved from a purely charitable and welfaristic profession into a rights-based and developmental profession premised upon social and economic justice. This section shall therefore examine the evolution of the profession from charity to welfare. Just like any other profession, social work needs to define its professional territory and earn recognition as a legitimate profession (Soydan, 2011). On this note, professional identity takes place over time and involves trial and error (Watson & West, 2006). As such, it is imperative that a few definitions of social work be presented in

E. Mtetwa · M. Muchacha (✉)
Department of Social Work, University of Zimbabwe, Harare, Zimbabwe

© The Author(s) 2021   237
S. S. M. et al. (eds.), *The Palgrave Handbook of Global Social Work Education*, https://doi.org/10.1007/978-3-030-39966-5_15

historical sequence. (For a comprehensive examination of the definitions of social work in historical sequence, see Soydan, 2011, pp. 12–13.)

Citing Richmond (1915, p. 43) and Soydan (2011) defined social work as the art of doing different things for and with different people by cooperating with them to achieve at one and the same time their own and society's betterment.

Given that social work is a contemporary profession, Richmond's definition has witnessed incremental extensions to reflect contemporary developments within the profession. On this note, the International Association of Schools of Social Work and the International Federation of Social Workers (2014, p. 19) define social work as "a practice-based profession and an academic discipline that promotes social change and development, social cohesion, and the empowerment and liberation of people. Principles of social justice, human rights, collective responsibility and respect for diversities are central to social work. Underpinned by theories of social work, social sciences, humanities and indigenous knowledge, social work engages people and structures to address life challenges and enhance well-being". The last definition situates social work as a contemporary and context specific profession. Trevithick (2000) emphasised this point by stating that social work is located within some of the most complex problems and perplexing areas of human experience, as such, social work is, and has to be a highly skilled activity.

The above definitions have made it clear that not only is it difficult to strike a consensus when it comes to defining social work, rather, the definition is entirely dependent on both context and a given historical moment. What is clear to all social workers, however, is what the profession seeks to achieve more than what it really is. In this context, there is growing consensus that the purpose of the social work profession is to promote human and community well-being. Guided by a person and environment construct, a global perspective, respect for human diversity, and knowledge based on scientific inquiry, social work's purpose is actualised through its quest for social and economic justice, the prevention of conditions that limit human rights, the alleviation of poverty, and the enhancement of the quality of life for all persons.

Social Work and Social Justice

Implicit in the definitions of social work given above is that social workers strive to end poverty, human misery, and social injustice for all in society. Freedom from oppression, want, and the right to a life with dignity are central to the social work profession. All this amounts to what has come to be known as social and economic justice. The question that remains, therefore, is: What really is meant by social justice? It is important to set the record clear that the current paper is bereft of both space and scope to intensely interrogate this concept. However, a brief description of the concept is given.

The concept of social justice first surfaced in Western thought and political language in the wake of the industrial revolution and the parallel development of the socialist doctrine. It emerged as an expression of protest against what was perceived as the capitalist exploitation of labour and as a focal point for the development of measures to improve the human condition. It was born as a revolutionary slogan embodying the ideals of progress and fraternity (Department of Economic and Social Affairs, 2006, p. 12). At that time, social justice represented the essence and the raison d'être of the social democrat doctrine and left its mark in the decades following the Second World War (ibid.). Social justice became more clearly defined when a distinction was drawn between the social sphere and the economic sphere. The concept developed into a mainstream preoccupation when a number of economists became convinced that it was their duty not only to describe phenomena but also to propose criteria for the distribution of the fruits of human activity (ibid.). (For a detailed examination of social justice and equity, see Roberts & McMahon, 2007.) In the modern social work parlance, the concepts social justice and redistributive justice have been used interchangeably. Social justice refers to the creation of social institutions that support the welfare of individuals and groups. The application of social justice requires a geographical, sociological, political, and cultural framework within which relations between individuals and groups can be understood, assessed, and characterised as just or unjust.

Social work thus seeks to intervene in ways that can remove the barriers or structural impediments to human well-being. Such interventions promote social development. Social development here is used to refer to progress or growth that encompasses both social and economic outcomes and impacts positively on human well-being (Midgley, 2014). Social work's mandates on empowerment and liberation speak to the notion of emancipating people from alienating social and economic conditions. Social justice therefore in its entirety has come to represent modern social work theory and practice. It is expressed through varied theoretical and practice orientations, such as empowerment, participation, liberation, respect for diversity as well as equality, and the anti-oppressive discourse. With all these social virtues in mind, the question that remains is whether social justice resonates with human rights or not. This paper shall simply highlight this relationship in order to pave way for an examination of the human rights discourse in Africa together with the place of the social work profession within it.

HUMAN RIGHTS

The field of human rights has incidentally become a contested terrain, especially in the political discourse of Africa. The major bone of contention being that this is largely a foreign concept brought forth by European and North American idealists in order to perpetuate their neocolonial agenda (Murithi, 2013). For social work however, social justice and human rights remain synonymous, with the latter being the precondition for fulfilling the former.

SOCIAL WORK AND HUMAN RIGHTS

According to Healy (2008), human rights are those rights that belong to all just because we are human. This paper, however, observes that unlike other professions, the social work profession has not acquitted itself well when it comes to the defence of human rights, especially in Africa. It is, nevertheless, here argued that if well indigenised and localised, the social work profession has got a wealth of opportunities and prospects to champion and promote human rights and social justice on the African continent than elsewhere. The rich cultural roots of tolerance, collectivism, and shared destiny stand as key vantage points upon which the social work profession should ride in its quest to champion the human rights and social justice agenda on the African continent. Whereas Westerners are able to carry out family life in the form of the nuclear family and often in isolation from other kin, Africans do not put much emphasis on the nuclear family. Rather, they operate within a broader arena of the extended family. Rather than the survival of the fittest and control over nature, the African worldview is tempered with the general guiding principle of the survival of the entire community and a sense of cooperation, interdependence, and collective responsibility (Heyns & Stefiszyn, 2006, p. 35). In many African societies, there is no distinction between a father and an uncle, or a brother and a cousin. For instance, within the Akan community of Ghana the English word "aunt" has no equivalent. As such, the Akan community treats all aunts as mothers (ibid.).

Riding on the African values and philosophy of collectivism, peace, and the emphasis on kinship solidarity expressed through the extended family, clan and tribe, social workers in Africa are strategically positioned to register immense gains on the social and political front. The African Philosophy of humanity is best summed up by Heyns and Stefiszyn (2006, p. 35) who say that "For the African, a philosophy of existence can be summed up as: I am because we are, and because we are therefore I am". The question that immediately comes to mind is why then are social workers in Africa not so competent when it comes to taking up the role of defending human rights and social justice? The answer as suggested here is not exhaustive. It is here argued that social workers in Africa are just but victims of the long cherished history of welfare and charity, values that triggered the development of the profession on the continent. It is here contended that social work was brought to Africa largely as a grand package of colonial pacifist agenda. As such social work instilled in its practitioners the highest sense of loyalty to the ruling elite. As Kaseke (1991) would have it, social work has always been treated as an instrument of social control. As such, the profession has, therefore, not been able to address the root causes of social problems. Couched in conservative ideals of access to social services, the profession propagated a pacifist ideology accompanied by the emphasis on philanthropy, charity, docility, "good behavior", social order, and respect for authority.

This paper further contends that the social work profession was brought forth to most African countries by religious institutions as part of evangelical works of charity, peace, and harmony amid growing social, economic, and political agitation and dissent by some Africans who gradually became disillusioned and could no longer withstand the weight of the yoke of servitude and oppression. Weighing in on the same point of view, Kaseke (1991) opines that the religious tradition left an indelible mark on the current practice wisdom in social work. On the same note, Leiby (1978) boldly asserts that "The Christian tradition was most important in the development of our institution for charity and correction because it furnished a cosmic drama, the story of creation, sin, judgment and salvation - in which suffering had a meaning and so did efforts to relieve and correct it. As such, the Helper and the helped could believe that their personal action counted for something in the very structure of the universe" (Leiby, 1978, p. 21). In such countries as Zimbabwe, Zambia, and Ghana, various religious organisations were at the forefront in establishing social work training colleges. In most of these countries, it took quite some time before local universities assimilated and incorporated these training institutions into their administrative structures. When African universities eventually embraced the social work training, they had little room to manoeuver other than to continue on the track of producing mainly for present regimes a docile and bureaucratic functionary whose prime responsibility was to sheepishly take orders in the provision of limited state charity to the most vulnerable in society. Very little if any option did exist for such bureaucrats to rise up to the policy formulation levels. Under such circumstances, the fight for social justice was largely seen as outright disobedience if not an unwitting attempt to plunge the social work profession into the unfamiliar waters of rebellion, political antagonism let alone technical quagmire in relation to other long established professions.

Africa's Human Rights and Political Synopsis

In order to squarely place the discussion into perspective, it remains all the more critical that a brief examination of Africa's political stability and human rights record be examined. Having interrogated African virtues couched in collectivism, communalism, and a philosophy of oneness, the question that immediately comes to the reader is: Why then does Africa rank so highly on the total disregard of human rights and social justice? Although it is not within the scope of the current discussion to exhaustively interrogate this question, let is suffice that the advent of western forms of capitalism are not far from blame. As such, the degree to which human rights are violated or protected entirely depends on the nature of the socio-economic system in place in each African country, their varied levels of development as well as the character of the ruling class (Heyns & Stefiszyn, 2006). The ruling class plays a critical role in influencing the degree of popular participation and democratisation (Bösl & Diescho, 2009).

Arguably, the deterioration of human rights on the African continent could in part be a result of the colonial legacy that supplanted the traditional and customary ways of life. The ultimate result was a new form of nationhood characterised by inter-tribal and intercultural forms of relationships as well as the demise of familiar customary ways of economic and social life. As such, the African continent is now littered with conflicts, avarice, and undemocratic forms of governance that serve to fuel human rights violations. In far too many places, freedoms of expression, association, and peaceful assembly continued to be severely curtailed (Amnesty International, 2015, p. 7). Following a deepening campaign of violence by the Islamist armed group Boko Haram during 2013, the armed conflict in Nigeria's north-east intensified in scope casualties, powerfully illustrating the threats to the stability of Africa's most populous nation and to regional peace and security. The abduction in April of 276 schoolgirls by Boko Haram was one emblematic case of the group's campaign of terror against civilians, which continued unabated. On the other hand, communities already terrorised for years by Boko Haram became increasingly vulnerable to repeated human rights violations by the state security forces, which regularly responded with heavy-handed and indiscriminate attacks and with mass arbitrary arrests, beatings, and torture (Amnesty International, 2015, p. 1).

The situation in Nigeria is no news to the conflict ridden African continent. For instance, millions of people perished in the civil war in the Democratic Republic of Congo (Commission for Africa, 2005, p. 107). Besides, according to the African Development Bank et al. (2014, p. 106), Africa's score on the Ibrahim Index of "political participation and respect for human rights" changed little between 2000 and 2012. Thirty-four countries made progress, but 17 lost ground in governance indicators. According to the same report, by 2013, 35 African countries had registered some marked improvement on the human rights record yet 17 countries even experienced a reversal in democratic gains. Although the number of leaders ousted unconstitutionally has decreased over the last two decades, five have been forced out since 2010 (African Development Bank et al., 2014, p. 106). In the Central African Republic, more than 5 000 civilians were killed in sectarian violence despite the presence of international forces. Similarly, in South Sudan tens of thousands of civilians were killed with more than 2 million fleeing their homes in the armed conflict between government and opposition forces (ibid.).

Arguably, political unrest and democratic deficits characteristic of most African countries are borne largely out of greed and corruption on the part of African leaders. This has led many scholars among them Chitereka (2009) to contend that poverty in Africa is mainly caused by corrupt regimes which do not care for the welfare of their citizens. Regimes bent on amassing wealth absorbed the region's resources into patrimonial power structures (United Nations Development Programme, 2012). For example, history has it that the late Presidents Sani Abacha of Nigeria and Mobutu Sese Seko of the former Zaire looted their countries' resources and had off-shore accounts (Chitereka, 2009). Some current African leaders are still plundering their countries' resources leading to the majority of their citizens wallowing in poverty (Chitereka, 2009).

In the middle of all these political, economic, and social injustices, the place of social work in standing up and protecting the most vulnerable in society remains blurred. Once again, social workers as advocates of the poor and downtrodden members of society remained silent. Having as its basic tenet the intrinsic value of every human being and as one of its main aims the promotion of equitable social structures, which can offer people security and development while upholding their dignity, the deafening silence of social workers during such human rights abuses remains a matter of concern (Mtetwa & Muchacha, 2013). This raises critical questions regarding whether or not social justice in social work is a real goal to strive towards or is just nothing short of an obsolete anthem devoid of any practical realisation. In addition to social justice, it is here contended that social workers have to start bothering themselves with economic justice if ever their plea to fight poverty is to register any degree of success. By economic justice is meant those aspects of social justice that relate to economic well-being, such as a livable wage, pay equity, job discrimination, and social security (Hepworth, Rooney, & Larsen, 2002).

THE EXTENT OF POVERTY AND INEQUALITY

As a profession, social work has always focused attention on poverty and the difficulties faced by persons who do not have enough resources to obtain the basics of life such as food, shelter, and medical and dental care. Such a professional preoccupation stems from the fact that poverty has devastating effects on individuals, families, and communities (Chitereka, 2009). It is a contributing factor to many other problems, such as the breakup of families, violence, crime, substance abuse, suicide, and a multitude of health problems. This led Handley, Higgins, Sharma, Bird, & Cammack (2009) to contend that poverty could as well be viewed as a sense of helplessness, dependency and lack of opportunities, self-confidence, and self-respect on the part of the poor. As such, the poor themselves see powerlessness and voicelessness as key aspects of their poverty (Narayan, Patel, Schafft, Rademacher, & Koch-Schulte, 1999).

One of the most critical goals of the social work profession is the eradication of extreme poverty, marginality, and powerlessness. From its formative phases in the UK right from the Elizabethan poor laws to the Charity Organisation Society, the social work profession embraces the virtues of dignity, equality, and justice at the economic, political, and social spheres of life (Becket, 2006). It is worth of note that extreme poverty does not entail just having unsatisfied material needs or being undernourished. It is often accompanied by a degrading state of powerlessness (Department of Economic and Social Affairs, 2006). Even in democratic and relatively well-governed countries, poor people have to accept daily humiliations without pro-test. Often, they cannot provide for their children and have a strong sense of shame and failure. When they are trapped in poverty, the poor lose hope of ever escaping from their hard work for which they often have nothing to show beyond bare survival (Singer, 2009). It is here argued that poverty is the worst of all evils, with many professionals and academics laying claim on their mission as that of eradicating extreme poverty and social deprivation. Social workers are in no way strangers to the war on poverty, with the very foundation upon which the profession is anchored being the need to fight urban poverty that became manifest in Europe and the United States mainly due to the industrial revolution that greeted those societies in the eight-eenth century (Kaseke, 1991). With respect to Africa, the paramount trig-ger of social problems is the scourge of poverty (Muzaale, 1987). Despite the fact that Africa is potentially the richest continent on the planet, it is actu-ally the poorest (Chitereka, 2009). Since 1990, income poverty has fallen in all regions of the world except in sub-Saharan Africa, where there has been an increase both in the incidence and absolute number of people living in income poverty (Handley et al., 2009). At least 28 of the 31 low human development countries are in sub-Saharan Africa (UNDP, 2006: 265 quoted in Handley et al., 2009). Further to that, 315 million people: one in two people in sub-Saharan Africa survive on less than one dollar per day. Also, 184 million people: 33% of the African population suffers from malnutrition (United Nations Development Programme, 2007). Another critical indica-tor of absolute poverty in Africa is food insecurity. To this, various scholars have keenly observed that no sustainable democracy has ever been built on empty stomachs and rampant poverty. In other words, food and nutrition security has had a far-reaching impact on democratisation processes. It has been a sound road map to rural development and political stability. On the same note, it is here contended that rapid economic progress in Africa has not brought food security to the substantial proportion of the population still gripped by hunger (UNDP, 2012). In fact, it is estimated that in late 2002 the lives and livelihoods of as many as 16 million people in Lesotho, Malawi, Mozambique, Swaziland, Zambia, and Zimbabwe were threatened by food insecurity (Handley et al., 2009). Therefore, the issue of assuring food and nutrition security for all in Africa is a critical concern not only for African governments, but also for the international community (International Food Policy Research Institute, 2004).

By implication, this paper contends that social justice and human rights are difficult to attain in the middle of poverty and inequality characteristic of most African societies. As such, the social work profession still remains drowned in the mashes of charity, poverty, and welfare mostly at the detri-ment of propagating the human rights agenda on the African continent. Put simply, social work practice, policy, and education all suffer in the "absence of conceptual or historical clarity or agreement" on the meaning of social justice

(Reisch, 2002, p. 349). On this note, the paper concludes the discussion by arguing that social justice and human rights remain a pie in the sky for the poor in Africa, with social workers doing very little if anything to put a foot on the ground in this area.

Implications on Social Work Education.

It is here contended that social work educators must equip practitioners with lobbing and advocacy skills if their quest to deal with poverty and deprivation is to succeed (Kaseke, 2001). Regrettably, the social work curricular of most African universities remains bereft of such an academic orientation, preferring the "traditional" social work methods of casework, group work, and community work.

If social work educators are to avoid creating cardboard people to fit particular stereotypes, they have to engage with the complexities of both their own contexts and those of the individual or groups with whom they are working (Dominelli, 2002, p. 23). The theories, methods, and domains of social work education should therefore reflect actual practice contexts of Africa. At present Western theories and methods have remained pre-eminent in most African schools of social work. These theories and methods represent nothing short of the intellectual achievements based upon foreign experiences.

Admittedly, they are useful in pointing to many common human problems, but they do not necessarily address the relevant problems or have all the answers to the problems in the rapidly changing African social and geopolitical space. Given this situation, the field will continue to struggle because of its weak commitment to the development of its exclusive knowledge base—which means limited standing among other related helping professions and academic disciplines.

The contextual imperatives of Africa therefore demand a paradigm shift from the social work curriculum predicated upon casework and group work towards a more proactive and rights-based orientation. Social work educators therefore should priorities the acquisition of such skills and competences as advocacy skills, community mobilising, and economic literacy.

Needless to emphasise, African schools of social work should refocus their curricular towards a rights-based model. Such social work curricular would serve as the critical crucible upon which the anthem of social justice is predicated. The human rights dimension to social work education should in turn capitalise on the eclectic nature of the profession to instil in future practitioners the skills and ethos of advocacy, human rights activism, and economic literacy together with the international legal competences expected of social justice practitioners.

Social work education should also instil an understanding of policy practice in regard to political, economic, and institutional systems and apply these in formulation, implementation and advocate for policy change consistent with the values and ethics of the profession.

Due to the eclectic nature of the profession, there is indeed potential for social work educators to enrich the curriculum by tapping from the rich experiences of such disciplines as political science, human rights law as well as feminist teachings. It is only when advocacy skills from these disciplines are universally adopted into the social work curriculum that the plea for social equity and poverty reduction are likely to see the light of day.

Conclusion

Evidently, human rights violation, poverty, and food insecurity have since come to characterise the African way of life. Whereas many African governments have tended to blame those mainly on the neocolonial overtures of their former colonial masters, other stakeholders including civil society organisations and intergovernmental agencies seem to place the blame on corruption, misgovernance, and the pursuit of selfish motives on the part of African leaders. In the middle of this debate, this paper argues that it is mainly the poor and most vulnerable members of society who suffer the most. It is those without the means for survival that go without food. It is primarily the powerless that find themselves caught up in conflicts, that lose lives in the process or who find themselves uprooted and alienated from their familiar environments (Mupedziswa, 1992). On the whole, it is the poor and most vulnerable members of African societies that suffer from the adverse effects of corrupt leadership, inequality, and poor service delivery. Once again, the visibility of social workers in defence of the underprivileged in society is called into question. Emphasising the place of the social work profession in defence of human rights and social justice, Pincus and Minahan (1973) observe that the responsibilities of social workers to become involved in public issues that have an impact on the private troubles of people and to influence people within the social system to make them more responsive to present and potential consumers is crucial. In this light, social workers contribute to the development and modification of social policies promulgated by legislative bodies, elected heads of government, public administrative agencies, and even private agencies (Mtetwa & Muchacha, 2013).

The Way Forward

In the light of the above state of affairs, it is here argued that social work academics and practitioners in Africa have not fully embraced the developmental thrust called for by such scholars as Mupedziswa (1992, 1995), Mupedziswa (2005), Midgley, and Chitereka (2009) among others. Following from such an observation is the question: Why do social workers take so long to embrace a developmental practice trajectory amid growing calls and compelling evidence that this is the panacea to dealing with the political, economic, and structural challenges confronting Africa? It is here argued that the reasons are manifold. Chief among these reasons is the way social work curricular for most African universities are designed.

Following from the above theoretical demands is the esoteric call for social justice that has become an anthem within the social work parlance. Once more, the call for social justice has meant a dramatic shift towards a political and grass-roots approach to community mobilising to fight oppression, inequality, and dilettantism. Basically, it is here contended that Africa's social problems now demand a dramatic shift from the traditional residual and welfaristic approach to problem solving towards a human rights or citizen of the world approach. Therefore, the profession's call for social justice is an indictment on the schools of social work in particular to take a fresh look at their curriculum and determine whether they are delivering as expected. Focus should therefore be placed on capacity building both students and practitioners on issues of human rights and social justice. This entails revisiting the social work curriculum with a view to inculcating values of empowerment, accountability, human rights, citizenship rights as well as entrepreneurship. This can help students, new professionals as well as experienced practitioners in implementing human rights and social justice strategies. Last but not least, social workers in Africa should strive to work in multidisciplinary teams in defence of human rights and social justice. On this note, Becket (2006) posits that social workers must endeavour to pursue policies, services, resources, and programmes through organisational and administrative advocacy and social and political action so as to empower groups at risk and promote social and economic justice. In the middle of such social challenges, social workers should be seen joining other progressive forces in speaking out against corrupt, inefficient, and repressive governments.

References

African Development Bank, Organisation for Economic Co-operation and Development, & United Nations Development Programme. (2014). *African economic outlook 2013/14*. Paris and Tunis: AfDB, OECD, UNDP and UNECA.

Amnesty International. (2015). *The state of the world's human rights*. London: Amnesty International Limited.

Becket, C. (2006). *Ethics and values in social work* (3rd ed.). Basingstoke: Palgrave Macmillan.

Bösl, A., & Diescho, J. (2009). *Human rights in Africa: Legal perspectives on their protection and promotion*. Windhoek: Macmillan Education Press.

Chitereka, C. (2009). Social work practice in a developing continent: The case of Africa. *Advances in Social Work, 10*(2), 144–156.

Commission for Africa. (2005). *Our common interest: Report of the commission for Africa*. Retrieved from http://www.commissionforafrica.info/wp-content/uploads/2005-report/11-03-05_cr_report.pdf.

Department of Economic and Social Affairs. (2006). *Social justice in an open world: The role of the United Nations.* New York: United Nations Publications.

Dominelli, L. (2002). Anti-oppressive practise in context. In R. Adams, L. Dominelli, & M. Payne (Eds.), *Social work: Themes issues and critical debates* (2nd ed.). Basingstoke: Palgrave.

Handley, G., Higgins, K., Sharma, B., Bird, K., & Cammack, D. (2009). *Poverty and poverty reduction in sub-Saharan Africa: An overview of Keyissues* (Working Paper 299). Results of ODI research presented in preliminary form for discussion and critical comment. London: Overseas Development Institute.

Healy, L. (2008). Exploring the history of social work as a human rights profession. *International Social Work 51*(6), 735–748.

Hepworth, D. H., Rooney, R. H., & Larsen, J. A. (2002). *Direct social work practice: Theory and skills* (6th ed.). Pacific Grove, CA: Brooks/Cole Publishing.

Heyns, C., & Stefiszyn, K. (2006). *Human rights, peace and justice in Africa: A reader.* Pretoria: University of Pretoria Law Press.

International Association of Schools of Social Work and International Federation of Social Workers. (2014). *The global agenda for social work and social development progress report.* Retrieved March 22, 2016, from http://www.nasow.org/wp-content/uploads/2016/05/IFSWReport2014.pdf.

International Food Policy Research Institute. (2004). Sustainable solutions for ending hunger and poverty. Assuring Food and Nutrition Security in Africa by 2020: Prioritizing Actions, Strengthening Actors, and Facilitating Partnerships. Proceedings of an All-Africa Conference.

Kaseke, E. (1991). Social work practice in Zimbabwe. *Journal of Social Development in Africa, 6,* 33–45.

Kaseke, E. (2001). *Social development as a model of social work practice: The experience of Zimbabwe* (SSW Staff Papers). Harare: School of Social Work. https://opendocs.ids.ac.uk/opendocs/handle/123456789/9576 Accessed 8 February 2019.

Leiby, J. (1978). *A history of social welfare and social work in the United States.* New York: Columbia University Press.

Midgley, J. (2014). *Social development: Theory and practice.* London: Sage.

Mtetwa, E., & Muchacha, M. (2013). The price of professional silence: Social work and human rights in Zimbabwe. *African Journal of Social Work, 3*(1), 19–43.

Mupedziswa, R. (1992). Africa at the crossroads: Major challenges for social work education and practice towards the year 2000. *Journal of Social Development in Africa, 7*(2), 19–38.

Mupedziswa, R. (1995). Social welfare services. In N. Hall & R. Mupedziswa (Eds.), *Social policy and administration in Zimbabwe* (pp. 81–105). School of Social Work: Harare.

Mupedziswa, R. (2005). Challenges and prospects of social work services in Africa. In J. C. Akeibunor & E. E. Anugwom (Eds.), *The social sciences and socio-economic transformation in Africa* (pp. 271–317). Nsukka: Great AP Express Publishing.

Murithi, T. (2013, March). *The African Union and the International Criminal Court: An embattled relationship?* (Policy Brief Number 8). Cape Town: Institute of Justice and Reconciliation.

Muzaale, P. (1987). Social development, rural poverty, and implications for fieldwork practice. *Journal of Social Development in Africa, 2*(1), 75–85.

Narayan, D., Patel, R., Schafft, K., Rademacher, A., & Koch-Schulte, S. (1999, December). *Voices of the poor, can anyone hear us? Voices from 47 countries* (Vol. I). World Bank, Poverty Group, PREM.

Payne, M. (1997). *Modern social work theory*. Chicago, Il: Lyseum books limited.

Pincus, A., & Minahan, A. (1973). *Social work practice: Model and methods*. Itasca, IL: F. E Peacock Publishers.

Reisch, M. (2002). Defining social justice in a socially unjust world. *Families in Society: The Journal of Contemporary Human Services, 83,* 343–346.

Richmond, M. (1915). The social case worker in a changing world. *Proceedings of the National Conference of Charities and Corrections*. Chicago, IL: National Conference of Charities and Corrections.

Roberts, R., & McMahon, W. (2007). *Social justice and criminal justice*. London: Centre for Crime and Justice Studies.

Singer, P. (2009). *The life you can save: Acting now to end world poverty*. Melbourne, VIC: Text Publishing.

Soydan, H. (2011). *Understanding social work in the history of ideas*. Paper Prepared for the Conference on "Shaping a Science of Social Work", May 23–24, University of Southern California, Los Angeles.

Trevithick, P. (2000). *Social work skills: A practice handbook*. Buckingham and Philadelphia: Open University Press.

United Nations Development Program. (2007). *Facts on poverty in Africa*. Retrieved March 5, 2016, from www.africa2015.org/factspoverty.

United Nations Development Programme. (2012). *Africa human development report*. New York: The United Nations Development Programme Regional Bureau for Africa (RBA).

Watson, D., & West, J. (2006). *Social work process and practice: Approaches, knowledge and skills*. New York: Palgrave Macmillan.

CHAPTER 16

The Context of Social Work Profession and Education in Transitional Countries: The Case of Georgia

Shorena Sadzaglishvili

INTRODUCTION

Transitional countries are termed as such due to their transitional nature, typically during recovery from an extended conflict or war. The social work profession is a newly emerging discipline in Georgia, the former Soviet Union country which developed as a response to the severe socio-economic crisis following the collapse of the USSR in 1991.

History shows that social work practice developed disparately in separate countries and is idiosyncratic to the cultures in those separate countries (Penna, Paylor, & Washington, 2000). At the same time, it is a global profession with broad, global concerns. These include children separated from their families, refugees, poverty, public health, violence, and disability, among others. Following Penna and colleagues (2000), these issues may be best studied and addressed from within the ecological context of each country, while placed in a global perspective. Best practices and social interventions should be informed by comparative cross-national research, through the application of an ecological systems perspective (IASSW, IFSW, & ICWS, 2012; Penna et al., 2000). This perspective has become a core concept in social work worldwide (Hare, 2004). According to this approach, an individual and his or her multiple environments are viewed as dynamic, interactive systems.

S. Sadzaglishvili (✉)
Ilia State University, Tbilisi, Georgia
e-mail: shorena_sadzaglishvili@iliauni.edu.ge

S. S. M. et al. (eds.), *The Palgrave Handbook of Global Social Work Education*, https://doi.org/10.1007/978-3-030-39966-5_16

Problems of any system cannot be solved without taking into account all the factors that influence the system and its components (Bronfenbrenner, 1986).

Brim (1975) and Bronfenbrenner (1977) identified four levels of ecological components useful in understanding how individual processes are influenced by the hierarchical environmental systems in which they function. These four levels are: microsystems (face-to-face or direct contact among the individual, family, peers, church members, social workers, etc.), mesosystem (interconnections between microsystems, "the network of personal settings", such as the relationship between the person's peers and the family), exosystem (social structure linkages in which the individual does not have an active role, e.g. local policies, social services, etc.), and macrosystem (the culture in which individuals live, including prevailing values, attitudes, and ideologies).

After its collapse in 1991, individual countries of the Soviet Union moved from having a tradition of "no social problems" towards facing major social and economic challenges (IFSW, 2014). These macro-level "large scale ecological changes" from a communist utopian social-economic system to a market-oriented one, from a federated central government to individual national (and potentially democratic) governments, and from collectivist responsibility towards individual responsibility instigated changes at meso- and micro-levels, transitioning the individual from a citizen of a "super country" to one of a so-called newly emerged developing country with its own transitional social-political-economic system lacking structures conceptually devoted to "social welfare". In Georgia, from the mid-1990s to the present, both Social Welfare services and the profession of social work have undergone and continue to undergo significant changes.

This chapter will present these changes using an ecological systems framework, identifying idiosyncratic factors shaping the development of social work profession and education in Georgia.

REFORMS IN CHILD WELFARE SYSTEM

Particularly idiosyncratic for Georgia at the macro-level was the extreme political turmoil and civil unrest of the period from 1991 to 2003. Ethnic conflicts both reflected and exacerbated the general socio-economic decline. More than 300,000 people were internally displaced as a consequence of the fighting between Georgia and the separatist regions of South Ossetia and especially Abkhazia in the early 1990s. Sustained military conflicts and corrupt, ineffective political practices impeded societal stability until the Rose Revolution of November 2003, which afforded the opportunity for greater democratisation and the introduction of reforms. However, with the Russian-Georgian War of 2008, Georgia saw one-third of its territory occupied by the Russian Federation. Political disorganisation and renewed concerns about governmental corruption—despite the acknowledged progress achieved during the middle of the decade—led to the ascendancy of the Georgian Dream, a coalition political party, in 2013.

In the face of deteriorating economic and social conditions, more children were cared for with fewer resources, and fewer options were available to them once they were too old to qualify for residential care. Some international donors tried to improve conditions in these institutions but these efforts unintentionally reinforced local reliance on residential care (Tobis, 2000).

Within this context, the first social reforms in the county were targeted at the most vulnerable microsystem—children in residential institutions. A well-organised deinstitutionalisation process of special residential institutions was considered to be the most appropriate solution to assist this most disadvantaged group by all stakeholders including government ministries, NGOs, local advocates, and others.

The deinstitutionalisation process was accelerated by the 2001 Law on Foster Care and Adoption. Passage of this law signalled the government's willingness to assume greater responsibility for the deinstitutionalisation process and other child welfare reforms, with the technical assistance of UNICEF and international NGOs.

By 2009, the number of institutionalised children declined to 4600, and by 2015, to only 100—a 98.6% reduction from the late-Soviet period estimate of over 7000. Also by 2015, the number of state institutions dropped from 46 to just three (an almost 94% reduction). There are today roughly 3700-dependent children receiving services, across a growing range of alternate care and community-based settings (SSA, 2015).[1]

These accomplishments resulted from policy level changes such as the government child welfare action plans and legislation supporting establishment of a host of enhanced operations including alternative care services, "gate-keeping" policy guiding principles (focused on prevention and family-strengthening services), state childcare standards and monitoring mechanisms, a child protection referral system with mandatory reporting, operational Child Care and Guardianship Councils composed of key NGO and government representatives, and a system of professional social work supervision and performance appraisal system, among others (Namicheishvili, 2014; Shatebrashvili et al., 2012).

In terms of developing a workforce to support the deinstitutionalisation process, a non-degree course was provided to 18 people in 1999, by the British International NGO"Every Child". This course provided instruction on normal and abnormal child development, the mechanics of promoting and sustaining foster care and small group home programmes, and on legal matters bearing on adoption. Workers completing the programme were called "sotsialuri mushaki", or "social worker".

In 2000, the Open Society Foundation (OSF) launched the Social Work Fellowship Program. Within the broad goal of creating skilled human capital in the region in general, the development of a professionally trained social work workforce was specifically supported by the provision of grants enabling students to study at American universities.

In 2004, the first group of American-educated social workers established the Georgian Association of Social Workers (GASW) as a local non-governmental organisation (NGO) to support the continued development of the profession within Georgia. In particular, it advocated for the legal and policy infrastructure necessary to extend professional expertise to local social service providers and to establish a strong educational framework based on recognised professional standards. The GASW also actively contributed to the development of operational procedures and standards integral to the administration and practice of a large child welfare system. Over the subsequent years, GASW published and disseminated a Social Work Code of Ethics (2005), an educational paper on Social Work Professional Terminology (2006), and a set of Social Work Practice Standards (2007) (GASW, 2014).

In close collaboration with international and local stakeholders including the Government of Georgia, GASW participated in policy formulation, instigating reforms that affected the legislative framework supporting new social work establishments in the country. In addition to helping raise the profile of social work within the country, it supported the development of social work education as well as the establishment and enforcement of a professional code of ethics, a key characteristic of the profession (IFSW, 2014).

In 2004, social work was included under the Law of Higher Education as a new interdisciplinary profession, listed among the other professions. In 2006, with support of the European Union (EU), OSF Academic Fellowship Program/Higher Education Support Program, and other international actors, the first social work degree programmes were established at Tbilisi State and Ilia State Universities. Also in 2006, social work was granted further official and legal recognition by the Law of Social Assistance (Shatberashvili, 2011), which specifies "a social worker – a person specially authorized by custody and guardianship authorities" (SSA, 2013). At the micro-level of practical operations in Child Welfare services, social workers must adhere to "gatekeeping" principals to restrict intake of children into out-of-home services. The system distinguishes children at high, middle, and low levels of risk for harm. Defined as those victimised or in danger of being victimised, lacking parental care, orphans without guardians, those whose parents are sent for involuntary treatment or who are in the criminal justice system, or being in severely dysfunctional families, only high-risk children are eligible for out-of-home care services. Priority is given to kinship care, then foster care, and lastly to small group homes. The cases of children in state care are reviewed regularly, on a 6-month basis.

Middle-risk children are provided with family support and rehabilitation services, such as day centres, food assistance, targeted social assistance, a government reintegration benefit, and crisis intervention funding to prevent further family deterioration. Low-risk children and their parents are provided with information about social assistance programmes and referred to other services provided by different agencies.

The Georgian child protection referral system obligates every institution and a range of professional and public employees including: schools, medical institutions, country doctors, the Social Service Agency, district services, and patrol police, to detect and report facts or threats of violence on a child. However, the application may be made by any citizen (SSA, 2013).

Disabled children are eligible for early child development programmes, rehabilitation programmes, and provision of supporting equipment and day centres. Today, these services are extended to upwards of 1800 children. A law on inclusive education (passed in 2005) made public schools available for children with special needs. Today, 3445 students with special education needs—ranging from hearing impairment to autism and cerebral palsy—attend Georgian public schools (MoES, 2015).

In 2009, the Childcare Unit under the Ministry of Education and Science moved to the Social Service Agency (SSA) under the Ministry of Labor, Health and Social Affairs (MoLHSA), a reorganised state body responsible for the provision of state social and health protection programmes for beneficiaries. The SSA administers a range of social and health protection programmes such as state pension, targeted social assistance, universal health insurance, provisions for persons with disabilities, the elderly, people with mental disorders, guardianship, and custody of children deprived of care (SSA, 2013). As a result, the functions of state social workers were extended beyond providing bio-psycho-social assessment for children. Their new responsibilities extend to making decisions regarding the care and guardianship of other vulnerable groups such as the elderly and disabled, including their placement in newly established community organisations and houses, day centres, and institutions (SSA, 2013). Today, approximately 1000 adults receive such services. At the macro-level, on December 26, 2013, the Georgian parliament ratified "The Convention on the Rights of Persons with Disabilities". After ratification, the government adopted a set of legal acts in order to protect rights of people with disabilities as well as to establish state programmes aimed at civil reintegration and social rehabilitation of people from vulnerable groups.

In total, there are 2000 employees of the SSA serving approximately 2.5 million Georgian citizens (approximately 60% of Georgian citizens). Among other workers at the SSA, social workers are considered key players in the ongoing child welfare system reform, which has ensured almost full deinstitutionalisation in Georgia and is considered the best practice in the Region (Namicheishvili, 2014; Partskhaladze, 2014). By 2013, there were about 240 statutory child welfare social workers countrywide employed by the SSA (SSA, 2013).

GASW's Western-educated social workers provided expertise for the SSA to elaborate and pilot almost all key projects such as policy guiding the above-described "gatekeeping" principles, development of social work practice forms, social work supervision and performance appraisal systems, state childcare standards, childcare service monitoring, and inspection mechanisms. In addition, the vast majority of the social work graduates of the local academic programmes take up key positions at SSA, such as head social workers and supervisors.

Reforms in Criminal Justice System

After the Rose Revolution, Georgia embarked upon a comprehensive reformation process, with a view to promoting democracy. Fighting corruption and organised crime with its entrenched mentality became a matter of vital importance for the country ((MCLA, 2011). One way by which Georgia sought to achieve these goals was to dramatically expand criminal prosecutions for graft and related corruption based on mandatory custodial sentencing and "zero tolerance" policing (2006–2009). This produced an influx of some thousands of convicted felons into an already outdated and overcrowded penitentiary system. Prison census reached 21,079 persons in 2009, 23,684 in 2010, and 24,114 in 2011. From 2003 (9688 prisoners) to 2011, the number of prisoners increased by 300% (Slade, Kachkachishvili, Tsiskarishvili, Jeiranashvili, & Gobronidze, 2014). During the first four years of the reform (2006–2009), authorities spent $182 million on building European quality prisons. However, this did not keep pace with the rise in inmate population. The state committed considerable resources specifically aimed at improving inmates' conditions and promoting further rehabilitation and re-socialisation.

However, in 2012 a prison rape scandal documented in video recordings revealed that the old system of human rights abuse and violence still existed in the penitentiary system. Commenting on the shocking incident, then-President Saakashvili declared that, "It is not about some isolated cases, but about the failure of the penitentiary system itself", urging another complete reform in the sphere (RT News, 2012).

The opposition party "Georgian Dream" made prison reform their campaign promise. After being elected to the government in 2012, they initiated a new round of reforms supported by the EU that focused on re-socialisation, rehabilitation, and crime prevention. As a consequence, the number of persons employed as social workers increased by 40 and those as probation officers by 50. These improvements were in line with European standards aimed at ensuring humanisation of the system and the effective execution of sentences (MCLA, 2014). By 2015, the number of persons placed in the penitentiary system declined to 9716, which is a 49.9% reduction from the 19,349 inmates in 2012, at the time of the rape scandal. On the macro- and meso-levels, massive releases of inmates to alleviate overcrowding drove the need for more community-based and institutional supportive and rehabilitative services, in turn facilitating the opportunity for social work development.

Prison reform at the meso-level over the last three years includes the establishment of the Psycho-Social and Rehabilitation Programs Division of the National Agency (PSRPS) for the Execution of Non-Custodial Sentences and Probation. This Division is charged with the initiation and organisation of best practices in the rehabilitation of probationers and other offenders. These include diversion and mediation programmes, introduction of risks and needs assessment methodologies, individual sentence planning for the employment of inmates, involvement of probationers in rehabilitation programmes, implementation of professional standards in rehabilitation services, retraining of social workers, development of a monitoring and evaluation system, and so on. On micro-level, probationers and prisoners are connected to social services including psycho-rehabilitation, employment, education, vocational training, sport, cultural, and other activities. A social worker is available and provides individual-based case management.

Moreover, a new by-law reforming social service in the prisons implemented by the Department of Prisons added degreed social workers in the system. In addition, the Penitentiary and Probation Training Center, under the Ministry of Corrections, with the technical support of GASW, provided intensive training on the social worker's role in the criminal justice system for probation officers, social workers, and social service staff in the country's penitentiaries. Based on these trainings, social workers and probation officers are now equipped with advanced practice skills including motivational interviewing, cognitive behavioural therapy, task-centred casework, and others—all of which include an exploration and acknowledgement of the client's world view as a vital element in their working methods (Hohman, 2012).

Another agency, the Center for Crime Prevention of the Ministry of Justice (MOJ), established in 2012, plays a central role in reforming the criminal justice system (CCP, 2014). This Center aims to implement projects related to crime prevention, to work with high-risk groups, and to reduce recidivism. There are about 20 professional social workers employed by this agency working on re-socialisation and rehabilitation of former prisoners, creating a referral system, providing corresponding assistance, and managing the Diversion and Mediation Program and the Leadership House Program.

CHALLENGES TO SOCIAL WORK PROFESSION AND EDUCATION IN GEORGIA

As the above discussion shows, aggressive reforms and improved service, especially in the fields of Criminal Justice and Child Welfare but also in related fields, were both facilitated and promoted by the evolution of professional social work in Georgia. At the same time, development of the profession was itself enabled by governmental and other macro-level policy and programme reforms, reflecting a coordinated approach among international, local, state, and non-governmental organisations. These interacting factors laid the groundwork for a new social welfare system with beneficial manifestations on the macro-, exo-, meso-, and micro-levels.

These achievements notwithstanding, it can be seen that they are currently being implemented without a holistic approach and can be characterised as a reactive system aimed at solving existing social problems spontaneously. The reforms are unbalanced and underdeveloped towards different target groups of vulnerable populations including Roma children, children leaving state care, and migrants, among others. There are gaps in geographic coverage and inconsistencies in the quality of services. Where Government collaboration with local NGOs and experts in the field has been shown to be very critical in the success of Child Welfare and Criminal Justice reforms, such engagement has not yet emerged in other domains. Similarly, while Georgia needed to rely upon, and benefitted greatly from, private funding from international NGOs, such funding is grant-dependent and not sustainable in the long term. For example, donor organisation support for the role of social workers in crisis situations during the Russian-Georgia War in 2008 was discontinued by 2010 (Shatberashvili, 2011).

Other macro-aspects contributing to failed social welfare efforts are connected with the posture of some populist politicians who advocate for social reforms that may not yet be feasible (e.g. comprehensive universal health care, universal access to quality preschool education, etc.) in a developing country undergoing industrialisation. Similarly, citizens of this post-communist country also require and expect more social welfare services from the government, as they still live with "socialist" views. For instance, research showed that majority of interviewed homeless people (90%) think the government is responsible for their free housing (Sadzaglishvili & Kalandadze, 2018). In addition, the majority of socially and economically disadvantaged people who get targeted social assistance refuse to be employed, as they do not consider themselves stigmatised by getting social assistance. Thus, traditional macrosystem or exosystem perspectives about social values and societal organisation appear to require modification driven by an increasing awareness of post-communist social welfare operations at mesosystem and microsystem levels, even while improvements are needed at those levels, as well.

For example, in the field of Child Welfare, lack of coordination between social agents (authorised persons of the SSA who deliver information to be registered in the unified database of socially vulnerable families), the SSA social workers, and primary health practitioners resulted in child fatalities including the highly publicised death of an infant (SSA, 2015).

In the field of disability, though "the social model of disability" (in contrast to the old "medical model") is approved on macro- and exo-levels, implementation of this policy is very challenging. For instance, macro-level changes require use of the new term "disabled" instead of "invalid", although the old classification is still used to designate the disability status of persons being severely, considerably or mildly impaired. Continued use of this outdated terminology reinforces stereotypical attitudes within the professional community.

Moreover, stigma continues to surround people with disabilities in Georgia, and many families with special needs children tend to keep them at home, with little or no exposure to the outside community even though these children qualify for inclusive education programmes. The SSA has a list of about 10,000 children who could qualify as special needs students, a far greater number than those currently attending Georgia's elementary and high schools (MoES, 2015). The three remaining residential institutions provide care to 100 disabled children, for whom community-based placements are hard to find. A contributing factor identified in a UNICEF study was the negative and pessimistic attitudes towards disabled children's placement in foster care held by 22% of social workers themselves (UNICEF, 2013).

Weak transactions across the macro, exo-, meso-, and microsystems can also be found in the mental health field. Macro- and exo-level changes such as Georgia's Law on Psychiatric Care (Law of Georgia on Psychiatric Care, 2006) and the National Health Care Strategy 2011–2015 (MoLHSA, 2011) prompted the deinstitutionalisation of patients in large-scale psychiatric institutions and the introduction of a balanced community and hospital-based mental health system. However, this did not result in increased numbers of social workers in the mental health field at the meso-level. GASW research showed that the main mental health professionals are physicians (primarily psychiatrists, but also narcologists and neurologists), nurses, and psychologists/psychotherapists, with the medical model of treatment still prevalent in Georgia (Shekriladze & Chkonia, 2015). Out of 42 interviewed social workers employed in mental health, only four held a social work degree. Direct social work practitioners in mental health settings are mostly involved in bureaucratic duties rather than performing functions such as counselling, crisis intervention, therapy, advocacy, coordination of resources, and discharge planning. They are not provided with professional supervision (Shekriladze & Chkonia, 2015).

One reason for the diminished role of the social worker in mental health is the availability of a large number of unemployed psychologists, psychiatrists, and other health professionals. Social networking of these other professionals assists unemployed colleagues to be hired to social work positions that would otherwise be given to social work professionals. The job description of mental health social workers is very ambiguous and does not require qualified social workers. Somewhat conversely, in Mental Health as well as other fields with minimal social work presence, many persons without an academic social work degree are hired for "social work" positions mostly in the rural regions due to the lack of a professional workforce (Shatberashvili, 2011).

Accordingly, specialisation in clinical social work practice and mental health has not become a priority for academic social work programmes. Meanwhile, new master degree programmes in "Addictology" and "Mental Health" are established and run by psychologists and psychiatrists, producing allied mental health professionals with titles like "social psychiatrists" and "addictologists". The role of the social worker is also relatively minimal in the fields of health, substance abuse, school and school-linked services, unemployment, homelessness, and refugee resettlement (Shatberashvili, 2011). More discrete training is also needed for social workers even in fields where they are better established. This is true for the SSA social workers, for example, who are responsible for fulfilling multiple roles, serving all at once children, the elderly and disabled, the mentally ill and others, while requiring expertise in family conflicts, domestic violence, and other problematic processes.

Today, there are more than two hundred generalist practice social workers graduated from the local academic (bachelor and master degree) social work programmes, specialised mostly in two concentrations—child welfare and criminal justice. Their ranks are increasing at the rate of about 50 graduates per year. In addition to these and about twenty Western-educated social workers, there are more than three hundred social work practitioners who have higher education in other disciplines but have been retrained as social workers (Partskhaladze, 2014). It has been estimated that approximately 334 (60%) are employed by state agencies, while the remainder are employed by non-state (NGO) agencies. While many of the latter work in child protection, a comparatively large subgroup works in substance abuse and others are found in a range of fields from health care to human rights and community mobilisation[2] (Partskhaladze, 2014). In general, social workers in the NGO sector consider themselves to be less qualified than state social workers (Shatberashvili, 2011). In the state agencies as well as non-state agencies, social workers mostly play the role of case manager. Roles such as supervisor, mediator, advocate, and broker are also practised. However, the roles of clinical counsellor, social researcher, policy analyst and planner, social activist, programme developer and evaluator, educator, facilitator, and community mobiliser are very rarely practised and when they are, it is only in the non-statutory sector (Namicheishvili, 2014).

A situational analysis of the social work profession in Georgia done in 2011 revealed that social workers also see themselves more in the role of micro practitioners (90.2%) than as macro practitioners (49.2%), corresponding to their employers' attitudes (micro practice—87.5% and macro practice—37.5%) (Shatberashvili, 2011). However, both social activism (macro practice) and casework (micro practice) are equally important for the promotion of social change, problem-solving in human relations, and the empowerment and liberation of people to enhance well-being (Hare, 2004). Thus, there is still need for more professional social work human resources. It is the position of the GASW that there is a need for quality social work services, establishing a "scope of work" for the profession, identifying and promoting its role among multidisciplinary teams in mental health, defining other areas of development, and strengthening competence (GASW, 2014). GASW follows the position of Uehara et al., who observe that social work in the twenty-first century "can and must play a more central, transformative, and collaborative role in society, if the future is to be a bright one for all" (2013, p. 6). Thus, a qualified social work workforce can continue to play a critical and increasingly effective role in building the social welfare system of Georgia.

In 2018, Parliament of Georgia approved the bill on social work initiated by GASW and the Human Rights and Civil Integration Committee of Parliament. The bill established the uniform social worker system and determined the key principles of social works obliging the social worker to adhere to the fundamental aspects upon her official duties: respect to human rights, social justice, equality, sector competence, proportionality, honesty, and professional ethics. The bill specifies rights and obligations to ensure maximal protection of the beneficiaries and social servants as well it defines professional qualification of the worker and the competences (Parliament of Georgia, 2018). This is a first step for advancing the professionalisation of social work in Georgia, as it ensures the development of professional expertise and the individual accountability of social workers and social work practitioners in Georgia. The bill on social work creates new challenges for social work education and training to be planned in ways that support the formation of professional workforce acquired with skills and expertise and adapting to new job roles, career structures, and local and international professional discourses. In this context, the role of social work as a transdisciplinary science reaches a critical importance in terms of connecting high-quality education and training to service needs and ensuring that social workers develop the expertise necessary to improve outcomes for service users and create effective services by using research and evidence to inform their practice decisions to meet rapid social-economical changes and complex needs of transitional societies.

The history of social work profession development in Georgia shows that this process is dynamic as it facilitates the growth of the profession. Professional identity of social workers is growing step by step. For instance, social workers become aware of the existing discrepancy between the social work theory, as it is taught at the universities and the actual practice that does not allow them to fully meet social worker's roles, responsibilities and professional ethics. They become change agents at their work places, which are reflected in their activism and protest against the official structures. Social workers are striving for their professional development, advancing better social policies, and maintaining professional standards of practice. In addition, they fight for their place in the social welfare field despite facing competition from the other helping professionals (psychologists, mental health specialists, etc.) by adding more scientific basis and professionalism to dealing with their beneficiaries. Georgian Association of Social Workers and Academia have pivotal roles in this promotion of scientifically based social work, professional development, and advancement of better social policies and educational opportunities in the field.

Table 16.1 summarises macro-, exo-, meso-, and micro-level impacts on the development of social work profession and education in Georgia.

Table 16.1 Macro-, exo-, meso-, and micro-level impacts on the development of social work profession and education in Georgia

Macro	Exo	Meso	Micro
The collapse of the USSR in 1991 Ethic conflicts Civic War 1/3 of Georgia's territories occupied by the Russian Federation	No established social care/welfare policies; No social protection system Market-oriented economy	Deteriorated and corrupted residential care No social institutions that could provide services for disadvantaged people	300,000 people were internally displaced Socially and economically impoverished people A citizen is left on his/her own 4600 children are at large state institutions managed by several state entities Trained 18 childcare social workers
	International Donors' support—UNICEF, Save the children to the Government of Georgia	Deinstitutionalisation process of 46 large state institutions Non-degree training course in 1999 to support the deinstitutionalisation process in Georgia	
	Law on Foster Care and Adoption (2001) Child welfare action plans and legislation	Child welfare reforms; Alternative care services are established	Declined number of institutionalised children
	Open Society Foundation Support	Social Work Fellowship Program is launched (2000) Professional Association of Social Workers (GASW, 2004) is established. Strengthening Social Work Profession	Creating human capital—social workers
	Open Society Foundation Support	The development and implementation of the necessary legal and policy infrastructure	Experts in the field are in place

(continued)

Table 16.1 (continued)

Macro	Exo	Meso	Micro
	The recognition of the social work profession in the Georgian legislation (The Law of Social Assistance) EU, OSF Academic Fellowship Program/Higher Education Support (2006)	The first educational programs (BSW, MSW, Certificate Course) were introduced (2006–2007) at the universities	Social work lecturers and students are in place
	The Social Service Agency (SSA) is established—the state body responsible for provision of state social and health protection programs for beneficiaries (2009) State Child Care Standards approved (2009, August, Decree # 281/N)	From 46 institutions, only 3 large institutions for disabled children are left; development of alternative out-of-home care services (kinship and foster care, small group homes), family support services (day care centres, food assistance, targeted social assistance, etc.)	Child-oriented services are established A number of social workers are increased (about 240)
	"Gate keeping" policy guiding principles; Childcare standards and monitoring mechanism; Child protection referral system—mandatory reporting (2009–2014)	Government reintegration benefit; Government crises intervention fund donor-supported social fund Establishment of childcare and guardianship councils; Social work professional supervision and performance appraisal systems; Social work practice forms, licensing of 24-hr services	Family strengthening is priority Only 100 disabled children are left at the large-scale institutions (2014)

(continued)

Table 16.1 (continued)

Macro	Exo	Meso	Micro
	"The Convention on the Rights of Persons with Disabilities" is ratified. A set of legal acts in order to protect rights of people with disabilities as well as to establish state programs are adopted (2013)	Services and programs for disabled are established. Social workers' new responsibilities regarding the care and guardianship of other vulnerable groups such as the elderly and disabled, including their placement in newly established community organisations and houses, day centres, and institutions	Disabled and elderly are involved in services
	EU support, Fulbright Program	2010–2013 doctoral programs in social work are introduced	The first doctoral graduates in SW
	A law on inclusive education (passed in 2005) made public schools available for children with special needs	Disabled children are eligible for early child development programs, rehabilitation programs, provision of supporting equipment and day centres (1800)	3445 students with special education needs—ranging from hearing impairment to autism and cerebral palsy—attend Georgian public schools. Disabled children (1800) involved in services
The prison crisis—2012	Psycho-Social and Rehabilitation Programs Division of the National Agency of the Execution of Non-Custodial Sentences and Probation are established Center for Crime Prevention of the Ministry of Justice of Georgia (MOJ) established in 2012 Bylaw regarding reforming social services in the prison EU support	Social work services introduced in criminal justice system reform process The best practices in rehabilitation of inmates including diversion and mediation programs, methods of risks and needs assessment and individual sentence planning for the employment of inmates, involvement of probationers in rehabilitation programmes, etc.	Professional social workers in the criminal justice field (about 75) Better services for inmates, probationers, and offenders

(continued)

Table 16.1 (continued)

Macro	Exo	Meso	Micro
	The bill on social work initiated by GASW and the Human Rights and Civil Integration Committee of Parliament is approved (2018) The uniform social worker system	Development of professional expertise and the individual accountability of social work practitioners in Georgia	Better outcomes for beneficiaries. More professional practitioners in the field

Source Authors work

ROLE OF SOCIAL WORK AS SCIENCE IN REFORMING SOCIAL WELFARE SYSTEM

Originating in 2006, bachelors, masters, and doctoral programmes were established in Georgia to prepare professionals in social work. However, there is a clear line of demarcation associated with the degree attained; bachelor's and master's degrees prepare social workers to be practitioners while social work doctoral education prepares social work professionals to teach at higher-level institutions. Despite the doctoral focus on the instruction of educators, the social work profession is significantly challenged within European academia and is not seen as a science or research discipline (Decker, Constantine-Brown, & Tapia, 2016).

Georgia, similar to the United States, believes social work education and practice must include a solid foundation of science, core skills, and social justice. Brekke (2012, 2013) defines the framework of the science of social work with (a) core constructs (biopsychosocial, person-in-environment and service systems for change); (b) core domains (to understand marginalisation, disenfranchisement, the individual and social factors in disease and individual and social factors supporting health; to foster change, empowerment, inclusion, reducing disease, and increasing health); and (c) aesthetic characteristics (complexity, synthesis, and pluralism). Brekke (2012) asserts evidence-based practice (EBP) which is the area where social work has an explicit relationship with science. In particular, EBP provides science-informed practice and includes the development and implementation of evidence-based or evidence-supported practice interventions. Thus, EBP can be seen as a central feature for a scientific, accountable, informed, and ethical approach to social work practice (Brekke, 2012).

While social work education has historically been grounded in professional practice, reconsideration of social work as a science has recently been urged (Fong, 2012). This dilemma is present within domestic and international social work. American and European colleagues have initiated discourse about increasing social work's visibility as a scientific discipline and making a more demonstrative contribution to expanding the scientific knowledge base in social and human services (Anastas, 2014; Brekke 2012, 2013; Longhofer & Floersch, 2012; Shaw, 2014; Sommerfeld, 2014). The gap between science and practice has long been noted in the literature (Backer, David, & Soucy, 1995; Clancy & Cronin, 2005; Morrissey et al., 1997). Brekke, Ell, and Palinkas (2007) describe numerous American reports showing a 20-year gap between knowledge generated from the best clinical research and utilisation of that knowledge in health and mental health sectors. This division between research-informed practice and practice-informed research provides an impetus for practitioners and researchers to collaborate in establishing research priorities, developing appropriate methodologies, and producing useful and relevant research findings (Plath, 2006).

Although increased practitioner/researcher alliances have been observed in both Britain and the United States (Cheetham, 1997; Mullen, 2002; Webb, 2002), there is considerable room for improvement. One way to minimise the gap between research and practice is to develop a "translational" science that will bridge findings from exceptional evidence-based research into direct care settings, while building partnerships between research and practice constituencies (Brekke et al., 2007). One challenge to the integration of research into practice concerns the congruence between research and social work values. In this context, Marsh (2012) argues that it is relevant to determine whether a particular study has markers consistent with social work's professional purpose and ethical code, or whether it is derived knowledge from psychology, psychiatry, public health, sociology, or other related fields. Analyses that consider whether research is consistent with the core constructs, values, and fundamental purposes of social work are critically important to advancing the scientific base of social work practice and establishing more clearly the identity of the profession (Marsh, 2012).

Guerrero (2014) asserts that the situational context offers more opportunities than challenges for social work to become a scientific enterprise, noting that social work is well situated to lead conceptual and methodological discussions of client-centred and community-based approaches among vulnerable populations. Social work seeks to resolve real-life challenges, often in collaboration with other disciplines. Social work, similar to sociology, psychiatry, public health, and psychology, is an applied integrative science, not a natural or core science that engages in the development of knowledge for its own sake (Anastas, 2014).

In contrast to the core or natural scientific disciplines (such as biology or chemistry), the integrative scientific disciplines seek to push disciplinary boundaries for solving "problems in living" (Brekke, 2013, p. 522). They are defined by their explicit focus on the application of disciplinary knowledge in integrative ways. Thus, their knowledge is always applied and technological (Brekke, 2013).

According to the International Federation of Social Workers (IFSW) and the International Association of Schools of Social Work (IASSW), social work is both interdisciplinary (several disciplines working jointly from their discipline-specific bases to integrate, combine, or synthesise perspectives, concepts, and/or theories to address a common problem) and transdisciplinary (a collaboration between several academic disciplines and practitioners in professional fields outside academe to address a complex real-world problem). Social work as an integrative applied discipline provides new applications of existing theories (from social sciences and humanities) to problems in life and develops new social work integrative theories, "indigenous knowledges" (IFSW, 2014) and models and guides in solving critical social work problems, which can be replicated.

Georgia is a fertile climate for integrative social work expansion. However, Georgian Social work is still lacking scientific shape. It is critical to promote an idea of social work as Science worldwide and especially, in the countries where social work is a newly emerging discipline. In this case, social work will be raised as a global profession and will meet ongoing globalisation discourse and global political and economic processes (Penna et al., 2000). At the same time, scientific social work will be able to answer national challenges considering its ecological contexts based on evidence-based practices and scientific innovations to shape effective and responsive social policy and intervention programmes in transitional countries.

As historical analysis of social work development showed one direct way of promoting social work as a science is to establish sound doctoral programmes in research university settings (Reid, 2001). These programmes should highlight the importance of academic research and not sacrifice "gold standards" for doctoral education in social work in the context where social work is considered as a vocational and practical profession and social work doctoral graduates are not accepted as "true" scientists among scientific communities. Sound doctoral education in social work should focus on teaching qualitative as well as on quantitative and positivistic approaches and comprehensive research methodologies to identify and study meaningful topics and social problems.

Doctoral students need to become scholars within the academy, which means that they should be required to take courses that make social work distinctive in the PhD programme along the lines of Social Justice and Human Behavior in the Social Environment (Fong, 2013). It is important to highlight intersectionality and transdisciplinary approach for faculty who are teaching courses for doctoral students. This approach expands the scope of learning and mitigates the dichotomy between basic and applied research (Fong, 2013). Thus, doctoral education needs multiple mentors from different disciplines to understand and use a multidisciplinary approach, and doctoral programmes should incorporate team-taught courses presenting a multidisciplinary framework (Fong, 2012). For instance, a best practice is designing multi-professional teaching clinics, bringing together expertise from different social sciences/disciplines, e.g. psychology, public health, mental health, social policy to advancing solutions to difficult social issues in the region.

In combination with establishing sound doctoral programmes in social work, it is necessary to form social work Research Lobbing Organizations and Funding Institutions that will support building a research infrastructure for Schools of Social Work and advance "Social Work Research" opportunities. Finally, Schools of Social Work should implement translational research as an advanced social work research modality that will open up ways of dialogue and collaboration between university and community. Consequently, social work will gain stronger position among other well-developed scientific disciplines by promoting its theoretical and practice basis comprehensively. Translational research opportunities in the transitional contexts of the post-Soviet countries will have a positive affect on dissemination practices of social interventions by facilitating evidence-based, sustainable solutions to emerging public health and social challenges.

CONCLUSION

Macro-level reforms in Georgia, including new legislative frameworks, strategies and action plans, and reorganisation of major social welfare institutions, evoked exo-systemic exchanges at both meso- and micro-levels. On the meso-level, new state bodies such as the SSA, the Guardianship and Care Panels, the Psycho-Social and Rehabilitation Programs Division of the National Agency of the Execution of Non-Custodial Sentences and Probation, and others were established, and the role of social worker was recognised. Micro-level impacts were thus felt in terms of the availability of more home-based services, safer conditions for children, prisoners and other vulnerable groups, improved access to welfare benefits, etc. The two major fields of child welfare and criminal justice were prioritised and well developed in Georgia by the coordination and active participation of international, local state, and non-governmental organisations.

However, the lack of holistic thinking and of a robust ecological perspective has contributed to sustained gaps in geographic coverage, and inconsistencies in the quality of services, with a number of vulnerable populations still in need of support. The Georgian social welfare system can be characterised as reactive rather than proactive due to the weaknesses of the transactional processes across macro-, exo-, meso-, and microsystems. The new bill on social work creates new challenges for advancing social work education and training and especially, for doctoral programmes in social work as there is a great need for improving outcomes for service users and creating effective services which can not be accomplished without acknowledging the potential of social work as a transdisciplinary science in building balanced social welfare system in the transitional country—Georgia.

Thus, there is a need for more active participation of social workers as change agents on macro-, meso-, and micro-levels, and in the fields of social research, social development, and policy practice in Georgia in order to promote an increasingly balanced social welfare system, broader social and economic equality, and the dignity and worth of all the Georgian people.

Notes

1. Kinship and foster care—1235 children; small group homes only for healthy children—337 children; day centres—1089 children, food assistance—996 children; government reintegration benefit—442 children; shelters for street connected youth—123 children; etc. (SSA, 2015).
2. In total, 334 social workers were employed by state agencies (Guardianship and care for children, elderly and people with disability—240; probation services—40, crime prevention services and correctional services—20; correctional settings—15; mental health services—14; trafficking and domestic violence—3 and social housing services—2) and 224 were employed by non-state agencies (child protection—93; harm reduction—63; violence—12; HIV/AIDS—11; youth work—10; mental health—9; violence against women—9; social protection—9; human rights—6; IDPs—1 and palliative care—1; community mobilisation—2) in 2014.

References

Anastas, J. W. (2014). The science if social work and its relationship to social work practice. *Research on Social Work Practice, 24*(5), 571–580. http://journals.sagepub.com/doi/abs/10.1177/1049731513511335.

Backer, T. E., David, S. L., & Soucy, G. (1995). Introduction. In T. E. Backer, S. L. David, & G. Soucy (Eds.), *Reviewing the behavioral science knowledge base on technology transfer* (Vol. 155, pp. 147–168). Rockville, MD: National Institute on Drug Abuse.

Brekke, J. S. (2012). Shaping a science of social work. *Research on Social Work Practice, 22*(5), 455–464. https://doi.org/10.1177/1049731512441263.

Brekke, J. S. (2013). A science of social work, and social work as an integrative scientific discipline: Have we gone too far, or not far enough? *Research on Social Work Practice, 24*(5), 517–523. https://doi.org/10.1177/1049731513511994.

Brekke, J. S., Ell, K., & Palinkas, L. A. (2007). Translational science at the National Institute of Mental Health: Can social work take its right place? *Research on Social Work Practice, 17*, 1–11. https://doi.org/10.1177/1049731506293693.

Brim, O. (1975). Macro-structural influences on child development and the need for childhood social indicators. *American Journal of Orthopsychiatry, 45*, 516–524.

Bronfenbrenner, U. (1977). Toward an experimental ecology of human development. *American Psychologist, 32*, 513–531.

Bronfenbrenner, U. (1986). Ecology of the family as a context for human development: Research perspectives. *Developmental Psychology, 22*(6), 723–742.

Center for Crime Prevention. (2014). *About us.* Available at http://prevention.gov.ge/page/4/eng. Accessed December 27, 2014.

Cheetham, J. (1997). Evaluating social work: Progress and prospects. *Research on Social Work Practice, 7*(3), 291–310. https://doi.org/10.1177/104973159700700301.

Clancy, C. M., & Cronin, K. (2005). Evidence-based decision making: Global evidence, local decisions. *Health Affairs, 24*(1), 151–162.

Decker, J. T., Constantine-Brown, J., & Tapia, J. (2016). Learning to work with trauma survivors: Lessons from Tbilisi, Georgia. *Social Work in Public Health.* https://doi.org/10.1080/19371918.2016.1188744.

Fong, R. (2012). Framing education for a science of social work: Missions, curriculum, and doctoral training. *Research on Social Work Practice, 22*(5), 529–536. https://doi.org/10.1177/1049731512452977.

Fong, R. (2013). Framing doctoral education for a science of social work: Positioning students for scientific career, promoting scholars for the academy, propagating scientists of the profession, and preparing stewards of the discipline. *Research on Social Work Practice, 24*(5), 607–615. https://doi.org/10.1177/1049731513515055.

Georgian Association of Social Workers. (2014). *History.* Available at www.gasw.org/en/about-us/history.html. Accessed December 27, 2014.

Guerrero, E. G. (2014). What does if take for social work to evolve to science status? Discussing definition, structure, and contextual challenges and opportunities. *Research on Social Work Practice, 24*(5), 601–606. https://doi.org/10.1177/1049731513511993.

Hare, I. (2004). Defining social work for the 21st century. The International Federation of Social Workers' revised definition of social work, *International Social Work, 47,* 407–424.

Hohman, M. (2012). *Motivational interviewing in social work practice.* London: Guildford Press.

IASSW, IFSW, & ICSW. (2012). *The global agenda: For social work and social development commitment to action.* Available at http://www.cswe.org/File.aspx-?id=60880. Accessed December 27, 2014.

International Federation of Social Workers. (2014). *Statement in support of social workers in South Caucasus region.* Available at http://ifsw.org/wpcontent/uploads/2014/09/Statement-of-IFSW-Europe-in-Support-of-Social-Workers-in-South-Caucasus-Region.pdf. Accessed December 27, 2014.

Law of Georgia on Psychiatric Care. (2006). *Patient's rights and protection guarantees.* Available at www.gmhc.ge/en/pdf/Law_of_Georgia_on_Psychiatric_Care_sit.ana-leng.pdf. Accessed November 23, 2015.

Longhofer, J., & Floersch, J. (2012). The coming crisis in social work: Some thoughts on social work and science. *Research on Social Work Practice, 22*(5), 499–519. https://doi.org/10.1177/1049731512445509.

Marsh, C. M. (2012). From fish and bicycles to a science of social work. *Research on Social Work Practice, 22*(5), 465–467. https://doi.org/10.1177/1049731512441837.

Ministry of Corrections and Legal Assistance of Georgia. (2011). *Annual report.* Available at www.mcla.gov.ge/cms/site_images/pdf1.pdf. Accessed December 27, 2014.

Ministry of Correction of Georgia. (2014). *Reforms.* Available at http://www.mcla.gov.ge/index.php?action=page&p_id=17&lang=eng. Accessed December 27, 2014.

Ministry of Education and Science of Georgia. (2015). *Inclusive education.* Available at http://www.inclusion.ge/eng. Accessed November 23, 2015.

Ministry of Labour, Health and Social Affairs. (2011). *Georgia—National Health Care Strategy 2011–2015: Access to quality health care*. Available at www.mindbank. info/item/2932. Accessed November 23, 2015.

Morrissey, E., Wandersman, A., Seybolt, D., Nation, M., Crusto, C., & Davino, K. (1997). Toward a framework for bridging the gap between science and practice in prevention: A focus on evaluator and practitioner perspectives. *Evaluation and Program Planning, 20,* 367–377. https://doi.org/10.1016/S0149-7189(97)00016-5.

Mullen, E. J. (2002, July 4/6). Evidence-based social work theory and practice: Historical and reflective perspective. In E. J. Mullen (Ed.), *Paper presented at the 4th International Conference on Evaluation for Practice*, University of Tampere, Finland. https://pdfs.semanticscholar.org/dd04/4e89d486d170adefdf4662c7cfd761541bd4.pdf.

Namicheishvili, S. (2014, July). Effects and impacts of research on participants. In *Summer school—MA in advanced development in social work (advances)*, University Paris Ouest La Defense Nanterre, Paris, France.

Parliament of Georgia. (2018). *The human rights and civil integration committee. Bill on social work*. Available at http://www.parliament.ge/en/. Accessed November 28, 2018.

Partskhalaladze, N. (2014). *History of social work in Georgia*. Unpublished internal document for Open Society Foundations, New York.

Penna, S., Paylor, I., & Washington, J. (2000). Globalization, social exclusion and the possibilities for global social work and welfare. *European Journal of Social Work, 3*(2), 109–122.

Plath, D. (2006). Evidence-based practice: Current issues and future directions. *Australian Social Work, 59*(1), 56–72. http://dx.doi.org/10.1080/03124070500449788.

Reid, J. R. (2001). The role of science in social work: The perennial debate. *Journal of Social Work, 1*(3), 273–293. https://doi.org/10.1177/146801730100100303.

RT News. (2012, September 19). *Georgia jail shock: Rape by rubber batons amid 'EU-quality prison' sham*. Available at http://rt.com/news/georgia-prison-reform-european-standard-510/. Accessed December 27, 2014.

Sadzaglishvili, S., & Kalandadze, T. (2018). The pathways to homelessness in the post soviet context. *Journal of Social Service Research*. https://doi.org/10.1080/01488376.2018.1487361.

Shatberashvili, N. (2011). *Situational analysis of social work* (Report). Georgia: Georgian Association of Social Workers.

Shatebrashvili, N, Sadzaglishvili, S., Gotsiridze, T., Demetreashvili, N., Namicheishvili S., & Cherkezishvili, E. (2012). *Child rights situation analysis of children at risk of losing parental care and children who have lost parental care* (Report). Georgia: SOS Children's Village.

Shaw, I. (2014). A science of social work? Response to John Brekke. *Research on Social Work Practice, 24*(5), 524–526. https://doi.org/10.1177/1049731514543408.

Shekriladze, I., & Chkonia, E. (2015, September 6–9). Social work in mental health: International experience and Georgian reality. In *IFSW European Conference and Social Services Expo*, Edinburgh, UK.

Slade, G., Kachkachishvili, I., Tsiskarishvili, L., Jeiranashvili, L., & Gobronidze, N. (2014). *Crime and excessive punishment: The prevalence and causes of human rights abuse in Georgia's prisons* (Report). Georgia: Open Society Georgian Foundation.

Social Service Agency. (2013). *About us.* Available at http://ssa.gov.ge/index.php?lang_id=ENG&sec_id=14. Accessed December 27, 2014.

Social Service Agency. (2015). *Statistics.* Available at http://ssa.gov.ge/index.php?lang_id=ENG&sec_id=610. Accessed November 28, 2015.

Sommerfeld, P. (2014). Social work as an action science: A perspective from Europe. *Research on Social Work Practice, 24,* 586–600. https://doi.org/10.1177/1049731514538523.

Tobis, D. (2000) *Moving from residential institutions to community-based social services in Central and Eastern Europe and the former soviet union.* Washington, DC: World Bank.

Uehara, E., Flynn, M., Fong, R., Brekke, J., Barth, R. P., Coulton, C., ... Walters, K. (2013). Grand challenges for social work differentiating. *Journal of the Society for Social Work and Research, 4*(3), 165–170.

UNICEF. (2013). *Annual report 2013—Georgia.* Available at http://www.unicef.org/about/annualreport/files/Georgia_COAR_2013.pdf. Accessed December 27, 2014.

Webb, S. (2002). Evidence-based practice and decision analysis in social work: An implementation model. *Journal of Social Work, 2*(1), 45–63. https://doi.org/10.1093/swr/34.2.94.

CHAPTER 17

Social Work Education in Ireland

Julie Byrne, Stephanie Holt and Gloria Kirwan

INTRODUCTION

Ireland is a small island in the northwest quadrant of Europe. The island of Ireland consists of two separate countries, Ireland and Northern Ireland (part of the United Kingdom of Great Britain and Northern Ireland), which are connected not only geographically but through a long and complicated history, contentious politics, and cultural intersectionalities (Burns, Devaney, Holt, & Marshall, forthcoming). With a shared land border of 310 miles, there are both unique challenges and opportunities for social work practice north and south of the internal Irish border, including the need for cross-border co-operation in service provision to families and other groups as well as the monitoring of registered offenders or those on probation who may move from one jurisdiction to another. In the light of the need for joined-up services, there is a need for joined-up approaches to social work education across the island of Ireland.

Moving from the local to the global, social work is a global activity (International Association of Schools of Social Work, 2014) shaped nationally in response to local forces but also influenced by international issues such as globalisation, by research, trends, practice, and international protocols and conventions. The forces that have shaped social work and, thus, social work education in Ireland include the domestic influences of the legacy of political

J. Byrne · S. Holt (✉)
Trinity College Dublin, The University of Dublin, Dublin, Ireland
e-mail: sholt@tcd.ie

G. Kirwan
National University of Ireland, Maynooth, Ireland

S. S. M. et al. (eds.), *The Palgrave Handbook of Global Social Work Education*, https://doi.org/10.1007/978-3-030-39966-5_17

275

and sectarian conflict on the island and significant social change including increasing levels of ethnic and cultural diversity within the Irish population (Wilson & Campbell, 2013; Halton & Wilson, 2013). Ireland has also experienced the rollercoaster ride of high levels of economic growth during the 'Celtic Tiger' years and the subsequent economic and financial crash during the recession period of 2008–2014. Throughout this period, as the Celtic Tiger rose and fell, there were other significant challenges to the child welfare service including retrospective disclosures of child abuse within Catholic-run institutions (Powell, Geoghan, Scanlon, & Swirak, 2012), failures of the child protection and welfare system to respond in a consistent manner to child abuse concerns (Health Services Executive, 2010) and the deaths of children known to the child protection and welfare service (Shannon & Gibbons, 2012). While social work is just one profession that operates in the multi-disciplinary field of child protection and welfare, and child welfare and protection practice is just one area of social work practice, these crises nonetheless resulted in the effectiveness of the profession being questioned and much professional soul searching and media-driven moral panic (Hughes & Houston, 2019). The resulting emphasis on professionalisation and regulation wields a significant influence on current social work education and practice in Ireland.

What is clear, and will be outlined in this chapter, is that social work education in Ireland is not static, rather dynamically evolving in response to both existing and emerging needs in society. This chapter begins in the nineteenth century with an historical overview of, and reflection on, the development of social work practice and social work education in Ireland, before reflecting on some of the key driving influences on both of those activities over the last three decades. Not least among those influences has been social workers themselves and the population of service users that the profession serves. In more recent times, the process of professionalisation and accompanying regulatory standards and frameworks have been key drivers in influencing both the practice and education of social work. Focusing on social, economic, and demographic changes, we highlight the influence of austerity and significant increases in inward migration on social work education and practice. Finally, this chapter takes a future-focused position, concluding with a selective reflection on the emerging issues that need to be considered if the standard of social work education is to be protected and the professionalism of social work practice is to be upheld.

This chapter does not seek to repeat analyses undertaken elsewhere of social work education in Ireland (see, e.g., Kearney & Skehill, 2005) and the reader will be referred to these sources for additional commentary throughout the chapter.

Social Work in Ireland

Social work in Ireland can trace its origins to the late nineteenth century and the emergence of employment opportunities for Welfare Secretaries in a range of factories such as the Guinness Brewery, the Jacob Biscuit Factory, and other businesses which adopted a welfare capitalist approach (Kirwan, 2005). Similar to other European countries, charities and organisations involved in addressing a range of needs in society, began to employ the services of trained welfare workers, although the growth of such employment was particularly piecemeal and slow in the Irish context. The genealogy of Irish social work also includes the work of the Alexandra Guild Tenement Company, established in 1899, which was modelled on Octavia Hill's work to address housing conditions in England (Delap & Kelleher, 2005). The Alexandra Guild appointed Miss Bagley who is regarded as one of the early social work forerunners in Ireland. Early developments also include the appointment of a small number of Hospital Almoners in a selection of Dublin hospitals in the early decades of the twentieth century (Horne & O'Connor, 2005). The number of paid social work posts in Ireland at present remains low in comparison with its closest geographical neighbours, evidenced by the low number of social workers (c.4000) registered by the Social Work Registration Board (Gartland, 2016). Despite the comparatively low numbers of social workers in paid positions, social work in Ireland has expanded greatly since the initial examples outlined above and it is now practised across a wide range of sectors including health, the criminal justice system, the disability sector, child and adult mental health services, child and family welfare services, as well as services for the protection of older people. New areas of practice are also opening up as awareness grows within Irish society regarding the need for services to assist groups such as victims of human trafficking, online abuse, youth suicide, and emerging intersectionalities including the LGBTQ community.

The vast majority of registered social workers are employed in the public sector. The Child and Family Agency (Tusla) and the Health Service Executive (HSE) are the two main employers. Figures from 2016 indicated that 2755 social workers were employed across the two organisations, at a time when 3935 social workers were registered with the Social Workers Registration Board (Gartland, 2016). A third public sector organisation which employs social workers, the Probation Service, has 266 Probation Officers who are also registered social workers but going forward it has committed to a policy of only employing social work registered staff in the role of Probation Officer and this is likely to increase the number of social workers employed in the field of criminal justice (Irish Probation Services, 2018).

Social Work Education in Ireland

The origins of social work education in Ireland can be traced back to a course in Civic and Social Work in Alexandra College, Dublin in 1912, set up to meet the increasing demand for the proper method of dealing with the important social and economic problems presented by modern society (O'Connor & Parkes, 1984). The course was closely followed by a Diploma in Social Science in 1915 in Queen's University Belfast in Northern Ireland and Diplomas in Social Studies in Trinity College Dublin and University College Dublin in 1934 (Kearney & Carmichael, 1987).

In 2020, five higher education institutions in Ireland (Republic of Ireland) now offer professional social work education programmes and qualifications approved by the Irish professional regulator (CORU) to gain access to registration in social work. Just two of these are undergraduate qualifications and the remaining ten are postgraduate qualifications. These programmes are offered at universities in three of Ireland's largest cities—Dublin, the capital city; Cork; Galway and in an Institute of Technology in Sligo (Table 17.1).

At the time of writing, an additional higher education institution, the National University of Ireland, Maynooth, located outside of the capital city Dublin, is currently introducing a postgraduate social work degree and seeking regulatory approval. This reflects the growing national and regional demand for qualified social workers in Ireland.

Social work education, including the curriculum upon which it is based, is not a fixed agreed entity, but rather a fluid and much-debated social action. Like the profession of social work itself, social work education in Ireland has been influenced by a variety of perspectives including the views of social workers working in the field, employers, academic institutions, policy-makers, regulatory requirements and also the guidance from global institutions (e.g. International Association of Schools of Social Work/International Federation of Social Work, 2004; Office of the High Commissioner for Human Rights, 1994). A newer source of influence which is increasingly discernible and

Table 17.1 Approved social work qualifications in Ireland

Institution	Postgraduate qualifications	Undergraduate qualifications
University College Cork	• Masters of Social Work • Postgraduate Diploma in Social Work Studies	• Bachelor of Social Work
University College Dublin	• Masters of Social Science (Social Work) • Graduate Diploma in Social Work • Masters in Science (Social Work) • Professional Master of Social Work	
Trinity College Dublin, The University of Dublin	• Masters in Social Work • Postgraduate Diploma in Social Work	• Bachelor in Social Studies
National University of Ireland, Galway	• Masters in Social Work	
Institute of Technology, Sligo	• Master of Arts in Social Work	

Source Authors preparation

generally welcomed by the profession is 'the service user perspective'. In reality, there is no one singular perspective, but rather a wide spectrum of experiences which inform a range of interpretations of what it is to be a recipient or user of services and how service usage can be experienced. In this next section, we look at a number of major influences on current delivery of social work education, commencing with the professionalisation and regulation of social work education, and also including economic, political, and social developments which have played their part in shaping the social work curriculum.

Professionalisation and Standards

Social work has been greatly influenced in the last two decades by the process of professionalisation and the national standards in social work education and practice are now well established. Social workers are subject to statutory regulation which was firstly administered by the National Social Work Qualifications Board and subsequently by the Social Workers Registration Board which comes under the auspices of CORU, a multi-professional regulator.

The National Social Work Qualifications Board was established under the Health (Corporate Bodies) Act, 1961 (as amended in 1996). As a statutory body, the National Social Work Qualifications Board had specific functions and powers in relation to the award and recognition of social work qualifications (National Social Work Qualifications Board, 2007). These functions including the granting of the National Qualification in Social Work (NQSW) to persons who had successfully completed recognised courses and recognition of qualifications awarded outside the State. The National Social Work Qualifications Board also acted in an advisory capacity to a range of stakeholders including government and higher education institutions on the standards which should inform the education and training of social workers in the State.

The Social Workers Registration Board was the first Board to be set up under the *Health and Social Care Professionals Act* (2005) which established CORU, a multi-professional regulator which consists of The Health and Social Care Professionals Council and a registration board for each of the 17 professions that CORU will ultimately regulate. The Social Workers Registration Board took on the functions of the National Social Work Qualifications Board but has a much wider remit with an overall objective to protect the public by fostering high standards of professional conduct and professional education, training, and competence among registrants (Section 27 of the Act). Thus, the Social Workers Registration Board has a critical role in shaping the standards for the profession and performs this role by developing standards and issuing them for input from the public through consultation processes. Having developed standards, the Registration Board monitors their implementation through its various functions which include the registration of members of the profession, conducting fitness to practise hearings and the approval and monitoring of education and training programmes under Section 48 and 49 of the 2005 Act.

Currently, registration with the Social Workers Registration Board is mandatory for those using the title 'social worker' in Ireland. To be listed on the Register of Social Workers, an individual must hold an approved qualification and satisfy the Social Work Registration Board that (i) he/she is fit and proper to practise the profession, (ii) has been vetted by the relevant police authority relevant to where they live, or have lived in the past and (iii) has sufficient knowledge of the English language to practise social work in the Irish context (CORU, 2018). All registered social workers must agree to abide by the Code of Professional Conduct and Ethics for Social Workers (CORU, 2019c). CORU also has the powers to investigate any complaint against a registered social worker and, if deemed appropriate, that social worker may become the subject of Fitness to Practise procedures. The Council of CORU may take action in respect of a registered social worker where the incidents complained of are serious and raise a concern about the registrant's fitness to practise his or her profession.

Regulation of Social Work Education Programmes

The Registration Board's purpose in regulating education and training programmes is to ensure that all graduates entering the register meet the necessary standards required to practise and have completed an approved programme of study and acquired the knowledge and skills to do the job. The approval of educational programmes is one of the tools that a registration board uses to ensure the delivery of safe and effective practice to the benefit of the service user.

Providers of social work education and training must meet the requirements set by the Registration Board if their programmes are to be approved as entry-level qualifications for the profession. These requirements are set out in two parts—(i) the standards of proficiency and (ii) the criteria for education and training programmes.

The standards of proficiency are the threshold knowledge and skills that anyone entering the register must possess. An approved programme must ensure that all those who successfully complete the programme meet the standards of proficiency. In addition, the Registration Board sets criteria which refer to the way an approved programme should manage its curriculum, assessment, and resources as well as the arrangements for practice placements.

When a programme is approved, the qualification that is awarded upon completion of the programme may be listed on a statutory instrument called the Approved Qualifications Bye-Law. Completion of an approved programme resulting in the possession of an approved qualification is the first step for those seeking to be listed on the social workers register and enter practice. There are currently twelve approved social work qualifications (see Table 17.1).

Education providers in Ireland are at liberty to decide whether they wish to offer a programme of professional education and training which acts as an entry route to the register. They have freedom to apply for programme approval by the Registration Board and to have the associated qualification listed on the bye-law. If they do apply and a programme is successful in its application for approval under section 48 of the *Health and Social Care Professionals Act* (2005), the programme will be monitored by the Registration Board no less than once every five years. Monitoring is conducted under section 49 of the Act and is designed to ensure that the programme continues to meet the Registration Board's requirements, which change in line with changes in social work practice and best practice in professional education and training. Thus, the decision to apply for programme approval requires an ongoing commitment to active management and resourcing of the social work programme to ensure that it continues to meet the Registration Board's requirements.

The Social Worker Registration Board's requirements for social work education programmes, originally published in 2013, were revised by the Registration Board in 2019 following public consultation. When new requirements are issued by the Registration Board, the providers of social work education and training programmes normally have a period of 12 months to make any changes required to ensure that their programmes continue to meet the requirements. A programme which does not continue to meet the requirements can have its qualification removed from the Approved Qualifications Bye-Law and students graduating from the programme are no longer eligible to apply for registration.

The regulatory requirements influence the nature of the social work curriculum in Ireland. Many education providers develop a curriculum that reflects their particular philosophy regarding social work education and which builds on their strengths, including community and employer partnerships, and aims for best practice. However, in order for a programme to be approved and for its graduates to be eligible to enter the register, it must meet the threshold standards set by the Registration Board which outline the minimum knowledge and skills required for entry to practice. Currently, the providers of social work education programmes have to ensure that their curricula meet over 80 standards (CORU, 2019a) set across the following domains;

i. Professional Autonomy and Accountability;
ii. Communication, Collaborative Practice, and Team Working;
iii. Safety and Quality;
iv. Professional Development *and*
v. Professional Knowledge and Skills.

The Registration Board does not specify curricula or require specific module outlines or assessments which leaves education providers with the freedom to integrate the required standards into their programmes as they see fit.

In addition to the standards of proficiency, the Registration Board also sets requirements for the design, organisation, and management of the programme. The providers of social work education programmes have to meet over 50 criteria for education and training programmes (CORU, 2019b) set across the following areas;

   i. Level of Qualification;
   ii. Practice Placements;
   iii. Programme Admission;
   iv. Programme Management;
   v. Curriculum;
   vi. Assessment Strategy.

The requirements in relation to practice placements are particularly detailed and reflect the centrality of practice learning in the social work education.

The curriculum of any programme is the enactment of multiple philosophies, beliefs, and pressures. Higher educational institutions in Ireland expect all graduates to display critical thinking and reasoning and to function in a complex and increasingly global world. Regulators tend to have shorter term, local goals focused on preparedness for practice, competency across a range of standardised domains in a given jurisdiction and a demonstrated ability to carry out the professional role to a minimum quality standard for public protection. Van Heugten (2011) highlights a similar difference between educators and employers pointing out that educators assume that the capacity to analyse and reflectively amend practice is a core requirement for social work but that employers increasingly seek graduates who are willing to simply follow guidelines and apply their assigned part of practice. Given the intersecting objectives of social work regulators, employers, and educators, it will be important to navigate these tensions to continue to provide social work education that is fit for purpose in the long and short term.

Recent Issues Impacting on Social Work Education

As noted earlier, the last 25 years have witnessed significant social, economic, and political changes to the Irish landscape, including the rise and fall of the Celtic Tiger, the resulting economic crash and period of extended austerity. With regard to economic changes, some observers note that these periods of financial crisis impact some sections of our society significantly more than others (McGregor & Quinn, 2015), with professional social workers often 'first responders' to families in need. This practice reality has added to the need for social work education to ensure that students are well versed in key skills of micro-social work such as individual and family counselling and mental health and substance abuse treatment. However, in the face of diminishing resources, the education of social work students must find ways to prepare them to carry the emotional labour of practising these skills in line with the values of social work but in a real-world context which is characterised by limited resources (Grootegoed & Smith, 2018). Austerity, and its impact on citizens, has brought with it a resultant need for the curriculum to enable social work students to engage critically with the impact of social exclusion, marginalisation, and discrimination through a more sophisticated theoretical and intersectional lens. It is essential that social work graduates enter their chosen field of practice fully informed on the impact of social inequality and neoliberalism on individual lives. It is now vital that social work education develops the capacity of students and graduates to engage in integrated approaches to practice which can address both individual difficulties and structural problems (Hingley-Jones & Ruch, 2016).

Significant social change in Ireland, including increased levels of inward migration and other demographic changes, has seen an awareness emerge in society regarding population diversity and a recognition of the impacts of stigma and oppression, human trafficking, gender-based violence, elder abuse, and the exploitation of children. Practising social work in modern Ireland means that there is further pressure on the social work curriculum to expand in order to cover an increasing number of complex but essential topics.

Due in part to the financial demands on students and higher education institutions and the high demand for graduates by employers, there is pressure on social work educators to 'deliver' the social work curriculum within a short and rigid timeframe. All but two of the currently approved social work qualifications are delivered as postgraduate programmes over a condensed, normally two-year, period. Just two of the qualifications are delivered as undergraduate programmes over a four-year period.

The intensification, in time and content, of the social work curriculum can seem to be the solution to the ever-increasing demands of practice, the complex needs of service users and the growing demand for social workers by employers. However, the curriculum is just one part of the pipeline to produce effective social workers. Newly qualified social workers, fresh from their qualifying programmes with up-to-date knowledge and skills, can sometimes struggle to operate in complex environments soon after graduation (Byrne & Kirwan, 2019) highlighting the need for significant support in practice from employers, colleagues, and professional bodies.

While child protection and welfare issues tend to headline media reports of perceived failure in professional practice (including social work), there are many other issues of concern for social work education and practice to reflect on. With the advent of Brexit and the challenges presented by the absence or rigid presence of borders on both sides of the Atlantic, the remainder of this section will focus on the issue of migration and its implications for social work practice and education in Ireland.

Migration

While history has recorded Ireland's long, and often tragic flight of outward migration for a myriad of reasons, largely economic; those trends have significantly changed in more recent times. Indeed, while Ireland was one of the last EU countries to become a country of inward migration (Mannion, 2016), more recently however, it has been the recipient of a significant number of immigrants, becoming an increasingly diverse country, reflecting similar trends across the European Union (Central Statistics Office, 2018). While international migration levels continue to peak, Ireland has not hosted an ever-increasing refugee population to the same extent as other EU countries (Mannion, 2016). While the island of Ireland's geographical location may in some way account for this, domestic legal obstacles to entering Ireland and the difficulties with resettlement have also influenced its low refugee numbers, relative to the EU. Nonetheless, while the advent of Brexit may have significant implications for inward migration in Northern Ireland, it is expected that for Ireland, inward migration will continue over the next decades and that cultural diversity will continue into the future.

Inward migration and the diversity that accompanies it does not, however, occur in a vacuum. It happens in the context of other complex and challenging societal changes both internationally and across the European Union, including the rise in fundamentalism and populism, the rise of extreme right-wing politics, racism, and xenophobia, in addition to global issues such as climate change.

Both adults and children migrate for a myriad of diverse and complex reasons, the triggers for migration are equally complex, for example, displacement by war and other violent conflicts, political unrest and genocide, military conscription and torture (International Organization for Migration, 2004), human trafficking and exploitation (United Nations, 2014). From a social work education and practice, perspective, migrants are identified as being at increased risk of poverty and social exclusion according to The National Intercultural Health Strategy (Health Services Executive, 2008), are twice as likely as Irish nationals to be in consistent poverty, with children from these families overly represented in the Irish childcare system (Health Service Executive, 2011).

For those involved in social work education and practice, issues of migration, immigration, ethnicity, and integration/inclusion are not only complex, they are also challenging regarding the need for culturally competent interventions and practice. Despite the long-term trend towards increasing population diversity, human services including social work services have not developed at the same pace. This is particularly evident in social work services with statutory responsibility for child protection and welfare where Coulter (2015), reporting on care proceedings in Ireland, found that children and families from minority ethnic backgrounds are over-represented in child protection proceedings. The report by Logan (2014) highlighted the need more broadly for organisations providing services to new migrant groups to equip and prepare staff for culturally competent practice through measures such as training. It emphasised how the 'existing deficit of cultural competence needs to be addressed across state agencies interacting with minority communities, including the Roma community' (p. 107) and that training needs to be provided to raise the cultural competence of staff in the public services. A recent small-scale study on the views of Irish social workers on their skills in cultural competence revealed gaps in social workers' knowledge and highlighted the need for agencies to invest in upskilling staff on this issue (Flavin, 2018). Of course, the support for culturally competent practice should not begin in work, it must be woven into the curriculum too. This can help to ensure that culturally competent practice is not an 'add-on' for practice but inculcated throughout the process of professional education and training. This can also help to ensure a smooth transition for graduates moving from the protected environment of the classroom into the intensity of practice.

The analysis by Walsh, Wilson, and O'Connor (2009) of trends in migration to Ireland of internationally qualified social workers highlights the potential of migration to create collective professional identities that merge the local with the global. Other challenges are more specific to particular migrant groups, for example, asylum seekers and the controversial use of direct provision (Foreman, 2018; Ni Raghallaigh, Foreman, & Feeley, 2016) and others still are gender specific impacting directly on females only (Foreman, 2018). While these experiences and challenges have received considered attention across policy, practice, and academic discourses, the experiences of particular ethnic minorities (Jacob & Kirwan, 2016), and the issues related to racial profiling (Logan, 2014; Shannon, 2017) remain a challenge going forward to delivering culturally competent social work education and practice.

FUTURE DIRECTIONS FOR SOCIAL WORK EDUCATION IN IRELAND

This chapter has reflected on the emergence and development of social work education and practice in Ireland, highlighting some of the key drivers and influences on that development. Drawing this chapter to a close, the final section takes a future-focused position to identify two current issues that social work education needs to embrace as practice evolves to meet the complex needs of an ever diversifying and challenging social and professional practice context.

Meeting Demand for Social Work Graduates

Ireland is currently experiencing a shortage of social work graduates and mainstream services are finding it difficult to fill social work vacancies. This trend is pronounced and acute in child welfare and protection services, a field of practice which expanded rapidly in the past quarter of a century. This expansion was fuelled by public pressure on the political system in the wake of revelations of historical residential care abuse, historical cases of clerical abuse and a number of other high-profile child abuse cases in which services appeared, in the public's view, to be slow to intervene. A new state agency,

Tusla, was established in 2014 with the remit to provide a national child and family welfare service. Since its establishment, significant progress has been made in delivering nationwide services to families in distress and to children at risk of abuse or neglect. With this expansion, the numbers of social work posts have also increased and, at the time of writing, there are many vacancies unfilled due to a shortage of qualified, registered social workers in Ireland. In tandem with the expansion of child and family support services, the social work workforce has also increased in other sectors such as mental health services, older peoples' services and disability services to name just a few. These factors combined have raised the demand for registered social workers and at present, the supply of new graduates from social work qualifying programmes in Ireland, estimated at 210 per annum, (Joint Committee on Children and Youth Affairs, 2019, p. 4) is failing to meet the employer demand.

In this context, there is something of a public spotlight on how social workers are educated in the Irish context. On the one hand, the need for more qualified social work graduates is opening up for debate the ways in which social workers are educated and the length of time it takes to produce a qualified social worker in the Irish system. On the other hand, research on the experiences of new social work graduates making the transition into their first social work jobs (Byrne & Kirwan, 2018), reveals the many pressures on social work practitioners positioned on the frontline of service delivery. In a context where there are pressures to produce more graduates in a shorter space of time, the need to protect the standard of social work education is indicated by this study.

Social Work and Technology

Technology is transforming all areas of social life, not just those in which social work plays a role. However, for social work, technology opens up many possibilities not only in the delivery of more effective and efficient services but also to support under-served and disadvantaged groups in society. Technology is a wide field including topics such as electronic communications, robotics, and information systems. Taken in this wider view, there is endless potential to use technological advances for the enhancement of social work practice and to meet the needs of groups served by social work. However, there are challenges for the profession in making best use of technology. These include the absence of technology-related inputs on the curriculum of many social work programmes (not just in Ireland but globally) and where it is present, it is often relegated to a peripheral position in the course programme. Secondly, there is a dearth of research on how social workers can innovate with technology to improve the services they offer. This is related to the low numbers of social work academics who specialise in the use of technology in social work and this impacts on the research output on this topic, although there are some very interesting examples of research coming through in more recent times (see, e.g., Brown & Dustman, 2019; Castillo de Mesa, Gomez Jacinto, Lopez Pelaez, & De las Olas Palma Garcia, 2019). The use of relationships is at the heart of social work practice and it is not easy for social workers to understand or grapple with the concept of relationship in online contexts although this is beginning to enter the social work literature (Kirwan, 2019).

It is essential for social workers to understand and be able to evaluate how relationships work through electronic communications but until recently they have been hampered by the lack of methodologies to measure issues such as relationship strength and interaction in online social work contexts. Pioneering work by authors such as Castillo de Mesa et al. (2019), Lopez Peldez and Marcuello-Servos (2018), and Teixeira (2018) is prompting the social work profession to not only think about how technology can enhance social work practice, but also how such innovation can be measured and evaluated.

A further layer to the use of technology is the emerging field of e-professionalism (Kirwan, 2012) and the need for social workers to think about the ethical dimensions of technology usage in their practice (Boddy & Dominelli, 2017; Reamer, 2013, 2015). A key consideration for social work is how to use technology to further its human rights agenda and to empower those who are marginalised and disadvantaged in society (La Mendola, 2018). There is much, therefore, for the social work curriculum to address and the use of technology by social workers touches on many issues that are well-established components of social work education. The challenge going forward is to bring technology more centre-stage into social work education and to prepare new graduates for a world in which technology is part of the everyday fabric of practice (Byrne & Kirwan, 2019).

Conclusion

As this chapter has illustrated, the education of professional social workers in Ireland has evolved in response to both domestic and global trends against an increasingly sophisticated and diverse sociocultural, demographic, economic, and political canvas. At the point of writing this chapter, the political landscape across Europe has also changed and continues to evolve, some would say critically and with a concerning degree of instability. The Brexit vote in the UK, alongside a growing anti-European politicism on this side of the Atlantic, combined with uncharted territory in the wake of the Trump administration on the other side of the Atlantic, may serve to challenge the achievements in global social work education in promoting the human right to a life free from violence, discrimination, social exclusion, and marginalisation. Against the backdrop of this uncertainty and as we simultaneously reflect on our past while looking towards our future, we celebrate the growth and evolving diversity of social work education in Ireland, while recognising that this change is steadfastly underpinned by the core principles and tenets of social justice and human rights.

REFERENCES

Boddy, J., & Dominelli, L. (2017). Social media and social work: The challenges of a new ethical space. *Australian Social Work, 70,* 172–184.

Brown, M. E., & Dustman, P. A. (2019). Identifying a project's greatest 'hits': Meaningful use of Facebook in an underserved community's development and mobilization effort. *Journal of Social Work Practice, 33*(2), 185–200.

Burns, K., Devaney, J., Holt, S., & Marshall, G. (forthcoming). Child protection and welfare on the Island of Ireland: Irish issues, global relevance. In J. D. Berrick, N. Gilbert, & M. Skivenes (Eds.), *International handbook of child protection systems.*

Byrne, J., & Kirwan, G. (2018, November 11–14). Learning in transition: Workplace learning for newly qualified social workers In L. Gómez Chova, A. López Martínez, & I. Candel Torres (Eds.), *11th International Conference on Education, Research and Innovation* (pp. 6676–6683). Seville, Spain.

Byrne, J., & Kirwan, G. (2019). Relationship-based social work and electronic communication technologies: Anticipation, adaptation and achievement. *Journal of Social Work Practice, 33*(2), 217–232.

Castillo de Mesa, J., Gomez Jacinto, L., Lopez Pelaez, A., & De las Olas Palma Garcia, M. (2019). Building relationships on social networking sites from a social work approach. *Journal of Social Work Practice, 33*(2), 201–216.

Central Statistics Office. (2018). *Population and migration estimates.* https://www.cso.ie/en/releasesandpublications/er/pme/populationandmigrationestimatesapril2018/.

CORU. (2018). *What is registration?* Available at http://coru.ie/en/registration/what_is_registration. Accessed on June 16, 2019.

CORU. (2019a). *Social workers registration board–standards of proficiency for social workers.* Available at https://www.coru.ie/files-education/swrb-standards-of-proficiency-for-social-workers.pdf. Accessed on June 11, 2020.

CORU. (2019b). *Social workers registration board–criteria for education and training programmes.* Available at https://www.coru.ie/files-education/swrb-profession-specific-criteria-for-education-and-training-programmes.pdf. Accessed on June 11, 2020.

CORU. (2019c). *Social workers registration board—code of professional conduct and ethics.* Available at http://coru.ie/uploads/documents/2019_03_06_SWRB_Code_for_Website.pdf. Accessed on April 1, 2019.

CORU. (2020). *Social workers approved qualifications.* Available at https://www.coru.ie/health-and-social-care-professionals/education/approved-qualifications/social-workers/social-workers-approved-qualifications.html. Accessed on June 11, 2020.

Coulter, C. (2015). *Final report, child care law reporting project.* Dublin: Child Care Reporting Project.

Delap, C., & Kelleher, T. (2005). Local authority social work in Ireland: Origins, issues and developments. In N. Kearney & C. Skehill (Eds.), *Social work in Ireland: Historical perspectives* (pp. 51–76). Dublin: Institute of Public Administration.

Flavin, E. (2018). *Working in a culturally competent way? Exploring the perceptions of social workers engaging with children and their families from minority ethnic groups.* Unpublished thesis submitted to Trinity College Dublin in partial fulfilment of the MSc. in Child Protection and Welfare.

Foreman, M. (2018). *Support services for victims of violence in asylum and migration: Comments paper Ireland*. European Commission on Justice.

Gartland, F. (2016). Fewer male social workers leads to gender bias, says TCD academic. *The Irish Times* [online], February 22. Available at https://www.irishtimes.com/news/social-affairs/fewer-male-social-workers-leads-to-gender-bias-says-tcd-academic-1.2543216. Accessed on August 31, 2017.

Grootegoed, E., & Smith, M. (2018). The Emotional labour of austerity: How social workers reflect and work on their feelings towards reducing support to needy children and families. *The British Journal of Social Work, 48*(7), 1929–1947.

Halton, C., & Wilson, G. (2013). Editorial: Changes in social work education in Ireland. *Social Work Education, 32*(8), 969–971.

Health and Social Care Professionals Act. (2005). S.I. No. 27 of 2005, Dublin: Stationery Office. Available at http://www.irishstatutebook.ie/eli/2005/act/27/enacted/en/html. Accessed on June 5, 2019.

Horne, M., & O'Connor, E. (2005). An overview of the development of health-related social work in Ireland. In N. Kearney & C. Skehill (Eds.), *Social work in Ireland: Historical perspectives* (pp. 165–183). Dublin: Institute of Public Administration.

Health Service Executive. (2008). *National intercultural health strategy.* Dublin: Health Service Executive.

Health Services Executive. (2010). *Roscommon child care case: Report of the inquiry team to the health services executive.* Dublin: Health Services Executive.

Health Services Executive. (2011). *Review of adequacy for HSE children and family services 2011.* Dublin: Health Service Executive.

Hingley-Jones, H., & Ruch, G. (2016). 'Stumbling through'? Relationship-based social work practice in austere times. *Journal of Social Work Practice, 30*(3), 235–248.

Hughes, M., & Houston, S. (2019). 'It's almost Kafkaesque': Newspaper coverage of social work's role in the 'Grace case' in the Republic of Ireland. *The British Journal of Social Work, 49,* 1376–1394.

International Association of Schools of Social Work. (2014). *Global definition of social work.* Available at https://www.iassw-aiets.org/global-definition-of-social-work-review-of-the-global-definition/. Accessed on March 9, 2019.

International Association of Schools of Social Work/International Federation of Social Work. (2004). *Global standards for the education and training of the social work profession.* Available at http://cdn.ifsw.org/assets/ifsw_65044-3.pdf. Accessed on March 9, 2019.

International Organization for Migration. (2004). *International migration law—Glossary on migration.* Available at http://www.iomvienna.at/sites/default/files/IML_1_EN.pdf; UN Population: Demographic factors, economic disparities and environmental change are major drivers of migration. Accessed on April 7, 2019.

Irish Probation Services. (2018). *Careers* [online]. Available at http://www.probation.ie/en/PB/Pages/WP16000058. Accessed on January 17, 2018.

Jacob, D., & Kirwan, G. (2016). *The Tallaght Roma integration project: Working for inclusion in health care through a community development model.* Dublin: Health Services Executive.

Joint Committee on Children and Youth Affairs. (2019). *Official report on recruitment and retention of social workers discussion.* Available at http://www.data.

oireachtas.ie/ie/oireachtas/debateRecord/joint_committee_on_children_and_youth_affairs/2019-04-10/debate/mul@/main.pdf. Accessed on June 11, 2020.

Kearney, N., & Carmichael, K. (1987). *Social work and social work training in Ireland: Yesterday and tomorrow occasional Paper No. 1.* Dublin: The Department of Social Studies University of Dublin.

Kearney, N., & Skehill, C. (Eds.). (2005). *Social work in Ireland: Historical perspectives.* Dublin: Institute of Public Administration.

Kirwan, G. (2005). Welfare and wedding cakes: An example of early occupational social work. In N. Kearney & C. Skehill (Eds.), *Social work in Ireland: Historical perspectives* (pp. 196–210). Dublin: Institute of Public Administration.

Kirwan, G. (2012). Social media, e-professionalism and netiquette in social work. *Irish Social Worker* (Autumn), 9–12.

Kirwan, G. (2019). Networked relationships in the digital age—Messages for social work. *Journal of Social Work Practice, 33*(2), 123–126.

La Mendola, W. (2018). Social work, social technologies, and sustainable community development. *Journal of Technology in Human Services, Published Online.* https://doi.org/10.1080/15228835.2018.1552905.

Logan, E. (2014). *Garda Siochana Act 2005 (Section 42) (Special inquiries relating to Garda Siochana) Order 2013.* Dublin: Office of the Ombudsman for Children.

Lopez Peldez, A., & Marcuello-Servos, C. (2018). E-Social work and digital society: Re-conceptualizing approaches, practices and technologies. *European Journal of Social Work, 21*(6), 801–803.

Mannion, K. (2016). *Child migration matters: Child and young people's experience of migration.* Dublin: Immigrant Council of Ireland.

Mc Gregor, C., & Quin, S. (2015). Revisiting our history post 'Celtic Tiger': So, what's new? In A. Christie, B. Featherstone, S. Quin, & T. Walsh (Eds.), *Social work in Ireland.* London: Palgrave.

National Social Work Qualifications Board. (2007). *National social work qualification Board annual report—2006.* Dublin: National Social Work Qualifications Board.

Ni Raghallaigh, M., Foreman, M., & Feeley, M. (2016). *Transition from direct provision to life in the community.* Dublin: Irish Research Council.

O'Connor, A. V., & Parkes, S. M. (1984). *Gladly learn and gladly teach: A history of Alexandra college and school 1899–1966.* Dublin: Alexandra College.

Office of the High Commissioner for Human Rights. (1994). *Human rights and social work.* New York: United Nations.

Powell, F., Geoghan, M., Scanlon, M., & Swirak, K. (2012). The Irish charity myth, child abuse and human rights. *The British Journal of Social Work, 43*(1), 7–23.

Reamer, F. G. (2013). Social work in a digital age: Ethical and risk management challenges. *Social Work, 58*(2), 163–172.

Reamer, F. G. (2015). Clinical social work in a digital environment: Ethical and risk management challenges. *Clinical Social Work Journal, 43*(2), 120–132.

Shannon, G., & Gibbons, N. (2012). *Report of the independent child death review group.* DCYA: Dublin.

Shannon, G. (2017). *Audit of the exercise by an Garda Siochana of the provisions of Section 12 of the Child Care Act 1991.* Dublin: Department of Children and Youth Affairs.

Teixeira, S. (2018). Qualitative geographic information systems (GIS): An untapped research approach for social work. *Qualitative Social Work, 17*, 9–23.

United Nations. (2014). *Offices on drugs and crime, global report on trafficking in persons.* Available at http://www.unodc.org/documents/data-and-analysis/glotip/GLOTIP_2014_full_report.pdf. Accessed on August 30, 2019.

Van Heugten, K. (2011). Registration and social work education: A golden opportunity or a Trojan Horse. *Journal of Social Work, 11*(2), 174–190.

Walsh, T., Wilson, G., & O'Connor, E. (2009). Local, European and global: An exploration of migration patterns of social workers into Ireland. *The British Journal of Social Work, 40*(6), 1978–1995.

Wilson, G., & Campbell, A. (2013). Developing social work education: Academic perspectives. *The British Journal of Social Work, 43,* 1005–1023.

CHAPTER 18

Social Work Education in Poland

Jarosław Przeperski

SOCIAL WORK EDUCATION IN POLAND FROM A HISTORICAL PERSPECTIVE

Conditions for the Development of Social Work in Poland

A characteristic feature of the educational system for social workers in Poland is its discontinuity. The history of social work education has been influenced by historical events experienced by the Poles. The processes of professionalisation of the social worker profession, whenever started, were interrupted by events such as the Second World War or the introduction of communist ideology in Poland and Poland's dependence on the Soviet Union. Therefore, we can distinguish several stages of the development of social work as a social practice and professional training for the profession of social worker. When starting the analysis of the education system, it is worth mentioning that the official name of the profession—social worker—appeared in Poland in 1966. Previously, this area of work was not called social work, but the terms "social works" and "social welfare" were used interchangeably. Similarly, employees were called social carers.[1]

The development of the profession of social worker has resulted from historical, ideological or religious conditions, but one of the most important factors shaping this profession is the development of social work itself, understood as a method of providing support to people who cannot overcome the difficulties they face in their lives by themselves.

J. Przeperski (✉)
Centre for Family Research,
Nicolaus Copernicus University, Torun, Poland
e-mail: jprzeperski@umk.pl

© The Author(s) 2021
S. S. M. et al. (eds.), *The Palgrave Handbook of Global Social Work Education*, https://doi.org/10.1007/978-3-030-39966-5_18

Analysing the history of social work, it should be noted that the first institutions that were responsible for aid were families and local communities. They were the original and natural source of support and assistance. Of course, this cannot be considered professional help, but it should be noted that often this selfless help resulted from attitudes originating in Christian values, where help for the other, sacrifice and responsibility for another person was the realisation of the ideal of a good Christian and citizen. Poland accepted Christianity in 966 and practically until the eighteenth century, helping other people was the task of people in their immediate vicinity or was carried out by the wealthy or rulers who in this way obeyed the orders of the Bible and the Church. With the development of Church structures in Poland, social assistance tasks were more and more often carried out as part of the Catholic Church's charitable activities (Leś, 2001). Such an approach significantly limited the involvement of state authorities in the sphere of social welfare. It was not until 1775 that the "Hospital Constitution" was issued, providing grounds for the establishment of a body dealing with charity issues, and then provincial commissions supervising the functioning of care facilities. In 1817, a law was passed in the Kingdom of Poland concerning the care provided by communes [*gmina*] for the poor and incapacitated. At the same time, the communes were allowed to impose taxes for public charity earmarked for the support of dependent persons (Dobkowski, 2009). The methods of professional help for the other also determined its semantic formulation. Until the 1880s (Brenk, 2017), the term social service was commonplace. Such a definition of aid resulted from the understanding of activities for the benefit of another human being as a service, and historical conditions which broadened the scope of activities assigned to classical social work. Most of the activities were grassroots activities, undertaken in the area of broadly understood charity by socially active people. Due to the fact that Poland at that time was not an independent state and was divided between Russia, Austria, and Prussia, social work (social service) expanded its scope. Characteristic for this period was activities aimed at preserving Polish national and social identity. Social work was closely connected with informal educational tasks such as organising publications for self-taught people, promoting education (Brenk, 2017). These activities contributed to Poles raising their level of education, changing the way of life and, as a result, maintaining the sense of national identity.

In 1918, as a result of the end of the First World War, Poland regained its independence. This made it possible to restore and build the structures of a modern European state. The task of creating a social welfare system was also undertaken. This was reflected in the Social Welfare Act passed on 16 August 1923. It defined the tasks of social welfare in the following way: "the satisfaction from public funds of the necessary life needs of those persons who permanently or temporarily cannot do so with their own material means or their own work".[2] It is worth stressing that this law was in force in Poland for almost 70 years until 1990 when, after the fall of communism, a new law was prepared and passed. The adoption of the Act can be called a milestone in the organisation and professionalisation of social assistance in Poland, because until then many activities had been undertaken on the basis of various legal acts, local laws (cf. Krzyszkowski, 2005). Often, they not only did not complement one another, but were clearly contradictory. It should be remembered that Poland, divided between three partitioning powers, operated under three legal systems which were supplemented by local laws. The Social Welfare Act (1923) brought order to the legislative area and first of all provided a strong impulse for the development of professional social work through new regulations.

The period of the Second World War (1939–1945) was the time when the development of professional social work was abruptly interrupted. At the same time, the Nazi regime exterminated in a methodical and organised manner those related to the world of science and members of the intellectual elite of Poland at that time (Wardzyńska, 2009).

The next period of development of social work in Poland encompassed the years 1945–1989. At that time, Poland was under the domination of the Soviet Union. The binding ideology was communism and socialism. This ideology determined the way social assistance was organised and tasks undertaken by social carers and social workers. The almost 50-year-long period can be divided into three stages: the rescue period (the first years after the end of the Second World War), the phase of stagnation in the development of social services (the time of the strong Stalinist regime), and the third stage of the return to the development of scientific activity (after the year 1958) (Kluzowa, 2006).

An important event for the development of social work and the profession of social worker arose when the Ministry of Labour and Social Welfare was dissolved in 1960 and its competences were transferred to the Ministry of Health which was renamed the Ministry of Health and Social Welfare. The activity of social carers was formally subordinated to the health service. They were employed in health centres. This led to a significant change in the way social work was provided. It was more in line with the medical, deficit model focused on the health aspects of clients' lives (Szumlicz, 1987) and less focus placed on empowering and strengthening activities. The period immediately preceding 1989 was a time when client needs and expectations were becoming more and more apparent and were articulated. In the face of the inevitable collapse of communism, there was an increase in demand for social services. At the same time, there were no legislative or organisational initiatives that would allow the state to respond to the growing needs of the clients (Zalewski, 2005).

Another breakthrough in the development of social work in Poland was the collapse of the Soviet Union and the liberation of Poland from its domination. Already during the Round Table (historic meetings of the communist authorities and the democratic opposition), a commission was set up to deal with issues related to the restoration of a modern social welfare system. The concepts developed at that time were reflected in the establishment of social welfare centres at the commune level and the adoption of the Social Assistance Act on 30 November 1990. The first years after 1989 were the time of political transformation, transition from a socialist state, and economy to a democratic state and a competitive economy. The Social Assistance Act of that time mainly focused on material and living support for people who had difficulties in gaining a footing in the new mode of operation of the state. The first demands were made not to duplicate the system that was in force in the People's Republic of Poland, but they were not widely introduced as systemic solutions. Therefore, less emphasis was placed on the implementation of tasks related to non-material support and aid. In order to build a social welfare system, a network of social carer centres dating back to the communist period was used (Rymsza, 2014). The proposed solutions clearly separated the healthcare sector from social assistance. This was reflected in the transfer of social assistance competences from the Ministry of Health to the Ministry of Labour and Social Policy (Dobkowski, 2009).

The beginning of the twenty-first century in Poland was characterised by a strong development of the social policy of the state. The solutions introduced after regaining independence were also reviewed. The initiated discussion on social assistance's effectiveness was an important impulse for changes in that sphere. This discussion was reflected in the adoption of a new Social Assistance Act on 12 March 2004. In addition to material support, the tasks of a social worker include to a greater extent obligations related to the provision of non-material aid.

The framework for social assistance in Poland is set out in the aforementioned Social Assistance Act of 2004. It indicates the areas of social life which have been specifically assigned to the tasks of social assistance. The Act specifies in detail in Article 7 the following problems: poverty, orphanhood, homelessness, unemployment, disability, long-term or serious illness, domestic violence, the need to protect victims of human trafficking, the need to protect motherhood or families with many children, incapacity in matters of care and education and running a household, especially in single-parent families or families with many children, difficulties in integrating foreigners who have obtained refugee status or subsidiary protection in the Republic of Poland, difficulties in adapting to life after being released from a penal institution, alcoholism or drug addiction, random events or crises, natural or ecological disasters. The indicated areas concern many different situations that require specialist and diverse competences from social workers. Legal commentaries indicate that this catalogue cannot be treated as a closed set. It gives directions of activities and areas which are obligatory for the social assistance system. In a situation of constant social transformations and emerging consequential problems, the catalogue of tasks for social assistance is also being modified. For example, we will not only be dealing with the problem of alcohol or drug addiction but, in the area of social work, there will be various types of addiction that go beyond these two categories.

The Social Assistance Act also indicates which activities should be undertaken within the framework of social assistance. Article 15 states that social assistance primarily concerns:

1. granting and paying benefits provided for by law;
2. social work;
3. running and developing the necessary social infrastructure;
4. analysing and evaluating phenomena generating demand for social assistance benefits;
5. implementing tasks resulting from discerned social needs;
6. developing new forms of social assistance and self-help within the framework of identified needs.

It is worth noting that the first task the legislator indicates is the granting and payment of benefits (mainly cash benefits). It seems that placing this task at the top of the list results in its prioritisation in the real life and everyday functioning of the social assistance system.

Education of Social Workers in Poland—A Historical Perspective

Together with the development of social work in Poland, the need for the development of the education system for social workers emerged. The history of the creation of this system is closely related to the implementation of social work and the place it occupied in particular historical periods. At the beginning, it should be emphasised that the education of social workers in Poland takes place at three levels: higher (bachelor's and master's degree), secondary (post-secondary schools) and supplementary education (e.g. courses). Historically, we are dealing with all types of education.

The development of institutions educating social workers in Poland can be divided into five significant and relatively easy to distinguish stages.

Stage I—Until 1918

As outlined above, until the year 1918 the main providers of social services were families, community representatives, and the Catholic Church. Shortly before the First World War, the organisation of short-term additional training courses in Poland was started. In 1907, the first "Social Courses" were organised in the Kingdom of Poland by a Catholic association, and they dealt with social work in the Kingdom of Poland. In 1916, the Faculty of Social Work at the Higher Courses for Women was established in Kraków (Mikulski, 1974). Generally speaking, it can be said that before Poland regained independence in 1918, there was no professional training for social workers.

Stage II—1918–1939

After Poland regained independence, the social welfare system was built (the aforementioned Social Welfare Act of 1923), and at the same time an attempt was made to educate staff who could undertake the tasks contained in this Act in a professional manner. Therefore, the organisation of the education system for future social carers began. In 1925, the Adrian Baraniecki School of Social Work was established in Kraków, educating social carers at secondary level. Girls with a secondary school-leaving certificate and over eighteen years of age were admitted to the school.

An important step in the professionalisation of social assistance personnel was the establishment of a higher education institution. The first such institution was the School of Social and Educational Work of the Free Polish University in Warsaw, founded in 1925 by Helena Radlińska. Initially, it was a year-long course. Relatively quickly, this proved to be insufficient, so it was decided to opt for a dual system of education. One was a two-year cycle of a course character, the other was a four-year cycle of higher education (Brenk, 2012). The school had two specialities: organiser of cultural life and social care, and organiser of social care for children and youth (Szmagalski, 2012). At this point, it is worth noting that unlike the first vocational social work schools in other European countries, in Poland the education of social workers was developed at the level of higher education.

Stage III—1939–1945—The Second World War

The education of social workers during the Second World War was practically suspended. The only form consisted in secret classes organised by former lecturers of social work. Since it was an activity forbidden by the German occupant, it was of a discontinuous and random character. It is therefore difficult to talk about regular and professional training for social workers in this period.

Stage IV—From the End of the Second World War to the Fall of Communism (1989)

After the war, an attempt was made to rebuild the social welfare system that had been functioning before the war. In the first phase, shortly after the war, institutions educating social carers were established. The first permanent institution focused on education and further training was the Training Centre for Social Welfare Workers in Łódź, established on 1 June 1945 by the Ministry of Labour and Social Welfare. At the beginning of 1946, the Workers' Universities Society opened the Higher School of Social Sciences in Kraków. A similar institution was established in Warsaw in 1948 and was called the Training Centre for Social Welfare Workers (Brenk, 2012). After 1948, with the increase in communist influences, education in the field of social welfare and assistance was hampered by the state authorities. The development of modern social assistance structures and education of social workers was practically halted. This resulted from the adopted state ideology, which showed socialism as a source of prosperity for every citizen. Therefore, it was assumed (contrary to reality) that the system itself and the socialist economy were sufficient measures to ensure the absence of poverty and social dysfunctions.

In Poland, the situation changed after Stalin's death and the recognition of the failures associated with the communist ideology (the Polish thaw). This helped start the process of creating a network of county [*powiat*] social carers. In March 1959, the institution of social carer was re-established, which was undoubtedly one of the strongest incentives for the development of social work education in the years to come (Brenk, 2014a). Measures were taken to professionalise the profession of social worker. Since 1956, social workers could obtain higher education at the University of Warsaw and since 1957 at the University of Łódź. At the beginning of the 1960s, the possibility of obtaining a master's degree with a specialisation in social policy was possible at the Warsaw School of Planning and Statistics (Brenk, 2012). An important step in the development of the profession and education was the introduction of the professional title of social worker instead of the previously used term of social carer. It took place on 4 November 1966. A description of the profession was also provided, defining a social worker as "a specialist professionally dealing with satisfying social needs by means of social work methods" (Biederman, 1998, p. 38). The title of social worker was included in the professional register of social work schools in 1971 (Jagodzińska, 2014).

The introduction of a separate profession of "social worker" in 1966 was combined with the opening of the State Schools of Social Workers in Warsaw and Poznań in the same year, providing secondary education. In 1967, similar schools were opened in Łódź and Kraków, a year later in Wrocław, and in the 1970s, institutions were established in other cities (Brenk, 2014b). The education in the State Schools of Social Workers took two years, initially only on a daily basis. People under 40 years of age with a secondary school diploma entitling them to higher education were accepted. In the 1970s, the education of social workers in schools (at the level of secondary education) was the most popular form of preparing social workers for professional work. At the same time, social workers were once again merged with medical education, and gradually from 1971 the inclusion of social work schools in Vocational Medical Schools was started, with the removal of separate names of social work schools (Brenk, 2014a).

Stage V—After 1989—The Period After the Fall of Communism
At the level of higher education, the course which directly prepares students for the profession of social work has been implemented since 2006. Initially, social work could be studied at the bachelor's level. Before 2006, social work functioned as a speciality within such fields as: pedagogy, sociology, social policy, psychology, and family sciences. Higher education institutions running

this specialisation had a certain autonomy in the development of curricula and in the selection of staff. But this autonomy was also conducive to the emergence within a single-state university of two entities providing education of the same speciality, but at different faculties (pedagogy and sociology at the same time) (Kotlarska-Michalska, 2013). It is worth noting that the right to practice the profession of social worker cannot be acquired by completing postgraduate studies, courses, and training and the only way is to study social work or graduate from a college of social service workers (Jagodzińska, 2014).

Legal Conditions for the Profession of Social Worker

The Social Assistance Act of 2004 also regulates who can become a social worker in Poland. Article 116 indicates several different situations. Section "Social Work Education in Poland from a Historical Perspective" specifies that a social worker may be a person who satisfies at least one of the following conditions:

1. holds a diploma of completion of a college of social service workers;
2. has completed higher education in the field of social work;
3. until 31 December 2013 completed higher education studies in a specialisation preparing for the profession of a social worker in one of the fields of study:
   (a) pedagogy,
   (b) special education,
   (c) political science,
   (d) social policy,
   (e) psychology,
   (f) sociology,
   (g) family studies.

At this point, it is worth noting the cut-off point set by the year 2013. From this year onwards, only persons that graduate from a college of social service workers (secondary education level) or from a university or college in the field of social work could be a social worker. Earlier it was permissible to graduate from the fields of study related to social work, e.g. family sciences, pedagogy, and sociology.

In Article 116(2), the Act also introduced the post-qualification degrees of professional specialisation in the occupation of social worker:

2. The following grades of professional specialisation in the occupation of social worker shall be determined:
   1) first degree of professional specialisation in the field of social work, aimed at complementing knowledge and improving professional skills of social workers;

2) second degree of professional specialisation in the field of social work, aimed at improving knowledge and skills in working with selected groups of persons benefiting from social assistance.

Achieving each degree of professional specialisation is accompanied by a slight increase in remuneration, and therefore many employees benefit from this form of professional development. Social work is usually carried out in Poland by local social assistance centres. The division of work results more from geographical conditions (cities are divided into districts, streets) than problems tackled. In this case, a worker works with families living in a particular street, village, and not with families with specific problems. Although specialisation is to lead to social workers dealing with people with specific problems, it seems that in the current legal and organisational conditions the potential of this type of education is not fully utilised. Specialisation certainly develops skills, increases the level of knowledge that a worker can use in his or her daily work.

Educational Programmes in the Field of Social Work (Based on the Example of the First Degree of Social Work)

In Poland, as in most European countries, the so-called development and competence model is implemented in academic education, focused on knowledge as well as competences and skills (Kantowicz, 2005). In 2006, the Ministry of Science and Higher Education developed educational standards for particular fields of study, which are binding for all universities. The framework educational content was divided into two blocks: the group of basic content and the group of specialised content. In the first group are offered content in the following fields: social sciences, pedagogy, psychology, research methodology of social studies, law, economics, and management. The content related to the following areas of social work was included within the framework of specialised content: introduction to social work, methods of social work, knowledge of human development in the life cycle, social problems, and social policy. The regulation also defines the learning outcomes in each of the content groups.

In the field of social sciences, the following learning outcomes are expected—skills and competences: analysing and solving basic philosophical problems; understanding and using basic concepts of ethics; understanding the function of ethics in social life; analysing statements taken from the press, legal acts, textbooks, and public disputes; using basic sociological concepts; understanding social phenomena; understanding the organisation and functioning of institutions of social life. In the field of pedagogy—skills and competences: understanding the links between social and special pedagogy (disability studies) and social work; understanding the contemporary role and tasks of pedagogy in the context of social changes and building civil society; understanding the ideas, forms, and problems of lifelong learning worldwide and in Poland. In the field of psychology—skills and competences: understanding psychological processes and phenomena that direct people's behaviour; distinguishing types and functions of individual differences in terms of psychological functioning of people and elements of personality structure; understanding mental disorders; understanding social phenomena; using psychological knowledge in formulating and solving social problems. In the field of social science research methodology—skills and competences: design, execution, and analysis of data. Within the scope of law—skills and competences: applying legal regulations in care activity and family assistance; applying law in social work. In economics and management—skills and competences: using basic concepts of economics and management; understanding socio-economic processes; solving organisational and management problems—formulating objectives, planning, and evaluating performance.

The following educational outcomes were indicated in the group of content related to the field of study:

> In terms of introduction to social work—skills and competences: understanding the history of social assistance and social work in the historical context; understanding the role of the social worker and social assistance in society; participating in various forms of care, assistance and support; recognising one's own limitations in working with others; preventing and managing conflict; helping others. In the field of social work methodology—skills and competences: applying social work techniques—contract signing, interviewing, document analysis, observation, motivating clients to undertake activity, problem-solving approaches; carrying out social work with an individual, family, group, and local community; creating evaluation procedures; recognising axiological problems of social work; understanding ethical aspects of the profession and social responsibility; resolving ethical issues based on an axiological consensus of the profession. In the scope of knowledge of human development in the life cycle—skills and competences: understanding the causes of individual and inter-personal variability; analysing developmental disorders from the viewpoint of relations between aetiology and symptomatology; recognising individual needs and human capabilities in particular stages of ontogenesis; applying biomedical knowledge in social work. In the scope of social problems and social policy institutions—skills and competences: understanding contemporary social policy and its economic conditions; analysing and implementing tasks in the scope of social policy on a local, national, and international scale; identifying social problems; distinguishing types and manifestations of social pathologies; understanding phenomena of marginalisation and social exclusion and problems of social inequalities.

At the same time, every student of social work is obliged to complete an internship under the guidance of a social worker, which should last no less than eight weeks.

CHALLENGES FACING SOCIAL WORK EDUCATION IN POLAND

Training of Social Workers in a Changing Society

In Poland, as in other countries, we are witnessing accelerating social changes. Globalisation, new technologies, and new social structures imply, on the one hand, the development of society and, on the other hand, the emergence of new problems that social assistance has to face. The education system faces a big challenge of how to educate social workers to prepare them to work in a constantly changing society. The traditional education system has provided future social workers with a specific package of knowledge and skills that can be used in future work. For many years, it has been relatively easy and accurate, including through research, to predict what kind of knowledge and skills future workers will need. Educational programmes in the field of social work were created on that basis. More and more often, however, those programmes do not match the changing reality. Educators of future social workers relatively rarely review the subjects taught and modify their scope. At this point, it should also be stressed that the higher education system in Poland is highly formalised and every change, including in the curriculum, requires complex and time-consuming procedures. The full course of a social worker at the level of higher education in Poland lasts 5 years. It seems that often the knowledge a student acquires at the beginning of his or her education is outdated or at least does not fully relate to the challenges faced by an employee taking up a job. An even greater challenge seems to lie in preparing social workers in such a way that, during their professional career, they will independently expand their knowledge and skills so that they can adequately and fully respond to the needs of their clients.

It should be stressed that the social worker belongs to a group of occupations in which it is not possible to fully prepare for work. It is also not possible to achieve a situation in which you can say that someone has achieved full professionalism and does not need to update their knowledge and skills (Szpunar, 2013). The social worker is one of those professions which are constantly updated according to the identified needs and problems in society. This update also applies to the methods of diagnosing or working with clients. Methods that have provided a high degree of efficiency in the past may, under changing circumstances, become obsolete and require modification or replacement by new solutions.

The educational model must therefore aim at preparing students for future roles and tasks. It is therefore necessary to move away from the formula of vocational training which can be called craftsmanship. It teaches how to reproduce work methods, work culture or the knowledge conveyed as faithfully as possible. It is a reproductive model that does not require any involvement in the search for new and up-to-date solutions (Michalska, 2016). In view of the above, it can be concluded that it is not possible to effectively provide support without continuous learning and constant revision of working methods (Józefczyk, 2013). It is therefore important to teach students not only specific knowledge modules and methods of social work, but it is also necessary to include in the curricula the acquisition of competences which will allow future social workers to adapt actions to changing needs and problems. One of the key areas is the attitude of social workers towards innovation. Research conducted by the Centre for Family Research of the Nicolaus Copernicus University in Toruń (Przeperski, 2019b) has shown that social workers perceive themselves as innovative in the self-assessment questionnaire. However, a survey on readiness for change (Kriegel & Brandt, 1996) showed that tolerance to uncertainty, risk-taking, and adaptability is low in more than 90% of social workers. Therefore, an important challenge facing the education system of employees concerns how to assist students to become open to innovation and actively undertake dialogue with the changing social world.

Education for Evidence-Based Practice in Social Work

In the context of education, it is important to answer the question about the basic assumptions on which social work is based. In reference to Kahneman's concept (Kahneman, 2011), we can speak of two different approaches. The first one is primarily based on the intuition and experience of the social worker, the second one draws on scientific knowledge and evidence. It seems that such a radical juxtaposition of these two approaches results in reductionism in everyday work. The optimal approach seems to be an integrated one where both "hard knowledge" and subjective employee assessments are important. In Poland, the dominant approach is based on intuitiveness and subjectivism. Analysing the results of a survey of social workers in the area of client diagnosis, it can be stated that out of 400 respondents only 5% use any tools (surveys, questionnaires) to evaluate the client. The rest of the workers base their judgement solely on unstructured conversation and filling in the official client information form (Przeperski, 2019b). In this context, an important challenge facing the system of education for social work is to strengthen education teaching evidence-based practice without diminishing the role of the intuitive approach.

It seems that evidence-based social work practice (EBP) is often wrongly associated with a kind of technocratic and reductionist approach by the social worker. Some authors are sceptical of the knowledge-based approach using hard scientific tools (Smolińska-Theiss, 2013). They fear that this will lead to the disappearance of individualised work with clients and families and to a lack of reflection on the part of social workers. Procedures and standardised tools for diagnosing and working with clients will become dominant. The problem in the relationship between people in both positions may lie in that they perceive each other in a distorted way. Many practitioners or those who perceive social work only in the context of practice are seen more as those who base their work more on intuition than on research. Personal experience becomes an important and often the only category that determines the mode of operation. Practitioners, on the other hand, see researchers responsible for hard data and as people who do not understand reality, and whose research is aimed at negating the work methods proposed by practitioners (Browning & Pasley, 2015).

Professionalisation of the profession of social worker will not be possible without bridging the gap between scientific knowledge and practice and streamlining the path of transfer of research results to practice (Kaźmierczak, 2012). The use of knowledge is particularly important at two stages of work: when creating new solutions, both with a single client and at the level of system solutions, as well as when assessing the effectiveness of actions taken (Przeperski, 2019a). Thus, in the education process the social worker must be equipped with a new type of knowledge and invited to be a researcher in his or her area of activity (cf. Taylor, Killick, & McGlade, 2015).

A particular problem that occurs in Poland is the lack of recognition of social work as a scientific discipline, as is the case in many Western European countries. Social work is situated only as a field of study and not as a separate discipline in which research can be carried out. As a consequence, it is impossible to become a doctor or professor in social work. The only available options are: a bachelor's degree and, more recently, a master's degree. Researchers who undertake research in areas where social work practices are implemented are forced to embed them in other scientific areas. This is usually sociology, social pedagogy, or social policy. In the absence of a clear definition of the research area of social work, it is difficult to achieve a significant development of this area of knowledge, all the more so as scientific work is assessed in other disciplines mentioned above. This situation results in researchers marginalising social work research, because it is necessary to embed it in other scientific disciplines due to professional advancement.

Teachers of Social Work

In the Polish system of education of social workers, there is a discussion about who should be teachers, who should be responsible for the education of future staff. The answer to this question is determined primarily by the location of the education. It is currently carried out mainly at universities, the staff of which, in accordance with the applicable law, is mostly composed of persons conducting didactic and scientific activity and holding academic titles. As a rule, they are not practitioners but scientists. An additional problem lies in the lack of social work specialists, as mentioned above. Classes are usually conducted by people from the departments of sociology, pedagogy, social sciences, psychology, or law. Although the lectures are often conducted at a high scientific level, they fail to incorporate connections with the practice of social work. Today's challenge is to embed important knowledge in the context of social work and to indicate how the theories of particular disciplines, knowledge that comes from them, can be applied in the practical work of social workers.

At the same time, there is a growing awareness of the need to supplement the theoretical basis of social work with activities teaching students specific skills of working with clients. As part of the existing solutions, the employment of practitioners for the education of students was hampered by regulations which clearly pointed to the obligatory binary nature of work at universities—scientific and didactic. Only in exceptional cases were people employed at universities who did not have academic titles but were specialists in the field of social work. The new law on higher education—the Law on Higher Education and Science of 20 July 2018—introduces a new division of higher education institutions into vocational and research ones. This opens up opportunities for some universities to focus on practical preparation for careers without having to carry out research on such a large scale. It will be possible to employ more practitioners and social work specialists than was previously the case.

An important change that may be relevant for the development of social work education takes the form of enabling social workers to develop their research skills in cooperation with universities. This could be implemented on the basis of postgraduate or doctoral studies as a scientific view of the reality in which these workers are immersed on a daily basis. Such an approach would in turn require an increased recognition of the importance of research in social work and the acquisition of skills to combine practice and learning. It also seems pivotal to equip students and train already practising social workers in research competences so that the technical side of science is not a barrier to scientific development (Whittaker, 2012).

Students of Social Work

The effectiveness of education of social work personnel depends on many factors, e.g. curricula, teachers, learning aids, type, and quality of internships. However, one of the key factors influencing the quality of education is the intellectual, social, and motivational potential of students undertaking studies. The profession of social worker in Poland is not seen as a highly prestigious type of work. In a study conducted in 2017 on a sample of 105 social workers, they assessed the prestige of their profession on a 5-point scale, where 1 meant the lowest position in the hierarchy of professions, and 5 the highest position. Most people rated the professional position of social workers at two

(40.95%), every third person (30.48%) chose three, and seven people (6.67%) marked a high rating of four. Only three people (2.86%) chose the highest option (5). Interestingly, as many as 19.05% of social workers rated their profession as the least prestigious. In the opinion of representatives of aid professions (40.95%), the prestige of the profession of social worker in Polish society is low, and in the opinion of 36.19% of respondents very low (Kanios & Herman, 2017). This study shows that even among the social workers themselves, the prestige of the profession is very low. Similar results apply to the general public which perceives social work as a low-profile activity.

The low prestige of the profession of social worker translates into the low prestige of the field of study. It seems that the choice of social work as a subject of study is a choice of chance or necessity rather than a first and dream choice. Social work does not attract the best students from a given year but in many cases those who did not manage to study their first-choice course. In the academic year 2008–2009, a study of motivation to study social work was performed on a sample of 150 students starting their studies (Lalak & Skiba, 2010). Among the six possible answers, the students most often indicated the willingness to help others—45%, the way of self-fulfilment—19%, interest in the needs of other people, working with people—13%, vocation, own experience—9%. It is also important that over 17% of students indicated that they were not admitted to other studies or were admitted to these studies by accident. As can be seen from the above data, a big challenge for institutions educating social workers in Poland is to attract good students, who in the future will decide about the quality and prestige of the profession. It is also a problem to break the existing stereotypes concerning social work, indicating its ineffectiveness and unprofessionalism. The worst-case scenario that could materialise is the admission of increasingly weak students who would be unable to fully exploit the potential of the knowledge and skills transferred during the learning process. A low level of studies could result in more frequent rejection of this field of study as an option for good students who could potentially promote social work in their communities in the future. It seems that such a scenario is derived from some cases of social work where low potential and exclusion are inherited generationally and active efforts are needed to break the cycle of exclusion (Karwacki, 2006).

Conclusion

Social work education in Poland at a higher level will celebrate its centenary in four years' time. It seems that if it were not for the history of Poland, full of turbulence and difficult times, this education could be an example for many countries. The modern training of social workers is a field that is constantly evolving and developing. Many of the proposed solutions are taken from other countries where education had a chance for evolutionary development, permanently striving for greater efficiency and better educational results. These challenging times seem to be significant for the professionalisation of the social work profession and knowledge- and evidence-based education. At the same time, it is a time of intensive development of social work as an area of research and scientific reflection.

At this point, it is worth indicating the special role of Poland in the transmission of values and education between Western and Eastern Europe. Geopolitical conditions often make the country a bridge between the ideas of Western and Eastern Europe. It seems that also in the case of social work education in Poland, there is an attempt to combine these two traditions which approach social work in different ways. Combining the often standardised western approach and the very intuitive eastern approach may contribute to the creation of an integral model of social work education.

Notes

1. In Polish, it is important to distinguish semantically between particular terms used to describe social work activities and the employee performing them. The use of a given term throughout history in a significant way defined the scope and methodologyof work. It gives rise to difficulties when trying to express these terms in English. *Opieka społeczna* (social welfare—more social care and less social work in terms of support, empowerment), *pomoc społeczna* (social assistance—more social work than social care), *służba społeczna* (social service—to be a servant for those who are in need).
2. Social Welfare Act of 16 August 1923 (Journal of Laws of 1923, No. 92, item 726).

Bibliography

Biederman, V. (1998). Problemy kształcenia pracowników socjalnych [Issues of the education of social workers]. In W. L. Malinowski & M. Orłowska (Eds.), *Praca socjalna służbą człowiekowi*. Warsaw: Wydawnictwo Akademickie „Żak".

Brenk, M. (2012). Od społecznika do profesjonalisty – ewolucja zawodu pracownika socjalnego w Polsce [From social activist to professional—Evolution of the profession of social worker in Poland]. *Kultura-Społeczeństwo-Edukacja*, (2), 135. https://doi.org/10.14746/kse.2012.2.10.

Brenk, M. (2014a). Kształcenie pracowników socjalnych w Polsce Ludowej [Education of social workers in the People's Republic of Poland]. *Studia Edukacyjne*, *31*, 233–248. https://doi.org/10.14746/se.2014.31.13.

Brenk, M. (2014b). Minęło 90 lat od uchwalenia Ustawy o opiece społecznej w Polsce [It has been 90 years since the Social Welfare Act in Poland was passed]. *Praca Socjalna*, (1).

Brenk, M. (2017). Filantropia, opieka społeczna, praca socjalna - ewolucja form pomocy potrzebującym na przestrzeni dziejów. Zarys problematyki [Philanthropy, social welfare, social work—Evolution of forms of assistance to the deprived throughout history. Outline of the problem]. In W. A. Knocińska & P. Frąckowiak (Eds.), *Pomoc, wsparcie, ratownictwo: o optymalizacji rozwoju i edukacji człowieka*.

Browning, S., & Pasley, K. (2015). *Contemporary families: Translating research into practice* (1st ed.). New York, NY: Routledge.

Dobkowski, J. (2009). Europejskie systemu pomocy społecznej (wybrane uwagi z zakresu komparatystyki administracyjnej) [European social assistance system (selected comments on administrative comparative statistics)]. *Studia Prawnoustrojowe*, (9).

Jagodzińska, M. (2014). Kształcenie i doskonalenie zawodowe pracownika socjalnego jako wyznacznik profesjonalnej pomocy wobec osób wykluczonych społecznie [Vocational education and training of a social worker as a determinant of professional assistance for socially excluded people]. *Społeczeństwo, Edukacja, Język, 2*.

Józefczyk, J. (2013). Wymiary edukacji instytucji pomocy społecznej i idea uczącej się organizacji [Dimensions of education of social welfare institutions and the idea of a learning organisation]. In W. M. Mendel & B. Skrzypczak (Eds.), *Praca socjalna jako edukacja ku zmianie. Od edukacji do polityki*. Warsaw.

Kahneman, D. (2011). *Thinking, fast and slow*. Downloaded from http://api. overdrive.com/v1/collections/v1L2BaQAAAJcBAAA1M/products/ 22ad35b1-b466-42b5-b366-7000ed333ac7.

Kanios, A., & Herman, A. (2017). Ranga i prestiż zawodu pracownika socjalnego [Ranking and prestige of the social worker profession]. *Annales Universitatis Mariae Curie-Skłodowska, 30*(2), 165. https://doi.org/10.17951/j.2017.30.2.165.

Kantowicz, E. (2005). *Praca socjalna w Europie. Inspiracje teoretyczne i standardy kształcenia* [Social work in Europe. Theoretical inspirations and standards of education]. Olsztyn: Wydawnictwo Uniwerstytetu Warmińsko-Mazurskiego w Olsztynie.

Karwacki, A. (2006). *Błędne koło: reprodukcja kultury podklasy społecznej* [Vicious circle: Reproduction of the culture of the social subclass] (1st ed.). Toruń: Wydawnictwo Uniwersytetu Mikołaja Kopernika.

Kaźmierczak, T. (2012). Pracownicy socjalni, kapitał ludzki, profesjonalna praktyka [Social workers, human capital, professional practice]. In W. M. Rymsza (Ed.), *Pracownicy socjalni i praca socjalna w Polsce. Między służbą społeczną i urzędem*. Warsaw.

Kluzowa, K. (2006). Historia pracy socjalnej na łamach „Pracy Socjalnej" [History of social work in "Social Work"]. In W. K. Małek, K. Slany, & I. Szczepaniak-Wiech (Eds.), *Z zagadnień historii pracy socjalnej w Polsce i na świecie*. Kraków: Wydawnictwo Uniwersytetu Jagiellońskiego.

Kotlarska-Michalska, A. (2013). Przykłady dysfunkcji w kształceniu pracowników socjalnych [Examples of dysfunction in the education of social workers]. *Annales Universitatis Mariae Curie-Skłodowska, sectio J – Paedagogia-Psychologia, 26*(1–2).

Kriegel, R. J., & Brandt, D. (1996). *Sacred cows make the best burgers: Developing change-ready people and organizations*. New York: Warner Books.

Krzyszkowski, J. (2005). *Między państwem opiekuńczym a opiekuńczym społeczeństwem: determinanty funkcjonowania środowiskowej pomocy społecznej na poziomie lokalnym* [Between the welfare state and the welfare society: Determinants of the functioning of community social assistance at the local level]. Wydawnictwo Uniwersytetu Łódzkiego.

Lalak, D., & Skiba, W. (2010). Profil społeczno-motywacyjny osób podejmujących studia na kierunku praca socjalna. Badania porównawcze [Socio-motivational profile of people taking up studies in the field of social work. Comparative research]. *Prace Instytutu Profilaktyki Społecznej i Resocjalizacji, 16*, 249–271.

Leś, E. (2001). *Zarys historii dobroczynności i filantropii w Polsce* [Outline of the history of charity and philanthropy in Poland].Warsaw: Prószyński i S-ka.

Michalska, A. (2016). Warunki efektywnego kształcenia pracowników socjalnych [Conditions for effective training of social workers]. *Annales Universitatis Mariae Curie-Skłodowska, sectio J – Paedagogia-Psychologia, 29*(1).

Mikulski, J. (1974). *Służby socjalne: stan, potrzeby, kształcenie* [Social services: State, needs, education]. Warsaw: Instytut Wydawniczy CRZZ.

Przeperski, J. (2019a). *Badania współczesnej rodziny w kontekście tworzenia polityk publicznych opartych na wiedzy i dowodach naukowych* [Research on the contemporary family in the context of creating knowledge- and evidence-based public policies]. Warsaw: Wydawnictwo Instytutu Wymiaru Sprawiedliwości.

Przeperski, J. (2019b). *Portray of social workers in Poland* (Unpublished Report). Torun: The Centre for Family Research, Nicolaus Copernicus University in Torun.

Rymsza, M. (2014). Pracownicy socjalni, służby społeczne - profesjonalizacja i rozwój zawodowy [Social workers, social services—Professionalisation and professional development]. *Polityka Społeczna*, (3).

Smolińska-Theiss, B. (2013). Edukacyjny charakter pracy socjalnej – badanie i działanie [Educational character of social work—Research and activity]. In W. M. Mendel & B. Skrzypczak (Eds.), *Praca socjalna jako edukacja ku zmianie. Od edukacji do polityki.* Warsaw.

Szmagalski, J. (2012). Kształcenie do pracy socjalnej w Polsce po 1989 roku [Social work education in Poland after 1989]. In W. M. Rymsza (Ed.), *Pracownicy socjalni i praca socjalna w Polsce. Między służbą społeczną a urzędem.* Warsaw.

Szpunar, M. (2013). Edukacyjne konfrontacje rzeczywistości w pracy socjalnej – asystenci rodzin wobec poczucia własnych kompetencji [Educational confrontations of reality in social work—Family assistants in the face of the sense of own competence]. In W. M. Mendel & B. Skrzypczak (Eds.), *Praca socjalna jako edukacja ku zmianie. Od edukacji do polityki.* Warsaw.

Szumlicz, J. (1987). *Pomoc społeczna w polskim systemie zabezpieczenia społecznego* [Social assistance in the Polish social security system]. IPiSS.

Taylor, B. J., Killick, C., & McGlade, A. (2015). *Understanding & using research in social work.* Los Angeles: Sage/Learning Matters.

Wardzyńska, M. (2009). *Był rok 1939. Operacja niemieckiej policji bezpieczeństwa w Polsce. Intelligenzaktion* [It was 1939. Operation of the German security police in Poland. Intelligenzaktion]. Warsaw: Instytut Pamięci Narodowej.

Whittaker, A. (2012). *Research skills for social work.* Los Angeles and London: Sage.

Zalewski, D. (2005). *Opieka i pomoc społeczna: dynamika instytucji* [Welfare and social assistance: The dynamics of institutions]. Wydawnictwo Uniwersytetu Warszawskiego.

CHAPTER 19

Socio-Economic and Political Contextual Realities in India: Implications for Social Work Practice

Sajid S. M. and Khalid Mohammad Tabish

INTRODUCTION

India is known worldwide for its physical, cultural, social, religious, and lingual diversity. Emerged as an Independent nation on world's map in 1947, today, India has established itself as one of the major economic players in the world in a short span of 70 years. With an impressive and consistent rate of economic growth, it is identified as one of the fastest growing economies of the world. India has introduced numerous policy level changes to accelerate its economic growth over the years. Right after independence, Indian economy operated as a moderately regulated economy till 1968; and a stringently regulated economy from 1969 to 1974; while since 1975 onwards, it gradually started liberalising its economy and finally adopted the new economic policy in form of structural adjustment programme in 1991. The rate of economic growth (measured in terms of GDP) has also been found varying in these different phases of Indian economy. The annual GDP growth rate was 3–4% between 1956 and 1974 (when India was a closed and highly regulated economy), while the same was around 5% during 1975–1990 (when India started giving more room to its domestic private sector). With operationalisation of new economic policy, the per annum GDP growth had been recorded over 6% between 1991 and 2004, and over 8.5% during 2003–2007 (Mukherji, 2009). Acknowledging the robust growth of Indian economy, the

S. S. M. (✉) · K. M. Tabish
Jamia Millia Islamia, New Delhi, India
e-mail: ssajid@jmi.ac.in

© The Author(s) 2021
S. S. M. et al. (eds.), *The Palgrave Handbook of Global Social Work Education*, https://doi.org/10.1007/978-3-030-39966-5_19

World Bank (in 2018) forecasted 7.3% GDP growth rate for India in financial year (FY) 2018/2019, and 7.5% in FY 2019/2020, which would have made India—the fastest growing country among major emerging economies of world (*Business World*, 6 June 2018). This rate of growth, however, could not be achieved.

However, a gloomy picture also existed on the other side in India. In pursuit of maximisation of economic growth, environmental considerations have been ignored; the standard of living is sidelined; regional, gender, and class inequalities have been neglected; and poverty is left to persist in India (Basu, 2000). With increasing (economic) growth, inequality among masses is rising in India, which proves that the benefits of gain have been inequitable and favouring few at the cost of many. Gini wealth coefficient (represent the income or wealth distribution of a nation's residents) in India has gone up from 81.2% in 2008 to 85.4% in 2018, which confirms that inequality has risen. During last 12 months, wealth of top 1% of population increased by 39%, whereas the same increased by a dismal 3% for the bottom 50% of India's population (Global Wealth Report, 2018). Chan et al. (2019) in 'The Public Good or Private Wealth?' Oxfam Inequality Report documented that top 10% of India's population holds 77.4% of the total national wealth. The contrast becomes even sharper, as we narrow the data; wherein the top 1% of India's population has been noted holding 51.53% of the national wealth, while the bottom 60% of the population, owns merely 4.8% of the national wealth. The total wealth of top 9 Indian billionaires is equivalent to the (total) wealth of the bottom 50% of India's population. While the gap between rich and poor is unsustainably high in India, there exists different trajectory of inequalities for different social groups, men and women, rural and urban population, for example, as per the latest available evidence (for the year 2011–2012), the Gender Pay Gap in India was 34% in 2012; means that women were receiving 34% less wages than their male counterparts for carrying out the same work. Moreover, it must be noted here that women are not the homogenous group of population—various intersections of caste, class, religion, age, and sexual orientation further accentuates inequality among women (Chan et al., 2019).

Moreover, the World Bank report titled "Piecing Together the Poverty Puzzle" (2018) documented that India has highest number of people (170 million) living under the international USD 1.90 a day poverty line in 2015, which accounts nearly a quarter of global poor population. Four out of five poor people of South Asia lives in India (South Asia comprise one-third of poor people of world—United Nations Statistical Division [UNSD], 2017). Likewise, the available data suggests that India's major section of population is struggling in all parameters of development per se education, employment, health care, gender disparity, extreme geographical differences, social and economic inequality in access to basic service. Though the rate of literacy (total percentage of population in the age group seven years and above who can read and write with understanding) has remarkably increased in India, from 12% in 1951 to 74% in 2011, but at the same time, India ranks first in world in terms of having the largest pool of illiterate adults—287 million, amounting 37% of the global total (Oxfam India, 8 September 2015). The status of education in India worsens as we move upward in the trajectory of education (NFHS, 2015–16). It has also been documented that the status of education at each level is severe for those living in rural areas, women, scheduled castes, scheduled tribes, and Muslims (the largest religious minority) than others, with persistent regional and interstate differences. Children and young people belonging to rural areas constitute almost double percentage of persons never enrolled in school (age group 5–29 years) than those residing in urban areas (NSSO, 71st round, 2014).

After education, the poor status of health is another major challenge, affecting large section of India's population. Despite accounting 1/5th of total global burden of diseases, the expenditure on health (as part of total GDP expenditure) continues to hover around a little over 1% (*The Times of India*, 20 June 2018). Forty-two per cent of India's tribal children are underweight, 1.5 times higher than non-tribal children (NFHS, 2015–16). Children born in poor families are three times more likely to die before their first birthday than children from rich families (NFHS, 2015–16). A scheduled caste woman in India is expected to live almost 14.6 years less than the one hailing from a high caste (NFHS, 2015–16). There is an acute shortage of health professionals in India, especially in rural areas. The World Bank estimated that India had 0.7 doctors per thousand people in 2012 against 2.8 doctors per 1000 persons in UK and 1.8 doctors per 1000 persons in China. In terms of public spending, India spends rupees 1112 per person on public health (per capita) every year, that is rupees 93 (per capita) per month or rupees 3 per day. Which is roughly less than the single consultation at the country's top private hospitals or much equal to the cost of a pizza at many restaurants. As a result, out of pocket expenditure on health is very high in India, pushing as many as 63 million people into the grip of poverty every year. Almost one-fifth of the total ill in India deny themselves treatment; 68% of patients in urban India and 57% in rural areas attributes financial constraints, in wake of which they take treatment without seeking medical advice. Ironically, every year, large number of foreign patients arrives in India in purview of "world class health services at low cost" ranking India 5th in Medical Tourism Index, on the other hand, only 11% of India's Sub-Health Centers (SHC) and 16% of Primary Health Centers (PHC) fulfil the requisite quality standard of Indian Public Health Standards (IPHS), placing India at 145th position among 195 countries of world, in terms of quality and accessibility of healthcare (Chan et al., 2019).

Rising rate of unemployment, especially among youths, is another major concern in India, challenging its model of economy and associated growth. The State of Working India report (2019) exposed that women are the worst sufferer affected by unemployment. As against 6.0% overall rate of unemployment in 2018, for men, it was 4.9%, whereas for women it was 14.2%. Similarly, among educated (degree/diploma beyond class 12), the overall rate of unemployment was 12.7% (9.7% for males and 34.0% for females). Compared with other countries, India has a poor percentage of working women. Merely 27% of women in India belongs to working group of population, compared to 56% (in USA), 57% (in Bangladesh), 63% (in China), and 80% (in Nepal). 67% of women graduates in rural India do not work, moreover, 68.3% of working women do not have paid jobs (India Skills Report, 2019). Highlighting the persistent gender gap in India, the World Economic Forum (WEF) in 2018 placed India at 108th position in gender gap ranking, among total 149 countries of the world (*Business Standard*, 19 December 2018). The female labor force participation rate (LFPR) in India was measured 23.41 % in 2019 (Modelled ILO estimate)—one of the poorest in world. Over the years, the female LFPR reduced significantly in India—from 37.71% in 2001 to merely 20.83% in 2018. Factors like one's geographical location further accentuates female LFPR, pushing rural females in a more disadvantageous position (Chan et al., 2019).

Discrimination on basis of caste and religion is yet another menace plaguing the Indian society. Despite the constitutional provision of equality for all Indians irrespective of their gender, caste, and religion, and prohibition of discrimination on such basis, the (religious) minority communities (like Muslims and Christians) and scheduled castes face discrimination and persecution in India. These incidents have escalated significantly in India during last several years (*The Economic Times*, 9 February 2017). The cases of religion-based killings, assaults, and vandalism against minorities especially Muslims and Christians by certain groups of Hindus, and thus, restricting their (Muslims and Christians) right to freely practice the religion and belief, is continuously rising in India (Deutsche Welle, 25 June 2019), which in turn is posing serious threat to the pluralistic character of Indian society.

While a democratic and fair society should offer equal opportunities to each of its citizenry, it is often observed that economic status or social identity of a person dictates his/her destiny, and thus the underprivileged and poor are deprived of the fair and equal opportunity to excel in social, economic, and educational spheres. Prevailing economic inequalities, social and religious discrimination and the nexus between social, economic, and political power and the resultant marginalisation of poor, women, lower castes, and minorities in Indian society, on the one hand, and the emphasis on social change, liberation, empowerment, and social justice in the global definition of social work 2014, on the other hand, lead one to wrongly believe that the profession of social work is actually an answer to these structural problems. Let us briefly examine the social work profession in India.

SOCIAL WORK PRACTICE IN INDIA

India is a multicultural, multireligious, and multilingual country. With more than 1.28 billion population, India encompasses diverse cultures, traditions, belief systems, cosmologies, norms, values, and practices. Broadly there are "six main ethnic groups and fifty-two major tribes in India; six major religions and 6,400 castes and sub-castes; eighteen major languages and 1,600 minor languages and dialects" (Supreme Court of India, in its Judgement in T.M.A. Pai Foundations and Others vs. State of Karnataka, 1993, para 158). Such diversities pose a unique challenge for the social work profession to accommodate and acknowledge the same in its practice. At the micro-level of practice, social, economic, and cultural diversities of India need to be or can be considered for designing interventions within the ambit of social work profession. But the other role of social work profession to address the structural problems of society remains questionable irrespective of the context. Culture and context, in which people from a similar background shape themselves through their life experiences and other related factors, make them who they are. For professionals such as doctors, lawyers, and social workers, it is an inherent and basic professional requirement to adjust themselves to different social and cultural contexts, because these professionals directly deal with unique and different set of problems of individuals that often have its root in societal functioning or sociocultural context of groups and communities. Though the role and functioning of doctors and lawyers are well defined and accepted by their clients, social workers do not have this privilege of being so specific, and resultingly, the profession is expected to fulfil unrealistic expectation on its own, to bring about revolutionary changes like social justice and liberation of people. Which is not possible for a profession to bring about, by remaining within the ambit of its professional role and intervention. The social work profession can obviously commit to values like, social change, liberation, empowerment, human rights, and social justice, but the onus for ensuring these values broadly lies on the State. A profession's claim to do so on its own can at best be termed as wishful thinking, as no evidence of transformational social work in the recent or distant past is available.

The global definition of social work therefore appears more like an agenda of nation-building or re-building exercise than a professional intervention. The possibility and effectiveness of such intervention by social work professionals will therefore be doubtful. Another problem with this definition is a very wide scope of profession, it suggests, ranging from micro- to macro-level practice.

Another aspect of social work education and practice in India is the borrowed nature of the profession. Like many other developing countries, genesis of social work education and practice in India is also rooted in the United States of America and some Western nations. Indian model of social work education and practice is considered a transplanted model (Ankrah, 1992; Cox, 1995, 1997; Hugman, 2010; Mazibuko, McKendrick, & Patel, 1992;

Midgley, 1981; Yan & Tsui, 2007). It is argued that such transplanted models do help in addressing some social issues and needs of developing countries like India, but these models are not competent enough to undertake the macro-level engagement with poor and deprived communities located beyond urban areas, where issues like poverty, unemployment, health, education, and community infrastructure are rampant and lies at the core. And, therefore, alternatively, local, indigenous, and contextual models in social work are often presented as a solution to diverse problems of different groups and communities, residing in different geographical location, speaking different language, and having a unique culture. The term local model in community work signifies those (social work) practices with local communities, which are initiated by the local people and nourished at local level. However, many authors tend to believe that structural change can be brought about at the local level of community organising as well. "It may be referred to as community practice encompassing the essential processes of community organizing, social planning, community development and advocacy, and progressive social change work" (Weil, 2013). With the help of community structure, it strives to enable local people and communities, by encouraging them to share responsibility for improving their social and economic conditions (Midgley, 1992; Pawar & Cox, 2010). Similarly, indigenous model of social work refers to those set of practices which originates from a particular geographical location relevant to the culture of that society. The contextual model of social work advocates that under various cultural contexts, the practice of social work should be different. Contextual social work argues that it is not justified to wholly import and apply knowledge and principles from the West and impose it on local people, who are socially, culturally, and traditionally very different than those living in Western societies, for example, there is no such caste classification and associated discrimination on basis of caste in Western societies, they do not have such religious and lingual diversity as can be seen in countries like India. And, hence, there is a need for indigenisation and particularisation of set of knowledge and practices, suited to local situations (Ugiagbe, 2015).

This, however, gives us a wrong impression that indigenous or contextual social work necessarily addresses the peculiar and largely structural problems which are the hallmark of developing societies. By replacing the 'transplanted' or borrowed model of social work by an indigenous model of education and practice does not mean the agenda and objectives of social work profession become transformational. The debate on relevance and effectiveness of universal social work vs. indigenous or contextual social work is a separate debate which can continue irrespective of social work profession's ability or inability to effectively attempt macro-level changes and addressing structural problems. And to arrive at such a conclusion, one needs to deeply analyse what goes into the processes of removing social, economic injustices, and the practice of discrimination from a society?

Another limitation of social work profession is its inadequate emphasis on the need for political engagement in community practice (particularly), at local level. Ritter (2019) noted that historically, social work profession has maintained a love-hate kind of relationship with politics, sometimes apparently very active in advocacy, while sometimes relatively absent from such action. However, in totality, neither the social work education and practice, nor the (social work) professionals have paid adequate attention to the need and importance of political engagement in community practice. This is one of the reason due to which social worker's engagement with communities has apparently lost its momentum over the years, however, its growing relevance has been well acknowledged in the literature (Mizrahi, 2001; NAPSWI, Code of Ethics, 2016; NASW's, Code of Ethics, 2017; Pawar, 2019; Ritter, 2019; Stepney & Popple, 2008).

Social workers within the ambit of their professional value orientation are more likely to identify themselves as a non-political and non-religious entity in their practice (Smyth & Campbell, 1996; Whiting, 2008). Their professional orientation expects them to remain neutral and non-judgemental, towards political or religious groups, irrespective of personal values and beliefs (Pawar, 2014). Smyth and Campbell (1996) argued that the complex principles of social work (in the UK context) such as "respect for persons", "individualization", and "confidentiality" (p. 78) have not given enough consideration on the association of such principles with wider personal, professional, and political ideologies.

The values and principles like human rights and social justice enshrined in the global definition of social work (of 2014), and global social work standards (Chu, Tsui, & Yan, 2009) suggest that "social workers' adherence to such values and principles in practice requires political engagement" (Ritter, 2019). "It is difficult to imagine the realization of human rights and social justice for local communities without political engagement" (Pawar, 2014, p. 6). We must admit that most of the local communities in developing countries (like India) are commonly characterised by "low income, low levels of living, poor health, inadequate education, low productivity, high rates of population growth, substantial dependence on agriculture, imperfect markets, gender-based discrimination, and vulnerability" (Todaro & Smith, 2003). These (local) communities live in deplorable conditions, which suggests that not just their human rights have been exploited, but also approves that they are victim of social injustices. Such realities (of developing countries like India) invoke question, like what are the ways through which social workers can engage politically to apply the concept of social justice in a community setting. Human rights and social justice are not an entirely apolitical issues, and therefore, social workers must strive to address the three broad group of rights (civil and political; economic, social, and cultural; and collective rights), in an interdependent and integrated way, so to achieve social change, equality, and social justice. As all human rights are closely connected in community practice (Ghai, 2001), such integrated and conscious use of human rights values/principles will help social workers to shift their focus on individual and community rights rather than individual and community needs.

Similarly, social work as a profession emphasises on awareness generation and sensitisation of people towards their unmet needs and rights. It also strives to encourage capacity building of the disadvantaged, marginalised, and oppressed groups, as well as of their organisations and institutions. Such an emphasis of the profession must not be taken as apolitical activities. Moreover, raising awareness just for sake of awareness is not going to yield anything, either to the profession or to those affected with certain disadvantages. Rather, it must translate into some action. It should encourage people to think and realise about their rights, the injustices surrounding them, the structures worsening their situation, and strive to enable them to act and transform their despair in hope, and dependence in independence (Freire, 1972). Social workers for ensuring such awareness and capacity building need to facilitate a sustainable social, cultural, economic, and political development among communities.

In developing countries (like India), dominant and dictatorial leadership styles, and the concentration of power in few hands, are critical challenges for most communities, as well as major causes of non-development of many communities. Such myopic leadership style cannot cultivate a participatory and people-centred approach of community practice. Hence, one of the gigantic tasks for social workers and their community practice is to alter and change such leadership across the diverse communities. It is pertinent to mention here that such leadership and community power structures have compelled most grass-roots-level communities (particularly in rural areas), to experience extreme deprivation, oppression, and discrimination since long. The current social, economic, and political arrangements regardless of political structure (democratic or otherwise) are generally advantageous to local elites and feudal leaders. Many a times, the existing (government) bureaucracies often comply with these leaders in order to please them. Hence, any change that aims to alter the current status quo of those in power is likely to face strong resistance, in lieu of their vested interests. Those resistance may sometime turn extreme as well, and may lead to violence or deaths, and thus has the capacity to further deteriorate the situation in a community setting. It is also possible that community members (oppressed and unoppressed) may not respond and participate in community activities meant for their welfare, owing to the strength and community power structures of such leaders, as these leaders most often succeed in subverting the democratic process. People, who are marginalised and poor, are mainly concerned about their current situation (involving apathy, indifference, helplessness, and powerlessness), as in many cases they have been suppressed and weakened over a long period of time. In order to effectively deal with such complex issues and dynamics prevalent in communities, on the one hand, social workers are required to tactfully engage with both monolithic (Hunter, 1953) and/or pluralistic (Dahl, 1961; Oommen, 1970; Rogers, 1964) community power structures while, on the other, they must try hard to enable the oppressed groups, to realise and understand that the root resulting to their present situation lies elsewhere in socio-economic and political structures, which can be improved if they are ready to redefine and hold responsibility for changing their situation. Apart from this, as part of political engagement, social workers along with people need to understand the reason leading to development of such leadership. They are also required to identify the ways through which such myopic leadership styles can be transformed and concentration of power be diffused and disbursed in the hand of common people.

Way Ahead for Social Work Practice

Social work as a profession needs to clearly define its area of work, commitment, and ways through which it claims to improve the well-being of individuals, groups, and communities. Though numerous studies have suggested different ways and models (e.g. the task centred model, problem-solving model, remedial or therapeutic model, etc.), but nowhere in world, the social work professionals have been able to bring the revolutionary changes, which the profession claims to achieve. And, therefore, as social work educators and researchers, we need to do brainstorming, on the following points:

1. Whether a profession on its own has the capacity to bring about such a huge social change which requires a political action and will, irrespective of the competing interests of the corporate sectors on the one hand and largely voiceless/unrepresented masses on the other?

2. Whether engagement with the structures are merely going to be defined by largely persuasive discourse to empower and liberate people from discrimination and exploitation or it will have to take a confrontational or conflictual approach, in which the State may assume an adversarial role?

3. What are those knowledge domains and skill sets along with attitudes and commitment levels required to become empowering and liberating and social change functionaries under the garb of professional social workers, and whether the institutions have the resources and capacities to transact these?

4. What are the motivations of young students who are joining social work education and how many of them are really interested and comfortable with undertaking arduous work of social change, empowerment, and liberation? This of course is based on the assumption that enough employment opportunities will be available to them for this kind of work.

We anticipate that future studies will seriously reflect upon above questions and will come out with effective solutions, which will ensure acceptance of social work as a professional activity, capable enough to achieve certain targeted goals on its own.

Conclusion

Whether in India or any corner of world, social work as a profession with such huge and unrealistic expectation of bringing on its own, changes like social justice, liberation, and empowerment will remain blurred and confused, until and unless it narrows its focus, and come out with specific and targeted aims, which can realistically be achieved. Also, the profession needs to widen its understanding about different problems and their close connection with different forces which give them a particular shape. For example, the emphasis in the Western literature on community work and work with grass-roots communities for realising human rights and social justice is apparently suffering from a lack of deeper understanding about forces, that resist empowerment and liberation of the exploited and discriminated people, and the relationship of these forces with the industry and the State.

Given the sociocultural, religious, and lingual diversity in India, and the uneven distribution of wealth and resources, as well as skewed nature of development, the role of social work profession becomes important. But, at the same time, the profession needs to draw out specific set of intervention which can be practised in Indian society, acknowledging its diversity. These may include interventions which are more focused in context of professional social work. The structural change as pointed out earlier is too challenging to be achieved by any profession, not even by social work.

References

10 facts on illiteracy in India that you must know, Published on 8 September 2015. Retrieved from https://www.oxfamindia.org/featuredstories/10-facts-illiteracy-india-you-must-know. Accessed July 15, 2019.

Ankrah, E. M. (1992). Social work in Uganda: Survival in the midst of turbulence. In M. C. Hokenstad, S. K. Khinduka, & J. Midgley (Eds.), *Profiles in international social work* (pp. 145–162). Washington, DC: NASW Press.

Basu, K. (2000). On the goals of development. In Gerald M. Meier & Joseph E. Stiglitz (Eds.), *Frontiers of development economics: The future in perspective*. Washington, DC: The World Bank.

Chan, M. K., et al. (2019). *Public good or private wealth?* Oxford, UK: Oxfam GB for Oxfam International.

Chu, W. C. K., Tsui, M., & Yan, M. (2009). Social work as a moral and political practice. *International Social Work, 52,* 287–298.

Confederation of Indian Industry. (2019). *The India Skills Report*. Retrieved from https://www.aicte-india.org/sites/default/files/India%20Skill%20Report-2019.pdf. Accessed September 5, 2019.

Cox, D. (1995). Asia and the Pacific. In T. D. Watts, D. Elliot, & N. S. Mayadas (Eds.), *International handbook on social work education* (pp. 321–338). Westport, CT: Greenwood Press.

Cox, D. (1997). Asia and the Pacific. In N. S. Mayadas, T. D. Watts, & D. Elliot (Eds.), *International handbook on social work theory and practice* (pp. 369–382). Westport, CT: Greenwood Press.

Dahl, R. A. (1961). *Who governs?* New Haven, CT: Yale University Press.

Freire, P. (1972). *Pedagogy of the oppressed*. London, UK: Sheed & Ward.

Ghai, Y. (2001). *Human rights and social development: Toward democratization and social justice*. Retrieved from http://www.unrisd.org/unrisd/website/document. nsf/(httpPublications)/ECD0417EB1177C5280256B5E004BCAFA?.

Global Definition of Social Work. (2014, August 6). Retrieved from https://www. ifsw.org/global-definition-of-social-work/. Accessed September 19, 2019.

Global Wealth Report. (2018, October). Retrieved from https://www.credit-suisse. com/corporate/en/articles/news-and-expertise/global-wealth-report-2018-us-andchina-in-the-lead201810.html. Accessed July 10, 2019.

Hugman, R. (2010). *Understanding international social work: A critical analysis*. Basingstoke, UK: Palgrave Macmillan.

Hunter, F. (1953). *Community power structure*. Chapel Hill: University of North Carolina Press.

India's health spend just over 1% of GDP, Published in *The Times of India* on 20 June 2018, written by Sushmi Dey. Retrieved from https://timesofindia.indiatimes. com/business/india-business/indias-health-spend-just-over-1-of-gdp/article-show/64655804.cms. Accessed August 21, 2019.

India ranks 108th in WEF gender gap index: Sores third-lowest on health, Published in *Business Standard*, on 19 December 2018, written by Indivjal Dhasmana. Retrieved from https://www.business-standard.com/article/cur-rent-affairs/india-ranks-108th-in-wef-gender-gap-index-scores-third-lowest-on-health-118121900039_1.html. Accessed September 19, 2019.

Indian religious minorities face increased violence under Modi—Report, Published in Deutsche Welle on 25 June 2019, written by Murali Krishnan. Retrieved from https://www.dw.com/en/indian-religious-minorities-face-increased-violence-un-der-modi-report/a-49346394. Accessed September 22, 2019.

International Institute for Population Sciences (IIPS) and ICF. (2017). National Family Health Survey (NFHS-4), 2015–16: India.

Labor force Participation rate, Female (% of Female population ages 15+) Modeled ILO Estimate of India. Retrieved from https://data.worldbank.org/indicator/ SL.TLF.CACT.FE.ZS. Accessed July 16, 2019.

Labor force Participation rate, Female (% of Female population ages 15+) National Estimate of India. Retrieved from https://data.worldbank.org/indicator/SL.TLF. CACT.FE.NE.ZS. Accessed July 15, 2019.

Mazibuko, F., McKendrick, B., & Patel, L. (1992). Social work in South Africa: Coping with Apartheid and change. In M. C. Hokenstad, S. K. Khinduka, & J. Midgley (Eds.), *Profiles in international social work* (pp. 115–127). Washington, DC: NASW Press.

Midgley, J. (1981). *Professional imperialism: Social work in the third world*. London, UK: Heinemann.

Midgley, J. (1992). Development theory, the state and social development in Asia. *Social Development Issues, 14*, 22–36.

Mizrahi, T. (2001). The status of community organizing in 2001: Community prac-tice context, complexities, contradictions, and contributions. *Research on Social Work Practice, 11*, 176–189.

Mukherji, R. (2009). The state, economic growth, and development in India. *India Review, 8*(1), 81–106.

National Association of Professional Social Workers in India (NAPSWI). (2016). *Code of ethics for professional social workers in India*. Retrieved from https://www.nap-swi.org/pdf/NAPSWI_Code_of_Ethics).pdf. Accessed October 30, 2019.

National Association Social Workers (NASW). (2017). *Code of ethics*. Retrieved from https://www.socialworkers.org/About/Ethics/Code-of-Ethics/Code-of-Ethics-English. Accessed October 30, 2019.

Office, National Sample Survey. (2016). *Education in India NSS 71st Round (Jan–Jun 2014)*. New Delhi: MoSPI Government of India.

Oommen, T. K. (1970). Rural community power structure in India. *Social Forces, 49,* 226–239.

Pawar, M. (2014). Social work practice with local communities in developing countries: Imperatives for political engagement. *Sage Open, 4*(2), 2158244014538640.

Pawar, M. (2019). Social work and social policy practice: Imperatives for political engagement. *The International Journal of Community and Social Development, 1*(1), 15–27.

Pawar, M., & Cox, D. (2010). Local level social development. In M. Pawar & D. Cox (Eds.), *Social development: Critical themes and perspectives* (pp. 14–53). New York, NY: Routledge.

Religious minorities, Dalits face discrimination in India: Report, Published by *The Economic Times*, on 9 February 2017. Retrieved from https://economictimes.indiatimes.com/news/politics-and-nation/religious-minorities-dalits-face-discrimination-in-india-report/articleshow/57055700.cms?from=mdr. Accessed September 27, 2019.

Ritter, J. A. (2019). *Social work policy practice: Changing our community, nation and the world*. San Diego, CA: Cognella Academic Publishing.

Rogers, D. (1964). Monolithic and pluralistic community power structure. In R. L. Simpson & I. H. Simpson (Eds.), *Social organization and behavior* (pp. 400–405). New York, NY: Wiley.

Smyth, M., & Campbell, J. (1996). Social work, sectarianism and anti-sectarian practice in Northern Ireland. *British Journal of Social Work, 26,* 77–92.

Stepney, P., & Popple, K. (2008). *Social work and the community: A critical context for practice*. London, UK: Palgrave Macmillan.

The World Bank. (2018). *Piecing together the poverty puzzle*. Washington, DC: The World Bank.

T.M.A. Pai Foundations and Others vs. State of Karnataka, para. 158, CASE NO.: Writ Petition (Civil) 317 Of 1993, Date of Judgment by The Honorable Supreme Court of India: 31 October 2002. Retrieved from https://indiankanoon.org/doc/512761/. Accessed August 9, 2019.

Todaro, M. P., & Smith, S. C. (2003). *Economic development* (8th ed.). Harlow, UK: Pearson.

Ugiagbe, E. O. (2015). Social work is context-bound: The need for indigenization of social work practice in Nigeria. *International Social Work, 58*(6), 790–801.

United Nations Statistical Division (UNSD). (2017). *The Sustainable Development Goals Report 2017*. Retrieved from https://unstats.un.org/sdgs/report/2017/overview/. Accessed October 28, 2019.

Weil, M. (2013). Introduction: Contexts and challenges for 21st century communities. In M. Weil, M. Reisch, & M. L. Ohmer (Eds.), *The handbook of community practice* (pp. 3–25). Los Angeles, CA: Sage.

Whiting, R. (2008). "No room for religion or spirituality or cooking tips": Exploring practical atheism as an unspoken consensus in the development of social work values in England. *Ethics & Social Welfare, 2,* 67–83.

World Bank forecasts 7.3 per cent growth for India; making it fastest growing economy, Published in *Business World* on 6 June 2018, written by Lalit K. Jha. Retrieved from http://www.businessworld.in/article/World-Bank-forecasts-7-3-per-cent-growth-for-India-making-it-fastest-growing-economy-/06-06-2018-151264/. Accessed July 9, 2019.

Yan, M. C., & Tsui, M. S. (2007). The quest for western social work knowledge: Literature in the USA and practice in China. *International Social Work, 50,* 641–653.

CHAPTER 20

Decolonising Social Work Education in Nepal

Raj Yadav and Amit Kumar Yadav

INTRODUCTION

Taylor, Bogo, Lefevre, and Teater (2016) argued that "[i]n the Global South, education for social work … is emerging rapidly"; however, it is not "rapidly developing to keep pace with the changing requirements for social services in light of far-reaching social change[s]" (Taylor et al., 2016, p. xxiii). In Nepal, for example, social work education was imported in its Western context during the mid-1990s and since then has grown from a single educational institution in 1996 to over 50 social work colleges teaching social work education today. Social work education was introduced against the backdrop of the Nepali people's struggle to institutionalise its young democracy, on the one hand, and respond to the then emerging violent Maoist insurgency, on the other (Yadav, 2017). Back in the 1990s Nepal had to face up to a number of issues such as a precarious economic situation in which most of the population lived below the poverty line, regional and linguistic divisions, a strict social hierarchy, and discrimination based on caste and ethnicity (Hangen, 2010; Lawoti, 2005, 2012; Pfaff-Czarnecka, 2004; Shakya, 2012). As a result of the shift from monarchical rule to a democratic republic with a federal system in 2006, Nepal's situation has been described as complex (even devastating) due inter alia to the ongoing debate on ethnocentric polity surrounding decentralisation, liberalisation, and administrative and political reforms (Bhandari, 2014; Breen, 2018; Lecours, 2013). In light of this Yadav (2016, 2017) argued that a profession like social work had a potential role to play in driving Nepal's ongoing social,

R. Yadav (✉)
University of the Sunshine Coast, Sunshine Coast, QLD, Australia

A. K. Yadav
Nava Kshitiz College, Bardibas, Nepal

© The Author(s) 2021
S. S. M. et al. (eds.), *The Palgrave Handbook of Global Social Work Education*, https://doi.org/10.1007/978-3-030-39966-5_20

cultural, and political transitions to bring about a fully fledged democracy. However, social work's failure to do so has been attributed to the fact that education underlying social work was imported from the West and hence does not synergise with Nepali social realities:

> The advent of social work [education from the West] in Nepal gave birth to scientific and modernised way of thinking about social services. It linked the young peoples, mainly urban elite, physically through social work institutes, ideologically through Western concepts, and technologically through universal skills and techniques ... It [also] brought Western texts, concepts, reasoning, and, above all, the idea of cultural production... An elite group of social work educators readily adopted the Western brand and embraced its fundamental tenets... the driving question ..., [then and even now is], 'are Nepali social workers happy with this'? (Taylor et al., 2016, pp. xxviii–xxix)

The history of social work education in Nepal is the basis for arguing in this chapter that social work education needs to be decolonised. We begin by viewing decolonisation of social work education as a local construct—in other words, a paradigm shift in Nepali social work. Then we examine the process and practice of social work education as an entry point and explore Nepali society from the standpoint of building the case for decolonisation of social work education in Nepal. Moreover, drawing on theoretical analysis we conceptualise the framework for decolonised Nepali social work education at the end of the chapter.

Defining Our Subjective Location

A discourse on "decolonization is a messy, dynamic, and a contradictory process" (Sium, Desai, & Ritskes, 2012, p. ii). Battiste and Henderson (2000, p. 36) argued that decolonisation is so much a part of the community and individual—so deeply embedded in their day-to-day life—"that it cannot be separated from the bearer [community or individual] to be codified into a definition." Thus, decolonisation and subsequently localisation of knowledge in social work is the product of negotiation resulting from individuals' conscious interactions with their own identification, belongingness, responsibility, and appropriation in the particular context or geography. Those who narrate or claim authorship of the decolonisation discourse should be subject to scrutiny (especially, their political positions and vested interests). Therefore, it is important that we begin with our own position and take an inward look at our own backgrounds, privileges, interests, experiences, and values when detailing an account of decolonised social work education in Nepal. In other words, doing so is about speaking for ourselves—our particular context and day-to-day experiences—when it comes to claiming social work education should be decolonised in light of its imported root. By no means is it a case of 'morally correcting others' nor is it an empty text. More than deliberately fashioning or intending to derive a purist form of social work education in Nepal the term "decolonising social work education" has emerged from engaging in the field of social work education and practice and from our concern as insiders as to what social work education should not be in Nepal.

In writing this chapter it is important to point out that we have personal and ideological interests in introducing decolonised social work education in Nepal. We have both advocated decolonised social work education in Nepal from our own position of being members of a marginalised category in Nepal. We belong to the Madheshi people who are among the most historically marginalised population categories alongside the Dalit people, indigenous peoples, and Muslims in Nepal. We have noted in our roles as social work students, academics, and practitioner (Amit Kumar Yadav) that social work education's imported models and strategies from the West do not sit well alongside the country's ongoing political agenda that is aimed at mainstreaming marginalised populations into society and politics. As one of us put it when evaluating social work education in Nepal:

> There was some concern about the Western roots of, and influences on, social work education imported from foreign universities and its inability to respond to ... Nepal's socio-political context ... knowledge about culture, caste, class, [and] social institutions, [and their interplays in producing marginalised categories] ... was lacking in the social work curriculum. (Yadav, 2017, pp. 217–219)

On the other hand, our position is embedded ideologically per se in ongoing debates on different models of social work such as "globalisation–localisation" (Gray, 2005; Gray & Fook, 2004), "universalisation–multiculturalism" (Gray, 2005), "westernisation–indigenisation" (Fejo-King, 2014; Nimmagadda & Balgopal, 2000), "colonisation–authentisation" (Ragab, 1982; Walton & Abo El Nasr, 1988), "one way technological transfer–two way dialogical model" (Yip, 2005; Nimmagadda & Martell, 2008), and "outsider initiated–homegrown" (Yadav, 2017). Perhaps it is more accurate to put our position conceptually from the perspective of the post-colonial narrative within which the notion that subalterns must have a voice informs our worldview (Spivak, 1988). It implies "a conscious process of repositioning" (Apple, Ball, & Gandin, 2010, p. 8) and of turning a "ghost curriculum" (Doll, 2002) and "white mythology" (Young, 1990) upside down in social work education in Nepal. We also advocate "... a way of seeing things differently [in imported social work education], a language and a politics in which ... [local Nepali] interests come first, not last" (Young, 2003, p. 2). To this end we take a position that is similar to what Gramsci (1971) described as "organic intellectual" that attempts to provide moral and intellectual leadership for Nepali social workers and equips them with pedagogical and political skills that are essential for political awareness in thinking about counterhegemonic education (Giroux, 1998) such as decolonised social work education in Nepal.

SOCIAL WORK EDUCATION PROCESS AND PRACTICE: AN ENTRY POINT

The question of how to outline the process and practice of social work education in Nepal is particularly challenging given that there is a lack of systematic studies on these topics. Despite this it is possible to theoretically conceptualise the process and practice of social work education in Nepal using Dale's (2006) framework on "the education question." This framework deals mainly with (i) who are the learners, (ii) who are the educators, (iii) what are the pedagogical issues, (iv) what are the dominant politics within education and whose interests does education serve, and (v) what are the outcomes of education. Thus, we examine social work education in Nepal through its colonial history, curriculums taught in universities, issues relating to pedagogy, and the way in which social work education fits into Nepali society.

A Brief Colonial History of Social Work Education in Nepal

Father Charles Law, a Chicago-based missionary, introduced Bachelor of Social Work education at St Xavier's College under the aegis of Kathmandu University in 1996 when Nepal was struggling to sustain its fledgling multiparty democratic system and at the same time respond to the Maoist insurgency. Earlier, in 1987 fellow missionary Brother James F. Gates had initiated social work training at the Social Work Institute in Kathmandu. Such a missionary-led initiative relied on the expertise of Indian academics from the Nirmala Niketan School of Social Work and heavily drew on the US paradigm of the individual dysfunction and clinical treatment model of social work education (Yadav, 2017). Thus began the colonial history of social work education in Nepal.

Colonial development of social work education continued through Bachelor of Social Work education at Kadambari Memorial College of Science and Management and Master of Social Work education at St Xavier's College under the aegis of Purbanchal University in 2005. Despite the claim that Purbanchal University's curriculum focussed on a social work approach based on rights (Nikku, 2010), it was barely different from Kathmandu University's social work curriculum other than its consideration of children's rights and gender-related issues (Purbanchal University, 2005). Kathmandu University included these units in its "Analysis of Nepali Society" course (Kathmandu University, 1996).

The two main architects behind the development of social work education at the Purbanchal University were Indian nationals trained in social work. The Indian leadership sought to include the voices of Nepali peoples in developing the social work curriculum at Purbanchal University. However, none of the Nepali representatives were professionally trained social workers. Therefore, they were oblivious to the "West versus the rest of the world" debate in social work, which is missing in discourses on indigenous, decolonisation, and homegrown models of social work evident in the curriculum they developed. Although it has been argued otherwise (Nikku, 2010; Nikku, Udas, & Adhikari, 2014), eventually "[t]he committee submitted a fully developed curriculum designed for both BSW and MSW programs based on ... international social work development to the Purbanchal University..." (Nikku, 2013, p. 235) neglecting the fact that Nepali sociocultural and sociopolitical scenarios were different from international contexts of social work. Rather than resisting the colonial sentiment in social work that was already in effect since 1996 these new curriculums at Purbanchal University on the contrary strengthened the foundation of imported West-centric social work and allowed the colonial legacy to prevail further in Nepali social work education. The only difference at this time was that the colonial enterprise had shifted from "centre-West" to "dominant satellite-India" (see "Satellite connections: Western cuisine with an Indian flavour" in Yadav, 2017, p. 4). Today St Xavier's College and Kadamabari Memorial College of Science and Management unequivocally but informally drive social work education in Nepal. The latter has also been able to establish international collaborations and partnerships and represent Nepali social work on international platforms.

The absence of a collective dialogue on social work education inside Nepal has allowed outsiders to continue to experiment with social work education in Nepali social workers' own backyard. For example, Nikku (2014) defined a Nepali social worker within the hegemonic tradition of corporatism and institutional sanctions without considering the fact that his definition would exclude most local Nepali social workers with social work qualifications that were not recognised by either the Singapore Association of Social Workers or the International Association of Schools of Social Work for economic reasons and such social workers' lack of familiarity with international social work agencies. Nikku (2014) wrote:

'[S]ocial Worker' in the context of Nepal refers to new graduates and current practitioners (both Nepalese and other nationals) with recognized social work qualifications, that is, Degree in Social Work (BSW or MSW) or a Graduate Diploma in Social Work or a recognized Social Work qualification. These qualifications should be recognized or acceptable to associations like the Singapore Association of Social Workers and or International Association of Schools of Social Work. (Nikku, 2014, p. 103)

Monocultural Logic and Prescribed Curriculums

Western monocultural logic is evident in imported social work curriculums in Nepal. Social work curriculums taught across schools of social work in Nepal are homogeneous in nature. They are mainly based on intervening in social work at the microlevel and on modernising outlooks. The contexts of social work curriculums are sheer replicas of those from Western universities, have been disseminated across Nepali social work schools, and done so without any critical analysis. Missing in these curriculums are local epistemologies and developmental and political approaches that best respond to the Nepali nation-state's diverse, multilayered sociocultural and sociopolitical context. This led Yadav (2017) to argue that social work graduates face difficulties in translating social work knowledge into practice in Nepal.

Issues Relating to Pedagogy and Educators

What social work education suffers from is "pedagogic inflation" (Bernstein, 2001) linked to West-centric enlightenment visions, modernising narratives, universalising missions, and scientific reasonings that focus on equipping students with professional knowledge and skills to deal with individuals' problems. However, missing in these pedagogies is the notion of critical discourse looked at through "culture and classroom, policy and practice, teacher and learner, knowledge both public and personal" lenses (Alexander, 2008, p. 3) and Freirean, indigenous, post-colonial, and post-development lenses (Freire, 1972; Gray, Coates, Yellow Bird, & Hetherington, 2013; Yadav, 2017). Instead of adopting pedagogies of social transformation and political change, social work education has been developing within a neoliberalist, managerialist version of social work. Developed in this way social work education has failed to comprehend the relationship among Nepali social hierarchies, political power, cultural rights, and the need for a decolonised, developmental approach to uplift Nepal's marginalised populations. Drawing on Bourdon's (1990) insights into curriculum we assert that Nepali social work education's inability to incorporate local and contemporary progressive pedagogies, discussed as "authentic pedagogy" (Newmann, 1996), "productive pedagogy" (Dimitriadis & McCarthy, 2001), and the "pedagogy of difference" (Lingard, 2010) in terms of sociology of education, is mainly due to the uncritical importation of the Western context.

Social Work Education Institutional Closure: Who Teaches and Who Learns?

Social work education is mainly taught in private colleges in the capital city Kathmandu. Inspired by a neoliberal knowledge economy these educational institutions are run with a business motif (Yadav, 2017). Many if not all of these institutions have been able to distinguish themselves from public educational institutions that reflect a high-brow, aristocratic, and bourgeois culture (Cookson & Persell, 1985), while at the same time being able to legitimise their existence through their symbolic, cultural, and social and economic capital (Bourdieu, 1996). Evaluating our own direct and indirect engagements with several social work institutes over time affirms that they are far from becoming both "a site of academic excellence and ... a site of equity, freedom and reshaped socialities" (Nair, 2017, p. 35). In other words, Nepali social work institutions have yet to view themselves as change agents that simultaneously serve and criticise society and state and hence consider themselves as "… a vital place of self-reflection … and place for simultaneously achieving goals of openness and equality" (Nair, 2017, p. 35).

Social work education remains firmly targetted at urban upper-class students in Nepal who regard graduating with a social work degree as entry to an elite club (Mikkonen, 2017). "Inassimilable" non-elite students from Nepali villages with lower socioeconomic backgrounds are excluded because courses are taught compulsorily in English language and standard admission criteria have a strongly Western bias such as participation in extracurricular activities, autobiographical essays, focussed group discussion, and interviews. Despite several "affirmative action" policies pursued by the state, social work education based on a knowledge economy has yet to give an edge to the nation's marginalised populations such as Dalits, indigenous populations, Madheshis, and Muslims. Consequently, social work education in Nepal suffers from a lack of diversity in its student makeup. This is borne out by graduates in social work from urban upper-class backgrounds never having had the chance to work with the rural poor who desperately need social work intervention (Yadav, 2017). Given such conditions of social work education in Nepal the driving question for many Nepali social work graduates is: Can "social work education" in Nepal justify its "social nature." The next section examines this.

Understanding Nepali Society—What Does "Social" in "Social Work Education" Entail: A Standpoint

Both native intellectuals (priests, wanderers, and sages) and modern social scientists (academics, researchers, and policy makers) participate in Nepali studies. However, making sense of Nepali society as an entity is complex owing to constantly competing sociocultural diversities and emerging new political dimensions. With this in mind we examine Nepali society using a critical sociospatial theory in which ideas are categorised as "perceived," "conceived," and "lived" (Lefebvre, 1991) and in "relative" and "relational" terms (Harvey, 2006). Such an approach allows us to juxtapose some critical questions in relation to decolonising social work education in Nepal such as: What does "social" entail in "social work education"? What sort of social work curriculum and whose worldview of it should be professed? Can social work education decide on its contextual scope by only considering Nepali history, cultures, traditions, and sociopolitical dynamics? Can social work education translate its borrowed language and concepts into solidarity with the most marginalised populations of Nepal?

In the nineteenth century Le Bon (1886, in Bell, 2014, p. 1) said about Nepal that "I doubt that an opium eater has ever dreamt, in his wildest dreams, of a more fantastic… [country] than … this strange [one]." Such wonderful complexity remains unchanged even today as Mikkonen (2017) noted that Nepal was:

… like a paradox of a really busy and extremely relaxed environment at the same time, where—within the chaos—everything was in its place, in a sort of messy order… Diversities penetrate Nepal on many levels… The differences between the rural and urban areas are evident in livelihoods, material resources, access to different services and social organising … social categories, along with other social identities [caste, ethnicity, gender, religion, and geographic affiliations] … overlap in various ways in people's lives, which makes the … [Nepali society] more complex. (Mikkonen, 2017, pp. 39–40)

One way of disentangling this complexity is to make a critical sociospatial analysis in terms of "territory, scale, network, and place" of Nepali society. Analysing Nepali society in both a polymorphic and heuristic way is empowering when thinking about decolonising social work education since it allows us to explore Nepali geography, structural variations, forms of interconnection, and social relations. Moreover, when combined together the evolving nature of sociopolitical restructuring of Nepali society can also be explored.

Mignolo (2009) argued that the first step in understanding epistemological disobedience (i.e., decolonising social work education in Nepal as proposed in this chapter) is to start by configuring the geohistorical and biographical processes of the context in question. Tucked in the foothills of the Himalayas, Nepal is a small landlocked country with a population of about 30 million. Its geostrategic position is commonly described as a "yam caught between two boulders" with China to the north and India to the west, south, and east—the two fastest rising global powers (von Einsiedel, Malone, & Pradhan, 2012). International relationship studies show that the bilateral stronghold of Beijing and New Delhi has dwarfed Nepali national interests (Chaturvedy & Malone, 2012; Kochar & Jaiswal, 2016; Upadhya, 2012). Moreover, as a result of the dominant roles played by Indians in driving Nepali social policies and political decisions, Nepal has never been able to derive its own independent domestic and foreign policy and achieve internal stability, peace, and economic development (Chaturvedy & Malone, 2012). Furthermore, Indian influence is common in social work too since the early leaders in two major social work institutes—St Xavier's College and Kadambari Memorial College of Science and Management—were Indians who assumed introducing Western social work via India was what was needed. They also brought in Indian academics who were tasked at the outset with training Nepali students and with representing Nepali social work on international platforms. Since this is an important point when thinking about decolonising social work education in Nepal we keep such an epistemology distinct in our analysis.

Robertson (2010, p. 19) said: "Scale represents social life as structured in particular ways." In the case of Nepal this relates geographically to the global, national, and local identities of Nepali society. Global development and monetary funding bodies such as the United Nations, the World Bank, the Asian Development Bank, and international non-government humanitarian aid agencies have categorised Nepal as underdeveloped and one of the poorest nations in the Global South. Such categories have given international development actors the self-proclaimed moral responsibility to penetrate and experiment with Nepali society—described as "dancing with development" by Collier (2013). However, at the national and the local level the "social production of scale" is itself complex due to layers of identities relating to Nepali geographies. Despite the popular national rhetoric of *ek desh*, *ek bhasa*, and *ek bhesh* (one country, one language, and one costume), the local identities of Nepali peoples vary according to their geographical affiliations. Nepal has three physiographic regions—the Himalayas, the Hills, and the Terai— in which not only the topography and climate but also social lives vary from each other (Shrestha, 2002). For instance, while most of the populations in the Himalayas are Tibeto-Burman Nepali-speaking groups, the flatland Terai mainly consists of people speaking north Indian dialects. Inhabitants in the Hills Region are predominantly Nepali-speaking groups. Analysing scales helps Nepali social workers to generate insights into the "making of regions" (or scale making) for the Nepali nation both in terms of interregionalism and intraregionalism.

Robertson (2010, p. 19) said: "Place, on the other hand, is constituted of spatialized social relations and the narrative about these relations." Viewed from the perspective of social production, place is the outcome of social "efforts to contain, immobilize, to claim as one's own, to include and therefore exclude" (Robertson, 2010, p. 19) and embodies distinct cultures, identities, multiple meanings, and social practices (Hudson, 2001; Massey, 1994). Understanding Nepali society in terms of place requires a discussion of caste and ethnic dynamics that have been a longstanding key social practice for inclusion and exclusion since the country was founded in 1769. The Muluki Ain of 1854 (the general code) further institutionalised caste and ethnicity-based inclusion and exclusion as a national norm. As the general code the Muluki Ain promoted the Hinduised way of life and classified Nepali society as *chokho jat* (pure caste) or water-acceptable caste and *pani nachalne jat* (impure caste) or water-unacceptable caste (Hofer, 2004). More recently, it has been argued that caste and ethnicity go beyond social practice and are political in nature giving a new meaning to Nepali society in a "place–time" sense (Gurung, 2009; Hangen, 2007, 2010; Lawoti, 2012). Lawoti (2012) listed the caste hill Hindu elite (Bahun, Chhetri, Thakuri, and Sanyasi), indigenous nationalities, Madheshis, and Dalits as the major caste/ethnic categories in terms of political dominance in Nepal. Noting variation in gaining access to political rights and resources Lawoti (2012) expressed that the dynamics played out between caste and ethnicity makes Nepal a challenging place when it comes to eradicating discrimination:

> Despite the diversity in religion and language, politics is underpinned by ethnicity and caste in Nepal... the CHHE [caste hill Hindu elite], accounting for 30.89% of Nepal's total population, is the ruling hill "upper" caste group and

... [dominates] Nepal's socio-political and cultural life ... Indigenous nation-alities... [Dalit, and Madheshi] make up around 36%, [14.99%, and 12.30% respectively] of the population... [and] face pervasive linguistic, religious, and sociocultural discrimination as well as unequal access to resources. (Lawoti, 2012, pp. 130–131)

Notwithstanding being a challenging place when it comes to eradicating discrimination, Nepali society has some positive characteristics too. A net-work consisting of what Robertson (2010, p. 20) termed "the porous nature of knots and clusters of social relations" has been significant in Nepali soci-ety right up to today. In response to this Yadav (2017) claimed the Nepali lifestyle remains an unfinished project of modernisation and Westernisation. Despite adopting some Western cultural practices, Nepali society continues to maintain its many original social rituals and rhythms such as traditional forms of communication, a deep sense of reverence for nature, unique agricul-tural activities, religious festivals, and seasonal gatherings (Luger & Hoivik, 2004). The interspatial interconnectivity of Nepali peoples draws on "spiritual reality" (Diemberger, 2000 in Luger & Hoivik, 2004), relies on a sense of communitarianism and reverence for keeping the environment and ecology sustainable (Parajuli et al., 2015), values mutually informed knowledge pro-cesses (Högger, 1997), and promotes the philosophical value of pause and reflection in life (Luger & Hoivik, 2004).

Social work education imported from the West with its West-centric foun-dation (as discussed above) has unfortunately failed to respond to the Nepali sociospatial scenario. Rather than critically responding to the needs to over-come geostrategic vulnerability, internal regional diversities and distinct cul-tures, and deep-rooted caste and ethnic-based structural issues, social work education has stereotyped Nepali society in a negative way regarding social case work, diagnosis, and investigation frameworks. This is because social work education is grounded in the values of "capitalism, Social Darwinism, the Protestant ethic and individualism" (Nagpaul, 1993, p. 214). Critiques have been published describing the contradiction between social work edu-cation and practice as colonialism, imperialism, cultural production, cultural appropriation, and as having a hegemonic worldview that run counter to local people's lived experience and limit their self-determination in framing their own world (see, e.g., Gray et al., 2013). This is the reason for arguing in this chapter to shift toward decolonised Nepalisation of social work education.

DECOLONISED SOCIAL WORK EDUCATION: A VANTAGE POINT

Having subjectively defined the location and context in which social work education should take place and Nepali society, we now turn to proposing a process model that can be used to decolonise social work education. The focus and aim of such a model is to shift the basis of social work education from imported West-centric to homegrown Nepalisation. Decolonised Nepali social work education should cover a wide scope including but not limited to Nepali territory, scale, place, and networks that chime with debates of decolonised pedagogies embracing Nepali cultural narratives and recognising the need of Nepali social workers for representation and rights to drive Nepali social work education in the future.

Process Model for Decolonising Social Work Education in Nepal

The process model is shown in Fig. 20.1 and begins with "thinking about Nepali society." It values Nepali society's pluralistic nature and considers the multiple meanings that Nepali society yields daily from its competing socio-cultural and sociopolitical interactions. Among other things it utilises knowledge about the social conditions and cultural practices that define not only the "being" but also the "becoming" of Nepali society. It studies broader structural social issues and problems and investigates their nature, how they came about, and how they affect the social functioning of Nepali peoples. It also analyses the structure and power of social categories and goes beyond the factual characteristics of Nepali society to providing a critical analysis of the factors that oppress Nepal's marginalised populations such as the Dalits, indigenous peoples, Madheshis, and Muslims. Thinking about Nepali society in terms of decolonising social work education also highlights the roles of formal human service organisations, both governmental and non-governmental, and considers informal grassroots movements and social change initiatives. Critical to decolonising social work education is building alliances with such

Fig. 20.1 The process model for decolonising social work education in Nepal (*Source* Authors work)

organisations and politicising human service efforts to meet peoples' developmental needs (Yadav, 2017).

The process model then considers local values and assumptions that should be used to view society in Nepal. This relates to knowledge about Nepali cultural and ethnic sensitivity, diversity, and local traditional norms and values. According to Yadav (2017) by including contextual and local assumptions in Nepali social work education social work students should be able to clearly identify the differences between Nepali society and that of the Western nation-states from which social work knowledge was imported. This should allow social work students to move beyond mere adoption of Western social work interventions to put in place a contextualised and people-centred social work practice that in fact responds to the unmet needs of Nepal's populations.

The process model for decolonising social work education then turns its emphasis to decolonising and local pedagogies that expand on critical theory approaches to enable social work educators and students to consider the ways in which Nepali epistemologies are represented and eliminated across social work education. It locally positions and critiques the hegemonic ideologies of social work's technological transfer from the West. Although such a transfer has contributed to cultural production in Nepali social work, it has prompted Nepali social workers to deconstruct the unequal relations of power between Nepali social workers and outsiders in the past and present. As part of decolonising pedagogy it draws on the Freirean concept of praxis (Freire, 1972, 1987) to equip Nepali social work educators and students with the wherewithal to focus on the activities of Nepali peoples and provide a better understanding of the Nepali world and its horizontal and vertical sociocultural and sociopolitical interactions. It also empowers social work educators and learners to re-claim, re-write, and re-right (Smith, 2012) and in a similar vein reposition Nepali social workers from being subject to history to agents of history (Kohn & McBride, 2011) in social work education.

The final stage in the process model of decolonising Nepali social work education should bring about an outcome that "... goes beyond mental gymnastics and Western conceptions of 'Reason'" (Sium et al., 2012, p. v) and results in locally responsive social work education. In other words, decolonised social work education pivotal to Nepali society, local assumptions, and decolonising pedagogy "...goes beyond, goes deeper, [and] goes further than reason can reach" (Sium et al., 2012, p. v) to legitimise the meaning of "social" in "social work education" (as questioned earlier in this chapter). Among other things decolonising social work education in Nepal involves:

- critically examining current Nepali social realities with a conceptual/political framework to make social work education transformative in Nepal;
- encouraging educators and students to engage and explore Nepali epistemologies and invest in research to develop practice models that chime with Nepali society;

- promoting the notion of organic intellectuals so that Nepali social workers can coordinate with other social agents such as development workers, activists, civil society, and grassroots leaders to learn and reflect about their own knowledge and practice;
- highlighting the politics of redistribution and the politics of recognition in Nepali social work education; and
- advocating that any Nepali social work model should go beyond the notion of the "free-floating" or "socially unattached intelligentsia" (Barboza, 2018) that "lives on the balcony" (Bakhtin, 1968). That is, social work education should equip students with the vision and skills to take the side of the most marginalised populations and ensure the Nepali peoples can live their lives free from fear and want.

The Focus and Implications of Decolonising Nepali Social Work

The decolonisation of Nepali social work education has both a conceptual and descriptive sense. It not only provides a broader focus in its conceptual sense but also guides curriculum development in its descriptive sense (see Table 20.1). It rests on the belief that social work education in Nepal should be inward-looking and only take into consideration the social welfare and social development needs of Nepali society. Despite claims about the success of "post-welfare capitalism" in Nepal, it is worth noting that the country's marginalised populations continue to be in need of welfare support from the government. Moreover, the government needs to take concerns about worsening development scenarios seriously (United Nations Development Programme, 2016). Such needs and concerns require a decolonised approach that advocates social work education be transformative in nature and utilise cross-sectional analysis of social, cultural, political, and developmental factors of Nepali society to ensure human rights and social justice for every citizen. Moreover, at the same time it should argue that change strategies should be locally informed.

Furthermore, the decolonisation of social work education should be used to guide the development of social work curriculums at Nepali social work institutes. Table 20.1 shows how a curriculum in social work should address Nepali society by looking at past and present scenarios (general contents) that include welfare and development models from the perspective of human rights and social justice (required contents), specialisation in the field of social welfare and social development (elective contents), and development-related fieldwork activities (fieldwork contents).

FINAL REMARKS

Our analysis on decolonising social work education in Nepal is tentative and certainly not exhaustive. We are aware that not everyone engaged in critical social work will agree with all the claims we have made in this chapter.

Table 20.1   The focus and implication of decolonised social work education in Nepal

Key focus of decolonised social work education		*Key implication for curriculum design*	
Assumption	Social work education should look inward and while doing so should be able to equip educators and learners with the knowledge about Nepali society in the broader context of social welfare, social development, and world polity	General contents	Social work education should infuse the general understanding of Nepali society in its curriculum. It should orient learners about Nepali society's past and present and should develop learners' ability to make sense of it
Goals	Social work education should be transformative in nature that analyses Nepali society not only as historically competing and contesting but also as continuously evolving space	Required contents	Social work education should have curriculum with its extensive focuses on social welfare and social development models. The idea of human rights and social justice should be incorporated in curriculum where necessary
Targets	Social work education should target the both 'being' and 'becoming' of Nepali nation-state and include analysis on factors such as social groups, geographic and linguistic identities of Nepali peoples, and formal and informal human service organisations	Elective contents	Social work education may develop additional curriculum to support learners to be specialised in the field of social welfare and social development
Change strategies	Social work education should emphasise on change strategies that are embedded in lived experiences of Nepali peoples. The meaning to welfare and social development, and careful engagement in the world polity should be derived from local Nepali position	Fieldwork contents	Social work education should emphasise on arranging fieldwork practices in development related social organisations

Source Authors work

Although this is to be expected, what we have attempted throughout this chapter is to begin a dialogue as to what social work in Nepal at present is and what should be done to situate it in the Nepali context. We conclude by declaring that decolonising social work education in Nepal is an act of becoming. However, further research and dialogue are required to focus minds on the need to decolonise social work education in Nepal.

References

Alexander, R. (2008). *Essays on pedagogy.* London: Routledge.

Apple, M. W., Ball, S. J., & Gandin, L. A. (2010). Mapping the sociolgoy of education: Social context, power and knowledge. In M. W. Apple, S. J. Ball, & L. A. Gandin (Eds.), *The Routledge international handbook of the sociology of education* (pp. 1–11). New York, NY: Routledge.

Bakhtin, M. M. (1968). *Rabelais and his world* (H. Iswolsky, Trans.). Cambridge: MIT Press.

Barboza, A. (2018). Karl Mannheim's sociology of self-reflexivity. In D. Kettler & V. Meja (Eds.), *The anthem companion to Karl Mannheim* (pp. 175–198). New York, NY: Anthem Press.

Battiste, M., & Henderson, J. Y. (2000). *Protecting indigenous knowledge and heritage: A global challenge.* Saskatoon, Canada: Purich Publishing Ltd.

Bell, T. (2014). *Kathmandu.* New Delhi, India: Random House India.

Bernstein, B. (2001). From pedagogies to knowledge. In A. Marais, I. Neves, B. Davies, & H. Daniels (Eds.), *Towards a sociology of pedagogy: The contribution of Basil Bernstein to research* (pp. 363–368). New York, NY: Peter Lang.

Bhandari, S. (2014). *Self-determination and constitution making in Nepal: Constituent assembly, inclusion, and ethnic federalism.* New York, NY: Springer.

Bourdieu, P. (1990). Principles for reflecting on the curriculum. *Curriculum Journal, 1*(3), 307–314.

Bourdieu, P. (1996). *The state nobility: Elite schools in the field of power.* Stanford, CA: Stanford University Press.

Breen, M. G. (2018). *The road to federalims in Nepal, Myanmar and Sri Lanka: Finding the middle ground.* New York, NY: Routledge.

Chaturvedy, R. R., & Malone, D. M. (2012). A yam between two boulders: Nepal's foreign policy caught between India and China. In S. von Einsiedel, D. M. Malone, & S. Pradhan (Eds.), *Nepal in transition: From people's war to fragile peace* (pp. 287–312). New Delhi, India: Cambridge University Press.

Collier, M. J. (2013). Dancing with development: UN and INGO community engagement in Nepal. In M. J. Collier (Ed.), *Community engagement and intercultural praxis: Dancing with difference in diverse contexts* (pp. 31–61). Bern, Switzerland: Peter Lang.

Cookson, P. W., & Persell, C. H. (1985). English and American residential secondary schools: A comparative study of the reproduction of social elites. *Comparative Education Review, 29*(3), 283–298.

Dale, R. (2006). From comparison to translation: Extending the research imagination? *Globalisation, Societies and Education, 4*(2), 179–192.

Dimitriadis, G., & McCarthy, C. (2001). *Reading and teaching the postcolonial: From Baldwin to Basquiat and beyond.* New York, NY: Teacher's College Press.

Doll, W. E. (2002). Ghosts and the curriculum. In W. E. Doll & N. Gough (Eds.), *Curriculum vision* (pp. 23–70). New York, NY: Peter Lang.

Fejo-King, C. (2014). Indigenism and Australian social work. In C. Noble, H. Strauss, & B. Littlechild (Eds.), *Global social work: Crossing boarders, blurring boundaries* (pp. 55–68). Sydney, NSW: Sydney University Press.

Freire, P. (1972). *Pedagogy of the oppressed* (M. B. Ramos, Trans.). Harmondsworth, UK: Penguin.

Freire, P. (1987). A critical understanding of social work. *Journal of Progressive Human Services, 1*(1), 3–9. https://doi.org/10.1300/J059v01n01_02.

Giroux, H. A. (1998). *Teachers as intellectuals: Toward a critical pedagogy of learning.* London: Bergin & Garvey.

Gramsci, A. (1971). *Selection from the prison notebooks* (Q. Hoare & G. N. Smith, Trans.). New York, NY: International Publishers.

Gray, M. (2005). Dilemmas of international social work: Paradoxical processes in indigenisation, universalism and imperialism. *International Journal of Social Welfare, 14*(3), 231–238.

Gray, M., Coates, J., Yellow Bird, M., & Hetherington, T. (Eds.). (2013). *Decolonizing social work.* Aldershot: Ashgate.

Gray, M., & Fook, J. (2004). The quest for a universal social work: Some issues and implications. *Social Work Education, 23*(5), 625–644.

Gurung, O. (2009). Social inclusion: Policies and practices in Nepal. *Occasional Papers in Sociology and Anthropology, 11*, 1–15.

Harvey, D. (2006). *Spaces of global capitalism: A theory of uneven geographical development.* London: Verso Books.

Hangen, S. I. (2007). *Creating a "New Nepal": The ethnic dimension.* Washington, DC: East-West Center Washington.

Hangen, S. I. (2010). *The Rise of ethnic politics in Nepal: Democracy in the margins.* New York, NY: Routledge.

Hofer, A. (2004). *The caste hierarchy and the state in Nepal: A study of the Mulki Ain of 1854.* Kathmandu, Nepal: Himal Books.

Högger, R. (1997). *Naga and Garuda: The other side of development aid.* Kathmandu, Nepal: Sahayogi Press.

Hudson, R. (2001). *Producing place.* London: Guilford Press.

Kathmandu University. (1996). *Bachelore of arts in social work curriculum.* Dhulikhel, Nepal: Kathmandu University.

Kochar, G., & Jaiswal, P. (Eds.). (2016). *Unique Asian triangle: India, China, Nepal.* New Delhi, India: G. B. Books.

Kohn, M., & McBride, K. (2011). *Political theories of decolonization: Postcolonialism and the problem of foundations.* New York, NY: Oxford University Press.

Lawoti, M. (2005). *Towards a democratic Nepal: Inclusive political institutions for multicultural society.* Thousand Oaks, CA: Sage.

Lawoti, M. (2012). Ethnic politics and the building of an inclusive state. In S. von Einsiedel, D. M. Malone, & S. Pradhan (Eds.), *Nepal in transition: From people's war to fragile peace* (pp. 129–152). New Delhi, India: Cambridge University Press.

Lecours, A. (2013). The question of federalism in Nepal. *Publius: the Journal of Federalism, 44*(4), 609–632.

Lefebvre, H. (1991). *The production of space.* Malden, MA: Blackwell.

Lingard, B. (2010). Towards a sociology of pedagogies. In M. W. Apple, S. J. Ball, & L. A. Gandin (Eds.), *The Routledge international handbook of the sociology of education* (pp. 167–178). New York, NY: Routledge.

Luger, K., & Hoivik, S. (2004). With reverence for culture and nature: Development and modernization in the Himalaya. In A. Loseries-Leick & F. Horvath (Eds.), *Path to nature's wisdom: Ecological dialogue Himalaya & Alps* (pp. 145–166). Graz, Austria: Naturschutzbund Steiermark.

Massey, D. (1994). *Space, place and gender*. Cambridge, UK: Polity Press.

Mignolo, W. D. (2009). Epistemic disobedience, independent thought and decolonial freedom. *Theory, Culture & Society, 26*(7–8), 159–181.

Mikkonen, E. (2017). *Bridges over the mountain ranges: Ethnography on the complexities of transition in women's social position in Nepalese rural communities.* Rovaniemi, Finland: University of Lapland.

Nagpaul, H. (1993). Analysis of social work teaching material in India: The need for indigenous foundations. *International Social Work, 36,* 207–220.

Nair, J. (2017). The provocations of the public university. *Economic and Political Weekly, 52*(37), 34–41.

Newmann, F. M. (1996). *Authentic achievement: Restructuring schools for intellectual quality.* San Francisco, CA: Jossey-Bass.

Nikku, B. R. (2010). Social work education in Nepal: Major opportunities and abundant challenges. *Social Work Education, 29*(8), 818–830. https://doi.org/10.1080/02615479.2010.516984.

Nikku, B. R. (2013). Social work education in south Asia: A Nepalese perspective. In C. Noble, M. Henrickson, & I. Y. Han (Eds.), *Social work education: Voices from the Asia Pacific* (pp. 227–244). Sydney, NSW: Sydney University Press.

Nikku, B. R. (2014). Social work education in South Asia: diverse, dynamic and disjointed? In C. Noble, H. Strauss, & B. Littlechild (Eds.), *Global social work: Crossing borders, blurring boundaries* (pp. 97–112). Sydney, NSW: Sydney University Press.

Nikku, B. R., Udas, P. B., & Adhikari, D. R. (2014). Grassroots innovations in social work teaching and learning: Case of Nepal School of Social Work. In B. R. Nikku & Z. A. Hatta (Eds.), *Social work education and practice: Scholarship and innovation in the Asia Pacific* (pp. 35–53). Brisbane, QLD: Primrose Hall Publishing Group.

Nimmagadda, J., & Balgopal, P. R. (2000). Transfer of knowledge: An exercise of adaption and indigenization. *Asia Pacific Journal of Social Work, 10*(2), 64–72.

Nimmagadda, J., & Martell, D. R. (2008). Home-made social work: The two-way transfer of social work practice knowledge between India and the USA. In M. Gray, J. Coates, & M. Yellow Bird (Eds.), *Indigenous social work around the world: Towards culturally relevant education and practice* (pp. 153–164). Aldershot: Ashgate.

Parajuli, M. N., Luitel, C., Upreti, B. R., Gautam, P. R., Bhandari, B. K., Dhakal, R. K., & Munakarmi, R. (2015). *Nepali society and development: Relevance of the Nordic model in Nepal.* Kathmandu, Nepal.

Pfaff-Czarnecka, J. (2004). High expectations, deep disappointment: Politics, state and society in Nepal after 1990. In M. Hutt (Ed.), *Himalayan people's war: Nepal's Maoist revolution* (pp. 166–191). Bloomington: Indiana University Press.

Purbanchal University. (2005). *Bachelore of social work curriculum*. Biratnagar, Nepal: Purbanchal University.

Ragab, I. (1982). *Authenitization of social work in developing countries*. Egypt: Tanta.

Robertson, S. L. (2010). 'Spatializing' the sociology of education: Stand-points, entry-points, vantage-points. In M. W. Apple, S. J. Ball, & L. A. Gandin (Eds.), *The Routledge international handbook of the sociology of education* (pp. 15–26). New York, NY: Routledge.

Shakya, S. (2012). Unleashing Nepal's economic potential: A business perspective. In S. von Einsiedel, D. M. Malone, & S. Pradhan (Eds.), *Nepal in transition: From people's war to fragile peace* (pp. 114–128). New Delhi, India: Cambridge University Press.

Shrestha, N. R. (2002). *Nepal and Bangladesh: A global studies handbook*. Santa Barbara, CA: ABC-CLIO.

Sium, A., Desai, C., & Ritskes, E. (2012). Towards the 'tangible unknown': Decolonization and the Indigenous future. *Decolonization: Indigeneity, Education & Society, 1*(1), i–xiii.

Smith, L. T. (2012). *Decolonizing methodologies: Research and indigenous peoples* (2nd ed.). London: Zed Books.

Spivak, G. C. (1988). Can the subaltern speak? In C. Nelson & L. Grossberg (Eds.), *Marxism and the interpretation of culture* (pp. 203–235). Urbana: University of Illinois Press.

Taylor, I., Bogo, M., Lefevre, M., & Teater, B. (2016). Introduction. In I. Taylor, M. Bogo, M. Lefevre, & B. Teater (Eds.), *Routledge international handbook of social work education* (pp. xxiii–xxxiii). London: Routledge.

United Nations Development Programme. (2016). *Human development report 2016: Human development for everyone*. New York, NY.

Upadhya, S. (2012). *Nepal and the geo-strategic rivalry between China and India*. New York, NY: Routledge.

von Einsiedel, S., Malone, D. M., & Pradhan, S. (2012). Introduction. In S. von Einsiedel, D. M. Malone, & S. Pradhan (Eds.), *Nepal in transition: From people's war to fragile peace* (pp. 1–33). New Delhi, India: Cambridge University Press.

Walton, R. G., & Abo El Nasr, M. M. (1988). Indigenization and authentization in terms of social work in Egypt. *International Social Work, 31*(1), 135–144.

Yadav, R. K. (2016). Social work(ers) in nation building. In P. Jaiswal (Ed.), *Understanding Nepal in contemporary times* (pp. 245–272). New Delhi, India: Synergy.

Yadav, R. K. (2017). *Decolonised, developmental Nepali social work: Making it matter* (Doctoral unpublished). The University of Newcastle, Callaghan, NSW.

Yip, K.-S. (2005). A dynamic Asian response to globalization in cross-cultural social work. *International Social Work, 48*(5), 593–607. https://doi.org/10.1177/0020872805055314.

Young, R. J. C. (1990). *White mythologies: Writing history and the west*. London: Routledge.

Young, R. J. C. (2003). *Postcolonialism*. New York, NY: Oxford University Press.

CHAPTER 21

Islamic-Based Social Work Practices for Social Development: Experience in Bangladesh

Isahaque Ali, Azlinda Azman
and Zulkarnain A. Hatta

INTRODUCTION

Asia is home to four major religious faiths: Islam, Judaism, Christianity, and Hinduism (Hatta, Ali, Subramaniam, & Salithamby, 2014). Once such religions became widespread there was a need to build mosques, temples, synagogues, and churches in an effort to control and organise them. Religion plays a major part in the welfare process in eastern culture (Yen, 2008). Although social work in a different guise has commonly been practised since the time of the ancients, it is widely accepted that modern day social work emerged in the West in the late nineteenth century as a charity-based practice and today has turned into a rights-based practice (Hatta et al., 2014). The primary mission of the social work profession is to enhance human well being and the efficacity with which they live their lives while helping people to

I. Ali (✉) · A. Azman
Social Work Section, School of Social Sciences,
Universiti Sains Malaysia, Penang, Malaysia
e-mail: ialisw@yahoo.com

A. Azman
e-mail: azlindaa@usm.my

Z. A. Hatta
Faculty of Social Science, Arts and Humanities, Lincoln University College,
Petaling Jaya, Malaysia
e-mail: zulkarnain@lincoln.edu.my

© The Author(s) 2021
S. S. M. et al. (eds.), *The Palgrave Handbook of Global Social Work Education*, https://doi.org/10.1007/978-3-030-39966-5_21

meet their basic needs (particularly, the needs of people who are vulnerable, oppressed, and living in poverty). Since social workers are also tasked with promoting social justice and social change affecting and on behalf of clients, they have to be sensitive to cultural and ethnic diversity to end discrimination, oppression, poverty, and other forms of social injustice (IFSW, 2000). Bangladesh is a relatively large and profoundly densely populated country in South Asia. Its population was estimated at 170 million in 2018 with male and female ratios of 50.41% and 49.59%, respectively. The religious makeup of the country is Muslim 89.1%, Hindu 10%, and others 0.9% (includes Buddhist and Christian) (BBS, 2018). Each ethnic group faithfully pursues its respective religious and cultural beliefs, which play a dominant role in their lives in the country. Religion is an indispensable part of Bangladeshi society and forms the basis of the core beliefs of individuals. Muslims have historically contributed to philanthropic matters to provide assistance to deprived classes of the community as the religion decrees *zakat* (almsgiving) as one of the five pillars of Islam[1] and calls for *waqf* (public charity) as a prime endeavour of this (Amin, 2016). Moreover, a verse from the *Hadith* is relevant and significant to social wellbeing where Prophet Muhammad (SM) instructed his followers:

> The Muslim that serve the diseased persons, provide food with the hungry-men, and make free the innocent prisoners. (Bukhari Sharif, 5649)

During the time of the Prophet Muhammad (peace be unto Him), mosques were not only places for communal gathering of Muslim society, but also centres for worship, education and training, social activities, society development, sharing information, judicial disputes, communication, society interaction, treatment and emergency, rehabilitation, and art. Mosques played a major role in the spread of education in the Muslim world and the close association between mosques and education remained one of its main characteristics throughout history (Samad & Hossain, 2016). Since mosques are used not only as centres where religious rites and rituals are performed but also where activities promoting development and faith-based social welfare in Muslim countries are carried out, they have recently been receiving attention in academia. As a result of the strict directives given in Islam to take special care of orphans, many orphanages have been established in Bangladesh as safe shelters where orphans can be brought up at the initiative of an individual or groups of individuals (*Encyclopaedia of Bangladesh*, 2014). Such orphanages are conventionally managed by contributions made by an individual or by funds raised collectively from *zakat* money or public charity. Such support allows orphanages to play an important role in the socioeconomic development of orphans in Bangladesh. Muslim religious institutions such as mosques, madrasas (Islamic educational institutions), orphanages, and *maajar* (shrines) engage in social work to improve the welfare of communities in Bangladesh. The objectives of this chapter are to examine Islamic social work practices operated by Muslim NGOs (mosques) and orphanages in Bangladesh.

Historical Roles Played by Mosques and Orphanages for Social Development

During the early days of Islam, mosques were used as headquarters for the state, accommodation for the needy and poor, information sharing, health-care centres, places where judicial disputes could be resolved, places of prayer, and places guiding Muslims to live in accordance with Islam at the family, community, country, and international level (Wahid, Kader, & Ahmad, 2011). During the early times of Islam, the poor and needy took shelter in mosques. Most mosques would provide the poor with food and lodging and give information about how to live their daily lives. In addition, *waqf* consisted in mosques apportioning charitable funds for the construction of hospitals to provide healthcare for the poor and needy. Although the roles of mosques have undergone profound changes from the position they held during the Prophet's time, they still have a great impact on the lives of Muslims and play a vital role in the cultural and social life of Muslims when it comes to social development (Mohit, Zahari, Eusuf, & Ali, 2013). Although mosques are sacred places of worship for Muslims, they generally serve as somewhere Muslims can get together for *solat* (Muslim prayer) and somewhere for dispute settlement negotiation by the Mosque management committee regarding issues occurring in the family, society, and community. From the earliest days of Islam, the mosque was the centre of the Muslim community, a place for prayer, meditation, religious instruction, political discussion, and where social and religious activities were organized for the community (Samad & Hossain, 2016). The mosque was seen as the nucleus for community development in various aspects during the golden age of the Prophet Muhammad (peace be upon Him). Mosques are not only sacred places for prayer, they also provide religious education, general primary education, and counselling to the people in the community to steer them away from anything that might hamper community development. The roles played by mosques are important and crucial to the wellbeing of the Muslim community when it comes to social development (Kausar, Alauddin, & Kabir, 2016). There are about 300,000 mosques in Bangladesh (*Dhaka Tribune*, 2016). Mosques are critical to Muslims learning the interpretations and judgements of Islam that help people live peacefully and harmoniously and achieve escape to Allah in their life hereafter. The meaning of "mosque" is derived in the *Quran* as:

> The Mosques of Allah shall be visited and maintained by such as believe in Allah and the Last Day, establish regular prayers, and practise regular charity, and fear none (at all) except Allah. It is they who are expected to be on true guidance. (Surah At-Taubah: 18)

Mosques currently influence all aspects of Muslim community. They are a symbol of morality and piety and are central of all functions of social and material life in Bangladeshi society. Although *Yateem* (orphan) refers to a child who has lost one or both of his parents, in some Muslim societies it also refers to children not wanted by their fathers. Many orphans around the world live in poor, underdeveloped, or developing countries. There are around 4,800,000 orphans living in Bangladesh, although the real figure is hard to know because of lack of censuses or proper official documents (Chowdhury et al., 2017). It is well known that orphanages are residential institutions for bringing up children whose parents are dead, but less well known that this also applies to children of financially insolvent parents. In most cases, the care given to orphans is by religious leaders without sufficient professional training in childcare. Most orphanages in Bangladesh are supported by *zakat* money or other religious endowments. The period of orphan life ends with the attainment of adulthood. One of the most important social problems in the initial days of Islam was bringing up children whose fathers did not want them. During British rule, provisions were made to grant endowments from the government exchequer to run orphanages and shelter homes for the needy. There are presently two types of orphanages in Bangladesh: those attached to a madrasa (i.e., an institution specially designed for Islamic education and culture); and those providing meals, lodgings, and education for orphans (simply any goodness given or done with the intent to please Allah) (*Encyclopaedia of Bangladesh*, 2014).

Materials and Methods

Interviews are considered principal data collection strategies of the qualitative research method and deliver a great degree of flexibility and a wide range of findings. A qualitative approach was taken in pursuing present research work to get a clear understanding of the trends and nature of Muslim social work practices in Bangladesh. The study was conducted in the Gaibandha District in Bangladesh between November 2018 and December 2018. To examine Islamic social work activities operated by teachers and *imams* in Muslim orphanages and mosques, data were collected from 10 orphanages (Islamic NGOs) and 10 mosques. A total of 810 orphan boys living in 10 orphanages were interviewed by the authors in 2018. The organisation collects financial assistance from different sources. It is run entirely through public donations receiving no funds from the state. Pious Muslims donate money to this organisation and do so motivated by the spirit of Islam. It also raises funds from *zakat, fitra,* and *sadaqah* (Muslim charities). Muslim orphanages and mosques were deliberately selected. Data were collected from *ustads/imams* (religious leaders) and teachers in mosques and orphanages. In-depth interviews and focus group discussions (FGDs) were the methods used to collect data and an interview guideline was used to conduct them. Interviews and FGDs were conducted by professional researchers (the authors) and digitally recorded. Each interview lasted 4–5 hours and respondents agreed to the interview being recorded. The interviews were transcribed from the local language (Bangla) to English with the support of a bilingual expert. Transcribed data were intensively analysed to identify the main themes running through answers to the research questions. The main themes were broken into subthemes that were finally grouped into different categories to answer relevant research objectives more specifically.

RESULTS

Comparison of the incorporation of standardised social work established in the West with that established in the religious settings of other areas is important. Each area of Bangladesh has its own culture and historical experience both of which have to be simplified when standard social work fails in such localities. Moreover, there is a distinct probability that local social work, the way in which everyday life is run, and social relationships that have been accomplished in these areas from early times may give major insights. Such activities may well chime with standard social work and may even be better (Akimoto, Fujioka, & Matsuo, 2016, p. 5). By investigating such activities we might discover real social work practices that that have been ignored in standardized social work. This research investigates social work activities operated by *imams* and teachers in two types of Muslim institutions—mosques and orphanages in Bangladesh. Tables 21.1 and 21.2 present the social work practices of these institutions in a different cultural and religious context.

DISCUSSION

Poverty Reduction by Mosques and Orphanages

The concepts of welfare and pensions were put into practice in early Islamic law in the form of *zakat* (almsgiving) in the seventh century. Taxes such as *jizya* (tax from non-Muslims) collected in the treasuries of Islamic governments coupled with *zakat* had long been used to provide income for those in need such as the poor, elderly, orphans, widows, and the disabled (Samad & Hossain, 2016). *Zakat* is one of the basic principles of Islamic economies based on social welfare and fair distribution of wealth (Ali & Hatta, 2014). Muslims are required to pay a fixed proportion of their possessions for the welfare of the whole community and the poor in particular. Orphanages and mosques are also places that collect public charity and *waqf* in the forms of wealth such as building and land (Wahid et al., 2011). Most of the study participants made statements like:

> We have established a poor fund made up of money coming from *zakat, waqf, fitra* (charity) and public donations. However, we don't receive any financial assistance from the government. We help the poor to get healthcare, to buy

Table 21.1 Social work provided by mosques in Bangladesh

Poverty reduction	Education and training	Religious functions	Social ills and social breakdown	Rights and ownership	Social control	Climate change and disaster management	Social movement	Social awareness
Setting up poor funds Collecting *zakat* (almsgiving), *sadaqah* (charity), and *fitra* (charity) Managing *waqf* (charity) Providing financial assistance to the poor, hard-up students, the sick, and young women about to get married whose parents are poor Distributing food during *Ramadan* (fasting) Distributing clothes to the poor Ensuring water supply and washroom facilities for people in the community	Making a library available to community people such that story books and general literature can be borrowed by young and old alike Providing school equipment to students who are poor Providing religious education to young and old alike, and general education to illiterate elderly people Teaching social values and norms Educating pilgrims about how to make the most of their pilgrimage	Leading prayers five times a week Arranging funerals for the poor Celebrating religious festivals Motivating Muslims to practise Islam in their daily lives	Delivering sermons at Friday prayer (by an *imam*) against drug impacts, the dowry system, child marriage, and fundamentalist and terrorist activities Teaching people in the community about creating harmony in society Preventing the breakdown of social norms and values Discussing social problem and issues within the community to bring about peace in society	Teaching parents and children about their roles and responsibilities toward each other Educating women about their roles and responsibilities as mothers	Settling family and community disputes Preventing the breakdown of society Discussing fundamentalist and terrorist activities (at Friday prayer) Teaching best practice Avoiding social ills (drugs, infidelity, etc.)	Planting trees to prevent or at least mitigate climate change and natural disasters Providing food, shelter, and relief during natural disasters or humanmade disasters	Organising demonstrations and human chains against violations of human rights nationally and internationally and coordinating them such that they are more effective Organising demonstrations against drugs, the dowry system, social problems, and social issues	Delivering sermons at Friday prayer (by an *imam*) about personal health and raising public awareness about bringing it about Discussing the ill effects brought on by drugs, the dowry system, child marriage Raising public awareness about bank interest, extramarital affairs, and living together while unmarried

Table 21.2 Social work provided by orphanages in Bangladesh

Basic assistance given to orphans	Wider poverty reduction	Education and training	Religious functions	Social ills and social breakdown	Rights and ownership	Cultural activities	Social control	Climate change and disaster management	Social movement	Social awareness
Providing food, lodging, clothes, and healthcare	Distributing warm clothes to the poor during winter Collecting zakat (almsgiving), fitra (charity) and other money to help the poor with food, lodging, and healthcare Providing employment opportunities for orphans and children of the poor Collecting funds for refugees (such as the Rohingya) Providing the poor with food during Ramadan (fasting)	Providing education (both religious and general) including Bengali, English, and mathematics Providing orphans and children of the poor with the opportunity of having higher education Making a library available to people in the community Educating pilgrims about how to make the most of their pilgrimage Training teachers and honing their skill	Conducting funerals for all including the poor and the unidentified Arranging marriage ceremonies for young women whose parents are poor Arranging prayers for the sick to give solace and help them recover Arranging Tafsir Mahfil (discussions from the Quran and the Hadith) to ensure Islam is practised correctly by promoting peace in society	Providing education about following social norms, values, respecting the elderly, and loving the young Inviting people to embrace Islam Organising seminars to discuss social issues, problems, and their impacts on society	Arranging and delivering sermons based on the Quran and the Hadith concerning the roles and responsibilities people have in the family, community, and society	Arranging and getting people to participate in local and national competitions such as reciting the Quran and singing Hamd and Naat (Islamic songs)	Minimising conflict in the family and community Teaching social values such as respecting the elderly and providing the young with love Preventing terrorist activities by providing the police with information about anyone acting suspiciously Raising public awareness on social issues and problems	Collecting money on behalf of flood-affected people Providing food and shelter for flood-affected people Helping to repair rural roads during natural disasters such as landslides by organising demonstrations and human chains Raising public awareness on environmental pollution	Organising demonstrations and human chains against violations of human rights nationally and internationally Raising public awareness of the impacts of drugs, the dowry system, and harassment of women	Organising seminars to raise public awareness of the evil of fundamentalist and terrorist activities Raising public awareness of human rights and the impact that drugs, the dowry system, and the harassment of women have on society Organising seminars on how to prevent early marriage and motivate people to get rid of the dowry system Organising seminars on social problems and their impacts on society Raising public awareness of the need to vaccinate children

food, to provide food during Ramadan, to give financial assistance to celebrate religious festivals, and to distribute clothes during winter seasons. In addition, we help parents who are poor to pay for the marriages of their daughters and try to get universities and colleges to award scholarships to bright students from poor families to continue their studies.

Mosques have relatively good cash savings and own assets (Razak, Hussin, Muhammad, & Mahjom, 2014). Moreover, they collect and distribute *zakat* and *fitra* (public donations) to enable the poor to celebrate religious festivals, to provide food for the poor during *Ramadan* (fasting), and to distribute clothes to the poor in the community in winter. The ultimate goals of *zakat* are to reduce inequality and to establish human rights, human dignity, social justice, and empowerment of the poor by reducing poverty in Muslim communities (Ali & Hatta, 2011). Moreover, *zakat* and *fitra* play major roles in providing the government with the necessary finance such that social assistance can be given to the poor and needy in various forms such as food subsidies for the poor and their children, housing, healthcare, public transport, and provision of the welfare state (Kausar et al., 2016). *Zakat, fitra,* and *waqf* are unique to Islam and are solely used to combat poverty (Damilola, Nassir, & Baba, 2015). Muslims are strongly encouraged to look after the poor in their communities consistent with the goodwill that Islam espouses. Additionally, mosques and orphanages provide stipends and scholarships to poor students who show potential and financial grants to destitute Muslims, to poor girls for marriage ceremonies, and newly converted Muslims for their instant assistance and rehabilitation.

Used in this way *zakat* helps to provide social and economic security to the poor and needy in Muslim communities and brings all its members closer together. Muslim countries use *zakat, sadaqah,* and *waqf* in the fight against poverty and encourage their members to pay *zakat* to balance things up in society. *Waqf* is one of the basics of Islamic economic systems and refers to making charitable endowments such as property that are unique to Islam. Islamic law was the first to define and regulate *waqf* as a civil societal institution. *Waqf* is used in much the same way as *zakat* in providing benefits such as free education, scholarships, orphanages, and free healthcare treatment. *Waqf* properties in Bangladesh predominantly consist of mosques, madrasas, cultivatable agricultural land, forests, hillocks, and housing. Major beneficiaries of *waqf* include the poor, needy, orphans, and prisoners (Kahf, 2007). Other users of *waqf* include health services that use such revenues to cover construction of hospitals and spending on doctors, nurses, patients, and medicines for poor people.

As citizens of one of the least developed countries in the world Bangladeshi orphans are subjected to poverty, malnutrition, poor living conditions, illiteracy, and of course broken families all of which may have negative effects on their physical and mental wellbeing (Chowdhury et al., 2017). Some of the study participants made statements like:

> We provide food, clothes, lodging, education, healthcare, and educational materials to orphans because they are neglected in society, live under miserable conditions, and don't have any alternative. Strong religious beliefs guided by the *Quran* and *Hadith* encourage us to get involved in much the same way as a kind of profession. In addition, we are inspired by feelings of sympathy and kind-heartedness to orphans and other destitute people.

Note that malnutrition, physical or mental abuse, food insecurity, and lack of parental care and protection are widespread among Bangladeshi orphans in state-run orphanages (Madumita, Mondol, Rahman, & Khan, 2017). In contrast, Muslim-run orphanages provide orphans with three meals a day and cover their education, healthcare, food, clothing and lodging expenses. Such orphanages also provide free health services such as medical advice, pathological services, and medicines. In these way, orphanages play major roles similar to madrasas in reducing poverty (Chowdhury et al., 2017). A congenial atmosphere exists in Muslim-run orphanages helped by their generally having sufficient finances. Mosques likewise have a positive impact on society (Razak et al., 2014). On the other hand, state-run social work practices are concerned with remedial services and focus on the treatment of social problems faced by individuals and families. These social problems include child abuse, drug addiction, juvenile delinquency, mental illness, alcohol dependency, family conflict, and poverty. Although state-run social workers have historically been the predominant profession working with and on behalf of poor people (Ali & Hatta, 2010), the aim is to get Islamic social work incorporated in professional social work practices.

Education and Training Programmes Undertaken by Mosques and Orphanages

The history of Islam from the very outset made education available to the Muslim community by providing mosques and madrasas that traditionally educated people in classes taught by persons of Islamic learning or *imams* hired by villagers to work in the mosque and teach the children (Al-Krenawi, 2016). Most of the study participants made statements like:

> In mosques and orphanages we basically teach religious subjects such as Arabic, the *Quran*, and the *Hadith* and general subjects such as Bengali, English, and Mathematics. There are also literary programmes for illiterate older people. We also teach social values and norms and issue books from our library to children and adults. Moreover, we provide training to pilgrims to improve their pilgrimage experience and to teachers to improve their skills in the classroom.

The Orphanage Authority is tasked with arranging modern educational facilities for orphans such that they become useful human resources and good citizens. It also takes necessary measures to ensure employment opportunities are created in the community. The Mosque-based Child Education and Mass Literacy Programme (MCMLP) is an important programme that aims to strengthen people's moral standards and to develop their socioeconomic conditions as far as possible. Moreover, MCMLP activities ensure children are provided at mosques with pre-primary education and knowledge on religious matters, moral values, and ethics. Mosques also provide adult education. The Adult Education Programme enhances the practical life skills of people by creating awareness about primary healthcare and by providing such diverse functional information about their daily lives as child education, child health, personal healthcare, tree planting, and vegetable cultivation (Samad & Hossain, 2016). As mentioned earlier, fundamental courses on Arabic, the *Quran*, and the *Hadith* are taught in mosques and orphanages. People are given free educational equipment such as exercise books and writing materials by mosques and orphanages and are taught religious education. In this way they have a greater understanding of their own religion (Samad & Hossain, 2016). Additionally, there are libraries in mosques and orphanages and people from the community can borrow books for reading. This is important because it develops people's minds, makes people more knowledgeable, and keeps their minds active. Benefits range from improving mental health to improving physical health. Making people aware of the importance of reading books is highly significant to building an enlightened society in Bangladesh. Along with bringing about moral education mosques and orphanages play active roles in creating a sense of togetherness through knowledge and awareness that stem from religious services. Mosques and orphanages strengthen the moral position of people to lead lives in a proper manner from religious and social points of views (Samad & Hossain, 2016). Mosques and madrasas also conduct *hajj* (pilgrimage) education and training courses for pilgrims before they depart for the Holy Land that cover basic knowledge related to *hajj* rituals, healthcare, and *hajj* management. The *hajj* education and training conducted by mosques and madrasas make *hajj* and *umrah* exercises accessible to the entire congregation rather than just the pilgrims.

Religious Rituals and Functions Carried Out by Mosques and Orphanages

Mosques and orphanages are the vital Muslim religious institutions provide a number of religious services in Bangladesh. The religious services included moral teaching, religious and child education, teaching the *Quran* and the *Hadith*, preaching religion through educating religious rites and rituals and conducting these rituals such as marriages, baptisms, and funerals (Samad & Hossain, 2016). Most of the study participants made statements like:

> As human beings we have a social obligation to others and as religious leaders we provide numerous services in the community such as leading prayer five times a day, arranging *namaj-e-janaza* and funerals for all Muslims in

the community, arranging *Tafsir Mahfil* (discussions from the *Quran* and the *Hadith*), celebrating *Shab-E-Barat* (night of good luck), *Shab-E-Qadr* (night of honour), *Shab-E-Miraj* (night of meeting the prophet with Allah), and the birthday of Prophet Muhammad (SAW), and motivating people to practise Islam. In addition, we lead prayers for sick people to recover soon, assist in celebrating religious festivals, and attempt to make people of the community happy and bring peace to society.

Mosques play an important role in getting Muslims to thank Him (Creator) for all His blessings and motivating people to practise Islam in their daily lives, pray regularly, and surrender themselves to God (Creator). *Solat* (prayer) encourages punctuality, self-discipline, self-control, and cleanliness and doing it five times a day brings them closer to God and improves their relationship with Him. It also teaches Muslims tolerance, unity, equality, and co-operation and helps them build a good character and develop qualities of patience and honesty. Moreover, mosques and orphanages organize annual get-togethers on *Shab-E-Barat* (night of good luck), *Shab-E-Qadr* (night of honour), *Shab-E-Miraj* (night of meeting the prophet with Allah), and the birthday of Prophet Muhammad (SAW). Mosques and madrasas teach and conduct *namaj-e-janaza* (rituals and prayers for salvation of a departed soul before burial of the dead body) (Samad & Hossain, 2016).

Prevention of Social Ills and Social Decay

Mosques and madrasas help to fulfil recreational needs and to build the good character of children in the light of Islam. In addition, *ustads/imams* teach followers about manners and customs, how to exchange *Salam* (greetings), and give blessings. In this respect a few of the study participants made statements like:

> We teach orphans and people of the community about social norms and values such that peace reigns in society and the community. On Fridays we deliver sermons on the impact of drugs, the custom of dowry, the impact of early child marriage, and warn against fundamentalist and terrorist activities in an attempt to prevent social illness and decay. Sometimes we also conduct seminars to discuss social issues, problems, and impacts on society.

Such practices strengthen social bonds among people and prevent social ills. All orphans are taught the principles of religious rites, rituals, social norms, and values that prevent social ills and decay. Islam considers education not only as a common process of socialisation, but also as a means to improve and develop the condition of society such that it conforms to Islamic teaching (Tamuri, Ismail, & Jasmi, 2012). It helps build orphans' moral characters and makes them worthy members of society.

Create Rights and Ownership

Ustads/imams deliver sermons on Fridays about various aspects of Islam such as the empowerment of women by building awareness about the status of women in Islam. They also deliver sermons about the roles and responsibilities parents have for their children and those children have for their parents in Islam. Additionally, sermons based on the *Quran* and the *Hadith* are delivered concerning people's roles and responsibilities in the family, community, and society. Since mosques, madrasas, and orphanages use resources to help orphans become well-balanced individuals by learning and literacy, such institutions also give meaning to their lives in relation to the cultural systems and social structures to which they belong (Rao & Hossain, 2011).

Cultural Activities Carried Out by Mosques and Orphanages

Mosques and madrasas have long provided an extensive array of religious and cultural services in the Muslim community (Al-Krenawi, 2016). This was borne out by a large number of the study participants making statements like:

> Every year we conduct annual get-togethers on *waaz mahfil* (religious speeches/ lectures) in mosques and madrasas. We also conduct annual competitions on reciting the *Quran*, singing *Hamd-O-Naat* (Islamic songs), and reciting poetry. At the same time religious sermons/lectures (*waaz*) are delivered to orphans and people of the community in an attempt to meet their recreational needs.

Mosques and madrasas are religious institutions providing sociocultural services aimed at strengthening Muslim cultural tradition and meeting the recreational needs of people in the community. As already mentioned, cultural functions include teaching *Hamd-O-Naat* (Islamic songs that praise the Creator), arranging *Qirat* competitions (reciting the *Quran* correctly), reciting poetry, delivering religious sermons/lectures (*waaz*), celebrating the birthday of Prophet Muhammad (SAW), and organising religious discussions (*waaz mahfil*). These are important sources of pleasure for the Muslim community.

Social Control by Mosques and Orphanages

The *Quran* is the basis on which Islamic law (Sharia law) is founded. It controls the lives and behaviour of Muslims (Al-Krenawi, 2016). The *Quran* is ultimately seen as the locus of both religious and worldly knowledge. It also teaches Muslims how to behave in a civilised and humane manner and in so doing controls human behaviour in society (Rao & Hossain, 2011). In this respect some of the study participants made statements like:

> As religious and spiritual leaders we provide counselling to solve familial/conjugal conflicts in communities. We also help to create public awareness on social

issues and problems, to ignore fundamentalist and terrorist activities, to teach moral values and norms, and to prevent the breakdown of society.

Muslims teach moral values in which sacrifice, hard work, and patience are encouraged in accordance with the *Quran* and the *Hadith*. Such moral values allow learners to become religious-minded, moral persons. Qualities such as tolerance, sacrifice, and care are valorised in a context in which livelihoods are uncertain and emphasis is given to property ownership and paying taxes to contribute to social control (Barton & Hamilton, 2000). Peace and discipline are prerequisites to a healthy society. Mosques as religious institutions play very crucial roles in this respect. *Imams/ustads* raise people's consciousness as to what is right and wrong, give people advice to prevent them from engaging in unfair, harmful, and wrong activities, build a feeling of belonging among people of all communities, and give advice on preventing drug addiction. Moreover, mosque and madrasa management committees resolve disputes through arbitration, highlight the importance of paying respect to all religions, and take legal initiatives in case of serious crime to maintain discipline and peace in society. *Imams* are not only responsible for counselling, mediating, and resolving conflicts but also charged with spiritual leadership and guidance in the Muslim community and in so doing directly help in social control.

The main responsibility of an *imam* is to identify the needs of a community and address these needs to provide psychological relief and a sense of community in social development (Al-Krenawi, 2016). Additionally, community members receive counselling from *imams* who mediate in familial/conjugal conflicts and in so doing help them to lead healthy conjugal lives. The role of the *imam* is that of a spiritual teacher in the community. His job is to ensure that Muslims are aware of their indebtedness to and need to worship Allah (Creator) directly. *Imams* are considered top-level religious leaders (Siddiqui, 2004). Findings from this study show that *imams* have succeeded in bringing about moral education and helped people differentiate between fair and unfair and between right and wrong through discussions and sermons at mosques on Fridays (speech in the light of the holy *Quran* and the *Hadith*).

Mitigation of Climate Change and Disaster Management by Mosques and Orphanages

During natural and humanmade disasters mosques and madrasas play significant roles in collecting money from the public, helping the communities affected, and assisting others around the world in rehabilitation work (Mohit et al., 2013). Bangladesh is one of the most vulnerable countries when it comes to natural disasters. Millions of people suffer different types of disasters almost every year; hence emergency relief and support services are vital to helping the poor and disaster victims. Most of the study participants made statements like:

When natural disasters happen we help victims by providing emotional support, collecting money for them, giving food and shelter, and distributing relief materials. In addition, as part of Friday sermons and by word of mouth we create public awareness of environmental pollution and emphasise the need to plant trees to prevent and mitigate climate change and natural disasters.

When people are in urgent need of help the Mosque and Madrasa Management Committee provides a number of services to help the poor and disaster victims that range from distributing relief materials to providing shelter, medicine, and healthcare. When disasters happen faith-based organisations (FBOs) along with other stakeholders help in a number of ways such as providing hungry people with food and medical care, giving clothes to the poor and destitute, finding shelter for those made homeless, and supporting communities in a holistic way. Moreover, mosques and madrasas collect and distribute whatever has been donated by the public. They also play a major part in persuading the general public to assist those affected and deliver psychosocial support through institutional or personal approaches taken at Friday sermons (Mohit et al., 2013). FBOs play a major role in developing social cohesion by constructing social and safety networks in society (Bano & Nair, 2007). Religious groups, communities, leaders, and institutions hold a lot of potential in minimising risk facing local communities (Wisner, 2010). There is a need to get religious communities involved in community awareness about how to prevent disasters or at least mitigate them. This could be done by making use of community experiences of previous disasters and could lead to lives being saved, reducing vulnerability, and limiting financial damage (Cheema, 2012).

Social Movement by Mosques and Orphanages

The main responsibilities of an *imam* is to lead prayer five times a week and give guidance and support to the community and society (Al-Krenawi, 2016). The purpose of the Islamic movement in society is to pursue changes in communities that it perceives as desirable. Some of the study participants made statements like:

> Nowadays, although the reporting of domestic violence, rape, and sexual harassment has been increasing both nationally and internationally, the trial and punishment of perpetrators leave much to be desired. Therefore, we educate the public about the impacts drugs, dowries, and the harassment of women have on the individuals concerned and on society generally. This is done by organising rallies, seminars, and human chains in support of national and international responses to human rights crises and crimes against humanity.

Women in Bangladesh continue to be subject to dowry-related violence, rape, sexual harassment, and domestic violence. As already mentioned, despite widespread incidents of violence against women and girls the trial and punishment of perpetrators leave a lot to be desired. More children are becoming victims of rape than adult women. Even though women are being subjected to sexual violence on public transport, no preventive measures let alone action are taken against such violations. Lots of people are facing humanitarian crises such as Rohingya refugees, Syrians fleeing war, and others around the world. Mosques and madrasas organise demonstrations, rallies, processions, and human chains in support of national and international responses to human rights crises and crimes against humanity.

Creating Social Awareness of Social Issues

FBOs and culture play an important role in influencing people's behaviour within Muslim society. There are many misconceptions related to family planning and vaccination of children because awareness remains low in Bangladesh. Resistance to family planning is often driven by health concerns regarding the side effects of contraceptive methods and by opposition from family members, particularly husbands (Hamri, 2010). Most of the study participants made statements like:

> There are many misconceptions related to family planning and vaccination of children because awareness remains low in Bangladesh. Therefore, we help to create public awareness on such matters of personal health, family planning, offering or accepting bribes, extramarital affairs, living together when unmarried, prevention of early child marriage, the dowry system, the urgent need to vaccinate children, and the health of adults.

Ustads/imams provide welfare services in the light of Islam intended to strengthen healthy familial lives and family planning such as family counselling, awareness building, empowerment of women, and delivering sermons at Friday prayer on personal health aimed at improving public awareness in Bangladesh. Since most women in Bangladesh do not use modern contraceptives, the ability of Muslim religious leaders to educate society concerning family planning in Bangladesh is clearly important (Bigalke, 2006). Due to the sensitivity of the topic there is a need for family planning and vaccination activities to be preceded by an inclusive process of consultation and sensitisation with local communities, *imams*, and community leaders (Hamri, 2010). Additionally, religious leaders organise seminars and discussions on the impact of drugs, the custom of dowry, the impact of early child marriage, the taking or offering of bribes, extramarital affairs, and living together when unmarried. They also raise awareness against fundamentalist and terrorist activities, human rights issues, and the harassment of women by offering advice and delivering sermons at Friday prayer. However, these are but a few of the services *imams* help to provide. They also arrange campaigns in support of extended programmes for immunisation (EPI) and observance of national vaccination days. They raise awareness of the importance of EPI, the prevention of diarrheal disease, and the use of oral saline. They arrange doctors and ambulances to satisfy the special needs of seriously ill patients. They also employ a faith healing system to restore mental strength when patients are recovering from illness as a religious backup to medical care given by doctors (Samad & Hossain, 2016).

Policy Recommendations

Although mosques and orphanages carry out substantial amounts of social work in the community aimed at social development, the present study found that they always face financial shortages and do not employ any trained social workers. Therefore, professional social work practice is not systematically employed for effective social development. Professional social work is based on scientific knowledge and follows specific methods and techniques that may help to modernise and systematise social services such that they are fit for social development (Samad & Hossain, 2016). The main limitation of education provided at mosques and orphanages is that it is informal and elementary. Therefore, the introduction of vocational, technical, secondary, and higher secondary education is recommended to take place in mosques and orphanages. *Ustads* and service providers do not have the requisite knowledge when it comes to programme planning and executing plans and programmes systematically. Therefore, expertise in social work is needed to get an in-depth understanding of the problem and to address it appropriately (Razak et al., 2014). Social workers should be familiar with the basic beliefs, values, and rituals of Islam as practised in the client's milieu. Social workers could learn the relative significance of religion and how it could be integrated to form part of social development. Training in professional social work can help the service providers of religious institutions to understand the nature and depth of problems and to improve their skills at rendering services for social development in Bangladesh (Damilola et al., 2015; Samad & Hossain, 2016).

Conclusions

Many children are deprived of their basic human rights because of poverty, the political conditions that prevail, and shortages such as human and financial resources, poor coordination, appropriate child governance bodies, comprehensive national plans, little independent monitoring, targetted resources for children, and policies and programmes. Furthermore, lack of sufficient educational facilities and social awareness coupled with traditional values, vested interest groups, ignorance, migration, parental separation, death/disability of the income provider in the family, social injustice, crime, and natural calamities have all combined to produce the extraordinarily high magnitude of hazards facing children in Bangladesh. Therefore, government and non-government agencies need to come together and play major roles in solving the difficulties orphans face in Bangladesh. Official and civil bodies should take the necessary protective steps to eliminate the life-threatening dangers that await orphans and make sure they get the chance to develop under conditions appropriate to integrating a child in society in Bangladesh. Compulsory regulations and initiatives should be implemented to ensure and defend the rights and lives of orphans (Kavak, 2014). Despite the enduring belief in the importance of mosques and madrasas, it is mainly undocumented and not recognised in development studies. Little study has been undertaken to document the roles they play as development in agents in Bangladesh, despite the roles they play in community development in many Muslim countries being evident and currently major in Bangladesh for social development (Cheema, 2012; Mohit et al., 2013). To abide by the instructions of Islam according to the *Quran* and the *Hadith*, *ustads/imams* and Muslim authorities provide social work services devoted to human wellbeing such that they can earn the grace of Almighty Allah for securing Heaven and eternal peace in the afterlife. Feelings of empathy and kindness to orphans, the elderly, and the destitute are the triggers that encourage *ustads/imams* to get involved in social service work in Bangladesh. Almost all the study participants mention that as human beings they have social responsibility to others. Therefore, they are willing to help each other to build a just society in accordance with the principles of Islam. Additionally, many of the study participants feel that helping the poor and disadvantaged brings social status and prestige that in turn create scope for both religious and sociopolitical leadership in their community; hence their involvement in humanitarian activities. Islam is a complete code of life. The five pillars of Islam help to bring people at all levels of society together in mutual support and in enhancing social development. Islam is a religion that has a theoretical framework that guides its followers to observe and adopt it as a system of life (Damilola et al., 2015). Religious forms of charity or "financial worship" have historically played a key role in funding charity and philanthropy at the individual and institutional level in South Asia with *zakat*, *fitra*, *sadaqah*, and *waqf* being the largest source of such funding in Muslim communities (Kirmani, 2012). Religious values and beliefs could play an important role in motivating social workers, individuals, and organisations to respond to people's immediate needs and partially fulfilling social services that have been deliberately overlooked by the state (Kirmani, 2012).

Acknowledgment The research project that has been funded by the Japan Society for the Promotion of Science, JSPS KAKENHI Grant Fund No. JP17K18586 (Project Head: Kana Matsuo).

NOTE

1. The five pillars of Islam are: declaring one's complete faith that Allah (God) is the only Supreme Being and Muhammad (SAW) is the messenger of Allah; performing five prayers a day; donating 2.5% of annual income through *zakat* (a charity tax to help the needy); fasting (which includes no eating, drinking, or intimacy) during the daytime in Ramadan; and making a pilgrimage to Mecca (Muhammad's birthplace) at least once in a person's life if that person is able.

REFERENCES

Ahmad, M. (2015). Role of waqf in sustainable economic development and poverty alleviation: Bangladesh perspective. *Journal of Law, Policy and Globalization, 42*(2), 118–130.

Akimoto, T., Fujioka, T., & Matsuo, K. (2016). *Islamic social work practice: Experiences of Muslim activities in Asia*. Chiba, Japan: Asian Center for Social Work Research (ACSWR), Shukutoku University.

Ali, I., & Hatta, Z. A. (2010). Microfinance and poverty alleviation in Bangladesh: Perspective from social work. *The Hong Kong Journal of Social Work, 44*(2), 121–134.

Ali, I., & Hatta, Z. A. (2011). The role of *zakat* in poverty reduction in Bangladesh from a community social work perspective. *International Journal of Business and Technopreneurship, 1*(3), 467–478.

Ali, I., & Hatta, Z. A. (2014). *Zakat* as a poverty reduction mechanism among Muslim community: Case study of Bangladesh, Malaysia and Indonesia. *Asian Social Work and Policy Review, 8*(1), 59–70.

Al-Krenawi, A. (2016). The role of the mosque and its relevance to social work. *International Social Work, 59*(3), 359–367.

Amin, F. (2016). *Social welfare program of Islamic political party: A case study of Bangladesh Jama'at-e-Islami* (Published PhD thesis). Western Sydney University, Sydney, Australia. Retrieved August 11, 2018, from https://researchdirect.west-ernsydney.edu.au/islandora/object/uws%3A36236.

Bangladesh Bureau of Statistics (BBS). (2018). Bangladesh statistics 2018. Bangladesh Bureau of Statistics (BBS). Statistics and Informatics Division (SID) Ministry of Planning. Dhaka: Bangladesh.

Bano, M., & Nair, P. (2007). *Faith-based organisations in South Asia: Historical evolution, current status and nature of interaction with the state*. Retrieved February 12, 2019, from https://berkleycenter.georgetown.edu/publications/faith-based-organisations-in-south-asia-historical-evolution-current-status-and-nature-of-inter-action-with-the-state.

Barton, D., & Hamilton, M. (Eds.). (2000). *Situated literacies: Reading and writing in context*. London and New York: Routledge.

Bigalke, R. (2006). Sexual and reproductive health in Islamic contexts. In E. Ganter (Ed.), *Development cooperation in Muslim countries: The experience of German technical cooperation* (pp. 65–74). Baden-Baden, Germany: Nomos.

Cheema, A. R. (2012). *Exploring the role of the mosque in dealing with disasters: A case study of the 2005 earthquake in Pakistan* (PhD dissertation). Massey University, New Zealand.

Chowdhury, A. B. M. A., Wasiullah, S., Haque, M. I., Muhammad, F., Hasan, M. M., Ahmed, K. R., et al. (2017). Nutritional status of children living in an orphanage in Dhaka city. *Bangladesh, Malaysian Journal of Nutrition, 23*(2), 291–298.

Dhaka Tribune. (2016). Mosque committees under scanner. Retrieved February 9, 2019, from https://www.dhakatribune.com/uncategorized/2016/01/10/mosque-committees-under-scanner.

Damilola, O. W., Nassir, B. A., & Baba, S. H. (2015). The role of zakat as a poverty alleviation strategy and a tool for sustainable development: Insights from the perspectives of the holy prophet (PBUH). *Arabian Journal of Business and Management Review, 5*(3), 8–17.

Encyclopaedia of Bangladesh. (2014). *Orphanage.* Retrieved February 8, 2019, from http://en.banglapedia.org/index.php?title=Orphanage.

Hamri, N. E. (2010). Approaches to family planning in Muslim communities. *Journal of Family Planning and Reproductive Health Care, 36*(1), 27–31.

Hatta, Z., Ali, A., Subramaniam, J., & Salithamby, A. R. (2014). Professional and functional alternative social workers: A case study of Malaysia. *Asian Social Work and Policy Review, 8*(2), 138–155.

Hodge, D. R. (2005). Social work and the house of Islam: Orienting practitioners to the beliefs and values of Muslims in the United States. *Social Work, 50*(2), 162–173.

International Federation of Social Work. (2000). IFSW general meeting in Montreal, Canada, July 2000. Retrieved from http://www.ifsw.org/f38000138.html.

Kahf, M. (2007). *Role of zakah and awqaf in reducing poverty: A case for zakah-awqaf—Based institutional setting of microfinance.* Paper presented at the Seminar on "Islamic Alternative to Poverty Alleviation: Zakat, Awqaf and Microfinance", Bangladesh.

Kausar, A., Alauddin, M., & Kabir, M. R. (2016). Masjid based zakat management model in alleviating poverty: Bangladesh perspective. *International Journal of Ethics in Social Sciences, 4*(2), 63–82.

Kavak, H. Z. (2014). *Report on world's orphans.* IHH Humanitarian and Social Researches Center. Retrieved February 13, 2019, from https://reliefweb.int/sites/reliefweb.int/files/resources/REPORT%20ON%20WORLD%27S%20 ORPHANS.pdf.

Kirmani, N. (2012). The role of religious values and beliefs in charitable and development organisations in Karachi and Sindh, Pakistan. *Development in Practice, 22*(5–6), 735–748.

Madumita, B. P. C., Mondol, R., Rahman, M. A., & Khan, M. A. M. (2017). Assessment of nutritional status of a government girls orphanage in Tangail District of Bangladesh. *SMU Medical Journal, 4*(1), 79–87.

Mohit, M. A., Zahari, R. K., Eusuf, M. A., & Ali, M. Y. (2013). Role of the masjid in disaster management: Preliminary investigation of evidences from Asia. *Journal of Architecture, Planning & Construction Management, 4*(1), 1–16.

Razak, A. A., Hussin, M. Y. M., Muhammad, F., & Mahjom, N. (2014). Economic significance of Mosque institution in Perak State, Malaysia. *Kyoto Bulletin of Islamic Area Studies, 7*(March), 98–109.

Rao, N., & Hossain, M. I. (2011). Confronting poverty and educational inequalities: Madrasas as a strategy for contesting dominant literacy in rural Bangladesh. *International Journal of Educational Development, 31*(6), 623–633.

Samad, M., & Hossain, M. A. (2016). *A study on social service activities of Muslim religious institutions in Bangladesh: Relevance with social work.* Chiba, Japan: Asian Center for Social Work Research (ACSWR), Shukutoku University.

Siddiqui, S. (2004). *A professional guide for Canadian Imams.* Winnipeg, MB, Canada: Islamic Social Services Association Inc.

Tamuri, A. H., Ismail, M. F., & Jasmi, K. A. (2012). A new approach in Islamic education: Mosque based teaching and learning. *Journal of Islamic and Arabic Education, 4*(1), 1–10.

Wahid, H., Kader, A. R., & Ahmad, S. (2011). *Localization of zakat distribution and the role of Mosque: Perceptions of amil and zakat recipients in Malaysia.* Retrieved February 19, 2019, from http://www.ukm.my/hairun/kertas%20kerja/Paper%20Hairunnizam,%20Radiah%20and%20Sanep-MALAYSIA%20_9_final_28062011.pdf.

Wisner, B. (2010). Untapped potential of the world's religious communities for disaster reduction in an age of accelerated climate change: An epilogue & prologue. *Religion, 40*(2), 128–131.

Yen, L. K. (2008). *Learning from our fathers: Prospects for ecumenism in the 21st century Asia.* Retrieved September 11, 2018, from http://eapi.admu.edu.ph/content/learning-our-fathers-prospectss-ecumenism-21st-century-asia.

CHAPTER 22

Social Work Education in Pakistan: Analysis of Past and Present Practices

Nasreen Aslam Shah

INTRODUCTION

Pakistan gained independence from the British in 1947. From the outset the country faced multifaceted issues from the legislative, monetary, sociopolitical to the ethnic. Since then military rule over the country created numerous problems that damaged the social structure of the country (Zaidi, 2009). Pakistan never put in place sustainable intellectual social advancement strategies for most of its people because power was held in a few urban areas by primitive rulers. They did not want the masses to have full access to improvements in human lifestyles. Even after 71 years of independence Pakistan is still considered not to have grown socially, monetarily, fiscally, or educationally to any great extent. A large portion of the populace experience hardships despite some fundamental social administrations in getting education, medical services, and safe drinking water. The difference between the haves and have nots is vast. Financial development cannot be accomplished without human productivity; hence the have nots cannot be viewed as minor when it comes to improving the finances of the country (Rizvi, 2016). There is an urgent need for social work to be overhauled in Pakistan. However, the question arises as to what constitutes social work. Although it is widely accepted there are two concepts of social work—the Pakistani perspective and the international perspective—we first have to discuss the past concept of social work.

In the past the responsibility for taking care of poverty-struck siblings, the handicapped, the elderly, and the unemployed fell to the family, caste,

N. A. Shah (✉)
Department of Social Work, Centre of Excellence for Women's Studies,
University of Karachi, Karachi, Pakistan

S. S. M. et al. (eds.), *The Palgrave Handbook of Global Social Work Education*, https://doi.org/10.1007/978-3-030-39966-5_22

society, and religious institutions. After industrialisation and rapid growth in economic development people started to move from rural to urban areas. Therefore, the role played by the old social security and welfare system had to adapt to the needs of people disadvantaged by such a move. However, although the role of academics has been little analysed in social work education, it is essential to get their opinion about what should be done to improve the standard of provision of services to the people (Wilson & Campbell, 2013). The term social worker is hard to define no matter where you are in the world. Its importance and degree extend from unadulterated religion-based philanthropy to the advanced present-day concept of social work. In Pakistan in the early years the term social specialist was given to any individual who thought about human needs beyond their immediate family or who generously parted with their own money to aid the poor. It was something anybody could do requiring no knowledge of the circumstances under which individuals lived. Rehmatullah (2002) pointed out that Pakistan had long been a nation with few experienced social specialists. It took about 6 months for the Pakistan government and UN experts to agree that a programme of "Training for Social Work" was the best way forward. This resulted in experienced social specialists and senior government authorities being tasked with designing a programme to achieve the following objectives:

- finding the most appropriate way of training social workers best suited to the case of Pakistan;
- studying the peculiar needs and social trends affecting social welfare in Asia;
- identifying Pakistani teachers of social sciences and social work;
- making accessible Pakistani literature on social work; and
- testing the motives, personality, character, and intellectual ability of a pioneer organisation to carry out such training in light of the initiative and early responsibility required for pioneer organisation of scientific social work in the East (Rehmatullah, 2002).

The modern concept of social work is generally new to people in Pakistan. Consequently, it is not delivered efficiently and has not been received well—at least not according to the genuine meaning of the term. Although some spadework has certainly been done, much of the ground remains undug. Social work is dynamic in that it is needed and impacted by the advancement of social, monetary, political, and social variables. Accordingly, the advancement of social work in Pakistan must be looked at through the lens of how it can be brought about in light of the nation's financial status (Khalid, 2001).

International Perspective

The concept of professional social work unlike usual charity practice was once based on an organized, systematic framework to eliminate socioeconomic problems and evils. After in-depth study of the problems, it was designed

to help individuals, families, and communities to not only cope with difficult conditions but to improve them in some way. In the 1870s Octavia Hill
introduced a scheme to train house managers to make life easier for tenants
in Britain. At that time it was generally felt that there was a need for professional social workers. Therefore, in the 1890s social work training was started
in London at the Women's University (Axinn & Levin, 1975).

Many definitions of social work explain social work as:

> ... it seeks two things for people: economic well being and the deeper source of
> happiness that is a self-realization, the stuff of its concern is human behavior and
> relationship. Its focus of attention is the individual and his self-adjustment to a
> recognized reality. Also, social work is an interaction between people and their
> social environment which affects the ability of people to accomplish their life
> tasks, alleviates distress, and realizes their aspirations and values. (Joshi, 2004)

> Social work is a practice-based profession and an academic discipline that pro-
> motes social change and development, social cohesion, and the empowerment
> and liberation of people. Principles of social justice, human rights, collective
> responsibility and respect for diversities are central to social work. Underpinned
> by theories of social work, social sciences, humanities, and indigenous knowl-
> edge, social work engages people and structures to address life challenges and
> enhance wellbeing. (Theobald, Gardner, & Long, 2014)

It is also explained as: "social work education is professional and based
upon research and practice which is systematic and evidence based" (Riaz,
2016). Early social work trends provided inadequate solutions to the mentally ill and to children in need inspired by Britain's framework of charity. At
the beginning of the nineteenth century nations offered assistance in urban
and rural areas (Shah, 2015). Therefore, "Social work believes in building a
social structure on strengths rather than building on weaknesses" (Watson
& Hoefer, 2016). The purpose of social work education is to make use of
knowledge and skills to assist people in their everyday lives and help them
spend satisfying lives (Hill, 1965). Due to the shortage of trained social workers it is often the case that other professions step in and train students to run
voluntary organizations. Social scientists believe professional social workers
are much better suited to manage welfare programmes for the simple reason
that qualified social workers not only have expertise at managing an agency
but are more committed to the mission and clients of such an agency (Watson
& Hoefer, 2014).

RESEARCH METHODOLOGY

The research methodology used in this research combines critical content
analysis with a qualitative approach. Qualitative methodologies are based
on a diversity of paradigms associated with research strategies (Sarantakos,
2005). The research topic was selected to explore the reasons behind the failure of social work education practice in Pakistan and why Pakistani society

underestimates the job of professional social worker. The study undertaken in this chapter is based on analysis of past and present practices of social work education in Pakistan since the 1950s. Qualitative content analysis was the method employed and was based on secondary data used to analyse the needs, issues, hurdles, and benefits of social work education practice. Heaton (2004) defines secondary data analysis as "a research strategy which makes use of pre-existing quantitative data or pre-existing qualitative data for the purposes of investigating new questions or verifying previous studies." In other words, secondary data analysis is the use of previously collected data for some other purpose. Since it is not a method of data analysis other methodologies such as grounded theory or statistical analysis, for example, can be applied to the process of secondary data analysis. Books and articles related to social work in Pakistan were carefully reviewed to understand the concept, history, and recent practice of social work education in educational institutions of Pakistan.

It is important to spend a moment defining content analysis. A method of social research widely used, content analysis is a documentary method that aims at quantitative and/or qualitative analysis of texts, pictures, films, and other forms of verbal, visual, or written communication. Content analysis can be one of four types: descriptive content analysis, contextual analysis, comparative content analysis, and procession or particularistic content analysis. The type used in this study is contextual analysis, which studies the research object in context and aims to understand the context through meaningful statements of authors found in texts. As part of my study I used books and journals related to social work education in Pakistan. There was no particular area from which text was selected because the literature on social work education is very limited. I selected the topic of social work education in Pakistan because I wanted to analyse differences between past and present practices to spot improvements. Methodological construction of the research topic was specifically designed to look into the Pakistani context because the concept of social work is so poorly perceived in Pakistan. Every available book, journal paper, and newspaper article was reviewed because of the limited research material related to the topic. Data were collected from books, journal papers, newspapers, and online magazines using a purposive and convenience sampling method and careful analysis (Sarantakos, 2005).

Objectives

Aims of the study were twofold:

- analysing the history of social work education in academic institutions and how it has evolved over time; and
- investigating the influence of the Western school of thought regarding social work education in Pakistan and its impact.

Historical Perspective

Professional education on the subject of social work began in 1936 when the Tata Group, one of the largest private business enterprises, established a school of social work in Mumbai. The idea behind setting up this school came from America and its founding director was an American. At that time the American system of graduate social work education was deemed the most successful model available compared with other systems operated in European societies. Social work education has been termed the greatest revolution of the twentieth century (Trivedi et al., 2013).

The Social Workers' Oath states:

"I shall serve to the best of my ability, the depressed, the handicapped and the needy,"

"I shall serve all the people I can, in all ways I can, as often as I can,"

"I shall look not back but forward until the goal is reached" (Rehmatullah, 2002).

A total of 65 social workers trained in the first in-service training course funded by the government of Pakistan and the UN Technical Assistance Administration (UNTAA). It took place on 2 April 1953 at Khalikdina Hall in Karachi. They swore the above oath at an inspiring ceremony presided over by the then Minister for Health, Labour and Works Dr. A. M. Malik. In the history of social work in Pakistan this was a turning point (Rehmatullah, 2002).

This training course was followed by another in Dhaka held during May, June, and July 1953. The two courses were instrumental in developing university-level courses in social welfare. Despite being experimental their objectives were clear and twofold:

- broadening the horizons and strengthening the skills of trainees; and
- discovering teachers and leaders capable of developing "a Pakistani pattern of social work."

The UN team was asked to plan the training. They were probably surprised to see the extreme poverty and underdevelopment of the country. However, designing a curriculum teaching social work has to be related to a society's psychological and social behaviour. Unfortunately, due to lack of time the UN team could not make an in-depth study and due to lack of indigenous literature Pakistani faculty members were also unable to develop a comprehensive outline of social work. Although these hurdles became problematic, efforts were made to draw on local material resulting in the curriculum being divided into three major phases.

The first phase was the orientation phase that included three lecture courses: "Social Work as a Profession," "Problems of Pakistan," and "Social Sciences as Related to Social Welfare." A series of 12 lectures were delivered including some on the following topics:

- developing charity into the science of social work;
- providing a brief historical review with special reference to world pioneers such as Jamshed Nusservanjee Mehta;
- outlining the philosophy and goals of social work training; and
- understanding the purposes of the Ministry of Health and Works in requesting a social welfare project.

The second phase dealt with a number of issues such as modern trends in social services in the East and West; new emphasis on rural welfare experiments in Egypt and Sri Lanka; national planning for social welfare under international leadership in Burma and India; university–government co-operation in Malaysia; training of auxiliary workers; training according to cultural, geographical, or economic patterns; and world organisations.

The third phase again dealt with a number of issues such as modern professional fields of social work whose specialisations could contribute to the development of indigenous patterns or institutions in Pakistan; rural welfare, labour welfare, medical social work, emergency relief, prevention and treatment of delinquency, institutional care of dependants, character-building organisations, fundamental education, child and family welfare, youthwork; preparing communities for social services and social action; the personality and character needed for someone to engage in effective social work; pioneers and engineers; the importance of voluntary workers; and the difficult transition to professional status. Such a tentative training programme had to try and overcome many problems. While national and international teaching staff were hired from diverse fields of experience, the latter were given extra responsibilities: training students and making suggestions to the government on setting up services. Selection of national staff was based on the progress they showed during various parts of the training process and on how well they understood the people and the social problems. They were trained as sociologists, psychologists, labour welfare administrators, and group leaders. Any of such social workers skilled in audiovisual techniques would be of great value in helping to adapt the contributions of international staff to the culture and aspirations of the country.

Lessons learned from the first training course at Karachi provided invaluable help in planning future courses. According to Dr Dumpson, who reviewed the results of the first training programme, there were discrepancies between actual training practices and imported practices. This was mainly because such practices were not always adaptable to the Pakistani case.

Second Training Course at Dhaka

September–November 1953

The training course at Karachi concluded on 2 April 1953. Soon after, the UN team was asked to prepare similar courses to be held in East Pakistan and Punjab. The Dhaka course started in September 1953 and its objectives were:

1. "An effort to introduce the concepts of modern social work, philosophy, and practice, and to help determine ways in which they may be adapted to meet the social needs of the country."
2. "To provide an introduction to the various fields of social work, the underlying philosophy of modern social work, and an opportunity for practical demonstration of its skills and practices."

Third Short-Term Training Course at Karachi

February–July 1954

In 1954 the central government of Pakistan announced its decision to recognise social work as a profession by declaring that government posts in social work will hold the status of class 11 gazetted officer.

> On 13 November 1954 the vice chancellor of the University of Punjab and the Secretary of Education had accepted the proposal and sanctioned formation of the Department of Social Work at the University of Punjab. The University of Dhaka started an MA course in 1958 and for the first time Pakistan had trained its own professional social workers. (Rehmatullah, 2002)

MA classes in social work began at Karachi University in 1962. Before this time Karachi University adopted the same curriculum as Punjab University, although some minor changes were made over the years. Comparison between the first curriculum introduced at Punjab University with that of Karachi University is appropriate here. The changes that stand out are "Social Thoughts on Islam," "Population Planning and Family Education," and "Rural Problems of Pakistan," but they are widely accepted as welcome additions to the curriculum.

Today 22 public universities offer MA social work programmes and 7 universities offer PhD programmes in social work including the University of Karachi, University of Punjab, University of Balochistan, University of Peshawar, Greenwich University, and Shaheed Benazir Bhutto Dewan University (eduvision, 2017).

Need and Importance of Social Work Education in Pakistan

Social work education in Pakistan finds it hard to reconcile a number of factors such as its objectives, limitations, academic practices, academic locations, and the methods and techniques used to acquire knowledge to improve the way it is practised (Green & Clarke, 2016). Before beginning a social work education programme it is essential to get a clear picture of the current social needs and problems of the country for which social workers are being trained. The 2014 Human Development Report Sustaining Human Progress: Reducing Vulnerabilities and Building Resilience published by the

UN Development Programme (UNDP) stated that Pakistan ranked 146 out of a total 187 countries on the index. According to the report 52% of Pakistani people live in poverty. According to the Human Development Index, a multidimensional poverty index used as an alternative way of estimating income-based poverty, the ratio of the population living under multilateral poverty in Pakistan increases by about 3% every year (Sheikh, 2014). According to the Asian Development Bank 12.4% of the population in Pakistan live below the poverty line, 50.7% of the population aged 15 years and above are employed, and for every 1000 babies born in Pakistan 66 die before their first birthday (Asian Development Bank, 2017). The situation within Pakistan is crying out for immediate changes to fulfil the needs of the people. Before attempting to change conditions in the country—from the local to the national level—it is essential to prepare qualified social work professionals well versed in the techniques and methods of social work. This means the basis of social work education should be extended to include comprehensive policies and strategies, which can only be done in collaboration with social work educators, experts, and researchers.

Professional social workers are of course fully aware of the philosophy underlying social work and trained to understand the culture, social philosophies, political ideologies, and ongoing pressures that accompany economic and social conditions (Livingstone, 1957). This begs the question as to what is the relationship between the philosophy underlying social work and the immediate needs of the people of Pakistan? Without developing an understanding of these factors it is difficult to resolve issues because the purpose of social work education is professional and meant to be utilized for the service of the people (Omer, 1960).

Although the main responsibility of social workers is to build a positive and sustainable rapport with the client, the relationship has to be built on genuine concern, empathy, faith, professionalism, and the ability to communicate well (Simock & Castle, 2016). This begs another question as to what a social worker can do in such a scenario. Professional social work has developed certain well-defined rules that originate from its basic liberal–democratic value framework and provide guidelines for practice. Accordingly, the role of the social worker as perceived from this approach is to establish a dynamic process of interaction that takes place at the social and the psychological level. The areas of knowledge covered in the curriculum of a school of social work can be broadly grouped as follows:

i. Knowledge about human beings and about society drawn primarily from psychology, sociology, social psychology, economics, and to a lesser degree political science.
ii. Knowledge of methods or techniques of social work such as casework, group work, community organization, social administration, and to a lesser degree social action.

  iii. Knowledge about and ancillary to particular fields of social work (e.g., medical social work, care of the physically handicapped, tribal welfare, etc.) (Gore, 1965).

  iv. Understanding the key demographic and socioeconomic characteristics of the poor is an essential prerequisite for the formulation of an effective and meaningful policy to eliminate social problems in Pakistan (Social Policy and Development Centre, 2016).

Social work education in Pakistan clearly needs to be enhanced if professionally trained individuals are to motivate people to overcome their problems, to organise different communities regarding how to bring about development, and to guide people as to how to solve problems themselves.

Any curriculum on social work education should describe the concepts of fieldwork and research such that professional social workers will find it easy to adapt these concepts to the Pakistani scenario.

Fieldwork

"Learning by doing" is the most important process in social work. Fieldwork provides an opportunity for students to work with individuals and the community and to deal with social problems practically in the field (i.e., within the community). The most authentic and genuine approach to social work can only be developed by fieldwork. Moreover, at the professional level it is an essential part of social work training. Since fieldwork has to be planned scientifically, performed precisely, and supervised carefully schools of social work take all measures necessary to improve the organisation, administration, and supervision of fieldwork. Most social work departments of public universities include in their courses 175 hours of fieldwork per semester for 2 years. Teachers in university departments of social work are expected to supervise fieldwork as part of their job. An efficient fieldwork programme depends on strong collaboration between social work departments and social agencies. Such a joint endeavour of university teachers and fieldworkers is vital to exchanging knowledge and experience with each other and achieving satisfactory standards in fieldwork supervision. Supervision is essentially a helping and enabling process (Khalid, 2001).

Research in Social Work

Social work education in Pakistan is heavily influenced by the Western model of social work. Although social work is a context-based profession, the concept and theories of social work are based on the Western framework and cannot be applied to the Pakistani people (Nikku & Hatta, 2014). Research has shown that social work cannot be carried out by professionals on their own, rather it should be a collective venture involving the entire community (Muhammad, 2008). Although research on social work has been done scientifically and logically, its major purpose is discovering the truth. The scientific method underlying research involves five steps. The first step is identifying the problem (i.e., the research question). The second step is gathering information related to the research question such as found in the literature. The third step is forming a hypothesis based on past research. The fourth step is testing the hypothesis through careful examination of the data collected. The fifth step is developing a theory should the hypothesis be proven to be true. Researchers use these methods to study people's thinking, actions, and behaviours. Since little research into social work has been undertaken in Pakistan the curriculum on social work needs to be improved and changed to match the needs of society. Curriculum development is more important at the classroom level than at the strategic level (Shah, 2015).

Discussion and Analysis

Although the situation in which professional social work in Pakistan finds itself is poor, the term social work education in Pakistani pedagogy has been widely discussed. A lot of people ask whether social work is a discipline or not. Despite being confused by the concept, its meaning, and the scope of it, most people are unaware that social work is a proficient subject that depends on logical information. It is interesting to note that people in Pakistan do not easily distinguish between trained and untrained social workers because they think that charity and helping needy people is a noble activity. In reality, professional social workers in Pakistan have a lower societal position than other professions and practitioners much like the case in other South Asian countries (Riaz, 2016).

Examining the history of Pakistani academia makes it abundantly clear that the university system has not only been starved of investments by governments but has been extremely politicized. That is why today only a few (but strong) social sciences faculty members are left in the country who can make a living by teaching at a university, feel safe, and operate free from any political harassment. Many people who became academics during the time of General Zia ul-Haq's military regime (1977–1988) left problematic campuses and set up their own non-governmental organisations (NGOs), advocated social and political revolution, and with the support of donor agencies launched small projects. What little social science research is done today comprises detailed ethnographic community-based studies and needs field researchers who can converse in at least two languages (Khan, 2007).

Pakistan is blessed to have good professional social workers (Khalid, 2007). Since the establishment of Pakistan social work has provided many types of human services to try and overcome many issues such as poverty, lack of financial sources, unemployment, illiteracy, crimes, child labour, destitution, and discrimination against women. The social work curriculum provides students with an understanding of the basic systems of social work such as preparing and organising people such that problems at the individual, group, and community level can be solved. The number of teachers teaching social work at universities is very low compared with the number of students. Therefore, the teacher to student ratio is particularly high and in need of immediate action (Watts, Elliott, & Mayadas, 1995). The objective of the latest social work programme is to promote the gathering of information and gain the support of individuals and the community to uncover problems and try to solve them. Although social work has a theoretical basis, its special focus is fieldwork. The main objective of social work courses is to prepare and train students to acquire managerial positions or work for NGOs, welfare organisations, and research institutes. Although social work as a discipline has struggled to overcome many hurdles over the past 50 years, it has earned a good reputation. Teachers improve their teaching methodology with the cooperation of the Higher Education Commission (HEC) and different national and international research and development organisations. Moreover, the curricula for BS, MA, MPhil, and PhD courses have not only been revised according to modern trends and societal requirements, they have been prepared by keeping society's future needs clearly in mind.

Important units of the BS program include fundamentals of social work, social problems of Pakistan, communication skills, human resource management, community development, social mobilisation, and research. Although the main areas of concern at the MS and PhD level are research and fieldwork, the writing of theses is essential of all levels. However, due to the obvious influence of the West on social work education in Pakistan that bears little similarity to Pakistani culture and traditions the scholarly code of ethics for professional social work has not developed satisfactorily (Zaman, 1977). It is important to conduct research into current social issues of Pakistani society to discover new aspects of social structure. Another important issue is updating BS and MA courses because students of social work are currently still being taught backward, old courses of social work that do not fulfil contemporary requirements.

Lack of Facilitative Attitudes Toward Teachers and Students

Social work education is now systematically taught at higher education institutions and practical internships are an essential part of it. Since teaching is an ongoing procedure it should take place alongside research and training in the workplace. Although the reasons for reduced interest in social science education in Pakistan have not been examined satisfactorily, some stand out such as funding shortages and the belief that gaining MBA and MBBS degrees lead to better paid jobs than social science degrees. Therefore, students prefer to study science subjects. The fact that social scientists are paid less gives momentum to the belief that social sciences are not worthwhile or useful for society. Underprivileged social science departments urgently need serious attention of the HEC and government.

University administrators and bureaucrats provide little support to social science departments and their attitude toward students and teachers of social sciences can only be described as derogatory. Although teachers and students of social work struggle hard in their professional and academic roles, alone they cannot make a big difference to quality education. Universities need to focus on fulfilling the working conditions, requirements, and academic facilities of social science departments. It is essential to provide academic and financial assistance to students and teachers of social work for quality education to move forward. Furthermore, something needs to be done to bolster the relationship between teachers and students because right now the environment in social work departments in public universities seems neither academic nor friendly as exemplified by students often missing morning classes due to transport problems and the poor academic environment (Shah, 2015).

We now turn to analysis of the five-year plans put in place by the Pakistan government to improve the conditions under which social work education took place. The practice of carefully preparing individuals for a life in social service has existed since ancient times (Gore, 1965). Educational problems were quickly recognised after the establishment of Pakistan. Male and female social workers were appointed as recommended by the *First Five-Year Plan* (1957), which was an experimental model aimed at tackling the irregular attendance of children at school and their withdrawal from schools by parents. This recommendation was based on the belief that school social workers could bridge the gaps between parents and teachers and improve matters. The *Second Five-Year Plan* (1960) recognised the importance of school social workers in decreasing absence, indiscipline, and failures in schools. The *Third Five-Year Plan* focussed on the responsibilities and performances of professional school social workers. It was accepted that as a result of overwork and low wages teachers had little incentive to involve themselves in the lives of their students and find out what lay behind non-attendance, failures in exams, and even the production of criminals. The hectic schedule of parents and their disregard for school and educational issues resulted in the connection between teachers and parents being frail. Therefore, the appointment of school social workers with casework and group work specialties was suggested in schools, colleges, and universities. School social workers would support students in a number of ways such as telling them the importance of learning, protecting them at school, informing them about economic support, helping them develop their own personality, assisting them to adjust to the home environment, supporting them in their schooling work, building up the parent–teacher connection, and helping them stay away from crime. The *Third Five-Year Plan* was revolutionary in that in East Pakistan 40 school social work units were set up funded to the tune of 2 million rupees by the government. It was believed that better relationships between education departments and school social workers would help to solve the school education problems of students. This idea was initially tested in West Pakistan where six social work schools were set up. The priority of the *Fourth Five-Year Plan*

(1970) in social welfare revolved around the practice of school social work and 18 more units were planned. It was proposed that the Directorate of Social Welfare would administer these units. Since the *Third Five-Year Plan* and the *Fourth Five-Year Plan* were considered perfect for the practice of school social work adequate finances were provided for them.

The *Fifth Five-Year Plan* (1978) anticipated setting up 10 more school social work projects (2 in Islamabad, 2 in Lahore, 2 in Azad Kashmir, 2 in Northern Areas, 1 in Quetta, and 1 in Peshawar) in different cities in West Pakistan. It was recommended that such units should initiate in slum areas where low-income groups lived in an attempt to overcome socioeconomic problems related to children's schooling. The plan also suggested that these projects should solve the issues of failure and absenteeism. The *Sixth Five-Year Plan* (1983) recognised that school social work practice should help improve the education system and the psychosocial development of 44.4% of children under the age of 14 years at that time in Pakistan. A revised version of the *Sixth Five-Year Plan* (1988) said that the objective of this practice was to help students remain at school, to reduce the ratio of children excluded, to escape from the old teaching system, and to develop connections among education institutions, the family unit, and society. During the *Sixth Five-Year Plan* school social work pilot units were started in Islamabad that were then planned to be extended to the provincial and local level in the next stage. The *Seventh Five-Year Plan* had provisions that would allow school social work units to be set up and provide better education services for low-income communities. Likewise, it was suggested in the *Eighth Five-Year Plan* (1993) that the system of school social work units would fall under the aegis of federal and provincial social welfare departments that would set up more schools in disadvantaged areas. Pakistan's *Fourth Social Welfare Policy* focussed on providing services that would allow school social workers to assist students by coordinating activities between parents, schools, and communities. Although the practice of school social work does not currently include schools of special education that previously fell under the aegis of the Federal Special Education Department, after 18 amendments it was incorporated in provincial special education departments (Ranjha, Shoukat, & Dilshad, 2014).

Many authors have pointed to the poor state of social sciences including social work in Pakistan. Although social work education has been discussed in various studies, few studies have reported on the poor state of social work teaching. The HEC needs to take urgent actions to improve social science education and social work in Pakistan.

Scope of Social Work Education in Pakistan

Social work education as a mainstream subject of higher education can point to a 100-year world history (Midgley, 2000). Although social work education is multidimensional in meeting the needs of individuals and communities, it is most important when it comes to culture. Since the cultures of Western countries and the Third World are very different, it is not possible to apply Western theories, knowledge, and models to developing countries. Midgley (1978) argued that developing countries have been used by Western countries by getting developing countries to adopt Western policies and programmes and establishing a new form of colonialism to have power over them. It is true that the Pakistani social work education system is inspired by the American concept of social work education philosophy. However, it is totally alien to that of the Pakistani people, history, culture, and issues (Anwer, 2008). Therefore, collecting knowledge about the aptitudes of people and identifying social problems is of the utmost importance.

The scope of social work relates to what can be done to help people and society at various levels. Different services provided to individuals, groups, and communities are contingent on the aims, thoughts, and ethics of social work. An important element of social work is the resolution of psychosocial issues that block an individual's social progression. Social work is a relatively new branch of information that step by step covers every part of an individual's life. Social work is steadily extending its influence throughout the world and has been adapted to suit various ethnicities. Although social work has a part to play in most aspects of an individual's life, its scope is constantly being modified with the passage of time and changing social conditions (Nayak, n.d.). Social work education in Pakistan is renowned for producing quality professional social workers who provide exceptional services to the people. However, such social workers are expected to perform new and different tasks. Pakistani society is facing difficult social situations especially regarding its young people (as mentioned earlier in this chapter). Although social work is sorely needed to solve such issues, this requirement can only be met by training professional social workers and expanding the reach of social work education in Pakistan. Furthermore, researchers, academia, and policymakers should get together to identity the need for social work and come up with strategies to implement a practical plan of action. Moreover, there is a need to enhance research into social worker issues and problems.

Conclusions

The journey undertaken by social work education has faced many problems in the 70 years since its establishment. Despite many achievements, there are many failures that require serious debate between educators, policymakers, and representatives of the HEC of Pakistan. "Social Work as a Profession" involves studying it as a profession and working on solving issues that crop up during the teaching and studying of social work. Other important findings are the lack of literature on social work education in Pakistan and the older generation of teachers of social work struggle to fulfil the need for social work education.

Suggestions

- Essential to building a network between all public and private sector universities is the formation of a framework in which all published and unpublished literature including material from non-profit organisations is shared.
- Policymakers, social work experts, academicians, and activists need to take part in discussions on improving the scope of social work in Pakistan and applying different social work techniques to various societal problems.
- A qualitative outline of social work education should be formed by getting all provincial and federal university teachers to reach a mutual understanding regarding a more realistic view of society and developing a meaningful and practical account of social work education in Pakistan.
- Since social work has proven to be a very useful tool to improve societal structure the government of Pakistan should take a keen interest in developing policies to spread social work education in the education sector and give it added value.
- Teachers and students of social work need to be encouraged by the provision of scholarships and interexchange programmes of faculty and students both of which should start at either the local or the national level.

References

Anwer, A. (2008). *Community development and social welfare*. Peshawar, Pakistan: New Awan Printers.

Axinn, J., & Levin, H. (1975). *Social welfare: A history of the American response to need*. New York: Harper & Row.

Gore, M. S. (1965). *Social work and social work education*. New Delhi: Asia Publishing House.

Green, L., & Clarke, K. (2016). *Social policy for social work*. Cambridge, MA: Polity Press.

Hill, C. (1965). *The field of social work*. New York, USA: Holt, Rinehart and Winston.

Heaton, J. (2004). *Reworking qualitative data*. London: Sage.

Joshi, S. C. (2004). *Handbook of social work*. New Delhi: Akansha Publishing House.

Khan, A. (2007, February 28–March 3). *The relevance of research: Social science as local/global resistance*. Paper presented at international studies association 48th Annual Convention Chicago, IL. http://www.Researchcollective.Org/Documents/The_Relevance_of_Research.pdf.

Khalid, M. (2001). *Social work theory and practice with special reference to Pakistan*. Lahore: Kifayat Academy Karachi.

Khalid, M. (2007). *Social work theory and practice with special reference to Pakistan*. Lahore: Kifayat Academy Karachi.

Livingstone, A. S. (1957). *Social work in Pakistan*. Punjab: The West Pakistan Council of Social Welfare.

Midgley, J. (1978). Developmental roles for social work in the third world countries: The prospect of social planning. *Journal of Social Policy, 7*(2), 173–188.

Midgley, G. (2000). *Systematic intervention: Philosophy, methodology and practice.* New York: Kluwer Academic.

Muhammad, A. T. (2008). Urbanization and the role of social work in schools of Karachi. *Journal of Social Sciences & Humanities, 47*(11), 50–51.

Nikku, B. R., & Hatta, Z. A. (Eds.). (2014). *Social work education and practice: scholarship and innovations in Asia and Pacific.* Brisbane, QLS, Australia: The Primrose Hall Publishing Group. http://www.eduvision.edu.pk/institutions-offering-social-work-with-field-social-sciences-at-master-ma-msc-level-in-pakistan-page-1.

Omer, S. (1960). *Professional education for social work.* Lahore: The Department of Social Work, University of the Punjab.

Poverty in Pakistan, Asian Development Bank. (2017). https://www.adb.org/countries/pakistan/poverty.

Ranjha, A. N., Shoukat, A., & Dilshad, M. (2014). Need of school social work in response to education related problems in Pakistan. *Journal of Educational Research, 17*(2), 58–70.

Rehmatullah, S. (2002). *Social welfare in Pakistan.* Karachi: Oxford University Press.

Riaz, S. (2016). Development of social work as a discipline in Pakistan: An evaluation. *New Horizons, 10*(1), 30–45.

Rizvi, A. J. (2016). *Social development in Pakistan: An analytical study of shaping public policy.* www.linkedin.com/pulse/social-development-pakistan-analytical-study-shaping-public-rizvi.

Sarantakos, S. (2005). *Social research.* New York: Palgrave Macmillan.

Shah, N. A. (2015). Social work teaching in Pakistan problems and remedies. *New Horizon, 9*(1), 97–112.

Sheikh, I. (2014). Pakistan remains stagnant at 146 Human Development Index. Retrieved from *The Express Tribune.* http://tribune.com.pk/story/740478/human-development-index-pakistan-remains-stagnant-at-146/.

Simcock, P., & Castle, R. (2016). *Social work and disability.* Cambridge, UK: Polity Press.

Theobald, J., Gardner, F., & Long, N. (2014). Teaching critical reflection in social work field education. *Journal of Social Work Education, 50*(3), 1–12.

The State of Social Development in Urban Pakistan. (2016). *Social development in Pakistan: Annual Review 2014–15.* Karachi: Social Policy and Development Centre.

Trivedi, P. R., Singh, U. K., Nayak, A. K., Salpekar, A., Sharma, K., & Ao, I. (2013). *Social work education.* New Delhi: Jnanada Prakashan.

Watson, L. D., & Hoefer, R. (2014). Social work values in human services administration: Implications for social work education. *Journal of Social Work Education, 50*(4), 623–629.

Watson, L. D., & Hoefer, R. (2016). The joy of social work administration: An exploratory qualitative study of human service administrators' positive perceptions of their Work. *Journal of Social Work Education, 52*(2), 178–185.

Watts, T. D., Elliott, D., & Mayadas, N. S. (Eds.). (1995). International handbook on social work education. *The Journal of Sociology & Social Welfare, 23*(3), 175–188.

Wilson, G., & Campbell, A. (2013). Developing social work education: Academic perspectives. *The British Journal of Social Work, 43*(5), 1005–1023.

Zaidi, A. S. (2009). *A short history of Pakistan.* The South Asian Institute at Columbia University. http://www.columbia.edu/cu/sai/outreach_files/Syllabus%20A%20Short%20History%20of%20Pakistan.pdf.

Zaman, S. (1977). *Community development.* Peshawar, Pakistan: Taj Publishers.

CHAPTER 23

Social Work Education in Contemporary Sri Lanka: Issues and Challenges

H. Unnathi S. Samaraweera

BACKGROUND

Social work as a profession is not yet deeply rooted as an ideology either among commoners or in the education system in contemporary Sri Lanka. In the long run the historical philanthropic mentality will lead to narrowing it down to social service or volunteerism where social reputation and social acceptance of social work as a profession are somehow overlooked. The impact of the Tsunami in 2004 triggered the resurgence of professional social work in the country to such an extent that it was even taken into consideration within the higher education curriculum. Thus, social work got incorporated in the higher education system largely in Bachelor-level degree programmes as a stream of social work. The fact remains that—as was the case in most social sciences including sociology—academic knowledge related to social work was borrowed from European contexts within which the origin of methods, ethical considerations, and theoretical perspectives and approaches were mostly developed. Against this backdrop, establishing social work as an academic discipline was quite difficult in the Sri Lankan context. One of the main reasons was the ideology that reduced social work to volunteerism and social services. This commonsensical understanding curtailed the space for theoretical and practical components of the social work discipline to emphasise its professionalism. Cultural attributes derived from Sri Lanka as a welfare state also play a major role in this regard. The main issue here is there is no clear understanding about the discipline.

H. U. S. Samaraweera (✉)
Department of Sociology, University of Colombo, Colombo, Sri Lanka

S. S. M. et al. (eds.), *The Palgrave Handbook of Global Social Work Education*, https://doi.org/10.1007/978-3-030-39966-5_23

To find a solution to this the role of the social worker and the importance of such a practical discipline in post-war and post-disaster contexts have first to be described. The problem is not only the shortage of material resources but also the absence of human resources as there are shortfalls that must be addressed in knowledgeable academics and practitioners, funding, built environment resources, and cooperation from officers in the government and other institutions. Therefore, any solution has to take such practical issues into consideration. Social work methods discussed in academia need to be used in the field at the individual, group, and community level appropriately as a way of empowering service users thereby identifying gaps and limitations rather than merely critiquing those incompatible areas of social work methods that were originally developed in the Western context.

Information about the issues and challenges discussed in this chapter were mainly collected during fieldwork and recorded in field diaries maintained by the author as a social worker in Sri Lanka over the last decade. Such information covered the experiences of different social institutions and urban communities such as universities, disability centres, residential homes for the elderly, children's homes, rehabilitation centres for drug addicts, sex worker rehabilitation centres, and a number of other underserved communities within the city of Colombo.

The main objective of the chapter is to discuss the issues and challenges facing Sri Lankan academia in relation to social work and to highlight some areas that need to be further developed for the betterment of social work education. Since the chapter is focussed on contemporary Sri Lanka the historical roots of social work education are briefly discussed as background information for the chapter. However, the main focus is the contemporary setting.

HISTORICAL ROOTS OF SOCIAL WORK EDUCATION IN SRI LANKA

Sri Lanka has long been a welfare society in which major significance has been given to social welfare of the country (Jayasuriya, 2000). The lengthy history of the social welfare system is one of the reasons social work education has been neglected in Sri Lanka. A distinction between the social welfare system and the professionalism of the social work field has not yet been properly made.

It is important to keep in mind that Sri Lankan social work education has also been influenced by international collaborations through the United Nations and countries such as India and member-states of the European Union, which has made it difficult to separate native and foreign social work theories and practices in the country (Ranaweera, 2013; Zaviršek & Herath, 2010). However, the literature available to study the historical roots of social work education in Sri Lanka is limited and sometimes contradictory. What is evident is that social work education has not been given due importance in the Sri Lankan context. Moreover, the few sources available on the topic do not adequately analyse the historical development of social work.

According to Herath (2017) the colonial regime in Ceylon appointed a social service commission in 1948. This was preceded by establishment of the Beveridge Commission in the United Kingdom. This influenced the Ceylon colonial regime to subsequently establish such a commission in the country. The commission was mainly focussed on wide-ranging issues related to poverty. Findings of the commission highlighted the significance of institutionalisation of social services that resulted in establishment of the Department of Social Services. The department mainly focussed on consolidating and employing numerous welfare activities that identified the need for professionally trained social workers in the country (ibid.).

Furthermore, initiatives taken by the United Nations at the global level highlighted the need to establish social work education and training in Sri Lanka. It was mainly non-governmental organisations (NGOs) working on the ground that raised the need for social work education and training (ibid.). Against this backdrop social work education was first introduced to Sri Lanka in 1952 (Dissanayake, 2003; Ranaweera, n.d.; Zaviršek & Herath, 2010). Launch of the Institute of Social Work is often identified as the first step toward social work education in the country (Zaviršek & Herath, 2010). Underlining the government's accountability for social work education the institute was subsequently put under the purview of the Ministry of Social Services (Weerasingham, 2003). In 1964 it was renamed the Ceylon School of Social Work when it became a government institution and later became the Sri Lanka School of Social Work in 1972 (The National Institute of Social Development (NISD) website, 2018).

Although the institute only offered short-term courses originally, in 1964 the institute introduced a 2-year full-time diploma programme conducted by internationally qualified staff (ibid.). The diploma programme was sustained by the United Nations and unlocked opportunities for international training and higher education (Zaviršek & Herath, 2010). From the beginning the institute aimed at teaching diverse subfields within social work and attempted to cover broader aspects such as voluntary organisations, the private sector, family welfare, probation and prisons, health and community, and rural work (ibid.).

Herath (2017, p. 44) claimed "the school, however, continued to be under the Ministry of Social Services administered by the civil service and never became a part of the higher educational system in the country." In contradiction to her view the NISD website (2018) reported that the Sri Lanka School of Social Work was instructed to upgrade as an independent institution in 1989 by the University Grants Commission (UGC) and after approval was granted by the Cabinet the school was upgraded and renamed as the National Institute of Social Development by an act of parliament (The National Institute of Social Development Act No. 41 of 1992). The main reason for the upgrade was to provide higher education in social work in the country (ibid.). This coupled with a recommendation made by the UGC in 2003 resulted in a memorandum of understanding (MoU) being signed between the National Institute of Social Development (NISD) and the University of Colombo to initiate collaboration with a local university to commence a Bachelor of social work programme under the NISD (ibid.).

In 2005 the institute was granted degree-awarding authority under Section 25A of the Universities Act No. 16 of 1978 published in the *Gazette Extraordinary* No. 1395/15 of 1 June 2005 by the Ministry of Social Services and Social Welfare (Herath, 2017; NISD website, 2018; Zaviršek & Herath, 2010). In December 2005 the NISD commenced a Bachelor's degree programme in social work (NISD website, 2018).

The NISD introduced the first social work Master's degree programme in Sri Lanka in 2008 (Zaviršek & Herath, 2010; NISD website, 2018). It was established under Section 25A of the Universities Act No. 16 of 1978 and published in the *Gazette Extraordinary* No. 1557/7 of 7 July 2008 (NISD website, 2018). The Master's programme was supported by the Canadian International Development Agency (CIDA) and entered the curriculum at the Queen's University, Kingston, Canada in collaboration with the Ministry of Social Services and Social welfare (NISD website, 2018; Ranaweera, 2013). Even though the Bachelor of social work degree programme was originally taught just in English, the institute has begun to run Diploma, Higher Diploma, and Bachelor's degree programmes in Sinhala, Tamil, and English as a way of opening up the space for undergraduates to work in their mother tongue (ibid.).

Today the NISD is the only institute focussing on social work education and offering Bachelor's and Master's degree programmes in Social Work (Ranaweera, n.d.). Presently, the NISD falls under the aegis of the Ministry of Social Empowerment and Welfare.

Even though the history of social work in Sri Lanka can be traced back to 1952, the social work degree programme under the NISD is more recent (commencing in 2005). This demonstrates that social work was never included in the curriculum of tertiary education. Simply put, despite social work celebrating a long historical path, the discipline as a profession in itself has unfortunately not evolved much ever since. It is important to point out that the Tsunami disaster in 2004 was the trigger recognizing the need for professional social workers in the country. During the Tsunami recovery period a team made up of professors and undergraduates from the Faculty of Social Work, University of Ljubljana, Slovenia conducted a project on social work practice at a summer camp in Sri Lanka along with staff and undergraduates from the Department of Sociology, University of Colombo (Herath, 2017). This was the trigger that highlighted the importance of establishing a robust professional social work network in the country and led to social work getting incorporated in other tertiary-level curricula in the country. As a result the Department of Sociology, University of Colombo initiated the development of a stream of social work undergraduates in 2009 in collaboration with the University of Ljubljana after signing an MoU that remained valid until the first batch of undergraduates in the social work stream completed their degree programme (Lešnik & Urek, 2010; Zaviršek & Herath, 2010). Supported by a team of qualified and trained staff from Ljubljana who visited as scholars the University of Colombo took the necessary steps to train their own staff in the field. The sustainability of the social work stream was thus ensured (Zaviršek & Herath, 2010). The author makes this point to show how social work was an untapped discipline in the public university system without even having qualified staff or a curriculum related to social work. The University of Ruhuna recently started a community development Diploma programme in social work (Zaviršek & Herath, 2010, p. 835). Moreover, the University of Sabaragamuwa and the University of Peradeniya now provide basic introductory social work courses for their undergraduates.

Although the introduction and establishment of social work have a long history in Sri Lanka (dating back to 1952), the way in which they have evolved and been sustained has unfortunately been poor. Nevertheless, we should not forget that community-based support systems are not new to Sri Lanka. "Community support and community living has been an inherent feature of the Sri Lankan culture throughout its long history" (Herath, 2017, p. 44). As a result of *Shramadana* (voluntarily donating labour) community-based religious and cultural services and functions have always been inherent historical features of Sri Lankan culture. Since professional social work was a new concept that could not reach its due level of professionalism, it was consequently reduced to social services or charity. On the other hand, such a philanthropic mentality actually minimised the prerequisites of relevant approaches to social work that could have been used for positive change in ground-level realities.

Misconceptions About the Social Work Discipline in Sri Lanka

Defining social work is a never-ending task since there are many features and objectives that vary spatiotemporally within which sociocultural patterns become highly important (Rode, 2017). Bartlett (1958/2003, cited in Rode, 2017) identified five interrelated parts under the definition of social work: purpose, knowledge, values, sanctions, and methods. Later Gordon (ibid.) revised the definition structuring it at a more conceptual level and highlighting social transactions as the main focus. In the Sri Lankan context social transactions are more communal and driven by cultural norms and values in which charity and volunteerism become inherent parts of society including social policies.

"Voluntary work creates inseparable part of [cannot be separated from] social policy" (Zozulakova & Kuzysin, 2012, p. 4). When it comes to differentiating between volunteerism and social work in the sociocultural context of Sri Lanka, practical issues beg the question as to whether social work is treated as a profession or whether it is simply defined as a part of volunteerism within the Sri Lankan context. Even though the role of a social worker extends beyond that of a volunteer in such sociocultural contexts, it has very often been rendered as a part of volunteerism.

Jirovec and Hyduk (1999) stated that there are two types of volunteerism: informal volunteerism and formal volunteerism. When a volunteer provides care within his or her own family it is defined as informal volunteerism. It becomes formal when a volunteer does it within an organisation. Although social work deals with both informal and formal volunteerism, it does so at a professional level that goes beyond mere volunteerism.

Tang and Morrow-Howell (2008) observed that older people tend to be recruited as volunteers within organisational structures in the United States because their experiences make them better suited to the American context. Coulshed and Orme (2006, p. 2) stated that "the social work profession promotes change, problem solving in human relationships and the empowerment and liberation of people to enhance well-being." Although a holistic approach to social work is universal, priorities, methods, and changes in social work practice differ according to cultural, historical, and socioeconomic conditions from one geopolitical location to another. It should be kept in mind that the matriarchal notion of volunteerism is arguably the most closely related to social work practice in Sri Lanka when trying to identify clear distinctions between social work practice and volunteerism.

Smith et al. (1995) noted that any activity which involves spending time, unpaid, doing something which aims to benefit someone (individuals or groups) other than or in addition to close relatives, or to benefit the environment could be defined as volunteerism. It explains five principles of volunteering: "mutually beneficial (to individual and organisation), independently chosen and freely given, enabling and flexible wherever possible, has a community or social benefit and offered to [for] not-for-profit activities." Gregorova (2012) explained that voluntarism is an inseparable part of the social work profession. Although such principles are related to social work practice in which volunteerism becomes a part of social work, social work is much more than volunteerism.

Although volunteerism is not a profession and can best be defined as an individual's dedication to improving a multitude of things in the environment, it is based on service-led programmes that have already been formulated. In contrast, social work is a profession that not only has service-led programmes but also methods that have already been devised. It is important to note that the usage of services and methods is based on professional requirements in the field of social work and the professionally built relationship between the social worker and the service receiver in such contexts. Note

Table 23.1   Summary of differences between social work and volunteerism

Social work	Volunteerism
Professional and academic discipline	Neither a professional nor an academic discipline
Involves theoretical and methodological interventions	Does not involve theoretical and methodological interventions
Aim is to empower	Aim has mainly to do with philanthropy
Service user ends up becoming an independent person	Service user is more likely to end up depending on volunteers
Social workers are professionals who can also be volunteers	Volunteers are not necessarily social workers
Professionally trained	Not always professionally trained

Source Field data gathered using the Semi-Structure Interview Method in 2014

also that social work is an internationally developed profession with a strong theoretical and methodological backdrop, whereas volunteerism is based on the willingness to provide care. Theoretical and methodological approaches that are critical to social work as an academic discipline and/or a profession are absent within volunteerism. Ironically, these elements are invisible in the social work setting in Sri Lanka due to the overwhelming charity and social welfare modes enabled in the Sri Lankan context.

Differences between social work and volunteerism according to social work graduates are indicated in Table 23.1.

Social work and volunteerism are two distinct fields (as mentioned above). However, in the Sri Lankan context a commonsensical understanding of these fields leads to misinterpreting the differences or homogenising them at the risk of social work being defined merely as volunteerism. Although volunteerism could not be completely treated as social work practice, it might in fact use a few social work professional interventions such as providing information, coordinating, and mediating. On the other hand, some volunteer activities such as making donations, providing material goods, and helping individuals go to the bathroom cause many to misinterpret social work as volunteerism, a misconception that commonly occurs within the Sri Lankan context. Even though social work and volunteerism are two different fields, in the Sri Lankan context there seems to be a hybridisation of social work and volunteerism resulting in the emergence of the notion that the two are interchangeable. Therefore, this misconception needs to be rectified such that the benefits from professional social work are clearly seen as optimised.

The reasons social work is treated as volunteerism in the Sri Lankan context include:

- professional social work is a concept new to the Sri Lankan context;
- the importance given to social work and its practice is low in Sri Lanka;
- the phrase "social work" is misunderstood as meaning "social services";

- proper recognition has not been given to social workers as professionals; and
- social work has yet to be recognised at the policy level.

Despite these reasons for the non-acceptance of social work as a profession and reducing it to volunteerism, there are some positive trends in the field of social work in contemporary Sri Lanka. There are institutions that teach social work at the tertiary level such as the NISD and certain government universities. Furthermore, there are a few cadre positions for social workers in some government and non-government institutions where they are given the august title psychosocial officers although their role is exactly that of a social worker. Awareness and sensibility to social work as a profession are gradually being established in contemporary Sri Lanka.

NEED FOR SOCIAL WORK EDUCATION IN SRI LANKA

Sri Lanka is a developing country where there is poverty and the disparity between rich and poor in urban and rural areas is large (Dundar et al., 2014). The Civil War that lasted 30 years added extreme inequality to socioeconomic conditions that further exacerbated matters. Poverty is intertwined with larger sociopolitical and cultural issues present in the country. The migration of Sri Lankan women as domestic workers to Middle East countries has become the highest foreign currency income source (Handapangoda, 2014). As a consequence interrelated social issues such as broken family ties, child abuse, and incest are high due to disintegration of the family and absence of a proper social security system. There are many other shortfalls of the social security system including people with disabilities who are given little visibility and few rights. Equally disempowered are sex workers and the LGBTQI community who are marginalised from the mainstream due to their sexual orientations and gender identities. Therefore, the need to establish a professional social work network is undeniable considering the social issues faced by these vulnerable communities in the country.

Relevant stakeholders including the government need to take the action needed to improve the standards of social work education while establishing a professional social work network in Sri Lanka. For instance, the Chinese government has taken steps to provide working opportunities to millions of low-paid workers in newly developed community services in Sri Lanka and has established a number of state-controlled community centres (Zaviršek & Herath, 2010).

ESTABLISHING SOCIAL WORK EDUCATION AS A PROFESSION

Social work is a practice-based profession and an academic discipline "that promotes social change and development, social cohesion, and the empowerment and liberation of people. Principles of social justice, human rights, collective responsibility and respect for diversities are central to social work. Underpinned by theories of social work, social sciences, humanities and indigenous knowledge, social work engages people and structures to address life challenges and enhance wellbeing" (International Federation of Social Workers, 2014).

Let us now turn to highlighting the ways in which social work education could be developed and established as a profession in Sri Lanka. Looking at the global context it is evident that social work education has proliferated in other countries and adapted the subject to local contexts while at the same time drawing on elements of the dominant Western model of social work. What is important though is the availability of some form of social work training and practice within local contexts. Noble (2004, p. 529) stated "Borrowing social work curriculum[s] from industrialised nations, such as the United Kingdom, the United States of America, Australia and New Zealand, social work programmes are evident in India, the Philippines, Singapore, Japan, Hong Kong and more recently in China, Korea, Vietnam, Thailand, Indonesia, Papua New Guinea, Samoa and other Pacific Islands." Although this subject mostly appears in the curriculum of tertiary-level education, there are different ways of incorporating social work into the curriculum of each country (Noble, 2004). However, there are difficulties here such as cultural and language barriers, geographical isolation, and lack of access to technologies that hinder the development of universal social work standards for social work education (ibid.). In parallel with his argument this chapter explains that adopting a predominantly Western universal social work model in Sri Lanka would be a mistake and that instead a social work curriculum should be developed that takes into consideration the sociocultural settings of the country.

Thus, while it is important to insert social work theoretical approaches and methods developed and used in the West into the curriculum, it is equally important for us as Sri Lankans to find ways to overcome the cultural, social, and language barriers that require social workers in Sri Lanka to come up with methods of our own that are socially and culturally specific.

In contemporary Sri Lanka the urgent need for professional help at the individual and the community level can clearly be seen when considering various social issues such as poverty, violence, and human rights violations and how they affect social actors including women, children, people with disabilities, prisoners, and sexual minority groups. Since education about social work as a profession is poorly understood any positive impact that it could have brought about is still absent.

In general, there are about 1500 social workers trained by the Sri Lanka School of Social Work under the aegis of the NISD. Yet, there is no proper mechanism to issue a licence to social workers or a system of registration (Ranaweera, n.d.). The only position directly linked to social work as a profession in the country is that of psychiatric social workers. Even though the social work profession is directly and indirectly connected with other professions such as social service officer, community officer, probation and child care officer, women's development officer and counsellor, the role of the social worker is not properly defined let alone adequately acknowledged. Such invisibility is also reflected in social work education where Sri Lankans have little awareness of the importance of such a discipline in the country.

While there is no precise estimate of the number of social workers and related employees required, Lešnik and Urek (2010, p. 273) refer to a figure of 30,000 social workers as Sri Lanka's current need as estimated by a former director of the NISD. However, the number of social workers engaged in practice is only 800 (Lešnik & Urek, 2010). This massive gap has been substantially filled by NGO sector employees who often lack the necessary education and training in social work (Herath, 2017).

The 2004 Tsunami highlighted the importance of establishing a strong professional social work network in the country since formal help for victims was clearly absent. Help was first provided by the military and then the Red Cross, local communities, NGOs, and other networks joined in the relief process (ibid.). The clear absence of state intervention in the form of professional care and support underscored not only the need for trained professional social workers in the country but also the lack of well-trained psychologists. As discussed earlier, this resulted in the establishment of an undergraduate social work programme that a group of social work students and lecturers visiting Sri Lanka to help with relief work in the aftermath of the Tsunami disaster played a major part in setting up (ibid.).

"Social work has absolutely no voice in shaping [a] country's policy framework" (Herath, 2017, p. 50). Given that context in this chapter the author would like to highlight some key areas that should be properly covered in Sri Lankan social work education. First and foremost, the social work discipline should be introduced at all tertiary-level higher education institutions not only as a core subject for undergraduates and postgraduates from social science backgrounds but also as an optional/non-credit course for undergraduates from other natural science backgrounds. This will allow developing the capacities and soft skills of graduate students who aspire to become professional social workers.

Social work theories such as the strengths perspective coupled with postmodern theories in social work and such methods as empowerment, individual mapping, risk analysis, community mapping, and narrative should be incorporated in the social work curriculum to tap into the practicalities of the subject. Furthermore, problem-solving mechanisms need to be carefully described before they can be applied. When incorporating these into the curriculum, it is equally important to pay attention to barriers such as language and problems of a sociocultural, political, and economic nature. Being a multiethnic and multireligious country it is equally important to develop language proficiency in Sinhala, Tamil, and English not just for communication between social workers and service users but also for official usage.

Although addressing sociocultural barriers would be extremely difficult and very subjective, developing an ideology in which studied theories and methods trickle down to the grassroot level of service users would be important. Such a level of application should be kept in mind while developing the curriculum further. In simple terms the curriculum has to identify and address sociocultural differences in the country.

CONCLUSION

The role of a social worker extends far beyond that of a volunteer. Social workers are professionals who can also be volunteers but volunteers are not necessarily social workers. As Department of Health in UK (2003, cited in Coulshed & Orme, 2006, p. 2) explained "the new award will require social workers to demonstrate their practical application of skills and knowledge and their ability to deliver a service that creates opportunities for service users." Therefore, what should be attempted is to create opportunities for service users at a professional level that needs to be reflected properly in the social work education system. However, within the existing sociocultural context in Sri Lanka the social work discipline has not evolved sufficiently to reach that level, which is why it has been treated simply as volunteerism. The misconception that social work is the same as volunteerism is a reductive and simplistic understanding that limits the role of professionalism among social workers. However, social work is an international professional discipline that has its own methods and theories as an academic discourse oriented toward the wellbeing of all service users.

Therefore, social work education should be aimed at bringing about possible changes within organisational structures and developing the wellbeing of service users. Empowerment, risk analysis, mapping, normalisation, individual planning, and recovery planning are a few theoretical implications that could have been used pragmatically as tools to move the subject on in a more appropriate way. Through these experiences the chapter has been able to recognise the barriers and limitations to establishing professional social work education in the Sri Lankan context that need to be overcome. As a final thought, the time has come for us to revisit and develop social work programmes in the country that are most likely to contribute to the betterment of society.

REFERENCES

Coulshed, V., & Orme, J. (2006). *Social work practice* (4th ed.). London: Palgrave Macmillan.

Dissanayake, D. (2003). The Sri Lanka school of social work: My life and times. In A. Ranaweera (Ed.), *Mathaka Satahan, Ninaiveduhal, memories of the past: 1952–2002* (pp. 57–111). Colombo: National Institute of Social Development.

Dundar, H., Millot, B., Savchenko, Y., Aturupane, H., & Piyasiri, T. A. (2014). *Building the skills for economic growth and competitiveness in Sri Lanka.* Washington: World Bank. https://doi.org/10.1596/978-1-4648-0158-7. Last Accessed on October 25, 2018.

Gregorova, A. B. (2012). The importance of volunteering in professional orientation: Spreading the knowledge and competencies among volunteers. *In Social work and voluntary activities H.E.L.P.* Published under Erasmus Project.

Handapangoda, W. S. (2014). Is transnational labour migration empowering for women? Re-evaluating the case of married Sri Lankan domestic maids. *Indian Journal of Gender Studies, 21*(3), 353–377. https://doi.org/10.1177/0971521514540704. Last Accessed on October 25, 2018.

Herath, S. M. K. (2017). Indian Ocean Tsunami and its influence on the resurgence of social work as an academic discipline in Sri Lanka. *European Journal of Social Work, 20*(1), 42–53. https://doi.org/10.1080/13691457.2016.1185706. Last Accessed on October 25, 2018.

International Federation of Social Workers. (2014). *International definition of social work.* Retrieved from http://ifsw.org/get-involved/global-definition-of-social-work/. Last Accessed on June 10, 2014.

Jayasuriya, L. (2000). *Sri Lanka: Experience of a third world welfare state.* Perth: The School of Social Work and Social Policy, The University of Western Australia.

Jirovec, R. L., & Hyduk, C. A. (1999). Type of volunteer experience and health among older adult volunteers. *Journal of Gerontological Social Work, 30*(3-4), 29–42. https://doi.org/10.1300/J083v30n03_04. Last Accessed on September 5, 2014.

Lešnik, B., & Urek, M. (2010). Traps of humanitarian aid: Observations from a village community in Sri Lanka. *European Journal of Social Work: Race, Ethnic Relations and Social Work, 13*(2), 271–2820. https://doi.org/10.1080/13691451003690908. Last Accessed on October 25, 2018.

NISD website. (2018). http://www.nisd.lk/web/. Colombo: National Institute of Social Development. Last Accessed on October 25, 2018.

Noble, C. (2004). Social work education, training and standards in the Asia–Pacific region. *Social Work Education, 23*(5), 527–536. https://doi.org/10.1080/0261547042000252262. Last Accessed on October 25, 2018.

Ranaweera, A. (2013). *Review and record of the history of social work education in Sri Lanka.* Colombo: National Institute of Social Development.

Ranaweera, A. (n.d.). *Social work education in Sri Lanka.* National Institute of Social Development web page. http://www.nisd.lk/web/index.php/en/component/content/article/122-article3.html. Last Accessed on March 2, 2018.

Rode, N. (2017). Defining social work is a never-ending story. *European Journal of Social Work, 20*(1), 64–75. https://doi.org/10.1080/13691457.2016.1185704. Last Accessed on October 25, 2018.

Smith, J. D., Rochester, C. & Hedley, R. (1995). Introduction. In J. D. Smith, C. Rochester & R. Hedley (Eds.), *An Introduction to the Voluntary Sector* (pp.1–8). London: Routledge.

Tang, F., & Morrow-Howell, N. (2008). Involvement in voluntary organizations: How older adults access volunteer roles? *Journal of Gerontological Social Work, 51*(3–4), 210–227. https://doi.org/10.1080/01634370802039494. Last Accessed on September 5, 2014.

Weerasingham, M. (2003). Wither social welfare, social work in Sri Lanka. In A. Ranaweera (Ed.), *Mathaka Satahan, Ninaiveduhal, memories of the past: 1952–2002* (pp. 49–55). Colombo: National Institute of Social Development.

Zaviršek, D., & Herath, S. M. K. (2010). 'I want to have my future, I have a dialogue': Social work in Sri Lanka between neo-capitalism and human rights. *Social Work Education, 29*(8), (pp. 831–842). https://doi.org/10.1080/02615479.2010.51698 7. Last Accessed on October 25, 2018.

Zozulakova, V., & Kuzysin, B. (2012). Forward. *In Social work and voluntary activities H.E.L.P.* Published under Erasmus Project.

CHAPTER 24

Movement Towards Indianisation of Social Work Education

Bishnu Mohan Dash

INTRODUCTION

In the last few years there has been serious debate among social work academia about the existing curriculum and pedagogy of social work education offered in Indian universities since it does not conform to *Bharatiya* ("Indian") social work values and culture and is hence alien to *Bharat* ("India"). Given the vast diversity and complexity of Indian society and the fast-changing socioeconomic and political situation social work professionals are expected to play a significant role in the resurgence of India as a modern developed democratic nation. The need for both indigenisation and universalisation of social work education has been gaining momentum in the past few years. Recently three conferences were organised. They took place at Bhim Rao Ambedkar College (University of Delhi, Delhi); Mahatma Gandhi Antarashtriya Hindi Vishwa Vidyalaya (Wardha, Maharashtra), and Tumkur University (Tumkur, Karnataka) where I acted as Convenor, Co-Convenor, and Co-Convenor, respectively. In this chapter I have made use of some of the literature in conference brochures and some of my writings in various newspapers.

The Indian social work curriculum has been primarily American-centric and Eurocentric since its inception in 1936. The effectiveness and universality of Western knowledge, homogenised curriculum in Indian universities has been questioned in several forums since it is not keeping pace with the changing socioeconomic and political contexts of India, is unable to address

B. M. Dash (✉)
Department of Social Work, Bhim Rao Ambedkar College,
University of Delhi, Delhi, India

© The Author(s) 2021
S. S. M. et al. (eds.), *The Palgrave Handbook of Global Social Work Education*, https://doi.org/10.1007/978-3-030-39966-5_24

changing societal needs and problems, and despite more than eight decades of social work education in India it is still not considered a profession. In my article "Is Social Work a Profession in Bharat 'India'?"[1] published in the *New Delhi Times* I categorically mentioned that:

> there are several structural and functional deficiencies in the social work curriculum and field work training in [the] Indian context; so it is the need of [the] hour to restructure and revise the entire social work syllabus to suit in [the] Indian context. However, formulation of the *Bharatiya* Model of Social Work will be vital necessity to groom professional social workers to effectively handle emerging social problems.

Against this backdrop, the movement for the *Bharatiyakaran*[2] ("Indianisation") of social work education aims to tweak the entire social work curriculum to create a synergy between Indian traditional social services and practices and global standards of social work education. The movement for the *Bharatiyakaran* of social work aims to give a new perspective and new direction to social work education in the Indian context through redesigning and redefining the social work curriculum by bringing about a synergy between Indian wisdom and international standards of social work education. Whatever changes were made in the social work curriculum over the past eight decades were done within the Western paradigm. India's ancient civilisational wisdom in the field of social service and community development have at last been included in the process of designing the new curriculum.

Need for the *Bharatiyakaran* of Social Work Curriculum

Social work education has been taught in India for the last 80 years. It has been taught at institutions scattered far and wide across the country in these years. Notwithstanding this, social work knowledge imparted in schools of social work across the country remain Eurocentric. Moreover, the social work curriculum at the BSW, MSW, and the PhD level is Eurocentric too. The curriculum includes very little content that can be termed Indian in spirit. The authors of Indian social science and social work literature included in the reference list of syllabuses by and large look at Indian social realities from the perspective of European realities. It is a major concern that the relevance and adequacy of social science theories and social work practice models taught in Indian classrooms have yet to be tested for their empirical validity or adequacy in Indian contexts. Moreover, the effectiveness of the social work models, methods, and techniques imparted in classrooms and through fieldwork training has yet to be proven to work in Indian contexts since they have never been tested and validated in such a context. The lofty claim that social work is a scientific discipline has yet to be validated in Indian contexts despite a number of research projects and the PhD research work undertaken in the country.

Social work educators from Africa and China are challenging Eurocentricism in social work education and practice. They are proposing Afrocentric and Sinocentric social science and social work education models and perspectives for use in practice. They have been attempting to develop social work paradigms inspired by the philosophical and cultural wisdom of their own countries. The Afrocentric and Sinocentric paradigms proposed are important parts of the global literature on social work education and practice. There are social work educators in the United States who are challenging the imposition of Western models of social work education as little short of professional imperialism. Internationally, the debate on indigenisation vis-à-vis universalisation of social work knowledge is continuing. In fact the International Federation of Social Workers' (IFSW) global definition of social work recognises indigenous knowledge as just as important as theories of social work, social sciences, and humanities in the knowledge base of the social work profession. Unfortunately, social work educators in India have not participated in the global debate on Eurocentricism or professional imperialism. Rather, some Indian social work educators are advocating giving greater weight to radical approaches to social work practice in social work education. Attempts have been made to rechristen anti-oppressive social work as dalit or tribal social work.

Understanding the reality and complexity of Indian society in light of ongoing socioeconomic and political trends and their impact on society clearly demonstrates that the social work profession has a significant role to play in the resurgence of India as an ancient civilisation and as a developed modern democratic nation. The broad concerns of the social work profession are equity, social justice, harmony, and directing activities to support marginalised groups to meet their needs. Social work professionals are expected to respond to the social realities of contemporary society. Social work training needs to take note of all these contextual issues and incorporate them in the curriculum, classroom teaching, field practice, and research studies to make the learning relevant and more applicable. It is in this national context that social work educators and practitioners need to review, critique, and reformulate Indian efforts at Indianising the social work knowledge base and methodological orientations.

India as a civilisation has a long and rich literary, artistic, philosophical, scientific, and technological heritage. Unfortunately, this rich heritage has been ignored in the development of social sciences or the social work knowledge base of the country. In the pre-independence period, nationalist thinkers and leaders of the freedom movement emphasised the ideals of the *Swadeshi* (efforts to develop indigenous social science), *Swatantra* (Indigenous methods/techniques), and *Swarajya* (self rule) in every sphere of life. Yet in the post-independence period such values were not taken into account when it came to building the nation, national development, or educational advancement. The post-independence political, administrative, academic, and media climate remained and still remains Eurocentric and looks down on Indian knowledge systems in every field. There have been efforts to replace Indian knowhow in every field with modern Western knowhow without scientifically assessing the relative costs and benefits of them. The Eurocentricist claim that Indian knowledge in the fields of agriculture, healthcare, and food processing is obsolete is increasingly being proved wrong.

The social work curriculum in India has not only excluded Indian knowledge systems and philosophy but also pioneering services done in the fields of social emancipation, welfare, and development by Indian nationalist organisations and spiritual organisations. Concerted efforts to tap the wisdom of Indian, dharmic, spiritual, and nationalist organisations in promoting the wellbeing of people would have contributed such a lot to a rich indigenous theory and value base in social work.

As a result of Eurocentricism prevailing in social work education, Indian experience being excluded from social welfare, and pseudo-scientific Western social science and social work theories being imparted instead, professional social workers lack emic perspective. Eurocentricism prevents social work educators from generating significant social science or social work theories or debating with Western counterparts for want of a national original theory or *Siddhanta*. This is not simply a problem with social work education in India but a global one prevailing throughout the Third World. There is widespread resentment toward Eurocentricism and European supremacism in the Third World today—this is particularly the case in India where there is a widespread movement behind the decolonisation and indigenisation of social work. A recent global definition of social work by the IFSW (2014) recognises indigenous knowledge as just as important as the theories of social sciences and social work in the knowledge base of the social work profession. The major lacuna in the definition is that the idea of indigenous knowledge has been confined to that of tribal people. The IFSW's global definition fails to recognise the uniqueness and relevance of knowledge systems embedded in the cultures and civilisations of the Third World and suffers from a Eurocentric mindset.

Despite serious debates taking place in the global arena on Eurocentricism, social work educators and professional associations have given scant regard to it in India where major debate has been confined to micro vs macro methods and therapeutic vs activist models. Such a debate is not just confined to social work educators located in Delhi and Mumbai, professional bodies led by social work educators also continue to promote Western concepts and theoretical frameworks through national conferences and seminars organised all over India and little space is given to proponents of the *Bharatiyakaran* of social work education in India.

However, members of the social work fraternity feel there is an urgent need for the *Bharatiyakaran* of *Samaj Karya* ("Indianization of social work"). To bring about the *Bharatiyakaran* of social work some members of the social work fraternity joined together and organized a national conference held at Dr B. R. Ambedkar College in Delhi with active support from Bharatiya Shikshan Mandal and Mahatma Gandhi Antarrashtriya Hindi Vishwavidyalaya (Wardha, Maharashtra) and later a national conference at Tumkur University (Tumkur, Karnataka). Efforts were made to build a *Bharatiyakaran* of social work curriculum by conducting a national workshop in Wardha. The workshop objectives were to challenge Eurocentricism and European supremacy and to promote the *Bharatiyakaran* of social work by drawing inspiration from India's rich knowledge systems, experiences, and experiments promoting wellbeing in varied Indian contexts. *Bharatiyakaran* of the social work curriculum is holistic, integrated, and anti-discriminatory in nature. The concept of *Bharatiyakaran* is based on three major premises: Indianisation, indigenisation, and decolonisation. It is important to note that *Bharatiyakaran* is not synonymous with Indianisation in the context of the *Bharatiyakaran* of social work. The Indianisation of social work strives to include Indian models, approaches, values, ethics, and practices of social work and integrate perspectives of Indian scriptures, culture and rituals, Indian experiences, and an Indocentric fieldwork practicum in social work education. Indigenisation is the process of developing local ideas, perspectives, regional experiences, and indigenous innovations in Third World countries. Indian indigenous models of sanitation, housing, and water harvesting have been added to *Bharatiyakaran* of the social work curriculum. In the process of decolonising the social work curriculum attempts were made to reject irrelevant and outdated knowledge imposed on India by Eurocentric and American-centric scholars who attempted to make it more relevant and applicable to Indian settings (Dash, 2018a). However, *Bharatiyakaran* of the social work curriculum is not entirely opposed to Western theories of social work and retains relevant Western material in the curriculum. *Bharatiyakaran* of the social work curriculum is an educative, continuous, and consultative process where more than 32 experts from various leading schools of social work actively participated in designing the curriculum that has been partially implemented in various universities in India.

The *Bharatiyakaran* of social work involves promoting *Swadeshi*, *Swatantra*, and *Swadrushti* ("self-sight"), respectively, when it comes to theory, method, and perspective. The *Bharatiyakaran* of social work calls for an emic perspective that is *Swadrushti* in nature to understand India's social reality and challenges embedded in it. *Swadeshi* is an effort to develop indigenous social science and social work theories and practice models that draw inspiration from Indian philosophy ancient, medieval, and modern. Vedic, Vedantic, Buddhist, Jain, and Sikh philosophies and worldviews are what lie behind promoting *Swadeshi* in social work theory building. They do help to challenge the universality of Western social work knowledge. *Swatantra* denotes the methodology of promoting the wellbeing of people inspired by dharmic values and Indian experiences in addressing Indian challenges.

Thus, the major challenge facing advocates of the *Bharatiyakaran* of social work theory and practice is building an Indian knowledge base for social work that is organically linked with India's rich intellectual, spiritual, and cultural heritage. There are two major ways of theory-building from the Indian point of view. One is theory-building from different schools of Indian philosophy and the other is to theorise from the experience of practitioners and dharmic organisations at work in varied fields. Since every school of Indian thought has been developed to address human problems there is little gap between theory and practice. Hence, theorising from philosophy and practice is feasible and possible. Likewise, theorising and building models from practice wisdom will generate knowledge and techniques that are highly effective.

The practice of social work is as old as human civilisation. Selfish instincts and greed for power have been responsible for a great deal of human suffering across the globe. Simultaneously, concern for the poor and providing assistance to people generally have been part and parcel of human civilisation. World religions such as Hinduism, Christianity, and Islam are the primary sources underlying the provision of welfare services to curb the suffering of people. *Bharat* ("India") under the broad aegis of Hinduism is strongly founded on concerns for human wellbeing. *Bharatiya* history is flooded with initiatives taken by kings, queens, and social reformers to improve the lot of vulnerable groups, in particular, and to elevate the wellbeing of everybody, in general. The idea of social work that emerged in the Western world under the influence of humanism, rationalism, welfarism, liberalism, democracy, secularism, and utilitarianism as a discipline and later as a profession was characteristically more strategic and less welfaristic. Hinduism, one of the oldest living religions, with a history stretching from around the second millennium BC to the present, is India's indigenous religious and cultural system. It encompasses a broad spectrum of philosophies ranging from pluralistic theism to absolute monism. It has no founder and no single code of beliefs; it has no central headquarters; it never had any religious organisation that wielded temporal power over its followers; nor does it have a single scripture as the source of its teachings. It possesses great power as a result of assimilating and absorbing numerous schools of thoughts that appeal to people of all communities. Every religion consists of three parts: philosophy, mythology, and ritual. Philosophy is an abstract spiritual idea found in religious scriptures and texts; mythology is a set of stories and beliefs about the legendary lives of great men and fables about wonderful things; and rituals are beliefs, customs, and symbols. Rituals provide philosophy with a much more concrete form so that everyone can grasp it. Historically, *Dharma* ("inherent nature of reality") has been the guiding force motivating and inspiring social concern in *Bharat*.

Although *Bharat* was one of the foremost richest cultures to take up social concerns, continuous foreign invasions and many centuries of alien rule and subsequent change in the social ethos and social structure resulted in family ties and community belonging starting to get weaker. The needs of individuals were no longer fulfilled and taken care of within the family and societal structure. It facilitated third-party intervention and *Bharatiya* society started accepting Western values and opened itself up to learning from their experiences. Furthermore, the two ultra-ideal *Bharatiya* concepts—namely, anonymity and selfless action—provided fertile ground for Western powers to seed their ideas in Indian minds.

Bharat first witnessed formal and modern social work trends through Christian missionaries. Missionaries in Serampore were the first evangelical Baptist missionaries in India. They identified a series of social issues within the Indian social structure. The first formal education of social work in *Bharat* started with the establishment of the Sir Dorabji Tata Graduate School of Social Work (presently known as the Tata Institute of Social Sciences) at Mumbai in 1936. Social work as a subject and as a profession is characteristically an alien concept. Early phases of the social work education curriculum were borrowed from the United Kingdom and the United States. Social work, curriculum, objectives, pedagogy, and overall practice do not conform with Indian basic values and culture. They cannot therefore address *Bharat*-specific social problems. Although it is claimed that the crux of social work is rooted in humanistic principles, in practice it appears more strategic, agenda based, and targeted at achieving certain personal illicit goals. In the *Bharatiya* context it is believed that helping should be performed in a silent manner without revealing the name of the person who helped (i.e., anonymously) or blowing their trumpet. It is also believed that social work should be extended without expectation of any personal gain. The notion of getting paid for services offered to the needy, publicising the help given, expecting the receivers of help to embrace the beliefs of the donor or service provider and in some cases even using social services as a covert drive to recruit a silent army for a particular purpose are characteristic features of Western professional social work that are antithetical to the *Bharatiya* value system. Ironically, despite 80 years of social work education in *Bharat* philosophies, most principles, theories, methods, and techniques taught at various levels continue to remain Western world dominated. Consequently, there is a continuing trend to look at *Bharatiya* life and problems from the perspective of outsiders. To make social work as a discipline academically and socially relevant the need of the hour is to understand the realities and complexities of *Bharatiya* society from an indigenous perspective in concurrence with being prepared to face upcoming socioeconomic and political challenges. Social work education has a significant role to play in the resurgence of *Bharat* and to re-establishing its glory as *Vishwa-Guru* ("reformer and teacher of the entire world"). The major challenges facing the social work profession are equality, equity, social justice, social harmony, and helping marginalised groups assert their identities. The solution to all these issues lies in adding rich *Bharatiya* wisdom to the social work curriculum, classroom teaching, and field practice and research studies to make learning more relevant and more applicable.

BHARATIYAKARAN OF THE INDIAN SOCIAL WORK CURRICULUM

Since its inception there has been no change in the curriculum, research, teaching, and training in social work education. Although there may be some elements of universality and utility in imparting the colonial model of social work education, applying Eurocentric models in their entirety is going to further deteriorate the quality of social work education in India. At this critical period social work academics should free themselves of the status quo and look instead at studying the traditional Indian roots of social work, initiatives of social reformers and philanthropists, models of rural reconstruction experiments, and Indian spiritual ideals and values (Dash, 2018b). What is worse, most schools/universities in India have adopted the Western model of the social work curriculum without examining its suitability to India characterised as it is by having a multiethnic, multicultural, multilingual, and multireligious environment. It is difficult to claim that any development in social work education in India was in response to any substantial expression of local need for such professional preparation. The sudden gap brought about by the introduction of a new professional mode of social work education and discontinuation of traditional social services has hampered growth of the social work profession. Although the American model of social work education was developed in a systematic manner on the foundations of Judeo-Christian values, democratic organisations, and theories of social change (Rao, 1969), Indian social work adopted Western imported material without testing its validity, suitability, and applicability. One of the major weaknesses of professional social work education in India is the lack of uniformity in the curriculum throughout the country; in fact, even within states there is lack of uniformity in the university curriculum as shown in the syllabi of autonomous colleges (Ilango & Francis, 2012 cited in Jyoti, 2015). According to Yasas (1971) systematic development of indigenous teaching material not only for method courses but also for every course in the curriculum is urgent. So, the social work profession in India still needs to eliminate American influences and methods of practice such that the student will possess a broad knowledge base and have solid practical skills (Howard, 1971). The absence of a coherent curriculum that challenges imported Eurocentric and American-centric knowledge, paradigms, theories, and methodologies urgently needs to be addressed. The observations made by Flexner more than 100 years ago still characterise the same situation in India. Consequently, there is a continuing trend to look at *Bharatiya* life and problems from the perspective of outsiders. The University Grants Commission (UGC) constituted the first review committee on social work education in 1960, and the second review committee on social work education in 1975 to promote and maintain the quality and standards of social work education, training, research, and practice in India. The third review committee on social work education was constituted by the UGC in 2001 and tasked with providing a model curriculum in social work education. Despite a small number of changes made in the curriculum, it has remained unfit for purpose to suit Indian realities as it has not been thoroughly indigenised. Overreliance on Western ideologies of social work has not only halted the *Bharatiyakaran* of social work education but also helped perpetuate Western curricula in Indian universities. Several social work academics have written extensively on the urgent need to indigenise the curriculum, strongly criticised the Western model, and made emphatic deliberations on the need for a newer and relevant curriculum for social work education in India (Nadkarni & Joseph, 2014). Various alarming situations have hampered the growth of social work in India that has led to the profession suffering a credibility problem (Dash, 2017). It is now widely felt that *Bharatiya* philosophy, values, wisdom, culture, and experiences need to be incorporated in the social work curriculum to make it inclusive, holistic, and relevant to the Indian context.

Efforts Towards *Bharatiyakaran* of the Social Work Curriculum

To Indianise the social work curriculum a national conference titled "Indian Social Work: Scope and Challenges"[3] was held over 14–15 March 2018 in Delhi. It was sponsored by the Indian Council of Social Science Research (Government of India) and was the first of its kind. The purpose of the conference was to rediscover Indian perspectives toward social work, decolonise academic discourse, and lay down the foundation stone for the *Bharatiyakaran* of social work education in India. The conference provided a platform for speakers to discuss the philosophical, ideological, and methodological strengths of *Bharatiya* perspectives in social work education in great depth and compare them with incompatible, inadequate, colonial American-centric and Eurocentric perspectives. Consequently, a national workshop[4] was held at Mahatma Gandhi Antarrashtriya Hindi Vishwa Vidyalaya (Wardha, Maharashtra) in academic partnership with Bharatiya Shikshan Mandal (a voluntary organisation working in education) on 29–30 June 2018 to draft a social work curriculum in which social work curriculum would have the aim of infusing Indian philosophical, cultural, and civilisational wisdom into social work literature, methods, techniques, and fields of practice. While identifying relevant sources of Indian indigenous knowledge that would strengthen social work education all writings, legends, and Indian rituals deemed relevant to social work practices as well as Indian experiences on rural development and reconstruction were to be kept in mind during preparation of the syllabus. Although restructuring the curriculum is of course an ongoing process undertaken by universities, revisions in the curriculum are not undertaken systematically. While preparing *Bharatiyakaran* of the social work curriculum, the overall structure of the programme was discussed, analysed, and finalised in consultation with experts and in line with UGC guidelines and framework. Core papers and discipline research papers listed by the UGC were retained and their contents developed on the basis of deliberation, discussion, and consultation. The idea was to get about 30% of the contents of the existing curriculum based on Indian wisdom.

Rich social service traditions, religion, and spirituality were given due place in the curriculum. The new *Bharatiya* curriculum includes lessons from ancient Indian texts such as *Shukra Niti*, *Vidur Niti*, *Nyaya Shastra*, and *Natyashastra*. It also contains the basic tenets of Hinduism, Buddhism, Jainism, Sikhism, Christianity, and other major religions. Social reform movements, rural reconstruction experiments, and the philosophical beliefs of leading philosophers in India such as Nanaji Deshmukh, Ambedkar, Gandhi, Vivekananda, Guru Nanak, Narayan Guru, Jyotiba Phule, and Vinoba Bhave were integrated in the social work curriculum so that students would understand the social transformations brought about in India by the initiatives of individuals and those of social movements. Each and every subject at the Master's level as part of the social work curriculum helped to get *Bharatiya* concepts, paradigms, and theories included in the syllabus. The newly structured curriculum incorporated concepts described in the paper entitled "Fundamentals of Social Work" regarding Kalyan, Mangal, Yogashema, Sukha, Dukha, Bakthi, Vedanta, the Sufi Movement, Indian traditional values, Purusharthas, Viduras, and the Golden Rules of Reciprocity. The curriculum included contributions about Arya Samaj (reform movement of modern Hinduism), Brahmo Samaj (the societal component of Brahmoism), the Ramakrishna Mission (Hindu religious and spiritual organisation), and the Sufi Movement. Indian components were taken paper "Psychology for Social Workers" and included in the curriculum. Such components covered the Indian approach to life, Ashrama, body, and mind; Pancha Koshas, Sankhya, and Yoga on mind; Antahkaranas, states of human consciousness; Yoga, Buddhism, Jainism, and Vedanta; the Triguna theory of personality; the concept of Self; and Buddhist, Vedantic, and humanistic models. Indian components such as Shukra Niti, Shantiparv, Chanakyaniti, the ideologies and perspectives of Swami Vivekananda, Mahatma Gandhi, and Vinoba Bhave were added in the paper social policy and added to the curriculum. When it came to urban community development the Indian approaches of sarvodaya, the contributions of Jaya Prakash Narayan (an Indian independence activist), the Health, Sanitation, and Livelihood Model of the Tamil Nadu Slum Clearance Board (Chennai), the Urban Renewal Mission, and *Swachh Bharat Abhiyan* (Clean India Mission)—flagship programmes of the government of India—were added to the syllabus. A paper on mental health included various Indian aspects included in the curriculum. Concepts and approaches such as prayer through *mantras* ("rhymes"), the Rig Veda, prayers for mental happiness, methods of increasing intelligence and power of mind in healing, mental health and Buddhism, mindfulness and its roots in eastern religions such as Buddhism, Taoism, and Hinduism, Buddhist teachings and mental health were also included in the curriculum. Buddhist approaches to mental illness and spiritual tradition, the doctrine and role of Ayurveda (a system of medicine with historical roots in India) in mental health also gained entry to the curriculum. Various Ayurvedic techniques, procedures, and regimes; the philosophy of *Pancha bhootas* ("five element theory") of living bodies; the Siddha system of medicine; the Unani system of medicine; herbal medicines; Yoga and naturopathy; Patanjali's Astanga Yoga, yogic therapies and meditations; and hydrotherapy were also included in the curriculum. The paper entitled "Rural Development" was used to get various Indian components such as peasant movements; Bhoodan and land reforms; green revolution and farmers' movements; backward classes and dalit movements; Gandhian approach to rural development; Indian traditional arts and crafts included in the curriculum. This paper also added Indian rural development initiatives such as natural farming; the Organic Consumption Model of Dhabolkar, Palekar, Shiva, and Nammazhvar; and the Water Harvesting and Renewable Energy Model of Anna Hazare and Rajendra Singh to the curriculum. The curriculum now also includes the Low-cost Housing and Sanitation Model of L. Baker and B. Pathak. Senior academics from the Tata Institute of Social Sciences (Mumbai), the Delhi School of Social Work, Jamia Millia Islamia, Central University of Rajasthan, Central University of Kerala, Bharathidasan University (Chennai, Tamil Nadu), Assam Central University, Central University of Karnataka, Udaipur School of Social Work, Nagpur University, Punjabi University, Mizoram University, Mysore University, Pondicherry University, and others participated in development of the curriculum. Several universities in India almost fully adopted the *Bharatiyakaran* of the social work curriculum at the Master's level in social work, while others partially adopted it. In addition to curriculum development the Fraternity of Social Work got together at a curriculum development workshop and decided to celebrate 11 October, the birthday of Nanaji Deshmukh,[5] who made major contributions to rural development and tribal empowerment in the states of Uttar Pradesh, Madhya Pradesh, Maharashtra, and Rajasthan, as *Bharatiya Samaj Karya Diwas* ("Indian Social Work Day"). The request to formally declare 11 October as Indian Social Work Day was sent to the government of India for consideration.

The curriculum was developed in such a way that students could familiarize themselves with the core values and philosophy of the social work profession and could embrace them in their professional selves. It was further developed to familiarize the student with Indian approaches to nature, human relations, wellbeing, and their relevance in social work education. It will enable them to understand Indian philosophical approaches to social welfare and the importance of religion in social work. The newly structured curriculum will also help them understand issues relating to professional imperialism, Eurocentrism, and the indigenous social work perspectives of Africa and China. The social work fraternity assembled in the curriculum development workshop pledged[6] themselves to continue contributing to the *Bharatiyakaran* of social work education in India.

Conclusion

Bharatiyakaran of the social work curriculum involved reawakening indigenous theoretical and practice frameworks and paradigms and making them part of the social work curriculum. Although *Bharatiyakaran* of the social work curriculum was a revolutionary step and a sudden departure from its earlier trajectory in an attempt to bring about social emancipation, it also gave utmost importance to the plurality of diverse social work traditions, paradigms, and theories that essentially chime with international standards in the discipline.

Acknowledgements The author acknowledges the constructive comments and suggestions of Prof. Kanagaraj Easwaran, Head, Department of Social Work, Mizoram University (Aizawl, Mizoram, India) and Shri Mukul Kanitkar, National Organising Secretary, BSM, Nagpur.

Notes

1. https://www.newdelhitimes.com/is-social-work-a-profession-in-bharat-india/.
2. Social Work Fraternity tasked with creating a new curriculum and an Indian Social Work Day, http://www.newdelhitimes.com/social-work-fraternity-to-get-new-curriculum-and-indian-social-work-day/, https://www.duexpress.in/masters-in-social-work-gets-bharatiya-curriculum/.
3. A national conference entitled "Indian Social Work: Scope and Challenges" was held in Delhi over 14–15 March 2018 jointly by Bhim Rao Ambedkar College (University of Delhi) and Mahatma Gandhi Antarrashtriya Hindi Viswa Vidyalaya (Wardha, Maharashtra) and sponsored by the Indian Council of Social Science Research (government of India), https://results.amarujala.com/career-diary/national-conference-in-delhi-university-to-decolonise-the-social-work-education.
4. National Workshop on the *Bharatiyakaran* of social work education, https://economictimes.indiatimes.com/news/politics-and-nation/remove-colonial-influences-in-courses-on-social-work-rss-to-tell-universities/articleshow/64581978.cms.
5. 11 October was approved to be celebrated as Indian Social Work Day by the government, https://www.newdelhitimes.com/social-work-fraternity-celebrated-nanaji-deshmukhs-birthday-as-bharatiya-social-work-day/, https://www.dailypioneer.com/2019/columnists/social-work-curriculum-gets-an-indian-icon.html.
6. Eleven-point action plan for the Indianisation of social work education, https://economictimes.indiatimes.com/news/politics-and-nation/rss-body-suggests-11-point-action-plan-for-indianisation-of-courses/articleshow/64834524.cms.

References

Dash, B. M. (2017). Revisiting eight decades of social work education in India. *Asian Social Work and Policy Review, 11*, 66–75.

Dash, B. M. (2018a). *Bharatiyakaran of social work education-understanding the meaning and concept.* Retrieved from https://www.newdelhitimes.com/bharati-yakaran-of-social-work-understanding-the-meaning-and-concept/. December 7, 2018.

Dash, B. M. (2018b). *Revamp social work education.* The Pioneer 14 March, 2018, Retrieved from https://www.dailypioneer.com/avenues/revamp-social-work-education.html. August 10, 2018.

Howard, J. (1971). Indian society, Indian social work-identifying Indian principles and methods of social work practice. *International Social Work, 14*(4), 16–31.

International Federation of Social Workers (IFSW). (2014). *Global Definition of Social Work.* Retrieved from https://www.ifsw.org/what-is-social-work/global-definition-of-social-work/. December 21, 2018.

Jyoti, H. P. (2015). Issues and challenges of social work education in Karnataka. *EPRA International Journal of Economic & Business Review, 3*(1), 61–70.

Nadkarni, V. V., & Joseph, S. (2014). *Envisioning a professional identity: Charting pathways through social work education in India.* In Noble et.al., Global Social Work, Sydney University Press, Sydney.

Rao, M. K. (1969). Cultural variants and social work practice in India. *Journal of Education for Social Work, 5*(1), 69–74.

Yasas, F. M. (1971). *Asian creative literature for social work education,* In V. Armaity, Development and Teaching, Proceedings of the South East Asian Seminar for Social Work Educators, School of Social Work, Nirmala Niketan, Bombay, pp. 88–106.

PART IV

Socio-political and Economic Conflicts and Social Work in a Contemporary World

The new millennium has brought major changes, challenges, and hardships in human service delivery. Communities across the globe are confronting hardships with regard to rapidly changing demography, widening disparities between poor and rich, concentration of wealth, reduced welfare spending by the state, and new challenges for human service profession in terms of identity, credibility, and efficacy. New progress, advancement, and growth in the new millennium brought in enormous social issues such as multiple disparities, widespread inequality, violence, poverty, climate change, the rise of extreme nationalism, racism, war, and human rights violation and terrorism. Industrial revolution initiated in the eighteenth century and rapid growth of science and technology lead by neoliberalism, globalization, and privatization expected to pull out a large number of poor from hunger and suffering across the world societies. However, a large number of poor populations in the new millennium are subjected to variety of discrimination and subjugation in different parts of the world. Increasing discrimination, poverty, hunger, and widening income gap are resulting in crime, distraction, violence, and societal imbalance.

Social work by default is a profession aspiring to achieve a just and equal society. Social justice, equality, and human dignity are the core areas where social work educators and practitioners are expected to focus during their professional practice. This part of the book looks at the social work educational programmes in the countries, which frequently face social, economic, and political crises or breakdown. It is largely acceptable that the social realities and the social issues that are experienced by a society influence the social work education as well as practice. Or in other words, the formation, implementation, and delivery of social work educational programmes including curriculum, pedagogy, research, teaching, and practice components, are largely decided by the social realities that a particular society experiences. Social workers ability to create a just and equal society depends to a large extent on the profession's ability to influence the political processes and accordingly gearing social work education and practice. Preventing conflicts in the society no-account of above-mentioned reasons is a complex phenomenon and may be beyond the professional reach of any single profession. However, there is a definite carved out field for post-conflict social work, which focuses on resilience, reconciliation, post-trauma counselling, confidence building, emotional strengthening, etc. This will require some core knowledge and skills but in addition to that a deeper understanding of the contextual social realities and dimensions of the conflict, kind of loses encountered and perceived victims and perpetrators along with a different set of skills and knowledge, to be effective in post-conflict social work interventions.

Despite advancement in many field and a relatively advanced standards of living in many countries, people across the globe are protesting, condemning, and critiquing state discrimination at different level. Irrespective of type of government, people in countries across the globe undergo crisis and face differential treatment at some point in their life. In particular, some geographical landscapes are more vulnerable because of both internal and external factors. Social work educations in these countries are more vulnerable and uncertain because of the social factors influencing education and practice. Further social, political, and economic instability contributes to the poor performance of social work programmes. This is further evident in a discussion by Ziad Fara, Razan Lahamm, and Majdi Nabahin on the development of social work education in Palestine. This is a politically uncertain and economically less developed country that shares its territory with the state of Israel.

Similar to most of the other countries in the world, social work curriculum in Palestine is westernized and hence preparing social workers who are unable to address the social realities and the problems faced by the Palestinian society. The authors argue that low competencies of social work cadre with lack of minimum required skill and knowledge, weak field training, very limited level of coordination between social work programs in the five universities is challenging the existence of social work in entire country. Inadequate admission policies to social work programs, outdated textbooks, low scientific research in the field of social work, and poor linkages to labour market demands and requirements are further weakening the opportunities of professionalization of social work and thus restricting the growth and advancement. Given the special political, economic, and social condition of Palestine and the surrounding states, social work in the Middle Eastern countries including Palestine and other politically uncertain states in the region needs special attention at the education and training level. There is a need for these social work programmes to focus on social realities that they face every day in training new generation of social workers who can then address then at both policy and practice levels.

The economic growth and development, and technological advancement in many countries lead to changes in social needs of the people. As a result of

these changing demands, the social problems and their solutions also changing and demanding new dimensions of approach. However, despite varied
social issues and social change, social work education in many parts of the
world is still unchanged and remains Western centric. *Oguzhan Zengin and
Bugra Yildirim* examine the situation in Turkey and note that despite decades of development, social work in present Turkey is largely unresponsive to
the social realities and the curriculum and the teaching programmes are still
Western centric and follow Western thoughts. Even though a rapid growth
of social work institutions is witnessed by the country, it largely failed to produce quality graduates because large number of educators are untrained with
no social work background. Open education system is really producing large
numbers of graduates with social work degree; however, the country is unable to provide decent employment to all the social workers currently graduating from about 70 social work programmes across the country. Similar to
this in many other countries social work stories are represented in this part
of the book. *Emilio Jose Gomez Ciriano* examines the changes in social work
education in Spain during the past forty years in line with political, demographic, and cultural transformation that is taking place in Spain and express a
hope that social work in the future is expected to make substantial changes in
the professional practice in Spain. However, the need of training adequately
skilled social work professionals with the knowledge of social and cultural
aspects of the country was reported in many previous studies and the challenge remains largely unaddressed.

Like many other countries in the world, South Africa has undergone
numerous socio-economic challenges over the years. However, since the
introduction of democratic political system, South African government has
developed policies which have focused on poverty, alleviation, and achieving equality. Several programmes for uplifting the population living in poverty and unemployment were initiated by the state. Advanced social assistance
provisions were made available to people in distress, especially people with
disability as part of initiative to achieve equality and social justice. Despite
these initiatives and interventions, many countries in the Southern African
region still face extreme poverty and social exclusion. Social work education in many South African countries addresses the issues related to social
inequality and discrimination. However, still researchers highlight growing challenges for social work education in many African countries. *Rodreck
Mupedziswa, K. Nthomang, and O. Jankey* provide such an evidence in relation to the recent development of social work education and training in
Botswana with an account of challenges and issues faced by the profession.
It makes clear that social work in Botswana still faces the issues around relevance and appropriateness of the curriculum in relation to largely existence
of inequality and discrimination in the society. Further, Md. Ismail Hossain
provides a contextual background of social work practice in Bangladesh. With
a brief description of the emergence and development of social work education and training in Bangladesh. Nevertheless, social work in Bangladesh

also faces many similar problems like social work in other developing countries; however, given the uniqueness of political system, cultural aspect, and religious background and population served by the profession, social work in Bangladesh needs an country-level intervention that imbibes the cultural and economic aspects of the country. *Bojana Mesec* provides an account of progress made by the social work programme in the University of Ljubljana, Slovenia, which is the only one institute in the country that offers social work education since 2003. In a nutshell, all these explorations provide us an understanding that social work in many countries is still in developing state and many countries yet to develop adequate social work educational programmes. The problems related to professional recognition, less number of programmes, lack of focus on social problems in the curriculum, and lack of adequate number of social work educators with social work educational background are actually hindering the growth of these countries social work academia and practice.

In sum, the Sustainable Development Goals developed by the world leaders aim for achieving empowerment of people, socio-economic development, protection of human rights, and the environment. Social work education in the new millennium has tremendous scope for its practice and representation at each goals set by Sustainable Development Goals, as all the goals that sustainable development address are covered in the core principle and definition of social work theory and practice developed by the IFSW/IASSW (IFSW, 2014). Social work in contemporary world across the globe should focus on producing graduates with skill and knowledge to work for the economic equality, political stability, and social change. Existence of social work education and profession without an effort to achieve these goals especially in the countries where political unrest, economic crisis, and social disparity affect the lives of common people will have no recognition.

REFERENCE

IFSW. (2014). *Global agenda for social work and social development*. Retrieved from http://cdn.ifsw.org/assets/ifsw_23031-6.pdf.

CHAPTER 25

Challenging Realities Facing Social Work Education in Palestine

Ziad Faraj, Yazan Laham and Majdy Nabahin

INTRODUCTION

The aim of this chapter is to shed some light on the challenging realities facing social work education in the West Bank, Jerusalem, and Gaza Strip as perceived by 213 social work graduates through structured survey field research conducted between January and March 2018. It was an exploratory study that applied the non-purposive random sampling method. The convenience sampling technique was applied due to the absence of any central databases about social work graduates in Palestine and to the fact that none of the universities in Palestine were prepared to provide data for security and privacy reasons. This chapter also includes some of the findings from other research conducted by Faraj (2018) as part of his PhD dissertation at the University of Birmingham about the challenges facing development of the social work profession in Palestine. The principal researcher (Ziad Faraj) designed the data collection tools used for both research studies for triangulation purposes. Survey findings were analysed by the SPSS package and PhD research findings were analysed by thematic analysis.

The significance of this research rests in the fact that it is the first time the views of social work graduates from all governorates of the West Bank and Gaza Strip have been systematically researched and heard. Incorporation in a book such as this gives Palestine equal treatment with countries throughout

Z. Faraj (✉)
University of Birmingham, Birmingham, UK

Y. Laham · M. Nabahin
Al-Quds Open University, Jerusalem, Palestine

© The Author(s) 2021
S. S. M. et al. (eds.), *The Palgrave Handbook of Global Social Work Education*, https://doi.org/10.1007/978-3-030-39966-5_25

the world. The findings of this research are fully consistent with the findings of research Ibrahim (2017) conducted about the same topic but with a smaller sample size in the West Bank only. Moreover, they are consistent with the research conducted by Faraj in 2012 about the views of 210 service providers in the West Bank, Jerusalem, and Gaza Strip who solicited the views of service providers in social work education at the time. Jane et al. (2007) and Abu Ras et al. (2013) confirmed that the social work profession has been playing a substantial role in helping hundreds of thousands of disadvantaged and oppressed Palestinians, particularly as a result of Israeli colonial occupation, to cope with many life challenges since the emergence of the social work profession in 1971. According to Faraj (2017) social work education became part of the curriculum of an academic institution for the first time in 1971 at Hind Al-Husseini College for Girls in Jerusalem. Throughout the 1970s and the following decades some other undergraduate and postgraduate programmes in social work emerged and are still offering BA and MA degrees in social work.

The gap in knowledge about the social work profession in Palestine due to lack of research has been a stumbling block to development of the profession in the country according to the findings of Faraj (2018). Moreover, many other challenges to development of the profession, in general, and social work education, in particular, were identified. The findings from Faraj's PhD research and those from the survey demonstrated a surprising level of consistency regarding the challenges facing the development of this profession and the impacts they have had on social work education and on academics, professionals, employers, and social work graduates. The latter research study was carried out by completely voluntary efforts from the three key researchers (the authors of this chapter) and social work instructors of Al-Quds Open University in the West Bank and Gaza Strip. This highlights their awareness of the dire need for this and other research and their commitment to the development of this profession in Palestine.

The findings of the two research studies have a great deal in common. They reflect the considerable level of concern about different elements of the social work education process in Palestinian universities such as field training, the competencies of social work academics and the teaching methods they apply, the mismatch between the theoretical curriculum and Palestinian realities such as the cultural context, the dearth of research in the field of social work, the disconnect between education and the labor market, and the absence of a shared national vision and strategies for social work education in Palestine.

This chapter presents a brief account of the socioeconomic and political context, the developmental history of social work education in Palestine, and findings relating to the challenges facing social work education in the West Bank and Gaza Strip. The chapter ends with a conclusion and recommendation section.

PALESTINE: ZONE OF CONFLICT

The quality of life of all Palestinians over the last 500 years including the period of Ottoman Empire domination (1516–2018) has been dictated by occupiers as a result of the absence of a Palestinian national independent state.[1] The Zionist colonial project in historic Palestine was established by the colonial British under the mandate given to the United Kingdom by the League of Nations at the end of World War I. The project started on the date of the Balfour Declaration on 2 November 1917 and resulted in devastating effects on Palestinian society. The period between 1917 and 1948 witnessed intensive popular resistance to the British Mandate and its role in facilitating the immigration of Jewish settlers from all over the world (mainly Europe) to Palestine using the capitulation system agreed with the Ottoman Empire (Angel, 1901; Khalidi, 2004; Kialy, 1990). However, the Palestinian National Authority (PNA) was established in 1994 and was given control over about 3% of historic Palestine that fell within the 22% that constituted the total area of the West Bank and Gaza Strip. The PNA[2] was established as a result of peace negotiations between the PLO[3] and Israel under the auspices of the United States,[4] which embodied a neoliberal capitalist agenda being set up in Palestine in the post-colonial era that started in the aftermath of World War II.

Palestine has been subject to Israeli colonial occupation since 1948 when the nation was handed over to the Zionist movement by the British Mandate that had administered the country since the end of World War I. This reality deeply influenced and profoundly shaped many of the socioeconomic characteristics of today's Palestinian society. This political reality put paid to the establishment of a Palestinian national state that should have taken responsibility for the welfare of its citizens. On the contrary, it created a community of Palestinian refugees who comprised two-thirds of the total population of Palestine (PCBC, 2007). They were subject to ethnic-cleansing and removed from 531 villages, towns, and cities in 1948. At the time about 800,000 Palestinians were forced to leave their homes to settle in the West Bank, Gaza Strip, Jordan, Syria, and Lebanon which are defined as the five fields of operations of the United Nations Relief and Works Agency (UNRWA) (2018).

As a result of security measures restricting the mobility of all Palestinians resident in the West Bank, Jerusalem, and the Gaza Strip since 1967 (refugees and non-refugees), the majority of the workforce became labourers in the Israeli labour market (mainly the construction sector). Ever since, what was left of the Palestinian economy was totally confiscated, annexed, and became part of the occupier's colonial economy. Over the last 110 years the welfare of Palestinian families has been subject to policies and practices of occupying powers that were often brutal. Even the unbalanced peace negotiations with the PLO, which resulted in the establishment of the PNA in 1994 as part of the Oslo Accords, exacerbated economic annexation through the Paris Economic Treaty that was signed in 1996 as part of the Oslo Accords. Palestinian national resistance to occupying powers started at the beginning of the last century, particularly resistance to the Zionist project of establishing a homeland for Jews in Palestine, a decision taken at the First Zionist Conference in Basel (Switzerland) in 1897. The immigration of Jewish individuals and families to Palestine started prior to that conference and increased steeply after World War I and imposition of the British Mandate on Palestine. The Balfour Declaration of 2 November 1917 brought about the open and unconditional support of the United Kingdom to the fulfillment of Zionist dreams in Palestine (Machover, 2006; Trueman, 2015).

That entire period witnessed continuous clashes between the Palestinians and the forces of the occupiers (mainly the British and the Zionists). The 1929 uprising, the 1936–1939 civil disobedience, the war of 1948, the armed resistance movement launched in 1965, the war of 1967, the First Intifada (1987–1994), the Second Intifada (2000–2005), wars in the Gaza Strip in 2008, 2012, and 2014 are salient events in the history of the Palestinian national liberation movement. However, those events were accompanied by another movement that emerged and evolved to support the national struggle of the Palestinian community and enhance its steadfastness. This was a grassroots movement comprising initiatives locally organized by women and formal and informal youth charities. Volunteerism constituted solely the spirit of that movement, which was rooted in Islam, Christianity, and nationalism (Abu Ras et al., 2013).

Confiscation of all the natural resources of Palestinian society (land and underground water) coupled with continuous confrontation between the national liberation movement and the occupiers resulted in severely deteriorating economic conditions (poverty and unemployment), imprisonment of and injuries to hundreds of thousands, the demolition of tens of thousands of houses, the deportation of millions from their home towns, the destruction of hundreds of towns, villages, and cities, and psychological trauma of the vast majority of the population. All these conditions necessitated the emergence of institutionalised interventions through local grassroots and other civil society organisations, international aid agencies (mainly after 1948) (BISAN, 2007), and the establishment of the first social work education programme in 1971 (Faraj, 2017).

Emergence and Evolution of the Social Work Profession

The establishment of the UNRWA[5] in the Middle East on 8 December 1950 provided a robust example of the need for organised social work intervention through its relief and social services programme. What distinguished the UNRWA in its relation to social work history is that it became the largest employer of social workers between the mid-1970s and the establishment of the PNA in 1994 when it grew even larger under the aegis of the Ministries of Social Affairs and Education. In fact, prior to the mid-1970s the UNRWA used to provide relief services to Palestine refugees by employing Palestinians educated in different humanity fields except social work or social sciences because no social work or social sciences academic programmes existed in Palestine. According to UNRWA relief instructions the job title given to relief services employees until 1992 was welfare worker (UNRWA Relief Instructions No. 1/95). In October 1992 the title was changed to social worker when a proposal to upgrade this position from grade 7 to grade 9 was approved by the agency. Approval was based on reviewing and modifying the job description and bringing it in line with similar positions in the country and other Arab countries, particularly in the five fields of operations where governmental welfare services were in place (UNRWA Relief Instructions No. 1/95).

Extensive review of many publications and references as to when social work first started revealed there had been no research let alone documentation about it (Faraj, 2017). However, through a series of 10 in-depth interviews with Palestinian social work professionals Faraj (2017) succeeded in tracking down the date. The first step to institutionalise the social work profession within the Palestinian educational system took place in 1971. The step was taken by the Palestinian woman Hind Al-Husseiny who pioneered the social work profession (Faraj, 2017; Hind Al-Husseiny College, 1994). However, it should be kept in mind that the political context between 1967 and 1971 helped greatly in bringing this about. In 1971 Hind Al-Husseiny contacted Prof. Abdul-Razeq (a well-known professional at the time, at least in Jerusalem) and consulted him about establishing a 3-year programme aimed at getting some of the female students of the Dar Ettifil El-Arabi School qualified for social services as well as paraprofessionals capable of helping other women cope with life challenges (Faraj, 2017; Hind Al-Husseiny College, 1994). He liked Al-Husseiny's request and proposed the programme be focussed on social work. In 1974 the first undergraduate 4-year social work programme was established in Bethlehem University (West Bank), followed by another in 1991 at Al-Quds Open University, another in 1998 at the Islamic University (Gaza Strip), and yet another in 2008 at Al-Ummah University (Gaza Strip) (Faraj, 2017).

EVOLUTION OF GOVERNMENTAL SOCIAL WELFARE SERVICES

During the period 1948–1967 the West Bank had been under the control of the Hashemite Jordanian government since 24 April 1950 (Cavendish, 2000; Milton, 2009) while the Gaza Strip had been under the control of the Egyptian government since 24 February 1949 (Birzeit University, 2006). During these 20 years social services were provided to Palestinian citizens through three main service providers: the government (through the Jordanian Ministry of Social Affairs in the West Bank), international agencies such as the UNRWA that mainly provided services to Palestine refugees inside and outside camps (West Bank and Gaza Strip), and Palestinian civil society organisations including Palestinian charitable societies under the aegis of the Jordanian Association of Charitable Societies in the West Bank and Egyptian Law in the Gaza Strip (Faraj, 2017). In October 1967 the Jerusalem Welfare Office fell under the formal administration of the Israeli occupation and was assigned to the Israeli Municipality of Jerusalem (Faraj, 2017). In 1994 governmental social welfare services were transferred to the PNA, as was the entire education system (Faraj, 2017). As a result of needed reforms in these two ministries (the Ministry of Social Affairs and the Ministry of Education and Higher Education) the number of social work positions increased markedly and job descriptions were reviewed and modified. This stimulated interest in the social work profession and its status (education and practice) (Abu Ras et al., 2013; Faraj, 2017).

CHALLENGES FACING SOCIAL WORK EDUCATION IN PALESTINE

Purpose

The purpose behind conducting this research was to explore how social workers in the West Bank, Jerusalem, and the Gaza Strip perceived the key challenges facing social work education and what actions they recommended to improve it.

Methodology

Exploratory quantitative research design using the social survey research method was applied for the purpose of this research. It targeted 213 participants from the West Bank, Jerusalem, and the Gaza Strip who completed their first university degree at one of the five universities teaching social work. The main selection criteria of participants were that they should be working as social workers at the time of the research. The data collection tool was a structured survey questionnaire that covered 57 items distributed across 6 areas related to social work (education, labour market, representation, professional development, social status, and other challenges facing development of the social work profession in Palestine). The survey included 13 items about social work education (Table 25.1). A five-point Likert scale was applied. Social work instructors from Al-Quds Open University who taught the targeted areas volunteered to collect the data from fourth-year social work students after steering them in the requisite direction and providing them with instructions. The convenience sampling technique was applied to data collection. Data were collected between 1 February and 31 March 2018.

Table 25.1 How social work graduates perceived the challenges facing social work education in the West Bank, Jerusalem, and the Gaza Strip

	Question	Mean	SD	%
1	The content of theoretical curriculum was convenient	3.19	0.667	79.75
2	The total number of credit hours were convenient	3.15	0.624	78.75
3	The competencies of academics teaching social work theoretical courses were convenient	3.06	0.789	76.5
4	The competencies of academics teaching social work field-training courses were convenient	2.95	0.787	73.75
5	The level of coordination between universities and field placement institutions was convenient	2.94	0.819	73.5
6	The content of field-training courses was convenient	2.93	0.786	73.25
7	The competencies of field supervisors in field placement institutions were convenient	2.89	0.796	72.25
8	University supervision over field training was convenient	2.85	0.829	71.25
9	Institutional supervision strategies were convenient	2.82	0.824	70.5
10	Total credit hours of field-training courses were convenient	2.8	0.778	70
11	The service programmes in which I received field training inside institutions were adequate for the course objectives and requirements	2.71	0.839	67.75
12	Social work curricula were more Westernised than localised	2.71	0.806	67.75
13	The admission policies of universities for the social work programme were effective and sufficient to select the most competent and motivated applicants	2.54	0.988	63.5

Source Author

Findings and Arguments

Some of the key general findings of the study were that 148 (69.6%) of the participants were holders of a BSW compared with 65 (30.4%) who were hired to social work positions but had qualifications in other fields (i.e., sociology, psychology, and organisational management); 86 (40.4%) were male and 127 (59.6%) were female; and 131 (61.5%) were from the West Bank and Jerusalem while 82 (38.5%) were from the Gaza Strip. About 54.0% of the participants were graduates of Al-Quds Open University while the other 46.0% were graduates from the other four universities (Bethlehem University, Al-Quds University, Islamic University, and Al-Ummah University for Open Learning).

Responses to the 13 questions about social work education are summarised in Table 25.1.

Table 25.1 provides an overview of the levels of satisfaction of the social work graduates to 13 aspects of the social work education programmes in Palestine (without any comparison between the West Bank, Jerusalem, and the Gaza Strip). The two aspects of the social work education programmes that received the highest levels of satisfaction were the content of the theoretical curriculum and the total number of credit hours. Both were identified as convenient to some extent. Remaining aspects of the social work programmes were identified as less satisfactory.

Table 25.1 illustrates that the main challenges facing the social work education programmes in the five universities as perceived by the graduates were in the competencies of academics teaching social work theoretical courses, the competencies of academics teaching social work field-training courses, the level of coordination between universities and field placement institutions, the content of field-training courses, the competencies of field supervisors in field placement institutions, institutional supervision strategies, total credit hours of field-training courses, the service programmes in which students receive their field training inside institutions, Westernized social work curricula, and the inadequate admission policies of universities toward social work programmes. Accordingly, the majority of participants believe that weaknesses in social work education are mainly in admission policies, which are perceived as inadequate at selecting applicants who clearly have the potential and interest to study social work and become competent social workers (mean = 2.54), social work field training (means varied between 2.71 and 2.89), and Westernised and irrelevant curricula to the Palestinian context (mean = 2.71). Figure 25.1 shows that the levels of satisfaction start to

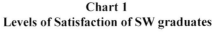

Chart 1
Levels of Satisfaction of SW graduates

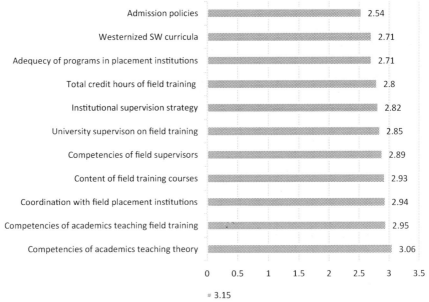

Admission policies	2.54
Westernized SW curricula	2.71
Adequecy of programs in placement institutions	2.71
Total credit hours of field training	2.8
Institutional supervision strategy	2.82
University supervison on field training	2.85
Competencies of field supervisors	2.89
Content of field training courses	2.93
Coordination with field placement institutions	2.94
Competencies of academics teaching field training	2.95
Competencies of academics teaching theory	3.06

⁎ 3.15

Fig. 25.1   Levels of satisfaction

drop as we move from theoretical aspects of the curricula to field training. However, the participants found the content of the curricula was poorly relevant to the Palestinian context. This implies that there could be a high level of satisfaction if the structures of theoretical courses were adjusted to chime with the fields they cover.

Abu Ras et al. (2013) reviewed the syllabi describing the courses in the five universities and found a high similarity between title and course descriptions. In this regard universities seem to copy the structure of programme design from universities in Western countries. This would explain the high level of satisfaction about this aspect of courses and does not contradict the low level of satisfaction about just how relevant the content of courses were to the local context. In fact, two other interrelated elements can be brought to bear to explain the findings about the issue of poor relevance: the limited number of specialised academics and the extreme weakness in research-based knowledge about the Palestinian context to make the curricula more relevant. Hanafi (2010) highlighted the concern about the dearth of research-based literature in social sciences in Arab countries including Palestine, while Abu Ras et al. (2013) highlighted the serious shortfall in the availability of qualified academics to teach social work education. Ibrahim (2017) confirmed not only the existence of such challenges but also those in the field-training element.

Inconsistencies in the design and the way in which field-training courses are applied among the five universities were confirmed by Abu Ras et al. (2013), Ibrahim (2017), and Faraj (2017). Each university developed and implemented its own modules, applied them with little or no attention to designing academic and field supervision in an appropriate way, poorly focussed on the qualifications of supervisors in the university and the field placement institution, and did so in the absence of a proper evaluation process. Faraj's (2017) notion that ties between social workers and psychologists in Palestine left much to be desired, weak coordination between universities, absence of a regulatory law, and the weak role played by the Palestinian Ministry of Education and Higher Education in ensuring social work programmes reached a certain level of national quality assurance are all key factors contributing to weaknesses in social work education programmes in the country. Yet, there is a significant difference in the quality of outcomes of social work education programmes between the West Bank and Jerusalem, on the one hand, and the Gaza Strip on the other.

The mean of all responses to the social work education question of participants from the West Bank was 3.04% compared with 2.64% in the Gaza Strip, which reflects the lower level or satisfaction of graduates from the Gaza Strip on different elements of the social work education system in the Gaza Strip compared with the level of satisfaction of graduates from the West Bank. Findings from qualitative research conducted by Faraj (2018) for his PhD thesis on the challenges facing development of the social work profession in Palestine confirmed that challenges facing social work education in Palestine outweighed those facing it in another five domains: community attitude, employability and labour market, policy and legal environment, professional representation, and the security and political environment. Findings from quantitative research in this sense were fully consistent with Faraj's (2018) qualitative research findings. Qualitative and quantitative research thus clearly confirm that the challenges facing social work education in the Gaza Strip are the same as those in the West Bank but more severe. This difference can be attributed to a variety of factors.

Universities in the West Bank started their social work programmes in the 1970s and 1980s while in the Gaza Strip they started in the late 1990s and early 2000s. The geographic proximity of Bethlehem and Al-Quds (Jerusalem), home to the two oldest social work programmes,[6] allowed them to benefit from qualified Palestinian staff from the Green Line area of historic Palestine (Israel), who had better chances to resume their postgraduate studies in social work in Israeli universities and abroad. Although access to universities in the West Bank remained open, it became stricter in the Gaza Strip due to the siege/blockade imposed on the Gaza Strip by the Israeli occupiers and ongoing wars there. Security restrictions imposed on the Gaza Strip made it very difficult for the two universities there, their graduates, and social service organisations to interact with the rest of the Arab world or internationally to exchange expertise, resume postgraduate education, and access other resources to develop their social work programmes. However, universities and social service organisations in the West Bank were able to interact with the rest of the world. This is the reason the number of qualified staff associated with social work programmes in the West Bank are higher than in the Gaza Strip, the quality of the social work programmes in West Bank universities is higher, and the number of specialised institutions providing social work services in the West Bank is much higher than in the Gaza Strip enabling them to provide better quality field training (Faraj, 2018, work in progress).

Not until 2008 were there postgraduate (PG) programmes in social work in the West Bank, Jerusalem, and the Gaza Strip. Before then the number of Palestinians with PG, MSW, and PhD degrees did not exceed 35 (30 with MSWs and 5 with PhDs) (Abu Ras et al., 2013; Faraj, 2017). They were able to resume their education in European or North American universities through scholarships. In 2008 the Al-Quds University in Jerusalem established its Master of Social Action degree and in 2013 the University of Bethlehem launched its Master of social work degree. As yet there are no PG programmes in social work in the Gaza Strip mainly due to the shortage of qualified personnel. In 2005 Al-Quds Open University (QOU) supported 25 Palestinians to get their Master of social work from Helwan University in Egypt through a partnership programme (18 were from the West Bank and 7 from the Gaza Strip). Ten of the 25 successfully completed their PhD in social work in Egyptian universities (Faraj, 2018, work in progress). The shortage is more acute in PhD degrees, which can only be acquired through scholarships and take much longer to complete than Master's degrees.

When it comes to continuing education there are no programmes in the West Bank and the Gaza Strip that provide social work graduates with any professional diplomas in specific fields in social work such as supervision, programme management, monitoring and evaluation, school social work, youth development, and advanced research. Such programmes would effectively contribute to enhancing the quality of existing social services and would provide better employment opportunities for thousands of graduates. At the very least they would enhance the number and skillsets of staff in temporary or short-term jobs in consultancies and in a research market that is desperately looking for social work graduates with specialised skills in specific fields such as local government development, market research, youth and child development programmes, and supervision.

At a more strategic level the social work profession in Palestine is seriously challenged by lack of vision, extremely weak professional leadership, and lack of a regulatory law (Faraj, 2018, work in progress). These and other factors are extremely important for the smooth running of social work education programmes. Lacking a clear definition of social work, its functions and clear roles coupled with a lack of standards as to who can practise social work and who cannot and a lack of standards for field-training programmes, as well as many other conditions contribute to making social work education in Palestine less responsive. A relevant finding from responses to questions relating to the labour market and social work education is that 58.7% of the graduates evaluated the content of social work curricula as responsive to demands of the labour market and 50.2% believed that universities invested sufficient efforts and resources to prepare students to integrate in the labour market. This reflects poor coordination between social work education programmes and the labour market and the absence of research in social work about issues that could contribute to the development of social work education that is more indigenised.

CONCLUSIONS AND RECOMMENDATIONS

Findings from the two studies illustrate that the main challenges facing social work education in Palestine are concentrated in the areas of field training, irrelevant and Westernized curricula, inadequate admission policies, poor research production, limited competencies of social work academics, and poor coordination between social work programmes and other external actors such as employers and professional representatives.

Based on these findings and the arguments presented in the chapter key recommended actions to improve the quality of social work education can be summarized as:

- establishing a Palestinian council of schools of social work that can take the lead in putting together a social work education development plan at the national level;
- establishing specialised training and further education centres that can provide professional development education opportunities for the vast majority of social work graduates;
- establishing specialised research centres in social work in universities that offer first degrees in social work (at least in the two that offer MSW degrees);
- establishing a Master's of social work degree programme and a professional development programme in the Gaza Strip; and
- allocating more resources and increasing university budgets for social work research, especially since such research was underbudgeted in existing universities and research centres when international donors guided by neoliberal policies and priorities neglected the need to increase budgets.

NOTES

1. Palestine was under the control of the Ottoman Empire between 1516 and 1917, the British Mandate between 1918 and 1948, Jordanian and Egyptian rule between 1948 and 1967, and Israeli colonial occupation between 1948 and 2018 (78% of historic Palestine) and between 1967 and 2018 (the remaining 22% of historic Palestine comprising the West Bank, Jerusalem, and the Gaza Strip).
2. Palestinian National Authority.
3. Palestinian Liberation Organisation.
4. United States of America.
5. The UNRWA was established by the UN General Assembly under Resolution 302 (IV) and tasked with taking responsibility for providing humanitarian relief, basic health, and education services to Palestine refugees who were forced to flee their homes and towns as a result of military action taken against them during the 1948 war when they lost their homes and livelihoods between 1 June 1946 and 15 May 1948 (unrwa.org).
6. At University of Bethlehem and Al-Quds University.

REFERENCES

Angel, J. (1901). The Turkish capitulations. *The American Historical Review* 6(2), 254–259. Oxford University Press, American Historical Association, UK.

Abu Ras, et al. (2013). The role of the political conflict in shaping the social welfare system in Palestine. *Social work in the Middle East* (pp. 53–81). New York and London: Routledge.

Birzeit University. (2006). Gaza after Israeli withdrawal: Evaluation study and future direction. www.birzeit.edu.dsp. Accessed October 9, 2018.

BISAN Center for Research and Development. (2007). *Community Base Organizations and Local Councils: Vision and Development Role* (1st ed.). Ramallah, Palestine.

Cavendish, R. (2000). Jordan formally annexes the West Bank. *History Today, 50*(4). www.historytoday.com/richard-cavendish/jordan-formally-annexes-west-bank.

Faraj, Z. (2017). *The emergence and development of social work profession in Palestine.* Bethlehem, Palestine: DOZAN.

Faraj, Z., et al. (2018). *Challenges facing social work education in Palestine; Social Work Graduates Perspective* (Unpublished Paper). Palestine.

Hanafi, S. (2010). *Donor Community and the Market of Research Production: Framing and De-Framing the Social Sciences.* www.staff.aub.edu.lb/~sh41/dr_sarry_website/publications/29_2010_Estime_Taiwan.pd. Accessed June 05, 2018.

Hind Al-Husseini College / Al-Quds University / Islamic Researches Center. (1994). *Commemoration of Hind Al-Hussein.* Jerusalem, Palestine.

Ibrahim, Q. (2017). Glocalization and international social work education: A comparative study of Palestine, Jordan, Saudi Arabia, Oman, Yemen, Egypt, Libya, and Morocco. *International Social Work, 60*(6), 1400–1417. Sage.

Jane, L., et al. (2007). The role of social work in Palestine in nation building. *International social work and the radical tradition* (pp. 163–188). Birmingham, UK: Venture Press.

Khalidi, W. (2004). *Before their Diaspora: A photographic history of the Palestinians, 1876–1948.* Studies, Washington/USA: Institute for Palestine.

Kialy, A. (1990). *The history of modern Palestine.* Beirut, Lebanon: Arab Institution for Studies and Publications.

Machover, M. (2006). *Israelis and Palestinians: Conflict & resolution.* The Center for Economic Research and Social Change: International Socialist Review (ISR). www.isreview.org/issue/65/israelis-and-palestinians-conflict-resolution. Accessed October 17, 2018.

Milton, E., et al. (2009). *Jordan: A Hashemite legacy* (2nd ed.). Contemporary Middle East Series. London and New York: Routledge.

PCBC. (2007). www.pcbs.org, Accessed: October 10, 2018.

Trueman, C. (2015). *Palestine 1918 to 1948,* The History Learning Site. www.historylearningsite.co.uk/modern-world-history-1918-to-1980/the-middle-east-1917-to-1973/palestine-1918-to-1948. Accessed October 15, 2018.

UNRWA. (2018). www.unrwa.org. Accessed August 15, 2018.

CHAPTER 26

Social Work Education in Botswana: Issues, Challenges, and Prospects

Rodreck Mupedziswa, Keitseope Nthomang and Odireleng Shehu

INTRODUCTION

Botswana is a landlocked country situated in southern Africa. It borders Zimbabwe, Zambia, South Africa, and Namibia on the north, east, and west, respectively. The chapter commences with a brief historical account of the evolution of Botswana as a country, as this is important for appreciating the evolution of social work profession in general and social work education and training in particular in the country. Osei-Hwedie (1995, p. 79) has correctly observed that "An understanding of the nature of social work education and practice must be sought in her (i.e. Botswana's) colonial history". For this reason, it is proper to commence by briefly surveying the country's sociopolitical and economic history.

Botswana started off as a British Protectorate and during the period 1895–1965, the country was being administered by the British High Commission in Cape Town and Mafeking, South Africa. The country attained Independence from Britain in 1966. Wass (1969) has noted that there was lack of commitment on the part of the colonial administrators to develop the country during the colonial era; hence, at the dawn of Independence in 1966, Botswana was ranked among the poorest countries in the entire world. The author further explained that British rule was characterised by neglect, with only rudimentary health and education services being in existence, and these were communally

R. Mupedziswa (✉) · K. Nthomang · O. Shehu
Department of Social Work, University of Botswana, Gaborone, Botswana
e-mail: mupedziswa@mopipi.ub.bw

© The Author(s) 2021
S. S. M. et al. (eds.), *The Palgrave Handbook of Global Social Work Education*, https://doi.org/10.1007/978-3-030-39966-5_26

oriented and administered essentially by tribal chiefs—*Dikgosi*. As Osei-Hwedie (1995, p. 80) has explained, whatever services were provided during this era did not develop into a coherent system of social protection across the country. During that time, the country depended mostly on agriculture, but over time the importance of agriculture decreased due to perennial drought, aridness of the land coupled with poor rainfall patterns (Waas, 1969). Many men in particular were forced by circumstances to fend for their families outside their country's borders, with most opting for neighbouring South Africa. It is instructive that at one point the number of Batswana employed in South Africa was much higher than that of those employed in the country's formal sector (Hoppers, 2003). Ngwenya (1992) observed that during those days, the country served as a reservoir of cheap labour, a development which suggested that the meagre resources available to the country derived essentially from remittances from migrant labour. Such a situation was obviously untenable.

The country's fortunes however changed markedly for the better in the 1970s when large deposits of diamonds were discovered. Over the years, prudent management of resources and political stability have seen the country maintain a high economic growth rate. The phenomenal economic growth trajectory resulted in the country attaining upper-middle-income status in 1991. Today, Botswana is a shining example of democracy, with a stable government, peace, and tranquillity (Mafela, Maundeni, & Mookodi, 2011). The country's GDP is estimated at USD 11.0 billion, while its international reserves stand at 7.5 billion, yet as the World Bank (2015) notes, Botswana remains the 3rd highest unequal country in the world. Inequality tends to be associated with poverty and high rates of unemployment, especially among the youth.

Over the years, the government has, however, worked hard to improve conditions of living of its people. Even so, while a considerable fraction of the population has been absorbed into the formal labour market, many citizens continue to languish outside the formal sector and in the quagmire of poverty. The unemployment rate has remained unacceptably high (at 17.7%) and with this the levels of poverty too (16.3%) (Statistics Botswana, 2018). A number of mitigating measures are in place; however, most of these are under the rubric of social safety nets. Whereas traditionally the country depended largely on the extended family support system, today several state-led social protection programmes exist, and these mostly target the marginalised (RHVP, 2011; World Bank & BIDPA, 2013). It is in this kind of environment that social work education and practice are rolled out in Botswana. Before we proceed to discuss social work education and training in Botswana it will be pertinent to briefly situate the social work profession in its Africa roots.

HISTORICAL DEVELOPMENT OF SOCIAL WORK EDUCATION IN AFRICA

In order to understand the historical development of social work education and training in Botswana, it is important to commence by taking a step back to consider the historical development of social work education on the

African continent. This is essential because the two (i.e. social work education in Africa and in Botswana) are intricately linked. It is instructive to note that social work education in Africa has a colonial heritage, having been imported from the Western World at the beginning of the last century. South Africa is credited with being one of the first countries on the African continent to introduce social work education, with the first school of social work emerging in Stellenbosch in 1931, followed by Cape Town and Pretoria in 1933 and 1934, respectively (Gray, Kreitzer, & Mupedziswa, 2014). This was apparently followed by Egypt which introduced social work education in 1936. It was not until the 1940s and 1950s that a couple of other countries across the continent began to offer social work education and training, and these included Algeria (1942), Ghana (1945), Uganda (1954), Tanzania (1958), Ethiopia (1959), Burkina Faso (1960), Tunisia and Zimbabwe (1964), Zambia (1965) and the Sudan (1969) (Gray et al., 2014; Mwansa, 2011). By 1973, the umbrella body of social work education and training institutions across the world, the International Association of Schools of Social Work (IASSW), had on its register, 25 schools of social work from the African continent. In the years that followed, a number of other countries on the continent established some form of social work education and training programmes of different configurations—at certificate, diploma, and much later degree and even post-graduate levels. Perhaps one of the youngest social work education and training programmes to be launched in Africa was that of Botswana, which was inaugurated in 1972 at the Botswana Agricultural College and later transferred to the University of Botswana as recently as 1985.

Before zeroing in on social work education in Botswana, it is worth briefly surveying the key tenets of the debate that has raged over the years pertaining to lack of relevance and appropriateness of social work in Africa (Mupedziswa, 2001, Mwansa, 2011). Concern has hinged on the fact that social work education and training's Western roots have meant that social work in Africa adopted a (remedial) Western orientation which some argued lacked relevance and appropriateness. The Western theories employed dealt with such (peripheral) issues as the "*crises of urban destitution and maladjustment and devote(d) their time to responding to requests for urgent material assistance, securing residential places and dealing with judicial child committal, probation and maintenance cases*" (Midgley, 1983, p. 154). Commentators (e.g. Osei-Hwedie, 1993) have opined that the lavish application of the remedial approach resulted in lack of fit between traditional social norms and Western processes of social welfare, resulting in the profession's dismal showing in Africa.

In the West and elsewhere, social work education was not imposed on the various countries: the profession grew "*through a process characterised by debate, dissent, negotiation, consultation, compromise, controversy, and sometimes confrontation*" (Mwansa, 2011). Its growth was also gradual, meaning important lessons were learnt every step of the way. Not so in the case of Africa—social work education and practice on this continent were, according to the critics, imposed from outside—a development which Midgley (1983) referred to as *professional imperialism*. This was characterised by a situation whereby social work education and training institutions in Africa were staffed mostly by teachers who were trained in the West and therefore peddled unbridled Western ideas, illustrations, textbooks, syllabi, and related teaching materials. Research done by several authors provides ample evidence of these anomalies. Gray et al. (2014, p. 103) have observed, "*Most early social workers had trained abroad either coming from or being educated in Western countries. Hence, Western ideas permeated these institutions, despite the ethical conflicts between traditional African cultures and values and the Western Judeo-Christian norms on which social work was based*". This, according to critics, has been the source of the concerns raised, as the argument has been that embracing of these ideas has resulted in ineffectiveness of social work on the African continent. Mwansa (2011, p. 7) corroborated the above contention by observing thus: "*....the evolution of social work education in Africa was influenced by foreign views and dictates unlike the process in Western communities*". The author (Mwansa) might as well have added that this has resulted in a blend of social work that, according to critics, lacked relevance and appropriateness, what Ngwenya (1992) correctly referred to as "*the agony of irrelevance*".

The configuration of social work education and training in Botswana has not been any different, as the paper will attempt to show. Certainly, if the criteria of staff profiles (trained in the west) and predominant use of Western literature and textbooks as well as preoccupation with promotion of direct practice is used, then social work in Botswana can be said to have remained predominantly Eurocentric, although of late there are signs of gradual change. The task of transforming social work education and training from its Western orientation (Eurocentric) to Afrocentric across Africa has proved to be a tall order, meaning the quest for relevance remains an issue of particular concern in Africa (Mupedziswa, 2001). Let us now consider social work education and training in Botswana, commencing with a historical note.

HISTORICAL EVOLUTION OF SOCIAL WORK BOTSWANA

There is very little information available on the history of social work education in Botswana. The limited information available which is presented in this chapter draws on the works of Hedenquist (1992), Wass (1969), Lucas (1994, 2017), Jongman (2015), and Ngwenya (1992), as well as anecdotal information derived from personal experiences. Social work is based on the intrinsic principles of social justice, compassion, and caring for the needy. In Botswana, traditionally social work draws its impetus from the cardinal principle of *botho* (or Ubuntu) which essentially relates to a natural call for assisting people in need or vulnerable groups such as children, older people, orphaned children, and the poor. The notion of *botho* has always been entrenched in traditional Tswana society. This natural calling did not require any formal training but there was a mutual, societal expectation that members of society would help each other—some kind of *quid pro quo* arrangement.

The recorded history of social work in Botswana (Wass, 1969) suggests that formal social work practice has a relatively short history and so is the concomitant education and training component thereof. The introduction, after World War II, of the social welfare scheme named Bechuanaland Soldiers Benefit Fund (BSBF) could be credited with triggering the commencement of formal social work education and training in Botswana in the sense that promotion of such initiatives required the services of professionally qualified people. The BSBF in particular was initiated by the British government with the main purpose of rehabilitating Botswana ex-servicemen who had fought in World War II on the side of the British. The BSBF scheme was adminis-tered by a British social welfare officer, and it had social work dimensions in the sense that it sought to restore social functioning of ex-servicemen (Lucas, 1994). Help was individualised by focusing on the ex-soldier and their family. The work of the BSBF could arguably be regarded as the forerunner to social casework because help was individualised. This is because in the 1960s, the prevailing social welfare activities put more emphasis on "rehabilitative case-work, investigating cases of indigence or other forms of hardship such as dis-ability and referrals where such existed and '*group work of a palliative nature, namely recreational activities among which youth group work featured promi-nently*'" (Lucas, 1994).

Throughout the pre-colonial and colonial (protectorate) period, provi-sion of social welfare and social support in Bechuanaland (now Botswana) was done by people without any formal training in social work. This task was largely confined to informal support systems involving extended family net-works, the community, *kgosi,* and later the church. In particular, the family extended kin and the community worked together to transmit values which included supporting and helping those in need. These educational tradi-tions and values have been aptly captured in numerous studies conducted by anthropologists, historians, and other researchers (cf Schapera, 1994; Tlou & Campbell, 1984).

Some of the traditional educational values passed from one generation to the next clearly geared towards assisting the poor included the practices of "*mafisa*", "*majako*", and "*go tshwara teu*". The "*mafisa*" system allowed able-bodied destitute persons to access cattle from rich households in return for looking after their cattle and using them as draft power, to supply milk, and to provide transportation. The "*majako*" system enabled poor people to work in the fields of the rich, in return for a share of the harvest, while "*go tshwara teu* or *badisa*" initiative provided able-bodied poor people with an opportunity to break the cycle of poverty by looking after cattle in return for receipt of a cow each year (cf BIDPA, 1997; Schapera, 1994; Tlou & Campbell, 1984).

Thus, during the pre-colonial and colonial periods, Tswana traditional society had a well-established informal education system meant to provide knowledge and skills in efforts to support the needy in society. Interestingly, very few people were classified as poor during that point in Botswana's history; in fact, poverty was associated with a polity rather than an individual. Thus, it can be categorically stated that traditional Tswana society had its own informal educational system characterised by structures that inculcated in both the young and the old, knowledge and skills to help and take care of the needy and vulnerable in society (Mupedziswa & Ntseane, 2012).

The above-narrated traditional practices resonate with the common African philosophy of "I am because you are". In other African societies, *Ujamaa, Ubuntu,* and *Harambee* all describe the common (African) philosophy of "I am because you are" (Aina & Moyo, 2013; Eze, 2008; Metz, 2007; Swanson, 2012). Schapera (1943) and Tlou and Campbell (1984) in their writings on the history of Botswana all underscored the principle of *botho* (alluded to earlier) and observed that through *botho* and/or *ubuntu,* people were able to support and help each other meet both their social and economic needs. These claims found legitimacy and have been supported by anthropological evidence in Tswana society (cf Schapera, 1943). European travellers, such as David Livingstone, also provided eyewitness accounts of these traditional practices anchored in the philosophy of *botho/ubuntu,* which could arguably be regarded as a precursor to modern-day social work education and training in Botswana (Schapera, 1943).

From the historical sources referred to above and anecdotal evidence, it is safe to conclude that during the pre-colonial and colonial period there was no formal social work education in Botswana. In existence were informal welfare structures that in various ways supported the needy and vulnerable. The major strength of the traditional social work approach, as noted, was that it was anchored on the principle of *botho* and as such could be said to have provided the foundation for professional social work practice in contemporary Botswana.

EVOLUTION OF FORMAL SOCIAL WORK EDUCATION AND TRAINING IN BOTSWANA

Professional social work education and training started in 1972 with the introduction of a community development programme run by the Botswana Agricultural College (Osei-Hwedie, 1995). At the time the college was training community development workers, meaning social work was subsumed in community work. Predictably, this resulted in the social work profession losing its identity. According to Osei-Hwedie (1995) in 1974, a few social work courses were introduced into the curriculum, resulting in the programme assuming the title *Certificate in Social and Community Development.* Apparently, the training was rather rudimentary, such that after graduation, *"the staff did not have the necessary skills, many appeared unsure of their duties and procedures, and that their job description as generalist fieldworkers was too vague and hence lacked focus"* (Osei-Hwedie 1995, p. 84).

In 1985, the social work education programme was transferred to the University of Botswana, and over the years a number of programmes have been launched at this institution. From 1985 up until 1995, the University of Botswana was offering a Certificate in Social Work, a Diploma in Social Work, and a Bachelor of Social Work degree. The Certificate in Social Work, which was regarded as a para-professional programme, was later phased out. Graduates of the Diploma and Bachelor degree programmes were both considered professionals. The Bachelor of Social Work degree has been regarded as the flagship of social work education and training in the country and has been the most subscribed. With time, a Masters in Social Work degree was launched, and this has 3 areas of specialisation, namely Social Policy and Administration, Clinical Social Work, and Youth and Community Work.

In 2011, the University of Botswana Senate approved the launching of a PhD in Social Work. The programmes offered by the University of Botswana have attracted both local and international students. At the time of writing, the Department of Social Work had a staff establishment of 17, made up of 3 Full professors, 4 Associate professors, several senior lecturers, and a few early career educators. The vast majority of the faculty members hold PhDs from reputable universities across the world. This serves to indicate that the Department of Social Work at the University of Botswana has come of age. Employment opportunities for graduates include in government service, in NGOs and FBOs, as well as the private sector. There are a number of former graduates of the programme in academia, and the service forces including the army and the police. The idea of private practice has still not yet quite caught the imagination of many professional social workers.

Be that as it may, there are a number of issues in social work education and training in Botswana today that need highlighting. Some of the key issues are explored briefly in the paragraphs that follow.

Issues in Social Work Education in Botswana Today

Issues Pertaining to Relevance and Appropriateness of Social Work Education Curricula

In Botswana, like in most African countries, questions around relevance and appropriateness continue to be an issue for intense debate. There is broad consensus that social work in Botswana is rather too remedial, and hence the debate has revolved around how to make social work more relevant to the local context (Mwansa, 2011). Critics say social work education continues to rely heavily on Western curricula, meaning there is overreliance on knowledge generated outside the African continent. It is instructive that what has evolved in Western countries over time continues to be deemed as suitable and transferable to the African context (Graham, 1999). It is critically important that social work education in Botswana ensures that the curriculum and teaching methods employed (should) reflect interventions that support indigenous knowledge and practice, while at the same time being consistent with the global standards.

Issues Pertaining to Fieldwork Practicum

In the context of Botswana, the fieldwork component has met with many challenges. One issue relates to the fact that there is still a shortage of qualified onsite (field) supervisors and this scenario means that some students are not provided with meaningful learning opportunities. In some instances, agency supervisors only grudgingly take on students (because their superiors have acceded to the request), meaning the students may not be welcome to practice in the agency (Xiong & Wang, 2007). Given the shortage of qualified supervisors, degree students in Botswana may find themselves being supervised by at best diploma holders, or certificate holders, or at worst non-social workers. This means that the student may not get the best out of their fieldwork experience given the different education levels (or even specialisations) of the supervisor and the supervisee. Many social work students have been supervised by officers who hold an adult education qualification—short-changing the students in the process.

Another challenge relates to the inadequate length of field placement. Because of the manner in which the university semesters are configured, it has not been easy to find a suitable slot for students to go on field attachment. The only time that has been convenient is the long vacation during the month of June/July each academic year, but even then the period does not offer enough latitude to do a longer placement. Consequently, the social work practicum curricula in Botswana, generally, do not meet the required international standard of at least 800 hours in practical training (Valentine, 2004). This therefore creates a fissure between the curriculum and the needs of the clientele. It also creates a challenge when former graduates want to register with professional bodies outside the country's borders such as South African Qualification Authority (SAQA) in South Africa.

Another challenge relates to low staffing levels. Elsewhere institutions recruit individuals dedicated to the field instruction component of social work education and training. In Botswana as elsewhere in Africa, social work education and training institutions do not have full-time field supervisors responsible for helping the students to identify the doubts, difficulties, and the emotional problems that they are bound to encounter during field practice. Due to resource scarcity, course instructors have been obliged to split their time between teaching, conducting research, and part-time fieldwork instruction. As noted by Edmond, Megivern, Williams, Rochman, and Howard

(2006), fieldwork education should provide an opportunity to integrate theory into practice. However, the kind of approach narrated above does not accord students the full benefit of field instruction, as in some cases supervision tends to be actually non-existent. The absence of full-time supervision has at times meant that there is no one to assist students (on placement) when they are in doubt, facing difficulties or when they encounter emotional problems (Xiong & Wang, 2007). Such a scenario does not augur well for professional growth as it has the potential to churn out half-baked professionals. Institutions, in particular the University of Botswana's Department of Social Work, are working on ensuring this anomaly is addressed, particularly within the context of the current BQA—Botswana Qualifications Authority—National Qualifications Framework.

Sometimes there is a mismatch between what students have learnt in class and the skills and knowledge that they need to problem-solve. This is usually a function of poor quality field instruction. Such a scenario might be a function of the fact that the field supervisor is not very sure of their own expected role, either because they have no professional social work background, have a lower level of social work education and training than the student, they have been in the field for so long that they have since become rusty, they are too lazy, or they are just not interested in student supervision. The University of Botswana in particular has tried to address these challenges by conducting regular field supervisors' workshops, both in Gaborone the capital city and in other areas. However, due to resource constraints, the workshops have hardly covered everyone who ought to benefit. Additionally, the placements have been for relatively short durations, meaning they have not been sufficiently comprehensive in their treatment of issues.

The Struggle to Promote Evidence-Based Practice Education

In Botswana, as elsewhere in the developing world, once social workers have graduated and have been deployed into the field, very often they have had to rely, not only on existing theories, but also on personal experiences and advice from colleagues and supervisors for practice direction in the field (Howard, McMillen & Polio, 2003). Today, social work education institutions are no longer challenged by the lack of skills and knowledge, but rather by the need to increase research outputs, which educators can use to assist students on how to cope with the complexities of the modern society. There is an increasing volume of scientific evidence-based research findings which social work educators and practitioners can easily incorporate into the menu of information they can use when imparting social work knowledge and skills to students. Perhaps the most critical question to ask in the context of Botswana's situation might be: Is there sufficient readiness and preparedness on the part of both practitioners and educators to fully utilise research in their teaching and professional practice? (Howard et al., 2003). The jury is still out in this regard.

Using evidence-based research is important for a number of reasons: firstly, it assists practitioners to meet their ethical obligations; secondly; with the increase in the laws that hold practitioners accountable for malpractice, evidence-based research will increase practitioner's effectiveness and enhance their credibility among other professions (National Association of Social Workers, 1996). Currently, in social work education and training in Botswana, while there is general agreement among scholars regarding the critical role of empirical research for effective practice, the social work curriculum at the University of Botswana in its present form does not provide students with the requisite skills to use and apply the scientific literature to their practice (Proctor & Rosen, 2000). This is therefore an aspect that requires strengthening, i.e. a gap that needs to be filled.

Research and Publications

Evidence-based practice is only possible where there is sufficient research being conducted. For any profession to meaningfully develop and acquire an appropriate knowledge base, research is paramount, and Botswana's institutions are no exception. For Botswana to develop locally relevant interventions, it will be important that institutions engage aggressively in research. To date, in Botswana as in many other African countries, only a limited number of empirical studies are being carried out (Mwansa, 2010). This is not because of shortage of skills to conduct research, but rather, the lack of resources for the purpose. Mwansa (2011) has argued that there is general frustration among students and educators alike regarding the lack of access to locally relevant knowledge.

In many instances, local experiences remain undocumented, meaning these remain only in people's heads. This suggests that some academics will even go to their graves with unshared knowledge, and this includes anecdotal information. In other cases, research findings have ended up gathering dust in office shelves due to the limited outlets for publishing. In yet other instances, the data were only accessible as grey materials, meaning very limited circulation. There may be a number of reasons why local academics have tended to churn out only limited amounts of research projects, but the key one is essentially difficulties in accessing funding (Osei-Hwedie, 1993). In cases where funding is availed, however, the research agenda is usually set by the sponsors such as donor agencies to achieve their own goals without being considerate of the demands of the curriculum and issues of concern in the host country. Botswana is no exception to experiencing these shenanigans.

Regulating Bodies

Across Africa the number of institutions offering social work education and training has continued to increase steadily over the years, with Uganda probably having the largest number at 21, followed by South Africa (17).

Zimbabwe currently has 4 such institutions, while Botswana, with a population approximately 2.2 million inhabitants, has a couple. Across the world, wherever a number of social work education and training institutions are operational, it becomes imperative to set up a regulating body or bodies. In the context of Botswana, two such bodies are well-worth mentioning. First, is the umbrella body of social workers in the country—the Botswana National Association of Social Workers (BNASW). This body has been functional for several years now. Unfortunately, the association has, over the years, tended to blow hot and cold, depending on who is at the helm at any given time. Membership is voluntary and this has probably rendered it a "toothless bulldog" in the sense that while it can appeal to the membership to maintain ethical standards, it has no power to enforce whatever resolutions it might come up with from time to time. There is near consensus that because of its *locus standi*, generally, the Botswana National Association of Social Workers has struggled to govern and enforce standards of practice.

Other than the BNASW is also the Botswana Health Professions Council (BHPC). In Botswana, social workers who wish to register to practice do so under the Health Act, essentially because there is no separate Act of Parliament governing the profession of social work. Not all social workers are registered under the Health Act. In any event, social workers unlike other professionals, such as doctors and nurses, are not obliged to register with this body in order to be admitted into the practice of social work. This means that this "body" also has not really governed the work of the social work profession.

Effectively, this means that in Botswana no regulatory or accreditation body exists at law that is responsible for ensuring social work professionals toe the line in terms of observing ethical conduct. Consequently, what is now evidenced is a *laissez-faire* approach towards the profession of social work (Mwansa, 2011). In the hiring institutions such as government and non-governmental organisations, many professionals such as adult educators, teachers, and nurses have been allowed to hold social work positions, and what more, to call themselves social workers since they are doing work ordinarily meant for qualified social workers. As observed by Hochfeld, Selipsky, Mupedziswa, and Chitereka (2009), across the African continent, this has then posed a threat to the well-being of social work as a profession as there is lack of relevant legislation, statutes, and accrediting bodies to bring about discipline into the profession.

Macro-Practice Versus Individual Therapy

Literature affirms (e.g. Osei-Hwedie, 1993) that social work in Africa has essentially promoted micro and mezzo as opposed to macro-practice, due to its Western residual orientation. In the context of Botswana, social workers essentially expend their energy mostly focusing on aspects of direct practice—in particular working with vulnerable groups such as destitute persons, orphaned children as well as people with disabilities. A limited number operate at the macro-level, where they mostly work as generalist officers covering social welfare, the youth, community development, procurement, poverty eradication, etc. One component of direct practice, that of the clinical approach, does not seem to have garnered sufficient traction or appeal among the authorities perhaps because this approach tends to use up meagre resources. The limited attention granted clinical social work has meant individual social problems that have a ripple effect on the wider community such as drug and alcohol abuse, intimate partner violence (IPV), mental health, among other social disorders, have been neglected by the social work profession.

The source of the problem might even be the classroom: some observers have argued that perhaps clinical intervention and methodologies have not received the attention they deserve in the classroom. As is the case elsewhere in the developing world (Yuen-Tsang & Wang, 2002), individualised social work practice (in Botswana) has thus over the years played a supplementary and secondary role in the social work curriculum. Counselling skills, in particular, may need greater attention at classroom level. Thus, while the social work curriculum at institutions in Botswana, as elsewhere in the developing world (Specht & Courtney, 1995; Mullay, 1997), does embrace elements of both macro- and micro-practice, the emphasis has apparently been on other forms of micro-practice that do not quite include the micro-practice called clinical social work. Needless to state that, consequently, vigorous efforts are currently underway to correct the anomaly by reclaiming this lost terrain. The Masters programme at the University of Botswana is currently churning out a few clinical social workers, and this development will certainly bear fruit in the long run.

CONCLUSIONS AND WAY FORWARD

Social work education in Botswana has clearly come of age. The University of Botswana (UB) is the leader in providing social work education and training in the country, although a couple of other institutions are also offering some kind of social work education and training. At the University of Botswana, curriculum review efforts continue to be a key item on the radar. The idea is to ensure the curriculum meaningfully responds to, not only current local needs, but also to regional needs as well, while the graduates produced ought to be capable of holding their own, on the international scene as well. To this end, concerted efforts have also gone into ensuring the curriculum measures up to international standards but without losing its indigenous touch. This is pertinent in the light of the argument made elsewhere that social work education and training in Botswana needs to strive to be Afrocentric if it is to be relevant and appropriate. Emerging issues on the international scene, in particular the slant towards promoting developmental social work, constitute a theme that the Department of Social Work remains ceased with. Apart from traditional social work themes such as family welfare, clinical social work, working with groups and communities, new topics that are increasingly gaining traction and currency on the international scene, and these include green social work (otherwise referred to as environmental social work) and issues around climate change, disaster risk management. These are slowly carving a niche in the curriculum of the University of Botswana as well.

In regard to the University of Botswana social work programme, an Advisory Board, made up of key stakeholders from the government, local government, the private sector, non-governmental and faith-based organisations, is firmly in place to give advice on the needs of communities out there. This arrangement has, over the years, helped shape the "menu" of courses on offer in the Department's curriculum, with a view to ensuring it realises relevance and appropriateness. Additionally, the Department of Social Work at University of Botswana also continues to cherish its association with international bodies such as the International Association of Schools of Social Work (IASSW) and the International Federation of Social Workers (IFSW). Needless to state that some critics have argued that while African countries continue to argue for indigenisation, the reality is that IASSW, IFSW, and similar organisations are dominated and funded by the West and as a result they continue to shape and determine the tempo of SW education in the world, with emphasis on the remedial approach. The point however is that these institutions, at least on paper, are not averse to indigenisation. It is against this backdrop that the Department has drawn inspiration from the international definition of social work crafted by the two bodies mentioned above, as well as international guidelines for social work education provided by the former organisation. All this is happening against a backdrop of the quest for relevance and appropriateness of social work education and training in Botswana.

References

Aina, T. A., & Moyo, B. (2013). *Giving to help, helping to give: The context and politics of African philanthropy.* Dakar: Amalion Publishing.

Botswana Institute for Developmemt Policy Analysis (BIDPA, 1997). *Poverty eradication in Botswana consultancy report.* Gaborone: Botswana Government/BIDPA.

Edmond, T., Megivern, D., Williams, C., Rochman, E., & Howard, M. (2006, March). Integrating evidence-based practice and social work field education. *Journal of Social Work Education, 42*(2), 377–396.

Eze, M. O. (2008). What is African communitarianism? Against consensus as a regulative ideal. *South African Journal of Philosophy, 27*(4), 386–399.

Graham, M. (1999). The African-centred world view: Developing a paradigm for social work. *The British Journal of Social Work, 29*(2), 251–267.

Gray, M., Kreitzer, L., & Mupedziswa, R. (2014). The enduring relevance of indige-nisation in African social work: A critical reflection on ASWEA's legacy. *Ethics and Social Welfare*, *8*(2), 101–116.

Hedenquist, J. (1992). *Introduction to social and community Development work in Botswana*. Gaborone: Ministry of Local Government, Lands and Housing.

Hochfeld, T., Selipsky, L., Mupedziswa, R., & Chitereka, C. (2009). *Developmental social work education in Southern and East Africa* (Research Report). Johannesburg: Centre for Social Development in Africa, University of Johannesburg.

Hoppers, C. O. (2003). *Indigenous knowledge systems: An invisible resource in literacy education*. Retrieved form http://www.sgiquaterly.org, Acessed October 9, 2007.

Howard, M. O., McMillen, C. J., & Pollio, D. E. (2003). Teaching evidence-based practice: Toward a new paradigm for social work education. *Research on Social Work Practice*, *13*(2), 234–259.

Jongman, K (2015). *Foretelling the history of social work: A Botswana perspective*. Geneva, Switzerland: International Federation of Social Workers.

Lucas, T. (1994). *Social work, social justice and empowerment: A case of Botswana*. Regina, SK, Canada: Social Administration Research Unit, University of Regina.

Lucas, T. (2017). Social work in Botswana: The struggles of a nascent profession. In R. Mupedziswa, G. Jacques, & L.-K. Mwansa (Eds.), *Social work and social development in Botswana* (pp. 38–53). Rheinfelden: IFSW.

Mafela, L., Maundeni, T., & Mookodi, H. (2011). Introduction: Socio-economic Development in Botswana. *Journal of Social Development in Africa*, *26*(1), 7–14.

Metz, T. (2007). Towards an African moral theory (Symposium). *South African Journal of Philosophy*, *26*(4), 332–336.

Midgley, J. (1983). *Professional imperialism: Social work in the third world*. London: Heinemann.

Mupedziswa, R. (2001, July). The quest for relevance: Towards a conceptual model of developmental social work education and training in Africa. *International Social Work*, *44*(3), 285–300.

Mupedziswa, R., & Ntseane, D. (2012, Autumn). Human security in the SADC region: Learning from Botswana [Special issue]. *Regional Development Dialogue*, *33*(2), 56–70. UNCRD: Adelaide, SA.

Mwansa, L. K. (2010). Challenges facing social work education in Africa. *International Work*, *53*(2), 129–136.

Mwansa, L. K. (2011). Social work education in Africa: Whence and whither. *Social Work Education*, *30*(1), 4–16.

Mullay, B. (1997). *Structural social work: Ideology, theory, practice—An empowering approach*. Boston, MA: Allyn & Bacon.

National Association of Social Workers. (1996). *Code of ethics: Revised and adopted by Delegate Assembly of National Association of Social Workers*. Washington, DC: NASW Press.

Ngwenya, B. (1992). *Social work in Botswana: The agony of irrelevance* [Monograph]. Gaborone: University of Botswana.

Osei-Hwedie, K. (1993). The challenge of social work in Africa: Starting the indigeni-zation process. *Journal of Social Development in Africa*, *8*(1), 19–30.

Osei-Hwedie, K. (1995). *A search for legitimate social development education and prac-tice models for Africa*. Queenston: The Edwin Mellen Press.

Proctor, E. K., & Rosen, A. (2000, May). *The structure and function of social work practice guidelines.* Paper presented at the Developing Practice Guidelines for Social Work Interventions: Issues, Methods, and Research Agenda Conference, George Warren Brown School of Social Work, St. Louis, Missouri.

Regional Hunger & Vulnerability Programme (RHVP). (2011). Social Protection in Botswana—A model for Africa? *Johannesburg: Regional Hunger and Vulnerability Programme.*

Schapera, I. (1943). *Native land tenure in Bechuanaland Protectorate.* Pretoria: Lovedale.

Schapera, I. (1994). *A handbook of Tswana law and custom.* Gaborone: Botswana Society.

Specht, H., & Courtney, M. (1995). *Unfaithful angels: How social work has aban- doned its mission.* New York: Free Press.

Statistics Botswana. (2018). *Botswana multi-purpose survey 2015/2016.* Gaborone: Poverty Stats Brief.

Swanson, D. M. (2012). Ubuntu, African epistemology and development: Contributions, tensions, contradictions and possibilities. In H. K. Wright & A. A. Abdi (Eds.), *The dialectics of African education and Western discoveries: Appropriation, ambivalence and alternatives.* New York: Peter Lang.

Tlou, T., & Campbell, A. (1984). *History of Botswana.* Gaborone: Macmillan.

Valentine, D. P. (2004). Field education: Exploring the future, expanding the vision. *Journal of Social Work Education, 40*(1), 3–12.

Wass, P. (1969). A case history: Community development gets established in Botswana. *International Review of Community Development, 16,* 181–198.

World Bank & Botswana Institute for Development Policy Analysis. (2013). *Botswana Social Protection Assessment Report.* Gaborone: World Bank & BIDPA.

World Bank. (2015). *Botswana poverty assessment: Despite significant decline in poverty, many, nearly half of them children, are still poor.* www.worldbank.org/en/country/ botswana/publication/books-poverty-assessment-decider-2015. Accessed May 29, 2018.

Xiong, Y., & Wang, S. (2007). Development of social work education in China in the context of new policy initiatives: Issues and challenges. *Social Work Education, 26*(6), 560–572.

Yueng- Tsang, A. W. K., & Wang, S. C. (2002). Tensions confronting the devel- opment of social work education in China: Challenges and opportunities. *International Social Work, 45*(3), 375–388.

CHAPTER 27

Evolution of Social Work Education in Turkey: A Critical Perspective

Oğuzhan Zengin and *Buğra Yıldırım*

INTRODUCTION

It is beyond doubt that every society, every country, and every individual are concerned about finding solutions to the social problems they experience and responding to their own needs. It was sometimes ensured with an individual reflex, sometimes with a work practice in small or large groups, and sometimes with education and social policy output. Regardless of the name, the developed solutions are natural; they depend on the political and social structure of that country, the level of economic development, the accumulation of culture and experience (Karataş & Erkan, 2005). Within this cultural and experience accumulation, the fact that religious organisations, foundations, social work, and aid practices carried out by individual initiatives have become a profession by developing and having rules and standards resulted from the coincidence of many historical events (Danışoğlu, 2011). Societies were undergoing a rapid technological development, industrialisation and urbanisation process. While ensuring material welfare in Turkey was getting harder with available resources, the search for new sources was continuing at full speed, and all attention was being drawn to settling social welfare for individuals and society (Kut, 2005). Social welfare has undergone a period of rapid growth and has also gained popularity in Turkey as in many parts of the world. Within the framework of

O. Zengin (✉)
Department of Social Work, Faculty of Economics
and Administrative Sciences, Karabük University, Karabük, Turkey

B. Yıldırım
Department of Social Work, Faculty of Health Sciences,
Manisa Celal Bayar University, Manisa, Turkey

S. S. M. et al. (eds.), *The Palgrave Handbook of Global Social Work Education*, https://doi.org/10.1007/978-3-030-39966-5_27

the principle of universalism, governments saw social work as an institution with the potential to treat social problems such as poverty, child, family, and old age welfare. As the field of social welfare expanded, the need for qualified professionals has come to the forefront. Demands have increased for scientific and professional standards for everyone with health and welfare services being in the first place. Thus, at the end of the 1950s, social work education has become an important concern of Turkey (Tuncay & Tufan, 2011).

The 1950s and 1960s are remembered as the years when a number of theoretical and social changes took place in Turkish society. At the beginning of the noteworthy transformation process, with the change of the Constitution of the Republic of Turkey, the increasing importance of the concept of "*social state*", the creation of new constitutional institutions required the national development to be provided with five-year planning programmes (Kut, 2005). The fact that social services and social work education were regarded as an effective policy and became a right of citizenship, and its application as a social service sector under the roof of the state coincided professionally during this period, but it was unlikely that social work education could be planned alone. Therefore, in Turkey, the elements that contributed most to the contemporary design of social welfare services both in the reorganisation of social services after the Second World War and in the structuring of social work education were external factors rather than internal social demands (Karataş & Erkan, 2005; Tuncay & Tufan, 2011). It is known that the United Nations Organization, which was founded after the Second World War, has undertaken a leading role in education not only in Turkey but also in many underdeveloped/developing countries (Karataş & Erkan, 2005).

Thus, the educational infrastructure of social work in Turkey was created in the 1950s by experts of the United Nations. When these experts met government officials, they decided to start social work education under the Ministry of Health and Social Assistance. After this decision, the Social Work Academy was established in 1959 to provide education for four years after high school graduation under the Ministry of Health and Social Assistance, in accordance with Law No. 7355 on the Establishment of the Social Work Institute. In 1961, social work education began in Turkey. The fact that the first school of social work in Turkey was established under the Ministry of Health and Social Assistance instead of the university is an important situation that needs to be emphasised. According to Karataş and Erkan (2005), Turkey's sociopolitical conditions during that period did not allow the provision of social work education within a university. The selection of the Ministry of Health and Social Assistance for education largely depended on the organisation of social assistance and social services in this ministry. As a matter of fact, six years after the Social Work Academy opened within the ministry started to provide education, a second school of social work was established within the scope of Hacettepe University. Later, these two schools united in 1982. Thus, the academy was admitted to Hacettepe University in accordance with the Law on Higher Education and received the name of Hacettepe University School of Social Work in 1982. In 2002, Baskent University also started social work education. This was a milestone because Hacettepe University School of Social work was the only organisation providing social work education in Turkey for 41 years. Since 2006, there has been a large increase in the number of social work departments, and there are now nearly 70 departments. However, nowadays, there are huge problems with the curriculum not specifically developed for Turkey (especially consisting of American thoughts), non-social work educated academicians, open education system, and increased unemployment in parallel with the increasing number of graduates. This chapter will focus on these problems.

Problems About the Curriculum

The quality of education/training of a social work programme can be achieved by first meeting the differentiating demands of individuals, groups, institutions, and societies that need a social work profession. Social work knowledge should be contemporary, constantly renewed, locally fed, and open to change (Yiğit, 2017). For example, social work practices for Turkish workers and their families who migrated from Turkey to Germany after the 1960s and still live in Germany have undergone three important stages. These stages are as follows: (1) the stage when German social workers tried to serve those coming from the Turkish culture, (2) the stage when German social workers served those who migrated from Turkey to Germany by learning Turkish, and (3) the stage when those who had previously migrated from Turkey to Germany and Turkish individuals living in Germany were educated as social workers in Germany. In Germany, it was observed that the approach to social work practices with Turkish immigrants is the third one and the approach which would be most appropriate to the new national culture forming in Germany with Turkish immigrants was preferred (Tomanbay, 2011). Cultural competence, as seen in this example, is a fundamental principle of the social work profession and education. It should evolve so as to respond to the needs of different populations under a multicultural umbrella and include differences belonging to others (Abrams & Moio, 2009).

Nowadays, the social work curriculum in Turkey is built on knowledge produced at a relatively international (mainly Anglo-Saxon) level rather than a local character. In the undergraduate programme of Hacettepe University, a pioneer in social work education in Turkey, the courses related to the local knowledge among 61 courses are the Social Structure of Turkey, Social Work Legislation I and Social Work Legislation II. Furthermore, courses such as the Social Work Theory and Practice and Social Problems, which should be loaded with local knowledge, are generally taught using sources belonging to Western countries (Zengin, 2017). In the Social Problems course, students see the problems of social adaptation of African-origin people in the United States rather than the problems in their lands, while in the Social Work

Theory and Practice courses, John's and Mary's social service needs and professional interventions aimed at these needs are studied (Akbaş, 2014).

The Turkish social work education curriculum does not comply with the standards set by the International Federation of Social Workers (IFSW) and the International Association of Schools of Social Work (IASSW) on social work education because according to the IFSW and IASSW (2004), the curriculum should address local, national, and international needs and priorities and be shaped by these needs and priorities. In the widely adopted curriculum in Turkey, there is no local or national emphasis at an adequate level. Tomanbay (2011) states that social work education and practice in Turkey are not integrated with the society and do not have a breathing vitality and activity because they are unfamiliar with the industry and culture stages involved in the society. Students who graduate with such an educational curriculum can develop hesitations about the theoretical application integrity in the field and experience cultural competence problems while working with clients coming from different ethnic and cultural backgrounds. It is expected that the application's content in Turkey will change and local actors and cultural motives will influence professional and academic methods.

This problem is not unique to Turkey since it is a problem at the universal level of social work. There are various tensions in social work education around westernisation, localisation, and assimilation subjects (Gray & Fook, 2004). In connection with the subject, Graham, Brownlee, Shier, and Doucette (2008) conducted a study entitled "*Localization of Social Work Knowledge Through Practitioner Adaptations in Northern Ontario and the Northwest Territories, Canada*", aimed at determining the functionality of the social work knowledge and intervention in this region with social workers serving in the northern part of Canada and working with local people. Social workers interviewed during the study indicated that they could not sufficiently use the knowledge they had learned during the undergraduate education, and they were trying to develop an understanding of social work unique to people there. As seen in this example, social work practices should differ according to countries and regions, the sociocultural structure in the regions, the values and intensity of the emerging problems should shape professional practices (Özmete, 2010). In parallel, Dominelli (2004) suggests that local knowledge has started to be based on social work knowledge and that the Western-based social work concept and practices are reshaping. The author presents a model of social work practice called "*Family Group Conference*", which was developed to address the Maori culture and value system in New Zealand as an example. This model refers to the process of making a formal decision on the care, protection, or criminal behaviour with regard to the child or adolescent by means of the cooperation of family members, social worker, and other workers (Pakura, 2004).

Just as micro- and macro-social work practice, international social work education and localisation seem to be opposite concepts, but they are complementary. The universal social work idea cannot match with a successful social work practice without the cultural motives that we all have, the socie-ties we are inspired by, and the states in which we live. Webb (2003) argues that social work is in favour of the habit of not ignoring the identity of its socialised essence since it must play a role in sustaining local cultural diver-sity. It is stated that it will become increasingly remote and difficult to work with our clients if we do not behave sensitively to the national cultural order (Webb, 2003). Similarly, Tomanbay (1999) emphasises that knowledge has a universal character and that the practice must exist in a locally fed and local-prioritising structure, and that the inclusion of both universal and local knowledge in social work education is healthier. Dominelli (1998), in the same direction with Tomanbay (1999), conceptualises the international social work knowledge as the globalisation of local activities and as the reduction of global activities to local activities by strengthening links between the local and global fields. In this way, the knowledge basis and application methods of social work will develop.

Graham et al. (2008) state that social work needs to adapt its knowledge to different geographies, change the professional behaviour of social work-ers and their relationships with clients coming from different societies, and re-examine appropriate and inappropriate social work theories and prac-tices, and that social service organisations face specific challenges in different regions and that such organisations need to rearrange their services according to social needs. On the other hand, regarding this issue, Dominelli (2004) states that dominant "*expertise*" knowledge at the national and international levels cannot be traced at the local level by questioning it with reference to the life experiences of people from different cultures. Based on this view of Dominelli, the shift of attitude from the problem-solving approach, which is the product of the positivist paradigm in which social workers see themselves as experts to the postmodern theories (solution-focused brief therapy, narra-tive therapy, etc.) that start from the argument that the client is regarded as an expert in his/her own life and that each individual has different subjective realities may be more appropriate in the reality of Turkey. Besides, the fact that scientific studies carried out in the field of social work are now directed from descriptive studies towards intervention studies is definitely very impor-tant for understanding whether the theories and approaches accepted in the social work intervention are appropriate for Turkey.

OTHER DETAILS ABOUT THE CURRICULUM

The institution responsible for the Turkish higher education system is the Turkish Council of Higher Education (CoHE). All private universities and state universities are affiliated to CoHE. CoHE is the institution that pro-vides universities with a wide range of services such as opening departments, providing academic staff, student quotas of universities, promotion crite-ria of academic staff, and also inspects universities in terms of these criteria. In this respect, the main addressee of the social work curriculum is CoHE, but it does not interfere with the content of the undergraduate curricula at universities.

The National Society of Social Workers, which was established in Ankara in 1988, is a solidarity network of social workers in general and has no significant focus on social work education. The Association of Turkish Social Work Schools, which is a newly established association, has some studies and suggestions related to the social work curriculum in Turkey, and these suggestions do not have any legal binding force. However, while there are many organisations that can accredit social work education at the international level, there is no organisation at the national level yet in our country. There are only initiatives undertaken by the Association of Turkish Social Work Schools in collaboration with CoHE regarding accreditation at the national level.

In Turkey, there are three important pillars of social work education: social work knowledge base, research, and practice. The bridge between these pillars is social work research. Social work research aims to integrate social service knowledge base with practice skills. The most important feature that differentiates social work research from other social science researches is that it addresses research issues for the solution of social problems, implements its suggestions, and provides a general perspective to society. The undergraduate curriculum of all social work departments in our country offers Social Work Research and Social Work Applied Research courses. Furthermore, students at the master's degree and doctorate level are expected to contribute to social work research in the country during the thesis period.

Zengin and Çalış (2017) examined the theses written in social work master's degree and doctorate programmes in Turkey in the last ten years and stated that the thesis topics were not related to the recent political events or current social problems in our region. In particular, there is a need for comprehensive doctoral research on Turkey and the human groups who come to Turkey due to forced migration from Syria and Iraq. We think that social work research should be focused on the current social problems experienced by Turkey and that this situation should be reflected on all social work curricula in Turkey at the undergraduate/graduate level.

NON-SOCIAL WORK EDUCATED ACADEMICIANS

The social work department, which has become a popular department in the last 10 years in Turkey, was dramatically opened in tens of universities. Universities that have opened this department have met their needs for academicians by employing academicians from different disciplines. Therefore, the profiles of lecturers and academicians working in social work departments in Turkey are another issue that needs to be focused on sensitively. Alptekin, Topuz, and Zengin (2017) examined the profile of social work department teaching staff through schools' Internet sites. More than two-thirds ($n = 121$) of all the teaching staff members ($n = 173$) that have the competence to give a lecture in the social work departments in Turkey do not have any degree in social work undergraduate education, the master of social work or doctorate, whereas the number of teaching staff with at least one of these degrees is less than one in three ($n=52$).

It should not be forgotten that social work education is eclectic. It is convenient for the acquisition of knowledge and the collection of academicians from different disciplines because it uses this knowledge cluster and academician community in line with the needs of social work education. The eclectic nature of social work should not mean that everyone can plan social work education or practice at the same time. In universities in Turkey that provide social work education, attention should be paid to the number of academicians. The main concern about the nature of social work education and the specificity of the social work discipline is the fact that the weight in the preferred academician profile in the education presentation is in the teaching staff that have not received any social work undergraduate education and/ or postgraduate education. At the moment, there are many academicians who have not received social work education in many social work departments in Turkey. The majority of teaching staff who have not received any social work undergraduate education and/or postgraduate education are the graduates of sociology, family, and consumer sciences and theology departments (Fig. 27.1).

When the examples outside Turkey are examined, the situation hardly seems to resemble Turkey. Alptekin et al. (2017) achieved the following conclusions as a result of a small-scale Internet search on social work departments in the United States and the UK, which are among the countries where social work education is widespread and developed: most of the teaching staff (26 out of 32 lecturers) serving at Columbia University School of Social Work, where social work education first started in the United States, and at Boston

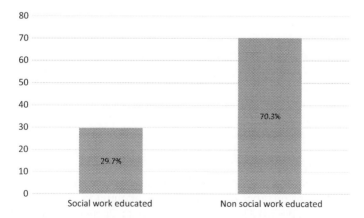

Fig. 27.1 The profile of lecturers and academicians in Turkish social work departments (Reference: Alptekin et al. [2017])

University School of Social Work (25 out of 29 lecturers) seem to have social work undergraduate education and/or postgraduate education. All of the teaching staff of the social work department of Durham University and the social work department of Oxford Brookes University in England have received social work undergraduate education and/or postgraduate education (Alptekin et al., 2017). The facts that the quantitative abundance of departments in universities is regarded as a source of prestige in Turkey, that social work departments do not need expensive inputs such as laboratories and experimental equipment like other science fields, the ease of collecting academicians from close disciplines (Zengin, 2011), although they do not have education in that field, with the thought that everyone can perform social work affect the distribution of the academician profile in social work departments.

OPEN EDUCATION SYSTEM

One of the biggest risks for social work education in Turkey is the presence of "open education programs". There is no obligation to attend any courses in these programmes. Open education programmes require a lower score, have less workforce and cost, and offer the opportunity to become a social worker easily. The absence of practice requirements, unlike formal education, is advantageous for those seeking to receive social work education through relatively easier tasks and exams. The most important problem in open education programmes is the low education quality and incompetence of graduates in terms of knowledge and skills. The nature of social work education can only be achieved through formal education. Although curricula have a theory-weighted structure, the practice dimension of the social work profession is an indispensable factor (Aydemir & Yiğit, 2017).

Two of the departments that offer social work education in Turkey are open education programmes. The first one of these programmes was opened in Atatürk University in 2011. The first programme accepts 1538 students each year. The second social work open education undergraduate programme was opened in Anadolu University, and its quota is 513 (ÖSYM 2017). These two programmes, which accept a total of 2053 students per year, accept the number of students nearly the same with the number of students accepted by all other departments in Turkey. Providing social work education based on an open education model as it is carried out in Turkey (quotas that are exaggerated from every aspect, the limited number of practice courses, and inadequate supervision support) does nothing other than devalues this profession (Alptekin et al., 2017). Achievement of the universal goals by social work depends on the professional qualifications of national social workers. Being a competent member of the profession requires quality education that blends the knowledge, skills, and values of the profession (Aydemir & Yiğit, 2017). It is, therefore, an essential responsibility to teach specific social work techniques, principles, and values to students correctly during social work education. On the contrary, the education given in some newly established universities in Turkey is considered to be insufficient in providing professional knowledge, skills, and techniques to social work students (Çifci, 2009).

At the focus of the social work education curriculum in Turkey, there are human, society, social work methods, social organisation, and social policy (Karataş & Erkan, 2005). On the other hand, the education technique that draws attention to put these titles, which are at the focus of social work education, into practice in addressing social problems is the professional and academic supervision. Furthermore, education, which is based on practice, provides skills, and requires mutual interaction, requires more in-class face-to-face education models. For example, supervision support, universal values, and ethical responsibilities of the profession, carried out by competent social work academicians in order to ensure the development and maturation of the knowledge and skills of a social worker candidate, and the strengthening of his/her work commitment and determination, can only be provided through in-class face-to-face interaction-based education (Alptekin, 2016).

Skill development is the compulsory curriculum content for social work education and is provided with supervision support. Through the teaching of professional skills, social work has been in an attempt to find a place in the modern university system (Papell & Skolnik, 1992) and has been called an academic discipline. The essence and application content of supervision support should be comprehended, and it should be well understood that supervision is a vital element in social work education programmes. In particular, provision of the highest benefit from theory and practice courses, integration with the social work profession and acquirement of the professional identity by students who practice social work (Akçay, 2011), and benefiting from the experience to be gained in the field at the highest level are closely associated with a quality supervision process. It is beyond doubt that diversity is richness, but at least it is necessary to conduct joint activities in the education process. Making local knowledge obtained from supervision and practice processes permanent, sharing and disseminating it will surely increase the efficiency of social work education in Turkey. Demiröz (2005) stated that every change made in the curriculum takes effect at least one generation later and that it is a rational approach to get feedback from supervision and practice instead of ignoring them. These conditions are unlikely to be fulfilled by the open education model in Turkey.

However, a part of social work education (especially courses that need to be given theoretically) can be given using open education technologies. In order to increase the quality of education in this period, when there is an inadequacy of teaching staff, this step may also meet an important need. However, trying to provide the whole of social work education on the basis of open education technologies will damage the nature and quality of education. There are some disadvantages as well as some advantages of open and distance education in social work education. Distance education offers a flexible education opportunity especially for disadvantaged groups that may be outside of social work education (Collins, 2008) and is thus considered as an outcome of equal opportunity in education. According to Abels (2005), the distance education of social work is a requirement of compliance with the principles of equality and social justice in the profession for those who will benefit from this opportunity. In a study emphasising the increased use of distance education (Siegel, Jennings, Conklin, & Napoletano Flynn, 1998), it was reported that the most common problems reported by academicians in relation to distance education are the preparation of the learning environment and the adaptation of training material for course presentations. For this reason, the knowledge and skill education provided by the method in question may also be inadequate at some point. There is a need for a new education curriculum unique to distance social work education.

INCREASED UNEMPLOYMENT FOR GRADUATES

The desire to market the social welfare system in Turkey and raise its standards caused the private sector and non-governmental organisations to begin to exist in this field in addition to the services provided by the government. However, a small number of social workers in Turkey received therapeutic education with their own initiatives, and a small number of them began to conduct couple and family therapy in private (Tuncay & Tufan, 2011). Despite all these developments, private organisations and NGOs in Turkey still play a limited role in the social service system. As a result, social workers are often employed by public institutions.

From the years when social work undergraduate education began in Turkey until 2010, when social workers, who graduated from the departments that gave at most 180 graduates each year, stepped on the field, they did not have any difficulties with finding a job. It is estimated that about 6000 social workers in total graduated by 2010. However, it is known that nowadays around 5000 students graduate from social work departments annually in Turkey. The public sector used to open social worker staff appointments, which ranged from about 200 to 500 in the period when there were 180 graduates per year. Over the years, the number of graduates could not meet the demand for employment. The employment quotas announced by the public sector since 2010, when the number of graduates began to increase, remained the same. Nowadays, while there are around 5000 graduates per year, only 500 graduates can be employed in the public sector.

Karakuş (2015) emphasises that social workers face the danger of being unable to be employed even in their own fields due to the rapid increase in social work departments and their capacities in recent years, indicating that social work has moved away from being a profession with no employment problem to joining those with employment problems. Therefore, unemployment appears to be a significant problem for newly graduated social workers. For this reason, a limit should be imposed on the number of students taken into social work departments, and also new employment opportunities should be investigated for social work graduates. Otherwise, social work may become a department that students do not prefer.

CONCLUSION

The social work profession, which has been in existence for more than a century, has become more important for reasons such as social problems, cultural development, poverty, and social change in the world. The education of such an important profession has been provided over a long period of 41 years by only one school in Turkey. With the understanding of the importance of the profession, new schools of social work have started to be opened. Indeed, the opening of new schools was an indication of the increasing demand for social workers in different fields in Turkish society. This situation was impossible to ignore, but the increase in the number of graduates provided new employment opportunities by the private sector and non-governmental organisations (NGOs) in the field of social services, creating a problem of unemployment and a significant change in the field of social work education. In recent years, there has been an increasing emphasis on cultural competences and local practices at the universal level of social work. Although the use of this term primarily refers to the practice related to ethnic and racial minorities, the concept has been expanded to include social work practice with other culturally different populations and solutions to national social problems.

All dimensions of social work education in Turkey (the education curriculum, the number of teaching staff, etc.) should be revised in accordance with local elements and national cultural needs and not only advance with the international standards. Against social work practices that are individually and structurally transformative at the global level, national practices in the local cultural order should be restructured, and the objectives and tasks of social work education should be defined correctly. Social work practices needed by the local culture should accept the understanding of a common depth in the special Turkey case, and an argument at the national level should be put forward against the established, concrete knowledge of social work and the global social problems that cannot be solved. In this way, social work education can develop national practice standards for the whole society and can support universal social work knowledge.

On the other hand, when national practice standards are developed, and valuable contributions are made to the curriculum, the professional self-assessment can also be mentioned. In both education and professional practice, the context that determines the place of learning is important. Questions should be asked as to how the content of social work education can respond to the challenges of clients facing various adverse situations and how to improve the professionalism of education and training programmes in Turkish universities. Furthermore, student education is a critical issue because it involves acquiring knowledge and skills. Since graduated students will be the exposed face of the profession, the status of the profession in the eyes of the society will be shaped according to the profile of graduates. In conclusion, the more qualified professionals we can raise in the profession, the higher the reputation of the profession will be. The main task for the future of social work education in Turkey is to improve its academic aspect and thus to strengthen its status.

References

Abels, P. (2005). The way to distance education. In P. Abels (Ed.), *Distance education in social work: Planning, teaching and learning* (pp. 3–22). New York: Springer.

Abrams, L. S., & Moio, J. A. (2009). Critical race theory and the cultural competence dilemma in social work education. *Journal of Social Work Education, 45*(2), 245–261.

Akbaş, E. (2014). *Sosyal çalışmada çağdaş eleştirel perspektifler.* Ankara: SABEV Yayınları.

Akçay, S. (2011). Sosyal hizmet uygulaması yapan öğrenciler için süpervizyonun önemi. In V. Işıkhan, T. Tuncay, & E. Erbay (Eds.), *50. Yılında Türkiye'de sosyal hizmet eğitimi: Sorunlar, öncelikler ve hedefler* (pp. 298–303). Ankara: Sosyal Hizmet Araştırma ve Geliştirme Derneği.

Alptekin, K. (2016). *Başlangıçtan bugüne ve yarına Türkiye'de sosyal hizmet eğitimi.* Ankara: Nobel Akademik Yayıncılık, Eğitim Danışmanlık Tic. Ltd., Şti.

Alptekin, K., Topuz, S., & Zengin, O. (2017). Türkiye'de Sosyal Hizmet Eğitiminde Neler Oluyor? *Toplum Ve Sosyal Hizmet, 28*(2), 50–69.

Aydemir, İ., & Yiğit, T. (2017). The social work education in Turkey. *International Journal of Social Work and Human Services Practice, 5*(3), 133–145.

Çifci, E. G. (2009). Social work profession and social work education in Turkey. *Procedia-Social and Behavioral Sciences, 1*(1), 2063–2065.

Collins, S. (2008). Open and distance learning in qualifying social work education in Britain and the USA: Celebrating diversity and difference? *Social Work Education, 27*(4), 422–439.

Danışoğlu, E. (2011). Sabiha Sertel'den günümüze sosyal hizmet eğitiminin 50. Yılı. In V. Işıkhan, T. Tuncay, & E. Erbay (Eds.), *50. Yılında Türkiye'de sosyal hizmet eğitimi: Sorunlar, öncelikler ve hedefler* (pp. 235–236). Ankara: Sosyal Hizmet Araştırma ve Geliştirme Derneği.

Demiröz, F. (2005). Sosyal hizmet eğitimi içinde uygulamaların yeri ve önemi. In Ü. Onat (Ed.), *Sosyal hizmet eğitiminde yeni yaklaşımlar* (pp. 134–141). Ankara: Aydınlar Matbaacılık Ltd., Şti.

Dominelli, L. (1998, December 8). *Culturally competent international social work in the 21st century: An analysis and critique.* Paper presented at the CSWE Conference on Culturally Competent Social Work, held at the University of Michigan, Ann Arbour.

Dominelli, L. (2004). International social work education at the crossroads. *Social Work & Society, 2*(1), 87–95.

Graham, J. R., Brownlee, K., Shier, M., & Doucette, E. (2008). Localization of social work knowledge through practitioner adaptations in Northern Ontario and the Northwest Territories, Canada. *ARCTIC, 61*(4), 399–406.

Gray, M., & Fook, J. (2004). The quest for a universal social work: Some issues and implications. *Social Work Education, 23*(5), 625–644.

IFSW & IASSW. (2004). *Global standards for the education and training of the social work profession.* http://cdn.ifsw.org/assets/ifsw_65044-3.pdf. Accessed March 23, 2018.

Karakuş, B. (2015). Sosyal hizmet mezunlarının kadro ve unvanı "Sosyal hizmet uzmanı/sosyal çalışmacı". *Toplum Ve Sosyal Hizmet, 26*(2), 169–190.

Karataş, K., & Erkan, G. (2005). Türkiye'de sosyal hizmet eğitiminin tarihçesi. In Ü. Onat (Ed.), *Sosyal hizmet eğitiminde yeni yaklaşımlar* (pp. 112–133). Ankara: Aydınlar Matbaacılık Ltd. Şti.

Kut, S. (2005). Türkiye'de sosyal hizmet mesleğinin eğitimi. In Ü. Onat (Ed.), *Sosyal hizmet eğitiminde yeni yaklaşımlar* (pp. 9–13). Ankara: Aydınlar Matbaacılık Ltd. Şti.

ÖSYM. (2017). *ÖSYS yükseköğretim programları ve kontenjanları kılavuzu.* http://www.osym.gov.tr/TR,13263/2017-osys-yuksekogretim-programlari-ve-kontenjanlari-kilavuzu.html Accessed March 24, 2018.

Özmete, E. (2010). Sosyal hizmette sürdürülebilir kalkınma anlayışı: Kavramsal analiz. *Aile Ve Toplum, 11*(6), 79–90.

Pakura, S. (2004, June). The family group conference 14-year journey: Celebrating the successes, learning the lessons, embracing the challenges. In *Proceedings American Humane Association's Family Group Decision Making Conference and Skills-Building Institute* (pp. 6–9).

Papell, C. P., & Skolnik, L. (1992). The reflective practitioner. *Journal of Social Work Education, 28*(1), 18–26.

Siegel, E., Jennings, J. G., Conklin, J., & Napoletano Flynn, S. A. (1998). Distance learning in social work education: Results and implications of a national survey. *Journal of Social Work Education, 34*(1), 71–80.

Tomanbay, İ. (1999). *Sosyal çalışmayı yapılandırmak.* Ankara: SABEV Yayınları.

Tomanbay, İ. (2011). Sosyal hizmet öğretiminde kaçan fırsatlar, kökenleri ve bugüne etkileri. In V. Işıkhan, T. Tuncay, & E. Erbay (Eds.), *50. Yılında Türkiye'de sosyal hizmet eğitimi: Sorunlar, öncelikler ve hedefler* (pp. 36–46). Ankara: Sosyal Hizmet Araştırma ve Geliştirme Derneği.

Tuncay, T., & Tufan, B. (2011). Social work education and training in Republican Turkey. In S. Stanley (Ed.), *Social work education in countries of the East: Issues and challenges* (pp. 543–562). New York: Nova.

Webb, S. (2003). Local orders and global chaos in social work. *European Journal of Social Work, 6*(2), 191–204.

Yiğit, T. (2017). Türkiye'de sosyal hizmet eğitim/öğretiminde kalite güvence sistemi ve akreditasyon standartlarına ilişkin bir model çerçeve önerisi. *Toplum Ve Sosyal Hizmet, 28*(1), 151–168.

Zengin, O. (2011). Sosyal hizmet eğitiminin eğitimci boyutu: Mevcut durum ve geleceğin sosyal hizmet akademisyenleri hakkında öngörüler. In V. Işıkhan, T. Tuncay, & E. Erbay (Eds.), *50. Yılında Türkiye'de sosyal hizmet eğitimi: Sorunlar, öncelikler ve hedefler* (pp. 193–199). Ankara: Sosyal Hizmet Araştırma ve Geliştirme Derneği.

Zengin, O. (2017). Sosyal hizmet eğitiminde ikilem: Uluslararası sosyal hizmet eğitimi ve yerelleşme. In A. İçağasıoğlu Çoban, B. Karakuş, A. Özdemir, M. Zubaroğlu Yanardağ, & M. C. Aktan (Eds.), *Türkiye'de sosyal politikanın dönüşümü: Yerelleşme ve sosyal hizmetler* (pp. 99–107). Ankara: Sosyal Hizmet Uzmanları Derneği Yayınları.

Zengin, O., & Çalış, N. (2017). Türkiye'de sosyal hizmet araştırması: Son 10 yılda sosyal hizmet anabilim dallarında yazılan tezler üzerine bir inceleme. *İnsan Ve Toplum Bilimleri Araştırmaları Dergisi, 6*(2), 1260–1273.

CHAPTER 28

Social Work Education and Practice in Bangladesh: Issues and Challenges

Md Ismail Hossain and Iftakhar Ahmad

INTRODUCTION

Social work is much more than an academic discipline; it is a professional practice that helps people solve problems that crop up in their lives. People only seek assistance when they are unable to solve problems on their own. The most effective way of addressing social problems is to seek help from professionals who have requisite knowledge of human relations, social and behavioural theories, and relevant skills in dealing with social problems. In developed countries where social work is recognised as a profession people seek help from social workers when they come up against psychosocial problems in their personal or social life. Bangladeshi people face a number of social problems such as poverty, school dropout, ill health, unemployment, gender inequality, violence against women, family disorganisation, drug addiction, crime and delinquency, and frequent natural disasters. However, getting help from social workers is the last thing they consider simply because they know so little about social work. Nevertheless, social work is treated just like other academic disciplines such as economics, sociology, political studies, public administration, and anthropology. People hold on to superstitious beliefs and misunderstand the nature and scope of social work (Singh, 2010). Although social work education was first introduced to Bangladesh

M. I. Hossain (✉) · I. Ahmad
Department of Social Work, Shahjalal University of Science and Technology, Sylhet, Bangladesh

© The Author(s) 2021
S. S. M. et al. (eds.), *The Palgrave Handbook of Global Social Work Education*, https://doi.org/10.1007/978-3-030-39966-5_28

almost 70 years ago, little progress has been made toward getting it generally accepted. Getting social work accepted by community people has been made worse because of the failure of the state to recognize it as a profession. The reasons responsible for the slow progress of professional social work practice in Bangladesh are addressed in this chapter. Based on a review of the literature and anecdotal evidence given to the authors this chapter discusses the history of social work practice, the current status of social work education, issues facing social workers in carrying out their jobs, and challenges facing social work practice in Bangladesh.

History of Social Work Practice in Bangladesh

Social welfare before the industrialised era was provided by charity, almsgiving, and poor relief influenced by philanthropic and religious beliefs. After the industrial revolution social problems became more complex due to the huge influx of people to city areas. Mary Richmond and Jane Addams were the first to conceive the importance of training social workers professionally and made significant contributions to the establishment of the Charity Organization Society (COS) in England and later in America (Franklin, 1986). The first training course for social workers in America was provided by the New York School of Social Work under Columbia University in 1898 (DiNitto & McNeece, 2007; Pierson, 2011). In subsequent years many schools throughout the world ran courses to train skilled social workers and provide them with Bachelor, Master's, M.Phil., and Ph.D. degrees in social work.

The history of the social work profession in Bangladesh started at two interlinked levels. The first was more academic in that it can be understood in the pre-qualifying sense (i.e., professional training) and the other was at the community development level that can be understood in the post-qualifying sense or non-government organisation (NGO) level sense (Hussain, 1999). The initial context behind social work practice in Bangladesh was basically the same as that in the developed world where problems resulting from the huge influx of peasants to city areas were being tackled by social workers. During the partition of India in 1947 Pakistan faced multifarious problems in economic development and social welfare due to the migration of millions of destitute refugees who urgently required elementary needs such as shelter, food, and clothes (Taher & Rahman, 1993). The huge influx of refugees to city areas, especially in Dhaka, worsened and continues to worsen the problem of social reintegration as a result of existing problems such as a lack of or poor habitation, joblessness, health and sanitation, and overall social reorganisation (Das, 2012). The resultant proliferation of lawlessness and dependency and their impact on socioeconomic development led the Pakistan government to seek assistance from the United Nations in 1952. The United Nations sent two teams to assess the actual situation in response to this call. The first UN expert team (namely, Lucky and Mr Dumpson) arrived the same year and hurriedly conducted a survey to assess the situation. At the initial phase they recommended a 3-month job-training programme to prepare people to effectively manage the situation. Immediately after, another two UN experts (namely, Dr. Shawky and Miss Anama Toll) organised a training programme comprising three teachers and three assistants at Bardwan House (Bangla Academy) in May 1955. This training programme led to the introduction of a 6-month training course to increase the number of professional social workers in the country (Sarker, 2015).

Based on a report assessing the situation provided by the expert team the United Nations set up a technical assistance project in the social service sector. Under the guidance of UN experts a programme implementation authority called the Urban Community Development Board was constituted to formulate, monitor, and supervise policies and programmes. Meanwhile the first pilot scheme of the Urban Community Development Programme (UCDP) was started in the Kayettuli area in the old part of Dhaka in 1953. In 1956 the National Council of Social Welfare was formed to monitor and supervise UCDP project activities and other allied social welfare programmes in the country. Thereafter, another two projects were initiated under the UCDP: one was in Gopibag—a relatively advanced area—and the other in Mohammadpur both of which had received large concentrations of non-Bengali refugees in 1957 and 1958, respectively (Sarker, 2015; Taher & Rahman, 1993).

The UN report led to a regular curriculum-based institution being set up called the College of Social Welfare and Research Centre with 15 students enrolled for a 2-year MA programme in social welfare in 1958 under the aegis of the University of Dhaka (Das, 2014). This college later became a constituent institution of the University of Dhaka as the Institute of Social Welfare and Research (ISWR) in 1973 (Ahmadullah, 1964; Das, 2013; Taher & Rahman, 1993). In 1964 another social work school the College of Social Welfare was established under the aegis of the University of Rajshahi. Initially, 3-year undergraduate courses were launched in 1964 and 1-year MA programmes in social work were introduced in 1966. This college later became part of the University of Rajshahi in 1973 as the Department of Social Work. Since then it has produced many graduates in social work. Almost 30 years later (1993) another school of social work was launched at Shahjalal University of Science & Technology by Professor Habibur Rahman. Currently, there are 7 public universities, 2 private universities, and 121 colleges under the aegis of national universities offering social work education in Bangladesh (Islam, 2017).

Social Work Curricula and Field Practicum

Social work tries to understand how the interaction between people and the social environment affects their ability to carry out their daily life tasks. A holistic understanding of the complex nature of the relationship between people and their social environment is a prerequisite to addressing social issues effectively. Given the necessities of understanding people and the environment, social work curricula in Bangladesh is a blend of Western and local knowledge. Since social work education was initiated in Bangladesh by the United Nations all the syllabi were based on Western curricula that knew little about the ground reality of Bangladeshi society (Das, 2014; Samad, 2013). Moreover, over the years there have been lots of changes in Bangladeshi society and many complex social issues have arisen where the application of Western social work knowledge did not chime with reality or was found to be irrelevant.

Acknowledging the importance of indigenising social work knowledge, social work curricula in Bangladesh now include courses focussed on both Western theory and approaches and locally emerging issues. Curricula are modified and updated before the start of each new academic year in line with the current needs of students. Every year social work departments arrange field practicum workshops involving students, faculties, and practitioners and get introduce with new areas of social work interventions from the working experiences of social work graduates. As for example, Department of Social Work at Shahjalal University introduced a course on 'Climate Change and Disaster Management' in 2013 based on the recommendation proposed by a workshop participant. Although it was down to practitioners to propose introducing new courses in such workshops, they were often well received by the department and included in the curricula. Newly included courses are designed in such a way that students can understand the local situation and context. Major courses focussed on American-centric or Eurocentric models and approaches include Social Work Practice with Individuals; Social Work Practice with Groups; Social Work Practice with Communities; Social Welfare Administration; Counseling in Social Work; International Social Work; Culture and Social Work Practice; and Strategies in Social Work Practice. Similarly, many courses have been developed in which the urgency and needs of community people are addressed such as Life and Society of Bangladesh; Culture and Social Work Contextualisation; Governance and Politics in Bangladesh; Socioeconomic Movements in Bangladesh; Approaches to Community Intervention; Social Problem Analysis; Human Rights and Social Justice; Social Welfare Services in Bangladesh; Social Work Camping; Climate Change, Disaster Management and Rehabilitation; Gender Issues and Social Work Practice; Guidance and Counseling in Social Work; Social Work Practice with Family and Children; Industrial Relations and Labor Welfare; and Social Work Practice with the Elderly. Currently 4-year Bachelor and 1-year Master's degree programmes are running in all universities and colleges. Students are required to complete 140–160 credits at the undergraduate level and 40 credits at the graduate level.

Another important component of social work curricula is fieldwork. Fieldwork can be defined as a process or approach in which social work knowledge, values, principles, and other social work–related concepts are exercised by apprentice social workers thrown into the "deep end" of social services, welfare, and sustainable development. Field placements provide students with the opportunity to apply their theoretical knowledge in actual practice. Field practicum is compulsory for social work students (without which degrees are not conferred). Social work students are supposed to carry out 60 working days (480 hours) of field practicum at both the undergraduate and graduate level. Fieldwork helps students understand how to target people living with problems and helps students acquire the basic skills necessary for working with an individual, group, or community. There are four types of fieldwork: (i) concurrent placement in which students engage with a fieldwork agency simultaneously with classroom instruction where students spend two or three days in the classroom and the remaining days of a week at the fieldwork agency; (ii) block placement in which social work students are engaged full-time at a fieldwork agency for a specific period ranging from at least a month to one year depending on the institution; (iii) a mixture of concurrent and block placement; and (iv) in-service placement in which students go back to their places of employment to gain fieldwork experience in the context of their existing jobs (Dhemba, 2012). Tightening the academic calendar, unwillingness of the agency to participate in such a placement, distance of the Social Work School from the agency and the working field, and lack of transportation facilities contribute to the reluctance of students to pursue concurrent placements. When there is a lack of resources and other logistic supports, block placement is preferred over concurrent placement. To overcome the lacuna caused by block placements, students are sent for social work camping to a community during the second year of their study. This enables students gain an initial understanding of a particular community including needs and problems, resources, community interaction, power structure, and social institutions.

Students are placed for training in both government and non-government organisations (NGOs). Since there is a scarcity of professional social work agencies students are usually placed for internships in such organisations because they provide students with ample opportunities for social work practice or the prospect of employment as future social workers. NGOs and development organisations are the primary institutions as it comes to absorbing large numbers of social workers. There are thousands of NGOs operating across the country involved in various socioeconomic and health programmes tasked with improving the lot of marginalized people. Students are placed here so that they can obtain practical training. Among the major NGOs are Grameen Bank, Bangladesh Rural Advancement Committee (BRAC), Association for Social Advancement (ASA), CARE Bangladesh, Underprivileged Children's Educational Programme (UCEP), Oparajeo Bangladesh, Bangladesh Women's Health Coalition (BWHC), Friends in Village Development of Bangladesh (FIVDB), Smiling Sun Clinic, Jagorani Chakra, RDRS Bangladesh, Family Planning Association of Bangladesh (FPAB) and other national and local NGOs. In addition, many government programmes are also chosen for field placement of trainee social workers including urban social services; rural social services; hospital social services; safe homes for older or vulnerable people; rehabilitation centres for socially disadvantaged women; children's homes (*Shishu Paribar*); babycare centres; rehabilitation centres for the disabled; adolescent development centres; schools for the blind, deaf and dumb; probation and aftercare services; department of youth; and women support programmes. The type of social work practice depends on the nature of each individual field. Practice is carried out at both the micro and macro level in such fields. Many settings in Bangladesh follow micro-level practice, particularly in hospital settings, correctional homes, babycare centres, and rehabilitation centres. Macro-level practice is done in community development settings, particularly in areas where NGO interventions predominate.

SOCIAL WORK PRACTICE SETTINGS IN BANGLADESH

Over the years the fields of practice of social work have widened. There has been a transformation from micro to macro practices. Social work is now viewed as an integral part of social development. Social work now integrates human rights with social justice and catchphrases such as "social work is for social development" and "social work is for social justice" are frequently heard. In the context of the developed world, particularly focussing on American society, Herbert Williams (2016) identified 12 emerging issues that need to be addressed by social workers: (i) ensure the healthy development of young people, (ii) close the health gap, (iii) stop family violence, (iv) advance long and productive lives, (v) eradicate social isolation, (vi) end homelessness, (vii) create social responses to a changing environment, (viii) harness technology for social good, (ix) promote smart decarceration, (x) reduce extreme economic inequality, (xi) build financial capability for all, and (xii) bring about equal opportunity and provide justice to all. By contrast, the nature and context of the problem in developing countries are largely connected with macro-level practice. Community development interventions are preferable when it comes to addressing problems in developing countries (Chitereka, 2009; Fahrudin & Yusuf, 2016; Pawar, 2014).

There are a number of issues prevalent in Bangladesh where knowledge of social work can be of use. The Seventh Five Year Plan of Bangladesh (2016–2020) mentioned major issues in a section on social welfare. It included the welfare of women, the welfare of young people, the welfare of children, health and family planning, the welfare of the workforce, disaster mitigation, the welfare of the elderly, social security, and the provision of safety nets. Major programmes offered by the Department of Social Services (DSS) under the Ministry of Social Welfare such as urban social services, rural social services, hospital social services, adolescent development centres, safe homes, baby homes, and *ShiShuParibar* ("safe havens for children") are in operation based on the philosophy of social work. However, there is little evidence of the application of social work knowledge because of the lack of professional social workers brought about by an open recruitment policy. The DSS are hiring graduates from different disciplines many of whom have no knowledge about social work. Alongside government programmes undertaken by different ministries there are thousands of NGOs operating in Bangladesh who started to engage in relief work shortly after the independence of Bangladesh. Within a few years NGO activities were transformed from relief to development work. NGOs became development partners for myriad interventions in socioeconomic development of Bangladesh (Hossain, Al-Amin, & Alam, 2012). Major areas in which NGOs intervene are poverty alleviation, maternal and child health, the development of women, rural and urban community development, the welfare of children, the development of young people, welfare of the workforce, drug addiction treatment, HIV/AIDS treatment, the welfare of the disabled, and the welfare of the elderly. All these issues can be addressed more effectively using social work knowledge. Unfortunately, social work knowledge is rarely practised in these fields because of a lack of professional recognition and professional social workers. When it comes to governmental and NGO interventions in the socioeconomic development of Bangladesh a number of major prospective fields of social work practice can be identified:

- **Health and medical care**: the healthcare system in Bangladesh is characterised by a shortage of doctors, nurses, medicine, and medical equipment. The gap between the rich and poor in public health access is also very significant and largely influenced by the high incidence of poverty among low-income people, the lack of social education, and the capacity of people to pay for healthcare (Islam, 2011). Bangladesh has experienced mushrooming growth in the number of private medical hospitals and diagnostic centres, mostly located in urban areas where only financially solvent people can afford to get services because of high cost (Hussain & Raihan, 2015). The poor prefer government hospitals for healthcare services. Hospital social service units are being operated in 90 government and private hospitals in district and city corporation areas under the DSS (MSW, 2018b) to bring healthcare facilities within the reach of the poor. Many NGOs operate in the health sector in both urban and rural areas to deliver healthcare services to the poor and underprivileged communities in Bangladesh (Hossain, Alam, & Islam, 2005). Major services delivered by such NGOs are primary healthcare and sexual and reproductive health services. Some NGOs also offer services to reduce HIV/AIDS and other sexually transmitted diseases (STDs) in the community. In the medical setting social workers can make various interventions in acute care, ambulatory care, and long-term care including high-risk screening, psychosocial assessment, coordinated patient care, counselling, education, discharge planning, and community outreach (Segal, Karen, Gerdes, & Steiner, 2010).

- **Gender development**: women make up half the population of Bangladesh. However, they are vulnerable in social, economic, and cultural areas since they are not given the same rights as men. The gender division of labour in which labour is socially demarcated by gender and social structure not only stops women from gaining employment but also makes them dependent. Moreover, the gender division of labour is the root cause of workplace exploitation influenced by gender-biased beliefs and practices (Hossain, Mathbor, & Semenza, 2013). Women are traditionally burdened with the reproductive responsibility of bearing and rearing children. They are politically suppressed, economically exploited, socially oppressed, legally ignored, and technologically deprived (MOWCA, 2011). Although gender-based violence such as physical assaults, dowry killing, acid burning, divorce and separation, and fatwa (verdict by a member of the local elite who has no legal judicial power regarding marriage) are increasing rapidly, women are reluctant to take legal measures because of social taboos. Since gender-based violence and inequality are deeply rooted in hegemonic patriarchal values and culture, this highlights the urgent need for feminist social work to be practised and confront existing social malpractices to ensure the safety and security of women in society. Government agencies such as the Department of Women Affairs and the Women Support Programme and NGOs such as Grameen Bank, BRAC, ASA, and Bangladesh Legal Aid and Services Trust provide a number of services including gender awareness, entrepreneurship development, microcredit, legal assistance, health and family planning, and training for capacity building. However, state policy makers and development practitioners are more inclined to adopt the views of liberal feminism rather than radical feminism (Hossain et al., 2012).

- **Child welfare**: a significant number of children end up living in the street after being abandoned by their parents or relatives. Deprived of love, care, and basic needs such children get involved in many anti-social and criminal activities. Although some government agencies and NGOs provide services to homeless, street, and abandoned children, these services are very limited and often provided by non-professional workers. Social work has a long tradition of working with children and families (Payne, 2015) and addresses many life circumstances and events such as violence, neglect, maltreatment, and poverty all of which play a part in preventing children's physical, emotional, social, and intellectual development (Noble & Ausbrooks, 2008). It is here in Bangladesh social workers can play a significant role by providing counselling, making associations, and linking them with existing child welfare services that are being delivered by different government agencies and NGOs.

- **Family welfare**: the family is the fundamental institution providing individual welfare and the place where socialisation is learnt. Individual peace and happiness are largely dependent on the relationship between family members. Family social work deals with a number of problems such as marital conflicts, parent–child relationships that have broken down, fatherless families, motherless children, single adults separated from their families, and problems in looking after elderly members (Das, 2012). The prime concern of social work is the family environment. One of the major objectives of family social work is to help individuals maintain harmonious relationships and protect the family from disorganisation (Konrad, 2013). Industrialisation had a devastating effect on traditional family patterns in Bangladesh and led to a number of negative consequences including the degradation of morality, loosening of family ties, aspirations for a Western lifestyle, improper socialisation, and self-centred attitudes (Samad, 2015). Such changes in family patterns produce difficult situations including anxiety, trauma, and mental breakdowns where psychiatric intervention may be necessary. Psychoeducational family counselling is designed to help people in difficult situations. It has both a preventative and treatment function (Van Hook, 2014). Apart from its use in marriage and family counselling it has also been used to address conflicts and other problems related to the family.

- **Community development**: Bangladesh is a developing country where many people live below the poverty line and most live in rural areas. Bangladesh has achieved its millennium development goals (MDGs) and is now struggling to attain sustainable development goals (SDGs). The DSS has introduced rural social services and urban social services that provide interest-free microcredit; motivate people for savings; encourage people to get involved in income-generating and economically profitable activities; provide informal education on health, nutrition, the welfare of mothers and children, sanitation, and safe drinking water; motivate people to engage in family planning, social afforestation, literacy, skill training, and adult education to improve their standard of living in both urban and rural areas (MSW, 2018a). Alongside government agencies there are many NGOs and voluntary organisations engaged in wide areas of social development in Bangladesh. The major objectives of NGOs include the formation of self-help groups, advocating awareness-raising to promote and identify social issues, arranging microcredit for the self-employed, and encouraging income-generating activities and social capital formation through training, community meetings, and public awareness campaigning (Hossain et al., 2012). Social work knowledge can be used to increase individual capabilities, to bring about solidarity, and extend mutual support. Advocacy and counselling are the main instruments used in individual, group, or community-level interventions (Rahman, 1977).

- **Disaster management**: gradual changes in the global climate are widely believed to have increased the risk of disasters. Bangladesh is very prone to natural disasters (Prodhan & Faruque, 2012). In the last 50 years Bangladesh has experienced many natural disasters such as floods, cyclones, river erosion, and droughts all of which have resulted in serious loss of human lives and property. The poor are more vulnerable than the rich during natural disasters mainly because of where they live but a lack of awareness and adaptive capabilities also contributes to such vulnerability. Challenges facing Bangladesh from natural disasters highlight the need for experts in disaster management. Community capacity building is viewed as a highly effective disaster management approach because it ensures the active participation of community people. Effective community participation is very much required in areas where natural disasters frequently happen, especially in coastal areas earmarked for development (Mathbor, 2008). Knowledge of social work, particularly group work and community work, can be used to create norms, build trust, and expand networks within the community and between communities that may enhance the capacity of community people to carry out successful disaster management (Mathbor, 2007).
- **Labor welfare**: acute poverty, unemployment, and frequent natural disasters are the principal reasons the poor migrate to city areas. Without suitable jobs in the city areas migrants are forced to work in construction firms as day labourers or to work as rickshaw pullers. As a result of trade liberalisation in the 1980s Bangladesh experienced a rapid boom in the readymade garments (RMG) industry, which created job opportunities for hundreds of thousands of people, particularly women. Currently 4 million people are working in this industry 90% of whom are women (BGMEA, 2018). Although it is true that the boom in RMG industries provided women with opportunities to gain employment, this sector is highly criticized for violating workers' rights (Islam & Hossain, 2016). The gender division of labour is at the forefront of workplace exploitation influenced as it is by gendered beliefs and practices (Hossain et al., 2013). Industrial disputes are constant in the absence of a fair process of collective bargaining and lack of knowledge about industrial relations. Lack of a decent income forces the poor to reside in low-cost areas such as slums, which are notoriously unhygienic and the root of many social and health problems. Industrial social work is a prospective field of social work practice in which social workers can address the human and social needs of the worker community through a variety of interventions. Its aim is to get individuals to adapt in the best possible way to their environments. Industrial social workers can counsel workers to solve personal problems such as absenteeism and alcoholism and to adjust to the work environment, educate and train workers' leaders, and negotiate between workers and employers. Like India, Industries in Bangladesh

are supposed to recruit social workers as labour welfare officers (often regarded as personnel/human resource managers) who can negotiate and improve the lot of workers in the industry.

- **Correctional services**: correctional services make up an important part of social work practice in Bangladesh. Juvenile delinquency is a matter of growing concern in Bangladesh because of the high involvement of children in criminal activities. Numerous social factors coupled with poor parenting, family troubles, and above all poverty push such children to take part in undesirable activities. In an attempt to rehabilitate juvenile delinquents "*Kishore Kishori Unnoyan Kendra*" (Children Development Centers) have been established and tasked with the responsibility of caring for and protecting such children, providing them with food, housing, clothing, medical care, education, vocational training, and counselling, and fulfilling other developmental needs (MSW, 2018a). There are three Children Development Centre in Bangladesh located at Tongi and Kona Bari (both in Gazipur) and Jashore (Khulna) that can hold 600 children. The main aim of these centres is to modify behaviour by involving family, community, and society instead of dishing out punishment. Psychosocial intervention and community engagement can be brought about by individuals with requisite knowledge of social case work, group work, and the systems theory of social work intervention.
- **Welfare for the elderly**: due to the way social and religious values have changed—some would say degraded—the elderly are not treated with the same respect by family members as they were before. Very often they are neglected and abused by immediate family members. Extreme poverty, poor healthcare provision, mistreatment by family members, unhygienic living conditions, isolation and loneliness, and poor transport and recreational facilities lead to the basic needs of the elderly being unmet and making the elderly more vulnerable (Hossain, Akthar, & Uddin, 2006). Breakdown of the joint or extended family compromised the provision of healthcare to the elderly. The rise of the nuclear family increased the need for old homes. Nevertheless, the number of such care homes in the country is still very few. What is worse, elderly people hate having to stay in old homes leaving their family members, friends, and the places that are close to their hearts and full of memories (Hossain et al., 2005). Social workers can employ micro- and macro-level counselling to change the way the elderly and community people look at things, motivate and persuade people to introduce new institutions, and advocate the need for elderly welfare and social security programmes through public–private partnerships.
- **Social protection system**: social protection is defined globally as a strategy to safeguard the economic security of vulnerable people including the poor and the marginalised. Social safety net programmes (SSNPs) play a part in social protection and are widely recognised instruments

that can be used by government and non-government agencies to ensure the economic wellbeing of the poor (Khan & Hasan, 2016). Major SSNPs in Bangladesh can be divided into four broad categories: (i) employment generation programmes; (ii) programmes to cope with natural disasters and other shocks; (iii) incentives provided to parents for their children's education; and (iv) incentives provided to families to improve their health status (Khuda, 2011). A number of SSNPs are taken by the Ministry of Social Welfare including elderly allowance, allowance for the socially disadvantaged women, disability allowance, living standard development program for *Hijra* community, living standard development program for *Bede* (gypsy) and under-privileged communities, living standard development program for tea garden laborers and financial support program for cancer, kidney and liver cirrhosis patients.

Challenges Facing the Social Work Profession in Bangladesh

Social work education in Bangladesh is much younger of course than that in First World countries. Bangladeshis first became familiar with the concept of social work during the 1950s after the partition of India. Social work has strived for 70 years to attain professional status. Unfortunately, it has still not received professional recognition by the state. This is because a number of factors pose barriers toward gaining the status of a profession. Moreover, such factors adversely affect how young social workers and other practitioners carry out their work. The major challenges facing the practice of social work in Bangladesh are:

- **Misconceptions about the Social Work Profession**: one of major challenges facing social work practice in Bangladesh is the degree to which it is misconceived. The term social work is very often interchangeably used with social welfare despite the significant difference between them. While social welfare should be understood as organised activities that seek to prevent, alleviate, or solve recognised social problems and improve the wellbeing of individuals and communities, social work is the delivery of social services by highly trained professionals. The majority of people in Bangladesh including policy makers and development practitioners consider social work as charitable or almsgiving work that can be done by any philanthropic or voluntary organisation. It is also believed that anyone wanting to do something for humankind can do social work as long as scientific knowledge is not required. Most social service agencies, both government and non-government, are managed and directed by people from other disciplines such as economics, sociology, anthropology, political science, physics, and mathematics who have no or very little knowledge about social work. Lack of knowledge about social work results in many development workers equating their own knowledge from totally different disciplines with professional social work and dramatically changing the concept and meaning of social work (Islam, 2011).

- **Lack of Consistent and Uniform Curricula**: curricula for social work education should be updated, made consistent, and standardised to produce efficient and competent social workers capable of meeting the challenges facing the world. Course curricula on social work are revised on a regular basis. However, inclusion or modification of a course in the curricula is largely at the whim of the interested faculty (Samad & Hossain, 2014). There is no accreditation council to monitor and maintain standards in social work curricula. Absence of an accreditation council results in respective schools of social work modifying and adapting curricula to suit their own needs without having any direction and guidance from the International Association of Schools of Social Work or other sister organisations (Fahrudin & Yusuf, 2016; Islam, 2017). The biggest challenge facing social work practice in Bangladesh is the lack of inclusion of indigenous knowledge in curricula (Das, 2014; Islam, 2017).

- **Absence of a Social Work Agency for Field Practicum**: fieldwork is an integral part of social work education without which such education remains incomplete. It is during fieldwork that students get the opportunity to apply theoretical knowledge. It is essential for apprentice social workers to undertake field training under the supervision of a professional social worker so that they can learn how to use theoretical knowledge effectively. Practitioners in any professional field such as lawyers, doctors and even social workers in the United States, the United Kingdom, Australia, and Canada need certification from respective professional bodies. However, there is no such body for social workers in Bangladesh. Despite having no prior training or knowledge in social work many people are working in specialised service delivery areas. As a result agency supervisors very often find it difficult impossible to relate social work knowledge with field practice. Faculty supervisors are limited in their ability to guide and supervise their students. Since they are not professional practitioners their experiences of applying social work knowledge when dealing with a case are few. In the absence of proper guidance from supervisors, students face difficulties in locating how and in what context knowledge of a particular item is applied.

- **Lack of Indigenous Knowledge**: the indigenisation of social work is essential because failing to grasp the local context appropriately would simply nullify social work. While many scholars have given more focus to indigenous social work rather than indigenised social work because the latter is often not best suited to different cultures and may produce little success (Gray, Coates, & Bird, 2008; Samad & Hossain, 2014), the focus of Bangladeshi scholars is on the indigenisation of social work. The main reason is that social work professionals and practitioners in have not managed to develop a new model or approach of social work best suited to addressing social problems in Bangladesh. Although indigenous literature has yet to be written, collaborative work between academics and field practitioners should be able to correct this. High-quality research could play a leading role in this regard (Hossain et al., 2013). Although social development activities started in Bangladesh with successful research work carried out at the College of Social Welfare (currently, the ISWR), they fell into disuse within a few years and have not since been revived.

- **Lack of a Professional Association**: the purpose of any professional organisation is to act as a vanguard improving the status of professionals. A professional organisation should be the knowledge base of the profession, disseminating knowledge, creating group cohesion among professionals, and working as a pressure group to attain professional status. Bangladesh is still lagging behind in this regard. Social work in Bangladesh has yet to be recognised as a profession because it lacks a professional organisation (Taher & Rahman, 1993). Although some professional organisations have been formed over the last few years by social work professionals to fulfill their own vested interests such as the Bangladesh Council of Social Work Education and the Bangladesh Association of Clinical Social Workers, they are little more than paper-based associations of social work. Professional representation is completely absent in both these organisations because membership is not open to all, but confined to a few (Hossain et al., 2013). Although another organisation the Bangladesh Social Work Teachers Association received a lot of praise for organising conferences during its initial years, it no longer exists. No initiatives of any note were put forward by these organisations to enhance the professional development of social work. Democratic and participatory organisations are indispensable to ensuring the professional development of social work in Bangladesh.

- **Limited Scope for Employment**: the prime aim of educational disciplines is to prepare graduates for employment. As mentioned earlier, major areas in which social work takes place in Bangladesh are the many programmes run by the DSS. However, it is to be regretted that jobs in these fields are not confined to social work graduates. As a result of the open recruitment policy DSS personnel are dominated by people with different academic backgrounds whose knowledge of social work falls short when it comes to dealing with social problems. Development activists need an in-depth understanding of the complex nature of the human problems, values, and ethics that social work addresses—something very difficult for graduates in mathematics, physics, or other disciplines to grasp. Social work graduates are also reluctant to develop their careers as social service professionals due to the status of the profession being perceived as low. Although social service officer (SSO) is not included as a cadre service job by the Bangladesh Civil Service (BCS), many jobs are included such as agriculture officer, Forest officer, Fisheries officer, Medical officer, engineers and Judge and these jobs are confined for the graduates from the respective disciplines. As a result the social service sector faces acute shortages of qualified professionals many of whom regard the job as a vocation.

Conclusions and Recommendations

Although social work is a recognised profession in almost all developed countries throughout the world, it has not gained the status of a profession in Bangladesh. Now that Bangladesh has achieved its MDGs and it is making progress in achieving its SDGs. However, SDGs can only be achieved when community people have the capacity to tackle problems using their own initiatives. There are many social issues in Bangladesh such as poverty and exclusion, lack of healthcare, crime and delinquency, gender inequality, violence against women, industrial disputes and strikes that need to be addressed properly for sustainable development to occur. These problems are best addressed by social work professionals who have thorough knowledge of social work. However, the acquisition of such knowledge is not possible and its application cannot make any substantial contribution to solving problems until it is experienced and practised in the field and viewed from a professional perspective.

Social work education and the practice of social work in Bangladesh face many challenges such as people's misconceptions about social work, lack of consistent and uniform curricula, absence of professional organisations, scant indigenous knowledge, shortage of professional organisations for fieldwork training, and limited job opportunities. Unless these challenges are confronted there is little chance of getting social work as a recognized profession. Once social work gains the status of a profession many issues will automatically be resolved. Moreover, this will motivate social workers to develop further as professional social workers. The few steps suggested here may help to overcome the many challenges:

i. The foremost need is to establish a professional association and bring all social workers under one umbrella. Such a body should be tasked with introducing social work knowledge and techniques in different service delivery systems. It should also be tasked with arranging seminars and symposia to propagate knowledge about the best way of addressing current problems.

ii. A professional association should be tasked with advocating and putting pressure on relevant authorities to ensure professional social workers are recruited in social service sectors. It should also be tasked with setting up a mass campaign about how the practice of social work will bring about socioeconomic development and in so doing boost the movement for professional recognition. The attitude of community people to social work will also change as a result of an awareness campaign.

iii. Social work scholars and practitioners need to collaborate to create and develop knowledge as to how indigenous social work might be of great value in the socioeconomic context of Bangladesh.

iv. Curricula should be updated and standards maintained by getting local and global issues and recent advances in social work knowledge through international collaboration and a scholar exchange programme included in them.

v. Partnership projects should be initiated by social work professionals such that the importance of social work interventions for sustainable development of Bangladesh can be brought home to stakeholders.

vi. Social work scholars and practitioners should be tasked with developing new approaches, models, and techniques of social work to address local problems. They have to be able to show how social work carried out by professional social workers makes a greater difference in bringing change to society than that undertaken by non-professionals. Comparative research in the local context is of great importance in finding the best-suited approach.

vii. Social work teachers and academics should be tasked with building social cohesion by arranging conferences or symposia on a regular basis through which social workers can be updated about new advances in social work knowledge.

viii. There should be an accreditation council in the country to monitor and control social work curricula. There should also be a licensing authority of social workers where they are to be registered. Licensing should be mandatory for all social work graduates who wish to recognize them as professional social workers. Registration from such an authority will depend on approval from the proposed accreditation council of social work curricula.

REFERENCES

Ahmadullah, A. K. (1964). Problems and prospects of social welfare education in Pakistan. In M. A. Momen (Ed.), *Social Work Education in Pakistan*. SWRC. Dhaka: University of Dhaka.

Bangladesh Garments Manufacturer and Exporters' Association (BGMEA). (2018). *Membership and employment*. Retrieved from https://www.indeed.com/q-Membership-jobs.html.

Chitereka, C. (2009). Social work in a developing continent: The case of Africa. *Advances in Social Work, 10*(2), 144–156.

Das, T. K. (2012). Applicability and relevance of social work knowledge and skills in the context of Bangladesh. *SUST Studies, 15*(1), 45–52.

Das, T. K. (2013). Internationalization of social work education in Bangladesh. In T. Akimoto & K. Matsuo (Eds.), *Internationalization of social work education in Asia*. ACWelS and APASWE: Tokyo.

Das, T. K. (2014). Indigenization of social work education in Bangladesh: History review. In A. Tatsuru (Ed.), *Internationalization and indigenization of social work education in Asia*. Kiyose, Japan: Japan College of Social Work.

Dhemba, J. (2012). Fieldwork in social work education and training: Issues and challenges in the case of Eastern and Southern Africa. *Social Work & Society, 10*(1), 1–10.

DiNitto, D. M., & McNeece, C. A. (2007). *Social work: Issues and opportunities in a challenging profession*. Englewood Cliffs, NJ: Prentice Hall.

Fahrudin, A., & Yusuf, H. (2016). Social work education in Indonesia: History and current situation. *International Journal of Social Work and Human Services Practice, 4*(1), 16–23.

Franklin, D. L. (1986). Mary Richmond and Jane Addams: From moral certainty to rational inquiry in social work practice. *Social Service Review, 60*(4), 504–525.

Gray, M., Coates, J., & Bird, M. Y. (2008). *Indigenous social work around the world: Towards culturally relevant education and practice*. Surrey, UK: Ashgate.

Herbert Williams, J. (2016). *Grand challenges for social work: Research, practice, and education*.

Hossain, I., Akthar, T., & Uddin, M. T. (2006). Elderly care services and their current situation in Bangladesh: An understanding from theoretical perspectives. *Journal of Medical Science, 6*(2), 131–138.

Hossain, I., Alam, M. J., & Islam, M. N. (2005). Medical social work practices for the improvement of health care system in Bangladesh. *Journal of Sociology, 1*(1), 63–74.

Hossain, I., Al-Amin, M., & Alam, M. J. (2012). NGO interventions and women development in Bangladesh: Do feminist theories work? *The Hong Kong Journal of Social Work, 46*(1&2), 13–29.

Hossain, I., & Mathbor, G. M. (2014). Social work practice for social development in Bangladesh: Issues and challenges. *Asian Social Work and Policy Review, 8*(2), 123–137.

Hossain, I., Mathbor, G. M., & Semenza, R. (2013). Feminization and labor vulnerability in global manufacturing industries: Does gendered discourse matter? *Asian Social Work and Policy Review, 7*(3), 197–212.

Hussain, A. (1999). A brief discussion on social work in Bangladesh. *International Journal of Social Work and Human Services Practice, 4*(1), 16–23.

Hussain, M. M., & Raihan, M. M. (2015). Patients' satisfaction with public health care services in Bangladesh: Some critical issues. *Malaysian Journal of Medical and Biological Research, 2*(2), 115–126.

Islam, F. (2011). Social work education and practice in Bangladesh: Past effort and present trends. In S. Selwyn (Ed.), *Social work in countries of the East* (pp. 27–45). Hauppauge, NY: Nova Publishers.

Islam, M. F. (2017). In quest for indigenization of social work education and practice in Bangladesh: Complexities and prospects. *Journal of Social Science, 1*(1), 69–92.

Islam, M. S., & Hossain, M. I. (2016). *Social justice in the globalization of production: Labor, gender, and the environment nexus*. Basingstoke, UK: Palgrave Macmillan.

Khan, T., & Hasan, M. M. (2016). *Social protection system in Bangladesh and the scope of social work: Learning from lessons on the ground* (Munich Personal RePEcArchive, MPRA Paper No. 70949). Posted 27 April 2016 14:12 UTC.

Khuda, B. E. (2011). Social safety net programs in Bangladesh: A review. *Bangladesh Development Studies, 34*(2), 87–108.

Konrad, S. C. (2013). *Child and family practice: A relational perspective.* Chicago, IL: Lyceum Books.

Mathbor, G. M. (2007). Enhancement of community preparedness for natural disasters: The role of social work in building capital for sustainable disaster relief and management. *International Social Work, 50*(3), 357–369.

Mathbor, G. M. (2008). *Effective community participation in coastal development.* Chicago, IL: Lyceum Books.

Ministry of Social Welfare (MSW). (2018a). *Children Development Centre.* Retrieved from https://msw.gov.bd/site/page/191db876-d6e2-4445-bff4-c5fdd07a330d/Children-development.

Ministry of Social Welfare (MSW). (2018b). *Hospital Social Services Program.* Retrieved from https://msw.gov.bd/site/page/2c320c86-b8b9-4a94-ba5d-64dc8e0fe942/Hospital-Social-Services.

Ministry of Women and Children Affairs (MOWCA). (2011). *National Women Development Policy.* People's Republic of Bangladesh.

Noble, D. N., & Ausbrooks, A. (2008). Social work with children and their families. In D. M. Dinitto & C. A. McNeece (Eds.), *Social work: Issues and opportunities in a challenging profession* (pp. 239–260). Chicago: Lyceum.

Pawar, M. (2014). *Social and community development practice.* SAGE Publications India.

Payne, M. (2015). *Modern social work theory.* Oxford: Oxford University Press.

Pierson, J. (2011). *Understanding social work: History and context.* England: Open University Press.

Prodhan, M., & Faruque, C. J. (2012). The importance of social welfare in the developing world. *Journal of International Social Issues, 1*(1), 11–21.

Rahman, H. (1977). Rural development and social services in Bangladesh. *Community Development Journal, 12*(1), 36–42.

Samad, M. (2013). Social work education in Bangladesh: Internationalization and challenges. In T. Akimoto & K. Matsuo (Eds.), *Internationalization of social work education in Asia.* Tokyo: ACWelS and APASWE.

Samad, M. (2015). Marriage in changing family pattern of Bangladesh: The present trends. *International Journal of Social Work and Human Services Practice, 3*(4), 155–161.

Samad, M., & Hossain, M. A. (2014). Indigenization of social work education in Bangladesh: Knowledge, perception and realities. In A. Tatsuru (Ed.), *Internationalization and indigenization of social work education in Asia.* Kiyose, Japan: Japan College of Social Work.

Sarker, H. A. (2015, February 20). History of social services in Bangladesh, *The Daily Observer,* Dhaka.

Segal, E., Karen, A., Gerdes, S., & Steiner, S. (2010). *Professional social work.* Rawat Publication.

Singh, A. N. (2010). Status of field work and research in social work education: With special reference to Hindi speaking areas in India. *Social Work Journal, 1*(1).

Taher, M., & Rahman, A. (1993). Social work in Bangladesh: Problems and prospects. *Indian Journal of Social Work, 54*(4), 567–577.

Van Hook, M. P. (2014). *Social work practice with families: A resiliency-based approach.* Chicago, IL: Lyceum Books.

CHAPTER 29

Social Work and Social Work Education in Spain

Emilio José Gómez-Ciriano

BIRTH OF A PROFESSION

In 1932, during the Second Spanish Republic,[1] the first school of social work opened its doors in Barcelona. It followed the same patterns as Belgian Catholic schools of social work and was inspired by the principles of social Catholicism.[2] The aim of the school as established in its charter was: "The formation of competent professionals that could organize social assistance in a scientific way so that energies could be concentrated, society could be improved and services, already existing in other industrialized countries, could be implemented through the technical and pedagogic formation of all th[o]se who would develop them" (Barbero & Feu, 2015).

The Barcelona social work programme included theoretical and practical training. Theoretical perspectives were taught by specialists from different academic disciplines. Practical elements of the course consisted of home visits, placements in care and health institutions, and study visits abroad to meet experts from other countries. The total number of teaching hours was 842 (202 practical and 640 theoretical). The programme was so intense that only 15 students in the first cohort and 16 in the second completed their studies out of the 60 that had started them. Unfortunately, this excellent initiative finished with the outbreak of the Spanish Civil War (1936–1939). Shortly after the end of the Civil War a new school opened its doors in Madrid (1939). Its name the *Escuela de Formación familiar y social* ("School of Family and Society Training") clearly reflected the conservative patriarchal

E. J. Gómez-Ciriano (✉)
Universidad de Castilla-La Mancha, Ciudad Real, Spain
e-mail: emiliojose.gomez@uclm.es

© The Author(s) 2021
S. S. M. et al. (eds.), *The Palgrave Handbook of Global Social Work Education*, https://doi.org/10.1007/978-3-030-39966-5_29

social values of the Franco regime. The school sought to train women for traditional roles such as good carers, good Christian wives, and good mothers.

The social work schools of the 1950s were linked to the Catholic Church
or the women's branch of the proto-fascist Falange. At the beginning of the
1960s a new awareness developed among social assistants. This argued that
there was a need to move from charitable schemes to community approaches
based on direct intervention with users and communities. This approach was
summarised in the editorial of the first issue of *Documentación Social*, the pioneering Spanish social studies and social work journal published in 1958: "It
is necessary to move in our actions from charitable to more social patterns for
three reasons. Firstly because charity is ephemeral (...) secondly because it is
never ending, and thirdly because it is [i]ncomplete" (Duocastella, 1958).

Several events would be crucial to broadening the minds of professionals
and raising awareness of the profession in the forthcoming years: creation of
the Federation of Schools of Social Assistants of the Catholic Church (1959);
the attendance of international experts at seminars and workshops[3] organised
by the associations of social workers throughout the country; and, last but not
least, the impact of new inspiring ideas about community work and reconcep-
tualisation by Marco Marchioni (Italy) and Paulo Freire (Brasil), respectively.
In 1964 a governmental decree granted official recognition to social assistance
studies and structured its curriculum over 3 years of theoretical and practical
training. By that time there were 33 schools in Spain (Vilas, 1958).

Consolidation of the schools of social work that followed official recognition was accompanied by a period of professional organisation. In 1967, still
at a time when the right to association was restricted by the Franco regime,
the Spanish Federation of Social Assistants (FEDAAS) was created and only
one year later the first National Congress of Social Assistants took place in
Barcelona. Sessions of the congress raised awareness of the importance and
strength of social assistants and highlighted three important issues that would
shape their future developments. The first was adoption of the term social
work instead of the previous term social assistance. The second was creation
of a code of ethics for practitioners. Finally, a revision proposal of the plan of
studies approved by the government in 1964 meant that social work could
achieve the status of a university degree in forthcoming years (De las Heras,
2012). The last years of the Franco regime saw significant social reforms the
most important being creation of the Social Security Service in 1963. Such
reforms were accompanied by huge social expenditure that reached 10% of
GDP in the mid-1970s (González Begega & Del Pino, 2017).

The initial optimism of the Second Republic disappeared under the social
conservatism of the Franco regime. However, the later period of Franco's rule
coincided with rebirth of the social work profession. This was undoubtedly
influenced by the relaxation of control measures at the end of Francoist government, by opening up to new ideas and conceptions from abroad (especially
from Latin America), by the professionalisation of social work studies, and by
the social reforms that took place in the last years of the Franco regime.

Political Transition and New Possibilities for Social Work, 1975–1985

During the transitional period to full democracy (1975–1978) substantial efforts were made by the National Association of Social Assistants to remove any remnants of old Francoist beneficence terminology from the constitutional draft. At the same time pressure was exerted to get economic, social, and cultural rights included as such in the new constitutional arrangements. It was argued that they should have the same status and protection as civil and political rights. It was a timely ambition because Spain had just ratified the International Covenant on Economic, Social and Cultural Rights (ICESCR) in 1977. However, this objective could not be reached (Gómez-Ciriano, 2012a). As a result many of the social rights acknowledged by the covenant were just termed guiding principles to be achieved provided that the economic situation allowed it.

Social work was inevitably affected by the profound changes that took place in post-Franco Spain: transition from a dictatorship to a democratic regime after Franco's death, the approval of a new constitutional chart with a decentralized scheme on which regions held devolved powers in crucial areas of welfare, and, last but not least, entry into force of the Basic Act on Local Competencies detailing the responsibilities of municipalities in welfare provision.

This new political and social scenario required new approaches and adequate resources that would enable professionals to cope with the effects of such significant changes. As a result of the pressure applied by the National Association of Social Assistants and the National Association of Schools of Social Work academic recognition was granted to social work studies by an act in 1981. Guidelines for the implementation of a diploma in social work considered a maximum of 3200 teaching hours would be required 40% of which would have to be practical.

As a consequence of the work undertaken by representative bodies that had been so important in raising awareness about social assistants during the dictatorship a new act (Act of 13 April 1982) paved the way for the creation of regional and provincial professional colleges of social work and the creation of the General Council of Social Work of Spain. The newly acquired academic status, new wider employment opportunities in the public sector, and the existence of a representative body that would protect professionals made the discipline attractive to students who foresaw a rewarding and stable profession in social work.

Golden Age of Social Work in Spain 1986–2008

The period 1986–2008 is generally acknowledged as a time of expansion and consolidation of social work studies in Spain. It coincided with the development of welfare structures by the central government and social service systems by the regions. As a result of such development thousands of social workers were recruited in what was considered a golden age for the profession.

The welfare model developed by Spain was Mediterranean in type (Ferrara, 1996) characterised by the strong presence of family structures in care provision based on cultural and religious traditions in which the state played a subsidiary role. This model was not exclusive to European countries but also included countries right at the edge of Europe like Turkey and in the Middle East like Israel (Gal, 2010). The entry of Spain into the European Economic Community in 1986 was the trigger for policy makers, academics, and practitioners to adapt and improve welfare systems to match the standards of neighbouring countries. As a result health and education became universalised and the pensions system increased its comprehensiveness by including both contributory and non-contributory schemes financed through public taxation. The social services system deployed in the regions in accordance with regional legislation was inspired by the principles of universalisation, proximity, equity, accessibility, and public responsibility. Although the expansion of welfare structures was remarkable, it was less so in terms of intensiveness (Rodriguez Cabrero, 2014).

By the mid-1990s third-sector organisations and private companies greatly strengthened their participation in welfare provision by specialising in areas of intervention not covered or poorly covered by the public sector. By 2008 the presence of non-government organisations (NGOs) had multiplied several fold: more than 30,000 entities and more than 2 million people (including volunteers) were involved (Fundación PWC, 2018), while precarity became commonplace among professionals.

So many changes required a new educational and institutional framework. The Decree of 1964 had been useful for structuring the contents of studies and providing them with official status during the time of the dictatorship. The Act of 1981 had been the cornerstone supporting the education and training of students in the new democratic period. However, since Spanish society had experienced so many changes, new needs were identified (migrants, ageing population, drug and substance misuse, the impact of poverty and inequality). Social workers were practising in new areas and with new groups of service users. The Sorbonne (1998) and Bologna (1999) Declarations and the Prague Communication (2001) paved the way for Spanish academic studies in social work to adapt to the European space of higher education. For social work studies this not only meant a different way of teaching and learning, but also conversion of the diploma in social work to a degree in social work.

By the end of 2007 Spain had caught up with most of the developed countries of the European Union in terms of per capita income, gross national product, and unemployment rates. The pensions system had a big surplus and the welfare model, despite its low intensity and commitment to traditional family and gender roles, had reached a high degree of excellence (National

Statistics Office, 2008). Meanwhile, the social services system had been expanded significantly even though its intensity was not as strong as desired (Rodriguez Cabrero, 2014).

Passing of the Dependency Act in 2006 by the central government and its implementation in Spanish territory triggered the enactment of new-generation social services laws by regional parliaments to update resources, structures, and personnel to the new requirements. The contents of courses taught in different subjects were modified by lecturers to comply with this crucial law.

The Dependency Act also produced a new category of social services user—dependant—and a new job title—carer—who could be informal (if he/she was a relative) or formal (if he/she was a professional), whose salary was covered by the public budget. This was a great advance toward decommodification (Esping-Andresen, 1990) and defamilisation (Lister, 1997)[4] that would have changed the family-based welfare model. However, due to retrenchment policies the process could not be completed.

NEW RESPONSES TO NEW NEEDS? NEW DEGREE IN SOCIAL WORK

The *Libro blanco del título de grado en trabajo social* ("White Book on Social Work Studies") (Vázquez Aguado, 2012) was agreed by representatives of the schools of social work of 32 universities and submitted to the Spanish National Accreditation Agency (ANECA) as a non-binding proposal. It aimed at guaranteeing enough formative background for the training of future social workers within the framework of a complex society. The Royal Decree of 2010 approved the new degree in social work in accordance with European Higher Education System guidelines. It consisted of 240 European Credit Transfer and Accumulation System (ECTS) credits and a Master's/doctoral degree of 60–120 ECTS credits, respectively. According to the White Book on Social Work Studies the new courses would provide undergraduates with enough skills to develop the following functions (Vázquez Aguado, 2012):

- **Prevention**: intervening early in causes that produce collective and individual problems; producing and elaborating on plans of intervention for populations at risk and those who have suffered human rights violations.
- **Direct attention**: paying close attention to vulnerable individuals and those at risk of social exclusion to help them develop their capacities and abilities so that they can be successfully integrated into social life in the future.
- **Planning**: directing a plan according to proposed objectives by analysing the reality of the situation and controlling the way it might evolve. Such a function could be implemented at two levels: the microsocial (regarding direct interventions) and the macrosocial (by designing programmes and social services).

- **Promotion and social inclusion**: finding ways of holding on to, raising awareness of, and promoting capacities and abilities for self-determination and the normal functioning of groups and individuals by designing and implementing social policies that favour the creation and adjustment of services capable of covering social needs.
- **Supervision**: enabling capacitation in which professionals of social work and social services receive the help of an expert with the objective of maximising their knowledge and abilities and perfectionating their attitudes so that they develop their professional abilities in the best possible and most satisfactory way—not just for themselves but also for the service they are involved in.
- **Evaluation**: being able to compare and contrast results obtained relating to the initial aims and objectives by taking into consideration techniques, means, and time.
- **Management**: taking responsibility for the way in which social services centres are planified, organized, managed, and controlled.
- **Research**: discovering, describing, interpreting, explaining, and valuing a reality by systematic data compilation; stabilising hypotheses and verifying systems using professional and scientific techniques that any planned action or adequate intervention can take into account.
- **Coordination**: determining the action of a group of professionals in a certain organisation or belonging to different organisations by using means, techniques, and resources so that an intervention line and common objectives will be determined in relation to a concrete professional group, community, and case.

As a result of the new act universities adapted their studies in social work to the new framework and schools of social work (transformed into faculties) began to offer a new 4-year degree in social work and doctoral programmes from the academic year 2010 onward to train future social work professionals to address the challenges Spanish society was facing.

SOCIAL WORK IN TIMES OF CRISIS

The economic and financial crisis of 2008 had a devastating effect on Spanish society. This impact was greatest on the most vulnerable: young people, immigrants, non-qualified workers, and single-parent families (Laparra & Pérez Eransus, 2010).

Instead of cushioning the effects of the crisis by increasing social protection, the government implemented a raft of retrenchment measures. These reduced welfare services and had a profound impact on the working conditions of social workers many of whom lost their jobs. Although many others experienced new uncertain forms of employment, it was not only the working conditions but the whole role of the profession that was at stake as a consequence of the neoliberal measures that affected them (Gómez-Ciriano, 2012a):

- Cuts in the public sector had a direct effect on social services diminishing the possibility of responding properly at a time of increasing needs of the people. Reduced services led to reduced social rights.
- Cuts led to deprofessionalizing social work by transferring some of the tasks that traditionally were the responsibility of social workers to non-professionals or to the voluntary sector in an attempt to reduce costs.
- Cuts led to the subsidiary role third-sector organizations (highly dependent on public funding) were playing in the provision of some services being seriously affected.
- Taken together these led to poorer working conditions for social workers, increased demand for services at a time of retrenchment, and increased the risk of stress and burnout of professionals (Bravo-Jiménez, 2002; Ravalier, 2019).

There were similar developments in universities. The recent cohort of social work graduate students found it really difficult to obtain posts offering fair and decent conditions. As a result many of them took the option of migrating abroad (Lima, 2014).

Orange Tide or How Social Workers Organise Themselves in Their Fight for Dignity

The retrenchment measures implemented between 2012 and 2014 were so drastic that initially there was little reaction to them by social workers or users out of a sense of shock. However, as cuts continued the rights of users were increasingly affected, the quality of benefits was substantially lowered and made conditional, many social workers were made redundant, and a feeling of anger developed and extended throughout the profession (Gomez-Ciriano, 2012a). The General Council of Social Work, together with the 37 different professional colleges of social work, set up the Orange Tide Movement as a way of raising concern among the population about the serious harm cuts were inflicting on the welfare state. The movement consisted in wearing every Friday an orange T-shirt as a way of raising awareness about how cuts were bringing about poverty, social exclusion, and human rights violations. There were also periodic demonstrations (Consejo General de Trabajo Social, 2015).

The Orange Tide Movement, together with other tide movements that protested against cuts in education (Green Tide), health (White Tide), and libraries (Yellow Tide), highlighted the impact of retrenchment policies.

The Orange Tide Movement did not receive the level of support among academics that might have been expected. Despite limited support from academies the Orange Tide Movement helped enormously to make the population aware of what social workers did and of the importance of social workers in promoting, defending, and implementing dignity and human rights.

CONCLUSION

From the very beginnings of the social work profession in the years of the Second Republic social workers have strongly advocated the need for social justice. Without their involvement the development of welfare and the social services system in Spain would have been impossible. One of the main challenges facing the social work profession and social work academics is to produce synergies that could be beneficial to students, users, practitioners, and lecturers in which social workers report and transmit their experiences and at the same time benefit from the theory and research developed by academics. The links between academics and practitioners are still in their infancy as a result of distrust traditionally underlying non-cooperation between academia and practice. It is important here to highlight how the European project Erasmus Key Action 2 (among others) is contributing greatly to filling the gap between practical and theoretical knowledge as it promotes interprofessional and multidisciplinary work (European Union, 2020).

Public-sector and private-sector retrenchment policies have meant that social work agencies have been focussed on eligibility criteria and conditionality at the expense of processes of social integration and defending human rights. Nevertheless, there are reasons to be optimistic. The global definition of social work is the promotion of social change, social cohesion, and the empowerment and liberation of people. They are the key principles of the profession. Social work in Spain not only emerged from the ashes of Francoism it also played a key role in the transition to democracy. This illustrates that change is always possible. Growing awareness of their rights prompted users as well as professionals to challenge the current neoliberal tendency of the Spanish welfare model. Finally, although movements are taking place within academia to adapt responses to needs from a gender-based and human rights perspective, we should also be positive and not lose sight of progressive values while recognising the challenges.

NOTES

1. The Second Spanish Republic lasted from 1931 to 1939, a period that included the Civil War (1936–1939). It was followed by the 40-year-long dictatorship of Francisco Franco.
2. The encyclicals *Rerum Novarum* issued in 1891 and *Quadragesimo Anno* issued in 1931 had a great influence in societies where the Catholic Church was preeminent.
3. In 1959 the Association of Social Assistants of Barcelona organised two courses, one on individual social work and the other on supervision. Both courses were taught by Gouvera Kfouri, a UN expert and director of the Sao Paulo School of Social Work.
4. Decommodification is defined as the degree to which individuals or families can retain a socially acceptable standard of living without participating in the

market, while defamilisation is defined as the degree to which individuals can retain a socially acceptable standard of living independently of family relationships either through paid work or through social security provisions.

REFERENCES

Barbero, J. M., & Feu, M. (2015). El origen del trabajo social en Cataluña. La escuela de asistencia social para la mujer (1932–1939). *Pedagogia i Treball Social. Revista de Ciències Socials Aplicades, 4*(2), 4–32.

Bravo-Jiménez, J. (2002). Trabajo social y burnout in. *Servicios Sociales y Política Social, 60,* 137–158.

Consejo General de Trabajo Social. (2015). *Marea Naranja.* Retrieved from www.cgtrabajosocial.es/marea_naranja.

De las Heras, P. (2012). Intervención social en la década de los 70. *Revista de Servicios Sociales y Política Social, 100,* 17–38.

Duocastella, R. (1958). Necesidad de una acción social en las Cáritas Diocesanas. *Documentacion Social, 1,* 5–9.

Esping-Andersen, G. (1990). *The three worlds of welfare capitalism.* Cambridge: Polity Press.

European Union. (1998, May 25). *Joint declaration on harmonization of the architecture of European Higher education system in Paris.* Retrieved from http://www.ehea.info/media.ehea.info/file/1998_Sorbonne/61/2/1998_Sorbonne_Declaration_English_552612.pdf.

European Union. (1999, June 19). *Joint declaration of the European Ministers of Education in Bologna (Italy).* Retrieved March 13, 2019, from http://www.ehea.info/media.ehea.info/file/Ministerial_conferences/02/8/1999_Bologna_Declaration_English_553028.pdf/.

European Union. (2001, May 19). *Towards the higher education area.* Communiqué of the meeting of the European ministers in charge of higher education in Prague. Retrieved from http://www.ehea.info/media.ehea.info/file/2001_Prague/44/2/2001_Prague_Communique_English_553442.pdf.

European Union, Directorate General Education and Culture. (2020). *Erasmus+ Programme guide.* Retrrieved from http://ec.europa.eu/erasmus-plus/resources/documents/erasmus-programme-guide-2020_en.

Ferrara, M. (1996). The southern model of welfare in social Europe. *Journal of European Social Policy, 6*(1), 17–37.

Fundación PWC. (2018). *Radiografía del tercer sector social en España: Retos y oportunidades en un entorno cambiante* (Resource Document). Plataforma Tercer Sector. http://www.plataformatercersector.es/sites/default/files/20180626%20estudio%20fundacion-pwc-tercer-sector-social-2018%20DEF.pdf. Accessed January 21, 2019.

Gal, J. (2010). Is there an extended family of Mediterranean welfare states? *Journal of European Social Policy, 20*(4), 283–300.

Gómez-Ciriano, E. J. (2012a). España se examina…y suspende en Derechos Sociales. El Estado Español ante el Comité de Derechos Económicos, Sociales y Culturales de las Naciones Unidas. *Documentación Social, 164,* 190–211.

Gómez-Ciriano, E. J. (2012b). Welfare cuts in Spain and the effects on the most vulnerable populations: Impact on the role of social workers. *Social Policy and Social Work in Transition, 3*(1), 121–139.

González Begega, S., & Del Pino, E. (2017). *From letting Europe into policy conditionality: Welfare reform in Spain under Austerity* (Instituto de Políticas y Bienes Públicos (IPP) CSIC, Working Paper, 2017-01). Resource document: Instituto de Políticas y Bienes Públicos. Consejo Superior de Investigaciones Científicas. Retrieved from http://ipp.csic.es/es/workpaper/letting-europe-policy-conditionality-welfare-reform-spain-under-austerity. Accessed February 6, 2019.

Laparra, M., & Pérez Eransus, B. (2010). *El primer impacto de la crisis en la cohesion social de España*. Colección Estudios 32. Madrid. Foessa.

Lima, A. I. (2014). *I Informe sobre los servicios sociales en España*. Investigaciones e informes del Consejo General de Trabajo Social, 1. Madrid

Lister, R. (1997). *Citizenship: Feminist perspectives*. London: Macmillan.

National Statistics Office of Spain. Instituto Nacional de Estadística. (2008). *Spain in figures 2008* (Resource Document). http://www.ine.es/ss/Satellite?c=INEPublicacion_C&cid=1259924856416&pagename=ProductosYServicios%2FPYSLayout&L=en_GB&p=1254735110672&param1=PYSDetalleGratuitas. Accessed February 3, 2019.

Ravalier, J. M. (2019). Psycho-social working conditions and stress in UK social workers. *The British Journal of Social Work, 49*(2), 371–390.

Rodriguez Cabrero, G., et al. (2014). Estado de bienestar en España: Transformaciones y tendencias de cambio en la Unión Europea en Lorenzo, F. VII *informe sobre exclusión y desarrollo social en España*, Madrid. Fundacion FOESSA, 300–393.

Vázquez Aguado, O. (2012). (coord) *Libro blanco del título de grado en trabajo social*. Retrieved from http://www.aneca.es/var/media/150376/libroblanco_trbjsocial_def.pdf/. Accessed March 3, 2019.

Vilas, M. (1958). El servicio social en España. *Documentacion Social, 3,* 103–132.

CHAPTER 30

Development of Social Work Education in Slovenia

Bojana Mesec

INTRODUCTION

It was in 1955 that the first generation of students was able to enrol in the first form of education for social work in Slovenia, with fifteen students taking part. The school, which was founded by the People's Assembly of The People's Republic of Slovenia did not have the official title of a school. It was defined as such only in 1958, under the Schools Founding Act. In 1960 legislation enabled the school to become the short-cycle College for Social Workers, with a total of 159 students (Rapoša Tajnšek, 2005).

The curriculum of the first year of education for social work included subjects that were divided into five groups, namely: the social and political order of the Federal People's Republic of Yugoslavia (four subjects); health care and social security (six subjects); psychology, pedagogy, and methods of social welfare work (five subjects); German and English languages; and preliminary military education (Rapoša Tajnšek, 2005).

In 1959 the school adopted a new curriculum that was more appropriate for that time, but it still did not include a single subject that would be called social work. The curriculum was divided into four subject groups: economic and sociological analysis (four subjects); psychological and health analysis (four subjects); substantive subjects (nine subjects); and methodological subjects (three subjects) (Rapoša Tajnšek, 2005).

The same year saw the publication of *The Methods of Social Work*, a manual written by Katja Vodopivec, which according to Gabi Čačinovič Vogrinčič

B. Mesec (✉)
University of Ljubljana, Ljubljana, Slovenia
e-mail: bojana.mesec@fsd.uni-lj.si

© The Author(s) 2021
S. S. M. et al. (eds.), *The Palgrave Handbook of Global Social Work Education*, https://doi.org/10.1007/978-3-030-39966-5_30

(2005) brought a high level of useful expert knowledge that was then new to Slovenia. While still very valuable today, at the time the manual was prohibited for use for the study purposes (Čačinovič Vogrinčič, 2005).

Of course, social work was known to Slovenia even before the foundation of the first school in the field. Social work was practised as family help which was carried out by the so-called lay social workers. The first centres for social work emerged after World War II, which even at the time had an organisational scheme which implied that family help was divided, into different thematic sets (Mešl, 2005).

In the late 1950s, the first social workers were employed in Slovenia. This took place within the context of "personnel and social services" that pointed to the humanisation of work and an integrated consideration of employees within their organisations. Social workers' tasks included care for the quality and security of employment. Due to these new forms of work the College for Social Workers developed a special department for social work in the economy and for the employment of social workers in "personnel and social services". The students taking this course were distinguished by their rich work experience, and typically they had strong union and political support in their own companies and society at large (Rapoša Tajnšek, 2005).

In its first decades the school experienced many changes and modernisations of the curriculum, as well as changes of name. From the short-cycle College for Social Workers, its name was changed to the College for Social Work, which was later replaced by the University College for Social Work, and finally, in 2003 it obtained the title of Faculty of Social Work that designed programmes at all three levels of study (undergraduate, master, and doctoral). Soon afterwards, Slovenian universities along with other European universities signed the Bologna Declaration that brought long-lasting changes to the field of European higher education. Moreover, since 1975 the school has also been an associated member of the University of Ljubljana, which in 2019 celebrates the 100th anniversary of its foundation (1919–2019).

The governments of the 29 European countries which signed the Bologna Declaration in 1999 (*The Bologna Declaration*, 1999) were committed to creating a common European higher education area. In this way, European higher education was to achieve a more unified structure. Within the Bologna reform, the study structures needed to be designed to enable mobility in at least two directions. The first refers to vertical mobility within a given discipline, and increasingly also between two or more different institutions, which before that was unknown in Slovenia. The second direction refers to horizontal mobility, which mainly takes place between related disciplines, and is to encourage co-operation between faculties and universities. These changes were intended to enable high student mobility and were supported by the European Credit Transfer and Accumulation System (ECTS). Moreover, universities were required to broaden their missions in education to encompass all forms of life-long learning in order to achieve a highly qualified population. Within Europe the reform of study programmes has led to the gradual development of European comparable and compatible national higher education systems (Pejovnik, 2012). This does not refer to comparability in terms of study programme contents, but primarily to the credit system. A programme evaluation system applying the same rules to the whole Europe was thus introduced for the first time. This, however, did not automatically mean that the quality of various programmes improved, as such developments would depend on the distribution of individual requirements within the credit evaluation. The Faculty of Social Work evaluated the comparability of its study programme from several aspects, with the detailed areas examined being the following:

1. Comparability of the concept, formal, and substantive structure of the study programme;
2. Comparability of the accessibility of the study programme and enrolment conditions;
3. Comparability of the duration, progression, and completion of the study programme, and the titles obtained;
4. Comparability of the types and forms of study;
5. Possibilities of including the programme in international co-operation projects (mobility) or the common; European higher education area
6. The differences between the proposed and foreign programmes with regard to specific needs and conditions of the national economy and public services;
7. Harmonisation with the EU regulations in regulated occupations.

The elements in which the accreditation application was compared with programmes from higher education institutions in other countries are defined by the Higher Education Act (1993), and the accreditation application was examined by the Slovenian Quality Assurance Agency for Higher Education (SQAA).

Before the adoption of the reform, each university or even faculty had their own evaluation and study recognition system. The programmes were almost impossible to compare, or their comparability was very difficult to establish. The European area required a higher degree of cohesion, as under the existing circumstances it was almost impossible to achieve any student or teacher mobility. Today a quick look at the progress in that direction reveals that mobility is virtually the only aspect of the entire higher education system in Europe that was realised according to the plan. Speaking of social work, between the 2008/2009 and 2014/2015 academic years (Majer, 2008–2015) 130 students of social work went to study abroad, while 196 foreign students came to study to Slovenia at the Faculty of Social Work. Since the Faculty of Social Work is a relatively small faculty, the growth in the number of Erasmus exchanges from the years prior to 2008 and until today can primarily be attributed to the comparability of social work studies across Europe, greater transparency, and better organisation of the Erasmus programme. Moreover, the Faculty of Social Work introduced a new staff position of coordinator of the Erasmus exchanges, with this person managing all student exchanges at the faculty, in terms of both contents and technical issues. Students as well as professors now visit other faculties with which it has bilateral agreements, with the list of such faculties growing longer every year (Mesec, 2015a).

However, the reform process that the faculty started over ten years ago has only just begun. The first generation of students, who tried out the entire cycle as well as successfully evaluated both the programmes and the effects of the study, left us with invaluable data. Their analyses should be the basis of the re-accreditations of the programmes needed for the reforms to start showing their first positive effects.

The Beginning of the Reform at the Faculty of Social Work

In 2004 Slovenia obtained the legislative grounds (Higher Education Act, 2004) needed to introduce new study programmes complying with the Bologna Declaration signed in 1999. Soon afterwards discussions first arose about what the declaration was actually about and what it would bring for the future of the higher education in Slovenia. We wondered whether this was the choice of individual faculties or a mandatory task for the whole higher education system. We listened to debates in the media and heard those both in favour of and against the changes (Mesec, 2015a).

It was only in 2006 that the first steps related to this reform were made at the Faculty of Social Work. At the time changes had been carried out in almost all other faculties and academies that were members of the University of Ljubljana. In contrast, we were still deciding which system was more acceptable for social work: 3+2 or 4+1 years of study. With the first possibility, students would acquire their diploma after three years of study, which they would then be able to continue with two years of master's study, while the second possibility would be more comparable to the past form of the study of social work, concluding with a diploma after four years of study, and enabling a continuation for a further year of master's study. Even today it is not clear which option is better, each having advantages as well as downsides. Our decision led social work to become a four-year first-cycle study and one-year second-cycle study. According to Andreja Kocijančič (2009), the former rector of the University of Ljubljana, the division of the university programmes according to the formula 3+2 or 4+1, may seem simple, but it is almost impossible to carry out in terms of contents. In her opinion, Slovenian universities were not able to carry out the substantive reform of their study programmes, because the EU guidelines were inadequately interpreted with regard to the country's specific higher education system.

However, the substantive renewal of its study programme was not a problem for the Faculty of Social Work: it was an opportunity to develop new contents that would be more intertwined with practical work. This was our framework and the basis for the design of the new curriculum. In the years that followed the self-evaluation of the quality of the study showed that in this period the faculty had made great progress in terms of the contents of the education for social work.

In the time just before the programme renewal, there were some graduate theses that researched the issues of renewing the study programmes and social workers' employability. Statistical data provided by these theses (Čalopa & Vedenik, 2007) revealed that around 20% of graduates found employment immediately after completing their studies at the Faculty of Social Work, with slightly over one half of them finding employment in the first year after leaving, and 20% in the second year.

In designing new programmes the wishes of the faculty's students who actively participated in groups that planned the changes were also taken into account. Based on the survey conducted by Čalopa and Vedenik (2007), most of them were interested in working with young people and with older people, follow various fields of work in education, health care, mental health care, addictions, and work with the family. Interestingly, almost none of them was interested in working in crisis centres, private companies, the police, or military.

The Bologna Declaration and new way of financing of higher education have strengthened the faculty and staff's wish to have the opportunity, after almost fifteen years, to renew study programmes that in many ways were deficient and outdated. Primarily we wanted to make up for the deficits in practical work and enable our students to immediately test out their knowledge in practice, and vice versa, enable them to continuously reflect on their experiences through theory, and thus build their knowledge through experience. This approach enables the faculty to be well-connected with practice, while at the same time promoting theoretical knowledge about social work. With the greater selectivity and flexibility of the study programmes, future graduates should be able to deepen their knowledge in accordance with their interests or broaden their horizons beyond the standard knowledge of social work, thus creating their own profiles of skills and knowledge. The renewal of programmes and changes in the system of social security also entailed the development of new profiles, primarily those bordering different disciplines (i.e. placed between social and health care, social work, and pedagogy), which is why at the time we planned to establish several joint programmes with other European faculties. Based on co-operation with the Faculty of Social Sciences of the University of Ljubljana, we thus successfully carried out the postgraduate master's programme Sociology—Social Work in the Community, while the planned joint master's programme Supervision, to be done in co-operation with the Faculty of Education in Ljubljana, remained unrealised. Completely new challenges were presented by student and teacher mobility to other countries of the European Union, and, increasing from year to year, an even bigger challenge was the mobility of our graduates who at the time, though with some reservation, looked to the possibility of finding employment outside Slovenia (Mesec, 2015a).

Throughout its history, the Faculty of Social Work has invested considerable effort to address the question of employability of its graduates, and in recent years started to follow the related statistics, which show that its graduates are employed in all areas of society.

However, according to the statistics the vast majority of the graduates in social work find employment in the area of social protection (Statopis, 2018). Moreover, recent data show that compared to all other areas of employment of social workers, their employment in the area of social protection has been on the increase. Social workers are the most represented professional profile at the centres for social work, they are employed in social care institutions, and in non-governmental voluntary organisations in the area of social protection, while outside that field, most social workers are employed in education and health care, as well as in public administration and justice, in private companies, the military, the police, and elsewhere. However, social work graduates do not only work in the job positions of social workers, but also in different areas that require knowledge and skills with regard to working with people (Mesec, 2018).

Undoubtedly, the actual demand for social workers is much greater both in the area of social protection and in many other fields (health care, education, employment, labour, etc.) than can be inferred from the existing job notifications. In Slovenia, there are approximately four social workers per 10,000 inhabitants, which—considering the need in social care—is not enough even today, while the expected demographic and social changes that are coming lead us to anticipate an increased need for social workers in the areas, including work with the family, ranging from providing help for parents and children to dealing with domestic violence, work with older people, in particular in the provision of long-term care, help for dying people and their relatives, work with children and youths in schools and in their spare time, work with the disabled, solving problems and distress in the contexts of mental health, addiction, stress reduction and abuse at work, work with migrants, and so on. Besides the specialised courses, as noted previously in this text, new and partly interdisciplinary profiles are expected to be developed as a result of new demands for experts, such as in the organisation and co-ordination of long-term care, individual planning, local co-ordination and prevention, harm reduction and addiction, and other areas (Mesec, 2018).

Data from a 2007 research study (Čalopa & Vedenik, 2007) also give a more detailed explanation of the employability problems in social work. Namely, the respondents' reports show that legislation covering the area of social protection enables professionals from other fields to obtain employment in the field of social work, although these individuals are not adequately qualified for this work and are taking up job positions designed for graduates of the Faculty of Social Work. In its Article 69, the Social Assistance Act lays down that recognised professionals in this field are graduates of short-cycle college or university college courses that educate for social work, although jobs in this field can also be performed by those who completed short-cycle college or university college courses in psychology or biopsychology, pedagogy and its special disciplines, public administration, law, sociology, health sciences, in particular work therapy, and theology (Social Assistance Act, 1992).

For all these reasons, the Faculty of Social Work embarked on the reform of its undergraduate and postgraduate study programmes very eagerly, seriously, and in an integrated manner. First we focused on better understanding of the basic ideas of the Bologna process and on planning the coherent vision of the programmes. Then, we continued our work in the individual departments which were invigorated by the reform process and started to work more intensely on the establishment of the competences that social work graduates needed to gain through their studies.

The establishment of a special workgroup for the renewal of the curriculum that followed led the renewal process through several phases to the final proposals for the lists of competences, the curriculum, and the first syllabuses. We acquired the means to carry out the ESS VS—06 project of pilot renewal of the practical work for 3rd and 4th years of study, and tested some pedagogical innovations (2005/2006/2007). In parallel we developed postgraduate programmes for the 2nd and 3rd cycle in accordance with the Bologna guidelines.

At the beginning of 2007, the Faculty of Social Work organised a working meeting with various social partners (representatives of the Ministry of Labour, Family and Social Affairs, the Social Chamber of Slovenia, the Association of Social Institutions of Slovenia, the Association of Occupational Activity Centres, the Slovenian Association of Social Work Centres, the Trade Union of Health and Social Services, the Association of Social Workers of Slovenia, the University of Ljubljana, the Faculty of Social Sciences, the students of the Faculty of Social Workers, and other groups) and established two additional working groups (the first for the analysis of the labour market and employability, competences, and profiles; and the second for the practice of social work, internship, and practical competences).

The suggestions of these two additional working bodies, composed of the representatives of the faculty's social partners, were then included into the proposed curriculum, after the latter was approved by the whole collective of the Faculty of Social Work, as well as by the Social Chamber of Slovenia. The work was continued at the related departments, within working groups and in the study affairs committee. This long and complex process required the participation of all the faculty's staff and associates and resulted in the development of all the required documents, namely: the list of general and subject-specific competences, the curriculum and syllabuses. The process had an important effect: all teachers and other employees at the Faculty were familiar with the reform and took his or her share of responsibility for its realisation.

Substantive Reform of Education for Social Work in Slovenia

In the process of renewing the undergraduate social work programme, special attention was paid to practical training. At the end of the 2006/2007 academic year, the Centre for Practical Study was established at the faculty. It is responsible for the implementation of practical education in accordance with the existing curriculum. In parallel the Centre prepared the conditions for the introduction of the renewed system of practical education. Our ambitions were high, and with our approach to practical work we wanted to come closer to the practical training programmes that exist at those higher education institutions of social work which have for years, in Europe and across the world, presented a model of excellence in education, and helped in the formation of competent graduates who are successful in the labour market.

After the process of designing new programmes was completed Srečo Dragoš wrote in the Quality Report (2008): "The largest quality shift was achieved in the area which we can influence the most, that is, the renewal of the study contents." In a relatively short period education for social work experienced extensive transformation of contents, as well as system, including the following turning points:

- 1991/1992 academic year: the curriculum's distinctive feature was that this was the last year in which the short-cycle College for Social Workers carried out its two-year professional programme;
- 1993/1994 academic year: the first university college four-year curriculum was introduced;
- 1996/1997 academic year: the university college programme was carried out under the institutional form of the four-year university College for Social Work until its transformation to the Faculty of Social Work;
- 2003/2004 academic year: the implementation of the first faculty programme after the university college became the Faculty of Social Work;
- 2009/2010 academic year: the reformed ("Bologna") programme was introduced.

In his 2008 Quality Report Srečo Dragoš along with the Quality Commission (2008) gave a detailed description of how the study programme of social work was developing and changing in its contents, and primarily, presented its main highlights and differences between them in the mentioned years. For those years the study programmes were analysed according to two criteria, the practical and theoretical. The first criterion involved the analysis of the share of compulsory practical work that takes place outside the faculty in different social care institutions and non-governmental organisations. The specificity of social work as opposed to other academic disciplines lies in the fact that concrete knowledge and the skills needed to work with people are equally important as the theoretical contents. As soon as practical work would cease to be an indispensable and equal part of such education, then social work would start losing its specific nature and would start becoming one of the numerous other social science profiles. This is why the share of practical work in the compulsory study programme, along with its relationship to other, more theoretical subjects, is a vital part of the identity and quality of social work. In this context, all subjects were divided into three groups, namely the group of non-social work subjects, the group of connective subjects, and the group of social work subjects:

The first, the group of non-social work subjects, includes those that provide the basic knowledge from other social sciences. Although these subjects do not contain social work-specific theoretical knowledge, they are still necessary in the programme because they provide social work with the broadness and analytical depth of the social sciences. These subjects involve contents based on various other "mother" faculties (such as psychology, sociology, education, constitutional order, and foreign language).

The group of connective subjects includes those that are closer to social work than the ones from the first group, but are still not considered specific social work subjects. The function of connective subjects is to highlight how general knowledge from other expert fields is transferred and applied to social work (such as social security, theories of deviance, management in social work, quality of work life).

The social workgroup of subjects is composed of those that cover specific theoretical knowledge from social work, with most of them reflecting the different and specific nature of education at the Faculty of Social Work. The subjects that are typical of the Faculty of Social Work and not found in any of the programmes of other faculties and schools include: the theory of help, addictions, introduction to social work, family social work, community social work, and others.

As Lea Šugman Bohinc (2008) wrote in the programme application for the faculty's first accreditation, since the very beginning the first-cycle Bologna programme was developed with the idea of achieving a synergistic effect in horizontal and vertical dimensions of individual elements of the curriculum at undergraduate level, and with the application of the logic of vertical integration in the development of numerous one-year programmes and their subjects at the second-cycle postgraduate level. A third dimension was added to those, which through a spiral movement that encompasses both the vertical and horizontal connection between the subjects is introduced by the logic of practical contents, and the way practical education is organised in seven semestral units or four practical subjects.

The people who designed individual syllabuses were continuously encouraged to relate these syllabuses to the practical training of students—through the training of generic and specific knowledge and skills within the study practicum, and through diverse developmental and research project tasks and tasks related to fieldwork and practical placement bases—and thereby contribute to practical testing of and giving meaning to the conceptual knowledge acquired in the class.

Through self-evaluation we succeeded in designing a programme whose main focus is placed on social work subjects and practical work, which gives the social work profession more status and standing. To illustrate this extremely important, difficult and long-term improvement it is useful to recall the very beginnings of the School for Social Work, which only included a small sample of social work subjects. According to the description of the history of the curriculum given by Pavla Rapoša Tajnšek in the book *It Was Easier for Me to Work with a Diploma* (Rapoša Tajnšek, 2005), in the first year of the existence of the School for Social Work in 1955/1956 there was not a single subject among the total of seventeen in the two-year programme that would qualify as social work, and even ten years later, in 1965, there was only one specific social work subject and only one connective subject among a total of fifteen subjects.

The recognition of practical work in the faculty programme, the increased share of specific social work subjects, and the increased share of elective contents within all three subject groups are considered to be among the most important achievements of the Faculty of Social Work within the Bologna reform. Moreover, the entire concept of the study for social work has been subjected to thorough rethinking, so that it now reflects those needs for social work knowledge that were suggested by the members of the strategic reform group who are practising professionals. The transformation of the study subjects continued for four years and encouraged many new ideas and connections that before this had been unexpressed. The entire process also largely impacted the quality of work at the faculty through redefining the relations among the staff, in the sense that we became more connected to each other.

In 2009 (Dragoš, 2009), most of the work was invested in the operation of the Centre for Practical Study. Its tasks now range from the most diverse aspects of content and organisation of practical social work to involving numerous other fields of work related to the Bologna reform. Practical work is very important for the profession of social work, which is why the faculty devotes much time and attention to this part of education.

With the reformed study programme, the faculty made a huge step forward in terms of the implementation of practical education, resulting in a much more elaborated programme of practical work, mainly due to the realisation that preparations for practical work involve more contact hours than it was possible to achieve in the old programme. The preparation for practice also involves the training of mentors from professional practice in accordance with the respective study years and modules.

The substantive renewal of the social work study programme involved the identification and compilation of a list of the competences of prospective social workers. Initially, faculty was faced with the question of what can be considered a competence, and in identifying individual competences it followed the definition suggested by Professor Ivan Svetlik (2005), who described competences not only in terms of "what" they are, but also of "how" they can be identified.

General competences of the programme were then defined, encompassing 15 elements which have remained unchanged until today. As agreed by all those who collaborated in the design of the programme, the common grounds of all these competences are that they define the scientific and expert field of social work and therefore refer to education and research in social work, thus following the mission of our work. Further, numerous subject-specific competences in different areas of social work were then designed referring to the teaching contents of individual subjects, and these are written in the subject syllabuses. The competences then get updated and changed depending on the way each individual teacher delivers the subject contents, which is the responsibility of individual teachers as holders of the subjects.

The general competences of the programme in the first cycle of the study are the following (Šugman Bohinc, 2008):

1. Knowledge and understanding of the concepts, theories, and phenomena, as well as methods and procedures of social work (e.g. social contexts, legal norms, institutions, public policy and administration, human resources management, etc.);
2. Ability to analyse and synthesise (e.g. analysis of social phenomena and developments, synthesis of professional skills, ability to understand the relations between the problems of individuals and wider social context, the ability to identify and remove systemic obstacles);
3. The use of knowledge, procedures, and methods (e.g. the use of knowledge and procedures to strengthen user power, joint finding and co-creation of support networks, co-creation of working relationship, advocacy and the inclusion of deprivileged persons, etc.; the use of knowledge on the structural characteristics of marginalisation, the use of diverse resources of support and help; the use of methodological research tools; the use of modern approaches and principles, co-ordination of work tasks and the selection of methods and modes of work in compliance with the professional standards);
4. Capability of strategic thinking and acting (e.g. the ability of joint planning and evaluation, anticipation of developments, distinguishing which issues are essential and which are not, co-creation of solutions for long-term fundamental problems, advocacy attitude);
5. Critical and ethical (self)reflection of thinking and acting (e.g. commitment to professional ethics in social environment with respecting the principle of non-discrimination and multi-culturalism, the ability to reflect on one's own participation);

6. Recognition and understanding of and response to diversity (e.g. the ability to reflect on one's own prejudices and discriminatory actions, identify any racist and discriminatory actions and social ideologies, and actively engage against them; flexibility of action in diverse social and cultural environments; identification, recording, and documenting of personal stories of users/their problems, needs, aims, resources, etc., differences among them and responses to them);

7. Recognition and understanding of human distress and crises related to social and personal circumstances (in the lives of individuals, families, groups, collectives, communities);

8. The ability to co-create the desired outcomes with taking into account the user perspective (the ability of monitoring and regulating given circumstances, such as articulating previously unreflected on conflicts, establishment of the working relationship and personal contact, joint definition of problems and desired outcomes, conversation management towards the agreed desired outcomes, negotiations);

9. Communication skills (skills of conveying a message, listening, summarising, writing, public presentations and argumentation, verbal expression, clear, active, public appearances, the use of ICT);

10. Innovation (ability to (co-)create authentic or alternative concepts, solutions, procedures—instead of leaning on regular procedures, when they do not work in given situations).

11. Ability of team, group, and project work (willingness to collaborate, respect others' opinions and fulfil the agreed role within the team and group, ability to collaborate and represent the views of the profession in an interdisciplinary environment);

12. Networking ability (e.g. making new connections in the organisation and outside it, management of formal and informal relationships, skilled use of networks in the context of the problem considered);

13. The ability of joint management and co-management (e.g. the ability to co-ordinate, organise, give advice, and manage users and professional co-workers);

14. The ability of working in international and pluralist professional environment (e.g.: the ability to understand global processes, the articulation and representation of the profession in international environment, work in international professional bodies, writing and publishing in international publications);

15. Professional attitude: the ability of professional discipline, care for one's own professional development, for the development and the reputation of profession, and the transfer of knowledge.

In the same year (2009) the faculty also started to evaluate the "Social work" study programme to be able to renew and improve it, even while it was being implemented during the studies of the first generation of students. The evaluation procedures used with the programme included:

- the reports of those who implemented the programme;
- student surveys;
- evaluation of the programme at the related departments;
- consideration of the programme in the internal evaluation group.

In 2010 (Dragoš, 2010) much work was devoted to the promotion of the study programme. While for the time being the enrolment in the full-time social science programme at other faculties was still satisfactory, there were the first signs of reduced demand for these fields, which could be seen in less students attending the study information days taking place each year before the call for enrolment. The reduced number of enrolled students was mainly recorded for part-time studies, where the positions were not quite filled even after the third call for applications, while the positions for full-time study were filled at the first call. This was attributed to the decreased interest in paying for the study, as a result of the 2008 financial crisis, as unlike in the socialist past the study was no longer free. The study programme was promoted on different occasions, also being presented in high schools, particularly those ending with a final matriculation exam.

In 2012 (Dragoš, 2012) intense work was devoted to different indicators of the quality of the study programme for social work (which was related to the re-accreditation of the University of Ljubljana, whose member is the Faculty of Social Work), and in closely co-operating with the university services the faculty was faced with many strengths and weaknesses of its own work. This co-operation resulted in the strengthened links between the faculty and the University of Ljubljana, as well as entailing the establishment of a completely new level of co-operation between the faculty's staff and its students. In terms of content, the faculty acquired much information that helped us in our work on the programme re-accreditation, immediately following the re-accreditation of the University of Ljubljana. Visits and reports of the evaluators from the University of Ljubljana as well as foreign evaluators were very positive and offered us invaluable insights into how the faculty is seen and perceived by our environment. We were positively surprised and happy about the response, which gave us new energy for further work.

In 2014/2015 the preparations were started for a re-accreditation of the programmes in all three study cycles, and again, within a year, the faculty did outstanding work at all three levels of study.

Advantages and Disadvantages of the Bologna Reform of the Programmes of Education for Social Work

This chapter presents brief summaries describing the specific changes, noting which of them were good and which were less effective, and what achievements were made as seen from today's point of view, based on the strategic plans that we have committed to eight years ago, after we had managed to grasp the idea of the Bologna reform as mandatory rather than a choice.

The three-cycle study was designed, as follows:

1. cycle—a four-year study of social work giving students the title "University Graduate Social Worker";
2. cycle—a one-year study that brings the title "Master of Social Work", and at the Faculty of Social Work there are five master's studies: Family Social Work, Social Work with the Elderly, Mental Health in the Community, Social Inclusion and Justice in Handicap, Ethnicity and Gender, and Social Work;
3. cycle—doctoral study of social work that brings the title Doctor of Philosophy, PhD.

For all three study cycles, the content plans of study were changed and a new credit system was introduced. However, while the study degrees have remained the same, the European reform guidelines were not adequately interpreted for the benefit of the Slovenian education system. Namely, under the Bologna reform students at Slovenian universities study for five years to achieve the same degree of education that they could previously obtain after only four years. This makes us unique in all of Europe. The goal of the Bologna reform was to make the length of study shorter and more connected with practice, so that the graduates would become employed more rapidly.

The faculty's integrated approach to the reform resulted in an increased quality of work among the faculty staff and mainly in the increased connections among the teaching and non-teaching staff. Moreover, the links between the Faculty of Social Work and the University of Ljubljana also strengthened. After many years of effort, the faculty gained a clearer view of the work of all the University's offices and of how the programmes should be implemented at all three levels. Feedback from the University with regard to the faculty's programmes and the institution as a whole brought us to the decision to make the inventory of all the processes in the entire study process (pedagogical and non-pedagogical), the result of which was a comprehensive document including recommendations and measures to improve the operation and implementation of the programmes at the Faculty of Social Work.

There are some other things to be pointed out, such as, reduced quality of work for the staff of all the Faculties of the University of Ljubljana due to the increased bureaucracy that followed the reform. To put this in another way, the autonomy of the University seems to be gradually reducing due to the unharmonised requirements of the recently established Slovenian Quality Assurance Agency (SQAA) and the Ministry of Higher Education that carry out quality control in higher education. The financial crisis even widened the gap between the University on the one side, and SQAA and government services in the field of education on the other. In order to obtain a positive opinion from this agency, all higher education institutions are required to follow a set of quality assurance recommendations that sometimes fail to be linked to improving the actual quality of study programmes.

Although the reform mainly took place at the content level, the framework outlined by the credit system made it impossible for students to be offered a programme that would be effective in terms of content, because even in the first years of its implementation it turned out that the number of contact hours was reduced to such a degree that it prevented the realisation of the core content of some subjects. Theoretical subjects suffered a deficit in the number of teaching hours, because they are now required to include less lectures and hours of practicum and provide for more independent individual work. On the bright side, there are the subjects of Practical Work 1, 2, 3, and 4 that have enough hours for the students to get to know the profession and its work in real-life situations. When the first generation of the Bologna graduates finished their studies, the evaluation showed that they had acquired less knowledge, although it was of higher quality. However, it did take one study year longer in the new system to acquire the 7th degree of education in Slovenia, with five years needed compared to four under the old system.

All this also influenced graduate social workers' employability. While with the first-degree diploma the graduates of social work can now enter the labour market, they automatically enter a lower pay class of their older colleagues who completed the old two-year professional programme of social work.

This also made the Faculty of Social Work question its role both in the promotion of the profession and in raising the faculty's reputation among the public. Currently, these are very topical issues, which the Faculty of Social Work as well as the whole of the University of Ljubljana are dealing with in the 2018/2019 academic year.

The establishment of the new tutor system the Alumni Club and the work of the University Career Center are of great help to us in resolving these questions.

The basic aim of the tutor system is to provide learning support, which has been shown to be an effective mechanism to help achieve a higher student progression rate, which is one of the indicators of the quality of study at the University of Ljubljana. There was also an important shift concerning the association of Slovenian and foreign tutors, which strengthens internationalisation. Strengthening the connections between Slovenian tutors, as well as between Slovenian and foreign tutors, also creates a number of new opportunities for student collaboration (Pulko, 2018).

Founded at the Faculty of Social work in 2017, the Alumni Club has the following goals (The Rules of the Organization and Work of the Alumni Club of the Faculty of Social Work, 2016):

- establishment of connections and social ties among graduates as professional colleagues and with the Faculty of Social Work, its teachers, and staff;
- promotion of professional and scientific collaboration between the Faculty of Social Work and its graduates, and the promotion of collaboration between the environments in which they work;

- monitoring and supporting the Faculty of Social Work's development;
- encouragement and promotion of connections between the teaching, and scientific-and-research work of the Faculty of Social Work and employers;
- care for the reputation of the profession and education provided by the Faculty of Social Work;
- promotion of social work in the social environment.

The Career Center of the Faculty of Social Work offers a personal approach to all students in their transition from study to the labour market, which includes activities such as:

- workshops for acquiring competences and other employment skills;
- visits and presentations of working environments in Slovenia and other EU countries;
- networking and meetings with employers;
- conferences and meetings regarding the challenges of working abroad, of working in private businesses, and of apprenticeships;
- Skype counselling with counsellors from other countries;
- fairs, career days, and many other activities.

The University of Ljubljana with its very strong activities in the development of human resources and the transition from studying to the labour market has been, and continues to be, of great help in this regard.

The University of Ljubljana also carries out its social responsibility by transferring knowledge into practice. This is achieved through research and development as well as expert work, through employment of its graduates in other organisations, promotion of entrepreneurship, through counselling work and the inclusion of experts from practice in teaching and research work, through programmes of life-long learning, further training and education.

Organisational forms for the transfer of knowledge include competence centres, excellence centres, research and development projects for businesses and other organisations, the Career Center, the Ljubljana University Incubator, Innovations and Development Institute, and the advising the Collegium of Businessmen of the University of Ljubljana.

This is the so-called third dimension of the University, which in the future will be further strengthened, as by 2020 it will increase the number and value of the projects for the private and public sector by one-third, as well as double the number of participants in the programmes of life-long learning (Strategy of the University of Ljubljana, 2012). This will be achieved through the following:

- formation of strategic and development partnerships and joint development groups, and through carrying out development projects in collaboration with both private companies and the public sector;

- strengthening the transfer of technology and establishing the role of managers of knowledge as promoters of the transfer of basic knowledge in practice, and concrete development issues ranging from the production environment to research and development teams;
- developing the supply of programmes of life-long learning for further training and education of graduates, including the possibility of achieving additional qualifications;
- strengthening the activities of the Career Center, whose task is to direct students to study programmes of the University of Ljubljana, help graduates plan their careers and find employment, collaboration with employers, the organisation of graduate clubs, and monitoring the employability and success of the graduates in their work environments;
- better connections and mutual collaboration among the Career Center, the Ljubljana University Incubator and the transfer of knowledge office, with the emphasis on the promotion of the creation of new businesses and jobs, and increasing employment opportunities.

Before the beginning of the reform, the Faculty of Social Work had strategically set some framework goals. While not all of them were achieved mainly due to legislative constraints and administrative obstacles, many of them were realised, which is also seen from the reports that the faculty submits annually to the University of Ljubljana. The goals included the following: a further reform until 2016; consideration of the evaluation of all five years of the study; the development of the integrated master's study programme; the development of the national doctoral study programme; and restoration of the autonomy of the faculty, mainly with regard to bureaucratic obstacles.

The re-accreditation process is now behind us, and it let us acquire substantial data with intermediate evaluations of the study subjects and their implementation, which were the basis for all the changes that are considered in the re-accreditation documents.

IMPROVING THE QUALITY OF STUDY

In all the years of its existence (since 1955) the Faculty of Social Work has been a pillar of the development of social work and the field of social care in general in Slovenia. Its workers and associates have developed a high level of education for social work that is mainly based on the faculty's own scientific and research activities, as well as good knowledge of international trends. The faculty is a holder and initiator of numerous innovations without which it would be difficult to even imagine social work in Slovenia.

The employees at the Faculty of Social Work have developed forms and methods of work that represent the basis of modern social work in Slovenia: counselling work, group work, community social work, street social work, and family social work, to name a few. We have established the basis of voluntary work, action research, and qualitative analysis, which have not only influenced the profession of social work, but have also had a broader meaning in Slovenian social and human sciences (Mesec, 2015b).

In 2007 the faculty made a conscious decision to explore our internal environment and try to introduce changes that in the era of general progress could help develop not only a fresh organisational culture, but would also influence the development of the study of social work according to the new, Bologna principles. A process of comprehensive strategic planning was started even before, in October 2006, which involved the participation of all employees at the Faculty of Social Work and the students (Mesec, 2007).

Research was started by exploring the existing internal environment, following the SWOT (strengths, weaknesses, opportunities, threats) principle. A comprehensive document was written which in the following years provided the faculty with support to build new approaches for quality and more professional work with students (Mesec, 2015b).

The most frequently mentioned virtues of the faculty were the friendly interpersonal relationships, good group dynamics, solidarity, sense of belonging, absence of competition, good relationship with students, democratic relationships, simplicity, tolerance, and similar qualities.

The departments highlighted their unity, broad knowledge, recognisability and strong connections, and as a faculty we were proud of our conference activities, public recognition, efficient transfer of knowledge to practice, and the adaptation of the study programmes for students with impairments.

The main advantage, as expressed by the staff at the Faculty of Social Work, is its smallness, which enables them to nurture good professional communication that generates a great variety of ideas along with the awareness that social work is a practical, active science that requires continuous transformation. This is largely because in Slovenia we have no competition in this field, as well as a result of the aforementioned nurturing of tradition and values that were left to us by our forerunners.

In 2009, the faculty decided to record all its processes, with the aim of helping to recognise any risks to its operations. All its staff answered different questions related to employment, organisation, professional competences and learning, attitude to quality assurance, payments, internal communication and information, internal relationships, management, sense of belonging, knowledge of the mission, vision and goals of the institution, motivation and engagement, career development, innovation and initiative, and the satisfaction (Mesec, 2015b).

The results showed that most of the employees had a clear idea about what is expected from them in their work and about their position in the organisational scheme of the faculty. It was noted that employees' tasks were clearly defined and that the decisions of leaders were timely.

With regard to training and learning, the great majority of employees agreed that they had enough opportunities for further education, that only people with adequate education were employed at the faculty, but that many people were not acquainted with the different kinds or contents of additional education available. These observations contributed to improvements in recent years, with the University of Ljubljana offering free education with diverse themes that are needed to raise the quality of pedagogical work (Project KUL, 2013–2014).

Teachers as well as support staff feel responsible for the quality of their work and for contributing to the best of their abilities to the joint achievement of the quality standards outlined in the Rules of Procedure of the University of Ljubljana. All departments have clearly defined goals and quality standards and agree on that the Faculty of Social Work considers the quality of work and the workload to be equally important issues.

SUMMARY

Throughout the years the institution has existed—under its various names, as a school, college, and faculty of social work—its staff and students have taken care to collect materials about its work, which today are a precious resource for research into the history and development of the professionalisation of social work in Slovenia. The institution also keeps documents that contain syllabuses and descriptions of the teaching process in the first years of the development of the social work programme. In 2005 all employees and students of the Faculty of Social Work participated in extensive research into the history of social work in Slovenia. Through collecting data and conducting interviews with the still living representatives of the early years of education for social work in Slovenia, the faculty was able to acquire new knowledge that later in the same year was presented at the scientific conference "History of Social Activities, Social Policy and Education for Social Work".

In 2006 the Bologna reform forced the Faculty of Social Work to give the form and content of the study of social work more in depth thought. It also triggered long debates about what we wanted for the future of our profession, and what the profession of social work represented in the social environment. The process of creation and formation of the new study programme at all three study levels was a huge challenge and raised questions related to the existence of the study of social work and independence of this higher education institution. In the not so distant past the School for Social Work had to strive for recognition in the world of science on several occasions, and with its persistence and good results finally acquired the title of the Faculty of Social Work, and with it a university title and the possibility of providing study programmes at 2nd and 3rd levels. It aimed at keeping and upgrading all its system and status gains, which is why it was very motivated to change. The entire process of programme design took four years, mainly because all syllabuses and curricula had to be transformed. The European credit transfer system was introduced for the first time, and completely new study programme was designed, taking into account the relevant aspects of student surveys and student opinions about past programmes, as well as employment indicators (based on these, new modules were introduced, and those that did not show a high degree of employability were abolished).

If today we ask ourselves what were the advantages of the reform for the Faculty of Social Work, it is difficult to decide whether the present situation is better or worse than was the past. Certainly, the study is more structured and of better quality, but there are many negative remarks with regard to the implementation of the Bologna system of education.

At the beginning, the reform had its supporters as well as strong opponents. Among the latter was Jože Mencinger (2008), the former rector of the University of Ljubljana, who in an interview suggested that the Bologna reform of higher education in Slovenia was yet another attempt to introduce the so-called study by stages, employment-oriented education or a similar form that in Slovenia (and the former Yugoslavia) had existed once before. As Mencinger critically pointed out, all those experiments had failed, and the introduction of the Bologna reform was not different from those past reforms in Slovenia but in that the latter had been dictated by the needs of our society, while the former was introduced due to the requirements of the labour market. At the very end, as he claimed, the Bologna reform was an attempt to produce human capital with a universally valid certificate to reduce employment risks for employers.

Faculties and other members of the University of Ljubljana have had many discussions in the years since the introduction of the reform about differences that arose during its implementation, from the first accreditation of the programmes to their re-accreditation after seven years. While "the spirit of Bologna" somehow did not draw much enthusiasm, it did, however, enable at least some faculties as university members to carefully and thoughtfully design new programmes complying with the employability data and needs that emerge in practice, and the Faculty of Social Work is among these.

References

Čačinovič Vogrinčič, G. (2005). Social work with family: Development of doctrine. In Lešnik, B. (Ed.), *Traditions, fractures, visions: Collection of abstracts/scientific congress/* [Zbornik povzetkov/*Kongres socialnega dela Tradicije, prelomo, vizije/*]. Ljubljana: Faculty of Social Work.

Čalopa, G., & Vedenik, M. (2007). *Graduates of the Faculty of Social Work in the labour market* [Diplomanti in diplomantke Fakultete za socialno delo na trgu delovne sile] (Graduate thesis). Ljubljana: Faculty of Social Work.

Dragoš, S. (Ed.). (2008). *Quality Report* [Poročilo o kakovosti]. Ljubljana: Faculty of Social Work.

Dragoš, S. (Ed.). (2009). *Quality Report* [Poročilo o kakovosti]. Ljubljana: Faculty of Social Work.

Dragoš, S. (Ed.). (2010). *Quality Report* [Poročilo o kakovosti]. Ljubljana: Faculty of Social Work.

Dragoš, S. (Ed.). (2011). *Quality Report* [Poročilo o kakovosti]. Ljubljana: Faculty of Social Work.

Dragoš, S. (Ed.). (2012). *Quality Report* [Poročilo o kakovosti]. Ljubljana: Faculty of Social Work.

Higher Education Act. (Official Gazette RS, No. 67/93, 1993).

Higher Education Act—Official Consolidated Text—ZViS- UBP2 (Official Gazette of the Republic of Slovenia [*Uradni list RS*], No. 100/04 of 13. September 2004).

Kocijančič, A. (2009). *The error of the Bologna process in Slovenia is its formalism* [Napaka bolonjskega procesa v Sloveniji je formalizem]. Ljubljana: Dnevnik Daily.

Majer, A. (Ed.). (2008). *Annual Report of the Faculty of Social Work* [Letno poročilo Fakultete za socialno delo]. Ljubljana: Faculty of Social Work.

Majer, A. (Ed.). (2009). *Annual Report of the Faculty of Social Work* [Letno poročilo Fakultete za socialno delo]. Ljubljana: Faculty of Social Work.

Majer, A. (Ed.). (2010). *Annual Report of the Faculty of Social Work* [Letno poročilo Fakultete za socialno delo]. Ljubljana: Faculty of Social Work.

Majer, A. (Ed.). (2011). *Annual Report of the Faculty of Social Work* [Letno poročilo Fakultete za socialno delo]. Ljubljana: Faculty of Social Work.

Majer, A. (Ed.). (2012). *Annual Report of the Faculty of Social Work* [Letno poročilo Fakultete za socialno delo]. Ljubljana: Faculty of Social Work.

Majer, A. (Ed.). (2013). *Annual Report of the Faculty of Social Work* [Letno poročilo Fakultete za socialno delo]. Ljubljana: Faculty of Social Work.

Majer, A. (Ed.). (2014). *Annual Report of the Faculty of Social Work* [Letno poročilo Fakultete za socialno delo]. Ljubljana: Faculty of Social Work.

Majer, A. (Ed.). (2015). *Annual Report of the Faculty of Social Work* [Letno poročilo Fakultete za socialno delo]. Ljubljana: Faculty of Social Work.

Mencinger, J. (2008). *Second Thoughts on Bologna* [Bolonjski pomisleki]. Ljubljana: Mladina Weekly—Supplement of Education.

Mesec, B. (2007). *Quality Report* [Poročilo o kakovosti]. Ljubljana: Faculty of Social Work.

Mesec, B. (2015a). Ten years of the Bologna Report at the Faculty of Social Work [Deset let Bolonjske reforme na Fakulteti za socialno delo]. *Socialno delo Journal,* 54(3/4), 169.

Mesec, B. (2015b). Quality of higher education and the Faculty of Social Work [Kakovost visokega šolstva in Fakulteta za socialno delo]. *Socialno delo Journal,* 54(3/4), 233.

Mesec, B. (2018). *Self-evaluation of the social work study programme* [Samoevalvacija študijskega programa Socialno delo]. Ljubljana: Faculty of Social Work.

Mešl, N. (2005). History of social work: Family support services from 1945–1962 (the case of Celje with its surroundings). In V. Leskošek, & D. Zaviršek (Eds.), *Collection of abstracts/scientific symposium history of social policy, social work and education for social work in Slovenia/* [Zbornik povzetkov/*Znanstveni posvet Zgodovina socialne politike, socialnega dela in izobraževanja za socialno delo v Sloveniji/*]. Ljubljana: Faculty of Social Work.

Pejovnik, R. S. (2012). *Bologna reform Ljubljana style* [Bolonjska prenova po ljubljansko]. Ljubljana: University of Ljubljana.

Project KUL (Quality of the University of Ljubljana [Kakovost Univerze v Ljubljani], 2013–2014). Retrieved from http://www.uni-lj.si/o_univerzi_v_ljubljani/kakovost/projekt_kul/. Accessed September 25, 2018.

Pulko, N. (2018). *Report on Tutor Work at the Faculty of Social Work* [Poročilo o tutorskem delu na Fakulteti za socialno delo]. Ljubljana: Faculty of Social Work.

Rapoša Tajnšek, P. (2005). Development fragments of study program in the first decades of education for social work. In D. Zaviršek (Ed.), *It was easier for me to work with a Diploma* [Z diplomo mi je bilo lažje delat] (pp. 135–145). Ljubljana: Faculty of Social Work.

Social Assistance Act (Official Gazette RS, No. 54/92, 1992).

Statopis—Statistical Review of Slovenia [Statopis – Statistični pregled Slovenije 2018]. (2018). Ljubljana: Statistical Office of the Republic of Slovenia.

Strategy of the University of Ljubljana 2012–2020 "Excellent and Creative" [Strategija Univerze v Ljubljani 2012–2020»Odlični in ustvarjalni«]. (2012). Ljubljana: University of Ljubljana.

Šugman Bohinc, L. (Ed.). (2008). *Accreditation of the first cycle social work program* [Akreditacija programa Socialno delo na 1. stopnji]. Ljubljana: University of Ljubljana.

Svetlik, I. (2005). *Competences in Human Resources Practice* [Kompetence v kadrovski praksi]. Ljubljana: GV Izobraževanje.

The Bologna Declaration of 19 June 1999. *Joint declaration of the European Ministers of Education.* Bologna.

The Rules of the Organization and Work of the Alumni Club of the University of Ljubljana, Faculty of Social Work [Pravilnik o organiziranosti in delovanju Alumni kluba Univerze v Ljubljani, Fakultete za socialno delo]. (2016). Ljubljana: Faculty of Social Work.

PART V

Researching Social Work in the Global South– Implications for Education

INTRODUCTION

Teaching and learning of research is one among the persistent challenges in social work education. This part of the volume casts new light on the emerging social work research in the Global South and tries to document its contribution to social work education. As evident in many chapters in this book, social work across the Global South is dominated by the Western knowledge and thoughts. Curriculum, pedagogy, teaching, and learning practices were directly borrowed from the Western origin during the establishment of social work as an academic discipline in many countries across the globe. Further minimal resources, lack of adequate knowledge, and lack of leadership in the social work institutions, favourable policies towards research and innovations by the state discouraged local innovation and Western replication for many decades in the Global South. Schools of social work across the world use a variety of approach for educating the students at different levels (Fook, 2003; Gibbs, 2001; Hardcastle & Bisman, 2003). Research is one of the methods of teaching mainly used by the educational institutions in the West with minimal emphasis in the South. In recent years, research and evidence-based teaching is getting more and more recognition at different levels of teaching across the globe and in the developing countries. *Liljan Rihter* provides an account of students and educators perspectives on research activities and its role in social work education in Slovenia. In Slovenia, educators are expected to use teaching materials drown from their scientific research and academic writing. However, existing literature shows that research is rarely used by the graduate students (Adam, Zosky, & Unrau, 2004; Bergmark & Lundstrom, 2002) in general and in social work poorly developed and rarely utilized particularly in the developing countries. Researchers have also noted a negative attitude of social work students towards research (Berger, 2002) and resistance to increase knowledge (Knee, 2002).

The chapters groped in this part are mainly resulting from the research activities happening in the social work academia in the Global South. Karene *Anne Nathaniel-Decaires* describes social work education at the University of the West Indies, St Augustine Campus, in the island Republic of Trinidad and Tobago in the Eastern Caribbean. The chapter outlines the challenges faced by social work educators at SAUWI and invites the educators in other regions to gain a deeper understanding of some of their own challenges and come up with innovative ways to address them. Development of social work across the globe is influenced by the contextual political realities. Further social work by its virtue is a political profession that strives for achieving social justice and bringing social change in the society it operates. Despite social works fundamental principle of working for social change and achieving social equality and justice, its connection with political ideologies and political regimes is not much researched, especially in the Global South. Every country is unique in its political system with different political administrative polices. These political 'regimes' largely define the social service and welfare delivery of the country. However, research exploring the 'political' influence on social work development is rarely focused and documented in the dominant literature. In this volume, Jaroslaw Przeperski provides an in-depth understanding of the development of social work education in the post-communist Poland. This helps the radars to understand the underlying assumption of the post-communist transformation of public education system developed for social workers in Poland. Further, the discussion of social work education in Romania by *Bela Szabo* provides an understanding of post-communist regimes social work and its professionalization in Romania. The chapter analyses different perspectives on social work development, and in addition, it presents the current challenges of social work in Romania. Given the social, political context, and institutional network in Romania, the growth of social work education and practice experiences numerous context-specific issue.

Changing global order had numerous impact on social work education across the globe. Further, neoliberalism had very specific effect on social work practice (Hasenfeld & Garrow, 2012) in many countries. Alice Gojova, Kateiina Glumbikova, and Soha Vavrova provide such an evidence of influences of globalization and neoliberalism on social wok education in the Czech Republic. The understanding developed in this chapter is based on a qualitative enquiry with the help of focused group discussion with social workers over a period of 7 years. The authors argue that the contemporary practice of social work places high demands on social workers due to an emphasis on efficiency, economization, and bureaucracy. Coming back to our discussion on social work research in the Global South, we argue that research as a teaching method for social work students is not well recognized and rarely utilized in many developing countries. The reason behaving this may be mostly, unavailability of financial resources for funding the research and in many cases non-availability of advanced literature related to the subject matter. We bring back our argument here again that the contributions in international scholarly journals are mostly dominated by the academics in the West and even the editorial boards of many leading social work journal are represented predominantly by Western academics including the chief editorships. Further low quality, local, in-house easily available publication, pay and publish or commercial publication has rampant in many developing countries academia, and thus, the quality of research and publication in these countries is deteriorating and not reaching the international networks. Further, there is a perception among both students and educators that research is mysterious and difficult (Cox & Jackson, 2003), whereas students interested in learning and applying research in their learning are very five (Berger, 2002; Knee, 2002; Montcalm, 1999).

Scholars and social work departments in the West initiated the establishment of social work education programmes in many developing and less developed countries. Perhaps this is the reason it was historically agreed that knowledge flow is always from the Global North to the Global South. However, the new definition of global social work challenged the dominance of Western ontology (Ornellas, Spolander, & Engelbrecht, 2018). In the past few decades, both at the local and international level scholars are critiquing the global dominance on knowledge production and the knowledge inequalities between the Global North and Global South. As a result, there has been a slower shift in the knowledge production patterns and Global South started getting little recognition. However as noted by Gibbs (2005) confusion and controversy continues to persist in the development and practice of social work research. Further, there are also discussions on disagreement in defining social work research and scholars often ask the question: 'is there anything unique and distinct about social work research?' (Shaw, 2007).

In sum, research plays an important role in the development of social work education as well as practice across the globe. The research conducted in the discipline helps to understand the progress and accomplishments whereas research in other disciplines provides an understanding of co-learning and collaboration in problem-solving. Social work education across the globe and especially in the Global South countries needs to take an urgent call on promoting quality and ethical ways of conducting research related to both practice and educational learning in social work. Supportive to this there was also a call in the literature for greater attention to social work research (Shaw, 2005). Further Dominelli (2005) highlighted, promoting social justice, social change and social inclusion in the society as the aim of social work research. In a nutshell, overthought the idea of social work academia in the Global South learning from the Global North is well agreed and followed since decade, the emerging idea of industrial countries learning from the third world countries is novel. If developed and accepted respectfully the developments and innovations origin from the Global South may help the Western world to solve many of their problems.

References

Adam, N., Zosky, D. L., & Unrau, Y. A. (2004). Improving the research climate in social work curricula: Clarifying learning expectations across BSW and MSW research courses. *Journal of Teaching in Social Work, 24*(3/4), 1–18.

Berger, R. (2002). Teaching research in practice courses. *Social Work Education, 23*(1), 247–258.

Bergmark, A., & Lundstrom, T. (2002). Education, practice and research. Knowledge and attitudes to knowledge of Swedish social workers. *Social Work Education, 21*(3), 359–373.

Cox, P., & Jackson, S. (2003). Editorial. *Social Work Education, 22*(1), 3–5.

Dominelli, L. (2005). Social work research: Contested knowledge for practice. In R. Adams, L. Dominelli & M. Payne (Eds.), *Social work futures. Crossing boundaries, transforming practice* (pp. 223–236). Basingstoke: Palgrave Macmillan.

Fook, J. (2003). Social work research in Australia. *Social Work Education, 22*(1), 45–57.

Gibbs, A. (2001). The changing nature and context of social work research. *British Journal of Social Work, 31*(5), 687–704.

Gibbs, A. (2005). The paradigms, contexts and enduring conflicts of social work research. In L. Stoneham (Ed.), *Advances in sociology research* (pp. 135–164). New York: Nova Publications.

Hardcastle, D. A., & Bisman, C. D. (2003). Innovations in teaching social work research. *Social Work Education, 22*(1), 31–43.

Hasenfeld, Y., & Garrow, E. E. (2012). Nonprofit human-service organizations, social rights, and advocacy in a neoliberal welfare state. *Social Service Review, 86*(2), 295–322.

Knee, R. (2002). Can service learning enhance student understanding of social work research? *Journal of Teaching in Social Work, 22*(1/2), 213–225.

Montcalm, D. M. (1999). Applying Bandura's theory of self efficacy to the teaching of research. *Journal of Teaching in Social Work, 19*(1/2), 93–107.

Ornellas, A., Spolander, G., & Engelbrecht, L. K. (2018). The global social work definition: Ontology, implications and challenges. *Journal of Social Work, 18*(2), 222–240.

Shaw, I. (2005). Practitioner research: Evidence or critique? *The British Journal of Social Work, 35*(8), 1231–1248.

Shaw, I. (2007). Is social work research distinctive? *Social Work Education, 26*(7), 659–669.

CHAPTER 31

Research in Social Work Education in Slovenia: From the Lateral to the Indispensable

Liljana Rihter

INTRODUCTION

Social work education has various forms and emphases in different parts of the world (Blakemore & Howard, 2015; Gredig & Bartelsen-Raemy, 2018; Lyons, 2000). Nevertheless, some common guidelines and global standards for social work education and training (IASSW, n.d.) are followed to some extent.

Current social work education deals with methods that are related to evidence-based practice (Lorenz, 2017). Social crises are responded to situationally and based on charity and in so doing weaken the social solidarity agenda. This has an impact on social work practice and social work education (Lorenz, 2017). Šugman Bohinc (2016) and Lorenz (2017) emphasised the importance of social work developing its own science-based principles of education on the basis of the complex practical demands and methodological demands of emergent academic paradigms of scientific research. Lorenz (2017, p. 317) argued for "… creating a space for reflection through practice-related education, reflection on the variety of experiences made in practice, reflection with regard to the best available explanatory theories concerning the nature of human behaviour and the nature of society." The main threats to social work education are the attempts being made to adjust to changes in social politics and economics. The Bologna Process

L. Rihter (✉)
Faculty of Social Work, University of Ljubljana, Ljubljana, Slovenia
e-mail: liljana.rihter@fsd.uni-lj.si

© The Author(s) 2021
S. S. M. et al. (eds.), *The Palgrave Handbook of Global Social Work Education*, https://doi.org/10.1007/978-3-030-39966-5_31

set up to reform the higher education system in Europe also contributed to that as did reductionist views on social problems and a general trend to risk reduction.

Šugman Bohinc (2016) argued that social workers should have an epistemologically reflexive, ethically sensitive, and self-critical attitude and possess narrative skills when it comes to collaboration in the education, research, and constructive dialogical practice of social work to create the necessary conditions to develop a culture of coexistence embodying the ideals of multiculturality, global citizenship, and a more just society. In social work curricula and research all levels of social work practice should be recognised and emphasised. Yet there is no clear answer about how to implement these professional and ethical values, missions, and highly valued global goals of social work in practice, education, and research. There is an even more crucial question: How do global standards of education and practice respond to local particularities (Ponnuswami & Harris, 2017)? Šugman Bohinc (2016, pp. 226–227) argued for an education system in which students should be encouraged to use different sources of knowledge and skills to enable them to make their own professional behaviour more appropriate and more sensible to answer complex questions posed by their own partners in cooperation projects. The exchange of knowledge between Western parts of the world and other parts should be bidirectional. Moreover, it is very important that educators respond to the criticism that postmodern practice and social work education are focussed mainly on directing work at people and less at the structural factors that affect their lives. There is a need to teach students to research how concrete user problems in oppressed groups correlate with structural sources of their oppression and how they interconnect with users if social workers are to participate in radical social change (Šugman Bohinc 2016, p. 229). Therefore, teaching students the importance of research should be an important part of social work curricula.

Although research is perceived as a traditional requirement for disciplinary development (Lyons, 2000), the development of professional disciplines should include being able to manage knowledge creation (research), knowledge transmission (education), and knowledge application (practice). However, research is not given great priority everywhere in social work education. This is reflected in a statement made by Habermas (1978, cited in Lyons, 2000, p. 435) that scientific knowledge (derived from positivistic epistemology) has long been prioritised at the expense of emancipatory forms of knowledge (predominant parts of research in social work). Moreover, due to the predominance of instrumental values in society knowledge has become more functional and has led to the weakening of disciplines and academic work has become training rather than the development of critical thought.

Gredig and Bartelsen-Raemy (2018) summarised information from various parts of the world about the importance of and necessity for research courses in social work education programmes. Although social work study programmes were launched at the academic level in the early years of the twentieth century (United States) and later after World War II (Australia and some European countries), various standards for accreditation of research courses were demanded much later. Challenges related to the part educators and/or the profession itself played in such courses. Research courses are important as a result of their short-term and long-term consequences. In the short term they should influence learning and in the long term they should provide the skills necessary to engage in research. Therefore, research courses in social work programmes should be developed in such a way as to enable critical, creative, and strategic thinking.

This chapter highlights the importance of the role research activities and research courses play in social work education in Slovenia both for professional work and curricula development. In the first section a short history of social work education in Slovenia is presented. The second section presents results of a meta-analysis of ongoing self-evaluations by students with the aim of identifying the advantages and disadvantages of social work education in Slovenia. Then the importance of research courses in social work education is considered from the students' points of view and the importance of research activities of educators when it comes to the development of contemporary curricula. Results presented in the chapter are based on the meta-analysis of secondary data (self-evaluation reports from 2008 on, available at the faculty website at https://www.fsd.uni-lj.si/fakulteta/dokumenti/porocila/) and students' assessments of teacher work (personal documents of the author of this chapter from the study year 2012/2013 on). The concluding section focusses on contemporary challenges that have to be addressed in research courses for social work education to be optimal.

Social Work Education in Slovenia

Although social work education in Slovenia has a relatively short history, it has experienced a number of changes. A 2-year course was established at the High School of Social Work in 1955. This was a political decision made at a time of socialism in response to various challenges facing Slovenia as a consequence of World War II that needed to be addressed by professionals. Although social work education had been under political supervision, some modern concepts were developed in the first few decades (social justice, equality of women) based on ideas put forward by individuals who believed in the importance of helping people (Zaviršek, 2005a, 2005b). As a result of the ideological break with the Soviet Union teachers from ex-Yugoslavian republics studied mainly in the United States to build their knowledge of social work (Zaviršek, 2005c). Although the High School of Social Work in Slovenia had been independent and not part of any faculty and/or university for two decades, in 1975 it became part of the University of Ljubljana (Flaker, 2005). However, it took 10 years for a specific course on social work to be included in the curriculum (Dragoš, 2008). Although the academic year 1991/1992 was the last year to have a 2-year professional programme, in 1993/1994 the first higher education (4-year) course was introduced and in 2003/2004 the first faculty programme was introduced when the High School of Social Work was renamed the Faculty of Social Work. Then, in the academic year 2009/2010 a renewed (Bologna) programme was introduced.

In 2004 the Faculty of Social Work adopted recommendations from the Bologna Process (1999), which initiated a process aimed at harmonising European systems of higher education. Although emphasis was put on the importance of international cooperation and academic exchange, the need to establish links between research institutions and higher education, and fostering research and development (explicitly at the third or tertiary level—vocational schools and universities of applied sciences), Leskošek (2011) acknowledged that not all countries had the same opportunities to develop social work Bologna programmes at all three levels as Slovenia did. The Bologna Process provided the Faculty of Social Work the opportunity to engage in complex programme renewal that would reflect contemporary needs in the practical field and integrate new concepts, paradigms, and advances in social work theories. The process was manifold in that primary teachers revealed and reviewed advances in social work theories and practices as well as the latest research findings regarding the needs of users and necessary changes and then social partners such as ministries, societies, and communities working in the field of social work were invited to analyse the labour market and come up with the necessary competencies that social workers should have. Three basic groups of courses were developed (Mesec, 2015b): non-social work subjects (basic knowledge from other social sciences such as psychology, sociology, and pedagogy), connecting courses (general knowledge applicable to social work such as social security, theories of deviance, and management of social work), and social work courses (specific knowledge of social work theories and concepts). A programme was prepared to bring about horizontal and vertical connectedness with the organisation of practical work. Renewing the programme provided a golden opportunity to include much more practical work with students and courses on research methods in specific fields (e.g., in the work environment) and/or specific groups (the elderly). Since the main disadvantage of previous programmes was the low number of hours for practical education this was changed to improve the practical competencies of students (Mesec, 2015b). Since 2007 the Centre for Practical Studies has provided support in getting teaching contents integrated, given support to mentors and students, and supported the coordination of practical placement. Practice is conceived in such a way that students in the first and second year learn about the lives of users from the users' perspective invaluable to students when they later work as social workers under supervision of a mentor (Mesec, 2015c).

Currently there are about 600 students (around 100 in each study year) and 27 teachers.

In addition to formal education the faculty provides a means of continuing professional development based on input-based models (Halton, Powell, &

Scanlon, 2014). Although professional social workers are not obliged to complete a certain amount of work, they cannot be promoted unless they keep fully up to date with further professional education. Courses and programmes are designed in such a way that new knowledge, advances in practical work, and research knowledge are paramount.

ADVANTAGES AND DISADVANTAGES OF SOCIAL WORK EDUCATION

In the past and, more systematically, after gaining accreditation for faculty-level programmes continuous self-evaluations were conducted at the Faculty of Social Work in Slovenia. Higgins (2015) criticised the role of evaluation in social work education as excessively linked to the trends of modernity, reflexive modernity, and an audit society. He argued that evaluation research should have the purpose of learning and improvement. Hughes (2012) presented unitary appreciative inquiry as a possible tool to research social work education. It is based on similar values to those of social work such as gaining insight and understanding of a situation, following anti-oppressive principles, recognising the expertise of personnel, allowing participants to express themselves in creative ways and benefit from research process, making knowledge generated from research accessible to the wider public, and creating a base for wider reflections from research findings.

Self-evaluations of social work education in Slovenia are carried out mainly for the purpose of learning and improvement. Although the methodology used cannot be described as unitary appreciative inquiry, self-evaluations are based on most of the above-mentioned values. All participants such as students, teachers, administrative workers, and mentors in the practical field are involved and benefit from self-evaluations since minor disadvantages are solved immediately and those that need programme changes are recognised early. Self-evaluations are the main factor bringing about programme changes.

The results of meta-analysis of self-evaluations highlight some of the main advantages. Mesec (2015b) emphasised that an important indicator of quality in higher education is the standard of teaching. Although it is primarily assessed on the content of courses, it should be remembered that courses are mainly based on teachers' own scientific and research activities. Teachers develop the concepts and methods on which contemporary social work in Slovenia is based. Such concepts and meanings have a wider meaning in Slovenian social sciences and humanities in such areas as counselling, work with groups, community work, street work, work with families, voluntary work, action research, and qualitative analysis.

Reform as a result of the Bologna Process has made more hours available for practical work. It is a core course where students, users, practitioners, and teachers meet (Mesec, 2015c). Practical work is constantly evaluated and is critical to success (from the viewpoint of mentors in the field), to motivating students, and to getting them to use their own initiative (Rape Žiberna & Žiberna, 2017). Practical work is an important part of the study. Since reform brought about by the Bologna Process practical work has gained additional attention and provided renewal to improve the quality of the course (Mesec, 2015c).

Other advantages are the rising number of foreign students and teachers at the faculty and the improved mobility of students and teachers (Mesec, 2015a).

The main disadvantage of the reform brought about by the Bologna Process was that it prolonged the length of the course. Although Bologna Process programmes were supposed to shorten the study process, in Slovenia this was not the case. Instead of adapting valid levels of education to Bologna Process programmes such as equating the 4-year undergraduate course to level VII (as was the case before), students now have to finish a Master's level to gain level VII. This had the consequence of not only lowering the salary levels of social workers who took the Bologna Process undergraduate programme compared with "old" undergraduate programme social workers but also fewer employment opportunities (Mesec, 2015b). Moreover, there are as yet no clear results regarding competencies or whether declared goals have been achieved.

Although reform brought about by the Bologna Process had some positive consequences for social work education in Slovenia, Leskošek (2011) called attention to dilemmas faced by other countries. It was not possible in all countries to establish third-level study. Mobility depends on the Erasmus Programme for exchange where different countries cover different portions of the costs. Moreover, the attempt at making social workers attractive and employable has done more harm than good. Social work is itself critical at a time of market domination.

RESEARCH COURSES AND ROLE RESEARCH ACTIVITY PLAYS IN CURRICULUM FOR SOCIAL WORK EDUCATION

Blakemore and Howard (2015) analysed the literature on the importance of research courses in social work and revealed that some social work programmes are more focussed on how to develop critical research students and others on training that enables students to produce and take research on board. The latter is usually only found at the postgraduate level. Research-orientated social work education received more attention as a result of reform brought about by the Bologna Process that raised a lot of discussion because of the introduction of a Master's and doctoral level in social work in a number of countries (Labonté-Roset, 2005). Before the Bologna Process research was not deemed important (except in some countries) despite social work programmes having some common characteristics such as academic focus, generalist programmes, and an international perspective that are connected to research. In countries where social work education is part of the curriculum of a classical university such as Poland, Sweden, Finland, the United Kingdom, Slovenia, and Estonia research methods are important parts of the curriculum. In other countries the situation regarding research can vary (Labonté-Roset, 2005).

This chapter presents the importance of including research courses in the curriculum for social work in Slovenia from the students' point of view and the importance of educators carrying out research to develop a contemporary curriculum. Compared with many other countries the importance of research though modest was recognised from the outset in Slovenia. It was also believed that both the goals and methods of teaching would respond to contemporary challenges.

The research results of more than 130 research projects as of 2010 (Kunič, 2011) guided most courses now taught at the faculty. Flaker (2005) described the importance of action and qualitative research in developing the country's own practical methods, concepts, and scientific knowledge that began in the 1970s when qualified teachers started getting involved in systematic research. International cooperation started in the 1960s. Research and teachers joining various research (and development) projects became important resources to develop methods (and courses) of social work adjusted to current needs. The first formal research into voluntary work was implemented in 1969. The research that followed contributed to the development of new methods of social work and to other forms of organisation. A great deal of new knowledge has been tested in practice. The development of social work education can be classified as having three phases (Flaker, 2005): between 1955 and 1972 there was a pioneer phase that developed the profession; between 1973 and 1987 a scientific base of social work was developed; and after 1987 scientific and educational institutions of social work were established. A further phase could be added: after 2009 with the renewed Bologna Process programme as a result of which the former programme and needs assessment in practice were thoroughly evaluated. Research played an important role in developing the scientific base.

Research methods have been taught as an important part of social work curricula in Slovenia from the outset primarily as part of general social sciences ("basics of statistics"), after 1959 in a group of methodical courses ("statistics"), and from 1965 in a group of professional courses as a "theoretical course" (Rapoša Tanjšek, 2005). Mesec (1997) and Čačinovič Vogrinčič (2006) explained that "statistics" was mainly a course with analytical purposes—not scientific ones. In the 1970s the course was given a new name "research in social work" and taught in the second year of study (Rapoša Tanjšek, 2005). In 1992 this course was divided into three: "methodology of research in social work I" (M1) that focussed on a research plan that enabled students to take research on board and become critical of it; "methodology of research in social work II" (M2) that focussed on qualitative research in which students already had experience of being researchers and being able to analyse qualitative and quantitative data; and a "research seminar" (RS4) in which students were encouraged and supervised while researching with the main goal of encouraging research-mindedness, research capacity, and making researchers reflective. This would be brought about by teachers guiding students in developing a research proposal, data collection, analysis through discussion, challenging assumptions, and promoting critical thinking and reflection. Reform brought about by the Bologna Process added extra courses to these three courses on first-level education for social work (actually divided into four—with "statistics" as a separate course). These extra courses were special in that they focussed on special populations "research methods in social work with the elderly" (RE4) or circumstances "research in the work environment" (RWO3) or research strategies "evaluation research in social work" (EV4)[1] all of which had the purpose of preparing students in specific education modules to select appropriate methods to address research problems. In the second-level programme "social work" there is a general course "research in social work" (SECRA) and yet another in the programme "social work with the elderly" with the title "innovation and research in social work with the elderly" (SECINOV). In the other three second-level programmes (intended only for part-time students) there are no specific research courses, although students have the chance to consult on research topics that are available in the course practicum. At the third level (doctoral study) students have a couple of courses "research in social work" (general topic) and "individual research work" (consultations). At the second and third level research courses are intended to encourage and support the active engagement of students in the research process. Students should develop critical and reflective thinking when it comes to research problems.

The content of research courses allows suggestions made by Ponnuswami and Harris (2017) and IASSW (2014) to be assessed regarding how social work research should proceed. Teachers should draw on their understanding of their own context and research traditions, adopt a student-centred approach, and help build the practical capacities of students. There should be a focus on a research nexus that teaches practice and has the goal of developing a "research-informed professional culture" (IASSW, 2014). However, using a variety of research methodologies and methods can only be informed from a critical standpoint anchored in principles of social justice and human rights (Ponnuswami & Harris, 2017). Baikady, Pulla, and Channaveer (2014) recommended that social work research education should be rooted in the culture and needs of a country's own society. Contrary to evidence from other countries (Ponnuswami & Harris, 2017), qualitative methods are used in most research projects in Slovenia (Kunič 2011) and students prefer to choose qualitative methodologies to research problems in practice. Nevertheless, financers of various social protection programmes prefer quantitative methods to monitor services. Compared with the models of teaching proposed by Fish (2015) research courses in social work in Slovenia are intended not only to teach students how best to be informed about research or be educated in the way they take research on board, but also want to encourage research-mindedness, research capacity, and making researchers reflective practitioners (even at the first level of education). Ponnuswami and Harris (2017) wrote about the necessity of guaranteeing a safe learning environment for students that not only connects with their life experiences in practice contexts while teaching research methods, but also with social work values and principles.

Although students' attitudes toward research courses in Slovenia were not systematically studied, a similar situation to elsewhere should be expected in which students approach research subjects with reluctance (Blakemore & Howard, 2015; Gredig & Bartelsen-Raemy, 2018; Ponnuswami & Harris, 2017). Although it is to be expected that assessment of their knowledge and competencies will result in lower grades at the beginning of their study, providing a safe environment for learning and a student-centred approach to their active engagement in the research process with continuous teacher support (as suggested by Blakemore & Howard, 2015) should result in higher grades at the end of the study.

By analysing secondary data (students' assessments of teachers' work) the main trends in the opinions of students in various years of the study can be presented. Assessments of teachers' work and some indicators of courses are available from the academic year 2012/2013 on. However, in the academic year 2015/2016 the methodology (and partly the study programme and the teachers) changed so the data are not entirely comparable. Nevertheless, similar trends can be noticed. In the first period a number of indicators for each course were assessed using the following scale –3 (poor), –1, 1, 3 (good): general indicators included information about realisation of the course, conditions for study, the number of credit points, exercises in relation to the content, study literature, on-the-spot verification, disciplinary knowledge acquired, and general competencies acquired; assessment of the performance of lectures: attendance at lectures, quality of lectures, promotion of discussion, attitude of and accessibility to discussion and help when a student wants to fulfil some other obligations with the help of the professor. For the purpose of this chapter (assessing knowledge and competencies) two indicators were analysed: disciplinary knowledge acquired and general competencies acquired. From the academic year 2015/2016 the indicators were assessed following a scale from 1 (poor) to 5 (good): general satisfaction, content compliance, autonomy, literature, information, online information, on-the-spot verification, course content, tasks, assessment, competence, number of credit points, quality, teachers' readiness, comprehensibility, interest, criticality, and correctness. For the purposes of this chapter the following indicators were analysed: general satisfaction, competence, and interest.

Trends from students' assessments of research courses (Figs. 31.1, 31.2, 31.3, 31.4, and 31.5) on completion of lessons in the first, second, third, and fourth year (marked 1–4 in the tables) show gradual improvement in that the grades are better for courses in the third and fourth year and, generally, for courses at the second level of education (marked with the prefix SEC). Higher grades for competencies, general satisfaction, and interest in the final years of the study may be (subject to further research) a consequence

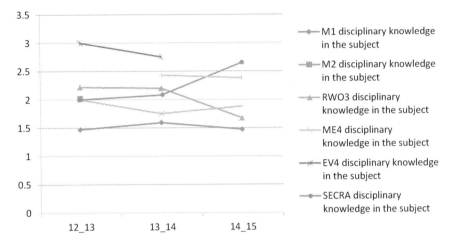

Fig. 31.1 Trends for acquired disciplinary knowledge (academic years 2012/2013–2014/2015)

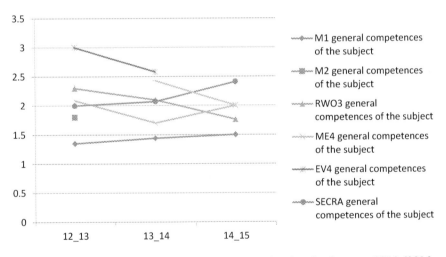

Fig. 31.2 Trends for acquired general competencies (academic years 2012/2013–2014/2015)

of progressive goals (from becoming informed about research in the early years to becoming reflective practitioner researchers in the final years and at the second level). Moreover, from the first to the last year of the study more experience-based or active learning approaches are increasingly used to help students recognise the importance of research, which is similar to the Blakemore and Howard (2015) study.

The main challenge now is to provide and teach research methods that would enable research in concrete user problems and structural sources, as

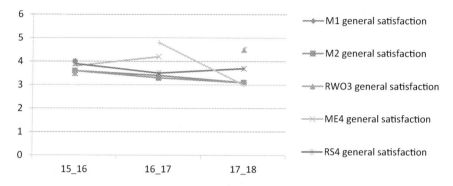

Fig. 31.3 Trends for assessing general satisfaction (academic years 2015/2016–2017/2018)

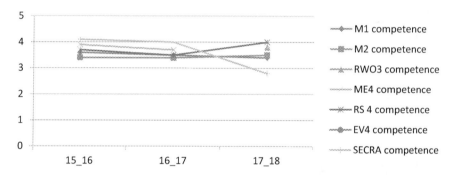

Fig. 31.4 Trends for assessing competency (academic years 2015/2016–2017/2018)

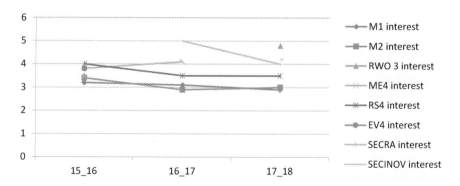

Fig. 31.5 Trends for assessing interest (academic years 2015/2016–2017/2018)

emphasised by Šugman Bohinc (2016). Research is important because it is closely connected with innovations in social work that are an ongoing necessity when it comes to social protection (Rape Žiberna, 2017). The task of social workers is to respond to the needs of individuals, groups, and communities, while looking for new (innovative) responses to new challenges Although there is not much Slovenian literature about innovation in social work (Rape Žiberna, 2017), research into innovation is becoming an important topic and is already included in some postgraduate programs such as "social work with the elderly."

CONCLUSION

Based on how students describe research courses in social work education in Slovenia and the importance of practicum it is possible to identify (as did Blakemore & Howard, 2015) the strong commitment to active experience made by engaging students in a process of learning to overcome any reluctance on their part as a result of negative beliefs and anxiety. The results of students' assessments show positive trends and present important evidence that the efforts of teachers (mainly in an environment that leaves much to be desired) can result in the achievement of better competencies. However, additional efforts should be made to directly connect practical work and research course. Blakemore and Howard (2015, p. 875) found that work-integrated learning opportunities in research courses, even more than experience-based or active learning approaches, help students recognise the importance of research, gain an additional skillset, and realise that research is "... an activity social workers routinely undertake to solve problems, generate workable solutions and establish connections with clients and colleagues." For this to come about students groups should be of a much smaller size than they are today.

There have been a number of joint endeavours in Europe regarding research-orientated social work education. For example, Hackett and Matthies (2005) wrote about the various activities undertaken by different universities trying to address the importance and challenges of social work education and research such as comparative social work research, threats to core social work values due to neoliberal politics, users' perspectives on social work, and local traditions within a context of Europeanisation and globalisation.

Videmšek (2017) pointed out the importance of including people who already had personal experience as members of research groups. There have been several research projects (mainly in the field of disability studies) at the Faculty of Social Work in Slovenia involving experts with experience. Videmšek (2017) described the advantages and possible barriers. A similar project carried out by Heule, Knutagård, and Kristiansen (2017) looked at the development of gap-mending strategies in research and education. The gap-mending concept is rooted in a movement advocating service user involvement in social work that has attracted the interest of researchers. The main challenges are power inequalities and the importance of recognition.

Nurius, Kemp, Köngeter, and Gehlert (2017) suggested that research in social work should develop the capacity to be multilevel and transdisciplinary, and at the same time be prioritised by funders and the public. Social work already has such capacities due to it being inherently a boundary-spanning discipline. Nurius et al. (2017, p. 908) "… see a need for strategic national and global investments in educational innovations that augment students' cross-disciplinary understanding of determinants of social and health problems, illuminate the potential advantages of interdisciplinary approaches to these problems, and—ultimately—enable them to develop and translate knowledge, in partnership with colleagues and community stakeholders, that improves the effectiveness and sustainability of social care and action." Therefore, there is a need for education programmes in which transdisciplinary preparation complements disciplinary preparation.

Although social work academics and professionals value and recognise the importance of research knowledge, the influences of contemporary neoliberal ideology can be a big obstacle. When it comes to research Ferguson (2017) emphasised that the business ethos prevails, research activities and themes financed require large amounts of time, and often critical research is not possible or is not financed. Similarly, Labonté-Roset (2005) pointed out crucial obstacles to social work research more generally such as lack of funding, small research projects (limitations to transferability), and topics founded are those that gain political attention and more practically orientated. Moreover, since the Faculty of Social Work in Slovenia is a public institution financial limitations are an important reason that more active methods of teaching (even in research courses) are omitted that would provide more support to students and bring about a context more suitable to work-integrated learning opportunities.

Academic research into social work coupled with professionals who are competent at planning and conducting research are needed to draw attention to the traps of neoliberalism and their consequences. If social work practice is not constantly researched and given careful reflection, then existing social policies and measures will end up serving only those groups with power. Therefore, a strong commitment to research courses (and their implementation as a way of teaching and carrying out research at the same time) is needed.

NOTE

1. "Research methods in social work with the elderly" and "evaluation research in social work" were removed from the programme at the first level, but some contents were transferred to the programme at the second level a few years ago as a result of rationalising programmes at all three levels as a consequence of the economic crisis.

REFERENCES

Baikady, R., Pulla, V., & Channaveer, R. M. (2014). Social work education in India and Australia. *International Journal of Social Work and Human Services Practice*, 2, 311–318. https://www.academia.edu/9818867/Social_Work_Education_in_India_and_Australia?auto=download. Accessed October 11, 2018.

Blakemore, T., & Howard, A. (2015). Engaging undergraduate social work students in research through experience-based learning. *Social Work Education*, 34(7), 861–880.

Bologna Declaration. (1999). *The Bologna Declaration of 19 June 1999*. Joint Declaration of the European Ministers of Education. http://www.magna-charta. org/resources/files/BOLOGNA_DECLARATION.pdf. Accessed November 16, 2015.

Čačinovič Vogrinčič, G. (2006). Izobraževanje za socialno delo v letu 1959: o metodiki socialnega dela pri Katji Vodopivec. In D. Zaviršek & V. Leskošek (Eds.), *Zgodovina socialnega dela v Sloveniji: med družbenimi gibanji in političnimi sistemi* (pp. 201–214). Ljubljana: Fakulteta za socialno delo.

Dragoš, S. (Ed.). (2008). *Poročilo o kakovosti* (Quality Report). Ljubljana: Fakulteta za socialno delo.

Ferguson, I. (2017). Hope over fear: Social work education towards 2025. *European Journal of Social Work*, 20(3), 322–332.

Fish, J. (2015). Investigating approaches to the teaching of research in undergraduate social workprograms: A research note. *British Journal of Social Work*, 45, 1060–1067.

Flaker, V. (2005). Od praktičnega poklica k dejavni znanosti. Memoarska analiza poti in prehodov izobraževanja za socialno delo (1975–2005). In D. Zaviršek (Ed.), *"Z diplomo mi je bilo lažje delat!": znanstveni zbornik ob 50-letnici izobraževanja za socialno delo v Sloveniji* (pp. 65–135). Ljubljana: Fakulteta za socialno delo.

Gredig, D., & Bartelsen-Raemy, A. (2018). Exploring social work students' attitudes toward research courses: Predictors of interest in research-related courses among first year students enrolled in a bachelor's programme in Switzerland. *Social Work Education*, 37(2), 190–208.

Hackett, S., & Matthies, A. (2005). Towards research-oriented social work education in Europe. *European Journal of Social Work*, 8(3), 245–246.

Halton, C., Powell, F. W., & Scanlon, M. (2014). *Continuing professional development in social work*. Bristol and Chicago: Policy Press.

Heule, C., Knutagård, M., & Kristiansen, A. (2017). Mending the gaps in social work education and research: Two examples from a Swedish context. *European Journal of Social Work*, 20(3), 396–408.

Higgins, M. (2015). Evaluations of social work education: A critical review. *Social Work Education*, 34(7), 771–784.

Hughes, M. (2012). Unitary Appreciative Inquiry (UAI): A new approach for researching social work education and practice. *The British Journal of Social Work*, 42(7), 1388–1405.

IASSW. (2014). *The IASSW statement on social work research*. http://www.iassw-aiets. org/the-iassw-statement-on-social-workresearch-july-2014/. Accessed October 5, 2018.

IASSW. (n.d.). *Global standards for social work education and training*. https:// www.iassw-aiets.org/global-standards-for-social-work-education-and-training/. Accessed October 5, 2018.

Kunič, L. (Ed.). (2011). *Pregled raziskovalnega dela 1969–2010*. Ljubljana: Fakulteta za socialno delo.

Labonté-Roset, C. (2005). The European higher education area and research-orientated social work education. *European Journal of Social Work, 8*(3), 285–296.

Leskošek, V. (2011). The Bologna process in social work education: Changes and impacts. *Social Policy and Social Work in Transition, 2*(1), 105–123.

Lorenz, W. (2017). Social work education in Europe: Towards 2025. *European Journal of Social Work, 20*(3), 311–321.

Lyons, K. (2000). The place of research in social work education. *The British Journal of Social Work, 30*(4), 433–447.

Mesec, B. (1997). *Metodologija raziskovanja v socialnem delu I*. Ljubljana: Visoka šola za socialno delo.

Mesec, B. (2015a). Deset let bolonjske reforme na Fakulteti za socialno delo. *Socialno delo, 54*(3–4), 169–179.

Mesec, B. (2015b). Kakovost visokega šolstva in Fakulteta za socialno delo. *Socialno delo, 54*(3–4), 233–239.

Mesec, M. (2015c). Praktični študij na Fakulteti za socialno delo. *Socialno delo, 54*(3–4), 239–249.

Nurius, P. S., Kemp, S. P., Köngeter, S., & Gehlert, S. (2017). Next generation social work research education: Fostering transdisciplinary readiness. *European Journal of Social Work, 20*(6), 907–920.

Ponnuswami, I., & Harris, N. (2017). Teaching research methods to social work students in India and Australia: Reflections and recommendations. *Social Work Education, 36*(6), 690–701.

Rape Žiberna, T. (2017). Konceptualizacija inovacij v socialnem delu. *Socialno delo, 56*(2), 111–129.

Rape Žiberna, T., & Žiberna, A. (2017). Kaj je pomembno za dobro študijsko prakso v socialnem delu: Pogled mentoric z učnih baz. *Socialno delo, 56*(3), 197–221.

Rapoša Tanjšek, P. (2005). Fragmenti razvoja študijskega programa v prvih desetletjih izobraževanja za socialno delo (). In D. Zaviršek (Ed.), *"Z diplomo mi je bilo lažje delat!": znanstveni zbornik ob 50-letnici izobraževanja za socialno delo v Sloveniji* (pp. 135–146). Ljubljana: Fakulteta za socialno delo.

Šugman Bohinc, L. (2016). Socialno delo v uresničevanju idealov pravične družbe. *Socialno delo, 55*(5–6), 221–239.

Videmšek, P. (2017). Expert by experience research as grounding for social work education. *Social Work Education, 36*(2), 172–187.

Zaviršek, D. (2005a). »Nekaj jih boste naučili vi, ostalo bo naredil socializem« Začetki izobraževanja za socialno delo v Sloveniji obdobju med 1945–1961. In D. Zaviršek (Ed.), *"Z diplomo mi je bilo lažje delat!": znanstveni zbornik ob 50-letnici izobraževanja za socialno delo v Sloveniji* (pp. 7–65). Ljubljana: Fakulteta za socialno delo.

Zaviršek, D. (2005b). Between unease and enthusiasm: The development of social work education in Yugoslavia. In S. Hessle (Ed.), *Sustainable development in social work: The case of a regional network in the Balkans* (pp. 26–43). Stockholm: Department of Social Work, Stockholm University.

Zaviršek, D. (2005c). Profesionalizacija socialnega dela med subverzijo in politično prilagoditvijo. In V. Leskošek & D. Zaviršek (Ed.), *Znanstveni posvet Zgodovina socialne politike, socialnega dela in izobraževanja za socialno delo v Sloveniji: zbornik povzetkov* (ppr. 13). Ljubljana: Fakulteta za socialno delo.

CHAPTER 32

Social Work in Romania: Education, Professional Life, and Challenges

Béla Szabó

HISTORICAL OVERVIEW

Although social work has a number of universal values and goals, when it comes to a concrete intervention plan such factors as the client's history, background, and resources need to be taken into consideration. Similarly, to better understand current trends and advances in social work and social work education in Romania reference should be made to its historical experience, its culture, and its laws.

Eastern Europe has a rich cultural and ethnic history as a result of numerous boundary changes that have taken place in the last millennium. As a consequence a number of nationalities live together within the borders of the country primarily made up of Romanians (88.9%), Hungarians (6.5%), Gypsies/Romas (3.3%), Ukrainians, Germans, and Turks (the last three less than 1% each). There are counties where Hungarians are in the majority such as Harghita (85.2%) and Covasna (73.75%) or make up a large ratio such as Mureş (38.1%), Satu Mare (34.7%), Bihor (25.3%), and Sălaj (23.3%). These counties are mainly situated in Transylvania, formerly a part of Hungary (recensamantromania.ro).

Describing the first evidence of social work practice in early Romanian princedoms Buzducea (2009) noted that voivodes (local officials) and rulers involved themselves with processes that nowadays are associated with social work such as dealing with poverty. Religious institutions also played an important role in developing the first forms of social work. Zamfir (1999) and Paşa and Paşa (2004) pointed to the first signs of social work being

B. Szabó (✉)
Babeş-Bolyai University, Cluj-Napoca, Romania

© The Author(s) 2021
S. S. M. et al. (eds.), *The Palgrave Handbook of Global Social Work Education*, https://doi.org/10.1007/978-3-030-39966-5_32

when the first child protection law appeared and when in 1775 certain specialised institutions were established for persons in need. However, it is widely agreed by authors dealing with the roots and origins of social work in Romania that the modern history of the specialisation can be laid at the door of Dimitrie Gusti, a Romanian sociologist, ethnologist, historian, and philosopher. Rădulescu (2007), Zamfir (1999), and Paşa and Paşa (2004) described Gusti's professional work. He held a number of different positions such as professor at different universities in the country, Minister of Education between 1932 and 1933, member of the Romanian Academy in 1919, and president of the academy between 1944 and 1946. He also set up multidisciplinary research teams to analyse and develop rural settlements.

In 1929 the Ministry of Health and Social Assistance, the Romanian Social Institute, and the Christian Women's Association got together to establish the first school of social work named the *Principesa Ileana*. The Ministry of Health bore the cost of organising and remunerating teaching staff, the Christian Women's Association made classrooms and a student dormitory available, and the Romanian Social Institute was tasked with developing and supervising the curriculum, organising seminars, and field practice (Sorescu, 2015).

The social worker profession was based on data accumulated during field research such as community development in rural areas and interventions in families with complex needs. Curricula included courses on psychology, public health and hygiene, intervention methods and techniques, legislation, and political economy. Training initially lasted 4 years, the same as university programmes (Rădulescu, 2007).

The 1930s and 1940s were decades in which social initiatives including legislation were rife. In addition to the School of Social Workers, other institutions and associations were established such as the Romanian Institution of Sociology and the Association for Social Work Progress. Between 1929 and 1936 scientific journals on sociology and social work were published such as *Sociologie Românească* and *Revista de Asistenţă Socială*. There were major legislative changes on health and protection (1930) and on social services (1939). In 1936 a general census was carried out into social care, child protection units, and social work. All these initiatives led to a paradigm shift in social problems and the spectacular development of social support (Buzducea, 2009; Rădulescu, 2007).

After World War II Romania fell under Soviet influence and any further development of social work was affected. Although political, economic, and social changes made by the Romanian Communist Party (the only party between 1947 and 1989) were made little by little, a change in the leadership of the party led to the Nicolae Ceausescu dictatorship emerging and changes becoming more significant. In 1952 social work education shifted from the university level to the post-secondary school level and the study period was reduced from 4 years to 3 years. In 1969 the programme was totally abolished since the regime's official discourse declared that no social problem existed. Many other measures were taken that led to deep structural change in society. One was Decree No. 770/1966 that outlawed abortion. Although more than 50 years have passed since this time—the decree was in force for half this period (i.e., 24 years)—Romanian society is still suffering from its effects. The immediate impact was a doubling of the fertility rate in less than a year (the main purposes of the decree). Compared with the fertility rate in those years in eastern Europe and the world at large the Romanian increase stood out. Although this is seen as the only positive (or at least not negative) effect of the decree, what followed still affects Romanian society (Szabó, 2014). The health, welfare, and the whole social protection system of Romania still suffer the consequences such as unwanted children, children living in the streets, the deaths of women as a result of non-clinical abortions, increase in poverty, and a significant emigration rate.

After World War II a series of measures were introduced with the aim of bringing about forced urbanisation and industrialisation. Before the war Romania's population lived mainly in rural settlements and worked in agriculture and animal husbandry (Rădulescu, 2007). After the nationalisation of private property the state became the owner of land and decided the direction of industrial developments. This brought about a number of negative effects such as a poor social and economic quality of life, low quality of urban housing, centralisation of the economy, strict social control, and decreased social responsibility of individuals. Despite all these social problems the state turned a blind eye and erased social work from the registry of professions and its role was forgotten.

Regeneration of Social Work

The euphoria that followed the removal of the communist regime at the end of 1989 slowly faded in the following months and years. Hopes for a welfare society appeared to be even more distant than they had been. Although the first measure of the interim government was to repeal the above-mentioned decree, its effects continued to bring new waves of social and health problems. The first year after abortion became legal more than one million abortions were carried out. Those having abortions were mainly born at the time of the decree. Having witnessed the disastrous effects the decree had on society they were desperate for family planning and to avoid repeating history. For every live birth 2.4 abortions were carried out. The media pointed to Romania as the country of abortions where women on average have 3 abortions in their lifetime (romanialibera.ro, who.int, provitabucuresti.ro).

The signs of an ageing society can also be seen with the number of people 60 years and older increasing every year. Women plan their first child at an older age reducing the probability of a second child. Over the 16-year period from 2000 to 2016 the average age of a mother at first birth increased more than 3 years (from 23.7 to 26.9). The same indicator analysed by settlement type shows not only that the average age in urban areas is higher in all these years, but also makes clear that the difference between the two areas increased every year from 2.6 in 2000 to 4.2 in 2016 (Romanian Statistical Yearbook, 2017).

The socioeconomic situation in Romania after the revolution was such that university experts discussed the possibility of relaunching social work education. The very first year after the revolution (1990) the University of Bucharest in collaboration with the Babeş-Bolyai University from Cluj-Napoca started a course in social work specialisation. The course was initially run as a college course and then gradually transformed into a university-level programme lasting 4 years. This was followed a year later by the other two major university centres in the country at Iaşi and Timişoara. The curricula of the different social work university programmes of this period predominantly included such subjects as sociology, research methodology, psychology, legislation, and social medicine and a few basic social work disciplines relating to theories and methods of intervention. Since it was a new specialisation the teaching stuff included sociologists, psychologists, lawyers, doctors, but no social workers. As different denominations of the Christian Church actively took part in the reconstruction of social care and an NGO network, since 1991 some university centres have introduced a double specialisation named "theology–social work." Such programmes were offered countrywide by three denominations of the Church: Orthodox, Roman Catholic, and Protestant. At the beginning of the new millennium distance learning was introduced as another way of receiving training in social work and involved 5 years of study. It was considered that students in the distance learning system needed an extra year of study than those enrolled in a full-time programme. Just before introduction of the Bologna Process[1] in the 2004–2005 academic year all university study programmes were transformed in Romania with the two educational forms in social work (full-time and distance learning) lasting equally 4 years. After the Bologna Process both programmes were shortened to 3 years. Reforms brought about by the Bologna Process introduced some confusion in university-level education, in general, and in social work education, in particular. Social work as a secondary specialisation (in the case of "theology–social work") became impossible. Theological faculties introduced a brand new specialisation that had no equal in other European universities called "social theology" (and in some cases "theological social work"). Although the double specialisation was reintroduced later, in the labour market such diplomas were often ignored. A temporary solution came from the Ministry of Education through an order (No. 6521/19.12.2012) declaring that those who completed the above-mentioned specialisations could become social workers if their curriculum coincided at least 70% with the social work curriculum. Universities were free to decide each case based on a request submitted by the diploma holder. There were no clear rules whether the number of disciplines or the number of study hours (or both) had to be considered. Without a clear and, even more important, unified methodology the decisions were divergent. Currently, the "theology–social work" specialisation curriculum follows the requirements of the National Professional Association of Social Workers meaning that graduates are fully entitled to work as social workers.

When it comes to where students have the opportunity to receive social work education in the country it is fair to say that compared with the inter-war period (when only one school of social work existed) the current situation is far better. Based on the latest governmental decision No. 158/2018 relating to the approval of university-level programmes in 2018 there are currently 21 universities offering 41 Bachelor-level social work programmes meaning that some universities run more than one programme (i.e., one full-time and one distance learning). Moreover, if there is a theological faculty, then there might also be a "theology–social work" programme. Most programmes take place at the Babeş-Bolyai University where seven programs are listed. This is the only state-owned university offering programmes in both Romanian and Hungarian. It is further unique in offering the only distance-learning programme for social work in Hungarian. There is also a private university running two Hungarian programmes and a state-owned university where there is a German programme. A detailed list of the programmes is presented in Table 32.1.

Comparing these data with the summarisation made by Sorescu (2015) of the situation in 2014 some changes in the structure and distribution of social work programmes can be seen. Private university programmes have almost halved (from 11 to 6) and the number of programmes in state-owned institutions slightly increased from 32 to 35. There is also a decrease in the number of theological social work programmes (from 18 to 15), but almost no difference in the number of secular programmes (from 25 to 26).

Analysing the chances of receiving social work education Neamţu (2007) specified 16 state universities when describing the situation in 2004. However, there are differences when compared with the present situation as evidenced by two ceased programmes (in Baia Mare and Târgovişte) and two newcomers (Galaţi and Suceava). He also noted the uneven regional distribution of these programmes underlining oversupply in the western and central parts of the country, while in the east where the population's income is the lowest and where there is a greater need of social intervention there are fewer programmes.

The opportunities given to candidates to study social work might not be sufficient for there to be a well-developed national social care system. Who can apply and what qualifications are needed are also interesting. At the national level the number of students generally decrease every year (Mitulescu & Florian, 2015). This trend might partially be explained by the negative natural increase rate of Romania since 1990 (higher death rate than birth rate).

Table 32.1   Romanian universities with social work specializations

University name/city	Type of university	Full time	DL	OT–SW	RCT–SW	GCT–SW	BT–SW	T–SW
Universitatea "Ovidius"/Constanța	State	1		1				
Universitatea din Craiova	State	1						
Universitatea "Dunărea de Jos"/Galați	State			1				
Universitatea "Al. I. Cuza"/Iași	State	1	1	1	1			
Universitatea din Oradea	State	1						
Universitatea din Petroșani	State	1						
Universitatea din Pitești	State	1		1				
Universitatea "Eftimie Murgu" din Reșița	State	1						
Universitatea "Lucian Blaga"/Sibiu	State	1		1				1[b]
Universitatea "Stefan cel Mare"/Suceava	State	1						
Universitatea de Vest/Timișoara	State	1	1					
Universitatea din București	State	1	1	1	1		1	
Universitatea "1 Decembrie 1918"/Alba	State	1		1				
Universitatea "Aurel Vlaicu"/Arad	State	1						
Universitatea "Transilvania"/Brașov	State	1						
Universitatea "Babeș-Bolyai"/Cluj	State	1+1[a]	1+1[a]	1	1	1		
Universitatea "Vasile Goldiș"/Arad	Private	1						
Universitatea "Petre Andrei"/Iași	Private	1						
Universitatea "Emanuel"/Oradea	Private	1						

(continued)

Table 32.1   (continued)

University name/city	Type of university	Full time	DL	OT–SW	RCT–SW	GCT–SW	BT–SW	T–SW
Universitatea Creştina "Partium"/Oradea	Private	1[a]						1[a]
Universitatea "Adventus"/ Cernica	Private	1						

Source Data in the table are based on Governmental Decision No. 158/2018

DL, Distance learning; *OT–SW*, Orthodox theology–social work; *RCT–SW*, Roman Catholic theology–social work; *GCT–SW*, Greco-Catholic theology–social work; *BT–SW*, Baptist theology–social work; *T–SW*, theology–social work

[a]In Hungarian

[b]In German

Despite rich offers made by the universities (including private institutions) it is often the case that there are more places available than candidates. The graduation exam introduced in 2011 was tightened up and further served as a strong filter evidenced by the success rate in 2018 being around 67%. Nevertheless, Mitulescu & Florian (2015) pointed out that only about 38% of youngsters directly transit from the 12th grade to the university annually. These conditions affected competition in gaining admission to courses on social work education. In the beginning (i.e., in the early 1990s) the admission process consisted of several exams. Limited payment-free places (at state universities the government covered the expenses) created high competition with some applicants trying several years in a row to get to university. Apart from exams usually in biology, philosophy, and psychology some universities such as Babeş-Bolyai introduced an eliminatory psychological ability test as well. This test lasted only until 1994. From 1995 more prominence was given to the decentralisation and expansion of universities. This culminated in 2001 with the number of places quadrupling and written exams being removed from most subjects (including social work). Since then entry to social work education has been based on marks in graduation exams and in some cases on motivational letters written by the applicants. The selection process is autonomously decided by each higher education institution. Although university education as a whole changed from being elite orientated to mass educated, a consistent part of available places for new applicants became payable.

Reporting on the success rate achieved in social work studies Neamţu (2007) estimated a success rate of around 90–95% of those who start studies. However, he did not present any statistical support to affirm this statement. In a PhD dissertation written in 2015 Botond Daniel presented the results of his research into social work students at Babeş-Bolyai University where he measured a dropout rate of approximately 25%. When it came to "theology–social work" these rates were somewhat higher (around 35%). The percentage of students postponing their studies (typically for one year) was around 10%. He also noticed that in years when a high number of places were offered there was a higher proportion of dropouts. A common finding was that students apply for a couple of specialisations only to decide at a later stage which one to choose.

The gender distribution of students generally shows the feminisation of higher education (59%) much as is the case in most European states (Mitulescu & Florian, 2015). When it comes to social sciences these rates are higher (63.3%). Dániel and Albert-Lorincz (2014) also measured a higher female presence among social work students (87.5%). Based on his research he also noted that male students have a significantly higher rate of dropout thus strengthening the feminisation of social work professionals in the national social care system.

In the social work education, under the equal opportunity principle there are special places for different disadvantaged social groups. The Roma ethnics for example, may apply on special places in several universities. After the admission, they usually follow their studies in Romanian language, or in the case of Babeş-Bolyai University, they might also choose to study in Hungarian. This university also offers reserved places in social work departments for people with sensory or motor disabilities or for students coming from foster homes.

The content of the initial training of social workers and the quality of the programmes are generally satisfactory. Neamţu (2007) pointed out that Romanian universities by and large use the Western experience borrowing well-established and verified models from the Anglo-Saxon space. In the 1990s study programmes were run by teachers/professors who had no social work background. They occupied related professional spaces such as psychology, philosophy, sociology, special education, and medicine. The curricula often reflected the competencies of local teaching staff rather than professional demands. In some cases the faculty hosting the course was a telltale sign of this such as "history and philosophy" or "psychology and sciences of education." Although there was little Romanian professional literature in the 1990s, the following years witnessed university libraries filling this gap with books and reading material written primarily by teachers. The process was helped by the Polirom publishing house producing a separate collection of books on social work called "Collegium—Asistenţă Socială." It also publishes the scientific journal *Social Work Review*, which is indexed in many scientific databases such as ProQuest, EBSCO, Social Work Abstracts, CEEOL, Index Copernicus, SCIPIO, GESIS, and IBS.

The quality of university programmes was assured by the National Council for Academic Evaluation and Accreditation (CNEAA) tasked with carrying out institutional and programme accreditation between 1993 and 2006. Once Romania agreed to participate in the Bologna Process in accordance with European higher education trends a new approach was needed regarding quality evaluation and assurance. The Romanian Agency for Quality Assurance in Higher Education (ARACIS) was established in 2005 to address this need. The new institution's mission and way of operation are defined to comply with European trends established by higher education ministers at conferences that have been held every two years since 2001 (www.aracis.ro).

ARACIS is the only institution allowed to set standards in social work education. Its standards mainly relate to enumerating different types of disciplines used in social work (such as fundamental disciplines, field disciplines, and specialised disciplines), calculating hours of work, and stipulating the qualifications teachers must possess. Sorescu (2015) pointed out that there are no specifications regarding the competencies to be formed, that fundamental disciplines differ from the internationally considered base, and that there are no directives regarding the content of the analytical programmes that disciplines should have. She concluded that quality assurance was based on the entrance side and that emphasis should be moved to results such as competencies, abilities, and values learnt by students.

The creation of the National College of Social Workers (CNASR) in 2005 represented a milestone in the development of the specialisation. Since the number of graduates in social work exceeded 16,000 at that time the need to protect the interests of professionals increased. There were multiple initiatives that led to the establishment of this college. Finally law No. 466/2004 created the framework for it and made it clear that only those with a Bachelor's degree had the right to practise as social workers. Although earlier there had been some other forms of education that existed in parallel with higher education, they had the effect of delaying the professionalisation of social work and created unnecessary confusion. A deontological code was adopted by the college in 2008 and published in the *Official Journal of Romania*. Based on the Registry of Social Workers there are currently 8240 registered social workers in the country (www.cnasr.ro).

According to law No. 466/2004, which paralleled the procedures of the CNASR, there are four stages to a social worker's career: debutant (less than a year of experience), practitioner (1–3 years of experience), specialist (3–5 years of experience), and principal (at least 5 years of experience). Despite there being little research conducted into social workers at the national level until recently, the CNASR collaborated in two research studies of this kind: Lazăr (2015) and Lazăr, Degi, and Iovu (2016). The first study (Lazăr, 2015) revealed that social workers mainly comprise the young, female generation since around 70% are below the age of 40 and the vast majority are female (only 12% are male). At a certain level their distribution countrywide follows that of universities with this specialisation. For example, in counties where there is a school of social work the number of registered professionals is higher. They mainly work for public agencies (75%), for NGOs (20%), and just 1% in the private sector. The rest either do not have jobs or are not working in the field. The major benefit of this research was that for the first time details of the makeup of this professional group came to the fore. The disadvantage of this research lied in the nature of the database analysed. It suffered from limited registered details about social workers and lack of data about those social workers who had a university degree, but did not enroll into the CNASR. Despite these weaknesses this is the most comprehensive database on social workers. To raise the accuracy of data and better protect professional interests, the CNASR reached agreements with higher education institutions that allowed fresh graduates to enroll into the national college free of charge.

To get a better understanding about practitioners another research study was conducted in collaboration with the CNASR in 2015. Lazăr et al. (2016) used a questionnaire on a representative sample of social workers to get to know their profiles, needs, challenges, and activity. The questionnaire was an adaptation of one used by the American National Association of Social Workers (NASW). The study revealed that a very low percentage of social workers (11%) were based in rural areas where almost half the population (46.3%) lived. Most worked in child protection (over 50%), elderly care (about 30%), adult and disabled person care, Roma programmes, and in the provision of benefits. They were less present in the social economy and in central government; therefore, they had little influence on social policy strategies. Social workers reported they mainly used public transport for fieldwork making it even more difficult to reach remote rural areas. Many social workers (42%) faced personal safety issues at the workplace, which is comparable with the percentage measured in the United States. When it came to workload, data from the Ministry of Labor (2013) showed that social workers had 2.5 times more cases (above 75) to deal with in the national social care system than the standard (30 cases). Despite these workplace challenges matters are made worse because a quarter of them have second jobs to augment their low income. Lazăr et al. (2016) also reported that lack of supervision was another major problem related by practitioners. One in four social workers reported professional exhaustion, while the proportion of those thinking of leaving the field was the same.

The accreditation of social service providers coupled with social services licensing are meant to be quality assurance tools used for social services in Romania verifying the fulfilment of the basic requirements and conditions necessary to meet the needs and expectations of beneficiaries and the government. Accreditation (of social care institutions) and licensing (of different types of activity) are mandatory procedures for all social service providers operating in Romania. The Ministry of Labour and Social Justice organizes, coordinates, and implements quality assurance processes for governmental and non-governmental organisations (NGOs). However, the management of NGOs often complain about bureaucracy and unequal treatment compared with governmental services. For example, the high number of non-accredited governmental services despite the law requiring them to be accredited since 2012.

The National Registry of Social Services (also managed by the Ministry of Labour and Social Justice) presently lists 2698 accredited social service providers (https://www.servicii-sociale.gov.ro/ro/registrul-electronic-unic). A superficial glance is all that is required to conclude that more than half belong to the NGO sector (foundations, associations, religious institutions, etc.). Although Romania has over 3000 mayors' offices where social services should be registered, only 580 are actually listed in the registry—let alone the other governmental structures with similar activities.

In Place of Conclusion

After almost 20 years of transition in social work in September 2009 the Special Commission of the Presidency made the following statement: "the Romanian social care system and social policy is still incoherent, inefficient, reactive, offering mainly ad hoc solutions to certain specific crisis, in some cases there are conflicting objectives, lack of vision, lack of strategic approach, they are not based on evidence[s] or social indicators" (Preda, 2009). Monitoring and evaluating current or previous programmes were the only exceptions to this statement regarding the Romanian social care system and social policy. Even if these tools were used, the main aim was to control matters, punish abuses, and reduce costs—as was the case with the governmental actions that followed this report. The main strategic approach was economic delivering as it did a clear message of cutting back the number of existing benefits and their value. Concrete measures are detailed in the Governmental Memorandum (2011).

Furthermore, the Special Commission of the Presidency stated that human resources working in social policy and social care institutions run by the state were in many cases not up to the job. At the lowest level (i.e., at the base of the system) they were insufficiently qualified, underpaid, immobile, and very often hired and controlled politically by local administrations (especially, in rural areas). At the central level (i.e., in ministries, national agencies, and directorates) decision makers tasked with formulating a strategic vision were changed continuously for political reasons—not on competencies—aggravating the temporary effects, incoherence, and inconsistency of planned measures and actions (Preda, 2009).

Zamfir (2014) stated that making the conclusions of social research into public policy decisions transparent was not as problem free as would have been expected in the 1990s in Romania. As former head of the Social Work Department in Bucharest she had strong ties with central government and a good overview on decisional mechanisms. She noted that sociologists were tasked with sorting out social problems during a confusing transition period in the early 1990s. The sociologists in turn hoped that their proposals about social policies in need of reform in the context of the new democracy would be appreciated and taken into account by political decision makers. However, coming up with social reforms during the transition period was made more difficult when the relationship between the academic environment of social researchers and decision makers at times lacked any semblance of collaboration and partnership. Sometimes this relationship was stretched during theoretical and scientific arguments mainly because decision makers were not won over by the results of Romanian research. There were also times when communications between decision makers and social researchers were totally interrupted, when research results were ignored, or when they were even contested. Lack of credibility in the conclusions reached by Romanian social researchers often encouraged political decision makers to engage external expertise to develop strategies to reform the system. Zamfir (2014) argued that there was more to this than merely a policy option to bring about changes in social care. On the contrary, the pressure applied by some international intervention institutions on social change delayed structural reform of the system. The import of models from the West and their non-selective takeover did not have the expected effect. Unable to adapt to internal socioeconomic and cultural life coupled with being costly and difficult to implement in the country, such models turned out to be unsustainable when it came to providing disadvantaged people with support.

Although the social work profession has undoubtedly improved significantly in Romania in recent decades, much remains to be done for the future. Future challenges include evening out the distribution of social services and improving the working conditions of professionals. There needs to be a multiparty approach to social policy in which the basic strategy is agreed and commitments and goals do not change as a result of changes in government.

NOTE

1. Further information about the Bologna Process can be found on the European Commission's webpage: https://ec.europa.eu/education/policies/higher-education/bologna-process-and-european-higher-education-area_en.

REFERENCES

Buzducea, S. (2009). *Sisteme moderne de asistentă socială. Tendinţe globale si practici locale*. Iaşi: Polirom.

Dániel, B., & Albert-Lőrincz, E. (2014). A román nyelvi kompetenciák fontossága a magyarul végzett szociális munkások munkaerő-piaci érvényesülésében. *Magyar Kisebbség, 2*, 33–59.

Governmental Memorandum. (2011). *The strategies regarding the reform in social care domain*. Issued by the Romanian government and the Ministry of Labour, Family, Social Protection and Elderly.

Lazăr, F. (2015). *Profilul asistenţilor sociali din România*. Timişoara: De Vest.

Lazăr, F., Degi, C., & Iovu, M. B. (2016). *Renaşterea unei profesii sau despre cum este să fii asistent social în România?* Bucureşti: Tritonic.

Ministerul Muncii, Familiei, Protecției Sociale și Persoanelor Vârstnice (MMFPSPV) & SERA România. (2013). Studiu concluziv bazat pe evaluarea la nivel național a DGASPC, SPAS și a altor instituții și organizații implicate în sistemul de protecție a copilului. Retrieved from https://www.sera.ro/seraromania/images/Raport-final-studiu-conclusiv.pdf. Accessed February 13, 2019.

Mitulescu, S., & Florian, B. (Eds.). (2015). *Condiții sociale si economice ale vieții studenților din Romania (EUROSTUDENT V 2012–2014, sinteza raportului național)*. București: Institutul de Științe ale Educației.

National Institute of Statistics. (2017). *Romanian statistical yearbook*. București.

Neamțu, G. (2007). Formarea profesională a asistentului social din perspectiva Declarației de la Bologna. In A. Muntean & J. Sagebiel (Eds.), *Practici în asistența socială. România și Germania*. Iași: Polirom.

Pașa, F., & Pașa, L. M. (2004). *Asistența socială în România*. Iași: Polirom.

Preda, M. (Ed.). (2009). *Riscuri și inechități sociale în România* [Social risks and inequities in Romania]. Iași: Polirom.

Pro Vita Bucuresti Association. Retrieved from https://provitabucuresti.ro/docs/stat/statistici.avort.ro.pdf. Accessed February 13, 2019.

Rădulescu, A. (2007). Dezvoltarea profesiei și rolului asistentului social în România. In A. Muntean & J. Sagebiel (Eds.), *Practici în asistența socială. România și Germania*. Iași: Polirom.

România Liberă Newspaper. Retrieved from https://romanialibera.ro/special/reportaje/cum-a-ajuns-romania-sa-aiba-22-milioane-de-avorturi-217321. Accessed February 13, 2019.

Sorescu, E.-M. (2015). Învățământul românesc de asistență socială – istoric, standarde și perspective. *Revista de asistență socială, XIV*, 23–34.

Szabó, B. (2014). The evolution of social work and social care in Romania. In J. Csoba, G. Grasshoff, & F. Hamburger (Eds.), *Sociale Arbeit in Europa - Discurse der Socialarbeit, Europaisierung, sociale Bewegungen und Sozialsaat* (pp. 189–208). Frankfurt: Wochen Schau Verlag.

World Health Organization. (2004). *Abortion and contraception in Romania*. Retrieved from https://apps.who.int/iris/bitstream/handle/10665/43113/9739953166.pdf;jsessionid=0C70D58F8FA33EA64E13CBB91086C82E?sequence=1. Accessed February 13, 2019.

Zamfir, C. (1999). *Politica socială: 1990–1998*. București: Expert.

Zamfir, E. (2014). În loc de prefață – De la succesul tradițional la inconsistența schimbării. In E. Zamfir, S. Stănescu, & D. Arpinte (Eds.), *Asistența socială în Romania după 25 de ani*. Eikon: Cluj-Napoca.

CHAPTER 33

Czech Social Work from the Social Workers' Perspective and the Consequences for Social Work Education

Alice Gojová, Kateřina Glumbíková and Soňa Vávrová

BACKGROUND

Social work in the Czech Republic is confronted with the impact of global neoliberalism; a political ideology with an economising paradigm that applies the rules of the free market. It is the implementation of market-oriented values, processes, and management into a non-profit sector and public administration. Global neoliberalism is demonstrated in the area of social work by the individuation of social risks (although many risks arise structurally, their solution is expected at an individual level), economisation, and rationalisation (social work is subject to market interests and efficiency requirements) as well as privatisation of social services. As a result of global neoliberalism, the legitimacy of social services is also questioned, with social workers being perceived as those who artificially create problems or help those who do not deserve their help (Chytil, 2011; Valová & Janebová, 2015). In this context, Šimíková (2015) describes the leakage of a corporate environment related terminology (e.g. customer, enterprise) into the Social Services Act.[1]

A. Gojová (✉) · K. Glumbíková · S. Vávrová
Faculty of Social Studies, University of Ostrava, Ostrava, Czechia
e-mail: Alice.Gojova@osu.cz

© The Author(s) 2021
S. S. M. et al. (eds.), *The Palgrave Handbook of Global Social Work Education*, https://doi.org/10.1007/978-3-030-39966-5_33

A similar development is described in a pan-European context. The client has been redefined from "*an individual with difficulties*" to "*a service user*" (Ruch, 2009). The prevailing focus on performance creates a social work environment where everything has to be done faster and faster in the terms of transparency and measurability of the result. Little attention is paid to the process and the associated emotions not only of social workers, to reflection, to development of a deep relationship with a client, to the work with a client driven by his/her needs. "*The soul is being squeezed out of the work, pulling workers and entire systems' attention away from understanding and developing the kinds of deep relationships...*" (Ferguson, 2005). The system of social work provision has become overproceduralised with a target mentality and a focus on performance indicators. However, unless the emphasis is on soft skills in social work, the procedure is completed, but the result is not achieved (Munro, 2011). Lipsky (2010) adds that, thanks to the above, a certain dichotomy of expected roles of social workers is created, where they are required to follow the rigid script emphasising organisational policies and goals on one hand, and on the other, the workers are expected to become compassionate with clients on a case by case basis.

According to a number of Czech authors, many social workers have adapted to the above described neoliberal trends in social work or perceive them as unchangeable (Hloušková, 2010; Janebová, Hudečková, Zapadlová, & Musilová, 2013; Musil, 2008; Šveřepa, 2008; Valová & Janebová, 2015). And thus, they perceive themselves as the mere executors of the social work setting that has been prescribed to them "*externally*" or "*from the top*" by those who have no direct link to the everyday practice of social work with clients (Glumbíková, Vávrová, & Nedělníková, 2018). The role of social workers (whether conscious or unconscious) is, however, different; they are implementers (street level bureaucrats) of the given setting rather than its executives "from the outside or the top". In order to process a large number of clients within the limits of very limited resources, street level bureaucrats develop routines and simplifications that can be understood as their coping mechanism and way of manifesting themselves in the process of decision making. Through these processes, social workers can shape public policy directly in interaction with citizens (Lipsky, 2010).

The context of the aforementioned aspects of contemporary social work influences the contradictory concept of "*doing social work*" and "*being a social worker*". The former is related to the compliance with external rules and guidelines regardless of their reflection or personal values. The latter perceives social workers as integrated, holistically informed, reflective practitioners. "*Being a social worker*" enables social workers to face the above-mentioned challenges of contemporary society (Harrison & Ruch, 2007).

AIMS

Czech social workers perceive that theoretical education in social work is somewhat disconnected from everyday practice and formulate the need to strengthen interconnection of these two levels (Glumbíková et al., 2018). A similar dichotomy between theory and practice is also described in a foreign context by e.g. Healy (2005) as a relationship between "*formal*" theory and "*practice wisdom*" or by Kane (2007), who distinguishes between "*know that*" and "*know how*". Fook (2016) states that knowledge of social work consists of a dialectical relationship between "*experience*" and "*education*". The social work practice can thus be perceived as a valuable resource of theories of social work and practical knowledge that improves or complements formal theories (Fook, 2016).

As part of the research, the authors aimed to understand how social workers perceive the position and role of social work (and themselves as social workers) in contemporary society in the social work practice and to make, on the basis of these findings, recommendations for the setting of educational process and goals so that it enables social workers for "*being a social worker*".

The aim of (long-term) research was to understand how social workers perceive and reflect the position and role of social work in the context of contemporary society.

METHODOLOGY

We used a qualitative research strategy to implement the research. We chose focus groups ($N=10$) as a data collection method. A total of 60 social workers participated in the focus groups from 2011 to 2018. The time interval of the focus groups implemented allows us to capture a more general trend of understanding social work and to limit the possibility of its influence by specific events. The informants were selected based on three criteria: (a) University degree in social work and related fields; (b) Practice in social work for at least one year; (c) Voluntary participation in research.

The research was attended by: 22 heads of social care departments and their deputies from municipalities with extended competence; 26 social workers active in social services targeted at a group of persons at risk of social exclusion; 12 social workers active in social services dealing with vulnerable children and their families.

The focus groups were run using a funnel method, so we proceeded from the most general themes to the most specific topics. The questions included four main thematic areas: (a) the position of social work in contemporary society; (b) the role of social workers; (c) the perception and reflection of everyday practice of social work; (d) the reflection of the position and role of social work in the context of contemporary society. The data gathered from the focus groups was literally transcribed. The obtained data was analysed using the cluster method, i.e. arranging data (statements) into different groups based on similarity (thematic overlap). As part of the data analysis, we proceeded with coding followed by the compilation of typology of perceived social work positions. We conducted our research on ethical principles published by the American Psychological Association (APA, 2010); special emphasis was placed on informing each participant about the research objectives, maintaining participant anonymity, data anonymisation, and adherence to confidentiality rules. Each participant's involvement in the research was voluntary and could be withdrawn at any stage of the research without stating a reason.

FINDINGS

Research results have shown that social problems have been perceived by the social workers involved in the research as multiple, interdependent and unsolvable or difficult to solve. According to social workers, the combination of individual and structural causes is behind their development. Social problems, their understanding, and ways of addressing them, therefore, need to be considered in the societal context.

The Societal Context of Social Work

One of the fundamental characteristics of society is, according to research participants, its polarisation, which, in their views, contributes to an increase in social tensions and conflicts "... *that must lead to some social conflict*" and the decline of solidarity in society, described by social workers as a consequence of individuation of society. "*This society puts a great deal of emphasis on itself, on individuality, and solidarity starts disappearing ... it means that I'm part of something, now there's just every man for himself ... just me, me, me, and everything else only if it is useful to me. If it's not useful to me, it's of no interest to me, or I'm distancing myself from it*". If there is solidarity in society, it's based on the logic of merit, according to communication partners. "*... and now you're trying to help those who don't deserve it (in quotation marks) ... what we define as solidarity is just often missing here*".

Another characteristic of today's society, according to social workers, is the uncertainty "*that society experiences on all fronts, and it does not matter if the system is set hard or soft but that it has not been set up. And the uncertainty does not only concern us as social workers but us as citizens in general... social uncertainty then also affects our work*".

In this context, social work is often perceived by society as a control of the "maladjusted". "*What's your job? ... once I reply "I'm a social worker". I can see the reactions of those people..."So, you take kids away?*" And I respond, "*No, I'm trying to keep the kids there*" "*Yeah, they perceive it like this...they lump it together. For them, you're just a person who comes to check on them, if their kids have a bed and a desk at home... if there's enough food for the kids ... and that's it for them... they don't distinguish any other services...*"

Economisation of Social Work and Its Consequences

Another phenomenon that research participants associate with social work is its economisation. According to them, it is mainly reflected in financial cutbacks to the welfare state and the introduction of austerity measures, which are interpreted as a controlled process of devastation of a social work which has become too autonomous. *"The more we became competent as social workers, the more we demanded more costly solutions. And the state just put a stop to it. I think it's a drop, and if the government pushes through the reforms, this process will be very hard to reverse"*.

As a result of economisation, there is an emerging trend to focus on working with the least costly (expensive) clients with the risk of the fall of certain social groups. *"The market has penetrated into social services, and we work in a way so that the organisation could survive. So if they work with the disabled, seniors…they choose a group that ensures them money. … Nobody's dealing with a group of people that is not lucrative enough. The market just cannot work in social services. The state should not allow this … there is a certain group of people who do not bring any finances"*.

The tendency to monitor and show work efficiency of social workers is associated with increasing bureaucratisation and administration, which is at the expense of the work with clients. *"When I see it now, how much paperwork, phone calls and problems they have…"* *"Half of the working hours is writing about what I have done. I'd rather work with clients, but instead – I have to write we did this and that, yeah. Those reports. To be able to prove to someone what I'm doing, so that he/she knows because someone is paying us. That's what irritates me the most"*.

The Position of Social Work in Society

The research participants described social work as a low-prestige profession that is not valued enough by society. *"Social work is a profession with rather low public prestige as seen by the public"*. They talked about the public having very distorted notions of their work. They can be perceived as those who side with socially maladjusted, troubled members of society and participate in the behaviour that is known as the abuse of social benefits. *"The public often does not even know what a social worker does, they think that we support those socially maladjusted who steal from the state"*. *"I would say that the public perceives social work within that social benefit system"*. *"There is such a generalization present that it is a lot about the Roma community and such"*. Communication partners reported that the perception of the social work prestige depends on which target group a social worker works with. *"So, I think, surely, as a dedication, it's just like families with children or maybe seniors. But what I can see or feel that it is not very well perceived is, for example, the work with minorities, homeless and so on"*.

Weaknesses in the Education of Social Workers

Education in social work was perceived by the participants as the "*theoretical base*" but they pointed out the differences between education and practice and the fact that education did not prepare them for the everyday practice of social work: "*Sometimes the theory is a little bit different from the practice*". "*There is always some naivety there*". "*We didn't have a very real idea when we left school, what it would look like…*" The research participants reflected that some of the knowledge could not be virtually gained only in the process of professional training. They distinguished between learning about values in a university and applying values in practice, and also emphasised the need for practice in order to develop one's identity with the profession. "*When I was studying from my study materials at university, they were just values. It didn't enrich me in any way. There were just a few words written about values of some organisation in general, and it didn't give me anything. As soon as I got my job here after school, then … you just start learning as you go and I'm thinking it's my job*". "*Well, you learn about values when working with a client. As you graduate from school and then start working somewhere, you just need to gain some values… and you get them in that practice and always in those different cases in specific situations*". Participants in research all put emphasis in social work education on high-quality practical training during the studies and on its subsequent reflection in interaction with the teacher.

Typology of Positions in Czech Social Work

Within the context of the social work described above in contemporary society and on the basis of the extensive data that we collected during the research (and which could not be fully presented herein), we identified four positions that explicitly or implicitly appear in contemporary Czech social work (see Fig. 33.1).

The first of these positions is the position associated with the powerlessness of social workers and the pressure on financial efficiency, which is the position of social workers who are doing social work and passively accepting assignments and imperatives from outside. The second position is associated with (re)construction of legislation in the context of achieving maximum financial efficiency, which is the perceived position of politicians, and is followed by strong political assignments. The third position is the position of a helpless practitioner, who is reflexive and aware of the system's weaknesses, but perceives his/her own helplessness in the possibilities to change this system. The fourth position is the position of being a social worker. This position is associated with reflexivity in relation to the practice of contemporary social work and the perceived ability to implement (re)construction of legislation through to street level bureaucracy. However, this position is rather a certain ideal in our data. Individual positions are further analysed in a mutual context.

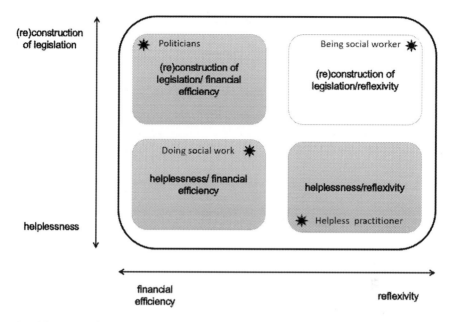

Fig. 33.1 Typology of positions in Czech social work (*Source* Author's own construction)

Political Assignments and the Resulting Helplessness: The Position of Politicians Versus Doing Social Work

Political ideologies, according to the social workers involved in the discussion, significantly affect the social work practice. They perceive the influence of the liberal approach as prevailing. "*The opinion of our politicians ... everyone is responsible for the situation he/she got himself/herself into, which means they can manage to help themselves*". It is the influence of politics that they consider to be the cause of discontinuity of social work. "*... rapid political changes, the governments and ministers change so often that it has no continuity*".

Social workers consider the social policy system to be highly determined by political interests, for which the social area is today "*somewhat on the brink of interest*". Legislation has often been seen in this context as "*something that tries to trip them up*". "*The biggest problem is in the laws. As if ... the social workers are doing well with the work, but sometimes are given obstacles by the state. For example now with GDPR...a lot of people have a problem how they should be sending those records*".

Another consequence of the politicisation of social work is the separation of social workers from its conception, which leads to their feeling of helplessness. "*It's not time to ask those people on the bottom, because the reforms need to be processed quickly*". "*And best of all, those from the top ...it should change... they should get a chance to try it out...*" "*And in the management there are people, who have neither idea nor interest, I'm afraid, in social matters*". However, the interviewed social workers tended to expect to be asked by "*those in management*" for their comments, opinions, and experiences. They did not mention their own initiatives and reactions, neither individual nor collective.

Financial Efficiency Versus Reflexivity: Helpless Practitioners and Ideal of Being Social Worker

A lack of instruments applicable in finding solutions to the situation of clients was perceived by the communication partners as the main obstacle in the work of social workers; they ask themselves the rhetorical question "*... what can a social worker do? What instruments does he/she have available?*" "*And we are in the situation that we have nothing to offer. ... a social worker is legally required to work with clients in a certain way, but adequate instruments are not being designed for him/her, not just the specific ones by the law that regulates his/her work, but on the whole societal level*". "*... the state legislatively removes the effective instruments*".

The communication partners considered the instruments in terms of financial and material assistance to be the main prerequisite for the performance of social work. "*... provided that there will be no instruments available, both the negative instruments such as sanctions, as well as the positive instruments such as social benefits ... Because, let's assume that some social workers remain in a municipality, but if the state takes away the social benefit instrument to municipalities, which can be used to motivate clients, then it'll be just about having a chat with clients*". Without the possibility and power of providing material assistance, social workers often feel helpless. "*We just, as we say here, have bare hands ... I can have understanding for them and everything...I know they are in trouble, but without financial means ... I really feel helpless*".

On the other hand, some communication partners saw the possibility of working with clients also in a reflexive approach. They did not regard this approach as saving but rather expanding the limited possibilities of practice. In this context, critical reflexivity was perceived as: (a) a self-reflective instrument; (b) an instrument for enhancing the social work practice with clients; (c) an instrument for a systemic change. Reflexivity was perceived by the communication partners as an instrument to work with the demands placed on them by a profession of social worker. "*It's a lot of individual work, there's a lot of the social worker's personality involved ... one is on his own in that moment, so it's important to reflect where my personal boundaries are, to where I can go and where I cannot go anymore*". Reflexivity was perceived as an instrument of social work interventions, which leads to enhancement of the quality of social work. "*I wonder ... if I was supposed to think of some technique that would be more effective for getting the job done*". "*And what I'm thinking about is that if some alternatives don't work out, if there's a chance that I contributed to it... that I was perhaps late with some advice...although one usually concludes that he/she couldn't do more, but there's always some doubt there*". In this context, critical reflexivity was perceived by the communication partners as an instrument for understanding client behaviour by the clients themselves. "*I think the clients appreciate a lot, and that is quite important to me, that they see some understanding from a social worker with no* a priori *judgment of the client's actions*". ... and also an instrument that will allow a social worker to work through empowering methods. "*We come together during our mutual relationship to the solution of how to deal with my client's problem ... I'm actually helping them ... or rather motivating them*".

Reflective communication was perceived by the communication partners as an instrument of social work interventions. "*And although those are unpleasant matters, I'm able to tell them without fear of any disruption of our relationship, which I consider to be a great benefit*".

Within the system level, social workers perceived the reflection as an important element. "*Right now, I think many of us are in our practice influenced by the pressure to shut down those hostels and convert them to rental housing. A lot of our families can't afford it. So this shutdown of hostels is often placed in the hands of people who act as the middlemen with those flats, if I say it in a harsh way...because they just can't go anywhere else. They can't officially apply through the organisation for a flat because of debts, and there's often no other option but through those dubious middlemen to get some housing. Now when those hostels are being converted into the rental flats*".

Consequences for Training of Social Workers

From the above data, it is clear that the social work as a profession places/lays high demands on social workers that require new knowledge and competencies (Fook, 2016; Thompson & Pascal, 2012). However, social workers perceived that professional training in social work did not prepare them for such demands. Social workers are expected to be able to work in (a) uncertain, (b) complex, (c) managerial work environments. The focus is on efficiency and outcome-focused practice rather than on professional values, flexibility and creativity in response to client issues (Gardner, 2006), which results in replacement of substantive accountability with clients for instrumental accountability to the organisation (Bauman, 1987), which limits autonomy and subjective decision making and does not capture the complexity of addressed problem situations (D'Cruz, Gillingam, & Melendez, 2007). The above results in strong feelings of failure, helplessness, and frustration of social workers.

In relation to the above, the key skill is the ability of reflexivity. We see reflexivity as a process of looking from the outside at social and cultural artefacts and forms of thinking that saturate the practice of social workers as well as the questioning and challenging processes that give sense to the world (Ferguson, 2003). A reflective tradition in social work seeks to connect both and analyse the functioning of formal knowledge in practice and the portability/applicability of practice knowledge into formal wisdom (Jones, 2010).

Reflexivity allows the following processes: dealing with messy or complex problems (Mathias, 2015); to cope with the doubts, anxieties, uncertainties (Gardner, 2006); develop professional confidence; articulate underlying and often implicit discourses, knowledge systems, assumptions and values; recognise how one's thinking may be restrictive (Fook, 2016). In relation to clients, the ability to use the reflexive approach allows to work in more empowering ways and to emphasise client agencies; to create more inclusive and less judgemental practice (Jones, 2010) as well as to create, rather than a less solution-focused practice, a client-skill building practice (Fook, 2016; Fook & Gardner, 2007).

As part of the education of social workers, and in line with the above noted there is an emerging need to incorporate reflexive approaches to social work into the curriculum.[2] According to some authors, for example, Valová and Janebová (2015), educators do not adequately develop critical reflexivity in social workers. At the same time, a number of authors believe that reflexive practices should be part of a standard educational curriculum (e.g. Council of Social Work Education, 2012; Gursansky, Quinn, & Le Sueur, 2010).

In the context of research carried out, we consider in line with Bay (2010) the inclusion of reflexivity into the educational process shall enable social work students to become autonomous and critical thinkers who can reflect on society, the role of social work, social work practices and their own experience developed in social work practice. The reflection process taught in this subject aims to assist students to recognise their own and other people's frames of reference, to identify the dominant discourses circulating in making sense of their experience, to problematise their taken for granted "*lived experience*", to reconceptualise identity categories, disrupt assumed causal relations and to reflect on how power relations are operating.

We consider the particular techniques important to introduce into the educational process in the context of professional training, namely the application of: (a) a critical incident method in teaching[3]; (b) reflexive logs in classes, to which students record their experience gained in the context of obligatory practical training as well as the feelings and ideas that these experiences have elicited in them and which are further reflected in cooperation with a teacher; (c) interviews that will evoke students to question the established way of thinking, "*well-known facts*" and prejudices through challenging questions regarding the functioning of the mechanisms of contemporary society and the social practice. The above-described techniques must be implemented in a stimulating and safe environment using non-judgmental questions and the formative character of teaching (Koole et al., 2012).

In the context of the above, we also believe that social work education should serve not only to acquire and internalise the necessary knowledge and skills, but also to enhance the identity of social work as a highly specialised profession (similarly, for example, Fook, 2016) and therefore we consider it desirable to incorporate the strengthening of social workers' identity across the entire educational process in social work. The particular techniques that can be used to achieve this goal are, for example, adaptation courses at the beginning of the first year of study, where students may not only get to know each other but also verbalise the reasons for their interest in the profession and confront their ideas of performing social work with specific settings of social work practice. Another factor reinforcing students' professional identity within their study could be, for example, student organisations that enable students to reinforce their identification with the profession and beyond the standard curriculum.

Professional identity of a social worker can be considered to be locked into aspects of organisational culture (Webb, 2017). Therefore, atmosphere of a workplace that has to support the (self-) reflection process for the further development of the social worker and workplace itself seems to be the most crucial element for the process of reflexivity. The techniques that need to be applied in social work practice include mentoring, supervision, and intervision (see e.g. Gibbons & Gray, 2004). The social workers themselves considered particularly beneficial the fact of the possibility to share their own experience from social work practice with (more experienced) colleagues, with a common sense of solidarity, but often also an idea how to solve the situation through social work interventions (Glumbíková et al., 2018).

The above consequences for the educational process have the potential to link the theory and practice already during training for the profession and also to strengthen this interconnection during the actual practice. The aim of the above is to enable social workers as for "*being social worker*", i.e. to create a reflexive professional identity, for which, willingness to be open to a (never-ending) self-examination is typical (Harrison & Ruch, 2007). As a result of strengthening of the "*being social worker*" identity, there could be the street level bureaucracy-strengthening, compared to current tendency to understand the current situation of social work as a status quo.

CONCLUSION

The research results prove that social workers consider social work a low-prestige job, and social work theory and education to be isolated from practice. They assess their work mostly in terms of "*doing social work*" because of (a) growing bureaucratisation in social work as a tool for minimising increasing uncertainty and (b) their own helplessness when solving clients' problems and changing the setting of social work at the systemic level. "*Being a social worker*" was perceived as a dream rather than day-to-day reality. The everyday practice means restricted autonomy and limited possibility to construct the profession through reflexivity. The social work education system should reflect the changes in the social work practice in terms of introducing elements such as exploration or questioning about experience, values, and political beliefs; to enable social workers not only to "*do social work*" but also to "*be social workers*".

NOTES

1. Social Services Act No. 108/2006 Coll. legislatively anchors the performance of all social services in the territory of the Czech Republic in the intentions of: the mission, goals, target group, provided services and their conditions, charging services, prerequisites for the performance of the social worker's profession, performance of public administration in social services, determination of entitlement to a care allowance.
2. We perceive education of social workers as training within professional education as well as further and specialised education during the course of the social work practice. Social work can be studied in the Czech Republic at colleges or universities of social work in Bachelor's, Master's and doctoral levels of study programmes. Two Czech universities have the right to hold habilitation and professorship degree procedures in the field of social work.
3. It is a systematic way of collecting and codifying a human activity. In the process of critical reflection people are asked to bring an experience that they view as significant to them (new, frustrated, upset) (Fook, 2016).

REFERENCES

American Psychological Association. (2010). *Ethical principles of psychologists and code of conduct.* http://www.apa.org/ethics/code/. Accessed July 29, 2014.

Bay, U. (2010). Teaching critical reflection: A tool for transformative learning in social work? *Social Work Education, 30*(7), 745–758.

Bauman, Z. (1987). *Legislators and interpreters: On modernity, post-modernity and intellectuals.* Oxford: Polity Press.

Chytil, O. (2011). *Proměny sociálních služeb a sociální práce. Resource document.* Ostrava: ACCENDO, Centrum pro vědu a výzkum, o. p. s. http://accendo.cz/wpcontent/uploads/chytil.pdf. Accessed July 29, 2014.

Council on Social Work Education. (2012). *Educational policy and accreditation standards.* www.cswe.org/File.aspx?id=41861. Accessed July 29, 2014.

D'Cruz, H., Gillingam, P., & Melendez, S. (2007). Reflexivity, its meanings and relevance for social work: A critical review of the literature. *The British Journal of Social Work, 37*(1), 73–90.

Ferguson, H. (2003). Welfare, social exclusion and reflexivity: The case of child and woman protection. *Journal of Social Policy, 32*(2), 199–216.

Ferguson, H. (2005). Working with violence, the emotions and the psychosocial dynamics of child protection: Reflections on the Victoria Climbié case. *Social Work Education, 24*(7), 781–795.

Fook, J. (2016). *Researching critical reflection: Multidisciplinary perspectives.* New York: Routledge.

Fook, J., & Gardner, F. (2007). *Practicing critical reflection: A resource handbook.* Berkshire: Open University Press.

Gardner, F. (2006). *Working with human service organisations: Creating connections for practice.* Melbourne: Oxford University Press.

Gibbons, J., & Gray, M. (2004). Critical thinking as integral to social work practice. *Journal of Teaching in Social Work, 24,* 19–38.

Glumbíková, K., Vávrová, S., & Nedělníková, D. (2018). Optiky posuzování v agendě sociálně-právní ochrany dětí. *Sociální Práce/Sociálná Práca, 18*(6), 78–88.

Gursansky, D., Quinn, D., & Le Sueur, E. (2010). Authenticity in reflection: Building reflective skills for social work. *Social Work Education, 29*(7), 778–791.

Harrison, K., & Ruch, G. (2007). Social work and the use of self: On becoming and being a social worker. In M. E. F. Lymbery & K. Postle (Eds.), *Social work: A companion to learning* (pp. 40–50). London, UK: Sage.

Healy, K. (2005). *Social work theories in context: Creating frameworks for practice.* Basingstoke: Palgrave Macmillan.

Hloušková, Z. (2010). Etické aspekty účasti poskytovatelů v procesech komunitního plánování sociálních služeb. In M. Kappl, M. Smutek, & Z, Truhlářová (Eds.), *Etika sociální práce* (pp. 223–228). Hradec Králové: Gaudeamus.

Janebová, R., Hudečková, M., Zapadlová, M., & Musilová, J. (2013). Příběhy sociálních pracovnic a pracovníků, kteří nemlčeli – Popis prožívaných dilemat. *Sociální práce/Sociálna práca, 13*(4), 66–83.

Jones, C. (2010). Voices from the front line: State social workers and new labour. *British Journal of Social Work, 31,* 547–562.

Kane, G. (2007). Step-by-step: A model for practice-based learning. *The Journal of Continuing Education in the Health Professions, 27*(4), 220–226.

Koole, S., Dorman, T., Aper, L., De Wever, B., Scherpbier, A., Valcke, M., ... Derese, A. (2012). Using video-cases to assess student reflection: Development and validation of an instrument. *BMC Medical Education, 12,* 22.

Lipsky, M. (2010). *Street level bureaucracy: Dilemmas of the individual in public services.* New York: The Russell Sage Foundation.

Mathias, J. (2015). Thinking like a social worker: Examining the meaning of critical thinking in social work. *Journal of Social Work Education, 51,* 457–474.

Munro, E. (2011). *The munro review of child protection: Final report—A child-centred system.* London: Department of Education.

Musil, L. (2008). Různorodost pojetí, nejasná nabídka a kontrola výkonu „sociální práce". *Sociální Práce/Sociálna Práca, 8*(2), 60–79.

Ruch, G. (2009). Identifying 'the critical' in a relationship-based model of reflection. *European Journal of Social Work, 12*(3), 349–362.

Šimíková, I. (2015). Možné důsledky implementace zákona o sociálních službách perspektivou kritiky modelu New Public Management. *Sociální Práce/Sociálna Práca, 15*(1), 24–35.

Švéřepa, M. (2008). Reforma sociálního systému v kontextu pomoci a kontroly. In R. Janebová, M. Kappl, & M. Smutek (Eds.), *Sociální práce mezi pomocí a kontrolou* (pp. 240–246). Hradec Králové: Gaudeamus.

Thompson, N., & Pascal, J. (2012). Developing critically reflective practice. *Reflective Practice, 13*(2), 311–325.

Valová, H., & Janebová, R. (2015). „Antiradikálnost" českých sociálních služeb aneb jak organizace sociálních služeb řeší pokles finančních prostředků. *Sociální Práce/Sociálna Práca, 15*(1), 5–23.

Webb, S. A. (2017). *Professional identity and social work.* London: Routledge.

Zákon č. 108/2006 O sociálních službách.

CHAPTER 34

Social Work in Poland: From the Marginal Position to the Professionalisation of Education and Social Work Practice

Jerzy Krzyszkowski and Mariola Mirowska

GENESIS AND EVOLUTION OF EDUCATION TO SOCIAL WORK BEFORE 1939

The analysis of the process of development of social work and social assistance in Poland before the partitions (1793–1918) indicates that it did not differ significantly from this type of organisation in other European countries. The dominating factor was the help of the family and church organisations, secular philanthropy (mainly magnate) and self-help of religious groups. In Poland, the Counter-Reformation strengthened the position of the Roman Catholic Church in the area of social work and social welfare and limited the state's participation in this area. Only the last years before the fall of the First Republic of Poland (1793) brought attempts at reform and increased involvement of the state authorities in helping those in need. The loss of statehood as a result of the partitions of Poland caused the development of social welfare in the Polish lands to be diversified. The loss of independence changed the possibilities of the functioning of the existing social welfare systems. Charity and philanthropy were continued by the church and secular institutions of Polish society, but their functioning was hampered by

J. Krzyszkowski (✉) · M. Mirowska
Department of Social Policy, Social Work and Tourism, Jan Dlugosz University in Czestochowa, Czestochowa, Poland
e-mail: jkrzysz@o2.pl

M. Mirowska
e-mail: mmirowska@interia.pl

© The Author(s) 2021
S. S. M. et al. (eds.), *The Palgrave Handbook of Global Social Work Education*, https://doi.org/10.1007/978-3-030-39966-5_34

the partitioning states. Philanthropic and charitable initiatives were treated not only as an aid to those in need but also as a patriotic duty. In the countryside, the main centres of charity activity were manors and parishes, which maintained parish hospitals and gave alms, financing their activities with public donations. The main subject of the charitable activity was still the Roman Catholic Church, which created its religious congregations during the period of the partitions in response to various social needs. Secular philanthropy, which was the domain of women, also developed, and a new kind of charity began to offer professional associations and institutions for charity, care, treatment, etc., established at the end of the nineteenth century. They were conducted by representatives of the intelligentsia and used modern forms of work with individuals and families (children's rest, legal aid, etc.). The social and philanthropic activity had a universal character and a common goal—national rebirth. The period of partitions caused the historical experiences and patterns of social intervention in Poland were different from those in other countries. The Polish path of social welfare development was non-public, based on philanthropy, religious and secular charity, social solidarity on patriotic grounds.

The critical role was played by informal aid organisations, mainly families. Social organisations were an instrument of political and economic resistance and social development, combining philanthropic activity with conspiratorial independence activities. In such conditions, the first forms of education for social work were also developed. In 1907, in the Kingdom of Poland (the then Russian partition) Catholic associations organised Social Courses on Social Work. In 1916, the Faculty of Social Work at the Higher Courses for Women was established in Cracow (the Austrian partition at that time). As it can be seen, the Polish system of education in the field of social work began to be created in the same period (the beginning of the twentieth century) as the American system, even though Poland was partitioned at that time. The beginning of the education was the courses created by non-governmental organisations.

Schools for social workers, followed by higher education, were established only after Poland regained its independence in 1918. In the first years after independence (1918), NGOs, associations, and foundations were the main actors in social welfare. Only the Constitution of 17 March 1921 [the Constitution of the Republic of Poland, 1921] granted the right to assistance to everyone in need, and the detailed rules of assistance were laid down in the Social Welfare Act of 16 August 1923 [the Act on Social Welfare, 1923]. The Act regulated the scope of social welfare activities, means of meeting needs, division of care duties of communities, counties, provinces, and central authorities. The conditions entitling to care and the rules of financing were defined, and social assistance was provided to infants, children and youth, mothers, elderly and disabled people, terminally ill, mentally handicapped and unable to work, homeless victims of war, especially the severely injured, prisoners after serving their sentences, beggars, vagrants, alcoholics, and harlots.

The forms of assistance specified in the Act were: providing necessary food, clothing, underwear, and footwear, providing a room with light and fuel and providing assistance in acquiring necessary tools for professional work, restoring or improving reduced fitness for work, assistance in the field of hygiene and sanitation as well as funerals. The state took over responsibility for social welfare, but the tasks were carried out by local governments. The central state administration body in the field of social welfare was the Minister of Labour and Social Welfare, with which the Social Welfare Council existed as an advisory and consultative body, composed of representatives of local government, social welfare institutions, and interested ministries. The state left the legislative and supervisory functions to itself, but the main financial burden rested with the municipalities, which could not refuse to help their permanent residents. The state paid for the care of those who did not have the right to it in the municipality. The subjective scope of social welfare created material aid, provided mainly in kind in the place of residence. The system was complemented by social guardians whose tasks included: initiating cooperation and the cooperation with community organisations, supervision over assisting, research on the family and property situation of social welfare recipients, providing immediate assistance, communication with the management board and reporting on their activities. The principles of social law in the Second Republic of Poland were the universality and obligation of benefits, and its distinctive feature was socialisation, i.e. the cooperation of the public sector with non-governmental organisations. Organisations established before 1918 continued their activity, and new ones appeared. A characteristic feature of the non-governmental sector in the Second Republic of Poland was the domination of religious and national organisations (Catholic, Jewish, Ukrainian, etc.). The adopted solution for the division of rights and obligations between state and local administration was modelled on the German dualistic political model, and the social welfare institution referred to the concepts adopted in the Austrian and German legislation and local solutions of some cities.

The beginning of the training of social workers at a higher level was the following creation in 1925 of the first higher school of social work—Study Center of Social and Educational Work at Free Polish University. Wolna Wszechnica Polska—Free Polish University (higher school of the universal education) was a private university established in Warsaw, 1918. Since 1929, it was included in the higher education institutions by the Parliament Act. The diplomas and degrees awarded by Free Polish University were equivalent to university degrees. The school aimed to promote and disseminate knowledge in all its fields. It had four departments: Mathematics and Natural Sciences, Humanities, Political, and Social Sciences and Pedagogy. The university specialised mainly in social sciences. It was also known as an educational unit for the cultural, educational, and economic life of the country, especially for its teachers. Among Polish universities, it was distinguished by a high percentage of female students (almost 75% in the academic year 1919/1920, with a decrease to 40% in 1928). The initiator was Helena Radlińska, who also became the first director of the study. Initially, it was a one-year study, then a two-year course of study and then a four-year higher education. Social workers with professional experience studied there. Among the students, there were those directed by workplaces and received a scholarship. All of them had two semesters of intellectual work technique and four semesters of visiting the institution. The school offered four specialisations: social welfare, social policy, librarianship, and adult education. The educational model adjusted the programme to the acquired education, theoretical, and practical knowledge. Helena Radlińska respected the principles of interdisciplinarity, multifacetedness, and polyvalence. She considered a theoretical elaboration, i.e. the setting of goals and direction of education, and only then the design of the curriculum and the curriculum plan, to be the primary theoretical elaboration. The whole educational model of Helena Radlińska was based on her original concept of social pedagogy referring to the theory of social environment and the use of social forces in the process of change.

EDUCATION FOR SOCIAL WORK IN THE YEARS OF COMMUNISM (1945–1989)

The qualitative change took place in the times of the People's Republic of Poland when the rules of market democracy were replaced by central planning and authoritarian power. In the years 1947–1956 in the period of reorganisation and rearranging of social welfare—the process of liquidation of independent organisations and associations took place. The previous system was replaced with taking the control over the social sphere by the state, passing a new law on local bodies of single state authority (1950), and abolishing of local government and the legal and organisational system of the interwar period. Social activities became the domain of state-owned companies and trade unions. The old foundations were liquidated, new state foundations were established to replace the old, independent ones, and inpatient care facilities were nationalised. In the period 1950–1957, the development of social welfare was hindered by political and doctrinal reasons. Social assistance was treated marginally because of the conviction that socialism, by guaranteeing work and company social assistance, social insurance, etc., eliminates the legitimacy of welfare institutions. The aid system only covered older adults who were unable to work and people with psychophysical dysfunctions, and the aid was limited to cash benefits or being placed in a closed care facility. The principle of localisation was abandoned, attempts at professional activation of persons in need of assistance were made, and support was granted in exceptional cases to selected categories of citizens. New institutions (e.g. the Polish Social Welfare Committee) were also established. In the years 1945–1953, in Łódź, the Social Welfare Employee Training Centre started its functioning. Then it transformed into the National Social Welfare Employee Training Centre, which dealt with education in the course system. In 1962, the Social Service Study Center at Warsaw University was established. It was not until the 1960s that the first schools of social workers were established, and the profession of social worker was introduced into the official nomenclature of professions by order of the Minister of Education of 24 November 1966. The first schools educating social workers were established in 1966 in Poznań and 1968 in Warsaw. Graduates of these schools could be employed in social policy institutions: national health care centres, community health centres, social welfare homes, specialist outpatient clinics and counselling centres (mental health, antituberculosis, anti-alcohol, etc.), hospitals, sanatoriums, crèches, rehabilitation counselling centres, departments of employee services of work establishments, etc. These were post-secondary extramural vocational studies, where the training lasted two years—four semesters. At the end of the training, the student took a diploma examination consisting of theoretical and practical parts and wrote a final thesis on the analysis of a specific case. A graduate of the school received a professional title of a social worker.

In the 1970s (1974), the Ministry of Health and Social Welfare adopted a programme for the development of professional social service for the years 1975–1990. It was intended to develop professionalism by increasing the number of full-time social workers and limiting the tasks of social carers to the role of representatives of their circles caring for their needs. The 1980s were a period of profound political and economic crisis, an increase in poverty areas, and new social problems (drug addiction, alcoholism, youth crime, etc.). Changes in the social welfare system in Poland during this period meant an increase in the role of informal philanthropic activities, self-help groups, and non-governmental organisations. Within the framework of the liberalisation of the system enforced by the inefficiency of public social assistance, church organisations were admitted to activities in this area, which was reflected in the relegalisation of the foundation. The Foundations Act 1984 [Foundations Act 1984] was introduced to regulate the distribution of gifts by the Church.

Throughout the Polish People's Republic, the policy of hiring non-professionals, wage pauperisation of social workers, and the lack of authorisation to grant benefits led to high turnover and professionalisation of human resources. The dominant substitution function of social welfare instead of complementary functions concerning other social security institutions, there was a lack of counselling and prevention. The centralist way of financing social welfare activities and the high level of state monopolisation of activities, including the nationalisation of social organisations, limited social activity and caused a lack of initiative in aid activities of individuals, groups and professional social services. Throughout the entire period of the Polish People's Republic, the distance between the rate of growth in demand for social assistance and the rate of development of the supply of social infrastructure increased.

In 1968, at the Faculty of Economics and Social Sciences of the Central School of Planning and Statistics, the education of social work organisers in enterprises and social workers of the state administration began. Graduates gained specialisation in labour economics and social policy.

A crucial moment in the development of academic education in the field of social work was the inauguration of a four-year extramural master's course in social work and social policy at the Institute of Social Policy at the Faculty of Political Sciences and Journalism of the University of Warsaw. In the academic year 1977/1978, the Social Service Employees' Study Centre was established at the Institute of Social Policy of the University of Warsaw. Its program provided for the education of three types of graduates: social assistance workers, disabled people employed in cooperatives and Social Insurance Institution employees. The last step towards the academicisation of education for social work in 1988 was the year when the Master's specialisation in social work at the extramural sociological studies at the Jagiellonian University in Kraków began.

MODELS OF EDUCATION FOR SOCIAL WORK AFTER 1989

In the 1990s, concepts for an integrated education system were developed, the main aim of which was to combine the vocational training of social workers with academic education, leading to a bachelor's and master's degree. Within such an integrated system of continuous education of social service employees, courses, trainings, and seminars for social service employees, a 6-semester bachelor's programme, a 4-semester master's programme and a 2-semester post-graduate programme in the field of social assistance organisation (Warzywoda-Kruszyńska & Krzyszkowski, 2000)[1] were included in the integrated system of continuous education of social service employees.

The progressive specialisation of working with a specific client and a specific catalogue of problems were the reasons for the introduction of professional specialisation. Specialisations in the profession of social worker of the first and second degree are intended for active social workers, while the first degree aims at supplementing the knowledge and improving professional skills of social workers, and the second degree aims at deepening knowledge and improving skills of work with selected groups of persons benefiting from social assistance. Specialisation training may be provided by units of vocational education or training after obtaining the consent of the Ministry of Family, Labour and Social Policy.

In 1993, the Ministry of Labour and Social Policy took over from the Ministry of Health the training of social workers and established 15 Schools of Post-Secondary Social Service Employees. The obtained special PHARE fund was allocated for the development and technical and didactic equipment of new schools. It was planned to transform these schools into higher vocational schools, but the local government reform (1999) resulted in the transition of these schools to the structures of the provincial self-government administration. In the Marshal's offices, specialised education departments have been established to deal with the existing departmental schools, including those of social workers. The pedagogical supervision is exercised by the education authorities. Unfortunately, local governments were not prepared to run such schools, although they were popular among young people. The current situation of these schools is complicated as most employers expect higher education from candidates for the position of a social worker, and an additional argument is the pan-European tendencies of higher education.

The development of education in the field of social work in Poland after 1989 was determined by two factors. The first of them was the administrative inclusion of Polish higher education in the so-called Bologna Process, started in 1990, which aims to create a common European Higher Education Area, with full permeability of education systems and three levels of higher education. The second factor was the European Union's decision on regulated professions, which set three-year higher education as the minimum condition for mutual recognition of diplomas of highly qualified specialists, including social workers, by the member states (Directive 2005/36/EC). As a result, a change concerning the introduction of three-year studies as a minimum education entitling to practice a profession was introduced in 2005. The regulation of the Ministry of National Education and the Ministry of Labour and Social Policy established three-year colleges of social service employees accessible to persons after graduation. The colleges replaced the post-secondary schools of social service employees, which did not comply with the principles of permeability of the educational system. However, as the colleges themselves did not meet these principles, but they could operate under the scientific care of universities which conducted social work specialising in one of the fields of study listed in the Act on Social Assistance. Until the end of the academic year 2014/2015, graduates received vocational diplomas, and the Bachelor's degree could be obtained at universities supervising colleges after completing additional classes required by the university. The next step of the academisation was the creation of social work as an autonomous field of study at universities in 2006 by the Ministry of Science and Higher Education. The training of social workers was limited to undergraduate studies only, which was not in line with the European principle of permeability of three-cycle higher education. In most EU countries, education for social work is provided at three levels. Vocational training of social workers only at Bachelor level deforms the idea of full academic education and indirectly affects the lower social status of the social worker profession compared to other social occupations.

In 2006, the Ministry of Science and Higher Education proposed standards of education in the field of social work, which were to guarantee the quality and profile of professional education at a higher level. A side effect of this was to make it easier for non-public universities without research and scientific and didactic facilities to obtain permission for this course. Simultaneously, the introduction of a separate field of study made difficult the operation of public universities which run specialisations of the same name, because the regulations made it impossible to run specialisations and fields of study simultaneously. The changed names of specialisations and programme derogations were a pretext for not recognising graduates' diplomas as entitling them to pursue the profession of a social worker. The amendment to the Act of 16 February 2007 specified that a social worker might be a graduate of a college or social work faculty or by the end of 2013, she completed studies in one of the recognised specialties: pedagogy, specialties, political science, social policy, psychology, sociology, family sciences. Currently, the only criterion for the qualification of a social worker is a university degree in social work or a specialisation preparing for the profession of a social worker.

SUMMARY—AN ATTEMPT TO EVALUATE THE MODEL OF EDUCATION FOR SOCIAL WORK

The Polish model of education in social work began to be developed in the same period (the beginning of the twentieth century) as other European and American education systems, even though Poland was partitioned at that time. Education started with courses created by NGOs, then schools for social workers emerged and then higher education developed. In recent years, there has been an increase in the overall level of qualifications and professional competences. In the research in 2010 (Staręga-Piasek & Herbst, 2010), it turned out that 42.7% have social work higher Master's degrees, 4.7% other Master's degrees, 11.3% Bachelor's degrees. As can be seen from the cited data, more than half (58.7%) of social workers had higher education, and 41.3% had secondary education. According to Anna Korlak (Korlak-Łukasiewicz, 2017), the problem of education for social work in Poland is the combination of theoretical issues and professional practice—there is still a disproportion between the number of lectures and exercises and the number of field classes. There is also a lack of so-called voluntary programmes for various groups (e.g. women in prisons, etc.). The selection of candidates for studies is also a problem. The only criterion is the passing of the baccalaureate, and once the entrance exams were passed positively. No interview with the candidate and no examination of his/her predispositions to perform the profession. Anna Kotlarska-Michalska (Kotlarska-Michalska, 2013) points to numerous dysfunctions in the education of social workers. They are seen in, among others, double standards of education (subject to two ministries), underdeveloped goals of education at the master's level, limiting the possibility of employing social work practitioners at universities, and the lack of requirements for linking scientific research with conducting education to social work at non-public universities. Other indicated dysfunctions are imperfections of the post-graduate education system, as well as irregularities in the selection of staff providing training and in the system of quality control of education. The same author also points to an over-marketing of this area, which is reflected in the presence of consulting entities in tenders for training services and non-educational companies in the process of publishing social work textbooks, as well as the ease of creating pseudo specialisations related to social work.

Among the postulates addressed to the creators and providers of education for social work, the following are mentioned: the need to accept social work as a scientific discipline and to develop full university education (including doctoral studies). It also points to the possibility of adopting European benchmarks in the form of external public examinations for social worker training graduates.

NOTE

1. Such an integrated education system was developed at the Institute of Sociology of the University of Łódź under the guidance of Wielisława Warzywoda-Kruszyńska and Jerzy Krzyszkowski as part of the "Public administration workers in the state welfare system" program financed by the European Union under the TEMPUS program (PHARE) (S. JEP9924/95). Cf. *Education of social workers on the eve of the European Union's enlargement*, edited by W. Warzywoda-Kruszyńska & J. Krzyszkowski, University of Lodz, Lodz, 2000.

REFERENCES

Bojanowska, E., & Krzyszkowski, J. (2018). Social assistance: From care to social services. *The Polish Monthly Journal "Social Policy" 100 Years Social Policy in Poland*, No1 ENG (14), Warsaw 2018, 31–35.

Brenk, M., Chaczko, K., & Pląsek, R. (2018). *The social services system in Poland 1918–2018*. Warszawa: Wydawnictwo Naukowe Scholar.

Kantowicz, E. (2016). Academic education for social work in Poland in perspective of new challenges. *Annales UMCS, Lublin—Polonia, XXIX*(1), 27–38.

Korlak-Łukasiewicz A. (2017). Vocational training of social workers in Poland and the USA. *Problems of Professionology, 2*, 103–116.

Kotlarska-Michalska, A. (2013). Examples of dysfunction in the education of social workers. *Annales Universitatis Mariae Curie-Skłodowska Lublin—Polonia, XXVI*(1–2), 147–165.

Krzyszkowski, J. (2005). *Between welfare state and welfare society*. Łódź: Wydawnictwo Uniwersytetu Łódzkiego.

Labonte-Roset, Ch., Marynowicz-Hetka, E., & Szmagalski, J. (Eds.). (2003). *Social work education and practice in today's Europe*. Katowice: Wydawnictwo Śląsk.

Staręga-Piasek, J., & Herbst, J. (Eds.). (2010). *Social services in numbers—2010*. Warszawa: Centrum Rozwoju Zasobów Ludzkich.

Szmagalski, J. (2012). Education for social work in Poland after 1989. In M. Rymsza (Ed.), *Social workers and social work in Poland*. Warszawa: Instytut Spraw Publicznych.

Warzywoda-Kruszyńska, W., & Krzyszkowski, J. (2000). *Education of social workers on the eve of the European Union's enlargement*. Lodz: University of Lodz.

CHAPTER 35

Sun, Sand, Sea and Social Work: Issues Facing Social Work Educators in the Republic of Trinidad and Tobago, West Indies

Karene-Anne Nathaniel

Context

Trinidad is the larger island of the twin-island Republic of Trinidad and Tobago located at the southern-most end of the chain of islands known as the Eastern Caribbean. Trinidad and Tobago gained independence from Britain in 1962, and many of its foundational structures have remained fashioned on the British system, for example, governance, justice, education, and welfare. The economy is driven mainly by the energy sector, that is, oil and gas reserves, ranking Trinidad and Tobago as having one of the highest GDP's in Latin America and the Caribbean (de Castro, 2012). However, economic and infrastructural development has not inoculated Trinidad and Tobago against harsh impacts of global economic recession and social problems including rising poverty rates, increasing disparity in income, high levels of unemployment and under-employment, and concurrent high rates of crime (de Castro, 2012). The Trinidad and Tobago Human Development Atlas (2012) identified a number of priority areas for attention for Trinidad and Tobago including poverty reduction, human security, human capital development, job creation, health care, and food security, all highlighted in the United Nations'

K.-A. Nathaniel (✉)
Department of Behavioural Sciences, Faculty of Social Sciences,
University of the West Indies, St Augustine, Republic of Trinidad and Tobago
e-mail: Karene.Nathaniel-DeCaires@sta.uwi.edu

© The Author(s) 2021
S. S. M. et al. (eds.), *The Palgrave Handbook of Global Social Work Education*, https://doi.org/10.1007/978-3-030-39966-5_35

Sustainable Development Goals 2015–2030 (UN 2015). These priorities are also reflected in the Global Agenda for Social Work and Social Development Commitment to Action (Jones & Truell 2012), as traditional concerns for the social work profession.

Trinidad and Tobago can be described as modern, largely influenced by North America, but is widely recognised as a multicultural and multiethnic society characterized by African and Indian descendants of slavery and indentureship, Chinese, Syrian-Lebanese and Portuguese entrepreneurs, European colonists, Venezuelan migrants, and persons of mixed racial heritage. It is a strongly faith-based society, consisting of Christian, Hindu, and Muslim followers. Racial sensitivities often play out in the political arena and there are noticeable class and socio-economic disparities on the basis of race, but in the social sphere there is racial and ethnic harmony for the most part. The composition of social work practitioners and students reflects this ethnic diversity, and education and practice embrace cultural competence as a skill and use multicultural approaches.

Social work in Trinidad has traditionally been practised through state agencies such as hospitals, clinics and health centres, mental health institutions including addiction services, social welfare services, children's homes, the court system, the prison and public schools. Over time, specialized areas of practice have also been introduced including youth services, poverty reduction, community development, HIV-AIDS and sexual and reproductive health, social displacement, disability affairs, elder care, family services, The Family Court, The Children Court, The Children's Authority, mediation, employee assistance, and services to victims of crime. Social work practitioners are involved in meeting basic needs, crisis and disaster management, child protection, domestic violence, individual therapy, group work, community organization, and policy development. Social workers in Trinidad and Tobago mainly provide ancillary services in the health/mental health, education, and justice systems.

In Trinidad and Tobago, social work positions are largely filled by persons who have tertiary-level qualifications in social work or related social science discipline, namely a certificate or bachelor's degree in social work, sociology, behavioural science or psychology, with few selected positions, save jobs in tertiary education and senior social service management, desiring Masters degrees. There is currently no registration, certification, or licensure requirement for professional social workers, but medical and psychiatric social workers seeking employment within the public health system, must be registered with the Board for Professions Allied to Medicine. Institutional accreditation for tertiary institutions is offered by the Accreditation Council of Trinidad & Tobago (ACTT), which is mandatory for programmes seeking approval for the State to cover student costs under the Government Assistance for Tertiary Education (GATE) programme.

Social Work Education in Trinidad

In 1990, The University of the West Indies St Augustine Campus in Trinidad (SAUWI) began offering tertiary-level training in social work, initially at the certificate level only, and quickly advancing to a Bachelor of Science degree. The Masters in Social Work (MSW) was introduced in 2002, and the MPhil/PhD Social Work soon followed in 2004. Since 2008, four other institutions have introduced undergraduate programmes in social work, and in the absence of a national or regional code of ethics or regulatory standards, there is an important opportunity for the profession as a whole to strengthen its mission, status, social identity, mandate and impact on which all education programmes might converge. SAUWI has a regional identity with three sister campuses in other parts of the Caribbean and an open campus offering a fully online bachelor's degree in social work. Two other institutions that offer BA's in social work are affiliates of well-established North American Christian universities, and the third is a public non-denominational institution. The ethos of each institution can inform philosophical differences in delivery, priorities, outcome, and impact. In the current climate of escalating social problems, there is need to harmonize understandings of the social mandate of social work in Trinidad and the terms of reference for professional training.

SAUWI is part of a larger institution with three regional campuses in Jamaica, Barbados, and Antigua (most recently) plus the Open Campus which offers pre-degree certificates, distance education, partial programmes, and fully online programmes (including a fully online social work degree). Deliberate efforts are made to ensure that programme offerings are aligned with each other and with international standards (UWI Strategic Plan 2017–2022). SAUWI is an institutional member of the International Association of Schools of Social Work (IASSW) and the social work programme reflects acceptance of the Global Standards for Education and Training for the Social Work profession (Sewpaul and Jones 2004). With the close social and cultural proximity to the USA, educators also refer to the Council for Social Work Education Educational Policy and Accreditation Standards list of core competencies for social workers (CSWE EPAS, 2015).

The UWI may be regarded as the subject leader in this field since its social work programmes date back almost sixty years, have evolved in keeping with the social needs of the territories, and have contributed significantly to shaping the practice of social work in traditional settings in particular (Maxwell, Williams, Ring, & Cambridge, 2003). Currently, holders of PhD's in social work are all employed at the UWI. Additionally, many faculty members in the programmes offered by other universities are graduates of the UWI so it would not be surprising if programme content and approaches used in other programmes reflect their UWI education. Therefore, UWI, and SAUWI by extension, may significantly impact social work education and practice in the region. Hence, this chapter will describe social work education offered at the University of the West Indies St Augustine Trinidad that include the challenges faced at different phases of the education process. This will be followed by a more in-depth discussion of the specific challenges for social work education in Trinidad and Tobago.

ADMISSIONS

Social work education at the UWI is governed by university regulations regarding matriculation and admission, course load, credit requirements, advancement through the programme and award of degrees. Literature on gatekeeping in social work refers to three different screening points in the education process—at admission, during training, and at exit/entry into professional practice (Elpers & Fitzgerald 2013; Finch & Taylor 2013; Holmström 2014; Sowbel, 2012). While the right and role of educators to 'gatekeep' has been debated, from its inception, the SAUWI saw it fit to include additional admissions screening for social work applicants. A two-level screening process was applied: matriculation and an in-person interview and essay. Applicants were able matriculate in the traditional way with requisite passes at the Caribbean Advanced Proficiency Examinations (CAPE), or a B+ average or above from the UWI Open Campus certificate programme. Students could also enter through the mature student route where, in lieu of CAPE, relevant work or voluntary experiences and other tertiary qualification or professional training in (for example) policing, prisons, nursing, or teaching, were acceptable alongside lower level matriculation requirements. The in-person interview allowed students to demonstrate their understanding of social work, awareness of ethical issues and clarity of academic and career purpose as well as non-academic factors such as interpersonal skills and maturity.

In 2015, there was debate among faculty regarding the usefulness of the in-person interview—did it ensure that the most suitable candidates were selected for social work education and training? While this was an aspect of social work education at SAUWI that set it apart from other social work programmes, it was also viewed as making it less competitive. The decision was taken to discontinue the interviews, and two years later, the essay requirement was also withdrawn. It is important to also note that outside of the admissions' phase, University regulations do not allow for enrollees to be 'counselled out' or 'required to withdraw' from social work for reasons of unsuitability or unfitness, unless they have committed a serious breach of University rules. Additionally, the prerequisite for entry into field is academic course completion which does not guarantee suitability or fitness for direct practice encounters. Social work faculty at SAUWI accept their duty to shape and mould future practitioners, but are also effectively powerless to gatekeep the profession at any stage. This has impacted the profile of the social work student and had implications for teaching and learning.

In its nearly thirty-year life span, the SAUWI social work programme has seen the demographics of each cohort change from predominantly mature students employed in social work and related jobs, to increasingly younger students coming into social work directly from secondary school. In the last three years, the mode age of the social work cohort has been 17–19 years at intake and the programme has consistently admitted on average 35–45 students per year. Another common concern for all social work education programmes and professional practice across the region is that the proportion of male enrollees has averaged less than 10% and has been seen as compromising professional effectiveness with gendered social problems such as gang activity, violent crime, and domestic violence. More targeted marketing of social work careers, such as outreach to all-male schools and motivational talks by male social workers from (e.g.) the prison and police services, are being used to address this shortfall.

Programme Structure

The SAUWI programme offers a three-year course of full-time study comprised of 30 three-credit courses. It is noteworthy that all other social work programmes in Trinidad and Tobago have lower matriculation requirements and are a minimum of four years with full-time and part-time options, with a higher number of credits. The UWI operates on a two-semester system, with the summer session being separate and self-funded. Students normally take five courses per semester over a minimum of three years, but may take longer if they have to repeat courses. The BSc Social Work is described in the SAUWI regulations as a 'special' degree, that is, it consists of a large complement of required or 'core' taught courses (twenty) and fewer elective courses (five), plus fifteen credits worth of field placement hours and assignments.

SAUWI offers a generalist social work degree meaning that the theories and methods taught may be applied across the spectrum of practice situations graduates may encounter, and prepares students with core knowledge, competencies and attitudes required for entry into generalist social work positions. The curriculum for the BSc is influenced by a combination of imperatives determined by stakeholders, including social work agencies and employers, the global agenda for social work, and the standards and competencies stated in the aims and objectives of the Social Work Unit. Core content covers theory and practice courses for working with all units of social work practice: individuals, families, groups, and communities, as well as social policy practice and management and administration of human service agencies. Other core areas are drawn from allied disciplines to inform the body of social work knowledge that supports social work assessments and interventions, for example, sociological, psychological, and organizational theories and research methodologies.

Students can also elect to take courses in special topic areas for example criminology, addictions, gender studies, disability studies, gerontology, international social work, and social policy analysis and formulation.

A clear difference between the SAUWI programme and others is that it emphasizes foundation knowledge with less emphasis on specific concentrations or fields of practice; practice with selected populations or social problems inform course content and case examples, and are infused throughout. The social work programme offers elective minors in Social Policy and Social Development Planning, but students also declare minors in other concentrated areas such as psychology, criminology, and gender studies.

Social work education is delivered using mixed methods: face-to-face interactive lectures, online activities, and active and cooperative learning projects. Human skills' laboratories—supportive group sessions specially designed to build inter-relational skills and reflectivity (Moss et al., 2007) are held concurrent with field placements. In the first year, students engage in social marketing/activism to commemorate World Social Work Day and final year students undertake a group community organizing project. Despite their young age, many social work students have confronted severe personal, family, and community trauma and are regarded as experts in their own survival and resilience. Approaches to teaching and learning actively accommodate students' lived experiences and provide opportunities for shared and reciprocal learning among students and educators.

The SAUWI programme is well-structured and course sequencing is important; many of the first year courses are prerequisites for the advanced courses. Additionally, social work theory and practice courses are offered only once per year and are prerequisites for later theory and practice courses, for example, Theory and Practice of Social Work I is a prerequisite for Theory and Practice of Social Work II which is a prerequisite for Theory and Practice of Social Work III, etc. The challenge for students is that if they fail any of these courses they cannot move on to the next, and they must wait until the following academic year to repeat. This means that a student who fails a Theory and Practice course effectively extends their degree duration by a year. While roughly 70% of social work students at SAUWI complete within three years, this presents a challenge for social work education throughput and outcome, and will be fully discussed later.

Field practice, or a practicum accounts for 1/6th of the course credit in the SAUWI programme (15/90 credits); students are assigned to social work agencies for 96 days over their last two years to get hands-on experience under the supervision and guidance of trained field instructors. Again, scheduling and administration of practicum is highly structured, and must be taken two days per week concurrent with Theory and Practice courses in a parallel learning modality: Wednesdays and Fridays in the second year, and Thursdays and Fridays in the final year. Students receive a dossier with rubrics and assessment forms that clearly outline their expectations. There is a formal agreement with agencies and field instructors to receive, train, mentor, and assess students. Students are placed in governmental and non-governmental organizations and a few private agencies. Field instructors are qualified social workers or experienced practitioners, but there have been concerns about parity in quality of instruction when some students are supervised by persons who are not social work-trained. SAUWI has field instructors' seminars every semester and also offers training in field instruction for non-social work-trained and new supervisors, so as to take advantage of the widest range of student learning opportunities at a time when the demand for social work field placements is high.

In their first year, students take an in-house preparation course designed to enhance their understanding of social work and its essential concepts, to develop appropriate attitudes and skills, and to improve their capacity to make full use of their later direct practice experiences in agencies. The changing student profile aforementioned led to the creation of a classroom-based programme of activities, discussions, role plays, and reflective exercises to replace the first year field placement (168 contact hours). The in-house practicum is built on four pillars: (i) team-building, reflecting a value for collegiality and cooperative learning; (ii) skills' building through role-playing and experiential learning; (iii) raising social consciousness and awareness of the social and social work environments through field activities and interactive discussions; and (iv) enhancing self-awareness and reflectivity through introspection and feedback. The students and field instructors have attested to enhanced learning, growth, and preparedness for direct practice experiences through the course. Students' journals and self-evaluation reports show enhanced insight and self-awareness as well as sound understanding of social work concepts, skills and abilities. Additionally, in the 2011 and 2019 quality assurance reviews of social work at SAUWI, the first year in-house practicum was noted to be a strength of the undergraduate programme.

Postgraduate Social Work Education

In the academic year 2002–2003, the Master of Science in Social Work (MSW) came on stream, marking the introduction of graduate studies in social work to Trinidad and Tobago. The graduate course of study provides the chance to acquire greater competence for contributing to the development of the profession, assuming leadership roles, and for addressing the distinct challenges facing the countries of the region. Applications to this programme reflect the high demand and need for advanced professional training, despite the fact that for the most part senior social work positions are filled by person with seniority in the organization and not tied to advanced qualifications. Candidates express the need for advanced knowledge and skills for dealing with contemporary social problems and seem to use the MSW for continuing education and development more than advanced academic qualification. This could provide an explanation for why candidates become 'stuck' at the research phase of the MSW taking between 1 and 2 years (or more) to complete a 6–9 month project and report: they place greater value on the knowledge and skill elements to enhance job performance with seeming less interest in research capacity. A group mentorship process has been introduced to assist with throughput in the research stages of the MSW programme.

In 2004, the MPhil and PhD degrees were introduced, marking another important development in social work education in Trinidad, and interest in the MPhil/PhD is also growing. Many candidates who apply for entry into the PhD programme are offered enrolment via the MPhil route. Candidates in higher education with good research experience enrol as PhD candidates and can take anywhere between three and eight years to complete the research degree. Holders of PhD's in social work are all employed in higher education and respected as experts in the field; however, research funding and institutional support are needed so that Caribbean research output can grow and strengthen the knowledge base for Caribbean social work.

SPECIFIC CHALLENGES FOR SOCIAL WORK EDUCATION IN TRINIDAD AND TOBAGO

In recent years, national security and violent crime, economic decline and unemployment, increase in domestic violence and child and elder abuse, the Venezuelan migrant crisis, and most recently the COVID 19 pandemic have consumed the attention of State agencies including social service providers, challenging social work practitioners to maintain proficiency and productivity in increasingly demanding situations in resource-strapped environments. By necessity, social work educators continue to monitor the dynamic context of social work practice in Trinidad and Tobago and find themselves in a state of continual adaptation in order to prepare professional social workers to meet these demands: educators have to prepare twenty-first century Caribbean social workers to do more with less. Social work educators can be viewed as experts in contemporary social issues and are involved in public fora, social and community engagement, and research activities, to help bridge gaps between theory and practice, and to keep content and methods contextually relevant; this can be an uphill battle in the current climate.

The governments of developing countries are drivers of economic development and stability, and social and human development. Those two elements can threaten each other, and in times of economic decline when social needs are highest, funding for social programmes is very limited. This is the reality facing Trinidad and Tobago, and social work services and jobs are harder to find; not that there are no positions, but the job market for social workers is effectively frozen. So, in addition to some 120 social work graduates 'hitting the streets' every year, many social work jobs are open to persons with any social science degree, so a stagnant job market is flooded with applicants. Social work educators are challenged to prepare graduates who can survive in this capitalist context and market themselves as self-directed innovative social work practitioners. Social entrepreneurship is fast becoming a premier option for social work graduates, and educators have to retool themselves to be able to prepare BSc graduates for self-employment.

Additionally, as the rates of crime, violence, and social problems have increased, the distinction between social work clients and social work students seems to be becoming blurred. A significant number of enrollees are drawn to social work because of their own experiences of extreme personal and family trauma, community violence and deep deprivation. These students seem to be driven by a desire to solve problems, prevent them, and save children and families from their impact. They tend to be eager for <u>the</u> answer, which the instructor often does not have because in social work, solutions are applied, not programmed or predetermined. Field instructors attest to having to support students through secondary traumatic stress reactions when client situations stimulate unresolved issues or difficult personal circumstances. Social work educators across Trinidad and Tobago concur that there are increasing demands for input into critical thinking and assessment skills for applying theory to real life practice situations, but more importantly for counselling therapy for students, and nurturing emotional awareness, self-acceptance, and self-regulation skills. The idea of mandatory counselling for all social work students has come up repeatedly, but there is no precedent for this at the undergraduate level. The Campus provides free voluntary counselling and psychological services to students and there is support available for those experiencing learning difficulties and financial problems. Nonetheless, there is a growing need for trauma-informed social work education to evolve alongside trauma-informed practice; in the meantime, social work educators at SAUWI are often called upon to provide support to vulnerable students.

Educators across all institutions and disciplines in Trinidad and Tobago lament the steady decline in students' foundational writing skills including use of English, comprehension, composition, and expressive skills. These challenges are attributable to changes in curriculum emphasis and exam structure at lower levels, and the digital era. Problems with writing skills are manifesting in professional practice with complaints from supervisors and allied professionals about the poor quality of social workers' assessment reports. This is a serious indictment against social work education and practice and educators have had to increase the scope of teaching beyond technical knowledge, skills development and formation, to basic mechanics of writing. SAUWI has put in a great deal of support to address this problem through the expansion of library services, the establishment of a writing centre, and a special needs programme that conducts educational assessments and interventions.

A common concern is the question of suitability for the demands of social work practice of the Generation Y (late millennial) and Generation Z students who tend to be more liberal, literal, digitally groomed, and future-oriented (Mohr & Mohr, 2017) and the pedagogical options for creating effective practitioners in this socially demanding, resource-strapped and uncertain environment. An obvious choice was to increase blended learning options, taking into consideration the importance of keeping connected to the students, maintaining open lines of communication and tangible support, and most importantly, facilitating development of learners' ability to apply theoretical knowledge to practice situations; however, outcomes from increased blended learning with respect to skills' development and practice applications are as yet undetermined. Faculty continue to experiment with interactive methods that provide opportunities for real-world problem solving and hands-on work using community engagement projects, case studies, and social activism. However, while students testify to having memorable experiences, there seems to be a challenge with transfer of learning to practice settings. Field instructors lament that some social work students display problematic and inappropriate behaviours that test professional ethics. Therefore, the ongoing challenge for educators lies in the formation aspect of social work education that moves theoretical and experiential learning to skills and attitude development demonstrated in practice.

To compound this, placement opportunities are becoming increasingly difficult to source because of high demand for spaces between institutions, the working conditions of social workers in agencies and the lack of incentive to accept students. The physical infrastructure in some organizations cannot safely accommodate students, departments are understaffed, the intensity of the work does not allow for adequate and effective supervision of students, and staff are over-stretched to near burnout. Experienced field instructors complain of exhaustion, plus field instruction is more and more demanding as students' needs expand. Additionally, senior administrators have become wary of students; on the one hand, they are nervous about exposing students/outsiders to the 'real world' of agency practice thereby opening the organization to criticism, and on the other hand, they are fearful of possible fall out if students make mistakes or breach ethics. Social work educators have had to become creative by developing projects, and community- and NGO-based practicum using long-arm field instructors. While these solve one problem, there is still the issue of relevance of practice learning experiences when the nature of social work practice in Trinidad and Tobago is predominantly welfare work and micro-practice with individuals and families. As direct practice placements become more scarce, graduates' readiness for professional practice can be compromised.

Social work practice in Trinidad and Tobago is not subject to statutory regulation—no registration, certification, or licensure requirements, and no agreed standards and accreditation for social work education programmes exist. There are currently five institutions offering social work education in Trinidad and Tobago that have different matriculation requirements and school ethos, and there can be variations in input, throughput, output, and outcome. Also, the educational environment is highly competitive, which can be antithetical to collaboration to ensure that there is alignment across institutions; yet graduates are competing for the same jobs. There are also no established standards for social work practice in the Caribbean, although all programmes use the ethical standards of the North American Association of Social Workers (NASW) and the International Federation of Social Workers (IFSW). Social work remains an unregulated profession with no clear performance indicators and sanctions for malpractice or dereliction of duty; the job title 'social worker' is not protected. These factors present significant challenges for social work educators.

Firstly, the policies and procedures governing social work practice can be dated and oppressive and out of step with international standards and best practices. Students' practicum can be limited by agency practice, which does not reflect classroom learning. In their field experience, students come face-to-face with the real 'unsanitised', unregulated world of social services delivery with human tragedy and social problems. They are exposed to practitioners' enduring frustrations (tantamount to burn-out) from working too long with difficult cases in under-resourced settings with very limited options to meet clients' need. This can be a harsh reality-check for young students excited about the promise of the human rights and social justice mission of social work, and longing to make a positive difference in society. When conditions of practice do not meet students' expectations, they can feel disheartened, demotivated, less cooperative, more complaintive, and can imbibe the agency climate of dissatisfaction. Educators at SAUWI are constantly challenged to bridge the widening gap between theory and practice, to keep students' motivation and morale up, strengthen their sense of agency and foster professional confidence. Regular field seminars, human skills' labs, skilled field supervisors and an open-door policy with faculty and the field coordinator play critical roles in this regard.

Secondly, because the title 'social worker' is not protected, social work positions in key social service agencies such as the Judiciary, probation services, child protection, and schools are open to multi-professionals. These are prime agencies for field placements, and agency managers and persons performing social work jobs may not be social work-trained. This places social work educators in a difficult dilemma because when their supervisors are not social work-trained, students have expressed feeling disadvantaged and seem less committed to the experience. Students and graduates alike have observed that non social work-trained supervisors do not demonstrate appreciation for what professional social work practice entails, and the gap between what they learned and what they are directed to do is widened even further. One of the ways that SAUWI has attempted to address this challenge is by providing field instructor training courses and interprofessional continuing education sessions to create communities of practice learning that support social work education. This has been very well received, but challenges persist as staff turnover in social work agencies can be high.

There are also challenges within the academic environment. SAUWI is governed by fairly strict regulations, to which social work is subject; the sequencing policy that prevents students who fail core prerequisites from advancing in the programme can be punitive and impose hardship on students who are struggling. In the case of social work, each theory and practice of social work course is offered once per academic year and is a prerequisite for the next, and a co-requisite for practicum. There have been instances where students have been withdrawn from field placement in semester two because they failed a core course in semester one and had to repeat the entire year. Adherence to rules and policies can supersede students' interests gives the impression of a harsh and insensitive institution; students can be left feeling depersonalized and aggrieved. There have been many debates in faculty meetings in response to appeals from students for special consideration, but the administration is very reluctant to relax the rules for selected cases thereby setting dangerous precedents, which, they fear, can leave the University open to litigation. Social work faculty at SAUWI are on the receiving end of students' grievances and find themselves balancing the explicit curriculum governed by strict university regulations, against the implicit curriculum informed by social work values and principles and students' expectations that social work educators will act consistent with what they teach (Bogo & Wayne, 2013; Miller, 2013) e.g. demonstrating empathy, and advocating for students' needs and considerate treatment. Special care is taken to ensure that students are regularly informed about university regulations and their rights and responsibilities within them.

Conclusion

In 2016, the Social Work Programme at The University of the West Indies St Augustine celebrated its 25th anniversary and has established itself as the leader in social work education in Trinidad and Tobago. The commemorative conference in March 2016 provided a platform for graduates and others to share knowledge and experience, and the overwhelmingly positive response to the conference was a testament to the reputation and contribution of the SAUWI social work programme. Field agencies have expressed satisfaction with the in-house preparation for field that students receive, and the clear and predictable structure of social work field practicum. SAUWI students have also been praised for their sound theoretical knowledge base. Despite the many challenges outlined above, at present, agencies, both in the public and NGO sectors, welcome the expertise that is offered to the field by the SAUWI programme. The current State initiatives to expand and increase access to social services and welfare hold definite potential as a timely investment in the well-being of the citizenry. Social work education plays a vital role in meeting the demands of practice and social development in Trinidad and Tobago and the wider Caribbean. Faculty and administration are not blind to these perennial challenges and efforts have been made to make representation to senior management, taking steps to avert them where possible by, for example, empowering student with information, and trying different strategies to address them. It is hoped that by outlining the challenges for social work educators at SAUWI, educators in other regions might gain a deeper understanding of some of their own challenges and come up with innovative ways to address them. Additionally, there is a lot to be gained by shared experience as it opens up opportunities for shared problem solving which SAUWI would welcome.

References

Bogo, M., & Wayne, J. (2013). The implicit curriculum in social work education: The culture of human interchange. *Journal of Teaching in Social Work, 33*(1), 2–14.

CSWE. (2015). 2015 *Educational policy and accreditation standards for baccalaureate and master's social work programs.* https://www.cswe.org/getattachment/ Accreditation/Accreditation-Process/2015-EPAS/2015EPAS_Web_FINAL.pdf. aspx. Accessed October 17, 2019.

de Castro, M. (2012). Preface by the UNDP. In *Trinidad and Tobago Human Development Atlas 2012,* vi. Port of Spain: Central Statistical Office (CSO). http://www.planning.gov.tt/sites/default/files/content/mediacentre/documents/ Human_Development_Atlas.pdf. Accessed March 14, 2014.

Elpers, K., & FitzGerald, E. A. (2013). Issues and challenges in gatekeeping: A framework for implementation. *Social Work Education, 32*(3), 286–300.

Finch, J., & Taylor, I. (2013). Failure to fail? Practice educators' emotional experiences of assessing failing social work students. *Social Work Education, 32*(2), 244–258.

Holmström, C. (2014). Suitability for professional practice: Assessing and developing moral character in social work education. *Social Work Education, 33*(4), 451–468.

Jones, David N., & Truell, R. (2012). The global agenda for social work and social development: A place to link together and be effective in a globalized world. *International Social Work, 55*(4), 454–472.

Maxwell, J., Williams, L., Ring, K., & Cambridge, I. (2003). Caribbean social work education. *Caribbean Journal of Social Work, 2,* 11–35.

Miller, S. E. (2013). Professional socialization: A bridge between the explicit and implicit curricula. *Journal of Social Work Education, 49*(3), 368–386.

Mohr, K. A. J., & Mohr, E. S. (2017). Understanding generation Z students to promote a contemporary learning environment. *Journal on Empowering Teaching Excellence, 1*(1), Article 9. Retrieved from https://digitalcommons.usu.edu/jete/vol1/iss1/9.

Moss, B. R., Dunkerly, M., Price, B., Sullivan, W., Reynolds, M., & Yates, B. (2007). Skills laboratories and the new social work degree: One small step towards best practice? Service users' and carers' perspectives. *Social Work Education: the International Journal, 26*(7), 708–722.

SDGs, UN. (2015). United Nations sustainable development goals. *UN.Org.*

Sowbel, L. R. (2012). Gatekeeping: why shouldn't we be ambivalent? *Journal of Social Work Education, 48*(1), 27–44.

Trinidad and Tobago Human Development Atlas 2012. (2012). Port of Spain: Central Statistical Office (CSO). Retrieved from http://www.planning.gov.tt/sites/default/files/content/mediacentre/documents/Human_Development_Atlas.pdf.

UWI. (2017). The UWI Triple A Strategy 2017–2022: Revitalizing Caribbean development. Retrieved from https://sta.uwi.edu/fss/heu/sites/default/files/heu/The%20UWI%20Triple%20A%20Strategic%20Plan%202017%20-%202022%20Full%20Plan%20.pdf.

PART VI

Social Work Education for Next Generation: Hope Over Fear

INTRODUCTION

In this part of the volume, authors from various part of the world address contemporary challenges for social work education across the borders. In many parts of the world, social work education, practice, and service had the impact of neoliberal ideology and policy. Further in some societies the impact of neoliberal ideology leads to marketization, managerialism, and consumerism (Dominelli, 1999, 2010; Fenton, 2014; Ferguson, 2009, 2012, 2013; Ferguson, Lavalette, & Whitmore, 2005; Garrett, 2010; Gray & Webb, 2013; Harris, 2014; Jones, 2001; Lorenz, 2005; Reisch & Andrews, 2002; Wallace & Pease, 2011). Further influence of neoliberalism, privatization, and globalization has resulted in sharp cuts in wages and pensions, social service delivery and welfare provisions in many countries across the globe. The effects of globalization are more adversely experienced by the developing and underdeveloped countries especially in the Global South. In order to deal with rapidly growing social problems across the globe, social work education needs to transfer the focus on training social work graduates with focus on social entrepreneurship approach. This idea is further discussed by *Kalyani K. Mehta* while discussing the recent growth and advancement of social work education in Singapore. Chapter argues that social workers in Singapore tend to shy away from social enterprise and social entrepreneurship approach and questions the general assumption that persists among the school of social work that the graduates would be employed in salaried jobs. By doing so, the author offers a fresh perspective to draw upon international figures that have ventured into social enterprise and offer that route as another productive option to students. Examples from developing countries such as India could inspire the local social workers.

In many parts of the world challenge for the social work in the future perhaps to develop a cordial relation with the 'state' and work in collaboration with 'state' for the development of service users. In many parts of the world, social work academia is maintaining a distance from the government or the 'state'. Perhaps in some cases the revolutionary role of social work or the activism aspect of the profession is keeping the profession away from the government machinery. In some countries, social workers are seen as troublemakers or the professionals who disturb the normal functioning of the 'government' through alerting the common people about their rights and entitlements. In the new millennium, changes have taken place in many countries social work delivery and educational programmes through international association and professional networks interventions, still coordination and co-working with government is not achieved in many parts of the world. Even in some countries social work education and profession is initiated and supported by the state, the government is just utilizing social work for social control and harmonization of the society rather than finding ethical and professional solution for the social problems. However, working along with the government and the governmental administration in policy formulation and policy implementation is a crucial area where social work academia needs to venture its experiments. Many scholars have already advocated for the importance political engagement of the social work education (Ferguson, 2017; Lorenz, 2017: 319). Further, *Janet T. Y. Leung* in this volume provides us a fresh understanding of social work development in Hong Kong. Social work education and its recent development in the Hong Kong are quite unique and interesting because of tremendous changes in the political and social arena in Hong Kong. Further, the lack of long-term welfare planning, increase in public accountability, change of operation mode, governance of non-government organizations, and development of social work have undergone various changes. As argued by many scholars, a more politically engaged social work profession may also lead to more focused understanding of the root cause of social problems such as poverty, unemployment, and inequality and social change (Ferguson, 2009; Ferguson & Woodward, 2009; Ferguson et al., 2005; Gray & Webb, 2013; Lavalette, 2011; Lavalette & Ferguson, 2007; Reisch, 2011; Reisch & Andrews, 2002).

Through the experience of editing this volume and reading the contributions from 42 countries in different parts of the world, we could note down some of the grand challenges for social work education that needs an immediate and systematic approach in the coming decades. Grand challenges for social work today may be bridging the widening gap between the Global South and Global North social work academia and bringing a harmonious learning relationship Gaining the public's confidence, building professional status and bringing legitimate changes in the lives of the people in the service context. This will help the social work profession across the globe to gain public recognition and thereby to get good working condition and better pay in many countries where social work is still not a well-paid job. In order to enhance the status of social work profession and educational standard, in many countries social work needs to establish minimum standard for educational programmes and practice standards in line with other human service professions. *Melike Tekindal and Seda Attepe Ozden* discuss the development of social work education in Turkey and express their concern about the uncontrolled increases of social work departments, the lack of skilled labour, the lack of standard training programmes, and the impact of globalization on the Turkish Social Work education system. The chapter calls for an inevitable renovation in the education system for training upcoming social service workforce that can effectively respond to the social issues of the local context. Capturing the public's attention, interest, and imagination to work together to address and solve pressing challenges will be the most demanded change in the social work service delivery and educational programmes in the coming decades. Further, social work needs to collaborate with individuals, community-based organizations, and professionals from all fields and disciplines to find doable solutions for the social issues that are slowing down the growth of developing and developed countries.

Futures are shaped by histories (Ferguson, 2016; Lorenz, 2016). A range of chapters in this volume discusses the historical growth of social work education in the respective country and then analyse the transformation that social work education and practice experienced since its inception. *Olga Borodkina* on Russian experience of social work development notes that social work education and social work practice have been developing under strong international influence, both from European countries and the United States. The institutionalization of social work in Russia began in 1991 after the collapse of the USSR and the constitution of the Russian Federation. The chapter proposes a strong international collaboration in the delivery of social work educational programme and training next-generation social workers who will then be able to address the social issues more effectively. An account of changes brought in by neoliberalism through transferring of market, business principles and management tools from the profit to the public sector, and changing welfare sector offered in the chapter provides the understanding on dramatical changes in social work system in Russia. This chapter serves as a starting point to understand the neoliberalism and its impact on changing social welfare delivery in Russia and then to an international context as neoliberalism, globalization, and privatisation of market have drastically changed the public service delivery in every parts of the world.

S. Shamila adopts a qualitative approach with in-depth interviews conducted to social work educators in Sri Lanka and demands for glocalization of social work education and practice in Sri Lanka. Social work as profession practised by many nonprofessional social workers which are leading to confusions and disrespect for the profession. Given the fact that the general public in Sri Lanka still perceives social work as a voluntary work that does not require professional education and training. Jonathan Parker proposes the importance of (re)developing and (re)imagining social work education in the international context. While offering a comparative analysis of social work education and its development in Malaysia and United Kingdom, the author explores potential futures for social work education in United Kingdom and Malaysia given the fact social work in both societies are made up of complex and somewhat contested definitions and practices. *Annamaria Campanini* provides an account of research-related developments in social work in Italy with reference to essential initiatives undertaken by the SOCISS (Italian Society for Social Work) in promoting and standardization of social work education.

In sum, social work schools across the globe should work together to tackle some of our toughest social problems. Bringing a common understanding, developing a working network where respect for our similarities and differences shapes the debates and discussions may be a workable solution for many countries in the Global South. Further nonbiased acceptance of untapped potentials of social work academics as well as practice fraternity in the Global South, especially in the underdeveloped countries is the key for the social work development in forthcoming decades. Peoples notion about ' west is best' should change and respect and acceptance of third world countries capacity and learning and replication from these third world may bring new era of growth and advancement for social work not only in developing world but also in the industrialized countries in the West.

References

Dominelli, L. (1999). Neo-liberalism, social exclusion and welfare clients in a global economy. *International Journal of Social Welfare, 8*(1), 14–22.

Dominelli, L. (2010). *Social work in a globalizing world.* Cambridge: Polity Press.

Fenton, J. (2014). Can social work education meet the neoliberal challenge head on? *Critical and Radical Social Work, 2*(3), 321–335.

Ferguson, I. (2009). Another social work is possible! Reclaiming the radical tradition. In V. Leskošek (Ed.), *Theories and methods of social work: Exploring different perspectives* (pp. 81–98). Ljubljana: University of Ljubljana.

Ferguson, I. (2012). From modernization to big society: Continuity and change in social work in the United Kingdom. *Cuadernos de Trabajo Social, 25*(1), 19–31. ISSN: 0214-0314.

Ferguson, I. (2013). Social workers as agents of change. In M. Gray & S. Webb (Eds.), *The new politics of social work* (pp. 195–208). Basingstoke: Palgrave Macmillan.

Ferguson, I. (2017). Hope over fear: Social work education towards 2025. *European Journal of Social Work, 20*(3), 322–332. https://doi.org/10.1080/13691457.2016. 1189402.

Ferguson, I., Lavalette, M., & Whitmore, E. (Eds). (2005). *Globalisation, global justice and social work.* New York, NY: Routledge.

Ferguson, I., & Woodward, R. (2009). *Radical social work in practice: Making a difference.* Bristol: Policy Press.

Garrett, P. M. (2010). Examining the 'conservative revolution': Neo-liberalism and social work education. *Social Work Education: The International Journal, 29*(4), 340–355.

Gray, M., & Webb, A. (Eds). (2013). *The new politics of social work*. Basingstoke: Palgrave Macmillan.

Harris, J. (2014). (Against) neoliberal social work. *Critical and Radical Social Work, 2*(1), 7–22.

Jones, C. (2001). Voices from the front-line: State social workers and new labor. *British Journal of Social Work, 31*(4), 547–562.

Lavalette, M. (2011). *Radical social work today: Social work at the crossroads*. Bristol: Policy Press.

Lavalette, M., & Ferguson, I. (Eds). (2007). *International social work and the radical tradition*. Birmingham: Venture Press.

Lorenz, W. (2005). Social work and a new social order—Challenging neo-liberalism's erosion of solidarity. *Social Work & Society, 3*(1), 93–101. ISSN 1613-8953. Retrieved from http://www.socwork.net/Lorenz2005.pdf.

Lorenz, W. (2017). European policy developments and their impact on social work. *European Journal of Social Work, 20*(1), 17–28. https://doi.org/10.1080/13691 457.2016.1185707.

Reisch, M. (2011). *Being a radical social worker in reactionary times, keynote address to the 25th anniversary conference of the Social Welfare Action Alliance, Washington, DC*. Retrieved from http://www.socialwelfareactionalliance.org/reisch_key-note_110610.pdf.

Reisch, M., & Andrews, J. (2002). *The road not taken: A history of radical social work in the United States*. London: Brunner-Routledge.

Wallace, J., & Pease, B. (2011). Neoliberalism and Australian social work: Accommodation or resistance? *Journal of Social Work, 11*(2), 132–142.

CHAPTER 36

Reinventing the Singapore Landscape of Social Work Education

Kalyani K. Mehta

INTRODUCTION

The history of Singapore as a former British colony in the nineteenth century significantly shaped the development of social work training and education. In the mid-nineteenth century, Singapore and Malaya were considered as one British territory; hence, the first University established by the British government in 1947 was named University of Malaya. The Social Welfare Department's Survey in 1947 made the strong recommendation that social work training be started at the University of Malaya, under the Economics Department (Tan & Mehta, 2002, p. 9). The first intake of students was admitted for the 2-year Diploma course in 1952.

In 1968, the 3-year degree programme in Social Work was established. It has produced numerous cohorts of graduates who have pioneered the social work profession, and through their advocacy and persistence today social workers in Singapore have been accorded due recognition from all sectors. Perhaps the most widely known among all the pioneers is late Mr S. R. Nathan, former President of Singapore, who, through his unstinting efforts and leadership, guided the nation to recognise the unmet needs of the disadvantaged in the society and garnered the support of all sectors to contribute towards their progress.

K. K. Mehta (✉)
S R Nathan School of Human Development, Singapore University of Social Sciences, Singapore 599494, Singapore
e-mail: kalyani@suss.edu.sg

© The Author(s) 2021
S. S. M. et al. (eds.), *The Palgrave Handbook of Global Social Work Education*, https://doi.org/10.1007/978-3-030-39966-5_36

THE SINGAPORE CONTEXT

Singapore, or 'the little red dot', as it is often referred to, gained its independence in 1965. Many of the social problems and issues that faced the nation in the twentieth century such as poverty and lack of sanitation, insufficient schools and hospitals, inadequate housing and tertiary institutions have been met to a great extent. Nonetheless, new social issues have emerged and social forces such as globalisation, inflow of labour migration, rapidly ageing society and growing income inequality are proving to be tough challenges for the government and society as a whole. We have come a long way from the post-colonial era described so vividly by Wee (2011), but the evolution of social problems in society inevitably demands a response from the social welfare sector. As the world order gets more complex and borders between countries get more porous, new challenges and adversities emerge.

Today, Singapore has about 1 million non-citizens who contribute economically and professionally towards its prosperity and stability in the region. The total population is approximately 6 million, and 12% consists of older people 65 years and above. It is projected that by 2030, the same segment will reach 25% of the total population. While the size of the older population will only be close to 1 million in 2030, in terms of the percentage Singapore would be classified as an 'aged society'. The social, economic, and health care implications of such a demographic shift in the population within a short period of three decades are staggering. To moderate the negative impact on the labour force of an ageing population, the government allowed the inflow of labour from the neighbouring developing countries. Today, as a result of rising sentiment by the local population who feel that employment opportunities are restricted for them due to the 'foreigners' in their midst, the government has cut down the quota of immigrants especially in certain sectors.

The recent President's address in the second session of the 13th Parliament (*Straits Times,* 8 May 2018a, p. A23) by Madam Halimah Yacob outlined the following five main areas of challenges for Singapore:

1. Challenges in securing a place in the world for Singapore
2. Building a well-connected world-class city for Singaporeans
3. Building a vibrant economy with more opportunities for workers
4. Forging a cohesive, caring, and inclusive society
5. Nurturing an identity we are proud of, with all Singaporeans

In the address, she asked the upcoming fourth generation of leaders to focus on the strengths of the nation, i.e. its multicultural diversity, sound political system, and unity as a nation.

The international arena is fraught with divisiveness along ethnic, religious, geopolitical, and economic lines. In the context of this volatile global scene, a small city-state, namely Singapore has proven over the last 52 years that it could survive. Not only was it successful in riding out economic recessions, but also in building a decent basket of reserves for a rainy day, and maintaining its respect among powerful nations such as USA and China.

The chapter will set out the concerns of the social work community and elucidate the main policy nodes that demand attention. The author has been active in the social work profession in Singapore for the past decade, and the chapter is based on her interactions with the community leaders, social service sector providers, undergraduate and graduate students as well as her observations as a volunteer in various government and non-government organisations.

LET'S LOOK AT THE CONTEMPORARY CHALLENGES

There are social and economic challenges that are common in most societies. To mention a few, poverty, homelessness, violence especially family violence, unemployment, delinquent youth, marginalisation of the less able (mental and physical), ageism, and so on. Singapore has its fair share of all of these. Being an Asian society, the 'collective' philosophy underlying the main cultural groups, i.e. Chinese, Malays, Indians as well as others such as Japanese, Koreans, etc. underpins the perceptions and the solutions that the residents adopt towards their problems. Informal sources of support are the first line of recourse before Singaporeans approach the formal agencies for help. The institution of 'family' is still strong and recent surveys have revealed that even the young generations find value in family relationships (Ministry of Social and Family Development, 2015).

Why did the President Madam Halimah Yacob emphasise the need for a cohesive, caring, and inclusive society? If families are close-knitted is it not logical to assume that the society would also be caring and cohesive, based on the rationale that families form the pillars of society?

It is at this juncture that the complications arise, and the inter-woven nature of social issues explains the current situation. Due to the ageing of the population, as well as the fact that many adult children are either staying apart or living overseas, there is an increasing dependence on 'foreign domestic workers' (FDW) for caregiving. There is also an increase in seniors living alone. The increase over the last five years has been from 31, 200 in 2012 to 47,400 in 2016 and the number is expected to double by 2030, based on the number of single adults in the age range 30–45 years in Singapore (https://www.moh.gov.sg/content/moh_web/home/pressRoom/Parliamentary_QA/2018/elderly-deaths.html).

Singapore being an urban environment, there is a growing distance developing between neighbours and community dwellers. To reduce this distance and develop community bonding, five Community Development Councils were set up in the 1990s. However, with the increasing complexity of the social fabric due to relatively high numbers of foreigners, the sense of trust that used to prevail in the 'kampongs' or villages of the past is more or less eroded. It is natural for people to hesitate from trusting strangers, especially if there is geographical mobility occurring simultaneously. Singaporeans are also moving overseas for better economic prospects or better quality of life. Globalisation brings with it many psychological and community effects, which are unavoidable. To address this, scholars have offered the concept of 'community resilience' (Tan, 2017, p. 69). Social scientists have discussed individual resilience for many centuries, but in the face of man-made and natural disasters community resilience is vital. In 2018, an interesting innovative design of integrated care and community was developed in Singapore called 'Kampong Admiralty'. It has eco-friendly features such as a roof garden, medical care and social day care facilities, child care centres, and housing for seniors. As it is an experiment in intergenerational living, multi-sector collaboration and multicultural diversity, the results will determine if it will be reproduced in other parts of Singapore.

Singapore is known for its long working hours (*Straits Times*, 13 June 2017). Being a financial hub and node, bankers, investment analysts, and traders work into the wee hours. Apart from the long working hours, the traffic jams and the five-day work week policy have also led to employees reaching home late and losing out on having dinner with the family members. There are many who sigh and say that they wish they had a better work-life balance. Technologies, such as smart phones, have also made it difficult to separate personal time from work responsibilities. If we put together all these factors, we can understand why there is a trend for more adults remaining single (unmarried), rising divorces and low fertility rates. The last point is a major factor explaining the increase in aged population in the society, as lower fertility rates imply a lower percentage of young versus the old in society.

The emphasis on tackling the widening inequalities in Singapore society was made by President Halimah Yacob. This is indeed a challenge that Singapore, as a meritocratic and capitalist state, has been facing for the last several years. It has been compounded by the policy of 'open' economy and willingness to allow foreigners to buy properties (albeit within some restrictions). Economists have debated on the implications of a lack of minimum wage guideline in Singapore, and the lack of universal pension. There are many social safety nets such as Public (or Social) Assistance, the Community Health Assist Scheme, Silver Support Scheme (especially for older persons who have low incomes); however, there could be lack of awareness of the schemes, or helplessness which prevents the person from seeking help (Low & Ngiam, 1998). Culturally, there is also a stigma attached to being dependent on the government for 'charity' and 'loss of face' (i.e. loss of self-respect) by Asians.

Singapore has risen from a Third World nation to a First World nation in a short span of time, and this progress has been achieved not without cost. The people have made plenty of sacrifices, directly or indirectly linked with high inflation, adjusting to a fast pace of modernisation and stiff economic competitiveness regionally and internationally. Alongside this transition, the society has witnessed a rapid increase in its ageing population profile, and issues such as depression, family breakdown, intergenerational social distance, and lack of societal cohesion have arisen.

To sum up, the government has tried its best to reduce inequalities through economic transfers to the lower income bands, e.g. workfare scheme for low income employees, but the gap still remains and it is a concern for social workers (Ng, Shen, & Ho, 2009, p. 110).

THE SOCIAL WORK EDUCATION LANDSCAPE

From 1952 to 1982, National University of Singapore (NUS) was the only tertiary institution training social workers in Singapore. From 2003 Monash University, which is established in Australia, offered a Bachelor degree programme in Singapore. It offered an alternative pathway for Singapore residents who could not be enrolled in National University of Singapore. It terminated its services in Singapore after about 8 years. In 2007, a Bachelor in Social Work was launched at the Singapore Institute of Management (SIM) University. In 2017, SIM University became an autonomous University (or public university) under the Ministry of Education. It was renamed Singapore University of Social Sciences (SUSS). These are the two main tertiary institutions offering social work education in Singapore. Alongside them, there are also other institutions of higher learning which offer diplomas in social/community services, e.g. Nanyang Polytechnic, Social Service Institute. Graduates from the Nanyang Polytechnic are known as Social Work Associates (SWA).

The Singapore Association of Social Workers (SASW), which has existed for more than five decades, works alongside with the Singapore Workers Accreditation Board (SWAB) which was set up by the Ministry of Social and Family Development in the premises of SASW. SWAB lays down the criteria for recognition of an accredited social worker. In Singapore, a graduate with a Bachelor of Social Work degree (or B.S.W.) is able to work as a social worker. In order to be fully accredited as a social worker, he/she has to accumulate 1000 practicum hours. A Social Work diploma holder can work as a social worker but he/she is encouraged to work towards a degree. A Social Work Associate may assist a social worker with functions such as intake assessment, but he/she cannot fulfil all the functions of a social worker. SWA are an important group as they help social workers to focus on the higher level functions. Social workers train the SWA and over time encourage them to gain a diploma or degree. Currently, only NUS offers PhD in Social Work through the research pathway.

CONCERNS AND CHALLENGES FACING THE SOCIAL WORK COMMUNITY

About ten years ago, one of the major issues that faced social workers was the low salary. In the range of salaries nationally, social workers were almost at the lowest rung. It was also found that almost half of the NUS graduating cohort from the Social Work Department exited from the social work sector and joined other sectors of the labour force. Since 2008, there has been serious efforts made by the Ministry of Social and Family Development to raise the salaries of qualified social workers, and today, a social work graduate earns a salary on par with an engineering graduate. While it is universally recognised that social workers do not join the sector for economic prospects, they should not be short-changed for choosing such a noble profession. During that time period from 2007 to 2009, the author was a Nominated Member of Parliament and recalls advocating on behalf of the social workers for better work national recognition! There are more than 1800 social workers today and through the Primary Conversion Programme (executed by the government), which offers sponsorships for adults to take up social work, a larger number of adults are being attracted to study and train as social workers.

In 2002, a few academics including myself and colleagues from the National University of Singapore compiled an edited book 'Extending Frontiers: Social Issues and Social Work in Singapore' in commemoration of the 50th Anniversary of the Department of Social Work. It was a volume that attempted to provide a comprehensive perspective of the social issues facing social workers as well the new frontiers as envisioned by the authors. A range of topics were addressed such as community development initiatives and policies, low income families, social policies focussing on the family, critique of policies relating to children, gender and cultural dynamics of retirement, drug abuse, inclusion of people with disability and the new frontiers. Some of these new frontiers were online teaching (or distant learning), internationalising the social work curriculum, development of leadership in the social work community, and multiculturalism. Since Singapore is a cosmopolitan city-state, harmony between different ethnic groups is essential for its cohesiveness and unity.

> Social work actively advocates policies that promote both social as well as economic development, social participation, and equality, which form the basis for collaborative and peaceful relations. (Tan & Mehta, 2002, p. 227)

The above quote is relevant even after 16 years, as the issues of inequality, cohesiveness, and inclusiveness are being raised by the president and are becoming the themes of public consultation and dialogue in 2018. On May 16, 2018, Minister Ong Ye Kung stated in Parliament that 'Fighting inequality is a national priority' (*Straits Times*, 16 May 2018b). The concept of 'redistributive justice' is one of the core social principles that is taught in social work curriculums worldwide. This is one of the chief foundations of a just and stable society because social equality gives everyone a fair chance to progress and improve their lives. For inequality to be reduced, one of the main strategies is to increase social mobility especially from the bottom upwards. Education offers one of the channels for this to take place, and social policies need to be crafted to encourage this to happen. To this end, social workers and counsellors intervene where necessary to assist children and youth from low income families to progress up the educational ladder.

Challenges such as elder abuse were tackled by the setting of a Golden Lifegroup comprising representatives from a comprehensive range of sectors, such as the Golden Lifegroups on Elder Abuse, and Suicide Prevention among older people. The SAGE Counselling Centre played a very active role in advocating for these causes in the 1990s (SAGE Counselling Centre, 2006).

Some local publications have emerged highlighting specific issues such as family violence and its impact on children (Nair, Pang, & Fong, 2001), juvenile delinquency (Veloo, 2004a, 2004b, 2004c, 2004d), and single parents (Mathews, 2013). Under the banner of one organisation, social workers are known to collaborate to publish on community-based problems they dealt with regularly (Tham & Balotta, 2002). Once in a while, a publication emerged on skills training such as support group facilitation skills (Thomas, 1999).

Reflections on the Social Work Landscape

Upon reflection of the past 66 years of social work education landscape in Singapore, I think that the thrust of social work education emphasises training social work graduates to manage social services and conduct clinical social work with individuals and families. A close look at the curriculums of the two tertiary institutions, i.e. Social Work Department of the National University of Singapore and the counterpart in Singapore University of Social Sciences, shows that at least 80% of the undergraduate courses focus on developing the skills at the micro level. However, there are a couple of courses dedicated to group work and community work skills development. As with other social work curricula in developed countries, there are compulsory Practicum and Policy modules. At postgraduate level, the students are given a wider variety of specialisation choices such as family therapy, health, and community social work.

From general observation, most of our social work graduates are employed at mid-level positions in government ministries, hospitals, prisons, community and family service centres, and social service offices. Most of the community services are run by voluntary welfare organisations, which are partially subsidised by the government. In tandem with the focus of the social work training programmes, majority of the social workers work at the micro level with individuals and families. However, these may be patients in hospitals, prisoners, parents, youth, children, or delinquent offenders. They may be in the primary, secondary, or tertiary settings. Social policy is an arena where very few social workers are involved. In the social policy sector, only a handful of social work trained professionals are found. Similarly, in the community development sector, few social work graduates leave their carbon imprint. One caveat is that many social workers are working with families, while simultaneously developing and delivering community-based schemes. In the social service offices, social workers are expected to do home visits and get to know their community well. Grassroots leaders and volunteers support the work of social workers in reaching out to the residents in the geographical community, and by referring cases that are complex and need professional assistance to formal social welfare organisations.

Social Research is mainly conducted by academics even though the government has been strongly encouraging practitioners to examine the readily available data in their organisations. One example is the research on medical and social issues faced by patients in hospitals. A joint effort by medical social workers led to the book 'Tapestry of Care: voices of medical social workers' published in 2009 by the Singhealth Academy Publishing Team.

Local research by Ms Anita Ho on foreign domestic helpers as part of her Master in Gerontology thesis at Singapore University of Social Sciences is an exceptional study as it examines the dynamics of relationships within the family where one of the players is the hired caregiver. Her thesis topic was 'Are Foreign Domestic Workers Indispensable? A Multi-Cultural Singapore Study' (2015). The study was timely as it was an in-depth qualitative study which shed light on the FDWs experience and family interactions; this complemented the findings of a survey commissioned by Ministry of Social and Family Development on Informal Caregiving (Ministry of Social and Family Development, 2014).

The publication of a Singapore-based journal, i.e. Asia Pacific Journal of Social Work (later renamed Asia Pacific Journal of Social Work and Social Development), encouraged local scholars to publish articles for example, on the importance of the skills of cross-cultural counselling (Ow & Osman, 2003) and cross-cultural social work (Mehta & Vasoo, 2003).

As the reality that Singapore was 'ageing' as a society, dawned on academics and practitioners, they joined hands and published on relevant topics such as Gerontological Counselling (Mehta & Ko, 2014).

REINVENTING THE SOCIAL WORK EDUCATION LANDSCAPE

Social work education has made inroads locally and in the Southeast Asia region. The National University of Singapore faculty have been involved in joint initiatives with the Singapore International Foundation to provide training to social workers in Vietnam and Myanmar. The textbooks written by social workers in Singapore are being used for educational purposes in other countries for example, Hong Kong (Mehta & Wee, 2011). The Singapore

Association of Social Workers has chapters such as the School Chapter, the Medical Chapter, and the Singapore government is providing financial grants for mid-career adults who wish to switch to social work careers. The Skills Future scheme and the National Silver Academy are large-scale national level innovative schemes that support lifelong learning and this paves the way for a better educated and engaged populace.

From my observations, social policy is an arena where more social workers could be involved to take leadership roles. Advocacy can be more impactful if it is based on applied research and evidence. The love of doing research can be effectively transferred to students by having more research projects jointly conducted by faculty and students such as Honours level or postgraduate students. If the social work profession is to create greater impact, it is necessary for more social workers to be visible in the applied research and policy making spheres. The seeds of such training and passion have to be planted in the tertiary institutions.

As compared to other developing countries, social workers in Singapore tend to shy away from social enterprise and social entrepreneurship. In the schools of social work education, there is a general assumption that the graduates would be employed in salaried jobs. It would be a fresh perspective to draw upon international figures who have ventured into social enterprise and offer that route as a viable option to students. Examples of social enterprises from developing countries such as India could inspire the local social workers.

Innovative pedagogy could be practised in the institutes of higher learning, to instil fresh perspectives and rich learning experiences to future generations of social workers. Online teaching methods such as videos, online discussions with students from the region, sharing of practicum learning by students on the digital space, and sharing of classroom presentations with students from underdeveloped countries could expand international social work. Social work education for the Singapore students could include topics such as impact of natural and man made disasters (which are so common in the world) as it would expand their horizon beyond national boundaries. Without compromising on the human relationships and social capital beliefs, a less classroom-oriented system of teaching and learning would benefit future cohorts of social workers. More experiential learning opportunities such as service learning projects in other environments would increase the passion for social work!

There is a strong need to expose the students to the perspectives of other cultures, especially since Singapore is an 'open economy' and we have people of many cultures living in our midst. Currently, the emphasis on cross-cultural social work and cross-cultural communication competency is limited.

The Singapore Mental Health Survey 2010, led by the Institute of Mental Health, was an important landmark research study which showed that the incidence of Major Depressive Disorder was 1 in 17 adults. 5.8% of the adult population in Singapore suffered from MDD at some time in their lifetime (Chong et al., 2012, pp. 54–55). Alcohol abuse and Obsessive-Compulsive disorders were two common mental health illnesses found in the population. Another key finding was that majority of the victims of mental health problems were not seeking help. Given this scenario, social workers have a clear role to play in creating greater awareness of the importance of seeking help early to prevent escalation of the mental condition. Another clear mandate is to advocate for better work-life effectiveness balance, to reduce the negative impact of long working hours. In an urban society such as Singapore, where land is scarce and competitiveness is pervasive, the importance of a balanced lifestyle is crucial.

Social policies are putting emphasis on community networks and community care, as the ageing of the population would place heavy responsibilities of care on families. Where the family is absent, the community has to substitute family care. Indeed, recently at the Global Conference on Integrated Care 2018, held in February 2018 at Sentosa, Singapore, there was a recognition of the key contribution of active social engagement and participation on the mental and physical health of all ages. Medical care has to be accompanied by social care in any population for effective maintenance of positive health and recovery from illnesses.

The future generations of social workers will be the product of our social work education system, so it behoves the current generation of social work teachers and leaders to put in place a forward looking curriculum that looks not only at current issues but also future trends.

REFERENCES

Chong, S. A., Abdin, E., Vaingankar, J., Heng, D., Sherbourne, C., Yap, M., ... Subramaniam, M. (2012). A population-based survey of mental disorders in Singapore. *Ann Acad Med, 41,* 49–66.

Ho, A. (2015). *Are foreign domestic workers indispensable? A multi-cultural Singapore study* (Unpublished master thesis). Master of Gerontology Programme, Nathan School of Human Development, Singapore University of Social Sciences.

Low, L., & Ngiam, T. L. (1998). An underclass among the overclass. In L. Low (Ed.), *Singapore: Towards a developed status.* Centre for Advanced Studies (pp. 226–249). Singapore: Oxford University Press.

Mathews, M. (2013). *Working with low-income Indian single mothers.* Singapore: Singapore Indian Development Association.

Mehta, K., & Ko, H. (2014). *Gerontological counselling: An introductory handbook.* Singapore: Write Editions.

Mehta, K., & Vasoo, S. (2003). Cross cultural social work in the Asia Pacific Rim. *Asia Pacific Journal of Social Work, 13*(2), 1–5.

Mehta, K., & Wee, A. (Eds.). (2011). *Social work in the Singapore context* (2nd ed.). Singapore: Pearson Custom Publishing.

Ministry of Health website, Parliamentary Questions. Retrieved from https://www.moh.gov.sg/content/moh_web/home/pressRoom/Parliamentary_QA/2018/elderly-deaths.html.

Ministry of Social and Family Development. (2014). *Survey on informal caregiving.* Singapore: Ministry of Social and Family Development.

Ministry of Social and Family Development. (2015). *Ageing families in Singapore: Insight Series 02/2015.* Singapore: Ministry of Social and Family Development.

Nair, S., Pang, K. T., & Fong, S. S. (2001). Children's resilience in living in violent families. *Asia Pacific Journal of Social Work, 11,* 63–77.

Ng, I. Y. H., Shen, X., & Ho, K. W. (2009). Intergenerational earnings mobility in Singapore and the United States. *Journal of Asian Economics, 20,* 110–119.

Ow, R., & Osman, M. M. (2003). Issues and challenges of cross-cultural counselling in Singapore. *Asia Pacific Journal of Social Work, 13*(1), 81–98.

SAGE Counselling Centre. (2006). *Aspects of elder abuse.* Singapore: SAGE Counselling Centre.

Singhealth Academy. (2009). *Tapestry of care: Voices of medical social workers.* Singapore: Singapore Health Services Pte Ltd.

Straits Times. (2018a, May 8). Singapore: The next chapter, pp. A23–24.

Straits Times. (2018b, May 16). Fighting inequality a national priority says Ong Ye Kung, p. 1.

Straits Times Review Forum. (2017, June 13). MOM: Singaporeans continue to clock longest working hours in the world.

Tan, N. T. (2017). What's so social? Change, integration, and social resilience. In Singapore University of Social Sciences's (Ed.), *The heart of learning* (pp. 61–72). Singapore: Singapore University of Social Sciences.

Tan, N. T., & Mehta, K. (Eds.). (2002). *Extending frontiers: Social issues and social work in Singapore.* Singapore: Eastern Universities Press.

Tham, L. K., & Balotta, L. (Eds.). (2002). *Hedges and edges: A compendium for social workers, counsellors & family therapists.* Singapore: Care Corner.

Thomas, J. (1999). *Facilitating support groups: A guide to growth and change.* Singapore: Family Resource and Training Centre.

Veloo, K. V. (2004a). *Juvenile delinquency in Singapore 1961–1980: Trends, programmes and outcome of probation and discharges.* Vol. 1: Rehabilitation of Offenders in Singapore Series. Singapore: Department of Social Work and Psychology, National University of Singapore.

Veloo, K. V. (2004b). *Probation for offenders in Singapore: History, growth and changes 1970–1993.* Vol. 2: Rehabilitation of Offenders in Singapore Series. Singapore: Department of Social Work and Psychology, National University of Singapore.

Veloo, K. V. (2004c). *Prison welfare service in Singapore: Social service to prisoners and their families.* Vol. 3: Rehabilitation of Offenders in Singapore Series. Singapore: Department of Social Work and Psychology, National University of Singapore.

Veloo, K. V. (2004d). *The uphill task of rehabilitating drug addicts 1973–1980.* Vol. 4: Rehabilitation of Offenders in Singapore Series. Singapore: Department of Social Work and Psychology, National University of Singapore.

Wee, A. (2011). Where we are coming from: Social and welfare interventions when Singapore was a British Colony. In K. Mehta & A. Wee (Eds.), *Social work in the Singapore context* (2nd ed.). Singapore: Pearson Custom Pub.

CHAPTER 37

Social Work Development Trends in Hong Kong: Implications for Social Work Education

Janet T. Y. Leung

INTRODUCTION

Welfare development in Hong Kong can be characterised as having both "a non-interventionist approach and residual nature" (Tsui, Lee, & Chui, 2013, p. 68). Since Hong Kong is a capitalist metropolitan city, the success of its economy relies on the laissez faire policies of the government. The fear of becoming a welfare state creating dependence and hampering economic success (Barry, 1999) led to the social welfare service being limited to serving residents in need. Chow (2008, p. 25) commented that social welfare was "short-term, conservative, passive, and discouraging." Despite such conservative welfare emphases social welfare services have been expanded rapidly in recent decades. In the 2016-2017 financial year the department's total annual expenditure was $61.5 billion of which $41.7 billion (67.8%) was for financial assistance payments (Information Services Department, 2018). Expenditure on social welfare was the third highest of all policy areas in Hong Kong. About 90% of social welfare services are provided by non-governmental organisations (NGOs) sharing annual subventions (grants) of $14.5 billion (23.6%) (Information Services Department, 2018). Social welfare services are mainly provided by professionally trained social workers in the province. Since 1997 anyone who practises social work has to be registered with the Social Workers Registration Board as a registered social worker. As of September 2018 the number of registered social workers in Hong Kong was 23,116.

J. T. Y. Leung (✉)
Department of Applied Social Sciences, The Hong Kong Polytechnic University, Hong Kong, Hong Kong
e-mail: janet.leung@polyu.edu.hk

© The Author(s) 2021
S. S. M. et al. (eds.), *The Palgrave Handbook of Global Social Work Education*, https://doi.org/10.1007/978-3-030-39966-5_37

595

Social work has undergone tremendous changes in Hong Kong during the past two decades. Analysing social work development in Hong Kong is crucial for four reasons. First, Hong Kong is a metropolitan city influenced by both Western and Chinese cultures (social work development trends may share global trends and some unique Chinese features). Second, social work is a profession that is highly responsive to a changing society (understanding social work development trends in Hong Kong in recent past decades would help to speculate about social work development in the future). Third, social work development trends in Hong Kong are important to social work education. Last but not the least, although social work in mainland China has a short history, it is now flourishing. Hong Kong has been a special administrative province of China since 1997 and acts as pioneer of social work practice in mainland China as a result of its rich practical experience. Thus, exploring social work development trends in Hong Kong can be expected to have a great impact on social work practice in China. It is also expected that social work expertise built up in Hong Kong will contribute to the design and implementation of social work practice in China.

SOCIAL WORK DEVELOPMENT TRENDS IN THE WEST

Reid (2002) highlighted six trends that social work practice has followed in the Western world during the past quarter of a century: the mushrooming of practice diversity in social work approaches; changing views of the worker–client relationship; the development of multilevel intervention models from the individual level to the societal level; the emergence of family therapy approaches; increasing focus on client actions, their meaning, and information gathered in the helping process; and growing emphasis of evidence-based practice. Reid (2002) and He and Chen (2005) further portrayed 10 trends that Western social work has followed: the growing use of multimethods in social work practice; the plurality of epistemology; the ongoing debate between the individual and the societal level of intervention; user (i.e., client) involvement that has altered the worker–client relationship; the emergence of evidence-based practice; change in the intervention focus from the deficit model to the strengths model; the increasing emphasis on research; the common use of short-term treatment and an eclectic intervention model; the expanding trend of new managerialism in social service organisation; and innovations in social work education. Social work development trends in the West have provided useful lenses through which to view social work development trends in Hong Kong during the past two decades.

Changes in the Social Welfare Climate of Hong Kong

The transfer of sovereignty in 1997 not only brought about tremendous changes in the political climate of Hong Kong, but also major transformations in government structure and machinery. Before 1997 the government was rather stable in its structure with civil servants tasked with service planning and policy implementation. Social welfare planning was directed by formulating and reviewing white papers and five-year social welfare development plans initiated by the Social Welfare Department in conjunction with the Hong Kong Council of Social Service (HKCSS) under the auspices of the Social Welfare Advisory Committee (SWAC) (Social Welfare Department, 1998). NGOs, social work professional bodies, and scholars from the academies were able to participate actively in social work welfare planning by participating in the HKCSS and the SWAC. However, after the transfer of sovereignty from the British in 1997 the Secretary for Labour and Welfare responsible for policy formulation and welfare planning was appointed by the Chief Executive of Hong Kong Special Administrative Region (HKSAR). The Chief Executive is elected by an election committee every five years according to the Basic Law. Such a political arrangement means the Labour and Welfare Bureau (and the government as a whole) might have less commitment to long-term social welfare planning in Hong Kong. The last five-year plan was conducted in 1998, a year after the transfer of sovereignty.

Inevitably, such a system leads to social demands that call for government responses and failure to address such demands may result in social protests or political disputes. The government met demands by establishing special funds. It would inject an amount to establish a fund and invite NGOs to submit project proposals. Some funds were a political gesture to respond to social agendas during Chief Executive elections, while others were responses to crises, traumas, and/or social demands that occurred. For instance, when the government faced great pressure as a result of criticisms of the enlarged Gini ratio and the adverse conditions of the working poor in 2011, the Community Care Fund was set up to provide tangible assistance to people who fell outside the social security safety net.

Another factor calling for changes in social work development was public accountability in the welfare sector. Since most welfare expenditure came from government revenues, charitable funds, or fees from service providers, NGOs needed to be accountable to different stakeholders such as the government, charitable funds, the public, service providers, and collaborators on the use of public spending.

Change in the subvention mode made by the Government in 2001 directly influenced the operation of NGOs and the climate under which they worked. In response to the previous inefficient and ineffective mode of subvention in meeting the demands of social needs, the government introduced the Lump Sum Grant, a mode of subvention that allowed more flexibility for NGOs in service operations. NGOs could delink from the government civil servant system and determine their own staffing ratios and remuneration systems as long as they fulfilled the requirements of standards set out in the Service Performance Monitoring System (SPMS) and service output and outcomes listed in the Funding and Service Agreement (FSA). Although NGOs had more autonomy to determine their staffing structure and payment systems in the new operation, adverse effects came to the surface such as reduced staff salaries, insecure jobs, large staff turnover, increased workload of social workers, and reduced staff morale (Lai & Chan, 2009). The turnover rate of social workers in 2016–2017 was 14.2%, 60.6% of whom had worked for 3 years or less (Joint Committee on Social Work Manpower Requirements, 2017). Operation of the Lump Sum Grant system altered the relationship between the government and NGOs. What was a partnership in the past became a funder–service operator relationship (Social Welfare Department, 2000). Together with competitive tendering for service contracts in some services, NGOs have undergone dramatic changes in their infrastructure and operations to adapt to the new environment.

Reform in the way NGOs were governed also impacted social work development. In the past most NGOs registered as charities or societies under the Societies Ordinance (Cap. 151) or under Hong Kong legislature as trusts or statutory bodies. However, more NGOs have recently registered as companies incorporated under the Companies Ordinance (Cap. 32), which clearly states the limited liability of the board of directors. Although in the past NGOs put their focus on conventional welfare deliverables for the needy, at present more NGOs operate their businesses and enterprises to generate income. Promoting the "user pays" principle, an increasing number of self-finance services appeared. Such changes facilitated the emergence of corporate management and entrepreneurship in NGOs.

Social Work Development Trends in Hong Kong

Such changes in the working climate allows the identification of seven social work development trends: (1) the emergence of project-based service deliverables under an integrative service model; (2) growing diversity of practice approaches; (3) development of multilevel intervention models; (4) multidisciplinary collaboration; (5) changes in client–worker relationships; (6) emergence of managerialism in social welfare settings; and (7) growing attention to evidence-based practice.

Emergence of Project-Based Service Deliverables
Under an Integrative Service Model

In response to the integrative approach of community-based service delivery outlined in the white paper *Social Welfare into the 1990s and Beyond* (Working Party on Social Welfare Policies and Services, 1991), most services in communities were reengineered into integrated services such as integrated family service centres, district elderly community centres, and integrated children and youth service centres. Integrated services serve as the main platform for service delivery at the district level, coordinate related services in the district, and handle ad hoc issues and problems that may arise. On the one hand, the integrated approach brings resources together and allows a variety of services to be delivered within a single unit. On the other hand, it needs to respond to diverse demands in the community in which service planning and provision becomes more reactive than proactive. Moreover, the bulky structure of integrated services introduces bureaucracy to staff communication and service coordination. The roles of supervisors have also changed. Rather than focusing on supervising social workers to deliver a professional service, they spend most of the time liaising with community leaders, collaborative partners, and other stakeholders in the community.

Integrated services can only be developed if there are sufficient funds to make projects deliverable in the community. Projects generated in integrated services are often small in scale and characterized by certain features. First, most projects are time limited lasting 2–3 years. Second, projects only employ a limited number of junior social workers due to restricted resources. Third, most projects are target specific such as elderly people with dementia and children with specific educational needs. Fourth, although different intervention strategies are expected, the outcomes should be concrete and measurable. Fifth, due to the short duration of projects, short-term treatment is expected. Last but not least, services have to confront the issue of sustainability.

Such projects bring a number of positive outcomes to integrated services such as innovation in service design and delivery (particularly, in services catering to specific clienteles) and encouraging practice diversity in integrated services. The projects allow intervention strategies to be more diverse and flexible to cater to the needs of service users. They also open up more channels for specific target users to gain access to the integrative service model and receive the service through it. Concrete intervention strategies and observable outcomes have the potential to make projects the flagship service of NGOs and in so doing attract more resources.

A project-based intervention approach creates challenges of its own to the way in which social work is developed. A critical issue is that service delivery is driven by funds rather than needs. To secure more resources, NGOs modify services according to the funding available. The issue is magnified if funding bodies intrude into the intervention approach and service operation and interfere with the professional autonomy of social workers. Another challenge is that projects require social workers to have the relevant experience and special skills. However, the funds may not be adequate to employ experienced social workers. Last but not the least, unstable financial support raises questions about continuity and sustainability.

Growing Diversity of Practice Approaches

Knowledge about the development of social science theories, psychotherapy, and community interventions has burgeoned and has given rise to a plurality of social work theories in recent decades. The theoretical foundations of such theories range from individual perspectives such as developmental theories, behavioural theories, and cognitive theories to getting a better understanding of the interactions between people and the environment such as the systemic approach and ecological perspectives. At the same time, social theories also extend from functional theories, structural models, and critical theories to the postmodern paradigm of post-structuralism, feminist perspectives, and hermeneutics. The diversity of theoretical foundations allows different therapeutic approaches and community interventions to thrive. Casework practice long influenced by individual psychotherapies has been challenged by the evolution of family therapy. Rather than perceiving individual problems from their own pathology, social workers attempt to look into disruptive patterns and interactions within the family (Minuchin, 1985). This is especially important to Chinese families where collective familism and interdependence are stressed (Chan & Lee, 1995; Chao & Tseng, 2002; Lau, 1982). Moreover, the postmodern paradigm seriously impacts social casework. Freedman & Combs (1996, p. 14) suggested that "[postmodernism] is not simply a further evolution of systems theory, it is a discontinuous paradigm, a different language." In narrative therapy in which constructivist epistemology is stressed, social workers listen to the stories of clients and the ways they perceive their problems. By reconstructing the stories of clients, social workers help clients discover new meanings about themselves (White & Epston, 1990). The diversity of intervention approaches not only applies to casework, but also to community development. Apart from conventional approaches (such as community organising, social planning, and social actions), innovative community intervention approaches also emerge. New community development models such as asset building, bonding and bridging of social capital, and community economic development not only empower individuals and families when it comes to their wellbeing, but also regenerate community resources and enhance community cohesion.

In addition to the rapid buildup of social science knowledge fostering the development of different intervention approaches, there are changing social environments triggering the diversity of social work practice. For instance, cyber-counselling has developed in recent decades as a result of the rapid development of information technology; financial counselling is provided to debtors to wean them off excessive use of credit cards and loans; and social enterprises have been developed to find ways of engaging deprived communities in job markets. To keep up with a changing world, social work practice is rapidly evolving in response to the diverse needs of people.

Practice diversity in social work approaches has three important implications. First, more voices are calling for social work practice to be strengths based. Rather than focussing on the client's pathologies and deficits social workers should explore the potential, assets, and strengths of clients (Saleebey, 2013). Second, the dialogue between social workers using different strategies and approaches needs to increase and be heard more widely. Fostering a genuine understanding of what their work involves and bringing about practice synergy among social workers in the workplace, the community, and the profession are urgently required. Third, pluralistic social work practice requires social workers to be more knowledgeable about different social work paradigms, the characteristics of specific service targets, and different therapeutic approaches and interventions. At the same time they need to keep abreast of the use of different intervention models.

Development of Multilevel Intervention Models

The integrative service model approach used to deliver certain social service projects gave rise to the development of multilevel intervention models. Integrative approaches have been made in social work settings to allow the synergy of practice across microlevels and macrolevels (Bartlett, 1970; Reid, 2002). For instance, one integrated family service centre (IFSC) employed "child-centered, family-focused and community-based" principles to operate a three-tiered model (resource unit, support unit, and counselling unit) in which a continuum of preventive, support, empowerment, advocacy, and remedial services were provided to families in need in the community (The Consultant Team, The University of Hong Kong, 2001).

Synthesising micropractice and macropractice allows different social work methods to be implemented in different social work settings. The traditional division of social work practice into casework, group work, and community work has been replaced by a matrix of multimethods in meeting the needs of service users in the community where the boundaries of casework, group work, and community work become blurred. In response to the criticism that social work exists as a "fragmented" profession rather than a coherent one (Meyer, 1983), social workers adopt a more holistic and eclectic approach in their intervention (Tsui et al., 2013).

Although the climate is favourable for the synthesis of different social work methods, there are also threats that are fundamental to social work practice such as the changing nature of casework. Rather than providing a counselling service to service users ever more caseworkers are acting as case managers who assess the eligibility of service users to other funds and services. They are obliged to monitor the progress of clients in so-called enhancement programmes: for instance, social workers involved in the Integrated Employment Assistance Programme for Self-reliance (IEAPS) are tasked with enhancing those receiving comprehensive social security assistance (CSSA) to overcome work barriers and enhance their employability to find paid employment. Service recipients who are non-compliant with the requirements run the risk of losing their CSSA payment. Thus, social workers are used as an apparatus of social control rather than as facilitators of the wellbeing of clients. Furthermore, due to the depoliticisation of social work in recent decades (Lam & Blyth, 2014) fewer social workers are prepared to take up the advocacy role, but assert the principle of social justice instead. Moreover, reliance on government funds determines social work intervention strategies in dealing with social problems at the microlevel rather than striving for social change that will empower the community to act against inequality and injustice.

Multidisciplinary Collaboration

The complexity of social problems makes multidisciplinary collaboration with other professions and service partners inevitable. As a consequence social workers work with other professionals in a number of settings. However, professional services in Hong Kong are discrete and lack much coordination. For instance, a child suffering from attention deficit hyperactivity disorder (ADHD) may need to receive medication from a psychiatrist at the local hospital, attend consultations with an educational psychologist of the Education Bureau, join a training group conducted by an occupational therapist from an NGO, and receive family counselling from a school social worker of another NGO. Social workers need to understand the roles played by, assessments made by, and treatment given by other professionals, collaborate with them, and coordinate services to suit the needs of clients and their families when necessary.

Moreover, social workers need to collaborate with other professionals who have little understanding of social welfare such as surveyors (residents facing urban renewal) and bankers (debtors receiving advice on financial management). Social workers need not only to be sensitive to the roles played by other professionals in the provision of social welfare, but also ready to negotiate with them on the needs of service users during such collaborative processes.

The government has recently promoted tripartite collaboration among the public sector, welfare sector, and business sector with a view to developing the social capital of deprived communities. The rise of social enterprises has been a catalyst for multidisciplinary collaboration. Although the values, principles, and approaches to work of social workers and businessmen may be different as evidenced by the business sector participating in welfare projects through donations and partnerships, social workers need to keep in mind the autonomy of professionals and the benefits received by clients in collaborative projects.

Changes in Client–Worker Relationships

The deficiency model conventionally used to assess the pathology of clients has thrown social workers and clients together in an unequal and hierarchical relationship. This is particularly problematic in Chinese communities since the Chinese perceive seeking help as losing face (Tsui et al., 2013). This contributes to the strong stigma attached to receiving welfare in Chinese culture (Mak & Cheung, 2008). Receiving welfare is perceived as a failure of self-reliance and of dishonouring the family name (Wong & Lou, 2010). De-emphasis of the deficiency model has reduced the authority-based relationship between social workers and clients to such an extent that it barely exists (Reid, 2002). The empowerment approach coupled with strengths-based practice encourage social workers to act as collaborators of clients in tackling their problems (Saleebey, 2013). The relationship between social workers and clients has become more mutual and less hierarchical.

User participation has recently become very popular in social service formulation and delivery. Some NGOs encourage service users to form advisory committees such that they can provide feedback that may be of use in service development. User participation in service formulation not only helps NGOs develop appropriate services for service users in the community, but also empowers participants to articulate their needs and opinions to NGOs and the government.

In contrast to there being a mutual relationship between service users and social workers, many social workers perform the role of case managers gatekeeping resources and services delivered to potential service users, and some act as a social control apparatus to assess and monitor the performance of participants in enhancement programmes, leading to the roles of social workers becoming hierarchical and coercive. The involuntary participation of clients also heightens tensions between service users and social workers.

Emergence of Managerialism in Social Welfare Settings

Requests for public accountability, changes in the Lump Sum Grant system, and the emergence of time-limited social service projects have brought about a rise in managerialism in social welfare settings. Such concepts as efficiency, cost-effectiveness, accountability, and consumer satisfaction are now the focus. Internal and external audits are performed to monitor the efficiency and cost-effectiveness of the delivery of services. The managerial orientation taken in social work development emphasises the standardisation of procedures and services thus minimising costs spent in the operation. Ritzer (2000) used the term McDonaldisation to characterise the emphasis put on efficiency, calculability, predictability, and control in different spheres of life. Dustin (2016) suggested that McDonaldisation has intruded into social welfare. In Hong Kong standardisation and McDonaldisation can be seen in the development of residential services for senior citizens and disabled persons. Under the competitive tender bidding mechanism applied to residential services, NGOs need to reduce operational costs, standardise operational procedures, and control staffing so that they can win the tender. As a consequence managerialism improves the efficiency of the service at the expense of impersonalising service delivery.

Growing Attention to Evidence-Based Practice

Evidence-based practice involves "integrating individual practice from systematic research as well as considering the values and expectations of clients" (Gambrill, 1999, p. 346). It is important since it allows social workers to assess whether the service delivered is beneficial to the wellbeing and social functioning of service users. However, it has been commented that evidence-based social work practice has its limitations in Hong Kong (Shek, Lam, & Tsoi, 2004). It was the emergence of project funds that facilitated the development of evidence-based practice as evidenced by the outcomes of projects such as the comprehensive research carried out during Project P.A.T.H.S. (Positive Adolescent Training through Holistic Social Programmes) supported by the Jockey Club Charitable Trust Fund (Shek & Sun, 2012) and a pilot study of Child Development Fund projects commissioned by the Welfare Bureau (The Hong Kong Polytechnic University, 2012). The government also encourages evidence-based practice in social work. In particular, one of the central pillars of the Social Welfare Development Fund (in which one billion Hong Kong dollars was given by the government to NGOs to cover a 9-year period) is the implementation of evaluative research into social work practice.

However, there are barriers to evidence-based practice in Hong Kong including a lack of awareness of service effectiveness by the public, the absence of a critical culture when it comes to social work practice, the heavy workload placed on social workers regarding tasks and output requirements, and little training given to social workers regarding research.

IMPLICATIONS OF SOCIAL WORK EDUCATION

Social work education is essential to building up the competencies of social workers in meeting the challenges ahead. The four aspects of social work education discussed in this chapter are the theory–practice relationship, the dual foci of social work, the professionalism of social work, and collaborations between academics and NGOs.

The relationship between the theory and practice of social work has been criticised as "inconsistent and muddled and needed to be put on a much firmer footing" (Parton, 2000, p. 451). There have been heated debates on whether social work is a rational technical activity (Sheldon, 1978) or a practical moral activity (Jordan, 1978; Schön, 1983). In the rational technical approach knowledge and skills are emphasised; knowledge is seen as objective, consensual, cumulative, and convergent while practice is describable, testable, and replicable; social work is regarded as a social science and social workers are rational practitioners who help clients in their proper functioning; outcomes are emphasized; and evidence-based practice and proliferation of procedures are the foci (Sheldon, 1978). In the practical moral approach, however, meanings and values are the foci; practice knowledge is derived from "reflection-in-action" and thus there is uncertainty, doubt, and ambiguity; practice is more practical, intuitive, flexible, and adaptable; social work is considered an art and social workers are reflective practitioners; interactions between social workers and clients are the foci; and reflective, informal negotiations are emphasised (Schön, 1983). The dichotomy of rational technical and practical moral approaches has resulted in heated debates in social work education. Although both approaches are not mutually exclusive, they are significant in that they allow a competent social worker to deal with the dynamic changes and complex environment that prevail nowadays. Although needs assessment and intervention requires social workers to be more knowledgeable of social science theories and concepts, the uniqueness of clients, the collaborative roles they play with service users, and value conflicts may call for social workers to be more reflective. Although the emphases on evidence-based practice, accountability, and standardisation favour technocratic rationality, situation ambiguities, doubts, and the ever-changing environment allow room for practical morality. Thus, a social worker should be equipped with knowledge of social science theories, but at the same time they need reflective vigour and practice wisdom. Rather than viewing the approaches of technical rationality and practical morality as a dichotomy that leads to a stalemate, it is important to look into the meaningful integration and creative synthesis of the two approaches that may arise.

Social work education has to emphasise the importance of pursuing the dual foci of social work: individual/family functioning and social change (Yan, Tsui, Chu, & Pak, 2012). Looked at from the functional perspective the mission of social work is to help clients enhance how they and their family function in daily life. The availability of different funds coupled with the depoliticisation of social work (Lam & Blyth, 2014) has put more emphasis on enhancing such functioning. However, this apparently harmonious scene masked the fact that oppressed communities were emerging. For instance, it was found that the Gini coefficient of Hong Kong in 2016 was 0.537 (Census and Statistics Department, 2017a) indicative of greater disparity between the rich and the poor. Taking the official poverty threshold as 50% of median monthly household income, there were 1.35 million people living beneath the poverty line including 19.0% of the child population of Hong Kong (Census and Statistics Department, 2017b). Many families were living in old and dilapidated buildings broken down into cubicles or in unauthorised congested flats located in factories where they faced daily threats regarding sanitation, fire, and security. According to the International Federation of Social Workers the primary mission of social work is to "promote social change and development, social cohesion, and the empowerment and liberation of people. Principles of social justice, human rights, collective responsibility and respect for diversities are central to social work" (International Federation of Social Workers, 2014, Definition of Social Work). Listening to oppressed communities, striving for social change, and pursuing social justice and human rights should be given greater emphasis in social work education.

It is important to uphold the professional standards of social work. On the one hand, the registration of social workers mandated by the Social Work Registration Ordinance was a major step toward the professionalisation of social work. On the other hand, the mass production of social workers through tertiary education coupled with a number of development trends regarding skills threatened the professionalism of social work. Fook, Ryan, and Hawkins (2000) highlighted eight threats to the professionalism of social work including the devaluation, disaggregation, and decontextualisation of professional knowledge and skills; the weakening of professional autonomy, control, identities, and boundaries; the representation of professional knowledge in terms of a managerial discourse rather than a professional discourse; illustrating the job of a social worker in fragmented skills programme-based terms rather than in holistic professional terms; blurring the domain boundaries between professional groupings; and increasing the competition between different professional groups for territory and dominance. In fact, growth in the number of short-term service projects brought about by diverse funds, the rise of managerialism, the competitive bidding mode of new services, and the emergence of the social control function in social work have subjected social work professionalism to serious risk. In addition, the rapid expansion of social work education programmes in response to the mandate of the Social Work Registration Ordinance requiring social workers to be registered raised alarms about the professional development of social work. As of 2018 there are six universities and five community colleges providing five Master's programmes, eight Bachelor programmes, three higher diploma programmes, and two associate degree programmes (recognised by the Social Workers Registration Board). The mass production of social workers may lead to such issues as the selection of appropriate candidates, quality of the curricula, fieldwork arrangement and coordination, qualifications of social work teachers, and the employment of graduate social work students. Despite the challenges these issues bring to the professional development of social work, similar to the situation in Western countries the professional training of social work has changed to vocational training under the new managerial regime of educational institutes (Rogowski, 2010). Thus, social work educators should be sensitive to changing environments and uphold professional standards in social work training.

Collaborations between universities and NGOs are important to the development of social work. Collaborative research into understanding the needs of deprived communities and enhancing evidence-based practice should be encouraged. Practical research and clinical consultation should be conducted to improve the quality of services and enhance the capacities and skills of frontline social workers. Furthermore, advanced training is necessary to get students to come up with new practice theories and models and help social workers consolidate what they have learned from their experiences in the field. Finally, scholars should collaborate with NGOs in bringing about long-term planning vital to social welfare and advocating changes in welfare policy when they deem it necessary.

CONCLUSIONS

Tremendous changes in political and social arenas have greatly influenced social work development trends in Hong Kong. Social work development has undergone a number of changes in facing a lack of long-term welfare planning, increased public accountability, and change in the operation mode and governance of NGOs. Some trends chime with those in Western society such as the growing diversity of practice approaches, the development of a multilevel intervention model, the emergence of managerialism in social welfare settings, and growing attention to evidence-based practice. Some are unique to social welfare development in Hong Kong such as the emergence of project-based service deliverables under an integrative service model, the tense client–worker relationship as a result of the social control function, and multidisciplinary collaborations with different sectors. Social work development trends have had insightful impacts on social work education (particularly, on theory–practice relationships), the dual foci of the social work mission, the professionalism of social work, and collaborations between academics and NGOs. Although social work in Hong Kong has undergone tremendous changes in dealing with the challenges and opportunities that have arisen, the mission of "helping people in need and striving to address social problems" (Social Workers Registration Board, 2018, Code of Practice) stands firm.

REFERENCES

Barry, N. (1999). Neoclassicism, the New Right and British social welfare. In R. M. Page & R. L. Silburn (Eds.), *British social welfare in the twentieth century* (pp. 55–79). New York: St. Martin's Press.

Bartlett, H. (1970). *The common base of social work practice*. New York: National Association of Social Workers.

Census and Statistics Department. (2017a). *2016 Population by-census—Main results*. Retrieved October 1, 2018, from https://www.bycensus2016.gov.hk/data/16bc-main-results.pdf.

Census and Statistics Department. (2017b). *Hong Kong poverty situation report 2016*. Retrieved October 1, 2018, from https://www.statistics.gov.hk/pub/B9XX0005E2016AN16E0100.pdf.

Chan, H., & Lee, R. P. L. (1995). Hong Kong families: At the crossroads of modernism and traditionalism. *Journal of Comparative Family Studies, 26*(1), 83–99.

Chao, R. K., & Tseng, V. (2002). Parenting in Asians'. In M. H. Bornstein (Ed.), *Handbook of parenting, vol. 4: Social conditions and applied parenting* (pp. 59–93). Mahwah, NJ: Lawrence Erlbaum Associates Publishers.

Chow, N. W. S. (2008). Social work in Hong Kong—Western practice in a Chinese context. *China Journal of Social Work, 1*(1), 23–35.

Dustin, D. (2016). *The McDonaldization of social work*. London: Routledge.

Fook, J., Ryan, M., & Hawkins, L. (2000). *Professional expertise: Practice, theory and education for working in uncertainty.* London: Whiting and Birch Ltd.

Freedman, J., & Combs, G. (1996). *Narrative therapy: The social construction of preferred realities.* New York: Norton.

Gambrill, E. (1999). Evidence-based practice: An alternative to authority-based practice. *Families in Society, 80,* 341–350.

He, X., & Chen, B. (2005). Ten development trends emerge in contemporary Western social work. *Journal of Nanjing Normal University (Social Science Edition),* 6 [in Chinese]. https://doi.org/10.3969/j.issn.1001-4608-b.2005.06.003.

Information Services Department, HKSAR. (2018). *Hong Kong 2017.* Retrieved October 1, 2018, from https://www.yearbook.gov.hk/2017/en/.

International Federation of Social Workers. (2014). *Global definition of social work.* Retrieved October 1, 2018, from https://www.ifsw.org/what-is-social-work/global-definition-of-social-work/.

Joint Committee on Social Work Manpower Requirements. (2017). *Social work manpower requirements system annual report 2017.* Retrieved October 1, 2018, from https://www.swd.gov.hk/storage/asset/section/296/en/SWMRS_Annual_Report_2017_Final(Clear).pdf.

Jordon, B. (1978). A comment on "Theory and practice of social work". *British Journal of Social Work, 8*(1), 23–25.

Lai, W. H. F., & Chan, K. T. T. (2009). Social work in Hong Kong: From professionalization to "reprofessionalization". *China Journal of Social Work, 2*(2), 95–108.

Lam, C. W., & Blyth, E. (2014). Re-engagement and negotiation in a changing political and economic context: Social work in Hong Kong. *British Journal of Social Work, 44,* 44–62.

Lau, S. K. (1982). *Society and politics in Hong Kong.* Hong Kong: Chinese University Press.

Mak, W. W. S., & Cheung, R. Y. M. (2008). Affiliate stigma among caregivers of people with intellectual disability or mental illness. *Journal of Applied Research in Intellectual Disabilities, 21,* 532–545.

Meyer, C. H. (1983). *Clinical social work in the eco-systems perspective.* New York: Columbia University Press.

Minuchin, P. (1985). Families and individual development: Provocations from the field of family therapy. *Child Development, 56,* 289–302.

Parton, N. (2000). Some thoughts on the relationship between theory and practice in and for social work. *British Journal of Social Work, 30*(4), 449–463.

Reid, W. J. (2002). Knowledge for direct social work practice: An analysis of trends. *Social Service Review, 76*(1), 6–33.

Ritzer, G. (2000). *The McDonaldization of society: New century edition.* Thousand Oaks, CA: Pine Forge Press.

Rogowski, S. (2010). *Social work: The rise and fall of a profession?.* Portland, OR: Policy Press.

Saleebey, D. (2013). *The strengths perspective in social work practice* (6th ed.). Upper Saddle River, NJ: Pearson Education.

Schön, D. A. (1983). *The reflective practitioner: How professionals think in action*. New York: Basic Books Inc.

Shek, D. T. L., Lam, M. C., & Tsoi, K. W. (2004). Evidence-based practice in Hong Kong. In B. Thyer & M. A. F. Kazi (Eds.), *International perspectives on evidence-based practice in social work* (pp. 167–181). London: Venture Press.

Shek, D. T. L., & Sun, R. C. F. (2012). Epilogue: The project P.A.T.H.S. in Hong Kong: Lessons learned and implications for positive youth development programs. *The Scientific World Journal*. Online publication. https://doi. org/10.1100/2012/687536.

Sheldon, M. E. P. (1978). Theory and practice of social work: A re-examination of a tenuous relationship. *British Journal of Social Work, 8*(1), 1–22.

Social Welfare Department. (1998). *The five year plan for social welfare development in Hong Kong—Review 1998*. Retrieved October 1, 2018, from http://www.swd. gov.hk/doc/pubctn_ch/e5yrplan.pdf.

Social Welfare Department. (2000). *Social welfare services lump sum grant manual* (2nd ed.). Hong Kong: Government Printer.

Social Work Registration Board. (2018). *Code of practice*. Retrieved October 1, 2018, from https://www.swrb.org.hk/en/Content.asp?Uid=14.

The Consultant Team, Department of Social Work and Social Administration, The University of Hong Kong. (2001). *Meeting the challenge: Strengthening families, report on the review of family services in Hong Kong*. Hong Kong: Social Welfare Department.

The Hong Kong Polytechnic University, Department of Applied Social Sciences. (2012). *Report of consultancy study on Child development fund Pioneer projects*. Retrieved October 1, 2018, from http://legco.gov.hk/yr14-15/english/panels/ ws/papers/ws20150112cb2-746-1-e.pdf.

Tsui, V., Lee, A. S., & Chui, E. W. (2013). Social welfare in Hong Kong. In S. Furuto (Ed.), *Social welfare in East Asia and the Pacific* (pp. 67–86). New York: Columbia University Press.

White, M., & Epston, D. (1990). *Narrative means to therapeutic ends*. New York: Norton.

Wong, C. K., & Lou, V. W. Q. (2010). "I wish to be self-reliant": Aspiration for self-reliance, need and life satisfaction, and exit dilemma of welfare recipients in Hong Kong. *Social Indicators Research, 95*(3), 519–534.

Yan, M. C., Tsui, M. S., Chu, C. K., & Pak, C. M. (2012). A profession with dual foci: Is social work losing the balance? *China Journal of Social Work, 5*(2), 163–172.

CHAPTER 38

Situation and Future of Social Work Education in Turkey

Melike Tekindal and *Seda Attepe Özden*

INTRODUCTION

Turkey is a developing country with a population of 80,810,525 (TUIK, 2018). Considering the social problems likely to be encountered with a population of this size the need for social workers in the country goes without saying. However, when wars fought in the immigration route from Asia to Europe and refugees immigrating to Turkey are taken into account, the need for social workers is clearly felt. Social workers play many roles when working with immigrants such as strength-givers, facilitators, planners, advocates, activators, accelerators, educators, society-informers, and researchers (Miley, O'Melia, & DuBois, 2001). Today there are 6150 social workers in Turkey. The limited number of social workers and their qualifications are matters of discussion in Turkey. Against this background the present chapter aims to provide information about social work education in Turkey, analyse current problems in social work education in Turkey, and look at the requirements necessary for social work education to be effective in a globalising world.

M. Tekindal (✉)
Department of Social Work, Faculty of Health Sciences, Izmir Katip Çelebi University, Izmir, Turkey
e-mail: melike.tunc@ikc.edu.tr

S. Attepe Özden
Department of Social Work, Faculty of Health Sciences, Baskent University, Ankara, Turkey

© The Author(s) 2021
S. S. M. et al. (eds.), *The Palgrave Handbook of Global Social Work Education*, https://doi.org/10.1007/978-3-030-39966-5_38

Social Work Education

Social work education is an education and training process carried out in 4-year undergraduate degree programmes that aim to turn students into professionals qualified for occupational interventions in client systems (individual, family, group, society).

Students are expected to gain the knowledge, skill, and value base of social work to become qualified professionals. Social work education comprises five main elements: the aim and scope of social work education (international, national, regional, local), the student dimension (student-centred approach), the instructor (facilitator) dimension (qualifications of the instructor), student–linguist interaction and whether it is a horizontal or vertical relationship, and the characteristics of the learning environment and whether they are facilitating or complicating.

"Social work is a practice-based profession and an academic discipline that promotes social change and development, social cohesion, and the empowerment and liberation of people. Principles of social justice, human rights, collective responsibility and respect for diversities are central to social work. Underpinned by theories of social work, social sciences, humanities and indigenous knowledge, social work engages people and structures to address life challenges and enhance wellbeing. The above definition may be amplified at national and/or regional levels" (IFSW, 2014). As indicated in the definition of social work, social workers aiming to enhance the wellbeing of clients have to take a number of decisions. When taking these decisions they make use of their professional knowledge. Experts can only obtain this professional knowledge by acquiring the necessary social work knowledge, skills, and value base while they are receiving social work education at university. Thus, the responsibility for delivering this knowledge lies with their instructors. In this regard Gökçearslan Çifci (2009) pointed out that education carried out in newly established universities in Turkey was not adequate enough to provide students with the requisite professional knowledge, skills, and techniques. Thus, it is considered essential that social work education is provided by instructors holding a degree in this field.

History of Social Work Education in Turkey

International organisations played an important role in Turkey in the reorganisation of social work and the initiation of social work education. For example, the United Nations (formed in the aftermath of World War II) assumed guiding and leading roles in underdeveloped and developing countries like Turkey.

Studies carried out by a UN advisor visiting Turkey in 1957 were significant to the way social work was organised in the country. They led to the enactment of a law establishing the Institute (Academy) of Social Work considered a significant turning point in terms of social work education in Turkey

(Karataş & Erkan, 2005). According to article 1 of this law "establishing an academy of social work in order to provide secondary and higher education for raising social workers and assistants" laid the legal basis of social work education. The UN advisor also played a role in the creation of the first curriculum at the academy (Koşar & Tufan, 1999, p. 3). The academy was accepted to the membership of the International Association of Schools of Social Work (IASSW) and renamed the Academy of Social Work at Hacettepe University in 1998. Koşar and Tufan (1999) pointed out that the Academy of Social Work would produce professionals armed with a discipline that could provide solutions to problems emerging under the fast-changing social and economic conditions of Turkey. Nevertheless, social work was developed in Turkey under the guidance of internal dynamics rather than external ones despite social work education in Turkey being the result of a project aimed at mainstreaming education in line with decisions taken by the United Nations in the aftermath of the war and despite students being sent to Western European countries and to the United States to receive education in this field. The first School of Social Work opened in 1961 in Ankara (Baycın, 1961, p. 11).

The history of social work education in Turkey clarifies the extent of structuring/organisation carried out in the second half of the nineteenth century as can be seen chronologically in Table 38.1.

As shown in the table, social work education was carried out under a single roof from 1967 to 2002. Such education started to be disseminated to other universities in 2002. In 2017 the number of universities in Turkey reached 193. Of these 35 public, 24 private, and 6 Northern Cyprus universities carried out social work education. At one time there were 89 social work departments in total. However, today only 65 of them are active.

Undergraduate Education

There were clearly insufficient resources to provide undergraduate, postgraduate, and doctorate education even though the Academy of Social Work had served as a higher education institution since its establishment. This was the reason alumni had difficulty in finding postgraduate opportunities. Thus, the small number of alumni either turned to other fields or chose to continue their education in other countries. Postgraduate education in social work was provided for the first time by the Social Work Department of Hacettepe University. When the Academy of Social Work merged with the Social Work Department of Hacettepe University in 1983 and began functioning as a separate school, this marked the start of postgraduate and doctorate education being carried out under a single roof (Karataş & Erkan, 2005).

Today there are 14 graduate social work programmes and 6 doctoral social work programmes running in the country (Çay, 2017). Despite these figures there are not this number of social work academics at universities casting a shadow over the quality of graduate education. According to Alptekin, Topuz, and Zengin (2017) more than a third of the teaching staff did not

Table 38.1   Development of social work education in Turkey (in chronological order)

Year	
1959	Institute of Social Work established under the Ministry of Health and Social Assistance
1961	According to law No. 7355 Academy of Social Work established under the Institute of Social Work
1963	Academy of Social Work established under the General Directorate of Social Work of the Ministry of Health and Social Assistance
1967	School of Social Work of Hacettepe University opened and 2 years later converted into Social Work Department under the Faculty of Social and Administrative Sciences at the university
1982	School of Social Work of Hacettepe University closed. According to law No. 2547 Academy of Social Work affiliated to Hacettepe University and the name and status of the academy changed to School of Social Work affiliated to the rectorship of Hacettepe University
2002	Social Work Department established under the Faculty of Health Sciences of Başkent University as a result of which the number of social work departments across the country increased to two
2006	This year represented a significant turning point for social work education because social work departments were established at a number of universities such as Selçuk University, Adnan Menderes University, Sakarya University, and Süleyman Demirel University. Apart from Süleyman Demirel University they all admitted students to start their social work education the same year. Up to this point social work education had been provided by individual educational institutions
	In 2006 School of Social Work affiliated to Hacettepe University was restructured as Social Work Department under the Faculty of Economics and Administrative Sciences of the same university
2007	Social Work Department of Ankara University established and admitted students
2009	Social Work Department established in Düzce University, Maltepe University, and Yalova University and students admitted to these universities the same year
2010	Social Work Department established in Kocaeli University and Cyprus International University and students admitted to these universities the same year
2011	Social Work Department established under the Faculty of Open Education (*Açıköğretim Fakültesi*) of Ankara University. Thus, social work education was provided distantly for the first time and uptake by students was extensive
2015	Social Work Department under the Faculty of Open Education of Anadolu University began to admit students
2016–2017	49 different social work departments (29 established in public universities and the remaining 20 in private universities) admitted students
	However, two social work departments at previously mentioned universities could not continue to provide education in this field due to the closure of certain universities in 2016

Source Çay (2017), available at https://idealsosyalhizmet.com/turkiyede-sosyal-hizmet-egitiminin-kisa-tarihi/, 9 April 2018 have any degree in social work at the undergraduate, graduate, or doctoral level. Although most faculty members did not receive undergraduate and/or graduate education in social work, they were graduates of sociology, family and consumer sciences, and theology.

Current Challenges Facing Social Workers in Turkey

Social work practice is currently attracting a lot of attention in Turkey as a result of the many problems that current global issues such as immigration, violence, and conflict have introduced to the country. Social workers fulfil a number of tasks in an effort to meet the requirements of current conditions and do so under such conditions as highly increased caseloads, long working hours, limited income, and lack of resources. In one study social workers stated that working conditions negatively affect service delivery (Gokcek Karaca, Karaca, & Dziegielewski, 2018).

Social workers in Turkey constantly face such problems as society does not know what they do, the need for the profession is not expressed by the people, and social workers consequently have occupational identity problems. Bolgün & Şahin (2018) found that nearly half the people had not heard of social work before, that social workers felt obligated to explain their jobs over and over again, and that in some agencies they just make social assessments— not social work interventions. Moreover, since there is a lack of social workers other professions have to step in and act as social workers.

Another problem social workers face is high occupational burnout as evidenced by a number of studies conducted by social workers in Turkey (Basım & Şeşen, 2005; İçağasıoğlu Çoban & Özbesler, 2016; Işıkhan, 1999). Although social workers in Turkey face much the same challenges as many other colleagues around the world as a result of globalisation and the problems accompanying it, the country "hosts the world's largest community of Syrians displaced by the ongoing conflict in their country" (İçduygu, 2015) and social workers are now assisting Syrian refugees to meet their needs with limited resources and services. It is another problem area for social workers in Turkey.

Requirements in Social Work Education in a Globalising World and the Situation of Turkey

There is no common definition of globalisation that everybody agrees on. The concept is defined differently according to the economic, social, political, and cultural perspective. Kıvılcım (2013) defined globalisation as an increase in communication, interaction, and bilateral connection between societies and countries in different parts of the world because of the increasing mobility of merchandise, services, and capital during transnational bilateral economic integration and of national economies engaging in the world market. This definition brings the economic dimension of the concept to the forefront by highlighting economic mobility across the world. Pointing to the increasing interaction between people living in different parts of the world and the emerging bilateral dependence among them the definition also indicates that the concept has a profound influence on the daily lives of individuals.

Globalisation is not only a system that enables organisations across the world to engage in commercial cooperation at the macrolevel, but also a local phenomenon that influences decisions taken at the political, family, education, employment, and health policy level (Alphonse, George, & Moffatt, 2008). Thus, it directly influences the implementation of social work. Reduction of the role played by the government in such areas as health, education, employment, and education and the increasing role played by the private sector in these areas because of globalisation makes it necessary for social work to take on new roles in all these areas. Shrinking of the public sector or its replacement by the private sector leads to inequalities and the marginalisation of vulnerable groups requiring social workers to tackle the negative effects of globalisation and look critically at points where local factors interact with one another (Alphonse et al., 2008). The chapter now looks at how social work practices and social work education are affected by globalisation starting with the effects globalisation has on higher education.

Dominelli (2005) stated that globalisation as a social phenomenon can be said to cause capitalist social relations to dominate in every area of life. This is true of universities. Fundamental changes seen in universities as a result of globalisation are the widespread use of technology, the dissemination of distance education, the globalisation of classrooms, the dissemination of specialisation education, and the increasing role played by the private sector in university education.

Meyer, Bushney, and Ukpere (2011) highlighted the fact that universities are global higher education institutions that react to a changing world order regardless of the country in which they are located rather than institutions that operate in certain cities or towns in isolation from society. Such structuring connects universities to the global world and obliges them to keep up with whatever competition the global world brings with it (Wright, 2007).

Globalisation brings about other changes in universities some of which are on a large scale such as the increase in cooperation between universities and accordingly the mobility of students (Robertson & Kedzierski, 2016) and connections between universities with the business world that have led to universities being considered institutions preparing personnel for the business world (Olssen & Peters, 2005). Institutions providing social work education are doubtless affected by such changes (as discussed in the following section).

EFFECT OF GLOBALISATION ON SOCIAL WORK EDUCATION

This section looks first at the effect globalisation has had on social work practices and then looks at the effect it has had on social work education. It was globalisation that led to neoliberal policies being implemented across

the world. The implementation of neoliberal policies emphasised individual evolution over structural evolution as the target of social work. Such a situation shifted the focus of social work from resistance to the discipline regime to adaptation to such a regime brought about by neoliberal policies (Reisch, 2013).

Dominelli (2005) believed globalisation imposed market discipline on social workers and changed their daily routine practices, working principles, and the system they used for service provision. Market discipline entailed the faster provision of services to more clients and required clients to become more participative. Since globalisation obliged many organisations and structures to operate on the basis of organisational logic, social work organisations could not avoid getting involved in this. Elements affecting the behaviour of social workers linked to globalisation were performance-based salary, the use of practice-orientated and qualification-based approaches, and new information technologies (Dominelli, 2005). It was unclear whether globalisation would lead to radical changes in social work or would preserve the status quo. The social work provision system is today stuck between non-governmental organisations and private institutions. What matters most when market discipline was imposed on social work was the provision of the service. However, there is a perception that anybody can carry out the work of social workers because the content of the service is not given importance. Such a situation brings a number of problems such as shrinkage of the number of areas covered by social work and trivialisation of the profession in the market discipline agenda as a result of changing the focus of the profession.

Another effect of globalisation on social work practice was the internationalisation of social problems such as immigration, sex trafficking of children, prostitution, kidnapping, drugs, and crime (Dominelli, 2005). Findlay & McCormack (2007) pointed out that social workers were tasked with tackling such serious matters as child abuse and pornography, the social effect of global viruses such as HIV/AIDS and SARS, the effects free trade agreements had on business life, and securing the wellbeing of international refugees and asylum seekers at the local scale.

Although globalisation had harmful effects when it came to the economy, it provided some opportunities too. Among these opportunities were the development of international cooperation, promotion of peace, and an increase in cultural understanding (Midgley, 2001). Moreover, the fact that the social worker profession now featured on the agenda as a profession ensuring human rights was another positive effect of globalisation.

Globalisation brought about many changes in social work practice. Since social work education was directly aimed at preparing practitioners for social work such changes had to be incorporated in the curriculum and encompassed by the profession in the future. The remainder of this chapter looks at changes in social work education brought about by globalisation.

The effects globalisation had on social work education came to the forefront after 2000. It was important for students in social work departments to get an education that was suitable to the needs of a fast-changing world (Gray & Fook, 2004). Sherman (2016) highlighted the importance of providing students in such departments with a curriculum that included the notion of global citizenship and increased global awareness. Therefore, subjects linked to international social work became obligatory parts of curricula.

Rotabi, Gammonley, Gamble, and Weil (2007) defined the characteristics a social work curriculum should include in their article on how globalisation should be reflected in such a curriculum: (1) the demographic, cultural, social, political, economic, environmental, and psychological reasons and advantages of globalisation; (2) ethical responsibilities; (3) intercultural competence; and (4) social justice and human rights.

Reisch (2013) believed that such topics as macroeconomy, social effects of a changing labour market, legal and regulatory frameworks for employment, and the increasing sociocultural importance of employment should also be included in the curriculum. However, students should also be taught about how the economic power of globalisation affected the daily lives of clients and their senses of self. In other words the individual dimension of such topics should be given pride of place in the curriculum and not subjugated to macrolevel topics.

The effect globalisation has on social work education is not limited to the curriculum. It also affects the way social work teachers carry out their work. Since there has been an increase in the number of students accessing higher education as a result of globalisation, social work academics now have little time to devote to research (Dominelli, 2005). They also need to be skilled in the use of new technologies such as PowerPoint and make use of them in lessons (Wright, 2007).

Another dimension of the effect globalisation has on social work education can be seen in applied lessons. Due to increasing workload social work educators have begun to limit the number of students they admit to the department (Dominelli, 2005). If they did otherwise, there would not be sufficient time to help them develop the necessary application skills. Such a situation led to limiting the content of applied lessons and students being unable to develop the applications skills they need.

As already mentioned, universities have begun to build cooperation at the international scale. The importance of schools of social work actively seeking cooperation has been highlighted (Merrill & Frost, 2011). Such cooperation is very significant in terms of understanding the effects of global issues at the local scale and of supporting increased student mobility at the global scale.

The greatest effect globalisation had on higher education was brought about by the Bologna Process. This process ensured standardisation in higher education and was launched by the European Commission with the aim of disseminating the concept of higher education across the world and increasing the employment expectations and geographical mobility of European citizens (Campanini, 2010). The Bologna Process brought about reforms in

many schools of social work in Europe. Labonté-Roset (2005, p. 286) broke down the changes taking place in schools of social work as: increased academic focus on training, generalist programmes, and international–European orientation. Accordingly, social work education began to be provided using a generalist approach in a system covering undergraduate, postgraduate, and doctorate degrees. The elimination of borders allowed international topics to be part of the agenda and included in the curriculum. In fact, the Bologna Process found a parallel in the marketisation logic of neoliberalism with its aim of ensuring standardisation of the higher education system.

Another matter worth attention when discussing social work education within the scope of globalisation is the process used to develop international standards in education. The International Association of Schools of Social Work (IASSW) and the International Federation of Social Workers (IFSW) are responsible for setting standards for inclusion in social work curricula at the global scale (Sewpaul & Jones, 2004). Such standards are very detailed in their structure and specially designed for schools of social work. They cover such factors as the importance of applied lessons in the curriculum, the qualifications educators should have, and social work principles and values. Although setting standards in education is important for social work education, it has prompted some discussion. For example, Wright (2007) argued that the standardisation of education and homogenisation of the content of the curriculum should be independent of application needs in other EU countries. Similarly, Alphonse et al. (2008) further argued that global standards should respond to local needs.

As well as determining the content and overall shape of curricula, global standards set within the scope of globalisation have brought cultural awareness and intercultural social work to the fore. In general terms intercultural social work can be defined as showing respect for the culture of clients who come from a different country while working with them (Yan & Wong, 2005). Jani, Osteen, and Shipe (2016) argued that the current education policy aimed at helping students gain application skills from people of different cultures should be extended to teaching concepts like social frameworks that form the multiple identities, subjectivities, and human behaviour of students and arise from the relationship between people and their surroundings. In other words, globalisation has brought to the fore the necessity to give pride of place to cultural frameworks and cultural sensitivity concepts in current education standards and to help students gain application skills in this area.

In short, globalisation has led to revision of the curricula used for social work education, change in the roles played by academics due to the increased student quota, the development of international standards in education, and the establishment of cooperation at the international level among schools of social work. Such effects are expected to be felt more profoundly in the coming years.

The Situation of Turkey

The higher education system in Turkey changed dramatically as a result of globalisation. The most striking change was the sharp increase in the number of universities and the number of students studying there. In 1982 there were 27 universities in Turkey. However, this number reached 175 at the end of 2013. While 50 new public and private universities were opened between 1982 and 2005, the following 7-year period (2006–2013) witnessed the establishment of 81 new public and private universities (Çetinsaya, 2014, p. 46). Running parallel to this situation the number of students also increased. There were 810,000 university students between 1982 and 1992 and 2,160,000 between 1993 and 2002. Some 4,250,000 higher education diplomas were awarded between 2003 and 2011 (Çetinsaya, 2014, p. 55). According to the latest data there are 186 universities in the country and 7,560,371 students studying there.

In addition to this dramatic change other changes took place such as internationalisation, the dissemination of distance education programmes, and the use of learning-based approaches and information technologies in education (Erdem, 2012). Social work education was seriously affected by the whole process.

After 2010 there was a notable increase in the number of schools providing social work education. According to the latest data there are 49 universities providing undergraduate education in social work. However, academics not in receipt of social work education themselves give lessons in departments of social work in many universities due to a shortage of qualified social work teachers.

Distance education programmes came about as a result of globalisation. Such programmes started in Turkey in the 1980s, rapidly increased in the 1990s, and ended up being taught in 47% of all universities in the country (Alptekin, 2016). Distance education programmes began to be provided in social work in Turkey in 2011 and student uptake of these programmes was fairly extensive (Alptekin, 2016). For example, annual uptakes of 2500 students were allocated to social work education within the scope of the distance education system. Social work education provided within the scope of this system falls short of the conditions set by international standards, the content of applied lessons is very limited in such programmes, and there is no supervision system. Although there are countries where the distance education method is successfully carried out in social work education across the world, there is a lot of room for improvement in Turkey in this regard.

Reforms brought about by the Bologna Process regarding social work education led to a series of workshops being held since 2011 in the country with the aim of defining the fundamental qualifications necessary to teach social work (Alptekin, 2016). In 2015 the Association of Schools of Social Work was established in an attempt to achieve international standards in social work in Turkey and to enhance national standards.

Conclusion and Discussion

Despite its deep-rooted history, the dissemination of social work education has not been managed well in Turkey. Attempts are still being made to continue with insufficiencies in the abovementioned five fundamental elements by getting scientists from different disciplines to deliver lessons. Although social work education structured without a proper plan continues to be provided, it contravenes the philosophy of the profession and the way it is taught especially through distance learning and open education methods. Although the initial provision of social work education in a single university and department from 1961 to 2002 was not sufficient to meet the needs of Turkey, increasing growth seen over recent years has led to engaging unqualified people in this field with the end result that such education is being provided by people who lack a degree in social work.

A social work education policy should be based on the fundamental principles and focus of social work. Moreover, international accreditation of a core education programme should be ensured even though such initiatives have gained momentum over recent years. It is also important that universities currently providing social work education subject themselves to such an accreditation process and thereby sustain the provision of such education—otherwise their closure should be considered.

There are other risks facing social work education in Turkey such as a shortage of qualified academics, limits to the education provided regarding content, deviations of applied lessons from the aim, and the problems alumni face in gaining employment due to increase in the number of graduates in this field.

References

Alptekin, K. (2016). *Başlangıçtan bugüne ve yarına Türkiye'de sosyal hizmet eğitimi* [*Social work education in Turkey from beginning to today and tomorrow*]. Ankara: Atlas Yayınevi.

Alptekin, K., Topuz, S., & Zengin, O. (2017). Türkiye'de sosyal hizmet eğitiminde neler oluyor? [What is happening in social work education in Turkey?]. *Toplum ve Sosyal Hizmet, 28*(2), 50–69.

Alphonse, M., George, P., & Moffatt, K. (2008). Redefining social work standards in the context of globalization lessons from India. *International Social Work, 51*(2), 145–158.

Basım, H. N., & Şeşen, H. (2005). Çalışma yaşamında tükenmişlik: Sosyal hizmet uzmanları ile hemşireler üzerine karşılaştırmalı bir çalışma [Burnout in work life: A comparative study on social workers and nurses]. *Toplum Ve Sosyal Hizmet, 16*(2), 57–70.

Baycın, F. (1961). Türkiye'de korunmaya muhtaç çocuklar ve koruyucu aile denemesi. *Sosyal Hizmet, 1*(2), 11–14.

Bolgün, C., & Şahin, F. (2018). Public perception and attitudes about social work in Turkey. *International Social Work*, 1–14. https://doi.org/10.1177/0020872818774105.

Campanini, A. (2010). The challenges of social work education in Europe. *Psychologica, 2*(52), 687–700.

Çay, M. (2017). *Sosyal hizmette yüksek lisans ve doktora* [*Graduate and doctorate in social work*]. https://idealsosyalhizmet.com/sosyal-hizmette-yuksek-lisans-ve-doktora/. Accessed May 28, 2018.

Çetinsaya, G. (2014). *Büyüme, kalite, uluslararasılaşma: Türkiye yükseköğretimi için bir yol haritası.* Anadolu Üniversitesi Basımevi. Accessed May 1, 2018. http://www.yok.gov.tr/documents/10279/2922270/B%C3%BCy%C3%BCme+Kalite+Uluslararas%C4%B1la%C5%9Fma+cetinsaya-19x27-12%2C5forma.pdf/e5681887-1560-4fc3-9bab-0402e7f3ec2b.

Dominelli, L. (2005). Social work education under globalisation: Trends and developments in The United Kingdom. *Portularia, 5*(1), 59–75.

Erdem, A. R. (2012). Küreselleşme: Türk Yükseköğretimine Etkisi [Globalization: Effects on Turkish higher education]. *Yükseköğretim Dergisi, 2*(2), 109–117.

Findlay, M., & McCormack, J. (2007). Globalization and social work education and practice: Exploring Australian practitioners' views. *The Journal of Sociology & Social Welfare, 34*(2), 123–142, Article 9.

Gokcek Karaca, N., Karaca, E., & Dziegielewski, S. F. (2018). Social workers in Turkey: Identifying and addressing professional problems and concerns. *Journal of Social Service Research.* https://doi.org/10.1080/01488376.2018.1477702.

Gökçearslan Çifci, E. (2009). Social work profession and social work education in Turkey. *Procedia Social and Behavioral Sciences, 1,* 2063–2065.

Gray, M., & Fook, J. (2004). The quest for universal social work: Some issues and implications. *Social Work Education, 23*(5), 625–644.

IFSW. (2014). https://www.ifsw.org/what-is-social-work/global-definition-of-social-work/. Accessed November 8, 2018.

Işıkhan, V. (1999). *Yönetim stresi* [*The stress of management*]. Ankara: Sosyal Sigortalar Kurumu Yayını.

İçağasıoğlu Çoban, A., & Özbesler, C. (2016). Hastanelerde çalışan sosyal hizmet uzmanlarında tükenmişlik ve iş doyumu [Burn-out and job satisfaction of social workers in hospitals]. *Başkent Üniversitesi Sağlık Bilimleri Dergisi (BUSBİD), 1*(2), 90–109.

İçduygu, A. (2015). *Syrian refugees in Turkey: The long road ahead.* Washington: Migration Policy Institute.

Jani, J. S., Osteen, P., & Shipe, S. (2016). Cultural competence and social work education: Moving toward assessment of practice behaviors. *Journal of Social Work Education, 52*(3), 311–324.

Karataş, K., & Erkan, G. (2005). Türkiye'de Sosyal Hizmet Eğitiminin Tarihçesi [History of social work education in Turkey] (Ümit Onat eds.). *Sosyal hizmet eğitiminde yeni yaklaşımlar, sosyal hizmet sempozyumu, 2002,* 112–133.

Kıvılcım, F. (2013). Küreselleşme kavramı ve küreselleşme sürecinin gelişmekte olan ülke Türkiye açısından değerlendirilmesi [Globalization and evaluation of globalization process in developing country Turkey]. *Sosyal ve Beşeri Bilimler Dergisi, 5*(1), 219–230.

Koşar, N., & Tufan, B. (1999). Sosyal Hizmetler Yüksekokulu Tarihçesine Bir Bakış [A look at the history of the school of social work]. Prof. Dr. Sema Kut'a Armağan: Yaşam Boyu Sosyal Hizmet. Editors: Nesrin Koşar and Veli Duyan, Ankara: Hacettepe Üniversitesi Sosyal Hizmetler Yüksekokulu Yayını. No. 4.

Labonté-Roset, C. (2005). The European higher education area and research-orientated social work education. *European Journal of Social Work, 8*(3), 285–296.

Merrill, M., & Frost, C. J. (2011). Internationalizing social work education: Models, methods and meanings. *Frontiers: The Interdisciplinary Journal of Study Abroad, 21*, 189–210.

Meyer, M., Bushney, M., & Ukpere, W. I. (2011). The impact of globalisation on higher education: Achieving a balance between local and global needs and realities. *African Journal of Business Management, 5*(15), 6569–6578.

Midgley, J. (2001). Issues in international social work resolving critical debates in the profession. *Journal of Social Work, 1*(1), 21–35.

Miley, K. K., O'Melia, M., & DuBois, B. (2001). *Generalist social work practice: An empowering approach.* Boston: Allyn Bacon.

Olssen, M., & Peters, M. A. (2005). Neoliberalism, higher education and the knowledge economy: From the free market to knowledge capitalism. *Journal of Education Policy, 20*(3), 313–345.

Reisch, M. (2013). Social work education and the neo-liberal challenge: The US response to increasing global inequality. *Social Work Education, 32*(6), 715–733.

Robertson, S. L., & Kedzierski, M. (2016). On the move: Globalising higher education in Europe and beyond. *The Language Learning Journal, 44*(3), 276–291.

Rotabi, K. S., Gammonley, D., Gamble, D. N., & Weil, M. O. (2007). Integrating globalization into the social work curriculum. *The Journal of Sociology & Social Welfare, 34*(2), 165–185, Article 11.

Sewpaul, V., & Jones, D. (2004). Global standards for social work education and training. *Social Work Education, 23*(5), 493–513.

Sherman, P. (2016). Preparing social workers for global gaze: Locating global citizenship within social work curricula. *Social Work Education, 35*(6), 632–642.

Turkish Statistical Institute (TUIK). (2018). http://www.tuik.gov.tr/PreTablo. do?alt_id=1059. Accessed May 25, 2018.

Wright, E. R. (2007). *Globalization and social work education: An initial international inquiry* (Electronic Thesis and Dissertations Paper 1594). https://doi. org/10.18297/ctd/1594. Accessed May 1, 2018.

Yan, M. C., & Wong, Y. R. (2005). Rethinking self-awareness in cultural competence: Toward a dialogic self in cross-cultural social work. *Families in Society: The Journal of Contemporary Social Services, 86*(2), 181–188.

CHAPTER 39

Social Work Education in Italy: Light and Shadows

Annamaria Campanini

Historical Context

Primitive forms of organised social aid date back to the fourteenth century in kingdoms that once ruled what is now Italy. This was a time when the state, alongside charitable work carried out predominantly by charities and community associations, began to set up bodies tasked with providing centrally organised care interventions to face the problem of trampism, the consequences of pauperisation (sixteenth century), increase in the population, and social conflicts linked to the emergence of capitalism (Stradi, 2013).

The answer to these problems was institutionalisation in which the Catholic church played a predominant role. Thus began the marginalising of certain categories of the population. In 1862 and 1890 two laws were introduced to regulate the *istituzioni pubbliche di assistenza e beneficienza* (IPAB, "charitable institutions") and place them under public control. After World War I the Italian state introduced a measure making it directly responsible for supporting specific categories of persons such as war invalids and orphans. Social legislation was even enacted during the years of the fascist government. The first legislation to protect the rights of children in the care of wet nurses, foundling homes, orphanages, reformatories, and prisons was introduced by the fascist government in 1927, which also established the Opera Nazionale Maternità e Infanzia (ONMI), which promoted benefits for mothers and

A. Campanini (✉)
International Association of Schools of Social Work (IASSW), Dipartimentodi Sociologia e Ricerca Sociale, Università Milano Bicocca, Milan, Italy
e-mail: annamaria.campanini@unimib.it

Senior Research Associate, University of Johannesburg, Johannesburg, South Africa

© The Author(s) 2021
S. S. M. et al. (eds.), *The Palgrave Handbook of Global Social Work Education*, https://doi.org/10.1007/978-3-030-39966-5_39

children, and the Ente Nazionale Assistenza Orfani Lavoratori (ENAOLI), which supported the orphans of workers.

These progressive acts were driven by the regime's aim to regenerate the Italian race by improving their welfare and promoting a higher birth rate so that Italy could become a great imperial power. Many other forms of social security in the area of work were subsequently introduced such as family allowances for salaried employees, provision of a family and demographic policy, control of urbanisation and internal mobility, and closing the urban labour market to the rural active population. More generally, all these norms had the specific objective of exercising greater social control by making such assistance political. It is in this context that the National Fascist Party along with the Industry Confederation first began to train *assistenti sociali del lavoro* ("social assistants of work") in San Gregorio al Celio school. According to Martinelli (2003, p. 6) the principal aim was to educate "technically and spiritually female personnel who [were] asked to support workers in factories... guiding and advising them in their private life events." However, this school was not considered the birthplace of social work education because its premises were too distant from the ideas and ideals that inspired the promoters of future schools in the post-war period—in any event the school closed in 1943.

Development of Social Work Education

After World War II a lively debate on the possibility of moving toward a social security system took place. The Ministry for Post-War Assistance (1945–1947) and the Administration for International Aid (AAI), a body connected with the UNRRA (United Nations Relief and Rehabilitation Administration), promoted initiatives to support and ensure standards of professionalism and competence in responding to welfare needs. During the Tremezzo Conference (1946) particular attention was paid to the role and function of the social worker defined as "the one who must be the architect of the great work of social rehabilitation."

The first school of social work in the country was the Scuola Pratica di Assistenza Sociale. It was established in Milan in 1944 by the Compagnia di San Paolo with the support of the Opera Cardinal Ferrari and directed by Odile Vallin, a young French anti-fascist social worker who modelled the school after the École Pratique de Service Social de Montparnasse (Cutini, 2000). Many other schools have opened in Italy since 1945 under the patronage of private organisations of Catholic or secular influence. All these schools were inspired by democratic values and the principles of social work such as having respect for fellow human beings, personalising intervention, and using psychological and social sciences as theoretical supports in identifying the causes of problems. Although many professors in social work schools came from the academic world, this did not stop a very lively discussion ensuing about the type of establishment in which such education should take place. Ultimately, it was decided that courses would not be integrated within the university education system.

The idea was that the private sector was better equipped to build a curriculum that focussed on both theoretical and practical training. This ambivalence profoundly impacted the development of social work education that at that time did not enjoy formal recognition from the government. However, students aspiring to follow social work courses were required to possess a *maturità* ("secondary school diploma") and pass many entrance exams.

Nevertheless, critical thinking persisted in several directors and teachers of social work schools who highlighted the lack of research and theorisation that had gone into the social work curriculum in addition to non-recognition of the course at the university level. These are the reasons seven universities set up "schools for special purposes" as part of their curricula. These universities included the University of Siena in 1956, the Statale University and the Santa Maria Assunta University in Rome in 1966, the University of Parma and the University of Florence in 1969, and the University of Pisa and the University of Perugia in the 1970s. A review initiated by the Minister for Universities discovered that this new type of education was being carried out not only by these seven universities but also by more than 100 private schools. This analysis led to the legalisation of social work education, which was slowly developed following the enactment of a series of decrees. These decrees state that the only formal training path for the profession would be offered by the university system (D.M. 30.05.1985 under the structure of "schools for special purposes").

Such schools were legally recognised on 15 January 1987 and the university diploma in social work was created on 23 July 1993. These led to the creation of a social workers' professional register (law No. 84, 23 March 1993) that regulates the profession. According to the professional register social work diploma holders are required to pass a state exam to become registered social workers. These state exams were to be held on university premises with examiners made up of academics and social workers appointed by Professional Order. The Research Doctorate in Sociology, Theory and Methodology of Social Work has been available at the University of Trieste since 1994 and an experimental Degree Course in Social Work has been available at the University of Trieste and the University of LUMSA in Rome since 1998. Together, they offered social workers the possibility of gaining a 3-year diploma from either a private or university institution and enrolling at the beginning of each integrative year to obtain a *laurea* (main post-secondary academic degree).

On 19 June 1999 an agreement regarding the European Higher Education Area (EHEA) was signed in Bologna by 29 European countries to harmonise diverse European higher education systems and thus increase the employment prospects and geographical mobility of European citizens

(Campanini, 2015). In accordance with the Bologna Process, Italy reformed its national higher education system and established three levels of degrees (BA/MA/PhD) at all university faculties. This resulted in a 3-year Bachelor degree in "sciences of social work" and a 2-year Master's degree in "planning and management of politics and social services."

The lengthy discussions between social work educators and sociologists that ensued eventually led to creation of an MA because many sociologists were opposed to naming the diploma "theory and methodology of social work," as was proposed at the beginning. As a consequence of reform brought about by the Bologna Process the professional register was split into two sections: Section A for those who completed a Master's degree and Section B for those who completed a Bachelor's degree. Consequently, two different exams were introduced. A further change (D.M. 22 October 2004, No. 270) modified the previous decree: the BA was named "social work" (L-39) and the MA "social work and social policies" (LM-87).

For the academic year 2018/2019 a total of 36 BA degrees were included in the L-39 and given different denominations: 22 in "social work," 7 in "social work sciences," 2 in "sociology and social work," and the other 5 in "science of society and social work," "science of social work and no profit," "science of education and social work," "theory, culture and techniques of social work," and "mediator of intercultural and social cohesion in Europe." Concerning the MA degrees there were 35 programmes included in the LM-87 with a vast array of different names such as "social work and social policies," "planning and organisation of social work," "work, social citizenship and interculturality," "social work in complex contexts," "methodology, organisation and evaluation of social services," "society and local development," and "innovation and social work."

Design of the Social Work Curriculum

The structure of the present curriculum can be better understood by presenting an overview of the changes that have taken place in recent decades as a consequence of the global inclusion of social work education in the university context. This has led to a reduction in the number of types of specific social work taught.

A typical programme at schools for special purposes such as the University of Parma includes a 1-year course on principles and fundaments; a 3-year course on casework; 2-year courses on groupwork, community work, and ethics; a 3-year course on applied social work research; and a 2-year course on the administration of social services.

The Decree of 30 April 1985 instituted a study plan that conferred uniformity on social work education in Italy. The decree foresaw a 1-year course on "fundaments and principles of social work" and a 3-year course on "methods and techniques." It also professionalised courses on "the administration and organisation of social work services" (2-year course), "applied social work research" (2-year course with a single exam at the end), and "social work policy" (1-year course).

Reforms brought about by the Bologna Process resulted in the structure of the curriculum in social work—as for all the other disciplines—being defined at the national level.

Despite strong positioning adopted by the Professional Register and the Association of Italian Teachers in Social Work and despite the orientation of international standards of social work education issued in 2004 by the International Association of Schools of Social Work (IASSW) and the International Federation of Social Workers (IFSW), the structure of social work curricula required by the Ministry of Education left much to be desired. Following ministerial requirements the social work BA curriculum (total 180 credits) is divided into primary and characterising disciplines where it is mandatory to fulfil a minimum number of credits. The primary disciplines cover 36 credits: 15 for sociology; 3 for law; 6 for psychology; 3 can be chosen from economics, politics, and history; and 9 can be chosen between historical, anthropological, and pedagogical studies. The characterising disciplines cover 54 credits: 15 for social work; 9 for sociology; 9 for law; 15 for psychology; and 6 for medical science. Moreover, there is a mandatory practice placement that can cover at least 18 credits while the remaining credits needed to reach a total of 180 can be allocated across all disciplinary areas.

The MA curriculum requires 120 credits of which 48 are mandatory for the characterising disciplines (15 for sociology; 12 for law; 12 between psychology, pedagogy, anthropology, and philosophy; and 12 between economics, politics, and statistics) and 10 for fieldwork placements. The remaining credits needed to reach a total of 120 can be allocated across all disciplinary areas.

Of the 180 credits needed for a BA the ministerial regulation requires a minimum of 15 mandatory credits for social work disciplines (quoted under sociology) and 18 credits for field placement. At the MA level 10 credits are allocated to field placements (very often spent conducting research activities related to the thesis) and no specific mention is given of social work disciplines. This means that students can earn a BA degree in social work after having completed only three exams over the course of their major. Generally speaking, one exam is more orientated toward defining "fundamentals and principles of social work" while the other two relate more to "methods and techniques." To reiterate, there is currently no specific social work course needed for students to gain an MA.

Such a curriculum structure clearly affects the preparedness of social workers who paradoxically require a greater breadth of competencies as a consequence of globalisation. Despite the few mandatory social work courses being very general, none of them deals with specific intervention methods or clients' problems. Further, none of the mandatory courses relates directly to human rights, social justice, advocacy, or policy practice.

Placements occupy a significant part of social work programmes (Dellavalle, 2011) perhaps because of the scarcity of social work–related courses. They are very limited in terms of hours compared with Italy's European homologues and arguably not as well structured (Campanini, 2009). The organisation of placements varies widely by institution. In some universities there are specific structures tasked with coordinating all activities linked to internships, while in others students are left to their own devices. In some cases supervision is carried out by designated persons located in students' placements, while in other cases supervision is not undertaken by social workers. In only a few universities is it possible for students to reflect on their placements in small groups under the supervision of field teachers. Such cases while rare are hugely beneficial for students to get feedback on their experiences and make links between theory and practice.

Other critical elements relate to curricula not focussing on the preparation needed to face the challenges that social workers are experiencing in social services despite the orientation of the Bologna Process and the Tuning Methodology (www.unideusto.org). Instead, curricula are often shaped by the resources available to faculty at the departmental level. These are the reasons there may be more courses related to sociology, law, political science, or pedagogy depending on the institution and its resources. The education process is not sufficiently orientated toward competencies and the teaching methods employed are still too teacher centred (as opposed to student centred). Italian universities still follow the traditional mode of lecturing (i.e., from the pulpit) while student-centred teaching methods tend to foster more critical thinking. Moreover, too many students get accepted onto courses (between 100 and 400 in some cases) for the number of teachers available. This is due to increased pressure faced by universities to enlarge the number of students to guarantee increments in the financing process. In the past the majority of social work schools accepted only 35–60 students per year. The current increase in the teacher/student ratio is hampering achieving a more student-focussed learning process.

An additional problem is the lack of analysis of the motivations and attitudes of students enrolling in social work programmes. The majority of universities conduct entrance examinations (general questions on culture) for students wishing to apply for social work courses. Scores obtained in this test and grades achieved at high school are the only criteria used to determine student selection. The issue is that selection based on the assessment of student motivations or their attitudes toward the social work profession in Italy is not possible because it is deemed a discriminatory approach. Such discrimination violates the Italian constitution that guarantees the right to all citizens of choosing their education. To improve the preparedness of students in scientific disciplines and to make up for deficiencies in the curricula more seminars or laboratories should be organised and proper supervision and tutorship in relation to placements should be provided (Dellavalle, 2011). However, the cost incurred in providing these for social work education is viewed as an additional burden universities' administrative bodies cannot afford. Further, the constraining structure of programmes makes it difficult to find the time to undertake such activities.

Despite all these problems there are many initiatives undertaken by social work professors in different universities to utilise more active teaching methodologies (Bertotti, 2012; Fazzi, 2016; Rizzo, 2012). Such professors find themselves juggling with various regulations (e.g., a security law stipulating that all furniture be affixed to the floor) creating difficulties in bringing about less formal ways of teaching. Some universities conduct workshops on a number of issues such as communication and writing skills, intercultural and interdisciplinary approaches, and seminars and groupwork. Doing so enables students to use the conceptual frameworks of different disciplines to understand the type and nature of social problems, to learn about good practice, to train themselves through role-playing activity, and to bring service users into the classroom to relate their experiences. These are but a few examples of good practice that are being carried out in different programmes of social work across the country. High-quality teaching is fundamental to approaching theory and praxis and to supporting students develop reflexivity and self-evaluation competencies. However, the economic crisis of 2007–2009 had an adverse impact on universities and existing policies for higher education in Italy make it even more challenging to maintain such activities.

Social Work: A Neglected Discipline?

Although discussion about the importance of a discipline being recognised as having an autonomy of its own has long been raised by social work representatives such as the National Association of Social Workers (ASSNAS), the Italian Association of Teachers of Social Work (AIDOSS), and the National Council of Social Workers (CNOAS), the result was half-hearted. The reasons for this can be attributed to the history of social work education and the culture of Italian academia and its relationship with sociologists. Getting social work courses taught at university was very problematic. Moreover, there was very strong resistance, especially from sociologists, to considering social work as an autonomous discipline. During social work education's transition from private schools to universities the Ministry of Education failed to adopt measures to protect chairs (professorships) in social work, much as was the case in Spain.[1]

Social work in Italy was thus firmly held in the grip of sociology. Precise reasons for this decision taken by the National University Council (CUN) were based on the so-called insufficient scientific rigour of social work. The long period when private entities ran social work education did not allow for the creation of a robust academic disciplinary background. Teachers in schools were more concerned in training social workers to respond to the needs of society than publishing theoretical essays or participating in research. American and British experts contributed a great deal to the social work discipline in the first years of social work education in Italy. Moreover, many textbooks from foreign scholars were translated into Italian. Nevertheless, the 1950s to the 1970s witnessed the start of indigenisation of social work when the contents of social work courses became more local-ised, as evidenced by articles in Italian journals and publications supported by the Amministrazione Aiuti Internazionali (AAI). The most significant move toward building specific scientific disciplinary knowledge came about as a result of analysing collaborative work carried out by the teachers who created AIDOSS. Many seminari and conferences were organised on differ-ent issues and topics by this association on different issues and topics rang-ing from: the processes of help and the unity of methods; the use of other disciplines to build up theoretical models; the concept of training as a part of the educational process and a representation of the theory-praxis relation; and themes concerning social work as a profession and discipline, as well as education in a university context. Such theoretical elaborations encouraged more contributions that once published became a point of reference for the evolution of social work in Italy (Coordinamento Nazionale Docenti di Servizio Sociale, 1987; Dal Pra Ponticelli, 1985a, 1985b, 1987; Giraldo & Riefolo, 1996; Neve & Niero, 1990; Università degli Studi di Siena, 1983). Thus, comparison with other disciplines became ever greater (Bianchi, Cavallone, Dal Pra Ponticelli, De Sandre, & Gius, 1988), particularly with sociology. Nevertheless, social workers teaching in schools were largely excluded from traditional university recruitment. Some continued to teach part-time while sociologists replaced social work professors because they had a chair in general sociology in which social work was included despite not having any specific theoretical knowledge or experience in the field of social work.

The 1980s marked the time when many publishers began to show interest in social work. As a consequence many books have been published in the last few decades. The most notable have been the publication of a social work dictionary edited by Maria Dal Pra Ponticelli (2005) and a new dictionary of social work put together by Annamaria Campanini (2013a). The dictionary is the result of a joint effort between professors, experts, and professionals from different generations and different regions in Italy. Although it is a dedicated work, it was deliberately made open to authors from other disciplines such as sociology, psychology, law, and political science. By doing so it contributes to enriching and better defining the social work discipline itself where events, ideas, and scenarios are deployed to illustrate the past, the present, and the future of social work.

Although this process could well testify to and consolidate the autonomy of social work as a credible discipline (Campanini, 1999; Gui, 1999); although it is now possible to affirm that social work has its own specific theoretical background (Dal Pra Ponticelli, 2005; Fargion, 2009; Gui, 2004); and although, as recognised in the words of Suzy Braye when she unveiled the dictionary in Rome,[2] "the volume brings a level of critical analysis that demonstrates the academic maturity and sophistication of the discipline of social work in Italy," social work is still not recognised within academia as a proper discipline.

In the academic year 2018–2019 only 16 teachers (1 full professor, 4 associate professors, and 11 associate researchers) appointed by universities in Italy (Torino, Piemonte Orientale, Milan Bicocca and Milan Cattolica, Verona, Trento, Trieste, Bolzano, Bologna, Ancona, Lecce, Palermo) are qualified social workers. As a result the majority of social work courses are not taught by tenured faculty, but by professionals working in social services or experts in the field with temporary contracts and without regular remuneration. A vicious circle has developed since the financial crisis: there are few teachers of social work in universities, few credits for social work disciplines, compounded by the impossibility of hiring new staff and the difficulty social workers have in obtaining research chairs since the conditions for such competition are defined in the context of sociology—not social work. Consequently, Italian social work research lags behind that of many other countries. Moreover, in its current form the Italian curriculum does not comply with guidelines regarding education standards (www.iassw-aiets.org) approved by the IASSW and the IFSW.

While unveiling the *Social Work Dictionary* in Rome in 2013 Suzy Braye stated "as the discipline takes shape and its scientific merit is established, so we have to ensure that professional education reflects these firm foundations, and that social work takes its rightful place in the curriculum for those wishing to enter the profession."

State of Social Work Research in Italy

The state of social work research in Italy is best analysed by looking at the historical development of social work education. Doctoral studies in Italy started in the 1980s as a response to D.P.R. No. 382/1980 (presidential decree) more than 20 years later than in other European countries. The first PhD in "sociology, theory and methodology of social work" (a 3-year programme) was instituted by the University of Trieste in the academic year 1993–1994.

At the time it was the only social work programme available. Students who were interested in enrolling in this programme needed to complete undergraduate and graduate studies in fields such as sociology, psychology, pedagogy, or social policy to be considered for the PhD programme. The establishment of a social work BA and MA in 2000 allowed for a more direct journey to a PhD.

Following the example of Trieste other universities introduced social work doctoral studies (Rome, Sassari, Milan Bicocca, Milan Cattolica, Bolzano, Bologna, Lecce, Trento, Calabria, and Marche Polytechnic University) with approximately 80 doctors having now graduated.

It is also worth noting that CNOAS financially supported doctoral studies by providing a bursary for students to help develop and promote a social work curriculum.

The development of third cycle education in social work has encountered many problems not only because of the lack of recognition of the discipline but also because of a new regulation that created doctoral schools between different departments or universities. This was done to connect fragmented disciplinary sectors and facilitate multidisciplinary research projects. Although social workers can apply, admissions are increasingly competitive.

PhD students mainly comprise professionals employed in social services interested in enhancing their professional skills or in pursuing their careers in academia. Since 1997, the year the first Italian social workers received their PhDs, four PhD graduates have been offered positions as associate professors and another four as researchers. All other graduates have continued their work in social services, while some have also been offered part-time teaching positions. This made it difficult to create social work research centres and to develop a strong network between these doctors who are spread across Italy but are not connected by an institutional framework.

The development of social work research can be divided into four periods (Ossicini Ciolfi, 1988):

a. 1945–1955 when particular focus was given to social investigation and the organisation of community projects;
b. 1955–1970 when focus was given to development of the profession and when there was a predilection for action research that allowed the participation of citizens in the processes of planning;
c. 1970–1985 when institutional changes were characterised by the establishment of a number of schools of social work, especially in northern Italy, and by a reduction in the participation of public institutions; and
d. 1980–2020 when peculiar conditions prevail.

Economic considerations have resulted in a number of organisational changes within universities that have impacted social work faculty and the curriculum, as explained in the previous section. There has been a reduction in the number of courses that really need to be part of the social work curriculum such as the research methodology course. Whittling down the number of teachers employed in universities has made it very difficult to develop and sustain research projects that can enhance the knowledge base and build up course material (Campanini, 2013b). Nevertheless, there are publications in the Italian context written by professors of social work at an individual level or by teams within specific universities sometimes in partnership with other European countries. Notable examples include the University of Verona conducting research on social worker training (Bressan, Pedrazza, & Neve, 2011); researchers at the University of Turin investigating the processes of professionalisation; the Interdepartmental Centre for Research and Services on Socio Health Integration (CRISS) of Marche Polytechnic University examining the role of social work; three international studies two involving the University of Calabria ("The Public Health Implications of Neoliberal Policy and Management on Professions and Vulnerable Rural Populations" and "Civil Engagement in Social Work: Developing Global Models") with partners worldwide and the third by the University of Genoa in collaboration with the University of Helsinki and Lund University on working conditions, welfare, and poverty.

Moreover, the last decade has witnessed some interuniversity research cofinanced by the Ministry of University and Research (MIUR). Such research has been carried out with the participation of some social work professors and has focussed on the following topics: the relationship between social work, social policy, and territory (Lazzari, 2008); the state of the profession of social work in Italy (Facchini, 2010); and the role played by social workers and educators in the promotion of active citizenship (Bifulco & Facchini, 2013).

The development of social work research in Italy took a major step when Italian social work professors participated in activities undertaken by the European Association for Social Work Research, its Board of Directors, and the boards of directors of international journals. Moreover, establishment of the Fondazione assistenti sociali (Social Workers' Foundation) and transformation of AIDOSS into the Social Work Society (SOCISS) contributed to developing this sector further. The Social Workers' Foundation played a prominent role in getting university teachers and doctors involved in extensive research into the reason social workers are subjected to aggression and violated by people they are trying to help. Since 2017 SOCISS has committed itself to organising biannual conferences on research into social work and publishing the best papers presented at such conferences in the journal *La Rivista di Servizio Sociale.*

CHALLENGES AND PERSPECTIVES

Comparison of the development of Italian social work with that at the European or international level not only highlights the lack of academic recognition of the social work discipline but also the fact that existing university policies structure social work courses within different areas—not as an independent academic subject. Although stringent provisions in ministerial documents prescribe openly discussing curricula with social actors, this is very often carried out bureaucratically—not as a constructive ongoing dialogue orientated at defining competence strategies fundamental to strengthening the preparedness of the next generation of social workers. Moreover, people using the services are not involved in this process, as happens in other parts of the world.

A law aimed at regulating social work education and the profession was proposed in 2013. The law had a number of objectives such as making it mandatory for social workers to complete 5 years of university studies (a 3-year BA and a 2-year MA), recognising social work as a disciplinary area, implementing specific social work courses in study programmes as agreed with the National Council of Social Workers, creating specific doctoral courses, and employing professors for social work disciplines who had specific social work backgrounds.

The driving force behind this initiative was recognition of the need for social workers to have robust and updated competencies to face challenges relating to the current situation in Italy. Such challenges include the increasing complexity, severity, and burdensomeness of social problems at a time of cuts in public expenditure as a result of a severe lack of resources; heavy caseloads causing both burnouts of social workers and higher levels of hostility toward them; and significant changes in the labour market with new employment opportunities in the third sector requiring active engagement in organisational, managerial, economic, and financial planning (Fazzi, 2012). The Conference of Heads of Social Work Degrees opposed this proposal, even though it was supported by the National Council of Social Workers. Although the bill has not yet been discussed in parliament and a new government having been elected, there is little prospect of any substantial upcoming change.

Another critical point has been the failure to internationalise the curricula despite many initiatives having been put forward in recent years. The inclusion of social work education in universities has made it possible to participate in a number of initiatives undertaken within the Socrates/Erasmus Programme where the participation of students is much more visible than that of professors. This may be because of their precarity in academia and limited proficiency in foreign languages (Campanini, 1999). Moreover, bibliographic material is generally limited to Italian publications therefore reducing the exposure of Italian scholarly work in European and international debates.

A European Thematic Network initiative comprising around 100 partners and spearheaded by the University of Parma (www.eusw.unipr.it) from 2002 to 2008 was important (Campanini, 2002, 2007) in supporting the integration of Italian and European social work.

Since 2010 social work education institutes have begun to actively participate in World Social Work Day by organising a number of initiatives in different Italian universities often in cooperation with regional professional registers. International conferences have been organised in which colleagues from different countries have participated such as "Social Work Education in a Changing Europe" (Turin, 1993); "Social Challenges and Social Profession" (Parma, 2007); "Social Work Education: Towards 2025" (Milan, 2015); and the "Joint Global Conference on Social Work Education and Social Development" in Rimini in 2020 that is being organised by the IASSW and the International Council on Social Welfare (ICSW).

Italian social work professors have not only been elected to the boards of the European Association of Schools of Social Work (EASSW), the European Social Work Research Association (ESWRA), and the International Association of Schools of Social Work (IASSW), but they have also assumed the presidency of these three international organisations. Nevertheless, limitations inherent in curricula make it very difficult to internationalise curricula, build up a strong knowledge base on human rights and social justice, and ensure social workers have a clear understanding of the effects of globalisation on local practice and be able to play a political role in society. Although social work education should be multidisciplinary, its core competencies need to have a strong scientific and methodological knowledge base and be capable of developing ethical professional attitudes. Critical reflection skills can be attained by integrating theory with practice, by adopting a modular structure, by activating the centrality of students in the learning process, and by utilising innovative teaching methodologies. The development and approval of new curricular structures hinge on the employment of additional professionally qualified teaching faculty in all BA and MA courses.

This chapter has presented the light and shadows found within social work education in Italy. Although it may appear that problems prevail over positive achievements, the social work community is committed to continuous engagement in improving the situation. Although this is widely believed to be an ethical question, only well-prepared professionals can work toward achieving the social work mission of enhancing human rights and social justice in the world.

NOTES

1. Real Decreto 1850/1981, de 20 de agosto, sobre la incorporación a la Universidad de Los Estudios de Asistentes Sociales como Escuelas Universitarias de Trabajo Social. BOE No. 206, de 28 de agosto de 1981; 5 Orden de 12 de abril de 1983 por la que se establecen las directrices para la elaboración de los Planes de Estudios de las Escuelas Universitarias de Trabajo Social. BOE No. 93, de 19 de abril de 1983.
2. Speech given by Suzy Braye when she unveiled the *Social Work Dictionary* on 18 March 2013 in Rome.

References

Bertotti, T. (2012). Specificità e proposte per una nuova didattica del servizio sociale. *Rassegna di Servizio Sociale, 4,* 105–127.

Bianchi, E., Cavallone, A. M., Dal Pra Ponticelli, M., De Sandre, I., & Gius, E. (1988). *Il lavoro sociale professionale tra soggetti e istituzioni.* Milano: Franco Angeli.

Bifulco, L., & Facchini, C. (a cura di). (2013). *Partecipazione sociale e competenze. Il ruolo delle Professioni nei Piani di Zona.* Milano: Franco Angeli.

Bressan, F., Pedrazza, M., & Neve, E. (2011). *Il percorso formativo dell'assistente sociale. Autovalutazione e benessere professionale.* Milano: Franco Angeli.

Campanini, A. (1999). *Servizio sociale e sociologia. Storia di un dialogo.* Trieste: Lint.

Campanini, A. (2002). EUSW. European social work. La rete tematica europea in servizio sociale. *Rassegna di Servizio Sociale, 4,* 144–152.

Campanini, A. (2007). Introduction: Educating social workers in the context of Europe. In E. Frost & M. J. Freitas (Eds.), *Social work education in Europe* (pp. 9–20). Roma: Carocci Editore.

Campanini, A. (2009). I mille volti del tirocinio in Italia e in Europa. In A. Campanini (a cura di), *Scenari di welfare e formazione al servizio sociale in un' Europa che cambia* (pp. 199–234). Milano: Unicopli.

Campanini, A. (diretto da). (2013a). *Nuovo Dizionario di servizio sociale.* Roma: Carocci Editore.

Campanini, A. (2013b). La Formazione al servizio sociale in Italia e in Europa: aspetti storici e prospettive. In Diomede M. Canevini & A. Campanini (Eds.), *Servizio sociale e lavoro sociale: questioni disciplinari e professionali* (pp. 161–179). Bologna: Il Mulino.

Campanini, A. (2015). Bologna process. In James D. Wright (editor-in-chief), *International encyclopedia of the social & behavioral sciences* (2nd ed., Vol 2., pp. 741–746). Oxford: Elsevier.

Coordinamento Nazionale Docenti di Servizio Sociale. (1987). *Il servizio sociale come processo di aiuto.* Milano: Franco Angeli.

Cutini, R. (2000). *Il servizio sociale nel secondo dopoguerra: contributi per una ricerca storica.* Roma: ISTISS.

Dal Pra Ponticelli, M. (a cura di). (1985a). *Metodologia del servizio sociale.* Milano: Franco Angeli.

Dal Pra Ponticelli, M. (1985b). *I modelli teorici del servizio sociale.* Roma: Astrolabio.

Dal Pra Ponticelli, M. (1987). *Lineamenti di servizio sociale.* Roma: Astrolabio.

Dal Pra Ponticelli, M. (diretto da). (2005). *Dizionario di servizio sociale.* Roma: Carocci.

Dellavalle, M. (2011). *Il tirocinio nella formazione al servizio sociale.* Roma: Carocci.

Facchini, C. (a cura di). (2010). *Tra impegno e professione. Gli assistenti sociali come soggetti del welfare.* Bologna: Il Mulino.

Fargion, S. (2009). *Il servizio sociale. Storia, temi e dibattiti.* Bari: Laterza.

Fazzi, L. (2012). Social work in the public and non-profit sectors in Italy: What are differences? *European Journal of Social Work, 5,* 629–644.

Fazzi, L. (2016). Are we educating creative professionals? The results of some experiments on the education of social work students in Italy. *Social Work Education, 1,* 89–99.

Giraldo, S., & Riefolo, E. (a cura di). (1996). *Il servizio sociale. Esperienza e costruzione del sapere*. Milano: Franco Angeli.

Gui, L. (1999). *Servizio sociale tra teoria e pratica. Il tirocinio, luogo di interazione*. Trieste: LINT.

Gui, L. (2004). *Le sfide teoriche del servizio sociale. I fondamenti teorici di una disciplina*. Roma: Carocci.

Lazzari, F. (2008). *Servizio sociale trifocale. Le azioni e gli attori delle nuove politiche sociali*. Milano: Franco Angeli.

Martinelli, F. (2003). Servizio sociale e democrazia. Il percorso delle scuole di servizio sociale. *La rivista di Servizio Sociale, 1*, 5–40.

Neve, E., & Niero, M. (1990). *Il tirocinio. Modelli e strumenti dell'esperienza delle scuole di servizio sociale italiane*. Milano: Franco Angeli.

Ossicini Ciolfi, T. (1988). *Ricerca e servizio sociale. Dalle prime inchieste alle ricerche contemporanee*. Roma: Carocci.

Rizzo, A. M. (2012). Una riflessione sugli approcci teorici che sottendono i metodi di insegnamento. *Rassegna di Servizio Sociale, 4*, 99–104.

Stradi, N. (2013). Assistenza (Storia della). In A. Campanini (diretto da), *Nuovo Dizionario di servizio sociale* (pp. 73–78). Roma: Carocci.

Università degli Studi di Siena. Ministero Dell' Interno. (1983). *Professionalità e formazione*. Atti del Convegno, Siena.

Websites

Alma Laurea—www.almalaurea.it.
CNOAS—www.cnoas.it.
EASSW—www.eassw.org.
ESWRA—www.eswra.org.
European Thematic Network—www.eusw.unipr.it.
EUSW—www.eusw.unipr.it.
Fondazione assistenti sociali—www.fondazioneassistentisociali.it.
IASSW—www.iassw-aiets.org.
ICSW—www.icsw.org.
IFSW—www.ifsw.org.
SOCISS—https://logintest.webnode.com.
Tuning Methodology—www.unideusto.org.

CHAPTER 40

Risks and Benefits of Convergences in Social Work Education: A Post-colonial Analysis of Malaysia and the UK

Jonathan Parker⊙

INTRODUCTION

Social work education globally has a diverse history with much influenced in its earlier growth by the Global North (Frampton, 2018; Gray, Coates, & Yellow Bird, 2010, 2013). This has skewed the development of social work thought and privileged certain discourses which may remain unspoken or may have created in appropriate forms of social work and welfare education. In this chapter, we are looking at social work education in the UK, which has a long history as developer and colonial exporter/influencer, and Malaysia, which has a shorter history of development, has been influenced by past colonial imports, and new assumed ideas whilst striving to develop an indigenous model within a neo-global context.

ISOMORPHIC CONVERGENCES

DiMaggio and Powell (1983) outlined a neo-Weberian organisational theory that identified some of the ways in which organisations display a tendency to adopt the strategies and structures of the powerful and successful. The approach outlines three ways in which organisations act to maintain their positions. These include coercive, mimetic, and normative processes

J. Parker (✉)
Department of Social Sciences and Social Work, Bournemouth University, Bournemouth, UK
e-mail: parkerj@bournemouth.ac.uk

© The Author(s) 2021
S. S. M. et al. (eds.), *The Palgrave Handbook of Global Social Work Education*, https://doi.org/10.1007/978-3-030-39966-5_40

employed by organisations to bring themselves in line with the assumed 'right ways of working'. This involves convergence across structures, processes, and practices.

The coercive processes concern those policies and procedures that derive from legislation or accepted standards within a particular profession. These processes must be followed and the organisations involved may suffer sanctions if they do not follow them. They represent the explicit external forces influencing a profession or organisation. Mimetic processes, on the other hand, concern the internal drivers of compliance: a wish to emulate or copy the practices of those organisations and/or professionals who represent the epitome of that group. Practices are adopted that follow those venerated organisations and professions and are gradually embedded within the copying organisation. These two processes have similarities to Bourdieu's concept of the *habitus* (Bourdieu, 1977). The external coercive behavioural drivers are *structuring structures*. They exert a pressure to conform to certain accepted standards which alter the culture and forms of the organisation or profession. Mimetic processes are perhaps more akin to Bourdieu's *structured structures*; those practices and organising behaviours which are moulded and shaped by copying those of an esteemed other.

The third isomorphic process occurs when the practices and behaviours become unspoken and assumed. They become the ways in which the practice is undertaken and any deviation from these normative standards is seen as bad practice or practice that is to be avoided. This normativity constructs a sense of belonging and a distinction from those professional organisations that do not conform.

These three processes can be identified in most professional organisations as they strive for recognition, acceptance as part of a larger entity and a seat at the table of influence. It is a process of convergence towards similar forms. There are a number of problems with isomorphic convergence. Firstly, it suggests that a one-size-fits-all approach is possible and desirable. For instance, standards in social work practice and education have been developed to ensure that those who use our services are protected, offered the very best practices and are not subject to differential treatment. These are laudable aims. However, social work is a human, relational profession that requires critical reflexivity and continual questioning of contexts and practices and a consideration of processes as much as outcomes, the latter of which may reflect professional rather than service user vested interests (Blom & Morén, 2019). Social work must be adaptable and plastic rather than rigidly adhering to prescribed standards. Therefore, understanding the model of isomorphic convergences allows social workers to weigh up the value of standard against the need for individual and localised plasticity. Adopting a situation ethic will help in which the rules of the game or standards are accepted as generally benign but need not be complied with where the contextual and individual needs are greater (Fletcher, 1966). This is something that is captured within the International Federation of Social Workers' (IFSW) revised definition of social work, which allows adaptation to local and indigenous conditions (IFSW, 2014).

Secondly, the normative aspects of isomorphic convergence in social work education suggest there is a correct way of doing it and that not conforming to these accepted practices implies deviance and lesser quality. The hidden imperialist tendencies within such an approach betray some of the history of social work education in its often (neo)-colonial transfer across countries (Frampton, 2018; Parker et al., 2014). Indeed, the models and standards that are copied, required, and become accepted have often derived from progenitors of social work education in the Global North, notably the UK and USA, although also including other European nations. This reinforces an unspoken assumption of hierarchy in education standards.

Allied to the point above is that being a structured structure, influenced by the lure of accepted standards, may prevent the development of appropriate indigenous and contextual approaches to social work practice and education (Ling, 2007). In turn, this may result in the development of a system of practice and education which fails to address the needs of local people.

In our analysis of social work education in the UK and Malaysia, these models provide a useful framework for understanding, and for recognising risk.

Social Work Education in the UK and Malaysia

Change and Reform in the UK

Change has permeated the development and delivery of social work education throughout its long history (over 100 years) within universities (Baron & McLaughlin, 2017; Parker, 2005, 2019). The Local Authority and Social Services Act in 1971 and subsequent formation of the Central Council for Education and Training in Social Work (CCETSW), however, heralded a more standardised and regulated qualifying education across the UK (Jones, 2006).

There were positive elements to this more organised approach to education standards. In the late 1980s, CCETSW emphasised political activism within qualifying education. However, a political backlash led to revisions to the qualification, which then sat at a sub-degree level, and a shift towards privileging employer needs. Whilst qualification levels increased from sub-degree to degree level from 2003, it also gave rise to enhanced surveillance and control, which instrumentalised social work education. Employer needs became paramount whilst relational and critical social work was diminished. Over time social work education shifted towards greater curricular prescription which, in turn, prevented universities from offering many of their specialist courses based on research expertise (Parker, 2019). The rationale for increased standardisation was to prevent tragedies such as high profile deaths of children. The insidious outcome, however, was to define social work as a 'state-sponsored' activity, located within local government in Britain whilst relegating community and radical aspects of social work that aligned with other international approaches. We have argued elsewhere that it also allowed social workers to be blamed when things went wrong and to suggest social work education and training was inadequate (Parker, 2019). The protective and social regulatory functions began to assume precedence in social work within a new context of mandatory registration with the professional body—at the time the General Social Care Council (GSCC) (see s.61 Care Standards Act 2000).

The pace of change increased under the New Labour Government (1997–2010), underpinned by the concept of New Public Management perspective (Jordan & Drakeford, 2012). The introduction of a minimum bachelor degree qualifying level allowed policy makers to introduce greater prescription into the curriculum and thereby influence the pedagogy underpinning it. The publication of the inquiry into the high profile death of 17-month old Peter Connelly in 2009 led to a growth in surveillance and scrutiny and education was again targeted with a great deal of curricula and pedagogical control being transferred to social work employers and policy makers (Balls, 2008; Jones, 2014; Shoesmith, 2016; Social Work Task Force, 2009). A Social Work Reform Board was developed that scrutinised practices in student selection, education, practice learning, and partnerships with practice agencies amongst other matters (Department for Education, 2010, 2012; Jones, 2014). This resulted in greater direction and reform for social work education (Higgins, 2016; Higgins & Goodyer, 2015). The power of the employer voice was clearly exemplified by some employer groups suggesting, even before the first cohort of students taking the 2003 programme in England had graduated, that student social workers were being failed by universities and not prepared adequately for practice (Evaluation of Social Work Degree Qualification in England Team, 2008). Perhaps this was not surprising given the metamorphosis of social work from a person-centred, social justice, and human rights-based entity to one concerned almost exclusively, at management and government directional level, with social regulation and protective function that had occurred almost by stealth as control and regulation became normalised (Parker, 2017; Parker & Ashencaen Crabtree, 2018a, 2018b). Reform and calls for reform have continued (Croisdale-Appleby, 2014; Narey, 2014; Maxwell et al., 2016; Smith, Stepanova, Venn, Carpenter, & Patsios, 2018).

The competency approach to social work education permeated the early qualifications and the qualifying degree was underpinned by National Occupational Standards in social work (BASW, 2003). This approach attracted many critics and an unholy alliance between government departments and educators led to change. The Social Work Reform Board envisaged social work as a life-long or career-long learning process that developed in breadth and depth of knowledge, skills, and practice and began with a student's initial application to an education programme. This was known as the Professional Capabilities Framework (PCF), a nine-domain overview of what were considered to represent the central characteristics of English social work (BASW, 2018; Higgins, 2016). Underpinning this conception was the capability approach (see Nussbaum, 2011; Sen 1999). However, as I have argued elsewhere the PCF to a large extent describes contemporary social work including national and international aspects in normative terms that reflect an instrumental, homogenised view of social work rather than offering a critical narrative on which one can reflexively develop (Parker, 2019).

As reform became ingrained within social work education, social work in England lost its professional and regulatory body the General Social Care Council with whom student social workers were registered. Responsibility for regulating social work was transferred to the Health Care Professions Council (HCPC). This led to social work education requiring students to meet key professional standards (Standards of Proficiency) (HCPC, 2012) revised in 2016 but no longer to be registered as students. The standards seemed to homogenise and replicate neoliberal concerns of performance measurement, targets, and outputs or productivity as well as an attempt to enhance the quality of the work. Regulation under the HCPC also relegated social work to a sub-set of health and the social science base became increasingly threatened. The reforms have also led to the development of core subject areas in qualifying social work education that creates a discourse outlining what social work means and what it is. The increasing focus on protection or 'safeguarding' and the legislative, regulatory aspects of social work are privileged whilst the campaigning, political, social justice, and relational elements are minimised however much lip-service is paid to them. A new regulatory body is planned for the end of 2019—Social Work England—which would realign social work in England with the other three countries in the UK in having a separate regulatory body. However, it also suggests that further changes in standards and requirements may also be coming in the near future. Further evidence suggesting this may be taken from the production of Knowledge and Skills Statements for both children and families and adult (Department of Education, 2014; Department of Health, 2015), and uncertainties for social work education in the light of the UK's planned withdrawal from the European Union (Parker, 2019).

These changes herald a definition of social work as a statutory service, as part of the state's organisational systems for the regulation of social and family life; social work is functional and functionary and students are being trained rather than educated into maintaining the practices of this system in a taken-for-granted manner (Bourdieu & Wacquant, 1992). This approach favours redistributing the power base towards employer organisations which have political as well as professional mandates to achieve.

The concept and practice of social work as an international entity are contested (Hugman, 2010; Hutchings & Taylor, 2007). Indeed, its social-historical-political construction leads to different morphologies and practices across the world. However, in an attempt to connect social work across the globe excellent work has been completed by the International Federation of Social Workers and the International Association of Schools of Social Work to reach agreement on a global definition (IASSW/IFSW, 2014). In turn, this has promoted the development of non-binding, yet important, global educational standards for social work (IFSW/IASSW, 2012). This is something of a 'double-edged sword'; however, it has both potential benefits and potential drawbacks. It provides a set of standards that social work educators in all countries can aspire to and can campaign to achieve within their universities, professional bodies, and policy-making bodies. It also has the potential to homogenise social work education around global isomorphs that may privilege certain countries more than others. Therefore, a critical eye has to be kept on the meanings that these standards create within each country and educational establishment and within social work organisations. However, if we approach these standards reflexively and critically, we can avoid their coercive and normative power and use these to campaign for an internationalised approach that preserves the central characteristics of social work and education—social justice and human rights—as the UK moves into a more insular and isolated approach to social work.

Malaysian Social Work Education

Social work, in Malaysia, is associated with its colonial past. Formal welfare services were developed, as in Britain, in the early twentieth century as a means of supporting the colonial economy (Parker et al., 2016). The first Department of Social Welfare was established in 1946 which was elevated to the Ministry of Social Welfare in 1964. In 1985, the Ministry was reduced again to departmental status under the Ministry of National Unity and Community Development, which was renamed in 2004 as the Ministry of Women, Family and Community Development (MWFCD). The MWFCD oversees four agencies—the Department for Development of Women (JPW), the Department of Social Welfare, Malaysia (JKM), the National Population and Family Development Board (LPPKN), and the Social Institute of Malaysia (ISM). The Department of Social Welfare (JKM) provides social services and implements government welfare policies. Services include casework, foster care and adoption, youth probation and parole, protective services for older people, and child protection. It is the largest government agency and employer of social workers in the country (Baba, 2002).

Social work education is offered at a number of universities in Malaysia, a middle-income country, where it is popular discipline and attracts high student numbers. However, compared with high-income countries, social work, as a regulated profession, remains an aspiration.

A two-year social welfare officer training course was offered by the London School of Economics following World War II; the majority of graduates during this period were British (Baba, 1998; Mair, 1944). Following *Merdeka* (independence) in 1963, social work education replicated its colonial heritage with many Malaysian social workers trained at the National University of Singapore, then known as the University of Malaya (Baba, 2002). Other social workers studied in Indonesia, the Philippines, India, and the UK, Australia and the USA. However, socio-economic, cultural, and political factors strongly encouraged the establishment of national social work education programmes. In 1973, the professional body, the Malaysian Association of Social Workers (MASW), was formed. Its main objective is to promote and maintain standards of social work in Malaysia. MASW has made a major contribution towards the development of the first social work education programmes in Malaysia.

The first social work undergraduate programme in Malaysia began at the Universiti Sains Malaysia (USM) in 1975. It was established by the Ministry of Social Welfare following the 1968 United Nations Conference of Ministers Responsible for Social Welfare and advice of the United Nation Economic and Social Commission for Asia and the Pacific (UNESCAP), owing to a recognised need for more professionally trained social and community workers (Ali, 1988; Baba, 1992, 2002).

In its first four years, the USM programme selected students via a special intake programme for staff at the Ministry of Social Welfare. The programme was opened to the staff of other relevant ministries as well and began to take in baccalaureate students in 2011. The student population is relatively small, no more than sixty students per intake, along with ten places for special intake students. However, both a masters and doctoral degree in Social Work was introduced in 1975. USM became the social work training hub for the many local and regional social work educators, especially those serving the other six HEI's that offering social work degree and like many other programmes across the world, programmes are located in the social sciences to give it a rigorous disciplinary base (Gray et al., 2008; Parker, 2007).

In the 1980s, social problems, such as HIV/AIDS and substance misuse, emerged in the context of a shortage of trained government-employed social work staff necessitating the development of further social work programmes. The changing social situation also provided an important social indicator that Malaysia needed to develop better services for its people. This need contributed towards the development of new social work education programmes in Malaysia in the 1990s (Baba, 1992; Cho & Salleh, 1992). Between 1993 and 2002 seven HEIs introduced their own social work education programmes, primarily at bachelor level.

The Professionalisation of Social Work in Malaysia and Implications for Education

Schools of social work globally have based their social work education on the criteria developed by the International Association of Schools of Social Work that also allows indigenous interpretation and application (IFSW/IASSW, 2012). The international standards for social work education developed by IASSW have been instrumental in developing Malaysian social work education (IFSW/IASSW, 2012). Evaluation of programmes is normally based on the philosophy of social work education and the global social work education criteria as laid down by IASSW (Hokenhead & Kendall, 1995; International Federation of Social Workers/International Association of Schools of Social Work, 2012).

The MASW, social work educators, practitioners, government, and non-government agencies who are concerned about the future of professional social work in Malaysia have debated regulation, standards, and professionalisation for four decades (MASW, n.d.). In order to maintain its standards, MASW set down specific criteria for candidates seeking full membership. To be a full member a candidate requires a social work degree (undergraduate or graduate) from a recognised or accredited HEI or social work education programme. However, Malaysia does not yet have an accreditation body that scrutinises professional issues, such as accreditation, standards, quality, and needs. Since there is no implemented Social Workers Act in Malaysia, accreditation standards of social work education has been primarily left to each respective institution offering social work education. This has resulted in a drive towards standardisation which, at times, is accepted simply as a 'received' good or panacea. These developments require critique and analysis, however, and a commitment to adopting the best local traditions in the context of global standards if they are to be authentic to the Malaysian context rather than replicating what is accepted, and often unquestioned practice in other countries.

A degree-level qualification has been promoted reflecting normative convergent approaches across the world. Whilst this has been tempered in Malaysia to include volunteers and existing practitioners, it shows the need to standardise has been accepted tacitly at least and explicates some of the pressures of conformity that need to be debated and understood. UNICEF, JKM, and MASW have collaborated in promoting an accredited system of appropriate education, training and qualifications for social work, particularly in working with children population. The premise was that creating a system of qualifying education based around accepted international competencies for social workers would bring Malaysian social work into line with other systems around the world, would protect the public by licensing, regulating and professionalising practice and provide the best social work services, in the end, for all (Parker et al., 2016).

Understanding the context is important when considering standardisation and regulation. It demonstrates the different contexts in the UK and Malaysia. For instance, social work is poorly understood amongst the general public in Malaysia and many of those employed in social work posts are unqualified as a result. Social work education programmes in Malaysia vary across universities. Most Malaysian universities offering social work education focus on undergraduate social work, with the exception of two universities where a masters programme is offered through course work and research. The majority of undergraduate students are aged between 19 and 21 and have very little experience of life and there is a wish to increase numbers of mature students. Some programmes still lack lecturers who are qualified social workers which are assumed to affect the standards and quality of social work education in the university-setting and also in understanding the centrality of practice or field education. In 2010, the majority of social work educators in Malaysia had no formal training or professional experience in social work prior to entering HEIs (Baba, Ashencaen Crabtree, & Parker, 2011). There are high student/staff ratios, stretching staff capacity, which further affects the quality of social work education and research. For these reasons, Baba et al. (2011) argued that Malaysia needs a unified, strong professional body, such as a council on social work education but adapted to Malaysian needs and an accreditation body that can monitor quality and standards for the profession (Baba, 2002).

Previously, we suggested a number of areas which need attention if social work education in Malaysia is to move forward (Parker et al., 2016). However, these must be seen in the context of risks, dangers, and unintended consequences of uncritically accepting normative standards and positionalities and ignoring or reducing the centrality of local indigenised needs.

Consistent standards are needed to guide the development of social work education. Some universities have used IASSW guidelines, but this has not been ubiquitous and a professional accrediting body could help in ensuring consistency. It is important that Malaysia develops locally specific standards which accord with IASSW's global guidelines. The experiences of other countries continue to hold important resonances for Malaysia; but these experiences should be looked at critically and lessons learned where stultification and over-prescription have resulted from the desire to professionalise. The potential problems of isomorphic convergence are stark within this call and for Malaysian social work to continue to develop its unique aspects awareness and reflexivity are key.

Universities need to increase qualified social work teaching staff to meet future needs in social work education and reduce reliance on overseas postgraduate education by developing masters and doctorate level programmes nationally (Desai, 1991). This may help in developing teaching and research capacity that focuses on Malaysian issues.

A central role of the MASW will be to work towards the complex identification of specific social work roles and tasks. Universities need to lobby government and non-government agencies to hire more qualified social workers.

International and intra-national staff exchanges should be encouraged, particularly between more experienced social work education programmes and those that are newly established. This would encourage closer working partnerships across institutions and promote good practice in social work education.

Traditional emphases on respect and deference for rank and hierarchy may hamper the acquisition and promotion of critical thinking skills and challenging. However, the development of professionalised education demands a sceptical approach to standards and competences and recognises the potential for instrumental political control of social work services as opposed to human-focused, fluid, and intuitive practice wisdom. Importantly, whilst the colonial legacy cannot all be seen in a negative light, Malaysia must develop its own unique approaches to social work education in the context of a post-colonial legacy and the development of global structures (Hew & Ashencaen Crabtree, 2012). Midgely (1990) condemned the transference of Western social work models, particularly US ones, to developing countries as a form of cultural imperialism. There has since been a body of literature discussing the question of the incongruence between the so-called Western focus on the cult of the individual as opposed to the interdependency and collective perspective prevalent in Asian societies (Fulcher, 2003; Ling, 2004; Ngai, 1996; Tsang, 1997, 2001).

Two particular social work paradigms have been identified as having emerged in countries of the Global South in order to meet local needs and thus diverge from the US-British models. These are 'indigenisation', which has adapted Westernised models to fit the local context, and 'authenticisation', which is fundamentally grounded in the cultural schema and knowledge base of ethnic groups (Ling, 2007). Due to the hegemony of professional literature, which continues to be dominated by Western authors and publishers, both indigenisation and authenticisation are primarily grass-roots phenomena, rather than regularly debated and analysed in social work curricula within developing countries (Ashencaen Crabtree, 2008; Parker et al., 2016).

Given the transitional state of social work education in Malaysia and the sociopolitical context in which it is practised, there are many challenges, but also many opportunities. Importantly, social work education and social work practice should reflect an authentic and appropriately indigenised approach befitting Malaysian society and its contemporary context.

Isomorphic Convergences and a Post-colonial Lens: Re-imaging Social Work Education Futures

The UK has a history as an exporter-coloniser in social work education whilst Malaysia's history is of an importer-colonised position. This has influenced the development and trajectory of social work education in each country respectively as we have seen above. Also, the historical needs to be set within the global turn; the drive towards internationalisation in professional and organisational matters in social work that has a rich and complex history from the early twentieth century onwards. It is important to recognise that practices are exported laden with values that may influence the construction of standards that assume policy or even quasi-legal and legal status. These are interpreted through the value lens of the importer country which may be influenced by assumptions of normalcy and 'rightness'. These values require exposure so that normative and mimetic forces can be seen and questioned for their appropriateness to the country wishing to adopt such education practices. For instance, moves towards professionalisation in Malaysian social work education and practice have sought to adapt a competence-based approach to assessment which builds upon Western normative practice which itself is fraught with questions and resistance. Asking the question 'why' we may want to do this is important if we are to remove modern-day professional imperialism and ensure adaptation to local circumstances.

Where there are such standards that must be complied with it is also imperative that social work, as a reflexive practice, interrogates the rationale behind them and challenges when they fail to meet needs. Social workers in the UK have a responsibility not to present practices simply as something to be copied, parrot-fashion but to be offered and adapted and the underlying normative discourses continually questioned. In Malaysia, questions of indigenity and authenticity are paramount.

Being aware of the underlying discourses that affect the assumptions we make of what is appropriate in social work education is important if we are to guard against a neo-colonial orthodoxy and to preserve a developing authenticity in both importer and exporter countries. Reflexivity, continual questioning of ourselves and our assumptions may also protect education from Merton's laws of unintended consequences that require us to consider whether we have adequate knowledge of the impact of adopting and adapting our social work education practices; to question potential errors of judgement; to consider long as well as short-term aspects in planning; to question normative and prescriptive demands and their consequences; and to recognise how predicting future practices and behaviours may set the conditions for that future.

Indeed, Merton's laws may help UK social work educators to challenge the unthinking politicisation of social work education that has potentially damaged its quality and adequacy. We must resist the political errors in re-positioning power towards employers who are, in the main, part of the state apparatus and therefore fundamentally politicised in their policies, guidance, and practice. The longer-term implications of changes in social work education have led to a focus on safeguarding practices and a rejection of the campaigning aspects of social work and education and service provision are now attuned to this residual approach. Recognising these problems and resisting them may help guard against an unquestioning adoption of assumed 'good' practices and a clear focus on the appropriateness and authenticity of social work education in all countries.

REFERENCES

Ali, S. H. (1988). *Social work education in Malaysia*. Paper presented at Seminar on Social Work Education in the Asian and Pacific Region. Organized by Sociology Department of Peking University, Beijing, China.

Ashencaen Crabtree, S. (2008). Dilemmas in international social work education in the United Arab Emirates: Islam, localization and social need. *Social Work Education, 27*(5), 536–548.

Baba, I. (1992). Social work: An effort towards building a caring society. In C. K. Sin & I. M. Salleh (Eds.), *Caring society: Emerging issues and future directions* (pp. 509–529). Kuala Lumpur, Malaysia: ISIS.

Baba, I. (1998, November 16–17). *The need for professionalism of social work in Malaysia*. A report on advancing social work education. Organized by Faculty of Social Sciences, Universiti Malaysia Sarawak.

Baba, I. (2002, January 17–18). *A report: The establishment of council on social work Malaysia. A first round-table meeting at the School of Social Sciences*. Universiti Sains Malaysia.

Baba, I., Ashencaen Crabtree, S., & Parker, J. (2011). Future indicative, past imperfect: A cross cultural comparison of social work education in Malaysia and England. In S. Stanley (Ed.), *Social work education in countries of the East: Issues and challenges* (pp. 276–301). New York: Nova.

Balls, E. (2008, December 1). Baby P: Ed Ball's statement in full. *The Guardian*. Available at https://www.theguardian.com/society/2008/dec/01/baby-p-ed-balls-statement. Accessed September, 2017.

Baron, S., & McLaughlin, H. (2017). Grand challenges: A way forward for social work? *Social Work Education, 36*(1), 1–5.

BASW. (2003). *The national occupational standards for social work*. Retrieved from https://www.basw.co.uk/resources/national-occupational-standards-social-work. Accessed July 4, 2019.

BASW. (2018). *Professional capabilities framework (PCF)*. Avaiable at https://www.basw.co.uk/social-work-training/professional-capabilities-framework-pcf.

Blom, B., & Morén, S. (2019). *Theory for social work practice*. Lund: Studentlitteratur AB.

Bourdieu, P. (1977). *Outline of a theory of practice*. Cambridge: Cambridge University Press.

Bourdieu, P., & Wacquant, L. J. D. (1992). *An invitation to reflexive sociology*. Chicago: University of Chicago Press.

Cho, K. S., & IM, Salleh. (1992). *Caring society: Emerging issues and future directions*. ISIS: Kuala Lumpur, Malaysia.

Croisdale-Appleby, D. (2014). *Re-visioning social work education: An independent review*. Available at https://www.gov.uk/government/uploads/system/uploads/attachment_data/file/285788/DCA_Accessible.pdf.

Department for Education. (2010). *Building a safe and confident future: One year on*. Detailed proposals from the Social Work Reform Board. Available at https://www.gov.uk/government/uploads/system/uploads/attachment_data/file/180787/DFE-00602-2010-1.pdf. Accessed August 2017.

Department for Education. (2012). *Building a safe and confident future: Maintaining momentum*. Progress report from the Social Work Reform Board. Available at https://www.gov.uk/government/uploads/system/uploads/attachment_data/file/175947/SWRB_progress_report_-_June_2012.pdf. Accessed August 2017.

Department of Education. (2014). *Knowledge and skills statements for child and family social work.* Available at https://www.gov.uk/government/publications/knowledge-and-skills-statements-for-child-and-family-social-work. Accessed September 6, 2016.

Department of Health. (2015). *Knowledge and skills for social workers in adult services.* Available at https://www.gov.uk/government/uploads/system/uploads/attachment_data/file/441643/Children_Act_Guidance_2015.pdf. Accessed October 9, 16.

Desai, A. S. (1991). Report of the academic assessor to the Social Development and Administration (SDA) Program, School of Social Sciences, Universiti Sains Malaysia, Octobr 27–November 2.

DiMaggio, P. J., & Powell, W. W. (1983). The iron cage revisited: Institutional isomorphism and collective rationality in organizational fields. *American Sociological Review, 48*(2), 147–160.

Evaluation of Social Work Degree Qualification in England Team. (2008). *Evaluation of the new social work degree qualification in England. Volume 1: Finding.* London: King' College London, Social Care Workforce Research Unit.

Fletcher, J. (1966). *Situation ethics: The new morality.* Louisville Kentucky: Westminster John Knox Press.

Frampton, M. (2018). *European and internatioanl social work: Ein Lehrbuch.* Weinheim Basel: Beltz Juventa.

Fulcher, L. (2003). The working definition of social work doesn't work very well in China and Malaysia. *Research on Social Work Practice, 13*(3), 376–387.

Gray, M., Coates, J., & Yellow Bird, M. (Eds.). (2010). *Indigenous social work around the world: Towards culturally relevant education and practice.* Abingdon: Ashgate.

Gray, M., Coates, J., Yellow Bird, M., & Hetherington, T. (Eds.). (2013). *Decolonising social work.* Abingdon: Ashgate.

Gray, I., Parker, J., & Immins, T. (2008). Leading communities of practice in social work: Groupwork or management? *Groupwork, 18*(2), 26–40.

HCPC. (2012). *Standards of proficiency for social workers in England.* Available at http://www.hpc-uk.org/assets/documents/10003b08standardsofproficiency-socialworkersinengland.pdf.

Hew, C. S., & Ashencaen Crabtree, S. (2012). The Islamic resurgence in Malaysia and the implications for multiculturalism. In S. Ashencaen Crabtree, J. Parker, & A. Azman (Eds.), *The cup, the gun and the crescent: Social welfare and civil unrest in Muslim societies* (pp. 82–100). London: Whiting & Birch.

Higgins, M. (2016). How has the professional capabilities framework changed social work education and practice in England. *British Journal of Social Work, 46*(8), 1981–1996.

Higgins, M., & Goodyer, A. (2015). The contradictions of contemporary social work: An ironic response. *British Journal of Social Work, 45*(4), 747–760.

Hokenhead, M. C., & Kendall, K. A. (1995). International social work education. In *Encyclopedia of Social Work* (19th Ed., pp. 1511–1527). Washington, DC: NASW Press.

Hugman, R. (2010). *Understanding international social work.* Basingstoke: Palgrave MacMillan.

Hutchings, A., & Taylor, I. (2007). Defining the profession? Exploring an international definition of social work in the China context. *International Journal of Social Welfare, 16*(4), 383–390.

IFSW (International Association of Schools of Social Work and International Federation of Social Workers). (2014). *Global definition of social work.* Available at http://ifsw.org/get-involved/global-definition-of-social-work/. Accessed June 6, 2016.

International Federation of Social Workers/International Association of Schools of Social Work (IFSW/IASSW). (2012). *Global standards for the education and training of the social work profession.* Available at http://ifsw.org/policies/global-standards/. Accessed June 6, 2016.

Jones, K. (2006). *The making of social policy in Britain: From the Poor Law to New Labour.* London and New York: Continuum.

Jones, R. (2014). *The story of Baby P: Setting the record straight.* Bristol: Policy Press.

Jordan, B., & Drakeford, M. (2012). *Social work and social policy under austerity.* Basingstoke: Palgrave Macmillan.

Ling, H. K. (2004). The search from within: Research issues in relation to developing culturally appropriate social work practice. *International Social Work, 47*(3), 336–345.

Ling, H. K. (2007). *Indigenising social work: Research and practice in Sarawak.* Selangor: Strategic Information and Research Development Centre.

Mair, L. P. (1944). *Welfare in the British colonies.* Great Britain: The Broadwater Press.

MASW. (n.d.). *History of Social Workers Act.* Accessed at www.masw.org.my/images/socailact.html. Accessed March 24, 2015.

Maxwell, N., Scourfield, J., Zhang, M. L., de Villiers, T., Hadfield, M., Kinnersley, P., ... Tayyaba, S. (2016, March). *Independent evaluation of the Frontline pilot: Research report.* London: Department for Education. Available at https://assets.publishing.service.gov.uk/government/uploads/system/uploads/attachment_data/file/560885/Evaluation_of_Frontline_pilot.pdf. Accessed October 1, 2017.

Midgely, J. (1990). International social work: Learning from the Third World. *Social Work, 35*(4), 295–299.

Narey, M. (2014). *Making the education of social workers consistently effective: Report of Sir Martin Narey's independent review of the education of children's social workers.* Available at https://www.gov.uk/government/uploads/system/uploads/attachment_data/file/287756/Making_the_education_of_social_workers_consistently_effective.pdf.

Ngai, N.-P. (1996). Revival of social work education in China. *International Social Work, 36*(2), 289–300.

Nussbaum, M. (2011). *Creating capabilities: The human development approach.* Harvard: Harvard University Press.

Parker, J. (2005). Social work education and palliative care. In J. Parker (Ed.), *Aspects of social work and palliative care.* London: Quay Books.

Parker, J. (2007). Developing effective practice learning for tomorrow's social workers. *Social Work Education, 26*(8), 763–779.

Parker, J. (2017). *Social work practice* (5th ed.). London: Sage.

Parker, J. (2019). Descent or dissent? A future of social work education in the UK post-Brexit. *European Journal of Social Work,*. https://doi.org/10.1080/13691457.2019.1578733.

Parker, J., & Ashencaen Crabtree, S. (2018a). *Social work with disadvantaged and marginalised people.* London: Sage.

Parker, J., & Ashencaen Crabtree, S. (2018b). Wisdom and skills in social work education: Promoting critical relational social work through ethnographic practice. *Relational Social Work, 2*(1), 13–29. https://doi.org/10.14605/rsw211802.

Parker, J., Ashencaen Crabtree, S., & Azman, A. (2016). Treading the long path: Social work education in Malaysia. In I. Taylor, M. Bogo, M. Lefevre, & B. Teater (Eds.) *The Routledge international handbook of social work education* (pp. 84–95). London and New York: Routledge.

Parker, J., Ashencaen Crabtree, S., Azman, A., Carlo, D. P., & Cutler, C. (2014). Problematising international placements as a site of intercultural learning. *European Journal of Social Work, 18*(3), 383–396.

Sen, A. (1999). *Development as freedom.* Oxford: Oxford University Press.

Shoesmith, S. (2016). *Learning from Baby P.* London: Jessica Kingsley.

Smith, R., Stepanova, E., Venn, L., Carpenter, J., & Patsios, D. (2018, May). *Evaluation of step up to social work, cohorts 1 and 2: 3-years and 5-years on research report.* London: Department for Education. Available at https://assets.publishing.service.gov.uk/government/uploads/system/uploads/attachment_data/file/707085/Step_Up_to_Social_Work_evaluation-3_and_5_years_on.pdf. Accessed October 2, 2018.

Social Work Task Force. (2009). *Building a safe confident future.* London: Department of Health/Department for Children, Schools and Families.

Tsang, N. M. (1997). Examining the cultural dimension of social work practice: The experience of teaching students on a social work course. *International Social Work, 40*(1), 133–144.

Tsang, A. K. T. (2001). Representation of ethnic identity in North American social work literature: A dossier of the Chinese people. *Social Work, 46*(3), 229–243.

CHAPTER 41

Social Work Transformation—National and International Dimensions: The Case of Russia

Olga I. Borodkina

INTRODUCTION

Social work has been called an institution closely linked to social policy (Colby, Dulmus, & Sowers, 2018; Green & Clarke, 2016). Sociopolitical transformations in Russia have greatly influenced the development of social work. One of the main contradictions lies in the preservation of paternalistic expectations of a large part of the population of Russia and neoliberal reforms that are carried out in an opaque way. The influence of the social policy of the Soviet Union remains quite strong in the post-Soviet period primarily when it comes to public opinion, expectations of the population, and the administrative structure of the social service system. This is happening against a background of increasing social inequality and at a time when the principles of social justice are being ignored. All this undoubtedly has an impact on the development of social work in Russia. The development of social work can only be understood by considering the sociopolitical context of ongoing social reforms in greater detail.

Russian social policy after the collapse of the Soviet Union underwent many reforms characterised by internal contradictions. The current stage of social policy is also characterised by significant contradictions such as Russian social policy, despite being aimed at social protection, has increased social and economic disparities and as a result social policy no longer fulfils the social security function. According to Russian official statistics the portion of poor

O. I. Borodkina (✉)
Saint Petersburg University, Saint Petersburg, Russian Federation

S. S. M. et al. (eds.), *The Palgrave Handbook of Global Social Work Education*, https://doi.org/10.1007/978-3-030-39966-5_41

households in 2014 was 41.1%, in 2015 47.1%, in 2016 48.7%, and in 2017 48.5% (Federal Statistic, 2019). Russia belongs to a group of countries where inequality is rife. Experts evaluate that 10% of the population own 65% of all wealth and 1% of the population owns almost half the country's wealth (Udin, 2019); hence the issue of social justice is particularly sensitive with the Russian population. Such a situation is much more than just a consequence of Russian society being transitional, it is also connected with the global trend of neoliberalisation of social policy and social work (Collier, 2011). Moreover, in many respects Russia is at the forefront of this trend that is transforming the social state.

Development of Social Work in Russia

In Russia the professional qualification of social worker was introduced in 1991, though different kinds of social service activities certainly existed before then. At the time of the Soviets there was a state social support system for the most vulnerable segments of the population such as the elderly, the disabled, and orphans. Moreover, social support was rigidly regulated by the state, the types of social assistance were limited, and basic support was all that was provided.

Development of the Russian system of social work occurred at the same time as a new social and economic system was created in Russia. At the beginning of the 1990s the primary task of social work was providing emergency help to citizens whose lives teetered on the edge of existence following disintegration of the Soviet Union and the transition of Russia into a market economy. At that time poverty, unemployment, and the breakdown in social relations were the problems that social work faced.

In the 1990s social work sought recognition as a scientific discipline that had a professional identity and as a result became established as an institution. One of the most important tasks that faced social work was the training of professional social workers. Since 1995 many Russian universities have offered educational programmes in social work. In the early 2000s the educational and methodological association of Russian universities providing training in social work included more than 120 universities and state educational standards had been developed according to which students were trained in different programmes such as specialists, Bachelors, and Masters (Starshinova, 2004). Russian universities also offered training programmes for social workers that were widespread in Western countries. At the same time intensive collaboration between Russian and European universities as well as Russian and US social agencies within the framework of social and educational programmes designed to help the process of social and economic reforms in partner countries helped to develop social work education in Russian higher education institutions. Russian universities in Moscow, St Petersburg, Saratov, Tomsk, Petrozavodsk, Arkhangelsk, Ekaterinburg, and other cities got involved in such programmes as the Trans-European Mobility Programme for University Studies (TEMPUS) and Technical Assistance for the Commonwealth of Independent States (TACIS) aimed at developing social work curricular and field educational programmes. However, there were always significant discrepancies not only between regions but also between those high schools involved in international cooperation and those that were not (Penn, 2007, p. 525). Many professionals critically assessed the TEMPUS programme as a one-way model of international knowledge transfer in which European partners were not sufficiently sensitive to the social and cultural context in Russia (Penn, 2007). Such programmes were not helpful in overcoming core shortcomings in the system of social work education. University courses were predominantly theory based and practical placement was not given sufficient priority and emphasis to prepare students for social work (Borodkina, 2015).

Since the beginning of the 1990s there has been systematic research into the theory and history of social work, social administration, and methods of providing assistance to different client groups. International influences on Russian social work have taken on rather specific forms whose characteristics are identified in what follows.

In the 1990s the theory of social work in Russia developed mostly under the influence of international social work. As a consequence Russian professionals understood social work methods and approaches such as crisis intervention, social casework, community work, and the task-centred approach through American models. For many years there was a significant gap between the theory and practice of Russian social work. However, practice in the late 20th and early twenty-first centuries underwent considerable changes as a result of the influence of international knowledge. These changes did not occur along normal lines such as from theory to practice or from practice to practice. Instead, social service international organisations came to Russia and significantly changed the practice of social work. Social work was introduced to client groups who were previously considered marginal and were treated solely as medical patients or offenders such as drug and alcohol users, homeless people, and people living with HIV (Borodkina, 2015).

Modern trends in social work education are related to the Bologna Process that created the European Higher Education Area based on uniform standards and quality of higher education qualifications. Russia joined the Bologna Process in 2003. This led in recent years to the active development of Bachelor programmes (4 years) and Master of social work programmes (2 years) in Russian universities the number of which is growing. Moreover, 5-year specialist of social work programmes that used to be traditional of the Russian higher education system became a thing of the past. Russia joining the Bologna Process gave new impetus to the modernisation of higher professional education and provided additional possibilities for academic mobility and the development of joint educational programmes in social work (Borodkina, 2015). However, some scholars still believe that Russia has entered the process of international education without taking into account the specifics of traditional Russian higher education and without thorough analysis of the consequences of transitioning to an international two-tier system of education (Bachelor and Master) including international academic mobility and the credit system (Kupriyanov, Vilensky, & Kupriyanova, 2014). At the same time joining the Bologna Process created the conditions necessary for Russian social work education to be integrated into the European system.

Modern trends in social work education are associated with professionalisation (i.e., the orientation of curricula with the professional needs of social work). In Russia contemporary social work education is based on so-called professional standards that reflect requirements needed for the professional competence of workers and regulate social work education programmes. Professional standards have been accepted as a way of integrating education systems with the labor market and of connecting social work theory with practice. However, although professionalisation and standardisation have now changed the social work educational system, they have not significantly affected the labour market. Social work is still not attractive to young people because of a number of issues such as poor social status, relatively low wages, high workload, and the robust way in which social work practice is administered. This has brought about a situation in which university graduates in social work end up being employed in completely different areas such as tourism, trade, and hospitality—a situation that is unfortunately quite typical of Russia.

Neoliberal Issues in Russian Social Policy and Social Work

The development of neoliberalism has been highly influential in making contemporary social work so essential. Neoliberalism and its effects on social work have been the focus of scientific research and the neoliberal restructuring of social security and social services has been widely discussed in recent years (Clarke, 2008; Ferguson, 2004; Garrett, 2008; Harvey, 2005; Pollack, 2010; Stark, 2008; Wacquant, 2009). Neoliberalism has come to be used in a wide variety of ways. For example, Garrett (2019) highlighted six main neoliberalist dimensions: the overturning of embedded liberalism; reconfiguration of the state to better serve the interests of capital; new patterns of income and wealth distribution to benefit the rich and superrich; insecurity and precariousness; the increase in mass incarceration; and strategic pragmatism.

The first crucial thesis that needs to be made about the common theoretical approach to neoliberalism is that in different countries neoliberal ideas are implemented in different ways. In other words, implementation of the global trend toward neoliberal reforms in social policy has distinct national characteristics. It should be mentioned that Russian authorities hardly ever refer to neoliberalism when they talk about reforms in the social sphere since neoliberalism, especially in the last decade, has a negative connotation. This is largely the result of liberal economic reforms carried out in Russia in the early 1990s that led to a significant drop in the standard of living of a significant part of the population—a drop that continues to increase to this day.

Institutions responsible for social policy should ensure the distribution of benefits that accrue from the development of a market economy is equitable such that the expectations of the population connect with their belief in having a strong state as an institute of social justice. Unfortunately, Russian social policy only nominally fulfils these functions of social security and social justice. Moreover, insecurity both social and economic has become one of the most common characteristics of Russian life. There are a number of reasons for the big differences between Russia and most European states. First, a contemporary developed state presupposes one in which there are legal solutions to controversial social conflicts including social work if necessary (Borodkina, 2019). Laws and legal norms in Russia are frequently violated in all spheres of life such as when the government passes laws that directly violate the interests of most of the population (e.g., Russian retirement reform in 2018) or social laws that do not have a practical mechanism for their enforcement. Second, a modern economic developed state presupposes one in which there is a democratic society whose civil society is strong. When liberal ideas were imported to Russia in the early 1990s much of the effort went into bringing about economic liberalism and little into liberalism itself (i.e., democracy and political liberalism were not engaged in a proper way). This has resulted in political freedom being significantly reduced in recent years. Such processes have had a direct impact on social policy and social work since civil society cannot be strong without political freedoms—and civil society is key to modern social policy and social work. The impact all of this has had on attempts to reform the social work system in Russia has been significant.

A significant characteristic of the neoliberal model of social work is considered to be reduction of the role played by the state. On this point we agree with Foucault who believed that neoliberal "state intervention is no less dense, frequent, active and continuous than in any other system" (Foucault, 2008, p. 145). However, although this activity in most Western countries was partly aimed at remaking or reconstituting the state such that it became more vigilant and active in promoting a market economy (Garrett, 2018), such activity in Russia witnessed the reconstruction of state social service organisations and the development of social non-governmental organisations (NGOs) strongly affiliated with the state and existing under its control. A particular model of social policy and social work is currently being developed in Russia that mixes certain features of neoliberalism aimed at reducing the role played by the state in social protection with the strengthening of state control.

Neoliberal trends generally deal with the transfer of market, business principle, and management tools from the private sector to the public sector including social work. Changing the role played by the state involves three important processes "marketisation, managerialism and consumerism"

(Harris, 2014) that qualify neoliberalism in social work. These three processes manifest themselves in unique ways in Russia.

(1) *Marketisation* involves creating a social services market and primarily implies development of the non-state sector in the provision of social services—a key characteristic of contemporary social work practice in most countries. Consequently, the social service system has become more flexible in that the social support and social services provided by state, NGO, and business organisations are much more variable in form. Although this process is also taking place in Russia, it reflects the main contradiction of Russia's social policy: the attempt to liberalize social work from strong state control (Borodkina, 2015).

In 2013 a legal base for developing the third sector in Russian social work was enacted by adoption of a law titled "On the fundamentals of social services in the Russian Federation" (28 December 2013). The law gave NGOs equal rights with state and municipal organisations to access state contracts for the provision of social services. Moreover, socially orientated NGOs were able to get state subsidies and grants for their activities. Amendments were made to the legislation to ensure equal conditions applied when accessing budget financing and, in particular, a register of social service providers was created made up of state and socially orientated NGOs providing social services to the population. Since joining this register was voluntary, it was not necessary for all NGOs acting in the social sphere to be registered as service providers. Russian authorities considered the register to be a mechanism to create competition in the market of social services that would lead to increasing the quality of these services. This register allowed social services provided by the state and NGOs to be compared in accordance with state standards, although inclusion on the register was not a guarantee of receiving funding. For example, in Moscow—the capital and largest city in Russia with a population of 11.92 million—more than 180 organisations are currently included on the register of suppliers more than 50 of which are NGOs (Why not all NGOs strive to get into the register of social service providers, 2019).

NGOs were allowed to be established in Russia after a law titled "The concept of long-term social and economic development of the Russian Federation for the period up to 2020" was enacted in 2008 in which getting NGOs involved in social services was considered a top priority. Implementation of this policy involved

transformation of the majority of state and municipal institutions of the social protection system that provide services to the elderly and disabled into non-profit organizations and creation of a mechanism for attracting them on a competitive basis to fulfill the state order for the provision of social services; ensuring equal conditions for taxation of providers of social services of various organizational and legal forms; reducing administrative barriers in the sphere of activity of non-governmental non-profit organizations; creation of a transparent and competitive system of state support for non-state non-profit organizations that provide social services to the population; implementation by government and local governments of programs to support the development of non-governmental non-profit organizations; reducing administrative barriers in the sphere of non-profit organizations; introducing tax preferences for non-state non-profit organizations. (The concept of long-term social and economic development of the Russian Federation for the period up to 2020, 2008, p. 70)

A major issue faced by NGOs is that they are often unable to compete with former state and municipal organisations because the latter are given strong administrative support by authorities. Another major problem is that the register rarely if ever selects small organizations providing only a few services; hence large and diverse organisations are usually selected. Such a situation makes competitive access difficult and diminishes the potential use of NGOs in particular cases. Although NGOs can get funding, they are currently reluctant to register. A number of reasons are given for this decision by the heads of organisations: (1) low state rates for social services that do not cover the expenses of NGOs; (2) NGOs have different reporting requirements than those of state organisations; (3) all manner of controls applied to organisation activities. An employee of one NGO said, "We have not provided any services yet, and there is already a huge queue of inspectors" (Why not all NGOs strive to get into the register of social service providers, 2019).

Nevertheless, the register of social service providers gives those services already regulated by law a chance to enter the market. However, this is often deemed a weak point of this system since experts say it is difficult to fit an individual and flexible approach reflecting the real needs of citizens into the standard. In other words, state social service standards very often do not meet people's needs. Therefore, NGOs should lobby the authorities to revise the register and standards, to make standards more flexible, to allow NGOs some leeway to make changes, and in particular to enable the most successful and popular projects to become social services.

A significant barrier to the development of a market providing social services is that the procedures for registration, regular reporting, and liquidation of NGOs are not only under the control of the Ministry of Justice but they are also quite complicated. On the one hand, the state declares its support for work to be undertaken by socially orientated NGOs while, on the other hand, a number of laws and legal norms have been adopted that make the process of creating and developing NGOs very difficult.

The most controversial widely discussed law dealing with NGOs is the so-called "Law on Foreign Agents." According to this law

a non-profit organization performing the functions of a foreign agent is understood as a Russian non-profit organization that receives money and other property from foreign states, their state bodies, international and foreign organizations, foreign citizens, stateless persons or persons authorized by them and (or) from Russian legal entities... receiving money and other property from these sources (except for open joint-stock companies with state participation and their subsidiaries) (hereinafter referred to as foreign sources), and which participates, including in the interests of foreign sources, in political activities carried out on the territory of the Russian Federation. (Federal Law 121-FL, 2012).

In other words, NGOs that receive funding from abroad in any form such as grants or sponsorships and engage in political activities are registered by the Ministry of Justice as foreign agents. Registration by itself does not mean cessation of the work carried out by such organisations, but it does discriminate against them in other ways by swamping them with paperwork, maintaining permanent control over them, making them overcome barriers to get funding, etc. In addition, uncertainty surrounding political activities allows authorities to consider any organisations whose activities are not approved by the current government as foreign agents. Altogether this creates obstacles to development of a market providing social services. Analysing development of the private sector in the country Borodkina (2015) noted:

> There is a limitation of competition in the social sphere and particularly in terms of creation of the real market of social services. In many respects this can be explained by officials striving to keep the sphere of social services and budget financing under control. Therefore, at the present time, as it was before, the providers of social services are mostly state and municipal organizations. The policy of high-pressure control over the activities of non-commercial organizations has been carried out by the state authorities. This policy seriously restricts the private initiative and development of non-governmental organizations (NGOs).

The situation has not changed dramatically in the last 5 years with the development of a market providing social services strongly controlled by the state. Despite new legislation, state and private partnerships have not yet been properly developed in the public sector.

(2) *Managerialism* is the second key characteristic associated with neoliberalism. It presupposes the models of administration, management, and delivery of social services are reformed by transferring business and market principles and techniques of management to the public sector (Pollitt & Bouckaert, 2011). In the 1980s the managerialism that developed in West European countries and the United States—connected with the concept of new public management—was an attempt to revise welfare state policies that were under pressure as a result of having to face economic, social, and demographic challenges. Later new approaches such as new public administration (Bourgon, 2009)

and new public governance (Osborne, 2006) were developed focussing on citizens as key social actors looking after the public interest.

Although changes to the administration and management of social work began later in Russia, it was mainly connected with restructuring the whole society in the 1990s. Moreover, much as was the case in other countries it was based on neoliberalism that included reducing the role of the state and transitioning business management models to the public sector to make the social service system more efficient. As a consequence of these reforms in social work new indicators aimed at reducing costs, new forms of measurability of social work, and new ways of monitoring and evaluating the activities of social workers were introduced. Mechanisms of management such as quality control and outsourcing were widely implemented in the public sector including in social work. However, the most important markers of a neoliberal agenda and managerialism such as decentralisation and transparency were not appropriately brought about in Russian social work. Social work in Russia is still somewhat closed to public scrutiny, although certain transparency instruments are being implemented (e.g., posting reports on the websites of organisations). However, they do not play a crucial role and are little more than decorative. When it came to decentralisation only a single major step was taken involving the transfer of administrative powers from the federal to the regional level. This was followed by an increase in state control and construction of a rigid power hierarchy that included the social service sphere.

Despite ongoing managerial reforms in Russia the effectiveness of the social service system is still a major issue. The existing system of social support for the population in Russia is complex, not transparent, and not well managed. In Russia there are many social programmes administered by different departments who are very often uncoordinated. It is difficult to estimate the cost of some programmes. According to experts there are currently 800 forms of social support at the federal level and an average of a further 100 in each Russian region. Sometimes federal and regional benefits intersect and in some regions this is exacerbated by there being a unitary register of recipients (Borodkina, 2019; Nazarov & Posharatz, 2017).

(3) *Consumerism* presupposes being orientated at clients/consumers. It means being able to choose a social service and a social service provider. Certain aspects of consumerism can be seen in social work practice in the country. The essential changes necessary to bring this about have to do with the federal law "On the Fundamentals of Social Services for Citizens in the Russian Federation." The law was enacted in 2013 and entered into practice in January 2015. The main reason for enacting this law was the need to make social services more cost-effective and to improve the quality of social services. The law establishes a new relationship between state and private organisations

on the basis of a social contract. In addition, the law changes the role of client since it introduces the concept of a "social service recipient" with the right to choose a provider of social services. Such a statement allows experts to conclude that "thus, clients of social work should not be understood anymore as passive recipients of social help, but as agents capable of making choices and being responsible for their own life situation" (Smirnova & Poluektova, 2018). This is a premature conclusion since the law creates a legal basis for clients of social services to engage in such activity while in practice they do not have this choice. Moreover, most recipients of social services are not ready to take responsibility for their social wellbeing as assumed by the new social policy. Paternalistic attitudes are still rather strong in Russia with most citizens believing the state has primary responsibility for their wellbeing. This attitude contrasts sharply with the current neoliberal tendency in social policy associated with strengthening individual responsibility. Current social work practice does not empower clients in any substantial way (Borodkina, Törrönen, & Samoylova, 2013).

Another important matter is that this law strictly defines who qualifies as being in need of social services. The law argues that Russian citizens feel their standard of living depends on many factors:

> (1) total or partial loss of ability or ability to provide self-care, to move independently, to provide basic necessities of life due to illness, injury, age or disability; (2) the presence in the family of a disabled person or persons with disabilities, including a disabled child or children with disabilities who need constant outside care; (3) the presence of a child or children (including those under guardianship) experiencing difficulties in social adaptation; (4) absence of possibility of providing care (including temporary) for the disabled person, the child, children, and also absence of care over them; (5) the presence of intra-family conflict, including with persons with drug or alcohol addiction, persons addicted to gambling, persons suffering from mental disorders, the presence of violence in the family; (6) the absence of a certain place of residence, including a person who has not reached the age of twenty-three years and completed his stay in the organization for orphans and children left without parental care; (7) lack of employment and livelihood; (8) existence of other circumstances which by regulatory legal acts of the subject of the Russian Federation are recognized [as] worsening or capable [of worsening the] conditions of activity of citizens. (Federal Law 442-FL, 2013)

According to the law a citizen must apply to the authorised organisation tasked with taking the decision whether the citizen is in need of social services or not within five working days from the date the application was submitted. Legal regulations like these make it difficult to recognise those in need. In other words, not all citizens who feel they need social support get it. This gap is partly covered by NGOs that provide assistance to citizens on their own terms, while not expecting state funding. In other words, while the state proclaims it is orientated toward the needs of the citizen, the citizen's rights as a potential recipient of social services are limited.

CONCLUSION

From this chapter's analysis of social work in Russia it is possible to conclude there is strong international influence on higher education and social work practice. Main global trends occurring in the development of social work are also taking place in Russia. Neoliberalism is critical to the contemporary concepts of social policy and social work. The rationality behind neoliberalism "reaches beyond the market, extending and disseminating market values to all institutions and social action so that individuals are conceptualized as rational, entrepreneurial actors whose moral authority is determined by their capacity for autonomy and self-care" (Baker, 2009, p. 277). In Russia as in many other countries there has recently been a tendency to rationalise resources and allow the private sector to manage the social state. The social state is understood as meaning a situation that provides minimum guarantees of social protection against the basic risks of a market economy. Managerial ideas stemming from neoliberalism such as the possibility of choosing a social service provider, increasing the professionalisation and skill sets of social workers, and strengthening the accountability of social service providers have had a significant impact on social work practice. Moreover, transitioning from a paternalistic model to a partnership model of social work between the state, private sector, and citizens has come up against a number of barriers in Russia because the paternalistic expectations of citizens are still strong, local community resources are limited, and social work fails in its efforts to empower consumers of social services.

Transformation of the welfare state and changes made to social work institutes in Russia have occurred relatively recently and are ongoing. Social policy in the country today presupposes developing a market providing social services in which NGOs and social entrepreneurs play major roles. Nevertheless, it has not led to reducing the role played by the state in the provision of social services primarily as a result of strong state control, bureaucracy, and a civil society that is weak. In general, contemporary Russian social policy is understood as inconsistent and dichotomous by experts and as unfair by much of the population. Moreover, all the contradictions of social policy clearly manifest themselves in social work.

Acknowledgements The research was conducted at St Petersburg University with the support of the Russian Science Foundation under project No. 19-18-00246 "Challenges of the transformation of welfare state in Russia: institutional changes, social investment, digitalization of social services."

REFERENCES

Baker, J. (2009). Young mothers in late modernity: Sacrifice, respectability and the transformation of the neoliberal subject. *Journal of Youth Studies, 12*(3), 275–288.

Borodkina, O. (2015). International trends in Russian. *European Journal of Social Work, 18*(4), 631–644. https://doi.org/10.1080/13691457.2015.1049588.

Borodkina, O. (2019). Social policy and social work under pressure in Russia. In K. Dunn & J. Fischer (Eds.), *Social work and social policy in the era of right-wing populism* (pp. 99–114). Opladen: Verlag Barbara Budrich.

Borodkina, O., Törrönen, M., & Samoylova, V. (2013). Empowerment as a current trend of social work in Russia. In M. Törrönen, O. Borodkina, V. Samoylova, & E. Heino (Eds.), *Empowering social work: Research & practice* (pp. 22–35). Helsinki: University of Helsinki, Kotka Unit Kopijyva Oy.

Bourgon, J. (2009). New Directions in public administration: Serving beyond the predictable public policy and administration. *Public Money & Management, 29*(1), 3–5.

Clarke, J. (2008). Living with/in and without neo-liberalism. *FOCAAL-Journal of Global and Historical Anthropoligy.* 135–147. https://doi.org/10.3167/fcl.2008.510110

Colby, I. C., Dulmus, C. N., & Sowers, K. M. (2018). *Social work and social policy: Advancing the principles of economic and social justice.* New York: Wiley.

Collier, S. J. (2011). *Post-soviet social: Neoliberalism, social modernity, biopolitics.* Princeton: Princeton University Press.

Concept of long-term social and economic development of the Russian Federation for the period up to 2020. (2008). Retrieved from http://www.consultant.ru/document/cons_doc_LAW_82134/28c7f9e359e8af09d7244d8033c66928fa27e527/.

Federal Law 121-FL "On Amending Certain Legislative Acts of the Russian Federation *Regarding Regulation of Activities of Non-Profit Organizations Performing Foreign Agent* Functions" (July 20, 2012). Retrieved from http://base.garant.ru/70204242/#ixzz5BRaaHq58.

Federal Law 442-FL *"On the Fundamentals of Social Services for Citizens in the Russian Federation"* (December 28, 2013). Retrieved from http://www.consultant.ru/document/cons_doc_LAW_156558/.

Ferguson, I. (2004). Neoliberalism, the third way and social work: The UK experience. *Social Work and Society.* http://www.socwork.net/sws/article/view/236/411.

Foucault, M. (2008). *The birth of biopolitics: Lectures at the college de France, 1978–79.* Houndsmill: Palgrave Macmillan.

Garrett, P. M. (2019). What are we talking about when we talk about 'neoliberalism'? *European Journal of Social Work, 22*(1), 1–13. https://doi.org/10.1080/1369145 7.2018.1530643.

Garrett, P. M. (2008). How to be modern: New labour's neoliberal modernity and the change for children programme. *British Journal of Social Work, 38*(2), 270–289. https://doi.org/10.1093/bjsw/bcl345.

Garrett, P. M. (2018). Revisiting 'The Birth of Biopolitics': Foucault's account of neoliberalism and the remaking of social policy. *Journal of Social Policy.* https://doi.org/10.1017/S0047279418000582.

Green, L., & Clarke, K. (2016). *Social policy for social work: Placing social work in its wider.* Cambridge: Policy Press.

Harris, J. (2014). (Against) neoliberal social work. *Critical and Radical Social Work, 2*(1), 7–22.

Harvey, D. (2005). *A brief history of neoliberalism*. Oxford: Oxford University.

Kupriyanov, R. V., Vilensky, A. A., & Kupriyanova, N. E. (2014). Bologna process in Russia: Specifics and difficulties of implementation. *Bulletin of Kazan Technological University, 20,* 412–415.

Nazarov, V., & Posharatz, A. (Eds.). (2017). *Development of effective social support of population in Russia: address, need, universality*. Moscow: Scientific Research Financial Institute, World Bank.

Osborne, S. (2006) The new public governance? *Public Management Review.* https://doi.org/10.1080/14719030600853022.

Penn, J. (2007). The development of social work education in Russia since 1995. *European Journal of Social Work.* https://doi.org/10.1080/13691450701356879.

Pollack, S. (2010). Labelling clients 'risky': Social work and the neo-liberal welfare state. *British Journal of Social Work, 40,* 1263–1278. https://doi.org/10.1093/bjsw/bcn079.

Pollitt, C., & Bouckaert, G. (2011). *Public management reform: A comparative analysis—NPM, governance and the neo-weberian state*. Oxford: Oxford University Press.

Population: Standard of living. Poverty level. (2017). Federal State Statistic Service. Retrieved from http://www.gks.ru/wps/wcm/connect/rosstat_main/rosstat/ru/statistics/population/poverty/. Accessed June 10, 2019.

Smirnova, A., & Poluektova, N. (2018). Professionalization of social work in Russia: Challenges for education system. *Social Work Education.* https://doi.org/10.1080/02615479.2018.1541978.

Stark, C. (2008). Neoliberalism and the consequences for social work. *IUC Journal of Social Work: Theory & Practice, 17*(4). https://www.bemidjistate.edu/academics/publications/social_work_journal/issue17/articles/stark_christian_final.html.

Starshinova, A. V. (2004). Education trends in social work: Studying the European experience. *Izvestia: Ural State University Journal, 32,* 69–80.

Udin, G. (2019). *Russia ceases to be a social state: Interview to on-line newspaper "Znak".* Retrieved from https://www.znak.com/2019-08-29/rossiya_perestaet_byt_socialnym_gosudarstvom_intervyu_sociologa_grigoriya_yudina. Accessed September 10, 2019.

Wacquant, L. (2009). *Punishing the poor: The neoliberal government of social insecurity*. Durham, NC: Duke University Press.

Why not all NGOs strive to get into the register of social service providers. (2019). *Social Information Agency.* https://www.asi.org.ru/news/2019/07/15/so-nko-reestr/. Accessed September 25, 2019.

CHAPTER 42

Impediments to Professionalising Social Work Education in Sri Lanka

S. Shamila

INTRODUCTION

Social work education in Sri Lanka is generic as evidenced by the National Institute of Social Development (NISD) having a monopoly over social work education. Since 1952 the aim has been to produce competent social workers and help the nation develop. NISD has had different names throughout its history. It was initially named the Ceylon School of Social Work when it was limited to training government and non-government staff in social services. It was administered and funded by non-governmental organisations and then handed over to the government. It was later named the Institute of Social Development. In 1992 NISD was reestablished as the Centre for Research and Development in the Field of Social Services under the purview of the Ministry of Bureaucracy. The hegemony of Sri Lankan bureaucracy is so overarching that a professional educational programme under the auspices of the Ministry of Social Services is virtually a contradiction in terms. It is important to point out that despite educational programmes in social work being initiated in the 1950s they were left isolated and failed to attract the attention of policy makers or the people concerned (Chandraratna, 2012).

The Ceylon Social Work Institute, subsequently renamed the Sri Lanka School of Social Work, was established in 1952. It initially offered a 2-year diploma programme in social work in English. It required an act of parliament—the National Institute of Social Development Act No. 41 of 1992—for the Sri Lanka School of Social Work to be upgraded. In 2005 the government of Sri Lanka took up a proposition made by the University

S. Shamila (✉)
School of Social Work, NISD, Colombo, Sri Lanka

© The Author(s) 2021
S. S. M. et al. (eds.), *The Palgrave Handbook of Global Social Work Education*, https://doi.org/10.1007/978-3-030-39966-5_42

Grants Commission and declared the NISD a degree-awarding higher learning institution. This development allowed the Bachelor of social work (BSW) programme to start in 2005. The technical support required to commence this programme mainly came from the University of Colombo. Sri Lanka's first Master's degree social work (MSW) programme was started in 2008 with funding from the Canadian International Development Agency. Queen's University at Kingston (Canada), the Ministry of Social Services in Sri Lanka, and senior scholars from Canada and Sri Lanka collaboratively launched the MSW programme (Rasanayagam, 2012).

Methodology

In the study forming the basis of this chapter a qualitative method was adopted to carry out interviews and garner in-depth information from social work academic staff, practitioners, and students. Literature review and an open-ended questionnaire were used to collect information from BSW students. Patterns of meaning (i.e., themes) were formulated and analyzed using thematic analysis and then triangulated with the literature (international and national) to fulfil the purpose of the research (Table 42.1).

Table 42.1   Profile of respondents selected for the study

Study No.	Designation	Social work qualification	Experience (years)
1	Lecturer I	PhD MSW	10
2	Lecturer II (field coordinator)	MSW	10
3	Lecturer II	MSW	7
4	Lecturer II	MSW	6
5	Lecturer II	MSW	4
6	Lecturer II	MSW	3
7	Practitioner (visiting lecturer and activist)	PhD	30
8	Practitioner (founder and director)	MSW	5
9	Practitioner/Teacher (career guidance officer)	MSW	
10	Practitioner (public health inspector)	MSW	7
11	President of SLAPSW	MSW	20
12	Students (35)	BSW	2nd and 3rd year
13	Students (32)	Diploma in social work	Enrolment

BSW, Bachelor of social work; MSW, Master of social work; PhD, Doctor of philosophy
Source Field study

ANALYSIS AND INTERPRETATION

Attitude of the Public to Social Work

Popular conventional wisdom among Sri Lankans believes that with a benevolent heart and energy anyone can do social work. Sri Lankans strongly believe that giving and helping others is the most meritorious act anyone can do on the planet (Chanthirasekere, 2012). Moreover, they do not see any difference between the terms social services and social work. They further believe that social work does not require special training, skills, or knowledge. Arguments emphasizing the distinction between social work profession and social services ended up getting heated and creating opponents to social and welfare services in government sectors. The vast majority of people do not understand the differences between social services and social work. The reasons are given in a student handbook documenting Sri Lankan experiences:

1. Social workers are unable to distinguish Western professional components from traditional religious components of social work.
2. Terminology has not developed sufficiently for people to understand the differences since social workers are preoccupied with solving problems of a day-to-day nature.
3. Precision and accuracy are lacking since most findings are drawn from social sciences.
4. Social work deals with problems about which laypeople have firmly fixed views.
5. Such confusion is exacerbated by politicians, film stars, and cricketers who describe some of their promotional campaigns as social work. Although trained social workers are paid and voluntary and untrained are not, when they work side by side laypeople often cannot understand the difference between activities that come under the label of social work undertaken by all manner of people.

The prevailing public attitude toward and understanding of social work are major constraints to an educational institution like the NISD being able to prove that social work is a profession. Although it is widely believed that there is a need for a profession like social work, the benefits of social work education and its practice still remain unrecognised at the local level (Ranaweera, 2012). Such a negative attitude needs to be eliminated by raising the image of social work education through quality teaching in a well-developed learning environment. For social work education in Sri Lanka to be professionalised it is necessary to assure the quality of teaching at all stages.

According to one practitioner the attitude and perception of laypeople and educated people in Sri Lanka is totally antagonistic to the social work profession:

People think that providing charity services or money, material and other help for those who are in need is social work. People also strongly believe that everybody can do it and [there is] no need of specific qualification and training to become a social worker. The term social work is confused with almsgiving/ donations/charity work/ social service/ social welfare/*shramadana* (volunteer work).

Attitude of Students During Enrolment in a Social Work Educational Programme

During interviews to see which students were suitable to take a course leading to a diploma in social work, students were asked about their reasons for taking the course. Of the 32 students who were interviewed the majority (30) stated they wanted to get a qualification that would lead to a job opportunity. However, none of them was aware of the concept underlying social work and social work education. Another point worthy of note is that their parents had no clue about what social work courses entail and had doubts about job opportunities in Sri Lanka after completion of such courses. In a nutshell, the purpose of social work education is to educate students about social work and train them to become social workers committed to work for the betterment of society. This statement emphasises that commitment is a core quality needed for anyone to take part in the social work educational programme and raises the issue of selection. Should students already know about social work or is it the job of a teacher to teach them what social work is?

Any student who has little understanding of social work and takes part in the course runs the risk of not being a competent social worker in the future.

Nature of Social Work Education Programmes at the National Institute of Social Development and Other Traditional Universities

The School of Social Work at the NISD conducts diploma, higher diploma, and Bachelor and Master's degree courses in social work. Although the Bachelor degree course was inaugurated in 2005, it was only conducted in English. In 2013 diploma and higher diploma courses were first conducted in Sinhala and Tamil. However, after successful completion of the higher diploma course those interested in degree programmes were required to sit a screening test conducted in English and continue the degree course again conducted in English from the third year. Although most students regarded language as a barrier, regardless of their language fluency they wanted to follow the degree. They also encountered difficulties in following a Bachelor degree course conducted in English, a scenario that considerably prevented students from acquiring the qualities needed for the social work profession. Maintaining the quality of the Bachelor degree programme became a great challenge for academic staff and the institution. Although the courses were conducted in Tamil and Sinhala, there were not enough textbooks available in these languages. This was also a significant challenge faced by the academic staff and the students. University academics have been found to be below par when it comes to teaching social work practice. The fact that the discipline could not even get tertiary acceptance for over half a century is testimony to the underdeveloped state of social science as a university discipline in the country.

The president of the Sri Lanka Association of Professional Social Workers (SLAPSW) stated:

> Yes. Absences of application of individual intervention techniques have hindered the development of the welfare of the people in this country.

Professionalism

History of Struggle

Evolution of the social work profession since its birth can be found in the literature accompanied by criticism that motivated social workers to commit to professional enhancement. The history of social work has been marked by uncertainties about it being given professional status and anxieties about whether social work is a legitimate profession. Social workers struggled for years to define the profession and develop a common conceptual framework that could house core elements of the definition (Ramsay, 1988). It is evident in this statement that the recognition of social work as a profession cannot be achieved without commitment and a lot of effort. Flexner (1915) claimed that social work lacked both a distinctive methodology and a scientific body of knowledge and was therefore not worthy of professional status. Flexner was an expert on professional education (particularly, on medical matters) in America and his statement was key to the development of social work as a profession later. He developed the classic statement outlining the sociological traits necessary to define a profession:

1. It must engage in intellectual operations involving individual responsibility;
2. It must derive its knowledge from science and learning;
3. It must apply its knowledge using techniques that are educationally communicable;
4. It must be self-organized; and
5. It must operate from altruistic motivations.

Social workers have tried ever since to establish their discipline according to the professional trait model set out by Flexner. This represented a historical milestone in the evolution of social work as a profession in America. This was exactly what social work and social workers needed to bring about in Sri Lanka. The struggle to achieve this has been experienced by Sri Lankan social workers since 1952, a period extending over 66 years. It was a critical time for all social workers to commit and participate fully to gain professional recognition. According to Practitioner I:

> The religion and culture of the country encourage helping the poor and the political system too encourages social welfare/free giving. The policy makers lack understanding about social work as a profession. The domination of Public Administration officers on social welfare and lack of understanding of Academics at the university level about social work are found to be major barriers for the professionalization of social work in Sri Lanka. Moreover, [there is a] lack of number of educational institutions providing social work education and lack of engagement of the professional social workers in developing the profession. With this social work education has become more knowledge based than ethical oriented.

Nature of Professional Education

Social workers are highly trained and experienced professionals. Only those who have earned social work degrees at the Bachelor, Master, or doctoral level and completed a minimum number of hours in supervised fieldwork are deemed professional social workers. Professional education programmes are provided by a few faculties in Sri Lanka such as those of medicine, engineering, law, and education. Some students with academic degrees follow professional courses conducted by other institutes after they graduate in an effort to find employment. Although medical colleges are part of the university system, law colleges are not. A Bachelor of law is an academic degree in which graduates have to follow a 3-month practical course at the law college for them to be qualified as lawyers. Chartered accountants, chartered engineers, and architects are some other professional arenas that offer professional education courses in their respective fields. Although social work education has still not been categorized as professional education, students train so that they can work at different levels and acquire many skills that they use to empower and help people find their own solutions to the problems they face (Ranaweera, 2013). Despite these statements by an expert in the field of social work education and despite social work education adapting to the international standard of providing knowledge and practical experience through different levels of fieldwork placement, the Organization of Professional Associations of Sri Lanka is reluctant to acknowledge social work as a profession equal to others. Social work as a discipline was never given a fair go in the country (Chandraratna, 2012). The following two facts provide evidence to support this argument. First, in the early days the terms social work and social service were totally interchangeable. Furthermore, social service was ultimately not considered a field needing a concrete knowledge base, but a charitable activity performed for a number of purposes such as gaining social or political popularity or delivering a religious vow. Second, social work was not initially accepted as an area with the essential characteristics of a scientific discipline.

Therefore, it encountered many obstacles to enjoying the level of social acceptance and professional recognition that other disciplines had. The struggle for social work to be recognised as a profession can clearly be seen in the historical evolution of social work.

Practitioners participating in this study remarked on the lack of professional organisations and a proper organisational network to build awareness and working relationships among social work educators and practitioners themselves. One of the reasons social work is not recognised as a profession is that the Association for Social Workers backs away from the fight for professional upgrading due to less enthusiastic and less committed members.

The academics and practitioners participating in this study said that social workers in Sri Lanka had failed to point out social inequalities and injustice. Bisman (2004) described this as malpractice, contrary to social work ethics, and a direct violation of the social work code of ethics. Responsibility toward the profession would be even greater if social workers were professionals and both formal and informal methods of social control would ensure that members conform to the code of ethics. Although a profession can only exist when it is recognized, recognition can be hard to achieve such as by reserving jobs for people with technical training, giving preference to those with the necessary qualifications to undertake the jobs, and making them aware of promotions and financial remuneration. The social work profession is built on a philosophy fundamentally based on a particular view of humanity and life. All these statements by experts in social work emphasise that it is the duty of every social worker as a professional to abide by the code of ethics and prove they have the qualities and competencies that distinguish them from non-professionals such as social service officers, welfare officers, and others who do not have the requisite educational qualifications or do not have experience of supervised field practice.

Admission Criteria

Existing admission criteria have been found to be inadequate at selecting students suitable for social work education programmes. Social work requires genuine passion and committed professional involvement wherever it is practised. Relying entirely on a candidate's academic performance will therefore not result in selection of students best fitted for social work. Academic members of the NISD stated that the easygoing manner of panel members and the shortage of applications resulted in unsuitable students being enrolled in social work degree programmes in recent years. Social work practitioners and academics strongly stated that passion toward the career must be demonstrated and given equal importance to academic achievements when it comes to selecting students for social work educational programmes. This enriches the quality of educational programmes and makes accreditation at the national and international level more likely. Social work is much more than carefully analysing situations, it involves a passion to make the world a better place, to express outrage at injustice and oppression, and to commit to bringing about change (Jim Ife, 2001). Jim Ife quite correctly felt that passion toward the profession was at the very heart of social work. Although academics have a major responsibility to make students passionate about social work, they pointed out the difficulties they encountered when trying to make students commit to and show interest in the profession due to it lacking a professional identity in the country.

Academic Freedom

Repercussions of Poor Recruitment, Study Leave, and Promotion Policies as Well as Academic Development at the National Institute of Social Development

A brain drain occurred as a result of the qualifications and commitments of academic staff being depreciated by the institute. Social work academics were not content like other academics in universities in Sri Lanka with the facilities available at the NISD. Staff shortages, inadequate salaries, poor staff development, lack of funds for research and related activities have characterised the history of the NISD (Ranaweera, 2013). At present there are 11 academic staff involved directly in teaching social work, each teaching fewer than two subjects and supervising more than 10 students. They strongly feel they are unable to exercise their academic freedom inside the premises as their movement is restricted by higher-ups responsible for academic administration. Academic staff are also required to report to the administration even when they need to visit libraries outside the premises or collect data for a research purpose. Moreover, academics face difficulties when they seek permission for leave to follow higher studies locally or outside the country. Some former academics who resigned from their positions acknowledge that they had little choice but to resign because administrative procedures are so rigid and unsystematic. They also went on to say that they were treated differently by administrators when they pushed policies they had picked up during study leave abroad about pay and promotion procedures. Like other administrative and non-academic officers, academic staff are obliged to report to the office Mondays to Fridays at 8.30 a.m. and again when they leave at 4.15 p.m. Such an environment greatly impacts their academic and personal development. They stated they hardly have time to conduct research or engage in academic writing. Due to a shortage of teaching staff they are compelled to conduct lectures on subjects other than those in which they are qualified. Additionally, they are expected to work for non-academic amenities as well. The professional satisfaction felt by academic staff involved in teaching has therefore significantly declined in recent years. It is through social work education that professionals acquire the knowledge, skills, and values that pertain to the profession (Gambrill, 1997). To maintain the quality of teaching, academics therefore need to have the freedom and time to engage in personal and professional development. Furthermore, Gambrill added that "... there is specialized knowledge and that accreditors can determine if this knowledge is being transferred to students." Quality of teaching is hence a component ensuring accreditation standards are reached. Accreditation is a process of external quality review created and used by higher education to scrutinise quality assurance and quality improvement in colleges, universities, and programmes (Eaton, 2015). Moreover, according to IASSW (2004) global standards it is the responsibility of the school to allocate workloads such as teaching, fieldwork instruction, supervision, and administration and to make provisions for research and publication.

Administrative Regulations and Procedures

Sri Lanka became a welfare state after gaining political independence from the British in 1948. The new government decided that health, education, and social services would be provided free by the state. Administrators of the social services sector and those engaged in social services were unaware of the need for professional education and training despite it being identified by the health and educational sectors (Chandraratna, 2008). Administrators are higher level officials appointed by ministers and departments of the Sri Lankan Administrative Service. They are obliged to consult respective ministers when it comes to decision making. However, they have little understanding of the social work profession and therefore it is hard to convince them to fulfil the needs of social work education. This is what lies behind the slow pace of development of social work as a profession in Sri Lanka.

Recognition of the Bachelor of social work degree by the University Grants Commission was made possible by lobbying rather than conceptually convincing the authorities (Ranaweera, 2013). This came about because the institute could not use its human resources in an effective and efficient manner to attain organisational goals due to unfit administrative procedures and regulations.

Field Placement and Supervision

Nature of Field Practice

Social work is a practice-based professional discipline anchored on a unified curriculum consisting of both theory and fieldwork components. Consequently, Hall (1990) asserted that a generally accepted view is that field instruction and education are of equal importance to theoretical academic instruction. Other concepts used to refer to fieldwork include field practicum, field placement, field instruction, fieldwork placement, internship, and field practice education. All these have the concept of linking theory to practice in common. Fieldwork placement is a critical method and phase of social work instruction that provides students with the opportunity to integrate classroom knowledge with experiential learning in a relevant social work setting. While acquiring experience students are supervised by professional staff members from agencies and supervisors from the academic institution. Field practice placements have changed over time based on course requirements. The first placements were given in agency settings and secondary placements were given in communities. Mental health hospitals, prisons, schools, and some organisations have provided students with opportunities to do their field placements. IASSW (2004) global standards for the education and training of social workers emphasise the importance of allocating time and selecting fields for placement. Such standards indicate that field education should be long enough, the tasks complex enough, and learning opportunities sufficient to ensure students are prepared for professional practice.

Allocation of Fieldwork Days

Students are expected to engage in fieldwork 2 days a week and do so for a minimum of 4 hours on each occasion. This means they are required to engage in fieldwork concurrently with lectures throughout the semester. Unlike lengthy periods spent doing fieldwork that exposes students to methods of working with individuals and communities, the purpose of concurrent fieldwork is to expose students to working therapeutic groups. They are expected to attend group meetings, make observations, and discuss, interview, and assist such groups to achieve their objectives or goals. Allocating full days for fieldwork has been found to be ineffective in many agency settings because students struggle to accomplish their fieldwork requirements such as social case work and group work.

Practical Obstacles

Field training in social work education lessened in importance when it was realised that students often failed to perform satisfactorily and found it difficult to apply the social work knowledge they had amassed. Students further stated that the knowledge learnt in the classroom is often out of context and clearly is aimed at Western society as a result of which students naturally struggle and are frequently confused about how to apply such knowledge in their field (Das, 2013). Moreover, Shaffie, and Baba (2013) stated that the shortage of trained personnel in most welfare agencies where students are placed for their field practice created a number of challenges. Students enter their field placements with the intention to gain experience, knowledge, and skills. Although they tend to have high expectations of agencies, they are often disappointed when they realise the agencies depend more on the student than the other way round. As is common in many Asian social work educational institutions such as those in Bangladesh, Indonesia, and Malaysia field practice education in Sri Lanka also faces numerous practical challenges in the field. A major handicap in fieldwork education in Indonesia is the lack of professionally qualified social workers to play the supervisory role for students on field placement. The lack of trained supervisors in field agencies has made the task of faculty supervisors much more difficult since they are often asked to fill the gap (Fahrudin & Yusuf, 2013).

Educational Background of the Field and Agency Supervisors

Supervision is an important part of social work education. It is essential for professional development and competent practice and has therefore been given particular attention in the literature (Jim Ife, 2001). The primary task of the supervisor is to maximise opportunities for students to learn for themselves within the context of a particular agency setting. Supervisors are professionally trained to provide students with protection, guidance, and control. Essentially, there are two types of supervisors: agency supervisors who are based at the agency and interact with the student regularly and academic supervisors who are appointed by the institute or university and have overall responsibility for supervising and reporting on the progress made by students. Agency supervisors are invariably social workers who are given such responsibilities not just because they are qualified but also because they are endorsed by the agency as a result of the training, expertise, and preparedness they have accrued in fieldwork. Unpublished research in the form of a thesis for a Bachelor of social work degree in 2016 revealed that of 30 agency supervisors 11 have either a degree or diploma in social work whereas the remaining 19 agency supervisors do not. Fahrudin and Yusuf (2013) reported that it was much the same in Indonesia where a major handicap in fieldwork education was lack of qualified social workers to take up a supervisory role for students on field placement.

As a result of the shortage of welfare agencies and agency supervisors qualified in professional social work, concurrent field placement has become a burden to students and faculty. Furthermore, although it is acknowledged that supervision plays a crucial role in fieldwork, supervisors are not able to provide effective supervision because of administrative and academic-related issues.

Fulfilment of Academic Requirements During Field Placement

Most respondents said they faced difficulties in completing their academic requirements during concurrent fieldwork in hospital settings. Unpublished research in the form of a thesis for a Bachelor of social work degree (Faslan, 2016) revealed that students and supervisors faced a number of challenges related to concurrent field placement when it was first introduced to the BSW curriculum.

Language Barrier

Students and faculty supervisors stated that language was a barrier to conducting supervisory discussions meaningfully. Since communication plays such an important role in the supervisory relationship, students conducting the degree in English face difficulty in communicating with the supervisor. Although English is used as the common language for students, it is done so against the academic background of students speaking Tamil or Sinhala. This means Sinhala-speaking students can be given Tamil-speaking supervisors and Sinhala-speaking supervisors can be assigned to Tamil-speaking students. Although this is not an ideal situation, such an initiative assists students to widen their horizons by learning alongside students of ethnic diversity. Knowing about the values and norms of a different culture helps them to be sensitive toward people of ethnic diversity. This also provides an opportunity to learn a new language or brush up on a language they are already familiar with.

Nature of Faculty Supervision
Number of Supervisees Assigned to a Supervisor

One supervisor said she supervised eight students and had other responsibilities such as conducting lectures, participating in academic and administration-related meetings, and attending workshops as a result of which she struggled to allocate time for individual supervision. Social work supervision can be broken down into several types such as formal, informal, group, individual, direct, and indirect. Supervisors stated that they mostly conducted group supervision because of the large number of students making individual supervision impossible. Therefore, supervision is not very effective and lets down students who have unique problems or challenges in their field of practice. Having to juggle three or four lectures with supervising a large number of students is something faculty supervisors struggle with.

Space Allocated for Supervision

For supervision to be successful the place where supervisors and supervisees meet is important. Supervisors described the places where they meet as cabins that are small and narrow. There is little privacy making them feel uncomfortable and affecting their supervision. There is nowhere else in the institute itself to conduct supervision because the institute building is quite small.

Visits by supervisors to agencies where students are placed are infrequent. Faculty supervisors gave work constraints and administrative procedures as reasons they were not able to visit all field agencies to evaluate the progress of students periodically. Students and faculty supervisors stated that the lack of field visits greatly impacted the learning process of students in the field and maximised the gap between fieldwork agencies and the institute.

Employment Opportunities

Without employment opportunities for social workers there will be little demand for social work education in Sri Lanka (Ranaweera, 2013). Such a statement was backed up by both the academic staff and students of the NISD. Decline in the number of student enrollments and lack of retention may well be the consequence of the negative impression people have of social work due to few recognised job opportunities and a drop in demand for courses. They added that counselling courses are in high demand because they are recognised and acknowledged as such in Sri Lanka and there are considerable job opportunities as well. The most frequently asked question by participants in the interview was whether they would get a job after completion of the course—a question met most of the time with silence.

Underdevelopment of Social Work Discipline

One expert in social work stated that it had not achieved proper disciplinary status in Sri Lanka for a number of reasons and pointed out that the term social worker used in common Sri Lankan parlance referred to people engaged in social philanthropy, charitable activity, and rendering services to the vulnerable and distressed and that such a commonality was a major impediment (Chandraratna, 2008). Moreover, the popularity of sociology in universities and lack of social work professionals in the country contributed to the slow pace at which social work advanced. Bureaucracy in social services and dependence on the state by the vulnerable are additional factors that held back professional recognition of social work. The history of the School of Social Work shows that it took 50 years for it to be promoted to being a degree-awarding institute. Ranaweera's (2013) statement is further evidence that universities paid little attention to social work until the Tsunami Disaster in Sri Lanka in 2004. Moreover, most people did not understand the difference between social work and sociology (Ranaweera, n.d.). The views of academic staff and practitioners participating in the study strongly emphasised such statements. For example, Practitioner III acknowledged that:

> Sri Lanka's academic and professional communities and the general public do not recognise social work as a profession. Sri Lanka's social work academics are reluctant to provide leadership in social work education (especially, when it comes to research). Furthermore, non-professionals identify themselves as social workers without having any idea of the purposes, principles, and ethics of social work. Moreover, those involved in sociology and psychology consider themselves to be psychosocial workers rather than social workers.

Dissemination of the Western Concept of Social Work and Social Work Theories

Dissemination of the Western concept of social work has been not very successful in Sri Lanka (Ranaweera, 2013). International joint research in 2013 revealed that the inability of the profession to gain recognition, the difficulty in finding jobs in social work, the public perception that social work is little more than a voluntary vocation requiring no professional training, and the need to have textbooks written in indigenous languages are challenges that have to be faced to internalise social work education in Asia. Indeed, these are obstacles encountered throughout the history of social work education in Sri Lanka. Despite many attempts made, contextualising appropriate knowledge of social work is still in question? Lacking textbooks in the indigenous languages (Tamil and Sinhala) students and academics have little option but to use Western textbooks. There is an additional difficulty here in that there is no word in Sinhala or Tamil synonymous with the English term social work.

Limitation of Resources

Insufficient funding of institutes is a further hindrance to the development of social work education in Sri Lanka. Major social work courses offered by the School of Social Work mainly rely on state funding. The funding allocated to the social work education programme has declined over the years and has impacted the quality of the programme. The absence of extracurricular activities for students is another reason social work education has lost popularity among students. Moreover, exchange programmes and exposure visits have been restricted as a result of financial constraints.

Local and international exposure to social work practicum is important to motivating students to become effective social workers in their respective countries. Bell and Anscombe (2013) stated that international study experience had significant positive impacts on social work students' learning, group cohesion, professional commitment, and motivation. It also enhanced their appreciation of international social work, grassroots community development work, cultural diversity, human rights, and social justice issues. International field experience has the potential to provide transformative learning and teaching experiences. Lyons (2006) stated that international field experience can broaden participants' perspectives on core social work values, ethics, and objectives by taking students and staff from familiar to unfamiliar contexts of practice. Cleak and Wilson (2004) emphasised that international fieldwork experience is critical to globalising the profession since it directly exposes participants to cross-cultural issues and diversity in theory and modes of practice. Financial assistance provided by the ministry has dropped dramatically leading to budgets suffering from fiscal instability. Academic staff also added that such financial constraints prevented academic-related activities (Chandraratna, 2008).

Sri Lanka Association of Professional Social Workers

The Sri Lanka Association of Professional Social Workers (SLAPSW) and the NISD are responsible for the accreditation of the social work profession in Sri Lanka. The association was registered as a voluntary social service organisation under the Voluntary Social Services Organizations Act No. 31 of 1980. Its general objectives are

a. to enhance and develop the concept of professional social work;
b. to create links between people engaged in social work; and
c. to provide training to social workers on how to conduct different categories of social work.

The president of the association stated that despite the objectives clearly identifying the need to enhance the social work profession, the speed of change was very slow and the efforts made were mostly done in vain. He added that they had not given up and were still striving to reach the goals. He felt that they could influence getting the act through parliament in 2015 by long-term lobbying.

CONCLUSIONS AND RECOMMENDATIONS

This chapter has discussed the obstacles that Sri Lankan social work academics and practitioners have been trying to overcome to upgrade social work as a profession and expand social work education by targetting potential student populations and bringing about change in the wellbeing of citizens in the country. The discussion clearly identifies factors that are barriers to the accreditation of social work education and the professionalisation of social work. The quality of social work education and its practice greatly impact recognition of the profession in Sri Lanka and professional recognition is determined by the quality of education programmes. The history of social work shows that the recognition and professionalisation of social work even in Western countries were only achieved after a great struggle. This highlights the need for social workers to continue making efforts and commitments to bring about such success. It is down to the NISD, the SLAPSW, alumni with Bachelor of social work degrees, and the ministry to accelerate progress in the accreditation and professionalisation of social work education in Sri Lanka. Although, these local bodies are at the forefront, international stakeholders need to get involved.

Despite the many challenges and obstacles, committed academic staff at the various institutes offer selfless services to produce competent social workers who abide by such values as human dignity and worth, equality and equity, social justice and human rights. The quality and commitment of students in the field are the only rewards they seek. International recognition and accreditation of the Sri Lankan social work degree would constitute a great achievement by the NISD. Moreover, academic staff at the NISD were offered PhD scholarships that they completed successfully in Malaysia, China, and the United Kingdom. They are now working as heads of departments and senior lecturers in Sri Lankan contemporary universities. Overcoming such challenges and obstacles can be done using internal and external remedies implemented by harnessing national and international expertise and engaging in constructive discussions with appropriate stakeholders such as the Association of Social Work Boards (ASWB), the SLAPSW, the Asian and Pacific Association for Social Work Education (APASWE), the International Association of Schools of Social Work (IASSW), and the OPA. International exposure, intellectual knowledge dissemination, and sharing experiences will enhance the quality of teaching and the practice of social work. It is imperative to localise Western concepts, approaches, models, and theories to the Sri Lankan sociocultural context and to translate them into the indigenous languages (Tamil and Sinhala) for social work practice to be effective.

The following statements are taken from the interviews to give an idea of the recommendations suggested by the respondents.

Practitioner I felt the following recommendations would promote professional social work in Sri Lanka:

> In my opinion there is an urgent need to revisit all existing social work curricula such that the specific needs of social work practice in Sri Lanka are not only met, but delivered professionally too. For this to be brought about many other things need to be put in place such as building strong alliances with academic associations/universities internationally, enhancing research, creating more opportunities for students to engage in social work practice in relevant settings, building own social work brand, adding value to social work education by promoting exchange programmes, creating robust selection criteria for diploma and degree programmes in consultation with the University Grants Commission (UGC), and lobbying the government to provide more employment opportunities from government sectors, particularly in medical and psychiatric social work settings and social services.

The president of the SLAPSW suggested that

> The social work profession should be recognised as a profession in the country and positions related to social work should be filled by people who have social work qualifications. Social work education should be provided by institutions recognised by other universities. The NISD should be prepared to embrace people committed to development of the profession. We need highly committed and motivated staff for such development to happen.

Practitioner II said his experience made it clear to him that

> Building strong professional associations with regional and international actors should be expedited and having a robust policy regarding the recruitment of people with the necessary professional social work background is vital.

Practitioner III suggested that

> Having competent and qualified social workers with academic credentials should be a prerequisite to running internationally accredited BSW and MSW degrees as should taking politics out of the equation to ensure suitable personnel are positioned appropriately.

References

Bell, K., & Anscombe, A. W. (2013). International field experience in social work: Outcomes of a short-term study abroad programme to India. *Social Work Education, 32*(8), 1032–1047.

Bisman, C. (2004). Social work values: The moral core of the profession. *The British Journal of Social Work, 34*(1), 109–123.

Chandraratna, D. (2008). *Social work education & practice: A Sri Lankan perspective.* Sri Lanka: VijiyhaYapa Publication.

Chandraratna, D. (2012). *Professionalization of social work in Sri Lanka.* 60th Anniversary 1952–2012. National Institute of Social Development, Rajagiriya, Sri Lanka.

Chanthirasekere, S. (2012). *Professionalization of social work in Sri Lanka.* 60th Anniversary 1952–2012. National Institute of Social Development, Rajagiriya, Sri Lanka.

Cleak, H., & Wilson, J. (2004). *Making the most of field placement.* South Melborne: Cengage.

Das, T. K. (2013). *Internalization of social work education in Asia.* Joint International Research Project.

Eaton, J. S. (2015). *An over view of U.S. accreditation.* Washington: Counsel for Higher Education Accreditation.

Fahrudin, A., & Yusuf, H. (2013). *Internalization of social work education in Asia.* Joint International Research Project.

Faslan, M. (2016). *A study on the evaluation of concurrent field placement at NID* (Unpublished).

Flexner, A. (1915). Is social work a profession? *Research on Social Work Practice, 11*(2), 152–165.

Gambrill, E. (1997). Social work education: Current concerns and possible futures. *Social work in the 21st century,* 317–327.

Hall, N. (1990). Social work training in Africa: A fieldwork manual. *Journal of Social Development in Africa.*

IASSW, I. (2004). *Global standards for the education and training of the social work profession.*

Ife, J. (2001). Local and global practice: Relocating social work as a human rights profession in the new global order. *European Journal of Social Work, 4*(1), 5–15.

Lyons, K. (2006). Globalization and social work: International and local implications. *British Journal of Social Work, 36,* 365–380.

Ramsay, R. (1988). *Is social work a profession?* A 21st Century Answer to 20th Century Question: Canadian Association of Social Worker, Canada.

Ranaweera, A. (2012). *Professionalization of social work in Sri Lanka*. 60th Anniversary 1952–2012. National Institute of Social Development, Rajagiriya, Sri Lanka.

Ranaweera, A. (n.d.). *Social work education in Sri Lanka*. National Institute of Social Development, Sri Lanka. http://www.nisd.lk/web/index.php/en/component/content/article/122-article3.html.

Ranaweera, A. (2013). *Review and record of the history of social work education in Sri Lanka: Internationalization of social work education in Asia*. Joint Research Project.

Rasanayagam, Y. (2012). *Professionalization of social work in Sri Lanka*. 60th Anniversary 1952–2012. National Institute of Social Development, Rajagiriya, Sri Lanka.

Shaffie, F., & Baba, I. (2013). *Internalization of social work education in Asia*. Joint International Research Project.

PART VII

Marginalized Communities in Diverse Contexts and Social Work Education

INTRODUCTION

Social work as a human service profession assists vulnerable population in fighting discrimination and stigma (Banks, 2008; Barnes, 2006; Burke & Parker, 2007; Cree, 2013; Dominelli, 2008; Fook, 2012; Thompson, 2006) by using the fundamental principles of social justice, equality, and diversity (Thompson, 2016). Contributions in this part of the book discuss about discriminatory practices in diverse context and social work response to these discriminations and assisting the marginalized sections in diverse context. *Claudia Reyes-Quilodran* is concerned about human rights status in Chile and provides an account of evidence-based account of how human rights are integrated into teaching social work graduates. The chapter discusses the challenge for social work education in a post-military intervention in government affairs and the torture and murder of thousands of people in Chile. Claudia Reyes-Quilodran proposes the much-required skill training for social workers which enables social work graduates to work with families affected by human rights violations, and strategies to support them during a judicial trial. Social workers intervene when a community, group, or individual experience marginalization (Rosen, McCall, & Goodkind, 2017), and thus, the intervention in human rights violation is one of the most important fundamental service offered by social work profession. However, in the contemporary society the concerns related to human rights in many societies across the globe are changing rapidly, and therefore, there is a need for training social work graduates to address these concerns within the social work framework. *This chapter by Claudia Reyes-Quilodran* by reviewing the results of an undergraduate social work course at Chilean universities provides the evidence for this claim and suggests for incorporating skill components in social work training to prepare graduates for interventions in contemporary human rights violation.

The Canadian Association of Social Workers' (CASW) Code of Ethics (2005) and the International Federation of Social Workers (2012) recognize 'pursuit of social justice' and 'diversity' as ethical principles of social work. Further both 'pursuit of social justice' and 'diversity' are recognized as core professional competences by the U Council on Social Work Education (CSWE, 2015). However, despite social work professions commitment in ensuring social justice and equality across the countries in the globe, a dilemma about the meaning of social justice in social work and its transformation from theory to practice is much debated (Dominelli, 2010) and continues to be debated. Mohd Shahid outlines the relevance of Gramsci's notion of common sense and hegemony and endeavours to delineate how professional social workers could use the Gramscian framework in making sense of the processes of marginalization. The author invites the practitioners working with the marginalized groups to identify and understand the normative framework and then to challenge the oppressive realities that are experienced by the service users. The author claims this understanding will help in development of the anti-oppressive social work practice.

Being responsive to other culture and societies may help the social work graduates to be effective in their service delivery. In order to ensure cultural competences among the social work graduates and equip them with required skills, studies have proposed for development and delivery of effective pedagogy on 'culturally competent social work' (Deal & Hyde, 2004; Hall & Theriot, 2007; Walls et al., 2009; Yee & Greene, 2004). *Hans Van Ewijk* builds a construct around the concept dignity, vulnerability, moral vulnerability, and social justice by exploring and connecting the concept 'dignity, social justice and vulnerability'. Understanding of these interplays is important to social work graduates as well as educators as we work with vulnerable communities, groups, and individual in ensuring a safe and dignified living. Further, research findings (Osteen, Vanidestine, & Sharpe, 2013) in this area revile that the student social workers who required to take courses on 'diversity' show more positive attitude towards marginalized people than the students who do not study the concept 'dignity'. M. Gilla Augustine makes an attempt to understand the philosophical framework that guides social work research on attrition and retention of marginalized population in higher education in the United States. The author uses four paradigms, i.e. positivism, post-positivism, interpretivism/constructivism, and critical theory in delineating the evidence-based practice with marginalized student populations.

Chapters in this part mostly focus on critical analysis of how social work education is responsive to marginalization and marginalized communities in a global context. Chapters from the Unites States, India, New Zealand, the Netherland, Germany, and Canada provide a wide variety of experiences on discriminatory practices and social work response in a multicultural context. *Ksenija Napan* based on an exploratory inquiry outlines the innovative teaching, learning and assessment practices at two tertiary providers in

Aotearoa/New Zealand. Policy influence by social work academia is limited and Gal and Weiss-Gal (2017) in a study found that the level of policy engagement by social work educators found to be 'moderate to low' (Gal & Weiss-Gal, 2017). The knowledge of social policy and their functional areas are important for social work practitioners; hence, the students need to be taught about policy formulation, policy influence, and policy evaluation during their social work programmes. Further social work educators have a critical role in providing the knowledge, motivation, and skills to future social workers (Weiss-Gal & Gal, 2017). Sylvia Parusel tries to influence the policies and practice through outlining the experiences of service users through life stories of women in treatment for opioid in British Columbia (BC), Canada. Author uses a critical feminist, social constructionist framework to analyze the intersections of agency and relational and structural forces, finding these clients' navigation of surveillance and support and their challenges to normative meanings illustrate an everyday politics of care. The chapter tries to become a voice to the women's who were in deep social exclusion and demands for polices and social work practice to assist these women's in marginalization. This discussion creates space for the service user's involvement in social work education. Many scholars have already noted that service users are already integrated to the social work education through admission process, student assessment, curriculum planning, co-teaching, and influencing student perspective (Cabiati & Raineri, 2016; Dorozenko, Ridley, Martin, & Mahboub, 2016; Robinson & Webber, 2013). However, the research related to outcome of service user's involvement in social work education is limited (Schön, 2015).

In sum, as is evident in this volume, social work education across the world is becoming sensitive towards the issues experienced by marginalized communities. New development in curriculum, pedagogy, and research in social work programmes encouraging new social workers to work in the areas of marginalized and disadvantaged communities' welfare and advocacy. Even though research shows that policy practice in social work is continued as sideline practice (Gal & Weiss-Gal, 2013) in many countries, social workers are working with the state and administrative machineries to ensure equality and social justice to every section of the society. *Caroline Schmitt and Matthias D. Witte* further this understanding through outlining the historic growth of social work education in Germany and its interweaving within nation-state structures. The chapter explores the central organizations and agencies in Germany and its working methods. At the same time, it also deals with transnational tendencies of social work

References

Banks, S. (2008). Critical commentary: Social work ethics. *British Journal of Social Work, 38*, 1238–1249, https://doi.org/10.1093/bjsw/bcn099.

Barnes, M. (2006). *Caring and social justice*. Basingstoke: Palgrave.

Burke, P., & Parker, J. (2007). *Social work and disadvantage: Addressing the roots of stigma through association.* London: Jessica Kingsley.

Cabiati, E., & Raineri, M. L. (2016). Learning from service users' involvement: A research about changing stigmatizing attitudes in social work students. *Social Work Education*, https://doi.org/10.1080/02615479.2016.117825.

Council on Social Work Education. (2015). *Education Policy and Accreditation Standards.* Washington, DC: Author.

Cree, V. E. (2013). Stigma in health and social work. In L. Beddoe & J. Maidment (Eds.), *Social work practice for promoting health and wellbeing: Critical issues* (pp. 76–85). London: Routledge.

Deal, K., & Hyde, C. (2004). Understanding MSW student anxiety and resistance to multicultural learning. *Journal of Teaching in Social Work, 24,* 73–86, https://doi.org/10.1300/j067v24n01_05.

Dominelli, L. (2008). *Anti-racist social work.* London: Palgrave Macmillan.

Dominelli, L. (2010). Globalization, contemporary challenges and social work practice. *International Social Work, 53,* 599–612, https://doi.org/10.1177/0020872810371201.

Dorozenko, K. P., Ridley, S., Martin, R., & Mahboub, L. (2016). A journey of embedding mental health lived experience in social work education. *Social Work Edcuation, 35*(8), 905–917.

Fook, J. (2012). *Social work: A critical approach to practice.* Thousand Oaks, CA: Sage.

Gal, J., & Weiss-Gal, I. (Eds.). (2013). *Social workers affecting social policy: An international perspective on policy practice.* Bristol: Policy Press.

Gal, J., & Weiss-Gal, I. (Eds.). (2017). *Where academia and policy meet: A cross-national perspective on the involvement of social work academic in social policy.* Bristol: Policy Press.

Hall, J., & Theriot, M. (2007). An exploratory study evaluating the effectiveness of an innovative model for teaching multicultural social work education. *Journal of Teaching in Social Work, 27,* 259–271, https://doi.org/10.1300/j067v27n03_16.

International Federation of Social Workers. (2012). *Statement of ethical principles.* Berne: International Federation of Social Workers.

Osteen, P. J., Vanidestine, T. J., & Sharpe, T. L. (2013). Multicultural curriculum and MSW students' attitudes about race and diversity. *Journal of Teaching in Social Work, 33,* 111–128, https://doi.org/10.1080/08841233.2013.775211.

Robinson, K., & Webber, M. (2013). Models and effectiveness of service user and carer involvement in social work education: A literature review. *British Journal of Social Work, 43,* 925–944. https://doi.org/10.1093/bjsw/bcs025.

Rosen, D., McCall, J., & Goodkind, S. (2017). Teaching critical selfreflection through the lens of cultural humility: An assignment in a social work diversity course. *Social Work Education, 36*(3), 289–298. https://doi.org/10.1080/02615479.2017.1287260.

Schön, U. K. (2015). User involvement in social work and education: Reasons for participation. *Scandinavian Journal of Disability Research, 18*(2), 1–10.

Thompson, N. (2006). *Anti-discriminatory practice.* Basingstoke: Palgrave Macmillan.

Thompson, N. (2016). *Anti-discriminatory practice: Equality, diversity and social justice* (6th ed.). London: Palgrave Macmillan. https://doi.org/10.1007/978-1-137-58666-7.

Walls, N. E., Griffin, R., Arnold-Renicker, H., Burson, M., Johnston, C., Moorman, N., ... Schutte, E. (2009). Mapping graduate social work student learning journeys about heterosexual privilege. *Journal of Social Work Education, 45,* 289–307. https://doi.org/10.5175/jswe.2009.200800004.

Weiss-Gal, I., & Gal, J. (2017). Social work educators and social policy: A cross-professional perspective. *European Journal of Social Work.* https://doi.org/10.1080/13691457.2017.1357026.

Yee, M. Y., & Greene, G. J. (2004). A teaching framework for transformative multicultural social work education. *Journal of Ethnic and Cultural Diversity in Social Work, 12*(3), 1–28.

CHAPTER 43

Social Work and Marginalisation in India: Questioning Frameworks

Mohd Shahid

Introduction

"Each case and each situation must be individualised," argued Octavia Hill in her *Letters to Fellow Workers* (Hill, 1875; Kendall, 2000). However, the argument in this chapter is that the role played by hegemony in the making of a social reality and its meaning-making by people needs to be examined. Each case and each situation must therefore be examined through the lenses of language, hegemony, and common sense. Professional social workers are obliged to work in diverse sociocultural settings many of which may be diametrically opposed to their own personally cherished sociocultural ideals. It is also possible that the practice setting and the community relationship that exists within it may be so structurally rooted that professionals may be unable to locate structural inequalities and oppressive realities in a specific sociocultural context.

India continues to witness virulent intolerance on the basis of caste and religious identities, aversion to diversities, and diminishing shared spaces. There is an increase in the incidence of conflicts on the basis of identity assertion and reactions to them, while age-old caste-based atrocities on people belonging to marginalised caste groups (now popularly and assertively referred to as Dalits) continue unabated. These are serious concerns for social workers and practices where they are employed. This is even more so when the social work fraternity at the global level is arguing for the empowerment

M. Shahid (✉)
Department of Social Work, School of Arts and Social Sciences, Maulana Azad National Urdu University, Hyderabad, Telangana, India
e-mail: shahid@manuu.edu.in

© The Author(s) 2021
S. S. M. et al. (eds.), *The Palgrave Handbook of Global Social Work Education*, https://doi.org/10.1007/978-3-030-39966-5_43

and liberation of people by engaging "people and structures" (IFSW & IASSW, 2014). The values of social justice, human rights, collective responsibility, and respect for diversities are projected as cardinal principles.

This requires social workers to find ways to locate and uncover their own trappings, their own social constructions, their ways of seeing, their gaze, their own make-up as a product of a particular sociocultural historical reality, and their own understanding of the journey they have to make to become a professional social worker committed to the cause of social justice. This necessitates revisiting the ontology of social work (social work as a being, a professional practice) and what is involved in becoming a social worker. Historians now (subalterns) argue that it is important to *search for ways* to *represent the remoteness in histories* that are written (Pandey, 2013 p. 30, emphasis added). In similar vein the consistent concern of social workers should be excavating their own constructions and searching for ways to locate the marginalities rather than structuralities in practices where they are employed.

This chapter argues, first, for the need to make social workers consistently revisit their own social constructions and, second, for the need to make use of indigenous knowledge sources in the meaning-making of sociocultural realities of any society. Together these two arguments point to a need to make use of critical social theories and theorists to examine complex structurally rooted sociocultural realities. In this chapter the theoretical framework of one such theorist Antonio Gramsci is used to understand how language, hegemony, and common sense work in tandem to make an oppressive social reality normal and natural and hence unquestionable.

Changing Nature of Social Work and Need to Change the Lens

Although social work as a profession has evolved over time, it has remained sufficiently dynamic in nature to address the changing needs and problems of human beings. Human needs and problems across time and space characterise the changing focus, concerns, and perspectives of social work. It has been aptly noted that social work is by nature a changing profession (Dominelli, 2004). From the legacy of basket-on-the-arm assistance to a profession committed to the cause of social justice, social work has a chequered history (Shahid, 2016a). Examples of this history are debates on social divisions; the increasing number of social workers challenging such divisions on the basis of class (radical perspective), gender (feminist perspective), and race (anti-racist/black perspective); discrimination arising from other forms of identities (anti-discriminatory practice); and arguments that take account of the oppressed and the interplay between power dynamics (anti-oppressive practice) (Bailey & Brake, 1975; Chambon, Irving, & Epstein, 1999; Davies, 2000; Desai, Jaswal, & Ganapathi, 2004; Dominelli, 1998, 2002; Mullaly,

2010; Shahid, 2016b). The latest global definition of social work is reflective of the journey travelled by the profession so far. It rightly argues that "underpinned by theories of social work, social sciences, humanities, and *indigenous knowledge*, social work *engages people and structures* to address life's challenges and enhance wellbeing" (IFSW & IASSW, 2014, emphasis added).

Despite debates on a single global definition of social work or on the processes that have to be followed to arrive at and generalise a single definition of social work, this definition marked a paradigm shift in the foci of social work education and practice from apolitical social work to profoundly political social work. The aspiration that "social work engages people and structures to address life challenges and enhance wellbeing" entrusts social workers with the responsibility to examine and expose inequalities and oppression inbuilt and inherent in social structures. The nature and quantum of structural inequalities and structurally rooted oppression may vary across sociocultural community contexts. The growing focus on indigenous knowledge is also interesting. Without entering into the debate on the appropriateness of eurocentric or indigenous knowledge and determining the specifics of what constitutes indigenous knowledge (Alvares, 2011; Bar-On, 2015; Deshpande, 2011; Dominelli, 2014), this chapter argues that indigenous knowledge could be an important source for social workers to make sense of sociocultural realities in a specific context. Indigenous knowledge sources of whatever form ranging from stories, novels, poems, films to stock narratives such as folktales, phrases, and proverbs could be an important source reflecting the critical realities of any society. However, this again requires the use of critical theories that may help in the meaning-making of sociocultural realities. The Gramscian theoretical framework is used in this chapter. This framework has recently been gaining significant ground in social work writings and scholars are appreciating the insights it provides in making social work practice less hegemonic and more anti-oppressive in nature (Agnimitra, Jha, & Shahid, 2015; Garrett, 2009; Ledwith, 2001; Shahid & Jha, 2014).

Theoretical Lens: Language, Hegemony, and Common Sense

Prison notes written by Antonio Gramsci (1891–1937) while he was incarcerated were later published as *Selections from the Prison Notebooks* and became a classic of social theory in contemporary times (Barrett, 1991; Gramsci, 1971/2014; Hobsbawm, 1977). The traditional conceptualisation of hegemony as leadership underwent much needed metamorphosis at the hands of Gramsci and became more analytical in elucidating "how seemingly private or personal aspects of daily life are politically important aspects of operation of power" (Ives, 2004, p. 71). Hegemony means that the terms of deliberation are framed in particular ways whereby certain ideas feel natural and prescribed actions appear as common sense (Shahid & Jha, 2014). Thus, Gramsci located hegemony in the daily and "molecular" operation of power and in the ways in which dominance is legitimised by the instrument of hegemony not by coercion but through consent (Ives, 2004). Gramsci insists that hegemony is dynamic and takes account of the interests and tendencies of groups over which hegemony is exercised (Forgacs, 2000).

Language is an important constituent of hegemony (Ives, 2004) because it is particularly in the realm of language use that the full implication of hegemony for structure and agency are most apparent (Sontag, 2003). Gramsci realised very early on that in a vital sense language is politics for it affects the way people think about power (Germino, 1990). For Gramsci language is therefore both an element in the exercise of power and a metaphor for how power operates (Ives, 2004). Gramsci (2014) described the link between the operation of hegemony and the insubordination of social groups as subaltern (oppressed). "One central aspect that makes all these social groups subaltern is that they lack a coherent philosophy or world view from which to understand and interpret the world. One could say they lack their own language" (Ives, 2004, p. 78).

Common sense comprises the diffuse uncoordinated features of a generic form of thought common to a particular period and environment (Gramsci, 2014, Notes, p. 330). Gramsci has a distinct meaning and understanding for common sense. "Unlike English, the Italian notion of common sense (*senso commune*) does not so much mean good, sound, practical sense rather it means normal or average understanding and refers simply to the belief and opinions supposedly shared by the mass of the population" (Crehan, 2011, p. 274). So good sense (*buon senso*) in Italian has a different meaning from common sense in English (Ives, 2004). Gramsci rightly pointed out that many elements in popular common sense contribute to people's subordination by making situations of inequality and oppression appear to them as natural and unchangeable (Forgacs, 2000). Such common sense contains elements of truth as well as elements of misrepresentation and helps in reproducing and maintaining not only existing power regimes, but also carries the seeds of transformation.

Social Work and Marginalisation

Social workers need to question the frameworks within which they work as a priori requisites to appreciating the role played by social work in challenging marginalisation. The fundamental question is how conscious are social workers of the meaning-making of their own constructions and of doing justice to diverse practice settings that are often diametrically opposite to their own normative beliefs and practices. Flexner (1915/2001) rightly argued that professions are essentially intellectual operations with large individual responsibility. How easy is it to uphold such professional responsibility? Paulo Freire, a leading advocate of critical pedagogy, had some answers for social workers. Speaking on *A Critical Understanding of Social Work* at the Social Workers' World Conference held in Stockholm (Sweden) on 30 July 1988 Freire argued (Moch, 2009) that:

> Social worker is not a neutral agent in his practice and in his action. ... The first virtue, or quality, that I would cite for a progressive social worker is the convergence between what is said and what is done. And it is not easy to work on diminishing the distance between discourse and action. It is much easier to talk than to do ... to diminish the distance between what I say, what I affirm, and what I do, I believe, would *require an effort every single day to realize*, for the educator, for the social worker, with a progressive obsession. And it is not even easy to measure when there is fantastic interference between the ideology and the weight of ideology, at the level of reflex and at the level of intellect. (Moch, 2009, p. 95, emphasis added)

Given the social conditioning of social workers they are always susceptible to doing injustice to themselves as professionals and to professional practice. An example of this susceptibility was given by the legendary social work educator Felix Biestek widely read and known for his work on the principles of social work and the case work relationship:

> ... Acceptance is a principle of action wherein the caseworker perceives and deals with the client as he really is, including his strengths and weaknesses, his congenial and uncongenial qualities, his positive and negative feelings, his constructive and destructive attitudes and behaviour, maintaining all the while a sense of the client's innate dignity and personal worth. ... *The role of the caseworker is to help the client proceed from a situation which is undesirable and unacceptable to a situation which is desirable and acceptable.* ... The violation of moral law by the *unmarried mother*, the violation of civil law by the *parolee*, ... the breakup of a family through divorce ... *all of these are undesirable*. It is therefore ridiculous to think that the caseworker's duty is to approve of everything about the client. (Biestek, 1957, p. 72)

Shahid and Jha (2014) argued that it is a case of professional hegemony and professional ambivalence on the part of Biestek to have the audacity to first frame the issues of unmarried mothers and the breakup of families (divorce) as undesirable and to then exhort that it is "ridiculous to think that the caseworker's duty is to approve of everything about the client." The instant an unmarried mother comes to a case worker is used as an occasion to judge and establish "ambivalence in sexual behaviour." Does not such disapproval by the worker conflict with values underlying the principle of acceptance? Do not unmarried mothers, divorcees, and parolees have the right to human dignity (Shahid & Jha, 2014, p. 31)? There is invariably the temptation to envisage Biestek's sermon in terms of some contemporary social workers promoting the rights of gays and lesbians, people living with HIV/AIDS, or people in live-in relationships.

A textbook widely referenced by social work educators and community development practitioners in India has a passage reflecting the process of community building in a village near New Delhi, the capital of India:

> A meeting of all the villagers was called with the help of the student worker. All the male members, especially the adults, were personally requested to attend the meeting. The meeting was attended by all the leaders. *There was no preferential order of sitting except for the fact that the lower caste people belonging to Jhimer, Chamar and Bhangi did not sit on the carpet.* (Gangrade, 1971, p. 59, emphasis added, cited in Shahid & Jha, 2016)

Stating "there was no preferential order of sitting" as a matter of fact is a blatant case of the untouchability and indignity some marginalised caste groups in India have to endure. Using derogatory names such as Chamar and Bhangi for marginalised caste groups constitutes a criminal offence in India. Nevertheless, normative social order in India, especially in rural India, has relegated marginalised caste groups like the Dalits to physical and symbolic segregation. Segregating caste clusters in Indian villages speaks volumes on inbuilt caste hegemony in social topography (Shahid, 2015). Although specific caste groups sitting "on the carpet" or "off the carpet" connotates a thin line marking the physical distance between caste groups, in reality they are explicit markers of subtle forms of untouchability (Shahid & Jha, 2016). This requires a prism through which to uncover hegemonisation of the vocabulary that normalises oppression and marginalisation (Shahid, Raza, & Alam, 2015, p. 10) and by the same token (see the following section) to use indigenous knowledge and critical social theories as a prism through which to uncover oppression and marginalisation rooted in structures and normalised in language used with reference to others such as marginalised caste groups in India like the Dalits.

INDIGENOUS KNOWLEDGE: A VALUABLE RESOURCE FOR SOCIAL WORKERS

Indigenous knowledge sources could represent the best possible resource for social workers to use to understand the sociocultural realities of any society. This is even more important because social workers traverse many cultural and geographical boundaries to work with the diverse groups that make up the population. Kakar (1989) rightly noted that there is a no better way to gain an understanding of a society than through its stock of stories such as myths, fables, parables, and tales. Indigenous knowledge sources in the form of stock narratives such as oral narratives, written stories, novels, real life stories, films, and other texts could help social workers understand the niceties of any society.

With the help of a story written by Munshi Premchand (1880–1936) an attempt is made in this section to argue that stories as indigenous knowledge sources could help social workers understand caste dynamics in Indian society and the subtle ways in which caste hegemony is normalised in popular common sense perceptions. Oppression and marginalisation can consequently be internalised by the subalterns (the oppressed groups) themselves who then apparently become flag bearers of those hegemonies. The Gramscian lens of language, hegemony, and common sense is used to help social workers in the meaning-making of indigenous knowledge sources and in locating the structural inequalities and oppressive realities rooted in sociocultural practices.

"Story as Text for Social Workers": Example from Premchand's Sadgati (Salvation)

Premchand is *the* legendary story writer and novelist of Urdu–Hindi canon in twentieth century India. Through his writings he achieved a stature during his own lifetime that was so distinguished it is still unmatched even in the twenty-first century. So much so that his writings are becoming ever more relevant to understanding contemporary Indian society, particularly with reference to the impoverished and the Dalits. This is also evident from academic work looking at the *Collected Works of Premchand* that do so from different vantage points such as caste, women, and village society and in different languages such as Urdu (Gopal, 2003), Hindi (Agarwal, 2013), or English (Asaduddin, 2018). Premchand wrote about people living on the margins of society and his stories and novels reflect the miseries of poverty intertwined with the stark realities of caste oppression and marginalisation. The plots, narratives, actors, and everyday forms of negotiations are so nuanced and woven with unmatched sensitivity that they provide a perfect prism through which to uncover injustice (subtle and blatant), indignity, and humiliation inflicted on the impoverished and the Dalits.

This section of the chapter is based on an ongoing endeavour to experiment and reflect on the importance of indigenous knowledge. The contention here is to argue that indigenous knowledge could be an important source for the meaning-making of sociocultural realities of any society across the globe. As part of pedagogical experiments with postgraduate students of social work, indigenous knowledge sources like Premchand's stories are subjected to group exercises by the students to analyse the text and reflect on the message the story delivers and the lessons that social workers could take from it. Many of these exercises over the years have helped cement the argument for using a "story as text for social workers." Furthermore, when the story is revisited through a critical theory lens like the Gramscian lens of language, hegemony, and common sense the story becomes ever more revealing.

The understanding gained using such pedagogical experiments relates specifically to Premchand's story *Sadgati* first published in 1930. In Urdu it appeared as *Najat* and more recently in English as *Salvation*. The Hindi compilation edited by Agarwal (2013) and an English translation done by the author of this chapter were used to gain such understanding.

Sadgati starts with poor parents Dukhi and Jhuria expressing concerns about arranging the marriage of their daughter. They seek help from a local religious person Pandit Baba who belongs to the higher Brahmin caste to fix the date based on good omens (divine messages from their gods). Dukhi and Jhuria belong to the Chamar caste. Chamar is a derogatory word inflicted on the caste group today called Jatav in northern India and collectively (as marginalised caste groups) called Dalits. They find themselves placed among the lowest castes in the caste hierarchy at the time the story was written and things have not changed much even today. They are considered untouchable by people belonging to higher castes. Dukhi and Jhuria are more concerned about their untouchable status (internalisation) than people generally. This leads to a lengthy discussion between them on what was the best seating arrangements for Pandit Baba should he agree to visit their house to fix the date for the marriage of their daughter. Dukhi while preparing to go to Pandit Baba's house to ask him to find and fix the marriage date is also equally concerned that he should not go empty handed since it was not the done thing. So he took a bundle of grass fodder, his only asset, as a tribute (*nazarana*) to Pandit Baba. Doing a bit of back-end planning and holding the bundle of grass as a gift Dukhi reached the house of Pandit Baba. The story beautifully reflects the niceties and intricacies with which Dukhi belonging to a lower caste greets the holy man and makes his submission before him. Although Pandit Baba first pretends to have a busy schedule, he does eventually agree to visit Dukhi's house in the afternoon provided Dukhi completes tasks Pandit Baba assigns to him such as cleaning his (Pandit Baba's) veranda, giving it a cow dung coat (to beat the heat), bringing husks in from the field, and chopping a wooden log into pieces. Immediately given the instructions Dukhi committed himself religiously to the tasks. Pandit Baba and his wife argue about whether to give some food to hungry Dukhi and Pandit Baba's wife gets angry because Dukhi entered a particular part of the house forbidden to him by virtue of belonging to a lower caste. While Pandit Baba had his lunch and went for a nap poor Dukhi (who went hungry) overexerted himself in completing the tasks demanded of him by Pandit Baba. Dukhi did everything except chop the wooden log. However, he lost his life in his efforts to do so through exhaustion and having an empty stomach. The story ends by reflecting on the inhuman treatment given to Dukhi's dead body. This was the unfortunate outcome of the lifelong belief, service, and commitment Dukhi had toward people of the higher Brahmin caste.

The story deals with the plight of people belonging to lower caste groups who are equally poor but more concerned about the rites, rituals, and obligations prescribed by society. This is reflected in poor Dukhi's concern about seeking the help of a religious person belonging to a higher caste (Brahmin) to identify good omens indicative of the best date for the marriage of their daughter. The back-end preparations Dukhi made are reflective of the internalisation of untouchability by lowest caste people. Dukhi's empty stomach represents the mass of poor people who spend much of their life half-hungry but are committed to the sacred duty of obliging upper caste groups. Dukhi lost his life completing the assignments (concealed forced labour) given to him by Pandit Baba simply because Pandit Baba asked him to do so. The language used in the whole story by people belonging to two different caste groups is also reflective of how language is an instrument in the operation of (caste) hegemony and that language in itself becomes a vector of power dynamics, oppression, and marginalisation. The meaning-making of this story by social workers requires revisiting the story through the Gramscian lens of language, hegemony, and common sense.

Language as an Instrument to Normalise Oppression

At the very start of the story Dukhi is introduced as Dukhi Chamar revealing his name and his caste. A little later Pandit Baba addresses Dukhi as *Dukhiya* deliberately altering the name to show the contempt with which higher caste people regard lower caste people. Then, while telling his wife about Dukhi's presence Pandit Baba referred to him as *Sasura Dukhiya Chamar* making the contempt shown far more derogatory and abusive. By contrast, all through the story the religious person is referred as *Pandit Baba* ("revered religious person"), *Pandit Ji* ("respected religious person"), or *Maharaj* ("emperor").

Such nomenclature reflects the caste hierarchy and manner in which language per se is hegemonised. Although upper castes and people belonging to them are addressed using words of praise and reverence, lower castes and people belonging to them are addressed using words of contempt. They are more often referred to by their caste names than their proper names. Furthermore, their caste names are often pejorative adjectives that have taken the form of derogatory names imposed on such caste groups to such an extent that even people belonging to the same caste group or other marginalised caste groups (Dalits) use such adjectives too. This is rightly argued as the basic marker of hegemonisation of the vocabulary (Shahid et al., 2015). Use of the word Chamar is today a criminal offence in India. Basically, the word Chamar is the derogatory name used against people belonging to lower caste groups correctly called Jatav (respectable proper noun) who have historically had to contend with caste-based untouchability and oppression (as reflected in the story of Dukhi). There is much derogatory use of the word Chamar in common parlance even today. Similarly, there are many marginalised caste groups in India who are still not called by their proper name. Instead, they have to put up with having the pejorative adjective imposed on them as the name by which they are called. Hence the need for meaning-making of caste names in common parlance and ensuring they are not used in a derogatory manner.

Caste Hegemony and Internalising Oppression

Returning to *Sadgati*, the story begins with a discussion Dukhi is having with his wife about inviting Pandit Baba to fix a suitable marriage date for their daughter. However, all he could concentrate on was how to handle a visit from a religious person belonging to the Brahmin caste to the house of an untouchable. He gave elaborate instructions to his wife about any presents (prescribed ritual gifts) that would be offered to Pandit Baba making sure none would be touched by Dukhi's family and finding a suitable person from another caste or tribal group not considered untouchable to hand the presents over. Dukhi is fully aware of what it means to belong to so-called lower or untouchable caste groups, convinced that Brahmins are made great by God, and hence all obligations must be followed strictly including the rules of untouchability. In the event of any violation God himself would punish the offender. His perception would be proven "right" shortly of course. While looking for fire balls (*angare*) to light a locally made tobacco pipe (*chilam*) Dukhi ventured too far into the house. As soon as Pandit Baba's wife became aware of Dukhi's caste she was outraged by his daring to came so close to their living room. Nevertheless, on her husband's insistence she gave Dukhi some fire balls, but aware of Dukhi's caste and annoyed by Dukhi entering her "sacred" house she simply threw the fire balls at him some of which fell on Dukhi's head. Nevertheless, Dukhi was happy to be punished for the sin he had just committed by entering the house of a Brahmin. He fully knew that divine retribution was the reason everyone feared Brahmins. This is reflective of how caste hegemony is internalised, normalised, and perpetuated unquestioned. These are the words of the underdog (Dukhi, the oppressed) speaking the language of the topdog (upper caste, the oppressor).

As pointed out earlier, despite Dukhi being very poor he was clear that he should not visit Pandit Baba empty handed and hence took with him a bundle of grass fodder as a gift or tribute. Although he was hungry and clearly not up to carrying out the tasks assigned by Pandit Baba, he knew it was his duty to do so and as a result lost his life through overexertion. This is indicative of caste hegemony and the fact that poor people belonging to lower caste groups live their lives serving and fulfilling the wishes of upper castes. Moreover, marginalised caste groups consider doing so their sacred duty. The manner in which Dukhi interpreted fire balls thrown at him and hitting his head as divine retribution for entering the house of a Brahmin is one small example of how popular common sense perceptions work in tandem to perpetuate caste hegemony and caste-based oppression. Had Dukhi been told such a story (i.e., of how a poor man died serving Pandit Baba) he would have considered it a great reward and would have said that the poor man would not only get salvation, but God would definitely reward him because he died serving a Brahmin. This is how caste hegemony colonises the mind and mannerisms of marginalised caste groups.

Conclusion

Social workers trying to uphold the values of human dignity and social justice need to identify the vectors of oppression and marginalisation. However, it is often difficult to locate oppression and marginalisation when concealed and normalised in sociocultural practices. This is especially so when social workers work in settings that are diametrically opposed to their own cherished sociocultural ideals. Stories like *Sadgati* could be used to help social workers understand the social dynamics of a particular society and differential and discriminatory variations in such dynamics across social identity markers. A theoretical lens like that of language, hegemony, and common sense could help them in the meaning-making of given sociocultural realities and locating subtle forms of oppression, mechanisms in which oppression is concealed, and ways to challenge oppression by making oppressed groups conscious of their own hegemonic sociocultural constructions. Thus indigenous knowledge sources in the form of novels, stories, and other writings from subalterns could be helpful in understanding marginalisation. Critical theories like that of Gramsci could help social workers in the meaning-making of sociocultural realities and making their practice anti-hegemonic in nature.

References

Agarwal, B. (Ed.). (2013). *Dalit Jeewan Ki Kahaniyan: Premchand*. Delhi: Sakshi Prakashan.

Agnimitra, N., Jha, M. K., & Shahid, M. (2015). Social work in India: Do we love being at crossroads? *Indian Journal of Social Work, 76*(3), 331–350.

Alvares, C. (2011). A critique of eurocentric social science and the question of alternatives. *Economic & Political Weekly, XLVI*(22), 72–81.

Asaduddin, M. (Ed.). (2018). *Stories on caste: Premchand*. New Delhi: Penguin Books.

Bailey, R., & Brake, M. (Eds.). (1975). *Radical social work*. London: Edward Arnold.

Bar-On, A. (2015). Indigenous knowledge: Ends or means? *International Social Work, 58*(6), 780–789.

Barrett, M. (1991). *The politics of truth: From Marx to Foucault*. Stanford, CA: Stanford University Press.

Biestek, F. P. (1957). *The casework relationship*. Chicago, IL: Loyola University Press.

Chambon, A. S., Irving, A., & Epstein, L. (Eds.). (1999). *Reading Foucault for social work*. New York: Columbia University Press.

Crehan, K. (2011). Gramsci's concept of common sense: A useful concept for antropologist? *Journal of Modern Italian Studies, 2*(16), 273–287.

Davies, M. (Ed.). (2000). *The Blackwell encyclopaedia of social work*. Oxford: Blackwell.

Desai, M., Jaswal, S., & Ganapathi, S. (Eds.). (2004). *The Indian Journal of Social Work* (Special Issue: Social Work Knowledge Development and Dissemination), *65*(1), 1–7.

Deshpande, A. (2011). Eurocentric versus indigenous. *Economic & Political Weekly, XLVI*(30), 87–88.

Dominelli, L. (1998). Anti-oppressive practice in context. In R. Adams, L. Dominelli, & M. Pyne (Eds.), *Social work: Themes, issues and critical debates* (pp. 3–22). Hampshire: Macmillan Press.

Dominelli, L. (2002). *Anti-oppressive social work theory and practice*. London: Palgrave.

Dominelli, L. (2004). *Social work: Theory and practice for a changing profession.* Cambridge and Malden: Polity Press (Indian Reprint, 2005).

Dominelli, L. (2014). Internationalizing professional practices: The place of social work in the international arena. *International Social Work, 57*(3), 258–267.

Flexner, A. (2001). Is social work a profession? *Research on Social Work Practice, 11*(2), 152–165 (Originally published in 1915).

Forgacs, D. (2000). *The Gramsci Reader: Selected writings 1916–1935.* New York: New York University Press (First Published in 1988).

Gangrade, K. D. (1971). *Community organization In India.* Bombay: Popular Prakasan.

Garrett, P. M. (2009). The 'whalebone' in the (social work) çorset'? Notes on Antonio Gramsci and social work educators. *Social Work Education, 11*(3), 237–250.

Germino, D. (1990). *Antonio Gramsci: Architect of a new politics.* Baton Rogue, LA: Louisiana State University Press.

Gopal, M. (Ed.). (2003). *Kulliyat-e-Premchand* (22 Vols.) (In Urdu). New Delhi: National Council for Promotion of Urdu Language.

Gramsci, A. (2014). *Selections from the Prison Notebooks* (Q. Hoare & G. Nowell Smith, Eds. and Trans). New Delhi: Orient Blackswan (First Published 1971).

Hill, Octavia. (1875). *Homes of the London poor.* London: Macmillan.

Hobsbawm, E. J. (1977, July). Gramsci and political theory. *Marxism Today,* pp. 205–213.

IFSW., & IASSW. (2014). *Social work definition.* Bern: International Federation of Social Workers & International Association of Schools of Social Work.

Ives, P. (2004). *Language and hegemony in Gramsci.* London and Manitoba: Pluto Press and Fernwood Publishing.

Jha, M. (2009). Community organization in split societies. *Community Development Journal, 44*(3), 305–319.

Kakar, S. (1989). *Intimate relations: Exploring Indian sexuality.* New Delhi: Penguin Boooks.

Kendall, K. A. (2000). World wide beginning of social work. *Indian Journal of Social Work, 61*(2), 141–156.

Ledwith, M. (2001). Community work as critical pedagogy: Re-envisioning Freire and Gramsci. *Community Development Journal, 36*(3), 171–182.

Moch, M. (2009). A critical understanding of social work by Paolo Freire. *Journal of Progressive Human Services, 20,* 92–97.

Mullaly, B. (2010). *Challenging oppression and confronting privilege: A critical social work approach* (2nd ed.). Don Mills, ON: Oxford University Press.

Pandey, G. (2013). In defense of the fragment: Writing about Hindu-Muslim Riots I India Today. In R. Guha (Ed.), *A Subaltern studies reader 1986–1995* (pp. 1-33). New Delhi: Oxford University Press (First published in 1997).

Shahid, M. (2015). Manual scavenging: Issues of caste, culture and violence. *Social Change, 42*(2), 242–255.

Shahid, M. (2016a). The art and science of social work. In G. Thomas & Saumya (Eds.), *Theoretical Framework and Review of Studies* (pp. 1–15). New Delhi: Indira Gandhi National Open University.

Shahid, M. (2016b). Social work practice frameworks. In G. Thomas & Saumya (Eds.), *Theoretical framework and review of studies* (pp. 16–32). New Delhi: Indira Gandhi National Open University.

Shahid, M., & Jha, M. K. (2014). Revisiting client worker relationship: Biestek through Gramscian Gaze. *Journal of Progressive Human Services, 25*(1), 18–36.

Shahid, M., & Jha, M. K. (2016). Community development practice in India: Interrogating caste and common sense. In Mae Shaw & Marjorie Mayo (Eds.), *Class, inequality and community development* (pp. 93–106). Bristol, UK: Policy Press, University of Bristol.

Shahid, M., Raza, M. S., & Alam, M. A. (2015). Disability and popular common-sense: Noun versus adjective. *International Journal of Disability, Development and Education, 62*(2), 151–162.

Sontag, S. (2003). *The local politics of global English: Case studies in linguistic globalisation.* Lanham: Lexington.

CHAPTER 44

Dignity and Social Justice

Hans van Ewijk

Introduction

Dignity and social justice are dominant overarching values in social work, social care, and social education. The argument in this theoretical and reflective chapter concerns the need to revalue vulnerability and take dignity and social justice as cornerstones for practice to be supportive. Although dignity and social justice are interdependent values, together they give direction to social work practice that is just and fair. Such values are not fixed and objective, rather they are always open to discussion. The main interest is to transfer such concepts to the context of local social practice when working with the most vulnerable people. The chapter ends with some reflections on tensions that exist between concepts and on some essentials in applying social justice and dignity. The chapter is split into five sections: vulnerability; moral vulnerability; dignity; social justice; and tensions and essentials.

Vulnerability

Vulnerability has long been perceived as belonging to the unworthy. The troubled, the leprous, the poor, the orphan were kept outside the city gates or were placed in madhouses, poorhouses (workhouses), and orphanages. Care and social services were meant for vulnerable people and even today vulnerable people are often perceived as weak, problematic, and needy. Neoliberal policies stressing personal responsibility and strength are not very helpful in bringing about a different perspective.

H. van Ewijk (✉)
Emeritus Professor Social Work Theory, University of Humanistic Studies, Utrecht, The Netherlands

Visiting Professor Social Work Policy, Tartu University, Tartu, Estonia

S. S. M. et al. (eds.), *The Palgrave Handbook of Global Social Work Education*, https://doi.org/10.1007/978-3-030-39966-5_44

Biographical

Vulnerability as such is very human and appealing. A world made up of invulnerable people feels like a nightmare. Vulnerability opens hearts, creates strong connections, and binds people to each other and their communities. However, vulnerability can be painful. We all have parts of our bodies (physical and mental) that hurt if they are touched. They are painful because of grief, shame, guilt, impotence, frustration, or anger. Sometimes they stop people from social functioning. They can develop into traumas. In this chapter they are coined "biographical vulnerabilities" or mental injuries that arise during people's lives.

Physically Handicapped

People start life physically vulnerable as babies and will be in later life when they become elderly. Accidents or serious illnesses can make people (temporally) vulnerable. Other people have a lasting impairment as a result of being blind, deaf, or lame.

Intellectually Disabled

Some people lack an adequate comprehension being intellectual disabled. In growing social complexity more people with an intellectual disability have serious problems to cope with daily life. It is not that the number intellectual disabled people is increasing, but they have increasing problems to cope with our complex society. Life's demands, temptations, choices, and threats are too overwhelming for them. The number of people intellectually disabled (albeit often slightly) in youth care, mental health, prisons, and homeless is rapidly increasing (Van Ewijk, 2010).

Mentally Disordered

Although all people feel mentally disordered at certain times of their lives, for some people the disorder seriously hinders them from social functioning. Despite well-ordered systems of education, health, housing, and social security the number of socially vulnerable people has not decreased. On the contrary, all over Europe the number of mentally disordered people in mental health services is growing (Witchen et al., 2011). This chapter argues this is due to the growing complexity of and reduced bonding in communities such as the family, the workplace, and the neighbourhood.

Socially Excluded

Finally, people become vulnerable when deprived access to systems and communities because they are too poor, or are illegals, stigmatized or too unknown with our society. Lack of resources hinders them from participating in communities, education, and work.

Self-Efficacy

Having a disability or disorder or being excluded hinders people from participating fully in society. However, vulnerable people can be exceedingly robust. Despite pain (physical and mental), disability, and disorders they manage their lives and find their own paths through it. Although they may need some extra resources such as a tool, an aid, personal care, a therapy, or a benefit, they are not in need of professional social support or serious interventions. Although vulnerabilities hinder people in living their lives, they do not by definition hinder people themselves. To see who are likely to be the users of professional social support there needs to be a second perspective in addition to vulnerability. This is referred to as self-efficacy (Bandura, 1982, 1995, 1997). Self-efficacy is the capacity to use knowledge, skills, experiences, and talents in such a way that a person is able to cope with daily life and participate in society and its communities. Although self-efficacy can be endangered by disabilities, disorders, and social exclusion, as already pointed out many of these people are able to manage their lives robustly. This is also true the other way around. People with hardly noticeable vulnerabilities often find it hard to cope with daily life. Self-neglect, addiction, isolation, and lack of motivation are commonly not due to a disorder or disability but come from a deep-layered inability to cope that differs from person to person (Polanyi, 1969, 2009). Self-efficacy is a personal disposition that is partly genetic and partly biographically developed (Bourdieu, 1984). It makes little sense to proclaim that people who lack self-efficacy should use what strength they have to participate adequately in society. It is like asking the blind to open their eyes.

MORAL VULNERABILITY

Moral vulnerability is another kind of vulnerability. Late modernity witnessed the disappearance from most societies of an overarching moral system linked to religion. Religion and morality are now perceived as personal choices and belong to the realm of private life. The world of sense-giving and moral choice has an open horizon (Taylor, 1989). It is up to individuals to find their own paths. This directing of the self is for many people demanding and quite often too demanding. Today's network society and risk society are overwhelming in their fragmentation, mobility, and speed. Although ongoing knowledge has brought tremendous progress in health, technology, and industries, it has also led to uncontrollable processes and a complexity that is disordered. Business and public administration consultants talk in terms of what they call the C-triangle made up of complexity, claims, and capacity (Noordegraaf, 2009). The more complex the market, the products, and the services, the more is asked of the capacity of the administration or enterprise. The same goes for claims. There are demands from consumers, financiers, quality systems, sustainability, safety, effectivity, efficiency, evidence, and so on calling for investment in specialised staff, procedures, and protocols. If complexity and demand increase, then an enterprise invests more in its capacity. What happens if this C-triangle is translated to the social domain, to the human being? If societies are growing in complexity and demands are rising, then what about human capacity? People cannot invest in more capacity since there is no market for self-efficacy, even though they can wonder whether they are able to control the complexity created and the increase in demand. Social stress felt by human beings and reduction in the bonding felt by communities together create a late-modern social vulnerability that is not easy to grasp or to categorise. It is everywhere, in all families and communities, and permeates societies. Growing complexity produces uncertainty. There is a great deal of uncertainty (e.g., in the upbringing of children) in the domain of morality and meaning of life. An open horizon and fewer bonding structures make more room for people with what is known as a thick ego who follow their own interests and do not feel responsible to others let alone the state or government (Kunneman, 2009).

Hannah Arendt

Hannah Arendt was a Jewish German philosopher who escaped from Germany to the United States just before World War II. Throughout her life she tried to find the reason her people were persecuted in the Holocaust. She thought it too easy just to blame Hitler and his accomplices. The Germans and to a certain extent even the Jews let it happen. She felt the answer might lie in modern societies failing to engage in critical dialogue. Citizens do not openly debate or discuss their aspirations, worries, and doubts sufficiently. She writes warmly about the Greek polis where citizens openly discussed politics and life in the marketplace. Such citizen power had a countervailing effect on rulers and systems. In modern (over)organised societies such a civil dialogue has all but disappeared. Maybe it is still there to some extent in the political arena. However, political parties in parliaments are more interested in claiming, counterclaiming, and engaging in power play. Professionals are unchallenged in how they run their systems of education, health, social services, and public administration. Moreover, civil dialogue on normative questions is almost lacking even in such systems. Everyone seems to be acting as wheels go round in a big machine reminiscent of complaints by community care teams about the lack of time to discuss what really matters. Until that happens everyone is just watching? wheels go round (Arendt, 1979).

Moreover, Arendt goes on to say that the right intonation is needed when discussing what matters. It is not about postulating truth and opinions, but rather a concerned and interested way of speaking and listening. It is about uncertain knowing, asking the other, and horizontal deliberating. Arendt refers to the Greek expression *dokei moi* ("it seems to me", "I think", "I presume") (Arendt, 1981, p. 21). A real civic dialogue should involve inviting, hesitating, and careful arguing. A citizen is not someone with a thick ego or someone watching a wheel go round—a citizen is critical and open for dialogue (Arendt, 1958, 1979, 1981).

The answer to growing moral uncertainty is dialogue that presumes to deliberate collectively about the good, the desirable, and the actions to take. Although universal truths and moral principles can no longer be claimed, it is possible to aim at civil dialogues inspired by concepts such as dignity and justice (Arendt, 1958).

DIGNITY

Dignity represents an alternative approach to social care and social work in which new public management language is expressed in words such as efficiency, effectivity, products, and time management. Care and social work have been excessively dominated by instrumental rationality. All professional activities have become framed in limited objectives and transformed into precisely defined products and services. People are seen in instrumental rationality as essential to bringing about economic objectives such as growth, increased productivity, and consumption. Moreover, dignity opposes turning people into objects to diagnose, to treat, and to measure progress and turning professionals into appliers of protocols and prescribed methods. Dignity respecting the very being of a person is also a decategorising concept. It opposes dividing populations into categories and comparing different categories of people as happens with class, gender, age, impairment, and disorder. Hundreds of categories are constructed leading to perceiving people as representatives of their specific category (Billig, 1991).

Intrinsic Dignity

In palliative care, in particular, intrinsic dignity often refers to showing respect for human beings at their most vulnerable and to avoiding perceiving them as objects of medical treatment (Leget, 2011). Intrinsic dignity is the belief that a human being is not a means but an objective. Human beings should not be seen as instrumental to higher objectives but as goals in themselves. Like all organisms human beings follow their own course in life and should be respected in that. Human beings should be considered subject, unique, and having a value of their own.

Moral Dignity

People are moral beings who understand the difference between good and bad, beautiful and ugly and suffer feelings such as shame, guilt, and pride. They are steered by what they value. Philosophers long perceived morality as unique to humankind diametrically opposite to nature's incapacity to recognise values and lack of feelings such as empathy and sympathy. According to this reasoning the human:nature ratio made it possible for people to distinguish between good and bad and to develop systems to explain the meaning of life. The same goes for religion with the God-given tree of knowledge making it possible for people to differentiate good from bad. However, bioscience and animal studies, particularly in the last decade, have shown that empathy and cooperation are essential to animals and even cells (Damásio, 2010). Frans de Waal (2009) demonstrated that apes and other mammals felt shame and guilt. Darwin himself stressed that competition *and* cooperation were essential to the survival of the fittest. Whatever the case may be, empathy and cooperation are definitely human qualities. It is not the case that humans are only steered by self-interest.

If moral feelings can be recognised as occupying a deeper layer in humankind, then amoral feelings should also be recognised. Human beings are not only sensitive to moral appeal but also to self-interest and to harming other people. Dignity calls for "peaceful confining" (Kunneman, 2017). People have to fight against indignity without losing their own dignity. This is an almost impossible task for moral people because in fighting indignity and evil they get very near the edge of indignity themselves. A utopian desire for dignity and justice calls for the evil tendencies inside and outside people to be confined making them vulnerable to acting dubiously. Dignity is not about being perfect but an ongoing appeal to human beings to restrict their evil tendencies and to strengthen good ones, all done without an objective compass in deciding what is good and what is bad. In that sense dignity is a relative concept dependent on choice and volition.

Relational Dignity

A third perspective additional to intrinsic and moral dignity is relational dignity. Dignity shows up in practice in the way people connect with each other (Van Heijst, 2006). Respectfulness and dignity in social practice are seen as conditional to a fair relationship with users. A relationship can only be dignified if both parties believe it to be so. A social worker's effectiveness is dependent on the user perceiving the professional as respectful and dignified. The first steps in bringing about such a valuable connection are the professional recognising the other as a person worthy of respect and being able to appeal to the moral feelings of that person.

Delving a little deeper, Ricoeur (1994) found what he termed the "idem" and "ipse" encounter doubled. When connecting with the other. Idem is the biographical identity people have become throughout their lives. It creates a feeling of certainty, gives some comfort, and says: "This is me." For most people this me-feeling is positive. Ipse is the capacity to react to the other appealing to us. Through our moral being and empathy others are asking for our sympathy, support, and help. When the ipse challenges our idem it very often disturbs our comfort zone. People recognise that such feelings of appeal take them out of their comfort zones. Action is called for even if it is just to ignore the appeal. Many professionals feel themselves overloaded by appeals from users and managers. Keeping the balance between idem and ipse is a major challenge in professional life as it is in private life too.

Social Justice

Dignity and Social Justice as Overarching United Nations Values

In the past century two world wars shocked the world. The strong belief in overarching meaning-making systems fell into disrepute as a result of the way their ideological power was abused in Fascism and Communism. This led to a global pursuit to find a new structural framework to bind all people together that was realised in the League of Nations and afterwards the United Nations. "Human dignity" became the shared hyper-value. "All human beings are born free and equal in dignity and rights. They are endowed with reason and conscience and should act towards one another in a spirit of brotherhood" (Article 1, Universal Declaration of Human Rights). This basic value led to several Declarations of Human Rights being accepted the last one being the Declaration on the Rights of Disabled Persons. Whole lists of rights like dignity put flesh on the bones of those declarations. By including dignity in sets of specific rights it took on a more political and rights-orientated appearance (Frost, 2011). The emphasis gradually changed from dignity to putting social justice into the foreground, as happened when setting the Global Agenda for Social Work and Social Development. The core question was "How to do justice to the other?" and the social-democratic answer was to share welfare and to create equal and fair opportunities for all (UN, 2006). In much the same way as happened with dignity, social justice developed into a system of rights, obligations, measuring instruments, and a growing number of indicators. This allowed nations and categories within populations to be compared and policies to be developed to diminish the gaps. Social justice became a distributive principle with an emphasis on the macrodistribution of welfare expressed in income, labour, housing, health, education, and so on. Although social justice and dignity were perceived as political instruments, their more appealing and inviting character lost something.

Social Work Definition

Social justice—not dignity—is the core value in the international definition of social work. The definition promotes social change, cohesion, empowerment, and liberation of all people (IFSW, 2018). Social workers are profiled as change agents contributing to social justice in terms of liberation and emancipation. Although the macrodistribution interpretation is dominant in most international discourses on social work, it sometimes leads to a certain arrogance in which almost the whole world is perceived as unjust with the exception of social workers. Apart from social workers and left-wing movements everybody else is on the wrong side (Price & Simpson, 2007). It all felt too simple. Apart from creating a "them and us" world, social workers were burdened with the weight of implementing change in political systems at the national and international level. To achieve structural change in systems is far beyond the reach of local social workers. In critical theory the challenging question for social workers "How to do justice to the other" (Rawls, 1999) was often overshadowed by an outspoken certainty of what was good and what was wrong in systems. It led to a judgemental way of speaking instead of posing the question "how to do justice to this person in his context" (Frost, 2011).

Change of Paradigm

Piet Hein Donner is vice chair of the Dutch Council of State, former Minister of Justice, and a respected lawyer. In a speech to representatives of the social domain in 2016 he argued that the wording "equal treatment" in the Dutch transformation or deinstitutional process in social care and social work should be changed to "to give each person what he needs." The argument here is that a social worker should start not from the perspective of objectivising and precisely measuring carried out by "objective" and "neutral" agencies that categorise people and diagnose disorders from the perspective of equal treatment, but from posing the question "what does this person need at this moment in this context?" The question is driven by need, context, and value. Donner argued for contextual responses to needs and problems and that professional care in the social domain should be started from scratch to build up new systems of accountability and contextual justice. New practices of fairness should be learnt by deliberation and argument rather than by quantitative and objective registrations. This could be an important criterion for interventions in that it answers what users value, need, and prefer within the discretional, legal, and financial room available for them to act appropriately. This perspective is close to that of Sen (2010) who argued that the needs and aspirations of people should be met by viewing resources and opportunities within the context of social justice as a moral horizon (2010). The character of social justice changes from a macrodistributional point of view to arguing for an open quest for "doing justice to a person in context." This is actually very close to the way social case work and community work was initially practised. Although this does not stop social workers from promoting change at the macro and economic level, it does mean that their core work should aim at contextual social justice (Van Ewijk, 2018). It deals with what is within the reach of social workers when carrying out their professional duties. In such a context, systems and personal life meet. Such meeting points or interference zones (Kunneman, 2017) are open to change by social workers since they are part of the world in between personal life and societal systems.

Another issue that needs consideration is the emphasis put on welfare distribution of *material* resources in social justice at the macro level. Social work is moving to a more contextual approach in which the *immaterial* distribution of social justice is also part of the job. In the family, the workplace, or the classroom unfairness can be seen in the immaterial distribution of trust, care, giving, and taking, or in the abuse of power. Social workers need to keep a weather eye not only on the just distribution of resources, access to them, and welfare itself but also on the just distribution of immaterial values. Social justice is a universal, political, and context-relational concept.

The context-relational meaning of social justice is similar to this chapter's treatment of dignity. However, social justice relates to distribution while dignity relates to attitude. Both perspectives are intertwined and interdependent in social and care practice where the professional focus is on fair distribution and a respectful relationship. They both recognise human beings as having an immanent value and the reciprocity between human beings as the ontological basis for perception and action.

BACK TO DIGNITY: TENSIONS AND ESSENTIALS

This chapter concludes with some personal reflections on the essentials and tensions found when applying both concepts to social work practice.

Dignity and Justice

Tensions between dignity and social justice can actually be observed. Dignity calls for people (citizens and social workers) to make the effort to be present, take time, be open and understanding—not pressed and stressed. Social justice calls for the fair distribution of professional support to a range of people including colleagues, managers, family, and friends. Although time and resources should not be limited, professionals have to make choices and fulfil obligations.

Dignity and Effectiveness

The demand for effectivity and efficiency cannot be ignored. Since citizens pay taxes and national insurance and expect value for money professional work invariably has to be carried out under conditions in which time and resources are restricted. "To give each person what he needs and values" (Donner, 2016) cannot be achieved by simply having a respectful attitude and way of working. However, if the pressure of efficiency and bureaucracy is too great and the professional is little more than a cog in some overheated machinery, the boundaries of professional work are surpassed. Social and care professionals not only need each other but also horizontal communities to resist such overheated machinery and the pressures applied by policy makers and public opinion. Moreover, support should be sought not only from other professionals but also from users, volunteers, and managers.

Dignity and Vulnerability

Vulnerability has no effect whatsoever on dignity. Dignity is much more than a standard to meet. It is the sincere recognition of the other's intrinsic value as a human being. The human race is made up of a wide range of people each of whom is unique—a variance of humankind. Whether people can lose their dignity, as is regularly expressed, when they become old, fragile, and fully dependent is a moot point. Dignity can be lost by people acting in a stupid way, but not by people with dementia. People calling a vulnerable person unworthy are making themselves unworthy. Dignity is the unconditional recognition and acceptance of the other.

Principles and Practice

Religions are often accused of not practising what they preach. Third-world countries argue that the reason they are unable to meet the objectives and standards of social justice is because rich countries fail to meet their commitments (Nussbaum, 2011; Sen, 2010). What the rich practise is often very different from the principles laid down in declarations, mission statements, and commitments. If dignity and justice do not emerge in practise, then dignity is worthless. Pride in the values of dignity and care can change into shame if words do not become action.

Whole and Detail

Philosophers and social scientists argue that the whole is often greater than the sum of its details (Morin, 2008; Polanyi, 1969, 2009). Taking all the details and bringing them together does not represent the whole. The whole consists of design, figure-ground, performance, and *Gestalt* ("form"). If a disorder or impairment is identified in someone, then this represents a detail. However, before it is identified the disorder is seen as representing the person. The whole is much more than the sum of the details. Ideas are wholes too that often even lack details. Dignity is such a whole that has inspiring power without knowing the details. Despite having a rough idea or intuition as to what it is, when it comes to transforming dignity into a policy and practice details are needed. Although dignity is transformed into declarations of human rights, protocols, methods, and theories, the risk is that the wholeness and inspiring power of the whole disappear behind the screen of details. There is and should be tension between the whole and details. A whole needs application and details need inspiration. Although professionals have their ethical codes, their protocols, and the law to fall back on, sometimes it feels unjust, unfair, and unworthy to follow a specific rule because it is not in line with the values of dignity and justice. Professionals need discretion to balance details and wholeness, to balance tensions between different values, and to balance values and prescriptions. Since professionals are ultimately steered by dignity and justice, they should keep a weather eye on and attitude toward protocols and prescriptions thus preventing them from being just a cog in an overheated machine just doing what they are told.

Being Vulnerable and Making Vulnerable

It is sometimes embarrassing to notice how caring and helping people focus on the presumed shortcomings of a vulnerable person. Such a person should be trained, supported, empowered, compensated, and informed. Presumed troublesome children are removed from their classes and treated in the office of a therapist. Although this is sometimes really necessary, it is often done too quickly. It makes little sense to treat vulnerable people outside the environment in which the vulnerability came about such as the classroom, the workplace, or the family. Quite often vulnerability becomes a problem because the people and physical environment surrounding it turn it into a problem. Social workers should focus on what makes people vulnerable (Beresford, Adshead, & Croft, 2007). Sometimes it is possible to reduce complexity in the workplace or classroom. Complex regulations in care and social security often create dependent citizens. Managing expectations is another thing to consider. Expectations that treatment will solve complex situations should be moderated. Although claims and demands have been known to decrease in a stressed society, in many cases material support (tools, benefits, income) is essential for vulnerable citizens to participate. Concepts such as activation and participation often overlook the necessary condition of embedment. People need a certain acceptance in communities. A society that demands people find and create their own personal profile and position begs the question: "But what if a person is not able to find a position, to participate, to adjust to all the claims, to be a member of different communities?" Justice and dignity presuppose an accepting attitude and making room for the most vulnerable.

Worthy Professionals

In the Netherlands there is evidence that respect for professionals is enjoying a revival. Such a revival hinges on there being generic, practical, wise professionals endowed with discretion and trust pushing the dialogue to adjust to the new paradigm in which teamwork is at the forefront. Professionals need to have a strong character to get things done since they carry out tasks on behalf of society and community. This applies to professionals working in care and social work because of their ability to get things done. Critical to this is recognising needs, connecting with users, convincing and supporting them, and finding resources and answers to the predicaments in which users find themselves. At the same time professionals are expected to be guided by principles of dignity and (contextual) justice. Professionals are characteristically value orientated. Professionals represent societal hyper goods. Normative professionals are those who act ethically in getting things done by doing good work in a good way (Van Ewijk & Kunneman, 2013). Such a "double good" is what positions professionals in our societies and applies to lawyers, doctors, and social workers alike. Instrumental and ethical normativity are often intertwined and complement each other. Sometimes they conflict resulting in technical perspectives overshadowing ethical ones, as regularly seen in the field of health. In other cases it is not so clear whether a decision is guided by instrumental or normative arguments. The decision about placing a child in an institute or in foster care is mostly a mix of ethical considerations (child rights) and risk assessment. Maybe there is room here for aesthetic normativity. Dignity includes many other factors such as sensitivity, taste, creating a pleasant climate, and being neatly dressed. Arts such as music and painting create conditions that bring harmony and beauty into people's lives.

Worthy Organisations, Managers, Working Conditions, and Social Policy

Professionals can only be worthy when they work in a worthy workplace and for a worthy organisation. The tone adopted, the dialogue used, and the resources available inspired by shared ideals such as dignity, justice, and good taste are necessary for professionals to do good work in a good way. Excellent organisations are those that do things together from management to shop floor, from policy makers to frontline workers. They make room available for dialogue and finding paths through complex contexts. When complexity reigns in society and in contexts, radical change is almost possible. However, change can be brought about by pathfinding, by making steps in the right direction in a shared process that restores justice and strengthens dignity. It does not start with certain knowledge or from a judgemental attitude, but from uncertain knowledge and openness inspired by ethical, instrumental, and aesthetic considerations and ambitions. It all comes down to asking the same question: "Is this just and worthy for this person in this context at this moment?"

Worthy Schools of Social Work

Contextual interpretations of social justice and dignity require schools of social work to spend time to explore values and acquire a value-based attitude. It requires what is called slow learning in which learning skills or gaining knowledge are accompanied by developing a deeper understanding by dialogue and reflection. Developing such an understanding calls for a non-judgemental attitude and uncertain knowledge that are open to exploration and contextual answers. Social work education should be an open invitation to discuss, think, and reflect on the question: "What is fair in this context at this moment and why?" This question is the core question for social workers, second only to: "What will work in this context at this moment?"

REFERENCES

Arendt, H. (1958). *The human condition*. Chicago: University of Chicago Press.

Arendt, H. (1979). *The origins of totalitarianism*. London: Harcourt, Brace & World (orig. 1951).

Arendt, H. (1981). *The life of the mind*. One Volume Edition (M. McCarthy, Ed.). San Diego, New York, London: Harcourt (orig. 1978).

Bandura, A. (1982). Self-efficacy mechanism in human agency. *American Psychologist, 37*(2), 122–147.

Bandura, A. (Ed.). (1995). *Self-efficacy in changing societies*. Cambridge, UK: Cambridge University Press.

Bandura, A. (1997). *Self-efficacy: The exercise of control*. New-York: W. H. Freeman.

Beresford, P., Adshead, L., & Croft, S. (2007). *Positive care, social work and service users: Making life possible*. London, UK: Jessica Kingsley.

Billig, M. (1991). *Arguing and thinking: A rhetorical approach to social psychology*. Cambridge, UK: Cambridge University Press (orig. 1987).

Bourdieu, P. (1984). *Distinction, a social critique of the judgement of taste*. Cambridge, MA: Harvard University Press.

Damásio, A. (2010). *Self comes to mind—Constructing the conscious brain: The evolution of consciousness*. Porthmouth, HN: Heinemann.

de Waal, F. (2009). *The age of empathy: Nature's lessons for a kinder society*. New York, NY: Harmony Books.

Donner, P. H. (2016). *Laat je niet gek maken*. https://www.raadvanstate.nl/publicaties/toespraken/tekst-toespraak.html?id=961&summary_only=&category_id=13. Accessed April 20, 2018.

Frost, R. (2011). *The right to justification: Elements of a constructivist theory of justice*. Columbia, NY: Columbia University Press.

IFSW. (2018). *Definition of social work*. http://ifsw.org/policies/definition-of-social-work/. Accessed April 20, 2018.

Kunneman, H. (2009). *Voorbij het dikke-ik. Bouwstenen voor een kritisch humanisme. Deel 1*. Amsterdam, The Netherlands: SWP.

Kunneman, H. (2017). *Amor complexitatis. Bouwstenen voor een kritisch humanisme. Deel 2*. Amsterdam, The Netherlands: SWP.

Leget, C. (2011). Menselijke waardigheid en humanisering van de zorg. *Tijdschrift Geestelijke Verzorging, 14*(62), 8–17.

Morin, E. (2008). *On complexity*. Cresskill, NJ: Hampton Press.

Noordegraaf, M. (2009). Managing by measuring? Professional organizing in and around public service delivery. In H. U. Otto, A. Polutta, & H. Ziegler (Eds.), *Evidence-based practice—Modernizing the knowledge base of social work?* (pp. 185–209). Leverkusen, Germany: Barbara Budrich.

Nussbaum, M. C. (2011). *Creating capabilities: The human development approach*. Cambridge, MA: Harvard University Press.

Polanyi, M. (1969). *Knowing and being*. Chicago, IL: University of Chicago Press.

Polanyi, M. (2009). *The tacit dimension*. Chicago, IL: University of Chicago Press.

Price, V., & Simpson, G. (2007). *Transforming society? Social work and sociology*. Bristol, UK: The Policy Press.

Rawls, J. B. (1999). *A theory of justice*. Cambridge, MA: Belknap Press of Harvard University Press, 1971 (1999, revised version).

Ricoeur, P. (1994). *Oneself as another*. Chicago: University of Chicago Press.

Sen, A. (2010). *The idea of justice*. London, UK: Penguin Books.

Taylor, C. (1989*). Sources of the self: The making of the modern identity*. Cambridge, MA: Harvard University Press.

UN, The International Forum for Social Development. (2006). *Social justice in an open world: The role of the United Nations*. New York : United Nations.

Van Ewijk, H. (2010). *Maatschappelijk werk in een sociaal gevoelige tijd*. Amsterdam: SWP/Humanistics University Press.

Van Ewijk, H. (2018). *Complexity and social work*. Abingdon: Routledge.

Van Ewijk, H., & Kunneman, H. (Eds.). (2013). *Praktijken van normatieve professionalisering*. Amsterdam, The Netherlands: SWP.

Van Heijst, A. (2006). Dignity as a relational concept: Arguments pro and contra from the ethics of care. In H. Goris (red.), *Bodiliness and human dignity* (pp. 89–97). Tilburg: Theological Studies 2.

Witchen, H. U, Jacobi, F., Rehm, J., Gustavsson, A., Svensson, M., Jönsson, B., & Olesen, J. (2011). The size and burden of mental disorders and other disorders of the brain in Europe 2010. *European Neuropsychopharmacology, 21*, 655–679.

CHAPTER 45

Professional: Yet Very Personal, Spiritual, and Unavoidably Political—Addressing Assessment in Social Work Education

Ksenija Napan

Instead of Introduction

This chapter poses a number of questions and tentatively proposes answers based on data collected over years while inventing and evaluating innovative teaching/learning methods in social work:

What are the ways of utilising students' learning styles and prior knowledge?

How can experiential activities including field trips enhance students' experience?

Can social work be taught on-line and what is required for effective transformative learning needed for competent social work practice?

Is there a space for art and spirituality in social work?

Do we still need exams and individualised essay writing?

Is there a space for self, peer, and group assessment and what is a safe way of doing it?

If students are assessed only based on academic merit of their work—are we producing academically capable but emotionally unavailable practitioners?

What are the alternative methods of assessing and how students respond to them?

K. Napan (✉)
School of Social Work, College of Health, Massey University, Auckland, New Zealand
e-mail: K.Napan@massey.ac.nz

© The Author(s) 2021
S. S. M. et al. (eds.), *The Palgrave Handbook of Global Social Work Education*, https://doi.org/10.1007/978-3-030-39966-5_45

How to ensure that basic competencies required for social work registration are addressed and assessed in a way that enhances learning as opposed to performativity?

How to explore personal indigenous with all social work students in order to develop cultural respectfulness and appreciation of diversity?

Introducing the Author and the Context

This chapter is based on author's 30 years of experience of being a social worker, educator, and creator of innovative social work education programmes and professional development courses. Her practice stretches from being a youngest social work teacher at University of Zagreb in Croatia, teaching an integrated Bachelor programme for social workers, counsellors and community developers in Aotearoa New Zealand, developing a Master of Social Practice transdisciplinary postgraduate course and coordinating a Master of Applied Social Work (a registrable qualification which in two years enables practitioners with degrees in related professions to become social workers) to development of professional development courses for social workers. The author developed two integrative methods of teaching and learning, the Contact-Challenge Method suitable for beginning students and the Academic Co-Creative Inquiry for advanced practitioners (Napan, 2015). She currently resides in Aotearoa New Zealand with deep appreciation of Māori culture and indigenous wisdom and is a lifelong curious learner committed to sustainability and whole people learning. This chapter attempts to share experiences from Aotearoa New Zealand and to showcase some alternative and novel assessment methods that enable achievement of core competencies required by Social Work Registration Board.

Critical Analysis of Assessment in Social Work Education

The exploration of questions listed in the introduction is not in any way definitive—it is intentionally tentative and it calls for discussion and critical reflection offering a potential for transformation of social work education across the globe.

Appropriate assessment is a prerequisite of effective social work practice and comparably, assessment in social work education will shape the way learning is consolidated, reflected on, and applied in practice. In social work education, two related fields of practice merge: tertiary education and social work. These two fields have some compatible and related principles and values and therefore the process of teaching can be utilised to embody and manifest some of the essential social work processes. Assessment is the core of social work practice and, when strengths based, it sets the intervention process that follows. Similarly, yet in a different way, assessment in social work education can set the context for students to learn by building on their strengths and abilities. This chapter proposes that assessment in social work education needs rejuvenation and potentially transformation which may bring forth better preparedness for ever-changing social work practice around the globe.

Various approaches to assessment in social work education are outlined and this chapter explores the relevance of 'whole people learning' (Heron, 1996) in social work. It places a focus on competencies required from Social Work Registration Board in Aotearoa New Zealand and offers practical examples of how these competencies can be achieved through innovative teaching and assessment methods aimed at creating transformative learning experiences in order to enable students to become competent social workers.

Comprehensive and detailed literature review on assessment is social work education (Crisp & Green Lister, 2002) emphasises the importance of encouragement of development of reflective and critical thinking and adequate assessment of acquisition of essential knowledge and skills. Alongside with knowledge and skills relevant to social work, students' values, beliefs, and attitudes significantly shape their ability to work competently and traditional assessment methods rarely address it.

Essays, tests, and closed book examinations predominantly focus on accumulation of knowledge and regurgitation of facts. Although potentially relevant for beginning students, these assessment methods are outdated for the digital age and rapidly changing social work practices. To address this problem, practical exams and skills tests have been used to assess social work practice skills with at times professional actors, students role playing with one another or authentically working on their real-life problems. Submission of video or audio recordings has been devised for assessment as well as a learning opportunity for students to self-assess their skills and ability to work with others and experience how is to be in a role of a client.

Creation of authentic case studies that evoke imaginative experiences and clinical reasoning (Bowers & Pack, 2017) enhanced teaching/learning processes and enabled students to explore ethical dilemmas and integrate theory and practice. This formative aspect of assessment contributes to development of reflective practitioners and promotes lifelong learning essential for effective social work practice.

Learning journals and portfolios (Rosegrant-Alvarez & Moxley, 2004) proved to be an excellent tool for reflection but challenging for assessment and evaluation in terms of clarity of what has actually been assessed—a student's progress, their transformation or prescribed learning outcomes? Pre-set marking criteria and rubrics commonly used at university for marking assignments often do not really suit the complexity of learning as one size does not fit all. Translating qualitative comments into percentages (required at most universities) has always been an arbitrary task flawed with randomness, open to interpretation and student complaints.

Group assignments, projects, skits, and presentations have a potential to reflect the reality of group work in social work organisations but have also created a lot of angst and conflict between low and high contributors and pose a challenge of fair mark distribution. Benefits of a range of internal assessment methods outweigh challenges they impose, however, preventative measures to improve group experience and investment of time before students embark on group projects proved to be beneficial (Postlethwait, 2016).

Self and peer assessment in social work education is not only a useful tool for development of reflective practice but essential for building relationships with colleagues and embedding reflexivity and lifelong learning in social work practice. However, although my students are always happy to give feedback to their peers, they are very reluctant to assign marks to each other. I was told repeatedly that they do not want to assign marks to one another, as "marks destroy relationships". However, they were happy for me to assign marks, as "this is my job". Today, in my courses I ask students to peer assess each other's work for the purpose of giving their colleagues a chance to improve it according to their feedback. Then, they self-assess and submit to me for marking. This threefold assessment process significantly improves the quality of their work and expands the achievement of prescribed learning outcomes. The benefit for assessors proved to be in discovering that there are many ways to cover the same learning outcomes and it completely eradicated plagiarism (Phillips & Napan, 2016). It also improves relationships and collaboration, so essential for effective social work practice. Through the process of self and peer assessment, students develop an understanding that personal is often closely interlinked with other three aspects of being—professional, spiritual, and political. It allows students to learn holistically and contextualise social problems in the light of their experiences without an unconscious urge to impose them or project them onto their clients. Enabling a colleague to improve their assignment by giving them feedback that at times addresses all four aspects of being creates a special kind of relationship that engenders trust, compassion and continuous improvement.

The main conditions for these 'soft' assessment methods to work are development of self-awareness, elimination of fear and creation of a context conducive to 'whole people learning'. These conditions equally relate to teachers as to students. In classrooms where 'whole people learning' is in action, teaching and learning are reciprocal and participants' involvement is at such high level that the same course cannot be taught twice. This does not preclude having prescribed learning outcomes, course aims, and outlines, but it requires skilful facilitation, wide knowledge, and emotional competence of a teacher who needs to be open to unpredictability this emergent type of facilitation brings.

WHOLE PEOPLE LEARNING IN SOCIAL WORK

The term 'whole people learning' was coined by John Heron at the end of last century (Heron, 1996) who offered experiential workshops at various universities, institutes of technology and private institutes on topics of facilitation, self, peer, and collaborative assessment, co-counselling, cooperative inquiry research and many other topics all relevant to social work education. I have been inspired with Heron's cooperative inquiry method, have modified it and applied it over years in my Bachelor and Master of social work classes. For a large period of my professional life, John has been my professional supervisor and currently he is my mentor and fellow participant in an inquiry group that I have been part of over 20 years.

I have written my PhD evaluating a Contact-Challenge method of teaching and learning in social work (Napan, 1998) and since then have researched and published extensively in the field of social work education. I am passionate about continuous improvement of processes that enable social workers to develop culturally and spiritually respectful, socially just, and sustainable integrated practice frameworks in order to bring forth the world (Ellis, Napan, & O'Donoghue, 2018). I want my students (and I model the same in my teaching) to:

- balance structure and flexibility and internal and contextual transformation,
- think globally but act locally,
- be aware of their beliefs and attitudes but not impose them on their clients,
- be authentically who they are and never stop learning or lose their compassion.

Yet, I want them to have clear boundaries, be critically reflective, not naïve, and advocate for their clients with sharpness and integrity.

For some of my students, this needs to happen in only two years as I teach on a Master of Applied Social Work programme, that transforms people with degrees in cognate disciplines into effective social workers. We accept practitioners with bachelor degrees in a range of humanistic professions and in two years of intensive Master course which includes two fieldwork placements and a lot of personal and professional growth, they become registered social workers capable of practising in New Zealand and many other countries. This context may be the reason why I find 'whole people learning' most relevant because it is engaging, experiential, personal, professional and political and also spiritual as my student's personal transformations challenge their beliefs and set them for a life of continuous inquiry, reflection and lifelong learning.

What Constitutes Becoming an Effective Social Worker?

Social workers are often described as 'dogooders', 'wounded healers' (Ashenberg-Straussner, Senreich, & Steen, 2018), 'baby snatchers', 'bleeding hearts', or 'saviours of the world'. There is a common understanding that many social work students join the profession because they have problems themselves, or they were at a receiving end of social welfare. At times, they are motivated by their wish to pay back what they received from their social workers and at times, they want to restore, repair, and transform social work practice because of the injustices that have been done to them. Social workers are also often motivated by their spiritual orientation and an inclusive definition of spirituality for social work and education becomes essential for development of respectful and relevant whole people teaching and learning practices (Senreich, 2013). A student may be attracted to social work because of their religious beliefs that may at times entail being judgemental and righteous which may prevent them to practice in non-discriminatory way, or a student may come to social work education with an open heart unaware of the necessity of clear professional boundaries. Similarly, to social work practice, in social work education there is no 'one size fits all' approach and personalised assessment methods may shape the way social workers turn out to be at the end of their professional education (Napan, 2015).

How Does It Look Like in Practice?

Current social work practice in Aotearoa New Zealand is regulated by the Social Work Registration Board (SWRB), which requires all social workers to demonstrate following competencies upon completing their social work degree, regardless if it is on a Bachelor or Master level. To practice as a social worker, these competencies need to be demonstrated in conjunction with the SWRB Code of Conduct and the Aotearoa New Zealand Association for Social Workers (ANZASW) Code of Ethics. These standards identify minimum standards of practice for the social work profession in New Zealand. They are not intended to describe all of the possible knowledge and practice skills required by social workers. They are the 'core' competencies for social work (Social Work Registration Board, 2016). The following section outlines these competencies and possible ways of achieving them through transformative learning processes.

Competence to Practise Social Work with Māori

Māori are indigenous people of Aotearoa New Zealand. Consequences of colonisation are still visible and palpable with disproportionate number of Māori clients and not enough Māori social workers. With increase of social workers from various parts of the world assessment of knowledge of Te Tiriti o Waitangi which is the founding document of the country, basic knowledge of Te Reo Māori (language) and tikanga (culturally appropriate and respectful way of doing things) becomes a prerequisite. This is not knowledge that can be merely acquired from reading historical documents. It is deeply experiential as Māori culture is profoundly connected to the land and based on reciprocal relationships. We enable students to experience this by taking them to the Marae Noho, which is an overnight stay at a meeting space (Marae) that includes a traditionally carved meeting house (wharenui) where they follow a specific protocol and learn within a culturally enhancing environment. Māori and non-Māori students equally benefit from this experience. They (those who do not know it already) learn how to introduce themselves by identifying their mountain, their river, the vessel they arrived in and their ancestry. They share their motivations and dreams, they eat together and sleep together, share facilities and their life stories. The process is deeply transformational and there is often no need to conduct any formal assessment as everybody engages and supports one another to thrive and learn. Although staff members offer workshops related to Māori models of practice, the line between the teacher and student is blurred and learning becomes mutual. Competent teaching methods ensure that the process enables students to continue learning about self-determining, respectful, and connecting practices that will be de-colonising on personal, professional, political, and spiritual levels. At times students are asked to do group presentations, but most of the time this work is not formally assessed, but celebrated and well supported. The effort and quality student put into this work is admirable. The whole process is facilitated by Māori teachers and non-Māori staff members participate as students.

Competence to Practise Social Work with Different Ethnic and Cultural Groups in Aotearoa New Zealand

Although primarily a bi-cultural country, based on an agreement between Māori and British in 1840 called Te Tiriti o Waitangi (The Treaty of Waitangi), Aotearoa New Zealand is a home to a number of cultures. Under three-quarters of population, who declare themselves European are coming with a range of cultural customs and norms. You can find people from far north to far south of Europe as well as from far west to far east, more specifically from Iceland to Turkey and from Portugal to Ukraine. This is followed by almost 15% of Māori, 7.4% of people coming from a range of Pacific Islands and a significant number of immigrants from Asia, Middle Eastern countries, Latin America, and Africa (Census New Zealand, 2013).

To develop competence to work with such a varied population in a culturally respectful way, I take my students to two festivals and engage them in an inquiry-based learning activity. Pasifika festival is an annual event that has been happening in Auckland for 26 years. It celebrates a range of pacific cultures through food, dance, workshops, engagement, showcase of social services and education. It is a family friendly event and students can bring their families if they wish to. It is an outdoor event (in 26 years it never rained on the day!) and prior to coming to the festival students need to research about pacific cultures and develop a set of three initial questions. On the day, they need to find three persons at the festival and interview them. During the day, they are invited to change or modify their questions in the light of their experience and at the end of the festival, they are asked to list new questions that emerged after the experience. A very similar activity needs to be completed before, during and after another field trip to the Auckland International Cultural Festival, which celebrates Auckland's cultural diversity with a range of cultural and educative activities from around the planet.

This is an assessed activity, it is the first assignment for the Social and Community work Theory and Practice course (within Master of Applied Social Work (MAppSW) programme) and it covers the following learning outcomes:

To develop an understanding of social work as a profession,
To examine and critique social work knowledge and practice,
To develop knowledge on practices relevant to social work with different cultural groups.

In order to achieve these outcomes students need to complete the following assignment (Table 45.1):

Table 45.1 First assignment for MAppSW class linking personal, professional, spiritual and political

Inquiry learning report—Is social work for me—Am I for social work?

- Explore and critically reflect on life experiences that have brought you to social work. Who were the role models that inspired you? Who were the people who taught you how <u>not</u> to do social work? Which events shaped you to become a person you are today? Explore your motivation for becoming a social worker and frame it in a wider context of your life (attend to personal, professional, and political aspects of your choice)
- Briefly explore your indigenous—what does it mean to you and how it will manifest in your inevitably transcultural social work—how will your beliefs shape your practice
- Include your own brief code of ethics which will be informed by ANZASW code of ethics and SWRB code of conduct. What are the main principles and values that will guide your practice?
- In what way or in what direction would you like to change, grow, and develop? What are your main challenges?
- Engage with literature and explore definitions of social work and find (or create) a most suitable definition of social work that matches your values and beliefs and reference it properly
- Use at least 3 books and 6 academic journal articles to back up your ideas and reference them APA style
- If you choose to be creative and produce a piece of art that metaphorically represents your relationship to social work, please write a short reflective piece linking it to learning outcomes needed to be covered in this assignment. Use literature and demonstrate your ability to reference properly and use academic resources adequately as well as being creative.

- Please reflect on the field trips (please fill the Inquiry learning sheet for each trip)

Students can present this assignment in any format they like; it can be an essay, a report, a creative piece, a short movie, a poem, and a rap. They are free to express themselves in a way that suits their learning style as long as they cover the prescribed learning outcomes.

Extensive feedback is given for this assessment activity, as this is the first assignment they are engaging in for their MAppSW programme.

This assignment enables them to ground themselves in their own culture and develop genuine interest and respect for a range of cultures that they may not know much about. For students who are from Pacific Islands, this activity provides an opportunity to guide and support their non-Pacific Island colleagues to navigate through unknown waters. At the same time, they have a chance to explore cultures from a range of Pacific Islands that are not their own.

Similarly, a second field trip to the annual International Cultural Festival enables students to link and connect with a range of people from a number of cultures and agencies that serve them.

Competence to Work Respectfully and Inclusively with Diversity and Difference in Practice

Ageism, sexism, disablism, racism, homophobia, or disrespect of beliefs are not acceptable at University, however, prejudices, 'unconscious biases' or covert or unaware discrimination are way too commonly present and need attention. As a first step to become aware of their prejudices and make the link between personal and professional, students are asked to complete the following activity (Table 45.2):

Table 45.2   Values and principles in action exercise

Values and principles in action

Please read the ten statements below and write 'yes' or 'no' next to each statement independently and quickly, almost without thinking

- Children from single-parent families disadvantaged in comparison with children from two-parent families
- Gay couples should not be allowed to adopt children
- Once an addict, always an addict
- Once a criminal, always a criminal
- Parents should realise that their children do not always want to practice the same cultural traditions as they do
- People with a disability should have the right to determine where they live
- Old people are best looked after at home by their families
- Young people should have the right to refuse to consent to medical treatment
- When people from very different cultural backgrounds decide to have children together, they impose many disadvantages on their children
- Children from economically deprived families are disadvantaged and would be better off if adopted by a wealthier family
- Children should have a right to refuse contact with a parent who used to abuse them

Table 45.2   (continued)

Values and principles in action

Then, try to justify your answer by linking it to at least one of the social work principles:
- *Self-determination*
- *Promoting the right to participation*
- *Treating each person as a whole and in their context*
- *Identifying and developing strengths*
- *Challenging discrimination*
- *Recognising diversity*
- *Distributing resources equitably*
- *Challenging unjust policies and practices*
- *Valuing diversity*

Discuss it in a small group by practising agreeing to disagree and listening without interrupting

Revisit your answers after the discussion and see if they have changed

This activity enables students to critically reflect on their own personal values and believes in order to manage influences of their personal biases in their social work practice. If their statement cannot be supported by at least one social work principle, it cannot be professionally justified. Vivid conversations and engagement while doing this exercise enables students to change their minds, realise the importance of the context in social work, and appreciate that simplistic dualistic thinking does not provide enough space for competent and ethical social work practice.

Competence to Promote the Principles of Human Rights and Social and Economic Justice

This competence is addressed and assessed through engagement with students and constant reflection on current events. Students bring newspaper articles and open the class with either a poem, sharing of a story, a prayer, or any kind of invocation creating a focus for the day. During the various world crises, political elections or celebrations of human spirit, there is space for students to address it in class and make links between social work and the context where it operates. Fieldwork placements provide time and space where students have a chance to advocate for their clients and the election of student representatives enables them to advocate for one another and offer support in case of need. Awareness of family violence in society, and at times in their own homes, often results in life-changing circumstances. Importance of sustainability in relation to competent social work practice is addressed as part of preparation for first fieldwork placement where students are taught to use the sustainability filter exercise before undertaking any intervention. It asks them to critically reflect on the purpose of the intervention, its cultural appropriateness, its necessity and how it affects the community and a planet as a whole (Ellis et al., 2018). This simple exercise encourages social workers to critically reflect on unsustainable assessment processes, adoption of unsustainable or colonising practices without awareness of the context or their cultural appropriateness and it has a potential to highlight injustices that may pass unnoticed in habitual way of working.

Competence to Engage in Practice That Promotes Social Change

Within the MAppSW programme in their second (and final) year students need to take the Management in Social Services course. This course was not very popular, as students have not seen it as relevant to their social work practice. They are just about to graduate and it is not likely that they will apply for management jobs. In order to make it more relevant to students' realities, Academic Co-Creative Inquiry (Napan, 2017) was employed to enhance student motivation and engagement with the topic. It also gave them a choice of assessment options as well as a possibility to do individual and group assignments and enabling them to create an imaginary socially just agency that would promote social change. One of the students developed a business plan and is currently working on bringing her dream to life after noticing what is needed in her community and developing skills and abilities necessary for bringing it to life. Others tailored their assignments in a way they found it useful for their future employment or future study.

For this particular course, all assignments are self- and peer-assessed which prepares students for deep reflection processes required at most social work agencies in the country as part of the appraisal process. It also has a double effect of enabling students to feel how it is to be assessed and learn to distance themselves from their work (in a similar way they need to learn to separate their clients from their problems) and still do their best. Sharing work with peers significantly improves the equality of student work.

Competence to Understand and Articulate Social Work Theories, Indigenous Practice Knowledge, Other Relevant Theories, and Social Work Practice Methods and Models

A range of orientations, worldviews, theories, and models of practice are taught within a programme and students need to develop their own Integrated Practice Framework that is in tune with who they are personally, professionally, politically and spiritually and how they prefer to practice social work. It tends to integrate what brought them to social work and how far they have come. They need to articulate what are their values and beliefs that will shape their professional practice and reflect on learnings from books, classes, experiences, and two fieldwork placements. They may revisit critical life experiences that are relevant for their future profession and express who they are, where they are coming from, where they belong and share a particularly interesting case they have encountered and learned from. This activity balances well with the Noho Marae where they learnt how to introduce themselves in Te Reo Māori (Māori language) at the beginning of the course and now, at the end they speak from the same place, but at a different, more professional level. They have a chance to explore their identity and their professional preferences, aspirations, views, and dreams. Students are encouraged to 'dance with theories' and mix and match them according to their compatibility as well as realising that they cannot fit clients into theories, but rather find a most appropriate model or method to support the client in a way that is most suitable to their reality. They also need to outline targets for their own growth understanding that being a social worker means being a lifelong learner. Critical reflection needs to be demonstrated and for these individual oral presentations students get extensive feedback from their peers. This assessment celebrates who students are and they can invite their field instructors, supervisors and family members to this event.

Competence to Apply Critical Thinking to Inform and Communicate Professional Judgements

Development of critical thinking is a core of effective social work practice and is encouraged throughout the course through thorough peer and self assessment and teacher's extensive feedback. Demonstration of clear boundaries and exploration of risk assessment in social work are taught in the class and expressed in the fieldwork placement. This is a pass or fail course and is assessed jointly by field educators (registered practising social workers) and university teachers. Although each placement agency has its unique features, the focus is on competencies listed here and students' ability to demonstrate them regardless of the field of practice they are engaged in. The aim is to develop practical wisdom and make autonomous and independent judgements grounded in social work theories and exemplified in competent application of a range of culturally respectful models. This includes competent use of information technology and their ability to refer clients to relevant agencies when needed. On top of that, critical thinking is assessed through a research report where students need to undertake an independent small research project in an area of interest. It would be ideal to conduct these projects in small groups which would reflect the reality of research projects in practice, however, current university policy for individual assessment does not allow for this yet.

Competence to Promote Empowerment of People and Communities to Enable Positive Change

A range of skills is taught during the programme, including management of interpersonal conflicts, giving negative and positive feedback all within a framework of non-violent, empathetic, and compassionate practice. Small classes (25–30 students) enable us to get to know one another and openly communicate in order to promote growth and development. Strong support from academic and counselling services enables us to retain most of our students until graduation. Careful selection is a significant contributing factor too. Each student is interviewed and upon acceptance, a four day orientation process brings students on board. During their studies, they develop a network of professional colleagues they will be able to rely on when they found employment. As students mirror Aotearoa New Zealand's multicultural reality, a lot of mutual learning happens in the class. Community development activities student engage in, testify to their ability to enable positive change. Through numerous self and peer reflection activities, reflection on their own practice becomes a second nature. The internal sense of competence replaces the constant strive for external validation.

Competence to Practise Within Legal and Ethical Boundaries of the Social Work Profession

As learning is deeply experiential, legal, and ethical boundaries are explored in depth. Students learn how to explore ethical dilemmas and how to utilise professional supervision required for all registered social workers. Challenging case studies are presented in lectures but also brought by students from their experience and reflected upon in their assignments. One of the examples is a case study they need to create and define a potential ethical dilemma demonstrating that they can differentiate between the real and false ethical dilemma. These experiential learning exercises entice students to think beyond right and wrong, open new possibilities to encompass a range of views, practice nonjudgementally and yet being able to make professional judgements. Awareness of what conflict of interest entails and how to uphold the right of privacy and confidentiality as well as being able to communicate clearly with clients when the information may need to be disclosed is practised in weekly skills training groups. Being conversant with the Code of Ethics and a Code of Conduct and writing their own code of ethics helps students to have clear guidelines for their future practice (see Table 45.1).

Competence to Represent the Social Work Profession with Integrity and Professionalism

It is my hope that social workers who have engaged with our programme are able to act with grace and integrity in the ever-changing field of social work. I know that when they graduate, if they forget all theories they have learnt, they at least know who they are and why they have chosen social work to be their profession. Through a number of experiential activities, they have learnt the importance of supervision being individual, group or peer, internal or external. By the end of the programme, they have learnt how to challenge social injustices and how to keep themselves safe. Practising problem-solving with one another in confidential small groups, they have experienced what it means to be in a role of a client and how genuine concern by another human being feels like. Development of compassion and genuine interest in improvement of human life on the planet becomes a reason of being or 'ikigai' (Nakanishi, 1999). This spiritual aspect of being a social worker has a potential of preventing burnout, job dissatisfaction, and sense of meaninglessness. Acting with integrity promotes well-being not only for communities we serve, but also for us as individuals, being part of a universe. Sensing these connections anchors social workers in ethical and grounded practice.

INSTEAD OF CONCLUSION

These competencies cannot be achieved through mere academic learning nor assessed through external examinations or essay writing, however, they can be achieved through deep transformational learning that requires intensive dialogue, debate, personalisation and full engagement from teachers and students. In order to satisfy the registering body, university requirements and my own integrity, I have developed a list of principles that permeate my teaching and out of these principles a specific teaching/learning methods emerged some of which have been described above. Teaching is a reciprocal process where every teaching is learning. In my country, Māori (indigenous people of Aotearoa New Zealand) have a term *ako* that depicts this. In my mother tongue, Croatian, a same word depicts teaching and learning and the context determines its meaning. The best way to learn something is to try to teach it and I feel privileged to be a teacher who is a lifelong learner. Knowledge cannot be copyrighted but only freely shared, enjoyed and enhanced as humans actually cannot posses it as it is fluid, contextual and everchanging. Knowledge is co-created through dialogical processes and experiences and in my classes, I attempt to create a context where people can grow personally, professionally, spiritually, and politically in order to become active citizens and agents of social transformation. In order to enable this to happen, fear needs to be eliminated as it blocks learning (Craske, Hermans, & Vansteenwegen, 2006). Assessment processes based on fear and regurgitation of material do not involve whole people and rarely contribute to development of critical thinking, which is an ability so essential for social work.

One of the characteristics of social work is that every one of us at some stage in life may become a social work client. The more respect and reciprocity we include in the social work process the more engagement and transformation will have a chance to occur.

I share my knowledge and encourage students to share theirs. I listen to my students and colleagues, we co-create and construct knowledge together, we evaluate the effectiveness of the process and propose ideas for improvement by co-creating new questions. I decided to devote my academic career to inspire students and other academics to do their best by doing my best. I am aware that education exists within a context and my devotion lies in transforming academic institutions from the inside. As these institutions are part of something bigger, my ultimate goal is to bring forth the environmentally sustainable, spiritually fulfilled, and socially just society to the best of my potential. I achieve this by developing a sense of purpose and meaning by asking students to personalise prescribed learning outcomes for courses I teach. These personalised learning outcomes are then translated into specific learning activities suited to a specific student's learning style. At the same time, students are encouraged to stretch their abilities and to expand their usual learning repertoire. Each student builds on their life experiences and sets out the direction, pace, and evidence of the achievement of their learning outcomes. There are no prescribed texts books, just recommended texts enhanced with students' choices of resources available at the university library, which is brimming with excellent resources. Each student tailors their learning programme according to personalised learning outcomes, teaching/learning activities they set themselves which are guided by prescribed learning outcomes and clearly set criteria for assessment that relate back to the prescribed outcomes (to ensure quality standards and compentencies are met). This personalised approach significantly increased student motivation. Engagement increased from doing a bare minimum to pass the course, to students doing their best. They do not do this in isolation; they do it in collaboration with their colleagues, field educators, and university staff members. Inclusion of field trips and the Marae Noho added joy and unexpected outcomes by enabling students to learn with their minds, bodies, guts, and hearts utilising their heads to think, their hearts to feel, hands to give, their legs to walk and visit their clients in their homes, and their bottoms to sit and reflect on their learning.

REFERENCES

Ashenberg-Straussner, S., Senreich, E., & Steen, J. (2018, April 1). Wounded healers: A multistate study of licensed social workers' behavioral health problems. *Social Work, 36*(2), 125–133.

Bowers, E., & Pack, M. (2017). Designing and embedding authentic learning opportunities in a social work curriculum: Reflections and lessons learned. *Aotearoa New Zealand Social Work, 29*(1), 99–110.

Census New Zealand. (2013). Ethnic groups in New Zealand. *Census QuickStats about culture and identity.* Retrieved from http://archive.stats.govt.nz/Census/2013-census/profile-and-summary-reports/quickstats-culture-identity/ethnic-groups-NZ.aspx.

Craske, M., Hermans, D., & Vansteenwegen, D. (2006). *Fear and learning: From basic processes to clinical implications.* Warriewood, NSW, Australia: Footrpint Books.

Crisp, B., & Green Lister, P. (2002). Assessment methods in social work education: A review of the literature. *Social Work Education, 21*(2), 259–269.

Ellis, L., Napan, K., & O'Donoghue, K. (2018). Greening social work education in Aotearoa/New Zealand. In L. Dominelli (Ed.), *The Routledge handbook of green social work* (pp. 535–546). New York, NY: Routledge.

Heron, J. (1996). Helping whole people learn. In D. Boud & N. Miller (Eds.), *Working with experience: Animating learning.* London: Routledge.

Nakanishi, N. (1999). 'Ikigai' in older Japanese people. *Age and Ageing, 28*(3), 323–324. https://doi.org/10.1093/ageing/28.3.323.

Napan, K. (1998, January 1). *Evaluation of the contact-challenge method in social work education.* Auckland, Aotearoa, New Zealand. Retrieved from https://mro.massey.ac.nz/bitstream/handle/10179/2440/02_whole.pdf.

Napan, K. (2015). Co-creative learning: A comparative analysis of two integrative and collaborative methods of teaching/learning social work (L. Press, Ed.). *International Journal of Innovation, Creativity and Change, 2*(1), 78–99.

Napan, K. (2017). Exploring practical wisdom: Teaching management in a spirit of co-creation. In W. Kupers & O. Gunnlaugson (Eds.), *Wisdom learning: Perspectives on wising-up business and management education* (pp. 248–272). London: Routledge.

Phillips, L., & Napan, K. (2016). What's in the 'co'? Tending the tensions in co-creative inquiry in social work education. *International Journal of Qualitative Studies in Education, 29*(6), 827–844.

Postlethwait, A. (2016). Group projects in social work education: The influence of group characteristics and moderators on undergraduate student outcomes. *Journal of Teaching in Social Work, 36*(3), 256–274.

Rosegrant-Alvarez, A., & Moxley, D. (2004). The student portfolio in social work education. *Journal of Teaching in Social Work, 1–2*(24), 87–103. https://doi.org/10.1300/J067v24n01_06.

Senreich, E. (2013). An inclusive definition of spirituality for social. *Journal of Social Work Education, 49*(4), 548–563.

Social Work Registration Board. (2016). *The SWRB ten core competence standards.* Wellington, Aotearoa, New Zealand.

CHAPTER 46

Social Work in Germany: Between a Nation State Focus and Transnational Horizons

Caroline Schmitt and Matthias D. Witte

INTRODUCTION

In many countries of the Global North, social work developed from historical roots in religious, neighbourly, and moral support to become its own profession (Rehklau & Lutz, 2011, p. 11). In Germany, social work gained recognition as a profession in the early twentieth century and had its precursors in voluntary activities devoted to poor relief. The origins of social work go back to what was termed the "social question". In the course of the far-reaching social process of industrialisation, the living conditions of the people underwent fundamental changes. Social risks such as poverty, immiseration, and job loss through illness were to be alleviated by sociopolitical support measures. Originally rooted in communal poor relief, over the course of its history, social work in Germany evolved into differentiated fields of practice. The concept of a professional support system exported from Northern countries in the course of their colonial appropriation of the countries of the South, where other forms of social work were not infrequently suppressed as a result. Only gradually are paradigm shifts, such as those being debated in the context of indigenisation, emerging as indications of a growing awareness of the multiple forms taken by social work worldwide (Straub, 2016).

C. Schmitt (✉) · M. D. Witte
Institute of Education Working Group "Social Work", Johannes Gutenberg-University Mainz, Mainz, Germany
e-mail: schmica@uni-mainz.de

M. D. Witte
e-mail: matthias.witte@uni-mainz.de

This paper reflects on the historical development of social work in Germany with its intrinsically heterogeneous strands of traditional social assistance; it also explores the contributions of other countries that influenced the development of social work in Germany. Even though social work is conceptually framed in Germany as having a national scope, it has always maintained transnational links to other countries (Treptow, 2004). The purpose of this paper is to engage in historical reflection (Köngeter & Reutlinger, 2014, p. 455) and trace the ways in which transnational interpretations of social work concepts came into being. After giving a brief historical outline, we will present an overview of the present-day organisation of social work in Germany, which involves a variety of different providers and fields of practice. We argue that one of the future tasks of the social work profession will be to extend its scope of practice across national borders, since people's lives are increasingly characterised by greater cross-border mobility and since global problems can no longer be addressed by the efforts of individual countries alone.

History of Social Work in Germany

The history of social work in Germany is not a history of linear progress. It is characterised by discontinuities, retrograde progress, and wrong turnings. However, it is necessary to review this history in order to distinguish new solutions from old mistakes (Hammerschmidt, Weber, & Seidenstücker, 2017, p. 7).

Since Germany has historically drawn a distinction between social service work (*Sozialarbeit*) and social pedagogy (*Sozialpädagogik*), the relevant aspects that come to the fore when we examine the history of the field may differ depending on whether we are viewing it from the perspective of social service work or of social pedagogy. Strictly speaking, therefore, we ought to speak of the *histories* (plural) of social assistance in Germany. While the roots of social service work are perceived to lie in poor relief, social pedagogy arose in the context of the youth movement—initially organised by young people themselves—of the early twentieth century. In our historical outline, we will consider both strands—social service work and social pedagogy—and stress that it is impossible to draw clear-cut lines of distinction between the two. Their histories, accordingly, are characterised not only by differences, but also by common factors (Eßer, 2018a). To highlight these common factors, researchers are increasingly adopting the term "social work" (*Soziale Arbeit*) as a blanket term for both social service work and social pedagogy (*Sozialpädagogik*). We endorse this practice. At the same time, various different terms have been used over the decades for different social activities. The words *Fürsorge* (welfare) and *Wohlfahrtspflege* (social welfare work) were widely in use in the past before being superseded by the new concepts of *Sozialarbeit* (social service work), *Sozialpädagogik* (social pedagogy), and *Soziale Arbeit* (social work). This multiplicity of terms demonstrates at a glance that the field of social assistance is not uniform, but an amalgamation of different traditions (Münchmeier, 2018, p. 527).

Our historical outline begins in the middle ages. During the *early middle ages*, material poverty was highly regarded, since the Christian tradition viewed an ascetic life as signifying closeness to Jesus and his disciples. Material poverty was distinct from personal poverty; those who were defenceless and at the mercy of the powerful could receive support in churches and monasteries and from private initiatives. This form of charitable poor relief[1] was not, however, a systematic strategy for combating poverty. In the hierarchy of the social estates, the poor occupied the lowest rank and their situation in life was deemed to be fated. While they were the recipients of religious charity, such charity was not intended to bring about a structural change of their situation (Sagebiel, 2005). For the wealthy population, almsgiving was a means of absolving one's sins and attaining a place in heaven. Life on earth was not focused on the "here and now", but on the expectation of a life after death.

The dissolution of the medieval estates began in the *early thirteenth century*. Towns were no longer obliged to pay duties to the clergy and princes and began to grow into centres of commerce and trade. More and more indigent people moved to the cities to look for work. In the *late middle ages*, population growth, along with wars and pestilence, caused a change in attitudes towards poor people and beggars and led to the reorganisation and secularisation of poor relief. The city of Nuremberg introduced a poor registry in 1370. Other cities followed suit, assessing and registering the poor among their population. Poor residents of the cities were issued pauper's papers and qualified for municipal welfare measures. People from other parts of the country and those who were not thought to qualify for assistance, since they were able to work, were not entitled to such aid. Those who were apprehended by the constables without their pauper's papers were expelled from the town. This measure shows that poor people were increasingly targeted by measures aimed at ensuring public order. As the social interpretation of poverty began to change, poverty was no longer regarded as ordained by God, but as a vice brought on by the sufferer's own fault. Work, in contrast, came to be regarded as the expression of a successful life and personal responsibility, as the Protestant work ethic began to gain traction.

The *sixteenth century* saw the gradual reorganisation of poor relief all over Europe. The Bridewell workhouse was established in London in 1555, while additional workhouses followed in Bristol and elsewhere. These English institutions were copied in continental Europe. In 1595, the city of Amsterdam opened a reformatory (*Tuchthuys*) for men. The inmates were predominantly beggars, but also included those who were destitute or disabled as well as convicts (Wendt, 2017, pp. 23–26). The concept subsequently spread to Germany, where workhouses were established in Bremen (1609), Lübeck (1613), and Hamburg (1620). Work was used as a disciplinary measure for poor people, who were tested in the workhouses for their fitness for work.

The punishment for begging in the streets was forced labour; poor relief was now geared towards discipline and "education" by means of work. Thus, it would be a mistake to regard these combined prison/workhouses as early expressions of middle-class social welfare policies. Rather, they were places where people were confined and segregated from the rest of society (Wendt, 2017, p. 27).

The "social question" acquired increasing urgency at the *dawn of industrialisation*. Technical innovations, such as the invention of the steam engine and the railway, triggered the rapid expansion of industry, and more and more people moved from rural areas into the cities, where they were employed with low wages in the new factories. However, not all of them found work. In the densely populated cities, the numbers of homeless people increased and famines ensued. In the *mid-nineteenth century*, wealthy urban residents called for a solution to the problem of the poor and demanded social reforms to foster social peace and prevent a "class struggle". Various German cities adopted what was known as the "Elberfeld system" as a new poor relief strategy. The cities were divided into small precincts, each of which was in the care of a volunteer almoner (i.e. local public official responsible for managing and administering social assistance) who lived in the precinct and cared for the people and families assigned to him. The almoner answered to the overseer of the district into which his precinct fell. The system was first introduced in 1853 in Elberfeld and spread rapidly thanks to its success. However, finding volunteer almoners was difficult in the large mass slums, which had their own specific and complex problems that differed from those of the areas where the middle-class families lived. The "Strasbourg system" emerged as a refined version of the Elberfeld system. The division of cities into precincts remained in place, but the Strasbourg system supplemented the volunteer almoners with paid professional almoners. The Poor Law authority was established as the administrative unit. For the first time in the history of social work in Germany, a distinction was drawn between practical, hands-on agencies and administrative, decision-making bodies in social assistance (Lambers, 2010, p. 149). Concurrently with municipal poor relief efforts, the churches and associations also laid the foundations of professional activities in the field of social assistance. The Protestant Church negotiated a division of labour with the municipal authorities and undertook to look after individual cases and to provide special institutions like orphanages and maternity homes (Hering & Münchmeier, 2003, p. 33). Johann Hinrich Wichern (1808–1881) founded the "Rauhes Haus" in Hamburg in 1833. One of the earliest facilities of the charitable organisation Diakonisches Werk in Germany, it was fundamentally different from the correctional institutions and workhouses that were widespread at the time. Wichern's aim was to give young people prospects for the future. In 1843, he opened an educational facility for training "Brothers", later termed "Deacons". In the Catholic Church, nuns were among the first in Germany to receive training in the field of poor relief

and nursing and to pursue these activities on a professional basis, also opening orphanages and schools.

In the *late nineteenth century*, more and more social services became
established. The Freiburg-based Caritas Association, founded by theologian
Lorenz Werthmann in 1897, was involved in various spheres of social assistance for seasonal workers, sailors, beggars, alcoholics, and disabled people.
Additionally, it established kindergartens, corrective training facilities, protection for girls, nursing programs, and women's work. On the level of the state,
Reich Chancellor Otto von Bismarck introduced social insurance. Medical
insurance was established in 1883, accident insurance in 1884, and disability and old-age pensions for workers in 1889. Unemployment insurance followed in 1927. Bismarck's reforms focused on two issues: firstly, preventing
workers and their party-political organisations from overthrowing the social
power structure and secondly, disburdening the state coffers from the high
costs of poor relief. Henceforth, two support systems existed side by side:
sociopolitical aid on the one hand and individual poor relief on the other.

Finally, *World War I* led to an increased demand for professional social
work (Lambers, 2010, p. 154). War relief for families without fathers and aid
for surviving dependents of soldiers increased the number of people qualifying for social assistance. Until 1918, Germany defined itself as a liberal constitutional state dedicated to minimal intervention in social and economic
processes. In 1918, however, there was a fundamental change (Schilling &
Klus, 2015, p. 34). The Prussian Ministry of Public Welfare was established as
the country's central welfare authority. Various laws were passed concerning
the care of war invalids and dependents of fallen soldiers, small social pensions
for victims of inflation, and youth welfare. The term *Armenfürsorge* ("poor
relief") was replaced by *Wohlfahrtspflege* ("public welfare"). Some institutions
that remain in existence to this day such as the youth welfare office (consisting of administrative services and what was then known as the youth welfare
committee, now the youth aid committee or *Jugendhilfeausschuss*) were established during this period. With the Weimar Constitution of 1919, the new
state consolidated its ideas of public welfare in a parliamentary constitutional
and welfare state. It was in this spirit that the women's movement, which had
been growing and fighting for recognition since the mid-nineteenth century,
came into play. It was modelled on the political women's movements that
had been active in France since the late eighteenth century (Lambers, 2010,
pp. 146–155). In particular, the social reformer Alice Salomon campaigned
for the participation of middle-class girls and women in social assistance in
Germany and helped to launch an independent training system. Salomon
became a member of the "Girls' and Womens' Groups for Social Assistance
Work" in 1893 and launched Germany's first Women's School of Social Work
in Berlin in 1908. She also founded the International Committee of Women's
Schools of Social Work in 1929. Her first textbook for welfare worker training was published in 1926. Salomon was highly active in transnational

networks and organised international congresses and exhibitions (Homfeldt, 2004, p. 5). At the culmination of her work, she served as the first female president of the International Association of Schools of Social Work (Healy, 2001, p. 29).

Salomon was powerfully influenced by the settlement movement, which had spread to the USA from its origins in London and also influenced social work in Germany. Proponents of the settlement movement sought not only to provide individual support for poor people, but also to effect social reforms and bring together poor and affluent people in order to foster mutual recognition and long-term improvements in living conditions (Köngeter, 2013, p. 81). The first settlement house, Toynbee Hall, opened its doors in London in 1883/1884. Jane Addams and Ellen Gates Starr discovered the concept in London, translated it into the context of the USA (Köngeter & Reutlinger, 2014, p. 459), and, in 1889, founded Hull House in Chicago. In Germany, the concept inspired not only Salomon, but also the Protestant pastor Friedrich Siegmund-Schultze, who founded the Soziale Arbeitsgemeinschaft (SAG) in Berlin in 1912. At approximately the same time as the work of the women's movement and the settlement movement, middle-class young people came together in the early twentieth century to form the youth movement. Actors in the field of social assistance adopted certain principles of this youth movement, such as the idea of (self-) education by a group, and developed concepts of reform pedagogy and the social pedagogy movement (Wagner, 2009, p. 111). The beginnings of the middle-class youth movement are generally dated to 1901, the year in which the *Wandervogel* youth groups were formed. This middle-class youth movement rebelled against school, parents, and society. They met for hiking trips and frequently subscribed to a romanticised view of nature. Distinct from this movement were the associations of working-class youth, which arose for political reasons and protested against poor working conditions. For these young people, urbanisation and industrialisation had brought numerous disadvantages (Münchmeier, 2018). The activities of the working-class youth movement were often international in scope, while parts of the middle-class youth movement had a nationalist, ethnic German focus. Like the international, emancipatory ideas of social work, nationalist and racist philosophies were in circulation across national borders. For example, the German anti-Semite Wilhelm Marr (Bruns, 2011), after spending several years in North and Central America in the late nineteenth century, approved the colonial racist division of people and the derogation of black people that he had encountered there. Associating binary, racialised modes of thought in terms of black vs. white with the anti-Jewish discourse in Germany, he constructed a kinship between Jews and black people and, thereby, sought to legitimise their devaluation.

With the rise to power of the Nazis and with the advent of *World War II*, nationalist mindsets became more entrenched and international exchange in women's networks and the international worker's youth came to an abrupt end. The Nazis installed the "Nationalsozialistische Volkswohlfahrt"

(NSV) as an organisation and replaced poor relief with "genetic and racial care" (Schilling & Klus, 2015, p. 40). Inhuman, destructive measures such as forced sterilisation and the murder of disabled people, homosexuals, and Jews aimed to protect the Nazis' imaginary "Aryan race" from "unhealthy genetic material". In many cases, people involved in social work both participated in and supported the murders and racist policies. Prominent representatives of the profession were murdered or forced to emigrate, including Alice Salomon, Adele Beerensson, Gertrud Israel, Hedwig Wachenheim, and Frieda Wunderlich (Paulini, 2013, p. 125).

After the *end of the war*, the social welfare system had to be rebuilt. Following Germany's surrender on 8 May 1945, the country was divided between the occupying forces of the USA, Great Britain, the Soviet Union, and later France. The main focus of practical social work was on caring for war orphans and war invalids, refugee services, and combating hunger and poverty (Hammerschmidt et al., 2017, p. 90). The surviving facilities of Caritas and Diakonisches Werk continued their activities. The "Hauptausschuss für Arbeiterwohlfahrt" (Main Committee for Workers' Welfare) and the "Zentralwohlfahrtsstelle der deutschen Juden" (Central Welfare Office of German Jews), which had been banned during the Nazi era, had to reorganise themselves from scratch.

In 1949, the occupation period ended with the *founding of the Federal Republic of Germany and the German Democratic Republic (GDR)*. From then on, different social assistance structures developed in the two states. In East Germany, Caritas and Diakonisches Werk were supplemented by the "Zentralausschuss für Volkssolidarität" (Central Committee for People's Solidarity), the central social welfare agency of the GDR. The Sozialistische Einheitspartei Deutschlands (SED), the GDR's ruling party, believed that overcoming capitalism and social problems were the task of the state. Accordingly, there was a well-developed network of state care services such as crèches (Eßer, 2018b). However, young people who failed to live up to the goals of the socialist party, and those whom the state regarded as having behavioural problems, were committed to special institutions for reeducation.

In West Germany, the Red Cross and the Deutsche Paritätische Wohlfahrtsverband developed additional welfare associations. The main associations of the Freie Wohlfahrtspflege[2] and a variety of other welfare providers came into being. Social service experts sought to build on the system of the Weimar Republic, whose social insurance and pension schemes they retained. The issue of insufficient funding for social work, which had already been a problem in the time of the Weimar Republic, likewise continued to exist. Practical social work modelled itself on methods imported from England and the USA, adopting the classical methodologies of help for individual casework, group work, and community work. It was mainly German emigrants returning from the USA who brought these methods back to Germany with them. From the 1950s onwards, the various training institutions began to be remodelled into social work colleges known as "Höhere Fachschulen für Soziale Arbeit" (Paulini, 2013, p. 127). Legal reforms followed, such as the Youth Welfare Act in 1961, which was reformulated as the Child and Youth Services Act in 1990. The Federal Social Assistance Act was passed in 1961/1962 as the precursor to the modern Social Security Statute Books.

In both East and West Germany, recipients of social services could be subjected to repressive treatment. The children's homes of the 1950s and 1960s employed many people without appropriate training, and many of these institutions emphasised discipline and control. Not until the rise of the student movement of 1968 did widespread criticism begin to be levelled at restrictive conditions in social work. The movement of 1968 was active in many countries worldwide from the mid-1960s onwards. Its emergence in Germany coincides roughly with the founding of the so-called Extra-Parliamentary Opposition as a political protest movement in the mid-1960s (Steinacker, 2018). In the course of the "children's home campaign", students associated with the movement of 1968 liberated adolescents from children's homes and offered them a place in their communes. They condemned the coercive and repressive measures to which children were subjected in homes and demonstrated for fundamental social and political change. The "sixty-eighters" were active in almost every field of social work. They established children's shops and child welfare facilities, independent schools, self-governed youth and cultural centres, alternative educational projects, and small group homes as alternatives to institutional youth service facilities. The movement of 1968 caused social work to engage in increased reflection about social conditions and promoted the academisation of social work training (Eßer, 2018b). Universities began to offer courses in social pedagogy with greater frequency. From the 1970s onwards, the social work colleges were upgraded to Universities of Applied Sciences. Increasing numbers of young people attended universities and colleges. In East Germany, meanwhile, protests against the political system were increasing. The mass demonstrations of 1989 called for regime change along with freedom of opinion and movement and exemplified the peaceful revolution in East Germany. The protests culminated in the fall of the Berlin Wall on 9 November 1989. On 3 October 1990, East and West Germany were officially reunified. In the reigning climate of rapid change, opportunities for comparative reflection about social work methodologies and approaches in East and West Germany were missed. Instead, *German unity* led to a one-sided export of the "western system" to eastern Germany (Bütow & Maurer, 2018).

SOCIAL WORK IN GERMANY TODAY AND ITS DIFFERENTIATION IN THE NATION STATE

Social work in Germany is differentiated into a varied landscape of multiple providers. The term *Träger*, here rendered as "provider", is a typically German concept referring to the way in which social work is organised and covers both *social insurance providers* and *providers of social services*. Social insurance providers are the agencies that cover the costs of social benefits. These may be the state of Germany, the federal states, the local authorities, or the health insurance funds. Providers of social services offer practical services and receive funding from the social insurance providers. They are the responsible legal entities entrusted with running social facilities on the professional, financial, and personnel levels. Providers of social services may be publicly or independently funded. Public providers are the child welfare services, welfare agencies, and public health authorities established by the state. Independent providers include free, nonprofit providers and private, commercial providers. Free, nonprofit providers are the large welfare associations, churches, self-help organisations, and foundations. Private, commercial providers were established in larger numbers in the early 1990s. They are profit-oriented and lack the overarching organisational structures of the free nonprofits. They are particularly heavily represented in the fields of inpatient and short-term health care, but they are not present in every field of social work. Just as the landscape of providers is differentiated and, at times, confusing, social work takes place in a variety of different *fields of action*. These can be divided according to their target groups such as social services for children and adolescents, families, older adults, people with mental health problems, and people with disabilities. Similarly, they can be grouped according to the social problems they address, such as homelessness, illness, and poverty. At the same time, social work experts are active in a variety of institutions, such as daycare facilities, residential groups, educational facilities, and migrant services. The degree of intervention can also help to systematise the different fields of action. This perspective can be used to distinguish between *activities supplementing the needs of people* (e.g. in youth camps or self-help groups), *activities supporting the needs of people* (educational aids or accommodation for people without fixed housing), and *activities replacing the normal environments of people* (such as prisons or retirement homes).

The history of social work in Germany and, in particular, its instrumentalisation during the Nazi era, has illustrated the importance and indispensability of a sound ethical basis. According to Böhnisch (2016), the core of social work is providing support for people in their quest for subjective agency in critical life circumstances. Social work seeks to prevent social exclusion and enable social, economic, cultural, and political participation (Bettinger, 2011). This view is compatible with the definition of social work according to the International Federation of Social Workers (IFSW) (2014):

> Social work is a practice-based profession and an academic discipline that promotes social change and development, social cohesion, and the empowerment and liberation of people. Principles of social justice, human rights, collective responsibility and respect for diversities are central to social work. Underpinned by theories of social work, social sciences, humanities and indigenous knowledge, Social Work engages people and structures to address life challenges and enhance wellbeing. The above definition may be amplified at national and/or regional levels.

In the view of the IFSW, it is crucial to regard social work as a field rooted in human rights. Social work is dedicated to empowering people and to designing and researching social structures that foster human development with the goal of human well-being. This view has been adopted by the German professional organisation Deutsche Berufsverband für Soziale Arbeit e.V. (DBSH). The DBSH is a member of the global umbrella organisation IFSW and IFSW Europe. Global social problems such as growing social inequality, poverty, natural disasters, wars, centres of conflict, and their concomitant migration and refugee phenomena illustrate the enduring urgency of cross-border communications in social work. In the early twenty-first century, social work in Germany (and elsewhere) is simultaneously encountering transnational solidarisation tendencies (e.g. with refugees) and demands for shoring up the nation state as a supervisory authority with the task of regulating and setting limits. Both the media discourse and the political debate are almost contemporaneously dominated in many countries of the world by the drawing of boundaries between "us" and "the others" based on racist discrimination and assumed "cultural differences" (Schmitt, Semu, & Witte, 2017). These problem areas can no longer be studied from the perspective of individual nation states alone, but must be examined in transnational networks and associations. They require the opening of social services and their work structures and patterns of action and interpretation.

Transnational Opening of Social Work in Germany

At the present time, the cross-border opening of social work is being discussed under the motto of "transnational social work" (e.g. Negi & Furman, 2010; Schwarzer, Kämmerer-Rütten, Schleyer-Lindenmann, & Wang, 2016). The terms "transnational", "transnationality", and "transnationalization", which have been gaining popularity since the 1980s in the context of migration research in the cultural and social sciences in the USA, denote processes that extend beyond individual nation states while still being influenced by national framings. In contrast to an international perspective that compares social services in different national contexts and seeks to achieve a border-crossing dialogue of different concepts of social work, a transnational perspective (also) takes the perspective of its recipients into account. It reflects the multi-national contexts of lived social work experiences from the perspective of the recipients themselves and discusses cross-border processes whenever they unfold in the persons' lives. Furman, Negi, and Salvador (2010, p. 8) define transnational social work as "an emerging field of practice that (a) is designed to serve transnational populations; (b) operates across nation state boundaries, whether physically or through new technologies; and (c) is informed by and addresses complex transnational problems and dilemmas". Schwarzer (2016) conceptualises transnational social work as an approach that critically reflects processes of boundary-drawing and demarcation such as "belonging to a country" and "not belonging to a country" as well as constructions of "us" and "the others". Transnational social work "challenges the underlying – often stereotypical – thinking that there are people who belong and that there are fundamentally different people like migrants and refugees" (ibid., p. 7). The German legislature regards social work as being primarily a service whose sphere of competence for addressing problems lies mainly on the national level and in the narrower social environment of its recipients (see, e.g., the laws in Social Code VIII, Section 27). Imposing such national limits on social work was, however, foreign to the pioneers of the field in the early twentieth century. Social work is challenged to learn from its history of exclusion and the extinction of human beings as practised by National Socialism, and to do justice to its human rights mandate. Against the background of the transnationalisation of social, cultural, and lived experiences, it is necessary to ask to what extent the liberating, cross-border history of social work can become an aid to orientation in the "here and now". For if social work wishes to do justice to its beneficiaries' requirements for support, it is challenged to open itself across borders in a networked world. In addition to the need for legislation to enable the expansion of social work's sphere of action, challenges can be formulated on (at least) three levels (Schmitt, 2016): (1) social work is required to perceive the significance of transnational processes and structures in the biographies of its recipients. Related to this is (2) the reflection of its own interpretive schemata and the development of a critically reflective diversity competence that reflects social work's field of action and that transcends the boundaries of the nation state. Furthermore, transnationally reflective social work must (3) address the institutional structures of its own facilities and examine whether they are adequately addressing and reaching people in transnational living situations. Such reflection is becoming increasingly urgent at the present time. Not only the migrant and refugee movements of recent times, but mobile family structures and the pluralisation of life circumstances also require the broadening of nationally framed concepts of social work. An examination of the history of social work can make a core contribution to such broadening and shows that transnational contacts between leading figures in the field can serve as crucial aids to dealing with current challenges.

NOTES

1. Since the history of "charity" is linked to the emergence of social service work in the context of poor relief, we begin our outline of history *before* the emergence of a form of an institutionalised social assistance.
2. Today, the "main associations of the Freie Wohlfahrtspflege" have been amalgamated within the "Bundesarbeitsgemeinschaft der Freien Wohlfahrtspflege (BAGFW)" ("Federal Committee for Free Social Welfare"). The BAGFW comprises six main associations, each with their own organisational structure: (1) the Workers' Welfare Association (Arbeiterwohlfahrt, AWO); (2) the Caritas Association (Deutsche Caritasverband, DCV); (3) the welfare organisation

Deutsche Paritätische Wohlfahrtsverband ("Der PARITÄTISCHE"); (4) the German Red Cross (DRK); (5) Diakonie Deutschland; and (6) the Central Jewish Welfare Office (Zentralwohlfahrtsstelle der Juden in Deutschland, ZWST).

REFERENCES

Bettinger, F. (2011). Bezugswissenschaften Sozialer Arbeit – ohne Bezug zur Sozialen Arbeit? [Disciplines related to social work—With no relationship to social work?]. *Forum Sozial, 2*, 41–42.

Böhnisch, L. (2016). *Lebensbewältigung* [Coping with life]. Weinheim and Basel: Beltz Juventa.

Bruns, C. (2011). Towards a transnational history of racism. Interrelationships between colonial racism and German anti-semitism? The example of Wilhelm Marr. In M. Berg & S. Wendt (Eds.), *Racism in the modern world: Historical perspectives on cultural transfer and adaptation* (pp. 122–139). Oxford: Berghahn Books.

Bütow, B., & Maurer, S. (2018). 1989/90 – Soziale Arbeit in DDR und BRD [1989/90—Social work in the GDR and the FRG]. In F. Eßer (Ed.), *Einführung in die Geschichte der Sozialen Arbeit* [Introduction to the history of social work] (pp. 133–150). Baltmannsweiler: Schneider Verlag Hohengehren.

Eßer, F. (2018a). Sozialpädagogik [Social pedagogy]. In G. Graßhoff, A. Renker, & W. Schröer (Eds.), *Soziale Arbeit. Eine elementare Einführung* [Social work: An elementary introduction] (pp. 273–286). Wiesbaden: VS.

Eßer, F. (2018b). Fünf Jahrhunderte Geschichte: ein kurzer Überblick [Five centuries of history: A brief overview]. In F. Eßer (Ed.), *Einführung in die Geschichte der Sozialen Arbeit* [Introduction to the history of social work] (pp. 15–32). Baltmannsweiler: Schneider Verlag Hohengehren.

Furman, R., Negi, N. J., & Salvador, R. (2010). An introduction to transnational social work. In N. J. Negi & R. Furman (Eds.), *Transnational Social Work Practice* (pp. 3–19). New York: Columbia University Press.

Hammerschmidt, P., Weber, S., & Seidenstücker, B. (2017). *Soziale Arbeit – die Geschichte* [Social work—Its history]. Opladen and Toronto: Barbara Budrich.

Healy, L. M. (2001). *International social work: Professional action in an interdependent world*. Oxford: Oxford University Press.

Hering, S., & Münchmeier, R. (2003). *Geschichte der Sozialen Arbeit. Eine Einführung* [History of social work: An introduction] (2nd ed.). Weinheim and München: Juventa.

Homfeldt, H. G. (2004). Soziale Arbeit – international und transnational [Social work—International and transnational]. In H. R. Yousefi & K. Fischer (Eds.), *Interkulturelle Orientierung – Grundlegung des Toleranzdialogs* [Intercultural orientation—Foundations of the dialogue of tolerance] (pp. 399–413). Nordhausen: Bautz.

International Federation of Social Workers (IFSW). (2014). *Global definition of social work*. https://www.ifsw.org/what-is-social-work/global-definition-of-social-work/. Accessed October 19, 2018.

Köngeter, S. (2013). Transnationales Wissen in der Geschichte der Sozialen Arbeit - Zur Bedeutung religiöser Verbindungen für die grenzüberschreitende Verbreitung der Settlement-Bewegung [Transnational knowledge in the history of social work—On the significance of religious ties for the transnational spread of the settlement movement]. In D. Bender, A. Duscha, L. Huber, & K. Klein-Zimmer (Eds.), *Transnationales Wissen und Soziale Arbeit* [Transnational knowledge and social work] (pp. 80–97). Weinheim: Beltz Juventa.

Köngeter, S., & Reutlinger, C. (2014). Community Connections - Die Vielstimmigkeit der transatlantischen Community-Orientierung zwischen 1890 und 1940 [Community connections—The many voices of transatlantic community orientation between 1890 and 1940]. Neue Praxis, 5, 455–477.

Lambers, H. (2010). Wie aus Helfen Soziale Arbeit wurde. Die Geschichte der Sozialen Arbeit [How helping became social work: The history of social work]. Bad Heilbrunn: Klinkhardt.

Münchmeier, R. (2018). Geschichte der Sozialen Arbeit [History of social work]. In H.-U. Otto, H. Thiersch, R. Treptow, & H. Ziegler (Eds.), *Handbuch Soziale Arbeit* [Handbook of social work] (6th rev. ed., pp. 527–539). München: Reinhardt.

Negi, N. J., & Furman, R. (Eds.). (2010). *Transnational social work practice*. New York: Columbia University Press.

Paulini, C. (2013). Soziale Arbeit als Beruf [Social work as a vocation]. In S. Hering (Ed.), *Was ist Soziale Arbeit? Traditionen – Widersprüche – Wirkungen* [What is social work? Traditions—Contradictions—Effects] (pp. 121–131). Opladen, Berlin, and Toronto: Barbara Budrich.

Rehklau, C., & Lutz, R. (2011). Andere Welten – andere Lösungen. Auf dem Weg zu einer Anthropologie des Helfens [Different worlds—Different solutions. Towards an anthropology of helping]. In C. Rehklau & R. Lutz (Eds.), *Sozialarbeit des Südens. Band 1 – Zugänge* [Social work of the South. Vol. 1—Approaches] (pp. 9–17). Oldenburg: Paulo Freire.

Sagebiel, J. (2005). *Geschichte der Sozialen Arbeit - Die Mütter der Sozialen Arbeit* [History of social work—The mothers of social work]. FH München, FB Soziale Arbeit.   http://w3-mediapool.hm.edu/mediapool/media/fk11/fk11_lokal/ forschungpublikationen/publikationen_4/dokumente_44/sagebiel/Sagebiel-Geschichte_der_Sozialen_Arbeit.pdf. Accessed August 15, 2018.

Schilling, J., & Klus, S. (2015). *Soziale Arbeit. Geschichte - Theorie – Profession* [Social work: History—Theory—Profession]. München and Basel: Ernst Reinhardt.

Schmitt, C. (2016). Transnational social work with young refugees. *Transnational Social Review—A Social Work Journal, 1*(2), 209–214. https://doi.org/10.1080/ 21931674.2016.1184024.

Schmitt, C., Semu, L., & Witte, M. D. (2017). Racism and transnationality. *Transnational Social Review—A Social Work Journal, 3*, 239–243. https://doi.org /10.1080/21931674.2017.1359959.

Schwarzer, B. (2016). Transnational social work: An introduction. In B. Schwarzer, U. Kämmerer-Rütten, A. Schleyer-Lindenmann, & Y. Wang (Eds.), *Transnational social work and social welfare: Challenges for the social work profession* (pp. 4–12). London and New York: Routledge.

Schwarzer, B., Kämmerer-Rütten, U., Schleyer-Lindenmann, A., & Wang, Y. (Eds.). (2016). *Transnational social work and social welfare: Challenges for the social work profession*. London and New York: Routledge.

Steinacker, S. (2018). 1968 ff. – Soziale Bewegung und Soziale Arbeit [Social movement and social work]. In F. Eßer (Ed.), *Einführung in die Geschichte der Sozialen Arbeit* [Introduction to the history of social work] (pp. 111–131). Baltmannsweiler: Schneider Verlag Hohengehren.

Straub, U. (2016). "All My Relations" – indigene Ansätze und Relationalität in der Sozialen Arbeit ["All my relations"—Indigenous approaches and relationality in social work]. In F. Früchtel & M. Strassner (Eds.), *Relationale Sozialarbeit* [Relational social work] (pp. 54–74). Weinheim: Beltz Juventa.

Treptow, R. (2004). Grenzüberschreitung und Globalisierung von Hilfe. Eine Skizze zur Internationalität Sozialer Arbeit [Border crossing and globalization of help: A sketch of the internationality of social work]. In H. G. Homfeldt & K. Brandhorst (Eds.), *International vergleichende Soziale Arbeit* [International comparative social work] (pp. 10–23). Baltmannsweiler: Schneider Verlag Hohengehren.

Wagner, L. (2009). Jugendbewegungen und Soziale Arbeit [Youth movements and social work]. In L. Wagner (Ed.), *Soziale Bewegung und Soziale Arbeit* [Social movement and social work]. Wiesbaden: VS.

Wendt, W. R. (2017). Geschichte der Sozialen Arbeit 1. Die Gesellschaft vor der sozialen Frage 1750 bis 1900 [History of social work 1: Society before the social question, 1750 to 1900] (6th ed.). Wiesbaden: VS.

CHAPTER 47

Decoding the Epistemological Framework of Social Work Research: Attrition of Under-represented Minority and Marginalised Students in Higher Education in the United States

M. Gail Augustine

Higher Education Minority and Marginalised Population Attrition Inquiries

The voluminous literature on attrition factors in higher education has provided variables and models to illustrate statistical evidence on minority and marginalised students drop out rates or failure to complete a college degree (e.g. Flynn, 2014; Jones, Barlow, & Villarejo, 2010; Murphy, Gaughan, & Moore, 2010). Responding to the attrition of minority and marginal groups in higher education cannot be done by merely using predetermine indicators used to measure all groups. For the most part, standardised measures have been constructed and tested around the higher education experiences of students from the dominant culture's paradigm as a base of knowledge production. For instance, the social and academic integration model constructed by Tinto (1975) has been used and referenced in over 777 studies for more than four decades and assumed to be universally applicable to measure attrition, retention, and success in higher education. From these previous and current

M. Gail Augustine (✉)
Associate Faculty (IUPUI), Indiana University-Purdue University Indianapolis, Indianapolis, IN, USA
e-mail: maraugus@iupui.edu

© The Author(s) 2021
S. S. M. et al. (eds.), *The Palgrave Handbook of Global Social Work Education*, https://doi.org/10.1007/978-3-030-39966-5_47

studies, we know that lack of social and academic integration, isolation, ill-preparedness, lack of faculty-student relationship all contribute to attrition.

Attrition has been defined as the act of premature departure from college before a degree completion. It is relatively difficult to discuss attrition without defining retention. *Retention* in educational settings is defined as students' continued study until successful completion of a degree. A *Minority* is defined as any ethnic or racial group who may typically be under-represented in higher education—colleges and universities. This definition may refer to but is not restricted to, Asian American, Hispanic, and African American students. Although Native Americans and women are historically under-represented, they are not included as specific or at-risk groups in higher education institutions. On the hand, *marginalised populations* in the United States have been coined as groups that are classified in social marginality. Historically, these groups were stigmatised as underclass as a result of low socio-economic status and continue to have the highest attrition rate in higher education institutions throughout the United States.

The knowledge base undergirding attrition rates of minority and marginalised students' experiences in higher education has been dominated by quantitative analyses. Using participatory action research and phenomenological approach to understand minority and marginalised students experiences in higher education will provide an opportunity for participants' voices in the research process. How social work researchers study the problem of attrition of minority and marginalised students in higher education requires an understanding of the historical dynamic of oppression and experiences of this population. No other discipline has the broad approach and understanding provided by social and psychological aspects of education. Decoding the epistemological framework based on predictors, such as lack of social and academic integration merely promotes the consequences of attrition factors. Thus, statistical outcomes on the population that dropped out and failed to complete a degree in higher education do not yield factors for the phenomenon. For a deepened understanding on attrition, social work inquiries must encompass phenomenological perspectives of under-represented minority and marginalised students' collegiate experiences.

Paradigms of Social Work Research

Social work research starts with three primary functions, which have been considered as critical from the inception of the profession: to create a framework for practice, to stipulate actions in specific situations, and to develop the knowledge base for professional information (Thyer, 2013). Social work research epistemological framework is formed across a wave of competing paradigms: positivism, post-positivism, constructivism, and critical theory. A paradigm is a comprehensive belief system, world view, or framework that guides research and practice in a field (Willis, 2007). The paradigmatic dimension of social work inquiry encompasses three perspectives: epistemology, ontology, and methodology. Each of these paradigmatic concepts merges, and ultimately defines, the way a social work inquiry is conducted and how a knowledge claim is accumulated within and across disciplines. In its broadest sense, if epistemology is defined as ways of knowing, ontology refers to ways of being or world view, and methodology is the means of knowing (Waismann, 2011) In this sense, to understand the philosophical framework that guides social work research and practice the following four paradigms will be discussed in the chapter: positivism, post-positivism, interpretivism/constructivism, and critical theory.

Positivistic Paradigm

Social work researchers utilise a positivistic paradigm function within the framework of knowledge production, which is based on empiricism, determinism, parsimony, and generalisation (Cohen, Manion, & Morrison, 2007). The epistemological foundation is based on dualism and objectivity; the inquirer and the subject are presumed to be separate entities (Waismann, 2011). This paradigm is based on prediction and control, with its focus being on empirical outcomes that are generalisable. As such, the empiricism, generalisation features of positivistic paradigm will not capture the subjective experience of the population. A growing body of knowledge in the social work literature on evidence-based practice has been generated in recent years, and some researchers have questioned whether the evidence from these studies can be counted as valid (e.g. Maschi & Youdin, 2010; Thyer, 2013; Van Wormer & Thyer, 2009). It is dissension such as this that led social work researchers to question whether absolute truth can be achieved in research inquiries. Equally important is that researchers' intent when using this paradigm is a concern with finding universal rules or truth, which do not accommodate cultural, social, and world view variations. McCoy and Rodricks (2015) criticised this paradigm on the basis of being depersonalised and responsible for reflecting the perpetual power relationships in society. When testing theories on human rights and social justice factors relating to marginal and multicultural student populations, variables must be examined within the context of their differences in the collegiate setting. Researchers are required to use theories of human behaviour and social systems, to intercede at the points where marginalised students interact with collegial environments. More specifically, the methodology used to collect data must encompass measures that allow the intended population an opportunity to tell their story rather and collecting data that just required a checkbox without an opportunity for narrative.

Given that a great majority of research on higher education to date has utilised quantitative methodologies for measuring marginalised or minority population's experiences in higher education using positivistic paradigms (e.g. Beck, Joshi, Nsiah, & Ryerson, 2014; Chen, 2012; Tinto, 1993). Higher education stakeholders, policymakers, funders, and institution administrators all rely on statistical outcomes as determinants of success. In fact, most studies done on collegial experiences of marginalised population over the last four decades have used quantitative methods (e.g. Harper & Quaye, 2009; Meeuwisse, Severiens, & Born, 2010).

Additionally, the National Center for Education Statistics (NCES) gathers data responding to the component of the mandate linked to producing reports, which documents gaps in access to and completion of higher education (Ross et al., 2012). The NCES is one of the main sources which track national data and reports on attrition and retention by using surveys and quantitative methods. More specifically, the Integrated Postsecondary Education Data System (IPEDS) is the mandatory Graduation Rate Survey used to determine institutional effectiveness, regarding attrition and retention.

The majority of studies on under-represented minority and marginalised student populations in higher education have used positivism approach. Outcomes from these studies display low graduation rates and attrition as generalisable outcomes. Studies on attritions using the positivist approach focus on tests and hypotheses to attain statistical outcomes, while neglecting human knowledge of the phenomena. Engel and Schutt (2009) explained that the positivistic paradigm assumes ontology that objective truth exists separately from human knowledge of that reality. Thus, the positivistic paradigm is limited in its ability to capture subjective experiences of minority and marginalised population; this fact demands further exploration.

Post-positivistic Paradigm

The paradigms of post-positivism and constructivism are also considered valuable in knowledge generation in social work research. The fundamental tenet of post-positivist ontology is that truth is not absolute but probabilistic. Within social work research, the assumption held by post-positivists is that observers can be influenced to some extent by what they observed in the inquiry. Post-positivists claim that truth must be subjected to a broad spectrum of critical investigations but "truth" cannot be conclusive because of the imperfections in human intelligence and the inflexibility of phenomena (Creswell, 2009) For example, when measuring graduation rates, a flaw is encountered by utilising studied achievement gaps reports, which are a limited measure because they mostly account for first-time, full-time students neglecting to consider the limitation of such measures. Post-positivist epistemology is based on deductive and inductive acquisitions, and objectivity is established through external authentication.

The post-positivism ontological argument is more nuanced in its generalisation of truth alluding to the need for triangulation and other research techniques to minimise biases (Engel & Schutt, 2009; Lever, 2013). Post-positivist characterises a methodology, which involves soliciting various emic viewpoints to understand and to gain the meanings, which minority and marginalised students attribute to their actions in higher education. Rubin and Babbie (2015) concluded that social work researchers who embarked on post-positivist approach largely contribute to the body of grounded theory studies in social sciences. From the social work research stance, knowledge base is not just looking for a truth to solve the problem, but that of post-positivism, where there are many ways to get to a truth. Embarking on research that is designed to engage in-depth interviewing with participants will help to identify and to understand patterns of behaviour, which lead to persistence from the perceptions of those who have successfully obtained an undergraduate degree.

Constructivism Paradigm

Constructivism informs social work knowledge base in that it suggests that research and other forms of data can inform how and why under-represented minority students succeed but that researchers must also infuse qualitative measures where the student's voice is heard. Constructivism inquiries theorise the importance of a subjective truth—realities constructed in parts as such social scientists seek to understand what meaning people give to multiple realities (Royse, 2011). More specifically, the constructivist ontological argument is that truth is relativism: formed on the basis of social, mental, and experiential constructs (Creswell, 2009). Social work researchers' inquiries using this method to understand multicultural students' experience in higher education are suitable to describe complex social phenomena, such as minority and marginalised students' attrition rate in higher education, within the context in which it is experienced.

In this sense, the impactful influence of contextual factors, such as time and culture can be recognized in the process of causes and effects of minority and marginalised students' higher education experiences. Thus, utilising constructivist approach, researchers are able to collect first-hand narrative data, which can be used to make empirical generalisations and to establish new theoretical frameworks rather than testing pre-existing theories on cultural factors. Fundamentally, the basis of constructivism is to incorporate a hermeneutic and dialectic approach to examine the phenomena of social work programs as it relates to cross-cultural perspectives (Sultan, 2018).

Critical Theory

Three factors characterise the epistemological framework of a critical theory inquiry: it deconstructs hierarchical ideology; the researcher's own ideology gives meaning to the critical issue; and its dialectical synthesis is based on a historical dualism (Greene, 2007). Similarly, the social work inquiry is espoused to deconstruct inequality across social, economic, and cultural statuses. Thus, social justice knowledge is not necessarily accumulated from the research experience, but it is accumulated in the process. Some researchers even argue that other paradigms lean towards the dominant ideological perspective and do not account for a world view (Kagawa-Singer, 2000; McCoy & Rodricks, 2015). In addition, the emergence of the critical approach provided a platform for marginalised groups to share their personal narratives in the research.

This philosophical stance suggests that if researchers are to acquire knowledge, they must be willing to become embedded in the culture in which the knowing and learning have meaning. For example, critical theorists Goodman (2011) and McCoy and Rodricks (2015) posited that academic institutions are designed to cater to the interests of the dominant social and educational elites. From this perspective, under-represented minority and marginalised students' attrition in higher education cannot be examined in isolation, but it must be viewed as part of a wider process of social stratification which functions to reinforce prevailing patterns of educational and social inequality. More specifically, the researcher must be connected with the process of the knowing, which in this stance is under-represented minority and marginalised students' persistence experiences in higher education. According to the National Association of Social Work (2008) (NASW), social work researcher must embark on inquiries that are aligned with the core values: service, justice, competence, and integrity. More importantly, social work research hinges on social problems that affect the marginalised, vulnerable, and disenfranchised population. The emergence of the critical approach provided a platform for marginalised groups to share their lived experiences, including storytelling, family histories, biographies, and narratives. More specifically, reflexivity is a very potent aspect of the research process in understanding and examining minority and marginalised population by using phenomenological approach. Previous studies used quantitative approaches to determine college failure and low graduation rates, while neglecting to examine the mechanism, which intercepts the decision to persist or to drop out of college. A qualitative research design allows students who are marginalised to describe their experiences, perceptions, and constructions of realities, providing a deeper understanding of their experience in higher education. Some studies have examined the experience of individual minority groups in higher education by utilising the critical theory paradigm. These studies (e.g. Ledesma & Calderon, 2015; Yosso, 2005) have examined the history of exclusion of minority students in higher education institutions as factors which impact under-represented undergraduate minority students' successes. Closson (2010) argued that there is a vital need for a change in viewpoint to the transformation of the inequities in the higher educational system.

Critical theory draws on the lived experiences of minority and marginalised groups by including methods of storytelling, family histories, biographies, and narratives (Yosso & Solorzano, 2007). Therefore, from a critical theorist perspective, to understand minority and marginalised students' perception of barriers in higher education, the researcher must be willing to become embedded in the culture.

Appropriateness of the Method Design

To guide an inquiry on the social-psychological attrition factors, and low graduation rates of marginalised and minority students in higher education, an appropriate design is critical. Qualitative research designs allow minority and marginalised students to describe their experiences, perceptions, and constructions of realities, providing a deeper understanding. In addition, Rubin and Babbie (2015) stated that this type of research method is very instrumental in helping the researcher to gain a deeper understanding of the experiences of the participants when attempting to reconstruct events in which the researcher did not participate.

In support of qualitative methods, Padgett (2016) pointed out that a quantitative research design restricts the scope of studies when seeking to gain an in-depth understanding. In addition, encoded categories based on standardised questionings are used in quantitative research methods, which limit the depth and width of participants' responses. More specifically, Creswell (2009) characterised quantitative research method as cause and effect factors through the collection of statistical data through questions and hypotheses in predetermined instruments for statistical data collection. Quantitative research embarks on a methodology, which yields numbers and statistics as a conclusion for research questions (Rubin & Babbie, 2015). Statistical analyses alone do not exemplify an in-depth picture of marginalised student population's experiences as qualitative research does. Thus, quantitative research methods are incapable of capturing the emotions and the meanings that participants attach to their lived experiences in the study (Padgett, 2016).

There is a need for increased knowledge of social and psychological factors and how they contribute to attrition, not only through methods which are positivistic but experiential qualitative. Indisputably, there is a place for a positivistic approach, which yields statistical outcomes. However, experiential qualitative knowledge from in-depth interviews will ensure that services and programs in higher education are responsive to the under-represented minority undergraduate needs as opposed to the assumed needs of the under-represented minority. Social work researchers do not get involved in biomedical or other research where invasive procedures or physical harm to subjects is likely to occur. However, social work researchers do have a general appreciation for the strength of both methods of inquiry—quantitative and qualitative. *Quantitative* research relies on the gathering of measurable data to analyse and explain the data in statistical manners. *Deductive* reasoning takes on the process of general principles for analysing specific phenomenon by that moving from a general assumption to the specific assumption. *Qualitative* research relies mostly on verbal data collections to be analysed subjectively. *Inductive* reasoning starts off with a specific statement or observation that progresses to a broader observation. This reasoning usually is perceived as moving from a specific principle and moving to a more general. This approach allows social work researchers to be engrossed in the study without preconceived assumptions of the outcomes. For the problem of attrition among minority and marginal students in higher education, it is necessary for researcher to welcome questions that have been neglected, ignored, or have been unexplored in research and in academia on the whole.

The research method chosen for a particular study depends mostly on the specific research topic and the question to be answered. It is not merely a matter of which method is better than the other but the appropriateness for the inquiry studied. The two methods are not opposed, but, instead, they tend to complement each other: both can be used to make a substantial contribution to the knowledge base on a given topic, although from different perspectives. However, to determine which method is best suited for the inquiry of social-psychological barriers, which impede minority students in higher education, it is necessary to examine critically the measures used in previous studies. Consequently, this notion requires an examination of measurements used in both quantitative and qualitative research studies on attrition and retention of under-represented minority students in higher education as a decisive factor. Regarding the data collection method to understand attrition factors of minority and marginalised students, survey or questionnaires which present Likert scales and yes or no responses cannot provide adequate information to understand the complexity of these groups' experiences in higher education. The choice of using semi-structured interviews is quite sufficient for understanding what mechanism can be employed to extract rich data and to capture participants' experiences. Royse (2011) posited that participants, when asked the same questions yet given the flexibility to explore individual experiences in-depth, often divulge more data that are purposeful. Therefore, a qualitative study is appropriate to examine the live experiences of marginal students in higher education, because it allows for the exploration of social-psychological barriers and attrition, which are not in the literature. Exploration studies will provide formative knowledge to understand better how resiliency intercepts attrition factors. More specifically, qualitative studies provide a more productive and more substantial data, which provide greater visibility of the phenomenon and point to a more in-depth dynamic of minority and marginalised students' retention and attrition in higher education. Also, Royse (2011) agreed that qualitative studies are more useful to understand the different theoretical and philosophical perspectives when using ethnography, phenomenology, and participatory action research methodologies. As such, using qualitative research to understand the experiences and mechanism through which social-psychological determinants impact minority and marginal students in higher education is necessary.

Decoding the Rigour, Reliability, and Validity

Qualitative Research

Neuman (2006) stated that most qualitative researchers accept the primary principles of reliability and validity but rarely use the terms because of their correlation with quantitative measurement. To understand qualitative methods adequately, researchers must be willing to explore to gain meaning. For instance, in a qualitative/naturalistic approach, the researcher embarks on prolonged engagement, participant observation, and in-depth interviews to understand the natives' realities. Qualitative inquiries primarily seek to gain the participants' perspectives from their realities. The listed criteria used in qualitative designs to establish trustworthiness as prolonged engagement, persistent observation, and triangulation. Padgett (2016) extended the list of criteria including member checking, audit trails, and negative case analysis. In qualitative research, the term rigour (often paired with reliability in quantitative research) is not often paired with triangulation. Royse (2011) stated that triangulation is used to illustrate that more than one method for data analysis/collection has been used, which provides grounds for reliability. Notably, triangulation illustrates the trustworthiness of the analysis. Other researchers introduced primary and secondary criteria for validating robustness in naturalistic inquiries (e.g. Whittemore, Chase, & Mandle, 2001) by listed authenticity, criticality, and integrity as primary measures and explicitness, vividness, creativity, thoroughness, congruence, and sensitivity as secondary measures. One reason for using a qualitative research method is to get a better understanding of the studied population experienced the social problem at hand. For example, how marginalised population and under-represented minority students voice their experience throughout their matriculation leading to attrition or completion of a degree. In qualitative, the participants can share the feelings attached to the experience linked to the problem studied. McGregor and Murnane (2010) stated that this interpretive approach helps researchers to understand how these aware and unaware feelings came to be, and how new, shared meanings affect the lives of those who experienced it. As such, the goal of embarking on this type of research is to explore how the participants' experienced, perceived, and constructed realities of the presenting phenomena. More specifically, the objective for using this research to decode an epistemological framework is to gain an understanding of how to create an all-inclusive collegial setting rather than a generalisation of cause and effect illustrating how a qualitative approach is more suitable. Talja, Tuominen, and Savolainen (2005) espoused that individuals form knowledge based on experience and observation, which have been influenced by their social ties, history, and interaction with significant others.

A phenomenological approach allows participants to interpret their experiences using their perceptions. Little is known about the phenomenon of persistence strategies and resiliencies of marginalised and under-represented minorities in universities; therefore, phenomenological lends itself to the appropriateness of a qualitative approach. More importantly, because attrition and retention of under-represented minority and marginalised students are complex socially, psychologically, and culturally, it is necessary to investigate this phenomenon within multiple contexts.

MAJOR MEASUREMENTS USED TO STUDY ATTRITION

Although standardised tests were commonly used to measure intelligence and to predict pedagogic performance since the early 1900s, today colleges and universities are beginning to embark on various measurements to predict academic success. Thus, the problem of attrition among college students has been the main issue for researchers, college educators, and administrators within the last decade. Accordingly, Sackett, Schmitt, Ellingson, and Kabin (2001) contended that there is an urgent need for the development of unbiased and valid determinants for college success, specifically for minority students. In the past, researchers looked at predictors such as standardised tests and the outcome variables (such as GPA) (e.g. Haynes, 2008; Nisbet, Ruble, & Schurr, 1982), while other researchers contended that measurement of non-academic predictors is necessary for determining which college students will persist or fail (e.g. Sedlacek, 2004).

School social workers have been at the front line in helping marginalised students to become acclimatised to the educational setting for years. More specifically, historically it was social workers who were instrumental in helping immigrant and other marginalised groups to be adjusted in the educational system in the United States, as school social workers. To foster an all-inclusive environment, higher education institution must be willing to be reconfigured to admit and educate a diverse student population.

The fact is that universities cannot be selective in what type of student populations enters their doors. As such, with a diverse student population, models and measures cannot be tailored to one specific group while isolating others such as under-represented minority and other marginalised groups. An emerging concern is that for many of years, studies on attrition have mainly compared and discussed the differences of attrition factors and low graduation rates between African American students and White students, failing to examine attrition variables across under-represented minority and other marginalised groups. Several theories, models, and measures have been used to discuss the educational gap between White students and minority students, particularly African American and Latino students. Thus, models, theories, and measures used as an explanation of minority students' retention and attrition must encompass all minority groups without consideration for cultural variations. Besides, it is necessary to be cognisant that there are nuanced dimensions within measures of both quantitative methods and qualitative approaches.

Academic Measurements

In studies measuring attrition in higher education, academic variables are almost always operationalised as levels of academic performances and achievements in terms of high school grade points. Numerous studies used SAT scores and ACT scores as academic variables; others use pre-college and first-year grade point to predict students' ability to persist in higher education (e.g. Ishitani, 2006). Accordingly, Wu, Flexner, and Oston (2007) noted four variables as attrition risk factors; the first-year college GPA, high school GPA, entry hours, and SAT composite scores are the most commonly used variables for operationalising academic constructs. Wu and colleagues' findings, similar to other researchers, supported the theory of academic assessments as important measures to determine college performance and persistence. Lotkowski et al. (2004) in their study found that academic measures alone cannot account for successful college performance, which leads to persistence. Schnell, Seashore Louis, and Doetkott (2003) in their longitudinal study found in addition to pre-college academic assessment; students' characteristics were a critical factor for persistence towards graduation in college. Notably, researchers have acknowledged academic assessment as an important measure for college students' successes, but they have also noted that academic measure alone cannot be used to determine college persistence. More specifically, studies using Tinto's academic and social integration constructs have been widely used in the literature on attrition and retention measures in higher education. The following highlights the social-psychological measures used in quantitative studies to measure attrition factors.

Social Psychological Measurements

Student Integration Measures

Most scholars operationalise student integration as student engagement, involvement, and/or integration measures based on the conceptualisation of theories and models from previous attrition studies using quantitative methods. Pascarella and Terenzini (2005) found that students who were involved and engaged in collegial activities also persisted and completed their degrees. Roberts and McNeese (2010) used an online questionnaire of a Student Satisfaction Likert scale to measure students' level of involvement and integration in the collegiate setting. Roberts and McNeese examined students' involvement and engagement based on their original educational pathway. The outcome from their study indicated that efforts must be made to improve students' acclimatisation to the collegiate setting.

Some researchers have raised criticisms; for example, Draper (2003) highlighted the problem with Tinto's model, that testing in the operationalisation of the key components is uncertain and that many studies use different questions. Other researchers criticised the operationalisation of these variables as inconsistent and lacking validity in empirical evidence.

Social Provisions Measures

Amid the many studies on college attrition, a few scholars have constructed social-psychological measures based on theories and models in an attempt to determine the cause and effect of attrition in higher education. For example, the Social Provisions Scale (SPS), developed by Cutrona and Russell (1987) to measure perceived social support, comprises 24 items on six subscales: attachment, social integration, reassurance of worth, a sense of reliable alliance, the obtaining of guidance, and opportunity for nurturance. The original authors tested the Social Provision Scale on a broad population, including college students, and reported that significant statistical variation occurred between age and sex among college students. For example, Cutrona and Russell noted that college students indicated greater levels of social integration; also, females indicated greater levels than males on all subsets. Empirically supported and constructed validity was also determined, indicating an association with measures of loneliness and social integrations.

Social Provisions Scale used to measure perceived social support showed a positive association with students' adjustment to the collegiate setting; however, because of low response rates, these studies cannot draw generalisability of their findings. Both Oppenheimer (1984) and Mattanah, Ayers, Brand, and Brooks (2010) found that SPS showed a positive association with students' persistence in their studies. A social support-based intervention program may boost social support and social adjustment at large universities with a diverse student population. Thus, studies using measures on SPS reported a positive correlation between social support and persistence but reveal uncertainty of whether the low response rates yielded in these studies are due to the populations sampled, the scales, or perhaps a combination of both factors (e.g. Mattanah et al., 2010).

Isolation Measures

Several scholars have operationalised loneliness, isolation, and alienation to measure social estrangement of students in the collegiate settings, particularly with students from minority groups (e.g. Aronson & Steele, 2005). For this cause, a few of these scholars have used the UCLA Loneliness Scale to examine students' sense of alienation in the college settings, which was developed by Russell, Peplau, and Cutrona (1980). Russell et al. assessed students' feelings of loneliness by administering a 20-item scale to measure the level of loneliness by rating responses such as "My social relationships as superficial" and "I feel isolated from others". The responses are a 5-point Likert scale, ranging from 0 (never) to 4 (often) with higher scores indicating a higher level of loneliness. Some scholars argued that it is as a result of isolation that under-represented minority students are unable to become socially and academically integrated into an academic environment (e.g. Hertel, 2002; Tatum, 2004). Researchers using this scale have shown positive associations with loneliness and depression and neuroticism with social self-efficacy, social support, and self-esteem showing adverse effects with loneliness (e.g. Kim & Sax, 2014; Wei, Shaffer, Young, & Zakalik, 2005). Others have found that loneliness correlates with attrition in college students (e.g. Anderson, 1987), suggesting that an important measure to study for decreasing students' attrition in higher education is loneliness. Some common concerns about attrition measurements and attrition factors' measurements relating to higher education occur from how these variables are operationalised. There are no standard definitions used by researchers and institutions; therefore, the manner in which attrition is determined is different for most researchers. Another concern highlighted in the literature is the reason established for students' withdrawal or attrition (Dodge, Mitchell, & Mensch, 2009; Tinto, 1975). More importantly, the challenge in measuring attrition and gathering data on the reasons for attrition is one that is apparent—most colleges do not have access to information on students when they prematurely leave the higher education institution.

In fact, when students drop out of colleges, these institutions do not make contact with students to determine the reason for their departure or whether those students transferred to other institutions. Student departure from college can occur at any time, making it virtually impossible to determine when any given student may prematurely leave the collegiate setting. For this reason, randomly choosing a time to pinpoint students' enrolment status when using a structural equation modelling cannot capture various departure behaviours because of the unpredictability of this behaviour. Most of the studies using structural equation modelling on premature college departure have not been able to accurately map the passage of attrition using this method (e.g. Braxton, Duster, & Pascarella, 1988). This lack of clarity has raised methodological concerns with attrition studies. Nonetheless, while a quantitative approach has been used extensively to measure attrition, very few studies over the last forty years have used qualitative methods to measure attrition in higher education. Accordingly, Tinto (1993) argued that students leave higher education for various reasons. Therefore, to determine and to address under-represented undergraduate students' attrition is even more complex without "an insider" perception, which can highlight the reason for the premature departure and/or persistence towards graduation.

Conclusion

To this end, one critical revelation towards this perspective is that numerous studies, predominantly quantitative studies, have identified what leads to minority and marginalised students' attrition over decades; none of these studies were able to end this phenomenon. Along that same continuum, these studies reflected how many minority students were dropping out of college; however, numbers alone do not tell the mechanism and perceptions of the target population. In addition, the landscape of US colleges and universities continues to grapple with how to retain and to successfully graduate minority students. What has been highlighted in it is virtually impossible to expect traditional paradigm to be effectively implemented to what can be termed as an ill-studied phenomenon, which is required to be further studied using qualitative approach. The ideal is that decoding epistemological framework is realised when social work researchers can engage in deliberate efforts to understand the complexity of social, economic, and cultural differences of marginalised groups to create an all-inclusive collegial setting. In conclusion, to study the complexity of higher education attrition the population most affected by this phenomena perception are required to set the research agenda for retention and to tackle equitable outcomes as put forth by the critical theory.

References

Anderson, E. (1987). Forces influencing student persistence and achievement. In L. Noel, R. Levitz, & D. Saluri (Eds.), *Increasing student retention* (pp. 44–61). San Francisco: Jossey-Bass.

Aronson, J., & Steele, C. M. (2005). Stereotypes and the fragility of academic competence, motivation, and self-concept. In A. J. Elliott & C. S. Dweck (Eds.), *Handbook of competence and motivation* (pp. 392–413). New York and London: Guilford Press.

Beck, K., Joshi, P., Nsiah, C., & Ryerson, A. (2014). The impact of sociability on college academic performance and retention of native Americans. *Journal of American Indian Education, 53*(1), 23–41. Retrieved from http://www.jstor.org/stable/43608712.

Braxton, J., Duster, M., & Pascarella, E. (1988). Causal modeling and path analysis: An introduction and illustration in student attrition research. *Journal of College Student Development, 29*, 263–272.

Chen, R. (2012). Institutional characteristics and college student dropout risks: A multilevel event history analysis. *Research in Higher Education, 53*(5), 487.

Closson, R. B. (2010). Critical race theory and adult education. *Adult Education Quarterly, 60*(3), 261–283.

Cohen, L., Manion, L., & Morrison, K. (2007). *Research methods in education* (6th ed.). London: Routledge.

Creswell, J. W. (2009). *Qualitative inquiry and research design: Choosing among five approaches.* Thousand Oaks, CA: Sage.

Cutrona, C. E., & Russell, D. (1987). The provisions of social relationships and adaptation to stress. In W. H. Jones & D. Perlman (Eds.), *Advances in personal relationships* (Vol. 1, pp. 37–67). Greenwich, CT: JAI Press.

Dodge, T. M., Mitchell, M. F., & Mensch, J. M. (2009). Student retention in athletic training education programs. *Journal of Athletic Training, 44*(2), 197.

Draper, J. (2003). Response to: Watson's guest editorial 'Scientific methods are the only credible way forward for nursing research', *Journal of Advanced Nursing 43*, 219–220.

Engel, R. J., & Schutt, R. K. (2009). *Fundamentals of social work research*. Thousand Oaks, CA: Sage.

Flynn, D. (2014). Baccalaureate attainment of college students at 4-year institutions as a function of student engagement behaviors: Social and academic student engagement behaviors matter. *Research in Higher Education, 55*(5), 467–493. Retrieved from http://www.jstor.org/stable/2457179.

Goodman, D. J. (2011). *Promoting diversity and social justice: Education people from privileged groups*. New York, NY: Routledge.

Greene, J. (2007). *Mixed methods in social inquiry*. San Francisco, CA: Jossey-Bass.

Harper, S. R., & Quaye, S. J. (Eds.). (2009). *Student engagement in higher education: Theoretical perspectives and practical approaches for diverse populations*. New York: Routledge.

Haynes, R. M. (2008). The impact of financial aid on postsecondary persistence: A review of literature. NASFAA *Journal of Student Financial Aid, 37*(3), 30–35.

Hertel, J. B. (2002). College student generational status: Similarities, differences, and factors in college adjustment. *The Psychological Record, 52*, 3–18.

Ishitani, T. T. (2006). Studying attrition and degree completion behavior among first-generation college students in the United States. *The Journal of Higher Education, 77*(5), 861–885. https://doi.org/10.1353/jhe.2006.0042.

Jones, M., Barlow, A., & Villarejo, M. (2010). Importance of undergraduate research for minority persistence and achievement in biology. *The Journal of Higher Education, 81*(1), 82–115. Retrieved from http://www.jstor.org/stable/27750767.

Kagawa-Singer, M. (2000). A socio-cultural perspective on cancer control issues for Asian Americans. *Asian American and Pacific Islander Journal of Health, 8*(1): 12–17.

Kim, Y., & Sax, L. (2014). The effects of student–faculty interaction on academic self-concept: Does academic major matter? *Research in Higher Education, 55*(8), 780–809. Retrieved from http://www.jstor.org/stable/24571816.

Ledesma, M. C., & Calderon, D. (2015). Critical race theory in education: A review of past literature and a look to the future. *Qualitative Inquiry, 21*(3), 206–222.

Lever, M. J. D. (2013). Philosophical paradigms, grounded theory, and perspectives on emergence. *SAGE Open*. Thousand Oaks.

Lotkowski, V. A., Robbins, S. B., & Noeth, R. J. (2004). *The role of academic and non-academic factors in improving college retention* (ACT policy report). Retrieved from https://www.act.org/content/dam/act/unsecured/documents/college_retention.pdf.

Maschi, T. & Youdin, R. (2010). *Social worker as researcher: Integrating research with advocacy*. Boston, MA: Pearson.

Mattanah, F. J., Ayers, F. J., Brand, L. B., & Brooks, J. L. (2010). A social support intervention to ease the college transition: Exploring main effects and moderators. *Journal of College Student Development, 51*(1), 93–108. https://doi.org/10.1353/csd.0.0116.

McCoy, D. L., & Rodricks, D. J. (2015). Critical race theory in higher education: 20 years theoretical and research innovations. *ASHE Higher Education Report, 41*(3), 1–117.

McGregor, S. L. T., & Murnane, J. A. (2010). Paradigm, methodology and method: Intellectual integrity in consumer scholarship. *International Journal of Consumer Studies, 34*(4), 419–427.

Meeuwisse, M., Severiens, S., & Born, M. (2010). Learning environment, interaction, sense of belonging and study success in ethnically diverse student groups. *Research in Higher Education, 51*(6), 528–545. Retrieved from http://www.jstor.org/stable/40785093.

Murphy, T., Gaughan, M., Hume, R., & Moore, S. (2010). College graduation rates for minority students in a selective technical university: Will participation in a summer bridge program contribute to success? *Educational Evaluation and Policy Analysis, 32*(1), 70–83. Retrieved from http://www.jstor.org/stable/40732410.

National Association of Social Workers. (2008). *NASW codes of ethics.* Retrieved from http://www.naswdc.org/pubs/code/code.asp.

Neuman, W. L. (2006). *Social research methods: Qualitative and quantitative approaches.* Toronto: Pearson.

Nisbet, J., Ruble, V. E., & Schurr, K. T. (1982). Predictors of academic success with high-risk college students. *Journal of College Student Personnel, 23,* 227–235.

Oppenheimer, B. (1984). Short-term small group intervention for college freshmen. *Journal of Counseling Psychology, 31,* 45–53. https://doi.org/10.1037/0022-0167.31.1.45.

Padgett, D. K. (2016). *Qualitative methods in social work research.* New York: New York University and Sage.

Pascarella, E. T., & Terenzini, P. T. (2005). *How college affects students: A third decade of research.* San Francisco: Jossey-Bass.

Roberts, J., & McNeese, N. M. (2010). Student involvement/engagement in higher education based on student origin. *Research in Higher Education, 7*(1), 1–11.

Ross, T., Kena, G., Rathbun, A., KewalRamani, A., Zhang, J., Kristapovich, P., & Manning, E. (2012). *Higher education: Gaps in access and persistence study* (NCES 2012-046). U.S. Department of Education, National Center for Education Statistics. Washington, DC: Government Printing Office.

Royse, D. (2011). *Research methods in social work* (6th ed.). Belmont, CA: Brooks, Cole, and Cengage.

Rubin, A., & Babbie, R. E. (2015). *Empowerment series: Essential research methods for social work* (4th Ed.). Boston: Cengage Learning.

Russell, D., Peplau, L., & Cutrona, C. (1980). The revised UCLA loneliness scale: Concurrent and discriminant validity evidence. *Journal of Personality and Social Psychology, 39*(3), 472–480. https://doi.org/10.1037/0022-3514.39.3.472.

Sackett, P. R., Schmitt, N., Ellingson, J. E., & Kabin, M. B. (2001). High-stakes testing in employment, credentialing, and higher education: Prospects in a post-affirmative-action world. *American Psychologist, 56*(4), 302–318. https://doi.org/10.1037/0003-066X.56.4.302.

Schnell, C. A., Seashore Louis, K., & Doetkott, C. (2003). The first-year seminar as a means of improving college graduation rates. *Journal of the First-Year Experience and Students in Transition, 15*(1), 53–75.

Sedlacek, W. E. (2004). *Beyond the big test: Noncognitive assessment in higher education.* San Francisco: Josey-Bass.

Sultan, N. (2018). *Heuristic inquiry: Researching human experience holistically.* London: Sage.

Talja, S., Tuominen, K., & Savolainen, R. (2005). Isms in information science: Constructivism, collectivism, and constructionism. *Journal of Documentation, 61*(1), 79–101. https://doi.org/10.1108/00220410510578023.

Tatum, B. D. (2004). Family life and school experience: Factors in the racial identity development of Black youth in White Communities. *Journal of Social Issues, 60*(1), 117–136. https://doi.org/10.1111/j.0022-4537.2004.00102.x.

Thyer, B. A. (2013). Evidence-based practice or evidence-guided practice: A rose by any other name would smell as sweet [Invited response to gitterman & knight's "evidence-guided practice"]. *Families in Society, 94*(2), 79–84. https://doi.org/10.1606/1044-3894.4283.

Tinto, V. (1975). Dropout from higher education: A theoretical synthesis of recent research. *Review of Educational Research, 45*, 89–125. https://doi.org/10.3102/00346543045001089.

Tinto, V. (1993). *Leaving college: Rethinking the causes and cures of student attrition* (2nd ed.). Chicago: University of Chicago Press.

Van Wormer, K. & Thyer, B. A. (2009). *Evidence-based practice or evidence-guided practice: A book of readings.* Thousand Oaks, CA: SAGE.

Waismann, F. (2011). Causality and logical positivism. In *Humanities, social science and law. Resource type: Springer eBooks.*

Wci, M., Shaffer, P., Young, S., & Zakalik, R. (2005). Adult attachment, shame, depression, and loneliness: The mediation role of basic psychological needs satisfaction. *Journal of Counseling Psychology, 52*(4), 591–601. https://doi.org/10.1037/0022-0167.52.4.60.

Whittemore, R., Chase, S. K., & Mandle, C. L. (2001). Validity in qualitative research. *Qualitative Health Research, 11*(4), 522–537. https://doi.org/10.1177/104973201129119299.

Willis, J. W. (2007). World views, paradigms and the practice of social science research. In J. Mukta & N. Rema (Eds.), *Foundations of qualitative research: Interpretive and critical approaches* (pp. 1–26). Thousand Oaks, CA: Sage.

Wu, D., Fletcher, K., & Olson, L. (2007). A study of college student attrition via probabilistic approach. *Journal of Mathematics Sociology, 31*, 89–95. https://doi.org/10.1080/00222500600561238.

Yosso, T. J. (2005). Whose culture has capital? A critical race theory discussion of community cultural wealth. *Race, Ethnicity and Education, 8*(1), 69–91.

Yosso, T. J., & Solorzano, D. G. (2007). *Conceptualizing a critical race theory in sociology: The Blackwell companion to social inequalities.* Malden, MA: Blackwell.

CHAPTER 48

Clientisation, Marginalised Identities, and the Politics of Care

Sylvia Parusel

Clientisation broadly concerns how people access and experience formal help as well as how professional work and social programming respond to their needs. As Gubrium and Järvinen (2014) describe the process from a social constructionist perspective, personal troubles are part of the human condition and when reinterpreted through expert knowledges at the level of services, troubles are reconstituted into observable social problems through rational, bureaucratic management. Texts, knowledges, and classifications play central roles, as do policies and practices. This chapter examines clientisation in the context of experiencing converging problems, drawing primarily on the life stories of five women who at the time of the study were taking part in methadone maintenance treatment (MMT) in British Columbia (BC), Canada. They were concurrently living with the effects of deep social exclusion which refers to multiple domains or aspects of social disadvantage, such as poverty, abuse, homelessness, and racialisation or other forms of discrimination (Levitas et al., 2007). In this case, the women's histories with drug use and their experiences of protracted and intersecting exclusions indicated the need for multiple formal supports to improve their material conditions, health situation, housing circumstances, and overall life chances.

S. Parusel (✉)
Qualitative and Community Based Research Unit, British Columbia Centre on Substance Use, Vancouver, BC, Canada
e-mail: sylvia.parusel@bccsu.ubc.ca

© The Author(s) 2021
S. S. M. et al. (eds.), *The Palgrave Handbook of Global Social Work Education*, https://doi.org/10.1007/978-3-030-39966-5_48

ACCOUNTING FOR SOCIAL AND LOCAL COMPLEXITIES OF DRUG USE AND TREATMENT

Methadone maintenance treatment is a medically administered, substitution drug treatment which treats chronic use of opioid substances. While conceived as a healthcare programme, it can also be a signifier of advanced social and economic marginalisation in societies (Bourgois & Schonberg, 2009; Fraser & valentine, 2008; Friedman & Alicea, 2001). Of note, figures reveal that MMT involvement in British Columbia often intersects with the experience of being poor. Of the 16,527 BC residents who were registered in this treatment in 2016, about 65% received some type of provincially funded income assistance (Parusel, 2017). Income assistance and disability clients receive inadequate benefit amounts, making it difficult for various recipient groups to move out of poverty (Klein, Ivanova, & Leyland, 2017; Pulkingham, Fuller, Morrow, & Parusel, 2016). The extent of hardship surrounding MMT participation in BC suggests the need to know more about complexities and contingencies of client experience in this context.

Social scientific research can illuminate social embeddedness and local perspectives of drug use and treatment. Early addiction studies examined drug use experiences in specific cultural settings (Dai, 1970) and helped build a social theory of addiction (Lindesmith, 1938). Others explored local environments, social learning about drug use, and the general social contexts and criminal policies that construct conditions in which drug use is more likely (Agar, 2002; Page & Singer, 2010; Reinarman & Granfield, 2014). Also, qualitative and ethnographic research on men and women in Western drug treatment, including studies of MMT programming, found clients' social marginalisation implicated governing policies, social control technologies, and laws to varying degrees (Bourgois & Schonberg, 2009; Boyd, 1999; Campbell & Ettorre, 2010; Friedman & Alicea, 2001; Garcia, 2008; Rosenbaum, 1981). Political dimensions especially illustrate continued need for MMT policies and practices that help repair classed, gendered, and racialised oppressions (Bourgois & Schonberg, 2009; Boyd, 1999; Boyd & MacPherson, 2019; Fraser & valentine, 2008; Smye, Browne, Varcoe, & Josewski, 2011). Overall, drug use and treatment experiences are shown to be complex social phenomena.

As Fraser and Moore (2011) argue, materiality also plays a part, as do the ways in which the material, ideas, discourses, practices, histories, and politics encounter each other to "produce each other and produce drugs, their effects and their circumstances" (p. 6). Furthermore, clients in turn display agency from their specific social locations, drawing on lived knowledge to actively navigate methadone maintenance treatment and negotiate social identities co-constructed through treatment practices and experiences (Fraser & valentine, 2008; Järvinen, 2014; Ning, 2005;

Smith, 2011). Järvinen (2014) points out that multi-directional practices and discourses influence both MMT providers and clients, and that varied outcomes reflect negotiation or even incomplete clientisation through resistance of expert practices. This chapter similarly examines MMT clientisation in BC as a site of complex, multiple, and sometimes competing practices and meanings, and further conceptualises MMT participation as one type among multiple forms of clientisation, presenting a case which renders visible the politics of care.

THE POLITICS OF CARE

Fine (2007) argues that care is a human service and public issue, and a "primary building block for social life" (p. 173). Formal care provision which broadly targets health and/or poverty through policies and human service intervention has a long history.[1] In recent decades, increased marketisation of care and declining public supports increasingly burden individuals and families (Fine, 2007; Offer, 2012). In this milieu, people comply with, navigate, negotiate, and contest knowledges, policies, and practices in their everyday efforts to locate resources for living (Fine 2007; Kerkvliet, 2009). This chapter addresses clientisation in the context of women seeking help through MMT and other local services and programmes. Specifically, what are some ways in which they navigated multiple formal services over time? How did they negotiate their identities and display agency in the process? Furthermore, with the decline of public funding for programmes and services in BC since the 1990s, the study participants also turned to and provided informal help, even if these approaches sometimes complicated their lived conditions and closest relationships. In such activities as turning to harm reduction services, seeking general medical treatment and social supports, and caring for and receiving help from family members and friends, how do the women's experiences with formal and informal supports illustrate an everyday politics of care? By examining women's experiences of methadone treatment and other services, it provides a nuanced understanding of the links between gendered MMT experience, identity, and marginality.

METHODS

The study utilised a social constructionist lens and critical feminist analysis. The multi-method research approach included multiple individual life story interviews conducted in 2011 and 2013 with five women participating in MMT in BC. At the beginning of the study, Camille, Debbie, Renee, Sarah, and Mariel (pseudonyms) were living in three distinct regions across the province and their ages ranged from 50 to 56. Camille identified as Aboriginal and the four other women identified as Caucasian. The 24 unstructured interviews took place in the participants' homes or at shelter locations and lasted between 30 minutes and 2 hours. Each woman received $50 for each interview. The study was designed to be collaborative with multiple sequential interviews allowing for ongoing negotiation of narratives (Gurstein, Pulkingham, & Vilches, 2011). As well, it offered the option to develop personal projects out of the research activities which two participants elected to complete.

Methods further included individual semi-structured interviews in 2012 with four methadone-prescribing physicians practising in Vancouver and content analysis of several documentary texts that guided physicians' MMT practices in the province. Analysis was an iterative and emergent process involving identifying and comparing themes at several stages of the study from the earliest interviewing and transcribing stages to close re-readings of all interview transcripts, through to the development of initial coding maps and redevelopment of coding frameworks. All interviews and field notes from 2011 to 2013 were coded using NVIVO software, first descriptively, then thematically. Overall, the study's interpretive approach paid close attention to different contexts and intersubjective relations. Additionally, an inductive and interpretive form of content analysis of the documentary texts drew on the language, meanings, and perspectives expressed in the documents.

Navigating Intersecting Problems

From the vantage point of mid-adult age, the five women's narratives richly detail unique life histories, varied social class backgrounds, and diverse substance use trajectories and household circumstances. Some issues, such as residential schooling (Camille) and lengthy employment history (Sarah), concern a single participant. As well, their length of participation in MMT varied, ranging from 20 years to less than 12 months. Notably, there is no common social location or path predicting their MMT experience and yet several experiential patterns can be discerned across the interview data. For example, participants were experiencing long-standing poverty due to job loss, long-term unemployment and underemployment, and meagre income assistance or disability benefits. They also had significant health problems which were related and unrelated to drug use, and they were dealing with the effects of multiple historical traumas, including trauma from physical and sexual abuse, injuries, and institutional violence. Thus, their troubles accumulated and intersected, illustrating the need for multiple services.

Under the Care and Surveillance of Physicians

Methadone maintenance aligns with neuroscientific approaches to opioid use, and in BC, it falls under the harm reduction umbrella of services. Noted for its "difference" among types of medical care (Reist, 2010), this treatment entails technologies and practices which construct its clients

(Bourgois & Schonberg, 2009; Fraser & valentine, 2008). MMT participation generally requires that clients daily ingest a prescribed dose of methadone,[2] typically under direct observation, as well as meet regularly with
their methadone-prescribing doctor and undergo blood or urine testing to
ensure compliance with treatment regulations (e.g. not using controlled
non-prescribed substances). Addressing the construction of addiction in society
and its effects, Reinarman and Granfield (2014) theorise that neuroscientific
claims have not reduced the moralising directed at drug use but can perpetuate individualising and responsibilising therapeutic controls. At the same time,
compliance within a care and surveillance treatment environment can in part
have practical benefits for those who use drugs (Keane, 2003, 2013).

People enter MMT for diverse reasons (Boyd, 1999; Reist, 2010). When
Camille, Debbie, Sarah, Renee, and Mariel first experienced MMT, they were
seeking help for their growing opioid habit and material deprivation, health
crises, family struggles, financial need, and their experiences of violence and/
or homelessness were among the problems that contributed to treatment
entry as well. To varying degrees, the participants appreciated the substance
of methadone as it reduced physical dependency on illicit opioids and they
found respite from associated pressures in the earliest days of programme
enrolment. Camille reported it helped her to temporarily stabilise her housing, be safer, and "...be good. I'm not running around looking for money for
heroin....", while Debbie remarked, "I used methadone as the way to stop
the other things...and [to] just concentrate on not being sick". Renee, Sarah,
and Mariel similarly reported that methadone provided significant relief from
frequent drug withdrawal as well as helped them improve their overall health.
Over time, all found the dosing regimen became a tiring routine and they
experienced frequent fatigue or lack of motivation. As well, travelling for dosing and testing could be an expense if one lived too far from pharmacies or
clinics to walk to them. Sarah who lived in a rural area stated, "You've got
to really watch, you have to think I need at least $40 dollars extra a month
for gas to get it. It's been tiresome, right down to the day before, we haven't
had a penny". Overall, the women's material conditions had not appreciably
improved since entering MMT, with some becoming homeless during the
study.

In purposeful ways, the participants strategised to make the most of valued
physician practices. They retained MMT providers who supported them
with the documentation for securing or maintaining income assistance status (Camille, Debbie, Renee, Mariel) or who helped defray costs of over
the counter medications (Debbie, Sarah). Life story data show that providers
can mediate within a broad system of health services to be of immediate practical benefit for women. In turn, the women sought out practitioners who
sympathised with their complex everyday struggles. Study findings also show
the four interviewed physicians expressed compassionate understandings of
the challenges that their women clients faced, including noting cumulative

effects of social trauma, homelessness, and gendered abuse on general health and treatment outcomes. Yet physician authority can be a complex and often contradictory presence in the lives of women who approach healthcare professionals with medical concerns, require timely referrals to primary health care or specialists, and seek counselling for gendered trauma.

Narrative data reveal lack of standardisation in MMT physician practices of counselling, referral, and case management. Practices responding to common issues were inconsistent, especially in the context of the women's emotional health or relapses; participants reported their interactions with their methadone doctors could be either frustrating or motivating, sometimes emotionally challenging or beneficial. Also, providers' mainly autonomous decisions and uneven documentation of their MMT practices suggest that they hold considerable power to shape their clients' experiences of MMT. Both Renee and Sarah shared a MMT physician with another member of their family, further navigating a specific identity that linked them to another MMT case file. Sarah who utilised the same physician and attended the same random testing appointments as her husband sometimes resented being treated as a co-client. Shared MMT consulting practices in this case often settled on her husband's unique health problems which left little time for Sarah to relate her Hepatitis C Virus (HCV) diagnosis and other treatment concerns. She stated, "that should be a separate case. I'm me, he's him. I have my own problem, right?". Overall, the women found at times that MMT care practices were quite supportive and at other times contradictory and "tiresome" to navigate. MMT participation could also be an expense for women who had little access to affordable transportation. These factors among others contributed to the women's overall ambivalence about MMT, even as they continued in the treatment programme in their active efforts to improve their circumstances.

NEGOTIATING THE "AT RISK" CLIENT LABEL

The health and safety of those who use opioids remain paramount concerns, especially given the recent increases in drug-related overdoses and deaths in BC (British Columbia Coroners Service, 2019). Within this situation of persistent drug use health crises, promotion and uptake of medically supervised programmes that prescribe methadone and other opioids as replacement therapies is on the rise (Damon et al., 2017). Given the power of all opioids to do harm, MMT physicians are responsible for monitoring the health risks of their clients through medical tests. In this programme environment, clients in turn reported excessive surveillance of their behaviours at times. For instance, Sarah recounted a consultation conversation after missing a random testing appointment with her husband:

> We've said to him, "We're not doing heroin." And finally, after about the fourth time [my husband] said it, and we repeated it ourselves, finally [the doctor] said, "Yeah, you have a point there." ... They don't want to give in to you, they

have to be strong. It's understandable. ... We're like, "We don't lie to you." He says, "Yeah, I know." But he still has to throw in, "Well, I assume that you're doing it and you don't want to see me."

On the one hand, Sarah understood her physician's distrust given that she had revealed infrequent cocaine use in the past to her doctor, and on the other hand, she challenged his unfounded suspicions of opioid use. Methadone dosing and testing reconstitutes women's marginality and contributes to a general climate of distrust (Boyd, 1999; Friedman & Alicea, 2001). Treatment emphasising control or governing of deviant women forecloses development of innovative and truly compassionate substance use treatments (Boyd, 1999; Campbell & Ettorre, 2010; Garcia, 2008). While participants typically complied with treatment rules, they sometimes resisted them and often questioned them. Control through clientisation can also hinge on competing notions of progress. Life stories show that successful MMT participation could be a step towards broader life goals that women had set for themselves, such as recovery or security, while providers typically prioritised the goal of maintenance, even as their counselling approaches varied. The four interviewed physicians did not indicate specific conflict with any of their patients, which contrasts to how life stories refer to sometimes conflictive client–physician encounters that foreclosed dialogue, opportunities, and clients' plans. Both texts and physicians were silent about how intense medical supervision of addiction treatment compliance can affect other areas of patients' lives. Debbie gave an example of how she encountered provider suspicions in MMT and across health services:

> ... he was always looking for a bit of the downfall in me, you know. ... Or the same treatment I would feel from just random doctors, at a hospital if they knew you were an addict, you know, the "different" treatment. And that's what I felt from him. Just, he was doubting me and not taking my aches and pains seriously and, you know, "What does she really want [that for]?"

The pejorative association between MMT client and "addict" could activate "different treatment" and make it difficult to access necessary medication for other ailments. MMT's overt disciplinary features and power differences are especially visible when women clients navigate risk management approaches (Fraser & valentine, 2008). Given its healthcare frame, MMT policies unsurprisingly and officially characterise participants as health treatment clients and not as citizens requiring care within society. Programmes targeting addiction-related harms were never designed to address multiple problems and oppressions surrounding drug use (Boyd, 2007). Yet MMT documents contain assumptions that MMT clients' health problems and social struggles highly relate to individual behaviours, and this narrow perspective can be problematic for clients. Physicians similarly drew on individualising language to describe practices of "management" and "monitoring", and sometimes "surveillance" of women clients' self-reported behaviour and social-related health risks (e.g. sex work, homelessness). When health policies and practices use risk language to interpret women's concerns about poverty and trauma, family circumstances, and inadequate housing, they render complex gendered experiences of harm and deep exclusion invisible. Notably, this "at risk" label followed the study participants into various human service sites and social relations, requiring them to actively self-manage their MMT identity, which was an additional struggle in their lives.

SEEKING HELP FOR HEALTH CHALLENGES

Participants sought help for health challenges arising from drug use (e.g. pneumonia, abscesses, injuries) or for chronic disorders related and unrelated to drug use (e.g. heart problems, diabetes, digestive disorders, depression, Hepatitis C (HCV), hearing loss, osteoarthritis, and chronic migraines). Initial contact with street nurses, local clinics or hospitals, and consultation with MMT physicians for general medical practice care helped the women to stabilise health conditions and connect to other health professionals. Camille and Debbie additionally took part in local research studies of people who inject illicit drugs, and their participation in these "fast-tracked" medical monitoring of their illnesses such as heart problems, hearing loss, and depression. Findings show that the client–health provider relationship also involved client challenges to advice and systemic barriers to accessing help. Sarah's MMT doctor was slow to provide her with supports for HCV or to refer her to other specialists for immune issues. Debbie, who took an exceptionally high dose of a mental health medication and was experiencing side effects, negotiated over several months for a dose reduction. Camille, Renee, and Sarah had exclusively drawn on their MMT doctors for drug use treatment and resisted their doctors' recommendations to take antidepressant medication. Camille, who was experiencing ongoing drug use and emotional problems arising from severe abuse over years, had not accessed counselling or effectively discussed effects of trauma with her successive MMT physicians or sought out specialists. Study findings show broad differences in health system involvement as Camille, Sarah, and Renee struggled over years to have a few physical and mental health issues addressed while Mariel and Debbie were actively locating and negotiating various types of medical care.

MMT identity can impact health care when participants either experienced or feared the stigma of being labelled an ex-substance user or suspected substance user. Debbie who faced the most health challenges had left methadone treatment at the beginning of this study, and then she elected to stay in the programme with her long-term MMT provider who monitored her exit out of the programme and provided general medical care for several months. Despite her successful recovery from drug use, Debbie found it time-consuming and frustrating to continually negotiate a MMT identity, spurring her to search for a new healthcare arrangement. Moreover, she reported that her methadone physician still suspected that she would relapse. By our third interview, she was considering how a new, yet unchosen family doctor might treat her long-term health problems:

> I want to move forward. But what I don't know about finding a doctor is, telling them everything. And then they get that little part in their head, "Oh, she used to be," "Will she still be?" "Will she always be?" That, I don't know what to do about yet.

A methadone client identity might negatively impact service experiences in mainstream health settings. For this reason, Debbie asked several physicians at her clinic to remove reference to her methadone treatment involvement from her medical file. It took some months before a physician agreed and once done, Debbie expressed relief:

> I don't have to tell anybody. It's going to be more of my past again. So, I don't need to tell anybody, I don't need to have to worry about having it. I don't have to worry about going down to get it. Miserable every morning. Crappy every morning. What a long journey.

Successful navigation and exit of MMT and normalising of medical identity were significant events illustrating tenacity in the face of recovery pressures and obstacles to equitable health care. Debbie preferred to keep her past private and yet in further reflecting on her wish to discard a lingering clinical identity, she remained worried about health outcomes and the effects of voluntary disclosure of her drug use past:

> I don't know. I'm scared to tell a new doctor. But yet I think the doctor needs to know everything about me, if they're going to take care of me. I don't know. I'm thinking there might still be some repercussions of poor health because of so long of it just being masked, I don't know. I'm stuck, I don't know. ... Maybe I'm not quite, I'm not proud of the past so I don't want to carry it with me wherever I go. But, of course I carry it with me wherever I go [brief laugh]. However, I don't know if a new doctor needs to do that, we could just start at zero. I don't know.

Worries about disclosing a chronic drug use past to a new doctor given serious health challenges contributed to new fears of being stigmatised in health care.

Mariel's entry into MMT is an example of negotiating identity to gain near-immediate help for withdrawal and health concerns. After ten years of hydromorphone use, Mariel sought out a physician who was licensed to prescribe methadone for pain as well as for opioid use. Her earliest consultation emphasised her need for pain management for undiagnosed health challenges. Mariel explained,

> I said I wanted to go on meth for the pain. And he said, "Yeah, you can do
> meth." And I said, "Okay, put me on it" ... and I said, "As long as I don't have
> the pain, I don't care," right. And he said, "Okay, we'll see how this works."

Approaching MMT as a health patient circumvented initial clinical discussions about her drug use but Mariel noted, "It's got a lot of stigma, you know, because if you're on methadone, they're just starting to use it as pain medication, so the stigma, it's like you're an addict. It's like anything". Here, methadone's blurred uses generated an opportunity to primarily self-identify as a medical patient rather than a person who used drugs, even as her involvement in MMT introduced controls and professional scrutiny of her drug use and she expected to experience stigma in the process. Stigma highlights the exercise of power in service provision and emerges from broad social and legal policies and processes, such as criminalisation of drug use and gender and racial inequalities. Status loss and discrimination are highly connected with broad consequences for housing, income, health, and education (Link & Phelan, 2001). Navigation of health care as a MMT client highlights identity work in the face of compliance expectations, discriminating or uneven MMT practices, documentation concerns, and new provider relationships.

Experiencing Poverty and Hierarchies of Identity

Camille, Debbie, Renee, Sarah, and Mariel were experiencing severe financial struggles while on any type of income assistance because their support benefits, including disability benefits, did not cover their monthly expenses. For some time, they had struggled to find basic resources for living each month whether they encountered income assistance as children or as adults, were infrequently using drugs or were abstinent for years, and whether they were living in shelters, shared housing, or social housing. They found it difficult to meet personal and nutritional needs, went without food at times, and relied on formal supports such as food banks and drop-ins for meals, and sometimes located free used clothing, household goods, or furniture at non-profit organisations. For several years, their struggles to make up monthly financial shortfalls included the activities of borrowing, pawning personal items, running tabs at local corner stores, walking instead of using transit, and multiple other approaches. Study findings reveal treatment clients' agency in their experience of material deprivation; study participants displayed resilience and resourcefulness, developed plans to reach goals and sometimes resisted rules or subverted expectations, all in their efforts to improve their circumstances (Lister, 2004).

Poverty experiences in the context of MMT participation strongly concern hierarchies of health statuses and income supports. For example, with documentation from her MMT provider, Renee gained the status of People with Persistent Multiple Barriers (PPMB) because of severe depression. Achieving the status required her to work well with her MMT doctor who also counselled her and prescribed psychiatric medication for her illness. The PPMB category mainly excused her from the standard income assistance work search requirement. Camille and Debbie similarly obtained documentation from their MMT doctors a few years earlier, working with their physicians to complete excessively long documentation that qualified each of them for disability status based on their mental health diagnoses and/or chronic physical ailments. They received the highest guaranteed benefit amount among the study participants. Clients especially valued disability status because the $500 earnings exemption allowed them to earn some income each month without having the money deducted from their benefits. Disability status-related experiences call attention to continuing struggles, even as participants appreciate the slightly higher household income they receive in comparison with other income assistance categories. For example, Sarah's co-client disability status (as in MMT, similarly placing her within a "family" file) constructed her as a dependent on her husband's income assistance classification. This service relationship authorised only her husband for the earnings exemption, and he was physically unable to work due to chronic illness.

Overall, study findings show that participants' intersecting health and social problems, the lack of affordable transportation, and/or lack of local opportunities made it difficult for them to participate in the labour market, whether this was categorically recognised by their income assistance workers or not. Sarah who lived in a rural area and had a long work history responded often to job advertisements but found it difficult to obtain employment. Her challenges to MMT rules, her doctor's authority, and income assistance policies most often revolved around her main life goal to find work and gain more financial security. By 2011, she was informally working for neighbours a few hours each week, receiving very small amounts of cash. For both Debbie and Sarah who actively searched for material resources at food banks and non-profit organisations, a worker identity had meaning because it signified to others, including their MMT service providers, their ability to make ends meet in a competitive market economy. Sarah's frustrations about not finding opportunities stated that one is more likely to qualify for disability-related support if you "say [that you're] mental or something, that's about the only thing". In suggesting that other clients are undeserving, Sarah echoed individualistic explanations for poverty-related problems and displayed awareness of growing competition among low-income groups for dwindling social supports (Lister, 2004). Disempowering poverty policies along with competition between low-income citizens for diminishing formal resources suggest that organising around poverty requires clients' extra efforts and advocates' involvement.

Accessing and providing help: Study findings reveal diverse experiences of coercive, governing, or stigmatising service environments and access to supportive programmes and inspiring professionals. Of note, participants' uptake of formal supports over the years was not directly related to the length of time one had been in MMT, although Debbie had been active over a decade in locating a range of supports from low-barrier services to supportive housing and employment training. Debbie and Camille required services to support long-term drug- and trauma-related problems. While both eventually found a specialised programme for women or disability clients, gaining coveted social housing resources in the process, Camille continued to resist longer-term services because they did not meet her needs. As she explained,

> ...there's not much else they can do for a person if they don't want to go to those places like uh, recovery houses and that. Like, I never wanted to do that. I wanted to do it myself, I guess.... I don't like group counseling, like, people there have no shame or pride.... It's not like they can give me some magic word that will make everything all right.

In this case, Camille feared service workers would push her into uncomfortable group counselling when she most needed specialised services to help her deal with historical colonial trauma and related gendered oppressions. Similarly, Renee had accessed few community or health services and infrequently sought out free or low-cost food resources, stating, "I don't ask for much". Furthermore, data reveal reduced uptake of services over time, typically after finding housing. While participants still required help, accessing formal services meant asking for assistance in institutionalised ways—often requiring people to fill out forms, share their story with a stranger, get along with other clients, and perform to programme expectations (Camille, Debbie, Sarah, Mariel). Service or label resistance sometimes concern efforts to avoid drug use triggers or protection of one's privacy and dignity. Over time, Debbie and Renee avoided useful addiction-related supports in those neighbourhoods considered less safe (Bourgois & Schonberg, 2009). Thus, challenges to clientisation can involve broad considerations of the fit between needs and programme design and delivery, as well as programme location.

Informal supports: Through their relationships with family members and friends, the study participants infrequently received and shared tangible and intangible resources for living such as cash, food, shelter, clothing, and transportation, childcare and eldercare, cleaning labour, and building maintenance work. They especially shared their meagre resources with their children or grandchildren and accepted help from parents or siblings, whether provided unconditionally or attached to obligations. This strategy of "give and take" support illustrated both interdependency and altruism and especially highlighted the women's identities as mothers, grandmothers, daughters, and sisters. Like harm reduction programmes, informal help of any type aided in times of severe crisis. Before she entered MMT, Renee's mother and sister provided crucial support. While Debbie increasingly helped her children in recent years, she had drawn on help from her parents, siblings, and her children during unstable periods of her recovery and during health challenges.

Renee, whose drug use history involved several family members, readily shared resources with her daughters when possible. However, when one daughter and granddaughter could not find shelter accommodation, they "sort of moved in", obliging Renee and her partner to share their small apartment for several months. Renee encouraged her daughter to keep applying for shelter beds and advised her not to disclose to front-line workers that she was getting help from family:

> She's been phoning [shelters and transition homes] every morning, and she's got the little one. Like I just say [to her], "Don't say you're staying with your mom ... or that you've been sleeping on people's couches." Because as soon as they think that mom will look after them, I mean, there's no room...we're not good for each other right now. Because I've been fooling around a bit and she's fooling around a little bit more than I am. Yeah, so it's not, not the scene.

With the lack of local shelter resources, tensions between Renee, her partner, and her daughter increased. Renee's narrative illustrates efforts to maintain her caring mother and grandmother identity, to keep substances out of her home, and to keep her closest family members physically safe. Similarly, Mariel drew on a friend for emotional support for several months after leaving a transition home, eventually moving to her home where she rented a room. Mariel left the home after not complying with her friend's expectations or schedule. Informal care especially emphasises the issue of reciprocity. Once considered to involve an economy of obligations and interdependencies, reciprocity is now a "force of fragmentation", burdening the poorest among citizens who have inadequate resources (Offer, 2012, p. 790).

Conclusion

Clientisation concerns a range of social phenomena from service-related classifications, institutionalised texts and knowledges, and policies to expert and therapeutic practices to various client-provider negotiations. This chapter explored how five women in methadone maintenance, a treatment for opioid use, broadly experienced clientisation and specifically navigated applied expert knowledges and the politics of care at various service sites. Importantly, the process also illustrated how clientisation can involve struggles for improved life chances and autonomy. To varying degrees, the participants appreciated the substance of methadone as it helped them manage their severe drug dependence problems. However, despite expectations, they had not found that MMT involvement significantly improved their social circumstances over time and this situation contributed to their ambivalence about the treatment. They narrated experiences of long-term poverty resulting from inadequate disability or income assistance, and their lives displayed the effects of social exclusion and traumas accrued over years, including trauma arising from institutional and gendered violence.

The participants encountered a distinct form of clientisation at the site of MMT, and in both obvious or subtle ways, they experienced surveillance and self-surveillance. Critical literature charts the effects of regulatory power of MMT on clients' lives, examining how technologies, addiction knowledge, and therapeutic practices individualise drug problems and inculcate self-discipline and responsibilisation (Bourgois & Schonberg, 2009; Boyd, 1999; Fraser & valentine, 2008; Friedman & Alicea, 2001). Numerous factors shape the everyday politics of MMT participation, including physician practices in concert with supervising technologies (e.g. dosing, urine and blood tests, and healthcare databases), and clients' social backgrounds and their expectations for their lives. Data show that clients have agency in this healthcare context. In various ways, clients navigated, negotiated, and contested norms or rules or expert knowledge (Fine, 2007; Kerkvliet, 2009). As Debbie and Sarah's experiences show, at times much effort is made to convince MMT physicians and other health workers to seriously consider requests or explanations, especially as institutional practices, such as labelling, categorisation, surveillance, and sidelining client concerns provide little scope for continuous clinical dialogue between clients and professionals.

Intersecting life troubles illustrated the need for and/or experience of a range of services. Access of formal supports among the participants varied and was not directly related to the length of time one had been in MMT but was shown to be related to a host of factors, involving severity of drug use, exposure to violence, navigation of application and programme procedures, the fit between programming and needs, and the diminishing availability of programmes due to economic restructuring policies. Findings illustrate women's identity work in the context of actively seeking help through MMT and local services and programmes targeting the poor. Participants also navigated informal care networks to access and share material and care resources, involving requests for and refusals of help to close and extended family members and friends. Reciprocal informal care practices and gifts were not common and could be alternately helpful or burdensome in the short term.

Overall, clients' lived perspectives on drug use can inform institutional knowledges and advise professional practice development (Raikhel & Garriott, 2013). For example, Graves, Csiernik, Foy, and Cesar (2009) call for broadening social work curriculum in Canada to include instruction of 18 core competencies they deem necessary for working with clients who use drugs. Jack et al. (2011) argue that experiential evidence can contribute in part to managers' evidence-based decision making on programming for women in addiction services. This chapter further highlighted need for more coordination of policies within health and social service fields in the context of women and their MMT participation.

NOTES

1. In Western countries, the concept of formal care arose from specialisation of occupations (e.g. medicine, nursing, social work) in the past two centuries and was shaped by bureaucratising and industrialising care provision, welfare state development, and feminism's influence on women's movement into paid work (Fine, 2007).
2. Although methadone is the primary substance utilised in MMT in BC, Suboxone prescriptions are rising.

REFERENCES

Agar, M. (2002). How the drug field turned my beard grey. *International Journal of Drug Policy, 13*, 249–258.

Bourgois, P., & Schonberg, J. (2009). *Righteous dopefiend.* Berkeley: University of California Press.

Boyd, S. C. (1999). *Mothers and illicit drugs: Transcending the myths.* Toronto, ON: University of Toronto Press.

Boyd, S. C. (2007). The journey to compassionate care: One woman's experience with early harm-reduction programs in BC. *Canadian Women's Health Network.* November 3, 2016. Retrieved from http://www.cwhn.ca/en/node/39390.

Boyd, S., & MacPherson, D. (2019). The harms of drug prohibition: Ongoing resistance in Vancouver's downtown eastside. *BC Studies, 200*, 87–308.

Campbell, N. D., & Ettorre, E. (2010). *Gendering addiction: The politics of drug treatment in a neurochemical world.* New York, NY: Palgrave Macmillan.

Dai, B. (1970). *Opium addiction in Chicago* (No. 126). Patterson Smith.

Damon, W., Small, W., Anderson, S., Maher, L., Wood, E., Kerr, T., & McNeil, R. (2017). 'Crisis' and 'everyday' initiators: A qualitative study of coercion and agency in the context of methadone maintenance treatment initiation. *Drug and Alcohol Review, 36*(2), 253–260.

Fine, M. D. (2007). *A caring society? Care and the dilemmas of human service in the 21st century.* New York, NY: Palgrave Macmillan.

Fraser, S., & Moore, D. (2011). Introduction. In S. Fraser & D. Moore (Eds.), *The drug effect: Health, crime and society* (pp. 1–16). New York, NY: Cambridge University Press.

Fraser, S., & valentine, k. (2008). *Substance and substitution: Methadone subjects in liberal societies.* New York, NY: Palgrave Macmillan.

Friedman, J., & Alicea, M. (2001). *Surviving heroin: Interviews with women in methadone clinics.* Gainesville: University Press of Florida.

Garcia, A. (2008). The elegiac addict: History, chronicity and the melancholic subject. *Cultural Anthropology, 23*(4), 718–746.

Government of British Columbia. Coroners Service. *Fentanyl-Detected Illicit Drug overdose Deaths.* January 1, 2012 to March 31, 2019. Retrieved from https://www2.gov.bc.ca/gov/content/life-events/death/coroners-service/statistical-reports.

Graves, G., Csiernik, R., Foy, J., & Cesar, J. (2009). An examination of Canadian social work program curriculum and the addiction core competencies. *Journal of Social Work Practice in the Addictions, 9*(4), 400–413.

Gubrium, J. F., & Järvinen, M. (2014). Troubles, problems, and clientization. In J. F. Gubrium & M. Järvinen (Eds.), *Turning troubles into problems: Clientization in human services* (pp. 1–13). New York, NY: Routledge.

Gurstein, P., Pulkingham, J., & Vilches, S. (2011). Challenging policies for lone mothers: Reflections on, and insights from, longitudinal qualitative interviewing. In W. Frisby & G. Creese (Eds.), *Feminist community research: Negotiating contested relationships* (pp. 127–146). Vancouver: University of British Columbia Press.

Jack, S. M., Dobbins, M., Sword, W., Novotna, G., Brooks, S., Lipman, E. L., et al. (2011). Evidence-informed decision-making by professionals working in addiction agencies serving women: A descriptive qualitative study. *Substance Abuse Treatment, Prevention, and Policy, 6*(1), 29.

Järvinen, M. (2014). Untidy clientization: Drug users resisting institutional identities. In J. Gubrium & M. Järvinen (Eds.), *Turning troubles into problems: Clientization in human services* (pp. 50–64). London, UK: Routledge.

Keane, H. (2003). Critiques of harm reduction, morality and the promise of human rights. *International Journal of Drug Policy, 14*(3), 227–232.

Keane, H. (2013). Categorising methadone: Addiction and analgesia. *International Journal of Drug Policy, 24*(6), e18–e24.

Kerkvliet, B. J. T. (2009). Everyday politics in peasant societies (and ours). *Journal of Peasant Studies, 36*(1), 227–243.

Klein, S., Ivanova, I., & Leyland, A. (2017). *Long overdue: Why BC needs a poverty reduction plan*. Canadian Center for Policy Alternatives. BC Office.

Levitas, R., Pantazis, C., Fahmy, E., Gordon, D., Lloyd, E., & Patsios, D. (2007). *The multi-dimensional analysis of social exclusion*. Bristol, UK: Department of Sociology and School for Social Policy, University of Bristol.

Lindesmith, A. R. (1938). A sociological theory of drug addiction. *American Journal of Sociology, 43*(4), 593–613.

Link, B. G., & Phelan, J. C. (2001). Conceptualizing stigma. *Annual Review of Sociology, 27*, 363–385.

Lister, R. (2004). *Poverty*. Cambridge, UK: Blackwell and Polity Press.

Ning, A. M. (2005). Games of truth: Rethinking conformity and resistance in narratives of heroin recovery. *Medical Anthropology, 24*, 349–382.

Offer, S. (2012). The burden of reciprocity: Processes of exclusion and withdrawal from personal networks among low-income families. *Current Sociology, 60*(6), 788–805.

Page, J. B., & Singer, M. (2010). *Comprehending drug use: Ethnographic research at the social margins*. New Brunswick, NJ: Rutgers University Press.

Parusel, S. (2017). *Women, methadone, and the politics of supervised exclusion* (Doctoral dissertation). Arts & Social Sciences: Department of Sociology and Anthropology, Simon Fraser University.

Pulkingham, J., Fuller, S., Morrow, M., & Parusel, S. (2016). *Walking the line to put their families first: Lone mothers navigating welfare and work in British Columbia*. First Call BC Child and Youth Advocacy Coalition; Simon Fraser University; Single Mothers' Alliance BC; Social Planning and Research Council of British Columbia (SPARC BC).

Raikhel, E., & Garriott, W. (2013). Introduction: Tracing new paths in the anthropology of addiction. In E. Raikhel & W. Garriott (Eds.), *Addiction trajectories* (pp. 1–35). London, UK: Duke University Press.

Reinarman, C., & Granfield, R. (2014). Addiction is not *just* a brain disease: Critical studies of addiction. In R. Granfield & C. Reinarman (Eds.), *Expanding addiction: Critical essays* (pp. 2–21). New York, NY: Routledge.

Reist, D. (2010). *Methadone maintenance treatment in British Columbia, 1996–2008: Analysis and recommendations.* Victoria: BC Centre for Addictions Research.

Rosenbaum, M. (1981). *Women on heroin.* New Brunswick, NJ: Rutgers University Press.

Smith, C. B. (2011). A users' guide to "juice bars" and "liquid handcuffs": Fluid negotiations of subjectivity, space and the substance of methadone treatment. *Space and Culture, 14*(3), 291–309.

Smye, V., Browne, A. J., Varcoe, C., & Josewski, V. (2011). Harm reduction, methadone maintenance treatment and the root causes of health and social inequities: An intersectional lens in the Canadian context. *Harm Reduction Journal, 8*(17), 1–12.

CHAPTER 49

How Do We Teach Human Rights in Social Work in the Undergraduate Level?

Claudia Reyes-Quilodrán

INTRODUCTION

The chapter presents a way to teach social work students, who are one year away from graduation. It reviews the process and constitution of current historical, ethical-judicial, and political dimensions of human rights both nationally and internationally. The course emerges from the need to ensure that students can identify and analyse factors that affect the massive perpetration of human rights and apply international and national mechanisms that guarantee the promotion of human rights. In the first section of this chapter, the Chilean context is presented, and in the second section, the objectives and contents of the course-programme are discussed.

CHILEAN MILITARY REGIMEN AND HUMAN RIGHTS VIOLATIONS

During the late 1960s and early 1970s, most Latin American countries experienced military coups and military intervention in government affairs. At that time, Latin America observed the birth of numerous military regimes (e.g. Never Again, 1986; Rettig et al., 1991; Uruguay Nunca Más, 1992). The military interventions severely damaged democratic institutions and affected the political and social evolution of each country. One of the worst consequences was a large volume of human rights violations, especially among vulnerable populations such as the poor and indigenous groups. Unfortunately,

C. Reyes-Quilodrán (✉)
Escuela de Trabajo Social, Pontificia Universidad Católica de Chile, Santiago, Chile
e-mail: claudiar@uc.cl

© The Author(s) 2021
S. S. M. et al. (eds.), *The Palgrave Handbook of Global Social Work Education*, https://doi.org/10.1007/978-3-030-39966-5_49

Chile was no exception. The military coup of 1973 established a military regime that lasted for seventeen years, from 1973 to 1990. As a result of the military dictatorship, an estimated 1322 people were killed and 957 people disappeared (Rettig et al., 1991). In addition, approximately 27,255 people were tortured but survived (Valech et al., 2004).

Throughout the Chilean dictatorship, people who opposed the regimen not only were unable to express their opinions, but also they felt threatened if they said anything against the regimen. At that time, the regular citizen did not feel safe expressing their ideas in more intimate social groups, since the risks were too high, in the sense that the mere fact of thinking differently was considered to be an enemy of the state. The military regime controlled public and intimate spheres. Social work was not out of this political persecution. Sixteen people died, including undergraduate students and social work practitioners (Rettig et al., 1991). Moreover, the most emblematic social work school offered by the state, the University of Chile, was closed; only in 2015, it has been reopened (Moreno, 2014).

The concept of national security argued that any person could be a threat to the regime and to society (Zagorski, 1992). Indeed, people who followed communist or socialist ideologies were considered terrorists, and also other civilians who could represent a threat, such as the case of the syndical leader, Tucapel Jiménez, who was murder by National Intelligence agents (Rettig et al., 1991). The concept of human rights also fell into the same category as communism. That is to say, the military regime put defenders of human rights in the category of enemies of the state. This negative connotation of human rights remained entrenched in Chile for many years, even after the dictatorship, and still remains so among some groups of people.

Social Work Role During and After the Chilean Military Regimen

In contrast to other Latin American countries, the Catholic Church through the Vicariate of Solidarity (1976–1992), led by Cardinal Raúl Silva Henríquez, was an instance that protected victims and their families from political persecution. This permitted the professionals who worked there (lawyers and social workers, among others) to save a significant number of people (Orellana & Hutchison, 1991). In addition, the Foundation of Social Assistance of the Christian Churches (FASIC) was created in 1975 with the purpose of providing assistance to the victims of the political repression of the military government. This foundation had and has an ecumenical nature, and brought together the Catholic, Evangelical Lutheran, and Jewish communities. The Lutheran bishop Helmut Frenz acted as the specialised operational agent of the United Nations High Commissioner for Human Rights. During the military regimen, FASIC extended its work to assist political prisoners and their families, through psychiatric, social, and psychological medical support, and later the foundation extended its functions to other victims of repression: tortured persons, former political prisoners, and relatives of politically executioned and of disappeared detainees. During the military regime, the international community gave strong financial support to non-governmental organisations (NGOs), which worked directly with the victims of human right violations even after the return of Chilean democracy in 1991 (Moyano, 2016). Social workers were present in this task and worked directly with the victims and their families in most of these institutions. This has allowed professionals to learn from them and offer a base to teach human rights under a new social-political scenario where the contemporary needs of Chilean and Latin American society are in constant transformation.

Undergraduate Teaching

Course Characteristics: Objectives and Contents

It is important to highlight that throughout the experience of teaching in social work at the university, it has been seen as a necessity to create a course that responds to the field of human rights. This vision incorporates the fact that human rights contents and meanings must be taught in a transversal way throughout the entire career of social work. However, in order to ensure that minimum contents of education in this area are met in social work education, a course was created to specifically address human rights issues.

Social work intervention focuses on people in their own environment. This person is a human being with specific needs and motivations, which require social work interventions to respond to the particular characteristics of the subjects from a legal framework. In this approach, social work must respect the dignity of the subjects, giving them the leading role that will mobilise them to respond to their own needs. This approach challenges the social worker to perceive and know others' needs, motivations, and aspirations, to prevent the violation of their rights, and to promote a dignified life.

The lessons examine the theoretical and historical bases of human rights; analyse the different generations of rights and the instruments used to guarantee their implementation; recognise the elements that affect the massive perpetration of human rights; and apply the international and national mechanisms that guarantee the promotion of human rights. Furthermore, the course problematises the relationship between human rights and the ethical commitment of social work.

The course-programme is structured in three modules. In the first module, students examine the historical, ethical-legal, and social-political foundations from which human rights emerge in contemporary society. They are able to identify the perpetration of rights and their implications in individual and societal dimensions. In the second module, students learn how to use and implement legal instruments to intervene in cases. Finally, in the third module, the specific role of social work is addressed as it relates to the perpetration and promotion of human rights. The three modules were constructed from a framework that allows the student to gradually gain a more in-depth understanding of the concepts learned, while applying them to professional activities. This implies that one module must precede the other. The following section describes the three modules in detail.

Module 1: The Emergence of a New Ethical-Legal Conscience

This phase of the course discusses the philosophical foundation of human rights. Here, the concepts of morals, ethics, dignity, and the origins of moral rights are reviewed. In this phase, the student should understand what the main tendencies are in defining and explaining human rights, based on their historical evolution.

Furthermore, this section discusses trends of legal realism and positivism and their relationship with the origin of human rights. Students are able to assess the tension between these two trends. They discuss and question legal instruments, because these legal instruments should support human rights based on the principle that human rights are inherent, universal, inviolable, and inalienable. Meanwhile, from the perspective of legal realism, a law is not required to respect these rights. This discussion leads them to question if legal instruments centre around human dignity.

The revision of legal realism brings forth the idea that they are able to advocate changes in laws to respond to the adherence of human rights. This aspect is crucial since in Chile there is a code law. This system makes judges dictate sentences attached to laws, assuming that these respect human rights. However, throughout Chilean history, the laws and the criminal justice system sometimes have not been efficient enough to respond to these demands. Such is the case of the military regime, where the judicial authorities protected practices that violated the rights of the people (Rettig et al., 1991). The code law implies a positivist position, in which rights must be written to be recognised. This aspect makes it very difficult to change the law, and it takes a long time to do so because it is necessary for all three state branches (executive, legislative, and judicial) to approve any modification to the law. Most of the time, social changes and citizen demands are required quickly, creating a gap between the people's needs and what the law offers them. In this context, another aspect examined is the struggle for recognition and shift from the "rights of the citizen" to "human rights".

In parallel, generations of rights are discussed: civil and political rights (first generation); economic, social, and cultural rights (second generation); and rights of people (third generation). At this stage, the students see the social-political and historical changes of humanity, and how these changes have influenced the vision of human rights throughout history. The tension between individual and collective rights is analysed within the context of social work.

To prevent human rights violations, it is necessary to know the causes that sustain the perpetration of human rights. These multiple causes and the complexity with which they express themselves at the individual and collective levels are examined. Here, a phenomenological approach based on social and political psychology is used. The students analyse the causes of violence in detail and observe the influence of social prejudice and stereotypes on aggressive behaviour. At this phase, it is expected that students are able to self-perceive their own prejudices and how these influence their word vision and their social relationships, and how their perceptions positively and/or negatively influence the social work intervention. The violations of human rights are examined by putting the focus on the action and omission of conducts that favour perpetration. Furthermore, factors that favour mass perpetration against human rights violations are exhaustively discussed.

The comprehension and discussion about the causes of violence can be a powerful tool for social workers, because they help students understand the factors that surround violence and can create strategies to reduce their impact and prevent future violations of human rights. Moreover, this knowledge can support an approach that promotes respect for social diversity and guiding principles to encourage a path for peace.

Module 2: Basic Human Rights Instruments

Several instruments that guarantee respect for human rights are studied, including:

Charter of the United Nations (1945);
Universal Declaration of Human Rights (1948);
International Covenants on Civil and Political Rights (1966);
International Covenants on Economic, Social and Cultural Rights (1966);
International Convention on the Elimination of All Forms of Racial Discrimination (1965);
Convention on the Elimination of All Forms of Discrimination against Women (1979);
Inter-American Convention on the Prevention, Punishment and Eradication of Violence against Women "Convention of Belem Do Para" (1995);
Convention against Torture and Other Cruel, Inhuman or Degrading Treatment or Punishment (1984);
Convention on the Rights of the Child (1989);
International Convention on the Protection of the Rights of All Migrant Workers and Members of Their Families (1990); and
American Convention on Human Rights (1969).

The selection of these legal instruments is based on several criteria. The first criterion refers to the fact that they are the fundaments of human rights both domestically and internationally. Second, the National Institute of Human Rights in Chile issues a national report annually about human rights violations and the state of advance on these matters. The report is a tool that allows one to know what areas are the most vulnerable for human rights perpetrations in Chile, and how the state has or has not adopted measures to handle them. Therefore, the course focuses on the main national needs. For instance, one of the issues refers to the indigenous conflict between Mapuches and the Chilean government. The complexity of the conflict emerges from the colonial time and is strongly related to the land rights and respect for the Mapuches' Cosmovision. Violent episodes have been reported, which have included the loss of human lives. Social work is called to comprehend indigenous needs and address how to enhance communication among the affected parties. Furthermore, social workers have to support families affected by violence. Although only some conventions are examined in the course-programme, the way in which the conventions are addressed permits the students to apply this knowledge to other international instruments. Here, the main point is to instil skills so that later the students can apply this knowledge in different scenarios. Third, Chile has ratified each human rights instrument previously mentioned and this act makes the professionals align with what the instruments establish. Fourth, Chile is one of the state members of the United Nations, the Economic Commission for Latin America (ECLA) is in Santiago, and Chile is one of the five regional commissions of the United Nations. This shows the Chilean commitment to overcome poverty in Latin America, despite the fact that according to the Organization for Economic Co-operation and Development (OECD, 2015). Chile is one of the countries in the region with the greatest economic disparity. These deep contradictions are discussed with the students.

Another element that this module covers is global, Latin American, and national organisations that guarantee respect for human rights based on international instruments. Those are:

- United Nations (UN);
- Organization of American States (OAS);
- International Courts: International Court of Justice, International Criminal Court, and Inter-American Court of Human Rights;
- Inter-American Commission on Human Rights; and
- National Criminal Justice System.

Students are able to examine the specific features of each organisation and to achieve a comprehension of their social-political origins and nature. The review of the structure and how human rights affairs are handled at each organisation is discussed. At this point, students are expected to be able to identify the organisations' politics and regulations, in such a way that they can see the international scopes and the impact that these have on the compliance with human rights.

Students learn how national and international judicial systems work. Here, civil and criminal matters are reviewed in order for the student to develop the ability to advise people about a legal procedure locally and internationally. Chile is also a member of the Organization of American States (OAS), and Chile has signed to submit to the resolutions and recommendations of the Inter-American Commission and Court on Human Rights led by OAS. This feature makes it possible for any Chilean to plead any human rights violations against the Chilean state to these institutions. It becomes a powerful tool for social workers who guide and support victims affected by human rights violations, in the event that the state does not respond to their demands or in cases where the state could become perpetration perpetrator. Indeed, in 2014, the Chilean state lost a legal case against a group of Mapuches (Corte Interamericana de Derechos Humanos, 2014). The Inter-American Court indicated that indigenous people should not be prosecuted by an anti-terrorist law but rather under the regular criminal law, which has less severe sentences than anti-terrorist law and requires the parties to follow the due process.

One of the great elements of the Inter-American Commission on Human Rights is that the Commission does not require a Chilean citizen to make the allegation with a legal representative such as a lawyer. This makes it easier for people with limited economic resources to plead their case; therefore, it gives access to any Chilean citizen who wants to demand that their rights be respected when the state fails to do so. Here, it is tremendously important for social workers to know the legal procedures to advise people both locally and internationally. Hence, students are trained to identify the different Chilean judicial system structures and the Inter-American Commission on Human Rights regulations and procedures.

In Chile, social work has an important role in the articulation of social and institutional networks. This means that professionals must know the network model when intervening with people, because it not only allows the person to visualise and access the support of other significant people in their lives when faced with the perpetration of human rights, but also enables them to access different organisations that can help them with their needs.

The network model taught in the course is based on focal or egocentric and open social or sociocentric networks. Students study works from two Latino American authors: Elina Dabas and Denisse Najmanovich (1999, 2001, 2006). The selection of these authors is based on the fact that they are able to apply and interpret the concepts of focal and social networks in the context of Latin American. The two dimensions are reviewed and applied to a case. The first example is a true and anonymous case, based on a person who has been a victim of perpetration of human rights. The students review which rights have been perpetrated in the light of the international instruments (i.e. Convention). Once the violated rights are identified, the student examines the egocentric networks that the subject possesses and identifies which individual social networks can be a support for the person to stop the rights' perpetration. Furthermore, students identify who could accompany the victim at the judicial trial, if need be. In addition, students must identify the institutional networks specialised in caring and treating victims according to the violation, and advise the person about the judicial procedures to which the victims must turn. The network model for social work also implies that professionals monitor the processes that the victims have to face, and coordinate and refer them to specialised institutions. For example, there is a case of a woman affected by domestic violence. Most of the time women are socially isolated, so their networks are precarious and homogeneous (Bush & Valentine, 2000; Hodson, 1983). This is a risk factor that makes a woman more vulnerable (Hoff, 2016). The social workers must support the victim throughout the judicialisation of the case and facilitate access to specialised institutions. In this stage, referral and accompaniment techniques are taught.

In this process, a group of students work on the case analysis, and not only they review the victims' resources and threats to support them in a possible judicial trial, but also the students examine the particular features of the case to determine what are the human rights violations, which affect the victim and her/his family or significant others. Moreover, the students identify how they have to stop the violations, and how to promote the strengths of the victims based on their own needs. During military regimen, the experience of the Chilean social workers tells us that when a victim suffers human right violations, the workers should focus on the case and examine the particular characteristics of the individual and her/his social context (Sánchez, 1990; Del Villar, 2018). Here, the case approach is studied and the students learn how to use the social and institutional networks, and how to use the legal tools to prevent and promote human right violations. Recall that a judicial sentence of the Inter-American Court mandates that the laws must be changed in the country sued, and the sentence establishes jurisprudence (Cavallaro & Brewer, 2008). The jurisprudence has the power to change laws and organisations; therefore, it has a direct impact on Latin American countries, because the Inter-American Court ruling demands modifications at the institutional level. This is the promotion of human rights.

Module 3: Human Rights and Social Work

As mentioned previously, sadly in Chile as well as other Latin American countries the perpetrations of human rights have historical roots, which become more severe during dictatorships. This led Latin American social workers to generate strategies to face state violence and offer a new view of how to approach human rights. Moreover, this has motivated a group of social workers to develop a formal position. One of them was Carlos Eroles (1997), who wrote the book Human Rights: The Ethical Commitment of Social Work (1997). The author argues that social work is a profession and its purpose is transformation of services and to help social subjects fully develop. In this view, people have to be perceived as individuals capable of managing their own personal, family, organisational, and community life. In other words, social workers must encourage self-determination provided that the client does not infringe the rights of others. Here, the tension between individual and collective rights is reviewed again.

Eroles argues that social work and human rights have deep historical, ethical-political, and scientific ties. In this context, rights have constitutional status, and there is no democracy without human development and access of all people to full citizenship. The author's arguments go further to claim that the organisational ideology of social work is also integrated with the affirmative action of rights, and as a central role of the professional interventions, which should take into account: unbalanced power relations, corruption, and fundamentalisms that deny the dignity of man in favour of an ideal, religion or other, promoting discrimination. Professionals must search democratic ways of social transformation, within a framework of social justice and an ethic of solidarity, which creates a culture of human rights. Eroles' approaches are discussed with the students in workshop, giving them the opportunity to debate different authors' views, what social justice means, and how these conceptualisations apply to professional practices.

Since human rights philosophy is strongly linked with ethics, the concept of dignity is examined from the view of the individual right to self-determination and the person's search for happiness. The strength perspective is reviewed (Saleeby, 2008) because it allows the student to leave the role of expert and create strategies to approach people from their own needs and co-construct interventions. That is to say, specialised knowledge is put at the service of the other.

The Chilean Social Work Ethical Code reedited in 2014 and Ethics in Social Work of the International Federation of Social Work and the International Association of Social Workers (2004) are examined, and special attention is given to the concept of social justice. The objective is that the students are able to develop concepts that help generate a culture of human rights that, in turn, can become the base of a new political culture.

CHALLENGES

Training professionals to lead social transformations is in itself a challenge. However, this challenge becomes more complex when future professionals must give voice to those who do not have it. In this context, they could experience their own violation of human rights, especially when the organisation where they work violates their rights. That is the reason why it is urgent that social workers have tools that allow them to face social problems and visualise the strengths of the judicial system and the international community as an ally in this defence of human rights.

Today, the Chileans are witnessing how mass citizenship has taken to the streets to claim their rights. In the thirty years since the dictatorship, the democratic government persisted in generating a system that privileges only a certain social group in this country (De Masi, 2019; "La marcha más grande de Chile", 2019). The vast majority must face a precarious health system, with long hours and days waiting for their attention, an unequal and standardised education that does not recognise the abilities and differences of children in their learning processes and their biopsychosocial context. A precarious public transport system that causes that people have to spend at least three hours in transit per day, in addition to their 45-hour workweek. A precarious retirement system that, on average, older adults receive an income of $200 USD per month. That is, when they retire, they remain in poverty. Chileans must pay for the use of highways. In circumstances that 60% of the population earns the minimum salary of $ 448 USD per month, from which 19% is then deducted in health and social security payments ("BBC: Las 6 grandes deudas", 2019). Human rights continue to be violated in our country, and today, the public protests have turned violent.

In this context, we have been able to observe how our students use their knowledge in the recognition of national and international organisations to support victims of police aggression, and how they use the Inter-American Court system to allege their cases. While we are aware that social transformation and the promotion of rights are not only a task of social work, but also of society as a whole, our students are capable of leading processes that prevent the violation of rights and in turn support the victims.

Today, our great challenge is to impact public policy in such a way that social inequality could be only a bad memory in Chilean history.

CONCLUSIONS

It has been highly rewarding to teach students the meaning of human rights. However, there are other proposals that would be important to understand, so as to enrich the discussion and share experiences. Therefore, here is an invitation to dialogue and mutually learn.

REFERENCES

American Convention on Human Rights. (1969). *Organization of American States.* https://www.oas.org/dil/treaties_b-32_american_convention_on_human_rights. pdf.

BBC: Las 6 grandes deudas. (2019, October 21). *BBC: Las 6 grandes deudas sociales por las que muchos chilenos dicen sentirse "abusados".* Tele13 Radio. https://www. t13.cl/noticia/nacional/bbc/protestas-en-chile-las-6-grandes-deudas-sociales-por-las-que-muchos-chilenos-dicen-sentirse-abusados.

Bush, N., & Valentine. D. (2000). Empowerment practice: A focus on battered women. *Journal of Women and Social Work, 15*(1), 82. https://doi.org/10.1177/08861090022093840.

Cavallaro, J. L., & Brewer, S. E. (2008). La función del litigio interamericano en la promoción de la justicia social. *Sur Revista Internacional de Direitos Humanos, 5*(8), 85–99. https://doi.org/10.1590/S1806-64452008000100005.

Charter of the United Nations and Statute of International Court of Justice. (1945). United Nations. https://treaties.un.org/doc/publication/ctc/uncharter.pdf.

Convention on the Elimination of All Forms of Discrimination Against Women. (1979). United Nations. http://www.ohchr.org/Documents/ProfessionalInterest/cedaw.pdf.

Convention Against Torture and Other Cruel, Inhuman or Degrading Treatment or Punishment. (1984). United Nations. http://www.ohchr.org/Documents/ProfessionalInterest/cat.pdf.

Convention on the Rights of the Child. (1989). United Nations. http://www.ohchr.org/Documents/ProfessionalInterest/crc.pdf.

Corte Interamericana de Derechos Humanos. (2014). *Caso Norín Catrimán y Otros: Dirigentes, Miembros y Activista del Pueblo Indígena Mapuche vs. Chile.* Sentencia de 29 de Mayo De 2014 (Fondo, Reparaciones y Costas). http://www.corteidh.or.cr/docs/casos/articulos/seriec_279_esp.pdf.

Dabas, E. (2001). *Redes Sociales: Niveles de Abordaje en la intervención y Organización en Red.* https://www.santafe.gov.ar/index.php/web/content/download/71292/345905/fi%20le/.

Dabas, E., & Najmanovich, D. (1999). *Redes: El Lenguaje de los Vínculos hacia la Construcción el Fortalecimiento de la Sociedad Civil.* Paidós.

Dabas, E., & Najmanovich, D. (2006). *Una, dos, muchas redes: itinerarios y afluentes del pensamiento y abordaje en redes.* Viviendo Redes. https://www.insumisos.com/lecturasinsumisas/Red%20de%20redes.pdf.

Del Villar, M. (2018). *Las asistentes sociales de la Vicaría de la Solidaridad: Una historia profesional.* Ediciones Universidad Alberto Hurtado. Santiago, Chile.

De Masi, V. (2019, October 26). *Estallido social: Levantan el toque de queda en Santiago de Chile tras la masiva marcha del viernes.* Clarín. https://www.clarin.com/mundo/levantan-toque-queda-santiago-chile-masiva-marcha-viernes_0_N16f8JZG.html.

Eroles, Carlos. (1997). *Los derechos humanos: Compromiso ético del Trabajo Social.* Buenos Aires: Espacio.

Hodson, C. A. (1983). Coping with domestic violence: Social support and psychological health among battered women. *American Journal of Community Psychology, 11*(6), 1573–2770. https://doi.org/10.1007/BF00896600.

Hoff, L. A. (2016). *Battered women as survivors.* New York, NY: Routledge.

IFSW/IASSW. (2004). International Federation Social Workers/International Association of Schools of Social Workers. *Ethics in Social Work: Statement of Principles.* Berne. IFSW/IASSW. Accessed June 8, 2020, from https://oldsite.iassw-aiets.org/wp-content/uploads/2015/10/Ethics-in-Social-Work-Statement-IFSW-IASSW-2004.pdf.

Inter-American Convention on the Prevention, Punishment and Eradication of Violence against Women "Convention of Belem Do Para". (1995). Organization of American States. http://www.oas.org/juridico/english/treaties/a-61.html.

International Covenants on Economic, Social and Cultural Rights. (1966). United Nations. http://www.ohchr.org/Documents/ProfessionalInterest/cescr.pdf.

International Convention on the Elimination of All Forms of Racial Discrimination. (1965). United Nations. http://www.ohchr.org/Documents/ProfessionalInterest/cerd.pdf.

International Convention on the Protection of the Rights of All Migrant Workers and Members of Their Families. (1990). United Nations. http://www.ohchr.org/Documents/ProfessionalInterest/cmw.pdf.

La marcha más grande de Chile. (2019, October 25). *La marcha más grande de Chile: Más de un millón de personas se manifiestan en Santiago.* Tele13 Radio. https://www.t13.cl/noticia/nacional/manifestantes-repletaron-plaza-italia-historica-marcha-mas-grande-chile.

Moreno, G. (2014). *Diario La Tercera.* Universidad de Chile reabre la carrera de Trabajo Social después de 40 años http://www.latercera.com/noticia/universidad-de-chile-reabre-carrera-de-trabajo-social-despues-de-40-anos/.

Moyano, C. (2016). ONG y conocimiento sociopolítico durante la Dictadura: la disputa por el tiempo histórico de la transición. El caso de los Talleres de Análisis de Coyuntura en ECO, 1987-1992. *Revista Izquierdas, 27,* 1–31.

Never Again. (1986). *Nunca Más: Never again: A report by Argentina's National Commission on disappeared people.* Somerset and London: Butter and Tanner Ltd., Frame.

OCDE. (2015). *Estudios Económicos de la OCDE Chile.* OCDE Mejore Políticas para una Vida Mejor. https://www.oecd.org/eco/surveys/Chile-2015-vision-general.pdf.

Orellana, P., & Hutchison, E. Q. (1991). *El movimiento de derechos humanos en Chile, 1973–1990.* Centro de Estudios Politicos Latinoamericanos Simón Bolivar (CEPLA). Chile.

Rettig, R., Castillo, J., Cea, J., Jiménez, M., Martín, R., Novoa, L., ... Zalaquett, J. (1991). *Informe de la nacional comisión de verdad y reconciliación.* Gobierno de Chile.

Saleeby, D. (2008). *The strength perspective in social work practice* (5th ed.). Boston: Allyn & Bacon.

Sánchez, D. (1990). *Trabajo social y derechos humanos: compromiso con la dignidad, la experiencia chilena.* Colectivo de Trabajo Social. Santiago, Chile. Ediciones Humanitas.

Universal Declaration of Human Rights. (1948). United Nations. http://www.ohchr.org/EN/UDHR/Documents/UDHR_Translations/eng.pdf.

Uruguay, Nunca Más. (1992). *Uruguay nunca más: Informe sobre violación de derechos humanos (1972–1985)* (2nd ed.). Servicio Paz y Justicia Uruguay.

Valech, S., Sepúlveda, M., Amunátegui, M., Fouillioux, L., Gómez, J., Lira, E., ... Varela, A. (2004). *Informe de la comisión nacional de prisión política y tortura.* Gobierno de Chile.

Zagorski, P. (1992). *Democracy vs. National security: Civil-military relations in Latin America.* Boulder: Lynne Rienner.

PART VIII

Pedagogical Issues in Social Work: Rethinking Practice Teaching

Introduction

The social work profession has gained recognition across the globe as a problem-solving profession where service users receive professional intervention by suitably trained professionals. The professional objectives and expected roles of professional social workers have undergone a tremendous change over the years. Universities offer a structured curriculum that equips social work professionals with the required knowledge, skills, and professional values. Universities also offer social work education at undergraduate, postgraduate, and doctoral levels. Distinct to social work education is its combination of theoretical components taught in the classroom, and field-based education involving the integration of the academic aspect and practice. The field-based education, commonly referred to across the globe as either fieldwork, field instruction, field placement, field education, practicum, or internship, is an integral component of social work education both at undergraduate and at postgraduate levels. This field instruction component offers students an opportunity to test and relate theoretical understanding to the real-life problems, situations, and challenges faced by individuals, groups, and communities. Many universities accord equal emphasis and weight to the theoretical component, and the field instruction components of social work education. Since the students are expected to work with human beings and intervene in their real-life situations, it is imperative that field education is implemented with the help of structured curriculum, tested situations, methods, tools under the close supervision of both the faculty and field supervisor.

Contributions in this part of the volume address the issues related to fieldwork education in different countries across the world. Despite well-established theoretical education in many countries, field education is somewhat neglected or not substantially taught or intensively practised. Further scan of available literature on fieldwork education shows an absence of service structure to support fieldwork education and employment of social work graduates in many countries (Gray, 2005; Gray & Yadav, 2015; Leung, 2007; Lin & Chen, 2005; Panic, 2016). Drawing from the work of Shulman (2005), the CSWE (2008a, b) framed field placements as signature pedagogy in social work for teaching and socializing future practitioners. However, the concept of signature pedagogy has been well discussed in the Western context, especially in America and Canada and rarely developed in the Global South. Further in many countries the service users' perspectives on field education are neither researched nor documented in the dominant literature. Such an effort by *Carolyn Gentle-Genitty* documents the voices of school social work interns in the field to describe the changing roles of school social work interns. The author argues that the school social work intern's ability to collaborate and communicate helps them navigate their changing roles and continues to provide the best possible care to the service users. The Council on Social Work Education (CSWE) standards expect the field education training to help the graduates to develop the competencies required for ethical behaviour; diversity and difference; advancement of human rights; research-informed practice, assessment, and intervention; practice with individuals, families, groups, communities, and organizations; and policy practice skills through fieldwork education (CSWE, 2015).

Carolyn Noble brings in the discussion, critical pedagogy, and its importance in social work. The argument put forward is, that in order to work critically, social workers need to be well versed in a pedagogy that equips them with the necessary knowledge, skills, and ability for lifelong learning and critical thinking. The unique characteristics of signature pedagogies help the students to understand a profession and prepare them for their future profession (Shulman, 2005). Further, *Carolyn Noble* examines the key concepts of a critical pedagogy, its theoretical underpinnings and associated learning strategies, and its centrality in framing a critical practice for use in professional social work supervision. The chapter further argues that critical pedagogy facilitates constant questioning and reflection and ongoing dialogue on, and critique of, the sociopolitical, economic, and cultural power relations within the organization as well as broadly in the community and society. Perhaps in the dominant literature the use of signature pedagogy for training the future professionals has been discussed widely in medicine, teaching, and law, while social work signature pedagogy being rarely and unclearly discussed (Bogo, 2015; Earls Larrison & Korr, 2013). In the context of social work, Carolyn Noble's arguments give a hope that the use of critical pedagogy in social work supervision may facilitate the exploration of new knowledge, theory, practice options, and broader societal concerns.

As noted in the literature, the use of signature pedagogy in social work as a method of teaching is not extensively discussed. Further several researchers were also pinioned that organizational level change is required for the effective implementation of fieldwork education as signature pedagogy in social work (Bogo, 2015; Holosko & Skinner, 2015). However, the recognition of signature pedagogy in social work is mostly successful in the West such as the United States and Canada. for example, in the United States, the Council on Social Work Education (CSWE) recognized signature pedagogy through 2008 Educational Policy and Accreditation Standards (EPAS) (Wayne, Bogo, & Raskin, 2010). Council on Social Work Education (CSWE) further states that the instructions and learning in the field practicum are the primary sources, where students are socialized to the professional roles (CSWE, 2008). Further in this direction *K. Anuradha* provides an understanding on the value of fieldwork experience(s), relevance of a constructivist approach, understanding and moving along with the pace of the learners in fieldwork teaching and learning. The chapter also argues for a process-oriented approach to promote effective theory and practice integration in social work education. Despite growing importance of discussion on fieldwork education in social work, five scholars have criticized the applicability of the term 'signature pedagogy' in social work (Holden, Barker, Rosenberg, Kuppens, & Ferrell, 2011; Wayne et al., 2010). However, an integrated model with fieldwork and classroom teaching was proposed by Armenta and Linseisen (2015) to promote field education as signature pedagogy in the United States.

Fieldwork education is an important site where future professionals learn, test, and acquire social justice, knowledge, and skills. Stavros K. Parlalis brings in the experiences of collaborative approach in field education by local authorities, NGOs, and civil society organizations. Qualitative interviews with social workers working as field placement supervisors for universities and social workers employed in organizations revile the importance of fieldwork education not only for the graduates but also for the larger society. *Gil Espenido* gives an account of community-level intervention as one of the social work interventions in addition to individual and group level interventions. The chapter argues that under neoliberalism, the process of community development has been depoliticized and has been 'sharpened' by instituting evidence-based practice (EBP) as the dominant process for guiding professional community practice.

In sum, for a better prospect for the social work graduates across the globe, schools of social work need to integrate theory and practice in their teaching and training. The departments of social work, social work educators, and field practitioners need to work together to develop modules for training future generation where experiences of the past shape the future social work professionals as ethical, moral, and skilled social workers. Further greater attention to be paid for the management of field education, programme structure, and broader university as these are identified as institutional factors influencing the social work curriculum (Grady, Powers, Despard, & Naylor, 2011).

References

Armenta, K. F., & Linseisen, T. B. (2015). The indispensable faculty liaison within the signature pedagogy: The Integrated Field/Classroom Model (IFCM) as an example. *Field Educator, 5*(1). Retrieved from http://fieldeducator.simmons.edu/article/the-indispensable-faculty-liaison-within-the-signature-pedagogy-the-integrated-fieldclassroom-model-ifcm-as-an-example/.

Bogo, M. (2015). Field education for clinical social work practice: Best practices and contemporary challenges. *Clinical Social Work Journal, 43*(3), 317–334.

Council on Social Work Education. (2008a). *2008 Educational Policy and Accreditation Standards.* Retrieved from http://www.cswe.org/Accreditation/2008EPASDescription.aspx.

Council on Social Work Education. (2008b). *Educational Policy and Accreditation Standards.* Washington, DC: Author.

Council on Social Work Education. (2015). *Education Policy and Accreditation Standards.* Washington, DC: Author.

Earls Larrison, T., & Korr, W. S. (2013). Does social work have a signature pedagogy? *Journal of Social Work Education, 49*(2), 194–206.

Gray, M. (2005). Dilemmas of international social work: Paradoxical processes in indigenisation, imperialism and universalism. *International Journal of Social Welfare, 14,* 230–237.

Gray, M., & Yadav, R. K. (2015). Social work without borders: A Janus-faced concept. *Social Dialogue, 11,* 26–27. Retrieved September 26, 2016, from http://data.axmag.com/data/201508/20150818/U114409_F349450/FLASH/index.html.

Grady, M. D., Powers, J., Despard, M., & Naylor, S. (2011). Measuring the implicit curriculum: Initial development and results of an MSW survey. *Journal of Social Work Education, 47,* 463–487, 10.5175/JSWE.2011.200900119.

Holden, G., Barker, K., Rosenberg, G., Kuppens, S., & Ferrell, L. W. (2011). The signature pedagogy of social work: An investigation of the evidence. *Research on Social Work Practice, 39,* 115–133.

Holosko, M., & Skinner, J. (2015). A call for field coordination leadership to implement the signature pedagogy. *Journal of Human Behavior in the Social Environment, 25*(3), 275–283.

Leung, J. C. B. (2007). An international definition of social work for China. *International Journal of Social Welfare, 16,* 391–397, 10.1111/j.1468-2397.2007.00495.x.

Lin, J., & Chen, X. (2005, September 6). The embarrassment prospects of seeking appropriate positions for social work graduates. *China Youth Daily,* p. 3.

Panic, G. (2016, August 19–21). *Mobilization of graduated social workers for alternatives in social work.* Paper presented at the 14th Annual TiSSA PhD Network, Gent, Belgium.

Shulman, L. S. (2005). Signature pedagogies in the professions. *Daedalus, 134*(3), 52–59.

Wayne, J., Bogo, M., & Raskin, M. (2010). Field education as the signature pedagogy of social work education. *Journal of Social Work Education, 46*(3), 327–339.

CHAPTER 50

Role of School Social Work Interns in the US: Voices from the Field

Carolyn Gentle-Genitty and Corinne Renguette

Introduction and Background

SCHOOL is a sacred place, a safe place, a learning environment, a space for growth, and a place for children to be socialised to the world around them. Ideally, it is a place filled with loving, supportive people. Yet, the COVID19 pandemic and current news of children shot to death at point-blank range, teachers using their bodies to shield children from flying bullets, the need for armed school teachers, principals, and personnel, and the marketing of children's bulletproof gear and backpacks is changing the roles for schools and their personnel. The shortage of social workers, including school social workers, continues to grow as the number of those entering the workforce is insufficient to meet demand (Fisher, 2010; Lin, Lin, & Zhang, 2015; Torpey, 2018). The village is now showing up to raise and educate the child after tragedy. The burden is heavy, but the commitment is obvious. "The school social worker is primarily concerned with every child whose coping capacity may not be well matched with the demands and resources of the education institution" (Constable, McDonald, & Flynn, 2006, p. 9). However, the number of children

Thank you to the contribution of our students especially Dan Moisoff and Tao Mowers.

C. Gentle-Genitty (✉)
Indiana University School of Social Work, Indianapolis, IN, USA
e-mail: cgentleg@iu.edu

C. Renguette
 Indianapolis School of Engineering and Technology,
Indiana University-Purdue University, Indianapolis, IN, USA

who need this type of assistance is also growing, which increases the load for the school social worker. There is no doubt that the roles of all school personnel have changed, including that of the school social worker. Today's school social worker needs to be able to function in many levels and domains and to stay focused on the priorities while serving larger numbers of youth (Berzin & O'Connor, 2010; Thompson, Reinke, Holmes, Danforth, Herman, 2017).

As a profession that equips schools with trained school social workers serving in these various capacities, we know that for the next cadre of school social work interns, the first step into a school placement site will bring emotions and a plan for change. This plan rests on the intern's knowledge, awareness of and openness to system nuances, and an advanced ability to collaborate and communicate. Preparing school social work students for this task becomes crucial. Competencies and standards exist as a guideline for what all students should achieve prior to graduation (CSWE, 2015; NASW, 2015). These competencies and standards can help guide interns' practice in schools both during the internship and later, when transitioning to practitioner. In addition, approaches for specific applications exist to aid practising in school settings (see, e.g., Kelly et al., 2010; Thompson et al., 2017). Graduate training has been provided in generalist practice issues specific to the school setting, but very little specialised training is provided in educational policies, the linking of services to academic outcomes, or practice and prevention programs (Bronstein, Ball, Mellin, Wade-Mdivanian, & Anderson-Butcher, 2011). Therefore, school social work interns must be able to find resources for the areas where they might need additional evidence-based guidelines. Another area that has not had a lot of investigation is that of the roles of student social work interns. To inform others of important observations and potentially help prepare those entering the field, this chapter will describe the role of school social work interns and identify foundations that must guide their work. The literature combined with the voices of school social work interns together offers a discussion of a graduated ability to effectively collaborate, communicate, and negotiate with all stakeholders in the school during normalcy, festivity, and tragedy in order to continue to provide the best care possible.

The Role of Student Social Work Interns

Social workers have been at the helm of schools' abilities to connect and maintain relationships with parents, teachers, and the community since the profession's inception. Social work services have been provided in schools dating back to the 1890s (Bronstein et al., 2011). Today, the roles of the school social worker have been enhanced and expanded, but have changed very little. Still exploring and responding to student challenges of behaviour, belonging, and connectivity while also responding to the need for resources from families and other school stakeholders, school social workers have now added to their list of daily duties the ability to create and provide individualised plans/counselling and functional behavioural assessments, to raise funds and compile resources, and to be a culturally competent school and community responder (Suppes & Wells, 2009). While the summary of the activities in Table 50.1 is short,

Table 50.1   Role of school social worker/intern: interactional and interpersonal skills

School social worker: Interactional skills	School social worker: Interpersonal skills
• Conduct informational or formal interviews • Learn student protocols and emergency plans • Review and help students be in compliance with school policies (dress code, technology, attendance, involvement, bullying, rules, interaction with other students, etc.) • Carry a caseload (basic counselling and problem-solving with an Individualized Education Plan) • Respond to violations of student rights and confidentiality • Provide direct school specialised services and interventions to promote student well-being • Conduct systematic and strength-based assessment to determine student needs (mental health, social, emotional, and academic needs) • Advocate for policies that promote student success and link families, schools, and community resources • Work as a member of multidisciplinary problem-solving teams to develop and implement solutions for student academic success • Find and implement research-informed school social work practices • Conduct record keeping through case reports and accountability through various forms of intake/assessment school-based tools • Articulate legal mandates and relevant historical, current, political, economic, social constraints, and local contexts of social work practice in school settings that guide standards and practice • Identify, analyse, and apply a range of prevention and intervention roles and methods and human behaviour theories with individuals, small groups, families, schools, and communities • Identify, evaluate, and apply a range of direct and specialised assessment, intervention, and evaluation strategies grounded in cultural competence with special populations (including but not limited to gifted students, learners with special needs, bullies, truants, dropouts, juveniles and at-risk populations, such as those distinguished by age, ethnicity, culture, class, religion and physical, emotional, or mental ability) in school settings • Develop strategies to conduct systematic and strength-based assessments to determine student needs • Apply research-informed practice skills to evaluate policy and program strengths and weaknesses • Identify and implement school context-specific program planning and evaluation • Articulate the influence of programs and policies, in the school setting, on populations distinguished by age, race, ethnicity, culture, class, religion, ability, and physical and mental ability. • Conduct multi-system level assessments, sensitive to developmental status, family context, culture and ethnicity, and larger system factors • Appraise the applicability and suitability of different treatment models	• Embrace flexibility and adaptability • Support students' academic success • Be a reliable resource • Possess warmth, empathy, respect, genuineness, listening, engagement • Manage a reflective and reflexive practice • Be culturally competent (appreciate the perspectives of each stakeholder) • Value the voices and views of stakeholders • Recognise the unique needs of special at-risk populations • Aid in providing safe student environment • Provide a conducive environment for students to learn • Use professional judgement, • Manage personal feelings with ethical models of practice • Practise integrity to respond to students and school personnel • Value all forms of communication beginning where the primary system is • Identify, within this setting, interpersonal methods of helping students achieve optimal success • Maintain personal and professional standards and personal needs • Be able to engage in the evaluation of one's own competence in practice with children and adolescents • Apply essential communication and relationship building skills in interactions with children and adolescents • Identify, evaluate, and apply critical thinking skills to practise confidentiality and ethical decision-making with integrity • Critically evaluate one's personal values to foster a self-disciplined, value-based professional practice in the school social work setting in working with students, parents, administration, and community partners • Apply critical thinking and knowledge of the political realities of a school service delivery system to define problems, identify social policy goals, and analyse major trends underlying US policy • Understand the contextual frameworks that inform practice with children and adolescents

when expanded, you can find a school social worker playing any of the 40 plus instructional and interpersonal roles compiled and identified, and a new school social work intern has to embrace most (if not all) of them as they acclimate to their new environment of practice (See Table 50.1). Students entering a school for their field placement must be aware of their roles, their own knowledge base of social work practice, and potential areas for further practice and growth to assess and plan for a successful field placement to fit their individual needs.

Despite the expectations of performing, learning, or carrying out many of these new tasks, many students entering the school as an intern are unaware of these expectations. Though the roles of social workers vary by school, and there is an expectation that each intern will be expected to work with individual students, student groups, families, the school community, staff members and the like, they rarely are given a detailed list of other expectations or what comes with carrying out these responsibilities. As such, some students leave not being fully immersed in the expected roles.

Experiencing a variety of new situations, both in practice and as members in a new organisation with no prior experience, and determining how a social work intern fits within the organisational culture of the school will continually be a challenge. Yet, professional presentation (semi-formal dress clothing, dress pants, shirt/blouse, khaki or dress pants with button-down or polo shirt), conveying a level of proficiency, respecting the structure of the school environment, modelling appropriate behaviour, and demonstrating care taken in self-presentation is a must. Many young students are intimidated by professionally dressed adults and think they may be in trouble when approached, especially by a new social work intern, but dispelling that myth is part of treating students with respect and courtesy, despite appearances. Much of the challenge in the early stages of entering the school as a social work intern begins with informing school personnel of who you are and what your role in the school will be. The success of the role of the intern rests largely on a supervisor who is fully aware of the roles and duties and has done an exceptional job of establishing and communicating those roles to the other staff and administrators in the building. This presents a platform for what will be learned and accomplished while in the school, but gives a glimpse into other tasks you may be able to perform randomly. For example, at the beginning of an intern experience, many students at the start of the school year were being sent home due to school uniforms not fitting properly from the previous year. Some pants had holes or were splitting, and the supervisor helped the students by sewing up their pants and keeping them in the classroom where they were able to continue learning.

Situations like these exhibit the flexibility, boundaries, and adaptability necessary in the role of the school social worker. Every student may be having difficulties that look similar, but it is not until speaking with them that you appreciate the uniqueness that each child has and the different ways and at different paces needed to work with each child. Treating the child as the "expert" of their own situation proves to be advantageously supported only by a competent school social worker finding their way in a new and challenging environment. The value of the work can be seen despite situations likes these highlighting more of the tedious work and growing caseload of the social worker, and despite the roles being intimidating to new interns. The job is about helping students in every way possible, and the role of the school social worker could be simple enough to help these children be more successful in the classroom through self-regulation and behavioural modification, especially if they are receiving social and mental health services outside of the school (Indiana School Social Work Association, 2010).

When it comes to school social work interns setting a plan to acquire these skills for themselves, it is best to prepare to fully participate in all the indirect and direct services and daily roles—shadow everything your supervisor and other social workers in the school do. This will better prepare any student intern for their independent career, and it will help them establish a presence at the practicum site while enabling professional networking. It is important also to observe and participate in aspects of school social work outside of direct service. This includes administrative work with the principals and other school professionals, such as record keeping, staff meetings, trainings, policy development, advocacy, and lunch duty. To some, these may be more of the mundane aspects of the school social workers' job and, because of that, particular field instructors may not insist on attendance. However, it is essential to engage in these activities because it will be required in your own career.

Establishing yourself as a professional in the school by studying and understanding the school organisation system and networking with school staff and administrators is essential, as administrators have hiring authority in their school and political clout within the larger school system. More so, it helps provide perspective to understand what is happening in the school. For instance, many schools are struggling and being classified as failing schools. Contributing to these difficulties, school districts are seeing huge funding cuts from their general operating fund. Students in these schools that have been "failing" according to traditional state and federal standards see more resources being cut. Due to the high poverty rate of some families, school receives Title I funding. This funding includes Supplemental Education Services (SES) in the form of voluntary tutoring for students in addition to classroom instruction time, but these, too, are at risk of cuts. Chapman (2003) found that strain on the adults in the family is increased for families living in poverty, which, in turn, reduces the resources available to the child and increases the likelihood that the child will fail in school. This information helps student interns understand the pressures of administrators and demands for outcomes while still actively playing supportive roles in being creative in acquiring services for students in their care. Demonstrating professional skills and work ethic as an intern will create positive connections and lasting relationships with people who have the power to advocate for you when applying for jobs. All this rests on interns entering the school with some foundation knowledge.

Knowledge Foundation of Student Social Work Interns

Essential abilities and personal attributes are necessary for a successful field placement and defining oneself within the system. The knowledge set that forms the foundation of any social work intern includes countless interpersonal and instructional skills. These skills can vary from ethical and professional practice using warmth, empathy, respect, listening, and genuineness to self-awareness, cultural competence, and commitment (NASW, 2015). Efficiently demonstrating these skills in field placement will make the evaluation process clearer for the field instructor and university and enhance the working relationships formed by the intern in the school. As such, the foundational knowledge set of every student entering the school as an intern rests in three specific areas *(1) self-assessment in the context of the school and multi-disciplinary teamwork, (2) research and assessment, and (3) theory application and evaluation.* The next section will define each of these and look more deeply at school social work intern reflections in all three of these areas based on their experiences.

Self-assessment and Multi-disciplinary Teamwork

Self-assessment involves learning about your own abilities and skills, reflecting on them regularly, and striving to continue self-development. This is part of the ethical and professional behaviour competency for practice in the field (CSWE, 2015; NASW, 2015). In any system, a social worker must self-assess. This could mean evaluating the privilege status from which you have been raised or educated and realising that it may be different from the students in the school where you now serve as an intern. It also could include the assessment of your personal values, biases, stereotypes, and discrimination about special populations, education, systems and policies, or methods of responding to the different needs of school stakeholders. For instance, through discussion with the students on your caseload you may learn that some may be living in poverty; some may be living with their grandparents due to their biological parents losing their parental rights; many may not have any contact with their fathers; and some have deceased parents. These conditions, in addition to other biological and environmental difficulties, provide greater context as to what is preventing these students from being successful in the classroom. Nevertheless, from a self-assessment perspective, it helps to inform the intern of the value of education and real barriers to success that may be beyond the students' control. These concerns may not have been explored in the intern's own college training or may not have been experienced personally. As an intern, you cannot fully relate to every challenge that your students may face; but, through the use of your social work skills, you can learn to actively listen and meet the client where they are. Thus, set aside your own experience, make evidence-based decisions, and treat your clients as the experts of their lives, keeping in mind their individuality, uniqueness, and personal values. Ethical decision-making models (see, e.g., Forester-Miller & Davis, 2016), in addition to supervision, help greatly in examining ethical dilemmas as they provide a systematic approach to an issue that can be very ambiguous.

Ultimately, interns must take personal responsibility for their own learning and gain as much knowledge from their experiences as possible. It would be ideal to have as much support from the field liaison, field instructor, and professors as possible; however, that is not always possible. Commit yourself to making the most of your practicum, regardless of the inherent stress of balancing school, work, the practicum, and personal obligations. Often this means researching on your own time, being available to work extra hours at the practicum site, and attending as many professional development trainings and staff meetings as possible, even if they are not all mandatory. Finding opportunities to learn from constant critical evaluation of all aspects of the process can help determine where you need to expand your knowledge or where you need improvement for your future practice.

In the practicum, you are learning how to become a school social worker through observation of your field instructor and by authentic practice. The field placement experience should be used to help you create and define your style and future social work practice (Columbia University School Social Work Field Manual, 2012). As MSW students, we have been taught to question, evaluate, and critically analyse different theories, models, and sources, and the same approach should be applied when evaluating practising professionals or field instructors. You may have anxiety knowing there is much to learn and experience, but you can take control by taking personal responsibility as adult learners, utilising supervision, investigating, and participating in all aspects of a school social worker daily responsibilities, presenting oneself professionally, networking, and evaluating the process, field instructor, and concentration curriculum.

Not only is self-assessment and feedback from supervisors and colleagues important, every intern must also know how to work on a multi-disciplinary team. Working on a team emphasises the group work experience from social work education and also requires constant communication about the reality of the school system and the needs of the stakeholders. To directly impact planning, collaboration, implementation, communication, and advocacy for students, you must pay attention to group processes, products, agendas, power, group diversity, and other group dynamics. Teamwork on multi-disciplinary teams also means that not everybody at the table may understand the role and purpose of the social worker or intern and verse versa, but must communicate for the benefit of the client. Thus, defining your role in an open context within the school helps others to know your purpose and legitimises the profession and the continued training of new school social workers (Frey et al., 2012).

Some of the collaboration that must take place centres around ethical concerns or direct programming for students. This type of collaboration requires the use of research and theory to ground your decisions and ideas. Ultimately, it will be a collaborative effort between you (on behalf of the school) and the student, family, teacher, tutors, and social worker to identify the need for the services, the areas in which the student needs the most assistance, and the delivery and evaluation of effectiveness of the services. As a result, school social work interns must constantly consult with supervisors and colleagues to determine the most effective course of action to benefit students and their families. Common areas of consultation include confidentiality, sharing resources, use of personal resources to respond to student concerns when the school cannot provide them, calling child protective services, and deciding when a case should be referred outside the school, especially if you are a mandated reporter. Keeping this information in mind will help maintain good professional boundaries with colleagues and minimise challenges experienced in the school context. The confidentiality of the student is imperative, and information should only be revealed to outside parties with the permission of the student, or on a minimal level if absolutely necessary when it is in the best interest of the student. Remember that student success is the most important thing, as this can weigh heavily on the decision and, when in doubt, if you are a mandated reporter, report.

RESEARCH AND ASSESSMENT

Research and assessment involves an evidence-based practice and involved continuous improvement based on empirical research methodologies and data, or, as stated in the professional competencies for social work, "engage in practice-informed research and research-informed practice" (CSWE, 2015, p. 8). As a school social worker, it is important to have basic research and assessment skills to be able to determine the most effective interventions as well as to read and conduct basic research. Evaluation is a common theme throughout the literature on the student's role in school social work practicums. Students will be better able to evaluate the data from the professional practice as they learn methodologies and critical thinking skills so they can assess "the effectiveness of agency policies and procedures" (Brigham Young University, 2012, p. 10). The social workers' intimate knowledge of personal skills and training as it applies to the school and community needs to be communicated to the staff in order to share in the control of the evaluation process. Basic research skills include information literacy skills and understanding statistical analysis and results, differences between populations, samples, interventions, and study and comparison groups. In the implementation, students should be able to carry out basic pre- and post-test assessments, surveys, and polls, in addition to collecting, analysing, interpreting, and sharing results. Much of this work determines the assessments chosen and used by school social workers.

For instance, Steinberg (2011) conducted a study to determine if the students in Chicago Public Schools (CPS) use SES and, if so, what type of student is more likely to utilise and benefit from these services. Through his research, Steinberg (2011) determined that prior-year cognitive achievement and disciplinary infractions strongly influenced the likelihood that a student would utilise SES with disciplinary infractions having a larger negative effect. He found that students with lower prior-year cognitive achievement and fewer disciplinary infractions were more likely to participate in SES (Steinberg, 2011). Steinberg suggests that "policies such as voluntary tutoring may help to reduce the achievement gap within (and between) schools, to the extent that participating students realize a positive educational benefit to their participation" (2011, p. 177).

He also notes that proactive efforts on the part of the SES program to communicate the services and benefits to parents of lower-achieving children may help to engage those students in services (Steinberg, 2011).

This type of study shapes the work of the school and the workers and can inform changes in your own school system. For instance, most students who have behavioural and disciplinary problems are less likely to be motivated to do well in school and may not be engaged in the learning process. On the other hand, the students who do not have a significant number of disciplinary infractions seem to be more motivated and engaged in their learning. This is promising, but at the same time frustrating. It is difficult to see so many children not succeeding and at the same time not willing to utilise additional resources to facilitate their learning. Therefore, research can be used as a way to introduce new interventions and services to the students and their families. Research can help determine how change can be made.

Assessment is essential to determining effective treatment; it prevents an uninformed approach and reduces the implementation of routine interventions. Assessment creates a framework to understand the clients' current situations and factors that may contribute to their presenting problems (Bisman, 2001). Accordingly, it sets the stage for the work that will be done with the client from the beginning to end (treatment planning to interventions). In social work, a popular form of assessment besides genograms, client self-reports, and ecomaps is biopsychosocial spiritual assessments. This form of assessment is based on the unique circumstances of an individual, group, or family. It is an ongoing process that often begins in the first or second session with a client. Information is gathered via qualitative and quantitative measures (goal attainment scaling and scaling questions or scales). Qualitative measures allow for a more detailed picture of a client's problem (a genogram) while quantitative techniques provide a way to operationally define a client's problem (a scale) (Jordan, 2008). Other information is gained via an in-depth interview aimed at understanding a client's situation, the use of critical thinking skills, knowledge of theory, and the experience of eliciting client input.

In schools, the Functional Behavioral Assessment (FBA) is the most common form of assessment. The FBA provides insight into where the behaviour was occurring, how often the behaviour was occurring, what was causing the behaviour, and some possible replacement behaviours. The FBA is also a good option because it requires input from multiple parties involved, including the student, the family, teachers, and staff, as a way of providing a well-rounded perspective of the problem behaviour. The assessment could include a classroom observation of the student to identify and help operationalise problem behaviour, an interview with the student to become more familiar with the student's academic abilities and attitudes towards school, and identification of strengths that can be used in the intervention phase. The questions included on the FBA form include inquiries about the child's strengths, what their behaviour is like at home, the parent or guardian's perception of the function of the behaviour, other health issues such as medications or mental health counselling, and student resources outside the school. The intern can also examine grades, attendance, and reports from teachers and include feedback from the teachers in the form of a Brief Functional Assessment Interview that they were to fill out. The feedback forms may provide valuable insight as to when and where the behaviours are occurring most often. In analysing the assessment, sitting down with the student and talking about what was found is helpful for developing a plan for the next steps. It is important to realise that if the assessment is not accurate, the intervention will not relate to the client's problems (Bisman, 2001); theory can help guide this assessment.

Theory Application and Evaluation

Theory application and evaluation involves not only a deep understanding of the accepted theories and models in the field including both human behaviour theories and practice theories, but also the ability to apply that theory in practice to identify important information, explain and evaluate contexts, and make effective decisions about interventions (CSWE, 2015; Gentle-Genitty, Chen, Karikari, & Barnett, 2014). Students entering a school for practicum placement must integrate theory. Integration relies on knowledge of the foundational concepts, theories, and skills of social work practice and the ability to integrate those into practicum placement through theory application. Theory application is a social worker's ability to examine a client situation by determining the best approach guided by theory research, the best course of assessment, the appropriate interventions for change and goal setting, and knowledge for termination, all guided by theory research. Together, the process forms a theory case plan based on theoretical knowledge to respond to the complex client situation.

A common theme throughout the literature is the students' understanding of systems theory and ecological perspective when entering a school. Payne states that systems theory and ecological perspective focus on the individual both as a part of and interacting with other systems in complex ways (2005). The ecological perspective has proven invaluable in gaining a better understanding of children's needs and how different each student's situation is.

However, it is not only theory knowledge and comprehension that is important. Each student entering the school social work practice world must be able to apply various theories to the school system and its members. The theories of importance range from life course, lifespan, and developmental and attachment theory to the foundation systems, ecological, empowerment, role, and structural functionalist theories. Each theory helps to explore and understand the student as they interact with their varied environments at multiple system levels (micro, meso, macro, exo).

An illustrative example is that of an intern using the ecological theory. The intern was asked to work with a local student to respond to a client situation. The intern not only spoke with the child, but also observed his behaviour in class, the lunchroom, and in the hallways during passing periods. He spoke with the child's mother over the phone to understand their relationship and his life at home, and he accessed school data that included his grades and attendance to determine how the student was performing. He used both systems theories to explore the various subsystems within which the client interacted and explored the relationships and interactions through the lens of ecological theory grounded in development theory. Following the assessment phase, he determined that the student was having difficulty in several different environments and decided to continue using the ecological theory for the intervention. This choice enabled him to intervene with the student, the child's mother, and the child's teacher to determine how interventions in each of these areas would benefit the child. He had buy-in from all parties so monitoring the effectiveness of the intervention was easily doable and provided prompt feedback about how the student interacted with his environment and vice versa. The collaborative process helped show the student all the different sources of support that were available to him. His family, teachers, administrators, and social workers also wanted to see him succeed and were working to helping him meet that goal. The process also kept all involved parties accountable, knowing that colleagues were aware of the work and progress. In the end, the family also felt empowered by the collaborative process, as their input was greatly needed and appreciated, and it was evident in the mother's sense of relief that there were so many people who were concerned with the academic, social, and behavioural well-being of her son. The ecological theory helps to identify and respond to many school situations. The systems that encompass the life of a student are complex and very interconnected. Therefore, it is important to assess the situation for the child from all angles to pinpoint the place for effective intervention. The inclusion of interdisciplinary staff as part of the ecological approach helps to provide multiple perspectives regarding the same situation. It is invaluable to have the insight of the child, the parent, the child's peers, his teachers, his administrators, and other school staff working towards helping a single struggling student.

Theory is at the centre of the work of social work interns, and they can rely on the strong research background and previous success that comes with effective theory application (Bye & Alvarez, 2007). The difference between an expert and a novice in practice is the infusion and constant use of theory. Entering student interns have theory knowledge readily available and can use this as their bridge to a flourishing school social work career. This comes with the responsibility to also analyse and evaluate theory effectiveness. For instance, Payne (2005) analysed the systems and ecological theories as often working to determine the best fit for an individual, but they fail to address necessary radical changes in the environment. There are times, when trying to create a good fit for the student in their own environment that the worker fails to change the environment to better suit the student. Yet, with continued practice and further knowledge, interns will be more cognisant of situations such as this one and work more effectively for larger, macro-level changes that can improve the environment for many clients. This change comes with a plan for continued collaboration, learning, and growth grounded in communication.

DISCUSSION ON A GRADUATED ABILITY TO COLLABORATE AND COMMUNICATE

In many systems of care, there is a discussion of graduated sanctions, and it is no different for school social work (see, e.g., NCJFCJ, 2015). This is the process that takes place when it is known that a person will either leave soon or enter a new system and will soon need to be prepared with a certain skill set or plan. In school social work, the concern is that interns will move into full-paid school social worker positions. In these positions, they must gradually move from their student roles, where they can ask the questions that some may think as obvious or unimportant, to roles where they will be the ones supervising new interns and should have answers to the interns' questions. In this process of graduated ability, the social work intern must learn the value of collaboration and communication and do so by learning the overt and covert expectations of collaborations and communication. This also means that rather than attending every meeting, sitting on every committee, meeting with every student, and following-up on each suggested meeting with a parent, school official, or related stakeholder, that you explore the who, what, where, why, and sustenance of these activities. Learning the administrative components of these processes and policies enables interns to easily transition to their new roles as school social workers. The transition then becomes clearer, and expectations are more evident. Interns can learn to plan the meetings, understand, and write policy; know when parents and teachers and other personnel should be invited to meetings; know what funds go into sustaining their position and offering programs; and know the who, what, when, where, and why of their school.

Collaboration is the next factor in this graduated ability. To collaborate well, interns must have social buy-in and know how to use the social credit of those that have been shared with you. Each new intern borrows the influence and social credit of their field supervisor to establish and maintain effective collaborations in the school. In every school, the new intern will be welcomed with a new group of students and staff and little knowledge of their relationships, but with the expectation that they will help to bring and bridge change. The roles may be different, some having more tasks, experiences, and exposure than others, but the primary task is to take responsibility and use the supervision of the field instructor as a crucial component to the learning process. Field instruction is an essential learning tool for students preparing to become professional social workers. The best way to use supervision and seminar education effectively and efficiently is to be prepared. For example, if you meet a student who is struggling with a particular issue for which you have no experience, research information regarding the issue, explore social work theories related to it, and evaluate best practices in assessment and intervention with the particular case. By doing so, you can return to supervision or seminar with specific questions and some basic knowledge of the issue. The school day can be unpredictable, and crises can arise at any moment—be prepared, and do not rely on the assumption that you will have long periods of supervision to teach you everything you need to know that was not covered in your education. Yet, limiting your exposure to only your own field instructor does not allow you to broaden your understanding of the field, nor is it effective for a good evaluation of the process. Take the opportunity to shadow, interview other school social workers, and observe different approaches, techniques, styles, and roles. Observing the different strengths and sometimes weaknesses of practising professionals and their varying roles and responsibilities will help you better evaluate your needs as a student learning to become a school social worker. It will provide insight on areas, skills, and competencies you want to develop further.

Collaboration and communication also require effective responses during crises. Interns will find themselves arguing for students' rights to confidentiality as they have built a bond and trust in the relationships they have with you. These concerns will also come as interns prepare to leave and come to the end of their placement at the school and terminate their caseloads. Supervisors can help you to respond the best way possible. In addition to a supervisor, the Social Work Code of Ethics can serve as a guide. Study and know the sections well enough to be able to quickly turn to the relevant section when responding to a situation. For instance, Section 1.07 of the NASW Code of Ethics (2011) details the right of the client to privacy and that information is to be kept confidential unless expressly permitted to be shared by the client, or if the practitioner has a duty to report abuse, neglect, or harm to self or others. At the same time, it is critical to be fully aware of the student's developmental level to be able to assess if they have advanced enough executive functioning to consent to sharing information that will better inform the teacher and help the student in their school performance and experience. The Code also helps us to know the value of self-determination (Section 1.02).

Having background knowledge of a model to respond to other dilemmas is also imperative to successful collaboration. The Congress (2008) ETHIC model (Examine, Think, Hypothesise, Identify, and Consult) can help assess the situation and provide recommendations concerning courses of action. The first step is to examine personal, societal, agency, client, and professional values. Our professional values state that the student has a right to privacy. Society may have a differing opinion, in that there may be a belief that children are not knowledgeable or aware enough to make their own decisions. The second step is to gather information about ethical standards, confidentiality, laws, legal obligations, etc. The third step is to hypothesise possible consequences and benefits of different decisions to take into account the relationship. The fourth step is to identify who may benefit and who may be harmed because of the decision. The last step is to consult and gather as much information as possible to make the best decisions and choices for a course of action. The teachers may feel like they cannot fully help the child to be successful if they do not have a full understanding of the situation; but, it is also important to evaluate how negatively the child could be affected if this information is shared or if it is not must also be evaluated.

Conclusion and Recommendations

After reviewing the literature, the social work student roles entering a school internship or practicum placement is an area that has not been adequately researched. The literature is focused more towards practitioners entering schools as social workers rather than social work students entering schools as part of their internships, practicums, and field instruction. This highlights the importance of more work in this area to educate interns. Social workers in the schools have many roles, as do the students placed in schools for their practicums or internships. In order to benefit from the practical internship, the student entering the school must have a clear definition of their roles in the school and expectations of those roles. Interns entering a school must have knowledge based on social work theory and application of that knowledge to practice, self-awareness of needs and skills, professional demonstration of personal attributes, and active involvement in the evaluation process. Despite the best preparation, inevitably, things may not always go as planned. When this happens, flexibility and adaptation become crucial skills for the interns to practice. Therefore, there is value in continuing to collect data in the field so we can inform practitioners and those preparing to enter the field about the changing roles of school social work interns and the foundations that must continue to guide their work. The literature and the voices of the interns in this work showcase the need for a graduated ability to effectively collaborate, communicate, and negotiate with all stakeholders in the school to continue to provide the best care possible.

REFERENCES

Berzin, S. C., & O'Connor, S. (2010). Educating today's school social workers. *Children & Schools, 32*(4), 237–249.

Bisman, C. D. (2001). Teaching social work's bio-psycho-social assessment. *Journal of Teaching in Social Work, 21*(3/4), 75–89.

Brigham Young University School of Social Work. (2012). *MSW field internship manual.* Retrieved on December 1, 2012 from https://socialwork.byu.edu/SiteAssets/Field/Internships/2012_2013%20MSW%20Field%20Internship%20Manual.pdf.

Bronstein, L. R., Ball, A., Mellin, E. A., Wade-Mdivanian, R., & Anderson-Butcher, D. (2011). Advancing collaboration between school-and agency-employed school-based social workers: A mixed-methods comparison of competencies and preparedness. *Children & Schools, 33*(2), 83–95.

Bye, L., & Alvarez, M. (Eds.). (2007). *School social work: Theory to practice* (1st ed.). Pacific Grove, CA: Brooks and Cole.

Chapman, M. V. (2003). Poverty level and school performance: Using contextual and self-report measures to inform intervention. *Children & Schools, 25*(1), 5–17. Retrieved from EBSCOhost.

Columbia University School of Social Work. (2012). *Field education manual.* Retrieved from http://www.columbia.edu/cu/ssw/field/manual/fe-manual.pdf.

Congress, E. P. (2008). What social workers should know about ethics: Understanding and resolving ethical dilemmas. *Advances in Social Work, 1*(1), 1–22.

Constable, R., McDonald, S., & Flynn, J. P. (2006). *School social work: Practice, policy, and research perspectives* (4th ed.). Chicago, IL: Lyceum Books.

CSWE. (2015). *Educational policy and accreditation standards for Baccalaureate and Master's social work programs.* Council on Social Work Education Commission on Accreditation Commission on Educational Policy.

Fisher, R. A. (2010). Supply and demand in school social work. *Children & Schools, 32*(3), 131–133.

Forester-Miller, H., & Davis, T. E. (2016). *Practitioner's guide to ethical decision making* (Rev. ed.). Retrieved from http://www.counseling.org/docs/default-source/ethics/practitioner's-guide-to-ethical-decision-making.pdf.

Frey, A. J., Alvarez, M. E., Sabatino, C., Lindsey, B., Dupper, D. R., Raines, J. C., et al. (2012). The development of a national school social work practice model. *Children & Schools, 34*(3), 131–134. https://doi.org/10.1093/cs/cds025.

Gentle-Genitty, C., Chen, H., Karikari, I., & Barnett, C. (2014). Social work theory and application to practice: The students' perspectives. *Journal of Higher Education Theory and Practice, 14*(1), 36–47.

Indiana School Social Work Association. (2010). *The Indiana school social work manual.* Retrieved from http://www.insswa.org/Manual/SSW_Manual_1_revised_2012.pdf.

Jordan, C. (2008). Assessment. In T. Mizrahi & L. E. Davis (Eds.), *Encyclopedia of social work.* Retrieved from http://www.oxford-naswsocialwork.com/entry?entry=t203.e24.

Kelly, M. S., Frey, A. J., Alvarez, M., Berzin, S. C., Shaffer, G., & O'Brien, K. (2010). School social work practice and response to intervention. *Children & Schools, 32*(4), 201–209.

Lin, V. W., Lin J., & Zhang, X. (2015). U.S. social worker workforce report card: Forecasting nationwide shortages. *Social Work, 61*(1), 7–15.

NASW. (2011). *Code of ethics of the National Association of Social Workers.* Retrieved from http://www.socialworkers.org/pubs/code/code.asp.

NASW. (2015). *Cultural competence in social work practice.* National Association of Social Workers. Retrieved from https://www.socialworkers.org/LinkClick. aspx?fileticket=PonPTDEBrn4%3D&portalid=0.

NCJFCJ. (2015). *Graduated sanctions for juvenile offenders, v. 2,: A program model and planning guide—Dispositional court hearing to case closure* (R. DeComo & E. Wiebush, Eds.). Office of Juvenile Justice and Delinquency Prevention, Juvenile Sanctions Center.

Payne, M. (2005). *Modern social work theory* (3rd ed.). Chicago, IL: Lyceum Books Inc.

Steinberg, M. P. (2011). Educational choice and student participation: The case of the supplemental services provision in Chicago Public Schools. *Journal of Educational evaluation and policy. 33*(2), 159–182. https://doi.org/10.3102/0162373711402991.

Suppes, M. A., & Cressy-Wells, C. (2009). *The social work experience: An introduction to social work and social welfare* (5th ed.). New York: Pearson.

Thompson, A. M., Reinke, W., Holmes, S., Danforth, L., & Herman, K. (2017). The county schools mental health coalition. *Children & Schools, 39*(4), 209–218.

Torpey, E. (2018, March). Careers in social work: Outlook, pay, and more. *Career Outlook*, U.S. Bureau of Labor Statistics, 1–9.

CHAPTER 51

Critical Pedagogy
and Social Work Supervision

Carolyn Noble

INTRODUCTION

This chapter examines the key concepts of a critical pedagogy, its theoretical underpinnings and associated learning strategies as both a process and teaching tool to support critically informed social work practitioners. Social workers are concerned with the 'social spaces' where injustices occur, where people are marginalised, excluded, or stigmatised as 'bludgers' and the like and opportunities for their well-being are denied (Mendes, 2017; Noble, Gray, & Johnston, 2016). Working in the 'social' involves empowering and liberating people from the margins, who are denied justice and human rights. It involves looking at the system of local and global governance, economic, political, and social relations that contribute to their oppression (Baines, 2011). If social work's mission is to foster human rights and social justice outcomes for service users then they require the means and processes to ensure they are equipped for the task (Noble et al., 2016; Noble & Irwin, 2009).

Critical social work focuses on the elimination of domination, exploitation, oppression (internally and externally held) and all undemocratic and inequitable social, political, and economic relations that marginalise and oppress many groups in society; privileging a few, while oppressing the many (Baines 2011; Lundy 2011; Morley, Macfarlane, & Ablett, 2014). So, the questions are: How are practitioners supported in this mission? How do social work teachers

C. Noble (✉)
Australian College of Applied Psychology (ACAP), Sydney, Australia
e-mail: carolyn.noble@acap.edu.au

© The Author(s) 2021
S. S. M. et al. (eds.), *The Palgrave Handbook of Global Social Work Education*, https://doi.org/10.1007/978-3-030-39966-5_51

prepare their students for this task? What educational material, teaching tools, processes and practices are available to equip new graduates with the practice skills to "promote social change and development, social cohesion, and the empowerment and liberation of people" (IASSW Global definition, 2014)?

The answer to the above questions is, I suggest, incorporating a critical pedagogy informed by critical theory for use in social work supervision. This then requires supervision to have a critical lens embedded in its practice. For critical supervision to work an understanding of the context that shapes the nature and context of social work and its impact on what it does, the how and the why is paramount. If social workers don't mark out the social spaces that impact directly on their work and that of the service users, then all this activity and impact is rendered invisible. When invisible the politicians and power elites can exclude the poorer and marginalised members of society and leave them excluded, impoverished. They can cut services, deny there is a problem with poverty, inequality, violence, discrimination and minimise or hide the very real impact these practices have on the lives of service users. Not only do the service users suffer but social work goes unnoticed and marginalised too (Hair, 2015; Noble et al., 2016; Noble & Irwin 2009). The first question to address though is what are the challenges in the current welfare landscape that would demand a critical response? What is the broader social landscape and challenges that unilaterally impact on both service delivery and service user's experiences, their issues and circumstances, and how well-placed organisations and practitioners are to address them through the use of a critical approach to supervision? (Noble et al., 2016, p. 40). The following sections explore these challenges.

CHALLENGES

National and Organisational Influences

It is generally acknowledged that the culture and context in which social work is currently practiced is complex, unstable, and increasingly governed by fiscal restraints characteristic of neoliberal economics enshrined in the new public management (NPM) (Chenoweth & McAuliffe, 2015; Hughes & Wearing, 2013). NPM as a practice of economic conservatism has brought with it a new set of management practices that has transformed workplace culture in the human services. NPM management argues in favour of the private sector providing welfare services. It promotes private over public, profit over people, corporations over state supported services, individual responsibility over the social contract. Proponents argue that the private sector is more lean, efficient, productive, and cost effective in providing services and delivering programs. NPM discourse argues that citizenship and economic and social benefits are more efficiently determined by labour market participation, economic productivity, and useful employment! In fact, many who have embraced the NPM discourse publicly abhor the idea of universal or even targeted welfare.

The popularity of NPM is fast becoming the raison d'etre for delivering health and welfare services, assessing suitability attached to that assistance and evaluating their effectiveness. In other words, the human service sector has seen a return to a more conservative policy and a highly commercial agenda relying more on the 'market' than the state for the provision of welfare programs. Accompanying the neoliberal philosophy of market led services has been a gradual attack on the universality of welfare provisions previously supported by more progressive 'left-leaning' governments (Jamrozik, 2009). Calling for an end to the age of entitlement conservative discourse targets people who are unemployed, homeless, poor, disabled, sick and old as draining the limited welfare budget. Services that promote equality of opportunity and protection from poverty are considered too expensive for an underfunded welfare state; the private sector would achieve the same ends but more effectively with less pressure on the public purse. Ideally, the argument goes, is that the public sector should make way for a quasi-market enterprise to contractually deliver programs relieving the Government of any direct responsibility for its citizen's well-being (Mendes, 2017).

Further, proponents argue that welfare spending should be reduced, and some form of paternalistic government regulation should be employed to discourage reliance on welfare, and non-government and/or volunteer services should replace government as main providers of welfare services and assistance for those who fall between the cracks. Individuals should be more proactive in providing for themselves rather than relying on Government 'handouts' (Mendes, 2017.) Individuals and families are primarily seen as responsible for their well-being and productivity and are encouraged to save for, and purchase their own health care, education, social and welfare needs and are blamed if they are unable to provide the funds to buy such benefits that make for a good, healthy life (Gray & Webb, 2016; Mendes, 2017)

This attitude is instrumental in creating a culture of blame. It absolves the state its responsibility to ensure all citizens have access to adequate education, health care, social services, and employment opportunities. This culture of blame also pits people against each other as 'deserving' or 'undeserving' of government help when their individual resources and opportunities are depleted. Indigenous peoples, refugees and asylum seekers as well the unemployed, the aged, differently abled, homeless people, and single women face social stigma, discrimination, and marginalisation as they struggle to provide for themselves in a culture of diminishing government help (Chenoweth & McAuliffe, 2015; Lundy, 2011; Mendes, 2017). This move towards individualism has replaced the notion of the common good; self-regulation and self-management has replaced a collective responsibility for the well-being of people disadvantaged, marginalise, or discriminated in society especially those people deemed unproductive and 'idle'.

Organisational-Workplace

To achieve this efficiency and more productivity, NPM brings into the workplace stringent accountability practices including introducing performance monitoring and measurement indices and risk aversion policies, cost-cutting practices such as staff reduction and restructuring, sidelining or defunding previously available 'free' essential services (such as services for domestic violence, the homeless and indigenous communities) and prioritising other programs such as work-for-the dole (which sits more with its philosophy of work) (Baines, 2011). These changes in the workplace culture coincided with the weakening of the power of the unions to protect workers' rights. Working conditions now include flexible hours and pay and conditions, more reliance on a casualised workforce and use of agency staff, increasing use of volunteers, and relying more on offshore processing and call centres for service delivery rather than direct service provision from qualified welfare staff. Increases in accountability practices and workplace reviews led to other changes in government agencies and organisations delivering welfare services. These included restructures to streamline decision-making, increased profit incentives, clients were renamed as 'consumers', personalisation of services by offering 'consumer' choice and outsourcing services leading to competition among former welfare collaborators and colleagues (Hughes & Wearing, 2013).

The growth of IT services has reduced face-to-face interaction with service users and along with the changes listed above has created a new landscape for welfare delivery and the human service culture. As a result, efficiency, productivity, and cost-cutting have become the norm in providing human service work enabling the government to reduce its spending in this area. These changes have destabilised a previously stable workforce making it extremely difficult to provide service users with certainty, continuity and consistent policy and practice options and standards (Baines, 2011, 2013). This is the climate many social workers are working in thus making the pursuit of social justice informed human rights practice an almost daunting task.

Global Influences

Of course, these national developments are a mirror of the global stage where neoliberal policies of globalism are, via the activities of, for example, the International Monetary Fund (IMF), the World Bank (WB) and the European Union (EU) promoted and, in many cases, enforced globally. It is globalisation that has entrenched capitalism and free market economies throughout the world and has affected the way individual country's social welfare and health systems operate (Noble et al., 2016, p. 43). In fact, many argue that it's the global players that direct and govern (in absentia) western democratic governments (Gray & Webb, 2016; Lundy, 2011). We see this in the gradual adoption of welfare austerity, punitive approaches to individual and social problems and the incursions of for-profit-organisations and interests (such as Transfield and Serco) into service provision consolidating their place as key human service providers (Gray & Webb, 2013; Noble, 2007). This unfettered growth of privatisation of state funded welfare and health services has resulted in welfare provisions becoming lucrative business opportunities for these profit-making industries. Worryingly, not-for-profit organisations are also expanding their for-profit initiatives to cover depleted government budgets (Hughes & Wearing, 2013). A critique of how global multinationals are infringing on welfare and health services is yet to be fully evaluated as most 'Free' Trade Agreements are conduced out of the public gaze and scrutiny (Noble, 2007).

So, What Now?

These are some of the social spaces where injustices occur, where people are denied their basic human rights and placed on the margin or made invisible and thereby excluded from the benefits and opportunities essential to their well-being (Noble et al., 2016, p. 13). All these challenges and changes have had a deleterious impact on social work and how practitioners think about themselves as practicing professionals. These changes are exacerbated by the stressful nature of the human service work, high caseloads, increase work pressures to perform, less contact with service users and more administrative and computer-based work (Chenoweth & McAuliffe, 2015; Hughes & Wearing, 2013). Additionally, there are more pressures to hire less qualified workers. Left unresolved these changes and pressures have resulted in low morale and low job satisfaction, high staff turnover, poor practices, loss of professional standards, and a compromised ability to work productively with service users towards social change and empowerment outcomes. The consequence of a depleted welfare state means that under-resourced and over-stressed workers are the only ones left to battle for adequate services for those who are disadvantaged, marginalised, and discriminated against in mainstream society. Social workers are left alone and unsupported to advocate for those who bear the brunt of social stigma and discrimination from the cultural norms that promote economic productivity as the only means of securing citizens' rights (Chenoweth & McAuliffe, 2015; Mendes, 2017).

It is in this analysis that I argue, along with my more critically informed colleagues, that the human services are facing a moral and philosophical crisis (Hughes & Wearing, 2013; Ife, 2013; Noble et al., 2016). The problems get worse if workplaces do not provide for and support their workers to reflect, strategize, and encourage them to think and practice critically and help them stay true to their emancipatory and transformative values. One way these issues can be addressed is for organisations and managers to support and provide workers with regular and professional supervision. The other is for social work supervisors to adopt a critical pedagogy with a critically informed lens within the supervisory processes to encourage resistance and change in this conservative environment.

Social Work Supervision—Applying a Critical Lens

Social work supervision is generally accepted as a core activity of professional practice whose function is to oversee professional accountability, independent practice, ethical and moral standards and reflection of practice outcomes against professional and organisational goals, processes, policies, and practices (Beddoe & Davys, 2016; Hair, 2015; Noble et al., 2016). More conventional models of supervision draw attention to its administrative, supportive, educational, and mediative functions (Beddoe & Davys, 2016). It is practitioner-centred in relation to the workplace and involves the 'what' and 'how' of the daily work. There are many ways of reviewing the 'what' and 'how' of social work supervision from surveillance to support, from ensuring personal survival against stress to quality assurance, from professional development to organisational constraint, from reviewing and monitoring to improving service delivery and increasing job satisfaction and enhancing professional values and ethics (Beddoe & Davys, 2016; Hair, 2015).

Supervision functions well when organisations see themselves as learning organisations that encourage individual growth in order to maximise organisation's assets and standards. The content can cover practise issues and skill development, linking theory with practice, reviewing past and present cases and activities, refining and enhancing practice skills and knowledge development, reviewing policy initiatives and practice guidelines and planning for the future. Importantly, it provides a space for reflecting on key issues of concern to the practitioners and service users (Noble & Irwin, 2009).

To be effective, practitioners, supervisors, and supervisees must be open to explore a range of conversations, activities, interactions, events, political debates, and organisational behaviours that occur outside the practice domain, particularly those events that impact directly on service users circumstances and opportunities and the broader social work mission as well as those of their immediate practice context. It means that social workers be open to critically reflect on the 'web of connections' that are in play in the lives of service users, the organisations that interact with them and the politics that resource them (Morley et al., 2014; Noble et al., 2016).

Embedded in a working and helping relationship social work supervision provides a safe and supportive space to assist in the maintenance of hopeful, positive practice (Beddoe & Davys, 2016). An even stronger theme that emerges from the progressive debate is that supervision should promote 'deep' learning and critical reflection in preference to providing support, guidance, and professional survival (Noble et al., 2016; Smith, 2011). Its practice should never be reduced to professional surveillance and supporting conservative polices linked to (austere) welfare reform but as a means for practitioners to fulfil their critical mission to promote social change and development, social cohesion, and the empowerment and liberation of people (Hair, 2015, IASSW Global definition, 2014). The supervisors and supervisees who form the supervision relationship are often from the same discipline who share common ethics, values, norms and professional goals, which can help foster a critical dialogue and response (Hair, 2015; Noble & Irwin, 2009).

Critical Supervision—Foundations

A critical approach to social work supervision is to steep the practice and process in critical theory and seek its application so that practitioners and service users can reflect on their circumstances broadly as well as personally. The reflection is to find a path towards a resistance and a change in their circumstances in a way that will enhance their well-being and create a more democratic and equitable social order. It acknowledges that people who are oppressed are subject to unjust systems that do not distribute society's benefits and opportunities equitably (Noble et al., 2016).

Critical supervision is informed by critical theory. Several critically informed options already exist that can inform a critical lens. These include structural and post-structural theory, feminism, social constructionism, constructivism, post-modernism, post-colonial theory and critical multiculturalism, post-conventional social work, new materialism and post-humanism (see Noble et al., 2016, pp. 117–123). Its focus is on understanding broader structural factors impacting on organizations, service users, practitioners, situations, and events. 'Using critical perspectives enables a view of the broader contexts in which organizations function, service users live, and practitioners do their work and the interplay within and among them' (Noble et al., 2016, p. 145). It also maps out a world view and the many facets comprising the socio-political and cultural and economic power plays influencing the broader structural context as well as organizational and professional contexts.

So how could social work supervision assist practitioners link critical theory with a critical practice and what skills and strategies would be useful in this endeavour? Importantly, what would supervision look like if we were to place service users their experiences, values, interests, ideas, and perspectives in the centre of the reflection. That is, what would its pedagogical practice entail? A key tool to get to the hidden context and influences is to engage in critical supervision within a critically informed pedagogy (also see Fook & Gardner, 2007; Smith, 2011).

Critical Supervision and Transformative Learning

Giroux (2011) and Brookfield (2005) as critical educationalists see education as a site of participatory democracy, civil activism, and social change. Knowledge production through learning and reflection has a social purpose. The purpose is to further social justice, keep democracy alive, and citizens engaged in securing their well-being. Its broad aim is to educate practitioners to question the "conditions giving rise to oppression, discrimination, human rights violations and social injustice, yet remain open to diverse perspectives, understandings and forms of knowledge to suit different purposes" (Noble et al., 2016, p. 130).

Critical supervision as a practice pursues social justice outcomes. It seeks anti-oppressive and culturally sensitive ways to review practice processes, context, and responses. The outcome is to create critical practitioners and the best interests of service users who bear the brunt of an oppressive capitalist social and economic system (Hair, 2015; Noble et al., 2016). A critical perspective is about seeing a bigger picture, naming the broader political, social, economic, cultural, environmental, technological factors shaping the immediate practice environment.

To undertake this process shifts the analysis from an individual view of social issues and solutions to the broader societal factors that shape the personal and professional lives of social workers and service users. It creates an openness to focus on social change and social justice outcomes. One aspect of critical supervision is to see individuals, families, groups, and communities as embedded within networks of social, political, economic, and cultural relations or webs of connection. Figure 51.1 sets out the parameters visually.

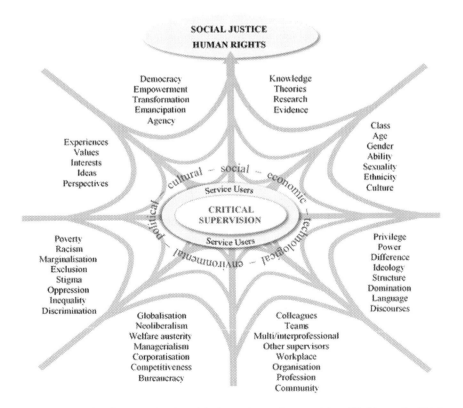

Fig. 51.1 Web of connection in critical practice and supervision (Noble et al., 2016, p. 148)

Critical supervision facilitates an openness by encouraging practitioners to revisit critical theory, explore new ideas, seek out underlying assumptions and motives as well as encouraging questioning of routinised, superficial knee-jerk responses to complex social problems (Noble et al., 2016, p. 131). It is transformative when a new perspective emerges from a critical rethinking of prior interpretations, biases, and assumptions to form new meanings to understand the world and our experiences in it. By reformulating prior knowledge and the meanings and practices attached to it; by critically reviewing the dominant view of practice, policy and socio-political discourses it is possible to emerge from this process as an autonomous, critically focused practitioner (op. cit., p. 138).

Fundamentally, critical supervision is formed through conversations, that are thoughtful, reflective, and use an array of strategic processes, tools, techniques, and skills. Without the appropriate skills and tools linked to an understanding of critical theory and used in a particular way, a critical approach to supervision may stand or fall in its desire to develop critically informed and active practitioners.

Critical Pedagogy

Critical pedagogy is a teaching approach informed by critical and other radical and post-conventional theories and practices which helps practitioners and service users critique and challenge the oppressive structures of the status quo. It is a pedagogy that equips supervisors with the necessary knowledge, skills, and ability for critical thinking, critical reflection, and critical practice. It requires that a critical lens is placed on all practice and organisational interactions from the local to the global; from the individual to the structural. Its practice incorporates constant questioning and reflection and ongoing dialogue and critique of, the socio-political, economic and cultural power relations within the organisation as well as more broadly in the community and society at large (Fook & Gardner, 2007; Noble et al., 2016).

By applying a critical lens to the work and process of supervision practitioners as well as teachers can explore a critically reflective view of the socio-political landscape to support social works' social justice and human rights agenda for societal and individual empowerment as well as its work, interactions, and practice outcomes. A critical pedagogy offers a framework for critical supervision to support the development of critical practitioners to untangle these webs in such a way as to free practitioners and service users from the political, economic, social, cultural, and organisational restraints that limit opportunities for a good life. Critical supervision sees the learning opportunities from this interaction as having a performing and empowering, transformative and emancipatory function (Freire, 1972; Noble et al., 2016; Noble & Irwin, 2009).

It is the position of marginalization that becomes the source of resistance, hope, and focus for supervision. It is the deliberate exploration of stories, collective histories, sense of community, culture, language, and social practices that become the source of power and resistance (Brookfield, 2005; Freire, 1972; Smith, 2011). This is true when reflecting on organizational behaviour as well as interacting with service users. A critical perspective is about questions, reflection, questions, reflection, questions, and so on. Critically informed questions shape the basis of critical pedagogies and encourage open and inclusive dialogues to "help those who seek greater control over their lives to envisage ways to achieve a better future" (Noble et al., 2016, p. 129).

Critical pedagogies seek to:

- *Engage* in forms of reasoning that challenge dominant ideologies and question the socio-cultural and political-economic order maintaining oppression
- *Interpret* experiences of marginalisation and oppression in ways that emphases our relational connections to others and the need for solidarity and collective organisation to others
- *Unmask* the unequal flow of power in our lives and communities
- *Understand* hegemony and our complicity in its continued existence
- *Contest* the all-pervasive effect of oppressive ideologies
- *Recognise* when an embrace of alternative views might support the *status quo* it appears to be challenging
- *Embrace, accept* and *exercise* whatever freedoms they have to change the world
- *Participate* in democracy despite its contradictions (adapted from Giroux 2011; Brookfield 2005 in Noble et al., 2016, p. 129).

The emphasis on using critical pedagogies in supervision assumes that professional supervision is a significant place for learning, review, reflection, and social change. It seeks to open up new avenues for exploration and through a process Carroll (2010) calls 'transformational openness' where we can create 'shifts in mentality' for new voices, perspectives, and understandings to emerge. Models are useful but without appropriate tools and skills used in a particular way and towards a particular end it may not achieve their intention. Indeed, supervision that is unreflective and unchallenging may just support the conservative and NPM status quo. Critical supervision is aimed at developing critically informed and critically active practitioners from a process of learning. This process must be informed by a critical lens.

Linked to critical analysis critical pedagogies are used to draw out our thinking, assumptions, use of language, power relations, biases, prejudices, conflicts, resistances, and beliefs. By placing our practice under a microscope, we open up previously closed spaces to make way for new practice approaches in supervision—practices that help practitioners as well as service users free themselves from oppressive daily habits and customs to create a 'big picture' interaction; one that sees and challenges existing power relations and structure that oppress, marginalise, and discriminate in order to promote human rights and social justice and empowerment outcomes (Hair, 2015; Noble et al., 2016).

Pedagogical Skills and Tools

Here, I identify six pedagogical skills and strategies that will help in establishing a critical narrative for use in professional supervision. These include the use of *critical questions*, *critical thinking*, *critical analysis*, *critical reading*, *critical reflection*, and finally *modelling critical practice*.

Critical questions can encourage deep, sustained, reflective discussions. Open-ended questions can generate new thinking and dialogue as well as reflection and can move the conversations forward. Questions that link to prior discussions can lead to deeper reflection. Hypothetical, cause and effect questions, summary and synthesis questions and challenging questions are all part of the repertoire available for use. Examples include

Me and my supervision

- What do you think a 'transformative supervisor' might look, sound, and feel like?
- How do I feel about being supervised by a 'transformative supervisor'?
- How do you feel about being a transformative supervisor/supervisee?
- What feedback might you invite from service users to enable your practice to be a medium in which all parties might shift perspectives, learn, and grow?

Supervision

- What previous experiences informed your/my decisions/actions?
- What knowledge did you draw on? Explore source, author, date, context, etc.
- What particular theory or theories did you use?
- What values guided your decision/action?
- How did you feel?
- What does this mean? To you, the service user, others involved?
- What were the consequences of your decision/action??
- Who benefitted from your actions and how?
- Who was disadvantaged by your actions and how?
- Were there alternatives and, if so, what are they?
- Were there any constraints on your action, e.g., time, resources, agency policy, agency culture, and your own skills?
- What, if anything, would you do differently next time?
- Was there a desired outcome which was different from the actual outcome? (see Fook & Gardner, 2007; Noble et al., 2016; Noble & Irwin, 2009)

Critical thinking signals a willingness to open our actions and motivations to scrutiny to enable fresh perspectives and understandings to emerge and help form new learning and perspectives. Underpinned by a sense of curiosity and discovery, critical thinking uses analysis to examine in detail what happened and its consequences. Critical thinkers challenge values, ethics, assumptions, beliefs, theories, and practice knowledge to assess the veracity of information, research, and knowledge form diverse sources (Noble et al., 2016, p. 109). For example, it espouses differences between facts and values; between assumptions and assertions, between arguments and actions. Discerning their differences and exploring the impact can create critical conversations, reduce error in assumptions, and identify difference between facts and biases. Some reflection exercises when reviewing practice include;

- What assertions, assumptions and biases are implicit and explicit in my analysis and action?
- Where do these assumptions and biases originate from?
- Is there another way to approach the situation or problem?
- Was my judgement fair and balanced? Is it defensible?
- Are the facts accurate?
- What are the dominant discourses at play here?
- Did I exercise enough curiosity and scepticism while examining them?
- What are alternative responses? and have I explored them fully?
- What was useful, helpful, affirming in what happened?
- Has my thinking changed after this analysis? How? (also see Brookfield, 2005)

Critical analysis seeks to identify the structural factors leading to social inequalities and multiple oppressions in society. It involves breaking down those structures that are seen as harmful divisions with a view of overcoming them for a more equal and just society (Baines 2011). Its strategic analysis seeks to expose vested interests, power monopolies, inherited and 'white' privilege, gender, age and ability bias, elitist practices and unjust redistribution of resources and uneven access to knowledge sources (Baines, 2011; Lundy, 2011). Again Freire's (1972) thesis on how 'education for the oppress' can be a tool for empowerment and social change is still an influential guide to transformative practice. In critiquing the existing social, political, and cultural arrangements it is hoped something better will be achieved. Critical analysis is informed by structural analysis steeped in social justice and human rights tradition (Ife, 2012).

Critical reading can be useful in going over case notes, reviewing research studies, literature, book chapters, journal articles, policy documents, media stories and agency and ethical guidelines. 'Critical reading of our knowledge base enhances understanding, improves thinking, expands horizons and reveals a whole new world of thought and imagining' (Noble et al., 2016, p. 192). It highlights ambiguities, inconsistencies, incoherencies, different cultural and gender basis and the appreciation of these complexities in practice and knowledge construction (Brookfield, 2005). For example, by examining a text for contradictions, biases, unsupported assumptions, social practices and language that oppress others we have the ability to uncover and expose perspectives and interpretations that need challenging, exposing, and repositioning (Fook & Gardner, 2007; Smith, 2011).

Critical reflection places emphasis and importance on uncovering values, assumptions, biases, and how and why power relations and structures of domination are created and maintained and who benefits. According to Fook and Gardner (2007) 'a critical reflective approach holds the potential for emancipatory practice in that it first questions and then disrupts dominant structures and relations and lays the ground for (social) change' (p. 47). Questions focusing on reflection include:

- What are some of the key messages in this text?
- Who is the intended audience?
- What words, language, and statements do you see and hear?
- What are their meanings? and what are the underlying assumptions?
- Whose knowledge is privileged? How?
- What power relations can be identified? To what end?
- What strategies are available for challenging knowledge construction?

Modelling critical practice is about leading with action not words! Supervisors should model critical practice in various supervisory events. They should demonstrate the appropriate use of questions and encourage deep learning and reflection. In modelling a critical practice, supervisors can play an important role in creating and fostering a learning culture in their organisation—a culture that values knowledge, supports learning, and fosters worker expertise. Critical supervisors are also critical practitioners. The key intention in creating a critical perspective for use in supervision is to develop

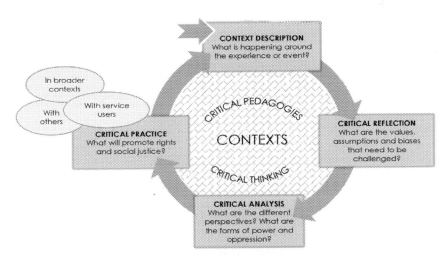

Fig. 51.2 A critical supervision and practice process (Noble et al., 2016, p. 152)

practitioners' ability to counteract the socio-political and cultural constraints currently influencing a more conservative practice—that is to promote a social justice, anti-oppressive informed practice (Baines, 2011). Figure 51.2 outlines the process diagrammatically for a clear statement of how a critical approach for use in professional supervision can unfold.

CONCLUSION

In this chapter, I have outlined key elements for supporting critical supervision and practice. It goes without saying that this process is complex and challenging and requires time, trust, commitment, and professional space to dig deeply into the way power relations and unjust social practices oppress practitioners and service users equally. If practiced with a critical lens professional supervision can provide an opportunity for both supervisor and supervisee to reflect on ways to disengage from oppressive structures with the aim of empowering social work practice and service users alike.

In the current context of neo-conservative politics and NPM discourse professional supervision may be the only available forum to reflect on practice, research and to explore and experiment new sites of resistance and social change. Its use in supervision has the potential to open up discussions and interaction beyond what is known to spaces where new knowledge, theory, practice options, and broader societal concerns are explored. It encourages 'deep learning' that can shepherd a transformational opportunity for new learning. Indeed, nothing begets learning that stimulates curiosity and the desire to learn more when a good supervisor and eager learner meet in a supervisory relationship with an ultimate end to achieve justice for all.

REFERENCES

Baines, D. (2011). *Doing anti-oppressive practice: Social justice social work*. Halifax, NS: Fernwood Press.

Baines, D. (2013). Unions in the non-profit social services sector. In S. Ross & L. Savage (Eds.), *Public sector unions in the age of austerity*. Halifax, NS: Fernwood Publishing.

Beddoe, L., & Davys, A. (2016). *Challenges in professional supervision*. London: Jessica Kingsley.

Brookfield, S. (2005). *The power of critical theory: Liberating adult learning and teaching*. San Francisco, CA: Jossey-Bass.

Carroll, M. (2010). Supervision: Critical reflection for transformational learning (Part 2). *The Critical Supervisor, 29*(1), 1–19.

Chenoweth, L., & McAuliffe, D. (2015). *The road to social work and human service practice* (4th ed.). South Melbourne, VIC, Australia: Cengage Learning.

Fook, J., & Gardner, F. (2007). *Practicing critical reflection: A resource handbook*. Maidenhead: Open University Press.

Freire, P. (1972). *Pedagogy of the oppressed*. Harmondsworth: Penguin.

Giroux, H. (2011). *On critical pedagogy*. New York: Continuum.

Gray, M., & Webb, S. (Eds.). (2013). *Social work theories and methods.* UK: Sage Publications.

Gray, M., & Webb, S. (Eds.). (2016). *The new politics of social work.* Basingstoke: Palgrave Macmillan.

Hair, H. J. (2015). Supervision conservations about social justice and social work practice. *Administration in Social Work., 15*(4), 349–370.

Hughes, M., & Wearing, M. (2013). *Organisations and management in social work.* London: Sage.

IASSW Global definition of social work. (2014). https://www.iassw-aiets.org/global-definition-of-social-work-review-of-the-global-definition/.

Ife, J. (2012). *Human rights and social work: Towards rights-based practice.* GB: Cambridge University Press.

Ife, J. (2013). *Community development in an uncertain world: Visions, analysis and practice.* Port Melbourne, VIC: Cambridge University Press.

Jamrozik, A. (2009). *Social policy in the post welfare state: Australian society in a changing world* (3rd ed.). Frenchs Forest, NSW: Pearson Education Australia.

Lundy, L. (2011). *Social work, social justice and human rights: A structural approach to practice.* Toronto, ON: University of Toronto Press.

Mendes, P. (2017). The Australian welfare state system. In C. Aspalter. (Ed.), *The Routledge international handbook to welfare state systems* Abingdon, Oxon, UK: Routledge.

Morley, C., Macfarlane, S., & Ablett, P. (2014). *Engaging with social work: A critical introduction.* North Melbourne: Cambridge University Press.

Noble, C. (2007). Social work, collective action and social movements. In L. Dominelli (Ed.), *Revitalising communities in a globalising world.* Aldershot: Ashgate.

Noble, C., Gray, M., & Johnston, L. (2016). *Critical supervision for the human services: A socialmodel to promote learning and value-based practice.* London: Jessica Kingsley.

Noble, C., & Irwin, J. (2009). Social work supervision: An exploration of the current challenges in a rapidly changing social, economic and political environment. *Journal of Social Work, 9*(3), 345–358.

Smith, E. (2011). Teaching critical reflection. *Teaching in Higher Education, 16*(2), 211–223. https://doi.org/10.1080/13562517.2010.515022.

CHAPTER 52

Fieldwork Revived in the Classroom: Integrating Theory and Practice

K. Anuradha

INTRODUCTION

Fieldwork plays a pivotal role in the professional development of a social work trainee. There has been a sizeable increase in the literature on this topic and social workers are increasingly getting a better handle on promoting the effectiveness of fieldwork in social work education (Adsule, 2005; Alphonse, 1999; Das & Roy, 2019; Dhemba, 2012; D'Mello & Monteiro, 2016; D'Souza & Sebastin, 2012; Johnson, Bailey, & Padmore, 2012; Mallick, 2007; Roy, 2012; Schmidt & Rauntenbach, 2016; Singh, 1985; Subhedar, 2001). Although fieldwork is considered a medium that ensures professional development, it has time and again been reiterated that fieldwork in social work calls for rigorous integration of theory and practice. It is also pointed out that social work courses often do not prepare students for real world practice (Clapton & Cree, 2004). Hence bridging the gap between theory and practice has been a major preoccupation in social work education since the very beginning (Clapton et al., 2006; Wrenn & Wrenn, 2009). Clapton and Cree (2004) also mentioned that there is a need for learning models that not only integrate theory and practice in ways that bring the field into the classroom but also take the classroom into the field. They further stated that this goal should be pursued throughout students' educational experience and not relegated to a single clinical internship course.

Although discussion on the role of theory and practice in the profession is ongoing, the benefits of applying and integrating theory with practice have

K. Anuradha (✉)
Department of Social Work, Sri Padmavati Mahila Visvavidyalayam
(Women's University), Tirupati, India

© The Author(s) 2021   837
S. S. M. et al. (eds.), *The Palgrave Handbook of Global Social Work Education*, https://doi.org/10.1007/978-3-030-39966-5_52

also been considered beneficial by others (Gilson & DePoy, 2002; Kendall, Adler, Adler, Cargan, & Ballantine, 2008; Royse, 2011; Turner, 1996; Walsh, 2010). It has also been observed that social workers are easily and overly affected by their own attitudes, moods, and reactions when theory and practice are not integrated. This may result in ineffectiveness and inefficiency and even harm clients (Walsh, 2010). There are others who opine that students often experience a disconnect between theory and practice (Vayda & Bogo, 1991) and find it difficult to apply theory in practice (Munro, 2002).

The Need

While pursuing a course in social work it is often observed that students give anecdotal accounts of the nature of their fieldwork. They are unable to make the transition from theory to practice with confidence and effectiveness. This may be due to a number of factors such as belonging to disadvantaged groups or being academically unprepared and lacking familiarity with the academic discourse. It may also be due to subjects chosen during a lower degree level, teaching pedagogies they are exposed to, and failure of the teacher to integrate theory and practice in the same course in the curriculum in ways that are relevant and meaningful to students (Wrenn & Wrenn, 2009). Such students require a carefully selected model or set of methods to achieve expected learning outcomes. So, it is rewarding for a teacher working under such conditions when students show the required growth and development in their knowledge, skills, and attitude. Ramsden (2003) observed that teaching is an important vehicle to promote learning and that teachers must always consider who their students are (Ramsden, 1992); try to understand them in all their complexities, strengths, and weaknesses; and work out how to influence their learning processes.

Hence it is essential that students in professional programmes like social work be able to put into practice what they have learnt in the classroom (Hutchings, 1990) and have training in self-awareness, knowledge acquisition, and skill building (Kramer, 1998). Shebib (2003) also maintained that practitioners need to have skills in four areas: relationship building; exploring or probing; empowering; and challenging. On the other hand, another essential skill is the ability to gain and utilise knowledge from practice (Dorfman, 1996). Mendenhall (2007) opined that for students to develop these skills they need and expect education at the Master's level as well as practical experience.

Gentle-Genitty, Chen, Karikari, and Barnett (2014) mentioned four major benefits of integrating theory with practice: it increases the effectiveness of social work interventions; it promotes confidence among social workers; it provides a valuable opportunity to transfer theoretical knowledge to solve practical problems; and it promotes in-depth reflection and evaluation of theories learnt and their application.

Thus, the primary objective of all professions is that practitioners should be able to integrate their formal knowledge base with fieldwork practice and embed it in their practice (Clapton et al., 2008).

This is an appropriate juncture to define integration. Carelse and Dykes (2013) cited the meaning of integration given by the University of Minnesota as: "Integrating theory and practice refers to the process whereby connections are made between the social work knowledge, values and skills learned in the classroom and the practice experience that individuals face in the field. Students must be given the opportunity to understand what are the skills needed during the interaction, the knowledge that informs the action and the social work values that influence the interaction" (University of Minnesota Duluth, 2013).

It is against this backdrop that the author of this chapter draws from her experience as a social work educator for the past three decades to highlight the scope that exists to integrate theory and practice in social work education through fieldwork seminar presentations, engaging in fieldwork labs, conducting an intervention-based dissertation in fieldwork, and having a theory course on fieldwork as part of the social work curriculum (see next section). Although no research has been conducted into integrating theory and practice in these ways, experience shows that students have begun to understand the need to integrate classroom learning with fieldwork practice. Moreover, since the integration of theory and practice is mandatory, students bend over backwards to make a beginning and every small attempt is appreciated by the faculty.

FIELDWORK SEMINARS (2 CREDITS)

Introduction

Fieldwork seminars are considered a valuable part of fieldwork programmes. They are indeed constructivist in the sense that a learning environment is constructed in which learners are given an opportunity to reflect on their own experiences. They are also viewed as a platform to bring students from different settings together to share any learning, challenges, or issues encountered during their placements (Bushfield, 2005; Garthwait, 2008). Such seminars basically aim to assist students to integrate theory with the work they are doing at their placements and to encourage group support. They also provide opportunities to integrate social work knowledge, skills, and values (Bohanon, 2007) as students interact with each other. Such seminars also forge and strengthen the dialogue and relationship between the training institution, the agency supervisor, and the agency (Sunirose, 2013) and promote cooperation. One study in which students participated pointed out that they were able to reflect upon the usefulness of the learning that occurs during field instruction programmes. Learning like this takes place in many forms such as observations, reviewing case files and documents, report writing, presentations, doing work with clients, and during supervision (Rautenbach & Schmidt, 2016).

Although well-structured fieldwork seminars (while absent in India) are an added advantage for students in Trinidad and Tobago (Johnson et al., 2012), presentation of a fieldwork seminar by students at the end of a semester provides a stimulating and interactive environment.

At the beginning of a semester in a Master of social work (MSW) degree programme the stage is prepared for presentation of the fieldwork seminar. The teacher-cum-fieldwork supervisor assists students to prepare the seminar based on the evaluation criteria given in the following list. Fieldwork done in an agency during the semester is presented by students in the presence of fellow students, faculty, and agency staff. Evaluation criteria fall into three categories:

1. *Preparation*
   - Organisation, structure, knowledge, and understanding of seminar contents (students may quote relevant references as appropriate)
   - Appropriateness and quality of visual aids.
2. *Presentation*
   - Understanding the fieldwork setting
   - Process of work done
     - Identification of needs
     - Planning, involvement, and intervention
   - Integrating theory with practice (as appropriate)
   - Professional development and evaluation (as appropriate)
   - Clarity, presentation style, confidence, etc.
3. *Resourcefulness and thoroughness*
   - Ability to handle questions/comments raised by students and faculty.

Seminar presentation by students using the above criteria has been found to be useful and fruitful for the best part of two decades now.

An Illustration

A seminar on, say, "Fieldwork experience with cervical cancer patients in the Oncology Unit, ABCD Hospital, Tirupati" would typically consist of information related to:

- Details about duration of fieldwork in the agency
- Objectives of fieldwork in the agency (hospital)
- Overview of the hospital and the Oncology Unit in particular
- Overview of cancer
- In-depth overview of cervical cancer

- Psychosocial concerns of patients with cervical cancer
- Practising the methods of social work used in the agency
- Case work
- Group work
- Other activities undertaken in the agency
- Integrating theory in light of the work done
- Describing how knowledge acquired in the classroom and from medical staff in the hospital about cancer was useful in working with cancer patients and their caregivers
- Discharging the roles and functions of a social worker in a health setting and working effectively as part of a team in the hospital
- Dealing with some of the psychosocial issues of patients such as anxiety, anger, helplessness, fear of being abandoned, inability to discuss gynecologic symptoms associated with the illness, worries about family, and lack of awareness of the disease.

Professional Development and Evaluation

- *Knowledge*: connecting with and presenting theoretical knowledge and practical aspects of the disease
- *Attitude*: showing a positive attitude toward fieldwork and clientele and adjusting to the fieldwork setting
- *Practice*: maintaining a strong belief in the worth and dignity of individuals.

Outcome

Students

- Students listen to each other's experiences, ask questions, appreciate the work of the presenters, give suggestions, and on the whole get involved in higher order thinking.
- An environment is created in which students are encouraged to be creative and independent. They write, read, and discuss the material they are going to present with their faculty supervisors before making their presentation. They learn how to make PowerPoint charts and use white boards to explain their work. Many students report improvements in their presentation skills by the end of the course.
- Students also benefit from suggestions given by faculty broadening their perspectives from a theoretical and practical point of view.
- Healthy competition prevails among the students motivating them to present the best of their work from the field and link it to classroom learning.

Teachers

- Teachers learn and assist students in keeping their seminars focussed. This is in tune with Wrenn and Wrenn (2009) who observed that a teacher is both a teacher and learner in the classroom and in the field.
- Discussion sessions that follow seminars bring out the best in teachers. They give teachers an opportunity to share their knowledge and offer concrete suggestions about integrating a concept with work done in the field.

FIELDWORK LABS (2 CREDITS)

Fieldwork based on the philosophy of "learning by doing" provides an opportunity for students to observe and understand the ground realities of the world around them and apply theory learnt in the classroom to such real life situations (Sunirose, 2013). In a lab session less emphasis is placed on transmitting information and more on developing students' skills. This kind of learning promotes issue-based learning that provides an opportunity for learners to think critically and analytically (Oko, 2008) about what they have learnt and how that knowledge can be used in practice (Whittaker, 2009). Moreover, students are given an opportunity to work in groups when it comes to delivering presentations of their lab session and in so doing promotes cooperative learning by maximizing the student's learning and that of others in the group (Carelse & Dykes, 2013).

Lab sessions also promote active learning (Bonwell & Eison, 1991; Coulshed, 1993) and focus on experience (Felder & Brent, 2003; Miller & Boud, 1996). Singh (2013) argued that skill laboratories help students gain insight into the need for skill development and provides ample scope for experimentation. Such simulated situations give scope for learning in a relatively safe environment. Skill laboratories help students learn the skills of planning and organising; develop professional attitudes and skills; make use of various tools such as role-play, simulations, and exercises; develop communication skills, self-awareness, self-evaluation, and time management; and understand the skill development process and the need for module development.

An array of issues related to fieldwork can be brought into the lab situation when looking at matters in knowledge and skills mode such as dealing with a reluctant patient with tuberculosis (TB) who is not adhering to his treatment regimen and alcoholism in the community. Whereas use of certain specific case work principles, understanding the process of working with individuals, the essentials of a home visit, etc. were some of the simplest subjects dealt with in a lab when looking at matters in role-play mode. Use of assessment tools such as genograms, ecomaps, or social network maps (during fieldwork) can be effectively demonstrated to other students and faculty attending the presentation.

Example

- Practice of case work principles (presentation title)
- Lab session sequence
- Objective of the lab
- Brief inputs on different case work principles
- Role-play of case work sessions
- Deroling and discussing the contexts of principles adhered to in sessions
- Discussion and feedback from other students and faculty.

Since fieldwork labs are evaluative they make students realise the seriousness of their task, helps them practise the process of reflection, and helps them build skills related to development of the professional self. The criteria used for faculty evaluation of a student's lab presentation (which carries 2 credits) are:

I. *Introduction of the theme/topic chosen*
   - Background explaining why the topic/theme has been chosen
   - Structure of the session for the day
   - Expected learning outcome
II. *Presentation of the topic and skills displayed*
   - Planning and organisation (as appropriate)
   - Medium chosen (oral, role-play, discussion, case record, etc.)
   - Confidence
   - Clarity
   - Ability to answer questions raised
III. *Content*
   - Information
   - Quantity and quality
IV. *Relevance of the theme/topic to fieldwork*
   - Knowledge
   - Practice

Outcome

Students

- Students usually use role-play mode to present their experiences in the field. This helps them shed their inhibitions and shyness and become more active in the classroom.
- When presenting a lab session students are trained to outline the processes involved in their work.
- Helps students realise that experience is the best way to understand theory.
- Gives students an opportunity to explore their attitudes and values.

Teachers

- Enables teachers to relate theory to practice more effectively in lab sessions.
- Helps teachers become grounded in practice.
- Helps teachers serve as positive role models by encouraging and being enthusiastic about the learning abilities of students.
- Helps teachers acknowledge the feelings of students while doing the assignment.

INTERVENTION-BASED DISSERTATION (4 CREDITS)

Although students at all higher education institutions should experience learning through research and inquiry, this can only be possible if fieldwork experience is integrated into the curriculum (Jenkins & Healey, 2012). Focus should also be on developing students' knowledge of and ability to carry out research methodologies and methods appropriate to their discipline(s) or profession (Healey, Flint, & Harrington, 2014, p. 42). Intervention is one of the core concepts used in social work practice. Although it has not been subjected to conceptual analysis, the emergence of evidence-based research and practice has led to interest in psychosocial interventions (Mittelman, 2008; Salem et al., 2017; Shean, 2014; Thiese, 2014; Waldorff et al., 2012; Wight, Wimbush, Jepson, & Doi, 2015) and reinvigorated interest among social work academics and researchers. Doctoral students are doing research based on social work methods (Sonali Jhanjee, 2014; Baruah, 2014; Amaresha, 2016; John, 2017) Supervising students' research involves a great deal of mentoring by the supervisor. Gershenfeld (2014) in a systematic review of the literature on student research discovered that mentoring involved more than academic support. She found that psychological/emotional support, goal setting, career paths, and role modeling were also involved and made the case for carrying out evidence-based research for each function. She pointed out that mentors in many institutions are themselves students and that this role has often been overlooked. The research relationship between staff and students can be viewed as a continuum with supervision at one end and mentoring at the other (Johnson, 2002).

For some time now there has been an increase in the use of single-subject designs in social work research. Prior to single-subject designs social work researchers had no alternative but to use conventional experimental research designs such as comparing an experimental group with a control group. Such experimental research has often been found to be inappropriate or impossible to conduct in social work practice settings (Das Lal, 2000). Although conventional experimental research is appropriate for some purposes, the drawbacks associated with the method have led social work researchers to look for an alternative approach to evaluate the effects of social work intervention. This is the reason single-subject designs have gradually gained popularity as instruments to merge research and practice.

Although there are different types of single-subject designs, all involve measurements during baseline and intervention phases and comparison across phases as evidence of intervention effects. The simplest and most popular design among social work researchers is "AB: the basic single-subject design" because it involves only one baseline phase (A) and one intervention phase (B). This design is more commonly known as AB design. The letter A signifies the baseline phase and the letter B indicates an intervention phase during which some specific intervention is introduced. In research design such as this the effect of intervention is ascertained by comparing the client's condition during the intervention phase with that of the baseline phase.

Students are encouraged to adopt intervention-based research when writing their dissertations on a topic related to their fieldwork during the final year of their Master's course in social work. Such a dissertation is equivalent to a theory paper carrying 4 credits and has well-defined inputs that are discussed in the classroom to facilitate completion of the work. The following schedule has been shown to help formulate effective intervention-based research:

- Identifying the theme/topic and target group for social work intervention
- Reviewing the relevant literature and finalising the title/topic for the dissertation
- Framing specific objectives and identifying an appropriate tool for pre-intervention assessment
- Deciding on the social work framework/approach to be adopted for intervention
- Preparing intervention modules keeping in mind the pre-intervention assessment tool and the social work framework/approach to be adopted
- Conducting pre-assessment session(s) by administering the tool
- Starting intervention session(s) as per the social work framework/approach and the intervention modules prepared beforehand
- Conducting post-intervention assessment session(s)
- Conducting post-intervention assessment after a gap of 1 week/15 days to gauge the efficacy of the intervention process
- Undertaking statistical analysis and interpreting pre- and post-intervention data, summary, and conclusions
- Submitting the final report on the dissertation.

Intervention-based research adopted by students has been undertaken on dissertation topics entitled:

- Enhancing Awareness in Patients with Cervical Cancer: Use of a Social Case Work Approach
- Efficacy of an Empowerment-based Case Work Approach in Enhancing Subjective Wellbeing of Women Suffering from HIV/AIDS

- Understanding the Self-esteem of Cancer Patients: Use of a Case Work Approach
- Providing Hope for Cancer Patients: Use of a Case Work Approach
- Efficacy of an Empowerment-based Case Work Approach in Enhancing Subjective Wellbeing of Male TB Patients
- Coping in Women with Cervical Cancer: A Social Case Work Approach
- Social Support of Women with Cervical Cancer: A Social Case Work Approach
- Academic Stress in Adolescence: Efficacy of a Social Case Work Approach
- Caregivers' Knowledge about Schizophrenia: Use of a Social Case Work Approach.

Outcome

Students

- Students began to learn the art of higher level thinking and the need for evidence-based fieldwork practice.
- They learnt to integrate the values, principles, and processes of social work methods while doing research.
- They learnt to appreciate the fact that the process of intervention is important and not the outcome.
- Conducting social work intervention-based dissertations helped students understand the nuances of social work theory with specific reference to its methods, inherent skills, and techniques.

Teachers

- Teachers functioned as mentors. Since dissertations carried 4 credits students met the supervisor regularly as per the time schedule. They acted like students. They read, searched the literature, and undertook research during the process to help students identify the appropriate instruments for pre- and post-assessment and to gauge the efficacy of the social work method employed during conduct of the research study.
- Teachers assisted students in synthesising and organising their ideas, information, or experiences into new, more complex interpretations and relationships—such dissertation work was done as a collaborative enterprise between mentee and mentor.

COURSE ON SOCIAL WORK PRACTICUM

A well-defined and uniform curriculum with a strong theoretical base on fieldwork is an absolute necessity in social work education. Although a few schools of social work in India do have a theory course, most have only the practicum. A basic foundation course on social work practicum (fieldwork) will help students integrate theory with practice. Some Indian authors have very clearly laid down the components of fieldwork (Roy, 2012; Subhedar, 2001).

The course content of papers on social work practicum should involve:

1. Highlighting the importance of fieldwork in social work education and how it differs from other disciplines that entail fieldwork
2. Pointing out the components that make up fieldwork such as concurrent fieldwork, observation visits, study tours, rural camp, and block fieldwork—guidelines and processes
3. Practice learning the methods of working with individuals and groups, working with individuals in difficult situations, and the method of community organisation
4. Practice learning the recording in case work, group, and community organisation
5. Capacity building and training programmes
6. Development communication
7. Citizen participation and governance
8. Professional development and evaluation during fieldwork.

This course carries 4 credits and students answer 2 periodic tests, present a seminar, and submit an assignment as part of internal assessment for 20 marks while the end semester examination is for 80 marks. The teaching methodology includes lectures, individual and group activities, and practice sessions on methods.

Outcome

Students

- Students developed more clarity about fieldwork concepts when they were discussed prior to fieldwork practice.
- They learnt the importance of professional development in terms of their attitude and practice. The need to reflect the values of social work and show responsibility and commitment toward themselves and the profession were reiterated time and again during the course. This was duly presented by students in their seminars and lab sessions.
- Above all, students began to learn the need to translate values into practice.

Teachers

- Teachers became more focussed during classes in the sense that teaching this course made them more grounded in their presentation of concrete examples while discussing skills and techniques.
- They were able to relate theory more effectively when they accompanied students in their concurrent fieldwork, study tour, rural camps, and block fieldwork.
- A sense of satisfaction and fulfilment prevailed in teachers since they found the classes more meaningful.

CONCLUSIONS

Social work is a professional course in which educators endeavour to assist students in gaining a solid grounding in theory so that they can be effective practitioners. The classroom is the ideal place to strike a balance between theory and practice so that excellence can be attained in professional practice. This chapter has presented some models that have helped teachers and students maximise their learning. Although no research has been carried out into studying the efficacy of such models, students' communication and presentation skills have improved considerably over the years. Although it is difficult to gauge how much both parties have learnt, nonetheless listening, observing, sharing, and exploring have promoted a sense of camaraderie and healthy competition that are important to professional development.

REFERENCES

Adsule, J. (2005). Fieldwork training for radical settings. *Perspectives in Social Work, 20*(2), 18–24.

Alphonse, M. (1999). Evolution of field action projects. *Perspectives in Social Work, 14*(2), 2–9.

Amaresha C. (2016). *Efficacy of psycho social intervention with siblings of persons with schizophrenia* (Unpublished PhD dissertation). NIMHANS, Bangalore.

Baruah, U. (2014). *A randomized controlled study of brief family based intervention in obsessive compulsive disorder* (Unpublished PhD Dissertation). NIMHANS, Bangalore.

Bohanon, J. (2007). *The perceived advantages of varied delivery methods for field integrative seminar among social work administrators and faculty* (Dissertation). The University of Southern Mississippi.

Bonwell, C. C., & Eison, J. A. (1991). *Active learning; Creating excitement in the classroom* (ASHE-ERIC Higher Education Report No. 1). Washington, DC: The George Washington University, School of Education and Human Development.

Bushfield, S. (2005). Field clusters online. *Journal of Technology in Human Services, 23*(3–4), 215–227.

Carelse, S., & Dykes, G. (2013). Integration of theory and practice in social work: Challenges and triumphs. *Social Work/MaatskaplikeWerk, 49*(2), 165–182.

Clapton, G., & Cree, V. (2004). Integration of learning for practice: Literature review. In *Learning for effective and ethical practice*. Edinburgh: Scottish Institute for Excellence in Social Work Education. Retrieved from http://www.iriss.org.uk/files/LEEP11LitRev.pdf.

Clapton, G., Cree, V. E., Allan, M., Edwards, R., Forbes, R., Irwin, M., ... Perry, R. (2006). Grasping the nettle: Integrating learning and practice revisit and re-imagined. *Social Work Education, 25*(6), 645–656.

Clapton, G. T., Cree, V. E., Allan, M., Edwards, R., Forbes, R., Irwin, M., ... Perry, R. W. (2008). Thinking 'outside the box': A new approach to integration of learning for practice. *Social Work Education, 27*(3), 334–340.

Coulshed, V. (1993). Active learning: Implications for teaching in social work education. *British Journal of Social Work, 23*(1), 1–13.

D'Mello, L., & Monteiro, M. (2016). The need and importance of field practicum for social work students. *International Journal of Engineering Research and Modern Education., 1*(1), 292–297.

D'Souza, A., & Sebastin, K. (2012). Field practicum: Need for evolving best practices. *Deeksha, 10*(2), 33–42.

Das Lal, D. K. (2000). *Practice of social research: Social work perspective*. Jaipur: Rawat publications.

Das, B. M., & Roy, S. (2019). *Field work training in social work*. New York: Routledge.

Dhemba, J. (2012). Field work in social work education and training: Issues and challenges in the case of Eastern and Southern Africa. *Social Work and Society, 10*(1), 1–16.

Dorfman, R. A. (1996). *Clinical social work: Definition, practice and vision*. New York, NY: Brunner/Mazel.

Felder, R., & Brent, R. (2003). Learning by doing. *Chemical Engineering Education, 37*(4), 282–283.

Garthwait, C. L. (2008). *The social work practicum: A guide and work book for students*. Boston: Allyn and Bacon.

Gentle-Genitty, C., Chen, H., Karikari, I., & Barnett, C. (2014). Social work theory and application to practice: The students' perspectives. *Journal of Higher Education Theory and Practice, 14*(1), 36–47.

Gershenfeld, S. (2014). A review of undergraduate mentoring programs. *Review of Educational Research, 84*(3), 365–391.

Gilson, S. F., & DePoy, E. (2002). Theoretical approaches to disability content in social work education. *Journal of Social Work Education, 38*(1), 153–165.

Healey, M., Flint, A., & Harrington, K. (2014). *Engagement through partnership: Students as partners in learning and teaching in higher education*. York: HEA.

Hodge, P., Wright, S., Barraket, J., Scott, M., Melville, R., Richardson, S. (2011). Revisiting 'how we learn' in academia: practice-based learning exchanges in three Australian universities. *Studies in Higher Education, 36*(2), 167–183.

Hutchings, P. (1990, June). *Assessment and the way it works: Closing plenary address*. Association of Higher Education Conference on Assessment, Washington, DC.

Jenkins, A., & Healey, M. (2012). Research-led or research-based undergraduate curricula. In D. Chalmers & L. Hunt (Eds.), *University teaching in focus: A learning centred approach* (pp. 128–144). Camberwell, VIC: Acer.

Jhanjee, S. (2014). Evidence based psycho social interventions' in substance use. *Indian Journal of Psychological Medicine., 36*(2), 112–118.

John, J. M. (2017). *Efficacy of group intervention module for adolescent girls on self awareness* (Unpublished PhD Dissertation). NIMHANS, Bangalore.

Johnson, E., Bailey, R., & Padmore, J. (2012). Issues and challenges of social work practicum in Trinidad and Tobago and India. *Caribbean Teaching Scholar, 2*(1), 19–29.

Johnson, W. B. (2002). The intentional mentor: Strategies and guidelines for the practice of mentoring. *Professional Psychology: Research and Practice, 33*(1), 88–96.

Kendall, Adler, Adler, Cargan, & Ballantine. (2008). *Sociology in our times with contemporary readings* (Custom ed.). Mason, OH: Cengage Learning.

Kramer, B. J. (1998). Preparing social workers for the inevitable: A preliminary investigation of a course on death, grief, and loss. *Journal of Social Work Education, 34*(2), 211–227.

Mallick, A. (2007). Fieldwork training in social work curriculum. *The Indian Journal of Social Work, 68*(4), 573–580.

Mendenhall, A. M. (2007). Switching hats: Transitioning from the role of clinician to the role of researcher in social work doctoral education. *Journal of Teaching in Social Work, 27*(3/4), 273–290.

Miller, N., & Boud, D. (1996). Animating learning from experience. In D. Boud & N. Miller (Eds.), *Working with experience* (pp. 3–13). New York, NY: Routledge.

Mittelman, M. S. (2008). Psycho social intervention research: Challenges, strategies and measurement issues. *Aging and Mental Health, 12*(1), 1–4.

Munro, E. (2002). The role of theory in social work research: A future contribution of the debate. *Journal of Social Work Education, 38*(3), 461–470.

Oko, J. (2008). *Understanding and using theory in social work.* London: Learning Matters Ltd.

Ramsden, P. (1992). *Learning to teach in higher education.* London: RoutledgeFalmer.

Ramsden, P. (2003). *Learning to teach in higher education* (2nd ed.). London: RoutledgeFalmer.

Rautenbach, J. V., & Black-Hughes, C. (2012). Bridging the hemispheres through the use of technology. *Journal of Social Work Education, 48*(4), 797–815.

Rautenbach, J. V., & Schmidt, K. (2016). Field instruction: Is the heart of social work education still beating in the Eastern Cape? *Social Work* (Stellenbosch. Online), *52*(14).

Roy, S. (2012). *Field work in social work.* New Delhi: Rawat Publications.

Royse, D. (2011). *Research methods in social work* (6th ed.). Belmont, CA: Brooks/Cole.

Salem, H., Johansen, C., Schmiegelow, K., Winther, J. F., Wehner, P. S., Hasle, H., … Bidstrup, P. (2017). Family-Oriented Support (FAMOS): development and feasibility of a psychosocial intervention for families of childhood cancer survivors. *Acta Oncologica, 56*(2), 367–374. https://doi.org/10.1080/02841 86x.2016.1269194. Epub 2017, January 12.

Schmidt, K., & Rauntenbach, J. V. (2016). Field instruction: Is the heart of social work education still beating in the Eastern Cape? *Social Work/Maatskaplike Werk, 52*(4), 589–610.

Shean, G. (2014). Limitations of randomized control designs in psychotherapy research. *Advances in Psychiatry, 2014.* Article ID: 561452, 5 pp. https://doi.org/10.1155/2014/561452.

Shebib, B. (2003). *Choices: Counseling skills for social workers and other professionals.* Boston, MA: Allyn & Bacon.

Singh, A. P. (2013). Skill laboratory in social work: An effective tool for developing professional attitude. *Journal of Social Work & Development Issues, 2.* Udaipur School of Social Work. ISSN: 2279-0411.

Singh, R. R. (1985). *Field work in social work education: A perspective for human service profession.* New Delhi: Concept Publication Co.

Subhedar, I. S. (2001). *Field work training in social work.* New Delhi: Rawat Publications.

Sunirose, I. P. (2013). Field work in social work education: Challenges, issues and best practices. *Rajagiri Journal of Social Development, 5*(1), 57–66.

Thiese, M. S. (2014). Observational and interventional study designs: An overview. *Biochemical Medicine, 24*(2), 199–210.

Turner, F. (1996). *Social work treatment: Interlocking theoretical approaches* (4th ed.). New York, NY: The Free Press.

Vayda, E., & Bogo, M. (1991). A teaching model to unite classroom and field. *Journal of Social Work Education, 27*(3), 271–278.

Waldorff, F. B., Buss, D. V., Eckermann, A., Rasmussen, M. H., Keiding, N., Rishøj, S., ... Waldemar, G. (2012). Efficacy of psychosocial intervention in patients with mild Alzheimer's disease: The multicentre, rater blinded, randomized Danish Alzheimer Intervention Study (DAISY). *BMJ, 345,* e4693.

Walsh, J. (2010). *Theories for direct social work practice* (2nd ed.). Belmont, CA: Wadsworth Cengage Learning.

Whittaker, A. (2009). *Research skills for social worker: Transforming social work practice.* Exeter, UK: Learning Matters Ltd.

Wight, D., Wimbush, E., Jepson, R., & Doi, L. (2015). Six steps in quality intervention development. *Journal of Epidemiology & Community Health, 70*(5), 520–525.

Wrenn, J., & Wrenn, B. (2009). Enhancing learning by integrating theory and practice. *International Journal of Teaching and Learning in Higher Education, 21*(2), 258–265.

CHAPTER 53

Civil Society, Non-governmental Organisations, and Social Work Education

Stavros K. Parlalis◉

Background

Social work education and the profession itself internationally have always embraced academic and practical components. Social work as an applied science finds applications in every society around the globe regardless of its kind (urban vs rural) or its level of development (agricultural, industrialised, post-industrial). In addition, social work intervenes in various fields of practice such as use of drugs, domestic violence, and juvenile delinquency and at different levels such as micro, meso, and macro, while working with a variety of vulnerable groups of people or people in need such as those with disabilities and unaccompanied minors. Social workers should clearly have a great range of theoretical knowledge to be able to respond to the needs of their job (Teater, 2014). Moreover, they should have working experience while still in education thus enabling them to test their skills, abilities, and knowledge in practice. Therefore, field placement is considered to be equally important to courses taught in the classroom (Dhemba, 2012). Once this reality is recognised the importance of having good field placements for social work students should be underlined (Williams, 2013). Although field placements should be protective environments for social work students, they should at the same time give them enough space to be productive, promote their ideas and initiatives, explore their knowledge and abilities, and finally test their practical capabilities (Poulin, Matis, & Witt, 2018).

S. K. Parlalis (✉)
Department of Psychology and Social Sciences, School of Education and Social Sciences, Frederick University, Nicosia, Cyprus
e-mail: soc.ps@frederick.ac.cy

S. S. M. et al. (eds.), *The Palgrave Handbook of Global Social Work Education*, https://doi.org/10.1007/978-3-030-39966-5_53

Since the very beginning of the social work profession worldwide the foundation of education and training in the profession was based on theoretical study and practical experience (Freund & Guez, 2018). In most countries and their models agencies voluntarily provide professional social work staff who teach, support, and mentor students as they learn to apply theory to practice, to function in an agency setting, and to develop professional competence (Bogo & Sewell, 2018). Moreover, international social work literature focusses on the importance of one-to-one relationships and how they impact the experience of field education (Vassos, Harms, & Rose, 2018). It should first be underlined that the establishment of clear goals and learning opportunities results in a better placement experience for the student and more productive outcomes for the host organisation (Madigan, Johnstone, Cook, & Brandson, 2018). Social work students in field placement more readily identify professional values, social work knowledge, and ethical action for social work practice (QiuLing & Szto, 2018) and they start to build up their own knowledge of how to engage in relevant, culturally appropriate, and socially responsive social work practice (Gray, Agllias, Mupedziswa, & Mugumbate, 2018). Furthermore, students have the opportunity to respond to the profession's ability to dynamically adapt their roles to meet the needs of different patient populations, employment settings, and interprofessional teams—important elements for social workers in a rapidly changing system (Fraher, Richman, Zerden, & Lombardi, 2018). Lastly, arguments in international literature about best practice principles in social work education have included international field placements (Fox & Hungman, 2018). International field placements "can be instrumental in preparing students for a future career in international practice, providing them with critical cross-cultural learning experiences, different systems of welfare and different perspectives on addressing social issues, as well as providing them with valuable overseas experience, often a prerequisite to securing a professional position upon graduation" (Fox & Hungman, 2018).

Field placements in social work education are not only beneficial for social work students, there are also benefits for stakeholders such as universities, agencies, and organisations offering field placements and wider society too. Nevertheless, preparation is clearly required to have a successful field placement since a number of problems might occur.

The study presented in this chapter scrutinises how organisations and agencies such as local authorities, non-governmental organisations (NGOs), and civil society contribute to social work education by offering and supporting field placements for social workers. Moreover, the chapter discusses the benefits of doing so for organisations and students and explores barriers and opportunities for proposals. The aims of the study and methodological issues are further elaborated in the following two sections.

AIMS/OBJECTIVES

This study aims to identify how organisations and agencies such as local authorities, civil society, and NGOs contribute to social work education by offering field placements to social work students,. Although the key focus of the study was to underline the benefits gained through field placements for the education of social workers, benefits for organisations and service users were also sought. Finally, the study investigated the main problems faced in social worker field placement and how it could be improved.

METHODOLOGY

The current research involved a qualitative study aimed at investigating the importance of field placements for social work education. The decision to employ a qualitative methodology in this study was based on a number of considerations. First, the aim was to explore professional social workers' perceptions of the importance of field placements for social work education rather than testing specific hypotheses. Adoption of an inductive approach could therefore draw conclusions beyond information that can be directly observed (Singleton & Straits, 1999). Adoption of a qualitative methodology allowed investigating the whole process over several years and getting the "insider's perspective [... and] the meanings people attach to things and events" (Punch, 1998). Moreover, a qualitative method enables the researcher to make an in-depth, detailed study rather than making statistical generalisations (Esterberg, 2002). Using such an approach the study aimed to collect data that could answer research questions and could lead to proposals and suggestions on how field placements in social work education could be improved. Therefore, adoption of a qualitative methodology in this study allowed the researcher to capture the perspectives and experience of professional social workers through their testimonies.

Data were collected by means of interviews, which allows the researcher to elicit participants' perceptions and experiences of the issues under investigation and understand *how* and *why* they come to have particular perspectives (King, cited in Cassell & Symon, 2004).

Open-ended questions were used to gain richness and depth allowing the case to be viewed from the participants' perspective (Gillham, 2000). Using open-ended questions gives professionals the opportunity to openly express their views and perceptions on research questions. In this way the collection of data regarding the issues investigated could be more easily achieved. Moreover, such a methodology gives professionals the appropriate space to focus and expand on any issue they consider significant and relevant to the questions posed. Finally, such an approach gives richness and pluralism to the data allowing for the formation of more fully developed answers to research questions. Interview guides comprised 10 questions covering different aspects of knowledge around social worker field placements.

Table 53.1 Participants' working profile

Name	Identity	Years in supervision
1. Uni1	University supervisor	12
2. Uni2	University supervisor	12
6. Uni3	University supervisor	12
5. Uni4	University supervisor	6
3. Agen1	Agency supervisor	10
4. Agen2	Agency supervisor	11
7. Agen3	Agency supervisor	13
8. Agen4	Agency supervisor	14

The scope of this study could not have been achieved by recruiting a probabilistic sample rather than a purposive sample. The only criterion set by the researcher in this framework was professional identity—the respondents had to be social workers either working as field placement supervisors for universities or as agency supervisors. Finally, eight interviews were conducted four of which with social workers working as field placement supervisors for universities sending out students and four with social workers employed in organisations that receive/accept students such as local authorities and NGOs (see Table 53.1). The interviews were conducted between December 2018 and January 2019 most lasting between 20 and 40 minutes.

METHOD OF DATA ANALYSIS: CHOICE OF GROUNDED THEORY APPROACH

The grounded theory approach was adopted for data analysis. An attempt was made in the study to understand the perceptions and ideas of professional social workers working either as field placement supervisors for universities or as agency supervisors.

The first stage of analysis involved transcribing the interviews into the N6 software program. The next step was to work with each individual interview separately. The unit of analysis was the sentence each of which was focussed on separately (Kelle, 2007, cited in Bryant & Charmaz, 2007). Every single item of data was coded. Such a method allowed the researcher to stay close to the data collected and ensure the reliability and validity of findings exported. This was the first step in using so-called open coding—"the basic grounding approach to the data [that] leads to emergent discoveries" (Glaser, 1992)—rather than testing the theory (Dey, 1999). A total of 1586 nodes were created.

The next step involved nodes of the same or similar concepts being identified (Glaser, 1992) and grouped to form categories of nodes with the same content. This led to the creation of 15 categories (see Table 53.2) divided according to their content and based on the properties and dimensions of each node.

Table 53.2   The 15 categories of nodes that have the same content (based on their properties and dimensions)

Human resources increasing the number of working hours available to agencies (1)	*Students are free to take up new initiatives (2)*	*Development of basic social worker skills (3)*
Knowledge update of students (4)	Continuous student flow (5)	Lack of specialised settings (6)
Students become doers (7)	Help given to immature students (8)	Personalised plan for each individual student (9)
Creation of new jobs (10)	Reduction of bureaucracy (11)	Emergency cases (12)
Search and try (13)	Official cooperation between universities and agencies (14)	Students become mature and professional (15)

Table 53.3   Four themes that emerged

Themes	*Categories*				
1. Benefits of field placement	1	2	4	8	10
2. Problems of field placement	5	6	8		
3. Knowledge/Skills gained in field placement	37	7	12	13	15
4. Proposals for improvement	5	6	9	11	14

Connections between some of these categories became clear through analysis. Subsequently, coding occurred around the axis of each category (axial coding). The last level of analysis was selective coding in which categories were integrated to form a theoretical scheme capable of leading to the formation of a *substantive* theory about the field of study (Wester & Peters, 2004, cited in Richardson & Kramer, 2006). Strauss and Corbin (1998) stressed that "if theory building is indeed the goal of a research project, findings should be presented as a set of interrelated concepts, not just a listing of themes." Application of this process led to the emergence of four broad themes (see Table 53.3) enabling the researcher to build a theory capable of answering the main research question.

QSR's NUD*IST (version N6) software program was used as the technical tool to facilitate data analysis. The main benefit of using such computer software was that it allowed the huge mass of data to be manipulated in a more controlled way (Eilbert & Lafronza, 2005; Webb, 1999). It also made categorizing the data much easier and faster than doing it manually. To avoid problems identified in the literature[1] the coding of each interview once finished was reviewed to avoid the problem of misinterpreting the data. This practice allowed the researcher to proceed with other analytical activities such as axial coding and avoided using the software only for coding and retrieving data, one of the main concerns about the impact of computerisation on qualitative analysis (Bazeley, 2007, p. 8).

FINDINGS

The study's findings are presented in this section. An attempt is made to elaborate categories and themes in this section as well. The theme titled "Benefits of Field Placement" comprises categories that explain interviewees' perceptions regarding the benefits gained by both students and agencies during field placement. The theme titled "Problems in Field Placement" contains data regarding problems met during field placement. The theme titled "Knowledge/Skills" focusses on categories that refer to the skills that can be gained by social work students and the opportunities provided for new working experiences. The theme titled "Proposals for Improvement" reflects professionals' perceptions of how field placement could be improved to offer greater education experiences to future social work students. The data are presented under these four themes.

Benefits of Field Placement

Interviewees stated that social work students who spend their field placement in agencies are a very useful source of human resources since "they increase the number of working hours available to an organisation and fulfil some of the organisation's responsibilities" (Agen1). The reality is that since "students are faced and treated as professionals regarding their responsibilities and their rights they intervene in cases and are not just observers" (Agen2). It was also stated that social work students get to realise in real terms how professionals work in all aspects of the job—not only typical cases but also even in emergency cases in which crisis intervention is required. They get a clear picture of wider aspects of the job, "they get to know what is involved in the profession and implement in practice their theoretical knowledge" (Uni2). Interviewees stated that when students are given opportunities by agency supervisors to take more initiatives, they actually act as professionals (Uni1). Moreover, they have the chance to work with different groups of people allowing them to choose those area(s) of work that interest them most. Interviewees widely stated that students have the chance to work on their prejudices and stereotypes such that by the end of field placement they become more mature. Finally, the creation of new social work posts is considered to be one of the best outcomes of field placement (Uni4). This happened in some cases in the past in settings where there was not a full social services agency such as in local authorities or in settings in which social work students had a great impact through their work and interventions.

Problems in Field Placement

Interviewees stated that there are always problems and barriers in field placement. They pointed out the great lack of specialist social service workers, something in which social work students could be given training (Uni1). For example, there are not enough mental health services, something in which students could get involved. Another barrier was that agency supervisors "do not have enough time to offer to a student and do not give them enough responsibilities" (Uni3). Yet other problems are that "some students are not mature enough when they are placed in field placement" (Agen4) and "they cannot respond to the demands of fieldwork" (Agen1). One of the main problems faced by agency supervisors is that there is not a continuous flow of students. As a consequence, by the time field placement is finalised some of the students' responsibilities return to agency supervisors who have to undertake this additional workload. This is a continuous challenge for agencies since they have to carefully design how social work students fit into their workload.

Knowledge/Skills

There are numerous references in the international literature regarding the skills gained through field placement. In line with the literature the interviewees declared that social work field placement arms students with a great variety of skills such as communication, flexibility, interview techniques, improving documents/forms (Agen3), professional identity, and practical techniques. They include getting to know how to handle an interview or how to make home visits (Uni1), actual listening/observation, search, evaluation, information collection/gathering, information cross-checking, cooperation, professional relations, and networking (Uni3). Moreover, social work students get experience in social work with groups, with individuals, and with the wider community. It was widely stated that "it is a great opportunity to personally progress through field placement" (Agen2) and "students have to become doers" (Agen4).

Proposals for Improvement

In this last theme of the study the participants came up with some proposals regarding how social work field placements could be improved. One such proposal referred to the need to reduce bureaucracy (Agen2) like the daily calendar that students have to complete (considered a repetitive practice). A second proposal was the need to create "a personalised plan for each individual student that could be designed during the first 2 weeks of the placement and be followed for the rest of the placement" (Uni4). Another participant stated that "there should be official cooperation between the university and organisations/agencies to agree on all aspects of field placements" (Uni2). Moreover, participants stated that there is a need in Cyprus for specialist agencies such as services for drug users and mental health services. This could enable students to gain experience in settings they did not have the chance to visit in the past.

Discussion

Benefits of Field Placement

To reiterate, social work field placements offer social work students great opportunities to gain experience and in so doing complete their education. What students learn during placement has a direct impact on how they will behave in the future as professional social workers. So it is essential that the learning environment is positive and one in which they can gain as much experience as possible (Flanagan & Wilson, 2018). Parallel with field placement, social work supervision is a crucial part of social work education since supervisors are responsible for monitoring and guiding interns to become effective professional practitioners (QiuLing & Szto, 2018). Supervision provides space for critical analysis to identify and alter the dynamics of power, privilege, and social oppression (O'Neill & Farina, 2018). Moreover, "close supervision based on critical and global perspectives and critical pedagogical practices will be necessary to support and challenge students in entering into critical reflection processes" (Jönsson & Flem, 2018). Therefore, it is essential to stress that supervision has to be provided by a supervisor who works closely with the student (Ibrahim, MacPhail, Chadwick, & Jeffcott, 2014), has the expertise to provide quality feedback (Bernard & Goodyear, 2013), and is committed to assessing learning rather than simply complying with it (Peach, Ruinard, & Webb, 2014). Agency supervisors clearly have to allocate adequate time to social work students for supervision to be qualitative and for the above objectives to be fulfilled. Overall, many studies show that students positively value regular formal supervision and emphasise the importance of a supportive supervisory environment (Roulston, Cleak, & Vreugdenhil, 2018).

Another issue raised quite often in field placement is the creation of new social work posts. Student placements have been viewed as an opportunity to assess the competence of students in practice and whether they would be suitable to recruit (Hay & Brown, 2015). Placement creation involves considerable work to establish and to show agencies how they and their clientele might benefit from such an arrangement (Gray et al., 2018). This is considered one of the most important outcomes of field placements since social worker interventions are valued and recognised. Moreover, it reflects well on the education provider (university). In addition, there are studies showing the advantages of employing students immediately after placement such as they would have already undertaken induction processes, they would be integrated into the organisation, and they would be familiar with staff and with some of the work tasks (Hay & Brown, 2015). Similar cases occurred in one local authority and two NGOs in Cyprus in which new social work posts were created after social work students finished their field placement. In all these cases the professionals concerned (having been previously engaged as students) are still in their posts and continue to offer valuable services. Even though these are exceptional and rare cases, they reveal the importance of field placements not only for social work students but also for the organisations/agencies.

Moreover, field placements offer great opportunities for schools to collaborate with organisations and entities that may have little understanding of the social work role or the needs of the student. For example, Gray et al. (2018) stated that "some social work programmes had developed significant partnerships with schools allowing for a number of students to be placed simultaneously, conducting activities such as assessments, providing group and community education, awareness campaigns and developmental projects." This is also true in the Cypriot context where many attempts have been made for universities to collaborate with organisations that had little understanding of the social work role in recent years. Such organisations included the armed forces and public schools. Although there are many references in the international literature regarding social work in both fields, they are considered to be totally new social work field placements in Cyprus. The experience of supervisors and supervisees revealed that both placements are challenging and demanding. Furthermore, while these environments offered considerable benefits to students and service users, it has been pointed out that students sometimes are exposed to situations that they are too inexperienced to address. Moreover, students who were not given the chance of social work placements missed important opportunities to get involved in social work. They suggested that any opportunity to observe social workers in practice would have helped to define their understanding of what is involved in professional social work (Roulston et al., 2018). Therefore, in similar cases it is necessary to offer adequate supervision to prevent students from feeling vulnerable and stressed (Gray et al., 2018).

Problems in Fieldwork Placement

Student immaturity was raised as a problem that agency supervisors have to face in field placement. The international literature states that some students have difficulties in translating theory to practice in the field (Beytell, 2014; De Jager, 2013) or in translating academic competencies to the practice setting in a designated and constrained period (Molina et al., 2018, p. 19). Students who struggle to develop positive relationships with colleagues or do not seem suited to the work are often less open to the learning opportunities available, do not take responsibility for their actions, or exhibit a lack of adaptability (Hay & Brown, 2015). Moreover, there are studies showing that when social work students start an internship they are given a short time frame in which to complete the learning contract (Molina et al., 2018). Moreover, the international literature states that universities make efforts to prepare students through a range of experience-based, practical, on-campus activities, excursions, and projects in which students are linked with key agencies (Gray et al., 2018).

In addition to these problems a recent study across six Australian universities "has highlighted how compulsory field placements for social work students can heighten the financial hardship already experienced by many students" (Baglow & Gair, 2018). This is sometimes the case in Cyprus since students have to travel many kilometers to reach field placement settings. One of the main problems raised in the literature is that there are difficulties in finding suitable field practice placements for students (Ross & Ncube, 2018). Such a situation is common to postgraduate students who have little option but to attend specialised field placement settings as a result of there being so few field placements with these characteristics (e.g., there is only one mental health hospital in the Republic of Cyprus). They are obliged to visit these settings regardless of the distance from their home/hometown.

Another problem raised by agency supervisors is that the flow of students placed with them is not continuous. As a consequence professional social workers have to take on the workload of students when their field placement comes to an end. Although such a problem could be resolved by allocating social work students to specific organisations on an ongoing basis, this could prevent them from having the opportunity to visit different field placements where they could gain valuable experience.

Knowledge/Skills

The skills acquired during field placement are one of the main advantages of social work education. Training given in how to function in the field demands skills that differ from those necessary for success academically (Levinger & Segev, 2018). Social work education therefore depends on field placement to equip future social workers with all the necessary skills. Placement experience is critical to the development of practice skills and to integrating students into the social work profession (Elpers & FitzGerald, 2013). An important skill for students to acquire is the ability to self-assess (Jackson, 2018) that gradually builds as students hone their ability to evaluate performance. Other skills acquired through supervision include goal setting, report writing, learning how to integrate theory with practice through the provision of examples, role-play, and group discussions (Ross & Ncube, 2018). Moreover, students often feel that feedback received through supervision is constructive and motivates them to learn new skills and acquire new knowledge (Ross & Ncube, 2018). Finally, the commitment supervisors demonstrate to ensuring that students are able to grow, learn, and become more professional social workers is itself a success that should be highlighted and further explored (Canavera & Akesson, 2018).

Proposals for Improvement

Lastly, participants made very interesting and useful proposals about how to improve field placement in social work education. One proposal pointed out the need for there to be agencies that offer specialised services such as mental health services in which social work students could do their placements. Moreover, agencies should be relevant to the course and support and understand the reasons for student placements (Ross & Ncube, 2018). Such a need could be covered by promoting international field placements that "provide a crucial link between the underlying principles of international social work practice and the demands of an internationalised educational environment" (Fox & Hungman, 2018). This represents a new trend internationally that could be extremely beneficial to students.

Another proposal referred to the need to create a personalised plan for each individual student. This proposal chimes with references found in the international literature according to one of which "these individual learning contracts are twofold. Firstly, the process of developing a learning contract facilitates communication and the engagement of all stakeholders. Secondly, the learning contract aligns with the learning objectives and ensures that the activities undertaken are appropriate for building OHS capability" (Madigan et al., 2018). Such engagement requires supervisors to understand internship requirements, to be more supportive and less judgemental of students, to be briefed on what is expected in reports, and to be aware of the need to assist students with theory integration (Ross & Ncube, 2018). Yet another proposal called for the grading of practice skills within social work education to be introduced (Domakin & Forrester, 2018) such that there is a common understanding of the tasks students should carry out and the responsibilities they should be given.

Another suggestion made by participants was the need to get universities and agencies to cooperate on an official basis. The aim here was to create close bonds between the two entities and bring education closer to the realities of doing the job. For example, there are studies arguing for closer collaboration between employers and educators so that academic institutions can modify the curriculum to respond to the needs of, say, a rapidly changing healthcare system (Fraher et al., 2018). Along the same lines social work education needs to prepare students to work in a new global environment (Jönsson & Flem, 2018).

CONCLUSION

This chapter focussed on how organisations and agencies such as local authorities, NGOs, and civil society contribute to social work education by offering and supporting social worker field placements. Field placements in social work education clearly offer many benefits to the stakeholders involved (universities, organisations, and civil society). Nevertheless, there are still many problems and barriers that all parties will have to overcome to improve such an educational process. With this end in mind the study presented in the chapter concluded by making some proposals aimed at improving overall social worker field placement. The adoption of such proposals will enable social work students to gain more experience and lead to their becoming better qualified social work practitioners (Bogo, 2015).

NOTE

1. Such problems include: "distancing" the researcher from the data (Bazeley, 2007, p. 8; Morison & Moir, 1998, p. 115); the danger of "forgetting that all analysis should be well grounded in the data" (Gibbs, 2002, p. 12; Webb, 1999, p. 325); "the researcher must keep going back and forth between the complete text and the codes in order not to fragment or decontextualise data and thus misinterpret them" (Webb, 1999, p. 325).

REFERENCES

Baglow, L., & Gair, S. (2018). Australian social work students: Balancing tertiary studies, paid work and poverty. *Journal of Social Work, 19*, 1–20.

Bazeley, P. (2007). *Qualitative data analysis with NVivo*. London: Sage.

Beytell, A. M. (2014). Fieldwork education in health contexts: Experiences of fourth-year BSW students'. *Social Work/MaatskaplikeWerk, 50*(2), 170–193.

Bernard, J., & Goodyear, R. (2013). *Fundamentals of clinical supervision* (5th ed.). Boston, MA: Pearson.

Bogo, M. (2015). Field education for clinical social work practice: Best practices and contemporary challenges. *Clinical Social Work Journal, 43*(3), 317–324.

Bogo, M., & Sewell, K. M. (2018). Introduction to the special issues on the supervision of staff and field education of students. *Clinical Social Work Journal, 46*, 249–251.

Bryant, A., & Charmaz, K. (2007). *The SAGE handbook of grounded theory*. London: Sage.

Canavera, M., & Akesson, B. (2018). Supervision during social work education and training in Francophone West Africa: Conceptual frameworks and empirical evidence from Burkina Faso and Côte d'Ivoire. *European Journal of Social Work, 21*(3), 467–482.

Cassell, C., & Symon, G. (2004). *Essential guide to qualitative methods in organizational research*. London: Sage.

Dhemba, J. (2012). Fieldwork in social work education and training: Issues and challenges in the case of Eastern and Southern Africa. *Social Work and Society, 10*(1), 1–16.

De Jager, M. (2013). How prepared are social work practitioners for beginners' practice? Reflections of Newly Qualified BSW Graduates'. *Social Work/ MaatskaplikeWerk, 49*(4), 469–480.

Dey, I. (1999). *Grounding grounded theory: Guidelines for qualitative inquiry*. San Diego, CA: Academic Press.

Domakin, A., & Forrester, D. (2018). Putting practice at the heart of social work education: Can practice skills be reliably graded by different markers in child and family social work contexts? *Social Work Education, 37*(1), 66–77.

Eilbert, K. W., & Lafronza, V. (2005). Working together for community health— A model and case studies. *Evaluation and Program Planning, 28*, 185–199.

Elpers, K., & Fitzgerald, E. A. (2013). Issues and challenges in gatekeeping: A framework forimplementation. *Social Work Education, 32*, 286–300.

Esterberg, K. G. (2002). *Qualitative methods in social research*. Boston, MA: McGraw-Hill.

Flanagan, N., & Wilson, E. (2018). What makes a good placement? Findings of a social work student-to-student research study. *Social Work Education, 37*(5), 565–580.

Fox, M., & Hugman, R. (2018). International field placements: The models Australian social work programmes are currently using. *International Social Work, 62*, 1–13.

Fraher, E. P., Richman, E. L., Zerden, L., & Lombardi, B. (2018). Social work student and practitioner roles in integrated care settings. *American Journal of Preventive Medicine, 54*(653), 281–289.

Freund, A., & Guez, G. (2018). Intentions to leave supervision among social work supervisors: contributing factors. *Social Work Education, 37*(4), 458–471.

Gibbs, G. (2002). *Qualitative Data Analysis Explorations with NVivo*. Buckingham: Open University Press.

Gillham, B. (2000). *Case study research methods*. London: Continuum.

Glaser, B. G. (1992). *Basics of grounded theory analysis*. California: Sociology Press.

Gray, M., Agllias, K., Mupedziswa, R., & Mugumbate, J. (2018). The expansion of developmental social work in Southern and East Africa: Opportunities and challenges for social work field programmes. *International Social Work, 61*(6), 974–987.

Hay, K., & Brown, K. (2015). Social work practice placements in Aotearoa New Zealand: Agency managers perspectives. *Social Work Education, 34*(6), 700–715.

Ibrahim, J., MacPhail, A., Chadwick, L., & Jeffcott, S. (2014). Interns' perceptions of performance feedback. *Medical Education, 48*(4), 417–429.

Jackson, D. (2018). Challenges and strategies for assessing student workplace performance during work-integrated learning. *Assessment & Evaluation in Higher Education, 43*(4), 555–570.

Jönsson, J. H., & Flem, A. L. (2018). International field training in social work education: Beyond colonial divides. *Social Work Education, 37*(7), 895–908.

Levinger, M., & Segev, E. (2018). Admission and completion of social work programs: Who drops out and who finishes? *Journal of Social Work, 18*(1), 23–45.

Madigan, C., Johnstone, K., Cook, M., & Brandson, J. (2018). Do student internships build capability?—What OHS graduate really think. *Safety Science, 111*, 102–110.

Molina, V., Molina-Moore, T., Smith, M. G., & Pratt, F. E. (2018). Bridging education and practice with a competency-based learning contract. *Journal of Teaching in Social Work, 38*(1), 18–27.

Morison, M., & Moir, J. (1998). The role of computer software in the analysis of qualitative data: Efficient clerk, research assistant or Trojan horse? *Journal of Advanced Nursing, 28*(1), 106–116.

O'Neill, P., & Fariña, M. (2018). Constructing critical conversations in social work supervision: Creating change. *Clinical Social Work Journal, 46*, 298–309.

Peach, D., Ruinard, E., & Webb, F. (2014). Feedback on student performance in the workplace: The role of the workplace supervisors. *Asia-Pacific Journal of Cooperative Education, 15*(3), 239–249.

Poulin, J., Matis, S., & Witt, H. (2018). *The social work field placement: A competency-based approach*. London: Springer.

Punch, K. F. (1998). *Introduction to Social Research: Quantitative and Qualitative Approaches*. London: Sage.

QiuLing, A., & Szto, P. (2018). Research on the relationship between supervisor and social work interns in China: A Shanghai case study. *International Social Work, 62,* 1–13.

Richardson, R., & Kramer, E. H. (2006). Abduction as the type of inference that characterizes the development of a grounded theory. *Qualitative Research, 6*(4), 497–513.

Ross, E., & Ncube, M. E. (2018). Student social workers' experiences of supervision. *The Indian Journal of Social Work, 79*(1), 31–54.

Roulston, A., Cleak, H., & Vreugdenhil, A. (2018). Promoting readiness to practice: Which learning activities promote competence and professional identity for student social workers during practice learning? *Journal of Social Work Education, 54*(2), 364–378.

Singleton, R. A., & Straits, B. C. (1999). *Approaches to social research.* Oxford: Oxford University Press.

Strauss, A., & Corbin, J. (1998). *Basics of qualitative research.* Thousand Oaks, CA: Sage.

Teater, B. (2014). *An introduction to applying social work theories and methods.* London: Open University Press.

Vassos, S., Harms, L., & Rose, D. (2018). Supervision and social work students: Relationships in a team-based rotation placement model. *Social Work Education, 37*(3), 328–341.

Webb, C. (1999). Analysing qualitative data: Computerized and other approaches. *Journal of Advanced Nursing, 29*(2), 323–330.

Williams, K. (2013). Field placement: What students need from their field supervisors: a student's perspective. *The New Social Worker, 20*(3), 6.

CHAPTER 54

Community Organising in Transformative Social Work Practice

Gil "Jake" I. Espenido

Context

The 2014 International Federation of Social Work (IFSW) definition of social work states:

> It is a practice-based profession and an academic discipline that promotes social change and development, social cohesion, and the empowerment and liberation of people. Principles of social justice, human rights, collective responsibility and respect for diversities are central to Social Work. Underpinned by theories of Social Work, social sciences, humanities and indigenous knowledge, social work engages people and structures to address life challenges and enhance wellbeing. The Social Work profession promotes social change, problem solving in human relationships and the empowerment and liberation of people to enhance wellbeing. (IFSW, 2014)

Practitioners recognise that intervention at the community level is another type of social work intervention in addition to those at the individual and group level. Key to this intervention is community organising.

Community organising in professional practice refers to various activities aimed at helping develop communities, challenge unjust systems and policies, and promote interconnectedness among community members (Brady & O'Connor, 2014).

Although community organising is pursued and can only be realised by people, its content, contours, and direction in organising work, in general,

G. "Jake" I. Espenido (✉)
Department of Social Work, College of Social Work and Community Development, University of the Philippines, Quezon City, Philippines

© The Author(s) 2021
S. S. M. et al. (eds.), *The Palgrave Handbook of Global Social Work Education*, https://doi.org/10.1007/978-3-030-39966-5_54

and social work, in particular, range from progressive to reactionary dependent upon whose interests it should serve. The mainstreaming of community organising into public consciousness by political forces, non-profit organisations, and social and mainstream media creates fundamental power shifts in the methods, directions, and priorities of practice (Brady, Schoeneman, & Sawyer, 2014).

Community organising in the Philippines started as mutual aid mechanisms set up by local people in the pre-colonial period and was employed in a number of people's revolts during colonial and neocolonial periods (Manalili, 1984). Since the 1970s it has been incorporated in development work and in the profession. Community organising was further refined and enriched using Marxist structural analysis and the thinking of Saul Alinsky and Paolo Freire (COM, n.d.). Even liberation theology from Latin America influenced the organising efforts of some churchpeople and institutions. When the practice of community organising later became part of the anti-dictatorship movement, its history was filled with people's narratives of emancipatory practice addressing oppressive structures and exploitative conditions. A large part of the anti-dictatorship movement can be traced back to community organising. Much of the anti-dictatorship movement helped sustain and advance the people's revolutionary movement. At any rate political organising had had its heyday. Community organising showed that it was indeed a potent process in empowering the people.

Individual social work practitioners also became part of the anti-dictatorship movement. Some are still members of the revolutionary movement. Many experienced torture and long periods of detention. A number died in the struggle. Purificación Pedro was a social work graduate who endured torture before she was killed. Others who survived the Marcos dictatorship took pioneering and innovative steps that led to building genuine collective strength of the people.

When the hated Marcos dictatorship was ousted through people power in 1986, President Corazón Aquino restored the so-called democratic space in the mid-1980s and in so doing a section of the Philippine left was coopted.

With people power instituted via the party-list system and the people's initiative enshrined in the fundamental law of the land, community development work in the twenty-first century became a multibillion dollar industry in the country encompassing practically all areas of social concerns and services. It evolved into a very complex phenomenon in which players came from both ends of the political spectrum of Philippine society. This is now referred to as mainstream development work. Within this ambit "the 'community development' approach ... under neocolonial conditions, was modified to suit the objectives of the national government; facilitate control of depressed or remote areas; persuade the masses to conform to government policies and goals; and institutionalize a system of patronage anchored on government bureaucracy ... It became a counter-insurgency measure ... and emphasized the involvement of target groups only in the implementation stage of the program/project primarily through the contribution of labor" (NCPD, 1988).

However, the heart and soul of community development is community organising.

At the international level there was a strategic retreat of revolutionary and progressive forces that were supplanted by the neoliberal paradigm. Although the focus of community organising in the 1960s and 1970s was on systematic reforms and transformation, social movements, and building collective power, since the 1980s community organising emphasised collaboration, capacity building, social planning, and working within the system (Brady et al., 2014). Community organising shifting from more critical and radical practice to more conservative approaches led to funded initiatives, community collaborative groups, and tax incentive programmes for small businesses (Defilippis & Saegert, 2012).

Community organising slowly lost its political and progressive content and process only for the politics of cooptation to become the trend.

RESEARCH DESIGN

Research design describes recent societal contexts where cooptation and depoliticisation occurred as well as the concepts and practice that have to be reaffirmed for community organising to be truly transformative. The research method used is a systematic review of secondary data that covers critical appraisal, summary, and an attempt to reconcile the evidence. This identified and synthesised all the available research evidence of sufficient quality concerning the topics covered in this study (Victor, 2008).

The methodology follows that proposed by Victor (2008). The first step defines the scope and aim of the chapter. The second step involves searching for and selecting research evidence. Such evidence came from published journals and books. The search and selection processes were tempered by quality appraisal of the limited materials available. The last step involves data extraction and data synthesis.

HIJACKING OF COMMUNITY ORGANISING

The hijacking of community organising is a logical consequence of the politics of cooptation. History shows that legitimacy is established through cooptation. Antonio Gramsci described cooptation "as a state in which 'spontaneous consent' is given by civil society to the general direction imposed on social life." Cooptation permits the confinement of class struggle to demands that can be accommodated with existing social relations. It requires the formation and acceptance of a hegemonic ideology that legitimises the new function of the state (De Janvry, 1981). In the case of a state like the Philippines that has long pretended to be the arbiter between contending forces this is not a new function. Such cooptation further buttressed the old political posturing of the state as an adherent and promoter of people's rights.

Since social work has the legitimate and strategic interests of the people at heart it needs to understand how cooptation occurs and how consent should be managed to struggle effectively for a better world (Carroll & Greeno, 2013). In the Philippines cooptation is specially targetted at those who are part of the broad people's movement that rejected long ago the existing system and fought to transform it and build a new one. The overarching objective is to deny progressive forces in their efforts to recruit supporters from the ranks of the people. Riding high on the issue of pervasive poverty the government came up with anti-poverty programmes specifically to lure the victims of poverty who professed allegiance to the other side (people's resistance) back to the government. Some call it building a new social contract between the state and its citizens (Oppenheim, 2012).

Community organising is used to show the exemplary role a civil society plays in linking the people with the government, the delivery of government services, facilitating peace in conflict-torn areas, and taking counter-insurgency measures in hard and recalcitrant rural areas. In the economic realm community organising was employed to facilitate the entry of foreign capital into the country (development aggression), individual and community entrepreneurship to extract social capital from the informal sector, private–public partnerships (PPPs), and get corporations to engage in public relations via corporate social responsibility.

The mushrooming of non-government organisations (NGOs) was no accident intended as it was to supplant mass movements (Petras, 1999). NGOs emphasise projects not movements and mobilise people to produce at the margins and not struggle with controlling the basic means of production (Petras, 1999). NGOs coopt the language of the left with such phrases as "popular power," "empowerment," "gender equality," "sustainable development," and "bottom–up leadership" (Petras, 1999). The problem is that such language is linked to a collaborative framework with donors and government agencies that subordinate activity to non-confrontational politics (Petras, 1999).

When mainstream development work hijacked the concepts and practice of community organising and sanitised it to serve its own purposes, it had difficulty in asserting itself and following its original purpose. Community organising has completely become an instrument and a process in which unequal relations are promoted and legitimacy is rendered to an oppressive and exploitative situation at the community level.

Community organising became almost complete when it moved from the politics of resistance to the politics of cooptation.

Depoliticising Community Organising

A key problem for ruling elites seeking to maintain their grip is the apparent paradox of how to maintain legitimacy in an economic system that continually undermines the stated basis of such legitimacy. The problem here is essentially one of how to maintain enough popular support to guarantee stable rule (Whyte, 2013).

Deception is one of two classical tactics (the other being repression) brought about by the ruling class creating a buffer zone (Kivel, 2006). The ruling class have always wanted to prevent people at the bottom of the pyramid from organising themselves to take power. They are desperate to maintain the power, control, and most importantly the wealth they have accumulated (Kivel, 2006). To maintain the separation and prevent themselves from becoming the object of people's anger they use legal, educational, and professional systems to create a network of occupations, careers, and professionals to deal directly with the rest of the population (Kivel, 2006). Such a buffer zone comprises all occupations that carry out the agenda of the ruling class without requiring the presence or visibility of that class (Kivel, 2006).

The buffer zone has three functions (Kivel, 2006). The first is taking care of people at the bottom of the pyramid. Conventional social work operates within existing social institutions to assist individuals to adjust and adapt to the status quo (George et al., 2013). The second function is keeping hope alive by distributing opportunities for a few people to become better off financially. When economic inequality is high and growing, upward mobility between social classes has to be seen to be attainable. This is achieved by proliferating such messages as "work hard and you'll be rewarded." If these messages permeate to the masses who do not enjoy much of the spoils, then they are more likely to tolerate the riches that a few enjoy within that society (Hill & Kumar, 2009). The final function is to maintain the system by controlling those who want to make changes.

In addition to deception there is depoliticisation. Depoliticisation is when the political content and consideration of any problem, individual, phenomenon, or process is glossed over, hidden, or even denied. People who have disdain for politics even raise it to the level of absurdity by arguing that ordinary people are tired of struggles.

Depoliticisation of the current hegemony was facilitated by neoliberalism. The uprooting of indigenous peoples from their ancestral domains, dispossessing peasants of their land, and eviction of the urban poor from their communities have severely ruptured the connectivity and closeness of individuals, families, and clans. Long-established social relations (before the onslaught of neoliberalism) contributed substantially to building the mass base of legitimate protests and movements in which organising efforts proceeded smoothly in earlier years. Such social relations also provided the so-called infrastructure of dissent via neighbourhood and workplace associations for radical dialogue (Dauvergne & LeBaron, 2014).

Moreover, neoliberalism promotes economic inequality, dependency, and individualistic values all of which can restrict community organising and social change (Brady et al., 2014).

Neoliberalism has negatively impacted community organising in a number of ways such as promoting evidence-based practice (EBP) as the dominant process to guide professional community practice, decreasing attention on and misrepresenting social movements in the community organising literature and in education, and increasing the professionalisation of community organising (Brady et al., 2014).

EBP is a major force in professional community organising (Brady et al., 2014) and is the direct manifestation and result of post-positivistic values (Brady et al., 2014). When EBP is used, it looks like an attempt is being made to extend a medical model to community organising, social work, and other professions in that it calls on practitioners to identify causal connections between interventions and to alleviate specific problems (Brady et al., 2014). Although EBP provides a worldview on how to arrive at best practice, it fails to address contextual and historical dimensions often at play in community organising or to provide room for radical change and system transformation that are common aims of critical community practice (Brady et al., 2014). Medical models obviously cannot approximate a correct appreciation of how embedded oppression and exploitation unfold or how class contradictions inherent in any community are heightened.

Community organising is currently becoming a sought-after profession or area of practice. It has created a new layer of professional community organisers some of whom profess to be experts or consultants (Brady et al., 2014). This introduces a subtle layer of elitism in which people are made to believe that others are better than they are.

Professionalisation like this impacts community organising because it reshapes how people understand what it means to participate in democracy (Speer & Han, 2018). Many organising campaigns run by consultants and experts are described as a kind of "shallow" mobilising (Speer & Han, 2018, citing McAlevey, 2016). Such campaigns rarely suggest that the actions of people are linked to social change (Speer & Han, 2018, citing McAlevey, 2016). What are needed are relational processes that build trust, stimulate the imagination, and develop into collective structures for exercising social power (Speer & Han, 2018, citing McAlevey, 2016). This includes the need for power analysis that is thoughtful and systematic and that people can conduct themselves (Speer & Han, 2018, citing McAlevey, 2016).

One problem with outsourcing such work to experts is that some organisers internalise such practices and privileged positions (Speer & Han, 2018, citing McAlevey, 2016). Professional staff direct, manipulate, and control mobilisation. They see themselves—not the ordinary people—as key agents of change (Speer & Han, 2018, citing McAlevey, 2016). To them it matters little who shows up or why as long as sufficient numbers turn up for a photo good enough to tweet and maybe generate interest in the media (Speer & Han, 2018, citing McAlevey, 2016). Although committed activists in the photo play no part in power analysis since they are not told about it or the resulting strategy, they dutifully show up at protests that rarely matter to power holders (Speer & Han, 2018, citing McAlevey, 2016).

Complicating matters further, professional community practitioners and scholars in the field need to question a number of key aspects of the status quo that help maintain the professionalisation of community organising (Brady et al., 2014). Professional community organisers need to question the motivation behind the professionalisation of community organising. They need to question the role that privilege plays in maintaining inequality between professional and non-professional organisers and find out how the systems and institutions we invest in, work for, and belong to through professional membership help to further coopt non-professional community organising to legitimise professional organising (Brady et al., 2014).

The claim made by professional community organisers that they are experts is highly contentious and borders on intellectual dishonesty. Central to community organising is the assertion that people can and should always empower themselves. Organising the work they carry out is central to people's lives and struggles and nobody knows this better than the people involved. The key task of any organiser is to get people to take control of organising their own lives. The best community organisers are those who are no longer needed in the lives and struggles of the people they have helped to organise. When such a situation is reached, it is the organiser's responsibility to move on and find other people in need to organisation.

Community Organising in Transformative Social Work

Practice is much more than stringing techniques and methods around a theoretical framework. It also reflects and promotes values and beliefs (Bricker-Jenkins, 1997). In other words, every practice model has an ideological core in which ideology is the glue that holds a practice system together and binds it to human conditions, institutions, and practices (Bricker-Jenkins, 1997).

Although social work is not a neutral profession, ideology is inherent to social work values, principles, and commitments and to its theories and approaches (Duarte, 2017). Reshaping and assuming a clear political ideology for social work constitutes a commitment to getting social work to actively participate in political and public arenas (Duarte, 2017). Such commitments are necessary for social workers to represent and speak on behalf of the most vulnerable who fall outside neoliberal normativity such as the poor and homeless, the unemployed, racialised people, women, children and young people, the LGBTQ community, indigenous peoples, the elderly, people with disabilities, and refugees and migrants moving across borders fleeing conflicts and persecution or other life-threatening situations (Duarte, 2017, citing Gray & Webb, 2013; McKendrick & Webb, 2014).

Social workers in the work they do and the commitment they show are human rights workers who advocate individual and collective rights everyday (Lundy, 2011). Human rights are intrinsic to social work and closely connected to economic, political, environmental, and social forces (Lundy, 2011). Such rights are fought for and realized collectively in community organising.

Community organising at its most elemental is the action of bringing people together and mobilising communities to meet common goals (Hale, 2014). Another definition of community organising is "the process that engages people, organizations, and communities toward increased individual and community control, political efficacy, improved quality of life, and social justice" (Hall, 2008). A central feature of community organising is that it is a process and strategy designed to build political power (Hall, 2008).

The basic tenets of transformative social work are moorings wherein community organising can redeem itself and align its practice in building people's organisations and people's movements against neoliberalism and for emancipation. From this framework, community organising can redefine its content, process, parameters for strategic objectives, and specific tactical engagements. Retracing its earlier progressive practices, community organising can ably chart once again its course in developing a comprehensive people's resistance.

Key Role of Raising Political Consciousness

Community organising is both a political act and a political process. It is first of all a political act because it aspires to tilt the balance between the forces of reaction (represented by the ruling class together with the sophisticated arsenal that government bureaucracy entails) and forces for change (the oppressed and exploited sections of society). Organising is geared to tilt the balance between forces that aspire to bring about transformation and change.

Community organising never was, is, or ever will be a neutral activity. Social work together with community organising is a contested and highly politicised practice (Baines, 2011). According to her, "everything is political despite the relatively widespread sentiment that most of everyday life is completely apolitical. For the holders of power, social problems are conventionally understood to be results of individual difficulties and poor decision making rather than unequal distribution of power, resources and affirming identities. They seek solutions by tinkering with the existing social system, applying managerial techniques to most or all social questions, or encouraging individuals to seek medical or psychological interventions for the problems they experience. As we try to bridge practice and social activism, it is important to ask who benefits from the way things operate at any given point in time, who can help make the changes we want, how we can help ourselves and others see the many ways in which issues are political, and how multiple strands of power are operating in any given scenario. At the very core of Social Work's existence are conflicts amongst competing social political groups, forces, and classes over defining needs and how to interpret and meet them."

Raising political consciousness is the process in which people are made to truly and deeply understand the fundamental reasons for their problems by linking their personal lives with how the system operates. This means taking hold of the forces and structures that cause their misery and deprivation, working out how they operate, and understanding such factors as the commonality of their problems together with those of other oppressed and exploited people; the need for collective struggle; the requirements necessary to fundamentally change the structures, risks, and dangers involved; and the inevitability of success that comes from a mass-based movement. Such a framework allows people to reach a resolution to act that will push them to participate at first gradually and then actively in building people's resistance.

It is only from the conscious conduct of political discussions that advanced elements can be identified from the ranks of the masses. Advanced elements share common traits such as sensitivity to the plight of the people, relative political sharpness, deep-seated interest in progressive ideas, and unceasing pursuit of long-established solutions to the problems of the exploited and oppressed. Political activists will logically emerge from the ranks of advanced elements. Such political activists will assume key and important responsibilities in organising work. This is the process in which organisers motivate others in the community to act in a similar manner and leaders will emerge from the ranks of the organised.

Use of Class Analysis and Centrality of Class Struggle

The proponents of cooptation and collaboration have deliberately buried class analysis and removed class content from community organising. They misrepresent reality by asserting that all communities are homogeneous. Classes exist and class relations operate in highly stratified societies. Community organisers should be able to recognise the different classes, their interests, and corollary standpoints based on such interests. Class analysis will help community organisers identify the most reliable forces, the forces to win over, those to be neutralised, and the target for the main attack. This should all be done in the process of building and strengthening the movement's forces.

Classes are not static economic categories. Rather they are social relations that are in the process of constant change and connected to and affected by other associations (Lundy, 2011). Not all social relations are class relations. However, class affects all social relations such as gender, religion, and ethnicity. They are all relational concepts that are affected by class (Lundy, 2011).

Social workers should always remember that social relations are enacted by human beings and are responsible for the ongoing oppression of many groups and individuals (Baines, 2011). That social relations are enacted by people means that such oppressive relationships can also be changed by people themselves (Baines, 2011). Implicit in the term social relations is that such relations are organised and operated by people. Hence they can be arrested or reorganised by people. They are wholly social relations—not inevitable conditions of modern life that cannot be changed (Baines, 2011).

The history of the world is full of class struggles that have motivated advances in humanity. However, genuine transformation to an ideal society can only be achieved when the masses (the most oppressed and exploited) assume and fulfil their historic responsibility to change the world and rid it of the evil of class.

Arouse–Organise–Mobilise (AOM) Framework

Mainstream social work education is split, on the one hand, *between* casework for social care and community work for social change *and*, on the other hand, a centred generalist model of intervention that is rooted in eclectic knowledge based on systems theory arising from a perspective that is status quo orientated (George & Marlowe, 2005).

However, use of the AOM framework in political organising is strongly promoted and rigorously implemented.

The arousing aspect of AOM relates to leaders of the masses understanding their situation, interests, and roots of their problems; firing them up to promote and fight for their interests; and developing the skills for effective and sustained struggle.

Propaganda work and education work fall within the remit of the arousing aspect. Propaganda work is designed to arouse people and make them aware of a particular situation or issue. The gravity of the situation and its meaning for the people are factors organisers should present, explain, analyse, and get the masses to understand. Depending on the level of work and the situation propaganda can be broken down into various forms. For example, propaganda that explains is called explicative propaganda and propaganda that stirs emotions is called agitational propaganda. Propaganda can range from written (statements, manifestos, briefing papers), verbal (forums, teach-ins, mass meetings, mobile propaganda), cultural (plays, skits, songs, poems, and dance), and informal propaganda such as storytelling and anecdotes.

Education work is designed to deepen understanding on any issue. It involves analysis and systematic, extensive, and structured study in defined courses (specific courses, mass courses, and ladderised courses). Education is pursued to answer a particular need for knowledge/skills of the rallying forces being organised and should be pursued promptly given the requirements involved in organising and struggles.

The organising aspect of AOM relates to gathering and organising people into formal and unified structures. Such structures provide a channel through which individuals can unite to advance and achieve their objectives. Organising is important to consolidating the individual strengths of each member and systematising and directing their movements to a single objective. Two elements of an organisation are developed in the process of organising. One is unity of objective and is based on the condition of the masses and the objective to be understood and nurtured among those being organised. The other is unity in the particular role of the organisation since each organisation is conscious of its particular condition, its role in society, and its role in social transformation.

The mobilising aspect of AOM relates to an increasing number of people participating in tasks geared toward strengthening the people's movement and advancing struggles in different arenas. The most important objective of mobilisation is to get the masses organised enough to participate in the tasks and activities of the movement. The capacity of the movement to fulfil its tasks and struggles is then immediately raised to a higher level. Getting the masses to act in this way hastens their understanding of politics and organisations by shattering their submissiveness and developing their combative spirit; strengthening their unity by mentally preparing themselves in their collective struggle against misery and in confronting the enemy; sharpening their understanding of their problems, conditions, and struggles and their knowledge of the enemy; highlighting the utmost importance of the collective struggle, the movement and its organisations; heightening their belief in themselves and their combined strength; and shattering individualism in the process.

The AOM framework has its own integrity because the three mutually reinforce each other.

Relationship Between Economic and Political Struggles

Politics in command is a phrase used to indicate that politics itself is relatively dominant when it comes to building a genuine people's movement since it is in the political sphere where different forces (from right to left) are examined and class alignment determined, where political directions are clearly defined, and where tactical leadership is continuously honed. However, politics of every persuasion is detrimental to the movement. Any people's movement should also pay serious attention to the actual needs of its forces to mitigate the devastating effects of the continuing economic crisis by engaging in tactical campaigns to achieve economic demands. Victories from such engagements definitely change class relations between contending forces. Peasants successful in lowering land rent and workers in obtaining an increase in wages slowly change the class relations they have with their oppressors.

Pure economic struggles without the political framework naturally fall into the trap of reformism. This is the character of any type of projects implemented in the community devoid of political framework. Reformism prolongs the life of the system. Community organising aspires to transform the system.

Using community organising to build social movements should have the effect of challenging dominant structures and in some cases mobilising participants to dramatically transform or eliminate such structures altogether. In other words, the concept of community organising should be extended not only to include a greater sustained effort over time, but also examine assumptions regarding the goals of such sustained efforts. Social movements can help chart courses of action and mobilise people to take alternative cultural and sociopolitical courses of action. They do not need to be restricted to confronting aspects of what currently exists (Brady et al., 2014).

Danger of Localism

A fragmented and superficial understanding of realities on the ground can also lead to unwarranted tactical engagements. Unfortunately, this promotes a model of power that is in harmony with and becomes the basis of such a conceptualisation of participation and empowerment (Mohan & Stokke, 2000). Power resides in individual members of a community and can increase with the successful pursuit of individual and collective goals. This implies that empowerment of the powerless could be achieved within the existing social order without any significant negative effects upon the power of the powerful (Mohan & Stokke, 2000). Such a mindset shows an almost total lack of understanding and critique of the underlying reality and forces of capital, its social relations, its historical development, its imperatives and tendencies, and its conditions of permanent historical crisis in the present period (Wage Slave X, 2002).

There are problems though such as the tendency to essentialise and romanticise the local (Mohan & Stokke, 2000). Another problem is the tendency to view the local in isolation from broader economic and political structures. This means underplaying the context of place such as national and translational economic and political forces (Mohan & Stokke, 2000).

An expression of such localism is the view that an action or an activity by even a small group of people is always more important and always more politically valuable than any political discussion or debate on political positions, orientations, or strategies between fellow militants (Wage Slave X, 2002). Such an attitude exemplifies a hidden—or not so hidden—elitism and vanguardism in that it implies that a small group of people can effect significant social change as opposed to the reality that only mass actions can do so. Under conditions of social passivity of most of the masses the activism of a small minority tends to merely become part of the capitalist political spectacle thus reinforcing the passivity of most of the masses (Wage Slave X, 2002).

A study of political economy will always provide a framework for class relations and class interests. It also provides an understanding of the nature of contradictions as they unfold. Although issues can definitely be resolved at the local level, economic and environmental crises are offshoots of the operations of capital at the international and national level.

Intervention at the local level should also be contextualised within the framework of power relations. There is too much confusion between reforms and revolution. Some community development practitioners assert that "relative transformation" is possible even when necessary changes at the macro level are not quite in place and that "reforms and revolution feed on each other; one forms part of a continuum of empowerment of the people and communities" (NPS, 1995). Hence either reforms and revolution are mixed up or revolution is seen as the accumulation of reforms (NPS, 1995).

The difference between revolution and reforms is clear. Reforms per se are changes within the context of the existing system, whereas revolution is a change in the system (NPS, 1995). Reforms replicated endlessly do not make a revolution. Reforms by themselves simply "improve" an exploitative system and help it to survive. Genuine revolutionaries know that the struggle for reforms must be deliberately and consciously linked to the struggle to overthrow the system for it to serve the revolution. Revolutionaries engage in the struggle for reforms in pursuit of and not as a substitute for revolution (NPS, 1995).

Social Justice–Oriented Social Work Assists Individuals While Simultaneously Seeking to Transform Society

The problem is not with providing social services, but with all time and energy being diverted toward social services to the detriment of long-term social change (Kivel, 2006). Instead of having an exclusive emphasis on changing individuals, social justice–oriented social work should be used to assist individuals in meeting their needs whenever possible in participatory and transformative ways and simultaneously to focus on challenging and transforming those forces within society that benefit from and perpetuate inequity and oppression. Placing the masses at the centre of a struggle for comprehensive human rights and popular democracy is problematic. Although the masses are not born with some special genes that grant them human rights and popular democracy, the place they occupy in society as it exists today makes the masses the potential force for reorganising society. This dictates the need for organisation, mobilisation, and broadening of political awareness among the popular classes, something that can only be won through struggle (Gutto, 1993).

The exploitative and oppressive relations inherent in Philippine society create a dominant narrative with which social work practice should engage. Understanding the relationship between the socially powerful (the ruling class) and the disenfranchised (the poor, deprived, and oppressed) will always generate a critique connected with class structure and economic division. Structural inequality and oppression are the contexts within which social workers practise their professions. However, if they do not deliberately seek to be part of the solution, then the work they do will inevitably become part of the problem (Ife, 2008). All social workers must therefore incorporate a multidimensional analysis of structural disadvantage in their work. This must be at the forefront of social work thinking at every level of practice (Ife, 2008). Questions on the causes of social problems, how to address them, and how to prevent them are central to the development of a strand of social work emerging from a people's movement and aimed at fundamentally transforming the political, economic, social, and cultural factors underlying and generating inequality and injustice (Baines, 2011). The need for a people's movement conflicts with the ideals of authoritarianism and neoliberal logic. The promotion and fulfilment of the human right to health, education, housing, and work cannot be a result of transactions in the market.

This calls for the creation or restrengthening of a real human rights movement. Although the state will officially guarantee the rights of the people as enshrined in its constitution, only the people can truly guarantee that their fundamental, democratic, and sovereign rights are respected. The way the system operates and the character of the state has shown "that the struggle even for human rights emanates, is contested and resolved within the relations of contending classes. The struggle for human rights cannot be fully understood and tenaciously fought for the interests of the oppressed outside of class struggle ... [For human rights] are products of social interactions and struggle. People's individual and collective initiatives and struggles for their rights do not consider themselves confined to existing international instruments and local laws. The people consider they have the inherent right, and potential power, of creating and extending the frontiers of rights on the basis of their life experiences" (Gutto, 1993).

COMMUNITY ORGANISING AS PART OF BUILDING A BROAD PEOPLE'S MOVEMENT

It is not enough simply to engage in community organising as social work professionals. Social work as a frontline profession should seek unity and chime with people-based movements to bring about political and social transformation. The key task is how to engage service users and carers in political organising and wield such organised strength to support people's resistance. This is necessary for it is only through such a movement that people can build organisational strength, secure tangible victories, and gradually realise their legitimate and strategic interests. Although tangible victories (whether economic or political) by the people are building blocks in nurturing their political power, the need remains for a vibrant and aggressive political movement to provide direction in any tactical engagement. Without making the organic relationship between tactical engagements and strategic objectives clear to the masses and by limiting the fight to specific economic and political issues runs the risk of making the masses focus on the pursuit of rights that can easily be snatched away from them because they would not have secured the necessary political power to defend and expand the rights they have won (Gutto, 1993).

The strong anti-dictatorship movement during the Marcos regime should be seen as a major contribution to the political isolation of the dictatorship and eventual downfall. Similarly, under President Duterte's regime social workers engaged in transformative social work had the task of helping the people realise that without their participation the struggle to uphold and defend human rights and democracy would be unattainable. The tasks at hand are not simple and involve painstaking work that requires organising, mobilising, and broadening the political awareness of the marginalised. The logic of transformative social work is not that of the market and profit. Its progressive discourse and practice have "the potential to flame the resistance against neoliberalism" including, of course, the resistance against President Duterte's oppressive regime.

CONCLUSION

Education has never been a neutral activity. It is in fact a subversive activity whose primary purpose is liberation.

Liberative education at the community level is complex because the social forces it addresses are complex (Nelson, Palonsky, & McCarthy, 2007). The central purpose is to liberate the individual and society and to distribute liberating power broadly (Freire, 1970). It requires a set of values that include justice and equality to serve as ideals to oppose oppression and authoritarianism and provide a critical understanding of the many cultural cross-currents in contemporary society, mechanisms of manipulation, and hidden ideological purposes (Nelson et al., 2007). Liberative education and critical pedagogy uncover myths and injustices evident in the dominant culture (Nelson et al., 2007). They also embrace the expectation that the powerless can develop power through education (Nelson et al., 2007). This once again requires recognising that forms of knowledge are not neutral but utilised by the dominant culture to secure its power (Nelson et al., 2007).

Community organising must become once more the place where conflicts of humankind are examined in increasing depth to understand the ideological and cultural bases on which societies operate. The purpose is not merely to recognise such conflicts or ideologies, but to engage in actions that constrain oppression and expand personal power (Nelson et al., 2007).

There is a need for social work educators, mentors, and practitioners "who exercise forms of intellectual and pedagogical practice which attempt to insert teaching and learning directly into the political sphere by arguing that communities represent both a struggle for meaning and a struggle over power relations. This also refers to one whose intellectual preferences are necessarily grounded in forms of moral and ethical discourse exhibiting a preferential concern for the suffering and the struggles of the disadvantaged and oppressed" (Giroux & McLaren, 1986).

At the end of the day theories are best understood in the crucible of practice and practice is always the final arbiter of truth.

REFERENCES

Baines, D. (2011). *Doing anti-oppressive practice* (2nd ed.). Winnipeg, MB: Fernwood Publishing.

Brady, S. R., & O'Connor, M. K. (2014). Understanding how community organizing leads to social change: The beginning of formal practice theory. *Journal of community practice, 22,* 210–228.

Brady, S. R., Schoeneman, A. C., & Sawyer, J. (2014). Critiquing and analyzing the effects of neoliberalism on community organizing: Implications and recommendations for practitioners and educators. *Journal for Social Action in Counseling and Psychology, 6*(1), 25.

Bricker-Jenkins, M. (1997). Hidden treasures: Unlocking strengths in the public social services. In D. Saleebey (Ed.), *The strengths perspective in social work practice* (pp. 133–138). New York: Addison-Wesley Longman Inc.

Carroll, W. K., & Greeno, M. (2013). Neoliberal hegemony and the organisation of consent. In R. Fisher (Ed.), *Managing democracy managing dissent* (pp. 121–135). London: Corporate Watch.

Dauvergne, P., & Lebaron, G. (2014). *Protest Inc.: The corporatization of activism.* Cambridge: Polity Press.

DeFilippis, J., & Saegert, S. (2012). *The community development reader* (J. DeFilippis & S. Saegert, Eds.). New York: Routledge.

De Janvry, A. (1981). *The agrarian question and reformism in Latin America.* Chicago: University of Chicago Press.

Duarte, F. (2017). Reshaping political ideology in social work: A critical perspective. *Aotearoa New Zealand Social Work, 29,* 34–44.

Freire, P. (1970). *The pedagogy of the oppressed.* New York: Herder and Herder.

George, P., & Marlowe, S. (2005). Structural social work in action. *Journal of Progressive Human Services, 16,* 24.

George, P., Silver, S., & Preston. S. (2013, November 1). Reimagining filed education on social work: The promise unveiled. *Advances in Social Work, 14,* 642–657.

Giroux, H. A., & McLaren, P. (1986). Teacher education and the politics of engagement: The case for democratic schooling. *Harvard Educational Review, 56*(3), 213–238.

Gutto, S. (1993). *Human and peoples' rights for the oppressed: Critical essays on theory and practice from sociology of law perspectives.* Lund: Lund University Press.

Hale, M. R. (2014, March). Community organizing: For resource provision or transformation? A review of the literature. *Global Journal of Community Psychology Practice, 5*(1), 1–9. Retrieved from www.gjcpp.org; https://www.gjcpp.org/pdfs/2013-004-final-20140205.pdf.

Hall, P. D. (2008, September 1). Transforming the city: Community organizing and the challenges of political change. *American Journal of Sociology, 114*(2), 555–558.

Hill, D., & Kumar, R. (2009). *Global neoliberalism and education and its consequences.* New York: Routledge.

Ife, J. (2008). *Human rights and social work: Towards rights-based practice.* New York: Cambridge University Press.

International Federation of Social Workers (IFSW). (2014, August 6). *Global Definition of Social Work.* Retrieved from www.ifsw.org: https://www.ifsw.org/global-definition-of-social-work/.

Kivel, P. (2006). *Social service or social change*. Retrieved from www.southwestern.edu; https://www.southwestern.edu/live/files/1151.

Lundy, C. (2011). *Social work, social justice & human rights: A structural approach to practice* (2nd ed.). Toronto: University of Toronto Press.

Manalili, A. (1984). *Community organizing for people's empowerment*. Manila: Kapatiran-Kaunlaran Foundation Inc.

Mohan, G., & Stokke, K. (2000). Participatory development and empowerment: The dangers of localism. *Third World Quarterly, 21*(2), 247–268. Retrieved from http://www.jstor.org/stable/3993419.

Multiversity, C. O. (n.d.). *History of community organizing in the Philippines*. Retrieved from www.comultiversity.org.ph; http://www.hartford-hwp.com/archives/54a/063.html.

National Council for People's Development. (1988). Review of Development Work.

National Peasant Secretariat, Community Party of the Philippines. (1995). Reformism in the peasant movement.

Nelson, J. L., Palonsky, S. B., & McCarthy, M. R. (2007). *Critical issues in education: Dialogues and dialetics* (6th ed.). New York: McGraw-Hill Education.

Oppenheim, B. (2012). Community and counterinsurgency. *Humanity: An International Journal of Human Rights, Humanitarianism, and Development, 3*(2), 249–265.

Petras, J. (1999, January 1). NGOs: In the service of imperialism. *Journal of Contemporary Asia, 29*(4), 429–440.

Speer, P., & Han, H. (2018). Re-engaging social relationships and collective dimensions of organizing to revive democratic practice. *Journal of Political Psychology, 6*, 745–758.

Wage Slave X. (2002). *A marxist critique of anti-globalization movement*.

Victor, L. (2008). *Social research update: Systematic reviewing*. Retrieved from http://www.sru.soc.surrey.ac.uk; http://sru.soc.surrey.ac.uk/SRU54.pdf.

Whyte, D. (2013). Market patriotism: Liberal democracy unmasked. In R. Fisher (Ed.), *Maaging democracy managing dissent* (pp. 46–62). London: Corporate Watch.

PART IX

Social Work with People in Difficult Circumstances: A Step Towards Sustainability

INTRODUCTION

This part discusses and advances cutting-edge analysis of social work education with people in difficult circumstances in multicultural context. Chapters in this part help to understand the social work response to social problems or societal sufferings across seven countries in the globe. Enormous global changes taking place across the world lead societies to become more diverse. The process of globalization, privatization, and neoliberalism resulted in multicultural society where people belonging to diverse culture live together and interact often. There are seven-chapter contributions across the seven countries in the world. Authors from United Kingdom, Ethiopia, Australia, Czech Republic, Romania, Italy, and Bangladesh present their research pertaining to social work education and the role of social work in the welfare of people in difficult circumstances. With the introduction of neoliberalism, globalization and privatization lead by rapid and unplanned social change, social work education has become more narrow, conservative and focused with much focus on social control rather than social change. Scholars have documented the social control function of social work in different contexts (see, e.g., Fenton, 2014; Hanesworth, 2017; Morley, Macfarlane, & Ablett, 2017). Further in many context, social work as a social service profession is working for the 'state' and state welfare than the welfare and empowerment of vulnerable and disadvantaged.

Social work, the helping profession in the new millennium, has enormous challenges. Yet finding a way out of ill effects of neoliberal policy and work with the core principles of the profession, i.e. social justice, equality, and human dignity. Further despite state control and market influence, working for the protection of human rights, social justice and equality with focus to bring positive social change, and the liberation of people in contemporary society is a challenge ahead of social work in the next generation. However, enormous global and demographic change across the globe is resulting in diverse societies with complex problems. These changes have brought dramatic influence on the helping profession both in the West and in the North. The issues related to poverty, inequality, unemployment, and crime are ever increased in the developing and underdeveloped economies since the introduction of free and liberal market. As a result of these changes in the past four decades, social work profession is increasingly working with multicultural societies with diverse and challenging population and issues.

In time when state is withdrawing from its welfare responsibility in a systematic way, many underdeveloped and developing countries are finding it difficult to support their population with special needs and care. It is this time when non-governmental organizations, not-for-profit organizations, and civil society organizations across the globe emerged in a larger number as alternative welfare provider to the needy people. However these organizations and not for profits are finding enormous challenges themselves in establishing and functioning across different regimes. *M. Rezaul Islam* provides an account of alternative care provisions provided by SOS Children's village in Bangladesh. The chapter explores the challenges and interventions of alternative care for children along with reviewing the existing child welfare laws and international conventions while justifying the position of alterative care. While M. Rezaul Islam argues in this chapter, SOS children village is an ideal organization for alternative care in Bangladesh. There are numerous other studies that have proved evidence of non-profits and human service non-profits in addressing persistent and emerging social needs of vulnerable social groups (Berzin & Camarena, 2018; Cnaan & Vinokur-Kaplan, 2015; Lawrence, Dover, & Gallagher, 2013; Nandan, London, & Bent-Goodley, 2015; Shier & Handy, 2016, 2015). *Helen Casey, Bini Araia, and Peter Beresford* bring in the discussion of refugee population, an issue disturbing the whole world irrespective of economic development achievements in the recent years. The authors explore how to promote human relationships through identifying and co-producing practical strategies for mending gaps that exist between people, policy, and practice.

The globalized society at present needs human service professionals more than ever before in the history. The need for the professionals has of course changed from problem-solving to problem prevention approach and in many countries problem avoiding and social control approach. Despite many challenges social work profession encounters presently, there is a need for exploring how student, service user, and social work educator partnership can lead to social change and social transformation. Wassie Kebede discusses the role played by social work in the social change in Ethiopia and notes the success of social change initiatives in Ethiopia, i.e. mass campaign against illiteracy through adult learning program that contributed for the formation of new social order during the socialist regime. The author argues that social work in post-1991 Ethiopia is responding to a social change process by unfolding and revisiting its teaching curricula and practice models to fit into the current needs of social change. Despite social work being a new profession, and suffering from lack of professional identity, author claims that social work in contemporary Ethiopia is exhibiting promising efforts in bringing social change. *Oldrich Chytil and Ivana Kowalikova* find an answer for the question whether education in social work in the Czech Republic critically reflects the changes in society. Using quantitative approach, the authors undertook a critical analysis of the academic texts and university curricula of social work and found that despite social work's long existence, the social change function performed by social work in Czech Republic has its own limitations and needs special attention in social work pedagogy. Indeed, social work across the globe need to do away with its complete dependency on traditional teaching method and focus more on newer and technology friendly methods of teaching social work. Further, it is noted with satisfaction that social work schools across the globe in the recent years are adopting the creative teaching methods (such as creative crafts, story making, role-play, drama, art, creative writing, and simulation games) as instruction method at different levels of programme delivery (Jackson & Burgess, 2005; Kirkendall & Krishen, 2014; Papouli, 2017).

Further in this volume many authors call for social work education to address the issues of marginalized and vulnerable population across the border as mandated in the ethical principles of the profession. Tatiana Saruis and Stella Volturo present the findings of their study on the effects of the welfare crisis and the transformations that have occurred in social work, applying a street-level perspective. The chapter analyses the decision-making process of caseworkers through field research methods in a north-eastern region of Italy. *Mayio Konidaris and Melissa Petrakis* demand for a social work approach that recognizes the marginalization of students and support their integration into peer group and discipline in social work educational programmes. The authors also recommend the better preparing of social work students for empathic and skilled work with minorities. In the end, there is a hope, as Maria Roth provides a detailed understanding of challenges faced by social work education in post-communist Romania, need for professionalization and documents a strong hope on social work profession working for the betterment of Romania society and elimination of social problems. Based on both literature review and the author's own experiences, the article parallels social problems, social policies, and the expectations attached to the social work profession in the last three decades.

References

Berzin, S. C., & Camarena, H. (2018). *Innovation from within: Redefining how nonprofits solve problems.* New York: Oxford University Press.

Cnaan, R. A., & Vinokur-Kaplan, D. (2015). *Social innovation: Definitions, clarifications, and a new model.* In R. A. Cnaan & D. Vinokur-Kaplan (Eds.), *Cases in innovative nonprofits: Organizations that make a difference.* Thousand Oaks, CA: Sage.

Fenton, J. (2014). Can social work education meet the neoliberal challenge head on? *Critical and Radical Social Work, 2*(3), 321–335.

Hanesworth, C. (2017). Neoliberal influences on American higher education and the consequences for social work programmes. *Critical and Radical Social Work, 5*(1), 41–57.

Jackson, N. J., & Burgess, H. (2005). *Creativity in social work and social work education.* Imaginative Curriculum Working Paper. Retrieved from http://www.creativeacademic.uk/uploads/1/3/5/4/13542890/creativity_in_social_work.pdf.

Kirkendall, A., & Krishen, A. S. (2014). Encouraging creativity in the social work classroom: Insights from a qualitative exploration. *Social Work Education, The International Journal, 34*(3), 341–354.

Lawrence, T. B., Dover, G., & Gallagher, B. (2013). Managing social innovation. In M. Dodgson, D. M. Gann, & N. Phillips (Eds.), *The Oxford handbook of innovation management* (Online edition). Oxford, UK: Oxford University Press.

Morley, C., Macfarlane, S., & Ablett, P. (2017). The neoliberal colonisation of social work education: A critical analysis and practices for resistance. *Advances in Social Work and Welfare Education, 19*(2), 25–40.

Nandan, M., London, M., & Bent-Goodley, T. (2015). Social workers as social change agents: Social innovation, social intrapreneurship, and social entrepreneurship. *Human Service Organizations: Management, Leadership & Governance, 39*(1), 38–56.

Papouli, E. (2017). The role of arts in raising ethical awareness and knowledge of the European refugee crisis among social work students. An example from the classroom. *Social Work Education, The International Journal, 36*(7), 775–793.

Shier, M. L., & Handy, F. (2015). From advocacy to social innovation: A typology of social change efforts by nonprofits. *Voluntas: International Journal of Voluntary and Nonprofit Organizations, 26*(6), 2581–2603.

Shier, M. L., & Handy, F. (2016). Executive leadership and social innovation in direct service nonprofits: Shaping the organizational culture to create social change. *Journal of Progressive Human Services, 27*(2), 111–130.

CHAPTER 55

Advancing Relationship-Based Social Work Through Mending Gaps Between Service Users, Carers, Social Work Students, and Practitioners: A Case Study Involving Refugees

Helen Casey, Bini Araia and Peter Beresford

THE UK CONTEXT

Social work in the United Kingdom has a long history stretching back to Victorian times. Two overlapping but often conflicting strands in its development were utilitarian philanthropy, associated with pioneers like Octavia Hill and the settlement movement, linked with Canon Samuel and Henrietta Barnett. While the first was associated with the regulation of charity and its recipients, the other sought to bridge the divide between privileged and disadvantaged people. The context for modern social work—within and indeed

H. Casey
Faculty of Wellbeing, Education and Language Studies, The Open University, Milton Keynes, UK

B. Araia
Investing in People and Culture, London, UK

P. Beresford (✉)
Brunel University London, London, UK
e-mail: Peter.Beresford@brunel.ac.uk
URL: https://en.wikipedia.org/wiki/Peter_Beresford

University of Essex, Essex, UK

© The Author(s) 2021
S. S. M. et al. (eds.), *The Palgrave Handbook of Global Social Work Education*, https://doi.org/10.1007/978-3-030-39966-5_55

beyond the United Kingdom—was the post-war welfare state with its commitment to social citizenship and the equalisation of opportunity (Beresford, 2016).

Social work underwent an expansion in the 1970s. Again conflicting strands can be identified in its development. In the early 1970s there were pressures to bureaucratisation, professionalisation, and managerialism associated with the creation of local authority social service departments. By the mid-1970s the "radical social work" movement had emerged to challenge this and committed itself to participation and structural change through social work. This gave further impetus to social work committed to challenging inequality and discrimination, supporting social justice, and valuing diversity. This was reflected both in the formal structures of social work as well as the increasing right-wing political and media opposition social work encountered (Bailey & Brake, 1975; Dominelli, 2010).

However, the two conflicting ideologies, one embodied in identity-based movements including the disabled people and service user movement, and the other committed to the private market embodied in increasingly dominant neoliberalism had one important meeting point in public policy. This was a new common interest in public participation and user involvement. Social work internationally was at the vanguard of this development and by the early 1990s had begun to establish provisions for user involvement in policy and practice (Beresford & Croft, 1990). A particularly important development was the pressure for more user (and carer[1]) involvement in social work education. In 2003 when UK social work education became degree based such involvement became a requirement supported with central funding for all qualifying (and subsequently post-qualifying) education and training offering an international precedent (Branfield, 2009).

Concept of "Mend the Gap"

Such an approach to learning has become a gateway to participatory social work for both practitioners and service users. For those committed to emancipation, social work is or should be concerned with working alongside people disempowered and oppressed in society, steeped in principles of human rights and social justice and the values of anti-discriminatory and anti-oppressive practice. This is what attracts many students to the profession: to work with people to "address the problems and difficulties in their lives" (SWAN, 2009). Unfortunately, this aspect of social work has for too many years now been increasingly undermined by managerialism, privatisation, austerity, and the ever-growing dominance of market forces already touched on. Social workers themselves and social work students have also felt oppressed through the encroachment of marketisation on their practice (Ferguson, 2008). This has led to increasing stigmatisation and pathologising of service users and carers and an ever-widening gap between them and social work practitioners—anathema to those who value relationship-based practice and effective partnership working.

There is however an antidote to this. It lies in the effective involvement and active participation of service users and carers in the ongoing education of social work students and practitioners. This has been growing in scale and sophistication through the twenty-first century. The reasons for this are manifold as are the added value benefits of such involvement. Meaningful service user and carer involvement acts as a consistent reminder to students and practitioners of the motivating factors that brought them into social work and the fact that emotional intelligence can be just as important as academic or analytical intelligence. It ensures that we never lose sight of the fact that service users and carers are human beings (Advocacy in Action, 2006; Branfield, 2007; Morrow et al., 2012). As far back as 2006 Advocacy in Action highlighted that effective involvement also "provides valuable correctives to bureaucratic and procedure driven practice that can characterise much of statutory social work" (Advocacy in Action, 2006, p. 342).

To bring these common goals to fruition has to involve breaking down perceived and often all-too-real barriers between practitioners, students, academics, service providers, and service users as well as mending the gaps between them to produce social work courses fit for purpose. "In social work education, more than in any other area, there are common aims between the individuals providing services, the teaching staff, the service users and the students. We should use these common aims to develop the courses together" (service user, cited in Branfield, 2007, p. 1).

Extensive research has been undertaken into how service users and carers are involved in social work education some of the best of it emanating from the Social Care Institute for Excellence (SCIE)[2] and the service user umbrella organisation Shaping Our Lives. Much of this research has looked at the service user and carer experience and how it can be improved, as well as the barriers and challenges that face academics, service users, and carers when facilitating this vital aspect of a social worker's education. For example, Taylor, Braye, and Cheng (2009) and Branfield (2009) highlight the fact that sharing information and improving supportive infrastructures are vital to sustainable involvement. There are discussions in their work and those of Beresford (2013) and Branfield, Beresford, and Levin (2007) into the resourcing of service user and carer involvement both in terms of payment for involvement and in terms of staff support. Interestingly, these publications all stress the importance of *reciprocity* in terms of service user satisfaction—something that lies at the heart of the more recent gap-mending approach to teaching under discussion here.

Mending the Gaps Between Service Users, Students, and Practitioners

The introduction to "gap-mending" approaches and involvement with PowerUs has enabled realisation of the potential for changing the way service users are involved in the delivery of social work education and the range of different ways in which this can be brought about. The gap-mending approach in social work education originates from Lund University, Sweden (since 2005) and was developed by the social work learning partnership PowerUs in 2012 (www.powerus.se) to promote new ways of learning that can come from sharing experiences, knowledge, and skills within professional education. By creating a learning environment where people share their experiences and knowledge, traditional barriers that exist between people on the receiving end of professional support and those providing it can be removed. PowerUs is a growing organisation with active gap-mending practices operating in 15 countries (Belgium, Canada, Spain, Croatia, Denmark, England/Wales, France, Germany, The Netherlands, Norway, Poland, Scotland, South Africa, Sweden, Switzerland). For further information about international gap-mending programmes see Chiapparini (2016).

Definition of Mend the Gap

> The gap-mending concept can be characterized as a reflective tool that helps teachers and researchers to consider what, in their practice increases, maintains or mends gaps between policies, services and professionals—as well as service users. Gaps always exist in a context. Gaps can develop and be maintained because of prejudices based on social work's categorization of people, because of language barriers, because of institutional hierarchies and the roles we have created for people within them. They can also exist because of lack of knowledge. Contextual knowledge is therefore essential in gap-mending reflections, as well as a good understanding of existing gaps. (Askheim, Beresford, & Heule, 2016).

To this quote from the three founding members of PowerUs writing in the *British Journal of Social Work* can be added "as a reflective tool, the gap mending concept helps service users, students and practitioners as well as teachers and researchers. There is a growing evidence base to demonstrate how the gap mending approach provides an alternative model for social work education which meets the needs of communities, not just professionals" (Chiapparini, 2016; Beresford & Carr, 2018; Community Care, 2018).

This chapter explores how to promote human relationships through identifying and coproducing practical strategies for mending gaps that exist between people, policy, and practice. The hoped-for outcome is to promote further interest and offer support from PowerUs to readers who would also be interested in taking forward this transformative approach in their work.

The first gap-mending programme in the United Kingdom was piloted at London South Bank University (LSBU) in 2012 and at New College Durham (NCD) in 2014. The second programme was piloted in response to barriers identified by parents at a children's centre where social work students were on placement and excluded by parents from their support groups.

Parents who were united by their negative experiences of having lost or been separated from their children by social workers agreed to pioneer the gap-mending approach. The aim of the first programme was to listen to parent's experiences and identify the gaps that created barriers between themselves and those in roles to support them. The programme content was defined by their identifying gaps as core themes around

- communication
- professional values
- information
- partnership working
- different roles
- mutual understanding and respect.

One parent summed it up: "I'll never forget the way the social worker spoke to me, as if I wasn't even a human being, let alone a mother to my children. She made me feel this (fingers demonstrating extremely small) big" (Chiapparini, 2016, p. 76).

This unique empowering experience putting parents in a lead role and prioritising their views was the start of a ground- breaking programme the outcome of which has created a legacy for other parents and changed the way that professionals learn from those they are seeking to support. For example:

- social workers from the local children and families team got involved in the programme and agreed areas for improvement such as supervised contact arrangements;
- a creative writing group was established resulting in one parent getting award-winning poetry published; and
- parents contributed to teaching social work students in universities and presenting at conferences.

The success of the first programme paved the way for subsequent gap-mending programmes in a wide range of contexts including mending gaps with young care leavers, with young people with mental health problems, with parents who are refugees and asylum seekers, and more recently with unaccompanied asylum-seeking children.

Each programme has explored different issues based upon people's experiences. However, all have centred around the core themes first identified by parents. These themes were pertinent gaps for students and practitioners to identify with. This has been most strongly demonstrated when bringing people together from diverse cultures. Mending gaps with those who have no recourse to public funds whose human rights are constantly eroded has brought participants together as partners in learning and transformed educational methods in the North East of England where a high proportion of refugees, asylum seekers, and unaccompanied children have been placed by the government. This need for a new and innovative approach to working with migrants was identified by Investing in People and Culture, a leading support organisation working with refugees and asylum seekers across the United Kingdom. Working with the North East Social Work Alliance (a government-funded teaching partnership made up of 6 universities and 12 local authorities) the gap-mending approach has been adopted to break away from the traditional classroom-based learning model and to promote coparticipatory learning and research—testimony to how practitioners, managers, and academics are seeking to find more effective ways of learning with and from those who are traditionally unheard and marginalised in educational processes (Robson, Sampson, Dine, Hernandez, & Litherland, 2008).

An outline of the programme with young people is provided by way of explaining the approach. It is important to introduce the concept of mend the gap and convey how this applies in practice. This programme has been part of a coparticipatory (PHD/Durham University) research project in a larger study exploring the effectiveness of service user and carer involvement in social work education.

Over a 6-week period participants met weekly (12 young people, 6 students, 6 facilitators, and 3 interpreters)—mostly on Saturdays to avoid conflicting with school arrangements—to identify key gaps and explore these through conversations and activities around the following themes the young people identified prior to the programme commencing. As was the case with parents this was a significant starting point for young people to set the agenda instead of professionals:

- children's rights in the United Kingdom
- education
- age assessments
- professional roles
- reviews and care plans
- funding and resources.

Introducing the programme

The first session focussed on introductions since the key aim of the mend-the-gap approach is to meet as people first. Everybody therefore introduced themselves and shared a little about themselves in terms of interests and where they are from. The nature of coworking, research, and coproduction, which are essential components of gap mending, were explained illustrating the transformative capacity of coproduction that Needham and Carr (2009) defined as: "a potentially transformative way of thinking about power, resources, partnerships, risks and outcomes, not an off-the-shelf model of service provision or a single magic solution."

This presented a new opportunity for young people to participate equally in the group. As they had already met to learn about the mend-the-gap approach and set the agenda for the programme they were starting to understand and feel the difference between formal and informal learning.

Gaps Identified in the First Session

Having Too Much Time on Your Hands
Most young people attend school 2–3 days a week meaning they spend a lot of time in their accommodation. All young people said they would like to improve their English and have more to do. One young person gave an example of speaking Kurdish 5 days a week and English on 2.

They have no access to Wi-Fi/internet or TV, although that would help them all greatly with their English. One helpful teacher offered to email extra work to students to help improve their English outside college demonstrating a lack of understanding about young people having no online access whatsoever when they are not in college.

Not Understanding Systems/Local Culture Increases Vulnerability
Discussion around what it means to be a young unaccompanied minor showed how vulnerable young people are when they arrive in the United Kingdom. Without support they are sometimes told they do not belong here or they don't have value making it easy for extremists to prey upon them and take them into their care.

A recent newspaper report highlighted the risks young people seeking asylum have to face on their journey and when they arrive in the United Kingdom. Many young people have "disappeared."

The report concluded that there is growing evidence that young unaccompanied minors are more prone to the risks of radicalisation and that these risks intensify when youngsters have fewer opportunities for education and as a result "are particularly prone to propaganda" (*Telegraph*, 2017).

Lack of Preparation of Local Authorities and Foster Carers
A suggestion was made in the programme that young people need a plan that they can understand and follow step by step to ensure they get everything they need and are entitled to. One social work student explained how hard it was to find out what young people were entitled to and felt she "had to fight for everything." Plans should reflect the needs and experiences of young people, be followed up, and be signed off.

How Can These Gaps Be Mended?

Discussions throughout the programme revealed gaps in the knowledge and understanding of the roles played by young people, students, and practitioners. They shared a lack of clarity about some procedures and processes in which they were involved such as age assessment. The processes and training of social workers around age assessment varies greatly between local authorities. Young people are often asked personal questions without being told why. The process of assessing age is not informed by the young person's culture. For example, a child who has walked barefoot for 6 years could have a very strong body and appear older. This is the same for a child who has lots of facial hair. **Findings show that age assessment methods are particularly unreliable with boys who come from countries around the Middle East. The early onset of facial hair can make some look older than their European or east Asian counterparts** (Dehaghani, 2017). Although all the children were confident they knew their age, they were not believed.

Although children have a right to advocacy support, no one had told them about advocacy or the National Youth Advocacy Service (NYAS).

The role of an advocate is to promote the wishes and feelings of children and young people, as set out in The Children Act 1989 (s22) and Article 12 of the UN Convention on the Rights of the Child: "Children have the right to have their views considered when adults are making decisions about them, such as where they live, who with, who they have contact with and where they go to school." In 1991, the UK Government ratified the UN Convention on the Rights of the Child (UNCRC). This human rights treaty guarantees to all children and young people1 the right to express their views freely in all matters affecting them and for these views to be given due weight in accordance with the child's age and maturity (Article 12). There is a gap between this commitment and young people's experiences.

There is a 7-year difference between the Ethiopian calendar and the Western calendar. At the time of writing it is 2011 in Ethiopia. If social workers/other professionals having conversations with young people about when they were born are unaware of this, then this may explain why they think the young people are lying.

There are significant practice implications where social workers and other professionals doubt young people because the do not fit the western cultural perception of what children look like. This would amount to Western cultural bias.

> Social work education and practice need to be informed by wider social, political, economic, cultural and environmental ideas and a genuine dialogue about the appropriateness of knowledge based on western cultural values (Cook in Community Care, 2020).

As summed up by one young person: "Mend the Gap helps to make processes simpler and helps us understand what our rights are" (Community Care, 2018).

Building Positive Relationships

A key characteristic of the gap-mending approach lies in building relationships and trust. This was brought about by getting the young people following the discussion to engage in sharing activities such as table tennis, football, and scaling a climbing wall. This helped to show what young people are good at as well as having fun and enjoying physical exercise.

Outcomes

A distinct feature of the gap-mending approach is its aim to transform service provision. Unlike many other models to get service users involved in social work education, this approach brings everyone together in the same physical space establishing an equal platform to connect and learn from each other and influence policy and practice.

Outcomes from this programme have led to young people getting involved in training social work practitioners about how best to work with unaccompanied asylum-seeking children. Resources are being coproduced as guidance for local authorities about best practice in supporting young people upon arrival in the United Kingdom.

The programme has given young people the confidence and sufficiently improved their English language skills to present at educational and professional conferences.

For a good flavour of the research see the following 5-minute film: https://vimeo.com/254536784/805ac454cc.

Conclusions

There are strongly competing strands in modern UK social work as there have been in social work from its early founding. There are currently powerful ideological and political pressures on privatisation, managerialism, and increased managerial control, as well as an emphasis on academic ability and the need for "elite" social work education courses to feed this perceived need for more closely controlled practice and provision. At the same time neoliberal politics have emphasised the importance of reducing state spending, cutting public services, and getting people off welfare benefits into employment. This has been associated with the increased stigmatisation and "othering" of groups such as single and poor parents, disabled people and mental health service users, and refugees and asylum seekers—groups that are also closely associated with receipt of social work services. The effect of these developments is to privilege the control rather than support the role of social work and emphasise the distance between service users, practitioners, and citizens more generally.

Pioneering initiatives developed in the United Kingdom show the part a gap-mending approach in social work (and indeed potentially in other helping professions) can play in challenging the divisions that are increasingly being highlighted politically and in rehumanising social work as well as other health and care professions.

For example, divisions between people in the United Kingdom who are reliant on welfare benefits characterised by some politicians and media as skivers and people in paid employment have been deliberately played up by right-wing politicians and media. The same has been done to distance citizens from refugees and asylum seekers and so on. Social work practice and practitioners correspondingly are being increasingly distanced from the people they work with by the imposition of layers of bureaucracy, rationing processes that include mechanical call centres and prewritten scripts in the assessment process, and practitioners who have to spend more and more time in front of computer screens recording the minutiae of their activities.

The gap-mending approach highlights that there is an alternative. Moreover, the evidence currently available—although it needs to be built on—indicates that it is valued by both service users and providers and can achieve the formal personal and social goals established for social work. Based on the idea of supporting understanding, contact, and relationship between service users and workers it provides a critical starting point for relationship-based social work in preliminary learning that models such a relationship in its own process. It offers a much bigger international beacon for progressive and effective social work learning and practice that offers an effective challenge to the regressive direction of travel of social work under neoliberal politics and ideology.

NOTES

1. Carers are family members or friends providing unpaid support to someone close to them.
2. The Social Care Institute for Excellence is a charitable company independent of government in its operations although it receives core funding from government grants. The main aim of the SCIE is to collate and disseminate knowledge about good practice in social care in the United Kingdom (SCIE, 2011).

REFERENCES

Advocacy in Action. (2006, June). Making it our own ball game: Learning and assessment in social work education. *Social Work Education, 25*(4), pp. 332–346.

Askheim, O. P., Beresford, P., & Heule, C. (2016). Mend the gap-strategies for user involvement in social work education. *International Social work Journal,* 128–140.

Bailey, R., & Brake, M. (1975). *Radical Social Work,* London: Hodder and Stoughton Educational.

Beresford, P. (2013). Service User Issues: Rights, needs and expectations. In Littlechild, B. and Smith, R. (Eds.), *A Handbook for Interprofessional Practice in The Human Services: Learning to work together* (pp.187–199). London, Routledge.

Beresford, P. (2016). *All our welfare: Towards participatory social policy.* Bristol: Policy Press.

Beresford, P., & Carr, S. (2018). *Social policy first hand: An International Introduction to participatory Social Welfare.* Bristol: Policy Press.

Beresford, P., & Croft, S. (1990). *From Paternalism to participation: Involving people in social services*. London: Joseph Rowntree Foundation and Open Services Project.

Branfield, F. (2007, February). *User involvement in social work education*. London: Social Care Institute for Excellence.

Branfield, F. (2009). *Developing user involvement in social work education* (Workforce Development Report 29). London: Social Care Institute for Excellence.

Branfield, F., Beresford, P., & Levin, L. (2007). *Common aims: A strategy to support service user involvement in social work education*. London: Social Care Institute for Excellence.

Casey, H., Shenton, F., Araia, B., Simpson, J. (2018, April 13). Learning from people: The training method bringing service users and social workers together. *Community Care*. http://www.communitycare.co.uk/2018/04/13/learning-people-newtraining-method-brings-together-service-users-social-workers/.

Chiapparini, E. (2016). *The service user as a partner in social work projects and education*. London: Barbara Budrich Publishers. http://www.communitycare.co.uk/2018/04/13/learning-people-new-training-method-brings-together-service-users-social-workers/.

Cook in Community Care. (2020). https://www.communitycare.co.uk/2020/02/03/social-work-knowledge-still-based-western-values-can-practice-really-anti-oppressive/.

Dehaghani, R. (2017). *Challenging Childhood: Vulnerability and Age Assessments*. Available at: https://www.law.ox.ac.uk/research-subject-groups/centre-criminology/centreborder-criminologies/blog/2017/02/challenging. Accessed June 16, 2020.

Dominelli, L. (2010). *Social work in a globalizing world*. Cambridge: Polity.

Ferguson, I. (2008). *Reclaiming social work: Challenging neo-liberalism and promoting social justice*. London: Sage.

Morrow, E., et al. (2012). *Handbook of service user involvement in nursing and healthcare research*. Chichester: Wiley-Blackwell.

Needham, C., & Carr, S. (2009). https://www.scie.org.uk/publications/briefings/briefing31. Accessed August 28, 2018.

Robson, P., Sampson A., Dine N., Hernandez L., & Litherland, R. (2008). *Seldom heard—Developing inclusive participation in social care* (SCIE Positon Paper 10). https://www.scie.org.uk/publications/positionpapers/pp10.asp.

SCIE. (2011). *'We are more than our story': Service user and carer participation in social work education*. London: Social Care Institute for Excellence.

SWAN. (2009). *The social work action network constitution* [online]. Available at http://socialworkfuture.org/who-we-are/constitution. Accessed January 8, 2016.

Taylor, I., Braye, S., & Cheng, A. (2009). *Carers as partners (CaPs) in social work education*. London: Social Care Institute for Excellence https://www.telegraph.co.uk/news/2017/02/06/islamic-state-recruiting-child-refugees-head-europe/.

Telegraph. (2017). https://www.telegraph.co.uk/news/2017/04/28/radicalisation-doesnt-happen-private-need-open-spot-signs/.

CHAPTER 56

Social Change in Ethiopia and Social Work Responses

Wassie Kebede

INTRODUCTION

Although the world around us is changing we rarely sense the process of social change. A simple definition of social change is a shift in attitude and behaviour characterising society (Greenwood & Guner, 2008). Change can be also conceived an alteration that occurs in a social structure and/or social relationship. It is a change in the nature of society, its social institutions, behaviour, and relations. Historically, the study of social change originated with the ancient Greeks. The basic characteristics of social change being "alterations in social actions and interactions, human relationships and attitudes" (Goodwin, 2008, p. 2). Social work is supposedly responding to this social change process by unfolding and revisiting its teaching curricula and practice models to fit current needs. Social workers are social change agents, who drive change processes and at the same time respond to the challenges facing people. Social change may be to the benefit of individuals, groups, and/or communities or may challenge such groups in cases where community welfare deteriorates. In either case social workers have important roles to play as agents of change or leaders resolving social problems (Nandan, London, & Goodley, 2014). Though social work contributes to social change its involvement in engaging people to adjust to existing circumstances finds the profession struggling between containment and change.

Abramovitz (1998) describes the changing mandate of social work, claiming that "social workers' commitment to both individual and social change stems from at least three sources: (1) the mandates of our professional

W. Kebede (✉)
School of Social Work, Addis Ababa University, Addis Ababa, Ethiopia

S. S. M. et al. (eds.), *The Palgrave Handbook of Global Social Work Education*, https://doi.org/10.1007/978-3-030-39966-5_56

organizations, (2) the professional literature, and (3) the long history of activism among social workers themselves" (p. 513). Activism is an inherent principle of social work, whereby professionals engage to advocate on behalf of the disadvantaged. Until the late nineteenth century the individual change paradigm took the lead in the agenda for social work change (Abramovitz, 1998). However, later it was recognized that in the rapidly changing environment, the focus on individual change did not bring comprehensive and successful results to restoring the wellbeing of members of society. Social change, as a focus for social work, became more prominent between the 1930s and 1960s and reached its peak in the 1970s during the period of reformism. During this period, structural social work became part of a social work intervention model. Structural social work focused social change processes on institutional and structural levels rather than holding individuals responsible for their own problems. Rather, "structural social work links 'individual problems' to broader societal injustice", something that can be addressed by bringing social change and social adjustment (George & Marlowe, 2005, p. 7).

According to advocates of structural social work, social change and social movements form the core of social work action in its drive to overcome the root causes of injustice and oppression. Structural social work applies similar assumptions to radical social work, both of which believe in the need for social change to improve societal life. Radical social workers ally themselves with the powerless in order to challenge an existing system and seek radical change. Both structural and radical social workers believe that "the interlocking structure of patriarchy, racism, capitalism, heterosexualism, ageism, and ableism ... referred here to as 'primary structures' reproduced various forms of inequality" (Carniol, 1992, p. 4) which have to be changed for the good of society. Changes in all these aspects of capitalist structure, contribute towards achieving social change for the benefit of the disadvantaged. This is the gem of social work, as a profession and as an academic discipline, that is, to bring about social change.

Social work is supposedly linked to social development in developing countries, where development encompasses a social change process. However, due to its orientation to industrialized countries, social work education and practice in many developing countries seem to focus on individual work (case work) and therapy/clinical work (Pawar, 2014), overlooking that social work requires community level engagement to mobilize communities for social transformation/change. As Dominelli (1997, p. 29) defines it, social development is "... a dynamic way of organising resources and human interactions to create opportunities through which the potentials of all peoples—individually and collectively—can be developed to the full." According to this definition, it is through social development that there is an interaction of people, which drives the agenda for social change. Social development liberates people through a positive economic, social, cultural, and spiritual transformation/change. Liberating people from all forms of operation, and ensuring a prospective social change is one of the principles of social work. Therefore, social work, social development, and social change are inseparable. This means that whenever there is proper social work intervention, it contributes to social development; and social development is one of the drivers of social change.

This chapter presents both the social change that has occurred in Ethiopia and the social work responses to it. The next section discusses the theoretical foundations of social change under two subsections: theoretical foundations and social change processes. Section three considers the history and current tides of social change in Ethiopia over three periods of time: pre-1974, mainly covering the 1940s, 1950s, and 1960s—until the last emperor of Ethiopia was overthrown by the coup in 1974; between 1974 and 1991, during which a socialist/military government ruled the country; and from 1991 to the present day, during which the country was ruled by a monopoly comprising a coalition of four rebel fronts under ethnic federalism. During these three distinct periods social change took on specific features shaped by the ideology and politics of the time. Section four provides details about social work in Ethiopia and considers its responses to social change. The final section is a summary of the chapter.

THEORETICAL FOUNDATIONS OF THE SOCIAL CHANGE PROCESS

Theoretical Foundations

Before considering the theoretical foundations of social change, it is sensible to describe the essence of society and an individual's place in society. According to Karl Marx the fundamental entities that compose society are individuals in relationships. Therefore, society consists of individuals in constant relationships. Individuals in relationships with one another create history. Relations do not exist apart from between individuals who are related. Human beings have been essentially social throughout all historical periods because of their relationships (Gould, 1978). Human relationships constantly change temporally and spatially as society progresses from one stage of development to the next. In this regard change in society is natural and dynamic—it is a consequence of human relationships and occurs continuously, moving from a lower and simpler stage to a higher and more complex stage. From this perspective, social change is broadly described as "a significant change of structured social action or of the culture in a given society, community, or context" (Servaes, 2011, p. 1).

Nisbet (1969) noted that change is natural, directional, immanent, and continuous. Social evolutionists, according to Nisbet, assume that change over time is natural and normal. The author (p. 168) further summarises social change as directional in that "change is a succession of differences in time within a persisting identity," continuing with "a mere array of differences is not necessarily a change, a passing of time is just that, not a change, and persisting identity apart from anything else is the opposite of change." These three elements, considered as a whole, comprise what is called change. Further, social evolutionists claim social change is inevitable. This leads to the continuity of social change. Darity (2008, p. 568), comments that "change is an inherent feature of society rather than a periodic event that they undergo or something extraneous that acts upon or happens to them." Social change may occur in short dramatic bursts (revolutionary) or more gradually over a longer term (evolutionary). As evolutionary social change is gradual and occurs over a long period of time it is difficult to pinpoint the change process. On the other hand, revolutionary social change happens in a dramatic burst with an observable style. Three factors are responsible for driving social change: economic, political, and cultural change. Cultural influences play a particularly important role in social change. Secularisation and the development of science (as components of cultural changes) influence rapid processes of social change. The role of individuals, groups, and organisations in effecting social change is undisputable (Leat, 2005).

There are different ways of classifying the theories of social change, distinguishing between sociocultural, institutional, and individual change. Theories of social change can be also classified on the basis of broad concepts that consider general trends, with others that claim "if certain conditions allow, something else happen" (Goodwin, 2008, p. 4). For some theorists, the form of social change is most important while for others it is the cause or factors driving social change, for example, the psychological values that individuals hold that lead to a particular social process. According to Reeler (2007, p. 9) there are three theories of social change, namely, emergent change, transformative change, and projectable change: "...emerging change describes the day-today unfolding of life, adaptive and uneven process of unconscious and conscious learning from experience and the change that results from that." The unconscious or less conscious emerging changes are not as predictable, and are more chaotic and haphazard than conscious emerging changes. On the other hand, more conscious emerging changes occur when identity, relationships, structure, and leadership are formed—the environment being relatively stable and less contradictory. Transformative change occurs through crises and unlearning. Reeler maintains that "... unlike emerging change, which is characterized as a learning process, transformative change is more about unlearning, of freeing the social being from those relationships and identities, inner and outer" (p. 11). The third theory of social change, a projectable change, focuses on working with a plan. According to this model of social change, there are two orientations of change. The first is change characterised by a problem-based approach, working logically according to plans from the present day into the future. The second orientation, within a projectable change, states that social change "... is characterized by a creative approach of people imagining or visioning desired results, not as a direct solution but as a new situation in which old problems are less or no longer relevant" (p. 13).

Social Change Processes

Social change is multidimensional—considered in terms of space, time, speed, direction, content, and impact. Each dimension has a specific content (Table 56.1).

Sources of social change vary temporally and spatially. Healy (1998) identified demography, the economy, technology, planning, organisations, institutions, and culture as sources of social change. Demographic processes drive change at all levels of society. Technological innovations and the introduction of computers, cellular phones, the internet, and social media have brought dramatic social change at the local and global level. Economic transformations to globalised markets have instigated changes to relationships between nations and in doing so have brought about tremendous social transformation. Economic concentration in cities has attracted immense rural-to-urban migration, which in turn, has brought fast social change. Planned changes have contributed to effective social change by transforming non-organised communities into well-organised and outcome-focused entities. All these processes have facilitated rapid social change. Organisations have a direct effect on social change. Institutions operate according to set rules which affect the effectiveness of operations, directly influencing social change processes. Culture can also provoke social change but may constrain change too if not properly managed.

Goodwin (2008) poses the question "What happens to people's everyday relationships when there are significant changes in their society?" (p. 1). The author goes on to suggest that change may be dramatic, due to war and civil conflict; sudden, resulting from political collapse; or planned, where a handover of power from one political group to another occurs. In all cases, people as individuals, groups, or society at large experience shock, anxiety, and fear much, if not all, of the time. According to Macionis (1997), social change has four characteristics. First, social change happens everywhere, but the rate of change varies from place to place; second, social change is sometimes intentional but often unplanned; third, social change often generates controversy;

Table 56.1 Social change dimensions and content

Dimensions of social change	Content
Space	Micro, meso, and macro
Time	Short, medium, and long term
Speed	Slow, incremental, evolutionary versus fast, fundamental, and revolutionary
Direction	Forward or backward
Content	Sociocultural, psychological, sociological, organizational, anthropological, economic, and so forth
Impact	Peaceful versus violent

Source Adapted from Servaes (2011)

and fourth, some changes matter more than others. A number of factors drive social change: culture, conflict, idealistic factors, the need to adapt, environmental factors, economic and political factors, demographic change, and social movements. Technological factors and education may also cause social change. These drivers may occur concurrently or individually. The greater the number acting at any time, the stronger and faster the social change.

History and Current Tides of Social Change in Ethiopia

Ethiopia's society is multiethnic and multilinguistic. The country is endowed with a rich culture and diversity, integrating customs, traditions, and way of life across more than 80 linguistic groups. Currently, the country is experiencing both opportunities and challenges to its socio-cultural, economic, political, and ideological standing. The process of social change in contemporary Ethiopia is related to transition from a feudal system to a socialist revolutionary government to its present-day ethnic-based federal system of government. In Ethiopia, the history of social change can be broken down into three periods of time: the pre-1974 period, dominated by feudal legacy; the 1974–1991 socialist period; and the post-1991 ethnic-based federal government operating a "capitalist" system.

Social Change in Pre-1974 Ethiopia

Contemporary Ethiopia can be split into three historical stages—imperial, socialist, and federal (Záhorík, 2014). Before the rise of the socialist regime in 1974 (which was the Ethiopian version of Marxism), and its later replacement in 1991 by an ethnic-based federal government (which also took its initial political ideology from Albanian socialism) (Girma, 2012), Ethiopia was a predominantly feudal society which had been led by kings crowned by patriarchs of the Orthodox Church. During the pre-1974 period social changes were characterised by evolutionary processes often demonstrating contradictory intentions in terms of modernisation and the traditional doctrine of religion—which wanted to maintain the Solomonic Dynasty (those with ancestral lines dating back to King Solomon of Israel). Relatively rapid social changes in pre-1974 Ethiopia took place after the reign of Emperor Menelik II (1889–1913). The idea of social transformation from a clergy-led feudal society to a secular centralised government system was initiated a decade after Menelik II's reign by Emperor Tewodros (1855–1868). However, the secularisation of the state and separation from the church's influence became fully realised during the reign of Emperor Haile Selassie (1930–1974) (Ofcansky & Berry, 1991).

When considering social change in Ethiopia it is sensible to reference, as a starting point, the reign of Emperor Menelik II, since present-day Ethiopia was shaped during this period. The process of social change during the reign of Emperor Menelik II, and subsequent kings, took on cultural, economic, political, demographic, and psychosocial (attitude, perception, and value) perspectives. The establishment of Addis Ababa in 1886 (Garreston, 2000), as the capital city of Ethiopia, transformed many social arrangements including trade routes, settlement patterns, occupations, and population compositions. Social administration, taxation, and government structures were transformed from the traditional feudal system to a modern European-style bureaucracy (Wolde-Giorgis, 2012). The stabilised capital of Ethiopia brought about a successful transformation in market infrastructure, the formation of a standing army, and the growth of additional infrastructure such as railways, telecommunications, and water supplies (Záhorík, 2014)—all of which accelerated social change processes. Earlier developments during the reign of Menelik II and Lij Iyasu (1913–1916) (Záhorík, 2012) that contributed significantly to social change included the "establishment of Djibouti-Addis Ababa railway, the telephone, telegraph system, a Russian run hospital, the Bank of Abyssinia, the Menelik II school, the postal service, mechanical flour mill, printing press, a sewing mill, a tannery and a soap factory" (Ege, Aspen, Teferra, & Bekele, 2009, p. 137).

Ethiopia applied for membership to the League of Nations under Empress Zewditu in 1919, which brought with it international importance. To be accepted as a member of the League, Ethiopia had to officially abolish slavery, which brought about significant change to the social status of many groups in society—the actual cessation of the slave trade was a drawn out process however. When Haile Selassie established a constitutional Monarchy in 1931, the nation transformed from a regionally divided feudal society to a sovereign nation state. This initiated a wide range of social change processes accompanied by social disorientation and crises due to the Italian occupation during World War II. During this occupation the whole nation was in a state of war during which significant socio-cultural change occurred, including the displacement of people, the emergence of single parent families due to the deaths of hundreds of men in the war, the fusion of Ethiopian and Italian cultures, and the exile of King Haile Selassie—which instigated the emergence of regional war lords once again, albeit for a short period only (Watkins, Valley, & Alley, 1978).

The establishment of a system of modern education, government bureaucracies, infrastructure (road, telecommunications, etc.), the health service, urbanisation, and other elements of modern life continued during the Haile Selassie period. These socio-economic and cultural transformations were further facilitated by the Italian occupation, during which road networks, the health service, and trade were developed. The post-World War II protectorate of the British over the Ethiopian government administration, foreign diplomacy, and foreign trade, etc.—in additional to aid from the United States in the 1950s—brought more social transformations than ever before (Asayehgn, 1979).

The advancement of education meant that many young people attended modern schools and were able to enjoy government employment until the

1960s, after which the capacity of the government to employ people became limited due to saturation (Asayehgn, 1979). Social crises were critical to bringing the rule of Haile Selassie to an end. The farmers movement in some parts of Ethiopia fought against the land tenure system, the youth movement demanded an end to the monarchy and supported a Marxist–Leninist ideology, and more importantly, the hidden famine in the Wello region, filmed by British filmmaker Jonathan Dimbleby and broadcast under the title "the Unknown Famine" (Vestal, 2013, p. 47), precipitated rapid social change—from a monarchy to a revolutionary regime. The 1972–1975 famine hit many areas in the northeast regions of Ethiopia and brought changes in attitude and behaviour to those affected. For example, "[b]y early 1973, there were signs of the distress in *Wello* spilling over to other regions in the form of migration and roadside destitution: sick and hungry people…stopping vehicles to beg for food…marching to Addis Ababa to plead for food were turned away by the police…who denounced reports of the distress as 'fabrication'" (Kumar, 1987, p. 10). The famine was the turning point—young intellectuals (especially university students), the military, and farmers in some regions revolted against the Emperor.

Social Change in Ethiopia Between 1974 and 1991

In 1974 a coup d'état took place overthrowing the Haile Selassie regime, replacing it with a military junta. The political ideology transformed to socialism, land ownership shifted from private to state, and the confiscation of extra urban housing from renters and rural land from landlords was accompanied by atrocities resulting from civil conflict and internal instability. The conflict that cost thousands of lives was popularly known as the "Red Terror." According to Tareke (2016, p. 184) "the Red Terror was an outcome of the interlacing of three factors: contingent circumstances, ideological motivations and political ambition." During the "Red Terror" over 100,000 well-educated and idealistic young people were killed and further thousands forced to seek asylum in foreign countries. This signalled dramatic social change including a massive migration of intellectuals, the precipitation of various factions, and militarisation of the country (Marcus, Mehretu, & Crummey, 2019). Apart from the "Red Terror" the wars between Ethiopia and Somalia (1963–1964 and 1977–1978) (Kigen, 2002) claimed thousands of lives, caused further internal displacement, and created a vast number of single parent families. These wars fuelled social change processes that had already started because of changes in ideology, internal conflicts, and other associated socio-cultural and even religious dynamics.

In addition to the ideological transformations of Ethiopia, which brought a transition from a feudal society to a revolutionary state where the military maintained control of social change processes, other incidents took place during the socialist regime that significantly perpetuated progressive social change. One of the social actions that contributed to the formation of the new social order during the socialist regime was a mass campaign against illiteracy through an adult-learning program. This program had two phases. The first phase, known as the "development in cooperation" campaign, was declared soon after the 1974 revolution. In this program 60,000 people joined the campaign and over 160,000 citizens became literate over a two-year period. The second phase was a campaign known as the "National Literacy Campaign," which remained in action from 1979 to 1988. The commitment of this campaign was the eradication of illiteracy in Ethiopia. It reached over 22 million people, providing them with a basic level of reading and writing. Over 2 million campaigners (mostly high school graduates) participated across the entire country (Shenkut, 2006). The national literacy campaign was paralleled by an expansion of formal schools to rural Ethiopia. This opened up opportunities for many rural children and youths to enter into formal education. This increased the number of educated citizens in the country by thousands, if not millions. The expansion of formal education during the socialist regime contributed a continuity of evolutionary social transformation in areas of culture, religion, way of life, social occupation, and family. There was an increase in the migration of the educated from rural to urban areas and the formation of nuclear families in urban settings became more common.

The recurrent drought that affected Ethiopia in 1984/1985 brought another level of social change, especially in terms of demographic composition and settlement patterns. The 1984/1985 famine, which some scholars compared with the great famine of the late nineteenth century, claimed over 175,000 lives (Kumar, 1987) and changed the demographics of drought affected communities. The famine that occurred in the northern central regions of Ethiopia forced the socialist government to mobilise over 600,000 people to other parts of the country (mostly western and northwestern parts) for permanent resettlement (Helmut & Adugna, 1989). The resettlement program brought with it cultural and linguistic dynamics, where new settlers mixed with recipient communities. Although the resettlement program was criticised for its coercive nature—moving people from localities they grew-up into new foreign destinations—it contributed to the social change processes that existed until very recently.

Another famous government-sponsored social change process was the villagisation programme, which touched almost every farming village. Villagisation is defined as "the concentration of the population in villages as opposed to scattered settlements, typically to ensure more efficient control and distribution of services such as health care and education" (Grunditz, 2015, p. 9; Holm, n.d., p. 7). The villagisation of farmers was aimed at improving accessibility to basic infrastructure including water, electricity, road networks, and other services. More than 12 million farmers and their families were moved to core villages (Grunditz, 2015). The programme was criticised for taking place without the consent of farmers, lacking facilities for exercising spiritual life, like places of worship (churches and mosques), and detaching households from their generationally anchored mental maps (Lorgen, 1999). People often had to use communal latrines and live in shared premises with small backyards. They were encouraged to develop a sense of communitarianism. This once again contributed to the evolutionary transformation of society with some villages going on to develop into towns. This in turn brought economic changes with improvements to the livelihoods of many farmers. However, many other farmers suffered a deterioration of livelihood, resulting from loss of property and identity and a tougher way of life—representing digressive social change.

Post-1991 Social Change in Ethiopia

May 1991 witnessed the collapse of the socialist regime. The long-standing guerrilla fighters, collectively known as the Ethiopian Peoples' Democratic Revolutionary Front (EPDRF), defeated the most powerful military regime in East Africa and established a transitional government. The EPDRF rearranged the country's administrative divisions, including the constitution, on the basis of ethnic settlement, which brought a new social classification based on ethnic belongingness or ethnic identity. Ethnic identity or nationality gained recognition above Ethiopianism. "Civic Ethiopian identity and sovereignty was not placed in the Ethiopian people but in the various nations, nationalities and peoples" (Abbink, 2010, p. 1). Ethnically divided Ethiopia remained under conflict, and ethnic tensions contributed to a new line of social division—one primarily based on ethnic belongingness rather than any other arrangement. This ethnic-based federalism was rarely encountered globally, especially after the downfall of the socialist camp. Ethiopia, Nepal, South Sudan, Pakistan, and the former Yugoslavia, all adopted ethnic federalism and all experienced ethnic conflict and civil war.

Post-1991 Ethiopia underwent changes to its borders. The country became land-locked after Eritrea declared itself an independent state in 1993—bringing about significant change to its social landscape. The constitution (Transitional Government of Ethiopia, 1995) provided more power to group thinking (based on ethnicity and politics) than individual and/or national thinking. This also shifted social change with societies forced to identify themselves in terms of language and ethnicity rather than other forms of social identity, such as education, income, geographical location, occupation, or even gender. All other areas of social classification remained secondary to language and ethnic identity. For the first time in the history of the country, ethnic identity appeared on national identification cards—later becoming a means to scrutinise specific ethnic groups, with both good and bad outcomes.

From 1991 onwards, ethnic identity dictated the country's politics, economy, education, and way of thinking. In its true sense, ethnic-based administration "constrains the political, economic and social sense" (Abbink, 2012, p. 598), bringing about some important positive social changes and unspeakable social crises too, a summary of which is provided here. The positive results of the ethno-federal arrangement in post-1991 Ethiopia included freedom of ethnic and linguistic self-expression, incentives to study local languages and folklores, a decentralisation and devolution of federal power (at least theoretically), the establishment of state bodies to deal with inter-ethnic conflicts, and so on. However, the crises that arose in post-1991 ethno-federal Ethiopia outweighed the positive outcomes. Leaving economic and political challenges aside, the unexpected social challenges and changes post 1991 included, for example, "strong normative social and cultural pressure on minority ethnic groups to conform [the majority of which are considered as owners of a particular region]" (Abbink, 2012, p. 604). Naturally speaking, Ethiopia is not an ethnically divided country. The reality is that a mix of different linguistic[1] groups exists, not only at regional or sub-regional levels but also community and even family levels. Therefore, the ethnic-based divisions between regional administrations have remained unclear, with no means of identifying where so-called "pure" ethnic groups live in any particular region. As such, ethnic minorities became subjects of subjugation and in the worst-case scenarios suffered mass persecution due to ethnicity. Limited information from news media and online sources exists about such persecutions, identifying processes as ethnic cleansing.[2] Citing sources such as Voice of America (October 21, 2014), Sahara TV (February 1, 2014), Zehabesha. com (October 29, 2014), and Ethiopian Satellite Television (April 8, 2013), Atnafu (2018) reported some of the more recent incidences of ethnic cleansing in Ethiopia.

Relative deprivation, as noted by Yeshiwas (2018, p. 75), created a number of challenges including ethnic cleansing and segregation at work, school, and even in social spheres. Relative deprivation refers to the "feeling of being excluded from social, economic, and political benefits in contrast to other referent groups." Such feelings, coupled with negative pressure from referent groups, force ethnic minorities to leave their places of residence and migrate to their so-called "places of origin." Many are of course unaware of their "origin"—with parents, grandparents, or earlier ancestors having migrated during the post-1991 period due to the persecution of linguistic minorities. This ethnically agitated segregation alone caused significant social dynamics, including sustained inter-regional migration, inter-ethnic conflict, increased rural-to-urban migration, lack of employment in urban areas, increased crime and gender-based violence, and the deaths of hundreds and thousands of citizens.

Another area of social dynamism in post-1991 Ethiopia was the weakening of Ethiopian nationalism and the triumph of ethnic nationalism. Ethnicism became a reason for competition and conflict among different language groups, not only at the national level but also the regional and local levels. The Crises Group Africa Report (2009, p. 22) states that "ethnic conflicts have not disappeared [in the post-1991 period], but have been either transferred from the national to the regional, district and *kebele*[3] levels or been contained by the security forces." The intensification of ethnic tension changed peoples' views from favouring nationalism to devoting themselves to their ethnic identity. This contributed to a weakening of the sentiment of nation building. Those who rallied for a nation-building agenda were categorised as anti-ethnic, anti-democratic, and in extreme cases were accused of being terrorist supporters and jailed. The current regime has been criticised by many nationalists for "… disintegration [of the nation] through ethnic nationalism" (Belachew, 2009, p. 88).

The continuous ethnic tension in post-1991 Ethiopia has been accompanied by political, economic, and social tides, accelerating social change in both a positive and negative manner. The concentration of power among ethnic affiliated elites, the strong bond between politics and economic ownership, the unobstructed power of government officials to influence not only politics but also the economy, rampant corruption, and the unbearably high cost of living (especially in cities) have ensured the majority of people remain in poverty, struggling to survive from one day to another. These challenges have acted to promote unusual social behaviour, such as individualism, misbehaviour, systemic corruption, a loosening of bonds within families and communities, intolerance, and inter-religious conflict—all new social phenomena never experienced before by Ethiopians. Many believe that such tensions have been deliberately fabricated by the political elite to maintain stresses among groups of people—a divide-and-rule tactic adopted by the current government. In this regard, "Ethiopian officials acknowledge that the [above mentioned] tense situations are … at least partly the government's fault" (Committee on Foreign Affairs, House of Representatives, 2017, p. 1). Since 2015 the tension between the ruling party/government and demonstrators (backed by activists and some political opposition parties) has heightened and the government has "undergone deep reformation with an aim towards national reconciliation" (Cultural Survival, 2018, p. 2).

The tensions and unprecedented actions by the government, including the indiscriminate detention of young protesters, the declaration and subsequent state of emergency since 2016, and the internal pressure within the ruling party and external pressure from the Ethiopian Diaspora community and the world at large, have changed social dynamics in Ethiopia in a number of ways. The so called "opposing ethnic groups" of Oromo and Amhara, supported by other groups like the Guraghe, joined in their struggle against the government, an action that shocked the country. The three-year demonstration to seek political and economic reforms left many dead—killed by government forces—and thousands detained with further millions displaced from their homes. This resulted in changes to many social patterns. Perhaps most significantly the violence meant that many farmers were unable work, succumbing to famine and hunger. Cultural Survival (2018, p. 3) noted that "the displacement [in recent years] is a result of scarcity of food, farmland, and livestock as a result of the violent clashes."

Some members of the ruling party sought change and facilitated processes from within government that contributed strongly to the political and social changes observed in Ethiopia since March 2018. On 27 March 2018 the then prime minister resigned and the ruling party was forced to elect a new chair for the party, who then automatically became prime minster. The new prime minister called for reconciliation, integrity, and belongingness—in a sense Ethiopianism—over ethno-centric nationalism. This signalled a peaceful collaboration with Ethiopia's neighbouring countries including Eretria, a country considered an enemy for over 20 years (Gottlieb, 2018). Upon coming to power the new prime minister (Abiy Ahmed) has made commendable political decisions, such as the release of all political prisoners, including journalists, a lifting of the repressive state of emergency, promises for national reconciliation, and a reformation in government structures including deposing authoritative security workers, judges, and other civil servants who have exercised all sorts of human rights violations. These active steps have, in a very short period of time (since April 2018), brought about rapid changes to the social landscape, for example, the gender balance of political power has been addressed, ensuring that pertinent government offices including president, head of the supreme court, and electoral board are occupied by women. The country declared a peaceful reconciliation with all opposition parties ("competitor parties" to use the Prime Minister's words), some of which were armed. As a result, almost all opposition parties accepted and agreed to continue their political opposition peacefully. Further, all media, including social-media platforms, were given full freedom of expression.

Although the above political action, in terms of government restructuring, reconciliation with opposition parties and the media, and the release of all political prisoners, was applauded by Ethiopians and the international community, tensions relating to inter-ethnic conflicts still exist, with the political, economic, and social landscape remaining volatile. In the first six months after the new Prime Minister came to power (in April 2018) there were 420 recorded protests compared with 388 in the six months pre-April 2018 (Matfess, 2018).

SOCIAL WORK IN ETHIOPIA AND ITS RESPONSES TO SOCIAL CHANGE

As in any other developing country, social work represents a very new profession. In Ethiopia the first school of social work was opened in 1959 and educated students to the diploma level. Social work education was interrupted in 1974 by the military regime and ceased for three decades until 2004. By considering this 30-year[4] period of social work training in Ethiopia, it is possible to critique the responses of social work and social workers to social change. Since the imperial period in Ethiopia's history social change has been dynamic, especially after the 1960s when drought and famine severely affected the country. Both farmer and student movements against imperial rule peaked during this period.

The Ethiopian student movement was recognised as the most prominent process that contributed to the socio-political change that transformed the country from an "imperialist" to "socialist" ideology—recognised as a radical social change. Since the 1940s—after the end of World War II and the reinstatement of the Emperor to power by the British protectorate—the country moved from a purely agrarian economy to an industrial one, specifically, agriculture became industrialised. Distribution of agricultural products to domestic and international markets was monopolised by Ethiopia's royal family. Labour unions emerged to support individual industries and commercial farms—driven by the proletariat. However, these unions were not allowed to establish a national infrastructure. In the 1950s and 1960s, the student movement challenged the government on three levels—culturally, structurally, and politically (Darch, 1976). This contributed to the precipitation of a significant class struggle that overthrew the imperial regime in 1974. Students pushed for land reforms, the elimination of illiteracy, and the eradication of elitism in educational opportunity. This all contributed to a complete social transformation during the imperial era. One quote from student leader's speech, made in 1974, reads:

> We are supposed to prepare the people for change, but they are ready for change. Peasants have started shooting their landlords. They know that landlords are the cause of most of their hardships... We want the establishment of [a] provisional people's republic, the grant of all democratic rights, and a fundamental change of the socio-economic structure of society. (Darch, 1976, p. 7)

The above statement suggests that students and farmers were joint drivers of the overall social change process in the 1960s and 1970s. A reasonable contribution also came from the proletariat and, of course, the military, which later stole power from the real drivers of change—students and farmers. The focus of this section is to critique how the contribution of social work and social work professionals was significant in the social change process during the student movement and subsequent years.

There is no documentation available to show what social work education looked like between 1959 and 1974. In terms of post-2004 social work in Ethiopia, few attempts were made to document the process of development within the profession or its contribution to social change (Ayalew, 2016; Gregoire, 2014; Kebede, 2011, 2014, 2019; Temesgen, 2016). Some research has addressed the specific details of social work, but little has explored the role social work plays in social change or the responses of social work to social change processes. However, the small amount of research that does exist has helped introduce social work as a profession and identify its role in specific areas of social life, such as health, justice, and community partnership—all of which significantly impact social change.

For example, Kebede (2011) noted that prior to the re-birth of the social work profession in 2004, there were only a few social workers in the country. Social work was, by and large, practiced by non-qualified individuals. Under such circumstances it is naïve to even consider exploring its contribution or response to social change. The same author, in an article entitled *Social Work Education in Ethiopia: Celebrating the Re-birth of the Profession* (Kebede, 2014), suggests that social work in Ethiopia is in its infancy and that evaluation of its contribution to social development is premature. However, an indication of the role social work in Ethiopia might play to catalyse social change was given: "...the need to put more emphasis on rural social work ... Trained social workers with the basic skills to work in rural settings will empower communities to make a difference within their own home village" (p. 164). Empowerment, as described elsewhere in this chapter, is part and parcel of social change.

Gregoire (2014), dean at the Ohio State College of Social Work, identified some challenges to social work in Ethiopia but also recognised its promising future during a visit to one Ethiopian university. Gregoire noted that the benefits of social work in Ehiopia to the health and wellbeing of its citizens was not well understood. The author made a comparative analysis of the number of social work programs in Ethiopia, of which there were six during his visit, and the number in the United States—400 undergraduate and 220 graduate programmes. This small number of social work educational programmes in Ethiopia affects the total number of qualified social workers, expected by society to show leadership in social change processes and responses to societal change. Another important analogy made by Gregoire was that of social work staff in hospitals in Ethiopia and United States. He noted that physicians and nurses understood that social factors helped to increase the recovery time of patients. At the same time, however, he noted that these professionals have a reduced understanding of the role of social work in society. In one hospital he visited, Gregoire found only four social workers, whereas in the United States, in a similar sized hospital to the one he visited in Ethiopia, one would expect to find 50 social workers. With such an insignificant number of social workers in important social settings like hospitals, it is impossible for the profession to provide a seasoned response to social change.

One study conducted by Temesgen (2016) on hospital social workers demonstrated another challenge, one which in many ways negates assumptions that social work responds in any way to social change in Ethiopia. Of the 12 participants in the study, only one had a social work qualification. The others were either qualified in nursing, sociology, social anthropology, psychology, or management training but were employed as hospital social workers. Social work intervention is a model of practice that contributes to social change or that responds to social change in an appropriate manner. In hospital settings where Temesgen conducted her study, half the participants commented that they were unaware of the concept of social work intervention. Such a lack of basic social work knowledge contributes to the gap we observe today in Ethiopia's social work response to social change. In addition to the shortage of trained social workers in the country, social work positions are inappropriately occupied by professionals from other disciplines, contributing highly to the misconceptions society has about social work in Ethiopia.

Another researcher conducting a study in a court setting identified judges who misunderstood the role of social work (Ayalew, 2016). It was found that judges, specifically new graduate judges, misunderstood the role of social work in addressing pertinent social issues facing those in conflict with the law. These judges passed judgements without considering court reports prepared by social workers. Research showed that of the eight professionals who participated in Ayalew's in-depth interviews, only two had social work training—similar to the findings in hospitals. The rest were either lawyers or psychologists who held social work positions.

In contrast to this challenge of a lack of professionalisation in social service centres, there are promising instances of social work professionals taking responsibility to drive social change. However, there is still a shortage of research papers to cite on the subject. Many qualified social workers are employed by non-governmental organisations (NGOs). They work in areas of community development, therapeutic care, and other social services such as health, education, water and sanitation, and livelihood and family empowerment. Some graduates of the former school of social work in the late 1960s are current leaders of NGOs, contributing critically to social change processes. Such senior social workers also employ new graduates and train them on the job in community settings where real social change is happening.

It is important to point out that social work schools actively engage their post-graduate students whenever a community crisis occurs. Examples of intervention by social work schools and their students include activities related to the rehabilitation of migrants, victims of landslides, and victims of internal displacement resulting from internal conflict. For example, in 2013 Saudi Arabia decided to expel about 163,000 Ethiopian migrants (Mengistu, 2015) over a very short period of time. The Ethiopian government was forced to arrange over 10 flights a day to return these so-called illegal migrants (illegal according to Saudi Arabia's Labour law). Many returnees were sheltered in tents adjacent to Bole International Airport. Many suffered psychological stress and social crises as a result of their sudden expulsion—a significant number had limited resources and some women were pregnant. Furthermore, the group included a significant number of children (about 8600). Those with rural backgrounds were unaware of the whereabouts of their families. Social work students and social work faculties from Addis Ababa University worked with them 24/7 over a period of several weeks and provided psychosocial support, family tracing, and reintegration.

Vast amounts of city trash that had been pilled-up for decades in the southwest of Addis Ababa suddenly collapsed in 2017 burying squatter houses built upon loose foundations. Many residents either lost property, were injured, or in some sad cases, lost their lives. The School of Social Work at Addis Ababa University was asked by Addis Ababa City Administration to volunteer psychosocial support and rehabilitation services to residents. Both the students and faculty provided commendable support to those people hit by the crisis. This represents a good example of the response of social work to social change, albeit a negative social change. This intervention meant that community members were able to rehabilitate themselves and were less affected by post-traumatic stress disorder. Other responses by social workers to unexpected social crises may have occurred in other regions of the country as well. However, due to a lack of documentation other examples are scarce, with only engagements by social work students and social work faculty members from Addis Ababa University being identified.

University–community engagements that focus on resource mobilisation and livelihood improvement are other good examples of social work responding to social change. One such example was a university–community partnership project run by Addis Ababa University's School of Social Work and the Gedam Sefer community in Addis Ababa. This project was initiated by post-graduate social work students and was able to create a partnership between the local community, university, and NGOs to mobilise local resources for community development. A report compiled on this community–university engagement stated "[this] community–university partnership is unique in that it not only brings together very different kinds of people—researchers, government officials, adult residents, children and youths—but also because it must integrate the perspectives of representative groups and bring them together according to the principles of ABCD" (Butterfield, Yeneabat, Kordesh, & Kebede, 2011, p. 12). The project brought about a complete shift in the attitudes and beliefs of community members with development models shifting from needs-based to asset-based and correlated to social transformation or social change as a strategy for livelihood improvement. Social work students played a critical role in bringing community members, local government officials, and the city's administration together to address local poverty, demonstrating how social work could bring about, and responds to, changes in society.

Poor communities are initially more appreciative of social change than improvements in physical infrastructure like roads. One community member from Gedam Sefer, who participated in the community–university partnership mentioned above, provided a powerful statement—it became the title of a research article on the accomplishments achieved by social workers engaging with the community—"we can't eat a road" she said (Yeneabat & Butterfield, 2012, p. 135). These words were an expression of grievance about the government's initiative to construct local roads without first considering the levels of poverty in local communities, highlighting that change should be real and should make a difference to the poor in society. Social work's response to social change should deliver on these words.

SUMMARY

Three factors are responsible for driving social change, that is, economic, political, and cultural change. The role of individuals, groups, and organisations in effecting social change is undisputable. For some theorists, the precise form of social change is most important, while for others, it is the cause or factors driving social change. Social change is multidimensional, measured in terms of space, time, speed, direction, content, and impact. Sources of social change vary spatially and temporally. The process of social change in contemporary Ethiopia is related to the country's history of transition from a feudal system to a socialist revolutionary government and its present-day ethnically based federal system of government. Relatively rapid social change in pre-1974 Ethiopia took place after the reign of Emperor Menelik II (1889–1913). When Haile Selassie established a constitutional Monarchy in 1931, the whole picture of the nation transformed from a regionally divided feudal society to a sovereign nation state. In 1974 a coup d'état overthrew the Haile Selassie regime replacing it with a military junta which brought revolutionary social change to the entire country. The political ideology transformed to socialism, land ownership shifted from private to state, confiscation of extra urban housing from renters and rural lands from landlords were quickly accompanied by the mass atrocities of civil conflict and internal instability. One of the social actions that contributed to the formation of a new social order during the socialist regime was the mass campaign against illiteracy through the adult learning programme. Another famous government sponsored social change process was the villagisation programme, which touched almost every farming village.

In post-1991 Ethiopia, ethnic identity or nationality gained recognition, "civic Ethiopian identity and sovereignty was not placed in the Ethiopian people but in the various nations, nationalities and peoples." Ethnically divided Ethiopia remained under conflict and ethnic tension contributed to a new line of social division, one primarily based on ethnic belongingness. Ethnic minorities became subjects of subjugation and in some worst-case scenarios mass persecution due to their ethnic identity. Ethnicism became the grounds for competition and conflict among different language groups, not only at the national level but also regional and local levels. The tensions and unprecedented actions by the government, including the indiscriminate detention of young protesters, the declaration and subsequent state of emergency since 2016, the internal pressure within the ruling party and external pressure from the Ethiopian Diaspora community and the world at large, changed the social dynamics in Ethiopia. Social work in Ethiopia is in its early stages. In addition to Ethiopia's shortage of trained social workers, many social work positions are inappropriately occupied by other professions—contributing to the public's misconceptions about social work.

NOTES

1. Language is the main criterion for ethnically driven regional administrations in Ethiopia.
2. "Ethnic cleansing is the systematic annihilation or forced removal of the members of an ethnic, racial, or religious group from a community in order to change the ethnic, racial, or religious composition of a given region" (Davis, 2000, cited in Atnafu, 2018).
3. *Kebele* is the lowest government administrative structure.
4. 15 years prior to 1974 and 15 years since 2004.

REFERENCES

Abbink, J. (2010). *Political culture in Ethiopia: A balance sheet of post 1991 ethnically-based federalism.* The Netherlands: African Study Centre (ACS Info Sheet 8/2010).

Abbink, J. (2012). Ethnic-based federalism and ethnicity in Ethiopia: Reassessing the experiment after 20 years. *Journal of Eastern African Studies, 5*(4), 596–618.

Abramovitz, M. (1998). Social work and social reform: An arena of struggle. *National Association of Social Workers, 43,* 512–526.

Asayehgn, D. (1979). *Socio-economic and educational reforms in Ethiopia (1942–1974): Correspondence and contradiction.* Paris: International Institute for Educational Planning.

Atnafu, B. (2018). Ethnic cleansing in Ethiopia. *The Canadian Journal of Peace and Conflict Studies, 50*(1), 77–104.

Ayalew, S. (2016, September). *Role and contribution of social work practice in court settings and its support system: The case of Lideta first instant court Addis Ababa* (Master thesis). Addis Ababa University.

Belachew, G. (2009). Ethiopian nationalism: An ideology to transcend all odds. *African Spectrum, 44*(1), 79–97.

Butterfield, K. A., Yeneabat, M., Kordesh, R., & Kebede, W. (2011, January). *A partnership for improving the lives of poor families in Gedam Sefer community in Ethiopia: Opportunities, challenges and lessons learned* (Final Report). Addis Ababa.

Carniol, B. (1992). Structural social work: Maurice Moreau's challenge to social work practice. *Journal of Progressive Human Services, 3*(1), 1–20.

Committee on Foreign Affairs, House of Representatives. (2017). *Democracy under threat in Ethiopia.* Washington, DC: US Government Publication Office.

Crises Group Africa Report. (2009, September). *Ethiopia: Ethnic federalism and its discontents* (Africa Report No. 153–4).

Cultural Survival. (2018, October). *Observation on the state of indigenous human rights in Ethiopia.* The 33rd session of the United Nations Human Rights Council, Universal Period Review 2019, Submission Date.

Darch, C. (1976, December 20–22). *The Ethiopian student movement in the struggle against imperialism 1960–1974.* Paper presented to the Annual Social Science Conference of the East African Universities (12th: Dar es Salaam).

Darity, A. W., Jr. (Ed.). (2008). *International encyclopaedia of the social sciences* (2nd ed.). New York: Course Technology Cengage Learning.

Dominelli, L. (1997). Social work and social development: A partnership for social change. *Journal of Social Development in Africa, 12*(1), 29–38.

Ege, S., Aspen, H., Teferra, B., & Bekele, S. (Eds.) (2009). Proceedings of the 16th international conference of Ethiopian studies (volume 1). Trondheim: Norwegian University of Science and Technology, Department of Anthropology.

Garreston, P. P. (2000). *A history of Addis Ababa from its foundation in 1886 to 1910*. Germany: Otto Harrassowitz.

George, P., & Marlowe, S. (2005). Structural social work in action: Experience from rural India. *Journal of Progressive Human Services.* https://doi.org/10.1300/J059v16n01_02.

Girma, M. (2012). *Understanding religion and social change in Ethiopia*. New York: Palgrave Macmillan.

Goodwin, R. (2008). *Changing relations: Achieving intimacy in a time of social transition*. Cambridge: Cambridge University Press.

Gottlieb, D. (2018, September). *Ethiopia 2018: The transition of power and its implications* (Volume 4, No. 3). Tel Aviv University: Africa Research Program.

Gould, C. C. (1978). *Marx's ontology individuality and community in Marx's theory of social reality*. Cambridge: The MIT Press.

Greenwood, J., & Guner, N. (2008). *Social change*. Madrid: Department of Economics Universidad Carlos III de Madrid.

Gregoire, T. (2014). *The future of social work in Ethiopia*. Retrieved from https://u.osu.edu/onehealth/2014/03/13/the-future-of-social-work-in-ethiopia-its-students/.

Grunditz, M. (2015). *Is villagization an acceptable solution? An analysis of villagization programmes in Ethiopia in relation to the fulfilment of state obligations under the ICESCR and the concept of self-determination of indigenous people* (Master thesis). Faculty of Law, Lund University.

Healy, K. (1998). *Social change: Mechanisms and Metaphors*. Princeton: Princeton University.

Helmut, K., & Adugna, A. (1989). Settler migration during the 1984/85 resettlement programme in Ethiopia. *GeoJournal, 19*(2), 113–127.

Holm, M. (n.d.). *Villagization: A case study of Ethiopia's villagization programme*. Retrieved from https://projekter.aau.dk/projekter/files/237239193/Thesis_Villagization_Mads_Holm.pdf.

Kebede, W. (2011). The challenges of re-establishing social work education at Addis Ababa University: A personal reflection. *Reflections-Winter, 2011,* 65–67.

Kebede, W. (2014). Social work education in Ethiopia: Celebrating the re-birth of the profession. In H. Spitzer, J. Twikirize, & G. Wairire (Eds.), *Professional social work in East Africa: Towards social Development, poverty reduction and gender equality* (pp. 161–172). Kampala: Foundation Publishers.

Kebede, W. (2019). Social work education in Ethiopia: Past, present and future. *International Journal of Social Work, 6*(1). https://doi.org/10.5296/ijsw.v6i1.14175.

Kigen, C. E. (2002). *The impact of the cold war on the Ethiopia-Somalia relations, 1960–1990* (MA dissertation submitted to the institute of diplomacy and international studies). University of Nirobi, Kenya.

Kumar, G. (1987). *Ethiopian famines 1973–1985*. World Institute for Development Economic Research of the United Nations University.

Leat, D. (2005). *Theories of social change.* Gütersloh: Bertelsmann Foundation.

Lorgen, C. C. (1999). *The experience of villagization: Lessons from Ethiopia, Mozambique and Tanzania.* Oxafam-GB. Retrieved from https://www.google. com/search?q=Challenges+of+Ethiopian+villagization+programe%2C+PD-F&oq=Challenges+of+Ethiopian+villagization+programe%2C+PD-F&aqs=chrome..69i57.12067j0j7&sourceid=chrome&ie=UTF-8.

Macionis, J. J. (1997). *Sociology.* Upper Saddle River, NJ: Pearson Education.

Marcus, G. H, Mehretu A., & Crummey, E. D. (February 2019). *Federal Democratic Republic of Ethiopia: Encyclopaedia Britannica.* Retrieved from https://www.britannica.com/place/Ethiopia.

Matfess, H. (2018). *Change and continuity in protests and political violence PM Abiy's Ethiopia.* Retrieved from https://reliefweb.int/report/ethiopia/change-and-continuity-protests-and-political-violence-pm-abiy-s-ethiopia.

Mengistu, B. (2015, June). *An assessment of rehabilitation and reintegration of female returnees: A case of Kingdome of Saudi Arabia returnees* (Master thesis). Addis Ababa University.

Nandan, M., London, M., & Bent-Goodley, T. (2014). *Social workers as social change agents: innovation, social entrepreneurship and entrepreneurship.* Retrieved from https://digitalcommons.kennesaw.edu/cgi/viewcontent.cgi?article=4780&context=facpubs.

Nisbet, A. R. (1969). *Social change and history: Aspects of the western theory of development.* New York: Oxford University Press.

Ofcansky, P. T., & Berry, L. (1991). *Ethiopia, a county study.* Federal Research Division Library of Congress: Kessinger Publishing LLC.

Pawar, M. (2014). Social work practice with local communities in developing countries: Imperatives for political engagement. *Sage Open,* 1–11. https://doi.org/10.1177/2158244014538640.

Reeler, D. (2007). *A three-fold theory of social change: Implication for practice, planning, monitoring and evaluation.* CDRA: Centre for Developmental Practice.

Servaes, J. (2011). *Social change.* Retrieved from https://www.researchgate.net/publication/274193404.

Shenkut, K. M. (2006). *Ethiopia: where and who are the world's illiterates? United Nations Educational, Scientific and Cultural organization.* Background Paper Prepared for the Education for All Global Monitoring Report.

Tareke, G. (2016). The red terror in Ethiopia: A historical aberration. *Journal of Development Societies, 24*(2), 206.

Temesgen, H. (2016, June). *Social work practice: Roles and challenges of social workers in selected public hospitals in Addis Ababa* (A Master thesis in Social Work). Addis Ababa University.

The Transitional Government of Ethiopia. (1995). Constitution: Federal *Negarit Gazetta,* Proclamation number 1/1995.

Vestal, M. T. (2013). The lost opportunity for Ethiopia: The failure to move toward democratic governance. *International Journal of African Development, 1*(1), 40–56.

Watkins, T., Valley, S., & Alley T. (1978). *Political and economic history of Ethiopia.* USA: San José State University, Department of Economics. Retrieved from http://www.sjsu.edu/faculty/watkins/ethiopia.htm.

Wold-Giorgis, E. (Ed.). (2012). *What is "Zemenawinet?" perspective son Ethiopian modernity*. Addis Ababa: Friedrich-Ebert-Stiftung.

Yeneabat, M., & Butterfield, K. A. (2012). "We can't a road:" Assest-based community development and the Gedam Sefer community partnership in Ethiopia. *Journal of Community Practice, 20*(1–2), 134–153.

Yeshiwas, A. D. (2018). Transactive approach: Explaining dynamics of ethnicity and inter-ethnic conflicts in post 1991 Ethiopia. *International Journal of Education, Culture and Society, 3*(4), 68–77.

Záhorík, J. (2012). *Iyasu V of Ethiopia (1913–1916): Perilous traitor or a true modernizer?* Retrieved from https://dspace5.zcu.cz/bitstream/11025/11847/1/Zahorik.pdf.

Záhorík, J. (2014). *Colonial perspective and nationalism(s) in Ethiopia in the context of African decolonization*. Pilsen: Department of Historical Sciences, Faculty of philosophy and Arts, University of West Bohemia.

CHAPTER 57

Developing Self-Reflexivity in Students Regarding Awareness of Racial Inequalities in Mental Health Service Provision

Mayio Konidaris◉ *and Melissa Petrakis*◉

BACKGROUND

Mariam had migrated from her home country 20 years ago but due to a number of reasons, and circumstances beyond her control, did not speak English. She had experienced a significant mental health decline over the years and had been hospitalised into a psychiatric facility due to an acute psychotic presentation, where she remained feeling alone and very isolated. Despite being admitted for over a week she was not provided with an interpreter during treatment. The rationale provided reflected racial bias, suggesting that since Mariam had migrated over 20 years ago there was no excuse for her to not be fluent in English and therefore no need for an interpreter.

The case of *Mariam* is based on a true example. Unfortunately, Mariam's scenario is not unique and clinical encounters such as this (and others) fuelled by white privilege and oppression for the most marginalised are continuously

M. Konidaris
Department of Social Work, Monash University, Melbourne, VIC, Australia

M. Petrakis (✉)
Senior Lecturer at the Department of Social Work,
Monash University, Melbourne, VIC, Australia
e-mail: melissa.petrakis@monash.edu

Senior Research Fellow at St Vincent's Hospital (Melbourne),
Mental Health Service, Melbourne, VIC, Australia

© The Author(s) 2021
S. S. M. et al. (eds.), *The Palgrave Handbook of Global Social Work Education*, https://doi.org/10.1007/978-3-030-39966-5_57

perpetuated, raising alarming concerns for appropriate mental health treatment and outcomes.

Such racialised clinical encounters heighten the advocacy and necessity for personal insight and self-awareness and its ongoing cultivation to consistently address implicit racial bias in social work practice. As noted in the case of *Mariam* the consequences of such racially influenced clinical decisions may also lead to enhancing the accuracy of psychiatric assessments and diagnoses— the implications being improved therapeutic engagement, more appropriate treatments, and an enhanced trust and rapport resulting in improved medication compliance. This may alleviate triggering depression and anxiety, common with implicit racial bias or setting-specific racism (Paradies et al., 2014). Overall, this may enhance consumer and service provider satisfaction, attend to cultural influences in recovery, and reduce negative cultural assumptions and stereotypes (Ascoli, Palinski, Owiti, De Jongh, & Bhui, 2012).

"STARTING WHERE THE CLIENT IS": SELF-REFLEXIVITY, CULTURAL HUMILITY, AND SOCIAL WORK EDUCATION

In deconstructing *self-reflexivity* in social work education, or as described throughout this chapter as *critical self-awareness*, the notion of "starting where the client is" resonates (Pilsecker, 1994). That is, the practitioner is challenged to consider how they are impacted by the client and all they bring to the therapeutic space and to remain critically aware of the influence of their own values, attitudes, and biases. Pilsecker (1994) therefore extends the notion of *starting where the client is* to one embedded in transparency and humility, inclusive of *starting where both the client and therapist are*. A true commitment to this therapeutic process with culturally diverse clients is inclusive of both positions, enabling an open and honest dialogue—the principles key to *cultural humility*. It is acknowledged that this is a practice for both social work academics and their students. This approach will no doubt suit some better than others—some will be more comfortable and confident to engage in such an earnest reflective process. Thus, in order to enhance and cultivate confidence in levelling this power differential it is vital to introduce this paradigm early on in social work education.

Engaging in *self-reflexivity* and critical self-awareness is particularly pertinent for practitioners in the mental health field and is therefore of relevance within social work education. Yip (2006, p. 393) elaborates, emphasising "the manifestation of mental illness and mental health problems are culturally bounded," highlighting as a consequence the importance of practitioners' understanding of *cultural indigenisation*. That is, in terms of how Western models of mental healthcare fit (or do not fit) into non-Western modalities. Therefore, it is paramount for trainees (*trainees* are utilised interchangeably with *social work students* throughout this chapter) and practitioners to be aware of their own explanatory models of mental illness and their influence on direct practice and ultimately treatment outcomes. It is thus emphasised that *self-reflexivity* is key given the tensions and complexities which arise from students and practitioners as they straddle *cultural* clashes or *sameness* (in terms of *overidentification*) in practice with cultural diversity.

Similar tensions are also identified in a practice context, that is, dealing with colleagues from different cultural backgrounds. Consequently, *self-reflexivity* aims to address a range of biases (not merely pertaining to racial bias), cultural assumptions, and negative stereotypes both within practice and organisational settings. Within the field of social work, self-reflexivity or critical reflexivity (both terms are utilised synonymously and interchangeably) are essentially considered two pronged (Allan, 2009). First, it encourages clients of services to be open about their thoughts and feelings in order to enhance and optimise self-growth and healing throughout the therapeutic process. Second, it aims to encourage the openness and self-reflection of social work students and practitioners, particularly as client information is gathered and their position of power influences the therapeutic process. Therefore, professional social workers and trainees develop the ability to reflect on their own position of power and critical self-awareness in relation to their practice and the influence of their own personal self in the helping domain.

According to Azzopardi and McNeill (2016), a growing sense of *cultural consciousness* and awareness of issues related to *oppression* and power are significant to self-reflexivity—they state that it is "akin to a culturally humility framework, ongoing reflection on how one is positioned within the continuum of power and its effects on practice, perceptions about clients, and the framing of problems and solutions is essential to this process" (p. 294). This is pertinent in the Australian social work context given the history of colonisation and ongoing oppression, poor health outcomes, and transgenerational transmission of trauma for Aboriginal Australians. Thus, students working with difference and diversity, as well as those who are marginalised, are encouraged to be conscious of organisational structures perpetuating notions of *institutional racism* where racial bias is either overt or covert, inherent in policy, and often translates into poor clinical outcomes. Following a police enquiry in the United Kingdom as a result of a substantiated racist homicide, *Institutional Racism* was defined as:

> The collective failure of an organization to provide an appropriate and professional service to people because of their colour, culture or ethnic origin. It can be seen or detected in processes, attitudes and behaviour, which amounts to discrimination through unwitting prejudice, ignorance, thoughtlessness and racist stereotyping which disadvantages minority ethnic people. (Fernando, 2010, p. 11)

Given the introspective focus of *cultural humility* it further promotes and cultivates the learning of cultural competence as preparation for the clinical practice of social work students. As already inferred, this is particularly pertinent in challenging notions of colonisation and *institutional racism*, and is of specific relevance to the authors' Australian historical context and Aboriginal people. Hence, it is important to note the relevance of *cultural safety* with Aboriginal Australians (and other Indigenous populations globally) as a consequence of historical socio-political subjugation, colonisation, and white oppression (Kirmayer, 2012). As an overarching framework however *cultural humility* is not deemed a one-stop framework, rather an approach to working with cultural diversity that is inclusive of difference.

AIMS/OBJECTIVES

In this chapter the authors have aimed to synthesise and critically appraise some of the literature regarding self-reflexivity, cultural competence, and cultural humility. These concepts, and related practices used to educate staff, have been considered in relation to their current and potential application to training social work practitioners.

The methodological approach taken was incremental, comprising two stages.

Stage 1: As part of a broader research initiative a scoping literature review was undertaken to synthesise and critically appraise the literature regarding self-reflexivity, cultural competence, and cultural humility, as per the aims/objectives.

The databases utilised were PsycInfo, ProQuest central, CINAHL plus, Informit, Google scholar, Taylor & Francis online, and Ovid MEDLINE. The publication dates considered were between 1997 and 2017, although some publications outside this period were included. This timespan was chosen to include publications about cultural training during the initial use and training of cultural humility principles in health service provision and the period of emergence of cultural competence training initiatives.

Stage 2: Subsequently a needs analysis was carried out to examine the views of social work students regarding their interest in, and current sense of, competency regarding cultural humility approaches.

CRITICAL LITERATURE REVIEW

Through the critical review, the broader theme of *self-reflexivity* underpins the findings in the literature grouped under the following headings:

- Social work education, research, and practice.
- Cultural competency, cultural humility in social work, and health service provision.

Social Work Education, Research, and Practice

While students are on clinical placement it is acknowledged that they are in fact *service providers*. In spite of students being in a less powerful position, themes of power and advantage in relation to cultural issues remain at the fore with clients being in a less powerful and more disadvantaged position. Therefore, addressing cultural and racial inequalities through dialogue in educational paradigms is helpful in reducing the propensity for racial bias and power differentials that impact negatively on clinical outcomes. A useful approach is to utilise critical self-awareness between service providers and culturally diverse populations. Addressing implicit racial bias may assist in various ways. It may promote equity and social inclusion in organisational processes and policies. It may enhance the accuracy of psychiatric assessments and diagnoses, leading to the implementation of more appropriate treatments. It may improve therapeutic engagement, trust, and rapport building resulting in improved medication compliance. It may alleviate the propensity of triggering additional symptoms of depression and anxiety, commonly associated with implicit racial bias in organisations or setting-specific racism (Paradies et al., 2014). These benefits may enhance consumer and service provider satisfaction and attend to cultural influences in recovery, inhibiting negative cultural assumptions and stereotypes (Ascoli et al., 2012).

Confronting such concerns in any system, particularly health and mental health systems, is a challenge—people often hold strong views about the subject, but little knowledge about the theory and practice regarding race and racism. Therefore, exploring ways in which to prepare students entering mental health services, in order to better address disparities impacting culturally diverse populations, will have merit. Relevant education and training, including a process that is *internal* and not *external* to the student, should raise awareness and build skills. A *cultural humility* framework will further support the *internal process*, promoting dialogue around racial awareness. Developing a student's ability to self-reflect will be a critical tool towards enhancing racial literacy and breaking the barriers between future service providers and culturally diverse communities.

Various schools within the helping professions draw upon processes of self-reflexivity in order to support trainee self-growth, particularly when personal issues and emotional vulnerabilities arise. This process sometimes results in trainees themselves engaging in therapy, providing a parallel process of learning—allowing them to empathise with clients *in therapy* by experiencing the emotional vulnerability that often exists when seeking help. The first author recalls a small group-learning exercise when training as a family therapist, whereby students were encouraged to reflect on the underlying reasons for working in the helping professions. That is, trainees were asked to consider whether their motivation was primarily *voyeuristic* or if they were themselves *wounded healers*. The latter acknowledges that many of those drawn into the helping professions (whether social work or work in a related field) have suffered a deeply held emotional struggle or a search for answers.

For the first author, the challenges encountered growing up in a migrant background in a Western context determined their passion to address the cultural issues, tensions, and struggles felt by both clinicians and clients and inspired further exploration of the role that cultural issues play for those living with mental illness (Konidaris, 2001), and subsequently, research into the benefits of providing the principles of *cultural humility* as part of the training regime for mental health practitioners (Konidaris & Petrakis, 2018). Despite the initial development of this concept coming from medical fields it can be strongly correlated to critical social work theory.

It is of particular relevance in challenging Australia's history of colonisation and notions of *institutional racism* as well as working within a framework that is inclusive of difference and diversity. Thus its relevance in social work education is twofold: first, to encourage future practitioners to address their own cultural biases and assumptions in order to enhance cultural competence; second, to enhance culturally safe social work learning environments for student cohorts from diverse, marginalised, and minority backgrounds.

Students are often at different stages of maturity and emotional development during social work education. Some require greater coaching and mentoring to engage in processes of enhanced self-awareness, particularly since some find themselves being personally challenged as part of their learning and practice. Others—the mature students or those who have encountered significant adversity in life—may have been pre-exposed to a range of healing experiences promoting critical self-reflection, personal growth, and development. Students also struggle when challenged by curriculum and placement experiences that trigger mental health symptoms—a process described as a "juggling act" by social work educators (Todd, Asakura, Morris, Eagle, & Park, 2019, p. 2).

In order to ensure the mental health of social work students and to further their education, Todd et al. (2019) proposed a set of reflective questions aimed at assisting students in their "readiness for practice" (as opposed to their ability to diagnose and be diagnosed) and suggested that educators have a responsibility to be proactive about such matters. Despite the limitations of these reflective questions—not specifically targeting the cultural needs of indigenous student cohorts (Todd et al., 2019) and not a focus on meeting social work competencies—they are aimed at encouraging students to talk about their underlying mental health needs and concerns. Such developmental opportunities for social work student cohorts also enable trainees to reflect on other concepts related to social work practice. Emphasis is placed on students enhancing their understanding of notions of *inclusiveness* and *diversity*.

This is evident in the *intersectionality* paradigm, describing ways in which differing aspects of identity interact with one another in terms of gender, religion, race, skin colour, and sexuality. According to Crenshaw (1991, p. 1245) such "intersections of race and gender only highlights the need to account for multiple grounds of identity when considering how the social world is constructed." For students, when facilitating learning around socially constructed concepts regarding race and the role of *whiteness* in organisations and social work practice with culturally diverse populations, this inadvertently invites a process of self-exploration and ultimately personal development—both central and inherent to *critical social work* practice.

Cultural Competency, Cultural Humility in Social Work, and Health Service Provision

Commonly used rhetoric—being *culturally sensitive* or working in a *culturally competent* manner—within therapeutic and mental health practice is used to describe working effectively with mental health consumers and their families. Such groups are often referred to as culturally and linguistically diverse (CALD) or as *culturally diverse communities.* Historically, many questioned whether cultural competency was achievable and not merely a myth (Dean, 2001). It was thought impossible for future social workers within the field of mental health to be capable of dealing with, in terms of knowledge and skill base, such an array of cultures they might encounter during their assessments and interventions with culturally diverse clients and families.

In order to further explore *cultural competency*, it is important to first define "culture" as representing a set of human beliefs, values, and behaviours associated with a particular heritage or social identity. Historically, such a definition implied culture as being static and not changeable (Dean, 2001). However, over time—particularly given the influences of globalisation and the effects of migration—culture has adopted a more politically and socially constructed meaning, suggesting cultures are transformative and continuously changing (Dean, 2001). Second, *competency* refers to having a certain level of capability, in terms of knowledge and skill base, and thus striving towards *cultural competence* is a "developmental process" (Cross, Bazron, Dennis, & Isaacs, 1989, p. v).

In addition it is paradoxically argued that clinicians should be informed "not-knowers" emphasising the importance of being mindful "of our own cultural baggage," further emphasising the perspective of Laird (1998) and others on the importance for clinicians "to engage in an ongoing process of learning about others and to operate, as much as possible from a 'not knowing position'" (Dean, 2001, p. 625). Therefore, the absence of a true process of critical self-awareness may lead to practice being subjected to negative cultural stereotypes and racialised responses resulting in racism. This can lead to inaccurate clinical assessments, further perpetuating "othering" and reinforcing power imbalances within the therapeutic context.

Finally, other social work literature, attending to cultural competency in practice with culturally diverse families, further addresses the importance of self-reflection in social work education and is heavily embedded in a number of modalities. Qualitative studies focusing on the principle of *self-awareness* form a common thread running through relevant social work education literature (Bender, Negi, & Fowler, 2010; Feize & Gonzalez, 2018). Such work includes focusing on the commitment of social work trainees to the struggle and importance of *self-awareness* and culturally responsive practice (Bender et al., 2010); the relevance of teaching methods that directly teach a level of discomfort while identifying issues such as othering, racial bias, race and racism, and the history of white privilege and oppression; and promoting the *cultural humility* paradigm (Feize & Gonzalez, 2018; Greeno et al., 2017; Nadan & Stark, 2017; Sloane, David, Davies, Stamper, & Woodward, 2018).

Social workers have been involved in institutional practices in the past that are now considered insensitive to cultural difference. Consequently, the profession has at times supported practices of discrimination. A measured historical analysis enables social work students and educators to begin to reveal such blindness in the past thereby helping provide insight into current implicit bias and unintentional injustice. Such an analysis promotes the idea that "the act of partnering social work with cultural history is a demonstration of cultural humility by learning directly from the past stories of the marginalized." According to Walter and Baltra-Ulloa (2016) *The Race Gap* in Indigenous Australia continues and is due to the overarching dominant paradigm of *whiteness* and *colonialism* within the Australian context. It highlights that in Australia social work education has a long way to go in terms of being inclusive of Indigenous perspectives and being less dominated by pedagogies embedded in whiteness and colonisation. Overall, this is a key theme in social work education and is central to critical self-awareness and its implications for future social workers.

The Voices of Social Work Trainees on Cultural Humility—A Needs Analysis

In recent years a number of studies embedded in social work education have explored the role of the student voice in enhancing and cultivating the importance of self-awareness in learning and ultimately practice with clients and families (Bender et al., 2010; Feize & Gonzalez, 2018; Greeno et al., 2017; Nadan & Stark, 2017; Sloane et al., 2018; Walter & Baltra-Ulloa, 2016). The relevance of *cultural humility* principles within the context of social work education was further examined in a *needs analysis* pilot study. The aim was to use the results to assist in the development of further training in cultural humility for practitioners in the mental health service (Table 57.1). The *needs analysis* was conducted using postgraduate social work students enrolled in a mental health unit in an Australian university setting following their receipt of an introductory lecture entitled "*A Cultural Humility Approach to Reflective Practice in Mental Health.*" This was a lecture that aimed to introduce the key tenets of *cultural humility* originating from the paediatric profession in the United States (Tervalon & Murray-Garcia, 1998), and included content from Fisher-Borne, Cain, and Martin (2015) which further explored *cultural humility utilizing a number of strategic questions targeted towards practitioners, organisations, and social work educators*. Following the initial lecture students were invited to participate in a needs analysis questionnaire, surveying their knowledge of *cultural humility* in terms of its relevance to individual practice as well as on the broader organisational level. From approximately 40 students, the results from 13 who chose to offer feedback are outlined in Fig. 57.1. While the authors recognise the limitations of such a small sample size they consider it represents a snapshot of trainee responses in relation to the tenets of greater self-awareness and critical self-reflection embedded in the *cultural humility* paradigm.

Results from the 13 respondents demonstrate a shift in cultural awareness—emphasising the importance of cultural humility in social work education and in future clinical social work practice. The respondents also recognised the importance of building cultural knowledge and that a shift in cultural practice needs to occur on the broader organisational level. Most respondents highlighted the significance of enhancing confidence in the application of cultural humility practice.

Figure 57.2 shows that the majority of respondents that already had experience with CALD clients and families felt they would benefit from further training in this area of practice; and that further implementation of such training in social work education, including training in cultural humility, would be beneficial. Finally, a single response by one trainee was that "Whiteness theory and decolonizing social work and political and historical critical analysis is necessary." Therefore, although the pilot had not aimed to influence change directly it did receive favourable responses from respondents, driving the development of similar workshop training content for broader research initiatives designed for mental health practitioners.

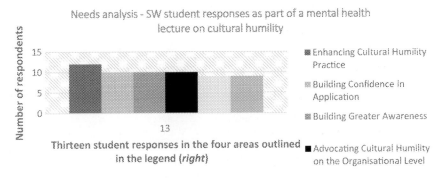

Fig. 57.1   Key areas of identified learning in relation to cultural practice

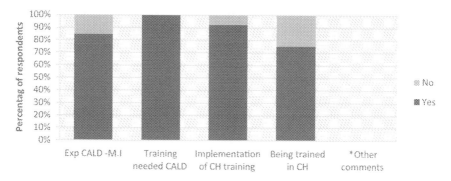

Fig. 57.2 Student responses regarding mental health, cultural and linguistically diverse (CALD) groups, and cultural humility training (*M.I.*: mental illness; *CH*, cultural humility)

Cultural Training in Mental Health Service Provision

Following the *needs analysis* pilot a workshop was developed for mental health practitioners across a number of professional disciplines, including social workers. Elements of its content were informed by the positive responses from students in the needs analysis pilot. The workshop aimed to challenge traditional notions of cultural competence training by promoting the principles of *cultural humility* and prompting practitioners to be aware of their own values, attitudes, stories of migration, ethnicity, and identity and how these might influence their professional practice (Konidaris & Petrakis, 2018). An outline of the workshop's content is provided in Table 57.1. A prominent feature of the training was the introduction of *whiteness theory* and the importance of having an awareness of white privilege—attendees being challenged to investigate the significance of this in their practice.

Table 57.1 Cultural humility workshop overview

Session 1	Session 2	Session 3	Session 4
Introduction: background to the facilitator's personal acculturation journey; and dealing with difference and being "the other" Professional: Discussion about barriers to engagement; Family therapy; and research influences	Use of videos Defining key concepts of: • Race • "Racialised" • Whiteness • Microaggressions • Cultural competence • Cultural responsiveness • Cultural safety • Ethnocentrism • *Cultural humility*	Practical and applied learning: Use of cultural humility principles and frameworks; and Utilising case scenarios and videos	Reflective summary evaluation: NEVIL and post-workshop survey

Konidaris and Petrakis (2018)

Conclusion

Strengths in Cultural Student Narratives and the Hopes for Social Work Practice

This text considers the importance of greater self-awareness and reflexivity as an optimum process of growth and student development, promoting a sense of hope in the field. Social work trainees from culturally diverse, and in some cases marginalised, backgrounds are challenged when dealing with dominant discourse and paradigms, embedded in structures historically influenced by whiteness and colonisation practices. For social work education, fostering a safe and inclusive environment influenced by intersectionality frameworks and cultural humility paradigms will assist in providing a sense of nurturing and acceptance of cultural diversity, including for students from Indigenous backgrounds. Essentially, supporting and empowering the voice of these students requires a *cultural humility* learning environment and pedagogy. This will enable students to find strength in their own voices and historical narratives. In addition, this may also alleviate the effects of adversity related to experiences such as being "othered," negative cultural stereotypes, and racism.

As already outlined, Walter and Baltra-Ulloa (2016) argue that issues of race continue to be neglected by the social work profession, further perpetuating *white privilege* and *othering*, particularly in relation to Aboriginal and Pacific Island people. Bennett and Gates (2019) apply a *cultural humility* framework to the teaching of social workers supporting LGBTQI Aboriginal Australian communities, which essentially relies on critical reflective practice and a strengths-based perspective. Essentially, they identify the importance of maintaining *cultural humility* in courteous conversations while remaining open and self-reflective. Although on the one hand it is hopeful that the Australian Association of Social Workers (AASW) Code of Ethics 2010 included *Culturally Competent, Safe and Sensitive Practice*; challenged prescriptive notions of *cultural competency*; and alternatively promoted critical self-reflection and the importance of attending to racial bias, often such rhetoric is not translated into practice. Walter and Baltra-Ulloa (2016) emphasise that ensuring *white vulnerability* is experienced within the profession is key, along with the shedding of *power* and *privilege*.

Thus, the role and challenge for social work educators is to engage vulnerable students with mental health needs in a safe and inclusive learning space. That is, one that relies on their own self-awareness, and accepting their discomfort regarding their own *whiteness, sense of power, and privilege*. This relies on their ability to speak openly about such topics with trainees. It is therefore important that trainees and educators, not necessarily persons of colour but individuals that have experienced adverse circumstances including racism or have come from minority cultural groups (in a dominant Western society), also identify with their own sense of *whiteness and privilege* (DiAngelo, 2012). Working with and strengthening the voice of social work trainees, despite their own challenges and vulnerabilities, is imperative to ensure that the future social work workforce can manage their discomfort around issues related to race, racism, and white privilege. One can but hope that such a strengthened student voice will combat the racism experienced by Mariam and others like her. Finally, while the construct of *cultural humility* has reached Australian shores and social work classrooms, prompting challenging conversations, an inconsistent cultural approach to practice and learning prevails globally, warranting greater attention.

References

Allan, J. (2009). Doing critical social work. In J. Allan, L. Briskman & B. Pease (Eds.), *Critical Social Work* (pp. 70–87). Crows Nest, NSW: Allen & Unwin.

Ascoli, M., Palinski, A., Owiti, J. A., De Jongh, B., & Bhui, K. S. (2012). The culture of care within psychiatric services: Tackling inequalities and improving clinical and organisational capabilities. *Philosophy, Ethics and Humanities in Medicine, 7*(1), 12. https://doi.org/10.1186/1747-5341-7-12.

Azzopardi, C., & McNeill, T. (2016). From cultural competence to cultural consciousness: Transitioning to a critical approach to working across differences in social work. *Journal of Ethnic & Cultural Diversity in Social Work, 25*(4), 282–299. https://doi.org/10.1080/15313204.2016.1206494.

Bender, K., Negi, N., & Fowler, N. D. (2010). Exploring the relationship between self-awareness and student commitment and understanding of culturally responsive social work practice. *Journal of Ethnic and Cultural Diversity in Social Work, 19*(1), 34–53. https://doi.org/10.1080/15313200903531990.

Bennett, B., & Gates, T. G. (2019). Teaching cultural humility for social workers serving LGBTQI Aboriginal communities in Australia. *Social Work Education*, 1–14. https://doi.org/10.1080/02615479.2019.1588872.

Crenshaw, K. (1991). Mapping the margins: Intersectionality, identity politics, and violence against women of color. *Stanford law review, 43*(6), 1241–1299.

Cross, L. T., Bazron, J. B., Dennis, W. K., & Isaacs, R. M. (1989). *Towards a culturally competent system of care: A Monograph on effective services for minority children who are severely emotionally disturbed volume 1.* Washington, DC: G. U. C. D. C. CASSP Technical Assistance Center.

Dean, R. (2001). The myth of cross-cultural competence. *Families in Society: the Journal of Contemporary Social Services, 82*(6), 623–630. https://doi.org/10.1606/1044-3894.151.

DiAngelo, R. (2012). *What does it mean to be White?: Developing white racial literacy.* New York, NY: Peter Lang.

Eley, D., Young, L., Hunter, K., Baker, P., Hunter, E., & Hannah, D. (2007). Perceptions of mental health service delivery among staff and indigenous consumers: It's still about communication. *Australasian Psychiatry, 15*(2), 130–134. https://doi.org/10.1080/10398560601121017.

Feize, L., & Gonzalez, J. (2018). A model of cultural competency in social work as seen through the lens of self-awareness. *Social Work Education*, 1–18. https://doi.org/10.1080/02615479.2017.1423049.

Fernando, S. (2010). *Mental health, race and culture* (3rd ed.). New York, NY: Palgrave Macmillan.

Fisher-Borne, M., Cain, J. M., & Martin, S. L. (2015). From mastery to accountability: Cultural humility as an alternative to cultural competence [References]. *Social Work Education: The International Journal, 34*(2), 165–181. http://dx.doi.org/1 0.1080/02615479.2014.977244.

Greeno, E. J., Fedina, L., Rushovich, B., Moore, J. E., Linsenmeyer, D., & Wirt, C. (2017). "They tippy toe around the race issue": The impact of a Title IV-E program on culturally informed practice for child welfare students. *Child and Family Social Work, 22*(4), 1374–1382. https://doi.org/10.1111/cfs.12355.

Helms, J. E. (2015). An examination of the evidence in culturally adapted evidence-based or empirically supported interventions. *Transcultural Psychiatry, 52*(2), 174–197. https://doi.org/10.1177/1363461514563642.

Kirmayer, L. J. (2012). Rethinking cultural competence. *Transcultural Psychiatry, 49*(2), 149–164. https://doi.org/10.1177/1363461512444673.

Konidaris, M. (2001). *Being second-generation of non-English speaking background: the neglected dimension in mental health and family therapy practice* (Minor thesis). School of Public Health, Faculty of Health Sciences, Latrobe University, Bundoora, Melbourne.

Konidaris, M., & Petrakis, M. (2018). Cultural humility training in mental health service provision. *New Paradigm. Research into Practice. The Australian Journal on Psychosocial Rehabilitation* (Summer 2017/2018), 30–33.

Laird, J. (1998). Theorizing culture: Narrative ideas and practice principles. In M. McGoldrick (Ed.), *Revisioning family therapy: Race, culture and gender in clinical practice* (Chap. 2, pp. 20–36). New York: The Guilford Press.

Nadan, Y., & Stark, M. (2017). The pedagogy of discomfort: Enhancing Reflectivity on stereotypes and bias. *The British Journal of Social Work, 47*(3), 683–700. https://doi.org/10.1093/bjsw/bcw023.

Paradies, Y. (2006). A systematic review of empirical research on self-reported racism and health. *International Journal of Epidemiology, 35*(4), 888–901. https://doi.org/10.1093/ije/dyl056.

Paradies, Y. P., Truong, M. M. P. H., & Priest, N. P. (2014). A systematic review of the extent and measurement of healthcare provider racism. *Journal of General Internal Medicine, 29*(2), 364–387. https://doi.org/10.1007/s11606-013-2583-1.

Pilsecker, C. (1994). Starting where the client is. *Families in Society, 75*(7), 447–452.

Sloane, H. M., David, K., Davies, J., Stamper, D., & Woodward, S. (2018). Cultural history analysis and professional humility: Historical context and social work practice. *Social Work Education,* 1–13. https://doi.org/10.1080/02615479.2018.14 90710.

Tervalon, M., & Murray-Garcia, J. (1998). Cultural humility versus cultural competence: A critical distinction in defining physician training outcomes in multicultural education. *Journal of Health Care for the Poor and Underserved, 9*(2), 117–125.

Todd, S., Asakura, K., Morris, B., Eagle, B., & Park, G. (2019). Responding to student mental health concerns in social work education: reflective questions for social work educators. *Social Work Education*, 1–18. https://doi.org/10.1080/0261547 9.2018.1563591.

Walter, M., & Baltra-Ulloa, J. (2016). The race gap: An indigenous perspective, on whiteness, colonialism and social work in Australia. *Social Dialogue*, 4(15), 29–32.

Yip, K. (2006). Developing social work students' reflectivity in cultural indigeniza-tion of mental health practice. *Reflective Practice*, 7(3), 393–408. https://doi. org/10.1080/14623940600839828.

CHAPTER 58

Changes in Society and Their Reflections in Social Work Education in the Czech Republic

Oldřich Chytil and Ivana Kowaliková

INTRODUCTION

The chapter aims to answer the question whether education in social work in the Czech Republic critically reflects the changes in society. If we want to answer this question, we must first define social work. The base for our concept of social work is a term 'the Social'.

Keller (2007) distinguishes between the two basic meanings of 'the Social'. Everything that concerns people's world is included in 'the Social' in the broadest sense. In the other, narrower definition, 'the Social' means different ties of mutual assistance and protection in critical situations. The relationship between society as a whole and the Social, understood as a network of support and protection, has significantly changed over the course of history. Keller points to a gradual historical transition from naturally assigned, primary sources of social security to secondary, artificially created sources.

> If we accept the thesis that 'the Social' as a variety of ties of mutual assistance and protection in critical situations has gone through the transition from naturally assigned primary sources of security (family, community) to secondary, artificially generated sources, then we have the answer to when social work was born. Social work can be defined as a "work tool" of a secondary sociability

O. Chytil (✉) · I. Kowaliková
Faculty of Social Studies, University of Ostrava, Ostrava, Czech Republic
e-mail: oldrich.chytil@osu.cz

© The Author(s) 2021
S. S. M. et al. (eds.), *The Palgrave Handbook of Global Social Work Education*, https://doi.org/10.1007/978-3-030-39966-5_58

institution whose task is to solve the problems of modern society generated by the process of modernisation, which has separated people from their traditional social support. (Chytil, 2007, p. 66)

Social Work and Changes in Society

Social work is very closely linked to the environment of organised modernity and when constructing its theories and methods it uses this concept of the world. Therefore, it entered a precarious situation when organised modernity transitioned into a qualitatively different modernity stage. Although different authors we cite herein (Bauman, 2002; Beck, 2004; Keller, 2005, 2007, 2009, 2011, 2013, 2014) name it differently, e.g. post-industrial modern, reflexive or liquid modernity, they have each identified a number of features and processes that distinguish it from organised modernity.

In order to answer the question whether education in social work in the Czech Republic critically reflects changes in society, we have identified the following set of features and processes with help from the works of the above theoreticians of post-industrial modernity, reflexive or fluid modernity.

Features of Post-industrial Modern Society

Individualisation

People are condemned to individualisation. Everyone faces a complex reality as its equal partner. People face the challenge of solving their own problems while having limited resources as individuals. Threats and risks are produced socially, and the need to cope with them is strictly individualised. At the social level, individualisation leads to an increasing dependence of individuals on social systems (Bauman, 2002; Beck, 2004; Keller, 2007).

Functional Differentiation

The increase in functional differentiation is intended to increase the performance of society in all areas of its activities. At the social level this leads to mutual assistance and support among people becoming only one of the specialised areas whose importance does not go beyond any other specialisation. Social protection and assistance in critical life situations are not more important than economic, political, military, and other issues. As a result of mutual competition for funding, other subsystems behave in a competitive manner towards the social field (Bauman, 2002; Beck, 2004; Keller, 2007).

Rationalisation and Economics

The system rationalisation model, which corresponds to the logic of increasing efficiency, is also applied to the social field. The social level is entitled to exist if it pays to society. Social assistance is to be organised on the principles of the market economy (Keller, 2007).

Commodification

Consumption has become symptomatic for post-industrial modernity, which does not only concern products and services, but also culture and social work. Social work is to be offered as "attractive service packages" that are consumed after purchase (Keller, 2007).

Generalisation

People's actions are liberated from local contexts and focus on ever more general and more universal relationships, norms, and values. Global integration is accompanied by local disintegration. The onset of generalised utilitarianism leads to the areas of education, social protection, family, politics, and science being transformed into mere branches of economics. Economics acts as a paradigm common to all humanities and social sciences (Bauman, 2002; Beck, 2004; Keller, 2007).

Changes of Society

Classes disappear while social inequalities intensify. Poverty is individualised; it stops uniting people, dividing them instead. Labour (as a result of the flexibility of work contracts) ceases to provide for the workers. Institutions that stabilise industrial modernity—both family and state—are being questioned. The family ceases to function as a reliable support for its members. Modernisation of the welfare state means that the public sector retreats to the market to solve social problems (Bauman, 2002; Beck, 2004; Keller, 2007).

Changes of 'the Social'

'The Social' in terms of various ties of assistance and protection in critical situations in modern society has transformed into the institutions of secondary sociability. Modernisation is directed against secondary ties of protection and requires their reduction and degradation (Keller, 2007).

Colonisation of the Public by the Private

Whereas in the first stage of modernity the private was colonised by public authorities, the public sphere is now colonised by private enterprises. Privatisation of public services such as education, health, social services, but also the judiciary, the police and the prison system is the motto of modernisation (Bauman, 2002; Keller, 2007).

Uncertainty

The modernisation of society brings all pervading uncertainty. Certainty, continuity, and trust as the basis of stable relationships are fading away. Coping with every-day life is so burdened by the uncertainty that it becomes a risky task (Bauman, 2002; Beck, 2004; Keller, 2009).

Increasing Inequality

Whereas organised modernity attempted for graded inequality, which has been legitimised, the subsequent modernity breaks down this system and generates enormous social inequalities that are unjustified (Keller, 2011).

Social Construction of Reality

Postmodern constructionism overlooks the social conditionality of those who perceive and interpret reality differently, emphasising the uniqueness of each subject and his/her absolute autonomy in interpreting and reinterpreting of the world. Similarly, there is no power structure that could restrict freedom of conception, which has a potentially fatal consequence, since people with such views deny the existence of a power structure that could undermine their "vision of the world" without admitting it at all (Keller, 2013).

According to Keller (2013), postmodernism defines itself against a modern way of thinking and is directed against the enlightened understanding of reason and science, which can be easily misused, according to the theoreticians of postmodernism, to control people and instil their discipline. Postmodernism promotes defending of oppressed and marginalised groups, in particular by helping to deregulate the power that in their eyes leads to this marginalisation. The problem is in a situation, where any power is considered oppressive, can arise too easily.

SOCIAL WORK EDUCATION

The system of education in social work is ensured at colleges and universities in the Czech Republic. Colleges of social work provide three-year post-secondary training in the field of social work, and graduates receive a diploma degree.

University education in social work has three levels: three-year Bachelor's, two-year follow-up Master's, and four-year doctoral degree programmes.

Performance of the profession of a social worker under the Act on Social Services (Act No. 108/2006 Coll.) is conditioned by graduation from at least a social work college or by having a university Bachelor's degree.

METHODOLOGY

Using quantitative content analysis (Gavora, 2010, 2015; Hendl & Remr, 2017) we investigated whether the texts of academics educating social workers published in the journal Sociální práce/Sociálna práca (Czech and Slovak Social Work) (the only reviewed professional journal published in the Czech Republic, included in the SCOPUS database) critically reflect the changes in society. Quantitative content analysis is a standard method of research aimed at evaluation and interpretion of textual content (Gavora, 2015). Therefore, we have chosen this method to analyse the content of our professional journal and university curricula. According to Berelson (1952), it is a research technique for the objective, systematic, and quantitative description of the manifest content of communication. Quantitative content analysis according to Hendl and Remr (2017) begins with defining a research question and selecting data for analysis. In our research we investigated whether the texts of academics educating future social workers published in the journal Sociální práce/Sociálna práca critically reflect the changes in society. We also investigated whether university curricula educating social workers critically reflect the changes in society. The reason for the selection of texts from 2012 to 2018 was to analyse the contemporary discourse of social work on the background of critical reflection of societal changes in relation to education in social work over the past five years. The quantitative content analysis included all the expert articles from the journal, the issues from 1/2012 through 6/2018. The basic unit of quantitative content analysis was the individual articles that we selected, based on one criterion, which was the professional articles reflecting the influence of societal changes on social work.

The content analysis included all the expert articles in the journal Sociální práce/Sociálna práca—issues 1/2012 through 6/2018. We set up analytical categories based on identification of the features and processes of contemporary society as defined by the theorists of modernisation Beck (2004), Bauman (2002), and Keller (2005, 2007, 2009, 2011, 2013, 2014). The analytical categories according to these authors include the following features and processes: individualisation, functional differentiation, rationalisation and economisation, commodification, generalisation, changes of society, changes of 'the Social', colonisation of the public by the private, uncertainty, increasing inequality and social construction of reality. Analytical categories for quantitative content analysis constituted a mutually exclusive system with clearly defined indicators.

Semantic units that were searched for in the articles of the journal Sociální práce/Sociálna práca included topics that critically reflect the impact of changes in society on social work. We then divided the identified semantic units—the topics—in different analytical categories. Subsequently, those analytical categories were quantified and interpreted (Gavora, 2010).

We also used quantitative content analysis (Gavora, 2010, 2015; Hendl & Remr, 2017) for the analysis of curriculum plans of the universities that have accredited education in social work. The same analytical categories that were used for content analysis of the texts in the journal Sociální práce/Sociálna práca were used to analyse curricula plans. The basic unit of quantitative content analysis were the individual university curricula and the course descriptions that were part of them.

Topics Characterising Post-industrial Modern Society Identified in the Journal Sociální Práce/Sociálna Práca

We used the method of content analysis of professional articles published in the 1/2012 through 6/2018 issues of the journal Sociální práce/Sociálna práca to search through professional articles written by educators of future social workers, in which the authors critically reflected the impact of changes in society on social work. A total of 205 articles were analysed, of which only 38 discussed topics of social work in the context of a critical reflection of the changes in society.

In 38 analysed articles, the following analytical categories were identified, characterising contemporary society:

- Rationalisation and economisation in 21 articles (out of 38)
- Commodification in 19 articles (out of 38)
- Changes of society in 15 articles (out of 38)
- Changes of 'the Social' in 10 articles (out of 38)
- Increasing inequalities in 8 articles (out of 38)
- Uncertainty in 5 articles (out of 38)
- Social construction of reality in 3 articles (out of 38)
- Individualisation in 3 articles (out of 38)

Regarding the frequency of topics that characterise contemporary society, the two most frequently discussed topics are **rationalisation** and related **economisation** and commodification.

The authors of analysed articles have correctly pointed to the consequences of rationalisation for social work that are closely related to efficiency, meaning that social work must only use "rational methods" for which high efficiency is guaranteed.

Social work is a fundamental activity offered by social services. Therefore, the character of social work in the Czech Republic is a significant concept of social services. The Social Services Act No. 108/2006 Coll. was conceived based on the UK social services model. There, as in the Czech Republic, the dominant bearer of social work was in care management (Baláž, 2012).

Baláž (2012), citing the British author Donna Dustin, describes the principles of care management implementation, which have been also adopted by Czech social work in social services.

1. Principle of efficiency in care management

Efficiency is achieved by recording and comparing what one does and how long he/she has been doing it.

2. Principle of predictability in care management

Predictability is achieved through the introduction of standardisation—for example, standardised forms for assessing the life situation are introduced.

3. Principle of calculability in care management

In the care management, resources are calculated from the perspective of inputs and outputs. Emphasis is placed on easily numerable, concrete, and measurable results.

4. Principle of care management control

The control is mainly through managers, who are at the same time law interpreters, constructing and controlling the workload in the organisation. They define the meanings of client groups for the organisation and determine employee responses to clients.

The American author Ritzer (1996) calls the above principles, adopted from McDonald's corporation, *McDonaldization*. The phenomenon of McDonaldization, according to Baláž (2012) and Holasová (2012), uncritically develops in Czech social work.

Social work in the social services system is quite standardised. Starting January 2012, based on the amendment to the Act on Material Need Assistance No. 111/2006, Coll. the work of social workers, and officials employed by the municipalities and the state that have not yet been subjected to standardisation of social services (Baláž, 2012) is now also standardised. According to Hiekischová (2015), starting from 1 January 2012, the performance of social work has been divided, with some social workers becoming employees of the state and thus being transferred from the municipalities to the Employment Office of the Czech Republic. As a result of this political decision aimed at rationalising and directness of public expenditures, social work with persons in material need has been reduced to the payment of benefits. The role of the social worker has been thus limited to bureaucratic, above all impersonal and routine actions that take the form of awarding or non-awarding that is retention or withdrawal of social benefits.

The amendment to the Act on Social and Legal Protection of Children also provides standardised child social and legal protection. The purpose of standardisation is to routinise work to a certain level of quality and to produce specific and measurable data that is predictable and easily quantifiable. The work of social workers is then assessed based on the produced data (Baláž, 2012).

One of the quality standards for providing social services is individual planning. The individual planning aims to plan out the course of provision of social services according to the individuals' goals, needs, and abilities to whom social services are provided, to keep written individual records of the course of service provision and to evaluate it with the participation of these individuals, provided that their state of health and the type of social service provided allows (Act No. 108/2006 Coll.).

Research carried out by Glumbíková and Vávrová (2018) concerning individual planning with people in homeless shelters shows that tying the methods of social work by legislation does not always produce the intended outcomes. There is often a paradoxical situation where a social worker is forced by the law to do an individual planning and the client is forced to set his/her individual goals in order to obtain accommodation in his/her situation of homelessness. The need for individual planning when arriving at an accommodation facility does not take into account: (a) the client's current psychological situation that can be associated with stress, crisis, or even trauma; (b) the fact that the client uses the service only to obtain emergency accommodation, i.e. he/she does not want to set any additional goals in the service. The goals set in the process of individual planning are therefore often only formal; satisfying the need for its determination. In addition, the process of individual planning in homeless shelters has become a process centred on the past and on the causes of the homelessness situation; the above mentioned can be described as an incapacitating concept of individual planning because it is oriented to the client's former "failure" resulting in the loss of home, and implicitly may refer to the fact that the client has lost not only the housing but also his/her ability to have a home.

As for the principle of control, it is even present in the Czech social work than the above principles. As noted by Holasová (2012), the power of managers is growing, focusing mainly on data reporting.

The findings of the cited authors show, rational actions in social work do not have to lead to rational results.

Economisation and commodification are closely related to rationalisation and making the social services a commodity market. At the same time, it is connected to the colonisation of the public by the private where public services, including social services, are to be privatised. The client of social work becomes a customer who purchases social services. The result of this process is interchanging of social work with social services (Keller, 2014).

Changes in social services systems have been brought by transformation processes that started in the Czech Republic together with the public administration reform following upon changes in the financing of social services. As Holasová (2012) notes, social work in the Czech Republic has been economised and its services have become commodities. Welfare provision has become a commodity in the context of economisation. The increasing commodification in the provision of social care has brought a focus on generating profits in the provision of social services. Holasová (2012) talks about economic rationality as a marketisation of social work. The social work client is now viewed as a customer who is supposed to decide about services between various providers who will compete to get him/her, for example, by expanding and improving their services offered. Customer-oriented approach includes viewing the clients as eligible economic and social participants who are able to follow their best interests in the market.

Šimíková (2015) writes that both in the Social Services Act and in the important elements of its implementation in the context of the Czech Republic we can find numerous similarities with the New Public Management model. This means in particular the involvement of market and business principles, typical for the private sector until now, moving into the public sector. Documents on how to implement the Social Services Act, for example Quality Standards for Social Services—Glossary of Terms for the Social Service Providers released by the Ministry of Labour and Social Affairs in 2008, emphasise in several parts transformation of the recipient of services (from a client to a customer), while the environment of providers is compared to the business using terminology that is associated with the corporate environment.

Another most frequent topic is the **changes of society** that are characterised by changes in the following three areas:

1. Changes in the labour market (which include flexibilization of labour)

Flexibilisation of labour means that instead of full-value standard employment contracts, partial and short-term contracts for limited working hours are preferred, and there is a growing tendency to transition from the classical employment relationship to the "looser" relationships between the company and formally independent suppliers and subcontractors, the effect of which shows in shifting of an increasing portion of market uncertainty from companies to employees or subcontractors. Labour flexibilisation seemingly reduces the unemployment rate, but the proportion of low-paid work is rising as is the risk that the income of an economically active person will be on the brink of poverty. This results in a phenomenon called "working poverty" (Keller, 2005). Minimal welfare benefits by the welfare state are conditioned by the willingness to take any, even poorly paid, work (Keller, 2009).

2. The decline in solidarity in society and changes in insurance systems

According to Keller (2005), there is lack in solidarity of labour among those who have any job and those who cannot enter the labour market. New forms of a lack of solidarity also arise as a result of increased family fragility and changes in its character. The source of tension in this area is a contradiction between those who have reduced the number of their children thus gaining an advantage over those who have more children. Similarly, intergenerational solidarity is threatened too. Those who contribute from their salaries for today's pensioners will have a significantly lower retirement pension in future. Privatisation of insurance systems, their individualisation and accompanying lack of solidarity of insured persons makes it difficult to cover individuals at the stages of their life cycle when they are not economically active.

3. Growing fragility of the family

The growing fragility of the family is a very frequent topic in the journal Sociální práce/Sociálna práca. The growing family fragility is manifested in the flexibilisation of the family, which is shown in increased divorce rates, an increasing share of single-parent families, and single-parent households that are more at risk of poverty than two-income households. Another manifestation of the growing fragility of the family is the participation of women in the labour market, which affects the extent of care for young children, the elderly and disabled persons traditionally provided by women in their households (Klimplová and Winkler, 2010; Sirovátka, Winkler, & Žižlavský 2009).

Processes of demographic changes and changes of the society's structure may have negative consequences that increase the family fragility in the area of elderly care, especially for women who are more frequent caregivers of an ageing parent (Dudová, 2015). Keller (1990) talks about how family care about the elderly has transformed during the development of society. One of the main functions of the traditional family, that is provision of care for the elderly, was gradually replaced by artificially created and specialised formal organisations. The arrival of the post-industrial society brought again a change in the organisation of family life. "*The family often splits and changes from a solid point of cohabitation of different generations to a relatively unstable walk-through space*" (Keller, 2011, p. 127). According to Beck (2004), the family is being stripped off its traditional values and networks of family cohabitation; therefore, providing care for the elderly due to the growing fragility of the family becomes unrealistic.

One of the options of social work in providing care for the elderly in their natural environment is domiciliary care. However, it is clear from the Kubalčíková's research (2012) that domiciliary care cannot be seen as a full-value alternative to care provided by institutions, especially when it comes to providing care to seniors with reduced self-sufficiency. Other research Kubalčíková (2016) states that the availability of care for the elderly in their natural environment is currently declining despite the increasing number of seniors in the population and the political preference of deinstitutionalisation. At the same time, she draws attention to the unintended consequences of deinstitutionalisation, such as the occurrence of unregistered social services, poor working conditions for care workers in these services, and missing care quality control bodies.

Mošová, Pulkertová, and Chytil (2018), who are interested to find out whether social services for the elderly are accessible in terms of time, location, and finances. The results of their research show that services are financially inaccessible, as they are too expensive according to the seniors. The results also show that local and time accessibility of social services is inadequate for this age group.

Another frequently discussed topic in the journal Sociální práce/Sociálna práca is the **changes of 'the Social'**. As we have already noted, 'the Social' in the sense of various ties of assistance and protection in emergency situations has transformed in modern societies into institutions of secondary sociability, especially in the form of a welfare state. Post-industrial modern era requires the reduction and removal of the welfare state. The arguments used for this requirement are summarised by the Czech author Keller (2014).

There are many unsubstantiated claims in the discussions about the causes of the welfare state crisis. Neoliberals, for example, believe that the existence and operation of this institution is the main cause of the indebtedness of the entire countries. However, the most indebted countries in Europe do not include the ones with the most developed welfare state (such as Sweden, Denmark) (Keller, 2014).

According to one claim, the welfare state is the main reason for us living beyond means. Indebtedness of both the state and households continues to grow faster, the process already initiated in the 1970s. Starting in the 1970s, the richest have ceased to share their profits with the rest of society. The post-war income agreement lasted only thirty years. Over the next thirty years, a serious income asymmetry has been growing. While the astronomical wealth is accumulated on the one hand, huge debts are accumulated on the other (Keller, 2014).

The topic of **increasing inequalities** was identified in only eight articles. Social inequality has always existed. Organised modernity has attempted to replace social inequalities with gradually phased and legitimate inequalities. For example, there were differences between the salaries of general staff and managers, with these differences being in the order of multiples. Since the 1980s, there has been a steep increase in inequality, where wealth is distributed primarily to the richest. Keller (2009) talks about the age of social incommensurability. Big enterprises and shareholders manage to make their profits at the expense of employee salaries. Top management remunerations are rising sharply. Employee salaries are stagnating or dropping (Keller, 2009).

Social incommensurability is illustrated by the research results carried out by Gojová, A., Gojová, V., Lindovská, Špiláčková, & Vondroušová (2014). Researchers analysed and compared the life situations of poor families and families at risk of poverty, especially in areas of finances, housing, employment, attitudes toward addressing of their risk of poverty or poverty, subjective assessment of their life situation and social relationships. Research has shown that the gap between poor families and families at risk of poverty is not significant, and that the risk of poverty is not limited to exclusively unemployed, single mothers, and families with three or more children who are considered to be the most at risk of poverty group. Another significant finding by the authors is that families feel threatened by external factors that they cannot really affect, and that the labour market will not protect them from poverty.

In the research, the example of the city of Ostrava shows the ways which families use to deal with the poverty situation or the risk of poverty. The 2014 research found that poor families have a monthly income of up to 8000 CZK, of which the highest source of income is welfare benefits. It is not enough for these families to make a living, and 86% of them have loans and problems with their repayment. Simultaneously, these families spend most funds on securing basic needs such as housing and food. The families lack money for the household and children (Gojová et al., 2014).

Families at risk of poverty have a monthly income of more than 20,000 CZK, of which the highest source of income is wages along with welfare benefits. These sources of income are not enough for these families to make a living, which is evidenced by the fact that 81% of them have loans and problems with their repayment. These families as well as poor families spend most funds on basic needs such as housing and food. Similarly, these families do not have enough money for household and holiday (Gojová et al., 2014).

Another article published in the journal Sociální práce/Sociálna práca reflecting the rise of inequality presents the research results by a group of authors, Kroutilová Nováková, Vaculíková, and Podaná (2016). This research portrays single mothers as a group that is more likely exposed to the risk of poverty and social exclusion. The cost of living and the services associated with single motherhood represent the largest item in the single-mother budgets. The management of housing funds is therefore closely related to the overall management of any potential social disadvantage and the risk of poverty. Kroutilová Nováková et al. (2016) reflect that the welfare state has little means to effectively cover by insurance large groups of persons against the increasing labour and life insecurity.

Only five articles deal with the topic of **uncertainty**. Uncertainty spreads in society together with mistrust in institutions that no longer ensure optimal performance and development as it was in traditional society. People feel tremendous uncertainty, especially in the labour market, education area, but also in the family life. Uncertainty also spreads to the upper levels of society and increasingly controls the life of the middle-class people. This modernisation is for a growing number of persons the transition from the world with clear rules to an unstable, unpredictable, flexible, and uncertain world. "*It is not about adapting to another world but rather accepting the world in permanent uncertainty*" (Keller, 2009, p. 19). The topic of uncertainty in social work is dealt with, for example, by Nečasová, Dohnalová, and Rídlová (2012). According to the authors, the contemporary social work is defined by the fact that the boundaries in the professional relationship between a social worker and a social service user are difficult to set. Emphasising of the rights of social service users, who are viewed as customers, leads to social workers feeling uncertain about their professional role, because they fear that they will be sanctioned because of the complaints from users of social services.

One of the two least frequented topics is the **social construction of reality**. According to Keller (2013), social constructivism can be divided into realist constructivism and postmodern constructivism. Realist constructivism emphasises that every individual or group of people interprets the world in their own way, but at the same time states that the outer world is influenced by man's position in the structure of society, the opportunities and limits associated with that position and reflected in man's view of the world. On the other hand, postmodern constructivism overlooks the influence of man's position in the structure of society and emphasises the uniqueness of all individuals, their autonomy and creativity, with which each person interprets and reinterprets their world. Any interpretation of the world is as arbitrary and non-committal as any other interpretation, they are all equally fleeting. For postmodern constructivism, there is no other reality than our concepts embodied in the respective discourses.

Only the authors of three articles take into account that the concept of constructing social reality can be used to suppress the question of the degree of veracity of different constructions, and also that postmodern constructivism, according to Keller (2013), tends to ignore the question of existing power inequality.

An example of a critical reflection of social constructivism in the practice of social work is the publication of research results by Hubíková and Havlíková (2017), which aimed to understand the essence of the reflexive practice and the importance of its application by social workers in practice, using an example of social work with persons in material need. The authors define the reflective practice in agreement with Thomas' concept and his definition of the situation. According to Thomas, the behaviour is heavily influenced by how one interprets the situation he/she is exposed to and how he/she perceives himself/herself and other people. The authors of the article point out that the idea of constructing the situation and its meanings is adopted and applied without analysing ways of constructing the reality of individual social participants and understanding the implications of social constructivism itself. This can lead to overlooking the social conditionality of one's own actions, thinking, life situation, and individualistic belief that we are the ones who completely construct the conditions and circumstances of our life situation. Research results show that social workers working with people in material need have difficulty in planning and reflecting their own practice. According to the authors, social workers do not realise the changes in society and that they have a significant impact on their performance.

Another less frequent topic is **individualisation**. According to Keller (2011), individualisation can be understood as a forced strategy. Individualism deprives a person from an earlier attachment to a group, but at the same time reinforces his/her need of the state if an individual needs help. A state that supports individualisation does not have enough tools to treat its consequences. Those in charge of the state advise those in need to help themselves. Thus, it may happen that the other side of individual responsibility is the irresponsibility of politics. Janebová (2018) deals with a topic of individualisation stating that the neoliberal state participates in the masking of the causes of social problems, while concentrating on emphasising individual causes of problems, without considering the broader contextual causes. According to this neoliberal ideology, everyone bears his own responsibility for the risks that arise in society. Individualisation is also the main subject of Dvořáková and Mertl (2018). Research on child borrowers criticises the emphasis on personal responsibility, which is part of this neoliberal revolution whose main goal is the pressure on commodification and privatisation of public services and the individualisation of societal risks. The authors point out that the case of child borrowers is a typical example of structural and systemic reproduction of marginalised individuals who social workers are supposed to "remedy" incorporating them back in the structures that make marginalised individuals out of society members.

Topics Characterising Post-industrial Modern Society Identified in University Curricula with Accreditation of Social Work Education

We have completed a content analysis of 13 university curricula with a total of 17 accredited Bachelor's degree programmes of social work and 9 accredited follow-up Master's degree programmes of social work.

Based on the content analysis of the curricula of 17 Bachelor's degree programmes, no courses that critically reflect the impact of changes in society on social work have been identified.

The curricula of 9 follow-up Master's degree programmes of social work were analysed. The researchers identified only four universities with five courses in their curricula that contained topics of critical reflection on the impact of changes in society on social work. Identified topics were ranked into the analytical categories—features and processes of contemporary society as defined by modernisation theorists.

In the analysed five courses included in four university curricula, the following analytical categories were identified, characterising the current society:

- Social construction of reality in 4 study courses (out of 5)
- Rationalisation and economisation in 2 study courses (out of 5)
- Changes of society in 2 study courses (out of 5)
- Changes of 'the Social' in 2 study courses (out of 5).

Other analytical categories individualisation, functional differentiation, generalisation, commodification, colonisation of the public by the private, uncertainty and increasing of inequalities were identified in the course content only in one of the universities.

The most frequent topic identified in the study course curricula was the **social construction of reality**. Based on the literature recommended to students, it can be said that in two courses only, students are led to think about the fact that the concept of constructing social reality can be used to suppress the degree of truth of different constructions and also that postmodern constructivism, according to Keller (2013), tends to ignore the question of existing power inequality.

CONCLUSION

The chapter has aimed to answer the question whether social work education in the Czech Republic critically reflects changes in society. Using quantitative content analysis (Gavora, 2010), we investigated whether the texts of academics educating social workers and curricula of universities educating social workers critically reflect those changes.

In order to assess whether the texts of academics educating future social workers critically reflect the changes in society in relation to social work, we used a method of quantitative content analysis of the articles included in the 1/2012 through 6/2018 issues of journal Sociální práce/Sociálna práca.

We found out that only 38 out of 205 articles published by Czech authors in 2012–2018 critically reflect the changes in society and discuss their impact on social work. What comes as surprising is not only the low number of articles reflecting the changes in society but also the low number of topics characterising the contemporary society discussed in these 38 articles, although we take into account that not all the topics contained in the articles allow reflection on society's transformation.

We have come to the conclusion that the discourse of social work led by the academics in expert articles of the journal Sociální práce/Sociálna práca does not sufficiently reflect the changes in society in relation to social work.

Based on the content analysis of 13 university curricula educating social workers we found that only five study courses in four universities critically reflect the changes in society in relation to social work.

The results of the quantitative content analysis of the texts of academics educating social workers and the university curricula educating social workers suggest that social work education in the Czech Republic inadequately critically reflects the changes in society. It is the critical analysis of societal changes that will help students to understand the changes in social work and to think about to what extent the values such as responsibility, professional mission, and an ethos to help are compatible with increasing pressures on calculability, efficiency, and purely technical rationality of social work activities.

One of our research limits may be that the journal Sociální práce/Sociálna práca does not provide a full picture of publication output by the academics at universities to reflect societal changes in relation to social work, since they also publish abroad and in monographs.

REFERENCES

Baláž, R. (2012). Společenské kontexty sociální práce a jejich vliv na práci s cizinci. *Sociální práce/Sociálna práca, 12*(4), 134–149.

Bauman, Z. (2002). *Tekutá modernita.* Praha: Mladá Fronta.

Beck, U. (2004). *Riziková společnost. Na cestě k jiné moderně.* Praha: Sociologické nakladatelství.

Berelson, B. (1952). Content analysis in communication research. *The Free Press.* New York.

Chytil, O. (2007). Důsledky modernizace pro sociální práci. *Sociální práce/Sociálna práca, 7*(4), 64–71.

Dudová, R. (2015). *Postarat se ve stáří.* Praha: Sociologické nakladatelství.

Dvořáková, T., & Mertl, J. (2018). Důstojná existence kontra osobní zodpovědnost: případ dětských dlužníků v Plzni. *Sociální práce/Sociálna práca, 18*(3), 54–69.

Gavora, P. (2010). *Úvod do pedagogického výzkumu.* Brno: Paido.

Gavora, P. (2015). Obsahová analýza v pedagogickom výzkume: Pohľad na jej súčasné podoby. *Pedagogická orientace, 25*(3), 345–371.

Glumbíková, K., & Vávrová, S. (2018). Koncept naděje a žádoucí budoucnosti jako nástroj redukce instrumentální odpovědnosti v individuálním plánování v azylových domech v České republice. *Sociální práce/Sociálna práca, 18*(5), 52–64.

Gojová, A., Gojová, V., Lindovská, E., Špiláčková, M., & Vondroušová, K. (2014). Způsoby zvládání chudoby a ohrožení chudobou rodinami s nezletilými dětmi. *Sociální práce/Sociálna práca, 14*(2), 44–60.

Hendl, J., & Remr, J. (2017). *Metody výzkumu a evaluace.* Praha: Portál.

Hiekischová, M. (2015). Sociální práce na úřadech práce – od stresu k bezmoci? *Sociální práce/Sociálna práca, 15*(5), 79–88.

Holasová, V. (2012). Sociální práce jako nová tržní příležitost? *Sociální práce/Sociálna práca, 12*(2), 126–137.

Hubíková, O., & Havlíková, J. (2017). Reflektivní praxe v sociální práci: diskuse na příkladu sociální práce s lidmi v hmotné nouzi. *Sociální práce/Sociálna práca, 17*(2), 42–57.

Janebová, R. (2018). Posedlost sociální práce managementem rizik a rezignace na potřeby. *Sociální práce/Sociálna práca, 18*(6), 39–56.

Keller, J. (1990). Makrosociální souvislosti krize rodiny. *Sborník prací Filosofické fakulty Brněnské univerzity, 33*, 15–26. Resource document. https://digilib.phil.muni.cz/bitstream/handle/11222.digilib/111869/G_Sociologica_33-1989-1_3.pdf?sequence=1. Accessed January 14, 2019.

Keller, J. (2005). *Soumrak sociálního státu.* Praha: Sociologické nakladatelství.

Keller, J. (2007). *Teorie modernizace.* Praha: Slon.

Keller, J. (2009). *Nejistota a důvěra: aneb k čemu je modernitě dobrá tradice.* Praha: Slon.

Keller, J. (2011). *Tři sociální světy. Sociální struktura postindustriální společnosti.* Praha: Slon.

Keller, J. (2013). *Posvícení bezdomovců: úvod do sociologie domova.* Praha: Sociologické nakladatelství.

Keller, J. (2014). Sociální stát ve věku přístupu. *Institucionální sborník Fakulty sociálních studií Ostravské univerzity v Ostravě.* Resource document. Ostrava: Fakulta sociálních studií. http://dokumenty.osu.cz/fss/fss-institucionalni-sbornik.pdf. Accessed January 14, 2019.

Klimplová, L., & Winkler, J. (2010). *Nová sociální rizika na trhu práce a potřeby reformy české veřejné politiky.* Brno: Masarykova univerzita.

Kroutilová Nováková, R., Vaculíková, J., & Podaná, A. (2016). Jak si žijí „samoživy" (?): spokojenost s bydlením pohledem samoživitelek. *Sociální práce/Sociálna práca,* 16(3), 5–20.

Kubalčíková, K. (2012). Podpora neformálních pečovatelů v podmínkách poskytování sociálních služeb pro seniory v ČR: příklad pečovatelské služby. *Sociální práce/ Sociálna práca,* 12(4), 89–101.

Kubalčíková, K. (2016). Current developments in social care services for older adults in the Czech Republic: Trends towards deinstitutionalization and marketization. *Journal of Social Service Research, 42*(2), 180–198.

Mošová, M., Pulkertová, M., & Chytil, O. (2018). To what extent are social services in the Ostrava region Available to senior citizens? *Czech and Slovak Social Work, 18*(1), 53–66.

Nečasová, M., Dohnalová, Z., & Rídlová, R. (2012). User of social services in postmodern times. *Sociální práce/Sociálna práca, 12*(5), 13–23.

Šimíková, I. (2015). Možné důsledky imlplementace zákona o sociálních službách perspektivou kritiky modelu New Public Management. *Sociální práce/Sociálna práca, 15*(1), 24–35.

Sirovátka, T., Winkler, J., & Žižlavský, M. (2009). *Nejistoty na trhu práce.* Brno: Masarykova univerzita.

Ritzer, G. (1996). *McDonaldizace společnosti.* Praha: Academia.

Zákon o sociálních službách č. 108/2006 Sb.

CHAPTER 59

Romanian Social Work Education, Past and Present Crossroads

Maria Roth

INTRODUCTION

In the first decade after the 1989 Revolution, economic downturn and restructuring, inflation, unemployment, and polarisation were painful experiences for a large category of the Romanian population: the elderly, children, members of the Roma minority, people with disabilities, and many others. Immediately after the demise of the Romanian communist regime, after 20 years of total absence, social work education was reinvented as a higher education professional training. After 1990, in the transition process from dictatorship to democracy and from a communist economy to capitalism, social workers were expected to play an important role by contributing to the reduction of the effects of the transition from a centralised and controlled economy to a market economy. Professionals in social services were supposed to empower vulnerable people, foster their participation in decision-making, and engage institutions in supporting families and communities.

Therefore, this article scrutinises the past and present processes of aligning the structures and contents of Romanian social work education with the needs of the social welfare workforce and how it manages to incorporate global tendencies with culturally relevant knowledge and practices. Methodologically, the analysis is taking into account the dynamics of the Four Pillar Framework (Davis, 2006; Rutgers University Center for International Social Work, 2008) which describes social work education in relation to the policy and legal framework, to the structure of services and practice

M. Roth (✉)
Social Work Department, Babes-Bolyai University, Cluj-Napoca, Romania
e-mail: mroth@socasis.ubbcluj.ro

© The Author(s) 2021
S. S. M. et al. (eds.), *The Palgrave Handbook of Global Social Work Education*, https://doi.org/10.1007/978-3-030-39966-5_59

environment, and to the chosen outcomes and performance measures. This chapter adopts both a historical and a critical perspective, to uncover the strengths and weaknesses of the Romanian social work education in its efforts to prepare future social workers to respond to the challenges of Romanian social transformation.

HISTORICAL CONTEXT

In the aftermath of the First World War (ended in 1918) and later in the modernisation period between the two world wars, social assistance activities became a stringent necessity in Romania, a country that had to deal with more than 350,000 orphaned children, a large number of invalid veterans, without adequate funds, professionals, or means to respond to such needs. As a rapid response, the social institutional network has been extended in order to offer housing to abandoned and unhoused children, as well as to people with disabilities, the homeless, and the unemployed. From an administrative point of view, social and health services and assistance were directed by the same ministry, functioning since 1920 under the name of the Ministry of Public Health, Work and Social Protection (Lambru, 2002). This led to the influence of public health concepts of the time on emerging social work conceptual framework. For example, in the assistance of "beggars and homeless", the founder of the Romanian legal medicine, physician Nicolae Minovici, categorised these people as either healthy and capable to work ('valid', in Romanian, meaning able bodied), to be placed in work units, mostly agricultural farms, or disabled, i.e. 'invalids', to be placed in asylums. In the same period, around the 1920s, in the capital Bucharest and in other cities of the country new orphanages were founded. The orphaned and abandoned babies were accommodated in social-medical institutions called cradles; after a short period of supervision in institutions, children were placed with paid nurse-maidens ('crescătoare' [ro]) literal translation nurturers) (Banu, 2016). Although this system of paid foster care seems—at least in principle—similar to the one promoted today as the desired alternative to institutionalisation (Eurochild & Hopes and Homes for Children, 2012/2014), there were high rates of child mortality and abuse and the survivors often were put to work at a very young age (Banu, 2016). The cradles and orphanages, as well as asylums, special schools, some community centres (kinder)'gardens' were funded, or partially run by the state, although in the interwar period the different confessions competed in philanthropic demonstrations, and fundraising, especially for children and war veterans (Majuru, 2006). Women's associations brought together higher or lower classes, generally educated women, or professionals, who immersed themselves in charity, or became professional social activists. Due to the activity of the National Council of Romanian Women, in 1929 a school of social caregivers was founded,[1] which offered theoretical knowledge to young women, but also practical skills to care for patients, medical dispensaries, cradles (residential units) for babies, schools, prisons, psychiatric asylums and to collect data in communities, by surveying families. The debut of the first Romanian higher education institution for social workers—called 'Principesa Ileana Superior School for Social Assistance'[2] (later transformed into the Institute for Social Assistance)—has been registered in Bucharest, in the same year. The profession of 'social assistants' as well as education for their professionalisation was sustained by the Law of Social Services issued in 1930, which initiated the development of a territorial public system of community services to alleviate the aftermath of the war and of the poverty affecting vulnerable children and adults. The whole period between the end of the First World War (1918) and Romania's entering the war on the side of the Nazi Germany (1942), the social policies were marked by the ideas of Eugenism, with dramatic consequences on its population of Jewish and Roma families. As shown here, the concepts of the pure, superior race also left powerful imprints on the social work concepts and instruments. Its ideology claimed the need to help the deserving poor, against those labelled as undeserving lazy, alcoholic, psychic ill, immoral, and with other similar categories (Turda & Quine, 2018).

After the country was overtaken by the communist regime in 1945, progressively lost its democratic aspect. All forms of social support, civic movements, and charity organisations were dismantled, social policies being organised by the state based on universal, egalitarian measures (Popescu & Roth, 2008). Some of the socialist reforms were in line with the much-needed modernisation of the nation, for example the introduction of free education and health care. The educational reform[3] introduced 7 grades of compulsory education for children, free of cost (later raised to 8, and then to 10 grades), and launched effective campaigns, managing to raise literacy rates to 90% by the end of the 1950s. Large vaccination and child healthcare campaigns were organised, with the voluntary participation of professionals. Early childcare settings were organised by age group for children of the working class (for babies, toddlers, and preschool children, for day care, for the week, and for long-term, residential care), so women could participate in the labour division. From the 1950s, social work became more and more dominated by the medical system, and slowly lost its social dimension. Social problems like illiteracy and high child mortality, classified as reminiscences of capitalism, were targeted either as exclusively educational or as medical issues. Large-scale voluntary activities were also organised by the state, as campaigns, as for alphabetisation, when intellectuals from cities were mobilised to teach villagers to read and write; for health education; for building railways towards regions difficult to access; or to adopt orphaned children in the post-war and famine period, mostly at the end of the 1940s (Roth-Szamoskozi, 2009).

From 1957 to 1968, social assistance was enacted under the responsibility of the Ministry of Health, which resulted in the medicalisation of social care for many categories of dependent people, in special little children and those with disabilities. Since the overtake of the communist regime, social work education was reduced in dimensions and moved to nursing schools, and in 1969 all forms of social work education were ended. Under Romania's communist regime, especially under Ceausescu's dictatorial ruling (1964–1989) ideology required individuals to subdue their needs to those of the society. Social support was equalised; decision-making was centralised; and economy and social protection principles and practices were strongly interrelated (Pasti, 1997, p. 6). In 1969, all the social work schools were closed by the communist regime, and later in 1975, all social science educations for psychologists and sociologists were also closed, based on the conviction that social problems were under control and there is no justification for formal social services or for the profession of social worker (Patterson, 2004; Roth-Szamoskozi, 2009; Roth-Szamoskozi, 1998).

After 45 years of communism and isolation from the West, and partially from other socialist countries too, the 1989 December Revolution set Romania on the path to democracy, opening the country to the outside view for the first time in decades. The demise of the communist regime permitted the world to see not only the odd face of political dictatorship, but also the inhuman policies aimed at orphan and abandoned children and people with disabilities, who were placed in residential care. In the following years, problems were not acknowledged under Romania's communist regime, as child maltreatment and abandonment, domestic violence, alcohol abuse, institutional abuse of children and persons with disabilities, and chronic mental health patients began to be acknowledged. As social problems became more and more acknowledged and aired in the mass media, it became obvious to national and international politicians and civil organisations that the serious social problems confronting the country required new kinds of public policies, different organisations to deliver social services and specialised workforce. It is in this context that the social work education and social work profession began to re-emerge in the universities of the country. With the help of international organisations, schools of social work were reopened in 1991 in the four major universities (Bucharest, Cluj-Napoca, Iaşi, and Timişoara), and in 1994, Romania had the first class of social work graduates. Later, new public and private universities emerged, and social work training was developed in many of the newly founded faculties of social sciences. As typical for social work education, it has "mainly been influenced by outside factors due to its frame of reference, its goals and role in society" (Júlíusdóttir, 2006, p. 39). As described by the same author, social work evolves "in a context of radical social change and as a reaction to problems of individual adjustment in the turbulence of industrial revolution" (Júlíusdóttir, 2006, p. 39). This has also been true for Romania, but the evolution started later, in the interwar period, stopped during communism, and resurrected from its ashes only after the Romanian revolution in 1989. The lack of qualified social workers and the favourable opportunities for developing new social science academic programmes in Romania were strong external motivations for the development of social work education in Romania.

POLICY CONTEXT IN THE POST-COMMUNIST PERIOD

The Romanian political change from the dictatorship of the Ceausescu regime was expected to be accompanied by the restructuring of a democratic society, with equal chances for all its citizens, with respect to human rights. This included rights which were limited or prohibited by the former regime, as for example freedom of speech, political and religious freedom, freedom of abortion, or freedom to travel abroad. Citizens also wished for welfare provisions to increase at the same pace with economic and democratic development to meet people's needs for decent salaries and pensions, free and quality health care and education. Early in the 90's, in the period 1990–1992, Romania was labelled 'post-communist conservative corporatist' (Deacon, 1993, p. 193), while later Romania tried to catch up with the Central European EU countries in their advancement towards liberalism (Deacon, 2000). Adopting the main UN and European Union recommendations for children's rights,[4] women's rights,[5] rights for people with disabilities,[6] the EU's strategies to reduce poverty,[7] and the European Roma strategies,[8] in principle Romania accepted governmental responsibilities for its most vulnerable citizens. In the Romanian social security system, universal benefits coexisted with insurance-based benefits and with means-tested provisions (Roth-Szamoskozi, Popescu, & Raţ, 2006). In spite of the existing legal basis, in practice, many of the functions of the welfare state were left to the goodwill of local authorities (mayoralties) and to civil society organisations, supported mainly by international funding agencies. During the post-revolution transition from the communist regime to capitalism, the need for social protection grew far beyond the previously existing social protection measures. While some socialist state entitlements continued or were converted into insurance-based benefit entitlements, new services and forms of financial assistance were claimed to protect people in a number of conditions, as unemployment, vulnerable childhood, disability, sickness, single parenthood, and old age. In Romania, post-communist state regulations concerning both the distributive and the redistributive policies—like strengthening individual property by allowing the acquisition of former state properties with financial resources accumulated legally or illegally had created significant advantages for some, which contrasted with the official pro-egalitarian discourse (Popescu & Roth, 2008).

Chronologically, the first and major universal social protection measures consisted of compensations for price increases and subsidies on essential food products, energy, transportation, and housing. Those who owned more goods profited more than the majority who suffered the main impacts of the market conditions, and who lost the capacity to spend and invest. For example, in the public housing system, until 2000, the state rents for the few who benefitted of them were kept at the former level, before 1989, while the rents for the privately owned dwellings increased disproportionately. The social transfers had a significant impact on the income of the households (in 2002, the average reached 29 per cent), with even higher share for those of pensioners, unemployed persons, and families with numerous children (CASPIS, 2002a). There were too few social policy measures directed to the most disadvantaged groups of people (e.g. the elderly with low pensions, women exposed to domestic violence, vulnerable children and youngsters, disabled people, Roma families living in poor communities, and the homeless), or have been ineffective in reducing gaps (Roth-Szamoskozi et al., 2006). At the same time, there were few social work services and social workers who could empower the people belonging to these groups to access their rights and become autonomous (Lazăr, Dégi & Iovu, 2016).

Despite the growing needs and the international pressure, the reform of the social protection system was slow and investment in public social services came only in the second decade after the political shift. The reconstruction of social assistance became more powerful with the social assistance laws (705/2001 and 47/2006), the Law against marginalisation (116/2002), the Child Law (272/2004), the law banning international adoptions (273/2004), the law on Guaranteed Minimum Income (276/2010),[9] and the law for People with Disabilities (448/2006). Nonetheless in spite of the existence of the legal foundation, the Social protection expenditures ratio in Romania's GDP remained throughout 2000–2008 approximately half of the average in the EU (around 13% in Romania, compared to the average 26% of the EU) (Lazăr, 2015). Before 2007, in the period before the accession to the European Union, both non-profit and public social services developed, and the basis for an administrative monitoring system for quality assurance of public services had been established. In the social security system, the passive social measures exceeded the active measures, with 74% of the financial resources spent on benefits and only 26% being directed to social services (Lambru & Vameşu, 2010).

The Romanian Government's Strategy on Social Inclusion and Poverty Reduction (2014–2020) states the fundamental principles of modern democracies based on human rights: equal opportunities for all citizens to participate in society, meeting basic needs, the respect of differences, valuing all people, and respecting their dignity (Teşliuc, Grigoraş, & Stănculescu, 2015). Romanian welfare policies, public social services and community development practices have often been criticised in Romania for not being successful in the social inclusion of people with disabilities, for maintaining a high number of children in care institutions, for not engaging individuals from poor communities, as well as for not increasing the education level and employability of Roma people (Alston, 2015; Commissioner for Human Rights, 2014; Roth & Toma, 2014). Facing the economic competition within the globalised market, the country continues to be confronted with poverty, Romania occupying one of the leading positions for overall poverty indicators in the EU[10] (Eurostat, 2018). The share of those severely financially deprived in 2017 in Romania was 19.7% (Eurostat, 2018). Severe social, educational, and medical problems, like the lack of social housing, highest child poverty rates in the EU, high rates of child abandonment and foster care, of infant mortality, of early school abandonment, of teenage pregnancy, and low rate of employment among people with low educational attainment, especially for those of Roma origin, continue to impede the social protection system, without any significant progress for these indicators. In spite of the reduction in absolute poverty (since 2015), statistically significant improvement was registered for fewer social protection indicators than for deterioration (Social Protection Committee, 2018, Table 4, p. 19). On behalf of the World Bank Group, Teşliuc et al. (2015) summarised Romania's objectives for improving social problems around several axes: increasing co-decision and participation of beneficiaries in the social services provision; improving needs assessments and information management system and ensuring their alignment with local decision-making policies and practices; improving financing for social services, which might include education of workforce to better attract, manage, reimburse, and account for the financial basis of public and private social services; strengthening and enhancing social assistance at the community level; developing integrated community intervention teams, particularly in poor and marginalised communities; and developing services for vulnerable groups, including children and people with disabilities (mental health problems included), elderly people, and other vulnerable groups. All of these greatly depend on the training and professional conduct of the workforce; therefore, they constitute relevant directives for the education of social workers.

INTERNATIONAL INFLUENCES AND THE DEVELOPMENT OF THE ROMANIAN SOCIAL WORKFORCE

In the search for the identity of Romanian social work, one has to acknowledge the contribution of the international civil sector, non-governmental organisations and aid-movement targeting Romania's orphanages, homes for the elderly and people with disability, or poor villages. They not only delivered basic services, but were also the ones to contribute to the development of the civil sector of non-governmental social services in the first phases after the political shift. The Western social workforce reaching Romania in the 90s had various ideological backgrounds, some being representatives of faith-based organisations, others of local or regional civil society initiatives, others of international human rights organisations (Dümling, 2004; Edwards, Roth, Popescu, & Davis, 2000). Initially delivering aid at a grassroots level, they became more and more involved in community development and the training of the Romanian social workforce, influencing the development of social work practice and education. As such, the effects of the social work practices delivered in Romania after the demise of communism can be seen as examples of internationalisation. Analysing this process from the point of view of the evolution of Romanian social work practice and education, one could assist to the delivery of functional Western practices for Romanian social problems, and their adaptation to the local needs and cultures, corresponding to what the literature calls internationalisation and localisation (Gray & Coates, 2008). International aid organisations and Western social workers/ staff were generally not contested, but appreciated by fellow Romanians for alleviating human suffering (Edwards et al., 2000; Lazar, 2015). At the same time, as Dümling (2004) shows, they felt disempowered by not being involved in the decision-making and by the expanding grant system, which imposed competition among agents active in the social arena. Romanian experts also felt disempowered by the alliances of Western organisations with public authorities, whom were often seen by local civic society as resistant to change, but whom were seen by international NGOs as guarantees of sustainability (Edwards et al., 2000; Popescu & Roth, 2008). On their turn, public authorities, representatives of local political power structures elected their partners according to the financial advantages, so local civic society, with little resources, and eventual greater local expertise had little chances to prove their competences. This might have contributed to the perpetuation of some tensions between local and international workforce, until in the recent years, when the NGOs have become sufficiently autonomous, due especially to the EU funding opportunities.[11]

In the Romanian social context, where communist ideology had been denying for years the existence of social problems and their influence on mental health and social integration, the adoption of international training models promoting inclusion and non-discrimination, by using individualised direct practice with people affected by poverty, discrimination and social exclusion had to face many practical and cultural obstacles (Patterson, 2004; Friedman, 2009). The scarcity of effective and culturally appropriate models that would promote the social inclusion of children or adults (as people with mental health issues, victims of violence, children at risk, people with disabilities, offenders, elderly, unemployed, substance abusers, etc.) acted as barriers to the effective adoption of inclusive models and the persistence of the biomedical one (Antal, 2010; Friedman, 2009). Case management was a new way to respond to beneficiaries' needs, and it required working with human relations in families, groups, and communities, as well as mobilising social and public resources. Later, when social services began to flourish and became competitive, deinstitutionalisation became an overall model, often applied without providing adequate community services, and as such, it has been criticised as copying the Western models without criticism, under the pressure of a neoliberal managerial drive for increased efficiency and effectiveness, thus avoiding again individualised practices (Friedman, 2009). As for the adopted models, their delivery often differed from the initial ones, due to insufficient resources, staffing, workforce mobility, or lack of supervision (Voicu, 2017).

As mentioned by Gray and Coates (2008), in the competition of practice models those that were situated closer and had a culturally more relevant conceptual framework were easier to adopt, which in case of Romania were the models based on spirituality, and charity or on family networks, in the detriment of the models that foster rights, empowerment, and self-determination of the vulnerable (Edwards et al., 2000; Dümling, 2004; Roth-Szamoskozi, 1998; Roth & Toma, 2014).

According to a recent study (Lazăr, Mihai, et al., 2019), the authors note that international agencies, such as the World Bank, the International Monetary Fund (IMF), and the World Trade Organization contributed to the grounding of the neoliberal ideology in the Romanian social protection institutions. Although the influences of the mentioned institutions in framing social protection policies cannot be denied, the tendencies towards neoliberal ways of decentralised, economically driven, impersonal, and less competence-based social work cannot only be explained by such international influences. According to Alston, the UN human rights, and poverty commissioner, the neoliberal interpretation that "poverty is a choice" is often voiced by stakeholders but in fact "that choice is too often made by government policies rather than by those living in poverty" (Alston, 2015, p. 1). According to the UNHRC commissioner, the low performance of Romania on all human development, human rights, and social protection indicators compared to other EU states is directly linked to the substandard funding of social services (only 0.6% of the GDP), so "the reduction of poverty and social exclusion remains a major challenge for Romania" (Alston, 2015, p. 2).

Taking into consideration the large international mobilisation throughout the period following the demise of the communist regime, both before and after the accession to the European Union aiming to assist Romania in developing a social protection and a social service system to benefit its vulnerable citizens, under a continuous monitoring for human rights, one would expect major improvements in the social situation of vulnerable citizens. However, the recent evaluation of the Commissioner for Human Rights indicates that "the decentralization of social services, in the absence of adequate resources and efficient monitoring mechanisms concerning the implementation of social protection standards, has diminished the accountability of local authorities in the implementation of these standards" (Commissioner for Human Rights, 2014, p. 6). The Commissioner for Human Rights on behalf of the Council of Europe also reports severe human rights problems in three main domains of social work: persons with disabilities (barriers to independent living and inclusive education, inadequate residential care), human rights of children (children living in institutions, abandoned and homeless children, victims of violence, children in contact with juvenile justice), and human rights of Roma people (institutionalised anti-gypsyism, discrimination related to access to housing, mainstream education, health services, and employment of Roma).

The recent report of UNHRC (2017) on the application of human rights in Romania confirms these issues and adds a larger constellation of aspects where human rights and access to adequate services need strengthening.

The examples below are often expected to be performed by social workers employed in the education, health and mental health, child welfare, disability, or justice sectors, for example: to elaborate procedures to include Roma children in mainstream education; to promote the equal access of Roma to health and housing services; to assure access of people with HIV/AIDS to specialised medical care; to ensure non-discriminatory access for people with disabilities to education, to public transportation, and public buildings; to encourage employment of people with disabilities; to promote gender equality and the access of women to high status and decision-making positions; to stand up against violence, raise awareness of its unacceptability and adverse impact; to enforce the prohibition of corporal punishment and domestic violence; to ensure thorough investigation and effective response to all victims of violence; to organise training for state officials; to design age-appropriate educational programmes in schools on sexual and reproductive health to prevent the high number of early pregnancies and unsafe abortions; to improve quality of life, living conditions, treatment and implement a deinstitutionalisation policy for persons with disabilities, psychiatric patients and for looked after children and young people from residential care; and to provide legal support for victims of trafficking, therapy and social assistance (listed by UNHRC [2017]).

CHALLENGES OF THE SOCIAL WORKFORCE AND SOCIAL WORK EDUCATION

As it results from the comments above, one of the main challenges of adopting policy and practice models and to culturally adjust them to the local needs—besides funding and logistic issues—includes training and qualification of the workforce in both public and private sectors (Davis, 2006; Iovu, 2019; Iovu & Runcan, 2012; Lazăr, 2015). Some authors linked the failure of anti-discrimination laws and policies and of the response to human right challenges to protect those most exposed to poverty and other risks to the inadequate training and insufficient qualifications of generalists social workers, who fail to adequately connect and respond to their needs (Alston, 2015; Roth & Toma, 2014). The inefficiency of social work services is also linked with structural issues, like understaffing of public services and discontinuity with financing at NGO level (Lazăr, 2015), but analysts also indicate the lack of competences of social workers to communicate, analyse, understand, and respond to cases of marginalisation and discrimination (Tonk, Adorjáni, & László, 2012).

According to the analysis on behalf of the World Bank, social workers do not know what specialised public or non-governmental services exist at the national level so they cannot make informed referrals. The referral system for people with disabilities is outdated. With no mapping of existing services, the referral commissions do not know what network of services is available at the local level (Teşliuc et al., 2015).

The cultural barriers in addressing needs of beneficiaries are the highest in case of working with Roma communities. Exploring the attitudes and values of social workers towards members of poor Roma communities, Roth and Toma (2014) noted the social distance between beneficiaries of Roma ethnicity and the social workers, especially in public services, insufficient interest in involving beneficiaries in decision-making, barriers in communications, and frequent deviation from the code of ethical professional behaviour. Similar obstacles were mentioned by Popoviciu, Popoviciu, Bara, Costea, and Drăgan (2012), who reported little investment of case managers in understanding of the resources of their clients, as well as ineffective communication with mothers separated from their children, or at risk of abandonment. Other data showed insufficient competencies of child protection workers, who often fail to involve children in communication and in decision-making (Roth, Antal, Kacsó, László, & Mureşan, 2018).

Inadequate professional training has been blamed by several studies for preventing staff from applying legal regulations to prevent and respond to situation of domestic violence and violence against children, or to turn to effective case management and behavioural management methods (Câmpean, Constantin, & Mihalache, 2010; Roth et al., 2018). According to a case-based analysis of files in a sample of the child protection departments, Tonk et al. 2012) found a shortage of information concerning social, behavioural, educational, or substance abuse problems faced by families and children, treatment plans indicating services not available to the beneficiaries, and no information regarding the outcome of the case management. A great number of children psychiatric services are provided, but less counselling or other therapeutic services. These authors explained the extended use of psychiatric medication, especially in cases of violence, with the dominance of the medical model used by professionals from the child protection system in the detriment of the ecological model. All these signalled weaknesses in the competences of the professionals point to the shortcomings in the training process of the workforce.

Besides cultural issues, the preference for still using bureaucratic, rather than direct and personalised practices with beneficiaries can be partly explained by the high workload of social workers. The data collected by the Romanian National College of Social Workers[12] show that there is an average of 3350 inhabitants per single social worker (at approx 6000 active social workers—of whom 4125 are registered by the professional body—and a total population up to approx. 20 million people) (Lazăr, Dégi et al., 2016). Social services are chronically understaffed, and it is estimated that approximately 20,000 more social workers would be needed (Iovu, 2019), especially in rural public services. Another explanation is the large proportion of social workers who do not have a university degree and only one in four is qualified (Lazăr, Dégi et al., 2016). In spite of the need for specialisation in different fields of social work, participation of social workers in ongoing training programmes is still low (Lazăr, Dégi et al., 2016), and supervision of professional work within the public and many private services is still hierarchical, having more an aspect of internal control, rather than becoming a learning opportunity and support for improving the quality of case management (Davis, 2010, Voicu, 2017). Both the cultural gaps and the insufficient workforce could and should be addressed by social work education.

Social Work Education Under Scrutiny

"The education and training of social workers is inevitably linked to the type of organization in which social work is carried out" (Gill, 2011, p. 54). Looking for the characteristics of the Romanian social work education, one has to consider all the above-mentioned influences that marked its development: the national historical origins, its anchors in the social and cultural context, and the global social work influences.

The modern era of social work education began in Romania in January of 1991 in three universities. The first social work programmes were modelled partly on the old Romanian social assistance training programmes that existed prior to the Second World War and partly on the Western European or US models. The initial curriculum consisted of a listing of social science courses already taught in the universities, with the addition of a few social work-related courses, taught by sociologists, psychologists, special educators, economists, or lawyers who lacked both theoretical knowledge of social work, and had no or little experience in social services. The generic and theoretical teaching based on outdated library literature—as during the communism no international literature has been brought into the country—was slowly updated and complemented with translations and later with writings by home-grown academics. The field practicum was initially planned as blocks of a couple of weeks placements in which students would have contact with emerging public or private services, with very few, if any, staff members, who neither had in those years any practice experience in social work nor any specialised training, which made it difficult to arrange adequate supervision for students placed in those settings. In addition, there was almost no social work literature—books or journals—available in Romanian, or any other language. Therefore, international aid which contributed to training, donated academic literature, and fostered exchanges of social service staff and academics was essential in the first decade after the political shift (Edwards et al., 2000). Faced with the choice to follow either the model of baccalaureate and masters level education that exists in the USA, UK, and Canada, or the applied high school model of France, Belgium or Germany that was initially implemented, the academics of Romania have chosen the first one, in order to transmit the message that the complexity of social problems in the post-communist period required highly skilled professionals trained in an academic setting, on an equal footing and social status as other professions in social sciences: psychologists, sociologists, special educators, and anthropologists. Placing social work studies on a university foundation was also considered a guarantee to increase the effective interventions of social workers to act for change at the individual, family, group, and community levels, applying knowledge from an interdisciplinary domain. The expectation was to enable social work graduates to successfully provide support for a diversity of vulnerable individuals, families, groups, and communities at risk, affected by poverty, physical, or mental illness, etc., and to become social agents at societal level (Zamfir, 1992). According to the role expectations, social workers would assess complex social problems and consecutively apply social policy measures, which has been the model inherited from the communist period, but also to go further than administering benefits by enabling beneficiaries to become autonomous (Zamfir, 1992).

During its initial developmental phase, social work education had to address gaps that existed on various levels (Edwards et al., 2000): between the communist model of state-care and institutionalisation of the so-called unfit individuals, and the modern forms of case management, group and community work, programme evaluation, evidence-based practices and social policy analysis; between the old forms of social assistance education that existed in Romania in the interwar period and the contemporary Western models of social work education; between the predominantly theoretical and practice disconnected Romanian higher education model, and the experiential, practice-based, conceptualised, and reflective social work education model; between the need of the society for licensing high numbers of social workers and the limits of developmental capacities of the newly created social work departments; and between the need for field practice and the scarcity of positive fieldwork models.

Bridging these gaps require restructuring both the social welfare system in Romania, but also changes in educational efforts, both on the side of academic staff and students, as well as more international collaboration. In the initial phase of the developmental process of social work education, the most important tasks were the development of course materials and of the practice component of the social work curriculum. The international agencies like USAID, UNICEF, WHO, and UNDP had a major influence throughout in identifying and investigating social problems, preparing detailed reports and recommendations towards change in social services. Besides the importance of such reports for the stakeholders and policymakers, both in the early years after the political change and today, they also represented important readings for students as well during their social work training. Non-profit organisations allowed students to see in practice the assessment processes and to participate in planning and delivering responses to problems they were studying in class. Beginning with the first years of rebuilding the democratic society, the flourishing civil sector (like Save the Children, SOS children's villages, Médecins Sans Frontières, Holt International, World Vision, Christian Children's Fund, Hope and Homes for Children, Terre des Hommes, the Order of Malta, the Red Cross, and many others) contributed to the development of Romanian social work education by offering functional social work training models to their own staff, but also to the personnel in the orphanages, homes for the elderly, Roma communities, poor communities, in cities and rural areas, and by offering placements for students enrolled in social work programmes. International social work not only influenced social work education by offering placements, the course work component was also largely influenced by the mobility of academics due to the Fulbright Exchange Program with the USA, and the staff and student mobility programmes within Europe. Gradually, the curriculum was enriched with specific social work methods courses (with individuals, groups, and communities), values and the ethical code, social policies and social problems, social work with practice courses with various populations (i.e. children, elderly, substance abusers, and delinquents), and health issues. Towards the end of the first decade of the transitioning state, social work graduates began to fill in positions also in public services and to develop new practices, to respond to the extensive social problems of the unemployed, the poor, the homeless children, and the victims of violence, the psychiatric patients. Social work jobs were founded on the renewed legal platforms for protecting and promoting the rights of the most vulnerable, like children, people with disabilities, psychiatric patients, the Roma, and for administering welfare provisions.

At the beginning of the Millennium, while preparing for the accession to the European Union, social workers advanced in their associative movement and pushed for a "Law on social assistance" to define the place and role of social protection and social workers in society. The initial law (Law 705/2001) has later gone through major changes (Law 47/2006; Law 2092/2011), advancing towards the recognition of the complexity of social problems, and of the subsequent necessity for professional response by quality social services, staffed with qualified personnel, including licensed social workers (with a bachelor's degree in social work). One regulation stated that all social services, including the civil sector, need to be accredited in order to offer services to clients and access public funds. Thus, this was a flourishing period for the professionalisation of the social services and its professionals. Due to the PHARE grant system of the EU, the Romanian social sector had accessed European funds aiming to reduce social inequalities. These opportunities favoured the launching of a large category of new public services and non-governmental organisations. In addition to their merit to alleviate human suffering by responding to the population's needs, the growth of the social service sector resulted in the creation of new jobs for graduates and placements for students, but it also required new courses for the preparation of social workers.

The process of developing competencies of social work academic staff was substantially supported by the opportunities to create and maintain a wide network of relationships with colleagues from many Western countries. The impact of Western social work depended on the efforts of both Romanian and international social work staff to reciprocally deepen their understanding of the organisational and social policy milieu as well as the applicability of intervention models.

THE ACCREDITATION OF SOCIAL WORK EDUCATION

As a result of internal development and collaborative initiatives, during the 30 years that passed since Romania has liberated itself from communism, the development of the content and structure of social work education has been marked by the major directions of the structural reform in Romania's higher education system. Since 2005, Romania is implementing the Bologna Convention (as formulated in the European Higher Education Area, 1999), and therefore, most of its bachelor programmes (except medicine and engineering) have changed from four to three years (six semesters) bachelor programmes, followed by two years master programmes. The requirements of the Bologna system gave a boost to the reforms to develop the high-level skills and *knowledge* that students and the *society* require, in order that they become more employable and mobile through Europe. During this process, learning becomes a continuous and an effective process, with important components of practice and doing, well integrated to the knowledge systems acquired by traditionally academic ways of teaching (Gibbs, 2013; Parker, 2007).

Actually in Romania, after 2010 there are around 30 public, private, or faith-based schools of social work, at bachelor level. Although in 2019 there are already 25 generations of national graduates, there are still no aggregate data on the total number of people who obtained a diploma in social work. During the 30 years of the democratic regime, the number of higher education institutions teaching social sciences increased from 4 universities in 1991, to 48 public universities and 29 private universities (Popescu, 2012), with 41 social work programmes in 2011 (Government Decision 966/2011), and 34 in 2018 (158/2018 29 March 2018), accepting 15–150 students annually.

As required by the national Law of Social Assistance (2011), and in agreement with the internationally accepted aims of social work education (Campanini, 2010), the bachelor programmes in Social Work aim to transmit an internationally and locally relevant body of knowledge, values, and skills of SW: to form the social work knowledge basis and consolidate the values promoting respect, non-discrimination, access to resources, equal chances and foster self-determination and participation of beneficiaries. The programmes running in different universities have a multidisciplinary foundation, teaching basics of sociology, psychology, law, social policies, research methods, and optionally health, anthropology, or economy. In the full social work curricula, the emphasis falls on learning SW methods with individuals and families, but some of the programmes also include group work and community development. Practice is highly valued in all bachelor programmes, the domain of social work being unique among Romanian bachelor studies for making space for at least one day of weekly practice time and a compact learning time of 60 hours/year on average (Popescu, 2012). Even compared to the other social science domains, social work programmes allocate the highest percentage of time to apprenticeship and service learning. Although the standards of 2018 have reduced the requirement for practice to only 10% of the total time allocated in the curriculum, most of the social work programmes seem to allocate more, data of 2012 showing an average of 15–20% of time allocated to fieldwork under the supervision of trained social workers, and faculty members, in order to immerse students in the real tasks of the profession. Students are also being encouraged and credited for volunteering. Different programmes can focus on specific aims, but the standards define the core general and specific competencies to be followed by all public and private programmes. As for the outcomes, in general students acquire good oral and written communication, as well as planning and evaluation skills. To illustrate the way social work competencies are formalised, a case example is presented.

Excerpts of the accreditation documents show the *mission, the goals and the teaching methods statement* of the Department of Social Work at Babeş-Bolyai University,[13]:

Mission: "*The Bachelor degree in Social Work is a generalist program that addresses and stimulates multicultural awareness and dialogue among cultures, scientific, technological and organizational competence and social responsibility*".

Goals: "*It promotes the development of students' critical thinking about social problems and policies and it focuses on responding to social problems by forming individual, familial, group and community level intervention skills. It aims to develop students' personality, by incorporating a multicultural perspective. It has a strong research orientation, by promoting collection of evidence for improving practice and by involving students in research. It gives a basic orientation to working in public services and NGOs, with individuals, families and communities, in child protection, with elderly people, the unemployed, people with disability, substance abusers as well as other vulnerable people and groups; it also includes the basics on social policies, management of social services and volunteering*".

"***Teaching methods:*** *Teachers and supervisors use a variety of methods, moving from lectures to interactive and reflective methods, stimulating students to cooperate and jointly work on projects.*"

As stated in the mission and goals, academic staff formulates its goals according to the expectations, aiming to develop student's critical thinking, multicultural perspective, and their capacity to become competent in working with individuals, families, groups, and communities, using evidence to build up and improve their practical competences.

Excerpt of the diploma supplement that accompanies the licensing certificate for successful graduation from the bachelor programmes of the Department of Social Work at BBU, as stated in the accreditation files, 2014[14]

Professional competencies:
- *to identify, collect, document, evaluate, and record data for the analysis, assessment, and specialised interventions to assist individuals, families, groups, and communities;*
- *to write, implement, and evaluate social work projects, programmes, and policies for different groups of vulnerable people;*
- *to develop prevention and support services for beneficiaries of social protection;*
- *to offer consultancy for people at risk of social exclusion for accessing community resources;*
- *to offer counselling and other specialised interventions delivered to individuals and families in their homes or in public or private institutions (e.g. hospitals, schools, prisons, anti-drug centres, specialised social work institutions, etc.);*
- *to communicate and develop a professional relationship with beneficiaries and other social actors while respecting the values and principles of social work.*

Transversal competencies:
- *to conceptualise social problems and analyse them by taking into account the social context and the views of the people themselves;*
- *to promote respect for all human beings, and social responsibility by multicultural awareness and dialogue among cultures, ethnicities, and religions;*
- *to promote scientific, technological, and organisational competence, by engaging efficient work technologies in a trans-disciplinary team, in a multiple hierarchical environment: within and between organisations;*
- *to understand the need for continuous, learning and professional training, and identify resources and ways to support personal and professional development for better employability on the job market;*
- *to understand and operate with research data.*

A specificity of the Romanian Quality Assurance regulations is that it allows double specialisation for theology-social work, awarding double licensing as social worker and a religion teacher. From the above-mentioned total number of institutions, in 2011 there were 17 (41%) theology schools, and in 2018, their number was maintained almost the same: 16 (46%), showing that double licensing persists, and it continues to be accredited, in spite of the scarcity of such degrees in Europe (Campanini, 2010). This demonstrates the influence of the church in East European countries: "The church has significant involvement in social work education in Eastern European countries such as Hungary and Romania where the social work training can be linked with the preparation to become a deacon" (Campanini, 2010, p. 688). The author has not managed to find literature to analyse the contradictions that might raise regarding overall accepted social work values like self-determination and non-discrimination for LGBT persons, women in situation of abortion, suicide, etc. On the contrary, there are publications to underly the importance of religious-based social work (Neagoe, 2013). The risks for double standards have often been voiced by academics[15] but were also documented based on the curricular structure of training by L. Popescu (2012). This author reports that apparently the curricula of the two programmes have a 85% overlap in the number of disciplines from the social work specialisation, but the real time (counted in number of planned courses and workshops) devoted by this curricular area in the whole study programme is 58% for the mono-specialisation and 35% for the double specialisation. Another important difference is the number of compact practice hours assigned in average: 80 hours for the mono-specialisation and 41 hours by the double specialisation in the evaluated programme. The author rightfully concludes that in spite of apparently respecting the regulations to cover 70% of the regular social work programmes specialised area, in fact the coverage is in average less than 60% for social methods and other specific disciplines, and 50% of the field learning component.

Bachelor programmes are generalists, and optional courses are limited by the number of maximum classes. Graduates can opt for a specialisation at the level of master programmes. Although the majority of employment opportunities are in the area of child protection, most of the courses offer specialisations in other areas, like: counselling and social work, probation, vulnerable and high-risk groups, social work supervision, social services management. There are some specializations in interdisciplinary areas (e.g. social work and social economy, gerontology, European master in children's rights, etc.) (Lazăr, 2015; Popescu, 2012).

Following an arbitrary decision at the level of the Romanian Higher Education Quality Assessment Body (ARACIS), through the governmental decree no. 581/2013,[16] all the mentioned master programmes defined until that time within the field of social work (Ministry of Education, 2013), had been transferred for the period 2013–2017 to the field of sociology. Although the master programmes continued to exist, the graduates could not be awarded the title of Masters in Social Work (MSW) any more. This did not affect the career paths of those who were seeking employment or career advancement in Romania, but it impacted those who had emigration plans in countries that valued MSW. This situation was a reflection of the scientific position of social work as lacking its own, solid epistemological and theoretical grounding. As a reaction, members of academic social work and the National College of Social Workers (which is the National Professional Association of the social workforce) have strengthened their structural relationships and recognised the need to reconstruct traditional social work practices and reinterpret narratives to increase professional integrity, visibility, and impact (Lazăr, Dégi et al., 2016). Academics collected data on the professional status of social workers (Lazăr, 2015; Ciocănel et al., 2018; Lazăr, Dégi et al., 2016; Lazar, Mihai et al., 2019) and advocated at political level, i.e. the parliament, for the improvement of the social and financial status of social work and social workers. As a consequence, the regulations in 2018 (Government Decision 185/2018)[17] reinstated the possibility for advanced master and doctoral studies in social work. Until 2019, successful research in topics as child protection, foster care, assistance for elderly, addictions, social policies related to poverty and disability, or community work was not awarded a doctoral degree in social work, but in related social sciences (e.g. sociology, psychology, political science). During this period, the National Professional Association launched a strong campaign for strengthening the public image of social work through the mass media and constructing structural links between academia and the National Professional Association.

As for the teaching content of the programmes, the requirement of the accreditation body imposed on the curriculum to integrate a varied set of values, institutional practices, theoretical backgrounds and expectations, as well as multiple international tendencies. In practice, accreditation lacks the effective instruments to assess the capacity of staff and schools to prepare their graduates with the competency to engage in research-informed practice and practice-informed research, as required by Sheafor (2011). Instead, standards define percentages of domain specific and specialised courses, of theoretical and practical activities, of exams versus other forms of evaluation. If at bachelor level the curriculum is required to follow the national guidelines with disciplines to be included in students' studies, at master level the curricula are entirely developed by the department running the programme, only the number of classes, the number of optional, and compulsory courses being standardised (ARACIS, 2011; ARACIS, 2017; Popescu, 2012). The accreditation procedures require evaluation of the application of the mission, the general objectives, and the teaching programmes of each study programme (ARACIS, 2017). In reality, there is no evaluation of the fulfilment of teaching objectives like forming analytical and critical thinking capacities of social work students, building up the students' research capacities, familiarising them with the evidence-based and human rights perspective, the comparative European and global perspective, as well as their acceptance of diversity, and their understanding of the links between social position and responsibility. One small-scale study run with 62 professionals found that only about thirty-eight per cent of graduates of social work stated that they had been informed in their training about the foundations of evidence-based practices, though 70% of them considered that they have the necessary searching skills to find the information they needed, 45.2% stated they were educated in critical appraisal of research literature. Only 35.5% of the respondents stated they agreed or strongly agreed that their facility supports the use of evidence in practice (Iovu & Runcan, 2012). Another research at the University in Timisoara on a sample of 100 students in social work demonstrated that respondents were putting efforts and time in studying research methods and statistical data analysis. Another small sample study showed promising results for front-line 80 social workers engagement in human rights and non-discriminatory practices, the use of the strengths perspective regarding their clients, as well as displaying collaborative skills and capacity to involve clients in decision-making, but less activism, defined as willingness to advocate in the benefit of their clients (Iovu, 2019). In order to evaluate social work education on these dimensions, more research is needed on much larger samples of bachelor and master students, as well as graduates.

CONCLUSION

The practice of social work and the training of its workforce in Romania, as well as in any other parts of the world are bound to national laws and training regulations, social contexts and cultural traditions. In the Romanian context, where in the recent past ideology declared the inexistence of social problems, and politics had ruled the demise of all civil society and blocked all education of social scientists, including social work training, and national social assistance models were far behind in history. Looking at the history of Romania, one could sense the abrupt interruption of the evolution of social work education and practice during communism, while communist social policies were seen as sufficient in raising quality of life for all its citizens. The high rate of poverty, child abandonment, and institutionalisation of disabled children, adults, and elderly proved the contrary.

Scrutinising the evolutions of the recent 30 years, one can see that in spite of the large international efforts to alleviate the effects of poverty and counteract institutionalisation, Romania has not yet defined the social policies and social work practices that best respond to the needs of its most vulnerable citizens, lagging behind in human development indicators compared to the European Union. These delays in responding to the ample social problems cannot be blamed on the international organisations; it was not their role to coordinate and synchronise their efforts.

Despite all efforts, reforms were enacted slowly and the previous organisational culture survived long after the political shift. According to Gill (2011, p. 38), "social work education has a central role to play in helping current and future social workers reclaim the profession from the organizations reacting to short term pressures". To fulfil this role, social work education, largely represented in universities, also needs to reflect on its progress. In spite of the complex administrative process of accreditation, data are scarce in demonstrating the competences of graduates in the area social change, activism, non-discriminatory practices, and use of individualised methods and of applicable evidence-based information. Although "the centrality of field-work practice is widely acknowledged in professional education" (Ghiţiu & Mago-Maghiar, 2011, p. 73), there is no large-scale information on the skills students can acquire and apply in practice in the different agencies, and how they incorporate practical knowledge in their conceptual upbringing. Principles of social justice, human rights, collective responsibility, and respect for diversity are central to social work. They need to be underpinned by theories of social work, social sciences, and humanities, and by connecting models to relevant cultural experiences of the workforce (IFSW & IASW, 2014). All these are intrinsic part of both education in bachelor and master programmes, in all universities, and accreditation needs tools to assess their existence. Beyond strengthening social work education at bachelor and master levels, a continuous education system needs to be developed, which should initially evaluate and eventually incorporate existing training organised by a large variety of agencies. Based on the observations of Iovu & Runcan (2012) and Lazăr, Mihai et al. (2019), in order to ensure the validation of social work education, research resources should be part of the services, accessible for workers. Continuous education would contribute to the specialisation of social workers and would be overlapping the generic education they receive at bachelor level, thus enabling social workers to deepen their understanding of specific fields. Supervision is another essential missing part of empowering the workforce, as for polishing and renewing its education (Davis, 2010; Voicu, 2017). The preferential supervisory relationship could be encouraged across disciplinary boundaries, and transfer of skills could get an impetus such as reflective practice, communicating with difference, shared decision-making, and working in partnership (Beresford et al., 2011).

The conclusions of this chapter again review the weaknesses, threats, strengths, and opportunities of social work education in Romanian context. As discussed, social work education should be aware of its own weaknesses in training the workforce, rooting first of all in the insufficient competences of social workers formed during their academic training, at bachelor and master levels, which impede on their capacity to engage in case management and is reflected in the low success level in the accompaniment of the most needy and vulnerable (Roth-Szamoskozi, 2000; Popoviciu et al., 2012; Tonk et al., 2012). The second level to improve is the further education programmes, at the level of either public or civil sector-run social services. Threats may further come from the exclusion people who are the neediest, and most marginalised, by the rest of the society, which place social workers in between, without equipping them with anti-discriminatory skills and models to successfully support their clients (Iovu, 2019; Roth & Toma, 2014). Threats come also from the waist of licensed social workforce, due to migration and low employment (Lazăr, Dégi et al., 2016). This adds to the insufficient resources existing in public or private agencies to improve the rate of beneficiary/social worker. Lack in intersectoral and interagency collaboration, as well as lack of political support to transpose laws into practices, resulting in the slowness of change in the social indicators for poverty, deinstitutionalisation, and all the other social problems revealed by comparing Romania to the other countries of the region (Pop, 2013; Teşliuc et al., 2015).

The strengths of the actual social work education lay in the awareness of its own needs and limits, as mentioned in the reports of the Romanian National College of Social Workers (Lazăr, Dégi et al., 2016) and the effort to identify its cultural roots and relevance. Social work education follows and advances in parallel with the consolidation of the national legislative grounding, which nowadays is aligned in their basic principles with the main international human rights platforms and the EU legislation (Lazăr, 2015; Lazăr, Dégi et al., 2016). The strengths of the social workforce are the existence of a large pool of university department accredited to train licensed professionals and the existence of a strong professional organisation embodied in the Romanian National College of Social Workers (CNASR). Besides, a large non-governmental organisation sector is active in the social area and is interested in social changes, in improving the laws and social policies, and in the competences of their workforce. As shown, in the process of internationalisation of the social sector, Romanian social work organisations linked with international bodies, at the level of academic, and practitioner exchanges, which have been formalised at the level of public services and civil society level (Lazăr, Dégi et al., 2016). Opportunities are also multifaceted: the capability and willingness of social workers to learn, develop, or adapt new social work practice models, to collect and share data on social work practices, to collaborate with other sectors and professionals, to develop assessment and evaluation instruments adapted to national and local cultural needs, to support prevention programmes (Iovu & Runcan, 2012; Iovu, 2019; Lazăr, Mihai et al., 2019).

As a recommendation, government, professional bodies and academics should partner for reforms in improving policies, in the area of deinstitutionalisation, poverty reduction, and service development. The four major elements of creating the social workforce have been identified by Roby (2016, p. 9) as: (1) political will and articulation with government priorities; (2) a clear legislative framework defining services and roles of each profession in the integrated social service workforce; (3) information systems that enable decision-making based on accurate data; and (4) a participatory implementation model of service delivery. These should be rigorously followed for improving the efficiency of the social workforce.

Better opportunities could result from a continuous common reflection of social work academics on the modalities to improve competencies of the workforce, by renewing education, integrating new models from connected fields, and improving interaction with allied professionals, as those working in health and education. Social work schools need to increase their own capacity to assess and plan for the further evolution of the social workforce, by continuously recalibrating education at organisational, academic content and field learning level, raising the quality requirements, and developing resources to improve outcomes.

NOTES

1. Initially, the Romanian name was *Şcoala de Auxiliare Sociale (School of Auxiliary Personnel)*, which later became *Şcoala de Surori de Ocrotire (School of Care-nurses)*.
2. The Romanian name was "*Şcoala Superioară pentru Asistenţă Socială „Principesa Ileana*" with its first publication being a bulletin with the curriculum, http://www.swreview.ro/uploads_ro/1515/1004/Social_Work_no._1-1929.pdf, accessed 13 April 2019.
3. Romanian Governmental Order 175, for the Reform of Education, 3 August 1948.
4. Romanian Parliament adopted the Children's Rights Convention in 1990.
5. The United Nations adopted the international bill of rights for women (CEDAW) on 18 December 1979, adopted in Romania in 1985. After the political shift, this was completed by the Romanian Law 202/2002 for equal opportunities and treatment between men and women, later completed by the Law 178/2018, and the law for the prevention of domestic violence adopted in 217/2003, published in the Official Monitor 367, 2003.
6. The 2006 UN Convention on the Rights of Persons with Disabilities was adopted and ratified by Romania through the Law 221/2010.
7. Following the Amsterdam Treaty (1997) in 1998 Romania established its first Presidential Commission to prevent and combat poverty, launching its first attempts to address poverty by structural social policy reforms. Following the Millennium Summit of the United Nations in 2000, and the Lisbon Treaty, in preparation of the access to the EU, Romania developed its first National Anti-Poverty Plan in 2002 (CASPIS, 2002b).
8. The first programming documents for Roma integration were the Strategy of the Government of Romania for improving the condition of the Roma (2001) and the Decade of Roma Inclusion 2005–2015, which focused on social inclusion, as required by the international political commitments of Romania.
9. The law 67/1995 legislated the right of citizens to social aid, but payment depended on the resources of the local authority; as a result, poor local authorities, often in rural areas, with higher percentages of unemployed persons and low-income families could not cover, were pressured to cut the payment of the due benefits. Only after 15 more years, the Law No. 276/2010 guaranteed a minimum income to every citizen (the law of the Guaranteed Minimum Income).

10. According to the Eurostat Newsrelease, 16 October 2018, Romania, with 35.7% of its population at risk of poverty and social exclusion, occupied in 2017 the second position by these criteria, with only Bulgaria having a higher percentage (38.9). https://ec.europa.eu/eurostat/documents/2995521/931 0033/3-16102018-BP-EN.pdf/16a1ad62-3af6-439e-ab9b-3729edd7b775.

11. The EU finding programme for Competitiveness Operational Programme (COP) targets, among other areas, social networking and social inclusion (https://ec.europa.eu/regional_policy/en/atlas/programmes/2014-2020/romania/2014ro16rfop001). In Romania, via POCU programs the EU funds support initiatives of the NGOs to propose amendments to the existing national social policies for vulnerable populations.

12. The National College of Social Workers (in Romanian Colegiul National al Asistentilor Sociali, acronym CNASR) is the largest membership organisation of professional social workers from Romania, with 5782 members. CNASR represents, defends, and promotes the rights and interests of members locally, nationally, and internationally, defends the honor, freedom, and independence of professional social workers in the profession, ensure the fulfill obligations that social workers have towards the beneficiaries, institutions and society, according to the professional ethics. http://www.cnasr.ro/en, 10 May 2019.

13. Excerpt of the accreditation file of the Department of Social Work at Babeș-Bolyai University (Universitatea Babes-Bolyai, with the acronym UBB), Cluj-Napoca, Romania, 2014.

14. Idem.

15. The author refers to discussions on electronic communication lists, in the period 2008–2010, and a proposition to change the license in theology-social work to pastoral theology or pastoral social work.

16. Government Decision 581/2013 on the accreditation of the domains of master programs and the maximum number of students, http://arhiva.gov.ro/upload/articles/120850/nf-hg-581-2013.pdf.

17. Governmental decision 185/2018, https://lege5.ro/Gratuit/gi3tmmzzgyzq/hotararea-nr-185-2018-privind-domeniile-si-programele-de-studii-univer-sitare-de-master-acreditate-si-numarul-maxim-de-studenti-ce-pot-fi-scolariz-ati-in-anul-universitar-2018-2019.

REFERENCES

Alston, P. (2015). *End-of-mission statement on Romania, United Nations Human Rights Council Special Rapporteur on extreme poverty and human rights.* Bucharest. Retrieved May 1, 2019, from https://www.ohchr.org/EN/NewsEvents/Pages/DisplayNews.aspx?NewsID=16737&LangID=E.

Antal, I. (2010). Aspecte privind excluderea socială şi ocupaţională a persoanelor cu probleme cronice de sănătate mentală [Aspects of social and vocational exclusion regarding adults with chronic mental health problems]. *Social Work Review/Revista de Asistenţă Socială, 9*(2), 87–99.

ARACIS. (2011). *Metodologia de evaluare externă, standardele, standardele de refer-inţă şi lista indicatorilor de performanţă a Agenţiei Române de Asigurare a Calităţii în Învăţământul Superior* [Methodology for the external evaluation, the standards and performance indicators of quality assurance for higher education].

Retrieved April 14, 2012, from http://www.aracis.ro/fileadmin/ARACIS/ Legislatie_-_Proceduri/Proiect_Metodologie.pdf.

ARACIS. (2017). *Standarde specifice privind evaluarea externă a calității academice a programelor de studii din domeniile de licență și master aferente comisiei de specialitate nr.4 științe sociale, politice și ale comunicării* [Specific standards for the external accreditation of bachelor and master programs for social, political and communication sciences]. Retrieved March 20, 2019, from http://www.aracis.ro/fileadmin/ ARACIS/Proceduri/2018/Standarde_specifice_C4.pdf.

Banu, Gh. (2016). *Asistența comunală a copiilor găsiți, orfani și săraci în București* [Communal assistance of foundlings, orphans and poor children in Bucharest]. In *Cooperativa Gusti*, 21st December, Retrieved January 20, 2019, from http://www.cooperativag.ro/asistenta-comunala-a-copiilor-gasiti-orfani-si-saraci-in-bucuresti-interbelic/.

Beresford, P., Fleming, J., Glynn, M., Bewley, C., Croft, S., Branfield, F., & Postle, K. (2011). *Supporting people: Towards a person-centred approach*. Bristol: Policy Press.

Campanini, A. M. (2010). The challenges of social work education in Europe. *Psychologica, 52*(2), 687–700. http://hdl.handle.net/10316.2/3491.

Câmpean, C., Constantin, P., & Mihalache, E. (2010). *Resources and needs in the social integration of children and youth from child protection residential services*. Iași: Fondul Român de Dezvoltare Socială [Romanian Developmental Social Funds]. Research Report Project ACTIN, Retrieved March 18, 2018, from http://www. crips.ro/doc/rfactin.pdf.

CASPIS. (2002a). *Planul Național Anti-Sărăcie și Promovarea Incluziunii Sociale* [National anti-poverty plan and promotion of social inclusion]. National Commission Against Poverty and for Social Inclusion, Romanian Government. Bucharest. Retrieved from www.caspis.ro.

CASPIS. (2002b). *Indicatorii de Incluziune/Excluziune Socială* [The indicators of social inclusion/exclusion]. National Commission Against Poverty and for Social Inclusion, Romanian Government. Bucharest. Retrieved from www.caspis.ro.

Ciocănel, A., Lazăr, F., Munch, S., Harmon, C., Rentea, G. C., Gaba, D., & Mihai, A. (2018). Helping, mediating, and gaining recognition: The everyday identity work of Romanian health social workers. *Social Work in Health Care, 57*(3), 206–219.

Commissioner for Human Rights. (2014). *Report by Nils Muznieks Commissioner for Human Rights of the Council of Europe*: Strasbourg. Retrieved from https:// rm.coe.int/16806db83b.

Davis, R. (2006). *A comparative country study of the evolution of community-based social services in the former Soviet Bloc*. Report for the Social Transition Team, Office of Democracy, Governance and Social Transition of USAID by Aguirre International.

Davis, R. (2010). Constructing a profession of social work: The role of social work supervision. *Social Work Review/Revista de Asistență Socială, 9*(1), 20–30.

Deacon, B. (1993). Developments in East European social policy. In C. Jones (Ed.), *New perspectives on the Welfare State in Europe* (pp. 177–197). London: Routlegde.

Deacon, B. (2000). Eastern European welfare states: The impact of the politics of globalization. *Journal of European Social Policy, 10*(2), 146–161.

Dümling, B. (2004). Country notes: The impact of western social workers in Romania—A fine line between empowerment and disempowerment. *Social Work and Society International Online Journal, 2*(2). Retrieved from https://www.socwork.net/sws/article/view/219/452.

Edwards, R. L., Roth, M., Davis, R., & Popescu, L. (2000). The role of global collaborative efforts to develop Romania's child protection and social work education systems. *Social Work and Globalization.* A special combined issue of *Canadian Social Work, 2*(1) and *Canadian Social Work Review, 17,* 162–183.

Eurochild & Hopes and Homes for Children. (2012/2014). *Opening doors for Europe's children.* Retrieved April 10, 2014, from https://www.openingdoors.eu/wp-content/uploads/2014/11/DI_Lessons_Learned_web_use.pdf.

Eurostat. (2018). *17 October: International day for the eradication of poverty downward trend in the share of persons at risk of poverty or social exclusion in the EU.* Newsrelease. Retrieved from https://ec.europa.eu/eurostat/documents/2995521/9310033/3-16102018-BP-EN.pdf/16a1ad62-3af6-439e-ab9b-3729edd7b775.

Friedman, J. R. (2009). The 'social case': Illness, psychiatry, and deinstitutionalization in post-socialist Romania. *Medical Anthropology Quarterly, 23*(4), 375–396.

Ghițiu, M., & Mago-Maghiar, A. (2011). Field instructors on key issues in social work education: A comparative approach. *Social Work Review/Revista de Asistență Socială, 4,* 73–84.

Gibbs, G. (2013). *Learning by doing* (1st Online ed.). Oxford Books University, Oxford Center for Staff and learning Development. Retrieved from https://thoughtsmostlyaboutlearning.files.wordpress.com/2015/12/learning-by-doing-graham-gibbs.pdf.

Gill, M. (2011). Educating the professional social worker: Challenges and prospects. *Social Work Review/Revista de Asistență Socială, 4,* 31–40.

Gray, M., & Coates, J. (2008). From indigenization to cultural relevance. In M. Gray, J. Coates, & M. Yellow Bird (Eds.), *Indigenous social work around the world: Towards culturally relevant education and practice* (pp. 13–29). Aldershot: Ashgate.

International Federation of Social Workers (IFSW) and IASSW. (2014). *Global definition of social work.* Retrieved December 2, 2018, from https://www.ifsw.org/what-is-social-work/global-definition-of-social-work/.

Iovu, M. B. (2019). Usage of human rights practice by Romanian social workers. *International Social Work, 27*(3), 1–15. Retrieved February 12, 2019, from https://journals.sagepub.com/doi/abs/10.1177/0020872819828429?journalCode=iswb.

Iovu M. B., & Runcan, P. (2012). Evidence-based practice: Knowledge, attitudes, and beliefs of social workers in Romania. *Revista de Cercetare si Intervenție Socială* [Review of research and social intervention], 38, 34–70. Retrieved March 15, 2019, from https://www.academia.edu/3189900/Evidence-Based_Practice_Knowledge_Attitudes_and_Beliefs_of_Social_Workers_In_Romania.

Júlíusdóttir, S. (2006). The emerging paradigm shift in social work—In the context of the current reforms of European social work education. *Social Work & Society, 4*(1). Retrieved March 3, 2019, from http://nbn-resolving.de/urn:nbn.

Lambru, M. (2002). *Asistenta sociala în România. Doua secole de evolutie institutionala* [Social Work in Romania. Two Centuries of Institutional Evolution]. In *Ligia Livada-Cadeschi* (Ed.). Saracie si asistenta sociala în spatiul românesc (sec. XVIII-XX)/Poverty and Social Work in Romanian space. College New Europe, 61–81.

Lambru, M., & Vameşu, A. (2010). *România 2010. Sectorul neguvernamental – profil, tendinţe, provocări* [Romania 2010: The non-profit sector. Profiles, tendencies, challenges]. Bucharest: Fundaţia pentru Dezvoltarea Societăţii Civile.

Lazăr, F. (2015). Social work and welfare policy in Romania: History and current challenges. *Visioni Latino Americane, VII*(13), 65–82.

Lazăr, F., Dégi, C. L., & Iovu, M. B. (2016). *Renaşterea unei profesii sau despre cum este să fii asistent social în România?* [Rebirth of a profession or what is like to be a social worker in Romania]. Bucharest: Tritonic. Retrieved from http://api.components.ro/uploads/12c6a09675620f589055800ba6ceceee/2017/02/Rena_terea_unei_profesii_sau_despre_cum_e_sa_fii_asistent_social_in_Romania.pdf.

Lazăr, F., Mihai, A., Gaba, D., Ciocănel, A., Rentea, G., & Munch, S. (2019). Romanian social workers facing the challenges of neo-liberalism. *European Journal of Social Work, 22*(2), 326–337. https://doi.org/10.1080/13691457.2018.1540405.

Majuru, A. (2006). *Copilaria la romani* [Childhood by Romanians]. Bucuresti: Compania.

Ministry of Education. (2013). *Governmental Decree no. 581/2013 on the accredited domains for master programs, study programs and the maximum number of students that can be enrolled for the 2013–2045 school year.* Published in the Official Gazette No. 500/08.08.2013.

Neagoe, A. (2013). Ethical dilemmas of the social work professional in a (post)secular society, with special reference to the Christian social worker. *International Social Work, 56*(3), 310–325.

Parker, J. (2007). Developing effective practice learning for tomorrow's social workers. *Social Work Education, 26*(8), 763–779. https://doi.org/10.1080/02615470601140476.

Pasti, S. (1997). *Principii de baza ale protectiei copilului si ale serviciilor de asistenta sociala pentru copiii si familiile aflate in situatii deosebit de dificile* [Principles of child protection and social services for children and families in extremely difficult situation]. In R. Vitillo and D. Tobis (Eds.), *Programul de consolidare a serviciilor pentru copii si familii aflate in situatii deosebit de dificile* [Consolidation of social services for children and families in extremely difficult situations], Ed. *Departamentul pentru protectia copilului si UNICEF* [The Department for Child Protection], UNICEF.

Patterson, E. (2004). Offering hope in Romania efforts to empower throughout cross-cultural social work. *Social Work and Christianity, 31*(2), 119–136.

Pop, L. (2013). The decoupling of social policy reforms in Romania. *Social Policy & Administration, 47*(2), 161–181.

Popescu, L. (2012). *Raport privind analiza curriculelor programelor de studii universitare de licenţă şi a formărilor nonuniversitare.* Internal report for the project Servicii de asistenţă tehnică pentru implementarea proiectului „Creşterea gradului de implementare a legislaţiei din domeniul serviciilor sociale în contextul procesului de descentralizare" (proiect al B&S, Berhard & Brunhes, and FDSC). Unpublished Manuscript.

Popescu, L., & Roth, M. (2008). Stress and coping among Romanian families in the post communist period. In C. B. Hennon & S. M. Wilson (Eds.), *Families in a global context* (pp. 99–126). Abingdon, UK: Routledge.

Popoviciu, S., Popoviciu, I., Bara, D., Costea, D., & Drăgan, E. (2012). Engaging mothers in Romanian child protection services: Caseworkers' perspectives. *Social Work Review/Revista de Asistenţă Socială, 2*, 103–111.

Roby, J. L. (2016). *The evidence base on the social service workforce: Current knowledge, gaps and future research direction.* Washington, DC: Global Social Service Workforce Alliance. Retrieved March 24, 2019, from http://www.socialservice-workforce.org/system/files/resource/files/Evidence%20Base%20on%20the%20Social%20Service%20Workforce_0.pdf.

Roth-Szamoskozi, M. (1998). *Intersection of tradition and need of change in Romanian Child protection system.* Research Report, Research funded by RSC—Open Society Foundation, Prague.

Roth-Szamoskozi, M. (2009). Child Protection in Communist Romania (1944–1989), In S. Hering (Ed.). *Social Care under State Socialism (1945–1989)* (pp. 201–212). Barbara Budrich Publisher, Opladen Ge, & Farmington Hills, MI, US.

Roth-Szamoskozi, M. (2000). Child welfare in Romania. In D. S. Iatridis (Ed.), *Social justice and the welfare state in central and eastern Europe-the impact of privatization* (pp. 220–232). Westport, CT and London: Praeger.

Roth-Szamoskozi, M., Popescu, L., & Raţ, C. (2006). Children and social policies in Romania. *Studia Universitatis Babes Bolyai. Sociologia, LI*(2), 69–94.

Roth, M., Antal, I., Dávid-Kacsó, Á., László-Bodrogi, É., & Mureşan, A. (2018). Violence and trauma in the Romanian residential child protection. *Social Work Review/Revista de Asistenţă Socială, 3*, 33–52.

Roth, M., & Toma, S. (2014). The plight of Romanian social protection: Addressing the vulnerabilities and well-being in Romanian Roma families. *The International Journal of Human Rights, 18*(6), 714–734.

Rutgers University Center for International Social Work. (2008). *Social work education and the practice environment in Europe and Eurasia.* USAID, Creative Associates International, Inc., and the Aguirre Division of JBS International, Inc.

Sheafor, W. B. (2011). Measuring effectiveness in direct social work practice. *Social Work Review/Revista de Asistenţă Socială, 1*, 25–33.

Social Protection Committee (SPC). (2018). *Annual review of the social protection performance monitor (SPPM) and developments in social protection policies report on key social challenges and main messages.* Social Protection Committee Annual Report 2018. Luxembourg: Publications Office of the European Union.

Teşliuc, E., Grigoraş, V., & Stănculescu, M. (Eds.). (2015). *Background study for the national strategy on social inclusion and poverty reduction 2015–2020.* Bucuresti: World Bank Group. Retrieved from http://documents.worldbank.org/curated/en/290551467995789441/pdf/103191-WP-P147269-Box394856B-PUBLIC-Background-Study-EN.pdf.

The European Higher Education Area. (1999). *Joint declaration of the European Ministers of Education.* Retrieved November 2016, from http://www.magna-charta.org/resources/files/text-of-the-bologna-declaration.

Tonk, G., Adorjáni, J., & László, É. (2012). Providing services to maltreated children and their families. Some findings of Romanian case based surveillance study. *Social Work Review/Revista de Asistenţă Socială, XI*(2), 91–103.

Turda, M., & Quine, M. S. (2018). *Historicizing Race*, UK, London.

United Nations Human Rights Committee (UNHRC). (2017). *Concluding observations on the fifth periodic report of Romania.* CCPR/C/ROU/CO/5. Retrieved March 11, 2019, from http://tbinternet.ohchr.org/_layouts/treatybodyexternal/Download.aspx?symbolno=CCPR%2fC%2fROU%2fCO%2f5&Lang=en.

Voicu, C. I. (2017). Importance of supervision in social work. Logos Universality mentality education novelty. *Section: Social Sciences, VI*(2), 19–30. https://doi.org/10.18662/lumenss.2017.0602.02.

Zamfir, E. (1992, July). *From the culture of silence to a culture of freedom: New directions in the practice of social work in Romania.* Paper presented at International Association of Schools of Social Work Conference, Washington, DC.

CHAPTER 60

Welfare Transformation and Social Work: A Learning-by-Doing Process Looking for New Balances

Tatiana Saruis and Stella Volturo

Introduction

Starting from the 1970s, European welfare systems have been in crisis and have experienced deep transformation. This is due to the transformation of social risks and the implementation of new policy aims and institutional configurations. Frontline social services must deal with the practical effects of these changes that alter the context that they work within, and consequently their role and tasks.

The present chapter studies this topic through a street-level perspective applied to a literature review about welfare transformation, and field research conducted on the implementation of minimum income in a region of Italy, to observe some of these effects more objectively.

The first paragraph analyses the potential effects of welfare transformation on social work. It focuses on how it is putting top-down and bottom-up

---

This chapter is the result of a joint work and exchange between the authors. However, paragraphs 1, 2, 3, and 5 shall be attributed to Tatiana Saruis and paragraph 4 shall be attributed to Stella Volturo.

T. Saruis (✉)
University of Modena and Reggio Emilia, Reggio Emilia, Italy
e-mail: tatiana.saruis@unimore.it

S. Volturo
University of Bologna, Bologna, Italy
e-mail: stella.volturo2@unibo.it

© The Author(s) 2021
S. S. M. et al. (eds.), *The Palgrave Handbook of Global Social Work Education*, https://doi.org/10.1007/978-3-030-39966-5_60

pressures on street-level bureaucrats (hereafter SLBs), tasking them, at least partially, with finding an adequate balance between new demands for intervention, policy aims, resources, and organisation assets.

In order to concretely analyse some of the effects of welfare transformation, the second paragraph presents a study on the implementation of the minimum income measure, which has recently been established in Italy. It focuses on how caseworkers are using their own discretion during the implementation process to achieve a new balance between activation, economic and social support, collectability, and personalisation of social intervention, coping with a changing context.

The final paragraph sums up the results of the field research, proposing some reflections on how the role of caseworkers and their relationship with welfare beneficiaries is changing within the transformation of welfare.

Welfare Transformation and Social Work

The European welfare crisis began in the middle of the 1970s. The economic slowdown linked to the oil crisis interrupted the positive virtuous circle between economic growth and increasing public expenditure that had ensured stability and growing resources for 30 years after the Second World War. An intense debate started about the sustainability and the improvement of efficiency and effectiveness of welfare systems and policies. It inspired a complex and silent process of structural reconfiguration of welfare systems (Gilbert, 2004; Jenson, 2004). The reforms have followed similar trends in all European countries, though with variations in timescales, national models, and local specifics (Armingeon & Bonoli, 2006; Barbier, 2008). They began as a reaction to the crisis, but were implemented gradually and differently in the different contexts, interacting with local assets and pre-existing welfare configurations.

As street-level theory has highlighted from Lipsky (1980) onwards, the conditions that services' frontline workers find themselves in influence the amount of discretion they have, and how much they use it. The transformations in welfare challenge the practices of consolidated services and cause uncertainties, gaps, and issues to emerge. This means SLBs must deal with new pressures and dilemmas and adapt to changing assets and demands for intervention.

On the one hand, the conditions of high employment stability, strong and stable family relationships, and gendered division of labour (Esping-Andersen, 1994; Esping-Andersen, Gallie, Hemerijck, & Myles, 2002) have been gradually destabilised by significant socio-demographic, sociocultural, and socio-economic changes (Ranci, 2010). The increasing complexity of post-industrial societies has challenged welfare policies, due to the increasing individualisation of biographies and flexibility of careers, and consequently a growing demand for tailored (personalised) intervention. A misalignment between welfare policies and new risk profiles in European societies has begun to rise (Ranci, 2010). The population of vulnerable people is growing. The *profiles* of welfare applicants are becoming more specific, complex, and unpredictable, requiring more adaptable, integrated, and personalised welfare measures to cope with social diversification (Ranci, 2010; Saraceno & Negri, 2003). This bottom-up pressure for personalised interventions could increase SLBs' discretion when assessing cases and allocating benefits.

On the other hand, the welfare systems have been transformed in order to respond to the crisis and now include new aims, organisation assets, and measures.

A first policy trend relates to the introduction of managerial logics in public institutions, particularly inspired by the philosophy of *New Public Management* (NPM). It aims to control public expenditure and increase services' efficiency and effectiveness through de-bureaucratisation. It started in the 1980s and has had various timescales and local effects. The strategy is to control the distribution of benefits, reduce the timescales for procedures, and make it possible for them to be managed by less skilled, lower-cost workers, with discretion moved to their supervisors. These reforms have achieved mixed results (Brodkin, 2008, 2011; Evans & Harris, 2004; Guidi, 2012; Hupe, Hill, & Buffat, 2015). Some basic contradictions affect discretion: first, the definition of rigid standards contradicts the (already highlighted) demand for tailored social interventions; second, low professional skills make SLBs' decisions more likely to be affected by their own perceptions and personal convictions (Carrington, 2005; Thorén, 2008).

A second policy trend concerns the transition from government to governance logics (Kazepov, 2010). Through outsourcing processes, private for-profit and non-profit organisations are involved in designing, planning, and implementing welfare policies. Furthermore, different organisations and public service sectors are asked to coordinate with one another. The aim is to offer more effective, efficient, varied, and personalised interventions. This means that the crucial relationship and interaction between services and citizens are shared among different organisations and partially moved away from the public institutions and workers. This builds on the idea of caseworkers as public bureaucrats and fragments the responsibility for policy implementation and outcomes.

A third policy trend aims to include or reinforce activation in the labour market in welfare reforms. Job activation has become increasingly important in the last few decades, but it is still interpreted and described differently through multiple policy labels: workfare, welfare to work, labour market activation, which depend on how the boundary between work and social support is shaped (Brodkin & Martson, 2013). Since the 1990s, European welfare systems have been committed to this aim, without abandoning their traditional social vocation, especially for the most vulnerable beneficiaries. These aims should be combined and support each other in specific combinations of active and passive measures, cash and in-kind benefits, as found in the different versions of the minimum income measure. Managing these complex and sometimes contradictory aims requires services to be flexible, allowing SLBs to have space for discretion.

To sum up, welfare systems are transforming due to changes that are both bottom-up (from demand for intervention) and top-down (from policy aims and organisation). These changes have been underway for several decades and have led to pressures both to increase SLBs' space for discretion (demand for personalisation, integration of social support and activation) and to limit and control it (de-professionalisation of SLBs, standardisation of measures, and managerialisation of public services). These incoherent pressures have potential consequences both for welfare beneficiaries, reducing their access to social rights, and for SLBs that have to adapt and redefine their role to cope with new tasks and conditions, heavy responsibilities, and the risk of blame.

A STUDY ON MINIMUM INCOME: RESEARCH CONTEXT AND METHOD

Considering the trends and reforms described above, this chapter aims to analyse the implementation of minimum income to understand how social services are affected, and caseworkers' activities in particular.

Minimum income measures were initially introduced in Europe as residual social protection for citizens not covered by the (varied but generally extensive) public and private insurance and pension systems (Bahle, Hubl, & Pfeifer, 2011). They were gradually implemented in most European Countries. While differently regulated, they basically all identified income thresholds to access a monetary benefit and provided personalised support for active social inclusion.

However, the aforementioned emergence of new social risks and retrenchment of the welfare state have, on the one hand, expanded the number of potential beneficiaries (overcoming the residual dimension and increasing public expenditure) and, on the other hand, given prominence (including through stricter conditionalities and sanctions) to activation in the labour market. The result has been lower protection and stricter requirements (Bahle et al., 2011).

Studying the implementation of this measure through a case study, conducted in Italy, helps to highlight how SLBs may interpret and use their discretion while coping with the effects of a changing welfare system. In particular, this study focuses on how caseworkers are interpreting and balancing the mandates of activation and social support, personalisation and eligibility conditions of the measure, dealing with limited resources and coordinating with external organisations.

The following paragraphs introduce the field research, providing background information and a presentation of the research strategy. There are two sections: first, it briefly describes the implementation process of the minimum income in Italy; then, it explains the method and technique applied in the field research.

Minimum Income in Italy: A Short Summary of a Long Debate and a Complicated Reform

Italy was one of the last European countries to introduce a national minimum income. This has been a topic in economic and political debate at least since the 1990s, when it was gradually implemented in the EU and included in the European policy agenda.

Beyond the national and subnational differences, minimum income is generally a measure aimed at combatting poverty, providing both an economic benefit and a personalised plan for social inclusion and job activation. The target population, the criteria for access, the amount of economic benefits, the foreseen in-kind interventions, and the stress on social or work aims can vary (ICF & ECSWPR, 2019; Marx & Nelson, 2013).

In Italy, a national trial of the measure was conducted between 1998 and 2001, involving a sample of municipalities and a group of regions that decided to co-finance it together with the central state. Despite the trial's positive results (IRS, CLES, Fondazione Zancan, 2001, 2005), in the following years the introduction of a minimum income became a local issue: some municipalities and regions (particularly the largest and richest) established their own specific measures, with different amounts, beneficiaries, conditionalities, aims, and provisions.

Only after several calls for alignment by the European Commission, Italy has finally implemented a national policy for minimum income: the *Support for Active Inclusion—SIA* (National Law 208/2015) was implemented starting from 2016 (after two years of experimentation). It immediately sparked several controversies due to the limited funding allocated and the narrow coverage of the population in poverty.

Less than two years later, a new measure was approved, the *Income for Inclusion—REI* (Legislative Decree 147/2017; National Law 33/2017), with the intent of addressing the previous one's weaknesses: in particular, it widened the target population and increased the benefit amounts (Alleanza contro la povertà, 2017). This was implemented in 2018. Meanwhile, some regions (such as the one studied here) have instigated their own measures when implementing the national policy, with the aim of extending the targets and amount of available resources for the poorest population. Thanks to European funds, municipalities could hire new caseworkers to increase the number of social services staff dedicated to the implementation.

However, the *REI* was also short-lived: in 2019, it was replaced by the *Citizenship Income— RdC* (National Law 4/2019) which is gradually being implemented. It further broadens the target population, increases the resources available, and reinforces the aim of job activation for the beneficiaries.

The rapid introduction and partial overlapping of the various reforms have complicated the implementation process. The three measures all assign a key role during implementation to the municipal social services, which (in consultation with other agencies such as job centres and health services) have the main responsibility for assessing applicants' needs and developing a personalised project focused on social and work inclusion for the most vulnerable beneficiaries. A pact signed by the caseworker and beneficiary contains a personalised project and establishes each party's commitment in order for the benefit to be allocated.

The street-level perspective appears to be the most useful approach to support the analysis of such a complicated framework that involves multiple institutional levels, agencies, and professionals. It allows us to focus on the point where the consequences of all macro- and micro-changes and a long chain of decisions tend to converge: at the street level, all the incoherent issues and unresolved problems must finally be resolved as practical solutions.

Research Strategy and Methods

The research reported here has included, in the first instance, a desk analysis aimed at defining the legal and organisational framework in which the reform is implemented[1] and highlights the relevant aspects for conducting the field research. Secondly, research was conducted based on a case study in a region of north-eastern Italy. It was mainly performed through observing 24 workshops where representatives of social service caseworkers from all the municipalities were called upon by the regional institution to discuss and share information about how they implement minimum income in practice. These meetings were carried out under the supervision of social policy experts and the support of facilitators. Their aim was to bring about peer-to-peer training where the sharing of interpretations, problems, and local solutions would result in dialogic learning to improve local practices and increase their homogenisation at the regional level.

About 200 social service caseworkers were involved in 24 workshops. Each of them participated in three of these meetings,[2] dedicated to a specific topic: (1) the criteria and procedures to access the minimum income, (2) the assignment and development of specific projects for social and work inclusion, and (3) the application of sanctions in cases of non-compliance or unadmitted behaviour.

The workshops were conducted using the *vignettes* technique (Brondani, MacEntee, Bryant, & O'Neill, 2008), applied in other studies of social policies (Kazepov, 2010; Trifiletti, 2004) and street-level practices (Saruis, 2015): a typology of (fictitious but based on previous research) cases was put together by social policy experts. The cases were about people with multidimensional needs and limited resources, who asked the services for the minimum income. The participants (social workers, educators, psychologists) had to discuss the cases and: (1) decide whether they could access the minimum income based on the formal criteria and then describe the realistic procedures for accessing it; (2) design a social support and (if possible) a job activation plan, indicating what benefits and interventions could realistically be provided; (3) describe the sanctions that could be assigned in relation to unadmitted behaviours and the conditions in which these could be realistically applied or ignored. This method aimed to provoke a discussion focused on concrete aspects and problems in implementing the minimum income. During the workshops, the *vignettes* were first discussed in sub-groups, then compared in plenaries, to share the differences and similarities in the cases' interpretations, difficulties, and local solutions. The facilitators had to explain the groups' tasks and steps and encourage the discussion.

The field research is mainly based on observing the conversations among the caseworkers. This strategy does not allow for direct contact with the actual practices, but information can be collected from caseworkers' opinions about their daily difficulties and dilemmas, the solutions they have identified and concrete examples.

This kind of observation has strengths and limitations. Firstly, it prevents the researchers' from influencing the context, as they participated in the workshops as facilitators and experts of social policies. In this sense, the approach is similar to covert observation, where the studied population is not aware that it is being observed. Even if the researchers' identity was known, the research aim and subject were not explicit. Secondly, this sort of indirect observation does not allow the beneficiaries' points of views to be collected, which were only represented by the caseworkers in their discussions. Thirdly, the observed sample was not selected at random, but chosen by the local social services with their own criteria. However, their high number and their distribution within the entire region make their points of view meaningful in this context.

This strategy for collecting information is defined by Riemer (1977) as *opportunistic research*. It allows for enhanced opportunities provided by specific circumstances and by familiarity with a context in order to obtain information and pursue research aims.

Participating in the meetings as facilitators allowed the researchers to collect formal and informal documents and field notes containing: descriptions of concrete procedures, interpretations of the law, organisational limitations, local opportunities and problems for social and work inclusion, difficulties posed by complex cases, information on the relationships with beneficiaries, and opinions about the effectiveness of the measure. A portion of this wealth of information is reported in the following paragraph.

The Field Research

In order to conduct the analysis, the implementation process has been unpacked into three steps: (1) the management of the access phase; (2) the pact between the caseworkers and beneficiaries of the measure, which includes a personalised project focused on social inclusion and activation;

and (3) the interpretation and use of sanctions in cases of non-compliance or unadmitted behaviours on the part of the beneficiaries. In the next paragraphs, the three steps are analysed from the caseworkers' perspective on the implementation practices.

Access

Firstly, access to the minimum income in Italy is subject to an assessment of the applicants' economic and family conditions. This verification and the calculation of the cash transfer amount are managed by the National Institute of Social Security (INPS). Eligibility is also subject to acceptance of a pact for activation and social inclusion that is managed by different public agencies, depending on an evaluation of the beneficiaries' conditions (see *The Pact and the Personalised Project*).

This standardised procedure gives caseworkers less space for discretion in comparison with traditional social intervention which allows more space in the professional assessment. The impact of this change on caseworkers is significant: they lose power when deciding whether to grant or refuse support to people and families, and what kind of support it should be.

The policy design of the measure envisages three specific situations which are directed to different public services: (1) *Complex* cases, which concern families who—in addition to material deprivation—present several needs, such as low education, fragile mental condition, relational isolation, negligence of child care, family conflict, and so on. They require support from social services and probably a multidimensional intervention; (2) cases with prevalent health problems (e.g. drug addiction or psychiatric fragility), which require the prior intervention of health services; and (3) cases with only labour problems, which are directed to job centres for activation and placement.

Once economic eligibility for the measure has been verified, the applicants are passed through a *pre-assessment* interview, managed within the social help desks of social services or the job centres, to establish the typology they belong to. The central government has developed a standardised tool to guide this evaluation; however, this tool only became ready many months after the beginning of the implementation. For this reason, especially during this phase, the caseworkers had to manage the assessment through their own professional experience and knowledge.

The professionals dedicated to managing access to the measure were, in some cases, administrative professionals moved to the task (ad hoc training was not always provided) or newly hired social workers or educators, who did not have experience of social work, and they therefore experienced difficulties carrying out the task. In other cases, they were experienced social workers who already worked in the services and were tasked with supporting new colleagues during this difficult phase. This choice has been a consequence of the scarce resources available. In contrast, municipalities with enough funds and favourable organisation assets hired new social workers or educators directly or through outsourcing; other municipalities drew professionals from their organisation to dedicate to the tasks needed to implement the new measure. The interviews in the pre-assessment phase were conducted by caseworkers belonging to mixed teams including the public and private sector, new and experienced professionals, administrators, social workers, and educators.

Two considerations can be made about this phase. Firstly, street-level literature reports that the less experienced the caseworkers are as social professionals, the more their decision tends to be guided by personal perceptions, judgements, and values (Thorén, 2008). In fact, professional knowledge influences the practices providing caseworkers with principles, models, and tools for social work (Carrington, 2005). Secondly, the caseworkers considered here not only had to learn how to manage the new tasks relating to minimum income, but they also had to adapt to new colleagues and support the less experienced through daily peer-to-peer training.

However, these caseworkers' ability to interview and analyse the case defined the applicants' pathways in the subsequent phases, directing them to the assigned service.

If they were directed to social services, they had a professional interview with a social worker who conducted a professional case analysis and defined a personalised project with them, with the emphasis on activation and social inclusion.

The Pact and the Personalised Project

As stated by the caseworkers involved in our field research, the relationship between social professionals and citizens was often mediated through a pact settling tasks and duties for both parties.[3] However, in the minimum income measure the pact is compulsory, regardless of the conditions of the beneficiary. Furthermore, the pact should be geared towards occupational activation rather than broader social inclusion aims. Indeed, according to the law (Legislative Decree 147/2017—Art. 6—subs. 2), the personalised project identifies: (1) the general goals and the specific results that are intended to be reached in the *pathway* to overcome the condition of poverty, in labour market activation and—more globally—in social inclusion; (2) the necessary resources in terms of interventions (which could also involve the beneficiary's family and community network) and services, beyond the monetary transfer provided by the measure; and (3) the tasks that must be accomplished by the beneficiary, as condition to maintain the right to the monetary support.

All the adult members of the families who have access to the measure must be submitted to needs assessment, take part in the project's definition, and sign a pact to engage in its fulfillment. The needs assessment should analyse the following areas: (a) personal and social conditions and functioning; (b) economic situation; (c) working status and employability profile; (d) level and type of education; (e) housing conditions; and (f) family and social relationships.

The law highlights that the project's goals and results must be defined through negotiation with the beneficiaries. In order to fully involve them and avoid the risk of misunderstanding, it should not contain technical, generic, or abstract language.

Three relevant aspects emerge in relation to space for discretion in this phase: (1) the *personalisation* of the interventions composing the project, which should be *tailored* to the needs and resources of the beneficiaries and their families; (2) the *relationship* between the beneficiary and the social service, that should be based on reciprocal trust; (3) the idea of activation devised by the caseworkers dealing with complex cases of vulnerability.

Due to the lack of time for case assessment, the risk is not only a superficial analysis of beneficiaries' needs, problems, desires, and resources, but also an overlap with the planning phase. In this sense, the personalised project is based more on the resources available than the needs and preferences of the beneficiary. For instance: if the municipality has a prior agreement with a gym that is willing to welcome poor children for free, this opportunity will probably be inserted into the project as an action to improve social inclusion, even if the family, and especially the children, do not desire this kind of activity.

Fulfilling a personalised project would require a coordinated system of private and public organisation providing opportunities for job and social inclusion for minimum income beneficiaries. Solid contacts and partnerships between social services and job centres, health services, for-profit, and non-profit organisations could support them in becoming independent. In many contexts, this infrastructural system still needs to be created or strengthened to be effective. Specific political attention and investments are needed to reach this aim. For the moment, caseworkers try to adapt the compulsory personalised projects to the limited resources and organisations available to them.

Another critical aspect relates to caseworkers' difficulty in emphasising the resources that beneficiaries have at their disposal. They rarely highlight that beneficiaries may have resources that can be developed within the project. They have a tendency to view them as people who are in need, and underline their vulnerability more than their potential resources.

Furthermore, caseworkers tend to have their own interpretation of the usefulness of the personalised project depending on the case's assessment and their concept of *activation*.

When the beneficiaries are in a very fragile psycho-social state, the caseworkers tend to interpret this concept in a broad sense, due to their 'social' mandate and in relation to beneficiaries' concrete ability for activation. They may envisage only limited or *protected* participation in the labour market, such as proposing that the beneficiaries engage in the community or in public service, participate in peer-support groups, or simply take care of their own children or assist elderly or disabled members of the family. It is a sort of social activation aimed at overcoming the concept of pure assistance, based on the premise that access to the labour market (or preparation for it) can be a very *distant* goal for some beneficiaries. Regarding this concern, the minimum income demonstrates the weakness of the concept of social inclusion which is actually only geared towards job activation, lacking coordination between social services and job centres and within a labour market still (partially) affected by the financial crises that began in 2008.

In addition, the aim of job activation is not always considered appropriate for all beneficiaries. In these situations, caseworkers use the aim of personalisation to overcome it. For example, they do not consider it appropriate to burden a lonely mother who is working for a low wage, pays her rent and bills, and takes care of her children. In cases like this, they simply write in the pact the commitments that the woman already has, as if they were aims to achieve. In other words, they do not consider it fair to ask her to do more than what she already does, and they find a way to adhere to the formal requirements established by the law.

In other situations, the economic benefit is so limited that they do not deem it fair to assign the applicants specific tasks: for example, if the amount of the monetary transfer is very low, they see the personalised project as uneconomic considering the organisation and resources required for it to be planned. Therefore, in these cases the project is only a formality where they simply write what the beneficiaries already do on their own to be included in society and in labour market. This happens especially for new cases (not known to the social services before the requirements for the minimum income) and for those which are not so complex: for them, the caseworkers would have to spend a lot of time on needs assessment and defining a project that they do not consider fair.

A further problematic aspect of the personalised project is linked to the difficulty monitoring the outputs and the actual compliance of the beneficiaries (and their family) to the aims and tasks defined in the project. This aspect is crucial because it can lead to the application of sanctions if the *pact* is neglected. The ample discretion left to the caseworkers in this phase has led to them feeling they have too much responsibility which has been highly problematic to manage. For example, to overcome this situation, one municipal social service devised an evaluation ladder for the project outputs.

At the end of the planning stage, the personalised project becomes part of a pact to be signed by the beneficiaries and all adult members of their family and the caseworker.[4] This stage is particularly appreciated by the caseworkers as a good innovative action, which clarifies the rules and reciprocal commitment and implies a shared responsibility for the success of the project. In fact, caseworkers consider a project *successful* if it brings about concrete joint responsibility, commitment, and motivation among the beneficiaries. They believe that a project *works* when it allows beneficiaries to (re)discover new, even residual, abilities, which were previously overwhelmed by economic and material deprivation.

Sanctions

Sanctions are one of the most controversial aspects which impact on the meaning caseworkers' give to their own work. In fact, even though conditionality has a tradition in social work, the idea of sanctioning introduced by the minimum income calls for *automatism* which caseworkers tend to avoid. In fact, in their opinion, this is in deep contrast with their *good* professional relationship with beneficiaries, which should be based on mutual trust and reciprocal adaptation.

According to the law, the beneficiaries of minimum income will see a reduction in the amount of monetary support in the event of unadmitted behaviour and, if they persist, suspension of the measure. Specifically, the sanctions are applied in case of: refusal to sign the pact containing the personalised project, break of the pact or practising of other behaviours that are incompatible with the personalised project.

According to the field research, the caseworkers do not tend to adopt a punitive approach towards the violations. They consider that their mandate is to support the beneficiaries; therefore, they hardly ever report unadmitted behaviours.

They tend to avoid sanctions, especially full suspension of the measure, through a variety of *preventive* actions. For example, if a beneficiary starts engaging in unadmitted behaviour that the caseworkers consider to be very serious, they tend to renegotiate the pact and reshape the personalised project to better meet the emerging problems. Another example is to incentivise beneficiaries' sense of responsibility, referring to their reputation/sense of honour in the community they belong to.

They mainly use the sanctions as *threats* in order to direct and control their behaviour. Usually only formal problems are reported, for instance, if the beneficiaries do not sign the pact despite many insistent reminders. An important deterrent to the application of the sanctions, especially the suspension of the economic support, is the fact that the minimum income is financed by the central government while, if people lose this support, their problems could fall within the local administration's budget. Municipal managers and politicians could therefore criticise the caseworkers for the application of sanctions.

Another interesting issue about sanctioning concerns caseworkers' decisions about beneficiaries' irregular work. When they discover these situations, they usually do not report them to the police as they should do according to law. Instead, they evaluate case by case how fair it is to allow it. If they decide to oppose it, a demanding commitment to the beneficiary will be required in the personalised project to prevent him from performing other work activities. Otherwise, if they think that the resources earned from the irregular work are too important for the beneficiaries and their families (as they do not have other options), they simply decide to ignore the information. Some cases were reported where applicants renounced the minimum income when they were informed they had to sign a pact and be involved in a personalised project.

Conclusions

The implementation of the minimum income in Italy has been analysed with the aim of surfacing the effects of the reform trends of European welfare systems at the street level.

This measure includes multiple and sometimes conflicting aims: reinforcing personalisation to respond to varying requirements; introducing automatisation to guarantee access and overcome professional caseworkers' evaluation (and their discretion); combining social and economic support and job activation; encouraging partnership between social services and other organisations; predicting pact logics; and breaking the *vertical* relationship with beneficiaries and assistance logics traditionally ascribed to social services.

The fieldwork shows that the implementation process is conducted in a context which basically has limited resources in terms of professional skills of new caseworkers—trained *on the job*—and scarce availability of opportunities for beneficiaries' activation, mainly due to weak contacts and coordination between social services and job centres and with private for-profit and non-profit organisations.

The caseworkers use their discretion to deal with these conditions, but what emerges is that they also play an important role in determining the concrete nature of the minimum income measure, influencing its application with their ideas. They have room to deeply reinterpret the minimum income measure's aims and practices. They devise their own concepts and designs in terms of activation, pacts, and sanctions, and they try to reconcile the new measure's approach with more traditional professional orientations and considerations in terms of concrete feasibility. Their decisions combine different concepts of minimum income, partly accepting and partly rejecting the change.

Four main strategies can be identified:

1. *Active subversion*. They could try to actively reconcile the innovative aspects of the new measures and the traditional idea of social assistance as support and guidance for the beneficiaries. They aim to personalise the interventions on the basis of beneficiaries' needs and resources, but usually they are perceived as people who are vulnerable or unable or unwilling to be activated.

2. *Passive subversion*. The innovative aspects of the measure are ignored or rejected. This is considered only as a bureaucratic accomplishment introducing automatisms and legal constraints that mainly produce ineffective or unfair effects. Activation and horizontal pacts are considered to be impossible aims in the actual conditions. Caseworkers try to preserve the vertical asset of the relationship with the beneficiaries.

3. *Passive adaptation*. Caseworkers interpret the measure as an *investment* to provide new opportunities for beneficiaries and promote their

independence and potential. They try to preserve the vertical relation-ship with the beneficiary to reach the new aims. For example, they may use or threaten sanctions, control or manipulate the beneficiaries to increase motivation to activation.

4. *Active adaptation*. They work on both innovating social work aims and the relationship with beneficiaries. The measure proposes a pact as an *exchange* aimed at recognising reciprocal trust and co-responsibility of both parties on common goals and promoting horizontal relationships involving rights and duties. The measure can be personalised balancing the new aims and beneficiaries' needs and resources.

These strategies are combined in the practices reported by the caseworkers. It is important to underline that all of them aim to produce fair interventions.

The most relevant innovations introduced by the reforms often look at *ideal* aims rather than concrete practices, mainly limited by the scarce resources available for their implementation. As change is in the making, what emerges is a mixture of path dependence and path discontinuity mechanisms. In this process, the caseworkers manage their everyday tasks and, at the same time, 'absorb' the innovative aspects of the new measure, in a process that combines learning and practice.

In this phase, caseworkers' discretion proves to be crucial as *professional tool* to adapt the measure to the conditions in which it is implemented. It also guarantees them flexible 'space' for learning how to interpret and apply new and complex key concepts, aims, tools, and organisation assets. However, there is also room for their personal and professional strategies.

Nevertheless, it must be said that too much discretion affects not only pol-icy outcomes but also caseworkers' roles and workloads, and tends to result in *heavy* responsibilities. They could feel overloaded and develop self-protection strategies on unsupported decisions.

Training provisions, experts' support, and/or peer-to-peer exchange could increase their awareness of discretion, and reflections on its potential (positive and negative) effects on their work, role, and tasks.

Finally, since discretion can have uncontrolled effects on the implementa-tion process and outcomes, all figures involved in the decision-making pro-cess on welfare policies, such as managers or policy makers, should be aware of caseworkers' discretion and its potential effects on policy implementation and outcomes.

NOTES

1. It is not possible to present the results of this rich analysis in detail in this chap-ter, but the collected information is used to explain and interpret the field research data.

2. Other meetings were dedicated to topics that are less consistent with the aims of this chapter.
3. Its practical expression is the so-called personalised project, which will be presented later.
4. Depending on the different local procedures, in some municipalities, the pact should also be signed by the other organisations involved (e.g. health services, third sector organisations, the job centre, and so on) that take part in the fulfilment of the personalised project as supporters of the beneficiaries in the planned interventions.

References

Alleanza contro la povertà. (2017). *Rapporto di valutazione: dal SIA al REI. Ricerca valutativa sulla prima fase di implementazione del programma di contrasto della povertà Sostegno per l'Inclusione Attiva.* https://bit.ly/2UJBXul.

Armingeon, K., & Bonoli, G. (Eds.). (2006). *The politics of postindustrial welfare states.* London: Routledge.

Bahle, T., Hubl, V., & Pfeifer, M. (2011). *The last safety net: A handbook of minimum income protection in Europe.* Bristol: Bristol Policy Press.

Barbier, J. C. (2008, September). *The puzzling resilience of nations in the context of Europeanized welfare states.* Communication to the RC19 Meeting "The future of social citizenship: Politics, institutions and outcomes". Stockholm.

Brodkin, E. Z. (2008). Accountability in street-level organizations. *Journal of Public Administration, 31,* 317–336.

Brodkin, E. Z. (2011). Policy work: Street-level organizations under new managerialism. *Journal of Public Administration Research and Theory, 21*(2), 253–277.

Brodkin, E. Z., & Martson, G. (2013). *Work and the welfare state.* Washington, DC: Georgetown University Press.

Brondani, M. A., MacEntee, M. I., Bryant, S. R., & O'Neill, B. (2008). Using written vignettes in focus groups among older adults to discuss oral health as a sensitive topic. *Qualitative Health Research, 18*(8), 145–153.

Carrington, K. (2005). Street-level discretion: Is there a need for control? *Public Administration Quarterly, 29*(2), 141–162.

Esping-Andersen, G. (1994). *After the golden age: The future of the welfare state in the new global order.* Geneve: UNRISD.

Esping-Andersen, G., Gallie, D., Hemerijck, A., & Myles, J. (Eds.). (2002). *Why we need a new welfare state.* Oxford: Oxford University.

Evans, T., & Harris, J. (2004). Street-level bureaucracy, social work and the (exaggerated) death of discretion. *British Journal of Social Work, 34*(6), 871–895.

Gilbert, N. (2004). *Transformation of the welfare state: The silent surrender of public responsibility.* Oxford: Oxford University Press.

ICF & European Centre for Social Welfare Policy and Research. (2019, November 15–16). Peer Review on *Minimum Income Benefits—Securing a life in dignity, enabling access to services and integration into the labour market* (Synthesis Report). Berlin.

IRS, CLES, Fondazione Zancan. (2001). *Valutazione di efficacia della I sperimentazione dell'istituto del Reddito Minimo di Inserimento in 39 Comuni italiani (1999–2001)*. Roma: Presidenza del Consiglio. Dipartimento per gli Affari Sociali.

IRS, CLES, Fondazione Labos. (2005). *Valutazione di efficacia della II sperimentazione dell'istituto del Reddito Minimo di Inserimento in Italia (2003–2004)*. Roma: Ministero del Lavoro e delle Politiche Sociali.

Guidi, R. (2012). «Effetti corrosivi?» Problematizzare l'impatto del New Public Management e della governance sui social workers del settore pubblico. *Rivista Trimestrale Di Scienza Dell'Amministrazione, 3*, 37–52.

Hupe, P., Hill, M., & Buffat, A. (2015). *Understanding street-level bureaucracy*. Bristol: Policy Press.

Jenson, J. (2004). *Catching up to reality: Building the case for a new social model* (CPRN Social Architecture Papers, Research Report F|35). Ottawa: Canadian Policy Research Networks Inc. (CPRN).

Kazepov, Y. (Ed.). (2010). *Rescaling social policies: Towards multilevel governance in Europe*. Burlington: Ashgate and European Centre Vienna.

Lipsky, M. (1980). *Street-level bureaucracies: Dilemmas of the individual in public services*. New York: Russell Sage Foundation.

Marx, I., & Nelson, K. (Eds.). (2013). *Minimum income protection in flux*. Basingstoke: Palgrave Macmillan.

Ranci, C. (Ed.). (2010). *Social vulnerability in Europe social vulnerability in Europe: The new configuration of social risks*. Basingstoke: Palgrave Macmillan.

Riemer, J. W. (1977). Varieties of opportunistic research. *Urban Life, 5*(4), 467–477.

Saraceno, C., & Negri, N. (Eds.). (2003). *Povertà e vulnerabilità sociale in aree sviluppate*. Roma: Carocci.

Saruis, T. (2015). *Gli operatori sociali nel nuovo welfare. Tra discrezionalità e responsabilità*. Roma: Carocci.

Thorén, K. H. (2008). *Activation policy in action: A street-level study of social assistance in the Swedish welfare state*. Växjö: Växjö University Press.

Trifiletti, R. (2004). Towards a qualitative research design? *Cross-National Research Papers, 7*(2), 7–11.

CHAPTER 61

Alternative Care for Children in Bangladesh: Challenges and Interventions

M. Rezaul Islam

INTRODUCTION

Bangladesh is a large and densely populated country in South Asia, bordering Myanmar, India, Nepal, and Bhutan. In 2019 its population was estimated at 168.07 million (World Population Review, 2019). About half its population is under the age of 18—considered children—and more than 20 million are under the age of 5. About 73% of its children live in rural areas (Mohajan, 2014). The Government of Bangladesh ratified the International Convention on the Rights of the Child (CRC) in August 1990, where it committed to respect, defend, and promote the rights of Bangladeshi children. Yet, despite its promise, the country faces serious problems that are currently hindering the rights of children (Humanium, 2019). More than 60 million children live in Bangladesh (eight times the number in France) and half of them grow up

This paper was presented as a keynote speech at the National Seminar on "Alternative Care of Children in Bangladesh: Challenges and Intervention" organised by SOS Children's Villages International in Bangladesh and the Institute of Social Welfare & Research, University of Dhaka, held on 28 March 2019 at Nabab Ali Chowdhury Senate Bhanban, University of Dhaka.

M. R. Islam (✉)
Institute of Social Welfare and Research, University of Dhaka, Dhaka, Bangladesh

© The Author(s) 2021   1001
S. S. M. et al. (eds.), *The Palgrave Handbook of Global Social Work Education*, https://doi.org/10.1007/978-3-030-39966-5_61

in abject poverty—the result of a high unemployment rate. This has severe repercussions on their ability to access a healthy diet, health services, education, financial resources, etc. Child malnutrition is a concern in Bangladesh, affecting poor families with no means of feeding themselves. In addition, severe weather, flooding, natural disasters, etc., in rural areas decreases food security. Waterborne diseases also represent a serious problem. Due to a general inaccessibility to drinkable water and sanitation systems, Bangladeshi children often suffer from diarrhoea.

One problem in Bangladesh is that parents rarely report births to the authorities. Without a birth certificate, a child's rights are not respected—they are not recognised as fully fledged members of society and as such cannot exercise their full rights. Unregistered children are not protected from abuse, such as forced labour, prostitution, early marriage, smuggling, and trafficking. Due to poverty, their right to an education is not respected—children among the poor communities (especially boys) must often abandon education to help their families financially. Because of extreme poverty, families are often forced to make their children work. They are generally employed in construction, battery recycling, road transport, car repairs, and tobacco manufacturing. These children grow up in miserable conditions: working long hours, receiving a low salary, no food, etc. Additionally, they face risks associated with prostitution, discrimination, and abuse. Child marriage has negative repercussions on the health, development, and rights of children. One example of exploitation is where girls in particular are initially employed as domestic servants and then often forced into prostitution. Child domestic work is widespread in Bangladesh. Baseline surveys by the Bangladesh Bureau of Statistics (BBS) and UNICEF in 2006 indicate there were approximately 400,000 child domestic workers aged between 6 and 17 in Bangladesh (Islam, 2013). In many cases, children under the influence of traffickers live and work on the streets. Factors related to such socioeconomic and cultural conditions include poverty, child labour, economic migration, domestic violence, economic and social insecurity, inadequate national child protection schemes, and war and the fragility of countries emerging from conflicts (Islam & Hossain, 2017).

There are no appropriate statistics about the vulnerable, marginalised, and destitute children in Bangladesh who are without parents or legal guardians due to death, war, disaster, displacement, etc. Martin and Zulaika (2016) provided the percentage of children in Asia aged between 0 and 14 years living with relatives and non-relatives but not biological parents (Fig. 61.1). According to the data, the Maldives has the highest percentage of children living with non-relatives, at nearly 18%, whereas in Bangladesh it is nearly 6%.

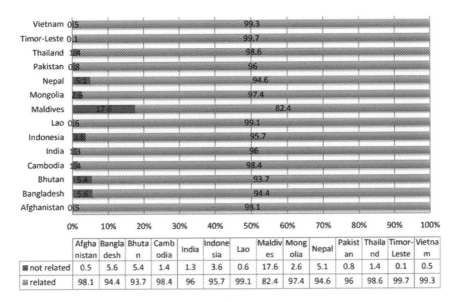

	Afgha nistan	Bangla desh	Bhuta n	Camb odia	India	Indone sia	Lao	Maldiv es	Mong olia	Nepal	Pakist an	Thaila nd	Timor- Leste	Vietna m
▓ not related	0.5	5.6	5.4	1.4	1.3	3.6	0.6	17.6	2.6	5.1	0.8	1.4	0.1	0.5
▓ related	98.1	94.4	93.7	98.4	96	95.7	99.1	82.4	97.4	94.6	96	98.6	99.7	99.3

Fig. 61.1 Percentage of children in Asia aged between 0 and 14 years living in households with relatives and non-relatives but not biological parents (*Source* Martin and Zulaika [2016])

CONCEPTUAL DEFINITION: ALTERNATIVE CARE

"Alternative care" is any arrangement, formal or informal, temporary or permanent, for a child who is living away from their parents. It is the care provided for children by caregivers who are not biological parents. Alternative care may be kinship care, foster care, other forms of family-based or family-like care placements, residential care, or supervised independent living arrangements (United Nations, 2010). Roby (2011) designed a model of both formal and informal alternative care, the main elements being statutory residential care, statutory foster care, unregistered group home care, other family-based care (requiring no State action), community-based care and support, and informal kinship care/non-statutory foster care. The alternative care concept has been drawn from the principles and standards set out in the key documents relating to separated children and out-of-home care, including: (1) The United Nations Convention on the Rights of the Child (CRC) (United Nations, 1989); (2) the Guidelines for the Alternative Care of Children (United Nations, 2009); (3) The Inter-agency Guiding Principles on Unaccompanied and Separated Children (ICRC, IRC, Save the Children, UNICEF, UNHCR, World Vision, 2004); and (4) IASC Guidelines for Mental Health and Psychosocial Support in Emergency Settings (Inter-agency Standing Committee, 2007). Article 20 of the CRC mandates that alternative care be provided when a child is "temporarily or permanently deprived of his or her family environment" (Part 2). The guidelines, however,

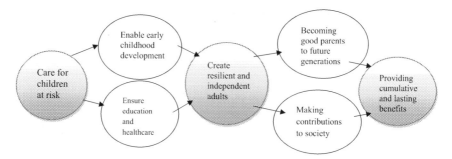

Fig. 61.2 Alternative care model (*Source* Developed by the author and adapted from SOS Children's Villages International [2017])

imply that a child's right to alternative care springs into effect when he or she is deprived of "parental care" (Part 1–1). The legal and policy framework for the delivery of high-quality alternative care for children emphasises the rights of all children to remain, or be reunited, with their families. Where this is neither possible nor in the child's best interest, alternative care should be provided in family-based settings. The challenge comes in realising these aims, given pressures resulting from emergency situations and potential pre-existing issues related to supporting families and the development of alternative family-based care.

SOS Children's Villages International (2017) have developed a model for the alternative care of children at risk, enabling early childhood development and ensuring child education and health care. This process helps children to become resilient and independent adults, to become good parents, and to contribute to, and thereby improve, society (Fig. 61.2).

One of the problems faced when writing this chapter was the lack of literature on alternative care for children. Figure 61.3 shows the number of global publications on the alternative care of children found on Web of Science and Scopus. Using these two search engines and the phrase "alternative care of children" (between 2014 and 2018) provided a limited number of publications—the Web of Science found 19 documents and Scopus listed 18, with the highest number of publications being in Africa and Europe. The Web of Science provided only one result from Bangladesh. This lack of published material represents a real challenge to any assessment of the alternative care of children in Bangladesh.

According to Save the Children (2013), the guiding principles of alternative care are to:

1. Base all decisions on the best interests of the individual child.
2. Respond to the care and protection needs of vulnerable children, families, and communities in an integrated manner.
3. Prevent, and respond to, family separation.

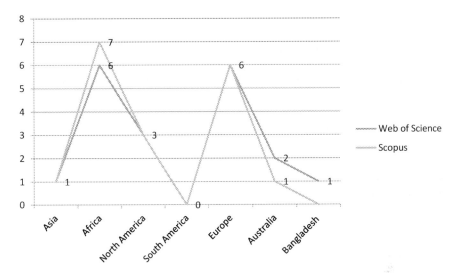

Fig. 61.3 Total number of published documents found on Web of Science and Scopus (2014–2018) (*Source* Developed by the author from the Web of Science [2019] and Scopus [2019])

4. Prioritise the reunification of all unaccompanied and separated children and find long-term stable placements for children unable to be reunified.
5. Ensure that emergency child protection responses are built on existing alternative care structures and capacities already in place.
6. Ensure that children and their caregivers have sufficient resources for their survival and maintenance.
7. Listen to and consider children's opinions.
8. Use and develop family-based care alternatives wherever possible.
9. Ensure that care placements meet agreed standards, especially before emergency placements.
10. Ensure that each child's care placement is registered, monitored, and reviewed.
11. Ensure that services are provided without discrimination and with attention to the specific needs of the child.

WHY PROVIDE ALTERNATIVE CARE FOR CHILDREN? A REVIEW FROM SOCIAL AND LEGAL PERSPECTIVES

Socioeconomic Perspective

A universal fact is that children need to be cared for. It is their fundamental right. The global community recognised this when it adopted the United Nations Convention on the Rights of the Child in 1989. No other human rights treaty has so many signatories, reflecting the belief that for a society to be considered civilised it must protect and care for its children. However, reality paints a different picture (SOS Children's Villages International, 2017). The absence of a stable and protective family exposes children to multiple risk factors. Their physical, psychological, and social development may be hindered by poor nutrition, a lack of access to education or healthcare, and the absence of emotional connections and the support every child needs. Without a caring and protective parent, a child is more vulnerable to abuse, discrimination, exploitation, and poverty. Research has even demonstrated that the lack of love, care, and support from a caregiver impairs the development of a child's brain.

Numerous factors contribute to placing children in vulnerable situations:

- Death of a parent—affecting 140 million children, with 15 million having lost both parents.
- Poverty—385 million children live in extreme poverty.
- Disability—affecting 93 million children.
- Lack of registration of births—230 million children have not been registered.
- Refugee status—half the world's 60 million refugees are children.

There are many socioeconomic and cultural factors that necessitate alternative care:

- Poverty.
- Lack of education.
- Orphanhood.
- Street children.
- Being affected by HIV/AIDS.
- Migration of one or both parents.
- War as well as natural and man-made disasters.
- Cultural factors.
- Gender inequality and discrimination.
- Violence, exploitation, abuse, neglect, and trafficking.
- Disability.
- Parental imprisonment.
- Illegal sex practices.

Other issues include:

- that many care placements are avoidable;
- that informal care is predominant but unsupervised;
- that there is a limited range of care options;
- the overuse of residential care;

- that inappropriate conditions exist in residential facilities, including issues associated with parental contact;
- that inadequacies exist in foster care systems;
- a lack of supervision at private facilities;
- an increased difficulty exiting the care system;
- a lack of preparedness for independent living; and
- additional problems linked to emergency situations.

Legal Perspective

The government of Bangladesh formulated a National Child Policy in 2011 in light of the number of child laws and international conventions it ratified (Table 61.1). The CRC is the main international document confirming the basic rights of children, including their right to safety and security. However, there is a question mark over why the UN Guidelines for the Alternative Care of Children (a resolution adopted by the UN General Assembly in 2010) were adopted—reviewing the CRC, we notice that while much of it is clear, detail is lacking for the provision of alternative care and the welfare of children without parents or legal guardians.

The CRC is clear on the following points:

- A family environment with an atmosphere of "happiness, love and understanding" is best for the child (Preamble).

Table 61.1 Legal tools available to support the rights of children in Bangladesh

Policies and laws for children in Bangladesh	International legal framework in Bangladesh
• National Children Policy (2011) • Bangladesh Child Act (2013) • National Child Labour Elimination Policy (2010) • Women and Children Violence Protection Law (2000) • Domestic Violence Prevention and Protection Rules (2013) • Domestic Violence Act (2010) • Child Marriage Restraint Act (2017) • Shishu Academy A (2018)	• The UN Convention on the Rights of the Child (UNCRC, 1989) • The Optional Protocol on the Sale of Children, Child Prostitution and Child Pornography • The Optional Protocol to the Convention on the Rights of the Child on the Involvement of Children in Armed Conflict (OPAC) • The Hague Convention on Protection of Children and Co-operation in Respect of Intercountry Adoption (1993) • The UN Convention on the Rights of Persons with Disabilities (2007) • The International Labour Organization's Minimum Age Convention and Worst Forms of Child Labour Convention • Guidelines for the Alternative Care of Children (resolution adopted by the UN General Assembly, 2010)

Source Compiled from many sources

- Children have the right to be brought up by parents where possible (Article 7.1).
- Assistance should be forthcoming to parents/legal guardians for upbringing and care (Articles 18, 27, etc.).
- A child should be removed from parental care if in the child's best interests and should be subject to judicial review (Article 9.1).
- The State is responsibility for "ensuring" alternative care for children who have been deprived of a family environment (Article 20).
- Family-based alternative care is preferable (Article 20).
- There should be a basic set of conditions for the provision of residential care (Article 3.3).
- A periodic review of placements is required (Article 25).

The CRC is less clear in its approach to:

- The relationship between "parental care" and a child's "family environment."
- Obligations regarding "informal" or "kinship" care.
- The principle of "best interests": going from "of paramount consideration" in the 1986 Declaration, to just "a primary consideration" in CRC Article 20.
- The goals of alternative care?
- What is meant by "institutions."
- Determination of "suitability."
- The definition of the word "necessary" in terms of placing children in institutions.

Reviewing the CRC further, we notice additional grey areas:

- A lack of clarity in terms of its definition of family.
- An outline of the State's role vis-à-vis informal care.
- Whether in child-headed households care options or "family preservation" is preferable.
- Its position on children being raised in prisons.
- Its approach to deinstitutionalisation.

Taking all this information into consideration allows the identification of some key areas for the development of alternative care:

- Placing major emphasis on promoting parental care, preventing family breakdowns, and facilitating family reintegration.
- Consulting with children at all stages.
- Ensuring children always have a legal guardian.
- Providing a strategy for care that relies as little as possible on institutions.
- The provision of permanency (that is, stable and durable solutions).

- Preparing and supporting those leaving care.
- The role of a civil society.
- Ensuring the oversight of all care providers.
- Recognising concerns for children abroad and those in emergency situations.

Key Challenges Facing Alternative Care in Bangladesh

It has been mentioned earlier that the term "alternative care of children" is not well documented in the literature. Only one entry was found for Bangladesh using the Web of Science search engine, highlighting the lack of evidence-based literature on the challenges associated with alternative care. Based on empirical observations, undocumented literature, unpublished reports, and authorised and unauthorised website articles, Bangladesh faces eight key challenges around alternative care, including not contextualising, or having a clear definition of, alternative care, the sheer number of children requiring care, cultural barriers, lack of government care, weak legislative frameworks, inadequate financial resources, a lack of research, and underdeveloped policies (Fig. 61.4).

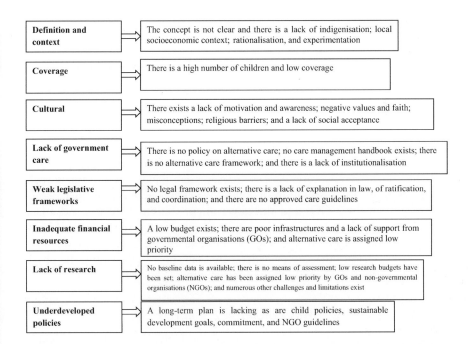

Fig. 61.4 Key challenges facing the alternative care of children (*Source* Developed by the author)

Definition and the Contextualisation of Alternative Care

It can be argued that no clear definition of the "alternative care of children" is provided in any of the current child policies, laws, or international conventions. There has been a lack of indigenisation, local socioeconomic context, rationalisation, and experimentation. As a result the issues facing alternative care have not come to light. Due to this unclear definition, governmental organisations (GOs) and non-governmental organisations (NGOs) have not taken the issue seriously. In addition, there has been a lack of contextualisation of the problem.

Wide Coverage

Initiatives by GOs and NGOs have provided limited alternative care for children. This is evidenced by the large number of children who still await the provision of care—many children still live on the streets or in homes that are used as brothels, with many of them working either at home or in industry. The initiatives simply do not meet the actual requirements.

Cultural Barriers

Cultural barriers represent a sensitive problem facing the provision of institutional alternative care. This is particularly true for charitable organisations like SOS Children's Villages. The general perception among the masses is that such organisations are operated by Christian funding. Consequently, they are greeted with a lack of motivation by the public and suffer misconceptions, religious barriers, and lack of social acceptance.

Lack of Government Care

Many NGO representatives claim that the response from government in terms of the alternative care of children is very poor. In Bangladesh, there is no policy on alternative care, no care management handbook and framework, and a lack of institutionalisation of alternative care. There is a distinct lack of orphanages run by NGOs and the government (Shishu Paribar), and a lack of madrasas, shelter homes, safe homes, government centres for disabled and autistic children, drop-in-centres for street children, and homes for vagrants. Additionally, services that are provided often fall short in providing the physical, mental, educational, and safety requirements of children.

Weak Legislative Framework

The Bangladesh Government has approved the UNCRC and UN Guidelines for Alternative Care of Children, but its legislative measures designed to fulfil them are poor. There is no legal framework and there is a lack of practical care guidelines. The main problem is that none of the documents, neither the Child Policy 2011 nor other child acts and laws, provide a clear definition and scope. The laws lack explanation. In addition, the Bangladesh Government has not ratified many important international conventions such as Convention 89 of the Decent Work Practice. A further issue is the lack of coordination among GO and NGO legislative services.

Inadequate Financial Resources

Alternative care has been assigned low priority in many areas of Bangladesh. Government budgetary allocation for alternative care is very limited. The alternative care budget of NGOs is also very limited and financial infrastructure is lacking across the entire sector.

Lack of Research

Research into the alternative care of children is very scarce. Questions have been raised about the quality of studies initiated by GOs and NGOs. Currently, there is a lack of baseline data—the number of children in alternative care is unknown and the limits and risks of care unclear. Additionally, no assessment of the needs of children in alternative care has been made. Research budgets and the assignment of alternative care as low priority by GOs and NGOs represent a significant challenge.

Underdeveloped Policies

Bangladesh has underdeveloped policies for the alternative care of children. The government of Bangladesh only included information about the alternative care of children in its Third Five Year Plan (1985–1990). This plan stated that all Sarkari Shishu Sadans and baby homes would be converted into Shishu Paribar in line with SOS Children's Villages, thereby securing the loving care and affection associated with family life (Planning Commission, 1985). Subsequent plans for alternative care, including specific child policies, Sustainable Development Goals (SDGs), commitments, and NGO guidelines, are non-existent.

ALTERNATIVE CARE: KEY INTERVENTIONS

Children are an integral part of a nation's development. They are the greatest asset of any country (Islam & Hossain, 2017). Therefore, proper childcare is of great significance to the development and safeguarding of children. Analysis of the alternative care framework allows the identification of a number of imperative interventions such as family reunification and family-based care, reintegration, community-based child protection, emergency shelters,

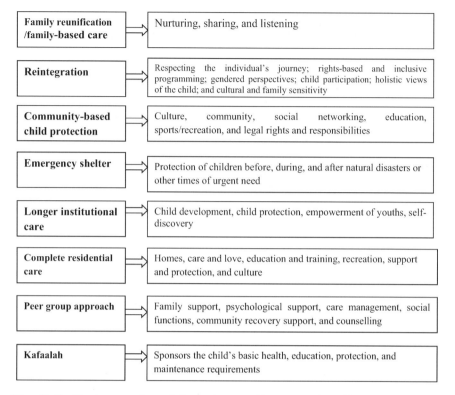

Family reunification /family-based care	→	Nurturing, sharing, and listening
Reintegration	→	Respecting the individual's journey; rights-based and inclusive programming; gendered perspectives; child participation; holistic views of the child; and cultural and family sensitivity
Community-based child protection	→	Culture, community, social networking, education, sports/recreation, and legal rights and responsibilities
Emergency shelter	→	Protection of children before, during, and after natural disasters or other times of urgent need
Longer institutional care	→	Child development, child protection, empowerment of youths, self-discovery
Complete residential care	→	Homes, care and love, education and training, recreation, support and protection, and culture
Peer group approach	→	Family support, psychological support, care management, social functions, community recovery support, and counselling
Kafaalah	→	Sponsors the child's basic health, education, protection, and maintenance requirements

Fig. 61.5 Key interventions of alternative care (*Source* Developed by the author)

longer periods of institutional care, complete residential care, peer group approaches, and the recognition of kafalah—all of which play a role in child welfare initiatives (Fig. 61.5).

Family reunification and family-based approaches. The cornerstones of family approaches are nurturing, sharing with, and listening to children. Children who have lost their parents can be cared for via alternative families through reunification.

Reintegration. This is an effective intervention where children are taught to respect one another's journeys, are provided with rights-based and inclusive programming, and gendered perspectives. This encourages their participation in different activities in institutional care. This approach is holistic, creating many ways for children to express their views and understanding through cultural and family sensitivity.

Community-based child protection mechanism. Here, children are allowed space and time to practice cultural activities, social networking, and sports/recreation. Under such a system they are provided with education and training, and knowledge about their legal rights and legal responsibilities.

Fig. 61.6 Institutional care model for the alternative care of children (*Source* Developed by the author and adapted from Wataneya Society for the Development of Orphanages [2019])

Fig. 61.7 Complete residential care model for the alternative care of children (*Source* Developed by the author)

Emergency shelter. One of the main interventions of alternative care is the accommodation of all children affected by disasters—either man made or natural. This intervention utilises response programmes specialising in the care and protection of children before, during, and after natural disasters and other instances requiring urgent action.

Longer periods of institutional care. Longer periods of institutional care are put in place for marginalised, vulnerable, and destitute children. This service ensures each child is enrolled in programmes of child protection, youth empowerment, and self-discovery (Fig. 61.6).

Complete residential care. This is where children are placed in safe and secure homes and receive care and love from mothers, brothers, and sisters. They also received education and training, access to sport and recreational activities, support and protection, and cultural education. In such instances children receive quality support with close supervision and monitoring from mothers and staff—a responsive, quick, and complete system (Fig. 61.7).

Peer group approach. In instances of residential care, the peer group approach ensures children receive lots of peer support. This intervention is

Fig. 61.8 Peer group approach to alternative care (*Source* Developed by the author)

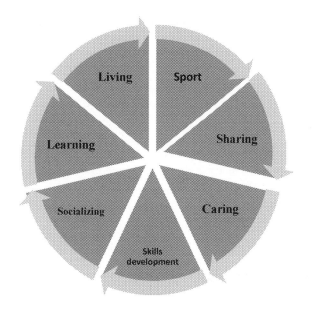

holistic and comprehensive—children are encouraged to socialise with one another in their learning environments and accommodation and also receive skills development training (Fig. 61.8).

Kafalah. The recognition of kafalah represents a landmark in the alternative care system of Muslim communities. Kafalah is the commitment by a person or family to voluntarily sponsor and care for an orphaned or abandoned child. The individual or family sponsors the child's basic needs for health, education, protection, and maintenance. Kafalah is recognised in the UNCRC.

Why SOS Children's Villages is an ideal organisation for child welfare in Bangladesh

SOS Children's Villages is one of the most successful organisations in the world. It was founded in Bangladesh by Professor Hermann Gmeiner in 1972. SOS is the main agency for children—especially the most marginalised. Examples of its founding principles are (1) that education is a human right that must be guaranteed, (2) that health is more than mere survival, (3) that employment measures create equal opportunities, and (4) that social protection structures are needed to tackle inequity and eradicate poverty. The following material justifies why SOS is an ideal organisation for driving through child welfare in Bangladesh.

1. *SOS is different from other agencies in that it*:
   • Provides a loving home for every child.
   • Cares for children who have lost parental care or are at risk of losing such care.

- Places children at the centre of the agenda for development.
- Considers education as a human right that must be guaranteed.
- Emphasises that health is more than mere survival.
- Champions employment measures to create equal opportunities.
- Puts in place social protection structures to tackle inequity and eradicate poverty.

2. *SOS is committed to*:
   - Amplifying the voice of children.
   - Quality childcare.
   - Tailored support.
   - Child safeguarding.
   - Learning and adapting.
   - Care integration.
   - Emergency response.
   - Employment and employability.

3. *Vision, values, strategy, and principles.* The vision of SOS is broad and wide. It considers that every child belongs to a family and should grow up surrounded by love, respect, and security. Its mission is to create families for children in need, help children shape their own futures, and share in the development of communities. Its values include courage, taking action, commitment, integrity, and belief in one another. SOS's strategies include providing the best care for children, innovating, and uniting more people so that no child grows up alone. Its programmes include quality care (alternative care and a strengthening of families), safeguarding, advocating children's rights, teaching and training, and protecting children in emergencies. SOS considers that every child is unique and deserves respect, every child needs caring for and stable parents, every child should grow up in a supportive family, and that every child should be a part of a safe and supportive community.

4. *Areas of risk.* SOS has identified health, economics, social and cultural factors, psychosocial aspects, and politics and the environment as risk factors for children who have no parental care. They consider the elimination of these risk factors essential to the physical and emotional development, economic and social wellbeing, and citizenship of children.

5. *SOS Strategy 2030—"No Child Should Grow Up Alone".* SOS Children's Villages has put the most disadvantaged children at the heart of its 2030 Strategy that directly relates to global SDGs in key areas such as poverty, inequality, education, health, society and child protection, and decent work. Achieving sustainable development by 2030 will require a renewed commitment to stronger partnerships among NGOs, the government, and the private sector. This must become a movement of like-minded and very determined partners that find common ground and noble ways to cultivate new forms of cooperation. Cooperation is paramount, as is supporting child and youth participation in this process. SOS Children's Villages believe that "No child should grow up

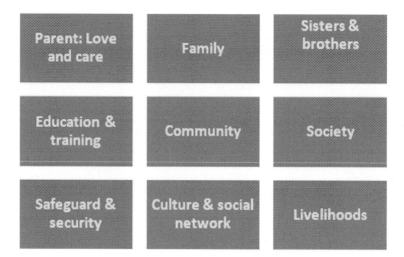

Fig. 61.9 The sustainability of SOS Children's Villages (*Source* Developed by the author)

alone," and embraces the challenge to secure a brighter and more sustainable future for the world's most vulnerable children (SOS Children's Villages International, 2017).

6. *Alternative care and social work interventions.* Alternative care interventions are similar to many other social work interventions, such as social case work, social group work, family social work, community social work, residential social work, school social work, crisis intervention, and child protection systems. These interventions can successfully be practiced as part of the interventions of alternative care.

7. *The sustainability of SOS Children's Villages.* When considering SOS's objectives, programmes, and principles it is clear that sustainability is attributed greater importance than other child development and child welfare organisations. It was mentioned earlier that SOS offers a comprehensive and complete programme for alternative care where children are offered the potential for full and rich lives—being provided with parents offering love and care, a family, sisters and brothers, an education, health and nutrition, training, a sense of community, a position in society, safeguarding and security, and the opportunity for cultural and social networking (Fig. 61.9), all of which are sustainable.

Conclusions and Suggestions

Based on a literature review, this chapter explores some ideas on the alternative care of children, particularly relating to its challenges and possible interventions. There were a number of challenges to writing this chapter, the principal one being the shortage of quality literature on the alternative care of children in Bangladesh. As a result, this chapter is based on empirical observations. This chapter is well organised, structured, and written in light of the model of the alternative care of children provided by SOS Children's Villages. First, this chapter considers the conceptual understanding of the issue in light of the CRC and UN Guidelines for the Alternative Care of Children. This chapter provides a background analysis of the perspective and rationale of UN Guidelines for the Alternative Care of Children according to the limitations imposed by the CRC and other legislatives. The chapter identifies some of the challenges facing the alternative care of children, including the unclear definition of alternative care, the lack of context, the number of children in the system, cultural barriers, the lack of governmental concern, the weak legislative frameworks in place, inadequate financial resources, the lack of research, and underdeveloped policies. This chapter incorporates a number of interesting interventions applied to the alternative care of children including family reunification/family approaches, reintegration, community-based child protection, emergency shelters, longer periods of institutional care, complete residential care, the peer group approach, and the recognition of kafalah. Finally, this chapter justifies why SOS Children's Villages represents an ideal organisation in light of its mission and vision, objectives and strategies, principles, innovative and comprehensive programmes, and well-structured model for the alternative care of children. This chapter critically argues that SOS Children's Villages has significant scope, is able to provide social work interventions utilised particularly through social case work, social group work, family social work, community social work, residential social work, school social work, crisis intervention, and child safeguarding systems. The chapter also identifies that SOS Children's Villages has a strategic relationship with global SDGs in key areas such as poverty, inequality, education, health, social and child protection, and decent work. The chapter argues that the alternative care service offered by SOS Children's Villages is sustainable, providing children with loving and caring parents, a family, sisters and brothers, education and training, a sense of community, a place in society, safeguarding and security, and cultural and social networking.

This chapter offers recommendations to overcome current challenges and implement interventions successfully.

- It is very important to formulate a uniform alternative care framework for practice in institutional care services. The government should formulate this framework in light of local contexts and culture.
- It is clear that insufficient research has been conducted on the alternative care of children. There is a lack of baseline data about the demographic and socioeconomic profile of alternative care for children. The government should do all it can to encourage such research.
- It is very important to consider alternative care in the long term. It should be included in the social sciences curriculum, particularly in social welfare/work.

- Increasing the budget set aside for alternative care should be a priority. Currently, there is no budget specifically for the alternative care of children in Bangladesh.
- It is important to include an approach to the alternative care system, including the SOS's role, in Bangladesh's Eighth Five Year Plan. The government recognised SOS's role in the Third Five Year Plan (1985–1990), but subsequently no long-term plans are mentioned.
- An alternative care management system is required in Bangladesh. Currently, the operational level of the existing alternative care system is underperforming. The government needs to show initiative and leadership to ensure the development of such a system.
- SDGs 1, 4, 8, 10, and 16 have close links to alternative care. It is important to recognise that without considering the proper wellbeing of marginalised, vulnerable, and destitute children, none of the goals will be achieved.
- The government, policy makers, and academics should encourage GOs and NGOs to show initiative by developing alternative care in terms of increased budgets, programmes, and research.
- The government should provide a serious commitment to "no child being left behind." This is an important message and should be the slogan adopted for child policy, planning, and laws.

References

Humanium. (2019). *Children of Bangladesh. Realizing children's rights in Bangladesh.* https://www.humanium.org/en/bangladesh. Accessed March 21, 2019.

Islam, M. R. (2013). Brighter future of child domestic workers in Bangladesh: Government initiatives and challenges. *Elixir International Journal, 60,* 16498–16503.

Islam, M. R., & Hossain, D. (2017). Protecting children from trafficking: Responses of the governmental and non-governmental organisations in Bangladesh. *The Malaysian Journal of Social Administration, 10*(1), 1–28.

Martin, F. S., & Zulaika, G. (2016). Who cares for children? A descriptive study of care-related data available through global household surveys and how these could be better mined to inform policies and services to strengthen family care. *Global Social Welfare, 3*(2), 51–74.

Mohajan, H. (2014). Child rights in Bangladesh. *Journal of Social Welfare and Human Rights, 2*(1), 207–238.

Planning Commission. (1985). *Third Five Year Plan 1985–1990.* Dhaka: Ministry of Planning, People's Republic of Bangladesh.

Roby, J. (2011). *Children in informal alternative care.* New York: UNICEF.

Scopus. (2019). *Total publication on 'alternative care of children'.* https://www.scopus.com/home.uri. Accessed March 22, 2019.

SOS Children's Villages International. (2017). *A world that cares how to support children without parental care through the sustainable development goal.* Vienna, Austria: SOS Children's Villages International.

United Nations. (2010). *Guidelines for the alternative care of children.* https://www.unicef.org/protection/alternative_care_Guidelines-English.pdf. Accessed March 18, 2019.

Wataneya Society for the Development of Orphanages. (2019). *Quality standard of alternative care.* https://amaanegypt.org/en/quality-standards-alternative-care. Accessed March 23, 2019.

Web of Science. (2019). *Total publication on 'alternative care of children'.* https://clarivate.com/products/web-of-science/. Accessed March 23, 2019.

World Population Review. (2019). *Bangladesh population 2019.* http://worldpopulationreview.com/countries/bangladesh-population/. Accessed March 20, 2019.

CHAPTER 62

Conclusion: Social Work Education in the Contemporary World—Issues, Challenges, and Concerns

Sajid S. M., Rajendra Baikady, Cheng Sheng-Li and Haruhiko Sakaguchi

As this book centres on the challenges faced by social work education in different socio-economic, political, and cultural contexts, authors in this volume have focused on addressing the issues concerning social work development in their respective countries. One unique feature of this volume is the non-Western-centric approach, which allowed for chapter contributions from countries which are not recorded in the dominant literature. This book also highlights the ongoing debate on professionalisation, curriculum

S. S. M.
Jamia Millia Islamia, New Delhi, Delhi, India
e-mail: ssajid@jmi.ac.in

R. Baikady (✉)
Paul Baerwald School of Social Work and Social Welfare, Hebrew University of Jerusalem, Jerusalem, Israel
e-mail: rajendra.baikady@mail.huji.ac.il

University of Johannesburg, Johannesburg, South Africa

C. Sheng-Li
Department of Social Work, Shandong University, Shandong, China
e-mail: chengsl@sdu.edu.cn

H. Sakaguchi
Department of Social Welfare, Ryukoku University, Kyoto, Kyoto, Japan
e-mail: antonkun@human.ryukoku.ac.jp

© The Author(s) 2021   1021
S. S. M. et al. (eds.), *The Palgrave Handbook of Global Social Work Education*, https://doi.org/10.1007/978-3-030-39966-5_62

development, development of teaching learning programmes around emerging areas, and, most importantly, the debates related to the internationalisation of social work education and practice around the globe. The book gives an account of the challenges, opportunities, and uniqueness of social work education and its delivery, as well as the prospects of the social work profession in 43 countries, covering each region of the world. Social work education across the globe is facing numerous challenges, of which some are common, while others are specific to regional or national contexts.

Schools of social work in the present world are continuously challenged to produce skilled and knowledgeable social work graduates who can effectively address contemporary societal issues across borders. However, at present, the focus is more on training social workers to meet in-house requirements rather than training social workers for practice in an international context. Apart from internships abroad, student and teacher exchange programmes; collaborative research projects take place only on a very small scale; and international teaching and learning programmes, joint degree programmes, and joint research programmes in the schools of social work are very minimal. A lack in the areas of trained and skilled teaching staff, favourable financial resources, administrative support, and student enthusiasm is the major setbacks that have resulted in failed internationalisation of social work in many countries in the world. In some cases, ideological differences and lack of coordination between educators, schools, and administration are also responsible for not initiating international collaboration and training. Furthermore, absence of debate among the social work educators on what 'indigenization' is, what is 'culturally relevant' social work practice, and what the advantages are of international collaboration in enhancing social work education and practice is also resulting in setting the boundaries for social work education and practice.

Many authors in this edited volume are critical of the development of social work in their countries. Authors have raised serious concerns about professional recognition of social work, as well as public support and acceptance of social work as a profession by society in their countries, although the issues are not very different in many other countries. The role of the state in social work development (Chapter 5 in this volume) and problems of accreditation in social work education and practice (Chapter 50 in this volume) are important in understanding the local, as well as the global, context. Irrespective of the development of the economy, social workers are poorly paid in many countries across the globe. Poor pay, low recognition, lack of support by the state, and failure to gain the confidence of the general public are affecting the profession's growth. Discussion on enhancing the academic status of social work education is in the forefront. Many authors in this volume are concerned about the academic status of social work programmes in their countries. In many parts of the world, social work education has been caught in a vicious circle. Poorly developed social work jobs with poor pay and limited job promotion prospects cannot attract motivated and quality students to enrol in social work programmes and enter social work jobs. As a result, the field of social work and social welfare is experiencing a very high dropout rate (Burns, 2011; Kim, 2011; Paat, 2016; Pösö & Forsman, 2013). Oftentimes, having receiving social work education from a loosely structured social work curriculum and non-specialised educators, and experiencing fieldwork arrangements taught by professionally incompetent teachers with limited direct social work practice experiences, social work graduates are ill-equipped for social welfare jobs. Bridging the gap between theory and practice in social work education is still an unsolved issue in many countries. Despite the advancement in social work research and development, educators across the globe find it difficult to combine theory and practice teaching in parallel (Komanduri, Chapter 52 in this volume). Untrained fieldwork supervisors and poor supervision, and undefined practice pedagogy further contributes to the growing challenge (Carolyn, Chapter 50 and Nobel, Chapter 51 in this volume).

Moving towards the accreditation of social work programmes is yet another issue discussed in the context of many countries. Social work, even after decades of practice and teaching in many countries, does not have an accredited teaching programme. Educators are not trained and educated in social work, and departments of social work are not independent and instead are affiliated with sociology or other more theory-based courses. In today's globalised society, with end number of technological enhancement and communication advancement, the profession of social work is still not very internationalised in many parts of the world. Authors in this volume address the importance of promoting international collaboration among the schools of social work across the globe. Learning from each other enables the growing profession in its service delivery and educational programmes. Learning from the mistakes of social work interventions in developed, Western countries help the developing and less developed countries to avoid heading in those directions, while the success stories and best practices can be replicated in social work teaching programmes around the world.

Marginalisation, inequality, and injustice still prevail in world societies. Social work, at its core, is expected to address the issues of injustice and assist people in their all-round development. Ensuring social justice and human dignity, accessibility and availability of resources to all sections of society, and enabling harmonious relationships between people are the expected professional roles of a social worker. As argued by Shaheed (Chapter 43 in this volume), social work in the new millennium needs to address issues of marginalisation, social justice, and human dignity (Ewijk, Chapter 44 in this volume). Social work needs to adopt an evidence-based programme delivery and programme evaluation in order to enhance its professional status and reputation. As argued by many authors in this volume, a low level of recognition, lack of reputation and respect among the public, lack of better job opportunities and poor working conditions exist largely because of the lack of evidence-based teaching and training programmes that are operating in the schools of social work across the globe.

A Call for North–South Collaboration
in Social Work Education

There has been effort to enhance the academic, research, and practice capacity of social work educators, researchers, students, and practitioners in the Global South through north–south collaboration. North–south research partnerships have contributed significantly to enhancing the social work research capacity in low- and middle-income countries. However, the academic research papers produced by the researchers in the Global South are significantly fewer compared to the numbers produced by scholars from the Global North. Evidence of this can be found in any scientific academic journal related to social work, where a considerable number of articles in each issue are contributed by scholars from the Global North. However, Roche and Flynn (2018, p. 14) noted that the increasing number of articles from the Global South is an indication of emerging scholarship in the Global South. Nurturing local scientific leadership and research capacity in the Global South is key to the development of international social work. Building capacity at both individual and institutional levels (Loukanova et al., 2014; Mayhew, Doherty, & Pitayarangsarit, 2008; Olaleye et al., 2014) will ensure scientific, innovative, and original contributions from the Global South to international social work academia. Internationalisation of social work has been supported by a large part of the social work academic community, significantly from the Global North; however, there is much less academic literature on the usefulness and effectiveness of international collaboration in social work. Apart from discussion by Brydon et al. (2012), nothing much has been written on the procedural aspects of international collaboration in social work; however, five studies have addressed the funding difficulties, language barriers, and methodological problems in international collaboration (Gardner, Katagiri, Parsons, Lee, & Thevannoor, 2012; Lombe, Newransky, Crea, & Stout, 2013). Furthermore, Aellah, Chantler, and Geissler (2016) and Lairumbi, Michael, Fitzpatrick, and English (2011) have argued that despite there being common goals, development and sharing of the benefits, resources, and knowledge in collaborative projects continue to be problematic.

The new millennium has brought major changes, challenges, and hardships in human service delivery. Neoliberalism, globalisation, and profit-centred development agendas have resulted in a complex pattern of widespread inequality, poverty, and social deviance across rich, poor, and middle-income countries. Social issues and chaos have developed in a more sophisticated way in both developed and developing societies, parallel to economic prosperity. In order to address this emerging social disorder, the discipline of social work needs to develop and nurture inter-professional collaboration in teaching, learning, practice, and research. Inter-professional collaboration happens when two or more professions work together to achieve common gaols and accomplishments. While there are concerns of loss of uniqueness of a profession or professional identity (Institute of Medicine, 2013) and potential challenges such as boundary disputes, status issues, language barriers, customer service orientation, and reporting structures (Lawlis, Anson, & Greenfield, 2014; Littlechild & Smith, 2013), inter-professional collaboration in social work is routinely used to address a variety of problems and complex issues that are encountered by modern society.

Since the colonial era, the Global North has assumed that knowledge, skills, and excellency are basically rooted in the rich Western countries, and a transfer of these skills, knowledge, and excellency needs to take place from the developed to developing countries in order to help the poor countries in the south to develop. As a result, cooperation, collaboration, and co-learning have flowed from Global North to Global South, and this has been practised, promoted, and debated for many years. To some extent, such cooperation from the Global North has also resulted in the development of the capacity, capability, and scientific knowledge produced in the Global South. At this time, the dominantly available literature on international collaboration represents this north–south collaboration, i.e. the flow of knowledge, literature, resources, and professional skills from the Global North to Global South, assuming that the Global South social work is poor in terms of knowledge, practice, and research base. We argue for a re-directed international collaboration, i.e. recognising the untapped capacity, skills, and knowledge of the Global South's social work academics and the building of a harmonious collaborative approach, where the Global North helps the Global South in developing its skills and capacities. And in principle, this approach will lead to sustainable changes in social work education in both the Global South and Global North. Furthermore, this collaboration will allow the profession to understand the social issues such as poverty and inequality across the boundaries of region, state, and nation. Thus, if rooted in the core principles of the profession, any collaborative processes can become the foundation for finding a new solution to serious global problems (McKay & Paikoff, 2007; Sperber et al., 2008).

On the whole, *The Palgrave Handbook of Global Social Work Education* is an effort towards contributing to the larger debate on enhancing the professional status of social work education and practice in the international context. The volume itself is a rich source of information that enables an international debate involving social work academics from both the Global South and the Global North. We primarily expect educators, students, and researchers—those who research and teach about social work programmes in an international context—to listen to the ideas of the authors in this volume and disseminate them to the larger social work community through their teaching and research programmes.

REFERENCES

Aellah, G., Chantler, T., & Geissler, P. W. (2016). *Global health research in an unequal world: Ethics case studies from Africa.* Oxfordshire: CAB International. Available from: https://www.ncbi.nlm.nih.gov/books/NBK458758/. Accessed December 15, 2019.

Brydon, K., Kamasua, J., Flynn, C., Mason, R., Au, R., Ayius, D., & Hampson, R. (2012). Developing an international social work education collaboration: A partnership approach between Monash University, Australia and University of Papua New Guinea. *International Social Work, 57*(6), 590–604. https://doi.org/10.1177/0020872812444939.

Burns, K. (2011). "Career Preference", "Transients" and "Converts": A study of social workers' retention in child protection and welfare. *British Journal of Social Work, 41*(3), 1–19.

Gardner, P., Katagiri, K., Parsons, J., Lee, L., & Thevannoor, R. (2012). "Not for the fainthearted": Engaging in cross-national comparative research. *Journal of Aging Studies, 26,* 253–261.

Institute of Medicine (US) Workshop. Cuff PA: Institute of Medicine (US), Board on Global Health, National Research Council (US); 2013. Global Forum on Innovation in Health Professional Education. (2012: Washington, DC).

Kim, H. (2011). Job conditions, unmet expectations, and burnout in public child welfare workers: How different from other social workers? *Children and Youth Services Review, 33*(2), 358–367.

Lairumbi, G. M., Michael, P., Fitzpatrick, R., & English, M. C. (2011). Ethics in practice: The state of the debate on promoting the social value of global health research in resource poor settings particularly Africa. *BMC Medical Ethics, 12*(1), 22. https://doi.org/10.1186/1472-6939-12-22.

Lawlis, T. R., Anson, J., & Greenfield, D. (2014). Barriers and enablers that influence sustainable interprofessional education: A literature review. *Journal of Interprofessional Care, 28*(4), 305–310.

Littlechild, B., & Smith, R. A. (2013). *Handbook for interprofessional practice in the human services: Learning to work together.* New York, NY: Routledge.

Lombe, M., Newransky, C., Crea, T., & Stout, A. (2013). From rhetoric to reality: Planning and conducting collaborations for international research in the global south. *Social Work, 58*(1), 31–40.

Loukanova, S., Prytherch, H., Blank, A., Duysburgh, E., Tomson, G., Gustafsson, L. L., ... Fonn, S. (2014). Nesting doctoral students in collaborative north–south partnerships for health systems research. *Global Health Action, 7*(1), 24070. http://dx.doi.org/10.3402/gha.v7.24070.

Mayhew, S. H., Doherty, J., & Pitayarangsarit, S. (2008). Developing health systems research capacities through north–south partnership: An evaluation of collaboration with South Africa and Thailand. *Health Research Policy Systems, 6,* 8.

McKay, M., & Paikoff, R. (2007). *Community collaborative partnerships: The foundation for HIV prevention research efforts in the United States and internationally.* West Hazleton: Haworth Press.

Olaleye, D. O., Odaibo, G. N., Carney, P., Agbaji, O., Sagay, A. S., Muktar, H., ... Murphy, R. L. (2014). Enhancement of health research capacity in Nigeria through north-south and in-country partnerships. *Academic Medicine, 89*(8 Suppl), 93–97.

Paat, Y.-F. (2016). Life course, altruism, rational choice, and aspirations in social work education. *Research Papers in Education, 31*(2), 234–253. https://doi.org/10.108 0/02671522.2015.1027725.

Pösö, T., & Forsman, S. (2013). Messages to social work education: What makes social workers continue and cope in child welfare? *Social Work Education: The International Journal, 32*(5), 650–661. https://doi.org/10.1080/02615479.201 2.694417.

Roche, S., & Flynn, C. (2018). Geographical inequity in social work research: A snapshot of research publications from the global South. *International Social Work.* https://doi.org/10.1177/0020872818797999.

Sperber, E., McKay, M. M., Bell, C. C., Petersen, I., Bhana, A., & Paikoff, R. (2008). Adapting and disseminating a community-collaborative, evidence-based HIV/AIDS prevention programme: Lessons from the history of CHAMP. *Vulnerable Children and Youth Studies, 3*(2), 150–158.

INDEX

Printed in the United States
by Baker & Taylor Publisher Services